THE ESSENTIAL WORKS OF

CHARLES SPURGEON

THE ESSENTIAL WORKS OF

CHARLES SPURGEON

SELECTED BOOKS, SERMONS, AND OTHER WRITINGS

INCLUDES SPURGEON'S AUTOBIOGRAPHY,
A COMPLETE SCRIPTURE INDEX,
AND RESOURCES FOR FURTHER STUDY

EDITED BY DANIEL PARTNER

BARBOUR
PUBLISHING

Published by Barbour Publishing, Inc., P.O. Box 719, Uhrichsville, Ohio 44683, www.barbourbooks.com

Our mission is to publish and distribute inspirational products offering exceptional value and biblical encouragement to the masses.

 Member of the
Evangelical Christian
Publishers Association

*The words of God have more power over me
than ever David's fingers had over his harp strings.*

CHARLES H. SPURGEON

CONTENTS

CONTENTS

INTRODUCTION

WHEN the coffin containing the remains of Charles Haddon Spurgeon was lowered into the grave at West Norwood Cemetery, London, on Thursday, February 12, 1892, a Bible lay upon its lid opened to Isaiah 45:22, which says, "Look to Me, and be saved, all you ends of the earth!"

That Bible may never have been there that day "had it not been for the goodness of God in sending a snowstorm" one Sunday morning forty-two years earlier while the fifteen-year-old Charles Spurgeon was making his way to church. As Spurgeon tells the story in his autobiography, "When I could go no further, I turned down a side street and came to a little Primitive Methodist chapel." The man preaching that day, "a very thin-looking man, a shoemaker or tailor or something of that sort," had chosen Isaiah 45:22 for his text. As his brief message ended, this man spoke directly to Spurgeon, who was the obvious visitor among the sparse congregation: "Young man, look to Jesus Christ. Look! Look! Look! You have nothin' to do but to look and live."

Years later, when people called him the "Prince of Preachers," C. H. Spurgeon testified, "When I heard that word *look*, what a charming word it seemed to me! Oh! I looked until I could almost have looked my eyes away." He then quoted William Cowper's well-known hymn:

> *E'er since by faith I saw the stream*
> *Thy flowing wounds supply,*
> *Redeeming love has been my theme,*
> *And shall be till I die.*

Born June 19, 1834, in Kelvedon, Essex, Spurgeon was baptized on May 3, 1850, in the river at Iselham. About six months later he delivered his first sermon in a cottage at Teversham, Cambridge. In 1851 he became pastor of a small Baptist church in Cambridgeshire, and his first literary work, a gospel tract, was printed in 1853. From there, it pleased God to speedily place him among the preeminent preachers of the nineteenth century. Of them all, Spurgeon is, in our day, arguably the best known and most influential.

It was April 1854 when C. H. Spurgeon assumed the pastorate of

London's New Park Street Chapel, the largest Baptist congregation in London. The "Boy Preacher," as he was known at the time, was soon renowned in London. Short and stout, not particularly well dressed, and with a face a contemporary described as homely, Spurgeon's flesh was evidently not the cause of his popularity. Like the apostle Paul, he also did not boast in fleshly wisdom, since he had no formal education in theology (2 Cor. 1:12). Rather, the reader will find in the selections from his sermons and writings collected in this book that Spurgeon's attraction is the grace of God conveyed by the sacred scriptures. As he said, "The words of God have more power over me than ever David's fingers had over his harp strings."

Yes, God gave Charles Spurgeon an ample portion of grace in gifts such as the word of wisdom and the word of knowledge (1 Cor. 12:4, 8), and he had significant oratorical powers—but again like the apostle, he did not use these gifts as some do, "peddling the word of God" (2 Cor. 2:17). Rather, he said, "It is better to preach five words of God's Word than five million words of man's wisdom."

The year 1855 saw the beginning of the publication of C. H. Spurgeon's sermons. Recorded by stenographers, these were reviewed by the preacher before being printed and distributed throughout the United Kingdom. In 1865 they sold twenty-five thousand copies a week at a penny each and were translated into twenty languages. At the time of his death, Spurgeon had preached nearly thirty-six hundred sermons. These were published in yearly bound volumes that eventually numbered sixty-three. Their publication ceased in 1917, but they are now available in reprint editions. Sixty of these sermons are collected in this book, lightly edited to modernize some language, spelling, and punctuation.

Numbering two to three hundred people when he arrived, the congregation of Park Street Chapel mushroomed until, at age twenty-two, Spurgeon found himself preaching to gatherings of ten thousand at Surrey Music Hall and was the most popular preacher of the day. His marriage to Susanna Thompson of London came in 1856. Twin sons soon followed.

That same year, he founded a pastors' college in Camberwell. It is now located in South Norwood Hill, London, and named Spurgeon's College. On October 7 the next year, an audience of 23,654 people heard him preach at London's Crystal Palace—the largest audience ever to hear his preaching of the gospel.

His congregation moved into the newly built Metropolitan Tabernacle in London's Southwark district on March 6, 1861; Charles Spurgeon was three years shy of his thirtieth birthday. Designed in the Greek revival style, this building accommodated gatherings of six thousand people blessed to hear the sermons of the Prince of Preachers and sing a cappella from *Our Own Hymnal*, a collection he selected.

The reader will notice that Spurgeon's sermons are laced with many lines and verses from hymns. He spoke from a brief outline only, so these sprang from the preacher's memory. His grandmother, who raised him in early childhood, encouraged the boy's faith by giving him a penny for each hymn he could memorize. Eventually his proficiency caused her to reduce the payment to a halfpenny to save expense. Years later, these hymns turned up in Spurgeon's sermons.

Naturally, controversy attended such a celebrated man. Newspapers caricatured and Christians opposed. After a controversy over deistic hymns, he said, "We shall soon have to handle truth, not with kid gloves, but with gauntlets—the gauntlets of holy courage and integrity." He challenged the practice of infant baptism as practiced by the Church of England and the Methodists and more significantly engaged in the Downgrade Controversy among the Baptists. He held that some Baptists downgraded the place of the Bible in the church by subscribing to the idea that the Pentateuch was not written by one person and by entertaining Darwin's theory of evolution by natural selection, among other things. As a result, on October 26, 1887, Spurgeon withdrew from the Baptist Union, the main association of Baptist ministers. In this way, his Metropolitan Tabernacle became the largest independent congregation in the world, anticipating the modern-day megachurch.

Still, he reached across sectarian divides. He was friend to James Hudson Taylor, founder of the China Inland Mission, and not only supported Taylor's work financially, but also encouraged people to serve with the seminal missionary. He admired George Müller and so emulated him by founding the Stockwell Orphanage. This establishment began to care for boys in 1867 and girls in 1879. It is now a charitable organization benefiting the world's children and is simply called Spurgeons.

In the later years of his life, Charles Spurgeon often retreated to Nice in the south of France for rest and recuperation from the sufferings of rheumatism, gout, and Bright's disease, and it was there, after he had served his own generation by the will of God, he fell asleep (Acts 13:36). One is tempted to call Spurgeon a great man, though he would certainly protest this in the humility of Christ. Therefore let us simply say that God operates all things in accord with the counsel of His will (Eph. 1:11), and therein greatly used this man for the advancement of the gospel.

C. H. Spurgeon was so prolific we cannot here list all the works in his bibliography. These include commentaries, books of illustrations for sermons, devotions, sermons, periodicals, hymns, speeches, lectures, an autobiography, and more. This volume includes a small selection of these. It is titled *The Essential Works of Charles Spurgeon* because we hope these selections will present to you the vitality of his spirit and the essence of his work.

Daniel Partner
Coos Bay, Oregon
November 2008

Selections from The Autobiography of Charles Spurgeon

CONTENTS

1

THE GREAT CHANGE—
CONVERSION

I have heard men tell the story of their conversion, and of their spiritual life, in such a way that my heart has loathed them and their story, too, for they have told of their sins as if they did boast in the greatness of their crime, and they have mentioned the love of God, not with a tear of gratitude, not with the simple thanksgiving of the really humble heart, but as if they as much exalted themselves as they exalted God. Oh! When we tell the story of our own conversion, I would have it done with great sorrow, remembering what we used to be, and with great joy and gratitude, remembering how little we deserve these things. I was once preaching upon conversion and salvation, and I felt within myself, as preachers often do, that it was but dry work to tell this story, and a dull, dull tale it was to me. But on a sudden, the thought crossed my mind, Why, you are a poor, lost, ruined sinner yourself. Tell it. Tell it as you received it. Begin to tell of the grace of God as you trust you feel it yourself. Why, then my eyes began to be fountains of tears; those hearers who had nodded their heads began to brighten up, and they listened, because they were hearing something that the speaker himself felt, and that they recognized as being true to him if it was not true to them.

Can you not remember, dearly beloved, that day of days, that best and brightest of hours, when first you saw the Lord, lost your burden, received the roll of promise, rejoiced in full salvation, and went on your way in peace? My soul can never forget that day. Dying, all but dead, diseased, pained, chained, scourged, bound in fetters of iron, in darkness and the shadow of death, Jesus appeared unto me. My eyes looked to Him; the disease was healed, the pains removed, chains were snapped, prison doors were opened, darkness gave place to light. What delight filled my soul! What mirth, what ecstasy, what sound of music and dancing, what soarings toward heaven, what heights and depths of ineffable delight! Scarcely ever since then have I known joys that surpassed the rapture of that first hour.

—*C. H. Spurgeon*

LET our lips crowd sonnets within the compass of a word; let our voice distill hours of melody into a single syllable; let our tongue utter in one letter the essence of the harmony of ages; for we write of an hour that as far excels all other days of our life as gold exceeds dross. As the night of Israel's Passover was a night to be remembered, a theme for bards, and an incessant fountain of grateful song, even so is the time of which we now tell, the never-to-be-forgotten hour of our emancipation from guilt and our justification in Jesus. Other days have mingled with their fellows till, like coins worn in circulation, their image and superscription are entirely obliterated; but this day remains new, fresh, bright, as distinct in all its parts as if it were but yesterday struck from the mint of time. Memory shall drop from the palsied hand full many a memento that now she cherishes, but she shall never, even when she totters to the grave, unbind from her heart the token of the thrice-happy hour of the redemption of our spirit. The emancipated galley slave may forget the day that heard his broken fetters rattle on the ground; the pardoned traitor may fail to remember the moment when the ax of the headsman was averted by a pardon; and the long-despairing mariner may not recollect the moment when a friendly hand snatched him from the hungry deep. But oh, hour of forgiven sin, moment of perfect pardon, our soul shall never forget you while within you, life and being find immortality! Each day of our life has had its attendant angel, but on this day, as with Jacob at Mahanaim, hosts of angels met us. The sun has risen every morning, but on that eventful morn he had the light of seven days. As the days of heaven upon earth, as the years of immortality, as the ages of glory, as the bliss of heaven, so were the hours of that thrice-happy day. Rapture divine, and ecstasy inexpressible, filled our soul. Fear, distress, and grief, with all their train of woes, fled hastily away, and in their place joys came without number.

When I was in the hand of the Holy Spirit, under conviction of sin, I had a clear and sharp sense of the justice of God. Sin, whatever it might be to other people, became to me an intolerable burden. It was not so much that I feared hell as that I feared sin; and all the while, I had upon my mind a deep concern for the honor of God's name and the integrity of His moral government. I felt that it would not satisfy my conscience if I could be forgiven unjustly. But then there came the question—"How could God be just, and yet justify me who had been so guilty?" I was worried and wearied with this question; neither could I see any answer to it. Certainly, I could never have invented an answer that would have satisfied my conscience. The doctrine of the atonement is to my mind one of the surest proofs of the divine inspiration of Holy Scripture. Who would or could have thought of the just ruler dying for the unjust rebel? This is no teaching of human mythology, or dream of poetical imagination. This method of expiation is only known among men because it is a fact: fiction could not have devised it. God Himself ordained it; it is not a matter that could have been imagined.

> *Oh, hour of forgiven sin, moment of perfect pardon, our soul shall never forget you while within you, life and being find immortality!*

I had heard of the plan of salvation by the sacrifice of Jesus from my youth up, but I did not know any more about it in my innermost soul than if I had been born and bred a Hottentot. The light was there, but I was blind. It was of necessity that the Lord Himself should make the matter plain to me. It came to me as a new revelation, as fresh as if I had never read in scripture that Jesus was declared to be the propitiation for sins that God might be just. I believe it will have to come as a revelation to every newborn child of God whenever he sees it; I mean that glorious doctrine of the substitution of the Lord Jesus. I came to understand that salvation was possible through vicarious sacrifice, and that provision had been made in the first constitution and arrangement of things for such a substitution. I was made to see that He who is the Son of God, coequal and coeternal with the Father, had of old been made the covenant head of a chosen people, that He might in that capacity suffer for them and save them. Inasmuch as our fall was not at the first a personal one, for we fell in our federal representative, the first Adam, it became possible for us to be recovered by a second Representative, even by Him who has undertaken to be the covenant head of His people, so as to be their second Adam. I saw that, before I actually sinned, I had fallen by my first father's sin; and I rejoiced that therefore it became possible in point of law for me to rise by a second head and representative. The fall by Adam left a loophole of escape; another Adam could undo the ruin wrought by the first.

When I was anxious about the possibility of a just God pardoning me, I understood and saw by faith that He who is the Son of God became man, and in His own blessed person bore my sin in His own body on the tree. I saw that the chastisement of my peace was laid on Him, and that with His stripes I was healed. It was because the Son of God, supremely glorious in His matchless person, undertook to vindicate the law by bearing the sentence due to me, that therefore God was able to pass by my sin. My sole hope for heaven lies in the full atonement made upon Calvary's cross for the ungodly. On that I firmly rely. I have not the shadow of a hope anywhere else. Personally, I could never have overcome my own sinfulness. I tried and failed. My evil propensities were too many for me, till, in the belief that Christ died for me, I cast my guilty soul on Him, and then I received a conquering principle by which I overcame my sinful self. The doctrine of the cross can be used to slay sin, even as the old warriors used their huge two-handed swords and mowed down their foes at every stroke. There is nothing like faith in the sinners' friend; it overcomes all evil. If Christ has died for me, ungodly as I am, without strength as I am, then I cannot live in sin any longer, but must arouse myself to love and serve Him who has redeemed me. I cannot trifle with the evil that slew my best friend. I must be holy for His sake. How can I live in sin when He has died to save me from it?

There was a day, as I took my walks abroad, when I came hard by a spot forever engraved upon my memory, for there I saw this friend, my best, my only friend, murdered. I stooped down in sad affright and looked at Him. I saw that His hands had been pierced with rough iron nails, and His feet had been rent in the same way. There was misery in His dead countenance so terrible that I scarcely dared to look upon it. His body was emaciated with hunger, His back was red with bloody scourges, and His brow had a circle of wounds about it. Clearly could one see that these had been pierced by thorns. I shuddered, for I had known this friend full well. He never had a fault; He was the purest of the pure, the holiest of the holy. Who could have injured Him? For He never injured any man. All His life long He went about doing good. He had healed the sick, He had fed the hungry, He had raised the dead. For which of these works did they kill Him? He had never breathed out anything but love, and as I looked into the poor sorrowful face, so full of agony and yet so full of love, I wondered who could have been a wretch so vile as to pierce hands like His. I said within myself, "Where can these traitors live? Who are these that could have smitten such a One as this?" Had they murdered an oppressor, we might have forgiven them; had they slain one who had indulged in vice or villainy, it might have been his desert; had it been a murderer and a rebel, or one who had committed sedition, we would have said, "Bury his corpse; justice has at last given him his due." But when you were slain, my best, my only beloved, where lodged the traitors? Let me seize them, and they shall be put to death. If there be torments that I can devise, surely they shall endure them all. Oh, what jealousy, what revenge I felt! If I might but find these murderers, what would I not do with them! And as I looked upon that corpse, I heard a footstep and wondered where it was. I listened, and I clearly perceived that the murderer was close at hand. It was dark, and I groped about to find him. I found that, somehow or other, wherever I put out my hand, I could not meet with him, for he was nearer to me than my hand would go. At last I put my hand upon my breast. "I have you now," said I. For lo! He was in my own heart; the murderer was hiding within my own bosom, dwelling in the recesses of my inmost soul. Ah! Then I wept indeed, that I, in the very presence of my murdered Master, should be harboring the murderer, and I felt myself most guilty while I bowed over His corpse and sang that plaintive hymn:

'Twas you, my sins, my cruel sins,
His chief tormentors were;
Each of my crimes became a nail,
And unbelief the spear.

Amid the rabble rout that hounded the Redeemer to His doom, there were some gracious souls whose bitter anguish sought vent in wailing and lamentations—fit music to accompany that march of woe. When my soul can, in imagination, see the Savior bearing His cross to Calvary, she joins the godly women and weeps with them, for indeed, there is true cause for grief—cause lying deeper than those mourning women thought. They bewailed innocence maltreated, goodness persecuted, love bleeding, meekness about to die; but my heart has a deeper and more bitter cause to mourn. My sins were the scourges that lacerated those blessed shoulders and crowned with thorns those bleeding brows. My sins cried, "Crucify Him! Crucify Him!" and laid the cross upon His gracious shoulders. His being led forth to die is sorrow enough for one eternity, but my having been His murderer is more, infinitely more grief than one poor fountain of tears can express.

> *He never injured any man. All His life long He went about doing good. He had healed the sick, He had fed the hungry, He had raised the dead. For which of these works did they kill Him?*

Why those women loved and wept, it was not hard to guess, but they could not have had greater reasons for love and grief than my heart has. Nain's widow saw her son restored, but I myself have been raised to newness of life. Peter's wife's mother was cured of the fever, but I of the greater plague of sin. Out of Magdalene seven devils were cast, but a whole legion out of me. Mary and Martha were favored with visits from Him, but He dwells with me. His mother bore His body, but He is formed in me the hope of glory. In nothing behind the holy women in debt, let me not be behind them in gratitude or sorrow.

> *Love and grief my heart dividing,*
> *With my tears His feet I'll lave;*
> *Constant still in heart abiding,*
> *Weep for Him who died to save.*

William Huntingdon says, in his autobiography, that one of the sharpest sensations of pain that he felt, after he had been quickened by divine grace, was this: "He felt such pity for God." I do not know that I ever met with the expression elsewhere, but it is a very striking one—although I might prefer to say that I have sympathy with God and grief that He should be treated so ill. Ah, there are many men who are forgotten, who are despised, and who are trampled on by their fellows, but there never was a man who was so despised as the everlasting God has been! Many a man has been slandered and abused, but never was man abused as God has been. Many have been treated cruelly and ungratefully, but never was one treated as our God has been. I, too, once despised Him. He knocked at the door of my heart, and I refused to open it. He came to me, times without number, morning by morning and night by night. He checked me in my conscience and spoke to me by His Spirit, and when, at last, the thunders of the law prevailed in my conscience, I thought that Christ was cruel and unkind. Oh, I can never forgive myself that I should have thought so ill of Him! But what a loving reception did I have when I went to Him! I thought He would smite me, but His hand was not clenched in anger but opened wide in mercy. I thought full sure that His eyes would dart lightning flashes of wrath upon me, but instead thereof, they were full of tears. He fell upon my neck and kissed me. He took off my rags and did clothe me with His righteousness, and caused my soul to sing aloud for joy. While in the house of my heart and in the house of His church, there were music and dancing, because His son whom He had lost was found, and he who had been dead was made alive again.

> *Many a man has been slandered and abused, but never was man abused as God has been. Many have been treated cruelly and ungratefully, but never was one treated as our God has been.*

There is a power in God's gospel beyond all description. Once I, like Mazeppa, lashed to the wild horse of my lust, bound hand and foot, incapable of resistance, was galloping on with hell's wolves behind me, howling for my body and my soul as their just and lawful prey. There came a mighty hand that stopped that wild horse, cut my bands, set me down, and brought me into liberty. Is there power in the gospel? Aye, there is, and he who has felt it must acknowledge it. There was a time when I lived in the strong old castle of my sins and rested in my own works. There came a trumpeter to the door and bade me open it. I with anger chided him from the porch and said he never should enter. Then there came a goodly Personage with loving countenance; His hands were marked with scars where nails had been driven, and His feet had nail prints, too. He lifted up His cross, using it as a hammer. At the first blow, the gate of my prejudice shook; at the second, it trembled more; at the third, down it fell, and in He came. And He said, "Arise, and stand upon your feet, for I have loved you with an everlasting love." The gospel a thing of power! Ah, that it is. It always wears the dew of its youth; it glitters with morning's freshness; its strength and its glory abide forever. I have felt its power in my own heart; I have the witness of the Spirit within my spirit, and I know it is a thing of might, because it has conquered me and bowed me down.

> *His free grace alone, from the first to the last,*
> *Hath won my affections and bound my soul fast.*

In my conversion, the very point lay in making the discovery that I had nothing to do but to look to Christ, and I should be saved. I believe that I had been a very good, attentive hearer; my own impression about myself was that nobody ever listened much better than I did. For years, as a child, I tried to learn the way of salvation, and either I did not hear it set forth, which I think cannot quite have been the case, or else I was spiritually blind and deaf and could not see it and could not hear it. But the good news that I was, as a sinner, to look away from myself to Christ as much startled me and came as fresh to me as any news I ever heard in my life. Had I never read my Bible? Yes, and read it earnestly. Had I never been taught by Christian people? Yes, I had, by mother and father and others. Had I not heard the gospel? Yes, I think I had, and yet, somehow, it was like a new revelation to me that I was to believe and live. I confess to have been tutored in piety, put into my cradle by prayerful hands, and lulled to sleep by songs concerning Jesus. But after having heard the gospel continually, with line upon line, precept upon precept, here much and there much, yet, when the Word of the Lord came to me with power, it was as new as if I had lived among the unvisited tribes of Central Africa and had never heard the tidings of the cleansing fountain filled with blood, drawn from the Savior's veins.

When, for the first time, I received the gospel to my soul's salvation, I thought that I had never really heard it before, and I began to think that the preachers to whom I had listened had not truly preached it. But on looking back, I am inclined to believe that I had heard the gospel fully preached many hundreds of times before, and that this was the difference: that I then heard it as though I heard it not, and when I did hear it, the message may not have been any clearer in itself than it had been at former times. But the power of the Holy Spirit was present to open my ear and to guide the message to my heart. I have no doubt that I heard, scores of times, such texts as these: "He who believes and is baptized will be saved" (Mark 16:16); "And as Moses lifted up the serpent in the wilderness, even so must the Son of man be lifted up" (John 3:14 KJV). Yet I had no intelligent idea of what faith meant. When I first discovered what faith really was, and exercised it, with me these two things came together: I believed as soon as ever I knew what believing meant; then I thought I had never before heard that truth preached. But now I am persuaded that the light often shone on my eyes, but I was blind, and therefore I thought that the light had never come there. The light was shining all the while, but there was no power to receive it; the eyeball of the soul was not sensitive to the divine beams.

I could not believe that it was possible that *my* sins could be forgiven. I do not know why, but I seemed to be the odd person in the world. When the catalog was made out, it appeared to me that, for some reason, I must have been left out. If God had saved me, and not the world, I should have wondered indeed; but if He had saved all the world except me, that would have seemed to me to be but right. And now, being saved by grace, I cannot help saying, "I am indeed a brand plucked out of the fire!" I believe that some of us who were kept by God a long while before we found Him love Him better perhaps than we should have done if we had received Him directly, and we can preach better to others—we can speak more of His loving-kindness and tender mercy. John Bunyan could not have written as he did if he had not been dragged about by the devil for many years. I love that picture of dear old Christian. I know, when I first read *The Pilgrim's Progress* and saw in it the woodcut of Christian carrying the burden on his back, I felt so interested in the poor fellow that I thought I should jump with joy when, after he had carried his heavy load so long, he at last got rid of it. And that was how I felt when the burden of guilt, which I had borne so long, was forever rolled away from my shoulders and my heart. I can recollect when, like the poor dove sent out by Noah from his hand, I flew over the wide expanse of waters and hoped to find some place where I might rest my wearied wing. Up toward the north I flew, and my eye looked keenly through the mist and darkness, if perhaps it might find some floating substance on which my soul might rest its foot, but it found nothing. Again it turned its wing and flapped it, but not so rapidly as before, across that deep water that knew no shore, but still there was no rest. The raven had found its resting place upon a floating body and was feeding itself upon the carrion of some drowned man's carcass, but my poor soul found no rest. I flew on; I fancied I saw a ship sailing out at sea. It was the ship of the law, and I thought I would put my feet on its canvas, or rest myself on its cordage for a time and find some refuge. But ah! It was an airy phantom, on which I could not rest; for my foot had no right to rest on the law. I had not kept it, and the soul who keeps it not must die. At last I saw the bark *Christ Jesus*, that happy ark, and I thought I would fly thither; but my poor wing was weary. I could fly no further, and down I sank. But as providence would have it, when my wings were flagging and I was falling into the flood to be drowned, just below me was the roof of the ark, and I saw a hand put out from it, and one took hold of me and said, "I have loved you with an everlasting love; therefore I have not delivered the soul of my turtledove unto the multitude of the wicked; come in, come in!" Then I found that I had in my mouth an olive leaf of peace with God, and peace with man, plucked off by Jesus' mighty power.

> *believe that some of us who were kept by God a long while before we found Him love Him better perhaps than we should have done if we had received Him directly.*

Once, God preached to me by a similitude in the depth of winter. The earth had been black, and there was scarcely a green thing or a flower to be seen. As I looked across the fields, there was nothing but barrenness, bare hedges, leafless trees, and black earth, wherever I gazed. On a sudden, God spoke and unlocked the treasures of the snow, and white flakes descended until there was no blackness to be seen, and all was one sheet of dazzling whiteness. It was at the time that I was seeking the Savior, and not long before I found Him, and I remember well that sermon that I saw before me in the snow: "Come now, and let us reason together, saith the LORD: though your sins be as scarlet, they shall be as white as snow; though they be red like crimson, they shall be as wool" (Isa. 1:18 KJV).

Personally, I have to bless God for many good books; I thank Him for Dr. Doddridge's *Rise and Progress of Religion in the Soul*; for Baxter's *Call to the Unconverted*; for Alleine's *Alarm to Sinners*; and for James's *Anxious*

Enquirer. But my gratitude most of all is due to God, not for books, but for the preached Word, and that, too, addressed to me by a poor, uneducated man, a man who had never received any training for the ministry, and probably will never be heard of in this life, a man engaged in business, no doubt of a humble kind, during the week, but who had just enough of grace to say on the Sabbath, "Look to Me, and be saved, all you ends of the earth! For I am God, and there is no other" (Isa. 45:22). The books were good, but the man was better. The revealed Word awakened me, but it was the preached Word that saved me, and I must ever attach peculiar value to the *hearing of the truth*, for by it I received the joy and peace in which my soul delights. While under concern of soul, I resolved that I would attend all the places of worship in the town where I lived, in order that I might find out the way of salvation. I was willing to do anything, and be anything, if God would only forgive my sin. I set off, determined to go round to all the chapels, and I did go to every place of worship; but for a long time I went in vain. I do not, however, blame the ministers. One man preached divine sovereignty; I could hear him with pleasure, but what was that sublime truth to a poor sinner who wished to know what he must do to be saved? There was another admirable man who always preached about the law, but what was the use of plowing up ground that needed to be sown? Another was a practical preacher. I heard him, but it was very much like a commanding officer teaching the maneuvers of war to a set of men without feet. What could I do? All his exhortations were lost on me. I knew it was said, "Believe on the Lord Jesus Christ, and you will be saved" (Acts 16:31), but I did not know what it was to believe on Christ. These good men all preached truths suited to many in their congregations who were spiritually minded people, but what I wanted to know was, "How can I get my sins forgiven?" They never told me that. I desired to hear how a poor sinner, under a sense of sin, might find peace with God; and when I went, I heard a sermon on "Do not be deceived, God is not mocked" (Gal. 6:7), which cut me up still worse but did not bring me into rest. I went again, another day, and the text was something about the glories of the righteous, nothing for poor me! I was like a dog under the table, not allowed to eat of the children's food. I went time after time, and I can honestly say that I do not know that I ever went without prayer to God, and I am sure there was not a more attentive hearer than myself in all the place, for I panted and longed to understand how I might be saved.

I sometimes think I might have been in darkness and despair until now had it not been for the goodness of God in sending a snowstorm one Sunday morning while I was going to a certain place of worship. When I could go no further, I turned down a side street and came to a little Primitive Methodist chapel. In that chapel there may have been a dozen or fifteen people. I had heard of the Primitive Methodists, how they sang so loudly that they made people's heads ache, but that did not matter to me. I wanted to know how I might be saved, and if they could tell me that, I did not care how much they made my head ache. The minister did not come that morning; he was snowed up, I suppose. At last, a very thin-looking man, a shoemaker or tailor or something of that sort, went up into the pulpit to preach. Now, it is well that preachers should be instructed, but this man was really stupid. He was obliged to stick to his text, for the simple reason that he had little else to say. The text was "Look to Me, and be saved, all you ends of the earth!" (Isa. 45:22). He did not even pronounce the words rightly, but that did not matter. There was, I thought, a glimpse of hope for me in that text. The preacher began thus: "My dear friends, this is a very simple text indeed. It says, 'Look.' Now lookin' don't take a deal of pains. It ain't liftin' your foot or your finger; it is just, 'Look.' Well, a man needn't go to college to learn to look. You may be the biggest fool, and yet you can look. A man needn't be worth a thousand a year to be able to look. Anyone can look; even a child can look. But then the text says, 'Look unto *Me*.' Aye," said he, in broad Essex, "many of ye are lookin' to yourselves, but it's no use lookin' there. You'll never find any comfort in yourselves. Some look to God the Father. No, look to Him by and by. Jesus Christ says, 'Look unto *Me*.' Some of ye say, 'We must wait for the Spirit's workin'.' You have no business with that just now. Look to *Christ*. The text says, 'Look unto *Me*.'"

> *I* am sure there was not a more attentive hearer than myself in all the place, for I panted and longed to understand how I might be saved.

Then the good man followed up his text in this way: "Look unto Me; I am sweatin' great drops of blood. Look unto Me; I am hangin' on the cross.

Look unto Me; I am dead and buried. Look unto Me; I rise again. Look unto Me; I ascend to heaven. Look unto Me; I am sittin' at the Father's right hand. O poor sinner, look unto Me! Look unto Me!"

When he had gone to about that length and managed to spin out ten minutes or so, he was at the end of his tether. Then he looked at me under the gallery, and I daresay, with so few present, he knew me to be a stranger. Just fixing his eyes on me, as if he knew all my heart, he said, "Young man, you look very miserable." Well, I did, but I had not been accustomed to have remarks made from the pulpit on my personal appearance before. However, it was a good blow, struck right home. He continued, "And you always will be miserable; miserable in life and miserable in death if you don't obey my text. But if you obey now, this moment, you will be saved." Then, lifting up his hands, he shouted, as only a Primitive Methodist could do, "Young man, look to Jesus Christ. Look! Look! Look! You have nothin' to do but to look and live." I saw at once the way of salvation. I know not what else he said. I did not take much notice of it, I was so possessed with that one thought. As when the brazen serpent was lifted up, the people only looked and were healed, so it was with me. I had been waiting to do fifty things, but when I heard that word, "Look!" what a charming word it seemed to me! Oh! I looked until I could almost have looked my eyes away. There and then the cloud was gone, the darkness had rolled away, and that moment I saw the sun; and I could have risen that instant and sung with the most enthusiastic of them of the precious blood of Christ, and the simple faith that looks alone to Him. Oh, that somebody had told me this before: "Trust Christ, and you shall be saved." Yet it was, no doubt, all wisely ordered, and now I can say:

> *E'er since by faith I saw the stream*
> *Your flowing wounds supply,*
> *Redeeming love has been my theme,*
> *And shall be till I die.*

I do from my soul confess that I never was satisfied till I came to Christ. When I was yet a child, I had far more wretchedness than ever I have now; I will even add more weariness, more care, more heartache than I know at this day. I may be singular in this confession, but I make it and know it to be the truth. Since that dear hour when my soul cast itself on Jesus, I have found solid joy and peace, but before that, all those supposed gaieties of early youth, all the imagined ease and joy of boyhood, were but vanity and vexation of spirit to me. That happy day when I found the Savior and learned to cling to His dear feet was a day never to be forgotten by me. An obscure child, unknown, unheard of, I listened to the Word of God, and that precious text led me to the cross of Christ. I can testify that the joy of that day was utterly indescribable. I could have leaped; I could have danced—there was no expression, however fanatical, that would have been out of keeping with the joy of my spirit at that hour. Many days of Christian experience have passed since then, but there has never been one that has had the full exhilaration, the sparkling delight that that first day had. I thought I could have sprung from the seat on which I sat and called out with the wildest of those Methodist brethren who were present, "I am forgiven! I am forgiven! A monument of grace! A sinner saved by blood!" My spirit saw its chains broken to pieces. I felt that I was an emancipated soul, an heir of heaven, a forgiven one, accepted in Christ Jesus, plucked out of the miry clay and out of the horrible pit, with my feet set upon a rock and my goings established. I thought I could dance all the way home. I could understand what John Bunyan meant when he declared he wanted to tell the crows on the plowed land all about his conversion. He was too full to hold—he felt he must tell somebody.

> *I felt that I was an emancipated soul, an heir of heaven, a forgiven one, accepted in Christ Jesus, plucked out of the miry clay and out of the horrible pit, with my feet set upon a rock and my goings established.*

It is not everyone who can remember the very day and hour of his deliverance, but, as Richard Knill said, "At such a time of the day, clang went every harp in heaven, for Richard Knill was born again," it was even so with me. The clock of mercy struck in heaven the hour and moment of my emancipation, for the time had come. Between half past ten o'clock, when I entered that chapel, and half past twelve o'clock, when I was back again at home, what a change had taken place in me! I had passed from darkness into marvelous light, from death to life. Simply by looking to Jesus, I had been delivered from despair, and I was brought into such a joyous state of mind that, when they saw me at home, they said to me, "Something wonderful has happened to you," and I was eager to tell them all about it. Oh! There was joy in the household that day, when all heard that the eldest son had found the Savior and knew himself to be forgiven, which was bliss compared with which all earth's joys are less than nothing and vanity. Yes, I had looked to Jesus as I was and found in Him my Savior. Thus had the eternal purpose of Jehovah decreed it. And as, the moment before, there was none more wretched than I was, so, within that second, there was none more joyous. It took no longer time than does the lightning flash; it was done, and never has it been undone. I looked, and lived, and leaped in joyful liberty as I beheld my sin punished upon the great Substitute and put away forever. I looked unto Him as He bled upon that tree. His eyes darted a glance of love unutterable into my spirit, and in a moment, I was saved. Looking unto Him, the bruises that my soul had suffered were healed, the gaping wounds were cured, the broken bones rejoiced, the rags that had covered me were all removed, my spirit was white as the spotless snows of the far-off North. I had melody within my spirit, for I was saved, washed, cleansed, forgiven through Him who did hang upon the tree. My Master, I cannot understand how you could stoop your awful head to such a death as the death of the cross, how you could take from your brow the coronet of stars that from old eternity had shone resplendent there. But how you should permit the thorn-crown to gird your temples astonishes me far more. That you should cast away the mantle of your glory, the azure of your everlasting empire, I cannot comprehend. But how you should have become veiled in the ignominious purple for a while and then be mocked by impious men who bowed to you as a pretended king; and how you should be stripped naked to your shame, without a single covering, and die a felon's death. This is still more incomprehensible. But the marvel is that you should have suffered all this for *me*! Truly, your love to me is wonderful, passing the love of women! Was ever grief like yours? Was ever love like yours, that could open the floodgates of such grief? Was ever love so mighty as to become the fount from which such an ocean of grief could come rolling down?

There was never anything so true to me as those bleeding hands and that thorn-crowned head. Home, friends, health, wealth, comforts—all lost their luster that day when He appeared, just as stars are hidden by the light of the sun. He was the only Lord and Giver of life's best bliss, the one well of living water springing up unto everlasting life. As I saw Jesus on His cross before me, and as I mused upon His sufferings and death, methought I saw Him cast a look of love upon me. And then I looked at Him and cried:

> *Jesus, lover of my soul,*
> *Let me to your bosom fly.*

He said, "Come," and I flew to Him and clasped Him, and when He let me go again, I wondered where my burden was. It was gone! There in the sepulcher it lay, and I felt light as air. Like a winged sylph, I could fly over mountains of trouble and despair, and oh, what liberty and joy I had! I could leap with ecstasy, for I had much forgiven, and I was freed from sin. With the spouse in the Canticles, I could say, "I found Him." I, a lad, found the Lord of glory. I, a slave to sin, found the great Deliverer. I, the child of darkness, found the Light of life. I, the uttermost of the lost, found my Savior and my God. I, widowed and desolate, found my friend, my beloved, my husband. Oh, how I wondered that *I* should be pardoned! It was not the pardon that I wondered at so much; the wonder was that it should come to *me*. I marveled that He should be able to pardon such sins as mine, such crimes, so numerous and so black; and that, after such an accusing conscience, He should have power to still every wave within my spirit and make my soul like the surface of a river, undisturbed, quiet, and at ease. It mattered not to me whether the day itself was gloomy or bright. I had found Christ; that was enough for me. He was my Savior, He was my all, and I can heartily say that one day of pardoned sin was a sufficient recompense for the whole five years of conviction. I have to bless God for every terror that ever scared me by night and for every foreboding that alarmed me by day. It has made me happier ever since, for now, if there be a trouble weighing upon my soul, I thank God it is not such a burden as that which bowed me to the very earth and made me creep upon the ground, like a beast, by reason of heavy distress and affliction. I know I never can again suffer what I have suffered; I never can, except I be sent to hell, know more of agony than I have known. And now, that ease, that joy and peace in believing, that no condemnation, which belongs to me as a child of God, is made doubly sweet and inexpressibly precious by the recollection of my past days of sorrow and grief. Blessed be you, O God, forever, who by those black days, like a dreary winter, has made these summer days all the fairer and the sweeter! I need not walk through the earth fearful of every shadow and afraid of every man I meet, for sin is washed away. My spirit is no more guilty; it is pure, it is holy. The frown of God no longer rests upon me, but my Father smiles. I see His eyes—they are glancing love; I hear His voice—it is full of sweetness. I am forgiven, I am forgiven, I am forgiven!

When I look back upon it, I can see one reason why the Word was blessed to me as I heard it preached in that Primitive Methodist chapel at Colchester. I had been up betimes crying to God for the blessing. As a lad, when I was seeking the Savior, I used to rise with the sun that I might get time to read gracious books and to seek the Lord. I can recall the kind of pleas I used when I took my arguments and came before the throne of grace: "Lord, save me; it will glorify your grace to save such a sinner as I am! Lord, save me; else I am lost to all eternity. Do not let me perish, Lord! Save me, O Lord, for Jesus died! By His agony and bloody sweat, by His cross and passion, save me!" I often proved that the early morning was the best part of the day; I liked those prayers of which the psalmist said, "In the morning my prayer comes before you" (Ps. 88:13).

> *If, beside the door of the place in which I met with Him, there had been a stake of blazing brushwood, I would have stood upon them without chains, glad to give my flesh and blood and bones to be ashes that should testify my love to Him.*

The Holy Spirit, who enabled me to believe, gave me peace through believing. I felt as sure that I was forgiven as before I felt sure of condemnation. I had been certain of my condemnation because the Word of God declared it, and my conscience bore witness to it; but when the Lord justified me, the same witnesses made me equally certain. The word of the Lord in the scripture says, "He who believes in Him is not condemned" (John 3:18), and my conscience bore witness that I believed, and that God in pardoning me was just. Thus I had the witness of the Holy Spirit and also of my own conscience, and these two agreed in one. That great and excellent man,

Dr. Johnson, used to hold the opinion that no man ever could know that he was pardoned; that there was no such thing as assurance of faith. Perhaps if Dr. Johnson had studied his Bible a little more, and had had a little more of the enlightenment of the Spirit, he, too, might have come to know his own pardon. Certainly, he was no very reliable judge of theology, any more than he was of porcelain, which he once attempted to make and never succeeded. I think both in theology and porcelain his opinion is of very little value.

How can a man know that he is pardoned? There is a text that says, "Believe on the Lord Jesus Christ, and thou shalt be saved" (Acts 16:31 KJV). I believe on the Lord Jesus Christ; is it irrational to believe that I am saved? I believe on Christ; am I absurd in believing that I have eternal life? I find the apostle Paul speaking by the Holy Spirit and saying, "Having been justified by faith, we have peace with God" (Rom. 5:1). If I know that my trust is fixed on Jesus only, and that I have faith in Him, were it not ten thousand times more absurd for me not to be at peace than for me to be filled with joy unspeakable? It is but taking God at His Word, when the soul knows as a necessary consequence of its faith that it is saved. I took Jesus as my Savior, and I was saved, and I can tell the reason why I took Him for my Savior. To my own humiliation, I must confess that I did it because I could not help it; I was shut up to it. That stern law work had hammered me into such a condition that, if there had been fifty other saviors, I could not have thought of them. I was driven to this One. I wanted a divine Savior. I wanted One who was made a curse for me, to expiate my guilt. I wanted One who had died, for I deserved to die. I wanted One who had risen again, who was able by His life to make me live. I wanted the exact Savior who stood before me in the Word, revealed to my heart; and I could not help having Him. I could realize then the language of Rutherford when, being full of love to Christ once upon a time in the dungeon of Aberdeen, he said, "O my Lord, if there were a broad hell betwixt me and you, if I could not get at you except by wading through it, I would not think twice, but I would go through it all, if I might but embrace you and call you mine!" Oh, how I loved Him! Passing all loves except His own was the love that I felt for Him then. If, beside the door of the place in which I met with Him, there had been a stake of blazing brushwood, I would have stood upon them without chains, glad to give my flesh and blood and bones to be ashes that should testify my love to Him. Had He asked me then to give all my substance to the poor, I would have given all and thought myself to be amazingly rich in having beggared myself for His name's sake. Had He commanded me then to preach in the midst of all His foes, I could have said:

> *There's not a lamb in all your flock*
> *I would disdain to feed,*
> *There's not a foe before whose face*
> *I'd fear your cause to plead.*

Has Jesus saved *me*? I dare not speak with any hesitation here; I *know* He has. His Word is true; therefore I *am* saved. My evidence that I am saved does not lie in the fact that I preach, or that I do this or that. All my hope lies in this, that Jesus Christ came to save sinners. I am a sinner, I trust Him, then He came to save me, and I am saved. I live habitually in the enjoyment of this blessed fact, and it is long since I have doubted the truth of it, for I have His own Word to sustain my faith. It is a very surprising thing, a thing to be marveled at most of all by those who enjoy it. I know that it is to me even to this day the greatest wonder that I ever heard of, that God should ever justify *me*. I feel myself to be a lump of unworthiness, a mass of corruption, and a heap of sin apart from His almighty love. Yet I know, by a full assurance, that I am justified by faith that is in Christ Jesus, and treated as if I had been perfectly just, and made an heir of God and a joint heir with Christ, though by nature I must take my place among the most sinful. I, who am altogether undeserving, am treated as if I had been deserving. I am loved with as much love as if I had always been godly, whereas aforetime I was ungodly.

I have always considered, with Luther and Calvin, that the sum and substance of the gospel lies in that word *substitution*: Christ standing in the stead of man. If I understand the gospel, it is this: I deserve to be lost forever. The only reason why I should not be damned is that Christ was punished in my stead, and there is no need to execute a sentence twice for sin. On the other hand, I know I cannot enter heaven unless I have a perfect righteousness. I am absolutely certain I shall never have one of my own, for I find I sin every day. But then Christ had a perfect righteousness, and He said,

"There, poor sinner, take my garment, and put it on; you shall stand before God as if you were Christ, and I will stand before God as if I had been the sinner; I will suffer in the sinner's stead, and you shall be rewarded for works that you did not do, but which I did for you." I find it very convenient every day to come to Christ as a sinner, as I came at the first. "You are no saint," says the devil. Well, if I am not, I am a sinner, and Jesus Christ came into the world to save sinners. Sink or swim, I go to Him; other hope I have none. By looking to Him, I received all the faith that inspired me with confidence in His grace, and the word that first drew my soul—"Look unto Me"—still rings its clarion note in my ears. There I once found conversion, and there I shall ever find refreshing and renewal.

> In life, He is my life, and in death, He shall be the death of death. In poverty, Christ is my riches. In sickness, He makes my bed. In darkness, He is my star. And in brightness, He is my sun.

Let me bear my personal testimony of what I have seen, what my own ears have heard and my own heart has tasted. First, Christ is the only begotten of the Father. He is divine to me, if He be human to all the world besides. He has done that for me which none but a God could do. He has subdued my stubborn will, melted a heart of adamant, broken a chain of steel, opened the gates of brass, and snapped the bars of iron. He has turned for me my mourning into laughter and my desolation into joy. He has led my captivity captive and made my heart rejoice with joy unspeakable and full of glory. Let others think as they will of Him; to me He must ever be the only begotten of the Father. Blessed be His holy name!

> Oh, that I could now adore Him,
> Like the heavenly host above,
> Who forever bow before Him,
> And unceasing sing His love!
> Happy songsters!
> When shall I your chorus join?

Again, I bear my testimony that He is full of grace. Ah, had He not been, I should never have beheld His glory. I was full of sin to overflowing.

I was condemned already, because I believed not upon Him. He drew me when I wanted not to come, and though I struggled hard, He continued still to draw. And when at last I came to His mercy seat, all trembling like a condemned culprit, He said, "Your sins, which are many, are all forgiven you. Be of good cheer." Let others despise Him, but I bear witness that He is full of grace.

Finally, I bear my witness that He is full of truth. True have His promises been; not one has failed. I have often doubted Him—for that I blush. He has never failed me; in this I must rejoice. His promises have been yea and amen. I do but speak the testimony of every believer in Christ, though I put it thus personally to make it the more forcible. I bear witness that never servant had such a Master as I have; never a brother had such a kinsman as He has been to me; never a spouse had such a husband as Christ has been to my soul; never a sinner a better Savior; never a soldier a better captain; never a mourner a better comforter than Christ has been to my spirit. I want none beside Him. In life, He is my life, and in death, He shall be the death of death. In poverty, Christ is my riches. In sickness, He makes my bed. In darkness, He is my star. And in brightness, He is my sun. By faith I understand that the blessed Son of God redeemed my soul with His own heart's blood, and by sweet experience I know that He raised me up from the pit of dark despair and set my feet on the rock. He died for me. This is the root of every satisfaction I have. He put all my transgressions away. He cleansed me with His precious blood; He covered me with His perfect righteousness; He wrapped me up in His own virtues. He has promised to keep me, while I abide in this world, from its temptations and snares. And when I depart from this world, He has already prepared for me a mansion in the heaven of unfading bliss, and a crown of everlasting joy that shall never, never fade away. To me, then, the days or years of my mortal sojourn on this earth are of little moment. Nor is the manner of my decease of much consequence. Should foemen sentence me to martyrdom, or physicians declare that I must soon depart this life, it is all alike:

> A few more rolling suns at most
> Shall land me on fair Canaan's coast.

What more can I wish than that, while my brief term on earth shall last, I should be the servant of Him who became the Servant of servants for me?

I can say, concerning Christ's religion, if I had to die like a dog and had no hope whatever of immortality, if I wanted to lead a happy life, let me serve my God with all my heart; let me be a follower of Jesus and walk in His footsteps. If there were no hereafter, I would still prefer to be a Christian, and the humblest Christian minister, to being a king or an emperor, for I am persuaded there are more delights in Christ, yea, more joy in one glimpse of His face than is to be found in all the praises of this harlot-world, and in all the delights that it can yield to us in its sunniest and brightest days. And I am persuaded that what He has been till now, He will be to the end; and where He has begun a good work, He will carry it on. In the religion of Jesus Christ, there are clusters even on earth too heavy for one man to carry. There are fruits that have been found so rich that even angel lips have never been sweetened with more luscious wine. There are joys to be had here so fair that even cates ambrosial and the nectared wine of paradise can scarcely excel the sweets of satisfaction that are to be found in the earthly banquets of the Lord. I have seen hundreds and thousands who have given their hearts to Jesus, but I never did see one who said he was disappointed with Him; I never met with one who said Jesus Christ was less than He was declared to be. When first my eyes beheld Him, when the burden slipped from off my heavy-laden shoulders and I was free from condemnation, I thought that all the preachers I had ever heard had not half preached—they had not told half the beauty of my Lord and Master. So good! So generous! So gracious! So willing to forgive! It seemed to me as if they had almost slandered Him; they painted His likeness, doubtless, as well as they could, but it was a mere smudge compared with the matchless beauties of His face. All who have ever seen Him will say the same. I go back to my home, many a time, mourning that I cannot preach my Master even as I myself know Him, and what I know of Him is very little compared with the matchlessness of His grace. Would that I knew more of Him, and that I could tell it out better!

2

EXPERIENCES AFTER CONVERSION

Our faith at times has to fight for its very existence. The old Adam within us rages mightily, and the new spirit within us, like a young lion, disdains to be vanquished; and so these two strong ones contend, till our spirit is full of agony. Some of us know what it is to be tempted with blasphemies we should not dare to repeat, to be vexed with horrid temptations that we have grappled with and overcome, but that have almost cost us resistance unto blood. In such inward conflicts, saints must be alone. They cannot tell their feelings to others—they would not dare. And if they did, their own brethren would despise or upbraid them, for the most of professors would not even know what they meant. Even those who have trodden other fiery ways would not be able to sympathize in all, but would answer the poor troubled soul, "These are points in which we cannot go with you." Christ alone was tempted in all points as we are, though without sin. No one man is tempted in all points exactly like another man, and each one has certain trials in which he must stand alone amid the rage of war, with not even a book to help him, or a biography to assist him—no man ever having gone that way before except that one Man whose trail reveals a nail-pierced foot. He alone knows all the devious paths of sorrow. Yet even in such byways, the Lord is with us, helping us, sustaining us, and giving us grace to conquer at the close.

—C. H. Spurgeon

WHEN my eyes first looked to Christ, He was a very real Christ to me; and when my burden of sin rolled from off my back, it was a real pardon and a real release from sin to me; and when that day I said for the first time, "Jesus Christ is mine," it was a real possession of Christ to me. When I went up to the sanctuary in that early dawn of youthful piety, every song was really a psalm, and when there was a prayer, oh, how I followed every word! It was prayer indeed! And so was it, too: in silent quietude, when I drew near to God, it was no mockery, no routine, no matter of mere duty; it was a real talking with my Father who is in heaven. And oh, how I loved my Savior Christ then! I would have given all I had for Him!

How I felt toward sinners that day! Lad that I was, I wanted to preach and

> *Tell to sinners round,*
> *What a dear Savior I had found.*

One of the greatest sorrows I had, when first I knew the Lord, was to think about certain persons with whom I knew right well that I had held ungodly conversations, and sundry others whom I had tempted to sin; and one of the prayers that I always offered, when I prayed for myself, was that such a one might not be lost through sins to which I had tempted him. This was the case also with George Whitefield, who never forgot those with whom, before his conversion, he used to play cards, and he had the joy of leading every one of them to the Savior.

I think about five days after I first found Christ, when my joy had been such that I could have danced for very mirth at the thought that Christ was mine, on a sudden I fell into a sad fit of despondency. I can tell now why it was so with me. When I first believed in Christ, I am not sure that I thought the devil was dead, but certainly I had a kind of notion that he was so mortally wounded that he could not disturb me. And then I also fancied that the corruption of my nature had received its deathblow. I read what Cowper said:

> *Since the dear hour that brought me to Thy foot,*
> *And cut up all my follies by the root.*

I really thought that the poet knew what he was saying; whereas, never did anyone blunder so terribly as Cowper did when he said that, for no man, I think, has all his follies thus cut up by the roots. However, I fondly dreamed that mine were; I felt persuaded they would never sprout again. I was going to be perfect. I fully calculated upon it, and lo, I found an intruder I had not reckoned upon, an evil heart of unbelief in departing from the living God. So I went to that same Primitive Methodist chapel where I first received peace with God through the simple preaching of the Word. The text happened to be "O wretched man that I am! Who will deliver me from this body of death?" (Rom. 7:24). *There,* I thought, *that's the text for me.* I had just got as far as that in the week. I knew that I had put my trust in Christ, and I knew that, when I sat in that house of prayer, my faith was simply and solely fixed on the atonement of the Redeemer. But I had a weight on my mind, because I could not be as holy as I wanted to be. I could not live without sin. When I rose in the morning, I thought I would abstain from every hard word, from every evil thought and look, and I came up to that chapel groaning because "when I would do good, evil is present with me" (Rom. 7:21 KJV). The minister began by saying, "Paul was not a believer when he said this." Well now, I knew I was a believer, and it seemed to me from the context that Paul must have been a believer, too. (Now, I am sure he was.) The man went on to say that no child of God ever did feel any conflict within. So I took up my hat and left the chapel, and I have very seldom attended such places since. They are very good for people who are unconverted to go to, but of very little use for children of God. That is my notion of Methodism. It is a noble thing to bring in strangers, but a terrible thing for those who are brought in to sit and feed there. It is like the parish pound: it is a good place to put sheep in when they have strayed, but there is no food inside. They had better be let out as soon as possible to find some grass. I maintain that that minister understood nothing of experimental divinity, or of practical heart theology, or else he would not have talked as he did. A good man he was, I do not doubt, but utterly incompetent to the task of dealing with a case like mine.

> *I* was going to be perfect. I fully calculated upon it, and lo, I found an intruder I had not reckoned upon, an evil heart of unbelief in departing from the living God.

Oh, what a horror I have had of sin ever since the day when I felt its power over my soul! O sin, *sin,* I have had enough of you! You never did bring me more than a moment's seeming joy, and with it there came a deep and awful bitterness that burns within me to this day! Well do I recollect when I was the subject of excessive tenderness. Some people called it morbid sensibility. How I shuddered and shivered at the very thought of sin, which then appeared exceedingly sinful! The first week after I was converted to God, I felt afraid to put one foot before the other for fear I should do wrong. When I thought over the day, if there had been a failure in my temper, or if there had been a frothy word spoken, or something done amiss, I did chasten myself sorely. Had I, at that time, known anything to be my Lord's will, I think I should not have hesitated to do it; to me it would not have mattered whether it was a fashionable thing or an unfashionable thing, if it was according to His Word. Oh, to do His will! To follow Him whithersoever He would have me go! It seemed then as though I should never, never, never be slack in keeping His commandments.

I do not know whether the experience of others agrees with mine, but I can say this, that the worst difficulty I ever met with, or I think I can ever meet with, happened a little time after my conversion to God. When I first knew the weight of sin, it was as a burden, as a labor, as a trouble; but when, the second time—

> *I asked the Lord that I might grow,*
> *In faith, and love, and every grace;*
> *Might more of His salvation know,*
> *And seek more earnestly His face—*

and when He answered me by letting all my sins loose upon me, they appeared more frightful than before. I thought the Egyptians in Egypt were not half so bad as the Egyptians out of Egypt; I thought the sins I knew before, though they were cruel taskmasters, were not half so much to be dreaded as those soldier-sins, armed with spears and axes, riding in iron chariots with scythes upon their axles, hastening to assault me. It is true, they did not come so near to me as heretofore; nevertheless, they occasioned me more fright even than when I was their slave. The Israelites went up harnessed, marching in their ranks and, I doubt not, singing as they went, because they were delivered from the daily task and from the cruel bondage. But suddenly they turned their heads while they were marching, for they heard a dreadful noise behind them, a noise of chariots and of men shouting for battle. And at last, when they could really see the Egyptians and the thick cloud of dust rising behind them, then they said that they should be destroyed—they should now fall by the hand of the enemy. I remember, after my conversion (it may not have happened to all, but it did to me), there came a time when the enemy said, "I will pursue, I will overtake, I will divide the spoil; my desire shall be satisfied on them. I will draw my sword, my hand shall destroy them" (Exod. 15:9). So Satan, loath to leave a soul, pursues it hotfoot. He will have it back if he can; and often, soon after conversion, there comes a time of dreadful conflict, when the soul seems as if it could not live. "Was it because there were no graves in Egypt that the Lord brought us into this condition of temporary freedom, that we might be all the more distressed by our adversaries?" So said unbelief. But God brought His people right out by one final stroke. Miriam knew it when she took her timbrel and went forth with the women and answered them in the jubilant song, "I will sing to the Lord, for He has triumphed gloriously! The horse and its rider He has thrown into the sea!" (Exod. 15:1). What gladness must have been in the hearts of the children of Israel when they knew that their enemies were all gone! I am sure it was so with me, for after my conversion, being again attacked by sin, I saw the mighty stream of redeeming love roll over all my sins, and this was my song: "Who shall lay any thing to the charge of God's elect? It is God that justifies. Who is he that condemneth? It is Christ that died, yea rather, that is risen again, who is even at the right hand of God, who also maketh intercession for us" (Rom. 8:33–34 kjv).

I was brought up, as a child, with such care that I knew but very little of foul or profane language, having scarcely ever heard a man swear. Yet do I remember times, in my earliest Christian days, when there came into my mind thoughts so evil that I clapped my hand to my mouth for fear I should be led to give utterance to them. This is one way in which Satan tortures those whom God has delivered out of his hand. Many of the choicest saints have been thus molested.

Once, when the tempter had grievously assailed me, I went to see my dear old grandfather. I told him about my terrible experience, and then I wound up by saying, "Grandfather, I am sure I cannot be a child of God, or else I should never have such evil thoughts as these."

"Nonsense, Charles," answered the good old man. "It is just because you are a Christian that you are thus tempted. These blasphemies are no children of yours; they are the devil's brats, which he delights to lay at the door of a Christian. Don't you own them as yours; give them neither house-room or heart-room."

I felt greatly comforted by what my grandfather said, especially as it confirmed what another old saint had told me when I was tempted in a similar manner while I was seeking the Savior.

A great many people make fun of that verse:

'Tis a point I long to know,
Oft it causes anxious thought,
Do I love the Lord, or no?
Am I His, or am I not?

If they ever find themselves where some of us have been, they will not do so anymore. I believe it is a shallow experience that makes people always confident of what they are, and where they are, for there are times of terrible trouble that make even the most confident child of God hardly know whether he is on his head or on his heels. It is the mariner who has done business on great waters who, in times of unusual stress and storm, reels to and fro and staggers like a drunken man and is at his wit's end. At such a time, if Jesus whispers that I am His, then the question is answered once for all, and my soul has received a token that it waves in the face of Satan, so that he disappears, and I can go on my way rejoicing.

> Who is he that condemneth? It is Christ that died, yea rather, that is risen again, who is even at the right hand of God, who also maketh intercession for us.

I have found, in my own spiritual life, that the more rules I lay down for myself, the more sins I commit. The habit of regular morning and evening prayer is one that is indispensable to a believer's life, but the prescribing of the length of prayer, and the constrained remembrance of so many persons and subjects, may gender unto bondage and strangle prayer rather than assist it. To say I will humble myself at such a time, and rejoice at such another season, is nearly as much an affectation as when the preacher wrote in the margin of his sermon, "Cry here," "Smile here." Why, if the man preached from his heart, he would be sure to cry in the right place and to smile at a suitable moment; and when the spiritual life is sound, it produces prayer at the right time, and humiliation of soul and sacred joy spring forth spontaneously, apart from rules and vows. The kind of religion that makes itself to order by the almanac and turns out its emotions like bricks from a machine, weeping on Good Friday and rejoicing two days afterward, measuring its motions by the moon, is too artificial to be worthy of my imitation.

Self-examination is a very great blessing, but I have known self-examination carried on in a most unbelieving, legal, and self-righteous manner; in fact, I have so carried it on myself. Time was when I used to think a vast deal more of marks and signs and evidences, for my own comfort, than I do now, for I find that I cannot be a match for the devil when I begin dealing in these things.

I am obliged to go day by day with this cry:

> *I the chief of sinners am,*
> *But Jesus died for me.*

While I can believe the promise of God, because it is His promise and because He is my God, and while I can trust my Savior because He is God, and therefore mighty to save, all goes well with me. But I do find, when I begin questioning myself about this and that perplexity, thus taking my eye off Christ, that all the virtue of my life seems oozing out at every pore. Any practice that detracts from faith is an evil practice, but especially that kind of self-examination that would take us away from the foot of the cross proceeds in a wrong direction.

I used, when I first knew the Savior, to try myself in a certain manner, and often did I throw stumbling blocks in my path through it, and therefore I can warn any who are doing the same. Sometimes I would go up into my chamber, and by way of self-examination, I used to ask myself this question: "Am I afraid to die? If I should drop down dead in my room, can I say that I should joyfully close my eyes?"

Well, it often happened that I could not honestly say so. I used to feel that death would be a very solemn thing. "Ah, then!" I said. "I have never believed in Christ, for if I had put my trust in the Lord Jesus, I should not be afraid to die, but I should be quite confident."

I do not doubt that many a person is saying, "I cannot follow Christ, because I am afraid to die; I cannot believe that Jesus Christ will save me, because the thought of death makes me tremble."

Ah, poor soul, there are many of God's blessed ones who through fear of death have been much of their lifetime subject to bondage! I know precious children of God now who, when they die, will die triumphantly; but I know this, that the thought of death is never pleasing to them. And this is accounted for because God has stamped on nature that law, the love of life and self-preservation, and it is natural enough that the man who has kindred and friends should scarcely like to leave behind those who are so dear. I know that, when he gets more grace, he will rejoice in the thought of death; but I do know that there are many quite safe who will die rejoicing in Christ, who now, in the prospect of death, feel afraid of it. My aged grandfather once preached a sermon that I have not yet forgotten. He was preaching from the text "The God of all grace" (1 Pet. 5:10), and he somewhat interested the assembly, after describing the different kinds of grace that God gave, by saying at the end of each period, "But there is one kind of grace that you do not want." After each part of his theme, there came the like sentence, "But there is one kind of grace you do not want." And then he wound up by saying, "*You* don't want dying grace in living moments, but you shall have dying grace when you need it. When you are in the condition to require it, you shall have grace enough if you put your trust in Christ." In a party of friends, we were discussing the question whether, if the days of martyrdom should come, we were prepared to be burned. I said, "I must frankly tell you that, speaking as I feel today, I am not prepared to be burned; but I do believe that if there were a stake at Smithfield, and I knew that I was to be burned there at one o'clock, I should have grace enough to be burned there when one o'clock came."

I was much impressed, in my younger days, by hearing a minister, blind with age, speak at the communion table and bear witness to us who had just joined the church that it was well for us that we had come to put our trust in a faithful God. And as the good man, with great feebleness and yet with great earnestness, said to us that he had never regretted having given himself to Christ as a boy, I felt my heart leap within me with delight that I had such a God to be my God. His testimony was such as a younger man could not have borne. He might have spoken more fluently, but the weight of those eighty years at the back of it made the old man eloquent to my young heart. For twenty years he had not seen the light of the sun. His snow-white locks hung from his brow and floated over his shoulders, and he stood up at the table of the Lord and thus addressed us: "Brethren and sisters, I shall soon be taken from you; in a few more months, I shall gather up my feet in my bed and sleep with my fathers. I have not the mind of the learned or the tongue of the eloquent, but I desire, before I go, to bear one public testimony to my God. Fifty and six years have I served Him, and I have never once found Him unfaithful. I can say, 'Surely goodness and mercy have followed me all the days of my life, and not one good thing has failed of all the Lord God has promised.'" There stood the dear old man, tottering into his tomb, deprived of the light of heaven naturally, and yet having the Light of heaven in a better sense shining into his soul. And though he could not look upon us, yet he turned toward us, and he seemed to say, "Young people, trust God in early life, for I have not to regret that I sought Him too soon. I have only to mourn that so many of my years ran to waste." There is nothing that more tends to strengthen the faith of the young believer than to hear the veteran Christian, covered with scars from the battle, testifying that the service of his Master is a happy service, and that, if he could have served any other master, he would not have done so, for His service is pleasant and His reward everlasting joy.

> *God has stamped on nature that law, the love of life and self-preservation, and it is natural enough that the man who has kindred and friends should scarcely like to leave behind those who are so dear.*

In my early days, I knew a good man who has now gone to his reward who was the means of producing, under God, a library of useful lives. I do not mean books in paper, but books in boots! Many young men were decided for the Lord by his means and became preachers, teachers, deacons, and other workers; and no one would wonder that it was so, if he knew the man who trained them. He was ready for every good word and work, but he gave special attention to his Bible class, in which he set forth the gospel with clearness and zeal. Whenever any one of his young men left the country town in which he lived, he would be sure to arrange a parting interview. There was a wide spreading oak down in the fields, and there he was wont to keep an early morning appointment with John, or Thomas, or William, and that appointment very much consisted of earnest pleading with the Lord that, in going up to the great city, the young man might be kept from sin and made useful. Under that tree several decided for the Savior. It was an impressive act and left its influence upon them, for many men came, in after years, to see the spot made sacred by their teacher's prayers.

Oh! How my young heart once ached in boyhood when I first loved the Savior. I was far away from father and mother and all I loved, and I thought my heart would burst; for I was an usher in a school, in a place where I could meet with little sympathy or help. Well, I went to my chamber and told my little griefs into the ears of Jesus. They were great griefs to me then, though they are nothing now. When on my knees I just whispered them into the ear of Him who had loved me with an everlasting love, oh, it was so sweet! If I had told them to others, they would have told them again, but He, my blessed confidant, knows all my secrets, and He never tells again.

There is one verse of scripture that, as a young believer, I used often to repeat, for it was very dear to me; it is this: "Bind the sacrifice with cords to the horns of the altar" (Ps. 118:27). I did feel then that I was wholly Christ's. In the marriage covenant of which the Lord speaks, when the husband put the ring upon his bride's finger, he said to her, "You have become mine"; and I remember when I felt upon my finger the ring of infinite, everlasting, covenant love that Christ put there. Oh, it was a joyful day, a blessed day! Happy day, happy day, when His choice was known to me, and He fixed my choice on Him! That blessed rest of soul, which comes of a sure possession of Christ, is not to be imitated, but it is greatly to be desired. I know that some good people, who I believe will be saved, nevertheless do not attain to this sweet rest. They keep on thinking that it is something that they may get when they are very old, or when they are about to die, but they look upon the full assurance of faith and the personal grasping of Christ and saying, "My Beloved is mine," as something very dangerous. I began my Christian life in this happy fashion as a boy fifteen years of age. I believed fully and without hesitation in the Lord Jesus Christ, and when I went to see a good Christian woman, I was simple enough to tell her that I believed in Christ, that He was mine, and that He had saved me. I expressed myself very confidently concerning the great truth that God would never forsake His people or leave His work undone. I was at once chided and told that I had no right to speak so confidently, for it was presumptuous. The good woman said to me, "Ah! I don't like such assurance as that," and then she added, "I trust you are believing in Christ. I hope so, but I have never got beyond a hope or a trust, and I am an old woman." Bless the old woman, she was no example for us who know whom we have believed; we ought to rise far above that groveling kind of life. The man who begins right, the boy who begins right, and the girl who begins right will begin by saying, "God has said it: 'He who believes in Him is not condemned' [see Mark 16:16]. I believe in Him; therefore I am not condemned. Christ is mine."

Before my conversion, I was accustomed to reading the scriptures to admire their grandeur, to feel the charm of their history and wonder at the majesty of their language, but I altogether missed the Lord's intent therein. But when the Spirit came with His divine life and quickened the entire book to my newly enlightened soul, the inner meaning shone forth with wondrous glory. I was not in a frame of mind to judge God's Word, but I accepted it all without demur. I did not venture to sit in judgment upon my judge and become the reviser of the unerring God.

I remember when I felt upon my finger the ring of infinite, everlasting, covenant love that Christ put there. Oh, it was a joyful day, a blessed day!

Whatever I found to be in His Word, I received with intense joy. From that hour, I bless God that, being not exempt from trouble, and especially not free from a tendency to despondency that is always with me, I yet rejoice and will rejoice, and am happy, unspeakably happy in resting upon Jesus Christ. Moreover, I have found that those points of my character that were most weak have been strengthened, while strong passions have been subdued, evil propensities have been kept under, and new principles have been implanted. I am changed; I am as different from what I was as a man could be who had been annihilated and had then been made over again. Nor do I claim any of the credit for this change—far from it. God has done great things for me, but He has done the same for others and is willing to do it for any soul who seeks His face through Jesus Christ and His great atoning sacrifice.

I have known some men who were almost idiots before conversion, but they afterward had their faculties wonderfully developed. Some time ago, there was a man who was so ignorant that he could not read, and he never spoke anything like grammar in his life, unless by mistake; and, moreover, he was considered to be what the people in his neighborhood called "daft." But when he was converted, the first thing he did was to pray. He stammered out a few words, and in a little time his powers of speaking began to develop themselves. Then he thought he would like to read the scriptures, and after long, long months of labor, he learned to read. And what was the next thing? He thought he could preach, and he did preach a little, in his own homely way, in his house. Then he thought, *I must read a few more books.* And so his mind expanded, until I believe he is at the present day a useful minister, settled in a country village, laboring for God.

> *It seemed to me as if, when I had discovered Christ and Him crucified, I had found the center of the system, so that I could see every other science revolving in due order.*

An idea has long possessed the public mind that a religious man can scarcely be a wise man. It has been the custom to talk of infidels, atheists, and deists as men of deep thought and comprehensive intellect, and to tremble for the Christian controversialist as if he must surely fall by the hand of his enemy. But this is purely a mistake, for the gospel is the sum of wisdom, an epitome of knowledge, a treasure house of truth, and a revelation of mysterious secrets. In it we see how justice and mercy may be married; here we behold inexorable law entirely satisfied and sovereign love bearing away the sinner in triumph. Our meditation upon it enlarges the mind, and as it opens to our soul in successive flashes of glory, we stand astonished at the profound wisdom manifest in it. I have often said that, before I knew the gospel, I had gathered up a heterogenous mass of all kinds of knowledge from here, there, and everywhere: a bit of chemistry, a bit of botany, a bit of astronomy, and a bit of this, that, and the other. I put them all together in one great, confused chaos, but when I learned the gospel, I got a shelf in my head to put everything upon just where it should be. It seemed to me as if, when I had discovered Christ and Him crucified, I had found the center of the system, so that I could see every other science revolving in due order. From the earth, the planets appear to move in a very irregular manner. They are progressive, retrograde, or stationary. But if you could get upon the sun, you would see them marching round in their constant, uniform, circular motion. So is it with knowledge. Begin with any other science you like, and truth will seem to be all awry. Begin with the science of Christ crucified, and you will begin with the sun; you will see every other science moving round it in complete harmony. The greatest mind in the world will be evolved by beginning at the right end. The old saying is "Go from nature up to nature's

God," but it is hard work going uphill. The best thing is to go from nature's God down to nature; and if you once get to nature's God and believe Him and love Him, it is surprising how easy it is to hear music in the waves and songs in the wild whisperings of the winds, to see God everywhere, in the stones, in the rocks, in the rippling brooks, and to hear Him everywhere, in the lowing of cattle, in the rolling of thunder, and in the fury of tempests. Christ is to me the wisdom of God. I can learn everything now that I know the science of Christ crucified.

3

Defense of Calvinism

*The old truth that Calvin preached, that Augustine preached,
that Paul preached, is the truth that I must preach today,
or else be false to my conscience and my God. I cannot
shape the truth; I know of no such thing as paring off the
rough edges of a doctrine. John Knox's gospel is my gospel.
That which thundered through Scotland must thunder through
England again.*

—C. H. Spurgeon

IT is a great thing to begin the Christian life by believing good solid doctrine. Some people have received twenty different "gospels" in as many years; how many more they will accept before they get to their journey's end, it would be difficult to predict. I thank God that He early taught me the gospel, and I have been so perfectly satisfied with it that I do not want to know any other. Constant change of creed is sure loss. If a tree has to be taken up two or three times a year, you will not need to build a very large loft in which to store the apples. When people are always shifting their doctrinal principles, they are not likely to bring forth much fruit to the glory of God. It is good for young believers to begin with a firm hold upon those great fundamental doctrines that the Lord has taught in His Word. Why, if I believed what some preach about the temporary, trumpery salvation that only lasts for a time, I would scarcely be at all grateful for it. But when I know that those whom God saves He saves with an everlasting salvation, when I know that He gives to them an everlasting righteousness, when I know that He settles them on an everlasting foundation of everlasting love and that He will bring them to His everlasting kingdom, oh, then I do wonder, and I am astonished that such a blessing as this should ever have been given to me!

Pause, my soul! Adore and wonder!
Ask, "Oh, why such love to me?"
Grace has put me in the number
Of the Savior's family:
Hallelujah!
Thanks, eternal thanks, to You.

I suppose there are some persons whose minds naturally incline toward the doctrine of free will. I can only say that mine inclines as naturally toward the doctrine of sovereign grace. Sometimes, when I see some of the worst characters in the street, I feel as if my heart must burst forth in tears of gratitude that God has never let me act as they have done! I have thought, if God had left me alone and had not touched me by His grace, what a great sinner I should have been! I should have run to the utmost lengths of sin, dived into the very depths of evil, nor should I have stopped at any vice or folly if God had not restrained me. I feel that I should have been a very king of sinners if God had let me alone. I cannot understand the reason why I am saved, except upon the ground that God would have it so. I cannot, if I look ever so earnestly, discover any kind of reason in myself why I should be a partaker of divine grace. If I am not at this moment without Christ, it is only because Christ Jesus would have His will with me, and that will was that I should be with Him where He is and should share His glory. I can put the crown nowhere but upon the head of Him whose mighty grace has saved me from going down into the pit. Looking back on my past life, I can see that the dawning of it all was of God, of God effectively. I took no torch with which to light the sun, but the sun enlightened me. I did not commence my spiritual life. No, I rather kicked and struggled against the things of the Spirit. When He drew me, for a time I did not run after Him; there was a natural hatred in my soul of everything holy and good. Wooings were lost upon me, warnings were cast to the wind, thunders were despised; and as for the whispers of His love, they were rejected as being less than nothing and vanity. But sure I am that I can say now, speaking on behalf of myself, "He only is my salvation" (Ps. 62:2). It was He who turned my heart and brought me down on my knees before Him. I can, in very deed, say with Doddridge and Toplady:

> *Grace taught my soul to pray,*
> *And made my eyes o'erflow.*

And, coming to this moment, I can add:

> *'Tis grace has kept me to this day,*
> *And will not let me go.*

Well can I remember the manner in which I learned the doctrines of grace in a single instant. Born, as all of us are by nature, an Arminian, I still believed the old things I had heard continually from the pulpit, and did not see the grace of God. When I was coming to Christ, I thought I was doing it all myself, and though I sought the Lord earnestly, I had no idea the Lord was seeking me. I do not think the young convert is at first aware of this. I can recall the very day and hour when first I received those truths in my own soul, when they were, as John Bunyan says, burned into my heart as with a hot iron. And I can recollect how I felt that I had grown on a sudden from a babe into a man, that I had made progress in scriptural knowledge, through having found, once for all, the clue to the truth of God. One weeknight, when I was sitting in the house of God, I was not thinking much about the preacher's sermon, for I did not believe it. The thought struck me, *How did you come to be a Christian?* I sought the Lord. *But how did you come to seek the Lord?* The truth flashed across my mind in a moment: I should not have sought Him unless there had been some previous influence in my mind to make me seek Him. *I prayed,* thought I, but then I asked myself, *How came I to pray?* I was induced to pray by reading the scriptures. *How came I to read the scriptures? I did read them, but what led me to do so?* Then, in a moment, I saw that God was at the bottom of it all, and that He was the author of my faith, and so the whole doctrine of grace opened up to me, and from that doctrine I have not departed to this day, and I desire to make this my constant confession: "I ascribe my change wholly to God."

I once attended a service where the text happened to be "He will choose our inheritance for us" (Ps. 47:4), and the good man who occupied the pulpit was more than a little of an Arminian. Therefore, when he commenced, he said, "This passage refers entirely to our temporal inheritance; it has nothing whatever to do with our everlasting destiny. For," said he, "we do not want

Christ to choose for us in the matter of heaven or hell. It is so plain and easy that every man who has a grain of common sense will choose heaven, and any person would know better than to choose hell. We have no need of any superior intelligence, or any greater being, to choose heaven or hell for us. It is left to our own free will, and we have enough wisdom given us, sufficiently correct means, to judge for ourselves." And therefore, as he very logically inferred, there was no necessity for Jesus Christ, or anyone, to make a choice for us. We could choose the inheritance for ourselves without any assistance. *Ah!* I thought. *But, my good brother, it may be very true that we could, but I think we should want something more than common sense before we should choose aright.*

suppose there are some persons whose minds naturally incline toward the doctrine of free will. I can only say that mine inclines as naturally toward the doctrine of sovereign grace.

First, let me ask, must we not all of us admit an overruling providence, and the appointment of Jehovah's hand, as to the means whereby we came into this world? Those men who think that, afterward, we are left to our own free will to choose this one or the other to direct our steps must admit that our entrance into the world was not of our own will, but that God had then to choose for us. What circumstances were those in our power that led us to elect certain persons to be our parents? Had we anything to do with it? Did not God Himself appoint our parents, native place, and friends? Could He not have caused me to be born with the skin of the Hottentot, brought forth by a filthy mother who would nurse me in her kraal and teach me to bow down to pagan gods, quite as easily as to have given me a pious mother, who would each morning and night bend her knee in prayer on my behalf? Or, might He not, if He had pleased, have given me some profligate to have been my parent, from whose lips I might have early heard fearful, filthy, and obscene language? Might He not have placed me where I should have had a drunken father, who would have immured me in a very dungeon of ignorance and brought me up in the chains of crime? Was it not God's providence that I had so happy a lot that both my parents were His children and endeavored to train me up in the fear of the Lord?

John Newton used to tell a whimsical story, and laugh at it, too, of a good woman who said, in order to prove the doctrine of election, "Ah, sir, the Lord must have loved me before I was born, or else He would not have seen anything in me to love afterward." I am sure it is true in my case; I believe the doctrine of election, because I am quite certain that if God had not chosen me, I should never have chosen Him; and I am sure He chose me before I was born, or else He never would have chosen me afterward; and He must have elected me for reasons unknown to me, for I never could find any reason in myself why He should have looked upon me with special love. So I am forced to accept that great biblical doctrine. I recollect an Arminian brother telling me that he had read the scriptures through a score or more times and could never find the doctrine of election in them. He added that he was sure he would have done so if it had been there, for he read the Word on his knees. I said to him, "I think you read the Bible in a very uncomfortable posture, and if you had read it in your easy chair, you would have been more likely to understand it. Pray, by all means, and the more, the better, but it is a piece of superstition to think there is anything in the posture in which a man puts himself for reading. And as to reading through the Bible twenty times without having found anything about the doctrine of election, the wonder is that you found anything at all. You must have galloped through it at such a rate that you were not likely to have any intelligible idea of the meaning of the scriptures."

> Must we not all of us admit an overruling providence, and the appointment of Jehovah's hand, as to the means whereby we came into this world?

If it would be marvelous to see one river leap up from the earth full grown, what would it be to gaze upon a vast spring from which all the rivers of the earth should at once come bubbling up, a million of them born at a birth? What a vision would it be! Who can conceive it? And yet the love of God is that fountain from which all the rivers of mercy that have ever gladdened our race, all the rivers of grace in time and of glory hereafter, take their rise. My soul, stand at that sacred fountainhead and adore and magnify for ever and ever God, even our Father, who has loved us! In the very beginning, when this great universe lay in the mind of God, like unborn forests in the acorn cup; long before the echoes awoke the solitudes; before the mountains were brought forth; and long before the light flashed through the sky, God loved His chosen creatures. Before there was any created being, when the ether was not fanned by an angel's wing, when space itself had not an existence, when there was nothing save God alone—even then, in that loneliness of deity and in that deep quiet and profundity, His bowels moved with love for His chosen. Their names were written on His heart, and then were they dear to His soul. Jesus loved His people before the foundation of the world, even from eternity! And when He called me by His grace, He said to me, "I have loved you with an everlasting love; therefore with lovingkindness I have drawn you" (Jer. 31:3).

> No Christian man will ever say that faith came of itself without the gift and without the working of the Holy Spirit.

Then, in the fullness of time, He purchased me with His blood; He let His heart run out in one deep gaping wound for me long before I loved Him. Yea, when He first came to me, did I not spurn Him? When He knocked at the door and asked for entrance, did I not drive Him away and do despite to His grace? Ah, I can remember that I full often did so until, at last, by the power of His effectual grace, He said, "I must, I will come in." And then He turned my heart and made me love Him. But even till now I should have resisted Him, had it not been for His grace. Well then, since He purchased me when I was dead in sins, does it not follow, as a consequence necessary and logical, that He must have loved me first? Did my Savior die for me because I believed on Him? No; I was not then in existence; I had then no being. Could the Savior therefore have died because I had faith, when I myself was not yet born? Could that have been possible? Could that have been the origin of the Savior's love toward me? Oh no; my Savior died for me long before I believed. "But," says someone, "He foresaw that you would have faith, and therefore He loved you." What did He foresee about my faith? Did He foresee that I should get that faith myself, and that I should believe on Him of myself? No; Christ could not foresee that, because no Christian man will ever say that faith came of itself without the gift and without the working of the Holy Spirit. I have met with a great many believers and talked with them about this matter, but I never knew one who could put his hand on his heart and say, "I believed in Jesus without the assistance of the Holy Spirit."

I am bound to the doctrine of the depravity of the human heart, because I find myself depraved in heart and have daily proofs that in my flesh there dwells no good thing. If God enters into covenant with unfallen man, man is so insignificant a creature that it must be an act of gracious condescension on the Lord's part; but if God enters into covenant with sinful man, he is then so offensive a creature that it must be, on God's part, an act of pure, free, rich, sovereign grace. When the Lord entered into covenant with me, I am sure that it was all of grace, nothing else but grace. When I remember what a den of unclean beasts and birds my heart was, and how strong was my unrenewed will, how obstinate and rebellious against the sovereignty of the divine rule, I always feel inclined to take the very lowest room in my Father's house. And when I enter heaven, it will be to go among the less than the least of all saints, and with the chief of sinners.

> God has a mastermind. He arranged everything in His gigantic intellect long before He did it, and once having settled it, He never alters it. "This shall be done," says He, and the iron hand of destiny marks it down, and it is brought to pass. "This is My purpose," and it stands. Nor can earth or hell alter it. "This is My decree,"

The late lamented Mr. Denham has put, at the foot of his portrait, a most admirable text, "Salvation is of the LORD" (Jonah 2:9). That is just an epitome of Calvinism; it is the sum and substance of it. If anyone should ask me what I mean by a Calvinist, I should reply, "He is one who says, Salvation is of the Lord." I cannot find in scripture any other doctrine than this. It is the essence of the Bible. Tell me anything contrary to this truth, and it will be a heresy; tell me a heresy, and I shall find its essence here, that it has departed from this great, this fundamental, this rock-truth, "God is my rock and my salvation." What is the heresy of Rome, but the addition of something to the perfect merits of Jesus Christ; the bringing in of the works of the flesh to assist in our justification? And what is the heresy of Arminianism but the addition of something to the work of the Redeemer?

Every heresy, if brought to the touchstone, will discover itself here. I have my own private opinion that there is no such thing as preaching Christ and Him crucified unless we preach what nowadays is called Calvinism. It is a nickname to call it Calvinism. Calvinism is the gospel, and nothing else. I do not believe we can preach the gospel if we do not preach justification by faith without works; or unless we preach the sovereignty of God in His dispensation of grace; or unless we exalt the electing, unchangeable, eternal, immutable, conquering love of Jehovah Nor do I think we can preach the gospel unless we base it upon the special and particular redemption of His elect and chosen people that Christ wrought out upon the cross. Nor can I comprehend a gospel that lets saints fall away after they are called, and suffers the children of God to be burned in the fires of damnation after having once believed in Jesus. Such a gospel I abhor.

> *If ever it should come to pass,*
> *That sheep of Christ might fall away,*
> *My fickle, feeble soul, alas!*
> *Would fall a thousand times a day*

If one dear saint of God had perished, so might all; if one of the covenant ones be lost, so may all be. And then there is no gospel promise true, but the Bible is a lie, and there is nothing in it worth my acceptance. I will be an infidel at once when I can believe that a saint of God can ever fall finally. If God has loved me once, then He will love me forever. God has a mastermind. He arranged everything in His gigantic intellect long before He did it, and once having settled it, He never alters it. "This shall be done," says He, and the iron hand of destiny marks it down, and it is brought to pass. "This is my purpose," and it stands. Nor can earth or hell alter it. "This is my decree," says He. "Promulgate it, you holy angels; rend it down from the gate of heaven, you devils, if you can; but you cannot alter the decree. It shall stand forever." God does not alter His plans; why should He? He is almighty and therefore can perform His pleasure. Why should He? He is the all-wise and therefore cannot have planned wrongly. Why should He? He is the everlasting God and therefore cannot die before His plan is accomplished. Why should He change? You worthless atoms of earth, ephemera of a day, you creeping insects upon this bay leaf of existence, you may change your plans, but He shall never, never change His. Has He told me that His plan is to save me? If so, I am forever safe.

> *My name from the palms of His hands*
> *Eternity will not erase;*
> *Impress'd on His heart it remains,*
> *In marks of indelible grace.*

I do not know how some people who believe that a Christian can fall from grace manage to be happy. It must be a very commendable thing in them to be able to get through a day without despair. If I did not believe the doctrine of the final perseverance of the saints, I think I should be of all men the most miserable, because I should lack any ground of comfort. I could not say, whatever state of heart I came into, that I should be like a wellspring of water whose stream fails not. I should rather have to take the comparison of an intermittent spring, which might stop on a sudden, or a reservoir, which I had no reason to expect would always be full. I believe that the happiest of Christians and the truest of Christians are those who never dare to doubt God, but who take His Word simply as it stands and believe it and ask no questions, just feeling assured that if God has said it, it will be so. I bear my willing testimony that I have no reason, or even the shadow of a reason, to doubt my Lord, and I challenge heaven and earth and hell to bring any proof that God is untrue. From the depths of hell I call the fiends, and from this earth I call the tried and afflicted believers, and to heaven I appeal, and challenge the long experience of the blood-washed host, and there is not to be found in the three realms a single person who can bear witness to one fact that can disprove the faithfulness of God or weaken His claim to be trusted by His servants. There are many things that may or may not happen, but this I know shall happen:

> *He shall present my soul,*
> *Unblemish'd and complete,*
> *Before the glory of His face,*
> *With joys divinely great.*

All the purposes of man have been defeated, but not the purposes of God. The promises of man may be broken. Many of them are made to be broken. But the promises of God shall all be fulfilled. He is a promise-maker, but He never was a promise-breaker; He is a promise-keeping God, and every one of His people shall prove it to be so. This is my grateful, personal confidence: the Lord will perfect that which concerns me, unworthy me, lost and ruined me. He will yet save me, and

> I, among the blood-wash'd throng,
> Shall wave the palm, and wear the crown,
> And shout loud victory.

I go to a land that the plow of earth has never upturned, where it is greener than earth's best pastures and richer than her most abundant harvests ever saw. I go to a building of more gorgeous architecture than man has ever built. It is not of mortal design; it is "a building from God, a house not made with hands, eternal in the heavens" (2 Cor. 5:1). All I shall know and enjoy in heaven will be given to me by the Lord, and I shall say, when at last I appear before Him:

> Grace all the work shall crown
> Through everlasting days;
> It lays in heaven the topmost stone,
> And well deserves the praise.

I know there are some who think it necessary to their system of theology to limit the merit of the blood of Jesus. If my theological system needed such a limitation, I would cast it to the winds. I cannot, I dare not allow the thought to find a lodging in my mind; it seems so near akin to blasphemy. In Christ's finished work I see an ocean of merit. My plummet finds no bottom; my eye discovers no shore. There must be sufficient efficacy in the blood of Christ, if God had so willed it, to have saved not only all in this world, but all in ten thousand worlds, had they transgressed their Maker's law. Once admit infinity into the matter, and limit is out of the question. Having a divine person for an offering, it is not consistent to conceive of limited value; *bound* and *measure* are terms inapplicable to the divine sacrifice. The intent of the divine purpose fixes the application of the infinite offering but does not change it into a finite work. Think of the numbers upon whom God has bestowed His grace already. Think of the countless hosts in heaven. If you were introduced there today, you would find it as easy to tell the stars, or the sands of the sea, as to count the multitudes who are before the throne even now. They have come from the east and from the west, from the north and from the south, and they are sitting down with Abraham and with Isaac and with Jacob in the kingdom of God. And beside those in heaven, think of the saved ones on earth. Blessed be God, His elect on earth are to be counted by millions, I believe, and the days are coming, brighter days than these, when there shall be multitudes upon multitudes brought to know the Savior and to rejoice in Him. The Father's love is not for a few only, but for an exceedingly great company. A great multitude that no man can number will be found in heaven. A man can reckon up to very high figures; set to work your Newtons, your mightiest calculators, and they can count great numbers, but God and God alone can tell the multitude of His redeemed. I believe there will be more in heaven than in hell. If anyone asks me why I think so, I answer, because Christ, in everything, is to have the preeminence, and I cannot conceive how He could have the preeminence if there are to be more in the dominions of Satan than in paradise. Moreover, I have never read that there is to be in hell a great multitude that no man could number. I rejoice to know that the souls of all infants, as soon as they die, speed their way to paradise. Think what a multitude there is of them! Then there are already in heaven unnumbered myriads of the spirits of just men made perfect—the redeemed of all nations, and kindreds, and people, and tongues up till now. And there are better times coming, when the religion of Christ shall be universal, when "He shall reign from pole to pole with illimitable sway"—when whole kingdoms shall bow down before Him and nations shall be born in a day, and in the thousand years of the great millennial state there will be enough saved to make up all the deficiencies of the thousands of years that have gone before. Christ shall be Master everywhere, and His praise shall be sounded in every land. Christ shall have the preeminence at last; His train shall be far larger than that which shall attend the chariot of the grim monarch of hell.

Some persons love the doctrine of universal atonement because they say, "It is so beautiful. It is a lovely idea that Christ should have died for all men. It commends itself," they say, "to the instincts of humanity; there is something in it full of joy and beauty." I admit there is, but beauty may be often associated with falsehood. There is much that I might admire in the theory of universal redemption, but I will just show what the supposition necessarily involves. If Christ on His cross intended to save every man, then He intended to save those who were lost before He died. If the doctrine were true, that He died for all men, then He died for some who were in hell before He came into this world, for doubtless there were even then myriads there who had been cast away because of their sins. Once again, if it was Christ's intention to save all men, how deplorably has He been disappointed, for we have His own testimony that there is a lake that burns with fire and brimstone, and into that pit of woe have been cast some of the very persons who, according to the theory of universal redemption, were bought with His blood. That seems to me a conception a thousand times more repulsive than any of those consequences that are said to be associated with the Calvinistic and Christian doctrine of special and particular redemption. To think that my Savior died for men who were or are in hell seems a supposition too horrible for me to entertain. To imagine for a moment that He was the substitute for all the sons of men, and that God, having first punished the substitute, afterward punished the sinners themselves, seems to conflict with all my ideas of divine justice. That Christ should offer an atonement and satisfaction for the sins of all men, and that afterward some of those very men should be punished for the sins for which Christ had already atoned, appears to me to be the most monstrous iniquity that could ever have been imputed to Saturn, to Janus, to the goddess of the Thugs, or to the most diabolical heathen deities. God forbid that we should ever think thus of Jehovah, the just and wise and good!

> *I do not know how some people who believe that a Christian can fall from grace manage to be happy. It must be a very commendable thing in them to be able to get through a day without despair.*

There is no soul living who holds more firmly to the doctrines of grace than I do. If any man asks me whether I am ashamed to be called a Calvinist, I answer, I wish to be called nothing but a Christian. But if you ask me, do I hold the doctrinal views that were held by John Calvin, I reply, I do in the main hold them, and rejoice to avow it. But far be it from me even to imagine that Zion contains none but Calvinistic Christians within her walls, or that there are none saved who do not hold our views. Most atrocious things have been spoken about the character and spiritual condition of John Wesley, the modern prince of Arminians. I can only say concerning him that, while I detest many of the doctrines that he preached, yet for the man himself I have a reverence second to no Wesleyan; and if there were wanted two apostles to be added to the number of the Twelve, I do not believe that there could be found two men more fit to be so added than George Whitefield and John Wesley. The character of John Wesley stands beyond all imputation for self-sacrifice, zeal, holiness, and communion with God; he lived far above the ordinary level of common Christians and was one of whom the world was not worthy. I believe there are multitudes of men who cannot see these truths, or at least cannot see them in the way in which we put them, who nevertheless have received Christ as their Savior and are as dear to the heart of the God of grace as the soundest Calvinist in or out of heaven.

I do not think I differ from any of my hyper-Calvinistic brethren in what I do believe, but I differ from them in what they do not believe. I do not hold any less than they do, but I hold a little more, and, I think, a little more of the truth revealed in the scriptures. Not only are there a few cardinal doctrines by which we can steer our ship north, south, east, or west, but as we study the Word, we shall begin to learn something about the northwest and northeast, and all else that lies between the four cardinal points. The system of truth revealed in the scriptures is not simply one straight line, but two, and no man will ever get a right view of the gospel until he knows how to look at the two lines at once. For instance, I read in one book of the Bible, "And the Spirit and the bride say, 'Come!' And let him who hears say, 'Come!' And let him who thirsts come. Whoever desires, let him take the water of life freely" (Rev. 22:17). Yet I am taught, in another part of the same inspired Word, that "it is not of him who wills, nor of him who runs, but of God who shows mercy" (Rom. 9:16). I see, in one place, God in providence presiding over all, and yet I see, and I cannot help seeing, that man acts as he pleases, and that God has left his actions, in a great measure, to his own free will. Now, if I were to declare that man was so free to act that there was no control of God over his actions, I should be driven very near to atheism; and if, on the other hand, I should declare that God so over-rules all things that man is not free enough to be responsible, I should be driven at once into antinomianism or fatalism. That God predestines, and yet that man is responsible, are two facts that few can see clearly. They are believed to be inconsistent and contradictory to each other. If, then, I find taught in one part of the Bible that everything is foreordained, that is true; and if I find, in another scripture, that man is responsible for all his actions, that is true. And it is only my folly that leads me to imagine that these two truths can ever contradict each other. I do not believe they can ever be welded into one upon any earthly anvil, but they certainly shall be one in eternity. They are two lines that are so nearly parallel that the human mind that pursues them farthest will never discover that they converge, but they do converge, and they will meet somewhere in eternity, close to the throne of God, whence all truth springs.

> We can run a golden line up to Jesus Christ Himself, through a holy succession of mighty fathers who all held these glorious truths, and we can ask concerning them, "Where will you find holier and better men in the world?" No doctrine is so calculated to preserve a man from sin as the doctrine of the grace of God.

It is often said that the doctrines we believe have a tendency to lead us to sin. I have heard it asserted most positively that those high doctrines that we love, and that we find in the scriptures, are licentious ones. I do not know who will have the hardihood to make that assertion when they consider that the holiest of men have been believers in them. I ask the man who dares to say that Calvinism is a licentious religion what he thinks of the character of Augustine, or Calvin, or Whitefield, who in successive ages were the great exponents of the system of grace; or what will he say of the Puritans, whose works are full of them? Had a man been an Arminian in those days, he would have been accounted the vilest heretic breathing, but now we are looked upon as the heretics, and they as the orthodox. We have gone back to the old school; we can trace our descent from the apostles. It is that vein of free grace, running through the sermonizing of Baptists, that has saved us as a denomination. Were it not for that, we should not stand where we are today. We can run a golden line up to Jesus Christ Himself, through a holy succession of mighty fathers who all held these glorious truths, and we can ask concerning them, "Where will you find holier and better men in the world?" No doctrine is so calculated to preserve a man from sin as the doctrine of the grace of God. Those who have called it a licentious doctrine did not know anything at all about it.

Poor ignorant things, they little knew that their own vile stuff was the most licentious doctrine under heaven. If they knew the grace of God in truth, they would soon see that there was no preservative from lying like a knowledge that we are elect of God from the foundation of the world. There is nothing like a belief in my eternal perseverance, and the immutability of my Father's affection, that can keep me near to Him from a motive of simple gratitude. Nothing makes a man so virtuous as belief of the truth. A lying doctrine will soon beget a lying practice. A man cannot have an erroneous belief without by and by having an erroneous life. I believe the one thing naturally begets the other. Of all men, those have the most disinterested piety, the sublimest reverence, the most ardent devotion, who believe that they are saved by grace, without works, through faith, and that not of themselves—it is the gift of God. Christians should take heed and see that it always is so, lest by any means Christ should be crucified afresh and put to an open shame.

In my early Christian days, I remember seeing a man about to enter a place of worldly amusement. Though he was a professing Christian, he was going to spend the evening in a dancing booth at the village fair, drinking and acting as other men did. I called out to him just as he was at the entrance, "What are you doing there, Elijah?"

"Why do you ask me such a question as that?" said he.

I asked again, "What are you doing there, Elijah? Are you going in there?"

"Yes," he replied with some sort of blush, "I am, but I can do so with impunity. I am a child of God, and I can go where I like and yet be safe."

"I could not," said I. "If I went there, I know I should commit sin. It is a place of danger, and I could not go there without great risk of sinning against God."

"Ah!" said he. "I could; I have been before, and I have had some sweet thoughts there. I find it enlarges the intellect. You are narrow-minded; you do not appreciate these good things. It is a rich treat, I assure you; I would go if I were you."

"No," I said, "it would be dangerous for me. From what I hear, the name of Jesus is profaned there, and there is much said that is altogether contrary to the religion I believe. The persons who attend there are none of the best, and it will surely be said that birds of a feather flock together."

"Ah, well!" he replied. "Perhaps you young men had better keep away. I am a strong man; I can go." And off he went to the place of amusement.

My soul revolted from the man ever afterward, for I felt that no child of God would ever be so wicked as to take poison in the faith that his Father would give him the antidote, or thrust himself into the fire in the hope that he should not be burned. That man was an apple of Sodom, and I guessed that there was something rotten at the core. And I found by experience that it was so, for he was a downright sensualist even then. He wore a mask, for he was a hypocrite and had none of the grace of God in his heart.

4

BEGINNING TO SERVE THE LORD

*As Jesus passed on from there, He saw a man
named Matthew sitting at the tax office. And He
said to him, "Follow Me." So he arose and followed Him.*
MATT. 9:9

*This is a little bit of autobiography. Matthew wrote this verse about
himself. I can fancy him, with his pen in his hand, writing all the
rest of this gospel. But I can imagine that, when he came to this very
personal passage, he laid the pen down a minute and wiped his eyes.
He was coming to a most memorable and pathetic incident in his own
life, and he recorded it with tremulous emotion. This verse reads to me
so tenderly that I do not know how to communicate to you just how
I feel about it. I have tried to imagine myself to be Matthew, and to
have to write this story, and I am sure that if I had not been inspired
as Matthew was, I should never have done it so beautifully as he has
done it, for it is so full of everything that is touching, tender, timid,
true, and gracious.*

*I know another man, not named Matthew, but Charles, and the
Lord said to him, "Follow me," and he also arose and followed Him.
I do not know all that He saw when He looked upon me. I fear that
He saw nothing in me but sin and evil and vanity, but I believe that
He did say to Himself concerning me, "I see one to whom I can teach
my truth, and who, when he gets ahold of it, will grip it fast and
never let it go, and one who will not be afraid to speak it wherever
he is." So the Lord saw what use He could make of me. There is an
adaptation in men, even while they are unconverted, that God has
put into them for their future service. Luke was qualified to write his
gospel because he had been a physician, and Matthew was qualified*

to write the particular gospel that he has left us because he had been a
publican. There may be something about your habits of life, and about
your constitution and your condition that will qualify you for some
special niche in the church of God in the years to come. Oh, happy day,
when Jesus shall look upon you and call you to follow Him! Happy
day, when He did look upon some of us, and saw in us what His love
meant to put there, that He might make of us vessels of mercy meet
for the Master's use!

—*C. H. Spurgeon*

I do not see how our sense of oneness to Christ could ever have been perfected if we had not been permitted to work for Him. If He had been pleased to save us by His precious blood and then leave us with nothing to do, we should have had fellowship with Christ up to a certain point, but (I speak from experience) there is no fellowship with Christ that seems to me to be so vivid, so real to the soul, as when I try to win a soul for Him. Oh, when I come to battle with that soul's difficulties, to weep over that soul's hardness; when I begin to set the arguments of divine mercy before it and find myself foiled; when I am in a very agony of spirit and feel that I could die sooner than that soul should perish; then I get to read the heart of Him whose flowing tears and bloody sweat and dying wounds showed how much He loved poor fallen mankind.

I think that when I was first converted to God, if the Lord had said, "I have taken you into my house, and I am going to make use of you, and you shall be a doormat for the saints to wipe their feet on," I should have said, "Ah, happy shall I be if I may but take the filth off their blessed feet, for I love God's people; and if I may minister to them in the slightest degree, it shall be my delight!" I know it did not come into my head, at that time, that I should be a leader in God's Israel. Ah, no. If I might but sit in the corner of His house, or be a doorkeeper, it had been enough for me! If, like the dog under the table, I might get a crumb of His mercy, were it but flavored by His hand because He had broken it off, that was all I wanted. In that day when I surrendered myself to my Savior, I gave Him my body, my soul, my spirit; I gave Him all I had, and all I shall have for time and for eternity. I gave Him all my talents, my powers, my faculties, my eyes, my ears, my limbs, my emotions, my judgment, my whole manhood, and all that could come of it, whatever fresh capacity or new capability I might be endowed with. Were I, at this good hour, to change the note of gladness for one of sadness, it would be to wail out my penitent confession of the times and circumstances in which I have failed to observe the strict and unwavering allegiance I promised to my Lord. So far from regretting what I then did, I would renew my vows and make them over again. I pray God, if I have a drop of blood in my body that is not His, to let it bleed away; and if there be one hair in my head that is not consecrated to Him, I would have it plucked out.

The very first service that my youthful heart rendered to Christ was the placing of tracts in envelopes and then sealing them up that I might send them, with the hope that, by choosing pertinent tracts applicable to persons I knew, God would bless them. And I well remember taking other tracts and distributing them in certain districts in the town of Newmarket, going from house to house and telling, in humble language, the things of the kingdom of God. I might have done nothing for Christ if finding myself able to do a little had not encouraged me. Then I sought to do something more, and from that something more, and I do not doubt that many of the servants of God have been led on to higher and nobler labors for their Lord because they began to serve Him in the right spirit and manner. I look upon the giving away of a religious tract as only the first step, not to be compared with many another deed done for Christ; but were it not for the first step, we might never reach to the second. That being attained, we are encouraged to take the next. And so, at the last, God helping us, we may be made extensively useful.

> *On that day when I surrendered myself to my Savior, I gave Him my body, my soul, my spirit; I gave Him all I had, and all I shall have for time and for eternity.*

I think I never felt so much earnestness after the souls of my fellow creatures as when I first loved the Savior's name, and though I could not preach and never thought I should be able to testify to the multitude, I used to write texts on little scraps of paper and drop them anywhere, that some poor creatures might pick them up and receive them as messages of mercy to their souls. I could scarcely content myself even for five minutes without trying to do something for Christ. If I walked along the street, I must have a few tracts with me; if I went into a railway carriage, I must drop a tract out of the window; if I had a moment's leisure, I must be upon my knees or at my Bible; if I were in company, I must turn the subject of conversation to Christ, that I might serve my Master. It may be that, in the young dawn of my Christian life, I did imprudent things in order to serve the cause of Christ, but I still say, give me back that time again, with all its imprudence and with all its hastiness, if I may but have the same love to my Master, the same overwhelming influence in my spirit, making me obey my Lord's commands because it was a pleasure to me to do anything to serve my God.

> *There is no time for work like the first hours of the day, and there is no time for serving the Lord like the very earliest days of youth.*

How I did then delight to sit in that upper room where stars looked between the tiles and hear the heavenly conversation that, from a miserable pallet surrounded by ragged hangings, an enfeebled saint of the Lord did hold with me! Like divers, I valued the pearl, even though the shell might be a broken one, nor did I care where I went to win it. When those creaking stairs trembled beneath my weight, when that bottomless chair afforded me uneasy rest, and when the heat and effluvia of that sick room drove my companion away, did I not feel more than doubly repaid while that friend of Jesus told me of all His love, His faithfulness, and His grace? It is frequently the case that the most despised servants of the Lord are made the chosen instruments of comforting distressed souls and building them up in the faith.

I love to see persons of some standing in society take an interest in Sabbath schools. One great fault in many of our churches is that the children are left for the young people to take care of; the older members, who have more wisdom, take but very little notice of them, and very often the wealthier members of the church stand aside as if the teaching of the poor were not (as indeed it is) the special business of the rich. I hope for the day when the mighty men of Israel shall be found helping in this great warfare against the enemy. In the United States, we have heard of presidents, judges, members of Congress, and persons in the highest positions, not condescending—for I scorn to use such a term—but honoring themselves by teaching little children in Sabbath schools. He who teaches a class in a Sabbath school has earned a good degree. I would rather receive the title of S.S.T. than M.A., B.A., or any other honor that ever was conferred by men.

There is no time for work like the first hours of the day, and there is no time for serving the Lord like the very earliest days of youth. I recollect the joy I had in the little service I was able to render to God when first I knew Him. I was engaged in a school all the week, but I had the Saturday afternoon at liberty, and though I was but a boy myself and might rightly have used that time for rest, it was given to a tract district and to visiting the very poor within my reach; and the Sabbath day was devoted to teaching a class and, later on, also to addressing the Sunday school. When I began to teach (I was very young in grace then), I said to the class of boys whom I was teaching that Jesus Christ saved all those who believed in Him.

One of them at once asked me the question, "Teacher, do *you* believe in Him?"

I replied, "Yes, I hope I do."

Then he inquired again, "But are you not sure?"

I had to think carefully what answer I should give. The lad was not content with my repeating, "I hope so." He would have it, "*If* you have believed in Christ, you *are* saved." And I felt at that time that I could not teach effectually until I could say positively, "*I* know that it is so. I must be able to speak of what I have heard and seen and tasted and handled of the good Word of life." The boy was right; there can be no true testimony except that which springs from assured conviction of our own safety and joy in the Lord. If I was ever a little dull, my scholars began to make wheels of themselves, twisting round on the forms on which they sat. That was a very plain intimation to me that I must give them an illustration or an anecdote, and I learned to tell stories partly by being obliged to tell them. One boy, whom I had in the class, used to say to me, "*This* is very dull, Teacher; can't you pitch us a yarn?" Of course he was a naughty boy, and it might be supposed that he went to the bad when he grew up, though I am not at all sure that he did, but I used to try to pitch him the yarn that he wanted in order to get his attention again.

At one of the teachers' meetings, the suggestion was adopted that the male teachers should, in turn, give a few words of address on the lesson at the close of the teaching, alternating in so doing with the superintendent. My turn came in due course. After I had spoken, the superintendent requested me to take his place in addressing the school on the following Sabbath, and when I had done this, he asked me, as I did so well, to speak to the children each Lord's day. But to this I demurred, not deeming it fair to the other teachers. "Well," he said, "on Sunday week, I shall expect you to give the address in my stead." The precedent thus instituted soon became a kind of usage, so that, for a time, it was usual for one of the teachers and myself to speak on alternate Sabbaths. Speedily something else followed. The older people also took to coming when I spoke; and that, before long, in such numbers that the auditory looked more like that of a chapel than a school—a circumstance that the old pastor, jealous of the seeming invasion of his province, did not quite like. I always spoke as best I could, after carefully preparing my subject. Though only a youth, I said, "I think I am bound to give myself unto reading and study and prayer, and not to grieve the Spirit by unthought-of effusions," and I soon found that my hearers appreciated what I said. Oh, but how earnestly I did it all! I often think that I spoke better then than I did in later years, for I spoke so tremblingly, but my heart went with it all. And when I began to talk a little in the villages on the Sunday, and afterward every night in the week, I know that I used to speak then what came fresh from my heart. There was little time for gathering much from books. My chief library was the Word of God and my own experience, but I spoke out from my very soul, no doubt with much blundering and much weakness and much youthful folly, but oh, with such an intense desire to bring men to Christ! I often felt that I could cheerfully lay down my life if I might but be the means of saving a poor old man, or bring a boy of my own age to the Savior's feet. I feel it a great joy to have been called to work for my Lord in the early hours of my life's day, and I hope by and by to be able to say, "O God, thou hast taught me from my youth: and hitherto have I declared thy wondrous works. Now also when I am old and gray-headed, O God, forsake me not; until I have shewed thy strength unto this generation, and thy power to every one that is to come" (Ps. 71:17–18 KJV). I do not think my Lord will turn His old servant off. When I get old, men may become tired of me, but He will not. He will hear my prayer: "Dismiss me not from your service, Lord."

I can truly say that I never did anything that was a blessing to my fellow creatures without feeling compelled to do it. For instance, before I thought of going to a Sabbath school to teach, someone called and asked me—begged me, prayed me—to take his class. I could not refuse to go, and there I was, held hand and foot by the superintendent, and was compelled to go on. Then I was asked to address the children. I thought I could not, but I stood up and stammered out a few words. It was the same on the first occasion when I attempted to preach to the people. I am sure I had no wish to do it, but there was no one else in the place who could, and the little congregation must have gone away without a single word of warning or invitation. How could I suffer it? I felt forced to address them, and so it has been with whatever I have laid my hand to. I have always felt a kind of impulse that I could not resist. But, moreover, I have felt placed by providence in such a position that I had no wish to avoid the duty, and if I had desired it, I could not have helped myself.

> *It is sadly true that even a Christian will grow by degrees so callous that the sin that once startled him and made his blood run cold does not alarm him in the least.*

I shall never forget standing by the bedside of a youth who had been in my Sunday school class. He had received very little good training at home, and though he was but a lad of seventeen, he became a drunkard and drank himself to death at one debauch. I saw him and talked to him and tried to point him to the Savior, and heard at last the death rattle in his throat, and as I went downstairs, I thought everybody a fool for doing anything except preparing to die. I began to look upon the men who drove the carts in the street, those who were busy at their shops and those who were selling their wares, as being all foolish for attending to anything except their eternal business, and myself most of all foolish for not pointing dying sinners to a living Christ and inviting them to trust in His precious blood. And yet, in an hour or so, all things took their usual shape, and I began to think that I was not dying after all, and I could go away and be as unconcerned as before. I could begin to think that men were, after all, wise in thinking of this world and not the next; I mean not that I really thought so, but I fear I acted as if I thought so; the impression of the deathbed was so soon obliterated. It is sadly true that even a Christian will grow by degrees so callous that the sin that once startled him and made his blood run cold does not alarm him in the least. I can speak from my own experience. When first I heard an oath, I stood aghast and knew not where to hide myself; yet now, if I hear an imprecation or blasphemy against God, though a shudder still runs through my veins, there is not that solemn feeling, that intense anguish that I felt when first I heard such evil utterances. By degrees we get familiar with sin. I am fearful that even preaching against sin may have an injurious effect upon the preacher. I frankly confess that there is a tendency, with those of us who have to speak upon these themes, to treat them professionally rather than to make application of them to ourselves, and thus we lose our dread of evil in some degree just as young doctors soon lose their tender nervousness in the dissecting room. We are compelled in our office to see ten thousand things that at first are heart breakers to us. In our young ministry, when we meet with hypocrisy and inconsistency, we are ready to lie down and die, but the tendency in after years is to take these terrible evils as matters of course. Worldliness, covetousness, and carnality shock us most at the outset of our work. Is not this a sad sign, that even God's ministers may feel the hardening effect of sin? I daily feel that the atmosphere of earth has as much a tendency to harden my heart as to harden plaster that is newly spread upon the wall, and unless I am baptized anew with the Spirit of God and constantly stand at the foot of the cross, reading the curse of sin in the crimson hieroglyphics of my Savior's dying agonies, I shall become as steeled and insensible as many professors already are.

5

REMINISCENCES AS A
VILLAGE PASTOR

*My witness is, and I speak it for the honor of God, that He is a good
provider. I have been cast upon the providence of God ever since I
left my father's house, and in all cases He has been my shepherd, and
I have known no lack. My first income as a Christian minister was
small enough in all conscience, never exceeding forty-five pounds a
year, yet I was as rich then as I am now, for I had enough; and I had
no more cares, nay, not half as many then as I have now; and when I
breathed my prayer to God then, as I do now, for all things temporal
and spiritual, I found Him ready to answer me at every pinch, and
full many pinches I have had. Many a pecuniary trial have I had in
connection with the college work, which depends for funds upon the
Lord's moving His people to liberality. My faith has been often tried,
but God has always been faithful and sent supplies in hours of need.
If any should tell me that prayer to God is a mere piece of excitement,
and that the idea of God answering human cries is absurd, I should
laugh the statement to scorn, for my experience is not that of one or two
singular instances, but that of hundreds of cases in which the Lord's
interposition, for the necessities of His work, has been as manifest as
if He had rent the clouds and thrust forth His own naked arm and
bounteous hand to supply the needs of His servant.*

—*C. H. Spurgeon*

WHEN I became pastor at Waterbeach, the people could do very little
for my support, and therefore I was an usher in a school at Cambridge at
the same time. After a while, I was obliged to give up the latter occupation and was thrown on the generosity of the people. They gave me a salary

of forty-five pounds a year, but as I had to pay twelve shillings a week for two rooms that I occupied, my income was not sufficient to support me. But the people, though they had not money, had produce, and I do not think there was a pig killed by any one of the congregation without my having some portion of it, and one or another of them, when coming to the market at Cambridge, would bring me bread, so that I had enough bread and meat to pay my rent with, and I often paid my landlady in that fashion.

There was one old man at Waterbeach who was a great miser. On one of my visits to the place, after I had removed to London, I heard that, in his last illness, he had a bed made up in the sitting room downstairs and ordered his grave to be dug just outside the window, so as to reduce the cost of his funeral as much as possible. One of the friends who was talking about him said, "*He* was never known to give anything to anybody."

"Well," I replied, "*I* know better than that, for one Sunday afternoon he gave me three half-crowns, and as I was wanting a new hat at the time, I got it with the money."

"Well," rejoined the friend, "I am quite sure he never forgave himself for such extravagance as that, and that he must have wanted his three half-crowns back again."

"Ah, but," I answered, "*you* have not heard the whole of the story yet, for the following Sunday, the old man came to me again and asked me to pray for him that he might be saved from the sin of covetousness—'For,' said he, 'the Lord told me to give you half a sovereign, but I kept back half a crown, and I can't rest of a night for thinking of it.'"

> *The* church owes an immeasurable debt of gratitude to those thousands of godly men who study her interests day and night

Of late years, I have heard a great deal against deacons and have read discussions as to their office, evidently suggested by no idolatrous reverence for their persons. Many of my brethren in the ministry bitterly rate them. Others tremble at the mention of their very name, and a few put on their armor and prepare to do battle with them wherever they go as if they were the dragons of ministerial life. I have been accused of saying that "a deacon is worse than a devil, for if you resist the devil, he will flee from you, but if you resist a deacon, he will fly at you." This is no saying of mine; I never had any cause to speak so severely, and although, in some cases, it may be true, I have never had any experimental proof that it is so. Not one in a hundred of the sayings that are fathered upon me are mine at all, and as to this one, it was in vogue before I was born. I pardon the man who preached from James 2:6 before that drunken Solomon, James I of England and VI of Scotland—the temptation was too great to be resisted. But let the wretch be forever execrated, if such a man really lived, who celebrated the decease of a deacon by a tirade from the words, "It came to pass, that the beggar died" (Luke 16:22 KJV). I forgive the liar who attributed such an outrage to me, but I hope he will not try his infamous arts upon anyone else.

My observation of deacons leads me to say that, as a rule, they are quite as good men as the pastors, and the bad and good in the ministry and the diaconate are to be found in very much the same proportions. If there be lordly deacons, are there not lordly pastors? If there be ignorant, crotchety men among deacons, are there not their rivals in our pulpits? The church owes an immeasurable debt of gratitude to those thousands of godly men who study her interests day and night, contribute largely of their substance, care for her poor, cheer her ministers, and in times of trouble as well as prosperity, remain faithfully at their posts. Whatever there may be here and there of mistake, infirmity, and even wrong, I am sure, from wide and close observation, that most of our deacons are an honor to our faith, and we may style them, as the apostle did his brethren, the glory of Christ. The deacons of my first village pastorate were in my esteem the excellent of the earth in whom I took great delight. Hardworking men on the weekday, they spared no toil for their Lord on the Sabbath. I loved them sincerely and do love them still. In my opinion, they were as nearly the perfection of deacons of a country church as the kingdom could afford.

Yet, good as my deacons were, they were not perfect in all respects. I proposed to them, on one occasion, that I should preach on the Sunday evening by the riverside, and the remark was made by one of them, "Ah! I do not like it; it is imitating the Methodists." To him, as a sound Calvinist, it was a dreadful thing to do anything that Methodists were guilty of. To me, however, that was rather a recommendation than otherwise, and I was happy to run the risk of being Methodistical. All over England, in our cities, towns, villages, and hamlets, there are tens of thousands who never will hear the gospel while open-air preaching is neglected. I rejoice that God *allows* us to preach in churches and chapels, but I do not pretend that we have any apostolical precedent for it, certainly none for confining our ministry to such places. I believe that we are permitted, if it promotes order and edification, to set apart buildings for our worship, but there is no warrant for calling these places sanctuaries and houses of God, for all places are alike holy where holy men assemble. It is altogether a mischievous thing that we should confine our preaching within walls. Our Lord, it is true, preached in the synagogues, but He often spoke on the mountainside or from a boat or in the court of a house or in the public thoroughfares. To Him, an audience was the only necessity. He was a fisher of souls of the true sort, and not like those who sit still in their houses and expect the fish to come to them to be caught. Did our Lord intend a minister to go on preaching from his pulpit to empty pews, when by standing on a chair or a table outside the meetinghouse he might be heard by hundreds? I believe not, and I held the same opinion at the very beginning of my ministry, so I preached by the riverside, even though my good deacon thought that, by so doing, I was imitating the Methodists.

Another of those worthy brethren, a dear old Christian man, said to me one day when I was at his house to dinner, "My dear sir, I wish you would not preach those *invitation sermons*. You are too general in your appeals; you seem to press the people so much to come to Christ. I do not like it, for it is not at all consistent with my doctrinal views." "Well," I replied, "what would you have me preach?" "Well, sir," he said, "though I don't like such preaching, yet it is evident that the Lord does, for my son-in-law was converted to God under one of those sermons, and when I came home the other Sunday, so angry with you for being such a Fullerite, there was my daughter crying fit to break her heart. So," he added, "don't you take any notice of an old man like me. As long as God blesses you, you go on in your own way."

I said to him, "But, my clear brother, don't you think, if God approves of this kind of preaching, that you ought to like it, too?"

"Well," he answered, "perhaps I ought, but I am an old man, and I have always been brought up in those views. I am afraid I shall not get out of them. But don't you take the slightest notice of what I say." That was exactly what I had determined in my own mind that I would do, so we agreed after all.

One of my Waterbeach deacons was named King. He was a very

methodical man and kept the accounts and the church books in admirable order. He was a calm, thoughtful, judicious brother, but he had a full proportion of zeal and warmth. His wife was made to match, and the pair were second to none in the village for grace and wisdom. Mr. King was a miller, and in his cottage by the mill I have often spent a happy night and have met his excellent son, who was then the pastor of the Baptist church in Aldres, Cambridgeshire. I remember our hearty laugh at the junior King for borrowing a horse to ride to a preaching engagement, and then appearing at the place *leading the horse*, having only ridden him a very little way and walked with him all the rest of the road because he seemed skittish. The elder Mr. King once gave me a kindly hint in a very delicate manner. He did not tell me that I should speak more guardedly in the pulpit, but when I left his house one Monday morning, I found a pin in my Bible, stuck through Titus 2:8: ". . .sound speech that cannot be condemned, that one who is an opponent may be ashamed, having nothing evil to say of you." Nothing could have been in better taste. The wise rebuke was well deserved and lovingly taken. It was so deftly given that its value was thereby increased indefinitely. Mr. King was a deacon of deacons to me and to the Waterbeach church, and his son was worthy of such a father.

On one occasion, there had been a meeting to raise money for home mission work. The collection had just been made, and the deacons had brought all the plates to the table pew, when an old gentleman entered. He could not help being late at the meeting, though his heart was there all the time. His feet would have carried him down to the chapel two hours before, only duty forbade. As soon, however, as he had concluded his business, off he walked, saying to himself, "I'm afraid I shall be too late, but I shall at least hear how they have gone on. The Lord grant blessings on the meeting and on the good work in hand!" It was Father Sewell, an Israelite indeed, the very image of Old Mr. Honest in Bunyan's *Pilgrim's Progress*. As soon as I caught sight of my aged friend, I said, "Our brother who has just come in will, I am sure, close the meeting by offering prayer for God's blessing on the proceedings of this evening." He stood up, but he did not pray. He did not shut his eyes; on the contrary, he seemed to be looking for something. He did not clasp his hands but put them into his pockets and fumbled there with much perseverance. "I am afraid," I said, "that my brother did not understand me. Friend Sewell, I did not ask you to *give*, but to *pray*."

"Ay, ay!" replied the straightforward, bluff old saint. "But I could not pray till I had given; it would be hypocrisy to ask a blessing on that which I did not think worth giving to." There was not the least ostentation in the good man; it was his honest heart pouring out its true feelings. And, odd as his behavior seemed, his conduct preached the whole congregation such a sermon as they would not readily forget.

In my first pastorate, I had often to battle with Antinomians, that is, people who held that, because they believed themselves to be elect, they might live as they liked. I hope that heresy has to a great extent died out, but it was sadly prevalent in my early ministerial days. I knew one man who stood on the table of a public house and held a glass of gin in his hand, declaring all the while that he was one of the chosen people of God. They kicked him out of the public house, and when I heard of it, I felt that it served him right. Even those ungodly men said that they did not want any such "elect" people there. There is no one who can live in sin—drinking, swearing, lying, and so on—who can truly declare that he is one of the Lord's chosen people. I recollect one such man—and he was a very bad fellow—yet he had the hardihood to say, "I know that I am one of God's dear people."

"So you are," said I. "Dear at any price, either to be given or thrown away!" He did not like my plain speaking, but it was true; for that was the only sense in which he was one of God's dear people. From my very soul, I detest everything that in the least savors of the Antinomianism that leads people to prate about being secure in Christ while they are living in sin. We cannot be saved *by* or *for* our good works; neither can we be saved *without* good works. Christ never will save any of His people *in* their sins; He saves His people *from* their sins. If a man does not desire to live a holy life in the sight of God, with the help of the Holy Spirit, he is still "poisoned by bitterness and bound by iniquity" (Acts 8:23). I used to know a man of this class, who talked a great deal about "saving faith." He was notorious for his evil life, so I could not make out what he meant by saving faith—until the collection was taken, and I noticed how carefully he put his fingernail round a threepenny piece for fear lest it should be a fourpenny. Then I understood his meaning. But the idea of saving faith apart from good works is ridiculous. The saved man is not a perfect man, but his heart's desire is to become perfect. He is always panting after perfection, and the day will come when he will be perfected after the image of his once crucified and now glorified Savior, in knowledge and true holiness.

While I was minister at Waterbeach, I used to have a man sitting in front of the gallery who would always nod his head when I was preaching what he considered sound doctrine, although he was about as bad an old hypocrite as ever lived. When I talked about justification, down went his head; when I preached about imputed righteousness, down it went again. I was a dear good man in his estimation, without doubt. So I thought I would cure him of nodding, or at least make his head keep still for once, so I remarked, "There is a great deal of difference between God electing you, and your electing yourself; a vast deal of difference between God justifying you by His Spirit, and your justifying yourself by a false belief, or presumption. This is the difference," said I—and the old man at once put me down as a rank Arminian—"you who have elected yourselves and justified yourselves have no marks of the Spirit of God, you have no evidence of genuine piety, you are not holy men and women, you can live in sin, you can walk as sinners walk, you have the image of the devil upon you, and yet you call yourselves the children of God. One of the first evidences that anyone is a child of God is that he hates sin with a perfect hatred and seeks to live a holy, Christlike life." The old Antinomian did not approve of that doctrine, but I knew that I was preaching what was revealed in the Word of God.

> *There is no one who can live in sin—drinking, swearing, lying, and so on—who can truly declare that he is one of the Lord's chosen people.*

There was another man of that sort who at one time frequently walked out with me into the villages where I was going to preach. I was glad of his company till I found out certain facts as to his manner of life, and then I shook him off, and I believe he hooked himself on to somebody else, for he must needs be gadding abroad every evening of the week. He had many children, and they grew up to be wicked men and women, and the reason was that the father, while he was constantly busy at this meeting and that, never tried to bring his own boys and girls to the Savior. He said to me one day, "I never laid my hand upon my children."

So I answered, "Then I think it is very likely that God will lay His hand upon you."

"Oh!" he said. "I have not even spoken sharply to them."

"Then," I replied, "it is highly probable that God will speak very sharply to you, for it is not His will that parents should leave their children unrestrained in their sin."

I knew another man, in those early days, who used to travel a long distance every Sabbath to hear what he called "the truth." Neither his wife nor any of his children went to any place of worship, and when I talked to him very seriously about them, he told me that "the Lord would save His own," to which I could not help replying that the Lord would not "own" him. He demanded my authority for that statement so I gave him this proof text, "If anyone does not provide for his own, and especially for those of his household, he has denied the faith and is worse than an unbeliever" (1 Tim. 5:8). One of his companions said to me one day that he knew how many children of God there were in the parish where he lived; there were exactly five. I was curious to learn their names, so I asked him who the five were, and much to my amusement he began by saying, "There is myself." I stopped him at this point with the query whether he was quite sure about the first one. Since then, his character has gone I know not where, but certainly he will get on better without it than with it, yet he was the first on his own list, and a few others of the same black sort made up the five. There were, in the other places of worship to which he did not go, men whose characters for integrity and uprightness, ay, and for spirituality and prayerfulness, would have been degraded by being put into comparison with his; yet he set himself up as judge in Israel and pretended to know exactly how many people of God were in the village. "The Lord knows those who are His" (2 Tim. 2:19). I bless God that I have learned to have very little respect for the vision of the man with the measuring line. When I see an angel with it, I am glad enough; but when I see a man with it, I tell him that he must give me a warrant from God and show me how he is to know the elect by any other method than that laid down by our Lord Jesus Christ: "Ye shall know them by their fruits" (Matt. 7:16 KJV).

I have sometimes been greatly obliged to a wicked world for what it has done to inconsistent professors of religion. While I was pastor at Waterbeach, a certain young man joined the church. We thought he was a changed character, but there used to be in the village, once a year, a great temptation in the form of a feast, and when the feast came round, this foolish fellow was there in very evil company. He was in the long room of a public house in the evening, and when I heard what happened, I really felt intense gratitude to the landlady of that place. When she came in and saw him there, she said, "Halloa, Jack So-and-So, are *you* here? Why, you are one of Spurgeon's lot, yet you are here. You ought to be ashamed of yourself. This is not fit company for you. Put him out of the window, boys." And they did put him out of the window on the Friday night, and we put him out of the door on the Sunday, for we removed his name from our church book. Where was he to go to? The world would not have him, and the church would not have him. If he had been all for the world, the world would have made something of him, and if he had been all for Christ, Christ would have made something of him. But as he tried to be a little for each, and so nothing to either, his life became a wretched one. As he walked the streets, people pointed at him with scorn. The Christians turned away, thinking him a hypocrite, as I fear he was, and the worldlings called him one and made his name a byword and a proverb.

> *I bless God that I have learned to have very little respect for the vision of the man with the measuring line. When I see an angel with it, I am glad enough; but when I see a man with it, I tell him that he must give me a warrant from God*

In those early days, I had sometimes to contend with the Antinominian preachers as well as with their people. I once found myself in the midst of a company of ministers and friends, who were disputing whether it was a sin in men that they did not believe the gospel. While they were discussing, I said, "Gentlemen, am I in the presence of Christians? Are you believers in the Bible, or are you not?"

They said, "We are Christians, of course."

"Then," said I, "does not the scripture say, 'of sin, because they believe not on me'? And is it not the damning sin of men that they do not believe on Christ?" I should not have imagined, if I had not myself heard them, that any persons would be so wicked as to venture to assert that "it is no sin for a sinner not to believe on Christ." I should have thought that, however far they might wish to push their sentiments, they would not tell a lie to uphold the truth, and in my opinion, this is what such men really do. Truth is a strong tower and never requires to be buttressed with error. God's Word will stand against all of man's devices. I would never invent a sophism to prove that it is no sin on the part of the ungodly not to believe, for I am sure it is. When I am taught in the scriptures that "this is the condemnation, that the light has come into the world, and men loved darkness rather than light, because their deeds were evil" (John 3:19), I affirm, and the Word declares it, *unbelief is a sin.* Surely, with rational and unprejudiced persons, it cannot require any reasoning to prove it. Is it not a sin for a creature to doubt the Word of its Maker? Is it not a crime and an insult to the Deity for me, an atom, a particle of dust, to dare to deny His words? Is it not the very summit of arrogance and the height of pride for a son of Adam to say, even in his heart, "God, I doubt your grace; God, I doubt your love; God, I doubt your power"? I feel that, could we roll all sins into one mass—could we take murder, blasphemy, lust, adultery, fornication, and everything that is vile and unite them all into one vast globe of black corruption—they would not even then equal the sin of unbelief. This is the monarch sin, the quintessence of guilt, the mixture of the venom of all crimes, the dregs of the wine of Gomorrah; it is the A1 sin, the masterpiece of Satan, the chief work of the devil. Unbelief hardened the heart of Pharaoh. It gave license to the tongue of blaspheming Rabshakeh. Yea, it became a deicide and murdered the Lord Jesus Christ. Unbelief! It has mixed many a cup of poison; it has brought thousands to the gallows and many to a shameful grave, who have murdered themselves and rushed with bloody hands before their Creator's tribunal, because of unbelief. Give me an unbeliever, let me know that he doubts God's Word, let me know that he distrusts His promise and His threatening, and with that for a premise I will conclude that the man shall, by and by, unless there is amazing restraining power exerted upon him, be guilty of the foulest and blackest crimes. Unbelief is a Beelzebub sin. Like Beelzebub, it is the leader of all evil spirits. It is said of Jeroboam that he sinned and made Israel to sin, and it may be said of unbelief that it not only itself sins, but it makes others sin. It is the egg of all crime, the seed of every offense; in fact, everything that is evil and vile lies couched in that one word *unbelief.*

In striking contrast to those apologists for sin, I met in my first pastorate, as I have often done since, a number of persons who professed to be perfect and who said that they had lived so many months or years without sinning against God. One man who told me that he was perfect was humpbacked, and when I remarked that I thought if he were a perfect man, he ought to have a perfect body, he became so angry that I said to him, "Well, my friend, if you are perfect, there are a great many more as near perfection as you are."

"Oh!" he exclaimed. "I shall feel it for having been betrayed into anger." He said that he had not been angry for many years. I had brought him back to his old state of infirmity, and painful as it might be for him, I have no doubt that it did him good to see himself as he really was.

When a man thinks that he is a full-grown Christian, he reminds me of a poor boy whom I used to see. He had such a splendid head for his body that he had often to lay it on a pillow, for it was too weighty for his shoulders to carry. His mother told me that when he tried to stand up, he often tumbled down, overbalanced by his heavy head. There are some people who appear to grow very fast, but they have water on the brain and are out of due proportion; but he who truly grows in grace does not say, "Dear me! I can feel that I am growing; bless the Lord! Let's sing a hymn. 'I'm a-growing! I'm a-growing!'" I have often felt that I was growing smaller; I think that is very probable, and a good thing, too. If we are very great in our own estimation, it is because we have a number of cancers, or foul gatherings, that need to be lanced, so as to let out the bad matter that causes us to boast of our bigness.

> It may be said of unbelief that it not only itself sins, but it makes others sin. It is the egg of all crime, the seed of every offense; in fact, everything that is evil and vile lies couched in that one word unbelief.

Our Wesleyan brethren have a notion that they are going to be perfect here on earth. I should be very glad to see them when they are perfect, and if any of them happen to be in the position of servants, wanting situations, I would be happy to give them any amount of wages I could spare, for I should feel myself highly honored and greatly blessed in having perfect servants. And what is more, if any of them are masters, and need servants, I would undertake to come and serve them without any wages at all if I could but find a perfect master. I have had one perfect Master ever since I first knew the Lord, and if I could be sure that there is another perfect master, I should be greatly pleased to have him as an undermaster, while the great Supreme must ever be chief of all.

One man who said he was perfect called upon me once and asked me to go and see him, for I should receive valuable instruction from him if I did. I said, "I have no doubt it would be so, but I should not like to go to your house. I think I should hardly be able to get into one of your rooms."

"How is that?" he inquired.

"Well," I replied, "I suppose that your house would be so full of angels that there would be no room for me." He did not like that remark, and when I made one or two other playful observations, he went into a towering rage.

"Well, friend," I said to him, "I think, after all, I am as perfect as you are; but do *perfect men* ever get angry?" He denied that he was angry, although there was a peculiar redness about his cheeks and a fiery flash in his eyes that is very common to persons when they are in a passion. At any rate, I think I rather spoiled his perfection, for he evidently went home much less satisfied with himself than when he came out.

> *While I am fully persuaded that perfection is absolutely impossible to any man beneath the sky, I feel equally sure that, to every believer, future perfection is certain beyond a doubt.*

I met another man who considered himself perfect, but he was thoroughly mad. And I do not believe that any of the pretenders to perfection are better than good maniacs, a superior kind of Bedlamites; for, while a man has got a spark of reason left in him, he cannot, unless he is the most impudent of impostors, talk about being perfect. He who imagines such a thing must be insane, for any man who examines himself for five minutes, in the light of God's Word, will find enough in his own heart to drive from him any shadow of a thought about being perfect in this world. I have little patience with such willfully blind people, and when I hear of some who are said to be perfectly holy, and of others who are utterly foolish, I think the two classes are wonderfully alike. I have met with a few people who seemed to me almost perfect, but they have been the very ones who have groaned most over their own imperfections, while those with whom I have come into contact, who have professed to be holy and without blemish, have been the most imperfect individuals I have ever known.

My own experience is a daily struggle with the evil within. I wish I could find in myself something friendly to grace. But hitherto I have searched my nature through and have found everything in rebellion against God. At one time, there comes the torpor of sloth, when one ought to be active every moment, having so much to do for God and for the souls of men, and so little time in which to do it. At another time, there comes the quickness of passion; when one should be calm and cool and play the Christian, bearing with patience whatever has to be endured, there come the unadvised word and the rash expression. Anon, I am troubled with conceit, the devilish whisper—I can call it no less—"How well you have done! How nobly you have played your part!" Then crawls out distrust, foul and faithless, suggesting that God does not regard the affairs of men and will not interpose on my behalf. Yet what would I not give if I might but be perfect! Sometimes I think that if God's people mentioned in the Old and New Testaments had all been perfect, I should have despaired. But because they seem to have had just the kind of faults I grieve over in myself, I do not feel any more lenient toward my faults, but I do rejoice that I also may say with each of them, "The Lord will *perfect* that which concerns *me*." He will most assuredly, beyond a doubt, bring to perfection my faith, my love, my hope, and every grace. He will perfect His own purposes. He will perfect His promises, He will perfect my body, and He will perfect my soul. While I am fully persuaded that perfection is absolutely impossible to any man beneath the sky, I feel equally sure that, to every believer, future perfection is certain beyond a doubt. The day shall come when the Lord shall not only make us better, but shall make us perfectly pure and holy; when He shall not merely subdue our lusts, but when He shall cast the demons out altogether; when He shall make us holy and blameless and irreprovable in His sight. That day, however, I believe, shall not come until we enter into the joy of our Lord and are glorified together with Christ in heaven. Then, but not till then, shall He present us "faultless before the presence of His glory with exceeding joy" (Jude 24).

While I was going about the Cambridgeshire villages, preaching and visiting, it often saddened me to see, especially in the houses of the poor, Roman Catholic pictures hanging on the walls, I suppose because they happened to be rather pretty and very cheap. Popish publishers have very cleverly managed to get up pictures of the virgin Mary, and the lying fable of her assumption to heaven, and all sorts of legends of saints and saintesses. Being brightly colored and sold at a low price, these vile productions have been introduced into thousands of houses. I have seen, to my horror, a picture of God the Father represented as an old man—a conception almost too hideous to mention—yet the picture is hung up in the cottages of England, whereas the Lord has expressly commanded us not to make any likeness or image of Him, or to try to represent His appearance in any way, and any attempt to do so is disobedient and even blasphemous.

It was grievous to find what gross ignorance prevailed among many of the villagers concerning the way of salvation. They seemed, somehow, to have got into their heads the notion that they could not be saved because they could not read and did not know much. Frequently, when I asked anything about personal salvation, I received the answer, "Oh, sir, I never had any learning," and that was supposed to be a sufficient excuse for not having repented of sin and trusted in the Savior. Yet the unlearned need not stay away from Christ. It was said of an old Greek philosopher that he wrote over his door, "None but the learned may enter here." But Christ writes over His door, "He who is simple, let him turn in hither." I can testify that great numbers of those humble country folk accepted the Savior's invitation, and it was delightful to see what a firm grip they afterward had of the verities of the faith. Many of them became perfect masters in divinity. I used to think, sometimes, that if they had degrees who deserved them, diplomas would often be transferred and given to those who hold the plow handle or work at the carpenter's bench; for there is often more divinity in the little finger of a plowman than there is in the whole body of some of our modern divines. "Don't they understand divinity?" someone asks. Yes, in the letter of it, but as to the spirit and life of it, D.D. often means Doubly Destitute.

> They still live; they still are blessed. While we weep, they are rejoicing; while we mourn, they are singing psalms of praise; and by and by, in God's good time, we shall meet them again, to be parted no more forever.

An incident that I once witnessed at Waterbeach furnished me with an illustration concerning death. A company of villagers, the younger branches of a family, was about to immigrate to another land. The aged mother, who had not for some years left her cottage fireside, came to the railway station from which they must start. I stood among the sorrowful group as their friend and minister. I think I see the many embraces that the fond mother gave to her son and daughter and her little grandchildren. I can picture them folding their arms about her aged neck and then saying farewell to all the friends in the village who had come to bid them adieu. A shrill sound is heard. It sends a pang through all hearts, as if it were the messenger of death to her who is about to lose the props of her household. In great haste, at the small village station, the passengers are hurried to their seats; they thrust their heads out of the carriage window. The aged parent stands on the very edge of the platform that she may take her last look at them. There is a whistle from the engine, and away goes the train. In an instant, the poor woman, jumping from the platform, rushes along the railway, with all her might crying, "My children! My children! My children! They are gone, and I shall never see them again." The illustration may not be classical; nevertheless, many a death, when I have seen the godly suddenly snatched away, has reminded me of it. They have gone from us, swiftly as the wind itself could bear them, or as the hasty waves of the sea could bury them out of our sight. It is our affliction and trouble that we must remain behind and weep, for they are gone beyond recall. Yet there is something pleasant in the picture. It is but a departure; they are not destroyed; they are not blown to atoms; they are not taken away to prison. 'Tis but a departure from one place to another. They still live; they still are blessed. While we weep, they are rejoicing; while we mourn, they are singing psalms of praise; and by and by, in God's good time, we shall meet them again, to be parted no more forever.

There was an amusing incident in my early Waterbeach ministry that I have never forgotten. One day, a gentleman, who was then mayor of Cambridge and who had more than once tried to correct my youthful mistakes, asked me if I really had told my congregation that if a thief got into heaven, he would begin picking the angels' pockets.

"Yes, sir," I replied, "I told them that if it were possible for an ungodly man to go to heaven without having his nature changed, he would be none the better for being there. And then, by way of illustration, I said that, were a thief to get in among the glorified, he would remain a thief still, and he would go round the place picking the angels' pockets!"

"But, my dear young friend," asked Mr. Brimley very seriously, "don't you know that the angels haven't any pockets?"

"No, sir," I replied with equal gravity, "I did not know that; but I am glad to be assured of the fact from a gentleman who does know. I will take care to put it all right the first opportunity I get."

The following Monday morning, I walked into Mr. Brimley's shop and said to him, "I set that matter right yesterday, sir."

"What matter?" he inquired.

"Why, about the angels' pockets!"

"What *did* you say?" he asked, in a tone almost of despair at what he might hear next.

"Oh, sir, I just told the people I was sorry to say that I had made a mistake the last time I preached to them, but that I had met a gentleman, the mayor of Cambridge, who had assured me that the angels had no pockets, so I must correct what I had said, as I did not want anybody to go away with a false notion about heaven. I would therefore say that if a thief got among the angels without having his nature changed, he would try to steal the feathers out of their wings!"

"Surely you did not say that?" said Mr. Brimley.

"I did, though," I replied.

"Then," he exclaimed, "I'll never try to set you right again," which was just exactly what I wanted him to say.

Once, while I was at Waterbeach, I had a sleepy congregation. It was on a Sabbath afternoon; those afternoon services in our English villages are usually a doleful waste of effort. Roast beef and pudding lie heavy on the hearers' souls, and the preacher himself is deadened in his mental processes while digestion claims the mastery of the hour. The people had been eating too much dinner, so they came to chapel heavy and dull, and before long many of them were nodding. So I tried an old expedient to rouse them. I shouted with all my might, "Fire! Fire! Fire!" When, starting from their seats, some of my hearers asked where it was, I answered, as other preachers had done in similar circumstances, "In hell, for sinners who will not accept the Savior."

On another occasion, I had a trouble of quite a different character. I had preached on the Sunday morning and gone home to dinner, as was my wont, with one of the congregation. The afternoon sermon came so close behind the morning one that it was difficult to prepare the soul, especially as the dinner was a necessary but serious inconvenience where a clear brain was required. By a careful measuring of diet, I remained in an earnest, lively condition, but to my dismay, I found that the prearranged line of thought was gone from me. I could not find the trail of my prepared sermon, and press my forehead as I might, the missing topic would not come. Time was brief, the hour was striking, and in some alarm I told the honest farmer that I could not for the life of me recollect what I had intended to preach about.

"Oh," he said, "never mind; you will be sure to have a good word for us." Just at that moment, a blazing block of wood fell out of the fire upon the hearth at my feet, smoking into my eyes and nose at a great rate.

"There," said the farmer, "there's a text for you, sir. 'Is not this a brand plucked out of the fire?'"

No, I thought it was not plucked out, for it fell out of itself. Here, however, was a text, an illustration, and a leading thought as a nest egg for more. Further light came, and the discourse was certainly not worse than my more prepared effusions; it was better in the best sense, for one or two came forward declaring themselves to have been aroused and converted through that afternoon's sermon. I have always considered that it was a happy circumstance that I had forgotten the text from which I had intended to preach.

6

THE LONG PASTORATE
COMMENCED, 1854

Here and there we meet with one to whom it is given to believe in God with mighty faith. As soon as such a man strikes out a project, or sets about a work that none but men of his mold would venture upon, straightway there arises a clamor: "The man is overzealous," or he will be charged with an innovating spirit, rashness, fanaticism, or absurdity. Should the work go on, the opposers whisper together, "Wait a little while, and you'll see the end of all this wildfire." What said the sober semi-faithful men to Luther? The monk had read in the scriptures this passage: "A man is not justified by the works of the law, but by the faith of Jesus Christ" (Gal. 2:16 KJV). He went to a venerable divine to ask him about it, and at the same time he complained of the enormities of Rome. What was the good but weak brother's reply? "Go to your cell, and pray and study for yourself, and leave these weighty matters alone." Here it would have ended had the brave reformer continued to consult with flesh and blood. But his faith enabled him to go forward alone, if none would accompany him. He nailed up his theses on the church door and showed that one man at least had faith in the gospel and in its God. Then trouble came, but Luther minded it not, because the Father was with him. We also must be prepared, if God gives us strong faith, to ride far ahead, like spiritual light cavalry, who bravely pioneer the way for the rank and file of the army. It were well if the church of God had more of the fleet-footed sons of Asahel—bolder than lions, swifter than eagles in their Lord's service—men who can do and dare alone till laggards take courage and follow in their track. These Valiant-for-Truths will pursue a solitary path full often, but let them console

themselves with this thought: "I am not alone, but I am with the
Father who sent me" (John 8:16). If we can believe in God, He will
never be in arrears with us; if we can dare, God will do; if we can
trust, God will never suffer us to be confounded, world without end.
It is sweet beyond expression to climb where only God can lead, and
to plant the standard on the highest towers of the foe.

—*C. H. Spurgeon*

WHEN I came to New Park Street Chapel, it was but a mere handful of people to whom I first preached; yet I can never forget how earnestly they prayed. Sometimes they seemed to plead as though they could really see the angel of the covenant present with them, and as if they must have a blessing from Him. More than once, we were all so awestruck with the solemnity of the meeting that we sat silent for some moments while the Lord's power appeared to overshadow us. All I could do on such occasions was to pronounce the benediction and say, "Dear friends, we have had the Spirit of God here very manifestly tonight; let us go home and take care not to lose His gracious influences." Then down came the blessing; the house was filled with hearers, and many souls were saved. I always give all the glory to God, but I do not forget that He gave me the privilege of ministering from the first to a praying people. We had prayer meetings in New Park Street that moved our very souls. Every man seemed like a crusader besieging the New Jerusalem. Each one appeared determined to storm the celestial city by the might of intercession, and soon the blessing came upon us in such abundance that we had not room to receive it.

> If we can believe in God, He will never be in arrears with us; if we can dare, God will do; if we can trust, God will never suffer us to be confounded.

There is a confidence in one's own powers that must ever be of service to those who are called to eminent positions, provided the confidence is well grounded, seasoned with humility, and attended with that holy gratitude that refers all honor and glory to the giver of every good and perfect gift. But at the same time, there is nothing truer than the fact that the self-confident are near a fall, that those who lean on themselves must be overthrown, and that carnal security has but a baseless fabric in which to dwell. When I first became a pastor in London, my success appalled me, and the thought of the career that it seemed to open up, so far from elating me, cast me into the lowest depth, out of which I uttered my *miserere* and found no room for a *gloria in excelsis*. Who was I that I should continue to lead so great a multitude? I would betake me to my village obscurity, or immigrate to America and find a solitary nest in the backwoods, where I might be sufficient for the things that would be demanded of me. It was just then that the curtain was rising upon my lifework, and I dreaded what it might reveal. I hope I was not faithless, but I was timorous and filled with a sense of my own unfitness. I dreaded the work that a gracious providence had prepared for me. I felt myself a mere child and trembled as I heard the voice that said, "You shall thresh the mountains and beat them small, and make the hills like chaff" (Isa. 41:15). This depression comes over me whenever the Lord is preparing a larger blessing for my ministry; the cloud is black before it breaks, and overshadows before it yields its deluge of mercy. Depression has now become to me as a prophet in rough clothing, a John the Baptist, heralding the nearer coming of my Lord's richer benison. So have far better men found it. The scouring of the vessel has fitted it for the Master's use. Immersion in suffering has preceded the baptism of the Holy Spirit. Fasting gives an appetite for the banquet. The Lord is revealed in the back side of the desert, while His servant keeps the sheep and waits in solitary awe. The wilderness is the way to Canaan. The low valley leads to the towering mountain. Defeat prepares for victory. The raven is sent forth before the dove. The darkest hour of the night precedes the day-dawn. The marine go down to the depths, but the next wave makes them mount toward the heavens and their soul is melted because of trouble before the Lord brings them to their desired haven.

Not long after I was chosen pastor at Park Street, I was interviewed by a good man who had left the church, having been, as he said, "treated shamefully." He mentioned the names of half a dozen persons, all prominent members of the church, who had behaved in a very unchristian manner to him—he, poor innocent sufferer, having been a model of patience and holiness! I learned his character at once from what he said about others (a mode of judging that has never misled me), and I made up my mind how to act. I told him that the church had been in a sadly unsettled state, and that the only way out of the snarl was for everyone to forget the past and begin again. He said that the lapse of years did not alter facts, and I replied that it would alter a man's view of them if in that time he had become a wiser and a better man. I added that all the past had gone away with my predecessors, that he must follow them to their new spheres and settle matters with *them*, for I would not touch the affair with a pair of tongs. He waxed somewhat warm, but I allowed him to radiate until he was cool again, and we shook hands and parted. He was a good man but constructed upon an uncomfortable principle, so that, at times, he crossed the path of other people in a very awkward manner, and if I had gone into his case and taken his side, there would have been no end to the strife. I am quite certain that, for my own success, and for the prosperity of the church, I took the wisest course by applying my blind eye to all disputes that dated previously to my advent. It is the extremity of unwisdom for a young man, fresh from college or from another charge, to suffer himself to be earwigged by a clique, and to be bribed by kindness and flattery to become a partisan, and so to ruin himself with one half of his people.

I do not find, at the present time, nearly so much advice being given to young men as when I first came to London. Dear me, what quantities I had! I believe I had as much as that American humorist, who said he found enough advice lying loose roundabout him to ruin three worlds at least. I am sure I had quite enough to have done that. But now, instead of advising our young brethren and hinting at their indiscretions, we rather rejoice in their impetuosity and earnestness. We like to see much freshness and vigor about them, and if they do kick over the traces now and then, we feel that time will moderate their zeal, and probably a very few years will add to them the prudence that they now lack.

I could tell many stories of the remarkable conversions that were wrought in those early days. Once, when I was in the vestry, an Irishman came to see me. Pat began by making a low bow and saying, "Now, your *riverence*, I have come to ask you a question."

"Oh!" said I. "Pat, I am not a *riverence*; it is not a title I care for. But what is your question and how is it you have not been to your priest about it?"

He said, "I have been to him, but I don't like his answer."

"Well, what is your question?"

Said he, "God is just, and if God be just, He must punish my sins. I deserve to be punished. If He is a just God, He ought to punish me. Yet you say God is merciful and will forgive sins. I cannot see how that is right. He has no right to do that. He ought to be just and punish those who deserve it. Tell me how God can be just, and yet be merciful."

I replied, "That is through the blood of Christ."

"Yes," said he, "that is what my priest said—you are very much alike there—but he said a good deal besides that I did not understand, and that short answer does not satisfy me. I want to know how it is that the blood of Jesus Christ enables God to be just, and yet to be merciful."

Then I saw what he wanted to know and explained the plan of salvation thus: "Now, Pat, suppose you had been killing a man, and the judge had said, 'That Irishman must be hanged.'"

He said quickly, "And I should have richly deserved to be hanged."

"But, Pat, suppose I was very fond of you—can you see any way by which I could save you from being hanged?"

"No, sir, I cannot."

"Then suppose I went to the queen and said, 'Please, Your Majesty, I am very fond of this Irishman. I think the judge was quite right in saying that he must be hanged, but let me be hanged instead, and you will then carry out the law.' Now, the queen could not agree to my proposal, but suppose she could—and God can, for He has power greater than all kings and queens—and suppose the queen should have me hanged instead of you. Do you think the policemen would take you up afterward?"

He at once said, "No, I should think not. They would not meddle with me; but if they did, I should say, 'What are you doing? Did not that gentleman condescend to be hung for me? Let me alone. Sure, you don't want to hang two people for the same thing, do you?'"

I replied to the Irishman, "Ah, my friend, you have hit it. That is the way whereby we are saved! God must punish sin. Christ said, 'My Father, punish me instead of the sinner,' and His Father did. God laid on His beloved Son, Jesus Christ, the whole burden of our sins, and all their punishment and chastisement, and now that Christ is punished instead of us, God would not be just if He were to punish any sinner who believes on the Lord Jesus Christ. If you believe in Jesus Christ, the well-beloved and only begotten Son of God, you are saved, and you may go on your way rejoicing."

"Faith," said the man, clapping his hands, "that's the gospel. Pat is safe now; with all his sins about him, he'll trust in the man that died for him, and so he shall be saved."

Another singular conversion wrought at New Park Street was that of a man who had been accustomed to going to a gin palace to fetch in gin for his Sunday evening's drinking. He saw a crowd round the door of the chapel, so he looked in and forced his way to the top of the gallery stairs. Just then, I turned in the direction where he stood; I do not know why I did so, but I remarked that there might be a man in the gallery who had come in with no very good motive, for even then he had a gin bottle in his pocket. The singularity of the expression struck the man. And being startled because the preacher so exactly described him, he listened attentively to the warnings that followed, the Word reached his heart, the grace of God met with him, he became converted, and soon he was walking humbly in the fear of God.

On another occasion, a poor harlot found the Savior in the same building. She had determined to go and take her own life on Blackfriars Bridge, but passing the chapel on a Sunday evening, she thought she would step in and for the last time hear something that might prepare her to stand before her Maker. She forced her way into the aisle, and being once in, she could not get out even if she had wanted to do so. The text that night was "Seest thou this woman?" (Luke 7:44 KJV). I described the woman in the city who was a notorious public sinner, and pictured her washing her Savior's feet with her tears and wiping them with the hair of her head, loving much because she had been forgiven much. While I was preaching, the wretched woman was melted to tears by the thought that her own evil life was being depicted to the congregation. It was, first, my great joy to be the means of saving the poor creature from death by suicide, and then to be the instrument of saving her soul from destruction.

God must punish sin. Christ said, 'My Father, punish Me instead of the sinner;' and His Father did. God laid on His beloved Son, Jesus Christ, the whole burden of our sins, and all their punishment and chastisement.

Deeds of grace have been wrought in the Tabernacle after the same fashion. Men and women have come in simply out of curiosity—a curiosity often created by some unfounded story or malicious slander of prejudiced minds. Yet Jesus Christ has called them and they have become both *His* disciples and *our* warmhearted friends. Some of the most unlikely recruits have been, in after days, our most valuable soldiers. They began with aversion and ended with enthusiasm. They came to scoff but remained to pray. Such cases are not at all uncommon.

They were not unusual in the days of Whitefield and Wesley. They tell us in their journals of persons who came with stones in their pockets to throw at the Methodists, but whose enmity was slain by a stone from the sling of the Son of David. Others came to create disturbances, but a disturbance was created in their hearts that could never be quelled till they came to Jesus Christ and found peace in Him. The history of the church of God is studded with the remarkable conversions of persons who did not wish to be converted, who were not looking for grace but were even opposed to it, and yet, by the interposing arm of eternal mercy, were struck down and transformed into earnest and devoted followers of the Lamb.

> *opened the Bible to find the text, which I had carefully studied as the topic of discourse, when, on the opposite page, another passage of scripture sprang upon me like a lion from a thicket.*

Ever since I have been in London, in order to get into the habit of speaking extemporaneously, I have never studied or prepared anything for the Monday evening prayer meeting. I have all along selected that occasion as the opportunity for off-hand exhortation, but I do not on such occasions select difficult expository topics or abstruse themes, but restrict myself to simple, homely talk about the elements of our faith. When standing up on such occasions, my mind makes a review and inquires, "What subject has already occupied my thought during the day? What have I met with in my reading during the past week? What is most laid upon my heart at this hour? What is suggested by the hymns or the prayers?" It is of no use to rise before an assembly and hope to be inspired upon subjects of which one knows nothing. If anyone is so unwise, the result will be that, as he knows nothing, he will probably say it, and the people will not be edified. But I do not see why a man cannot speak extemporaneously upon a subject that he fully understands. Any tradesman, well versed in his line of business, could explain it without needing to retire for meditation, and surely I ought to be equally familiar with the first principles of our holy faith. I ought not to feel at a loss when called upon to speak upon topics that constitute the daily bread of my soul. I do not see what benefit is gained, in such a case, by the mere manual labor of writing before speaking because, in so doing, a man would write extemporaneously, and extemporaneous writing is likely to be even feebler than extemporaneous speech. The gain of the writing lies in the opportunity of careful revision, but just as thoroughly able writers can express their thoughts correctly at the first, so also may able speakers. The thought of a man who finds himself upon his legs, dilating upon a theme with which he is familiar, may be very far from being his first thought. It may be the cream of his meditations warmed by the glow of his heart. He having studied the subject well before, though not at that moment, may deliver himself most powerfully, whereas another man, sitting down to write, may only be penning his first ideas, which may be vague and vapid.

> *cast myself upon God, and His arrangements quenched the light at the proper time for me. Some may ridicule, but I adore; others may even censure, but I rejoice.*

I once had a very singular experience while preaching at New Park Street Chapel. I had passed happily through all the early parts of divine service on the Sabbath evening and was giving out the hymn before the sermon. I opened the Bible to find the text, which I had carefully studied as the topic of discourse, when, on the opposite page, another passage of scripture sprang upon me like a lion from a thicket with vastly more power than I had felt when considering the text that I had chosen. The people were singing and I was sighing. I was in a strait between two, and my mind hung as in the balances. I was naturally desirous to run in the track that I had carefully planned, but the other text would take no refusal and seemed to tug at my skirts, crying, "No, no, you must preach from me! God would have you follow me." I deliberated within myself as to my duty, for I would neither be fanatical nor unbelieving, and at last I thought within myself, *Well, I should like to preach the sermon that I have prepared, and it is a great risk to run to strike out a new line of thought, but as this text constrains me, it may be of the Lord, and therefore I will venture upon it, come what may.* I almost always announce my divisions very soon after the introduction, but on this occasion, contrary to my usual custom, I did not do so for a very good reason. I passed through the first head with considerable liberty, speaking perfectly extemporaneously both as to thought and word. The second point was dwelt upon with a consciousness of unusual quiet efficient power, but I had no idea what the third would or could be, for the text yielded no more matter just then, nor can I tell even now what I could have done had not an event occurred upon which I had never calculated.

I had brought myself into great difficulty by obeying what I thought to be a divine impulse, and I felt comparatively easy about it, believing that God would help me and knowing that I could at least close the service should there be nothing more to be said. I had no need to deliberate, for in one moment we were in total darkness. The gas had gone out, and as the aisles were choked with people and the place was crowded everywhere, it was a great peril, but a great blessing. What was I to do then? The people were a little frightened, but I quieted them instantly by telling them not to be at all alarmed though the gas was out, for it would soon be relighted, and as for myself, having no manuscript, I could speak just as well in the dark as in the light, if they would be so good as to sit or stand still and listen. Had my discourse been ever so elaborate, it would have been absurd to have continued it; and as my plight was, I was all the less embarrassed. I turned at once mentally to the well-known text that speaks of the child of light walking in darkness, and of the child of darkness walking in the light, and found appropriate remarks and illustrations pouring in upon me. When the lamps were again lit, I saw before me an audience as rapt and subdued as ever a man beheld in his life. The odd thing of all was that, some few church meetings afterward, two persons came forward to make confession of their faith, who professed to have been converted that evening. The first owed her conversion to the former part of the discourse, which was on the new text that came to me, and the other traced his awakening to the latter part, which was occasioned by the sudden darkness. Thus, providence befriended me. I cast myself upon God, and His arrangements quenched the light at the proper time for me. Some may ridicule, but I adore; others may even censure, but I rejoice.

This illustration represents the pulpit stairs used by me at New Park Street Chapel after the enlargement. When that building was sold, I removed them to my garden at Nightingale Lane and fixed them to a huge willow tree. I remember reading, with some amusement, of Lorenzo

Dow, who is reported, many years ago, to have slipped down a tree in the backwoods in order to illustrate the easiness of backsliding. He had previously pulled himself up with extreme difficulty in order to show how hard a thing it is to regain lost ground. I was all the more diverted by the story because it has so happened that this pretty piece of nonsense has been imputed to myself. I was represented as sliding down the banisters of my pulpit, and that at a time when the pulpit was fixed in the wall and was entered from behind. I never gave even the remotest occasion for that falsehood, and yet it is daily repeated, and I have even heard of persons who have declared that they were present when I did so and, with their own eyes, saw me perform the silly trick.

> *It is possible for a person to repeat a falsehood so many times that he at length imposes it upon himself and believes that he is stating the truth.*

It is possible for a person to repeat a falsehood so many times that he at length imposes it upon himself and believes that he is stating the truth. When men mean to say what is untrue and unkind, they are not very careful as to the back upon which they stick the slander. For my own part, I have so long lived under a glass case that, like the bees that I have seen at the Crystal Palace, I go on with my work and try to be indifferent to spectators; and when my personal habits are truthfully reported, though they really are not the concern of anybody but myself, I feel utterly indifferent about it, except in times of depression, when I sigh for a lodge in some vast wilderness, where rumors of newspaper interviewers might never reach me more. I am quite willing to take my fair share of the current criticism allotted to public men, but I cannot help saying that I very seldom read in print any story connected with myself that has a shade of truth in it. Old Joe Miller's anecdotes of Rowland Hill, Sydney Smith, and John Berridge, and tales of remotest and fustiest antiquity, are imputed to me as they have been to men who went before, and will be to men who follow after. Many of the tales told about me, even to this day, are not only without a shadow of truth, but some of them border on blasphemy or are positively profane. On the whole, I am inclined to believe that the trade in falsehood is rather brisk, or so many untruths would not be manufactured. Why, I actually heard, not long since, of a minister who said that a certain thing occurred to him the other day, yet I told the original story twenty years ago! When I related it, I said it had been my experience the other day, and I believed it was so. But after hearing this man say that it happened to him, it makes me question whether it really did occur to me at all. I think it is a great pity for a preacher, or any speaker, to try to make a story appear interesting by saying that the incident related happened to him when it really did not. Scrupulous truthfulness should always characterize everyone who stands up to proclaim the truth of God.

> *Many of the tales told about me, even to this day, are not only without a shadow of truth, but some of them border on blasphemy or are positively profane.*

I mentioned to my New Park Street deacons, several times, my opinion that the upper panes of the iron-framed windows had better be taken out, as the windows were not made to open. Yet nothing came of my remarks. It providentially happened one Monday that somebody removed most of those panes in a masterly manner, almost as well as if they had been taken out by a glazier. There was considerable consternation and much conjecture as to who had committed the crime, and I proposed that a reward of five pounds should be offered for the discovery of the offender, who when found should receive the amount as a present. The reward was not forthcoming, and therefore I have not felt it to be my duty to inform against the individual. I trust none will suspect me. If they do, I shall have to confess that I have walked with the stick that let the oxygen into that stifling structure. In a very short time after I began to preach in London, the congregation so multiplied as to make the chapel, in the evening, when the gas was burning, like the Black Hole of Calcutta. One night in 1854, while preaching there, I exclaimed, "By faith, the walls of Jericho fell down; and by faith, this wall at the back shall come down, too." An aged and prudent deacon, in somewhat domineering terms, observed to me, at the close of the sermon, "Let us never hear of that again."

"What do you mean?" I inquired. "You will hear no more about it *when it is done*, and therefore the sooner you set about doing it, the better." The following extract from the church book shows that the members did set about doing it in real earnest:

CHURCH MEETING, 30TH AUGUST 1854

Resolved: That we desire, as a church, to record our devout and grateful acknowledgments to our heavenly Father for the success that has attended the ministry of our esteemed pastor, and we consider it important, at as early a period as possible, that increased accommodation should be provided for the numbers that flock to the chapel on Lord's days; and we would affectionately request our respected deacons to give the subject their full and careful consideration and to favor us with their report at the church meeting in October.

A considerable but unavoidable delay took place, in consequence of the vestry and school rooms being held on a different trust from that of the chapel, so that it became necessary to apply to the Charity Commissioners before including those rooms in the main building. After fully investigating the circumstances, they did not interpose any obstacle, so the alterations were commenced early in 1855, and in due course the chapel was enlarged as proposed and a new school room was erected along the side of the chapel, with windows that could be let down to allow those who were seated in the school to hear the preacher.

7

THE CHOLERA YEAR
IN LONDON

IN the year 1854, when I had scarcely been in London twelve months, the neighborhood in which I labored was visited by Asiatic cholera, and my congregation suffered from its inroads. Family after family summoned me to the bedside of the smitten, and almost every day I was called to visit the grave. At first, I gave myself up with youthful ardor to the visitation of the sick, and was sent for from all corners of the district by persons of all ranks and religions. But soon I became weary in body and sick at heart. My friends seemed falling one by one, and I felt or fancied that I was sickening like those around me. A little more work and weeping would have laid me low among the rest; I felt that my burden was heavier than I could bear, and I was ready to sink under it.

I was returning mournfully home from a funeral when, as God would have it, my curiosity led me to read a paper that was wafered up in a shoemaker's window in the Great Dover Road. It did not look like a trade announcement, nor was it, for it bore, in a good bold handwriting, these words: "Because thou hast made the LORD, which is my refuge, even the most High, thy habitation; there shall no evil befall thee, neither shall any plague come nigh thy dwelling" (Ps. 91:9–10 KJV).

> *A little more work and weeping would have laid me low among the rest; I felt that my burden was heavier than I could bear, and I was ready to sink under it.*

The effect upon my heart was immediate. Faith appropriated the passage as her own; I felt secure, refreshed, girded with immortality. I went on with my visitation of the dying in a calm and peaceful spirit; I felt no fear of evil, and I suffered no harm. The providence that moved the tradesman to place those verses in his window, I gratefully acknowledge, and in the remembrance of its marvelous power I adore the Lord my God.

> *stood by his side and spoke to him, but he gave me no answer. I spoke again, but the only consciousness he had was a foreboding of terror, mingled with the stupor of approaching death*

During that epidemic of cholera, though I had many engagements in the country, I gave them up that I might remain in London to visit the sick and the dying. I felt that it was my duty to be on the spot in such a time of disease and death and sorrow. One Monday morning I was awakened about three o'clock by a sharp ring of the doorbell. I was urged, without delay, to visit a house not very far from London Bridge. I went, and up two pairs of stairs I was shown into a room, the only occupants of which were a nurse and a dying man.

"Oh, sir!" exclaimed the nurse as I entered. "About half an hour ago, Mr. So-and-So begged me to send for you."

"What does he want?" I asked.

"He is dying, sir," she replied.

I said, "Yes, I see that he is; what sort of a man was he?"

The nurse answered, "He came home from Brighton last night, sir. He had been out all day. I looked for a Bible, sir, but there is not one in the house. I hope you have brought one with you."

"Oh," I said, "a Bible would be of no use to him now. If he could understand me, I could tell him the way of salvation in the very words of scripture."

I stood by his side and spoke to him, but he gave me no answer. I spoke again, but the only consciousness he had was a foreboding of terror, mingled with the stupor of approaching death. Soon even that was gone, for sense had fled, and I stood there a few minutes, sighing with the poor woman who had watched over him, and altogether hopeless about his soul. Gazing at his face, I perceived that he was dead and that his soul had departed.

That man, in his lifetime, had been wont to jeer at me. In strong language he had often denounced me as a hypocrite. Yet he was no sooner smitten by the darts of death than he sought my presence and counsel, no doubt feeling in his heart that I was a servant of God, though he did not care to own it with his lips. There I stood, unable to help him. Promptly as I had responded to his call, what could I do but look at his corpse and mourn over a lost soul? He had, when in health, wickedly refused Christ, yet in his death-agony he had superstitiously sent for me. Too late, he sighed for the ministry of reconciliation and sought to enter in at the closed door, but he was not able. There was no space left him then for repentance, for he had wasted the opportunities that God had long granted to him. I went home and was soon called away again, that time to see a young woman. She also was in the last extremity, but it was a fair, fair sight. She was singing—though she knew she was dying—and talking to those roundabout her, telling her brothers and sisters to follow her to heaven, bidding good-bye to her father, and all the while smiling as if it had been her marriage day. She was happy and blessed. I never saw more conspicuously in my life than I did that morning the difference there is between one who fears God and one who fears Him not.

SELECTED SERMONS OF CHARLES H. SPURGEON

CONTENTS

SERMONS RELATING TO GOD

THE IMMUTABILITY OF GOD

"For I am the LORD, *I do not change;*
therefore you are not consumed, O sons of Jacob."
MALACHI 3:6

IT has been said by someone that the proper study of mankind is man. I will not oppose the idea, but I believe it is equally true that the proper study of God's elect is God. The proper study of a Christian is the Godhead. The highest science, the loftiest speculation, the mightiest philosophy that can ever engage the attention of a child of God is the name, the nature, the person, the work, the doings, and the existence of the great God whom he calls his Father. There is something exceedingly improving to the mind in a contemplation of the divinity. It is a subject so vast that all our thoughts are lost in its immensity, so deep that our pride is drowned in its infinity.

Other subjects we can compass and grapple with; in them we feel a kind of self-content and go our way with the thought, *Behold, I am wise.* But when we come to this master science, finding that our plumb line cannot sound its depth and that our eagle eye cannot see its height, we turn away with the solemn exclamation, "For we were born yesterday, and know nothing" (Job 8:9). No subject of contemplation will tend more to humble the mind than thoughts of God. We will be obliged to feel—

Great God, how infinite are you,
What worthless worms are we!

But while the subject *humbles* the mind, it also *expands* it. He who often thinks of God will have a larger mind than the man who simply plods

113

around this narrow globe. He may be a naturalist, boasting of his ability to dissect a beetle, anatomize a fly, or arrange insects and animals in classes with well nigh unutterable names. He may be a geologist, able to discourse of the megatherium and the plesiosaurus and all kinds of extinct animals. He may imagine that his science, whatever it is, ennobles and enlarges his mind. I daresay it does, but after all, the most excellent study for expanding the soul is the science of Christ and Him crucified and the knowledge of the Godhead in the glorious Trinity.

Nothing will so enlarge the intellect, nothing so magnify the whole soul of man as a devout, earnest, continued investigation of the great subject of the Deity. And while humbling and expanding, this subject is eminently *consolatory*. Oh, there is, in contemplating Christ, a balm for every wound! In musing on the Father, there is a quietus for every grief, and in the influence of the Holy Spirit, there is a balsam for every sore. Would you lose your sorrows? Would you drown your cares? Then go plunge yourself in the Godhead's deepest sea—be lost in His immensity. And you will come forth as from a couch of rest, refreshed and invigorated.

I know nothing that can so comfort the soul, so calm the swelling billows of grief and sorrow, so speak peace to the winds of trial, as a devout musing upon the subject of the Godhead. It is to that subject that I invite you this morning. We will present you with one view of it: the *immutability* of the glorious Jehovah. "I am," says my text, "Jehovah" (for so it should be translated).

There are three things this morning. First of all, an *unchanging* God; second, the *persons* who derive benefit from this glorious attribute, "the sons of Jacob"; and third, the *benefit* they so derive—they "are not consumed." We address ourselves to these points.

I. First of all, we have set before us the doctrine of *the immutability of God*. Here I will attempt to expound, or rather to enlarge, the thought and then afterward to bring a few arguments to prove its truth.

1. I will offer some exposition of my text by first saying that God is Jehovah and He changes not *in His essence*. We cannot tell you what Godhead is. We do not know what substance that is that we call God. It is an existence, it is a being, but what that is we know not. However, whatever it is, we call it His essence and that essence never changes. The substance of mortal things is ever changing. The mountains with their

snow-white crowns doff their old diadems in summer, in rivers trickling down their sides, while the storm cloud gives them another coronation. The ocean, with its mighty floods, loses its water when the sunbeams kiss the waves and snatch them in mists to heaven. Even the sun itself requires fresh fuel from the hand of the infinite Almighty to replenish his ever-burning furnace.

All creatures change. Man, especially as to his body, is always undergoing revolution. Very probably there is not a single particle in my body that was in it a few years ago. This frame has been worn away by activity, its atoms have been removed by friction, fresh particles of matter have in the meantime constantly accrued to my body and so it has been replenished; its substance is altered. The fabric of which this world is made is ever passing away like a stream of water. Drops are running away and others are following after, keeping the river still full, but always changing in its elements.

But God is perpetually the same. He is not composed of any substance or material, but is spirit—pure, essential, and ethereal spirit—and therefore He is immutable. He remains everlastingly the same. There are no furrows on His eternal brow. No age has palsied Him—no years have marked Him with the mementoes of their flight. He sees ages pass, but with Him it is ever *now*. He is the great I Am—the great unchangeable. Mark you, His essence did not undergo a change when it became united with the manhood. When Christ in past years did gird Himself with mortal clay, the essence of His divinity was not changed—flesh did not become God, nor did God become flesh by a real actual change of nature.

> God is perpetually the same. He is not composed of any substance or material, but is spirit-pure, essential, and ethereal spirit—and therefore He is immutable.

The two were united in hypostatical union, but the Godhead was still the same. It was the same when He was a babe in the manger as it was when He stretched the curtains of heaven. It was the same God who hung upon the cross and whose blood flowed down in a purple river. The selfsame God who holds the world upon His everlasting shoulders and bears in His hands the keys of death and hell. He never has been changed in His essence, not even by His incarnation. He remains everlastingly, eternally, the one unchanging God, the Father of lights, with whom there is no variableness, neither the shadow of a change.

2. He changes not in His *attributes*. Whatever the attributes of God were of old, they are the same now. And of each of them we may sing, as it was in the beginning, is now and ever will be, world without end, amen. Was He *powerful?* Was He the mighty God when He spoke the world out of the womb of nonexistence? Was He the Omnipotent when He piled the mountains and scooped out the hollow places for the rolling deep? Yes, He was powerful then and His arm is unpalsied now. He is the same giant in His might. The sap of His nourishment is still wet and the strength of His soul stands the same forever.

Was He wise when He constituted this mighty globe, when He laid the foundations of the universe? Had He *wisdom* when He planned the way of our salvation and when from all eternity He marked out His awful plans? Yes, and He is wise now. He is not less skillful. He has not less knowledge. His eyes that see all things are undimmed. His ears that hear all the cries, sighs, sobs, and groans of His people are not rendered heavy by the years that He has heard their prayers. He is unchanged in His wisdom. He knows as much now as ever, neither more nor less.

He has the same consummate skill and the same infinite forecasting. He is unchanged, blessed be His name, in His *justice*. Just and holy was He in the past; just and holy is He now. He is unchanged in His truth. He has promised and He brings it to pass. He has said it and it will be done. He varies not in the *goodness*, generosity, and benevolence of His nature. He has not become an almighty tyrant, whereas He was once an almighty Father. His strong love stands like a granite rock unmoved by the hurricanes of our iniquity. And blessed be His dear name, He is unchanged in His *love*. When He first wrote the covenant, how full His heart was with affection to His people. He knew that His Son must die to ratify the articles of that agreement. He knew right well that He must rend His Best Beloved from His heart and send Him down to earth to bleed and die.

He did not hesitate to sign that mighty covenant. Nor did He shun its fulfillment. He loves as much now as He did then. And when suns will cease to shine and moons to show their feeble light, He still will love on forever and forever. Take any one attribute of God and I will write *semper idem* on it (always the same). Take any one thing you can say of God now and it may be said not only in the dark past, but also in the bright future. It will always remain the same: "I am the LORD, I do not change."

3. Then again, God changes not in His *plans*. Man began to build but was not able to finish, and therefore he changed his plan—as every wise man would do in such a case—and built upon a smaller foundation and commenced again. But has it ever been said that God began to build but was not able to finish? No. When He has boundless stores at His command and when His own right hand would create worlds as numerous as drops of morning dew, will He ever stay because He has not power? Or reverse, or alter, or disarrange His plan because He cannot carry it out?

"But," say some, "perhaps God never had a plan." Do you think God is more foolish than yourself then, sir? Do you go to work without a plan? "No," you say, "I have always a scheme." So has God. Every man has his plan, and God has a plan, too. God is a mastermind. He arranged everything in His gigantic intellect long before He did it, and mark you, once having settled it, He never alters it. "This will be done," says He, and the iron hand of destiny marks it down and it is brought to pass. "This is my purpose." It stands, and earth or hell cannot alter it. "This is my decree," says He. Promulgate it, angels; rend it down from the gate of heaven, you devils. But you cannot alter the decree. It will be done.

God alters not His plans. Why should He? He is almighty and therefore can perform His pleasure. Why should He? He is the All-Wise and therefore cannot have planned wrongly. Why should He? He is the everlasting God and therefore cannot die before His plan is accomplished. Why should He change? You worthless atoms of existence, ephemera of the day! You creeping insects upon this bay leaf of existence! You may change your plans, but He will never, never change *His*. Then has He told me that His plan is to save me? If so, I am safe:

> *My name from the palms of His hands*
> *Eternity will not erase;*
> *Impressed on His heart it remains,*
> *In marks of indelible grace.*

4. Yet again, God is unchanging in His *promises*. Ah, we love to speak about the sweet promises of God. But if we could ever suppose that one of them could be changed, we would not talk anything more about them. If I thought that the notes of the bank of England could not be cashed next

week, I should decline to take them, and if I thought that God's promises would never be fulfilled—if I thought that God would see it right to alter some word in His promises—farewell, scriptures! I want immutable things, and I find that I have immutable promises when I turn to the Bible, for "by two immutable things, in which it is impossible for God to lie" (Heb. 6:18), He has signed, confirmed, and sealed every promise of His.

The gospel is not "yes and no"; it is not promising today and denying tomorrow. The gospel is "yes, yes," to the glory of God (2 Cor. 1:16–20). Believer, there was a delightful promise that you had yesterday, and this morning, when you turned to the Bible, the promise was not sweet. Do you know why? Do you think the promise has changed? Ah, no, you changed; that is where the matter lies. You had been eating some of the grapes of Sodom, your mouth was thereby put out of taste, and you could not detect the sweetness. But there was the same honey there, depend upon it, the same preciousness. "Oh," says one child of God, "I had built my house firmly once upon some stable promises. There came a wind, and I said, O Lord, I am cast down and I will be lost."

Oh, the promises were *not* cast down. The foundations were not removed. You had been building your little wood, hay, and stubble hut. It was that which fell down. You have been shaken *on* the rock, not the rock *under you*. But let me tell you what is the best way of living in the world. I have heard that a gentleman said to a Negro, "I can't think how it is you are always so happy in the Lord and I am often downcast."

"Why, Massa," said he, "I throw myself flat down on the promise. There I lie. You stand on the promise. You have a little to do with it and down you go when the wind comes. And then you cry, 'Oh, I am down.' Whereas I go flat on the promise at once and that is why I fear no fall."

Then let us always say, "Lord, there is the promise. It is Your business to fulfill it." Down I go on the promise flat! No standing up for me. That is where you should go: prostrate on the promise. And remember, every promise is a rock, an unchanging thing. Therefore cast yourself at His feet and rest there forever.

5. But now comes one jarring note to spoil the theme. To some of you God is unchanging in His *threats*. If every promise stands fast and every oath of the covenant is fulfilled, hark you, sinner, mark the word, hear the death knell of your carnal hopes! See the funeral of the fleshly trusting. Every threat of God, as well as every promise, will be fulfilled.

Talk of decrees! I will tell you of a decree: "He who does not believe will be condemned" (Mark 16:16). That is a decree and a statute that can never change. Be as good as you please, be as moral as you can, be as honest as you will, walk as uprightly as you may, there stands the unchangeable threat: "He who does not believe will be condemned."

What do you say to that, moralist? Oh, you wish you could alter it and say, "He who does not live a holy life will be condemned." That will be true. But it does not say so. It says, "He who does not *believe*." Here is the stone of stumbling and the rock of offense. But you cannot alter it—you either believe or be damned, says the Bible. And mark: that threat of God is as unchangeable as God Himself. And when a thousand years of hell's torments will have passed away, you will look on high and see written in burning letters of fire, "He who does not believe will be condemned."

"But, Lord, I *am* condemned." Nevertheless, it says you *will be* still. And when a million years have rolled away and your pains and agonies exhaust you, you will turn up your eye and still read, "will be condemned," unchanged, unaltered. And when you will have thought that eternity must have spun out its last thread, that every particle of that which we call eternity must have run out, you will still see it written up there, "will be condemned." O terrible thought! How dare I utter it? But I must. You must be warned, sirs, lest you also come into this place of torment (Luke 16:28). You must be told rough things, for if God's gospel is not a rough thing, believe me, the law is a rough thing. Mount Sinai is a rough thing. Woe to the watchman who warns not the ungodly! God is unchanging in His threats. Beware, O sinner, for "it is a fearful thing to fall into the hands of the living God" (Heb. 10:31).

6. We must just hint at one thought before we pass on, and that is, God is unchanging in the *objects of His love*, and not only in His love, but also in the *objects* of it:

> *If ever it should come to pass*
> *That sheep of Christ might fall away,*
> *My fickle, feeble soul, alas,*
> *Would fall a thousand times a day.*

If one dear saint of God had perished, so might all. If one of the covenant ones is lost, so may all be, and then there is no gospel promise true. Then the Bible is a lie and there is nothing in it worth my acceptance. I will be an infidel at once when I can believe that a saint of God can ever fall finally. If God has loved me once, then He will love me forever:

> *Did Jesus once upon me shine,*
> *Then Jesus is forever mine.*

The objects of everlasting love never change. Those whom God has called, He will justify. Whom He has justified, He will sanctify. And whom He sanctifies, He will glorify (Rom. 8:30).

7. Thus having taken a great deal too much time, perhaps, in simply expanding the thought of an unchanging God, I will now try to prove that He *is* unchangeable. I am not much of an argumentative preacher, but one argument that I will mention is this: The very *existence and being of a God* seem to me to imply immutability. Let me think a moment. There is a God. This God rules and governs all things. This God fashioned the world. He upholds and maintains it. What kind of being must He be? It does strike me that you cannot think of a *changeable* God. I conceive that the thought is so repugnant to common sense that if you for one moment think of a changing God, the words seem to clash and you are obliged to say, "Then He must be a kind of man," and you have a Mormonism idea of God.

I imagine it is impossible to conceive of a changing God. It is so to me. Others may be capable of such an idea, but I could not entertain it. I could no more think of a changing God than I could of a round square, or any other absurdity. The thing seems so contrary that I am obliged, when once I say God, to include the idea of an unchanging being.

8. Well, I think that one argument will be enough, but another good argument may be found in the fact of *God's perfection*. I believe God to be a perfect being. Now, if He is a perfect being, He cannot change. Do you not see this? Suppose I am perfect today. If it were possible for me to change, should I be perfect tomorrow after the alteration? If I changed, I must change either from a good state to a better—and then, if I could get better, I could not be perfect *now*—or else from a better state to a worse. And if I were worse, I should not be perfect *then*. If I am perfect, I cannot be altered without being imperfect. If I am perfect today, I must be the same tomorrow if I am to be perfect then. So if God is perfect, He must be the same, for change would imply imperfection now, or imperfection then.

9. Again, there is the fact of *God's infinity*, which puts change out of the

question. God is an infinite being. What do you mean by that? There is no man who can tell you what he means by an infinite being. But there cannot be two infinities. If one thing is infinite, there is no room for anything else, for infinite means all. It means not bounded, not finite, having no end. Well, there cannot be two infinities. If God is infinite today and then should change and be infinite tomorrow, there would be two infinities. But that cannot be.

Suppose He is infinite and then changes; He must become finite and could not be God. Either He is finite today and finite tomorrow, or infinite today and finite tomorrow, or finite today and infinite tomorrow, all of which suppositions are equally absurd. The fact of His being an infinite being at once quashes the thought of His being a changeable being. Infinity has written on its very brow the word *immutability*.

10. But then, dear friends, let us look at *the past*, and there we will gather some proofs of God's immutable nature. Has He spoken and has He not done it? Has He sworn and has it not come to pass? Can it not be said of Jehovah, He has done all His will, and He has accomplished all His purpose? Turn you to Philistia; ask where she is. God said, "Gaza shall be forsaken, and Ashkelon desolate" (Zeph. 2:4). Where are they? Where is Edom? Ask Petra and its ruined walls. Where is Babel and where is Nineveh? Where is Moab and where is Ammon? Where are the nations God has said He would destroy? Has He not uprooted them and cast out the remembrance of them from the earth?

And has God cast off His people? Has He once been unmindful of His promise? Has He once broken His oath and covenant, or once departed from His plan? Ah, no. Point to one instance in history where God has changed! You cannot, sirs, for throughout all history there stands the fact: God has been immutable in His purposes. I think I hear someone say, "I can remember one passage in scripture where God changed!" And so did I think once. The case I mean is that of the death of Hezekiah. Isaiah came in and said, "Hezekiah, you must die. Your disease is incurable; set your house in order."

He turned his face to the wall and began to pray. And before Isaiah was in the outer court, he was told to go back and say, "You will live fifteen years more" (2 Kings 20:1–6). You may think that proves that God changes. But really, I cannot see in it the slightest proof in the world. How do you know that God did not know that? Oh, but God *did* know it. He knew that Hezekiah would live. Then He did not change, for if He knew that, how could He change? That is what I want to know. But do you know one little thing? Hezekiah's son Manasseh was not born at that time. And had Hezekiah died, there would have been no Manasseh and no Josiah and no Christ, because Christ came from that very line!

You will find that Manasseh was twelve years old when his father died—so that he must have been born three years after this. And do you not believe that God decreed the birth of Manasseh and foreknew it? Certainly. Then He decreed that Isaiah should go and tell Hezekiah that his disease was incurable and then say in the same breath, "But I will cure it and you will live." He said that to stir up Hezekiah to prayer. He spoke, in the first place, as a man. "According to all human probability, your disease is incurable and you must die." Then He waited till Hezekiah prayed. Then came a little "but" at the end of the sentence.

Isaiah had not finished the sentence. He said, "You must put your house in order, for there is no human cure. But—" And then he walked out. Hezekiah prayed a little, and then he came in again and said, "*But* I will heal you." Where is there any contradiction there, except in the brains of those who fight against the Lord and wish to make Him a changeable being?

II. Now second, let me say a word on *the persons to whom this unchangeable God is a benefit*. "I am the LORD, I do not change; therefore you are not consumed, O sons of Jacob." Now, who are "the sons of Jacob"? Who can rejoice in an immutable God?

1. First, they are the *sons of God's election*. For it is written, "Jacob I have loved, but Esau I have hated. . .the children not yet being born, nor having done any good or evil." It is written, "The older shall serve the younger" (Rom. 9:10–13). The sons of Jacob

> *Are the sons of God's election,*
> *Who through sovereign grace believe;*
> *By eternal destination*
> *Grace and glory they receive.*

The sons of Jacob here are God's elect, those whom He foreknew and foreordained to everlasting salvation.

2. By the sons of Jacob are meant, in the second place, *persons who enjoy peculiar rights and titles.* Jacob, you know, had no rights by birth, but he soon acquired them. He exchanged a mess of pottage with his brother, Esau, and thus gained the birthright. I do not justify the means. But he did also obtain the blessing and so acquired peculiar rights. By the sons of Jacob is meant persons who have peculiar rights and titles. Unto them that believe, He has given the right and power to become sons of God. They have an interest in the blood of Christ. They have a right to "enter through the gates into the city" (Rev. 22:14). They have a title to eternal honors. They have a promise to everlasting glory. They have a right to call themselves sons of God. Oh, there are peculiar rights and privileges belonging to the sons of Jacob.

3. Next, these sons of Jacob were *men of peculiar manifestations.* Jacob had had peculiar manifestations from his God, and thus he was highly honored. Once at night, he lay down and slept. He had the hedges for his curtains, the sky for his canopy, a stone for his pillow, and the earth for his bed. Oh, then he had a peculiar manifestation. There was a ladder and he saw the angels of God ascending and descending. He thus had a manifestation of Christ Jesus as the ladder that reaches from earth to heaven—up and down which angels came to bring us mercies (Gen. 28:10–12; John 1:51).

Then what a manifestation there was at Mahanaim when the angels of God met him, again at Peniel, when he wrestled with God and saw Him face-to-face (Gen. 32:1–2). Those were peculiar manifestations—and this passage refers to those who, like Jacob, have had peculiar manifestations.

Now then, how many of you have had personal manifestations? "Oh," you say, "that is enthusiasm; that is fanaticism." Well, it is a blessed enthusiasm, too, for the sons of Jacob have had peculiar manifestations. They have talked with God as a man talks with his friend; they have whispered in the ear of Jehovah. Christ has been with them to sup with them and they with Christ. And the Holy Spirit has shone into their souls with such a mighty radiance that they could not doubt about special manifestations. The sons of Jacob are the men who enjoy these manifestations.

4. Then again, they are *men of peculiar trials.* Ah, poor Jacob! I should not choose Jacob's lot if I had not the prospect of Jacob's blessing. For a hard lot his was. He had to run away from his father's house to Laban's, and then that surly old Laban cheated him all the years he was there; cheated him of his wife, cheated him in his wages, cheated him in his flocks, and cheated him all through the story. By and by he had to run away from Laban, who

pursued him and overtook him.

Next came Esau with four hundred men to cut him up root and branch. Then there was a season of prayer, and afterward he wrestled God and had to go all his life with his thigh out of joint. But a little further on, his daughter Dinah is led astray, and the sons murder the Shechemites. Then his dear son, Joseph, is sold into Egypt and a famine comes. Then Reuben goes up to his couch and pollutes it. Judah commits incest with his own daughter-in-law, and all his sons become a plague to him.

At last Benjamin is taken away, and the old man, almost brokenhearted, cries, "Joseph is no more, Simeon is no more, and you want to take Benjamin" (Gen. 42:36). Never was man more tried than Jacob, all through the one sin of cheating his brother. All through his life, God chastised him. But I believe there are many who can sympathize with dear old Jacob. They have had to pass through trials very much like his. Well, cross-bearers, God says, "I change not; therefore you sons of Jacob are not consumed." Poor tried souls! You are not consumed because of the unchanging nature of your God.

> *You do not understand what troubles mean. You have hardly sipped the cup of trouble; you have only had a drop or two, but Jesus drank the dregs.*

Now do not get to fretting and say, with the self-conceit of misery, "I am the man who has seen affliction." Why, the Man of sorrows was afflicted more than you! Jesus was indeed a mourner. You only see the skirts of the garments of affliction. You never have trials like His. You do not understand what troubles mean. You have hardly sipped the cup of trouble; you have only had a drop or two, but Jesus drank the dregs. Fear not, says God, "I am the LORD, I change not; therefore you sons of Jacob," men of peculiar trials, "are not consumed."

5. Then one more thought about who are the sons of Jacob, for I should like you to find out whether you are sons of Jacob yourselves. They are *men of peculiar character*. For though there were some things about Jacob's character that we cannot commend, there are one or two things that God commends. There was Jacob's faith, by which Jacob had his name written among the mighty worthies who obtained not the promises on earth but will obtain them in heaven (Heb. 11). Are you men of faith, beloved? Do you know what it is to walk by faith, to live by faith, to get your temporary food by

faith, to live on spiritual manna, all by faith? Is faith the rule of your life? If so, you are the sons of Jacob.

Then Jacob was a man of prayer—a man who wrestled, groaned, and prayed. There is a man up yonder who never prayed this morning, before coming up to the house of God. Ah, you poor heathen, don't you pray? "No!" he says. "I never thought of such a thing. For years I have not prayed." Well, I hope you may before you die. Live and die without prayer and you will pray long enough when you get to hell. There is a woman—she did not pray this morning. She was so busy sending her children to the Sunday school she had no time to pray. No time to pray? Had you time to dress? There is a time for every purpose under heaven, and if you had purposed to pray, you would have prayed.

Sons of God cannot live without prayer. They are wrestling Jacobs. They are men in whom the Holy Spirit so works that they can no more live without prayer than I can live without breathing. They must pray. Sirs, mark you, if you are living without prayer, you are living without Christ. And dying like that, your portion will be in the lake that burns with fire. God redeem you, God rescue you from such a lot! But you who are the sons of Jacob take comfort, for God is immutable.

III. Third, I can say only a word about the other point—*the benefit these sons of Jacob receive from an unchanging God.* "Therefore you sons of Jacob are not consumed." Consumed? How? How can man be consumed? Why, there are two ways. We might have been consumed in hell. If God had been a changing God, the sons of Jacob here this morning might have been consumed in hell. But for God's unchanging love, I should have been a stick in the fire. But there is a way of being consumed in this *world.* There is such a thing as being *condemned* before you die—"condemned already." There is such a thing as being alive and yet being absolutely dead. We might have been left to our own devices, and then where would we be?

Reveling with the drunkard, blaspheming Almighty God? Oh, had He left you, beloved and longed-for, had He been a changing God, you had been among the filthiest of the filthy and the vilest of the vile. Can you not remember in your life seasons similar to those I have felt? I have gone right to the edge of sin. Some strong temptation has taken hold of both my arms so that I could not wrestle with it. I have been pushed along, dragged as by an awful satanic power to the very edge of some horrid precipice. I have looked down, down, down and seen my portion. I quivered on the brink of ruin. I have been horrified as, with my hair upright, I have thought of the sin I was about to commit, the horrible pit into which I was about to fall.

> *S*ince He loved them without works, He loves them without works still. Since their good works did not win His affection, bad works cannot sever that affection.

A strong arm has saved me. I have started back and cried, "O God, could I have gone so near sin and yet come back again? Could I have walked right up to the furnace and not fallen down, like Nebuchadnezzar's strong men, devoured by the very heat? Oh, is it possible I should be here this morning, when I think of the sins I have committed and the crimes that have crossed my wicked imagination?" Yes, I am here, unconsumed, because the Lord changes not. Oh, if He had changed, we should have been consumed in a dozen ways. If the Lord had changed, you and I would have consumed ourselves. For after all, Mr. Self is the worst enemy a Christian has.

We should have proved suicides to our own souls. We should have mixed the cup of poison for our own spirits, if the Lord had not been an unchanging God and dashed the cup out of our hands when we were about to drink it. Then God Himself should have consumed us if He had not been a changeless God. We call God a Father, but there is not a father in this world who would not have killed all his children long ago, so provoked would he have been with them, if he had been half as much troubled as God has been with His family. He has the most troublesome family in the whole world: unbelieving, ungrateful, disobedient, forgetful, rebellious, wandering, murmuring, and stiff-necked. Well it is that He is long-suffering, or else He would have taken not only the rod, but also the sword to some of us long ago.

But there was nothing in us to love at first, so there cannot be less now. John Newton used to tell a whimsical story and laugh at it, too, of a good woman who said, in order to prove the doctrine of election, "Ah, sir, the Lord must have loved me before I was born, or else He would not have seen anything in me to love afterward." I am sure it is true in my case and true in respect to most of God's people. For there is little to love in them after they are born. If He had not loved them before, then He would have seen no reason to choose them after. But since He loved them without works,

He loves them without works still. Since their good works did not *win* His affection, bad works cannot *sever* that affection. Since their righteousness did not bind His love to them, so their wickedness cannot snap the golden links. He loved them out of pure sovereign grace, and He will love them still. But we should have been consumed by the devil and by our enemies; consumed by the world, consumed by our sins, by our trials, and in a hundred other ways if God had ever changed.

Well now, time fails us and I can say but little. I have only just cursorily touched on the text. I now hand it to you. May the Lord help you sons of Jacob to take home this portion of meat. Digest it well and feed upon it. May the Holy Spirit sweetly apply the glorious things that are written! And may you have "a feast of choice pieces, a feast of wines on the lees, of fat things full of marrow, of well-refined wines on the lees" (Isa. 25:6). Remember, God is the same, whatever is removed. Your friends may be disaffected, your ministers may be taken away, everything may change, but God does not. Your brethren may change and cast out your name as vile—but God will love you still. Let your station in life change and your property be gone. Let your whole life be shaken and you become weak and sickly. Let everything flee away—there is one place where change cannot put his finger. There is one name on which mutability can never be written. One heart never can alter. That heart is God's; that name Love.

> *Trust Him, He will ne'er deceive you.*
> *Though you hardly of Him deem,*
> *He will never, never leave you,*
> *Nor will let you quite leave Him.*

FOR FURTHER THOUGHT

1. *What is another way of saying "God is immutable"?*
2. *Spurgeon mentions several traits of people who can be considered sons of Jacob. With which of these do you most identify?*
3. *What is the main benefit to those who believe in the unchanging God?*

THE INFALLIBILITY OF
GOD'S PURPOSE

But he is in one mind, and who can turn him?
And what his soul desireth, even that he doeth.
JOB 23:13 KJV

IT is very advantageous to the Christian mind frequently to consider the deep and unsearchable attributes of God. The beneficial effect is palpable in two ways, exerting a sacred influence both on the judgment and the heart. In respect to the one, it tends to confirm us in those good old orthodox doctrines that lie as the basis of our faith. If we study man and make him the only object of our research, there will be a strong tendency in our minds to exaggerate his importance. We will think too much of the creature and too little of the Creator, preferring the knowledge that is to be found out by observation and reason to the divine truth that revelation alone could make known to us. The basis and groundwork of Arminian theology lies in attaching undue importance to man and giving God the second place rather than the first.

Let your mind dwell for a long time upon man as a free agent; upon man as a responsible being; upon man, not so much as being under God's claims as having claims upon God, and you will soon find in your thoughts a set of crude doctrines. You will support these doctrines with the letter of some few isolated texts in scripture that may be speciously quoted but that really in spirit are contrary to the whole tenor of the Word of God. Thus your orthodoxy will be shaken to its very foundations and your soul will be driven out to sea without peace or joy.

Brethren, I am not afraid that any man who thinks worthily about the Creator, stands in awe of His adorable perfections, and sees Him sitting upon the throne doing all things according to the counsel of His will, will go far wrong in his doctrinal sentiments. He may say, "My heart is steadfast,

O God" (Ps. 57:7), and when the heart is fixed with a firm conviction of the greatness, the omnipotence, the divinity of Him whom we call God, the head will not wander far from truth. Another happy result of such meditation is the steady peace, the grateful calm it gives to the soul. Have you been a long time at sea and has the continual motion of the ship sickened and disturbed you? Have you come to look upon everything as moving till you scarcely put one foot before the other without the fear of falling down because the floor rocks beneath your path? With what delight do you put your feet at last upon the shore and say, "Ah, this does not move. This is solid ground. Though the tempest howl, this island is safely moored. She will not start from her bearings. When I tread on her, she will not yield beneath my feet." Just so is it with us when we turn from the ever-shifting, often boisterous tide of earthly things to take refuge in the eternal God who has been "our dwelling place in all generations" (Ps. 90:1). The fleeting things of human life and the fickle thoughts and showy deeds of men are as movable and changeable as the waters of the treacherous deep. But when we mount up, as it were, with eagles' wings to Him who sits upon the circle of the earth, before whom all its inhabitants are as grasshoppers (Isa. 40:22), we nestle in the Rock of Ages that from its eternal socket never starts and in its fixed immovability never can be disturbed.

> *he fleeting things of human life and the fickle thoughts and showy deeds of men are as movable and changeable as the waters of the treacherous deep.*

Or to use another simile: You have seen little children running round and round and round till they get giddy. They stand still a moment and everything seems to be flying all around them. But by holding fast and still, and getting into their mind the fact that that to which they hold is firm, at last the world grows still again, and the world ceases to whirl. So you and I have been these six days like little children running round in circles and everything has been moving with us. Perhaps as we came to this place this morning, we felt as if the very promises of God had moved, as if providence had shifted, our friends had died, our kindred passed away. We came to look on everything as whirling; nothing firm, nothing fixed.

Brethren, let us get a good grip today of the immutability of God. Let us stand still awhile and know that the Lord is God. We will see at length that things do not move as we dreamed they did. "To everything there is a season, a time for every purpose under heaven" (Eccles. 3:1). There is still fixedness in that which seems most fickle. That which appears to be dreamiest has a reality. Inasmuch as it is a part of that divinely substantial scheme that God is working out, the end whereof will be His eternal glory. It will cool your brain; it will calm your heart, my brother. It will make you go back to the world's fight quiet and composed. It will make you stand fast in the day of temptation if now through divine grace you can come near to God, who is without variableness or shadow of turning, and offer Him the tribute of our devotion.

We will consider the text this morning, first as *enunciating a great general truth*. Second, out of that general truth we will fetch another upon which we will enlarge, I trust, to our comfort.

I. The text may be regarded as *teaching a general truth*. We will take the first clause of the sentence, "He is in one mind." Now the fact taught here is that in all the acts of God in providence, He has a fixed and a settled purpose. "He is in one mind." It is eminently consolatory to us, who are God's creatures, to know that He did not make us without a purpose and that now, in all His dealings with us, He has the same wise and gracious end to be served. We suffer, the head aches, the heart leaps with palpitations, and the blood creeps sluggishly along where its healthy flow should have been more rapid. We lose our limbs. Crushed by accident, some sense fails us.

The eye is eclipsed in perpetual night. Our mind is racked and disturbed. Our fortunes vary. Our goods disappear before our eyes. Our children, portions of ourselves, sicken and die. Our crosses are as continual as our lives; we are seldom long at ease. We are born to sorrow, and certainly it is an inheritance of which we are never deprived. We suffer continually. Will it not reconcile us to our sorrows that they serve some end? To be scourged needlessly we consider to be a disgrace, but to be scourged if our country were to be served we should consider an honor because there is a purpose in it. To suffer the maiming of our bodies because of some whim of a tyrant would be a thing hard to bear. But if we administer thereby to the weal of our families, or to the glory of our God, we would be content not to be mutilated once but to be cut piecemeal away so that His great purpose might be answered.

O believer, ever look, then, on all your sufferings as being parts of the divine plan and say, as wave upon wave rolls over you, "He is in one mind!" He is carrying out still His one great purpose. None of these comes by chance; none of these happens to me out of order; but everything comes to me according to the purpose of His own will and answers the purpose of His own great mind. We have to labor, too. How hard do some men labor who have to toil for their daily bread! Their bread is saturated with their sweat. They wear no garment that they have not woven out of their own nerves and muscles. How sternly, too, do others labor who have with their brains to serve their fellow men or their God!

How have some heroic missionaries spent themselves and been spent in their fond enterprise! How have many ministers of Christ exhausted not simply the body, but the mind! Their hilarity so natural to them has given place to despondency, and the natural effervescence of their spirits has at last died out into oneness of soul through the desperateness of their ardor. And sometimes this labor for God is unrequited. We plow, but the furrow yields no harvest. We sow, but the field refuses the grain, and the devouring bellies of the hungry birds alone are satisfied therewith. We build, but the storm casts down the stones that we had quarried with Herculean efforts, piling one on another.

> *O believer, ever look, then, on all your sufferings as being parts of the divine plan and say, as wave upon wave rolls over you, "He is in one mind!"*

We sweat, we toil, and we fail. How often do we come back weeping because we have toiled, as we think, without success! Yet, Christian man, you have not been without success, for "He is still in one mind." All this was necessary to the fulfillment of His one purpose. You are not lost; your labor has not rotted under the clods. All, though you see it not, has been working together toward the desired end. Stand upon the beach for a moment. A wave has just come up careening in its pride. Its crown of froth is spent. As it leaps beyond its fellow, it dies. It dies. And now another and it dies. And now another and it dies. Oh, weep not, deep sea! Be not sorrowful, for though each wave dies, yet you prevail!

O mighty ocean! Onward does the flood advance till it has covered all the sand and washed the feet of the white cliffs. So is it with God's purpose. You and I are only waves of His great sea. We wash up. We seem to retire as if there had been no advance. Another wave comes. Still each wave must retire as though there had been no progress. But the great divine sea of His purpose is still moving on. He is still of one mind and carrying out His plan. How sorrowful it often seems to think how good men die! They learn through the days of their youth, and often before they come to years to use their learning, they are gone. The blade is made and annealed in many a fire, but before the foeman uses it, it snaps!

How many laborers, too, in the Master's vineyard, who when by their experience they were getting more useful than ever have been taken away just when the church wanted them most! He who stood upright in the chariot guiding the steeds suddenly falls back, and we cry, "My father, my father, the chariot of Israel and its horsemen!" (2 Kings 2:12). Notwithstanding all this, we may console ourselves in the midst of our grief with the blessed reflection that everything is a part of God's plan. He is still of one mind; nothing happens that is not a part of the divine scheme. To enlarge our thoughts a moment, have you ever noticed, in reading history, how nations suddenly decay? When their civilization has advanced so far that we thought it would produce men of the highest mold, suddenly old age begins to wrinkle its brow, its arm grows weak, the scepter falls, the crown drops from the head, and we have to say, is not the world gone back again?

The barbarian has sacked the city, and where once everything was beauty, now there is nothing but ruthless bloodshed and destruction. But, my brethren, all those things were but the carrying out of the divine plan. Just as you may have seen sometimes upon the hard rock where the lichen spring, that as soon as the lichen grows grand, it dies. Why? It is because its death prepares the moss, and the moss, which is feebler, compared with the lichen growth, at last increases till you see before you the finest specimens of that genus. But then the moss decays. Yet weep not for its decaying. Its ashes will prepare a soil for some plants of a little higher growth, and as these decay, one after another, race after race, they at last prepare the soil upon which even the goodly cedar itself might stretch out its roots.

So has it been with the race of men; Egypt, Assyria, Babylon, Greece, and Rome have crumbled. A better succeeded each and all, when their hour had come. And if this race of ours should ever be eclipsed, if the Anglo-

Saxons' boasted pride should yet be stained, even then it will prove to be a link in the divine purpose. Still, in the end His one mind will be carried out. His one great result will be thereby achieved. Not only the decay of nations, but also the apparent degeneration of some races of men and even the total extinction of others, forms a part of the fixed purpose of God. In all those cases there may be reasons of sorrow, but faith sees grounds of rejoicing.

To gather up all in one (Eph. 1:10), the calamities of earthquake, the devastations of storm, the extirpations of war, and all the terrible catastrophes of plague have only been coworkers with God, slaves compelled to tug the galley of the divine purpose across the sea of time. From every evil, good has come. And the more the evil has accumulated, the more has God glorified Himself in bringing out at last His grand, His everlasting design. This, I take it, is the first general lesson of the text—in every event of providence, God has a purpose. "He is in one mind."

Mark, not only a purpose, but only *one* purpose—for all history is but one. There are many scenes, but it is one drama. There are many pages, but it is one book. There are many leaves, but it is one tree. There are many provinces, yes, and there are many lords and rulers, yet there is but one empire and God the only Potentate. "Let us come before His presence with thanksgiving; let us shout joyfully to Him with psalms. For the LORD is the great God, and the great King above all gods" (Ps. 95:2–3).

2. "Who can turn Him?" This is the second clause of the sentence, and here I think we are taught the doctrine that *the purpose of God is unchanged.* The first sentence shows that He has a purpose; the second shows that it is incapable of change. "Who can turn Him?" Some shallow thinkers dream that the great plan and design of God was thrown out of order by the fall of man. The fall they consider all accidental circumstances, not intended in the divine plan, and thus God, being placed in a delicate predicament of requiring to sacrifice His justice or His mercy, used the plan of the atonement of Christ as a divine expedient.

Brethren, it may be lawful to use such terms; that is, lawful to you, not to me. I am persuaded that the very fall of man was a part of the divine purpose: that even the sin of Adam, though he did it freely, was nevertheless contemplated in the divine scheme and was by no means such a thing as to involve a digression from His primary plan. Then came the deluge and the race of man was swept away, but God's purpose was not affected by the destruction of the race. In later years His people Israel forsook Him and worshipped Baal and Ashtaroth. But His purpose was not changed any more by the defection of His chosen nation than by the destruction of His creatures.

And when later the gospel was sent to the Jews, and they resisted it and Paul and Peter turned to the Gentiles, do not suppose that God had to take down His book and make an erasure or an amendment. No, the whole was written there from the beginning. He knew everything of it. He has never altered a single sentence nor changed a single line of the divine purpose. What He intended the great picture to be, that it will be at the end. And where you see some black strokes that seem not in keeping, these will yet be toned down. And where there are some brighter dashes, too bright for the somber picture, these will yet be brought into harmony. And when in the end God will exhibit the whole, He will elicit from both men and angels tremendous shouts of praise, while they say, "All the families of the nations shall worship before You. For the kingdom is the LORD's, and He rules over the nations" (Ps. 22:27–28).

> *I am persuaded that the very fall of man was a part of the divine purpose: that even the sin of Adam, though he did it freely, was nevertheless contemplated in the divine scheme.*

Where we have thought His government wrong, there will it prove most right, and where we dreamed He had forgotten to be good, there will His goodness be most clear. It is a sweet consolation to the mind of one who muses much upon these deep matters that God never has changed in any degree from His purpose. And the result will be, notwithstanding everything to the contrary, just precisely in every jot and tittle what He foreknew and foreordained it should be. Wars may rise and other Alexanders and Caesars may spring up, but He will not change. Now, nations and peoples, lift up yourselves and let your parliaments pass your decrees, but He changes not.

Now, rebels, foam at the mouth and let your fury boil. But He changes not for you. Oh, nations and peoples and tongues, and you round earth, you spin on your orbit still and all the fury of your inhabitants cannot make you move from your predestinated pathway. Creation is an arrow from the bow of God, and that arrow goes on, straight on, without deviation to the center of that target that God ordained that it should strike. Never varied is His plan. He is without variableness or shadow of turning. Albert Barnes very justly says, "It is, when properly understood, a matter of unspeakable consolation that God has a plan. For who could honor a God who had no plan, who did everything haphazardly? It is matter of rejoicing that He has one great purpose that extends through all ages and embraces all things. For then everything falls into its proper place and has its appropriate bearing on other events. It is a matter of joy that God does execute all His purposes. For as they are all good and wise, it is *desirable* that they should be executed. It could be a calamity if a good plan were not executed. Why, then, should men murmur at the purposes or the decrees of God?"

3. The text also teaches a third general truth. While God had a purpose and that purpose has never changed, the third clause teaches us that *this purpose is sure to be effected.* He made the world out of nothing. There was no resistance there. "Light be," said He, and light was. There was no resistance there. "Providence be," said He, and providence will be. And when you will come to see the end as well as the beginning, you will find that there was no resistance there. It is a wonderful thing how God effects His purpose while still *the creature is free.* They who think that predestination and the fulfillment of the divine purpose are contrary to the free agency of man know not what they say, nor what they affirm.

It would be no miracle for God to effect His own purpose if He were dealing with sticks and stones, with granite and with trees. But this is the miracle of miracles: that *the creatures are free*, absolutely free, and still the divine purpose stands! Herein is wisdom! This is a deep, unsearchable mystery. Man walks without a leash yet treads in the very steps that God ordained him to tread in as certainly as though manacles had bound him to the spot! Man chooses his own seat, selects his own position; guided by his will, he chooses sin, or guided by divine grace, he chooses right. And yet in his choice God sits as sovereign on the throne, not disturbing but still overruling and proving Himself to be as able to deal with free creatures as with creatures without freedom. As able to effect His purpose when He has endowed men with thought and reason and judgment, as when He had only to deal with the solid rocks and with the imbedded sea.

O Christians! You will never be able to fathom this, but you may wonder at it. I know there is an easy way of getting out of this great deep either by denying predestination altogether or by denying free agency altogether. But you can hold the two: You can say, "Yes, my consciousness teaches me that man does as he wills, but my faith teaches me that God does as He wills, and these two are not contrary the one to the other. And yet I cannot tell how it is. I cannot tell how God effects His end. I can only wonder, admire, and say, 'Oh, the depth of the riches both of the wisdom and knowledge of God! How unsearchable are His judgments and His ways past finding out!'" (Rom. 11:33). Every creature is free and doing as it wills, yet God is freer still and doing as He wills not only in heaven, but also among the inhabitants of this lower earth.

I have thus given you a general subject upon which I would invite you to spend your meditations in your quiet hours. I am persuaded that sometimes to think of these deep doctrines will be found very profitable. It will be to you like the advice of Christ to Simon Peter: "Launch out into the deep and let down your nets for a catch" (Luke 5:4). You will have a draught of exceeding great thoughts and exceeding great graces if you dare to launch out into this exceeding deep sea and let out the nets of your contemplation at the command of Christ.

"O Lord, how great are Your works! Your thoughts are very deep. A senseless man does not know, nor does a fool understand this" (Ps. 92:5–6).

II. I now come to the second part of my subject, which will be, I trust, cheering to the people of God. From the general doctrine that God has a plan—that this plan is invariable and that this plan is certain to be carried out—I drew the most precious doctrine that *in salvation God is of one mind*. And who can turn Him? And what His heart desires, that He does. Now, mark, I address myself at this hour only to you who are the people of God. Do you believe in the Lord Jesus Christ with all your heart? Is the spirit of adoption given to you whereby you can say, "Abba, Father" (Rom. 8:15)? If so, draw near, for this truth is for you.

Come then, my brethren; in the first place let us consider that *God is of one mind*. Of old, my soul, He determined to save you. Your calling proves your election, and your election teaches you that God ordained to save you. He is not a man that He should lie, nor the son of man that He should repent (Num. 32:19). He is of one mind. He saw you ruined in the fall of your father Adam, but His mind never changed from His purpose to save you. He saw you in your nativity. Your youthful follies and disobedience He saw, but never did that gracious mind alter in its designs of love to you. Then in your manhood you did plunge into vice and sin. Cover, O darkness, all our guilt, and let the night conceal it from our eyes forever! Though we added sin to sin and our pride waxed exceeding high and hot, yet He was of one mind:

Determined to save,
He watched over my path
When Satan's blind slave,
I sported with death.

At last, when the happy hour arrived, He came to our door and knocked, and He said, "Open to me." And do you remember, O my brother, how we said, "Go away, O Jesus! We want you not"? We scorned His grace. We defied His love! But He was of one mind and no hardness of heart could turn Him. He had determined to have us for His spouse and He would not take no for an answer. He said He would have us and He persevered. He knocked again. And do you remember how we half opened the door? But then some strong temptation came and we shut it in His very face. But even then, He said, "Open for me, my sister, my love, my dove, my perfect one; for my head is covered with dew, my locks with the drops of the night" (Song of Sol. 5:2). Yet we bolted and barred the door and would not let Him in. But He was of one mind and none could turn Him.

Oh, my soul weeps now when I think of the many convictions that I stifled, of the many moves of His Spirit that I rejected and those many times when conscience bade me repent and urged me to flee to Him but I would not. My soul weeps when I think of those seasons when a mother's tears united with all the intercession of the Savior, yet my heart was harder than granite, and I refused to move and would not yield. But He was of one mind.

He had no fickleness in Him. He said He would have us, and have us He would. He had written our names in His book and He would not cross them out. It was His solemn purpose that we should yield. And oh, that hour when, by His grace, we yielded at last! Then did He prove that in all our wanderings He had been of one mind. And oh, since then, how sorrowful the reflection! Since then how often have you and I turned? We have backslidden, and if we had the Arminians' god to deal with, we should either have been in hell or out of the covenant at this hour.

I know I should be in the covenant and out of the covenant a hundred times a day if I had a god who put me out every time I sinned and then restored me when I repented. But no, despite our sin, our unbelief, our backslidings, our forgetfulness of Him, He was of one mind. And, brethren, I know this, that though we will wander still, though in dark hours you and I may slip and often fall, yet His loving-kindness changes not. Your strong arm, O God, will bear us on. Your loving heart will never fail. You will not turn your love away from us or make it cease or pour upon us your fierce anger, but having begun you will complete the triumphs of your grace.

Nothing will make you change your mind. What joy is this to you, believers? For your mind changes every day; your experience varies like the wind, and if salvation were to be the result of any purpose on your part, certainly it never would be effected. But since it is God's work to save and we have proved that He is of one mind, our faith will revel in the thought that He will be of one thought even to the end—till all on glory's summit we will sing of that fixed purpose and that immutable love that never turned aside until the deed of grace was triumphantly achieved.

Now, believer, listen to the second lesson—"Who can turn Him?" While He is immutable from within, He is immovable from without. "Who can turn Him?" That is a splendid picture presented to us by Moses in the Book of Numbers. The children of Israel were encamped in the plains of Moab. Quietly and calmly they were resting in the valley, the tabernacle of the Lord in their midst and the pillar of cloud spread over them as a shield. But on the mountain range there were two men: Balak the son of Zippor, king of the Moabites, and Balaam the prophet of Pethor.

They had built seven altars and offered seven bullocks, and Balak said to Balaam, "Come, curse Jacob for me, and come, denounce Israel!" (Num. 23:7). Four times did the prophet take up his parable. Four times did he use his enchantments, offering the sacrifices of God on the altars of Baal. Four times did he vainly attempt a false divination. But I would have you mark that in each succeeding vision the mind of God is brought out in deeper characters. First, Balaam confesses his own impotence: "How shall I curse whom God has not cursed? And how shall I denounce whom the LORD has not denounced?" (23:8). Then the second oracle brings out more distinctly the divine blessing: "Behold, I have received a command to bless; He has blessed, and I cannot reverse it" (23:20). A third audacious attempt is not with a heavier repulse, for the stifled curse recoils on them: "Blessed is he who blesses you, and cursed is he who curses you" (24:9). Once again in the vision that closes the picture, the eyes of Balaam are opened till he gets a glimpse of the star that should come out of Jacob and the scepter that will rise out of Israel with the dawning glory of the latter days (24:17). Well might Balaam say, "For there is no sorcery against Jacob, nor any divination against Israel" (23:23).

> *Who can advise God? Who will counsel the Most High to cast off the darlings of His bosom or persuade the Savior to reject His spouse?*

And now transfer that picture in your mind to all your enemies and especially to that archfiend of hell. He comes before God today with the remembrance of your sins, and he desires that he may curse Israel. But he has found a hundred times that there is no enchantment against Jacob or divination against Israel. He took David into the sin of lust and he found that God would not curse him there, but bless him with a sorrowful chastisement and with a deep repentance. He took Peter into the sin of denying his Master and he denied Him with oaths and curses. But the Lord would not curse him even there, but turned and looked on Peter, not with a lightning glance that might have shivered him, but with a look of love that made him weep bitterly.

He has taken you and me many times into positions of unbelief and we have doubted God. Satan said, "Surely, surely God will curse him there," but never once has He done it. He has smitten, but the blow was full of love. He has chastised, but the chastisement was fraught with mercy. He has not cursed us nor will He. You cannot turn God's mind. Then, fiend of hell, your enchantments cannot prosper; your accusations will not prevail. "He is in one mind, and who can turn Him?" And, brethren, you know when men are turned, they are sometimes turned by advice. Now who can advise God? Who will counsel the Most High to cast off the darlings of His bosom or persuade the Savior to reject His spouse?

Such counsels offered were blasphemy and it would be not pungent to His soul. Or else men are turned by entreaties. But how will God listen to the entreaties of the evil one? Are not the prayers of the wicked an abomination to the Lord? Let them pray against us; let them entreat the Lord to curse us. But He is of one mind, and no revengeful prayer should change the purpose of His love. Sometimes the ties of relationships change men—a mother interposes and man yields—but in our case, who can interpose?

God's only begotten Son is as much concerned in our salvation as His Father, and instead of interposing to change, He would—if such a thing were needed—still continue to plead that the love and mercy of God might never be withdrawn. Oh, let us rejoice in this:

> *Midst all our sin and care and woe,*
> *His Spirit will not let us go.*

The Lord will not forsake His people for His great name's sake because it has pleased the Lord to make you His people. "He is in one mind, and who can turn Him?"

I know not how it is, but I feel that I cannot preach from this text as I should like. But oh, the text itself is music to my ears! It seems to sound like the martial trumpet of the battle, and my soul is ready for the fray. It seems now that if trials and troubles should come, if I could but hold my hand upon this precious text, I would laugh at them all. "Who can turn Him?" I would shout. "Who can turn Him?" Come on, earth and hell, come on, for "who can turn Him?" Come on, you boisterous troubles; come on, you innumerable temptations; come on, slanderer and liar: "Who can turn Him?" And since He cannot be changed, my soul must and will rejoice "with joy unspeakable and full of glory" (1 Pet. 1:8 KJV).

I wish I could throw the text like a bombshell into the midst of the army of doubters that that army might be routed at once, for when we get a text like this, it must be the *text* that takes effect and not our explanation. This surely is a most marvelous deathblow to our doubts and fears: "He is in one mind, and who can turn Him?"

III. And now with a few words upon the last sentence I will conclude: *God's purpose must be effected.* "What His soul desires, that He does." Beloved, what God's soul desires is *your salvation and mine*, if we are His chosen. And that He does. Part of that salvation consists in our perfect sanctification. We have had a long struggle with inbred sin, and as far as we can judge we have not made much progress. Still is the Philistine in the land, and still does the Canaanite invade us. We sin still and our hearts still have in them unbelief and proneness to depart from the living God. Can you think it possible that you will ever be without any tendency to sin?

Does it not seem a dream that you should ever be without fault before the throne of God—without spot or wrinkle or any such thing?

But yet you will be. His heart desires it and that He does. He would have His spouse without any defilement. He would have His chosen generation without anything to mar their perfection. Now, inasmuch as He spoke and it was done, He has but to speak and it will be done with you. You cannot rout your foes, but He can. You cannot overcome your besetting sins, but He can do it. You cannot drive out your corruptions, for they have chariots of iron, but He will drive out the last of them till the whole land will be without one enemy to disturb its perpetual peace. Oh, what a joy to know that it will be before long! Oh, it will be so soon with some of us, such a few weeks, though we perhaps are planning on years of life!

A few weeks or a few days, and we will have passed through Jordan's flood and stand complete in Him, accepted in the Beloved! And should it be many years, should we be spared till the snows of a century will have fallen upon our frosted hair, yet even then we must not doubt that His purpose will at last be fulfilled. We will be spotless and faultless and unblameable in His sight before long.

> *Come, you desponding ones. If salvation were to be your own work, you might despair, but since it is His and He changes not, you must not ever doubt.*

Another part of our salvation is that we should at last be without pain, without sorrow, gathered with the church of the firstborn before the Father's face. Does it not seem, when you sit down to think of yourself as being in heaven, as a pretty dream that never will be true? What? Shall these fingers one day smite the strings of a golden harp? O aching head! Shall you one day wear a crown of glory that fades not away? O toil-worn body! Shall you bathe yourself in seas of heavenly rest? Is not heaven too good for us, brothers and sisters? Can it be that we, poor we, will ever get inside those pearly gates or tread the golden streets? Oh, will we ever see His face? Will He ever kiss us with the kisses of His lips?

Will the King immortal, invisible, the only wise God, our Savior, take us to His bosom and call us all His own? Oh, will we ever drink out of the rivers of pleasure that are at the right hand of the Most High? Shall we be among that happy company who will be led to the living fountains of waters and all tears be wiped away from our eyes? Ah, that we will be! For "He is in one mind, and who can turn Him? And what His soul desires, that He does."

"Father, I desire that they also whom You gave Me may be with Me where I am, that they may behold My glory which You have given Me" (John 17:24). That is an immortal, omnipotent desire. We will be with Him where He is. His purpose will be effected and we will partake of His bliss.

Now rise, you who love the Savior, and put your trust in Him. Rise like men who have God within you and sit no longer down upon your dunghills. Come, you desponding ones. If salvation were to be your own work, you might despair, but since it is His and He changes not, you must not ever doubt.

> *Now let the feeble all be strong,*
> *And make Jehovah's power their song;*
> *His shield is spread o'er every saint.*
> *And thus supported, who can faint?*

If you perish, even the weakest of you, God's purpose cannot be effected. If you finally fall, His honor will be stained. If you perish, heaven itself will be dishonored; Christ will have lost one of His members. He will be a king whose regalia have been stolen. No, He will not be complete Himself, for the church is His fullness, and how can He be full if a part of His fullness will be cast away? Putting these things together, let us take courage, and in the name of God let us set up our banners. He who has been with us up to now will preserve us to the end, and we will soon sing in the fruition of glory as we now recite in the confidence of faith: that His purpose is completed and His love immutable.

I say by way of closing that such a subject ought to inspire every man with awe. I speak to some here who are unconverted. It is an awful thought: God's purpose will be subserved in you. You may hate Him, but as He got honor upon Pharaoh and all his hosts, so will He upon you. You may think that you will spoil His designs, but that will be your idea while your very acts, though guided with that intent, will only tend to subserve His glory. Think of that! To rebel against God is useless, for you cannot prevail. To resist Him is not only impertinence, but also folly. He will be as much glorified by you, whatever way you go. You will either yield Him willing honor or *unwilling honor*, but either way His purpose in you will be most certainly subserved.

Oh, that this thought might make you bow your heads and say, "Great God, glorify your mercy in me, for I have revolted. Show that you can forgive. I have sinned, deeply sinned. Prove the depths of your mercy by pardoning me. I know that Jesus died and that He is set forth as a propitiator. I believe on Him as such. O God! I trust Him. I pray you will glorify yourself in me by showing what your grace can do in casting sin behind your back and blotting out iniquity, transgression, and sin."

Sinner, He will do it. He will do it. If thus you plead and thus you pray, He will do it. There was never a sinner rejected yet who came to God with humble prayer and faith. Go to God today. Confess your sin and take hold of Christ as upon the horns of the altar of mercy and of sacrifice. If you do, you will find that it was a part of the divine plan to bring you here today, to strike your mind with awe, to lead you humbly to the cross, to lead you afterward joyfully to your God—and to bring you perfect at last before His throne!

God add His blessing for Christ's sake! Amen.

For Further Thought

1. *Genesis 1–3 tells of creation and the fall of humanity. Which of these is a part of God's plan?*
2. *How does Balaam's prophecy display God's immutability?*
3. *Does God ever change His mind concerning your salvation?*

God's Long-suffering:
An Appeal to the Conscience

*Consider that the longsuffering
of our Lord is salvation.*
2 Peter 3:15

JESUS is well called our Lord. Let us, at the commencement, adore Him. Let us, each one, cry to Him, "My Lord and my God!" (John 20:28). It is a long time since our Lord went up to heaven and He said that He would come again. Evidently, some of those who best understood Him *mis*understood Him and thought that He would surely come again even in their lifetime. He said that He would come, and faithful ones in all ages have looked for Him. It is not possible that our Lord can have deceived us. Because He is so sweetly our Lord, our brethren have made sure that He will keep His Word, and He will. But certain of them have gone beyond our Lord's promise and have felt sure that they knew when He would come. They have been bitterly disappointed because the hour that they fixed passed over and He did not appear. This does not prove that He will not come. The day is certainly nearer and every hour is hastening His coming. "They will see the Son of Man coming on the clouds of heaven with power and great glory" (Matt. 24:30).

But why are His chariots so long in coming? Why does He delay? The world grows gray, not only with age, but also with iniquity, and yet the Deliverer comes not. We have waited for His footfall at the dead of night and looked out for Him through the gates of the morning. We have expected Him in the heat of the day and reckoned that He might come before yet another sun went down. But He is not here! He waits. He waits very, very long. Will He not come?

Long-suffering is that which keeps Him from coming. He is bearing with men. Not yet the thunderbolt! Not yet the riven heavens and the

144

reeling earth! Not yet the great white throne and the Day of Judgment, for He is full of pity and bears long with men! Even to the cries of His own elect, who cry day and night to Him, He is not in haste to answer, for He is very patient, slow to anger, and plenteous in mercy.

But His patience sometimes greatly puzzles us. We cannot make it out. Eighteen, nineteen centuries and the world not converted! Nineteen centuries and Satan still to the front, and all manner of iniquity still wounding this poor, bleeding world! What does it mean? O Son of God, what does it mean? Seed of the woman, when will You appear with Your foot upon the serpent's head? We are puzzled at the long-suffering that causes so weary a delay.

> *We think that we do well to be angry at the rebellious, and so we prove ourselves to be more like Jonah than Jesus!*

One of the reasons is that we have not much long-suffering ourselves. We think that we do well to be angry at the rebellious, and so we prove ourselves to be more like Jonah than Jesus! A few have learned to be patient and show pity to the ungodly, but many more are of the mind of James and John who would have called fire from heaven upon those who rejected the Savior. We are in such a hurry! We have not the eternal leisure of God. We have but to live, like mayflies, our little day, and therefore we are in hot haste to see all things accomplished before the sun goes down. We are but leaves in the forest of existence, and if something is not done soon, and done quickly, we will fade and pass away amid unaccomplished hope! And so we are not patient. We are staggered when the Master tells us to forgive to seventy times seven. When He forgives to seventy times seven, and still waits, and still holds back His thunders, we are amazed because our mind is not in harmony with the mind of the infinitely patient God!

We are all the more puzzled, again, because the ungodly so sadly misuse this long-suffering of God as a reason for greater sin and as a motive for denying that there is a God at all! Because He gives them space for repentance, they make it into space for iniquity! And because He will not deal out His judgments immediately, they say, "Where is the promise of His coming?" (2 Pet. 3:4).

We have impatiently wished that He would break the silence. Have I not, in my heart of hearts, cried out, "O Lord, how long? Can this go on much longer? Can you bear it? Will you not come with the iron rod, breaking your foes before your face, most mighty Son of God?" It is hard to have the days of blasphemy and rebuke multiplied upon us, and to hear the adversary say in every corner, "Where is their God now?" Yet, dear friends, we ought not to be affected by the hissing of these serpents. Surely we would not have our God change His purposes because of the foolish taunts of men! One said, "If there is a God, let Him strike me dead!" But God did not smite him and from this he argued that there was no God! From the same fact I argue that there *is* a God and that this God is truly God, for if He had been less than divine, He might have struck him dead. But, being infinitely patient, He bore with him still. Who was that speck that he should cause God to move hand or foot even to crush him? God is not easily moved, even by the blasphemies of the ungodly. He may be provoked, one of these days, for long-suffering has its end, but for a while the Lord pauses in pity, not willing that any should perish, but that all should come to repentance.

Beloved brothers and sisters, God's long-suffering with a guilty world He may never explain to us. There are many things that we must not ask to have explained. We get into deep waters and into terrible troubles when we must have everything explained. For my part, I like to believe great truths that are beyond my reason. A religion without mysteries seems to me to be false on the face of it. If there is an infinite God, it is not possible that poor I, with my finite mind, will ever be able to understand everything about Him! If the Lord chooses to tarry till thousands of years have passed away, yes, till *millions* of years have elapsed, yet let Him do as He wills! Is He not infinitely wise and good? And who are we that we should put Him to the test? Let Him tarry His own time. Only let us watch and wait, for He will come, and they who wait for Him will have their reward!

At this time I am going to speak a little upon this point. First, *let us admire the long-suffering of God.* Second, *let us make a right account of it* by accounting it to be salvation.

I. First, I would conduct your minds hurriedly over a few points that may help you to *admire the long-suffering of God.*

Admire the long-suffering of God as to *peculiar sins.* Look, brothers and sisters, they make images of wood or stone and they say, "These are God."

They set up these things in the place of Him who made the heavens and the earth! How does He endure to see reasonable beings bowing down before idols, before fetishes, before the basest objects? How does He bear that men should even worship emblems of impurity and say that these are God? How does He bear it—He who sits in the heavens, in whose hands our breath is, and whose are all our ways?

> *Beloved brothers and sisters, God's long-suffering with a guilty world He may never explain to us. There are many things that we must not ask to have explained.*

Others, even in this country, blaspheme God! What an amount of profanity is poured out before God in this city! One can scarcely walk the streets today without hearing horrible language. An oath has often chilled me to the marrow; an oath that was not excused by any special circumstance, but rolled out of the man's mouth as a customary thing. We have, today, some among us who might match the devil in blasphemy, so foully do they talk! And oh, how is it that God bears it when they dare imprecate His curse upon their bodies and their souls? O Father, how do you bear it? How do you endure these profane persons who insult you to your face?

Besides, there are those who use fair speech and yet blaspheme most intolerably. Men of education and of science are often worse than the common folk because they blaspheme with fearful deliberation and solemnly speak against God and against His Son, and against the precious blood, and against the Holy Spirit! How is it that the Thrice-Holy One bears with them? Oh, wondrous long-suffering of a gracious God!

And then there are others who wallow in unmentionable impurity and uncleanness. No, I will not attempt any description, nor would I wish to take your thoughts to those things whereof men may blush to think, though they blush not to do them. The moon sees a world of foulness, fornication, and adultery! And yet, O God, you bear it! This great blot upon the face of the world, this huge city of London reeks in its filthiness, and yet you hold your peace!

And then, when I turn my thoughts another way, to the oppression of the poor, to the grinding down of those who, with the hardest labor, can scarcely earn enough bread to keep body and soul together, how does the just God permit it? When I mark the oppression of man by man—for among wild beasts there is none that equals the cruelty of man to man—how does the All-Merciful bear it? I think the Word of the Lord must often rattle in its scabbard and He must force it down and say, "Sword of the LORD. . .rest and be still!" (Jer. 47:6).

I will not go further, because the list is endless. The wonder is that a gracious God should continue to bear all this! Think of the sin involved in false teaching. I stood, one day, at the foot of Pilate's staircase in Rome, and saw the poor creatures go up and down, on their knees, on what they are taught was the very staircase on which the Lord Jesus Christ stood before Pilate! I noticed sundry priests looking on and I felt morally certain that they knew it to be an imposture. I thought that if the Lord would lend me His thunderbolts about five minutes, I would make a wonderful clearance thereabouts, but He did nothing of the kind. God is not in a hurry as we are! Sometimes this does suggest to a hot spirit to wish for speedy dealing with iniquity, but the Lord is patient and full of pity.

Especially notice, next, that this long-suffering of God is seen in *peculiar persons*. In certain persons sins are greater than the same sins would be in other people. They have been favored with a tender conscience and with good instruction, so that when they sin, they sin with a vengeance. I have known some who have stood at God's altar and have gone forth from His temple to transgress—they have been Levites of His sanctuary and yet first in transgressions! Yet the Lord spares the traitors and lets them live.

It is amazing that God should have such long-suffering when we look at the *peculiar circumstances* under which some men sin. Some men sin against God willfully when they have no temptation to do so and can plead no necessity. If the poor man steals, we half forgive him. But some do so who have all that the heart could wish. When the man driven to extremity has said the thing that was not true, we have half excused him. But some are willful liars, with no gain or profit therein. Some sin for the sheer love of sin, not for the pleasure they gain by it, nor for the profit they hope from it, but for mere wantonness! Born of godly parents, trained as you were in the very school of godliness, made to know, as you know in your own conscience, the Lord Jesus to be the Son of God, when you sin against Him, there is a painful emphasis in your transgressions! I speak to some who may well wonder that they are still alive after having sinned with such gross aggravations!

Some manifest the long-suffering of God very wonderfully in the length of time in which they have been spared to sin. Many men are provoked by one offense and think themselves miracles of patience if they forget it. But many have provoked God fifty, sixty, seventy, perhaps eighty years! You could not stand eighty *minutes* of provocation, and yet the Lord has put up with you throughout a lifetime! You tottered into this house tonight. You might have tottered more if you had remembered the weight of sin that clings to you! Yet the mercy of God spares you. Still, with outstretched arms, infinite mercy bids you come and receive, at the hands of God, your pardon bought with the blood of Jesus Christ! This long-suffering of God is marvelous!

> *God is not in a hurry as we are! Sometimes this does suggest to a hot spirit to wish for speedy dealing with iniquity, but the Lord is patient and full of pity.*

Remember that it would be easy on God's part to be rid of you. There is a text where He says, "I will rid Myself of My adversaries" (Isa. 1:24). Some men bear because they cannot help it. They are obliged to submit. But God is not in that condition! One wish, and the sinner will never provoke Him again, nor refuse His mercy again. He will be gone out of the land of hope. Therefore I say the long-suffering of God is enhanced in its wonderfulness by the fact that He is under no necessity to exercise it except in that which springs out of His own love.

I beg all of you who are unconverted to think earnestly upon God's long-suffering to you in permitting you to be here, still to hear from the cross of Christ the invitation, "Look to Me, and be saved, all you ends of the earth!" (Isa. 45:22).

II. Second, let us *take the right account of the long-suffering of God.* "Consider that the long-suffering of our Lord is salvation" (2 Peter 3:15). What does this mean?

Does it not mean, first, *as to the saving of the many?* The Lord Jesus Christ is, as I believe, to have the preeminence. I think that He will have the preeminence in the number of souls who will be saved as compared with those who will be lost, and that can scarcely be effected except by a lapse of time in which many will be brought to Christ. I am not, however, going into any speculations. I look at it this way: As long as this old hulk keeps beating up against the rocks, as long as she does not quite go down into the sea of fire, it means man's salvation. It means, "Out with the lifeboat! Man the lifeboat and let us take off from her all that we can and bring them to shore." God calls upon us, until the world is utterly destroyed with fire, to go on saving men with all our might and main. Every year that passes is meant to be a year of salvation. We rightly call each year the year of our Lord. Let us make it so by more and more earnest efforts for the bringing of sinners to the cross of Christ. I cannot think that the world is spared to increase its damnation. Christ came not to destroy the world, but that the world, through Him, might be saved. And so, as every year rolls by, let us account it salvation and spend and be spent in the hope that by any means we may save some.

And if we can indulge a still brighter hope that the kingdom of Christ will come, and that multitudes will be converted, and that the earth will be filled with the knowledge of God as the waters cover the sea, so let it be! But always let this be to the front: that this long-suffering of God means salvation, and at that we are to aim.

God's long-suffering is one of the great means by which He works for the salvation of His elect. He will not let them die till first they live to God.

So, dear friends, in the second place, the next meaning of this is *to any of you who are unconverted.* I want you to account that the long-suffering of God in sparing you means to you salvation! Why are you here tonight? Surely it is salvation! I met, years ago, a soldier who had ridden in the charge of Balaclava. He was one of the few who came back when the saddles were emptied right and left of him. I could not help getting into a corner and saying to him, "Dear sir, do you not think that God has some design of love to you in sparing you when so many fell? Have you given your heart to Him?" I felt that I had a right to say *that.* Perhaps I speak to some of you who were picked off a wreck years ago. Why was that? I hope it was that you might be saved! You have lately had a fever and have hardly been out before now. You have come here tonight still weak, scarcely recovered. Why were you saved from that fever when others were cut down? Surely it must mean salvation! At any rate, the God who was so full of pity as to spare you, now says to you, "Call upon Me in the day of trouble; I will deliver you, and you shall glorify Me" (Ps. 50:15).

When Master Bunyan was a lad, he was so foolhardy that when an adder rose against him, he took it in his hand and plucked the sting out of its mouth, but he was not harmed. It was his turn to stand sentinel at the siege of Nottingham, and as he was going forth, another man offered to take his place. That man was shot, and Master Bunyan thus escaped. We would have had no *Pilgrim's Progress* if it had not been for that. Did not God preserve him on purpose that he might be saved? There are special interpositions of divine providence by which God spares ungodly men whom He might have cut down long ago as cumberers of the ground. Should we not look upon these as having the intention that the barren tree may be cared for yet another year, if haply it may bring forth fruit? Some of you who are here tonight are wonders to yourselves that you are still in the land of the living—I pray you account the long-suffering of God to be salvation! See salvation in it! Be encouraged to look to Christ, and looking to Him, you will find salvation, for there is life in a look at the Crucified One. Account God's long-suffering to be salvation to you if to no one else!

God's long-suffering is one of the great means by which He works for the salvation of His elect. He will not let them die till first they live to God. He will not suffer them to pass into eternity till first His infinite love has justified them through the righteousness of Christ.

Thus I have said what I hope may be embraced by some here present.

But I must finish. This text seems to me to have a bearing upon *the people of God*. Indeed, it is for them that it is written, "Account that the longsuffering of God is salvation."

I must turn the text to give you what really lies in it. God hears the cry going up from His own elect and it is written, "And shall God not avenge His own elect who cry out day and night to Him, though He bears long with them?" (Luke 18:7). That long forbearance of God brings to His own people much trouble, pain, and sorrow, much amazement and soul distress. Brothers and sisters, you must learn to look upon that as salvation!

I hear you say, "What do you mean?" I mean this: The very fact that you are made to groan and cry by reason of God's long-suffering to guilty men gives you sympathy with Christ and union with Christ, who endured such contradiction of sinners against Himself! Reckon that in being brought into harmony, sympathy, and oneness with Christ through enduring the result of the divine long-suffering, you find salvation! It is salvation to a man to be put side by side with Christ. If you have to bear the jests and gibes of the ungodly—if God spares them and permits them to persecute you—be glad of it and reckon it as salvation, for now you are made partaker of Christ's sufferings. What more salvation do you desire?

> *R*ejoice and be exceedingly glad, for great is your reward in heaven, for so they persecuted the prophets who were before you."

Remember, too, that when the ungodly persecute the righteous, they give them the mark of salvation, for of old it was so. He who was born after the flesh persecuted him who was born after the spirit. If you were never reviled, if you were never slandered or traduced, who would know that you are a Christian? But when, through the long-suffering of God with the ungodly, you are made to suffer, account it to be a mark of your salvation. "Rejoice and be exceedingly glad, for great is your reward in heaven, for so they persecuted the prophets who were before you" (Matt. 5:12).

Once more. Reckon the long-suffering of God, when it permits the ungodly to slander and injure you, as salvation because it tends to your salvation by driving you nearer to the Lord. It prevents your making your home in this world. It forces you to be a stranger and a foreigner. It compels you to go outside the gate bearing Christ's reproach, and so, in this way, that which seemed so hard to bear brings salvation to you!

Therefore comfort one another, dear children of God! Be not overly cast down and troubled because of your Lord's delaying His coming, for He will yet help you and you will be delivered.

If the Lord has shown long-suffering to any of you and yet you have never repented or turned to Him, do so tonight! "The harvest is past, the summer is ended, and we are not saved!" (Jer. 8:20). But oh, that you might be saved before this service ends! The leaves are falling from the trees thick and fast, and before you fall from the tree of this mortal life, think of your God and turn to Him and live! "Believe on the Lord Jesus Christ, and you will be saved" (Acts 16:31). May He snatch you from the burning! Amen, and amen.

FOR FURTHER THOUGHT

1. *Why has God delayed in sending Christ to the earth the second time?*
2. *Why does God have patience with unrighteous people?*
3. *How does the long-suffering of God enable us to better understand Christ?*

ALL AND ALL IN ALL

Christ is all and in all.
COLOSSIANS 3:11

That God may be all in all.
1 CORINTHIANS 15:28

IN our two texts there are three *alls* rising, one out of the other: the first leading to the second and the second conducting to the third. You will notice at once that the first two are in the present tense. "Christ *is* all," and "Christ is in all." The third one refers to the future; it is yet to be fulfilled. When the great consummation will come, then will God be all in all. I will not detain you with any sort of preface, for my sole endeavor at this time will be to impress these texts upon your memory in the hope that the Spirit of God may make them a living and abiding influence upon your hearts and lives; that to you, Christ may be all, that Christ may be in you all, and that, in all that you do and say and are, God may be all in all.

I. We begin at the foundation where all blessing begins: "Christ is all." These are but few words, yet what divine will ever fully expound them? "Christ is all." Here is sea-room enough for all godly mariners! Yet with the best wind that ever blew to speed the ship along, and with every sail set and filled with the breeze from heaven, who will ever be able to go from one shore of this great truth of God to the other—"Christ is all"? I will not venture upon such a voyage! I can but look across this sea and ask you to kindly notice the connection in which the text stands that we may learn exactly what the apostle meant. Writing "to the saints and faithful brethren in Christ who are in Colosse" (Col. 1:2), Paul says, "There is neither Greek nor Jew, circumcised nor uncircumcised, barbarian, Scythian, slave nor free, but Christ is all and in all" (3:11).

That is to say, in the matter of salvation, "Christ is all." That which had often seemed the most important thing in the world is here thrown into the background by the apostolic declaration, "There is neither Greek nor Jew." For a long time it seemed as if the eternal light of God was only revealed to the eyes of the seed of the house of Israel. They sat in the brightness and all the rest of the world lay in dense darkness. But, behold, the Christ has come, "a light to bring revelation to the Gentiles" (Luke 2:32), and henceforth salvation is "not of blood, nor of the will of the flesh, nor of the will of man" (John 1:13), but "Christ is all."

It is a great privilege to be born of godly parents, to have come of a race that for generations has feared the Lord. But let no man trust merely in his natural descent. If you had sprung from a lineage of saints, if every one of your progenitors had feared God, still nothing of this could matter for your own salvation. "Christ is all." Now may the Gentile dog eat of the crumbs that fall from the Master's table where He feeds His Israel! No, the dog is transformed into a child; he who was far off is made near! In the person of the Lord Jesus Christ, both Jew and Gentile are made one, and all the sheep of the Good Shepherd are sheltered in the same fold! We who believe in Jesus are children of him who was called the father of the faithful, and though, according to the flesh, "Abraham was ignorant of us, and Israel does not acknowledge us" (Isa. 63:16), yet by faith we become the spiritual seed of the great father of all believers! As he believed in a son being born according to God's promise, and in a seed to which the covenant promises were given, even so do we. And entering into union with Christ Jesus, that blessed Son of the promise, we become joint heirs with Him, "heirs of God and joint heirs with Christ" (Rom. 8:17). You see, then, dear friends, that it is not *race*, or *pedigree*, or *descent* that saves the soul, but that "Christ is all."

> *L*et no man trust merely in his natural descent. If you had sprung from a lineage of saints, if every one of your progenitors had feared God, still nothing of this could matter for your own salvation.

Then Paul goes on to say, "There is neither circumcision nor uncircumcision," from which I gather that *there is nothing in outward ceremonies that can save*. Everything is still of Christ. "Christ is all." That circumcision in the flesh was ordained of God, and it was the mark of the seed that He had chosen. It was not therefore lightly to be spoken of. But now, "we are the circumcision, who worship God in the Spirit, rejoice in Christ Jesus, and have no confidence in the flesh" (Phil. 3:3). At this day even the ancient divine ordinance is put in the background, for "Christ is all." So is it with every other ordinance, whether ordained of God or of man. It must never be placed in the front as if it were the means of salvation! I say to you who may have been sprinkled, or to you who may have been immersed; to you who may bow at your altars, or to you who may come to the communion table, I do not place all these rites on a level, certainly, for some are of God and some are not. But I do place them all on a par in this respect: that they enter not into the essence of our salvation! And I say to all of you, "These things cannot save you, for 'Christ is all.'" Be you who you may, and do you what you may, you will not be saved because of your natural birth or because of any supposed holy acts that you may perform! Neither will you be saved by any transactions that may be the work of a human priest! You must have Christ as your Savior and you must rest in Him alone, or you cannot be saved! He is the one foundation, "for no other foundation can anyone lay than that which is laid, which is Jesus Christ" (1 Cor. 3:11), for "Christ is all." The Lord Jesus Christ sums up everything that ordinances can possibly mean and all that pedigree and descent can possibly bring, and He is infinitely more than all of them!

> *If the gospel of Christ were a matter so deep and profound that it could not be understood except by years of educated thought, where would they be who can scarcely read the letters of a boy's schoolbook?*

Read on in this epistle and you will find that as race and ceremonialism are both put into the background, so also is culture. "There is neither Barbarian nor Scythian, but Christ is all." Of course it was for many reasons much better to be a Roman citizen than to be a rude barbarian. And it is much better, now, to be a civilized man than an untutored Indian of the Wild West. But so far as vital godliness and the soul's salvation are concerned, there is no difference! The simplest and most illiterate, upon believing in Jesus Christ, will find that "Christ is all." And the most learned and most fully instructed, if they bring any of their learning and their culture and put it side by side with Christ as a ground of trust, will sorrowfully discover that none of those things can be placed on an equality with Him, but that "Christ is all."

I rejoice, brothers and sisters, in this truth of God! If the gospel of Christ were something eclectic that could only be received by a superior few, what a poor prospect there would be for the great mass of people among whom we dwell! If the gospel of Christ were a matter so deep and profound that it could not be understood except by years of educated thought, where would they be who have never had any culture and, perhaps, can scarcely read the letters of a boy's schoolbook, if, this day, they were lying upon the bed of sickness, expecting soon to stand before God? Blessed be God, we have a remedy for sin's sickness that the Great Physician understands! And if *He* is well acquainted with it, it matters not whether the patient fully comprehends it or not! Blessed be God, the effect of Christ's medicine does not depend upon the degree to which we can realize how it acts, but if we receive it by *faith*, if it penetrates into the *heart*, if it takes possession of the *affections*, it will work in us that wondrous change by which we will be delivered from the love of sin and saved both from its condemnation and its power! Thank God for a simple gospel! Blessed be His name that "Christ is all"! If, by the teaching of the Holy Spirit, you have learned that Christ died for the ungodly, if you know that He is the Son of God and the one great propitiation for sin, and if you accept Him as such, you have that which has delivered you from going down into the pit, for God has found a ransom even for you!

Once more. By this expression, Paul means us to understand that *all human conditions and positions in this life are put on a level before Christ*, for he adds, "There is neither bond nor free; but Christ is all." When the gospel of Jesus Christ came into the world, it contemplated the saving of bondmen as well as of freemen. Of course there was a great distinction between being bond or free, and the apostle wrote, "If you can be made free, rather use it" (1 Cor. 7:21). But as to the real power of God's grace, there was no distinction between the noblest citizen of Rome and the poor slave who wore an iron collar and was fastened, like a dog, at his master's gate! Christ's grace could enter into the heart of the servile as well as into the heart of the noble—and could work alike in each.

Now hear you, sirs! It is well that you should be industrious, that you should be thrifty, and that you should make your way in the world. But this is not the way to eternal life! What if you should work till your fingertips were raw? What if you labor during the livelong day and night and deprive yourselves of needed sustenance that you may hoard up gold and silver? With all this, you cannot buy salvation or be an inch nearer to it. "Christ is all." And if you lie penniless upon a workhouse bed, there it is that Christ can save you! If you beg your food from door to door, yet will you not stand at a disadvantage with this great and blessed gospel, for it comes freely to you with this message, and as it asks of you no *learning*, so it asks of you no wealth, no rank, and no position, for from first to last, "Christ is all."

Thus have I taken the words in their connection, and they are full of important teaching. Remember that they mean just this: that *to the man who is saved, Christ is all his trust.* Our healing lies in His stripes. Our life lies in His death. Our pardon lies in His having suffered the punishment due to us. Our eternal life is in the fact that He once died for us and that He now lives to make intercession for us. "Christ is all." You must not add anything to Christ as your ground of confidence, but just lean the weight of your sin, your sorrow, your needs, and your desires wholly and entirely upon Him who lives to stand for you before God. Christ, then, is all our trust!

And, as for our belief, *Christ is our entire creed.* What He has taught us personally and by His Holy Spirit through the Epistles—what He gives us in His Word—this is what we believe, and nothing else! The Bible and the Bible alone is the religion of a Christian! "Christ is all," and all the truth that there is in this book is in Him. This revelation of the Word of God is the same revelation as that which is made in the Christ Himself, who is the true Logos, the Word of God. "Christ is all" is our creed.

And, further, *Christ is all as our example.* You may safely do what He did, and you may *not* do what He would not have done. You may judge of the right or wrong of everything by this question: What would Jesus Christ do in these circumstances? You may thus know what you should do. And what you cannot suppose He would have thought of doing, you must not venture to do, for "Christ is all." He draws a ring around us, and we must not go outside that circumference. He is the atmosphere in which we are to live. He is about us. He is above us. He is beneath us. He is within us. He is everywhere, and to us, if we are Christians, "Christ is all."

There is the foundation of all our faith and hope—and I want you who preach and you who teach the children to always keep to this one truth of God—"Christ is all." Many other things have a measure of instruction in them, but Christ is all that is necessary. If you want to save men, if you truly wish to elevate men, if you desire still further to exalt them to the very highest degree of which human nature is capable, remember that "Christ is all" is your lever, and in Him is your fulcrum, and in Him is the power to use the lever! "Christ is all." You need not go abroad for anything, for "you are complete in Him" (Col. 2:10). The ship is furnished from stem to stern in Him. The house, from its foundation to its rooftop, is complete in Him. "Christ is all." Oh, to know Him! Oh, to have Him as our own! Oh, to live wholly upon Him! Oh, to grow like Him and always to keep before our mind's eyes this great truth that "Christ is all"!

II. Now we are going a step further to consider the second part of our first text—"Christ is all *and in all*." This is a matter of experience, and it reveals to us *how the work of grace proceeds*. Christ is in all His people; this gracious possession is the work of the Spirit of God, by whose means Christ is formed in us, the hope of glory.

To my mind it is a very beautiful thing that the Lord Jesus Christ, when He comes into the soul, does not annihilate any part of the personality, but shines in each separate being, for He is not only all, but He is *in* all His people! Very well, the grace of God does not turn the Gentile into a Jew. He remains a Gentile, but Christ is in him, and therefore he is made into a new creature. There have been some beautiful specimens of holiness and grace found in many of the Gentile nations dwelling in the islands of the sea, or among all sorts and conditions of men scattered up and down the world— and Christ has shone gloriously in them. Then comes the Jew. When he is saved, Christ is in him. The apostles of Jesus were mostly, at least, of that race, and many later believers have been of the seed of Abraham. But Christ has been in them and He has gloriously displayed Himself in them. The Lord Jesus Christ, dwelling in the Jew, leaves him still a member of the house of Abraham, but through the presence of the Lord Jesus within him, how wondrously his whole character is exalted!

Then you have the man who is circumcised and the man who is uncircumcised—and in each of these, if he is saved, Christ dwells. And each one therefore lives according to his light, his knowledge, and his standing. Christ enters into the barbarian, and though in certain natural respects he remains, to a large extent, what he was before, yet as soon as Christ enters into him, all of his barbarism that is *sinful* disappears! He retains the free spirit of the child of the wilderness or the son of the woods, but how grandly has Christ displayed Himself in such men as he is! The personal piety of a Red Indian, or of an African freshly taken from the wilds of the Dark Continent, has been as brilliant and as beautiful—certainly as fresh, bright, clear, and striking—as the piety of the most educated of the Caucasian race! Whether he is barbarian or Scythian, if Christ is formed in him, the hope of glory, it is only another form of the same exquisite beauty!

It is always a pity when our missionaries try to make other nations into English people. If we have pride enough to think so, we may regard ourselves as the model for others to imitate. But even if we could be a model, it would be a great pity for every native of India to copy the Englishman! I like the worship of our black friends in Jamaica and in the southern states of America, with its delightful simplicity, its vivacity. Yes, and I venture to say, even its grotesqueness. And I would not have a black man begin slavishly to imitate the white man. Let him continue to be a black man and let Christ shine in the black man's face right gloriously. Yes, let a man be a brown man, or a yellow man, or a red man, or whatever color God made him! The more he keeps to his own nationality and reflects the glory of Christ from that angle, the more will Christ's gospel triumph and the more will Christ Himself be honored!

> *C*hrist is all." You must not add anything to Christ as your ground of confidence, but just lean the weight of your sin, your sorrow, your needs, and your desires wholly and entirely upon Him who lives to stand for you before God.

The apostle adds, as we have already noticed, "Neither bond nor free, but Christ is all and in all." May the day speedily come when there will not be a bondsman under heaven! But in those days of the worst of all slavery, the Christian slaves were among the most brilliant gems in the Redeemer's diadem. Oh, what brave deeds they did for the Crucified One! I should think that it was harder to be a Christian freeman in those days than to be a Christian slave. But whether bond or free, whether the man took his place in the forum among the senators, or his lot was cast yonder among the slaves—either case, if Christ was in him—the light of God shone gloriously from Him and God was magnified thereby! Christ is all, and Christ is in all His people, each one remaining the same in His individuality, but Christ shining in each one!

I must again refer you to the connection of our text and ask you to read where Paul says, "You have put off the old man with his deeds, and have put on the new man who is renewed in knowledge according to the image of Him who created him" (Col. 3:9–10). You recollect that Adam was made in the image of God and that he lost that image by his sin. But when Christ enters into a man and he is created anew in Christ Jesus, then *he receives afresh the image of God*. The image of God is Christ Jesus, for He is the express image of His Father's glory. He who has seen Christ has seen the Father, and inasmuch as Christ enters into all believers and makes them like Himself, the image of God is thereby restored in all believers.

So note again that because Christ dwells in him, *every believer becomes a copy of Christ*. Read the thirteenth verse: "Bearing with one another, and forgiving one another, if anyone has a complaint against another; even as Christ forgave you, so you also must do" (Col 3:13). Isn't that beautiful? Christ in every believer means that Christ is the image of God and that the Christian is the image of Christ. So, just as Jesus freely forgave, so does every Christian freely forgive! Do you find it difficult to forgive one who has wronged you? Then you will find it difficult to get to heaven! If you cannot enter heaven unless you are like Christ, how can you be like Christ unless you can freely forgive? This seems a grand opportunity for you to stand on the same platform with Christ and, in some respects, to do the works of Christ when, having been slighted, ungratefully treated, misrepresented, slandered, and injured, you can say, "I as freely forgive you as the Lord Jesus Christ forgave me" (see Eph. 4:32). This is the token and evidence that Christ is in you: when you become imitators of Christ as dear children (Eph. 5:1).

It is a remarkable fact, as I have often said to you, that although our Lord Jesus Christ is more perfect than any other example—indeed, the *only perfect example*—yet it is easier to imitate Christ than it is to imitate some of the best of His people! That is curious, but it is a fact. I know a brother whom I greatly admire, an eminent Christian—I would not mention my own name in the same day with his, he lives so near to God and is such a truly gracious man—yet I could not imitate him. It is quite impossible that my nature should ever become exactly like his. Another brother, whom I used to know—he is now with God—was equally good, but he was as different from the other good man as anyone could be. They were as opposite as the poles in their temperament and behavior. The first brother I mentioned is solid, calm, quiet, and unexcitable. And I should think that he very seldom laughs and that even then, he does not know that he has done it!

My other friend sometimes used to literally roar with laughter! He was full of earnest love for the souls of men, and God blessed him greatly in his service. He had a merry vein and a humorous spirit, and I was more at home with him than I was with the first one. Yet the Lord Jesus Christ is far easier to imitate than either of my two friends, for sometimes I am so depressed that I cannot show all the cheerfulness of the one. And at other times, having such a humorous vein in my nature, I would be hypocritical and unnatural if I suppressed it and always acted as if I were as solemn as death itself! But in the case of our Lord Jesus Christ, albeit that there is never any mention of laughter, yet there were ripples of holy pleasantry in His life and in His character, though He was "a Man of sorrows and acquainted with grief" (Isa. 53:3). He is more of a man than the best of other men, and more imitable, though altogether inimitable, than those who can be imitated and, perhaps, can even be excelled.

> He who has seen Christ has seen the Father, and inasmuch as Christ enters into all believers and makes them like Himself, the image of God is thereby restored in all believers.

What is more, Christ in each one of these believers *creates them all into one body*. Read Colossians 3:14–15: "But above all these things put on love, which is the bond of perfection. And let the peace of God rule in your hearts, to which also you were called in one body; and be thankful." The same life is in all believers—in you and in me—well then, we are one! The same life is in ten thousand Christians; then they, also, are all one! If the same life quickens them and they live under the same influences, and they act according to the same rule, then are they one, and Christ becomes the glorious head of a body that He renders glorious by quickening it with His own indwelling!

I like to think of this blessed truth of God: Christ in all believers creating them into one body. This is the beginning of true unity. Here, for instance, is a man who says that he is baptized as I am, but if he has not the life of God within him, I cannot get on with him. Whatever he may call himself, I am not in union with him. There perhaps comes a Methodist, and we begin to talk about the Lord Jesus Christ, and I find that he loves Him with all his heart, and I know that I do, though I wish that I loved Him more. And directly we two get on together. We feel that we are one in Christ because of the one life that quickens us. Do you not feel it to be so? Have you not been reading a book and said to yourself, "Oh, what a blessed book this is! How full of the divine life?" Yes. And after you have read it, you have been surprised to find that the person who wrote it was a Romanist—for there are many books of that kind—or the writer was a member of some church that, in many respects, lies in very dangerous error! You say to yourself, "I do not care where this man lived, or what he did; I am one with him as far as he is one with Christ."

The one common feeling of union to Christ and Christ being in us makes us feel that we are one with each other. Wherever there is, as Augustine used to say, *aliquid Christi*, "anything of Christ," there our love must go forth—we cannot help it! Christ in you all makes you into one body and unites you together in a mysterious and unique manner. There is not a parallel to it anywhere else; it gives such a living, loving, abiding, undeniable unity that even if you wish to forget it, you cannot! If the man is in Christ, you must love him; do what you may, for you are one body with him.

Such is this manifestation of Christ in His people that it leads further to *the offering of one oblation*. Read Colossians 3:16: "Let the word of Christ dwell in you richly in all wisdom, teaching and admonishing one another in psalms and hymns and spiritual songs, singing with grace in your hearts to the Lord." Yes, all God's people love God's Word! They all find a great sweetness in "psalms and hymns and spiritual songs." They all delight to sing praises to the Most High. Montgomery truly wrote, "The saints in prayer appear as one." But it is equally true that the saints in *praise* appear as one. And the saints in love to the Word of God appear as one because Christ is in them and, Christ being one, they are knit to one another. Oh, how blessed it is for us to have Christ in us!

And lastly, upon this point, all that I have said leads up to *each one acting to the glory of one name*, for if Christ is in you, verse 17 is true of you: "And whatever you do in word or deed, do all in the name of the Lord Jesus, giving thanks to God the Father through Him." What a life to lead: Christ taking such entire possession of a man that everything he does, he does as if Christ Himself were doing it, because he does it in Christ's name and by Christ's power! As Paul wrote to the Corinthians, "Therefore, whether you eat or drink, or whatever you do, do all to the glory of God" (1 Cor. 10:31), so that it will no longer be yourselves who do it, but Christ who dwells in you. This will sanctify the most common actions of everyday life and make the whole of the Christian's career to be sublime, so that while he treads the earth beneath his feet, literally, he is also doing it *spiritually*, and all the while his conversation is in heaven.

I must just linger one minute here. You all agreed with me when I spoke about Christ being all. You understood clearly that He is the only ground of our hope. Can you also go with me in this part of my subject: Christ is in all His people? Is Christ formed in you, the hope of glory? Do you know anything about an *indwelling* Christ? Verily I say to you, the Christ on the cross will never save you unless there is also Christ *within you*! It is the Christ on the cross in whom we trust, but the outcome of that trust is that He is born in our hearts! His power comes from His love, His grace, His truth, Himself—and we live because He lives in us. Do you understand this? If you do not, I pray God that you may, for unless Christ is in you, you know what the apostle says: "Examine yourselves as to whether you are in the faith. Test yourselves. Do you not know yourselves, that Jesus Christ is in you?—unless indeed you are disqualified" (2 Cor. 13:5). If you are disapproved of God, Christ is not in you. If Christ is not in you, you are disapproved of God. But if He lives in you, you are "accepted in the Beloved" (Eph. 1:6) and that life of yours will never die out, but you shall, by and by, behold your Savior's face in the kingdom of His glory.

Brothers and sisters, we are not what we ought to be! We are not what we want to be; we are not what we will be! But we are something very different from what we used to be. The change in us is as great as in that blind man who said, "One thing I know: that though I was blind, now I see" (John 9:25). The change is not merely external, but it is vital! The Lord has taken away the heart of stone out of our flesh and given us back the heart of flesh that belonged to man in his unfallen nature. And then, upon this heart of flesh, He has also worked wondrously, making it conscious to spiritual influences that once did not affect it, and writing upon the fleshy tablets of that renewed heart His perfect law. Glory be to the name of Jehovah, a notable miracle has been performed upon us! A miracle so marvelous that it is comparable to the resurrection from the dead, and in some respects it even surpasses the wonders of creation itself! We will tell this story in the streets of the New Jerusalem, and we will draw around us attentive crowds as we narrate our experience and tell the tale of the sin that ruined us and of the mercy that reclaimed us!

Thus have we gone up the second rung of this golden ladder. First, "Christ is all." Next, "Christ is in all."

III. Now kindly turn back in your Bibles to our other text, 1 Corinthians 15:28, "That God may be all in all." First, Christ is all. Next, Christ is in all His people, but *the consummation*, the top-stone of all, is that God may be all in all.

The passage in which this text stands seems to be a very difficult one to understand. The common meaning that is given to it by nearly every interpreter I have ever met with, I do not believe or accept. It seems to a great many to be taught here that there is to come a time, called "the end," when the Lord Jesus Christ, having conquered all His enemies, is to resign His position, abdicate His throne, and cease to be King, "that God may be all in all."

Let us read the connection of the passage:

> For as in Adam all die, even so in Christ all shall be made alive. But each one in his own order: Christ the firstfruits, afterward those who are Christ's at His coming. Then comes the end, when He delivers the kingdom to God the Father, when He puts an end to all rule and all authority and power. For He must reign till He has put all enemies under His feet. The last enemy that will be destroyed is death. For "He has put all things under His feet." But when He says "all things are put under Him," it is evident that He who put all things under Him is excepted. Now when all things are made subject to Him, then the Son Himself will also be subject to Him who put all things under Him, that God may be all in all (1 Cor. 15:22–28).

The general meaning given to these words is that there is to be a time when the mediatorial kingdom of Christ will come to an end of itself and He will deliver up the kingdom to God, ceasing Himself to be King. I can only say that if this is the teaching of this text, it is not taught anywhere else in the whole Bible. Nobody can find any parallel passage to it, or anything like it. Neither do I believe that it is taught in the Bible at all, neither here nor anywhere else! And I can say that for this reason I cannot see that there is to be any end whatever to the mediatorial kingdom of Christ.

You perceive that *it is the Son who is to be subject to the Father*, but it is of the Son that we read in the first chapter of the epistle to the Hebrews, "To the Son He says: 'Your throne, O God, is forever and ever'" (Heb. 1:8). Here the Father, manifestly speaking to the Son, in His complex person declares that His throne is to be forever and ever. Brethren, in the day when the Christ will have overcome all His enemies, and death will be destroyed, there will be no abolition of His mediatorial kingdom! There still stands in the scriptures this promise of our Lord Jesus Christ: "To him who overcomes I will grant to sit with Me on My throne, as I also overcame and sat down with My Father on His throne" (Rev. 3:21). Does this mean that we are to have a temporary reign with a temporary Christ, a brief rule with a short-lived monarch? I do not believe it!

Moreover, the priesthood enters into the mediatorial office most eminently, yet "the LORD has sworn and will not relent, 'You are a priest forever according to the order of Melchizedek'" (Heb. 7:21). If the priesthood is to continue forever—and Melchizedek was king as well as priest—then the kingdom of Christ is to continue, world without end. Moreover, in the book of the Revelation—not to mention the almost innumerable passages to the same effect—we find that when the kingdoms of this world become the kingdoms of our Lord, it is added, "and of His Christ, and He shall reign forever and ever!" (Rev. 11:15). When the kingdoms are brought back, they will be the kingdoms of our God and of His Christ. Then we read of "the throne of God and of the Lamb" (22:1, 3). And when all kingdoms are subdued and the Lord God omnipotent reigns, then we are told to expect the announcement, "The marriage of the Lamb has come, and His wife has made herself ready" (19:7). What does all this mean but a continuance of that dispensation in which the Christ, the Son of man, as the Son of God, will be still at the head of His people, still their priest and still their king and still reigning? And that is exactly what this passage says, if you will kindly look at it again and dismiss all previous prejudices from your minds!

The fact is, our Lord Jesus Christ has performed and is still performing *a work that will end in putting everything into its proper order*. Now the proper order, according to 1 Corinthians 11:3, is this: "But I want you to know that the head of every man is Christ, the head of woman is man, and the head of

Christ is God." This is how it stands: the woman with the man for her head, the man with Christ for his head, and Christ with God for His head. Such is the scriptural order, an order that has been disturbed all through except with regard to the Father and the Son, for God has always been the head of Christ! Now Christ has come into the world to restore that right order from the bottom right up to the top! And it is to be so restored; first, by Christ becoming the head of men, when He will have put down all His enemies under His feet and when He will have put down all rule and all authority and power, "for He must reign till He has put all enemies under His feet. The last enemy that will be destroyed is death" (1 Cor. 15:25–26).

> *He who has seen Christ has seen the Father, and inasmuch as Christ enters into all believers and makes them like Himself, the image of God is thereby restored in all believers.*

Christ is come into the world that all the evil that is in the world should be subdued. And He will drive it out of the world. There will remain no power that will dare revolt against the majesty of heaven! Over the whole surface of this globe, beneath the new heavens and on the new earth, there will yet be the kingdom established of which Jesus Christ will be the supreme head and over which He will reign forever, King of kings and Lord of lords! The Lord hasten it in His own time!

"Well, and what then?" asks one. "Does it not say that He is to deliver up the kingdom to God, even the Father, and to be subject to the Father?" Exactly so. Suppose that India had been in revolt against our queen and that a viceroy had been sent there, and that he had warred against all the rebellious tribes and kingdoms, and they had all been conquered. He telegraphs to the queen, "Your Majesty's empire is at your feet." Does he therefore cease to be viceroy? Not necessarily in the least degree! He may remain as ruler and yet have delivered up the kingdom. I believe that to be the meaning of this passage: that Christ has so conquered the kingdom that it is all God's.

But what does it mean when it says that *then will* the Son also be subject to the Father? It means that He is subject now, and that *even then* He will continue to be subject to the Father, that is all. It cannot mean that at a certain time Christ will *become* subject to God, because He has been so ever since that day of His glorious humiliation when, for His people's redemption, He took upon Himself the form of a servant, and that condition is not to cease. He is still to be the representative of God even when He will have put down all power and all authority under His feet and when God has put all things under His feet. It is manifest that He who did put all things under Him is not, Himself, under Him. And it is clear from the text that even then, God will be the head of Christ. I do not know whether you catch my thought yet, but it is just this: all evil subdued, all the saints having Christ dwelling in them, Christ the head of all these saints, and then God, still as God, all the more surely and securely supreme over all things, or the head of Christ is God and God is all in all.

The conclusion of the whole matter is this: Every day the great consummation to be kept in view is "that God may be all in all." For this, the heroic labors of the Son of man here on earth! For this was His cruel death! For this was His rising again! For this, He grasps the mediatorial scepter! For this, He rules in providence! For this, He manages the world's affairs! For this will be His second coming and the glory of His saints! All this, while it continues to bring glory to Him, has been done in subjection to His great Father's will. He has accomplished it all as the Father's representative and messenger, sent by Him to do it, and then, when it is all done, and He will reign forever and ever, even then, the Son Himself will continue in that position in which He put Himself long, long ago, "that God may be all in all." Then will the whole universe, restored and brought back to its proper place, be ordered according to the eternal covenant arrangement.

> *I like to think of this blessed truth of God: Christ in all believers creating them into one body. This is the beginning of true unity.*

And the practical outcome of it all is this. I want you, beloved friends, so to live as to be persuaded that it will be so one day, that God will be all in all—that there will come a time when we will stand before the throne of God, God in us all, and everything in us of God, when all His elect, all His redeemed, all to whom Christ is all, and all in whom Christ is, will only know God as their All-in-All! God their all in their very existence. God their all in every hymn. God their all in every pulsing of their joy. God their all in every hope. God their all in every memory. God all to them, and

God *in* all of them to the very fullest. All redeemed, all delivered from the power of sin, all quickened into the divine and Godlike life, all summed up in Christ, Christ comprehending them all. And then, Christ Himself head over all things to His church, standing and giving to God the glory forever and ever, that God may be all in all.

I see no abdication of a throne here. I see not even a change of dispensation, and I do not believe in any! But as surely as God lives, our King lives, and our Priest still ministers before Him. And He will still be King over His people, though still, as the Christ, in His infinite goodness, abiding as subject to God Himself, God forever and ever, and yet, in His complex person, making the Father to be all in all. Looking forward to that glorious consummation, we can join again in the jubilant hymn we sang just now:

> *Hallelujah!—hark! the sound,*
> *From the center to the skies,*
> *Wakes above, beneath, around,*
> *All creation's harmonies!*
>
> *See Jehovah's banner furled,*
> *Sheathed His sword! He speaks—'tis done!*
> *And the kingdoms of this world*
> *Are the kingdoms of His Son.*
>
> *He will reign from pole to pole,*
> *With illimitable sway.*
> *He will reign when, like a scroll,*
> *Yonder heavens have passed away!*
>
> *Then the end—beneath His rod,*
> *Man's last enemy will fall!*
> *Hallelujah! Christ in God,*
> *God in Christ is all in all.*

Now let us begin at the beginning. This is very simple: *Christ is all.* Then may the Spirit of God help us to go on to the next rung of the ladder, *Christ is in all His people.* There is the difficulty! Is He in you, beloved? Have you received Him by faith? Then comes the third step—this may be, at present, full of mystery, but we will see it in brighter light, by and by—*God will be all in all.* So will He be to us even now! Amen and amen.

FOR FURTHER THOUGHT

1. *Since Christ is all, are some people more qualified for salvation than others?*
2. *What scriptural evidence does Spurgeon use to demonstrate that Christ is all in all the believers?*
3. *Which verse in the New Testament describes the consummation, or end, of God's purpose, when He becomes all in all?*

Mercy, Omnipotence, and Justice

The LORD is slow to anger and great in power,
and will not at all acquit the wicked.
NAHUM 1:3

WORKS of art require some education in the beholder before they can be thoroughly appreciated. We do not expect that the uninstructed should at once perceive the varied excellencies of a painting from some master hand. We do not imagine that the superlative glories of the harmonies of the princes of song will enrapture the ears of clownish listeners. There must be something in the man himself before he can understand the wonders either of nature or of art. Certainly this is true of character. Because of failures in our character and faults in our life, we are not capable of understanding all the separate beauties and the united perfection of the character of Christ, or of God, His Father.

Were we ourselves as pure as the angels in heaven, were we what our race once was in the Garden of Eden, immaculate and perfect, it is quite certain that we should have a far better and nobler idea of the character of God than we can by possibility attain to in our fallen state. But you cannot fail to notice that men, through the alienation of their natures, are continually misrepresenting God because they cannot appreciate His perfection. Does God at one time withhold His hand from wrath? Lo, they say that God has ceased to judge the world and looks upon it with listless phlegmatic indifference. Does He at another time punish the world for sin? They say He is severe and cruel. Men *will* misunderstand Him because they are imperfect themselves and are not capable of admiring the character of God.

Now, this is especially true with regard to certain lights and shadows in the character of God that He has so marvelously blended in the perfection of His nature. Although we cannot see the exact point of meeting, yet (if we have been at all enlightened by the Spirit) we are struck with wonder at the sacred harmony. In reading Holy Scripture you can say of Paul that he was noted for his zeal; of Peter that he will ever be memorable for his courage; of John that he was noted for his lovingness. But did you ever notice, when you read the history of Jesus Christ, that you never could say He was noble for any one virtue at all?

Why was that? It was because the boldness of Peter did so outgrow itself as to throw other virtues into the shade, or else the other virtues were so deficient that they set forth his boldness. The very feet of a man being noted for something is a sure sign that he is not so notable in other things. And it is because of the complete perfection of Jesus Christ that we are not accustomed to say of Him that He was eminent for His zeal, or for His love, or for His courage. We say of Him that He was a perfect character, but we are not able very easily to perceive where the shadows and the lights blended, where the meekness of Christ blended into His courage and where His loveliness blended into His boldness in denouncing sin.

> *Y*ou cannot fail to notice that men, through the alienation of their natures, are continually misrepresenting God because they cannot appreciate His perfection.

We are not able to detect the points where they meet. And I believe the more thoroughly we are sanctified, the more it will be a subject of wonder to us how it could be that virtues that seemed so diverse were in so majestic a manner united into one character. It is just the same of God. And I have been led to make the remarks I have made on my text because of the two clauses thereof that seem to describe contrary attributes. You will notice that there are two things in my text—He is "slow to anger," and yet He "will not at all acquit the wicked."

Our character is so imperfect that we cannot see the congruity of these two attributes. We are wondering, perhaps, and saying, "How is it He is slow to anger and yet will not acquit the wicked?" It is because His character is perfect that we do not see where these two things melt into each other: the infallible righteousness and severity of the ruler of the world and His loving-kindness, His long-suffering, and His tender mercies. The absence of any one of these things from the character of God would have rendered it imperfect. The presence of them both, though we may not see how they can be congruous with each other, stamps the character of God with a perfection elsewhere unknown.

And now I will endeavor this morning to set forth these two attributes of God and the connecting link. "The LORD is slow to anger"—then comes the connecting link, "and great in power." I will have to show you how "great in power" refers to the sentence foregoing and the sentence succeeding. And then we will consider the next attribute: "He will not at all acquit the wicked," an attribute of justice.

I. Let us begin with the first characteristic of God. He is said to be *slow to anger*. Let me declare the attribute and then trace it to its source. God is "slow to anger." When mercy comes into the world, she drives winged steeds. The axles of her chariot wheels are glowing hot with speed. But when wrath comes, she walks with tardy footsteps. She is not in haste to slay; she is not swift to condemn. God's rod of mercy is ever in His hands outstretched. God's sword of justice is in its scabbard, not rusted in it. It can be easily withdrawn, but is held there by that hand that presses it back into its sheath, crying, "Sleep, O sword, sleep. For I will have mercy upon sinners and will forgive their transgressions."

God has many orators in heaven; some of them speak with swift words. Gabriel, when he comes down to tell glad tidings, speaks swiftly. Angelic hosts, when they descend from glory, fly with wings of lightning when they proclaim, "On earth peace, good will toward men!" (Luke 2:14). But the dark angel of wrath is a slow orator. With many a pause between, where melting pity joins his languid notes, he speaks, and when but half his oration is completed, he often stays and withdraws himself from his rostrum, giving way to pardon and to mercy, he having but addressed the people that they might be driven to repentance and so might receive peace from the scepter of God's love.

Brethren, I will just try to show you now how God is slow to anger. First, I will prove that He is "slow to anger," because *He never smites without first threatening*. Men who are passionate and swift in anger give a word and a blow. Sometimes the blow comes first and the word afterward. Oftentimes kings, when subjects have rebelled against them, have crushed them first and then reasoned with them afterward. They have given no time of threat, no period of repentance. They have allowed no space for turning to their allegiance. They have at once crushed them in their hot displeasure, making a full end of them.

Not so God. He will not cut down the tree that much cumbers the ground until He has dug about it and fertilized it. He will not at once slay the man whose character is the vilest until He has first hewn him by the prophets. He will not hew him by judgments. He will warn the sinner before He condemns him. He will send his prophets, "rising up early" and late (Jer. 7:13, 25; 26:5; 29:19; 32:33; 35:15), giving him "precept upon precept, line upon line, here a little, there a little" (Isa. 28:13). He will not smite the city without warning. Sodom will not perish until Lot has been within her.

The world will not be drowned until eight prophets have been preaching in it, and Noah, the eighth, comes to prophesy of the coming of the Lord. He will not smite Nineveh till He has sent a Jonah. He will not crush Babylon till His prophets have cried through its streets. He will not slay a man until He has given many warnings, by sicknesses, by the pulpit, by providence, and by consequences. He smites not with a heavy blow at once. He threatens first. He does not in grace, as in nature, send lightning first and thunder afterward, but He sends the thunder of His law first and the lightning of execution follows it. The lictor of divine justice carries His ax, bound up in a bundle of rods, for He will not cut off men until He has reproved them, that they may repent. He is "slow to anger."

But again *God is also very slow to threaten.* Although He will threaten before He condemns, yet He is slow even in His threat. God's lips move swiftly when He promises but slowly when He threatens. Long rolls the pealing thunder and slowly roll the drums of heaven, when they sound the death march of sinners. Sweetly flows the music of the rapid notes that proclaim free grace and love and mercy. God is slow to threaten. He will not send a Jonah to Nineveh until Nineveh has become foul with sin. He will not even tell Sodom it will be burned with fire until Sodom has become a reeking dunghill, obnoxious to earth as well as heaven.

He will not drown the world with a deluge, or even threaten to do it, until the sons of God themselves make unholy alliances and begin to depart from Him. He does not even threaten the sinner by his conscience until the sinner has oftentimes sinned. He will often tell the sinner of his sins, often urge him to repent. But He will not make hell stare him hard in the face, with all its dreadful terror, until much sin has stirred up the lion from his lair and made God hot in wrath against the iniquities of man. He is slow even to threaten.

But best of all, when God threatens, *how slow He is to sentence the criminal*! When He has told them that He will punish unless they repent, how long a space He gives them in which to turn to Himself! "He does not afflict willingly, nor grieve the children of men" for nothing (Lam. 3:33). He stays His hand; He will not be in hot haste, when He has threatened them, to execute the sentence upon them. Have you ever observed that scene in the Garden of Eden at the time of the fall? God had threatened Adam that if he sinned he should surely die. Adam sinned. Did God make haste to sentence him? 'Tis sweetly said, "The LORD God [was] *walking* in the garden in the cool of the day" (Gen. 3:8, emphasis added).

Perhaps that fruit was plucked at early morn, maybe it was plucked at noontime. But God was in no haste to condemn. He waited till the sun was well near set and in the cool of the day came. And, as an old expositor has put it very beautifully, "when He did come, He did not come on wings of wrath but He 'walked in the garden in the cool of the day.'" He was in no haste to slay. I think I see Him, as He was represented then to Adam, in those glorious days when God walked with man. I think I see the wonderful similitude in which the unseen did veil Himself. I see Him walking among the trees so slowly. Yes, if it were right to give such a picture, beating His breast and shedding tears that He should have to condemn man.

At last I hear His doleful voice: "Adam, where are you? Where have you cast yourself, poor Adam? You have cast yourself from my favor; you have cast yourself into nakedness and into fear, for you are hiding yourself. Adam, where are you? I pity you. You thought to be God. Before I condemn you, I will give you one note of pity. Adam, where are you?" Yes, the Lord was slow to anger, slow to write the sentence even though the command had been broken and the threat was therefore of necessity brought into force.

It was so with the flood. He threatened the earth, but He would not fully seal the sentence and stamp it with the seal of heaven until He had given space for repentance. Noah must come, and through his hundred and twenty years must preach the Word. He must come and testify to an unthinking and an ungodly generation. The ark must be built to be a perpetual sermon. There it must be upon its mountaintop, waiting for the floods to float it, that it might be an everyday warning to the ungodly. O heavens, why did you not at once open your floods? Fountains of the great deep, why did you not burst up in a moment? God said, "I will sweep away the world with a flood."

Why, why did you not rise?

"Because," I hear them saying with gurgling notes, "because, although God had threatened, He was slow to sentence and He said in Himself, 'Haply they may repent. Perhaps they may turn from their sin.' And therefore did He bid us rest and be quiet, for He is slow to anger."

And yet, once more, even when the sentence against a sinner is signed and sealed by heaven's broad seal of condemnation, even then *God is slow to carry it out*. The doom of Sodom is sealed. God has declared it will be burned with fire. But God is tardy. He stops. He will Himself go down to Sodom that He may see the iniquity of it. And when He gets there, guilt is rife in the streets. 'Tis night, and the crew that is worse than beasts besieges the door. Does He then lift His hands? Does He then say, "Rain hell out of heaven, you skies?" No, He lets them pursue their riot all night, spares them to the last moment, and though when the sun was risen the burning hail began to fall, yet was the reprieve as long as possible.

God was not in haste to condemn. God had threatened to root out the Canaanites. He declared that all the children of Ammon should be cut off. He had promised Abraham that He would give their land to his seed forever, and they were to be utterly slain. But He made the children of Israel wait four hundred years in Egypt and He let these Canaanites live all through the days of the patriarchs. And even then, when He led His avenging ones out of Egypt, He stayed them forty years in the wilderness, because He was reluctant to slay poor Canaan.

"Yet," said He, "I will give them space. Though I have stamped their condemnation, though their death warrant has come forth from the court of the king's bench and must be executed, yet will I reprieve them as long as I can." And He stops, until at last mercy had had enough and Jericho's melting ashes and the destruction of Ai betokened that the sword was out of its scabbard and God had awaked like a mighty man and like a strong man full of wrath. God is slow to execute the sentence even when He has declared it.

And ah, my friends, there is a sorrowful thought that has just crossed my mind. Some men yet alive are sentenced now. I believe that scripture bears me out in a dreadful thought that I just wish to hint at. There are some men who are condemned before they are finally damned. Some men's sins go before them to judgment, who are given over to a seared conscience. Concerning these it may be said that repentance and salvation are impossible. Some few men in the world are like John Bunyan's man in the iron cage; they can never get out. They are like Esau; they find no place of repentance, though like he they do not seek it—for if they sought it they would find it.

Many there are who have sinned the "sin unto death" (1 John 5:16 KJV), concerning whom we cannot pray. But why, why, why are they not already in the flame? If they are condemned, if mercy has shut her eye forever upon them, if she never will stretch out her hand to give them pardon, why, why, why are they not cut down and swept away? Because God says, "I will not have mercy upon them, but I will let them live a little while longer. Though I have condemned them, I am reluctant to carry the sentence out. I will spare them as long as it is right that man should live. I will let them have a long life here, for they will have a fearful eternity of wrath forever." Yes, let them have their little whirl of pleasure. Their end will be most fearful. Let them beware, for although God is slow to anger, He is sure in it.

> God only knows the secret wickedness of this great city! It demands a loud and a trumpet voice. It needs a prophet to cry aloud, "Sound an alarm, sound an alarm, sound an alarm."

If God were not slow to anger, would He not have smitten this huge city of ours, this behemoth city? Would He not have smitten it into a thousand pieces and blotted out the remembrance of it from the earth? The iniquities of this city are so great that if God should dig up her very foundations and cast her into the sea, she well deserves it. Our streets at night present spectacles of vice that cannot be equaled. Surely no nation and no country can show a city so utterly debauched as this great city of London if our midnight streets are indications of our immorality.

You allow, in your public places of resort—I mean you, my lords and ladies—you allow things to be said in your hearing of which your modesty ought to be ashamed. You can sit in theaters to hear plays at which modesty should blush (I say nothing of piety). That the ruder sex should have listened to the obscenities of *La Traviata* is surely bad enough, but that ladies of the highest refinement and the most approved taste should dishonor themselves by such a patronage of vice is indeed intolerable. Let the sins of the lower theaters escape without your censure, you gentlemen of England. The lowest bestiality of the nethermost hell of a playhouse can look to your opera houses for their excuse.

I thought that with the pretensions this city makes to piety, for sure, they would not have gone so far, and that after such a warning as they have had from the press itself—a press that is certainly not too religious—they would not so indulge their evil passions. But because the pill is gilded, you suck down the poison. Because the thing is popular, you patronize it, though it is lustful, it is abominable, it is deceitful! You take your children to hear what yourselves never ought to listen to. You yourselves will sit in merry and grand company to listen to things from which your modesty ought to revolt. And I would surely hope it does, although the tide may, for a while, deceive you.

Ah, God only knows the secret wickedness of this great city! It demands a loud and a trumpet voice. It needs a prophet to cry aloud, "Sound an alarm, sound an alarm, sound an alarm" in this city (Joel 2:1). For verily the enemy grows upon us. The power of the evil one is mighty, and we are fast going to perdition, unless God will put forth His hand and roll back the black torrent of iniquity that streams down our streets. But God is slow to anger and does still stay His sword. Wrath said yesterday, "Unsheathe yourself, O sword," and the sword struggled to get free. Mercy put her hand upon the hilt and said, "Be still!"

"Unsheathe yourself, O sword!" Again, it struggled from its scabbard. Mercy put her hand on it and said, "Back!" and it rattled back again.

Wrath stamped his foot and said, "Awake, O sword, awake!" It struggled yet again, till half its blade was outdrawn. "Back, back!" said mercy, and with manly push she sent it back rattling into its sheath, and there it sleeps still, for the Lord is "slow to anger and plenteous in mercy."

Now I am to trace this attribute of God to its source. Why is He slow to anger? He is slow to anger *because He is infinitely good*. Good is His name: "good" God. Good in His nature. Because He is slow to anger. He is slow to anger, again, *because He is great*. Little things are always swift in anger; great things are not so. The silly dog barks at every passerby and bears no insult. The lion would bear a thousand times as much. And the bull sleeps in his pasture and will bear much before he lifts up his might. The leviathan in the sea, though he makes the deep to be hoary when he is enraged, yet is slow to be stirred up, while the little and puny are always swift in anger. God's greatness is one reason of the slowness of His wrath.

II. But to proceed at once to the link. A great reason why He is slow to anger is because He is *great in power*. This is to be the connecting link between this part of the subject and the last, and therefore I must beg your attention. I say that this word *great in power* connects the first sentence to the last. And it does so in this way. The Lord is slow to anger because He is great in power. "How say you so?" says one. I answer: He who is great in power has power over himself. And he who can keep his own temper down and subdue himself is greater than he who rules a city, or can conquer nations.

We heard but yesterday, or the day before, mighty displays of God's power in the rolling thunder that alarmed us. And when we saw the splendor of His might in the glistening lightning when He lifted up the gates of heaven and we saw the brightness thereof, and then He closed them again upon the dusty earth in a moment, even then we did not see anything but the crumbs of His power compared with the power that He has over Himself. When God's power does restrain Himself, then it is power indeed—the power to curb power. The power that binds omnipotence is omnipotence surpassed. God is great in power, and therefore does He keep in His anger.

> When God's power does restrain Himself, then it is power indeed—the power to curb power. The power that binds omnipotence is omnipotence surpassed. God is great in power, and therefore does He keep in His anger.

A man who has a strong mind can bear to be insulted, can bear offenses, because he is strong. The weak mind snaps and snarls at the little; the strong mind bears it like a rock. It moves not, though a thousand breakers dash upon it and cast their pitiful malice in the spray upon its summit. God marks His enemies, and yet He moves not. He stands still and lets them curse Him, yet He is not wrathful. If He were less of a God than He is, if He were less mighty than we know Him to be, He would long before this have sent forth the whole of His thunders and emptied the magazines of heaven. He would long before this have blasted the earth with the wondrous mines He has prepared in its lower surface. The flame that burns there would have consumed us and we should have been utterly destroyed. We bless God that the greatness of His power is just our protection! He is slow to anger because He is great in power.

And now there is no difficulty in showing how this link unites itself with the next part of the text. "He is great in power and will not at all acquit the wicked." This needs no demonstration in words. I have but to touch the feelings and you will see it. The greatness of His power is an assurance and insurance that He will not acquit the wicked. Who among you could witness the storm on Friday night without having thoughts concerning your own sinfulness stirred in your bosoms? Men do not think of God the Punisher, or Jehovah the Avenger, when the sun is shining and the weather calm. But in times of tempest, whose cheek is not blanched?

The Christian oftentimes rejoices in it. He can say, "My soul is well at ease amidst this revelry of earth. I do rejoice at it. It is a day of feasting in my Father's hall, a day of high feast and carnival in heaven, and I am glad:

> *The God that reigns on high,*
> *And thunders when He pleases,*
> *That rides upon the stormy sky*
> *And manages the seas,*
> *This awful God is ours.*
> *Our Father and our love,*
> *He will send down His heavenly powers*
> *To carry us above.*

But the man who is not of an easy conscience will be ill at ease when the timbers of the house are creaking and the foundations of the solid earth seem to groan. Ah, who is he then who does not tremble? Yonder lofty tree is split in half. That lightning flash has smitten its trunk and there it lies forever blasted, a monument of what God can do. Who stood there and saw it? Was he a swearer? Did he swear then? Was he a Sabbath-breaker? Did he love his Sabbath-breaking then? Was he haughty? Did he then despise God? Ah, how he shook then. Saw you not his hair stand on end? Did not his cheek blanch in an instant? Did he not close his eyes and start back in horror when he saw that dreadful spectacle and thought God would smite him, too?

Yes, the power of God, when seen in the tempest, on sea or on land, in the earthquake or in the hurricane, is instinctively a proof that He will not acquit the wicked. I know not how to explain the feeling, but it is nevertheless the truth: Majestic displays of omnipotence have an effect upon the mind of convincing even the hardened that God, who is so powerful, "will not at all acquit the wicked." Thus have I just tried to explain and make bare the link of the chain.

III. The last attribute and the most terrible one is "He will not at all acquit the wicked." Let me unfold this first, and then let me endeavor to trace it also to its source, as I did the first attribute.

God "will not acquit the wicked." How can I prove this? I prove it thus. Never once has He pardoned an unpunished sin. Not in all the years of the Most High, not in all the days of His right hand has He once blotted out sin without punishment. "What," you say, "were not those in heaven pardoned? Are there not many transgressors pardoned, and do they not escape without punishment? Has He not said, 'I have blotted out, like a thick cloud, your transgressions, and like a cloud, your sins' [Isa. 44:22]?" Yes, true, most true, and yet my assertion is true also: Not one of all those sins that have been pardoned was pardoned without punishment.

> The power of God, when seen in the tempest, on sea or on land, in the earthquake or in the hurricane, is instinctively a proof that He will not acquit the wicked.

Do you ask me why and how such a thing as that can be the truth? I point you to yonder dreadful sight on Calvary. The punishment that fell not on the forgiven sinner fell there. The cloud of justice that was charged with fiery hail—the sinner deserved it—fell on Him. But for all that, it fell and spent its fury. It fell there, in that great reservoir of misery. It fell into the Savior's heart. The plagues that should light on *our* ingratitude did not fall on us, but they fell somewhere, and who was it who was plagued? Tell me, Gethsemane. Tell me, O Calvary's summit, who was plagued? The doleful answer comes, " 'Eli, Eli, lama sabachthani?' that is, 'My God, My God, why have You forsaken Me?' " (Matt. 27:46). It is Jesus suffering all the plagues of sin. Sin is still punished, though the *sinner* is delivered.

But, you say, this has scarcely proven that He will not acquit the wicked. I hold it has proven it and proven it clearly. But do you want any further proof that God will not acquit the wicked? Need I lead you through a long list of terrible wonders that God has worked—the wonders of His vengeance? Shall I show you blighted Eden? Shall I let you see a world all drowned, sea monsters whelping and stabling in the palaces of kings? Shall I let you hear the last shriek of the last drowning man as he falls into the flood and dies, washed by that huge wave from the hilltop? Shall I let you see death riding upon the summit of a crested billow, upon a sea that knows no shore, and triumphing because his work is done? His quiver is empty, for all men are slain, save where life flows in the midst of death in yonder ark.

Need I let you see Sodom, with its terrified inhabitants, when the volcano of almighty wrath spouted fiery hail upon it? Shall I show you the earth opening its mouth to swallow up Korah, Dathan, and Abiram? Need I take you to the plagues of Egypt? Shall I again repeat the death shriek of Pharaoh and the drowning of his host? Surely we need not be told of cities that are in ruins, or of nations that have been cut off in a day. You need not be told how God has smitten the earth from one side to the other in His wrath and how He has melted mountains in His hot displeasure. No, we have proofs enough in history, proofs enough in scripture that "He will not at all acquit the wicked."

If you wanted the best proof, however, you should borrow the black wings of a miserable imagination and fly beyond the world through the dark realm of chaos on, far on, where those battlements of fire are gleaming with a horrid light. If through them, with a spirit's safety, you would fly and would behold the worm that never dies, the pit that knows no bottom, and could you there see the fire unquenchable and listen to the shrieks and wails of men and women who are banished forever from God; if, sirs, it were possible for you to hear the sullen groans and hollow moans and shrieks of tortured ghosts, then you would come back to this world amazed and petrified with horror, and you would say, "Indeed, He will not acquit the wicked." *Hell* is the argument of the text. May you never have to prove the text by feeling in yourselves the argument fully carried out. "He will not at all acquit the wicked."

And now we trace this terrible attribute to its source. Why is this? We reply, God will not acquit the wicked, *because He is good*. What? Does goodness demand that sinners will be punished? It does. The judge must condemn the murderer because he loves his nation. "I cannot let you go free. I cannot and I must not. You would slay others who belong to this fair commonwealth if I were to let you go free. No, I must condemn you from the very loveliness of my nature." The kindness of a king demands the punishment of those who are guilty. It is not wrathful in the legislature to make severe laws against great sinners. It is but love toward the rest that sin should be restrained.

Yonder great floodgates that keep back the torrent of sin are painted black and look right horrible, like horrid dungeon gates; they frighten my spirit. But are they proofs that God is not good? No, sirs. If you could open wide those gates and let the deluge of sin flow on us, then you would cry, "O God, O God! Shut the gates of punishment again! Let law again be established! Set up the pillars and swing the gates upon their hinges! Shut again the gates of punishment that this world may not again be utterly destroyed by men who have become worse than brutes." It needs for very goodness' sake that sin should be punished.

Mercy, with her weeping eyes (for she has wept for sinners), when she finds they will not repent, looks more terribly stern in her loveliness than justice in all his majesty. She drops the white flag from her hand and says, "No. I called and they refused. I stretched out my hand and no man regarded. Let them die, let them die," and that terrible word from the lip of mercy's self is harsher thunder than the very damnation of justice. Oh yes, the goodness of God demands that men should perish if they will sin.

And again, *the justice of God demands it.* God is infinitely just, and His justice demands that men should be punished unless they turn to Him with full purpose of heart. Need I pass through all the attributes of God to prove it? I think I need not. We must all of us believe that the God who is slow to anger and great in power is also sure not to acquit the wicked.

And now just a home thrust or two with you. What is your state this morning? My friend—man, woman—what is your state? Can you look up to heaven and say, "Though I have sinned greatly, I believe Christ was punished in my place?"

> *My faith looks back to see*
> *The burden He did bear*
> *When hanging on the cursed tree,*
> *And knows her guilt was there.*

Can you by humble faith look to Jesus and say, "My substitute, my refuge, and my shield; You are my rock, my trust. In you I do confide"? Then, beloved, to you I have nothing to say except never be afraid when you see God's power. For now that you are forgiven and accepted, now that by faith you have fled to Christ for refuge, the power of God need no more terrify you than the shield and sword of the warrior need terrify his wife or his child.

"No," says the woman. "Is he strong? He is strong for me. Is his arm brawny and are all his sinews fast and strong? Then are they fast and strong for me. While he lives and wears a shield, he will stretch it over my head. And while his good sword can cleave foes, it will cleave my foes, too, and ransom me." Be of good cheer. Fear not His power.

> *If it were possible for you to hear the sullen groans and hollow moans and shrieks of tortured ghosts, then you would come back to this world amazed and petrified with horror, and you would say, "Indeed, He will not acquit the wicked."*

But have some of you never fled to Christ for refuge? Do you not believe in the Redeemer? Have you never confided your soul to His hands? Then, my friends, hear me. In God's name, hear me just a moment. My friend, I would not stand in your position for an hour—for all the stars twice spelt in gold! For what is your position? You have sinned and God will not acquit you. He will punish you. He is letting you live; you are reprieved. Poor is the life of one who is reprieved without a pardon! Your reprieve will soon run out. Your hourglass is emptying every day. I see on some of you death has put his cold hand and frozen your hair to whiteness.

You need your staff; it is the only barrier between you and the grave now, and you are, all of you, old and young, standing on a narrow neck of land between two boundless seas; that neck of land, that isthmus of life, narrowing every moment, and you and you and you are yet unpardoned. There is a city to be sacked and you are in it. Soldiers are at the gates. The command is given that every man in the city is to be slaughtered save he who can give the password.

"Sleep on. Sleep on. The attack is not today. Sleep on. Sleep on."

"But it is tomorrow, sir."

"Yes, sleep on. Sleep on; it is not till tomorrow. Sleep on; procrastinate, procrastinate."

"Hark! I hear a rumbling at the gates; the battering ram is at them. The gates are tottering."

"Sleep on. Sleep on. The soldiers are not yet at your doors. Sleep on. Sleep on. Ask for no mercy yet. Sleep on. Sleep on!"

"Yes, but I hear the shrill clarion sound; they are in the streets. Listen to the shrieks of men and women! They are slaughtering them. They fall! They fall! They fall!"

"Sleep on; they are not yet at your door."

"But hark, they are at the gate! With heavy tramp I hear the soldiers marching up the stairs!"

"No. Sleep on. Sleep on; they are not yet in your room."

"Why, they are there; they have burst open the door that parted you from them and there they stand!"

"No. Sleep on! Sleep on; the sword is not yet at your throat. Sleep on! Sleep on!"

It is at your throat. You start with horror.

"Sleep on! Sleep on!"

But you are a goner.

"Demon, why did you tell me to slumber? It would have been wise in me to escape the city when first the gates were shaken. Why did I not ask for the password before the troops came? "Why, by all that is wise, why did I not rush into the streets and cry the password when the soldiers were there? Why stood I till the knife was at my throat? Yes, demon that you are, be cursed. But I am cursed with you forever!"

You know the application; it is a parable you can all expound. You need not that I should tell you that death is after you, that justice must devour you, that Christ crucified is the only password that can save you and yet you have not learned it! And with some of you, death is nearing, nearing, nearing, and with all of you he is close at hand!

I need not expound how Satan is the demon; how in hell you will curse him and curse yourselves because you procrastinated; how, in seeing that God was slow to anger, you were slow to repentance; how, because He was great in power and kept back His anger, therefore you kept back your steps from seeking Him. And here you are what you are!

Spirit of God, bless these words to some souls that they may be saved! May some sinners be brought to the Savior's feet and cry for mercy. We ask it for Jesus' sake. Amen.

For Further Thought

1. *Why has God not yet judged the earth?*
2. *What does God want us to understand when we see His power in nature?*
3. *Read Romans 1:20. What can be known through the things God has made?*

GOD, THE ALL-SEEING ONE

Hell and destruction are before the LORD:
how much more then the hearts of the children of men?
PROVERBS 15:11 KJV

YOU have often smiled at the ignorance of heathens who bow themselves before gods of wood and stone. You have quoted the words of scripture and you have said, "They have mouths, but they do not speak; eyes they have, but they do not see" (Ps. 115:5). You have therefore argued that they could not be gods at all, because they could neither see nor hear, and you have smiled contemptuously at the men who could so debase their understandings as to make such things objects of adoration. May I ask you one question, just one? Your God can both see and hear. Would your conduct be in any respect different if you had a god such as those that the heathen worship?

Suppose for one minute that Jehovah, who is nominally adored in this land, could be (though it is almost blasphemy to suppose it) smitten with such blindness that He could not see the works and know the thoughts of man. Would you then become more careless concerning Him than you are now? I think not. In nine cases out of ten, and perhaps in a far larger and sadder proportion, the doctrine of divine omniscience, although it is received and believed, has no practical effect upon our lives at all.

The mass of mankind forgets God. Whole nations who know His existence and believe that He beholds them live as if they had no God at all. Merchants, farmers, men in their shops and in their fields, husbands in their families, and wives in the midst of their households live as if there were no God. No eye inspecting them, no ear listening to the voice of their lips, and no eternal mind always treasuring up the recollection of their acts. Ah, we are practical atheists, the mass of us. Yes, all but those who have been born again and have passed from death to life, be their creeds what they may, are atheists, after all, in life. For if there were no God and no hereafter, multitudes of men would never be affected by the change. They would live the same as they do now, their lives being so full of disregard of God and His ways that the absence of a God could not affect them in any great degree.

Permit me, then, this morning, as God will help me, to stir up your hearts. And may God grant that something I may say may drive some of your practical atheism out of you. I would endeavor to set before you God, the All-Seeing One, and press upon your solemn consideration the tremendous fact that in all our acts, in all our ways, and in all our thoughts, we are continually under His observing eye. We have in our text, first, *a great fact declared*: "Hell and destruction are before the LORD." We have, second, *a great fact inferred*: "How much more then the hearts of the children of men?"

I. We will begin with the great fact that is declared, a fact that furnishes us with premises from which we deduce the practical conclusion of the second sentence: "How much more then the hearts of the children of men?" The best interpretation that you can give of those two words, *hell* and *destruction*, is, I think, comprehended in a sentence something like this: "Death and hell are before the Lord." The separate state of departed spirits and destruction⬚ *Abaddon*, as the Hebrew has it, the place of torment—are both of them, although solemnly mysterious to us, manifest enough to God.

> *I* would endeavor to set before you God, the All-Seeing One, and press upon your solemn consideration the tremendous fact that in all our acts, in all our ways, and in all our thoughts, we are continually under His observing eye.

1. First, then, the word translated "hell" might just as well be translated "death," or the state of departed spirits. Now, death, with all its solemn consequences, is visible before the Lord. Between here and the hereafter of departed spirits, a great black cloud is hanging. Here and there, the Holy Spirit has made chinks, as it were, in the black wall of separation, through which by faith we can see. For He has revealed to us by the Spirit the things that "eye has not seen, nor ear heard" (1 Cor. 2:9), and that the human intellect could never compass. Yet what we know is but very little. When men die, they pass beyond the realm of our knowledge;

both in body and in soul, they go beyond our understandings. But God understands all the secrets of death. Let us divide these into several heads and enumerate them.

> *God knows the thousands who have perished in battle, unnumbered and unnoticed; the many who have died alone amid dreary forests, frozen seas, and devouring snowstorms; all these and the places of their sepulcher.*

God knows the burial places of all His people. He notes as well the resting place of the man who is buried tombless and alone as the man over whom a mighty mausoleum has been raised. He saw the traveler who fell in the barren desert, whose body became the prey of the vulture and whose bones were bleached in the sun. He saw the mariner, who was wrecked far out at sea and over whose corpse no dirge was ever wailed, except the howling of the winds and the murmuring of the wild waves. God knows the thousands who have perished in battle, unnumbered and unnoticed; the many who have died alone amid dreary forests, frozen seas, and devouring snowstorms; all these and the places of their sepulcher. God has marked that silent grotto within the sea, where pearls lie deep, where now the shipwrecked one is sleeping, as the death place of one of His redeemed.

That place upon the mountainside, the deep ravine into which the traveler fell and was buried in a snowdrift, is marked in the memory of God as the tomb of one of the human race. No body of man, however it may have been interred or not interred, has passed beyond the range of God's knowledge. Blessed be His name, if I will die and lie where the rude forefathers of the hamlet sleep, in some neglected corner of the churchyard, I will be known as well, and rise as well recognized by my glorious Father as if interred in the cathedral, where forests of gothic pillars proudly stand erect and where the songs of myriads perpetually salute high heaven.

I will be known as well as if I had been buried there in solemn pomp and had been interred with music and with dread solemnities. And I will be recognized as well as if the marble trophy and the famous pillar had been raised to my remembrance. For God knows no such thing as forgetfulness of the burying places of His children. Moses sleeps in some spot that eye has not seen. God kissed away his soul and buried him where Israel could never find him, though they may have searched for him. But God knows where Moses sleeps, and if He knows that, He understands where all His children are hidden.

You cannot tell me where is the tomb of Adam. You could not point out to me the sleeping place of Abel. Is any man able to discover the tomb of Methuselah and those long-lived dwellers in the time before the flood? Who will tell where the once-treasured body of Joseph now sleeps in faith? Can any of you discover the tombs of the kings and mark the exact spot where David and Solomon rest in solitary grandeur? No, those things have passed from human recollection, and we know not where the great and mighty of the past are buried. But God knows, because death and Hades are open before the Lord.

And again: Not only does He know the place where they were buried, but also He is cognizant of the history of all their bodies after sepulture or after death. It has often been asked by the infidel, "How can the body of man be restored, when it may have been eaten by the cannibal, or devoured by wild beasts?" Our simple reply is that God can track every atom of it if He pleases. We do not think it necessary, in resurrection, that He should do so, but if He so willed it, He could bring every atom of every body that has ever died although it has passed through the most complicated machinery of nature and become entangled in its passage with plants and beasts. Yes, and with the bodies of other men. God has it still within the range of His knowledge to know where every atom is, and it is within the might of His omnipotence to call every atom from its wandering and restore it to its proper sphere and rebuild the body of which it was a part.

It is true; we could not track the dust that long since has moldered. Buried with the most exact care and preserved with the most scrupulous reverence, years passed away and a careless hand at last reached the body of the monarch who had long slept, well guarded and protected. The coffin had moldered and the metal was broken for the sake of its own value. A handful of dust was discovered, the last relics of one who was master of many nations. That dust by sacrilegious hand was cast in the aisle of the church, or thrown into the churchyard and blown by the winds into the neighboring field. It was impossible forever to preserve it. The greatest care was defeated. And at last the monarch was on a level with his slave, alike unknowing and unknown.

But God knows where every particle of the handful of dust has gone. He has marked in His book the wandering of every one of its atoms. He has death so open before His view that He can bring all these together, bone to bone, and clothe them with the very flesh that robed them in the days of yore and make them live again. Death is open before the Lord. And as the body, so the soul when separated from the body is before the Lord. We look upon the countenance of our dying friend, and on a sudden a mysterious change passes over his frame. "His soul has fled," we say. But have we any idea of what his soul is?

Can we form even a conjecture of what the flying of that soul may be and what the august presence into which it is ushered when it is disentangled from its earthly coil? Is it possible for us to guess what is that state where spirits without bodies, perpetually blessed, behold their God? Is it possible for us to compass some imagination of what heaven is to be, when bodies and souls, reunited, will before God's throne enjoy the highest bliss? I think that so gross are our conceptions, while we are in our bodies, that it is almost if not quite impossible for any of us to form any idea whatever as to the position of souls, while in the disembodied state, between the hour of death and the time of resurrection.

> *This much and this is all, we know,*
> *They are supremely blessed;*
> *Have done with sin and care and woe,*
> *And with their Savior rest.*

But the best of the saints can tell us nothing more than this. They are blessed, and in paradise they are reigning with their Lord. Brethren, God knows these things. The separate state of the dead, the heaven of disembodied spirits, is within the gaze of the Most High. And at this hour, if so He pleased, He could reveal to us the condition of every man who is dead—whether he has mounted to Elysian Fields to dwell forever in the sunlight of his Master's countenance, or has been plunged into hell, dragged down by iron chains, to wait in dreary woe the result of the awful trial, when "Depart from Me, you cursed" (Matt. 25:41) must be the reaffirmation of a sentence once pronounced and already in part endured. God understands the separate doom of every man's spirit before the great tribunal day, before the last sentence will have been pronounced. Death is open before the Lord.

2. The next word, *destruction*, signifies hell, or the place of the damned. That also is open before the Lord. Where hell is and what its miseries, we

know not except "in a mirror, dimly" (1 Cor. 13:12). We have never seen the invisible things of horror. That land of terror is a land unknown. We have much reason to thank God that He has put it so far off from the habitations of living mortals that the pains, the groans, the shrieks, the yells are not to be heard here, or else earth itself would have become a hell, the solemn prelude and actuality of unutterable torment.

> *God understands the separate doom of every man's spirit before the great tribunal day, before the last sentence will have been pronounced. Death is open before the Lord.*

God has put somewhere, far on the edge of His dominions, a fearful lake that burns with fire and brimstone, into which He cast the rebel angels, who (though by a license they are now allowed to walk the earth) do carry a hell within their bosoms. They are by and by to be bound with chains, reserved in blackness and darkness forever for them who kept not their first estate, but lifted the arm of their rebellion against God. Into that place we dare not look. Perhaps it would not be possible for any man to get a fair idea of the torments of the lost without at once becoming mad. Reason would reel at such a sight of horror.

One moment of listening to the shrill screams of spirits tortured might forever drive us into the depths of despair and make us only fit to be bound in chains while we lived on earth. Raving lunatics surely we must become. But while God has mercifully covered all these things from us, He knows them all. He looks upon them. Yes, His look makes hell what it is. His eyes, full of fury, flash the lightning that scathes His enemies. His lips, full of dreadful thunders, make the thunders that now frighten the wicked. Oh, could they escape the eye of God, could they shut out that dreary vision of the face of the incensed Majesty of heaven, then might hell be quenched, and then might the wheels of Ixion stand still! Then might doomed Tartarus quench its thirst and eat to his very full. But there, while they lie in their chains, they look upward and ever see that fearful vision of the Most High: the dreadful hands that grasp the thunderbolts, the dreadful lips that speak the thunders, and the fearful eyes that flash the flames that burn their souls with horrors deeper than despair. Yes, hell, horrible as it is and veiled in many clouds and covered over with darkness, is naked before the vision of the Most High.

There is the grand fact stated: "Hell and destruction are before the LORD." After this the inference seems to be easy: "How much more, then, the hearts of the children of men?"

II. We now come to the great fact inferred. In briefly entering upon this second part, I will discuss the subject thus: "How much more, then, the hearts of the children of men?" I will therefore begin by asking, why does it follow that God sees the hearts of men? *Why, how, what,* and *when* will be four questions into which we will divide what we have now to say.

1. *Why* is it so clear that if hell and destruction are open before the Lord, the hearts of men must be very plainly viewed by Him? We answer, because the hearts of men are not so extensive as the realms of death and torment. What is man's heart? What is man's self? Is he not in scripture compared to a grasshopper? Does not God declare that He "lifts up the isles"—whole islands full of men—"as a very little thing," and the nations before Him are but as the drop of a bucket (Isa. 40:15)? If, then, the all-seeing eye of God takes in at one glance the wide regions of death—and wide they are, wide enough to startle any man who will try to range them through—if, I say, with one glance God sees death and sees hell through, with all its bottomless depths, with all its boundlessness of misery, surely, then, He is quite able to behold all the actions of the little thing called man's heart.

Imagine a man so wise as to be able to know the wants of a nation and to remember the feelings of myriads of men; you cannot suppose it difficult for him to know the actions of his own family and to understand the emotions of his own household. If the man is able to stretch his arm over a great sphere and to say, "I am monarch of all this," surely he will be able to control the less. He who in his wisdom can walk through centuries will not say that he is ignorant of the history of a year. He who can dive into the depths of science and understand the history of the whole world from its creation is not to be alarmed by some small riddle that happens at his own door. No, the God who sees death and hell sees our hearts, for they are far less extensive.

Reflect, again, that they are far less aged, too. Death is an ancient monarch. He is the only king whose dynasty stands fast. Ever since the days of Adam, he has never been succeeded by another and has never had an interruption in his reign. His black ebon scepter has swept away generation after generation. His scythe has mowed the fair fields of this earth a hundred times and is sharp to mow us down. And when another crop will succeed us, he is still ready to devour the multitudes and sweep the earth clean again. The regions of death are old domains. His pillars of black granite are ancient as the eternal hills.

He is our ancient monarch, but ancient as he is, his whole monarchy is in the records of God, and until death itself is dead and swallowed up in victory, death will be open before the Lord. How old, too, is hell? Old as the first sin! In that day when Satan tempted the angels and led astray the third part of the stars of heaven, then hell was dug. Then was that bottomless pit first struck out of solid rocks of vengeance, that it might stand a marvelous record of what God's wrath can do. The fires of hell are not the kindling of yesterday. They are ancient flames that burned long before Vesuvius cast forth its lurid flame. Long before the first charred ashes fell upon the plain from earth's red volcanoes, hell's flames were burning. "For Tophet was established of old, yes, for the king it is prepared. He has made it deep and large; its pyre is fire with much wood; the breath of the Lord, like a stream of brimstone, kindles it" (Isa. 30:33).

If, then, the ancient things, these old ones, death and hell, have been observed by God and if their total history is known to Him, how much more then will He know the history of that mere animalcule, that ephemera of an hour that we call man? You are here today and gone tomorrow. Born yesterday, the next hour will see our tomb prepared, and another minute will hear the words "ashes to ashes, dust to dust," and the falling of the clod upon the coffin lid. We are the creatures of a day and know nothing. We are scarcely here. We are only living and dead. "Gone!" is the greatest part of our history. Scarcely have we time enough to tell the story before it comes to its end. Surely, then, God may easily understand the history of a man, when He knows the history of the monarchies of death and hell.

This is the *why*. I need not give further arguments, though there is abundance deducible from the text. "How much more then the hearts of the children of men?"

2. But now, *how* does God know the heart? I mean, to what degree and to what extent does He understand and know that which is in men? I answer, Holy Scripture in many places gives us most precise information. God knows the heart so well that He is said to search it. We all understand the figure of a search. There is a search warrant out against some man who

is supposed to be harboring a traitor in his house. The officer goes into the lower room, opens the door of every cupboard, looks into every closet, and peers into every cranny. He takes the key, descends into the cellar, turns over the coals, and disturbs the wood, lest anyone should be hidden there. Upstairs he goes.

There is an old room that has not been opened for years. It is opened. There is a huge chest; the lock is forced and it is broken open. The very top of the house is searched, lest upon the slates or upon the tiles someone should be concealed. At last, when the search is complete, the officer says, "It is impossible that there can be anybody here, for from the tiles to the foundation, I have searched the house thoroughly through. I know the very spiders well, for I have seen the house completely." Now, it is just so that God knows our heart. He searches it; searches into every nook, corner, crevice, and secret part. And the figure of the Lord is pushed further still. The Lord, we are told, "knows the secrets of the heart" (Ps. 44:21).

> *Born yesterday, the next hour will see our tomb prepared, and another minute will hear the words "ashes to ashes, dust to dust," and the falling of the clod upon the coffin lid.*

When we wish to find something, we take a candle, look down upon the ground with great care, and turn up the dust. If it is some little piece of money we desire to find, we light a candle, sweep the house, and search diligently till we find it. Even so it is with God. He searches Jerusalem with candles and pulls everything to daylight. No partial search, like that of Laban, when he went into Rachel's tent to look for his idols. She put them in the camel's furniture and sat upon them. But God looks into the camel's furniture and all. " 'Can anyone hide himself in secret places, so I shall not see him?' says the LORD" (Jer. 23:24). His eye searches the heart and looks into every part of it.

In another passage we are told that God tries the reins. That is even more than searching. The goldsmith when he takes gold looks at it and examines it carefully. "Ah," says he, "but I don't understand this gold yet. I must try it." He thrusts it into the furnace. There coals are heaped upon it and it is fused and melted till he knows what there is of dross and what there is of gold. Now, God knows to the very carat how much there is of sound gold in us and how much of dross. There is no deceiving Him. He has put our hearts into the furnace of His omniscience. The furnace, that is, His knowledge, tries us as completely as the goldsmith's crucible does try the gold: how much there is of hypocrisy, how much of truth, how much of sham, how much of real, how much of ignorance, how much of knowledge—how much of devotion, how much of blasphemy, how much of carefulness, how much of carelessness.

God knows the ingredients of the heart. He reduces the soul to its pristine metals. He divides it asunder: so much of quartz, so much of gold, so much of dung, of dross, of wood, of hay, of stubble. There is not so much of gold, silver, and precious stones because the Lord "searches the minds and hearts" of the children of men (Rev. 2:23).

Here is another description of God's knowledge of the heart. In one place of sacred writ (it will be well if you set your children to find out these places at home), God is said to ponder the heart. Now, you know, the Latin word *ponder* means "weigh." The Lord weighs the heart. Old Master Quarles has got a picture of a great one putting a heart into one scale and then putting the law, the Bible, into the other scale, to weigh it. This is what God does with men's hearts. They are often great, puffed up, blown-out things, and people say, "What a great-hearted man that is!"

But God does not judge by the appearance of a man's great heart, or the outside appearance of a good heart. But He puts it in the scales and weighs it; puts His own Word in one scale and the heart in the other. He knows the exact weight. He knows whether we have grace in the heart, which makes us good weight, or only presence in the heart, which makes us weigh light when put into the scale. He searches the heart in every possible way. He puts it into the fire and then thrusts it into the balances. Oh, might not God say of many of you, "I have searched your heart and I have found vanity therein"? Reprobate silver will men call you, for God has put you in the furnace and rejected you. And then He might conclude His verdict by saying, "Mene, Mene, Tekel, Upharsin. This is the interpretation of each word. Mene: God has numbered your kingdom, and finished it" (Dan. 5:25–26). This, then, is the answer to the question, how?

3. The next question is the *what*. What is it that God sees in man's heart? God sees in man's heart a great deal more than we think. God sees and has seen in our hearts lust and blasphemy and murder and adultery and malice and wrath and all uncharitableness. The heart never can be painted

too black unless you daub it with something blacker than the devil himself. It is as base as it can be. You have never committed murder, but you have had murder in your heart. You may never have stained your hands with lust and the aspersions of uncleanness, but still it is in the heart.

Have you never imagined an evil thing? Has your soul ever for a moment doted on a pleasure that you were too chaste to indulge in, but that for a moment you surveyed with at least some little complacency and delight? Has not imagination often pictured, even to the solitary monk in his cell, greater vice than men in public life have ever dreamed of? And may not even the divine in his closet be conscious that blasphemies, murders, and lusts of the vilest class can find a ready harbor even in the heart that he hopes is dedicated to God? Oh, beloved, no human eye could endure such a sight! The sight of a heart really laid bare before one's own inspection would startle us almost into insanity. But God sees the heart in all its bestial sensuousness, in all its wanderings and rebellions, in all its high-mindedness and pride. God has searched and knows it altogether.

God sees all the heart's imaginations, and what they are let us not presume to tell. O children of God, these have made you cry and groan many a time! And though the worldling groans not over them, yet He has. Oh, what a filthy sty of Stygian imaginations is the heart! All full of everything that is hideous, when it once begins to dance and make carnival and revelry concerning sin. But God sees the heart's imaginations.

Again: God sees the heart's devices. You, perhaps, O sinner, have determined to curse God. You have not done so, but you intend to do it. He knows your devices, heads them all. You perhaps will not be permitted to run into the excess of riotousness into which you purpose to go. But your very purpose is now undergoing the inspection of the Most High. There is never a design forged in the fires of the heart, before it is beaten on the anvil of resolve, that is not known and seen and noted by Jehovah our God.

He knows, next, the resolves of the heart. He knows, O sinner, how many times you have resolved to repent and have resolved and re-resolved and then have continued the same. He knows, O you who have been sick, how you did resolve to seek God, but how you did despise your own resolution when good health had put you beyond the temporary danger. Your resolves have been filed in heaven, and your broken promises, and your despised vows. All will be brought out in their order as swift witnesses for your condemnation. All these things are known of God.

We have often had very clear proof of God's knowing what is in man's heart, even in the ministry. Some months ago while standing here preaching, I deliberately pointed to a man in the midst of the crowd and said these words: "There is a man sitting there that is a shoemaker. He keeps his shop open on Sunday. He had his shop open last Sabbath morning, took nine pence and there was four pence profit out of it. His soul is sold to Satan for four pence." A city missionary, when going round the West End of the town, met with a poor man of whom he asked this question: "Do you know Mr. Spurgeon?" He found him reading a sermon. "Yes," he said, "I have every reason to know him. I have been to hear him, and under God's grace I have become a new man.

"But," said he, "shall I tell you how it was? I went to the Music Hall and took my seat in the middle of the place, and the man looked at me as if he knew me and deliberately told the congregation that I was a shoemaker and that I sold shoes on a Sunday. And I did, sir. But, sir, I should not have minded that. But he said I took nine pence the Sunday before and that there was four pence profit. And so I did take nine pence and four pence was just the profit, and how he should know that, I'm sure I cannot tell. It struck me it was God had spoken to my soul through him. And I shut up my shop last Sunday and was afraid to open it and go there lest he should split about me again."

I could tell as many as a dozen authentic stories of cases that have happened in this hall, where I have deliberately pointed at somebody without the slightest knowledge of the person, or ever having in the least degree any inkling or idea that what I said was right except that I believed I was moved thereto by the Spirit. And so striking has been the description that the persons have gone away and said, "Come, see a man who told me all things that ever I did. He was sent of God to my soul, beyond a doubt, or else he could not have painted my case so clearly."

And not only so, but we have known cases in which the thoughts of men have been revealed from the pulpit. I have sometimes seen persons nudge with their elbow, because they have got a smart hit. And I have heard them say, when they went out, "That is just what I said to you when I went in at the door."

"Ah!" says the other. "I was thinking of the very thing he said, and he told me of it." Now, if God thus proves His own omniscience by helping His poor, ignorant servant to state the very thing, thought and done, when he did not know it, then it must remain decisively proved that God does know everything that is secret, because we see He tells it to men and enables them to tell it to others.

Oh, you may endeavor as much as you can to hide your faults from God. But beyond a doubt, He will discover you. He discovers you this day. His Word "is living and powerful, and sharper than any two-edged sword, piercing even to the division of soul and spirit, and of joints and marrow, and is a discerner of the thoughts and intents of the heart" (Heb. 4:12). And in that last day, when the book will be opened and He will give to every man his sentence, then will it be seen how exact, how careful, how precious, how personal was God's knowledge of the heart of every man whom He had made.

4. And now the last question: *When?* When does God see us? The answer is, He sees us everywhere and in every place. O foolish man, who thinks to hide himself from the Most High, it is night and no human eye sees you. The curtain is drawn and you are hidden. There are His eyes lowering at you through the gloom. It is a far-off country. No one knows you. Parents and friends have been left behind; restraints are cast off. There is a Father near you, who looks upon you even now. It is a lone spot, and if the deed is done, no tongue will tell it.

There is a tongue in heaven that will tell it. Yes, the beam out of the wall and the stones in the field will rise up themselves as witnesses against you. Can you hide yourself anywhere where God will not detect you? Is not this whole world like a glass hive, wherein we put our bees? And does not God stand and see all our motions when we think we are hidden? Ah, it is but a glass hiding place. He looks from heaven and through stone walls and rocks. Yes, to the very center itself does His eye pierce, and in the thickest darkness He beholds our deeds.

Come then, let me make a personal application of the matter, and I am done. If this is true, hypocrite, what a fool you are! If God can read the heart, O man, what a sorry, sorry thing your fair pretense must be! Ah! Ah! Ah! What a change will come over some of you! This world is a masquerade, and you, many of you, wear the mask of religion. You dance your giddy hours and men think you to be the saints of God. How changed will you be when, at the door of eternity, you must drop the visor and must renounce the theatrics in which you live! How you will blush when the paint is washed from off your cheek, when you stand before God naked to your own shame, a hypocrite, unclean, diseased, covered up before with the gewgaws and the trickery of pretended formality in religion, but now standing there base, vile, and hideous! There are many men who bear about a cancer that would make one sick to see. Oh, how will hypocrites look when their cancerous hearts are laid bare!

> The sight of a heart really laid bare before one's own inspection would startle us almost into insanity. But God sees the heart in all its bestial sensuousness, in all its wanderings and rebellions, in all its high-mindedness and pride. God has searched and knows it altogether.

Deacon! How you will tremble when your old heart is torn open and your vile pretenses rent away! Minister! How black you will look when your surplice is off and when your grand pretensions are cast to the dogs! How you will tremble! There will be no sermonizing others then! You yourself will be preached to and the sermon will be from that text, "Depart, you cursed." O brethren, above all things shun hypocrisy. If you mean to be damned, make up your minds to it and be damned, like honest men. But do not, I beseech you, pretend to go to heaven while all the while you are going to hell. If you mean to make your abodes in torment forever, then serve the devil and do not be ashamed of it. Stand right out and let the world know what you are. But oh, never put on the cloak of religion. I beseech you, do not add to your eternal misery by being a wolf in sheep's clothing. Show the cloven foot. Do not hide it. If you mean to go to hell, say so. "If God is God, serve Him. If Baal is God, serve him." Do not serve Baal and then pretend to be serving God.

One other practical conclusion: If God sees and knows everything, how this ought to make you tremble, you who have lived in sin for many years! I have known a man who was once stopped from an act of sin by the fact of there being a cat in the room. He could not bear even the eyes of that poor creature to see him. Oh, I would you could carry about with you the recollection of those eyes that are always on you.

Swearer! Could you swear if you could see God's eye looking at you! Thief! Drunkard! Harlot! Could you indulge in your sins if you saw His eyes on you?

Oh, I think they would startle you and bid you pause before you did, in

God's own sight, rebel against His law. There is a story told of the American War, that one of the prisoners taken by the Americans was subjected to a torture of the most refined character. He says, "I was put into a narrow dungeon. I was comfortably provided for with all I needed. But there was a round slit in the wall and through that, both night and day, a soldier always looked at me." He says, "I could not rest; I could not eat nor drink, nor do anything in comfort, because there was always that eye—an eye that seemed never to be turned away and never shut, always following me round that little apartment. Nothing ever hidden from it."

Now take home that figure. Recollect that is your position: You are shut in by the narrow walls of time. When you eat and when you drink, when you rise and when you lie upon your beds, when you walk the streets, or when you sit at home, that eye is always fixed upon you. Go home now and sin against God, if you dare. Go home now, break His laws to His face, despise Him, and set Him at nothing! Rush on your own destruction, dash yourselves against the buckler of Jehovah, and destroy yourselves upon His sword! No! Rather, "Turn at my rebuke" (Prov. 1:23). Turn, you who have followed the ways of sin; turn to Christ and live! And then the same omniscience that is now your horror will be your pleasure. Sinner! If you now pray, He sees you. If you now weep, He sees you. "When he was still a great way off, his father saw him and had compassion, and ran and fell on his neck and kissed him" (Luke 15:20). It will be even so with you, if now you turn to God and do believe in His Son, Jesus Christ.

FOR FURTHER THOUGHT

1. *What is the doctrine of divine omniscience?*
2. *According to this sermon, in what way can the doctrine of divine omniscience affect your life?*
3. *Read Hebrews 4:12. What effect does the Word of God have on the human heart?*

The Righteous Father
Known and Loved

"O righteous Father! The world has not known You, but I have known You; and these have known that You sent Me. And I have declared to them Your name, and will declare it, that the love with which You loved Me may be in them, and I in them."
John 17:25–26

THESE are the last sentences of our Lord's most wonderful prayer. May they not be regarded as the flower and crown of the whole intercession? Minds usually burn and glow and reach their highest fervor as they proceed, and it will not be wrong to conceive of the Savior as having here reached the climax of His pleading, the summit of His supplication. He has kept the best wine until now and brings forth His richest sentences last. How, then, will our slender ability attain to the height of this great argument?

It is far beyond our little skill to draw forth all the sweets that lie within these words like ointment in a box of alabaster. For their full consideration, a lifetime would be too brief and the mind of the most grace-taught believer too feeble! Here are great deeps that neither reason nor thought can fathom nor experience fully know. Only the scholars of the New Jerusalem, who have for ages studied the manifold wisdom of God in the glorious work of redemption, and perhaps not even they, would be able to discover all that the Savior meant by these most simple but yet most pregnant words.

John's gospel is always easy for the child to read, but it is always hard for the man to understand. And these two verses, which are almost entirely made up of words of one syllable, contain mysteries that baffle the most enlightened understanding. When I consider what they veil, I am constrained to cry out, "Oh, the depths" (Rom. 11:33). I can only hope to present to you a few grains of gold that have been washed down by the streams of meditation; I cannot take you to the secret mines from which the treasures have been borne. It will need your own experience and the personal teaching of the Holy Spirit for you to know the height and depth of the truths of God spoken here. And even then it will require death and resurrection and a sight of the eternal glory to qualify you wholly to comprehend them!

There are two things in the text manifest to every careful reader. There is, first, a knowledge that is exceedingly peculiar and inestimably precious. "O righteous Father! The world has not known You, but I have known You; and these have known that You sent Me." In connection with this knowledge, you will observe that there is a great teacher who first knows for Himself that which He teaches: "I have known You." And then He communicates His knowledge: "And I have declared to them Your name, and will declare it." That fruitful theme will furnish the first topic of our meditation. May the Holy Spirit lead us into it.

The second part of the text is not knowledge. It is that to which all divine knowledge is intended to lead, namely, love. The twenty-sixth verse speaks of wonderful discoveries of a love of infinite excellence: "That the love with which You loved Me may be in them, and I in them." And you notice that in order to bring that love home to us, there is a divine indweller who goes with it, and without whom it could not be! As a teacher is required to bring us the choice knowledge, so an Indweller is necessary to infuse into us the infinite love: "And I in them." Jesus must teach us or we will not know the Father. He must dwell in us or we will not rejoice in His love.

Thus our first subject is divine knowledge and the divine instructor. Our second subject is indwelling love and the indwelling Lord. The two are one! The blessed person of our Lord Jesus is so connected with both and so unites both that the subject is one! To know God in Christ Jesus is to love Him, and to be loved of Him is the cause of our being made to know Him! When Jesus declares the Father's name, we both know and love. And when we see the Father in the Son, we are filled with both instruction and affection.

I. Our text speaks of *a knowledge of infinite value and its teacher*. What is that knowledge? Jesus tells us in verse 26, "I have declared to them your name." God has made man, and naturally, man ought to know his Maker. The creature should acquaint itself with its Creator. The subject should know the name of his King. But by reason of the blindness of our heart, through the depravity engendered by the fall, and also by reason of each man's personal sin, there is none who understands and none who seeks after God.

Whatever else fallen man desires to know (and by nature he is always ready to eat of the tree of the knowledge of good and evil), yet he desires not to know his God, but says to Him, "Depart from us. We desire not the knowledge of Your ways." Yet it is evident that a man can never be in a proper state till he knows his God and is at peace with Him. A man who is totally ignorant of God must be in a dark state of mind, and since he loves that darkness, it is plain that his mind is biased against good. His willful ignorance of God proves his enmity to Him. While man is opposed to God, he cannot be happy, holy, or safe. How can he be, when he fights against One who is perfect holiness and love?

> *o know God in Christ Jesus is to love Him, and to be loved of Him is the cause of our being made to know Him!*

Our Lord Jesus Christ, therefore, in coming to save us, makes it a part of His office to reveal the Father to us. He brings us the knowledge of the glory of God, for it shines in His own face. "God was manifested in the flesh" (1 Tim. 3:16). Man must know God in order to be saved, and therefore the Lord Jesus of old promised in Psalm 22, "I will declare Your name to My brethren" (v. 22), and here, in our text, He confesses, "I have declared to them your name, and will declare it." By the term *name*, He means the *existence* of God, the nature of God, the character of God, the work of God, the revelation of God, for the word *name* is a peculiarly expressive word in scripture and comprehends all that by which a person is properly described. In this case it comprehends the whole of God, and our Lord Jesus Christ has come to make God known to us to the fullest.

He says, "If you had known Me, you would have known My Father also" (John 14:7). This should suggest to each of us a searching question: Do I know the Lord? If you do not, it is quite certain that our Lord's words apply to you: "You must be born again." Without knowledge of God, you bear evidence that you are still in nature's darkness and in the natural alienation of your spirit. You belong to that world that lies in the wicked one, of which our Lord said, "O righteous Father! The world has not known You." Oh, that by the teaching of the Holy Spirit you may yet know the Father!

In verse 25 there is a testing name given to God, a name by which we may decide whether we know the name of the Lord or not. What is that? I call your particular attention to it, for my whole subject turns upon it. It is this: "righteous Father." I know of no other place in scripture where God is called by that name. In this prayer Jesus had not addressed His Father by that title before. He had spoken of Him as Father, and also as holy Father, but here alone it is righteous Father. I say that the knowledge of this name may serve as a test as to whether you truly and spiritually know God, or have only a notional and outward idea of Him. If you know Him aright, you know and understand what is comprehended under those two simple words that are so remarkable when found in combination: righteous Father.

He is righteous, having the attributes of a judge and ruler. He is just, impartial, by no means sparing the guilty. He is Father, near of kin, loving, tender, forgiving. In His character and in His dealings with His people, He blends the two as they were never combined before! How can the judge and the father be found in one? When guilty men are concerned, how can both characters be carried out to the fullest? How is it possible? There is but one answer, and that is found in the sacrifice of Jesus that has joined the two in one! In the atonement of our Lord Jesus, "mercy and truth have met together; righteousness and peace have kissed" (Ps. 85:10).

> This is the knowledge that our Lord has come to declare among the men whom He has chosen out of the world. And He assures us first that this is peculiar knowledge. "O righteous Father! The world has not known you."

In the sacred substitution we see declared how God is righteous, and yet also Father. In the sublime transactions of Calvary, He manifests all the love of a tender Father's heart and all the justice of an impartial ruler's sword! This is the knowledge that our Lord has come to declare among the men whom He has chosen out of the world. And He assures us first that this is peculiar knowledge. "O righteous Father! The world has not known You." The heathen world knew nothing of a righteous Father. It scarcely knew God as Father. Though here and there a line of a heathen poet might speak of men as the offspring of God, the true idea of divine Fatherhood was unknown to sages and philosophers. As to the righteousness of *God*, they had but clouded notions. A future judgment and a system of rewards and punishments they saw by the light of natural conscience. But true righteousness in the governing of the universe they had not discovered.

They knew not because they did not wish to know.

Their gods were generally monsters of iniquity. As to righteousness and love being combined, they imagined no such thing! The idea of a God who should be at once sternly righteous and yet infinitely tender had not occurred to them. How could it? Being themselves unrighteous, they sought not after a righteous God! He was not at all in their thoughts. Being themselves cruel and loveless, they could not discover a deity whose name is love. All the wisdom of antiquity went to fabricate gods of quite another kind. The world, by wisdom, knew not the God who is called righteous Father. It is more humbling to have to add that the Christian world does not know God as a righteous Father either, but persists in forsaking this grand, glorious, and scriptural view of Him.

Mark you: I draw a very grave distinction between the Christian church and the Christian world! The Christian world is a conglomeration of good and evil; the embodiment of the unreal and unspiritual that, nevertheless, desires to bear the Christian name. It is the world pretending to be the friend of Christ, and you know how hollow is the pretense. The Christian church, made up of the men taught of God and born of the Spirit, is another matter! There we have something very different, for these know the righteous Father. Skeptics labeled as thinkers reject the evangelical idea of God and the atonement that that idea involves. Worldly wisdom talks of the universal fatherhood of God and babbles forever about that mere dream, that fiction of folly against which the Bible is a plain and pointed protest.

Universal fatherhood indeed! Is it not described as a special wonder of love that we should be called the sons of God (1 John 3:1)? Did not the Holy Spirit say by His servant John, "In this the children of God and the children of the devil are manifest: Whoever does not practice righteousness is not of God, nor is he who does not love his brother" (1 John 3:10). The philosophic Christian world knows an effeminate, indiscriminate fatherhood, but not the righteous Father. It will not bow before the majesty of His justice.

According to the tenor of its teaching, sin is a misfortune, transgression a mere trifle, and the souls that suffer for willful guilt are objects to be pitied rather than to be blamed! The world's thinkers are continually drawing upon our feelings to make us pity those who are punished, but they have little to say in order to make us hate the evil that deserved the doom. Sin, according to them, does not, of itself, demand punishment, but penalties are to be exacted or remitted for the general good, if indeed they are to be executed at all! All necessary and inevitable connection between guilt and its punishment is denied. They dare to call justice *revenge*, and speak of atonement as if it were a compensation for private annoyance. The Christian *world* does not seem to have learned the truth that a God all mercy is a God unjust, and that a God unjust would soon be discovered to be a God without love, in fact, no God whatever.

Righteous Father! This is the peculiar revelation that is received by those who have been taught of the Holy Spirit, and to this day Jesus Christ may say, "O righteous Father! The world has not known You." Men kick against the doctrine of the atonement, they quarrel with substitution, they are fierce in their sarcasms against the mention of the precious blood of Christ, and they sneer superciliously at those who hold fast the old truths of God. They stumble at this stumbling stone and strive evermore to overthrow this rock of the truth of God! And yet, depend upon it, this is the test question by which we will know whether a man knows God aright or knows Him not!

> *A* God all mercy is a God unjust, and that a God unjust would soon be discovered to be a God without love, in fact, no God whatever.

There is much in this knowledge that renders it very distinctive, for it reveals the condition of the mind that receives it. A man who knows God as righteous Father shows that he has some knowledge of Himself. He has perceived the sin within his nature and it has burdened him. The righteousness of God has appeared to him in its threatening form, and he has been bowed before it under a sense of his guilt. You can see, too, that the man also knows something of his Savior. He has evidently seen the Son, or else he would not know the Father, for of old, Jesus said, "No one comes to the Father except through Me" (John 14:6). He has seen God's great gift to man and has learned His boundless love!

His knowledge of the righteous Father shows that his heart has submitted itself to the justice of God. He has been in the place where David stood when he said, "Against You, You only, have I sinned, and done this evil in Your sight—that You may be found just when You speak, and blameless when You judge" (Ps. 51:4). He has evidently bared his back to the lash of punishment and felt that he deserved all the blows that it could lay upon him. Inasmuch as it knows the Lord as a righteous Father, you can see that the heart has learned to trust God, for no man calls Him Father in spirit and in truth till first he possesses a living faith and some kindling of divine love. Submission and trust compose a condition of character that is peculiar to a renewed soul, but will surely be found in a man if he is indeed saved, for it is the mark of being saved from self-justification and from the hatred bred by despair.

When we see in a man an unconditional submission to the justice of God and yet a trustful hopefulness in His boundless love, we may be sure that he is a renewed man. He cries, "You are righteous, O my God, and if You destroy me, I can say nothing. But, Father, You will not destroy me, for I perceive that You are love. Though I see You grasp Your sword of fire, yet do I trust You, for I still believe You to be gracious and loving." The knowledge described in the text is not only peculiar to those who are taught of God, but it reveals peculiarities in them that grace has implanted there. They believe because they are Christ's sheep and know His voice. The life within them receives the living truth of God. They would not have come to know the righteous Father unless there had been a change in their character worked by the Spirit of God, and that once done, they know Him as of necessity.

I would next say that this knowledge is eminently consolatory. It is but little that I know, but I feel that I would cheerfully part with it all so long as I may be allowed to retain the knowledge contained in these two words, *righteous Father*. This is my life, my light, my love, my delight, and my heaven! If all the productions of wit and wisdom throughout all past ages could be as effectually consumed as the Alexandrian library when it was burned to ashes; if man did but retain the knowledge of these two words, *righteous Father*, he might be content to see the whole mass pass away in smoke! To know the only true God, and Jesus Christ whom He has sent, is the climax, the essence, and the sum total of wisdom! I said that it was consolatory, and so it is to the last degree. For a man to know that God is his Father is delightful beyond measure!

To feel that God forgives him as the father forgave the prodigal, to know that He has received him into His heart and home as the father did his once lost boy, is unspeakably delightful! But when we further learn that all this is done without the violation of justice—that all this deed of grace is done *righteously*—and so done that even justice demands it should be done, then are we full of wondering love! Beloved, God is as just in loving His sinful people as He could have been in manifesting His displeasure toward them!

He is as just in forgiving as He could have been in punishing—and this is the glory of the whole matter! This being understood, we see our position in Christ Jesus to be unassailable. We see that justice cannot punish us, for Jesus has borne our penalty! It cannot demand more at our hands, for our great Substitute has rendered to it the full tale of obedience. In Christ Jesus, God is just and yet our justifier! We are so safe that we begin to challenge opposition and cry, "Who shall bring a charge against God's elect?" (Rom. 8:33). We take up a triumphant note and sing with exceeding joy, "If God is for us, who can be against us?" If God is righteous and yet my Father, then I am saved and saved in such a way that the attributes of God are glorified by *my salvation*, and therefore I am most securely and certainly saved! Why should I not rejoice?

One more fact about this knowledge of God as a righteous Father: It is a knowledge that causes its possessor to enjoy much fellowship with Jesus. Notice how our Lord puts it. "O righteous Father! The world has not known You, but I have known You; and these have known that You sent Me."

"I have known You." Ah, yes, of old the Son of God knew the glorious character of the Godhead! Being Himself God, He knew that justice was an essential attribute of deity, which never, never could be tarnished or made to yield a hair's breadth! And He knew, also, that God is love and that His love would never cease to be His special glory and delight! He knew of old that, speaking after the manner of men, these two attributes were each resolved to suffer no eclipse. He knew that each of them must keep its place.

God must be just and must be a Father. Consequently, when dealing with sinners, He must smite and He must spare. Our Lord saw how these two necessities stood like the eternal hills and how our doom seemed to roll between—and it was He who condescended, for our sakes, to bring these two together by His own endurance of justice and manifestation of love. He determined to take upon Himself our nature and bear our sin that was the cause of the quarrel! And then, by enduring the punishment of our sins, He magnified justice—and to an equal degree glorified love. He came, He saw and solved the difficulty—and now the judge is as righteous as if He were not love and the Father is as loving as if righteousness had never been offended! This grand character of God as righteous Father was so dear to our Lord and so much admired by Him that He died to maintain and vindicate it! And when you and I come to know it, I am sure we so much delight in it that we feel we would sooner die than give up this truth of God!

This great revelation of God is not a dogma that may or may not be accepted—it must be so! I do, in my soul, believe this truth of God to be an article of a standing or of a falling of a Christian church. If you put away the doctrine of the substitutionary sacrifice of Christ, you have disemboweled the gospel and torn from it its very heart! Angels need no longer sing glory to God in the highest and peace on earth if it is not true that the union of the divine glory and human salvation is found in Jesus! The glad news dwindles down very lamentably if the atonement is denied! But it cannot be disproved—God is just and yet the justifier of him who believes! Christ has died that this truth of God may be clear and His people live to declare it and feel that it was worth a thousand martyrdoms to maintain it! Herein we have fellowship with Christ, for He knows the righteous Father and rejoices in Him—and *we* know the righteous Father, too, in Christ—and love and bless Him and wonder at Him every day more and more.

> *We see our position in Christ Jesus to be unassailable. We see that justice cannot punish us, for Jesus has borne our penalty!*

Thus I have, to the best of my power, described the invaluable knowledge. May we all be taught of the Lord and all know Him, from the least to the greatest.

Now, this knowledge comes to us by a teacher. That teacher is spoken of in verse 26: "I have declared to them Your name, and will declare it." Our beloved Lord has most fitly declared to us this name of righteous Father, for He Himself knows it as none other can know it! And He here confesses this intimate knowledge, saying, "But I have known You." No man knows the Father save the Son, and the Son knows the rectitude of the Father's government and the love of the Father's heart beyond all others. Is He not Himself very God of very God? And does He not perceive this wondrous union of the two ranges of attributes in the person of the Father with a clearness of vision that no one else possesses? Fit is it, therefore, that He should declare to us what He has seen and known of the Father.

He declared the righteous Father in His life, for in His life He incarnated truth and grace. Jesus Christ on earth was without sin in thought, in word, and in deed. Point me to a sin He ever committed, inculcated, or excused. Righteousness was about Him as the atmosphere that He breathed. Well did the psalmist say of Him, "You love righteousness and hate wickedness" (Ps. 45:7). And yet what love there was in Him and pity for the wandering sheep! He mingled with sinners and yet was separate from sinners. He touched their diseases and healed them and yet was not defiled by their impurities. He took their infirmities upon Himself and yet in Him, personally, there was no trace of sin. Our Lord was so righteous that you perceived at once that He was not of this world—and yet He was so lovingly human that He was altogether a man among men.

He was not at all separated from them in the way in which John the Baptist was, who "came neither eating nor drinking" (Matt. 11:18). Nor was He divided from His fellows, as many a man of genius has been, by eccentric modes of thought. He was man's brother and his Physician, his friend and his Savior! When you want to know the Father's righteousness and love, read the history of Jesus Christ—no, *know* the Lord Jesus Himself and you know the Father! His death, however, most gloriously illustrated this beyond everything else. Behold, He dies that the righteous Father may be seen! He has taken upon Himself man's sin and He is brought to the place where man must answer for his sin. He is silent before His accusers. He is condemned and numbered with the transgressors.

Now He must die the sinner's death. Look, He is nailed to the cross, and now God Himself forsakes Him, for He has laid the guilt of man upon Him and therefore cannot be present to make His spirit glad. The deserted Savior cries, "My God, My God, why have You forsaken Me?" (Matt. 27:46). And well He might, when His own Father in righteousness turned His face from Him! Beloved, when Jesus Christ died, there was a greater display of the righteousness and the fatherhood of God than could have been possible by any other means! Then the mystery was made plain and the depth opened up to its very bottom! O Lord our God, what an abyss of adorable goodness have You thus laid bare before us!

> *How our hearts tremble at your love immense!*
> *In love immense, inviolably just!*
> *You, rather than your justice should be stained,*
> *Did stain the cross with blood of your own Son.*

And now, today, it is the business of our Lord to continue to reveal the righteous fatherhood of God, and He does so by the work of His Holy

Spirit. Do you not remember when He revealed it to you? When you were bowed down with grief on account of sin? When you longed to be reconciled to God but could not see how, then the Spirit of God came to you and pointed you to the full atonement made, to the utmost ransom paid, and you clapped your hands for very joy as you perceived that God could be your Father and receive you as His child and yet His righteousness need not suffer the slightest decrease! That Spirit of God working on behalf of Christ is still declaring this among the nations! As the years roll on, He is opening the eyes of the blind and bringing His own chosen, one by one, to behold the glory of God in the face of Jesus Christ! And then they can say, "O righteous Father, I know You and rejoice in You."

To each one of us who is saved, Jesus is declaring this righteous Father more and more. I hope I know more of this than I did twenty years ago. Brothers and sisters, don't you, too? I trust that every day we see a little more of the righteous fatherhood of God and will continue to do so, world without end! We shall, as we grow in grace, look further and further into the wondrous mystery of the justice that was satisfied and the love that furnished the satisfaction! Beloved, it will be a part of our Lord's joy, even in eternity, to still declare to us the name of God, the righteous Father. Will it not be our joy to sit at His feet and learn of Him? Is He not a blessed teacher? Has He not been very patient with us? Blessed be His name for all His care and patience toward us. He has taught us much and means to teach us more. Let us bend a listening ear and bow a willing heart while, from day to day, He will continue to declare to us the righteous Father.

Now, if at any time I should seem to preach the doctrine of the substitution of Christ too often, and if you should say, "He is harping upon the old string," I will not hesitate to quote my Master's words and say, "I have declared to them Your name, and will declare it." This truth of God is one that needs continual declaration! It should be sounded often in the Christian's ears to keep alive his sense of obligation to the wisdom that devised and the love that carried out the plan of our salvation to the glory of the righteous Father.

II. Second, this heavenly knowledge is not given to us for its own sake alone. Even the high and blessed revelation of the righteous Father is not made to us that we may know it and end in knowing. Our Lord says, "I have declared to them Your name, and *will* declare it, that the love with which You have loved Me may be in them, and I in them." The objective of the knowledge bestowed upon us is the infusion of a *love unrivaled in value* and extraordinary to the last degree! Let us speak upon it. First, notice that this discovery of love that is spoken of in verse 26 is an inward discovery of it: "That the love with which You have loved Me may be *in* them." It was always *on* them, for the Father has always loved His people, but here it is spoken of as in them.

> *I* trust that every day we see a little more of the righteous fatherhood of God and will continue to do so, world without end!

What does that mean? I think it means that they may know it, be persuaded of it, believe it, and enjoy it, so that they, through knowing the righteous name, may come to perceive the love of God toward them. Do you not see the connection? Jesus Christ our Lord dies for us that God may be righteous and yet may save us! Is it not clear as a pikestaff to you that God loves His people with a very wonderful love when He gives His own Son to die and satisfy justice on their behalf? Nothing can prove that love so clearly. Nothing can bring it home so forcibly as the sacrificial death of the Only Begotten. Therefore does Christ declare the blessed name of the righteous Father, in order that it may come home to you with an unconquerable power that the Father loves you and loves you beyond conception, seeing that not even His dear Son was so loved as to be spared, but *He* must die that you might live and that the justice of God might be satisfied on your account!

There is no way of knowing the love of God like knowing the righteous Father and the atonement that that character necessitated. "By this we know love, because He laid down His life for us" (1 John 3:16). You may say, "I see His love in every flower that blooms and every breeze that blows." It is true, but it is the same love, after all, that He has toward a horse or a cow, for do not flowers bloom and breezes blow for them? "We see the love of God," say some, "in giving us meat to eat and raiment to put on." So do I, but this, also, is the same love that He bears to ravens and to lilies, for does He not feed the one and clothe the other? I need something more by way of love than this. "I see God's love," says one, "in Christ's coming to teach us and make us better." No doubt you do, and so do I, but I do not feel it one half so forcibly as when I gaze upon Calvary and see the innocent Victim bleeding for my crimes. "Herein is love!"

When the Father gives up His Best Beloved for guilty man, we may well say, "Behold how He loved Him!" Come and see this spectacle of love! It is none other than the Lord of heaven who must *die* to vindicate the jealous purity of the divine government! Is He God's only begotten Son and must He bear man's guilt? Miracle of miracles! Must the spotless Son bear human guilt? He must! He did! Tell it and let heaven be astonished still, though it has heard the wonder nearly two thousand years! Upon Him who never sinned the Lord has laid our iniquities! Bearing that guilt, must He suffer? He must. If God loves His people, His Son must suffer in their place—must suffer shame, must suffer desertion, must suffer death. What? Must He die? Incarnate deity is put to death? A felon's death? Can this be? It has been! It is finished! Such was the love of God that "did not spare His own Son, but delivered Him up for us all" (Rom. 8:32). Be astonished, O heavens, forever and ever, that love could accomplish such a feat as this!

Now then, Christ has come on purpose to declare the name of God that the love of God may be perceived by us, its power felt, its glory recognized, its greatness wondered at, its infinitude delighted in. But now notice, and here is the very heart of our subject: that this love was of a most extraordinary kind. "That the love with which You have loved Me may be in them." What is the love with which God loved His Son? Come, you philosophers and divines! Come, you who have learned to blend imagination with cool judgment—come and think this over—the love with which the Father loved His Son! Believer, He loves you as He loves His Best Beloved! He is His only begotten Son—Son in a very mysterious manner—for we cannot understand that divine filiation in which the Father is eternal and the Son also eternal.

He loves you as He loves such a Son. There is more than sonship; there is natural unity of essence, for the Father and Son are one God! And how the one God loves, how the Father loves, the Son, I know not, except that I know there can be no limit to such love. It must be altogether boundless and unspeakable! Now, if you fully know the righteous fatherhood of God, as Christ would have you know it, you will learn that God loved you as He loved His Son. Do you not see that it is so? If He had not loved you as He loved the Son, He would have spared His Son! Is not that clear? If He had not loved you as He loved His Son, He would have said to His Son, "Son, You will never leave heaven for that polluted planet. You will never descend to poverty and suffering. You will never have Your hands and feet pierced. You will never be despised and spit upon and put to a cruel death."

But because He loved us as He loved His Son, He gave His Son! Does not that fact warm your hearts? Does it not burn like coals of juniper within your bosoms? "Thanks be to God for His indescribable gift!" (2 Cor. 9:15). No, that is not all. We learn from the verse that precedes our text that the Father loved our Lord eternally: "For You loved Me before the foundation of the world." Perceive, then, that God has also loved you, dear child of His, from before the foundation of the world! Before you had a being, His prescient eye foresaw your existence and you were the object of His love! How or why, I cannot tell you, but He loved you and He still loves you as He loves His Son! May the power of that love be felt in your heart now! It was a love of complacency and delight!

Remember those words of the Lord that He spoke concerning His Son in the day of His baptism and at two other occasions when the heavens opened: "This is My beloved Son, in whom I am well pleased." Always draw a distinction between the love of benevolence, with which God loves *all* His creatures, and the love of *complacency* that is reserved for His own. He calls His church His Hephzibah because His delight is in her (Isa. 62:4). He says not so of the world! God never said concerning any wicked man, "This is My beloved Son, in whom I am well pleased" (Matt. 17:5), for He is *not* pleased with him, but angry with him every day! But concerning all those who know the righteous Father, it is the prayer of Christ that the love with which the Father loves Him may be in them, and by that He means that they may *feel* that the Lord has, *in them*, a father's content.

Do try, if you can, to realize this high privilege. It is true, O believer, that God, the infinite Father, takes pleasure in you! It is true, but it is very surprising! Often have I turned over that word in the Song of Songs where the bridegroom says to the bride, "You are all fair, my love, and there is no spot in you" (4:7). How can this be? Why, we are all spots! Yet does the eternal Father view us *in Christ*! And in Him He takes delight in us as a father does in his children. "My delight was with the sons of men" (Prov. 8:31). "He will quiet you with His love, He will rejoice over you with singing" (Zeph. 3:17). When you know God as righteous, and yet Father, then will you see that, inasmuch as the righteous way of salvation has put away all sin by laying it upon Christ, there is no reason why the Lord should be angry with us! And inasmuch as the righteousness of Christ is imputed to us, there is a legal reason why He should be satisfied with His people. And inasmuch as we have become one with Christ, there is good cause why He should take a delight in us, even for His Son's sake!

God the Father loves His Son infinitely! How could He do less? Without beginning has He loved Him, and without an end will He love Him, and also without change, without limit, and without degree! In the same way does He love His people, whose hope is fixed in Him as the righteous Father. This love, wherever it reigns in the heart, creates a return love to God. You cannot really know all this and enjoy it without feeling, "My God, I love you in return." And that high and noble passion works to the cleansing of the soul and the purging out of sin—and so it becomes a sanctifying influence by which a Christian is made to be "holiness to the LORD" (Jer. 2:3).

To close, this love within the soul comes through an Indweller. Observe the last words of the text, "That the love with which You have loved Me may be in them, and I in them." What does this mean? I cannot tell you all it means. Let us skim the surface just for a minute. It means this. The Holy Spirit is the representative of Christ now upon earth, and if ever the love of God the Father is to be known by any one of us, the Lord Jesus, by the Spirit, must be in us. Without the Spirit of God actually *resident in us*, we cannot know the righteous Father! We are as blind and dead men until He quickens and illuminates us—all the letter-teaching in the world will benefit us nothing—we must be born again!

My dear hearers, there may be some of you to whom all my talk this morning must seem very strange. You cannot see anything in it. Let the fact cause you to suspect that you must be in the dark. When even the love of God to His people becomes a dry theme to you, it looks suspicious! Surely you have no part or lot in it, or else you would relish a discourse upon it! The reason why you do not comprehend it is because you have not the Spirit of Christ—and if you have not the Spirit of Christ, you are none of His. May this convince you of your condition and may you be led to seek Christ and find everlasting life.

But when the text says that Christ is *in* His people, it means, besides the indwelling of the Spirit, that *Christ* is in us! He is in us by faith, for we have taken Christ Jesus as the great atoning sacrifice to be our sole and only confidence. Therefore He is in us, trusted and loved, fed upon and believed in. If He is so, then it is quite clear that we know the righteous Father! And when we know the righteous Father, then it follows that we must have some discoveries of His great love to us. Are you trusting Christ? Is Jesus, in you, the hope of glory? Do you trust in Him alone? If so, go and drink to the fullest the sweetness of the text, and let no man say you cannot! Christ is in you, moreover, by a real and vital union with you. You are in Him as a branch is in the vine, and He is in you as the sap is in the branch.

You are in Him as a member is in the body, and He is in you as the life is in all the members. We know that Jesus quickens us, and because He lives, we live also. From now on we are one with Christ! It must be so, because if God did not see us in Christ, He could not regard us with complacency or, in other words, love us as He loves His Son! If He did not, in looking upon a man, see the love and the nature of His Only Begotten in him, how could He love him? He views us as part and parcel of His own dear Son, and so His delight is in us!

Beloved, the Lord sees, in addition to all this, something of a likeness to Christ in us, worked by His Spirit, for if Jesus is indeed in us, we will grow to be like Him and will manifest somewhat of His spirit and nature. The more we have of likeness to Jesus, the more will it be evident that the love of God is in us and is working in us, "to will and to do for His good pleasure" (Phil. 2:13). May God grant that what I have spoken so feebly may, nevertheless, be sweetly enjoyed by you, for I am persuaded that in the text there lies many a banquet for saints who hunger and thirst after righteousness—and a depth of mystical teaching that it will be well for you to search into with all your powers. God bless you, my beloved, for Christ's sake. Amen.

For Further Thought

1. *According to 1 Timothy 3:16; Psalm 22:22; and John 17:26, why did the Lord Jesus Christ come to live among us?*
2. *What is the supreme expression of God's love for humankind?*
3. *Read Philippians 2:13. Why is God working in us?*

DIVINE SOVEREIGNTY

*"Is it not lawful for me to do what
I wish with my own things?"*
MATTHEW 20:15

THE householder says, "Is it not lawful for me to do what I wish with my own things?" And even so does the God of heaven and earth ask this question of you this morning: "Is it not lawful for Me to do what I wish with My own things?" There is no attribute of God more comforting to His children than the doctrine of divine sovereignty. Under the most adverse circumstances, in the most severe troubles, they believe that sovereignty has ordained their afflictions, and that sovereignty overrules them and that sovereignty will sanctify them all. There is nothing for which the children of God ought more earnestly to contend than the dominion of their Master over all creation—the kingship of God over all the works of His own hands—the throne of God and His right to sit upon that throne.

On the other hand, there is no doctrine more hated by worldlings, no truth of which they have made such a football, as the great, stupendous, but yet most certain doctrine of the sovereignty of the infinite Jehovah. Men will allow God to be everywhere except on His throne. They will allow Him to be in His workshop to fashion worlds and to make stars. They will allow Him to be in His almonry to dispense His alms and bestow His bounties. They will allow Him to sustain the earth and bear up the pillars thereof, or light the lamps of heaven, or rule the waves of the ever-moving ocean.

But when God ascends His throne, His creatures then gnash their teeth. And when we proclaim an *enthroned* God and His right to do as He wills with His own, to dispose of His creatures as He thinks well, without consulting them in the matter, then it is that we are hissed and execrated. And then it is that men turn a deaf ear to us, for God on His throne is not the God they love. They love Him anywhere better than they do when He sits with His scepter in His hand and His crown upon His head. But it is

God upon the throne whom we love to preach. It is God upon His throne whom we trust. It is God upon His throne of whom we have been singing this morning. And it is God upon His throne of whom we will speak in this discourse.

I will dwell only, however, upon one portion of God's sovereignty, and that is God's sovereignty in the distribution of His gifts. In this respect, I believe He has a right to do as He wills with His own and that He exercises that right. We must assume, before we commence our discourse, one thing certain—namely, that all blessings are gifts and that we have no claim to them by our own merit. This I think every considerate mind will grant. And this being admitted, we will endeavor to show that He has a right, seeing they are His own, to do what He wills with them; to withhold them wholly if He pleases; to distribute them all if He chooses; to give to some and not to others; to give to none or to give to all, just as seems good in His sight. "Is it not lawful for Me to do what I wish with My own things?"

We will divide God's gifts into five classes. First, we will have gifts *temporal*; second, gifts *saving*; third, gifts *honorable*; fourth, gifts *useful*; and fifth, gifts *comfortable*. Of all these we will say, "Is it not lawful for Me to do what I wish with My own things?"

I. In the first place, then, we notice *gifts temporal*. It is an indisputable fact that God has not, in temporal matters, given to every man alike. He has not distributed to all His creatures the same amount of happiness or the same standing in creation. There is a difference. Mark what a difference there is in men personally (for we will consider men chiefly). One is born like Saul a head and shoulders taller than the rest. Another will live all his life a Zacchaeus, a man short of stature. One has a muscular frame and a share of beauty; another is weak and far from having anything styled comeliness.

How many do we find whose eyes have never rejoiced in the sunlight, whose ears have never listened to the charms of music, and whose lips have never been moved to sounds intelligible or harmonious? Walk through the earth and you will find men superior to yourself in vigor, health, and fashion, and others who are your inferiors in the very same respects. Some here are preferred far above their fellows in their outward appearance, and some sink low in the scale and have nothing about them that can make them glory in the flesh.

Why has God given to one man beauty and to another none; to one all his senses and to another but a portion? Why, in some, has He quickened the sense of apprehension, while others are obliged to bear about them a dull and stubborn body? We reply, let men say what they will, that no answer can be given except this: "Even so, Father, for so it seemed good in Your sight" (Luke 10:21). The old Pharisee asked, "Who sinned, this man or his parents, that he was born blind?" (John 9:2). We know that there was sin in neither parents nor child, that he was nonetheless born blind and that others have suffered similar distresses, but that God has done as it has pleased Him in the distribution of His earthly benefits. And thus He has said to the world, "Is it not lawful for Me to do what I wish with My own things?"

Mark, also, in the distribution of *mental gifts*, what a difference exists. All men are not like Socrates. There are but few Platos. We can discover but here and there a Bacon. We will but every now and then converse with a Sir Isaac Newton. Some have stupendous intellects wherewith they can unravel secrets, fathom the depths of oceans, measure mountains, and dissect the sunbeams and weigh the stars. Others have but shallow minds. You may educate and educate but can never make them great. You cannot improve what is not there. They have not genius and you cannot impart it.

Anybody may see that there is an inherent difference in men from their very birth. Some, with a little education, do surpass those who have been elaborately trained. There are two boys educated, it may be, in the same school, by the same master, and they will apply themselves to their studies with the same diligence. Yet one will far outstrip his fellow. Why is this? It is because God has asserted His sovereignty over the intellect as well as the body. God has not made us all alike but diversified His gifts. One man is as eloquent as Whitefield. Another stammers if he but speaks three words of his mother tongue. What makes these various differences between man and man? We answer, we must refer it all to the sovereignty of God, who does as He wills with His own.

Note, again, the differences of men's *conditions in this world*: Mighty minds are from time to time discovered in men whose limbs are wearing the chains of slavery and whose backs are laid bare to the whip—they have black skins but are in mind vastly superior to their brutal masters. So it is in England as well. We find wise men often poor and rich men not seldom ignorant and vain. One comes into the world to be arrayed at once in the imperial purple—another will never wear anything but the humble garb of a peasant. One has a palace to dwell in and a bed of down for his repose, while another finds but a hard resting place and will never have a more sumptuous covering than the thatch of his own cottage.

If we ask the reason for this, the reply still is, "Even so, Father, for so it seemed good in Your sight" (Matt. 11:26). So in other ways you will observe in passing through life how sovereignty displays itself. To one man God gives a long life and uniform health so that he scarcely knows what it is to have a day's sickness, while another totters through the world and finds a grave at almost every step, feeling a thousand deaths in fearing one. One man, even in extreme old age, like Moses, has his eyes undimmed. And though his hair is gray, he stands as firmly on his feet as when a young man in his father's house. Again we ask, what is this difference? And the only adequate answer is this: It is the effect of Jehovah's sovereignty.

> *Why has God given to one man beauty and to another none; to one all his senses and to another but a portion?*

You find, too, that some men are cut off in the prime of their life—the very midst of their days—while others live beyond their threescore years and ten. One departs before he has reached the first stage of existence, and another has his life lengthened out until it becomes quite a burden. We must, I conceive, necessarily trace the cause of all these differences in life to the fact of God's sovereignty. He is Ruler and King, and will He not do as He wills with His own?

We pass from this point—but before we do so we must stop to improve it just a moment. O you who are gifted with a noble frame, a comely body—boast not yourself therein, for your gifts come from God. Oh, glory not, for if you glory you become uncomely in a moment. The flowers boast not of their beauty, nor do the birds sing of their plumage. Be not vain, you daughters of beauty. Be not exalted, you sons of comeliness. And, O you men of might and intellect, remember that a sovereign Lord bestows all you have. He did create. He can destroy. There are not many steps between the mightiest intellect and the helpless idiot—deep thought verges on insanity. Your brain may at any moment be smitten and you may be doomed henceforth to live a madman.

Boast not yourself of all that you know, for even the little knowledge you have has been given you. Therefore I say do not exalt yourself above measure, but use for God what God has given you, for it is a royal gift and you should not lay it aside. But if the sovereign Lord has given you one talent and no more, lay it not up in a napkin, but use it well. And then it may be that He will give you more. Bless God that you have more than others and thank Him also that He has given you less than others, for you have less to carry on your shoulders. And the lighter your burden, the less cause will you have to groan as you travel on toward the better land. Bless God, then, if you possess less than your fellows, and see His goodness in withholding as well as in giving.

II. So far most men probably have gone with us. But when we come to the second point, *saving gifts*, there will a large number go from us because they cannot receive our doctrine. When we apply this truth regarding the divine sovereignty to man's salvation, then we find men standing up to defend their poor fellow creatures whom they conceive to be injured by God's predestination. But I never heard of men standing up for the devil, and yet think if any of God's creatures have a right to complain of His dealings, it is the fallen angels.

> *Bless God, then, if you possess less than your fellows, and see His goodness in withholding as well as in giving.*

For their sin they were hurled from heaven *at once*, and we read not that any message of mercy was ever sent to them. Once cast out, their doom was sealed, while men were reprieved, redemption sent into their world, and a large number of them chosen to eternal life. Why not quarrel with sovereignty in the one case as well as the other? We say that God has elected a people out of the human race, and His right to do this is denied. But, I ask, why not equally dispute the fact that God has chosen men and not fallen angels, or His justice in such a choice? If salvation is a matter of right, surely the angels had as much claim to mercy as men.

Were they not seated in more than equal dignity? Did they sin more? We think not. Adam's sin was so willful and complete that we cannot suppose a greater sin than that which he committed. Would not the angels who were thrust out of heaven have been of greater service to their Maker if restored than we can ever be? Had we been the judges in this matter, we might have given deliverance to angels but not to men. Admire, then, divine sovereignty, and love that decree whereas the angels were broken into shivers. "But God has raised an elect number of the race of men to set them among princes, through the merits of Jesus Christ our Lord.

Note again the divine sovereignty in which *God chose the Israelite race and left the Gentiles for years in darkness.* Why was Israel instructed and saved, while Syria was left to perish in idolatry? Was the one race purer in its origin and better in its character than the other? Did not the Israelites take to themselves false gods a thousand times and provoke the true God to anger and loathing? Why, then, should they be favored above their fellows? Why did the sun of heaven shine upon them while all around the nations were left in darkness and were sinking into hell by myriads? Why? The only answer that can be given is this: God is sovereign and "has mercy on whom He wills, and whom He wills He hardens" (Rom. 9:18).

So now, why is it that God has sent His Word to us while a multitude of people are still without His Word? Why do we each come up to God's tabernacle, Sabbath after Sabbath, privileged to listen to the voice of the minister of Jesus, while other nations have not been visited thereby? Could not God have caused the light to shine in the darkness there as well as here? Could not He, if He had pleased, have sent forth messengers swift as the light to proclaim His gospel over the whole earth? He could have done it if He wanted. Since we know that He has not done it, we bow in meekness, confessing His right to do as He wills with His own.

But let me drive the doctrine home once more. Behold how God displays His sovereignty in this fact out of the same congregation. Of those who hear the same minister and listen to the same truth, one is taken and the other left. Why is it that one of my hearers will sit in yonder pew and her sister by her side and yet the effect of the preaching will be different upon each? They have been nursed on the same knee, rocked in the same cradle, educated under the same auspices. They hear the same minister, with the same attention—why is it that the one will be saved and the other left?

Far be it from us to weave any excuse for the man who is damned—we know of none—but also, far be it from us to take glory from God. We assert that God makes the difference; that the saved sister will not have to thank herself but her God. There will even be two men given to drunkenness. Some word spoken will pierce one of them through, but the other will sit unmoved, although they shall, in all respects, be equally the same both in constitution and education. What is the reason? You will reply, perhaps, because the one accepts and the other rejects the message of the gospel.

But must you not come back to the question, who made the one accept it and who made the other reject it? I *dare you* to say that the man made himself to differ. You *must* admit in your conscience that it is God alone to whom this power belongs. But those who dislike this doctrine are nevertheless up in arms against us, and they say, "How can God justly make such a difference between the members of His family? Suppose a father should have a certain number of children and he should give to one all his favors and consign the others to misery. Should we not say that he was a very unkind and cruel father?"

I answer you the cases are not the same. You have not a *father* to deal with, but a *judge*. You say all men are God's children. I demand of you to prove that. I never read it in my Bible. I dare not say, "Our Father in heaven," till I am regenerated. I cannot rejoice in the fatherhood of God toward me till I know that I am one with Him and a joint heir with Christ. I dare not claim the fatherhood of God as an unregenerate man. It is not father and child, for the child has a claim upon his father. It is king and subject. And not even so high a relationship as that, for there is a claim between subject and king. A sinful creature can have no claim upon God, for that would be to make salvation of works and not of grace.

If men can merit salvation, then to save them is only the payment of a debt and God gives them nothing more than He ought to give them. But we assert that grace must be distinguishing if it is grace at all. Oh, but some say, "Is it not written, 'He gives to every man a measure of grace to profit withal'?" If you like to repeat that wonderful quotation so often hurled at my head, you are very welcome, for it is *no quotation from scripture*, unless it is an Arminian edition. The only passage at all like it refers to the *spiritual* gifts of the saints and the saints only.

But I say, granted your supposition that a measure of grace is given to every man to profit withal, yet He has given to some a measure of particular grace to make that profit. For what do you mean by grace that I put out to profit? I can understand a man's improvement in the use of *grace*, but grace improved and made use of by the power of man I cannot comprehend. Grace is not a thing that I use; grace is something that uses me. But people talk of grace sometimes as if it were something they could use and not as an influence having power over them.

Grace is something not that I improve, but that improves me, employs me, works on me. And let people talk as they will about universal grace, it is all nonsense—there is no such thing, nor can there be. They may talk correctly of universal *blessings*, because we see that the natural gifts of God are scattered everywhere, more or less, and men may receive or reject them. It is not so, however, with grace. Men cannot take the grace of God and employ it in turning themselves from darkness to light. The light does not come to the darkness and say, "Use me." But the light comes and drives the darkness away. Life does not come to the dead man and say, "Use me and be restored to life."

No, it comes with a power of its own and restores to life. The spiritual influence does not come to the dry bones and say, "Use this power and clothe yourselves with flesh." But it comes and clothes them with flesh and the work is done. Grace is a thing that comes and exercises an influence on us.

> *The sovereign will of God alone*
> *Creates us heirs of grace*
> *Born in the image of His Son,*
> *A new-created race.*

And we say to all of you who gnash your teeth at this doctrine, whether you know it or not, you have a vast deal of enmity toward God in your hearts.

For until you can be brought to know this doctrine, there is something that you have not yet discovered that makes you opposed to the idea of God absolute, God unbounded, God unfettered, God unchanging, and God having a free will, which you are so fond of proving that the creature possesses. I am persuaded that we must hold the sovereignty of God if we would be in a healthy state of mind. Salvation is of the Lord alone, so give all the glory to His holy name, to which all glory belongs.

III. We now come, in the third place, to notice the differences that God

SERMONS RELATING TO GOD

often makes in His church in *honorable gifts*. There is a difference made between God's own children, when they are His children. Note what I mean: One has the honorable gift of *knowledge*; another knows but little. I meet, every now and then, with a dear Christian brother with whom I could talk for a month and learn something from him every day. He has had deep experience, he has seen into the deep things of God, and his whole life has been a perpetual study wherever he has been.

He seems to have gathered thoughts, not from books merely, but from men, from God, from his own heart. He knows all the intricacies and windings of Christian experience. He understands the heights, the depths, the lengths, and the breadths of the love of Christ that passes knowledge. He has gained a grand idea, an intimate knowledge of the system of grace, and can vindicate the dealings of the Lord with His people.

> *They* may talk correctly of universal blessings, because we see that the natural gifts of God are scattered everywhere, more or less, and men may receive or reject them. It is not so, however, with grace.

Then you meet with another who has passed through many troubles, but he has no deep acquaintance with Christian experience. He never learned a single secret by all his troubles. He just floundered out of one trouble into another, but never stopped to pick up any of the jewels that lay in the mire; never tried to discover the precious jewels that lay in his afflictions. He knows very little more of the heights and depths of the Savior's love than when he first came into the world. You may converse with such a man as long as you like, but you will get nothing from him. If you ask why it is, I answer, there is a sovereignty of God in giving knowledge to some and not to others.

I was walking the other day with an aged Christian who told me how he had profited by my ministry. There is nothing that humbles me like that thought of an old man deriving experience in the things of God, receiving instruction in the ways of the Lord from a mere babe in grace. But I expect that when I am an old man, if I should live to be such, some babe in grace will instruct me. God sometimes shuts the mouth of the old man and opens the mouth of the child. Why should we be a teacher to hundreds who are, in some respects, far abler to teach us? The only answer we can find is in the divine sovereignty, and we must bow before it, for has He not a right to do as He wills with His own?

Instead of being envious of those who have the gift of knowledge, we should seek to gain the same, if possible. Instead of sitting down and murmuring that we have not more knowledge, we should remember that the foot cannot say to the head, nor the head to the foot, "I have no need of you," for God has given us talents as it has pleased Him.

Note, again, when speaking of honorable gifts, that not only knowledge but also *office* is an honorable gift. There is nothing more honorable to a man than the office of a deacon or a minister. We magnify our office, though we would not magnify ourselves. We hold that nothing can dignify a man more than being appointed to an office in a Christian church. I would rather be a deacon of a church than lord mayor of London. A minister of Christ is, in my estimation, an infinitely higher honor than the world can bestow. My pulpit is to me more desirable than a throne, and my congregation is an empire more than large enough. An empire before which the empires of the earth dwindle into nothing in everlasting importance.

Why does God give to one man a special call by the Holy Spirit to be a minister and pass by another? There is another man more gifted, perhaps, but we dare not put him in a pulpit because he has not had a special call. So it is with the deaconship. The man whom some would perhaps think most suitable for the office is passed by and another chosen. There is a manifestation of God's sovereignty in the appointment to office in putting David on a throne, in making Moses the leader of the children of Israel through the wilderness, in choosing Daniel to stand among princes, in electing Paul to be the minister to the Gentiles and Peter to be the apostle of the circumcision. And you who have not the gift of honorable office must learn the great truth contained in the question of the Master, "Is it not lawful for Me to do what I wish with My own things?"

There is another honorable gift, the gift of *utterance*. Eloquence has more power over men than all else besides. If a man would have power over the multitude, he must seek to touch their hearts and chain their ears. There are some men who are like vessels full of knowledge to the brim but have no means of giving it forth to the world. They are rich in all gems of learning but know not how to set them in the golden ring of eloquence. They can collect the choicest of flowers but know not how to tie them up in a sweet garland to present them to the admirer's eye.

How is this? We say again, the sovereignty of God is here displayed in the distribution of gifts honorable. Learn here, O Christian man, if you have gifts, to cast the honor of them at the Savior's feet, and if you possess them not, learn not to murmur. Remember that God is equally as kind when He keeps back as when He distributes His favors. If any among you is exalted, let him not be puffed up. If any is lowly, let him not be despised. For God gives to every vessel his measure of grace. Serve Him after your measure and adore the King of heaven who does as He pleases.

IV. We notice, in the fourth place, the *gift of usefulness*. I have often done wrong in finding fault with brother ministers for not being useful. I have said you might have been as useful as I have been had you been in earnest. But surely there are others even more earnest and more efficient—others laboring as constantly but with far less effect. And therefore let me retract my accusation and in lieu thereof assert that the gift of usefulness is the result of God's sovereignty. It is not in man to be useful, but in God to make him useful. We may labor ourselves with all our might, but God alone can make us useful. We can put every stitch of canvas on when the wind blows, but we cannot make the wind blow.

The sovereignty of God is seen also in the diversity of ministerial gifts. You go to one minister and are fed with plenty of good food; another has not enough to feed a mouse. He has plenty of reproof but no food for the child of God. Another can comfort the child of God, but he cannot reprove a backslider. He has not strength of mind enough to give those earnest home strokes that are sometimes needed. And what is the reason? It is God's sovereignty. One can wield the sledgehammer but could not heal a broken heart. If he were to attempt it, you would be reminded of an elephant trying to thread a needle. Such a man can reprove, but he cannot apply oil and wine to a bruised conscience.

Why? It is because God has not given to him the gift. There is another one who always preaches experimental divinity and very rarely touches upon doctrine. Another is all doctrine and cannot preach much about Jesus Christ and Him crucified. Why? God has not given him the gift of doctrine. Another always preaches Jesus, blessed Jesus—men of the Hawker school—and many say, "Oh, they do not give us experience enough. They do not go into the deep experience of the corruption that vexes the children of God."

But we do not blame them for this. You will notice that out of the same man will at one time flow streams of living water, while at another time he will be as dry as possible. On one Sabbath you go away refreshed by the preaching, and the next you get no good. There is divine sovereignty in all this and we must learn to recognize and admire it. I was preaching on one occasion last week to a large crowd of people, and in one part of the sermon the people were very much affected. I felt that the power of God was there—one poor creature absolutely shrieked out because of the wrath of God against sin.

> *On one Sabbath you go away refreshed by the preaching, and the next you get no good. There is divine sovereignty in all this and we must learn to recognize and admire it.*

At another time the same words might have been uttered and there might have been the same desire in the minister's heart and yet no effect produced. We must trace, I say, divine sovereignty in all such cases. We ought to recognize God's hand in everything. But the present is the most godless generation that ever trod this earth, I verily believe. In our fathers' days there was hardly a shower but they declared that God caused it to fall. And they had prayers for rain, prayers for sunshine, and prayers for harvest. As well when a haystack was on fire, as when a famine desolated the land, our forefathers said, "The Lord has done it." But now our philosophers try to *explain* everything and trace all phenomena to second causes. But, brethren, let it be ours to ascribe the origin and direction of all things to the Lord and the Lord alone.

V. Lastly, *gifts comfortable* are of God. Oh, what comfortable gifts do some of us enjoy in the ordinances of God's house and in a ministry that is profitable. But how many churches have not a ministry of that kind? And why then have we? It is because God has made a difference. Some here have strong faith and can laugh at impossibilities. We can sing a song in all ill weathers—in the tempest as well as in the calm. But there is another with little faith who is in danger of tumbling down over every straw. We trace eminent faith entirely to God.

One is born with a melancholy temperament and he sees a tempest brewing even in the calm, while another is cheerful and sees a silver lining to every cloud, however black, and he is a happy man. But why is that? Comfortable gifts come from God. And then observe that we ourselves differ at times. For a season we may have blessed communion with heaven and are permitted to look within the veil. But perhaps these delightful enjoyments disappear. But do we murmur on that account? May He not do as He will with His own? May He not take back what He has given? The comforts we possess were His before they were ours—

> *And should you take them all away,*
> *Yet would I not repine,*
> *Before they were possessed by me*
> *They were entirely yours.*

There is no joy of the Spirit. There is no exceeding blessed hope, no strong faith, no burning desire, no close fellowship with Christ that is not *the gift of God* and that we must not trace to Him. When I am in darkness and suffer disappointment, I will look up and say He gives songs in the night. And when I am made to rejoice, I will say my mountain will stand fast forever. The Lord is the sovereign Jehovah, and therefore prostrate at His feet I lie, and if I perish, I will perish there.

> *F*or a season we may have blessed communion with heaven and are permitted to look within the veil. But perhaps these delightful enjoyments disappear. But do we murmur on that account? May He not do as He will with His own?

But let me say, brethren, that so far from this doctrine of divine sovereignty making you to sit down in sloth, I hope in God it will have a tendency to humble you and so to lead you to say, "I am unworthy of the least of all your mercies. I feel that you have a right to do with me as you will. If you do crush me, a helpless worm, you will not be dishonored. And I have no right to ask you to have compassion upon me, save this, that I want your mercy. Lord, if you will, you are able to pardon, and you never gave grace to one who wanted it more. Because I am empty, fill me with the bread of heaven. Because I am naked, clothe me with your robe. Because I am dead, give me life."

If you press that plea with all your soul and all your mind, though Jehovah is sovereign, He will stretch out His scepter and save, and you will live to worship Him in the beauty of holiness, loving and adoring His gracious sovereignty. "He who believes," is the declaration of scripture, "and is baptized will be saved; but he who does not believe will be condemned" (Mark 16:16). He who believes in Christ *alone* and is baptized with water in the name of the Father, the Son, and the Holy Spirit will be saved, but he who rejects Christ and believes not in Him will be damned.

That is the sovereign decree and proclamation of heaven. Bow to it, acknowledge it, obey it, and God bless you.

FOR FURTHER THOUGHT

1. *Why are some people more gifted in material things than others are?*
2. *What is the quality of God that describes why He chose Israel over other nations and races?*
3. *Members of the church, Christ's body, have different gifts, some greater than others. Why is this?*

GOD IN THE COVENANT

"I will be their God."
JEREMIAH 31:33

WHAT a glorious covenant the second covenant is! Well might it be called "a better covenant, which was established on better promises" (Heb. 8:6). It is so glorious that the very thought of it is enough to overwhelm the soul, when it discerns the amazing condescension and infinite love of God in having framed a covenant for such unworthy creatures, for such glorious purposes, with such disinterested motives. It is better than the other covenant, the covenant of works that was made with Adam. Or the covenant that was made with Israel, on the day when they came out of Egypt.

It is better, for it is founded upon a *better principle*. The old covenant was founded on the principle of merit. It was "Serve God and you will be rewarded for it. If you walk perfectly in the fear of the Lord, God will walk well toward you and all the blessings of Mount Gerizim will come upon you and you will be exceedingly blessed in this world and the world that is to come." But that covenant fell to the ground, because, although it was just that man should be rewarded for his good works, or punished for his evil ones, yet man being sure to sin and since the fall infallibly tending toward iniquity, the covenant was not suitable for his happiness, nor could it promote his eternal welfare.

But the new covenant is not founded on works at all. It is a covenant of pure unmingled grace. You may read it from its first word to its last, and there is not a solitary syllable as to anything to be done by us. The whole covenant is a covenant, not so much between man and his Maker, as between Jehovah and man's representative, the Lord Jesus Christ. The human side of the covenant has been already fulfilled by Jesus, and there remains nothing now but the covenant of giving, not the covenant of requirements. The whole covenant with regard to us, the people of God, now stands thus: "I will give this; I will bestow that. I will fulfill this promise. I will grant that favor."

And there is *nothing* for us to do. He will work all our works in us. And the very graces that are sometimes represented as being stipulations of the covenant are promised to us. He gives us faith. He promises to give us the law in our inward parts and to write it on our hearts. It is a glorious covenant, I say, because it is founded on simple mercy and unmixed grace, quite irrespective of creature-doings or anything that is to be performed by man, and hence this covenant surpasses the other in stability. Where there is anything of man, there is always a degree of mutability.

Where you have anything to do with creatures, there you have something to do with change. For creatures and change and uncertainty always go together. But since this new covenant has now nothing whatever to do with the creature, so far as the creature has to do anything, but only so far as he is to receive—the idea of change is utterly and entirely gone. It is God's covenant and therefore it is an unchanging covenant. If there be something that I am to do in the covenant, then is the covenant insecure. And although happy as Adam, I may yet become miserable as Satan. But if the covenant were all on God's part, then if my name is in that covenant, my soul is as secure as if I were now walking the golden streets.

And if any blessing is in the covenant, I am as certain to receive that blessing as if I already grasped it in my hands, for the promise of God is sure to be followed by fulfillment. The promise never fails. It always brings with it the whole of that which it is intended to convey, and the moment I receive it by faith, I am sure of the blessing itself. Oh! How infinitely superior is this covenant to the other in its manifest security! It is beyond the risk or hazard of the least uncertainty.

But I have been thinking for the last two or three days that the covenant of grace excels the other covenant most marvelously in the *mighty blessings* that it confers. What does the covenant of grace convey? I had thought this morning of preaching a sermon upon "the covenant of grace—what are the blessings it gives to God's children?" But when I began to think of it, there was so much in the covenant, that if I had only read a catalog of the great and glorious blessings wrapped up within its folds, I should have needed to occupy nearly the whole of the day in making a few simple observations upon each of them.

Consider the great things God has given in the covenant. He sums them up by saying He has given all things. He has given you eternal life in Christ Jesus. He has given Christ Jesus to be yours. He has made Christ heir of all things, and He has made you a joint heir with Him. Hence, He has given you everything. Were I to sum up that mighty mass of unutterable treasure that God has conveyed to every elect soul by that glorious covenant, time would fail me. I therefore commence with one great blessing conveyed to us by the covenant, and then on other Sabbaths I will, by divine permission, consider separately, one by one, sundry other things that the covenant conveys.

We commence then by the first thing, which is enough to startle us by its immense value. In fact, unless it had been written in God's Word, we never could have dreamed that such a blessing could have been ours. God Himself, by the covenant, becomes the believer's own portion and inheritance. "I will be their God."

And now we will begin with this subject in this way. We will show you first that this is a *special* blessing. God is the special possession of the elect, whose names are in the covenant. Second, for a moment or two we will speak of this as being an *exceedingly precious* blessing: "I will be their God." Third, we will dwell upon the *security* of this blessing, "I will be their God." And fourth, we will endeavor to stir you up to make *good use* of this blessing, so freely and liberally conveyed to you by the everlasting covenant of grace: "I will be their God."

Stop just one moment and think it over before we start. In the covenant of grace, God Himself conveys Himself to you and becomes yours. Understand it. God and all that is meant by that word—eternity, infinity, omnipotence, omniscience, perfect justice, infallible rectitude, and immutable love; all that is meant by God as Creator, guardian, preserver, governor, judge. All that that great word *God* can mean of goodness and of love, of bounty and of grace. All that this covenant gives you to be your absolute property as much as anything you can call your own: "I will be their God."

We say, pause over that thought. If I should not preach at all, there is enough in that, if opened up and applied by the all-glorious Spirit, to excite your joy during the whole of the Sabbath day. "I will be their God."

> *My God! How cheerful is the sound!*
> *How pleasant to repeat!*
> *Well may that heart with pleasure bound,*
> *Where God has fixed His seat.*

I. How is God especially the God of His own children? For God is the

God of all men, of all creatures. He is the God of the worm, of the flying eagle, of the star, and of the cloud. He is God everywhere. How then is He more my God and your God than He is God of all created things? We answer that in some things God is the God of all His creatures. But even there, there is a special relationship existing between Himself and His chosen creatures, whom He has loved with an everlasting love. And in the next place, there are certain relationships in which God does not exist toward the rest of His creatures, but only toward His own children.

1. First, God is the God of all His creatures, seeing that He has the right to decree to do with them as He pleases. He is the Creator of us all. He is the potter and has power over the clay, to make of the same lump one vessel to honor and another to dishonor. However men may sin against God, He is still their God in the sense that their destiny is immovably in His hand and He can do with them exactly as He chooses. However they may resent His will or spurn His good pleasure, yet He can make the wrath of man to praise Him and the remainder of that wrath He can restrain. He is the God of all creatures absolutely in the matter of predestination, seeing that He is their Creator and has an absolute right to do with them as He wills.

But here again He has a special regard to His children, and He is *their* God even in that sense. For to them, while He exercises the same sovereignty, He exercises it in the way of grace and grace only. He makes them the vessels of mercy, which will be to His honor forever. He chooses them out of the ruins of the fall and makes them heirs of everlasting life, while He suffers the rest of the world to continue in sin and to consummate their guilt by well-deserved punishment. And thus, while His relationship is the same, so far as His sovereignty is concerned and His right of decree, there is something special in its loving aspect toward His people. And in that sense He is *their* God.

Again, He is the God of all His creatures, in the sense that He has a right to command obedience of all. He is the God of every man who was ever born into this earth, in the sense that they are bound to obey Him. God can command the homage of all His creatures, because He is their Creator, governor, and preserver. And all men are, by the fact of their creation, so placed in subjection to Him that they cannot escape the obligation of submission to His laws. But even here there is something special in regard to the child of God. Though God is the ruler of all men, yet His rule is special toward His children. For He lays aside the sword of His rulership and in His hand He grasps the rod for His child, not the sword of punitive vengeance.

While He gives the world a law upon stone, He gives to His child a law in his heart. God is my governor and yours, but if you are unregenerate, He is your governor in a different sense from that in which He is mine. He has ten times as much claim to my obedience as He has to yours. Seeing that He has done more for me, I am bound to do more for Him. Seeing that He has loved me more, I am bound to love Him more. But should I disobey, the vengeance on my head will not fall so heavily as on yours if you are out of Christ, for that vengeance incurred by me has already fallen upon Christ, my Substitute. Only the chastisement will remain for me. There again you see where the relationship to all men is universal, there is something special in it in reference to God's children.

God has a universal power over all His creatures in the character of a judge. "With righteousness He shall judge the world, and the peoples with equity" (Ps. 98:9). He will judge all men with equity, it is true, but as if His people were not of the world, it is added afterward, "the peoples with equity." God is the God of all creatures, we repeat, in the sense that He is their judge. He will summon them all before His bar and condemn or acquit them all, but even there, there is something peculiar with regard to His children. For to them the condemnation sentence will never come, but only the acquittal.

While He is judge of all, He especially is *their judge* because He is the judge whom they love to reverence, the judge whom they long to approach because they know His lips will confirm that which their hearts have already felt, which is the sentence of their full acquittal through the merits of their glorious Savior. Our loving God is the judge who will acquit our souls, and in that respect we can say He is *our* God whether as sovereign, as governor enforcing law, or as judge punishing sin. Although God is in some sense the God of all men, yet in this matter there is something special toward His people so that they can say, "He is our God, even in those relationships."

2. But now, beloved, there are points to which the rest of God's creatures cannot come, and here the great center of the matter lies, the very soul of this glorious promise dwells. God is our God in a sense in which the unregenerate, the unconverted, the unholy can have no share whatever. We have just considered other points with regard to what God is to man generally. Let us now consider what He is to us, as He is to none other.

First, then, God is my God, seeing that He is the God of my *election*. If I am His child, then has He loved me from before all worlds and His infinite mind has been exercised with plans for my salvation. If He is my God, He has seen me when I have wandered far from Him, and when I have rebelled, His mind has determined when I will be arrested and turned from the error of my ways. He has been providing for me the means of grace; He has applied those means of grace in due time, but His everlasting purpose has been the basis and the foundation of it all. And thus He is my God as He is the God of none else beside His own children.

He is my glorious, gracious God in eternal election because He thought of me and chose me from before the foundation of the world, that I should be without blame before Him in love. Looking back, then, I see election's God, and election's God is my God if I am in election. But if I neither fear God nor regard Him, then He is another man's God and not mine. If I have no claim and participation in election, then I am compelled to look upon Him as being in that sense the God of a great body of men whom He has chosen, but not my God. If I can look back and see my name in life's fair book set down, then indeed He is my God in election.

Furthermore, the Christian can call God his God from the fact of his *justification*. A sinner can call God, God, but he must always put in an adjective and speak of God as an angry God, an incensed God, or an offended God. But the Christian can say "*my* God" without putting in any adjective except it be a sweet one wherewith to extol Him, for now we who were sometime afar off are made near by the blood of Christ. We who were enemies to God by wicked works are His friends, and looking up to Him, we can say "my God," for He is my friend, and I am His friend. Enoch could say "my God," for he walked with Him. Adam could not say "my God" when he hid himself beneath the trees of the garden, and while I, a sinner, run from God, I cannot call Him mine. But when I have peace with God and am brought near to Him by His grace, then indeed is He my God and my friend.

He is the believer's God by *adoption*, and in that, the sinner has no part. I have heard people represent God as the Father of the whole universe. It surprises me that any reader of the Bible should so talk. Paul once quoted a heathen poet, who said that we are His offspring. And it is true in some sense that we are, as having been created by Him. But in the high sense in which the term *childhood* is used in the scriptures to express the holy relationship of a regenerate child toward his Father, none can say "our Father" but those who have the "Abba Father" printed on their hearts by the Spirit of adoption. By this Spirit of adoption, God becomes my God, as He is not the God of others.

The Christian has a special claim to God because God is his Father just as He is not the Father of any else save his brethren. Beloved, these three things are quite enough to show you that God is in a special sense the God of His own people. But I must leave that to your own thoughts, which will suggest twenty different ways in which God is specially the God of His own children, more than He is of the rest of His creatures. "God," say the wicked, but "*my* God," say God's children. If then God is so specially your God, let your clothing be according to your feeding. Be clothed with the sun; put on the Lord Jesus. The King's daughter is (and so let all the King's sons be) all glorious within (Ps. 45:13). Let their clothing be of wrought gold. Be clothed with humility; put on love and bowels of compassion, gentleness, and meekness. Put on the garments of salvation.

> *He is my glorious, gracious God in eternal election because He thought of me and chose me from before the foundation of the world, that I should be without blame before Him in love.*

Let your company and conversation be according to your clothing. Live amongst the excellent, amongst the generation of the just. Get up to the general assembly and church of the firstborn, to that innumerable company of angels and the spirits of the just men made perfect. Live in the courts of the great King, behold His face, wait at His throne, bear His name, and show forth His virtues. Set forth His praises, advance His honor, and uphold His interest. Let vile persons and vile ways be condemned in your eyes. Be of nobler spirit than to be companions with them. Regard not their societies, their scorns, their flatteries, or their frowns.

Rejoice not with their joys, fear not their fears, care not their care, feed not on their dainties. Get up from among them, to your country, your city, where no unclean thing can enter or annoy. Live by faith in the power of the Spirit, in the beauty of holiness, in the hope of the gospel, in the joy of your God, in the magnificence and yet the humility of the children of the great King.

II. Now, for a moment, let us consider the exceeding preciousness of His great mercy: "I will be their God." I conceive that God Himself could say no more than that. I do not think, if the Infinite were to stretch His powers and magnify His grace by some stupendous promise that could outdo every other, that it could exceed in glory this promise: "I will be their God." Oh! Christian, do but consider what it is to have God to be your own! Consider what it is, compared with anything else.

Jacob's portion is the Lord;
What can Jacob more require?
What can heaven more afford—
Or a creature more desire?

Compare this portion with the lot of your fellow men! Some of them have their portion in the field. They are rich and increased in goods and their yellow harvests are even now ripening in the sun. But what are harvests compared with your God, the God of harvests? Or what are granaries compared with Him who is your husbandman and feeds you with the bread of heaven? Some have their portion in the city. Their wealth is superabundant and in constant streams it flows to them, until they become a very reservoir of gold. But what is gold compared with your God? You could not live on it; your spiritual life could not be sustained by it. Apply it to your aching head, and would it afford you any ease?

Put it on a troubled conscience, and could your gold allay its pangs? Put it on your desponding heart and see if it could stay a solitary groan or give you one grief the less. But you have God, and in Him you have more than gold or riches ever could buy, more than heaps of brilliant ore could ever purchase for you. Some have their portion in this world, in that which most men love—applause and fame—but ask yourself, is not your God more to you than that? What if a thousand trumpets should blow your praises and if a myriad clarions should be loud with your applause? What would it all be to you if you had lost your God?

Would this allay the turmoil of a soul ill at ease with itself? Would this prepare you to pass the Jordan and to breast those stormy waves that before long must be forded by every man, when he is called from this world to lands unknown? Would a puff of wind serve you then, or the clapping of the hands of your fellow creatures bless you on your dying bed? No, there are griefs here with which men cannot intermeddle, and there are griefs to come with which men cannot interfere to alleviate the pangs, pains, agonies, and dying strife. But when you have this: "I will be your God"—you have as much as all other men can have put together.

How little ought we to estimate the treasures of this world compared with God, when we consider that God frequently gives the most riches to the worst of His creatures! As Luther said, God gives food to His children and husks to His swine, and who are the swine that get the husks? It is not often that God's people get the riches of this world, and doesn't this prove that riches are of little worth? Otherwise, God would give them to us. Abraham gave the sons of Keturah a portion and sent them away. Let me be Isaac and have my Father, and the world may take all the rest. O Christian, ask for nothing in this world but that you may live on this and that you may die on this: "I will be their God." This exceeds all the world has to offer.

But compare this with what you require, Christian. What do you require? Is there not here all that you do require? To make you happy, you wanted something that will satisfy you. And come, I ask you, is not this enough? Will not this fill your pitcher to its very brim, aye, till it runs over? If you can put this promise inside your cup, will not you be forced to say, with David, "My cup runs over. I have more than heart can wish"? When this is fulfilled, "I am your God," let your cup be ever so empty of earthly things. Suppose you have not one solitary drop of creature joy, yet is not this enough to fill it until your unsteady hand cannot hold the cup because of its fullness?

I ask you if you are not complete when God is yours. Do you want anything but God? If you think you do, it is well for you still to want, for all you want save God is but to gratify your lust. O Christian, is not this enough to satisfy you if all else should fail?

But you want more than quiet satisfaction; you desire, sometimes, rapturous delight. Come, soul, is there not enough here to delight you? Put this promise to your lips. Did you ever drink wine one-half so sweet as this: "I will be their God"? Did ever harp or viol sound half so sweetly as this: "I will be their God"? Not all the music blown from sweet instruments, or drawn from living strings, could ever give such melody as this sweet promise, "I will be their God." Oh! Here is a very sea of bliss, a very ocean of delight! Come, bathe your spirit in it. You may swim to eternity and never find a shore. You may dive to the very infinite and never find the bottom. "I will be their God." Oh! If this does not make your eyes sparkle, if this makes not your foot dance for joy and your heart beat high with bliss, then assuredly your soul is not in a healthy state.

> *Let vile persons and vile ways be condemned in your eyes. Be of nobler spirit than to be companions with them. Regard not their societies, their scorns, their flatteries, or their frowns.*

But then you want something more than present delights, something concerning which you may exercise hope. And what more do you ever hope to get than the fulfillment of this great promise: "I will be their God"? Oh! Hope, you are a great-handed thing. You lay hold of mighty things, which even faith has not power to grasp. But though large your hand may be, this fills it so that you can carry nothing else. I protest, before God, I have not a hope beyond this promise. "Oh," say you, "you have a hope of heaven." Aye, I have a hope of heaven, but this *is* heaven: "I will be their God."

What is heaven but to be with God, to dwell with Him, to realize that God is mine and I am His? I see I have not a hope beyond that, there is not a promise beyond that, for all promises are couched in this, all hopes are included in this, "I will be their God." This is the masterpiece of all promises. It is the topstone of all the great and precious things that God has provided for His children: "I will be their God."

If we could really grasp it, if it could be applied to our soul and we could understand it, we might clap our hands and say, "Oh! The glory! Oh! The glory! Oh! The glory of that promise!" It makes a heaven below and it must make a heaven above, for nothing else will be wanted but that "I will be their God."

III. Now, for a moment, dwell on the certainty of this promise. It does not say, "I *may* be their God," but "I *will* be their God." Nor does the text say, "Perhaps I will be their God." No, it says, "I *will* be their God." A sinner says he won't have God for his God. He will have God to be his preserver, to take care of him and keep him from accidents. He does not object to having God to feed him, to give him his bread and water and raiment. Nor does he mind making God somewhat of a show thing, which he may take out on Sunday and bow before, but he will not have God for his *God*; he will not take Him to be his all.

He makes his belly his god, gold his god, the world his god. How then is this promise to be fulfilled? There is one of God's chosen people there. He does not know that he is chosen yet and he says he will not have God. How then is the promise to be carried out? "Oh!" say some. "If the man won't have God, then of course, God cannot get him." And we have heard it preached, and we read it frequently, that salvation entirely depends upon man's will. If man stands out and resists God's Holy Spirit, the creature can be the conqueror of the Creator, and finite power can overcome the Infinite.

Frequently I take up a book and I read, "O sinner, be willing, for unless you are, God cannot save you." And sometimes we are asked, "How is it that such a one is not saved?" And the answer is, "He is not willing to be. God strove with him but he would not be saved." Aye, but suppose he had striven with Him, as he did with those who *are* saved; would he have been saved then? "No, he would have resisted." Nay, we answer, it is not in man's will; it is not of the will of the flesh, nor of blood, but of the power of God. And we never can entertain such an absurd idea as man can conquer omnipotence, that the might of man is greater than the might of God.

> *W*hat is heaven but to be with God, to dwell with Him, to realize that God is mine and I am His?

We believe, indeed, that certain usual influences of the Holy Spirit may be overcome. We believe that there are general operations of the Spirit in many men's hearts that are resisted and rejected, but the *effectual* working of the Holy Spirit with the determination to save could not be resisted, unless you suppose God overcome by His creatures and the purpose of Deity frustrated by the will of man. That would be to suppose something akin to blasphemy. Beloved, God has power to fulfill the promise, "I will be their God."

"Oh!" cries the sinner. "I will not have you for a God."

"Will you not?" says He, and He gives him over to the hand of Moses.

Moses takes him and applies the club of the law, drags him to Sinai, where the mountain totters over his head, lightnings flash, and thunders bellow, and then the sinner cries, "O God, save me!"

"Ah! I thought you would not have me for a God."

"O Lord, you will be my God," says the poor trembling sinner. "I have put away my ornaments from me. O Lord, what will you do to me? Save me! I will give myself to you. Oh! Take me!"

"Aye," says the Lord, "I knew it. I said that I will be their God and I have made you willing in the day of my power."

"I will be their God and they will be my people."

IV. Now, lastly, I said we would conclude by urging you to make use of God, if He is yours. It is strange that spiritual blessings are our only possessions that we do not employ. We get a great spiritual blessing and we let the rest get on it for many a day. There is the mercy seat, for instance. Ah, my friends, if you had the cash box as full of riches as that mercy seat is, you would go often to it, as often as your necessities require. But you do not go to the mercy seat half so often as you need to go. Most precious things God has given to us, but we never overuse them. The truth is, they cannot be overused.

We cannot wear a promise threadbare. We can never burn out the incense of grace. We can never use up the infinite treasures of God's loving-kindness. But if the blessings God gives us are not used, perhaps God is the least used of all. Though He is our God, we apply ourselves less to Him than to any of His creatures, or any of His mercies that He bestows upon us. Look at the poor heathen. They use their gods, though they are no gods. They put up a piece of wood or stone and call it God, and how they use it! They want rain, so the people assemble and ask for rain in the firm but foolish hope that their god can give it.

There is a battle and their god is lifted up. He is brought out from the house, where he usually dwells, that he may go before them and lead them on to victory. But how seldom do we ask counsel at the hands of the Lord! How often do we go about our business without asking His guidance? In our troubles how constantly do we strive to bear our burdens, instead of casting them upon the Lord, that He may sustain us! And this is not because we may not, for the Lord seems to say, "I am yours, soul; come and make use of Me as you will. You may freely come to My store, and the oftener the better. Welcome."

Have you not a God lying by you to no purpose? Let not your God be as other gods, serving only for a show. Have not God in name only. Since He allows you to have such a friend, use Him daily. My God will supply all your wants. Never want while you have a God. Never fear or faint while you have a God. Go to your treasure and take whatever you need. There is bread and clothes, and health and life, and all that you need. O Christian, learn the divine skill to make God all things; to make bread of your God, and water, and health, and friends, and ease. He can supply you with all these.

What is better, He can *be* your food, your clothing, your friend, your life. All this He has said to you in this one word, "I am your God." And here you may say, as a heaven-born saint once did, "I have no husband, and yet I am no widow. My Maker is my husband. I have no father or friend, and yet I am neither fatherless nor friendless; my God is both my Father and my friend. I have no child, but is not He better to me than ten children? I have no house, but yet I have a home; I have made the Most High my habitation. I am left alone but yet I am not alone; my God is good company for me. With Him I can walk. With Him I can take sweet counsel, find sweet repose. At my lying down, at my rising up, while I am in the house, or as I walk by the way, my God is ever with me. With him I travel, I dwell, I lodge, and I live and will live forever."

Oh! Child of God, let me urge you to make use of your God. Make use of Him in prayer. I beseech you, go to Him often, because He is your God. If He were another man's God, you might weary Him. But He is your God. If He were my God and not yours, you would have no right to approach Him, but He is your God. He has made Himself one to you. If we may use such an expression (and we think we may), He has become the positive property of all His children, so that all He has and all He is, is theirs. O child, will you let your treasury lie idle when you want it? Go! Go and draw from it by prayer.

> To Him in every trouble flee,
> Your best, your only friend.

Fly to Him; tell Him all your wants; use Him constantly by faith, at all times. Oh! I beseech you, if some dark providence has come over you, use your God as a sun, for He is a sun. If some strong enemy has come out against you, use your God for a shield, for He is a shield to protect you. If you have lost your way in the mazes of life, use Him as a guide, for the great Jehovah will direct you. If you are in storms, use Him for the God who stills the raging of the sea and says to the waves, "Be still." If you are a poor thing, knowing not which way to turn, use Him for a shepherd, for the Lord is your shepherd, and you will not want.

Whatever you are, wherever you are, remember God is just what you want and He is just where you want. I beseech you, then, make use of your God. Do not forget Him in your trouble, but flee to Him in the midst of your distresses, and cry:

> *When all created streams are dried*
> *Your fullness is the same;*
> *May I with this be satisfied,*
> *And glory in your name!*

> *No good in creatures can be found*
> *But may be found in you;*
> *I must have all things, and abound,*
> *While God is God to me.*

Lastly, Christian, let me urge you again to use God to be your delight this day. It you have trial, or if you are free from it, I beseech you, make God your delight. Go from this house of prayer and be happy this day in the Lord. Remember it is a commandment: "Rejoice in the Lord always. Again I will say, rejoice!" (Phil. 4:4). Do not be content to be moderately happy. Seek to soar to the heights of bliss and to enjoy a heaven below. Get near to God and you will get near to heaven. It is not as it is with the sun here—the higher you go the colder you find it, because on the mountain there is nothing to reflect the rays of the sun. But with God, the nearer you go to Him the brighter He will shine upon you, and when there are no other creatures to reflect His goodness, His light will be all the brighter.

Child of God, let me urge you to make use of your God. Make use of Him in prayer. I beseech you, go to Him often, because He is your God.

Go to God continually, importunately, confidently. Delight yourself in the Lord, and He will bring it to pass. Commit your way to the Lord, and He will guide you by His counsel and afterward receive you to glory (Ps. 73:24).

Here is the first thing of the covenant. The second is like to it. We will consider that another Sabbath day. And now may God dismiss you with His blessing. Amen.

FOR FURTHER THOUGHT

1. *The scriptures picture God as a potter molding pots out of clay. What does this figure tell us about God in His dealings with His creation?*
2. *In this sermon, Spurgeon gives a definition of heaven. What is this?*
3. *Read Psalm 73:21–27, written by a person who has been grieved, foolish, and ignorant. What is God's relationship with that person?*

The Fatherhood of God

I think there is room for very great doubt whether our Savior intended the prayer, of which our text forms a part, to be used in the manner in which it is commonly employed among professing Christians. It is the custom of many persons to repeat it as their morning prayer, and they think that when they have repeated these sacred words, they have done enough. I believe that this prayer was never intended for universal use. Jesus Christ taught it not to all men, but to His disciples, and it is a prayer adapted only to those who are the possessors of grace and are truly converted. In the lips of an ungodly man, it is entirely out of place. Does not one say, "You are of your father the devil, and the desires of your father you want to do" (John 8:44)? Why then should you mock God by saying, "Our Father in heaven"?

For how can He be your Father? Have you two fathers? And if He is a Father, where is His honor? Where is His love? You neither honor nor love Him and yet you presumptuously and blasphemously approach Him and say, "Our Father," when your heart is attached still to sin, your life is opposed to His law, and you therefore prove yourself an heir of wrath and not a child of grace! Oh, I beseech you, leave off sacrilegiously employing these sacred words. And until you can in sincerity and truth say, "Our Father in heaven," and in your lives seek to honor His holy name, do not offer to Him the language of the hypocrite, which is an abomination to Him.

I very much question also whether this prayer was intended to be used by Christ's own disciples as a constant form of prayer. It seems to me that Christ gave it as a model whereby we are to fashion all our prayers, and I think we may use it to edification and with great sincerity and earnestness only at certain times and seasons. I have seen an architect form the model of a building he intends to erect of plaster or wood. But I never had an idea that it was intended for me to live in. I have seen an artist trace on a piece of brown paper, perhaps, a design that he intended afterward to work out on more costly stuff. But I never imagined the design to be the thing itself. This prayer of Christ is a great chart, as it were. But I cannot cross the sea on a chart. It is a map. But a man is not a traveler because he puts his fingers across a map. And so a man may use this form of prayer and yet be a total stranger to the great design of Christ in teaching it to His disciples.

I feel that I cannot use this prayer to the omission of others. Great as it is, it does not express all I desire to say to my Father who is in heaven. There are many sins that I must confess separately and distinctly. And the various other petitions that this prayer contains require, I feel, to be expanded when I come before God in private. And I must pour out my heart in the language that His Spirit gives me. And more than that, I must trust in the Spirit to speak the unutterable groans of my spirit when my lips cannot actually express all the emotions of my heart. Let none despise this prayer. It is matchless, and if we must have *forms* of prayer, let us have this first, foremost, and chief. But let none think that Christ would tie His disciples to the constant and only use of this. Let us rather draw near to the throne of heavenly grace with boldness, as children coming to a father, and let us tell forth our wants and our sorrows in the language that the Holy Spirit teaches us.

Coming to the text, there are several things to notice here. First, I will dwell for a few minutes upon the *double relationship* mentioned: "Our Father in heaven." There is *sonship* in "Father." There is also *brotherhood*, for it says, "*Our* Father." And if He is the common Father of us, then we must be brothers, for there are two relationships: sonship and brotherhood. In the next place, I will utter a few words about the spirit that is necessary to help us before we are able to utter this. It is the *spirit of adoption*, whereby we can cry, "Our Father in heaven." And then, third, I will conclude with the *double argument* of the text, for it is really an argument upon which the rest of the prayer is based. "Our Father in heaven" is, as it were, a strong argument used before supplication itself is presented.

I. First, the double relationship implied in the text. We take the first one. Here is *sonship*: "Our Father in heaven." How are we to understand this, and in what sense are we the sons and daughters of God? Some say that the fatherhood of God is universal and that every man, from the fact of his being created by God, is necessarily God's son. They say therefore that every man has a right to approach the throne of God and say, "Our Father in heaven." With that I must disagree. I believe that in this prayer we are to come before God, looking upon Him not as our Father through creation, but as our Father through *adoption* and the new birth. I will very briefly state my reasons for this.

I have never been able to see that creation necessarily implies father-hood. I believe God has made many things that are not His children. Has He not made the heavens and the earth, the sea and the fullness thereof? And are they His children? You say these are not rational and intelligent beings. But He made the angels who stand in an eminently high and holy position. Are they His children? "For to which of the angels did He ever say: 'You are My Son, today I have begotten You'?" (Heb. 1:5). I do not find, as a rule, that angels are called the children of God. And I must disagree with the idea that mere creation brings God necessarily into the relationship of a Father with us.

Does not the potter make vessels of clay? But is the potter the father of the vase or of the bottle? No, beloved, it needs something beyond creation to constitute the *relationship*, and those who can say, "Our Father in heaven," are something more than God's creatures. They have been *adopted* into His family. He has taken them out of the old sin family in which they were born. He has washed them, cleansed them, given them a new name and a new spirit, and made them "heirs of God and joint heirs with Christ" (Rom. 8:17). And all this is of His free, sovereign, unmerited, distinguishing grace.

And having adopted them to be His children, He has, in the next place, *regenerated* them by the Spirit of the living God. He has "begotten us again to a living hope through the resurrection of Jesus Christ from the dead" (1 Pet. 1:3). And no man has a right to claim God as his Father unless he feels in his soul and believes, solemnly, through the faith of God's election, that he has been adopted into the one family that is in heaven and earth and that he has been regenerated or born again.

This relationship also involves *love*. If God is my Father, He loves me, and oh, how He loves me! When God is a husband, He is the best of husbands. Widows, somehow or other, are always well cared for. When God is a friend, He is the best of friends and sticks closer than a brother. And when He is a Father, He is the best of fathers. O fathers, perhaps you do not know how much you love your children! When they are sick you know, for you stand by their couches and you pity them as their little frames are writhing in pain. Just "as a father pities his children, so the LORD pities those who fear

Him" (Ps. 103:13), you know how you love your children, too, when they grieve you by their sin. Anger arises and you are ready to chasten them, but no sooner is the tear in their eye than your hand is heavy and you feel that you would rather smite yourself than smite them. And every time you smite them, you seem to cry, "Oh, that I should have thus to afflict my child for his sin! Oh, that I could suffer in his place!" And God, even our Father, does not afflict willingly. Is not that a sweet thing? He is, as it were, *compelled* to do it. Even the eternal arm is not *willing* to do it. Only His great love and deep wisdom bring down the blow.

> *L*et us rather draw near to the throne of heavenly grace with boldness, as children coming to a father, and let us tell forth our wants and our sorrows in the language that the Holy Spirit teaches us.

But if you want to know your love to your children, you will know it most if they die. David knew that he loved his son Absalom, but he never knew how much he loved him till he heard that he had been slain and that Joshua had buried him. "Precious in the sight of the LORD is the death of His saints" (Ps. 116:15). He knows, then, how deep and pure is the love that death can never sever and the terrors of eternity can never unbind. But, parents, although you love your children much and you know it, you do not know and you cannot tell how deep is the unfathomable abyss of the love of God to you. Go out at midnight and consider the heavens, the work of God's fingers, the moon and the stars that He has ordained. And I am sure you will say, "What is man that You are mindful of him?" (Ps. 8:4). But more than all, you will wonder, not at your loving Him, but that while He has all these treasures, He should set His heart upon so insignificant a creature as man. And the sonship that God has given us is not a mere *name*. There is all our Father's great heart given to us in the moment when He claims us as His sons.

But if this sonship involves the love of God to us, it involves also the duty of *love to God*. O heir of heaven, if you are God's child, will you not love your Father? What son is there who loves not his father? Is he not less than human if he loves not his sire? Let his name be blotted from the book of remembrance who loves not the woman who brought him forth and the father who begat him. And we, the chosen favorites of heaven, adopted and regenerated, will not we love Him? Shall we not say, "Whom have I in heaven but You? And there is none upon earth that I desire besides You" (Ps. 73:25)?

"My Father, I will give you my heart. You will be the guide of my youth. You do love me, and the little heart that I have will be all yours forever."

Furthermore, if we say, "Our Father in heaven," we must remember that our being sons involves the duty of *obedience to God*. When I say "my Father," it is not for me to rise up and go in rebellion against His wishes. If He is my Father, let me note His commands and let me reverentially obey. If He has said, "Do this," let me do it, not because I dread Him, but because I love Him. And if He forbids me to do anything, let me avoid it. Some persons in the world have not the spirit of adoption, and they can never be brought to do a thing unless they see some advantage to themselves in it. But with the child of God, there is no motive at all. He can boldly say, "I have never done a right thing since I have followed Christ because I asked to get to heaven by it, nor have I ever avoided a wrong thing because I was afraid of being damned."

The child of God knows his good works do not make him acceptable to God, for he was acceptable to God by Jesus Christ long before he had any good works. And the fear of hell does not affect him, for he knows that he is delivered from that and will never come into condemnation, having passed from death to life. He acts from pure love and gratitude, and until we come to that state of mind, I do not think there is such a thing as virtue. For if a man has done what is called a virtuous action because he asked to get to heaven or to avoid hell by it, whom has he served? Has he not served himself? And what is that but selfishness? But the man who has no hell to fear and no heaven to gain, because heaven is his own and hell he never can enter—that man is capable of virtue. For he says:

> *Now for the love I bear His name,*
> *What was my gain I count my loss.*
> *I pour contempt on all my shame,*
> *And nail my glory to His cross.*

Nail it to His cross who loved and lived and died for me who loved Him not, but who desires *now* to love Him with all my heart and soul and strength.

And now permit me to draw your attention to one encouraging thought that may help to cheer the downcast and Satan-tempted child of God. *Sonship is a thing that all the infirmities of our flesh and all the sins into which we are hurried by temptation can never violate or weaken.* A man has a child—that child on a sudden is bereaved of its senses. It becomes an idiot. What a grief that is to a father, for a child to become a lunatic or an idiot and to exist only as an animal, apparently without a soul! But the idiot child is a child and the lunatic child is a child still. And if we are the fathers of such children, they are ours, and all the idiocy and all the lunacy that can possibly befall them can never shake the fact that they are our sons. Oh, what a mercy when we transfer this to God's case and ours! How foolish we are sometimes—how worse than foolish! We may say as David did, "I was like a beast before You" (Ps. 73:22). God brings before us the truths of His kingdom. We cannot see their beauty, and we cannot appreciate them. We seem to be as if we were totally demented, ignorant, unstable, weary, and apt to slide.

> *The child of God knows his good works do not make him acceptable to God, for he was acceptable to God by Jesus Christ long before he had any good works.*

But thanks be to God, we are His children still! And if there is anything worse that can happen to a father than his child becoming a lunatic or an idiot, it is when he grows up to be wicked. It is well said, "Children are doubtful blessings." I remember to have heard one say—and, as I thought, not very kindly—to a mother with an infant at her breast, "Woman, you may be suckling a viper there!" It stung the mother to the quick and it was not needful to have said it. But how often is it the fact that the child who has hung upon his mother's breast, when he grows up, brings that mother's gray hairs with sorrow to the grave! "Oh! Sharper than a serpent's tooth to have a thankless child!"—ungodly, vile, debauched—a blasphemer! But mark, brethren, if he is a child, he cannot lose his childship, nor we our fatherhood, be he who or what he may. Let him be transported beyond the seas; he is still our son. Let us deny him the house because his conversation might lead others of our children into sin. Yet our son he is and must be, and when the sod will cover his head and ours, "father and son" will still be on the tombstone. The relationship never can be severed as long as time will last. The prodigal was his father's son when he was among the harlots and when he was feeding swine. And God's children are God's children anywhere and everywhere and will be even to the end. Nothing can sever that sacred tie or divide us from His heart.

There is yet another thought that may cheer the Little-Faiths and Feeble-Minds. *The fatherhood of God is common to all His children.* Ah, Little-Faith, you have often looked up to Mr. Great-Heart and you have said, "Oh, that I had the courage of Great-Heart, that I could wield his sword and cut old giant Grim in pieces! Oh, that I could fight the dragons and that I could overcome the lions! But I am stumbling at every straw and a shadow makes me afraid." Listen, Little-Faith. Great-Heart is God's child and you are God's child, too. And Great-Heart is not a whit more God's child than you are. [Great-Heart and Little-Faith are characters in John Bunyan's *Pilgrim's Progress. Ed.*] David was the son of God, but not more the son of God than you. Peter and Paul, the highly favored apostles, were of the family of the Most High. And so are you. You have children yourselves—one is a son grown up and out in business, perhaps, and you have another, a little thing still in arms. Which is more your child, the little one or the big one? "Both alike," you say. "This little one is my child near my heart, and the big one is my child, too."

And so the little Christian is as much a child of God as the great one.

This covenant stands secure,
Though earth's old pillars bow.
The strong, the feeble, and the weak,
Are one in Jesus now.

And they are one in the family of God and no one is ahead of the other. One may have more grace than another, but God does not love one more than another. One may be an older child than another, but he is not more a child. One may do mightier works and may bring more glory to his Father, but he whose name is the least in the kingdom of heaven is as much the child of God as he who stands among the king's mighty men. Let this cheer and comfort us when we draw near to God and say, "Our Father in heaven."

I will make but one more remark before I leave this point, namely, this: that *our being the children of God brings with it innumerable privileges.* Time would fail me if I were to attempt to read the long roll of the Christian's joyous privileges. I am God's child—if so, He will clothe me. My shoes will be iron and brass. He will array me with the robe of my Savior's righteousness, for He has said, "Bring out the best robe and put it on him" (Luke 15:22). And He has said that He will put a crown of pure gold upon my head, and inasmuch as I am a king's son, I will have a royal crown. Am I His child? Then He will feed me. My bread will be given me and my water will be sure. He who feeds the ravens will never let His children starve. If a good husbandman feeds the barn-door fowl and the sheep and the bullocks, certainly God's children will not starve.

> *he prodigal was his father's son when he was among the harlots and when he was feeding swine. And God's children are God's children anywhere and everywhere and will be even to the end.*

Does my Father deck the lily and will I go naked? Does He feed the fowls that sow not, neither do they reap, and will I feel necessity? God forbid! My Father knows what things I have need of before I ask Him, and He will give me all I need. If I am His child, then I have a portion in His heart here and I will have a portion in His house above, for "if children, then heirs—heirs of God and joint heirs with Christ, if indeed we suffer with Him, that we may also be glorified together" (Rom. 8:17). And oh, brethren, what a prospect this opens up! The fact of our being heirs of God and joint heirs with Christ proves that all things are ours—the gift of God, the purchase of a Savior's blood.

> *This world is ours and worlds to come;*
> *Earth is our lodge and heaven our home.*

Are there crowns? They are mine if I am an heir. Are there thrones? Are there dominions? Are there harps, palm branches, white robes? Are there glories that eye has not seen? And is there music that ear has not heard? All these are mine, if I am a child of God. "It has not yet been revealed what we shall be, but we know that when He is revealed, we shall be like Him, for we shall see Him as He is" (1 John 3:2). Talk of princes, kings, and potentates. Their inheritance is but a pitiful foot of land across which the bird's wing can soon direct its flight. But the broad acres of the Christian cannot be measured by eternity. He is rich, without a limit to his wealth. He is blessed, without a boundary to his bliss. All this and more than I can enumerate is involved in our being able to say, "Our Father in heaven."

The second tie of the text is *brotherhood*. It does not say *my* Father, but *our* Father. Then it seems there are a great many in the family. I will be very brief on this point: "our Father." When you pray that prayer, remember you have a good many brothers and sisters who do not know their Father yet, and you must include them all. For all God's elect ones, though they are uncalled as yet, are still His children, though they know it not. In one of Krummacher's beautiful little parables there is a story like this:

> Abraham sat one day in the grove at Mamre, leaning his head on his hand and sorrowing. Then his son Isaac came to him and said, "My father, why do you mourn? What ails you?"
>
> Abraham answered and said, "My soul mourns for the people of Canaan, that they know not the Lord, but walk in their own ways, in darkness and foolishness."
>
> "Oh, my father," answered the son, "is it only this? Let not your heart be sorrowful. For are not these their own ways?"
>
> Then the patriarch rose up from his seat and said, "Come now, follow me." And he led the youth to a hut and said to him, "Behold." There was a child who was an imbecile and the mother sat weeping by him. Abraham asked her, "Why do you weep?"
>
> Then the mother said, "Alas, this my son eats and drinks and we minister to him. But he knows not the face of his father, or of his mother. Thus his life is lost and this source of joy is sealed to him."

Is not that a sweet little parable to teach us how we ought to pray for the many sheep that are not yet of the fold, but that must be brought in? We ought to pray for them, because they do not know their Father. Christ has bought them and they do not know Christ. The Father has loved them from before the foundation of the world, and yet they know not the face of their

Father. When you say "our Father," think of the many of your brothers and sisters who are in the backstreets of London, who are in the dens and caves of Satan. Think of your poor brother who is intoxicated with the spirit of the devil. Think of him led astray to infamy and lust and perhaps to murder, and in your prayer pray for them who know not the Lord.

"Our Father." That includes those of God's children who differ from us in their doctrine. Ah, some differ from us as wide as the poles, yet they are God's children.

"Come, Mr. Bigot, do not kneel down and say 'my Father,' but 'our Father.'"

"If you please, I cannot put in Mr. So-and-So, for I think he is a heretic."

"Put him in, sir. God has put him in and you must put him in, too, and say 'our Father.'"

Is it not remarkable how very much alike all God's people are upon their knees? Some time ago at a prayer meeting, I called upon two brothers in Christ to pray one after another. One was a Wesleyan and the other a strong Calvinist. And the Wesleyan prayed the most Calvinistic prayer of the two, I do believe. At least, I could not tell what was what. I listened to see if I could not discern some peculiarity even in their phraseology, but there was none. "Saints in prayer appear as one." For when they get on their knees, they are all compelled to say "our Father," and all their language afterward is of the same sort.

When you pray to God, put in the poor. For is He not the Father of many of the poor, rich in faith and heirs of the kingdom, though they are poor in this world? Come, my sister, if you bow your knee amid the rustling of silk and satin, yet remember the cotton and the print. My brother, is there wealth in your hand? Remember your brethren of the rough hand and the dusty brow. Remember those who could not wear what you wear, nor eat what you eat, but are as Lazarus compared with you, while you are as Dives. Pray for them. Put them all in the same prayer and say "our Father."

And pray for those who are divided from us by the sea; those who are in heathen lands, scattered like precious salt in the midst of this world's putrefaction. Pray for all who name the name of Jesus, and let your prayer be a great and comprehensive one. "Our Father in heaven." And after you have prayed that, rise up and act it. Say not "our Father" and then look upon your brethren with a sneer or a frown. I beseech you, live like a brother and act like a brother. Help the needy. Cheer the sick. Comfort the fainthearted. Go about doing good; minister to the suffering people of God wherever you find them. Let the world take notice of you—that you are when on your feet what you are upon your knees—that you are a brother to all the brotherhood of Christ, a brother born for adversity, like your Master Himself.

II. Having thus expounded the double relationship, I have left myself but little time for a very important part of the subject, namely, the *spirit of adoption*. I am extremely puzzled and bewildered how to explain to the ungodly what is the spirit with which we must be filled before we can pray this prayer. If I had a foundling here, one who had never seen either father or mother, I think I should have a very great difficulty in trying to make him understand what are the feelings of a child toward his father. Poor little thing, he has been under tutors and governors. He has learned to respect them for their kindness, or to fear them for their austerity, but there never can be in that child's heart that love toward tutor or governor, however kind he may be, that there is in the heart of another child toward his own mother or father.

There is a nameless charm there—we cannot describe or understand it. It is a sacred touch of nature, a throb in the breast that God has put there and cannot be taken away. The fatherhood is recognized by the childship of the child. And what is that spirit of a child—that sweet spirit that makes him recognize and love his father? I cannot tell you unless you are a child yourself and then you will know. And what is the spirit of adoption by which we cry out, "Abba, Father" (Rom. 8:15)? I cannot tell you. But if you have felt it, you will know it. It is a sweet compound of faith that knows God to be my Father, love that loves Him as my Father, joy that rejoices in Him as my Father, fear that trembles to disobey Him because He is my Father, and a confident affection and trustfulness that relies upon Him and casts itself wholly upon Him, because it knows by the infallible witness of the Holy Spirit that Jehovah, the God of earth and heaven, is the Father of my heart.

Oh, have you ever felt the spirit of adoption? There is nothing like it beneath the sky! Save heaven itself there is nothing more blissful than to enjoy that spirit of adoption. Oh, when the wind of trouble is blowing, waves of adversity are rising, and the ship is reeling to the rock, how sweet, then, to say "my Father" and to believe that His strong hand is on the helm! What joy when the bones are aching and when the loins are filled with pain and when the cup is brimming with wormwood and gall, to say "my Father," and seeing the Father's hand holding the cup to the lip, to drink it steadily to the very dregs because we can say, "My Father, not my will, but Yours be done." Martin Luther says, in his *Exposition of Galatians*, "There is more eloquence in that word, 'Abba, Father,' than in all the orations of Demosthenes or Cicero put together."

"My Father!" Oh, there is music there. There is eloquence there. There is the very essence of heaven's own bliss in that word, "my Father," when applied to God and when said by us with an unfaltering tongue through the inspiration of the Spirit of the living God.

> *S*ay not "our Father" and then look upon your brethren with a sneer or a frown. I beseech you, live like a brother and act like a brother.

My hearers, have you the spirit of adoption? If not, you are miserable men. May God Himself bring you to know Him! May He teach you your need of Him! May He lead you to the cross of Christ and help you to look to your dying brother! May He bathe you in the blood that flowed from His open wounds, and then, accepted in the Beloved, may you rejoice that you have the honor to be one of that sacred family.

III. And now, in the last place, I said that there was in the title a *double argument*. "Our Father." That is, "Lord, hear what I have got to say. You are my Father." If I come before a judge, I have no right to expect that he will hear me at any particular season in anything that I have to say. If I came merely to crave for some prize or benefit to myself, if the law were on my side, then I could demand an audience at his hands. But when I come as a law breaker and only come to crave for mercy, or for favors I deserve not, I have no right to expect to be heard. But a child, even though he is erring, always expects his father will hear what he has to say.

"Lord, if I call you King, you will say, 'You are a rebellious subject; get you gone.' If I call you Judge, you will say, 'Be still, or out of your own mouth will I condemn you.' If I call you Creator, you will say to me, 'It grieves me that I made man upon the earth.' If I call you my preserver, you will say to me, 'I have preserved you, but you have rebelled against me.' But if I call you

Father, all my sinfulness does not invalidate my claim. If you are my Father, then you love me. If I am your child, then you will regard me, and poor though my language is, you will not despise it."

If a child were called upon to speak in the presence of a number of persons, how very much alarmed he would be lest he should not use right language. I may sometimes fear when I have to address a mighty auditory, lest I should not select choice words, full well knowing that if I were to preach as I never shall, like the mightiest of orators, I should always have enough of carping critics to rail at me. But if I had my Father here and if you could all stand in the relationship of father to me, I should not be very particular what language I used. When I talk to my Father, I am not afraid He will misunderstand me. If I put my words a little out of place, He understands my meaning somehow.

> *When we come to God, our prayers are little broken things. We cannot put them together, but our Father, He will hear us.*

When we are little children, we only prattle; still our father understands us. Our children talk a great deal more like Dutchmen than Englishmen when they begin to talk, and strangers come in and say, "Dear me, what is the child talking about?" But we know what it is, and though in what they say there may not be an intelligible sound that anyone could print and a reader make it out, we know they have certain little wants and a way of expressing their desires so that we can understand them.

So when we come to God, our prayers are little broken things. We cannot put them together, but our Father, He will hear us. Oh, what a beginning is "our Father" to a prayer full of faults and a foolish prayer perhaps, a prayer in which we are going to ask what we ought not to ask for! "Father, forgive the language! Forgive the matter!"

As one dear brother said the other day at the prayer meeting, he could not get on in prayer, and he finished up on a sudden by saying, "Lord, I cannot pray tonight as I should wish. I cannot put the words together. Lord, take the meaning, take the meaning," and sat down. That is just what David said once: "Lord, all my desire is before You" (Ps. 38:9). Not my words, but my *desire*, and God could read it. We should say "our Father" because that is a reason why God should hear what we have to say.

But there is another argument. "Our Father, give me what I need." If I come to a stranger, I have no right to expect he will give it to me. He may out of his charity. But if I come to a *father*, I have a claim, a sacred claim. My Father, I will have no need to use arguments to move your bosom. I will not have to speak to you as the beggar who cries in the street. For because you *are* my Father, you know my needs and you are willing to relieve me. It is your business to relieve me. I can come confidently to you, knowing you will give me all I need.

If we ask our father for anything when we are little children, we are under an obligation certainly, but it is an obligation we never feel. If you were hungry and your father fed you, would you feel an obligation like you would if you went into the house of a stranger? You go into a stranger's house trembling and you tell him you are hungry. Will he feed you? He says yes, he will give you something. But if you go to your father's table, almost without asking, you sit down as a matter of course and feast to your full, and you rise and go and feel you are indebted to him. But there is not a grievous sense of obligation.

Now, we are all deeply under obligation to God, but it is a child's obligation that impels us to gratitude. That does not constrain us to feel that we have been demeaned by it. Oh, if He were not my Father, how could I expect that He would relieve my needs? But since He is my Father, He will; He must hear my prayers and answer the voice of my crying and supply all my needs out of the riches of His fullness in Christ Jesus the Lord.

Has your father treated you badly lately? I have this word to you, then. Your father loves you quite as much when he treats you roughly as when he treats you kindly. There is often more love in an angry father's heart than there is in the heart of a father who is too kind. I will suppose a case. Suppose there were two fathers and their two sons went away to some remote part of the earth where idolatry is still practiced. Suppose these two sons were decoyed and deluded into idolatry. The news comes to England and the first father is very angry. His son, his own son, has forsaken the religion of Christ and become an idolater.

The second father says, "Well, if it will help him in trade, I don't care. If he gets on the better by it, all well and good." Now, who loves more, the angry father or the father who treats the matter with complacency? Why, the angry father is the better. He loves his son—therefore he cannot give away his son's soul for gold. Give me a father who is angry about my sins and who seeks to bring me back, even though it is by chastisement. Thank God, you have a Father who can be angry, but who loves you as much when He is angry as when He smiles upon you.

Go away with that upon your mind and rejoice. But if you love not God and fear Him not, go home, I beseech you, to confess your sins and to seek mercy through the blood of Christ. And may this sermon be made useful in bringing you into the family of Christ though you have strayed from Him long. And though His love has followed you long in vain, may it now find you and bring you to His house rejoicing!

For Further Thought

1. *There is one qualification if a person is to be called a son of God. What is that qualification according to Galatians 3:26?*
2. *Two verses in the scriptures mention the cry "Abba, Father." Romans 8:15 says, "We cry out, 'Abba, Father.'" In Galatians 4:6, who is crying, "Abba, Father"?*
3. *In Ephesians 1:17, Paul prays to the Father. What does he ask for?*

SERMONS RELATING TO JESUS CHRIST

THE INCARNATION AND
BIRTH OF CHRIST

"But you, Bethlehem Ephrathah, though you are little among
the thousands of Judah, yet out of you shall come forth to
Me the One to be Ruler in Israel, whose goings forth
are from of old, from everlasting."
MICAH 5:2

THIS is the season of the year when, whether we wish it or not, we are compelled to think of the birth of Christ. I hold it to be one of the greatest absurdities under heaven to think that there is any religion in keeping Christmas Day. There are no probabilities whatever that our Savior Jesus Christ was born on that day, and the observance of it is purely of popish origin. Doubtless those who are Catholics have a right to hallow it, but I do not see how consistent Protestants can account it in the least sacred.

However, I wish there were ten or a dozen Christmas Days in the year—for there is work enough in the world and a little more rest would not hurt laboring people. Christmas Day is really a gift to us, particularly as it enables us to assemble round the family hearth and meet our friends once more. Still, although we do not fall exactly in the track of other people, I see no harm in thinking of the incarnation and birth of the Lord Jesus. We do not wish to be classed with those "who with more care keep holiday the wrong, than others the right way." The old Puritans made a parade of *work* on Christmas Day, just to show that they protested against the observance of it. But we believe they entered that protest so completely that we are willing, as their descendants, to take the good accidentally conferred by the day and leave its superstitions to the superstitious.

To proceed at once to what we have to say to you, we notice, first, who it was who sent Christ forth. God the Father here speaks and says, "Out of you shall come forth to Me the One to be Ruler in Israel" (Mic. 5:2). Second, where did He come to at the time of His incarnation? Third, what did He come for? "To be Ruler in Israel." Fourthly, had He ever come before? Yes, He had. "Whose goings forth are from of old, from everlasting" (Mic. 5:2).

I. First, then, *who sent Jesus Christ?* The answer is returned to us by the words of the text. "Out of you," says Jehovah, speaking by the mouth of Micah, "Out of you shall come forth to me the One." It is a sweet thought that Jesus Christ did not come forth without His Father's permission, authority, consent, and assistance. He was sent of the Father that He might be the Savior of men. We are, alas, too apt to forget that while there are distinctions as to the persons in the Trinity, there are no distinctions of *honor*—and we do very frequently ascribe the honor of our salvation, or at least the depths of its mercy and the extremity of its benevolence, more to Jesus Christ than we do to the Father. This is a very great mistake.

What if Jesus came? Did not His Father send Him? If He were made a child, did not the Holy Spirit beget Him? If He spoke wondrously, did not His Father pour grace into His lips that He might be an able minister of the new covenant? If His Father did forsake Him when He drank the bitter cup of gall, did He not love Him still? And did He not, by and by, after three days, raise Him from the dead and at last receive Him up on high, leading captivity captive?

Ah, beloved, He who knows the Father, the Son, and the Holy Spirit as he should know them never sets one before another. He is not more thankful to one than the other; he sees them at Bethlehem, at Gethsemane, and on Calvary all equally engaged in the work of salvation. "Out of you shall come forth to me the One." O Christian, have you put your confidence in the man Christ Jesus? Have you placed your reliance solely on Him? And are you united with Him? Then believe that you are united to the God of heaven, since to the man Christ Jesus you are brother and hold closest fellowship. You are linked thereby with God the eternal, and the Ancient of Days is your Father and your friend. "Out of you shall come forth to me the One."

Did you never see the depth of love there was in the heart of Jehovah, when God the Father equipped His Son for the great enterprise of mercy?

There had been a sad day in heaven once before, when Satan fell and dragged with him a third of the stars of heaven and when the Son of God, launching from His great right hand the omnipotent thunders, dashed the rebellious crew to the pit of perdition. But if we could conceive a grief in heaven, it must have been a sadder day when the Son of the Most High left His Father's bosom—where He had lain from before all worlds.

> *O Christian, have you put your confidence in the man Christ Jesus? Have you placed your reliance solely on Him? And are you united with Him? Then believe that you are united to the God of heaven, since to the man Christ Jesus you are brother and hold closest fellowship.*

"Go," says the Father, "and your Father's blessing on your head!" Then comes the disrobing. How do angels crowd around to see the Son of God take off His robes! He laid aside His crown. He said, "My Father, I am Lord over all, blessed forever. But I will lay my crown aside and be as mortal men are." He strips Himself of His bright vest of glory. "Father," He says, "I will wear a robe of clay, just such as men wear." Then He takes off all those jewels wherewith He was glorified. He lays aside His starry mantles and robes of light to dress Himself in the simple garments of the peasant of Galilee. What a solemn disrobing that must have been!

And next, can you picture the dismissal! The angels attend the Savior through the streets, until they approach the doors. An angel cries, "Lift up your heads, O you gates! And be lifted up, you everlasting doors! And the King of glory shall come in" (Ps. 24:7)! Oh, I think the angels must have wept when they lost the company of Jesus; when the Sun of heaven bereaved them of all its light. But they went after Him. They descended with Him. And when His spirit entered into flesh and He became a babe, He was attended by that mighty host of angels who, after they had been with Him to Bethlehem's manger and seen Him safely laid on His mother's breast, in their journey upward appeared to the shepherds and told them that He was born King of the Jews!

The *Father* sent Him! Contemplate that subject! Let your soul get hold of it and in every period of His life think that He suffered what the *Father* willed—that every step of His life was marked with the approval of the great I Am. Let every thought that you have of Jesus be also connected with the eternal, ever-blessed God, for "He," says Jehovah, "shall come forth to me." Who sent Him, then? The answer is His Father.

II. Now, second, *where did He come to?* A word or two concerning Bethlehem. It seemed meet and right that our Savior should be born in Bethlehem and that because of Bethlehem's history, Bethlehem's name, and Bethlehem's position—*little in Judah.*

First, it seemed necessary that Christ should be born in Bethlehem *because of Bethlehem's history.* Dear to every Israelite was the little village of Bethlehem. Jerusalem might outshine it in splendor, for there stood the temple, the glory of the whole earth, and "beautiful in elevation, the joy of the whole earth, is Mount Zion" (Ps. 48:2). Yet around Bethlehem there clustered a number of incidents that always made it a pleasant resting place to every Jewish mind. Even the Christian cannot help loving Bethlehem.

The very meanest of the family of God goes to Bethlehem for his bread, and the strongest man, who eats strong meat, goes to Bethlehem for it. House of bread! Where could come our nourishment but from you?

The first mention, I think, that we have of Bethlehem is a sorrowful one. There Rachel died. If you turn to the thirty-fifth chapter of Genesis, you will find it said in the sixteenth verse, "And they journeyed from Bethel; and there was but a little way to come to Ephrath: and Rachel travailed, and she had hard labour. And it came to pass, when she was in hard labour, that the midwife said unto her, Fear not; thou shalt have this son also. And it came to pass, as her soul was in departing, (for she died) that she called his name Benoni: but his father called him Benjamin. And Rachel died, and was buried in the way to Ephrath, which is Bethlehem. And Jacob set a pillar upon her grave: that is the pillar of Rachel's grave unto this day" (35:16–20 KJV).

This is a singular incident, almost prophetic. Might not Mary have called her own son Jesus, her Benoni, for He was to be the child of sorrow? Simeon said to her, "Yes, a sword will pierce through your own soul also, that the thoughts of many hearts may be revealed" (see Luke 2:35). But while she might have called Him Benoni, what did God His Father call Him? Benjamin, "the son of my right hand." He was Benoni as a man and Benjamin as to His Godhead. This little incident seems to be almost a prophecy that Benoni/Benjamin, the Lord Jesus, should be born in Bethlehem.

But another woman makes this place celebrated. That woman's name was Naomi. There lived at Bethlehem in after days, when perhaps the stone that Jacob's fondness had raised had been covered with moss and its inscription obliterated, another woman named Naomi. She, too, was a daughter of joy and yet a daughter of bitterness. Naomi was a woman whom the Lord had loved and blessed, but she had to go to a strange land and she said, "Do not call me Naomi [pleasant]; call me Mara [bitter], for the Almighty has dealt very bitterly with me" (Ruth 1:20).

Yet was she not alone amid all her losses, for there cleaved to her Ruth the Moabitess, whose Gentile blood should unite with the pure untainted stream of the Jew and should thus bring forth the Lord our Savior, the great King both of Jews and Gentiles. That very beautiful book of Ruth had all its scenery laid in Bethlehem. It was at Bethlehem that Ruth went forth to glean in the fields of Boaz. It was there that Boaz looked upon her and she bowed herself before her lord. It was there her marriage was celebrated. And in the streets of Bethlehem did Boaz and Ruth receive a blessing that made them fruitful, so that Boaz became the father of Obed and Obed the father of Jesse—and Jesse the father of David.

That last fact gilds Bethlehem with glory—the fact that David was born there—the mighty hero who smote the Philistine giant, who led the discontented of his land away from the tyranny of their monarch, and who afterward, by a full consent of a willing people, was crowned king of Israel and Judah. Bethlehem was a royal city, because the kings were there brought forth. Little as Bethlehem was, it was much to be esteemed because it was like certain principalities that we have in Europe, which are celebrated for nothing but for bringing forth the consorts of the royal families of England. It was right, then, from history, that Bethlehem should be the birthplace of Christ.

But again: *There is something in the name of the place.* Bethlehem Ephrathah. The word *Bethlehem* has a double meaning. It signifies "the house of bread" *and* "the house of war." Ought not Jesus Christ to be born in "the house of bread"? He is the bread of His people, on which they feed. As our fathers ate manna in the wilderness, so do we live on Jesus here below. Famished by the world, we cannot feed on its shadows. Its husks may gratify the swinish taste of worldlings, for they are swine, but we need something more substantial. In that blessed bread of heaven, made of the bruised body of our Lord Jesus and baked in the furnace of His agonies, we find a blessed food.

No food like Jesus to the desponding soul or to the strongest saint. The very meanest of the family of God goes to Bethlehem for his bread, and the strongest man, who eats strong meat, goes to Bethlehem for it. House of bread! Where could come our nourishment but from you? We have tried Sinai, but on her rugged steeps there grow no fruits, and her thorny heights yield no corn whereon we may feed. We have repaired even to Tabor itself, where Christ was transfigured, and yet there we have not been able to eat His flesh and drink His blood. But, Bethlehem, you house of bread, rightly were you called, for there the bread of life was first handed down for man to eat.

And it is called "the house of war," because Christ is to a man either "the house of bread" or else "the house of war." While He is food to the righteous, He causes war to the wicked, according to His own words: "Do not think that I came to bring peace on earth. I did not come to bring peace but a sword. For I have come to 'set a man against his father, a daughter against her mother, and a daughter-in-law against her mother-in-law'; and 'a man's enemies will be those of his own household'" (Matt. 10:34–36).

> *If we are like trees planted by the rivers of water, bringing forth our fruit in our season, it is not because we were naturally fruitful, but because of the rivers of water by which we were planted.*

Sinner, if you do not know Bethlehem as "the house of bread," it will be to you a "house of war." If from the lips of Jesus you never drink sweet honey—if you are not like the bee, which sips sweet luscious liquor from the Rose of Sharon, then out of the selfsame mouth there will go forth against you a two-edged sword! And that mouth from which the *righteous* draw their bread will be to you the mouth of *destruction* and the cause of your ill. Jesus of Bethlehem, house of bread and house of war, we trust we know you as our bread. Oh, that some who are now at war with you might hear in their hearts, as well as in their ears, the song "Peace on earth and mercy mild, God and sinners reconciled."

And now for that word *Ephrathah*, the old name of the place that the

Jews retained and loved. The meaning of it is "fruitfulness" or "abundance." Ah, well was Jesus born in the house of fruitfulness, for where come my fruitfulness and your fruitfulness, my brothers and sisters, but from Bethlehem? Our poor barren hearts never produced one fruit or flower till they were watered with the Savior's blood. It is His incarnation that fattens the soil of our hearts. There had been pricking thorns on all the ground—and mortal poisons, before He came—but our fruitfulness comes from Him. "I am like a green cypress tree; your fruit is found in Me" (Hosea 14:8). "All my springs are in you" (Ps. 87:7)

If we are like trees planted by the rivers of water, bringing forth our fruit in our season, it is not because we were naturally fruitful, but because of the rivers of water by which we were planted. It is Jesus who makes us fruitful. "If you abide in Me, and My words abide in you, you will ask what you desire, and it shall be done for you" (John 15:7). Glorious Bethlehem Ephrathah! Rightly named! Fruitful house of bread—the house of abundant provision for the people of God!

We notice, next, *the position of Bethlehem*. It is said to be "little among the thousands of Judah." Why is this? It is because Jesus Christ always goes among little ones. He was born in the little one "among the thousands of Judah." Not on Bashan's high hill, not on Hebron's royal mount, not in Jerusalem's palaces, but in the humble, yet illustrious, village of Bethlehem. There is a passage in Zechariah that teaches us a lesson—it is said that the man on the red horse stood among the myrtle trees. Now the myrtle trees grow at the bottom of the hill—and the man on the red horse always rides there. He does not ride on the mountaintop. He rides among the humble in heart.

"I dwell in the high and holy place, with him who has a contrite and humble spirit" (Isa. 57:15). There are some little ones here this morning; the "little among the thousands of Judah." No one ever heard your name, did they? If you were buried and had your name on your tombstone, it would never be noticed. Those who pass by would say, "It is nothing to me. I never knew him." You do not know much of yourself or think much of yourself. You can scarcely read, perhaps. Or if you have some talents and ability, you are despised among men. Or, if they do not despise you, you despise yourself. You are one of the little ones. Well, Christ is always born in Bethlehem among the little ones.

Big hearts never get Christ inside of them. Christ lies not in great hearts, but in little ones. Mighty and proud spirits never have Jesus Christ, for He comes in at low doors. He will not come in at high ones. He who has a broken heart and a low spirit will have the Savior, but none else. He heals not the prince and the king, but the broken in heart, and He binds up their wounds. Sweet thought! He is the Christ of the little ones. "But you, Bethlehem Ephrathah, though you are little among the thousands of Judah, yet out of you shall come forth to me the One to be Ruler in Israel."

We cannot pass away from this without another thought here, that is, how wonderfully mysterious was that providence that brought Jesus Christ's mother to Bethlehem at the very time when she was to be delivered! His parents were residing at Nazareth. And what should they want to travel at that time for? Naturally they would have remained at home. It was not at all likely that His mother would have taken a journey to Bethlehem while in so peculiar a condition. But Caesar Augustus issues a decree that they are to be taxed. Very well, then, let them be taxed at Nazareth. No. It pleases him that they should all go to their city.

But why should Caesar Augustus think of it just at that particular time? It is simply because man devises his way while the king's heart is in the hand of your Lord. Why, what a thousand chances—as the world has it— met together to bring about this event! First of all, Caesar quarreled with Herod. One of the Herods was deposed. Caesar says, "I will tax Judea and make it a province, instead of having it for a separate kingdom." Well, it must be done.

But when is it to be done? This taxing, it is said, was first commenced when Cyreneus was governor. But why is the census to be taken at *that* particular period—suppose—December? Why not have had it last October? And why could not the people be taxed where they were living? Was not their money just as good there as anywhere else? It was Caesar's whim, but it was God's decree. Oh, we love the sublime doctrine of eternal absolute predestination. Some have doubted its being consistent with the free agency of man. We know well it is so and we never saw any difficulty in the subject. We believe metaphysicians have made difficulties. We see none ourselves. It is for us to believe that man does as he pleases, yet notwithstanding he always does as God decrees. If Judas betrays Christ, it is because he was appointed to this. And if Pharaoh hardens his heart, "for this purpose I have raised you up, that I may show my power in you" (Exod. 9:16).

Man does as he wills, but God makes him do as He wills, too. No, not only is the will of man under the absolute predestination of Jehovah—but all things, great or little, are of Him. Well has the good poet said, "Doubtless the sailing of a cloud has providence as its pilot. Doubtless the root of an oak is gnarled for a special purpose. God compasses all things, mantling the globe like air." There is nothing great or little that is not from Him. The summer dust moves in its orbit, guided by the same hand that rolls the stars along. The dewdrops have their father and trickle on the rose leaf as God bids them. Yes, the sere leaves of the forest, when hurled along by the tempest, have their allotted position where they will fall; nor can they go beyond it.

In the great and in the little, there is God. God is in everything, working all things according to the counsel of His own will. And though man seeks to go against his Maker, yet he cannot. God has bound the sea with a barrier of sand, and if the seas mount up wave after wave, yet it will not exceed its allotted channel. Everything is of God. And to Him who guides the stars and wings sparrows, who rules planets and yet moves atoms, who speaks thunders and yet whispers zephyrs, to Him be glory. For there is God in everything.

III. This brings us to the third point: *What did Jesus come for?* He came to be "Ruler in Israel." A very singular thing is this, that Jesus Christ was said to have been "born King of the Jews" (Matt. 2:2). Very few have ever been born a king. Men are born princes, but they are seldom born kings. I do not think you can find an instance in history where any infant was born king. He was the Prince of Wales, perhaps. And he had to wait a number of years till his father died and then they manufactured him into a king by putting a crown on his head and a sacred chrism and other silly things. But he was not *born* a king. I remember no one who was born a king except Jesus. And there is emphatic meaning in that verse that we sing:

> *Born Your people to deliver*
> *Born a child and yet a king.*

The moment that He came on earth, He was a king. He did not wait till His majority that He might take His empire—but as soon as His eye greeted the sunshine, He was a king. From the moment that His little hands grasped anything, they grasped a scepter. As soon as His pulse beat and His blood began to flow, His heart beat royally and His pulse beat an imperial measure and His blood flowed in a kingly current. He was born a king. He came "to be Ruler in Israel."

"Ah," says one, "then He came in vain, for little did He exercise His rule."

"He came to His own, and His own did not receive Him" (John 1:11). He came to Israel and He was not their ruler, but He was despised and rejected, cast off by them all and forsaken by Israel, to whom He came.

Yes, but "they are not all Israel who are of Israel" (Rom. 9:6). Neither because they are the seed of Abraham will they all be called. Ah, no! He is not ruler of Israel after the *flesh*, but He is the ruler of Israel after the *spirit*. Many such have obeyed Him. Did not the apostles bow before Him and own Him as their King? And now, does not Israel salute Him as their ruler? Do not all the seed of Abraham after the spirit, even all the faithful (for He is the Father of the faithful), acknowledge that to Christ belong the shields of the mighty, for He is the King of the whole earth? Does He not rule over Israel? Yes, verily He does, and those who are not ruled over by Christ are not of Israel. He came to be a ruler over Israel.

> *God is in everything, working all things according to the counsel of His own will. And though man seeks to go against his Maker, yet he cannot.*

My brother, have you submitted to the sway of Jesus? Is He ruler in your heart, or is He not? We may know Israel by this: Christ is come into their hearts, to be ruler over them. "Oh," says one, "I do as I please. I was never in bondage to any man." Ah, then you base the rule of Christ. "Oh," says another, "I submit myself to my minister, to my clergyman, or to my priest, and I think that what he tells me is enough, for he is my ruler." Do you? Ah, poor slave, you know not your dignity, for nobody is your lawful ruler but the Lord Jesus Christ.

"Yes," says another, "I have professed His religion and I am His follower." But does He rule in your heart? Does He command your will? Does He guide your judgment? Do you ever seek counsel at His handling your difficulties? Are you desirous to honor Him and to put crowns upon His head? Is He your ruler? If so, then you are one of Israel, for it is written, He will "come forth to me the One to be Ruler in Israel." Blessed Lord Jesus! You are ruler in your people's hearts and you ever will be. We want no other ruler save you, and we will submit to none other.

We are free, because we are the servants of Christ. We are at liberty because He is our ruler and we know no bondage and no slavery, because Jesus Christ alone is monarch of our hearts. He came "to be Ruler in Israel," and mark you, that mission is not quite fulfilled yet and will not be till the latter-day glories. In a little while you will see Christ come again, to be ruler over His people Israel and ruler over them not only as spiritual Israel but even as natural Israel, for the Jews will be restored to their land and the tribes of Jacob will yet sing in the halls of their temple. Unto God there will yet again be offered Hebrew songs of praise, and the heart of the unbelieving Jew will be melted at the feet of the true Messiah.

In a short time, He who at His birth was hailed King of the Jews by Easterns and at His death was written King of the Jews by a Western, will be called King of the Jews everywhere—yes, King of the Jews and Gentiles also—in that universal monarchy whose dominion will be coextensive with the habitable globe and whose duration will be coeval with time itself. He came to be a ruler in Israel and a ruler most decidedly He will be, when He will reign among His people with His ancients gloriously.

IV. And now, the last thing: *Did Jesus Christ ever come before?* We answer, yes. For our text says, "Whose goings forth are from old, from everlasting." First, Christ has had His goings forth "from everlasting." He has not been a secret and a silent person up to this moment. That newborn child there has worked wonders long before now. That infant slumbering in His mother's arms is the infant of today, but He is the ancient of eternity. That child who is there has not made His appearance on the stage of this world; His name is not yet written in the calendar of the circumcised. But still, though you wish it not, His "goings forth are from old, from everlasting."

Of old He went forth as our covenant head in election, "just as He chose us in Him before the foundation of the world" (Eph. 1:4):

> *Christ be my first elect, He said,*
> *Then chose our souls in Christ our head.*

He had goings forth for His people as their representative before the throne even before they were begotten in the world. It was from everlasting that His mighty fingers grasped the pen, the stylus of ages, and wrote His own name, the name of the eternal Son of God. It was from everlasting that He signed the compact with His Father that He would pay blood for blood, wound for wound, suffering for suffering, agony for agony, and death for death on behalf of His people. It was from everlasting that He gave Himself up, without a murmuring word, that from the crown of His head to the sole of His foot He might sweat blood, that He might be spit upon, pierced, mocked, rent asunder, suffer the pain of death and the agonies of the cross.

> *Blessed Lord Jesus! You are ruler in your people's hearts and you ever will be. We want no other ruler save you, and we will submit to none other.*

His goings forth as our Surety were from everlasting. Pause, my soul, and wonder! You had goings forth in the person of Jesus from everlasting. Not only when you were born into the world did Christ love you, but His delights were with the sons of men before there were any sons of men! Often did He think of them; from everlasting to everlasting He had set His affection upon them. What? Believer, has He been so long about your salvation and will He not accomplish it? Has He from everlasting been going forth to save me and will He lose me now? What? Has He had me in His hand, as His precious jewel, and will He now let me slip between His precious fingers? Did He choose me before the mountains were brought forth, or the channels of the deep scooped out, and will He lose me now? Impossible!

> *My name from the palms of His hands*
> *Eternity cannot erase.*
> *Impressed on His heart it remains,*
> *In marks of indelible grace.*

I am sure He would not love me so long and then leave off loving me. If He intended to be tired of me, He would have been tired of me long before now. If He had not loved me with a love as deep as hell and as unutterable as the grave, if He had not given His whole heart to me, I am sure He would have turned from me long ago. He knew what I would be and He has had time enough to consider it—but I am His choice and that is the end of it.

And unworthy as I am, it is not mine to grumble if He is but contented with me. And He is contented with me—He must be contented with me—for He has known me long enough to know my faults.

He knew me before I knew myself—yes, He knew me before I *was* myself. Long before my members were fashioned, they were written in His book. When as yet there were none of them, His eyes of affection were set on them. He knew how badly I would act toward Him, and yet He has continued to love me.

> *His love in times past forbids me to think*
> *He'll leave me at last in trouble to sink.*

No. Since His goings forth were from everlasting, they will be to everlasting.

Second, we believe that Christ has come forth of old, even to men, so that men have beheld Him. I will not stop to tell you that it was Christ who walked in the Garden of Eden in the cool of the day, for His delights were with the sons of men. Nor will I detain you by pointing out all the various ways in that Christ came forth to His people in the form of the angel of the covenant, the paschal lamb, the brazen serpent, the burning bush, and ten thousand types with which the sacred history is so replete.

> *He knew me before I knew myself—yes, He knew me before I was myself. Long before my members were fashioned, they were written in His book.*

But I will rather point you to four occasions when Jesus Christ our Lord has appeared on earth as a man, before His great incarnation for our salvation. And, first, I beg to refer you to the eighteenth chapter of Genesis, where Jesus Christ appeared to *Abraham*, of whom we read, "And the LORD appeared unto him in the plains of Mamre: and he sat in the tent door in the heat of the day; and he lift up his eyes and looked, and, lo, three men stood by him: and when he saw them, he ran to meet them from the tent door, and bowed himself toward the ground" (18:1–2 KJV).

But to whom did he bow? He said "my LORD" only to one of them. There was one man between the other two, the most conspicuous for His glory, for He was the God-Man Christ. The other two were created angels who for a time had assumed the appearance of men. But this was the man Christ Jesus. "And said, My LORD, if now I have found favour in thy sight, pass not away, I pray thee, from thy servant: let a little water, I pray you, be fetched, and wash your feet, and rest yourselves under the tree" (vv. 3–4 KJV)

You will notice that this majestic man, this glorious person, stayed behind to talk with Abraham. In the twenty-second verse it is said, "Then the men turned away from there and went toward Sodom." That is, two of them, as you will see in the next chapter: "Abraham still stood before the LORD." You will notice that this man, the Lord, held sweet fellowship with Abraham and allowed Abraham to plead for the city He was about to destroy. He was in the positive form of man so that when He walked the streets of Judea, it was not the first time that He was a man. He was so before, in "the plains of Mamre, in the heat of the day."

Another instance is His appearing to Jacob, recorded in Genesis 32:24–28. All his family was gone.

> Then Jacob was left alone; and a Man wrestled with him until the breaking of day. Now when He saw that He did not prevail against him, He touched the socket of his hip; and the socket of Jacob's hip was out of joint as He wrestled with him. And He said, "Let Me go, for the day breaks."
>
> But he said, "I will not let You go unless You bless me!"
> So He said to him, "What is your name?"
> He said, "Jacob."
> And He said, "Your name shall no longer be called Jacob, but Israel; for you have struggled with God and with men, and have prevailed."

This was a man and yet God. And Jacob knew that this man was God, for he says in verse 30: "For I have seen God face to face, and my life is preserved."

Another instance you will find in the book of Joshua. When Joshua had crossed the narrow stream of Jordan, had entered the Promised Land, and was about to drive out the Canaanites, lo! God appeared to Joshua. In Joshua 5:13–15 we read, "And it came to pass, when Joshua was by Jericho, that he lifted his eyes and looked, and behold, a Man stood opposite him with His sword drawn in His hand. And Joshua went to Him and said to Him, 'Are you for us or for our adversaries?' So He said, 'No, but as Commander of the army of the LORD I have now come.'

Joshua saw at once that there was divinity in Him: "And Joshua fell on his face to the earth and worshiped, and said to Him, 'What does my Lord say to His servant?'" Now, if this had been a created angel, he would have reproved Joshua and said, "I am one of your fellow servants." But no: "Then the Commander of the LORD's army said to Joshua, 'Take your sandal off your foot, for the place where you stand is holy.' And Joshua did so."

Another remarkable instance is that recorded in the third chapter of the book of Daniel, where we read the account of Shadrach, Meshach, and Abednego being cast into the fiery furnace, which was so fierce that it destroyed the men who threw them in. "Then King Nebuchadnezzar was astonished; and he rose in haste and spoke, saying to his counselors, 'Did we not cast three men bound into the midst of the fire?' They answered and said to the king, 'True, O king.' 'Look!' he answered, 'I see four men loose, walking in the midst of the fire; and they are not hurt, and the form of the fourth is like the Son of God'" (Dan. 3:24–25).

> *A*re you little? He will go forth to you yet. Go home and seek Him by earnest prayer. If you have been made to weep because of sin and think yourself too little to be noticed, go home, little one! Jesus comes to little ones.

How could Nebuchadnezzar know this? There was something so noble and majestic in the way in which that wondrous man bore Himself, and some awful influence about Him who so marvelously broke the consuming teeth of that biting and devouring flame so that it could not so much as singe the children of God. Nebuchadnezzar recognized His humanity. He did not say, "I see three men and an angel." He said, "I see four men, and the form of the fourth is like the Son of God." You see, then, what is meant by His goings forth being from everlasting.

Observe for a moment here that each of these four great occurrences happened to the saints when they there engaged in very eminent duty, or when they were about to be engaged in it. Christ does not appear to His saints every day. He did not come to see Jacob till he was in affliction. He did not visit Joshua before he was about to be engaged in a righteous war. It is only in extraordinary seasons that Christ thus manifests Himself to His people. When Abraham interceded for Sodom, Christ was with him, for one of the highest and noblest employments of a Christian is that of intercession. And it is when he is so engaged that he will be likely to obtain a sight of Christ. Jacob was engaged in wrestling. That is a part of a Christian's duty to which some of you never did attain; consequently, you do not have many visits from Christ.

It was when Joshua was exercising bravery that the Lord met him. So with Shadrach, Meshach, and Abednego; they were in the high places of persecution on account of their adherence to duty when He came to them and said, "I will be with you, passing through the fire." There are certain peculiar places we must enter to meet with the Lord. We must be in great trouble, like Jacob. We must be in great labor, like Joshua. We must have great intercessory faith, like Abraham. We must be firm in the performance of duty, like Shadrach, Meshach, and Abednego, or else we will not know Him whose goings forth have been from everlasting. Or, if we know Him, we will not be able to comprehend with all the saints what is the height, depth, length, and breadth of the love of Christ that passes knowledge (Eph. 3:18–19).

Sweet Lord Jesus! You whose goings forth were of old, even from everlasting, you have not left your goings forth yet. Oh, that you would go forth this day to cheer the faint, to help the weary, to bind up our wounds, to comfort our distresses! Go forth, we beseech you, to conquer sinners, to subdue hard hearts, to break the iron gates of sinners' lusts and cut the iron bars of their sins in pieces! O Jesus! Go forth, and when you go forth, come to me! Am I a hardened sinner? Come to me. I want you.

Oh, let your grace my heart subdue;
I would be led in triumph, too.
A willing captive to my Lord,
To sing the honors of your Word.

Poor sinner! Christ has not left going forth yet. And when He goes forth, recollect He goes to Bethlehem. Have you a Bethlehem in your heart? Are you little? He will go forth to you yet. Go home and seek Him by earnest prayer. If you have been made to weep because of sin and think yourself too little to be noticed, go home, little one! Jesus comes to little ones. His goings forth are of old, and He is going forth now. He will come to your poor old house. He will come to your poor wretched heart. He will come, though you are in poverty and clothed in rags—though you are destitute, tormented, and afflicted—He will come, for His goings forth have been of old, from everlasting. Trust Him, trust Him, trust Him! And He will go forth to abide in your heart forever.

For Further Thought

1. *According to John 12:49, where did Jesus get the authority for the words He spoke?*
2. *Read Luke 2:1–4. What were the circumstances that caused Jesus to be born at Bethlehem?*
3. *In John 12:37–41, the Lord speaks about Israel's unbelief. What is the reason for that unbelief according to verses 39–40?*

THE BIRTH OF CHRIST

Behold, the virgin shall conceive and bear a Son, and shall call
His name Immanuel. Curds and honey He shall eat, that
He may know to refuse the evil and choose the good.
ISAIAH 7:14–15

THE kingdom of Judah was in a condition of imminent peril. Two monarchs had leagued themselves against her; two nations had risen up for her destruction. Syria and Israel had come up against the walls of Jerusalem with full intent to raze them to the ground and destroy the monarchy of Judah. Ahaz the king, in great trouble, exerted all his ingenuity to defend the city, and among the other contrivances that his wisdom taught him, he thought it fit to cut off the waters of the upper pool, so that the besiegers might be in distress for lack of water. He goes out in the morning, no doubt attended by his courtiers, makes his way to the conduit of the upper pool, intending to see after the stopping of the stream of water, but lo, he meets with something that sets aside his plans and renders them needless! Isaiah steps forward and tells him not to be afraid of the smoke of those two firebrands, for God should utterly destroy both the nations that had risen up against Judah. Ahaz need not fear the present invasion, for both he and his kingdom would be saved. The king looked at Isaiah with an eye of incredulity, as much as to say, "If the Lord were to send chariots from heaven, could such a thing as this be? Should He animate the dust and quicken every stone in Jerusalem to resist my foes, could this be done?"

The Lord, seeing the littleness of the king's faith, tells him to ask for a sign. "Ask it," He says, "either in the depth, or in the height above. Let the sun go backward ten degrees, or let the moon stop in her midnight marches. Let the stars move from one side to the other in the sky in grand procession! Ask any sign you please in the heaven above, or, if you wish, choose the earth beneath—let the depths give forth the sign; let some mighty waterspout lose its way across the pathless ocean and travel through the air to Jerusalem's very gates! Let the heavens shower a golden rain instead of the watery fluid that usually they distill. Ask that the fleece may be wet upon the dry floor, or dry in the midst of dew. Whatever you please to request, the Lord will grant it to you for the confirmation of your faith." Instead of accepting this offer with all gratitude, as Ahaz should have done, he, with a pretended humility, declares that he will not ask, neither will he tempt the Lord his God! Whereupon Isaiah, waxing indignant, tells him that since he will not, in obedience to God's command, ask for a sign, behold, the Lord Himself will give him one—not simply a sign, but *this* sign, the sign and wonder of the world, the mark of God's mightiest mystery and of His most consummate wisdom, for "the virgin shall conceive and bear a Son, and shall call His name Immanuel" (see Isa. 7:1–17).

It has been said that the passage I have taken for my text is one of the most difficult in all the Word of God. It may be so. I certainly did not think it was until I saw what the commentators had to say about it, and I rose up from reading them perfectly confused! One said one thing, and another denied what the other had said. And if there was anything that I liked, it was self-evident that it had been copied from one to the other and handed through the whole of them!

One set of commentators tells us that this passage refers entirely to some person who was to be born within a few months after this prophecy. They say, "It says here, 'Before the child will know to refuse the evil and choose the good, the land that you abhor will be forsaken of both her kings.'"

"Now," say they, "this was an immediate delivery that Ahaz required, and there was a promise of a speedy rescue, that before a few years had elapsed, before the child should be able to know right from wrong, Syria and Israel should both lose their kings."

Well, that seems a strange frittering away of a wonderful passage, full of meaning, and I cannot see how they can substantiate their view when we find the evangelist Matthew quoting this very passage in reference to the birth of Christ and saying, "So all this was done that it might be fulfilled which was spoken by the Lord through the prophet, saying: 'Behold, the virgin shall be with child, and bear a Son, and they shall call His name Immanuel'" (Matt. 1:22–23).

It strikes me that this Immanuel, who was to be born, could not be a mere simple man and nothing else, for if you turn to Isaiah 8:8, you will find it said, "He [the king of Assyria] will pass through Judah, he will overflow and pass over, he will reach up to the neck; and the stretching out of his wings will fill the breadth of Your land, *O Immanuel*" (emphasis added). Here is a *government* ascribed to Immanuel that could not be His if we were to suppose that the Immanuel here spoken of was either Shear-Jashub, or Maher-Shalal-Hash-Baz, or any other of the sons of Isaiah! I therefore reject that view of the matter. It is, to my mind, far below the height of this great argument. It does not speak or allow us to speak one-half of the wondrous depth that lies beneath this mighty passage!

I find, moreover, that many of the commentators divide the sixteenth verse from the fourteenth and fifteenth verses, and they read the forteenth and fifteenth verses exclusively of Christ, and the sixteenth verse of Shear-Jashub, the son of Isaiah. They say that there were two signs, one was the conception by the virgin of a Son, who was to be called Immanuel, who is none other than Christ, but the second sign was Shear-Jashub, the prophet's son, of whom Isaiah said, "Before the Child will know to refuse the evil and choose the good, the land that you dread will be forsaken by both her kings" (Isa. 7:16). But I do not like that explanation because it seems to me to be plain that the same child is spoken of in the one verse as in the others. "Before the child" means the same child. It does not say that child in one verse and then this child in another verse, but before the child, this one of whom I have spoken, the Immanuel, before He "shall know to refuse the evil and choose the good, the land that you dread will be forsaken by both her kings."

Then another view, which is the most popular of all, is to refer the passage, first of all, to some child who was then to be born, and afterward, in the highest sense, to our blessed Lord Jesus Christ. Perhaps that is the true sense of it. Perhaps that is the best way of smoothing difficulties. But I think that if I had never read those books at all, but had simply come to the Bible without knowing what any man had written upon it, I would have said, "There is Christ here as plainly as possible! Never could His name have been written more legibly than I see it here. 'Behold, a virgin shall conceive and bear a Son.' It is an unheard-of thing, it is a miraculous thing, and therefore it must be a Godlike thing! She 'shall call His name Immanuel. Curds and honey He shall eat, that He may know to refuse the evil and choose the good.' And before that child, Prince Immanuel, will know to refuse the evil and choose the good, the land that you abhor will be forsaken of both her kings, and Judah will smile upon their ruined palaces."

This morning, then, I will take my text as relating to our Lord Jesus Christ, and here we have three things about Him: First, *the birth*; second, *the food*; and, third, *the name of Christ*.

I. Let us commence with *the birth of Christ*—"Behold, the virgin shall conceive and bear a Son." "Let us now go to Bethlehem and see this thing that has come to pass," said the shepherds (Luke 2:15). "Let us follow the star in the sky," said the eastern magi, and so say we this morning. So near the day when we, as a nation, celebrate the birthday of Christ, let us go and stand by the manger to behold the commencement of the incarnation of Jesus! Let us recall the time when God first enveloped Himself in mortal form and tabernacled among the sons of men! Let us not blush to go to so humble a spot. Let us stand by that village inn and let us see Jesus Christ, the God-Man, become an infant of only a span long!

This sign, the sign and wonder of the world, the mark of God's mightiest mystery and of His most consummate wisdom, for "the virgin shall conceive and bear a Son, and shall call His name Immanuel

And, first, we see here, in speaking of this birth of Christ, a *miraculous conception*. The text says expressly, "Behold, the virgin shall conceive and bear a Son." This expression is unparalleled even in sacred writ! Of no other woman could it be said beside the virgin Mary, and of no other man could it be written that his mother was a virgin. The Greek word and the Hebrew are both very expressive of the true and real virginity of the mother, to show us that Jesus Christ was born of woman and *not of man*. We will not enlarge upon the thought, but still, it is an important one and ought not to be passed over without mentioning. Just as the woman, by her venturous spirit, stepped first into transgression—lest she should be despised and trampled on, God, in His wisdom, devised that the woman, and the woman alone, should be the author of the body of the God-Man who should redeem mankind! Albeit that she herself first tasted the accursed fruit and tempted her husband (it may be that Adam, out of love to her, tasted that fruit lest she should be degraded, lest she should not stand on an equality with him), God has ordained that so it should be that His Son should be sent forth "born of a woman" (Gal. 4:4). And the first promise was that the seed of the woman, *not* the seed of the man, should bruise the serpent's head (Gen. 3:15).

Moreover, there was a peculiar wisdom ordaining that Jesus Christ should be the Son of the woman, and not of the man, because "that which is born of the flesh is flesh" (John 3:6). Had He been born of the flesh, and merely flesh, He would, naturally, by carnal generation, have inherited all the frailties and the *sins* and the infirmities that man has from his birth. He would have been conceived in sin and shaped in iniquity, even as the rest of us. Therefore He was not born of man, but the Holy Spirit overshadowed the virgin Mary and Christ stands as the one man, save one other, who came forth pure from His Maker's hands, who could ever say, "I am pure." Yes, and He could say far more than that other Adam could say concerning *his* purity, for He maintained His integrity and never let it go! And from His birth down to His death He knew no sin, neither was guile found in His mouth. Oh, marvelous sight! Let us stand and look at it. A child of a virgin, what a mixture!

There is the finite and the infinite; there is the mortal and the immortal, corruption and incorruption, the manhood and the Godhead, time married to eternity! There is God linked with a creature, the infinity of the august Maker come to tabernacle on this speck of earth—the vast unbounded One whom earth could not hold and the heavens cannot contain—lying in His mother's arms! He who fastened the pillars of the universe and riveted the nails of creation, hanging on a mortal breast, depending on a creature for nourishment! Oh, marvelous birth! Oh, miraculous conception! We stand and gaze and admire. Verily, angels may wish to look into a subject too dark for us to speak of! There we leave it—a virgin has conceived and borne a Son.

In this birth, moreover, having noticed the miraculous conception, we must notice, next, *the humble parentage*. It does not say, "A princess shall conceive and bear a Son," but a virgin. Her virginity was her highest honor; she had no other. True, she was of royal lineage; she could reckon David among her forefathers, and Solomon among those who stood in the tree of her genealogy. She was a woman not to be despised, albeit that I speak of humble parentage, for she was of the blood-royal of Judah. O babe, in Your veins there runs the blood of kings! The blood of an ancient monarchy found its way from Your heart all through the courses of Your body! You were born, not of mean parents, if we look at their ancient ancestry, for You are the Son of him who ruled the mightiest monarchy in his day, even

Solomon, and You are the descendant of one who devised in his heart to build a temple for the mighty God of Jacob!

Nor was Christ's mother, in point of intellect, an inferior woman. I take it that she had great strength of mind; otherwise she could not have composed so sweet a piece of poetry as that which is called the Virgin's Song, beginning, "My soul magnifies the Lord" (Luke 1:46). She is not a person to be despised. I would, this morning, especially utter my thoughts on one thing that I consider to be a fault among us Protestants. Because Roman Catholics pay too much respect to the virgin Mary, and offer prayer to her, we are too apt to speak of her in a slighting manner. She ought not to be placed under the ban of contempt, for she could truly sing, "Henceforth all generations will call me blessed" (1:48). I suppose Protestant generations are among the "all generations" who ought to call her blessed. Her name is Mary, and quaint George Herbert wrote an anagram upon it:

> *How well her name an army does present,*
> *In whom the Lord of hosts did pitch His tent.*

Though she was not a princess, yet her name, Mary, by interpretation, signifies a princess, and though she is not the queen of heaven, yet she has a right to be reckoned among the queens of earth. And though she is not the lady of our Lord, she does walk among the renowned and mighty women of scripture.

Yet Jesus Christ's birth was a humble one. Strange that the Lord of glory was not born in a palace! Princes, Christ owes you nothing! Princes, Christ is not your debtor! You did not swaddle Him, He was not wrapped in purple, and you had not prepared a golden cradle for Him to be rocked in! Queens, you did not dandle Him on your knees; He hung not at your breasts! And you mighty cities, which then were great and famous, your marble halls were not blessed with His little footsteps! He came out of a village, poor and despised, even Bethlehem! When there, He was not born in the governor's house, or in the mansion of the chief man, but in a manger! Tradition tells us that His manger was cut in solid rock—there was He laid and the oxen likely enough came to feed from the same manger, the hay and the fodder of which was His only bed. Oh, wondrous stoop of condescension, that our blessed Jesus should be girded with humility and stoop so low! Ah, if He stooped, why should He bend to such a lowly birth? And if He bowed, why should He submit, not simply to become the son of poor parents, but to be born in so miserable a place?

Let us take courage here. If Jesus Christ was born in a manger in a rock, why should He not come and live in our rocky hearts? If He was born in a stable, why should not the stable of our souls be made into a house for Him? If He was born in poverty, may not the poor in spirit expect that He will be their friend? If He thus endured degradation at the first, will He count it any dishonor to come to the very poorest and humblest of His creatures and tabernacle in the souls of His children? Oh no! We can gather a lesson of comfort from His humble parentage, and we can rejoice that not a queen, or an empress, but a humble woman became the mother of the Lord of glory!

We must make one more remark upon this birth of Christ before we pass on, and that remark will be concerning *a glorious birthday*. With all the humility that surrounded the birth of Christ, there was yet very much that was glorious, very much that was honorable. No other man ever had such a birthday as Jesus Christ had! Of whom had prophets and seers ever written as they wrote of Him? Whose name is engraved on so many tablets as His? Who had such a scroll of prophecy, all pointing to Him as Jesus Christ, the God-Man? Then remember, concerning His birth, when did God ever hang a fresh lamp in the sky to announce the birth of a Caesar? Caesars may come and they may die, but stars will never prophesy their birth! When did angels ever stoop from heaven and sing choral symphonies on the birth of a mighty man? No, all others are passed by. But look, in heaven there is a great light shining and a song is heard: "Glory to God in the highest, and on earth peace, goodwill toward men!" (Luke 2:14).

Christ's birth is not despicable, even if we consider the visitors who came around His cradle. Shepherds came first, and as an old divine, the shepherds did not lose their way, but the wise men have quaintly remarked it did! Shepherds came first, unguided and unfed, to Bethlehem. The wise men, directed by the star, came next. The representative men of the two bodies of mankind—the rich and the poor—knelt around the manger—and gold, and frankincense, and myrrh, and all manner of precious gifts were offered to the child who was the Prince of the kings of the earth, who in ancient times was ordained to sit upon the throne of His father, David, and in the wondrous future to rule all nations with His rod of iron!

"Behold, a virgin shall conceive and bear a Son." Thus have we spoken of the birth of Christ.

II. The second thing that we have to speak of is *the food of Christ*—"Curds and honey He shall eat, that He may know to refuse the evil and choose the good." Our translators were certainly very good scholars, and God gave them much wisdom so that they craned up our language to the majesty of the original, but here they were guilty of very great inconsistency. I do not see how butter and honey can make a child choose good and refuse evil. If it is so, I am sure butter and honey ought to go up greatly in price, for good men are very much required! But it does not say, in the original, "Butter and honey shall He eat, that He may know to refuse the evil, and choose the good," but "Butter and honey shall he eat, till he shall know how to refuse the evil, and choose the good" (Isa. 7:15 KJV). Better still, "Butter and honey shall He eat when He will know how to refuse the evil and choose the good."

We will take that translation and just try to make clear the meaning couched in the words. They should teach us, first, *Christ's proper humanity*. When He would convince His disciples that He was flesh and not spirit, He took a piece of a broiled fish and of a honeycomb, and ate as others did. "Handle Me," He said, "and see, for a spirit does not have flesh and bones as you see I have" (Luke 24:39). Some heretics taught, even a little after the death of Christ, that His body was a mere shadow, that He was not an actual, real man. But here we are told He ate butter and honey just as other men did. While other men were nourished with food, so was Jesus! He was very man as certainly as He was verily and eternally God. "Therefore, in all things He had to be made like His brethren, that He might be a merciful and faithful High Priest in things pertaining to God, to make propitiation for the sins of the people" (Heb. 2:17). Therefore we are told that He ate butter and honey to teach us that it was actually a real man who, afterward, died on Calvary.

The butter and honey teach us, again, that Christ was to be *born in times of peace*. Such products are not to be found in Judea in times of strife. The ravages of war sweep away all the fair fruits of industry; the unwatered pastures yield no grass, and therefore there could be no butter. The bees may make their hive in the lion's carcass and there may be honey there, but when the land is disturbed, who will go to gather the sweetness? How will the babe eat butter when its mother flees away, even in the wintertime, with the child clinging to her breast? In times of war, we have no choice of food. Then men eat whatever they can procure, and the supply is often very scanty.

Let us thank God that we live in the land of peace, and let us see a mystery in this text: that Christ was born in times of peace.

The temple of Janis was shut before the temple of heaven was opened! Before the King of peace came to the temple of Jerusalem, the horrid mouth of war was stopped! Mars had sheathed his sword and all was still. Augustus Caesar was emperor of the world, none other ruled it, and therefore wars had ceased, the earth was still, the leaves quivered not upon the trees of the field, the ocean of strife was undisturbed by a ripple, the hot winds of war blew not upon man to trouble him. All was peaceful and quiet! And then came the Prince of peace, who in later days will break the bow, cut the spear in sunder, and burn the chariot in the fire.

There is another thought here. He ate butter and honey when He knew how to refuse the evil and choose the good. This is to teach us *the precocity of Christ.* By that I mean that even when He was a child, even when He lived upon butter and honey, the food of children, He knew the evil from the good. It is, usually, not until children leave off the food of their infancy that they can discern good from evil in the fullest sense. It requires years to ripen the faculties, to develop the judgment, to give full play to the man, to *make* him a man. But Christ, even while He was a baby, even while He lived upon butter and honey, knew the evil from the good, refused the one, and chose the other. Oh, what a mighty intellect there was in that brain! While He was an infant, surely there must have been sparklings of genius from His eyes! The fire of intellect must have often lit up that brow! He was not an ordinary child. How would His mother talk about the wonderful things the little Prattler said? He played not as others did. He cared not to spend His time in idle amusements. His thoughts were lofty and wondrous. He understood mysteries, and when He went up to the temple in His early days, He was not found, like the other children, playing about the courts or the markets, but sitting among the doctors, both hearing and asking them questions! His was a mastermind. "No man ever spoke like this Man!" (John 7:46), so never child thought like this child. He was an astonishing one, the wonder and the marvel of all children, the Prince of children, and the God-Man even when He was a child! I think this is taught us in the words, "Curds and honey He shall eat, that He may know to refuse the evil and choose the good."

Perhaps it may seem somewhat playful, but before I close speaking upon this part of the subject, I must say how sweet it is to my soul to believe that as Christ lived upon butter and honey, surely *butter and honey drop from His lips.* Sweet are His words to our souls, more to be desired than honey or the honeycomb! Well might He eat butter whose words are smooth to the tried, whose utterances are like oil upon the waters of our sorrows! Well might He eat butter, who came to bind up the brokenhearted, and well did He live upon the fat of the land, who came to restore the earth to its old fertility and make all flesh soft with milk and honey, ah, honey in the heart.

> *Where can such sweetness be*
> *As I have tasted in Your love,*
> *As I have found in Thee?*

Your words, O Christ, are like honey! I, like a bee, have flown from flower to flower to gather sweets and concoct some precious essence that will be fragrant to me, but I have found honey drop from your lips, I have touched your mouth with my finger and put the honey to my lips, and my eyes have been enlightened, sweet Jesus! Every word of yours is precious to my soul—no honey can compare with you. Well did you eat butter and honey!

> *Your words, O Christ, are like honey! I, like a bee, have flown from flower to flower to gather sweets and concoct some precious essence that will be fragrant to me, but I have found honey drop from your lips.*

And perhaps I ought not to have forgotten to say that the effect of Christ's eating butter and honey was to show us that *He would not, in His lifetime, differ from other men* in His outward guise. Other prophets, when they came, were dressed in rough garments and were austere and solemn in manner. Christ came not so—He came to be a man among men, a feaster with those who feast, an eater of honey with eaters of honey. He differed from none, and therefore He was called a gluttonous man and a wine-bibber. Why did Christ do so? Why did He so commit Himself, as men said, though it was verily a slander? It was because He would have His disciples not regard meats and drinks, but despise these things and live as others do. It was because He would teach them that it is not that which goes *into* a man but that which comes out that defiles him! It is not what a man eats with temperance that does him injury; it is what a man *says* and *thinks*. It is not abstaining from meat; it is not the carnal ordinance of "Do not touch, do not taste, do not handle" (Col. 2:21) that makes the fundamentals of our religion, albeit it may be good addenda thereunto. Butter and honey Christ ate, and butter and honey may His people eat! No, whatever God in His providence gives to them, that is to be the food of the children of Christ.

III. Now we come to close with *the name of Christ*—"and shall call His name Immanuel."

I hoped, dear friends, that I would have my voice this morning, that I might talk about my Master's name. I hoped to be allowed to drive along in my swift chariot, but as the wheels are taken off, I must be content to go as I can. We sometimes creep when we cannot go and go when we cannot run, but oh, here is a sweet name to close up with: "She shall call His name Immanuel." Others in the olden time called their children by names that had meaning in them. They did not give them the names of eminent persons whom they would very likely grow up to hate, and wish they had never heard of! They had names full of meaning that recorded some circumstance of their birth. There was Cain. "I have gotten a man from the LORD" (Gen. 4:1 KJV), said his mother, and she called him Cain, that is, "gotten" or "acquired." There was Seth, which means "appointed," for his mother said, "for God has appointed another seed for me instead of Abel, whom Cain killed" (4:25). Noah means "rest" or "comfort." Ishmael was so called by his mother because God had heard her. Isaac was called "laughter," because he brought laughter to Abraham's home. Jacob was called the supplanter, or the crafty one, because he would supplant his brother. We might point out many similar instances. Perhaps this custom was a good one among the Hebrews, though the peculiar formation of our language might not allow us to do the same, except in a certain measure.

We see therefore that the virgin Mary called her Son Immanuel that there might be *a meaning in His name*, "God with us." My soul, ring these words again, "God with us." Oh, it is one of the bells of heaven! Let us strike it yet again, "God with us." Oh, it is a stray note from the sonnets of paradise! "God with us." Oh, it is the lisping of a seraph! "God with us." Oh, it is one of the notes of the singing of Jehovah when He rejoices over His church with singing! "God with us." Tell it, tell it, tell it. This is the name of Him who is born today—"Hark! the herald angels sing."

This is His name, "God with us." God with us, by His incarnation, for the august Creator of the world did walk upon this globe! He who made ten thousand orbs, each of them mightier and vaster than this earth, became the inhabitant of this tiny atom! He who was from everlasting to everlasting came to this world of time and stood upon the narrow neck of land between the two unbounded seas! "God with us." He has not lost that name. Jesus had that name on earth, and He has it now in heaven! He is *now* "God with us."

Believer, He is God with you to protect you! You are not alone, because the Savior is with you! Put me in the desert, where vegetation grows not; I can still say, "God with us." Put me on the wild ocean and let my ship dance madly on the waves, and I would still say, "Immanuel, God with us." Mount me on the sunbeam and let me fly beyond the western sea; still I would say, "God with us." Let my body dive down into the depths of the ocean and let me hide in its caverns. Still I could, as a child of God, say, "God with us." Yes, and in the grave, sleeping there in corruption, still I can see the footmarks of Jesus! He trod the path of all His people, and His name is still "God with us."

But if you would know this name most sweetly, you must *know it by the teaching of the Holy Spirit*. Has God been with us this morning? What is the use of coming to chapel if God is not there? We might as well be at home if we have no visits of Jesus Christ, and certainly we may come, and come, and come as regularly as that door turns on its hinges unless it is "God with us," by the influence of the Holy Spirit! Unless the Holy Spirit takes the things of Christ and applies them to our heart, it is *not* "God with us." Otherwise, God is a consuming fire. It is "God with us" that I love.

Till God in human flesh I see,
My thoughts no comfort find.

Now ask yourselves, do you know what "God with us" means? Has it been God with you in your tribulations, by the Holy Spirit's comforting influence? Has it been God with you in searching the scriptures? Has the Holy Spirit shone upon the Word? Has it been God with you in conviction, bringing you to Sinai? Has it been God with you in comforting you, by bringing you, again, to Calvary? Do you know the full meaning of that name Immanuel, "God with us"? No. He who knows it best knows little of it! Alas, he who knows it not at all is ignorant indeed, so ignorant that his ignorance is not bliss but will be his damnation! Oh, may God teach you the meaning of that name Immanuel, "God with us"!

Now let us close. Immanuel—it is wisdom's mystery, "God with us." Sages look at it and wonder. Angels desire to see it. The plumb line of reason cannot reach halfway into its depths. The eagle wings of science cannot fly so high, and the piercing eye of the vulture of research cannot see it! "God with us." It is hell's terror! Satan trembles at the sound of it. His legions fly apace; the black-winged dragon of the pit quails before it! Let Satan come to you suddenly and do you but whisper that word, "God with us," and back he falls, confounded and confused! Satan trembles when he hears that name, "God with us." It is the laborer's strength. How could he preach the gospel, how could he bend his knees in prayer, how could the missionary go into foreign lands, how could the martyr stand at the stake, how could the confessor acknowledge his Master, how could men labor if that one word were taken away? "God with us" is the sufferer's comfort, is the balm of his woe, is the alleviation of his misery, is the sleep that God gives to His beloved, is their rest after exertion and toil.

Ah, and to finish, "God with us" is eternity's sonnet, is heaven's hallelujah, is the shout of the glorified, is the song of the redeemed, is the chorus of angels, and is the everlasting oratorio of the great orchestra of the sky! "God with us":

> *Hail you, Immanuel, all divine,*
> *In you your Father's glories shine!*
> *You brightest, sweetest, fairest One,*
> *That eyes have seen or angels known.*

Now, a happy Christmas to you all, and it *will* be a happy Christmas if you have God with you! I will say nothing, today, against festivities on this great birthday of Christ. I hold that perhaps it is not right to have the birthday celebrated, but we will never be among those who think it as much a duty to celebrate it the wrong way as others the right! But we will, tomorrow, think of Christ's birthday. We will be obliged to do it, I am sure, however sturdily we may hold to our rough Puritanism. "Therefore let us keep the feast, not with old leaven, nor with the leaven of malice and wickedness, but with the unleavened bread of sincerity and truth" (1 Cor. 5:8). Do not feast as if you wished to keep the festival of Bacchus! Do not live, tomorrow, as if you adored some heathen divinity. Feast, Christians, feast! You have a right to feast. Go to the house of feasting tomorrow! Celebrate your Savior's birth. Do not be ashamed to be glad—you have a right to be happy. Solomon says, "Go, eat your bread with joy, and drink your wine with a merry heart; for God has already accepted your works. Let your garments always be white, and let your head lack no oil" (Eccles. 9:7–8).

> *Religion never was designed*
> *To make our pleasures less.*

Remember that your Master ate butter and honey. Go your way, rejoice tomorrow, but in your feasting, think of the man in Bethlehem. Let Him have a place in your hearts, give Him the glory, think of the virgin who conceived Him. But think, most of all, of the man born, the child given! I finish by again saying, "A happy Christmas to you all!"

FOR FURTHER THOUGHT

1. *According to Philippians 2:6, what was Christ's position before He was born of Mary? What did he become after His birth? (See verse 7.)*
2. *First Timothy 2:5 says, "There is one God and one Mediator between God and men." What does this verse say is the outstanding aspect of the Mediator?*
3. *The name Immanuel translates as "God with us" (Matt. 1:23). How does Colossians 1:15 interpret this name?*

"My God, My God, Why Have You Forsaken Me?"

And about the ninth hour Jesus cried out with a loud voice,
saying, "Eli, Eli, lama sabachthani?" that is, "My God,
My God, why have You forsaken Me?"
MATTHEW 27:46

THERE was darkness over all the land to the ninth hour, and this cry came out of that darkness! Expect not to see through its every word, as though it came from on high as a beam from the unclouded sun of righteousness. There is light in it—bright, flashing light—but there is a center of impenetrable gloom where the soul is ready to faint because of the terrible darkness. Our Lord was then in the darkest part of His way. He had trodden the winepress now for hours and the work was almost finished. He had reached the culminating point of His anguish. This is His dolorous lament from the lowest pit of misery: "My God, My God, why have You forsaken Me?"

I do not think that the records of time, or even of eternity, contain a sentence more full of anguish. Here the wormwood, the gall, and all the other bitterness are outdone. Here you may look as into a vast abyss—and though you strain your eyes and gaze till sight fails you, yet you perceive no bottom—it is measureless, unfathomable, inconceivable. This anguish of the Savior on your behalf and mine is no more to be measured and weighed than the sin that needed it or the love that endured it. We will adore where we cannot comprehend.

I have chosen this subject that it may help the children of God to understand a little of their infinite obligations to their redeeming Lord. You will measure the height of His love, if the depth of His grief can measure it, if that can ever be known. See with what a price He has redeemed us from the curse of the law! As you see this, say to yourselves, what manner of people ought we to be? What measure of love ought we to return to One who bore the utmost penalty that we might be delivered from the wrath to come? I do not profess that I can dive *into* this deep. I will only venture to the edge of the precipice and bid you look down and pray the Spirit of God to concentrate your mind upon this lamentation of our dying Lord as it rises up through the thick darkness: "My God, My God, why have You forsaken Me?"

Our first subject of thought will be *the fact*, or what He suffered: God had forsaken Him. Second, we will note *the inquiry*, or why He suffered. This word *why* is the edge of the text. "Why have You forsaken Me?" Then, third, we will consider *the answer*, or what came of His suffering. The answer flowed softly into the soul of the Lord Jesus without the need of words, for He ceased from His anguish with the triumphant shout of "It is finished." His work was finished, and His bearing of desertion was a chief part of the work He had undertaken for our sake.

I. By the help of the Holy Spirit, let us first dwell upon *the fact*, or what our Lord suffered. God had forsaken Him. Grief of mind is harder to bear than pain of body. You can pluck up courage and endure the pang of sickness and pain so long as the spirit is hale and brave. But if the soul itself is touched and the mind becomes diseased with anguish, then every pain is increased in severity and there is nothing with which to sustain it. Spiritual sorrows are the worst of mental miseries.

A man may bear great depression of spirit about worldly matters if he feels that he has his God to go to. He is cast down, but not in despair. Like David he dialogues with himself and he inquires, "Why are you cast down, O my soul? And why are you disquieted within me? Hope in God, for I shall yet praise Him for the help of His countenance" (Ps. 42:5). But if the Lord is once withdrawn, if the comfortable light of His presence is shadowed even for an *hour*, there is a torment within the breast that I can only liken to the prelude of hell. This is the greatest of all weights that can press upon the heart. This made the psalmist plead, "Do not hide Your face from me; do not turn Your servant away in anger" (Ps. 27:9).

We can bear a bleeding body and even a wounded spirit, but a soul conscious of desertion by God is beyond conception. It is unendurable! When He holds back the face of His throne and spreads His cloud upon it, who can endure the darkness? This voice out of the belly of hell marks the lowest depth of the Savior's grief. *The desertion was real.* Though under some aspects our Lord could say the Father was with Him, yet was it solemnly true that God did forsake Him. It was not a failure of faith on His part that led Him to imagine what was not actual fact. Our faith fails us and then we think that God has forsaken us—but our Lord's faith did not, for a moment, falter, for He says twice, "*My* God, *My* God."

Oh, the mighty double grip of His unhesitating faith! He seems to say, "Even if you have forsaken me, I have not forsaken you." Faith triumphs and there is no sign of any faintness of heart toward the living God. Yet, strong as is His faith, He feels that God has withdrawn His comfortable fellowship, and He shivers under the terrible deprivation. It was no fancy or delirium of mind caused by His weakness of body, the heat of the fever, the depression of His spirit, or the near approach of death. He was clear of mind even to this last. He bore up under pain, loss of blood, scorn, thirst, and desolation—making no complaint of the cross, the nails, or the scoffing.

> *T*he testimony of the church has always been that while the Lord has permitted His saints to suffer in body, He has so divinely sustained their spirits that they have been more than conquerors and have treated their sufferings as light afflictions!

We read not in the Gospels of anything more than the natural cry of weakness, "I thirst!" (John 19:28). All the tortures of His body He endured in silence. But when it came to being forsaken of God, *then* His great heart burst out into its "lama sabachthani?" His one moan is concerning His God! It is not, "Why has Peter forsaken me? Why has Judas betrayed me?" These were sharp griefs, but this is the sharpest. This stroke has cut Him to the quick—"My God, My God, why have You forsaken Me?"

It was no phantom of the gloom. It was a real absence that He mourned. This was *a very remarkable desertion.* It is not the way of God to leave either His sons or His servants. His saints, when they come to die in their great weakness and pain, find Him near. They are made to sing because of the presence of God—"Yea, though I walk through the valley of the shadow of death, I will fear no evil: for You are with me." Dying saints have clear visions of the living God! Our observation has taught us that if the Lord is away at other times, He is *never* absent from His people in the article of death or in the furnace of affliction.

Concerning the three holy children, we do not read that the Lord was ever visibly with them till they walked the fires of Nebuchadnezzar's furnace—but then and there the Lord met with them. Yes, beloved, it is God's way and habit to keep company with His afflicted people. And yet He forsook His Son in the hour of His tribulation! How usual it is to see the Lord with His faithful witnesses when resisting even to blood! Read the *Book of Martyrs* and I care not whether you study the former or the later persecutions; you will find them all lit up with the evident presence of the Lord with His witnesses.

Did the Lord ever fail to support a martyr at the stake? Did He ever forsake one of His testifiers upon the scaffold? The testimony of the church has always been that while the Lord has permitted His saints to suffer in body, He has so divinely sustained their spirits that they have been more than conquerors and have treated their sufferings as light afflictions! The fire has not been a bed of roses, but it has been a chariot of victory! The sword is sharp and death is bitter—but the love of Christ is sweet, and to die for Him has been turned into glory! No, it is not God's way to forsake His champions or to leave even the least of His children in their hour of trial.

As to our Lord, this forsaking was *singular*. Did His Father ever leave Him before? Will you read the four evangelists through and find any previous instance in which He complains of His Father for having forsaken Him? No. He said, "I know that You always hear Me" (John 11:42). He lived in constant touch with God. His fellowship with the Father was always near and dear and clear. But now, for the first time, He cries, "Why have You forsaken Me?" It was very remarkable! It was a riddle only to be solved by the fact that He loved us and gave Himself for us and in the execution of His loving purpose came even to this sorrow of mourning the absence of His God.

This forsaking was *very terrible*. Who can fully tell what it is to be forsaken of God? We can only form a guess by what we have ourselves felt under temporary and partial desertion. God has never left us altogether, for He has expressly said, "I will never leave you nor forsake you" (Heb. 13:5). Yet we have sometimes felt as if He had cast us off. We have cried, "Oh, that I knew where I might find Him!" The clear shining rays of His love have been withdrawn. Thus we are able to form some little idea of how the Savior felt when His God had forsaken Him.

The mind of Jesus was left to dwell upon one dark subject, and no cheering theme consoled Him. It was the hour in which He was made to stand before God as consciously the sin-bearer according to that ancient prophecy, "He shall bear their iniquities" (Isa. 53:11). Then was it true, "He made Him who knew no sin to be sin for us" (2 Cor. 5:21). Peter puts it, "[He] Himself bore our sins in His own body on the tree" (1 Pet. 2:24). Sin was everywhere around and about Christ. He had no sin of His own, but the Lord had "laid on Him the iniquity of us all" (Isa. 53:6). He had no strength given Him from on high, no secret oil and wine poured into His wounds. He was simply the Lamb of God who takes away the sin of the world. Therefore He must feel the weight of sin and the turning away of that sacred face that cannot look thereon.

His Father, at that time, gave Him no open acknowledgment. On certain other occasions a voice had been heard, saying, "This is My beloved Son, in whom I am well pleased" (Matt. 3:17). But now, when such a testimony seemed most of all required, the oracle was not there! He was hung up as an accursed thing upon the cross, for He was made a "curse for us (for it is written, 'Cursed is everyone who hangs on a tree')" (Gal. 3:13).

And the Lord His God did not own Him before men. If it had pleased the Father, He might have sent Him twelve legions of angels—but not an angel came after Christ had left Gethsemane. His despisers might spit in His face, but no swift seraph came to avenge the indignity. They might bind Him and scourge Him, but none of the entire heavenly host would interpose to screen His shoulders from the lash. They might fasten him to the tree with nails and lift Him up and scoff at Him, but no cohort of ministering spirits hastened to drive back the rabble and release the Prince of life. No, He appeared to be forsaken, "smitten by God, and afflicted" (Isa. 53:4), delivered into the hands of cruel men whose wicked hands worked Him misery without stint. Well might He ask, "My God, My God, why have You forsaken Me?"

But this was not all. His Father now dried up that sacred stream of peaceful communion and loving fellowship that had flowed, up to now, throughout His whole earthly life. He said Himself, as you remember, "You will be scattered, each to his own, and will leave Me alone. And yet I am not alone, because the Father is with Me" (John 16:32). Here was His constant comfort—but all comfort from this source was to be withdrawn. The divine Spirit did not minister to His human spirit. No communications with His

Father's love poured into His heart. It was not possible that the judge should smile upon one who represented the prisoner at the bar.

Our Lord's *faith* did not fail Him, as I have already shown you, for He said, "My God, My God," yet no sensible supports were given to His heart and no comforts were poured into His mind. One writer declares that Jesus did not taste of divine wrath but only suffered a withdrawal of divine fellowship. What is the difference? Whether God withdraws heat or creates cold is all the same! He was not smiled upon nor allowed to feel that He was near to God—and this, to His tender spirit, was grief of the keenest order!

> *Our Lord's heart and all His nature were, morally and spiritually, so delicately formed, so sensitive, so tender, that to be without God was to Him a grief that could not be weighed.*

A certain saint once said that in his sorrow he had from God "that which was meet, but not that which was sweet." Our Lord suffered to the extreme point of deprivation. He had not the light that makes existence to be life and life to be a blessing. You who know, in your degree, what it is to lose the conscious presence and love of God, you can faintly guess what the sorrow of the Savior was now that He felt He had been forsaken of His God. "If the foundations are destroyed, what can the righteous do?" (Ps. 11:3). To our Lord, the Father's love was the foundation of everything, and when that was gone, all was gone. Nothing remained, within, without, above, when His own God, the God of His entire confidence, turned from Him.

Yes, God in very deed forsook our Savior. To be forsaken of God was *much more a source of anguish to Jesus than it would be to us.* "Oh," you say, "how is that?" I answer, because He was perfectly holy. A rupture between a perfectly holy being and the thrice-holy God must be in the highest degree strange, abnormal, perplexing, and painful. If any man here who is not at peace with God could only know His true condition, he would swoon with fright! If you unforgiven ones only knew where you are and what you are at this moment, in the sight of God, you would never smile again till you were reconciled to Him. Alas, we are insensible—hardened by the deceitfulness of sin—and therefore we do not feel our true condition!

His perfect holiness made it to our Lord a dreadful calamity to be forsaken of the thrice-holy God. I remember, also, that our blessed Lord had lived in unbroken fellowship with God, and to be forsaken was a new grief to Him. He had never known what the dark was till then—His life had been lived in the light of God. Think, dear child of God, if you had always dwelt in full communion with God, your days would have been as the days of heaven upon earth! And how cold it would strike your heart to find yourself in the darkness of desertion. If you can conceive such a thing as happening to a *perfect* man, you can see why, to our Well Beloved, it was a special trial.

Remember, He had enjoyed fellowship with God more richly, as well as more constantly, than any of us. His fellowship with the Father was of the highest, deepest, fullest order—and what must the loss of it have been? We lose but drops when we lose our joyful experience of heavenly fellowship, and yet the loss is killing! But to our Lord Jesus Christ the sea was dried up—I mean His sea of fellowship with the infinite God. Do not forget that He was such a one that to Him to be without God must have been an overwhelming calamity. In every part He was perfect and in every part fitted for communion with God to a supreme degree.

A sinful man has an awful need of God, but he does not know it and therefore he does not feel that hunger and thirst after God that would come upon a perfect man could he be deprived of God. The very perfection of his nature renders it inevitable that the holy man must either be in communion with God or be desolate. Imagine a stray angel—a seraph who has lost his God! Conceive him to be perfect in holiness and yet to have fallen into a condition in which he cannot find his God! I cannot picture him! Perhaps Milton might have done so. He is sinless and trustful, and yet he has an overpowering feeling that God is absent from him.

He has drifted into the nowhere—the unimaginable region behind the back of God. I think I hear the wailing of the cherub, "My God, my God, my God, where are you?" What a sorrow for one of the sons of the morning! But here we have the lament of a being far more capable of fellowship with the Godhead! In proportion as He is more fitted to receive the love of the great Father, in that proportion is His pining after it the more intense. As a Son, He is abler to commune with God than ever a servant angel could be, and now that He is forsaken of God, the void within is greater and the anguish more bitter.

Our Lord's heart and all His nature were, morally and spiritually, so delicately formed, so sensitive, so tender, that to be without God was to Him a grief that could not be weighed. I see Him in the text bearing desertion and yet I perceive that He cannot bear it. I know not how to express my meaning except by such a paradox. He cannot endure to be without God. He had surrendered Himself to be left of God, as the representative of sinners must be, but His pure and holy nature, after three hours of silence, finds the position unendurable to love and purity! And breaking forth from it, now that the hour was over, He exclaims, "Why have You forsaken Me?"

He quarrels not with the suffering, but He cannot abide in the position that caused it. He seems as if He must end the ordeal—not because of the pain, but because of the moral shock! We have here the repetition after His passion of that loathing that He felt before it, when He cried, "If it is possible, let this cup pass from Me; nevertheless, not as I will, but as You will" (Matt. 26:39). "My God, My God, why have You forsaken Me?" is the holiness of Christ amazed at the position of substitute for guilty men!

There, friends. I have done my best, but I seem to myself to have been prattling like a little child talking about something infinitely above me. So I leave the solemn fact that our Lord Jesus was on the cross, forsaken of His God.

II. This brings us to consider *the inquiry*, or *why* He suffered. Note carefully this cry: "My God, My God, why have You forsaken Me?" It is pure anguish, undiluted agony, that cries like this, but it is the agony of a godly soul—for only a man of that order would have used such an expression.

Let us learn from it useful lessons. This cry is taken from "the book." Does it not show our Lord's love of the sacred volume, that when He felt His sharpest grief, He turned to the scripture to find a fit utterance for it? Here we have the opening sentence of the twenty-second psalm. Oh, that we may so love the inspired Word that we may not only sing to its score but even weep to its music! Note, again, that our Lord's lament is an address to *God*. The godly, in their anguish, turn to the hand that smites them.

The Savior's outcry is not *against* God, but *to* God. "My God, My God." He makes a double effort to draw near. True Sonship is here! The Child in the dark is crying after His Father. "My God, My God." Both the Bible and prayer were dear to Jesus in His agony. Still, observe it is a faith-cry, for though it asks, "Why have You forsaken Me?" it first says, twice, "My God, My God." The grip of appropriation is in the word *my*. But the reverence of humility is in the word *God*. It is, "My *God*, my *God*, you are ever God to me, and I a poor creature. I do not quarrel with you. Your rights are unquestioned, for you are my God. You can do as you will and I yield to your sacred sovereignty. I kiss the hand that smites me, and with all my heart I cry, 'My God, My God.'"

When you are delirious with pain, think of your Bible. When your mind wonders, let it roam toward the mercy seat. And when your heart and your flesh fail, still live by faith and still cry, "My God, my God." Let us come close to the inquiry. It looked to me, at first sight, like a question as of One distraught, driven from the balance of His mind—not unreasonable, but too much reasoning and therefore tossed about. "Why have You forsaken Me?" Did not Jesus know? Did He not know why He was forsaken? He knew it most distinctly, and yet His *manhood*, while it was being crushed, pounded, and dissolved, seemed as though it could not understand the reason for so great a grief.

He must be forsaken—but could there be a sufficient cause for so sickening a sorrow? The cup must be bitter—but why this most nauseous of ingredients? I tremble lest I say what I ought not to say. I have said it and I think there is truth—the Man of Sorrows was overborne with horror! At that moment the finite soul of the man Christ Jesus came into awful contact with the infinite justice of God! The one mediator between God and man, the man Christ Jesus, beheld the holiness of God in arms against the sin of man whose nature He had espoused.

God was for Him and with Him in a certain unquestionable sense, but for the time—so far as His feelings went—God was against Him and necessarily withdrawn from Him. It is not surprising that the holy soul of Christ should shudder at finding itself brought into painful contact with the infinite justice of God, even though its design was only to vindicate that justice and glorify the lawgiver. Our Lord could now say, "All Your waves and billows have gone over me" (Ps. 42:7), and therefore He uses language that is all too hot with anguish to be dissected by the cold hand of a logical criticism.

Grief has small regard for the laws of the grammarian. Even the holiest, when in extreme agony, though they cannot speak otherwise than according to purity and truth, yet use a language of their own that only the ear of sympathy can fully receive. I see not all that is here, but what I can see I am not able to put in words for you. I think I see in the expression *submission and resolve*. Our Lord does not draw back. There is a forward movement in the question. They who quit a business ask no more questions about it.

He does not ask that the forsaking may end prematurely; He would only understand anew its meaning. He does not shrink, but dedicates Himself anew to God by speaking the words "My God, My God," and by seeking to review the ground and reason of that anguish that He is resolute to bear even to the bitter end.

He would gladly feel anew the motive that has sustained Him and must sustain Him to the end. The cry sounds to me like deep submission and strong resolve, pleading with God. Do you not think that the amazement of our Lord, when He was "made sin for us" (2 Cor. 5:21), led Him thus to cry out? For such a sacred and pure being to be made a sin offering was an amazing experience! Sin was laid on Him and He was treated as if He had been guilty, though He had personally *never sinned.*

And now the infinite horror of rebellion against the most holy God fills His holy soul, the unrighteousness of sin breaks His heart, and He starts back from it, crying, "My God, My God, why have You forsaken Me?" Why must I bear the dread result of conduct I so much abhor? Do you not see, moreover, there was here a glance at His eternal purpose and at His secret source of joy? That *why* is the silver lining of the dark cloud, and our Lord looked wishfully at it. He knew that the desertion was necessary in order that He might save the guilty, and He had an eye to that salvation as His comfort.

He is not forsaken needlessly, nor without a worthy design. The design is in itself so dear to His heart that He yields to the passing evil, even though that evil is like death to Him. He looks at that *why,* and through that narrow window the light of heaven comes streaming into His darkened life! "My God, My God, why have You forsaken Me?" Surely our Lord dwelt on that *why,* that we might also turn our eyes that way. He would have us see the why and the why of His grief. He would have us mark the gracious motive for its endurance. Think much of all your Lord suffered, but do not overlook the *reason* for it. If you cannot always understand how this or that grief worked toward the great end of the whole passion, yet believe that it has its share in the grand *why.* Make a life-study of that bitter but blessed question, "Why have You forsaken Me?"

Thus the Savior raises an inquiry not so much for Himself as for *us*—and not so much because of any despair within *His* heart as because of a hope and a joy set before Him that were wells of comfort to Him in His wilderness of woe. Think, for a moment, that the Lord God, in the broadest and most unreserved sense, could never, in very deed, have forsaken His most obedient Son. He was ever with Him in the grand design of salvation. Toward the Lord Jesus, personally, God Himself, personally, must ever have stood on terms of infinite love. Truly the Only Begotten was never lovelier to the Father than when He was obedient to death, even the death of the cross!

> *or such a sacred and pure being to be made a sin offering was an amazing experience! Sin was laid on Him and He was treated as if He had been guilty, though He had personally never sinned.*

But we must look upon God here as the judge of all the earth, and we must look upon the Lord Jesus in His official capacity as the surety of the covenant and the sacrifice for sin. The great judge of all cannot smile upon Him who has become the substitute for the guilty. Sin is loathed of God, and if, in order for its removal, His own Son is made to bear it, yet, as sin, it is still loathsome and He who bears it cannot be in happy communion with God! This was the dread necessity of expiation—but in the *essence* of things the love of the great Father to His Son never ceased, nor ever knew a diminution. Restrained in its flow it must be, but lessened at its fountainhead it could not be. Therefore wonder not at the question, "Why have You forsaken Me?"

III. Hoping to be guided by the Holy Spirit, I am coming to *the answer* concerning which I can only use the few minutes that remain to me. "My God, My God, why have You forsaken Me?" What is the outcome of this suffering? What was the reason for it? Our Savior could answer His own question. If for a moment His manhood was perplexed, yet His mind soon came to clear apprehension, for He said, "It is finished." And as I have already said, He then referred to the work that in His lonely agony He had been performing.

Why, then, did God forsake His Son? I cannot conceive any other answer than this: *He stood in our place.* There was no reason in Christ why the Father should forsake Him—He was *perfect* and His life was without spot. God never acts without reason, and since there were no reasons in the character and person of the Lord Jesus why His Father should forsake Him, we must look elsewhere. I do not know how others answer the question. I can only answer it in this one way:

All the griefs He felt were ours,
Ours were the woes He bore.
Pang not His own, His spotless soul
With bitter anguish bore.

We held Him as condemned of heaven,
An outcast from His God,
While for our sins He groaned, He bled,
Beneath His Father's rod.

He bore the sinner's sin and He had to be treated, therefore, as though He were a sinner, though sinner He could never be! With His own full consent He suffered as though He had committed the transgressions that were laid on Him. Our sin and His taking it upon Himself are the answer to the question, "Why have You forsaken Me?"

In this case we now see that *His obedience was perfect.* He came into the world to obey the Father, and He rendered that obedience to the very uttermost. The spirit of obedience could go no further than for one who feels forsaken of God still to cling to Him in solemn, avowed allegiance; still declaring before a mocking multitude His confidence in the afflicting God! It is noble to cry, "My God, my God," when one is asking, "Why have you forsaken me?" How much further can obedience go? I see nothing beyond it. The soldier at the gate of Pompeii, remaining at his post as sentry when the shower of burning ashes was falling, was not truer to his trust than He who adheres to a forsaking God with loyalty of hope.

Our Lord's suffering in this particular form was appropriate and necessary. It would not have sufficed for our Lord merely to have been pained in body, nor even to have been grieved in mind in other ways. He must suffer in this particular way. He must feel forsaken of God because *this* is the necessary consequence of sin. For a man to be forsaken of God is the penalty that naturally and inevitably follows upon his breaking his relationship with God. What is death? What was the death that was threatened to Adam? "In the day that you eat of it you shall surely die" (Gen. 2:17). Is death annihilation? Was Adam annihilated that day?

Assuredly not! He lived many a year afterward. But in the day in which he ate of the forbidden fruit, he died by being *separated* from God. The separation of the soul from God is *spiritual* death, just as the separation of the soul from the body is *natural* death. The sacrifice for sin must be put in the place of separation and must bow to the penalty of death. By this placing of the great sacrifice under forsaking and death, it would be seen by all creatures throughout the universe that God cannot have fellowship with sin. If even the Holy One, who stood as the just for the unjust, found God forsaking Him—what must the doom of the actual sinner be? Sin is evidently always, in every case, a dividing influence, putting even the Christ Himself, as a sin-bearer, in the place of distance.

This was necessary for another reason—there could have been no laying on of suffering for sin without the forsaking of the vicarious sacrifice by the Lord God. So long as the smile of God rests on the man, the law is not afflicting him. The approving look of the great judge cannot fall upon a man who is viewed as standing in the place of the guilty. Christ suffered not only *from* sin, but *for* sin. If God will cheer and sustain Him, He is not suffering for sin. The judge is not inflicting suffering for sin if He is manifestly encouraging the smitten one. There could have been no vicarious suffering on the part of Christ for human guilt if He had continued, consciously, to enjoy the full sunshine of the Father's presence. It was essential to being a victim in our place that He should cry, "My God, My God, why have You forsaken Me?"

Beloved, see how marvelously, in the person of Christ, the Lord our God has vindicated His law? If to make His law glorious He had said, "These multitudes of men have broken my law, and therefore they will perish," the law would have been terribly magnified. But instead, He says, "Here is my only begotten Son, my other self. He takes on Himself the nature of these rebellious creatures and He consents that I should lay on Him the load of their iniquity and visit in His person the offenses that might have been punished in the persons of all these multitudes of men, and I will have it so."

When Jesus bows His head to the stroke of the law—when He submissively consents that His Father will turn away His face from Him—then myriads of worlds are astonished at the perfect holiness and stern justice of the lawgiver! There are, probably, worlds innumerable throughout the boundless creation of God, and all these will see, in the death of God's dear Son, a declaration of His determination never to allow sin to be trifled with! If His own Son is brought before Him, bearing the sin of others upon Him, He will hide His face from Him as well as from the actually guilty. In God infinite love shines over all—but it does not eclipse His absolute justice any more than His justice is permitted to destroy His love. God has all perfections in Perfection, and in Christ Jesus we see the reflection of them.

> *I* know that I deserve the deepest hell at the hand of God's vengeance, but I am not afraid! He will never forsake me, for He forsook His Son on my behalf.

Beloved, this is a wonderful theme! Oh, that I had a tongue worthy of this subject! But who could ever reach the height of this great argument? Once more, when inquiring, "Why did Jesus suffer to be forsaken of the Father?" we see the fact that *the captain of our salvation was thus made perfect through suffering*. Every part of the road has been traversed by our Lord's own feet. Suppose, beloved, the Lord Jesus had never been thus forsaken, then one of His disciples might have been called to that sharp endurance and the Lord Jesus could not have sympathized with him in it.

He would turn to his leader and captain and say to Him, "Did You, my Lord, ever feel this darkness?" Then the Lord Jesus would answer, "No. This is a descent such as I never made." What a dreadful lack would the tried one have felt! For the servant to bear a grief his Master never knew would be sad indeed. There would have been a wound for which there was no ointment; a pain for which there was no balm. But it is not so now. In all their affliction, He was afflicted. He "was in all points tempted as we are, yet without sin" (Heb. 4:15). Whereas we greatly rejoice at this time and as often as we are cast down, underneath us is the deep experience of our forsaken Lord.

I am done when I have said three things. The first is, you and I who are believers in the Lord Jesus Christ and are resting in Him alone for salvation, *let us lean hard*. Let us bear all our weight on our Lord. He will bear the full weight of all our sin and care. As to my sin, I hear its harsh accusations no more when I hear Jesus cry, "Why have You forsaken Me?" I know that I deserve the deepest hell at the hand of God's vengeance, but I am not afraid! He will never forsake me, for He *forsook His Son on my behalf*. I will not suffer for my sin, for Jesus has suffered to the full in my place—yes, suffered so far as to cry, "My God, My God, why have You forsaken Me?" Behind this brazen wall of substitution a sinner is safe! These "munitions of rock" guard all believers and they may rest secure. The rock is cleft for me; I hide in its rifts and no harm can reach me. You have a full atonement, a great sacrifice, a glorious vindication of the law—you can rest at peace, all you who put your trust in Jesus.

Next, if ever, from now on, in our lives we should think that God has deserted us, *let us learn from our Lord's example how to behave ourselves.* If God has left you, do not shut up your Bible—no, open it as your Lord did, and find a text that will suit you. If God has left you, or you think so, do not give up prayer! No, pray as your Lord did and be more earnest than ever. If you think God has forsaken you, do not give up your faith in Him, but like your Lord cry, "My God, my God," again and again! If you have had one anchor before, cast out two anchors now and double the hold of your faith. If you cannot call Jehovah Father, as was Christ's habit, yet call Him your God.

Let the personal pronouns take their hold—"My God, my God." Let nothing drive you from your faith. Still hold on to Jesus, sink or swim. As for me, if ever I am lost, it will be at the foot of the cross! To this pass have I come, that if I never see the face of God with acceptance, yet I will believe that He will be faithful to His Son and true to the covenant sealed by oaths and blood. He who believes in Jesus has everlasting life—there I cling, like the limpet to the rock. There is but one gate of heaven, and even if I may not enter it, I will cling to the posts of its door! What am I saying? I will enter in, for that gate was never shut against a soul who accepted Jesus! And Jesus says, "The one who comes to Me I will by no means cast out" (John 6:37).

The last of the three points is this: *Let us abhor the sin that brought such agony upon our beloved Lord.* What an accursed thing is sin that crucified the Lord Jesus! Do you laugh at it? Will you go and spend an evening to see a mimic performance of it? Do you roll sin under your tongue as a sweet morsel and then come to God's house on the Lord's day morning and think to worship Him? Worship Him? Worship Him with sin indulged in your breast? Worship Him with sin loved and pampered in your life? O sirs, if I had a dear brother who had been murdered, what would you think of me if I valued the knife that had been crimsoned with his blood—if I made a friend of the murderer and daily consorted with the assassin who drove the dagger into my brother's heart?

Surely I, too, must be an accomplice in the crime! Sin murdered Christ—

will you be a friend to it? Sin pierced the heart of the incarnate God—can you love it? Oh, that there was an abyss as deep as Christ's misery, that I might at once hurl this dagger of sin into its depths, where it might never be brought to light again! Begone, O sin! You are banished from the heart where Jesus reigns! Begone, for you have crucified my Lord and made Him cry, "Why have You forsaken Me?"

O my hearers, if you did but know yourselves and know the love of Christ, you would each one vow that you would harbor sin no longer! You would be indignant at sin and cry:

The dearest idol I have known,
Whatever that idol is, Lord,
I will tear it from its throne,
And worship only you.

May that be the issue of my morning's discourse, and then I will be well content. The Lord bless you! May the Christ who suffered for you bless you, and out of His darkness may your light arise! Amen.

For Further Thought

1. *Read 2 Corinthians 5:21. What did God make Christ at the Crucifixion? Why did God do this?*
2. *As He died, Jesus asked God, "Why have You forsaken Me?" What is the reason for this forsaking that is given in Galatians 3:13? (See also Deuteronomy 21:23.)*
3. *Mark 15:27 tells us that two robbers were crucified with Jesus Christ. According to Romans 6:8, who else died with Him?*

OUR LORD'S

TRIUMPHANT ASCENSION

You have ascended on high, You have led captivity captive;
You have received gifts among men, even from the
rebellious, that the LORD God might dwell there.
PSALM 68:18

THE hill of Zion had been taken out of the hand of the Jebusites. They had held it long after the rest of the country had been subdued, but David, at last, had taken it from them. This was the mountain ordained of Jehovah of old to be the place of the temple. David, therefore, with songs and shouts of rejoicing, brought up the ark from the house of Obed-Edom to the place where it should remain. That is the literal fact upon which the figure of the text is based. We are at no loss for the *spiritual* interpretation, for we turn to Ephesians 4:8 where, quoting rather the *sense* of the passage than the exact words, Paul says, "When He ascended on high, He led captivity captive, and gave gifts to men."

The same sense is found in Colossians 2:15: "Having disarmed principalities and powers, He made a public spectacle of them, triumphing over them in it." Not misled by the will-o'-the-wisp of fancy, but guided by the clear light of the infallible Word, we see our way to expound our text. To paraphrase the words of David, we have an address to our Lord Jesus Christ concerning His ascent to His glory: "You have ascended on high, You have led captivity captive; You have received gifts among men, even from the rebellious, that the LORD God might dwell there" (Ps. 68:18).

Our Savior *descended* when He came to the manger of Bethlehem, and further descended when He became "a Man of sorrows and acquainted with grief" (Isa. 53:3). He descended lower still when He was obedient to death, even the death of the cross—and further yet when His dead body was laid in the grave. "Now this," says our apostle, " 'He ascended'—what does it mean but that He also first descended into the lower parts of the earth?" (Eph. 4:9). Long and dark was the descent. There were no depths of humiliation, temptation, or affliction that He did not fathom. Seeing He stood in their place, He went as low as justice required that sinners should go who had dared to violate the law of God.

> *he fact that Jesus died was put beyond question by the thrust of the spear, and the fact that He was alive, in a material form, was equally well established by the touch of Thomas.*

The utmost abyss of desertion heard Him cry, "My God, My God, why have You forsaken Me?" Low in the grave He lay, but He had His face upward, for He could not see corruption. On the third day He left the couch of the dead and rose to the light of the living! He had commenced His glorious ascent! To prove how real was His resurrection, He stayed on earth some forty days and showed Himself to many witnesses. Magdalene and Peter saw Him alone. The eleven beheld Him in their midst. The two on the road conversed with Him. Five hundred brethren at once beheld Him! He gave infallible proofs that He was really raised from the dead, and these remain with us to this day as *historic facts.*

He ate a piece of a broiled fish and honeycomb to prove that He was no phantom. He said to the apostles, "Handle Me and see, for a spirit does not have flesh and bones as you see I have" (Luke 24:39). One laid his finger in the print of the nails and even thrust his hand into His side! Their very doubts were used to make the evidence clearer. The fact that Jesus died was put beyond question by the thrust of the spear, and the fact that He was alive, in a material form, was equally well established by the touch of Thomas.

Beyond a doubt, Christ Jesus has risen from the dead and become the firstfruits of those who slept. This being settled beyond question, the time came for our Lord to continue His homeward, upward journey and return to the glory from which He had come down. From the Mount of Olives, "while they watched, He was taken up, and a cloud received Him out of their sight" (Acts 1:9). The rest of His upward progress we cannot describe. Imagination and faith step in and conceive of Him as rising beyond all regions known to us, far above all imaginable height. He draws near to the suburbs of heaven, and surely the poet is not wrong when he says of the angels:

> *They brought His chariot from on high*
> *To bear Him to His throne;*
> *Clapped their triumphant wings and cried,*
> *"The glorious work is done."*

"Lift up your heads, O you gates! And be lifted up, you everlasting doors! And the King of glory shall come in" (Ps. 24:7). How high He ascended after He passed the pearly portal Paul cannot tell us, save that he says God "seated Him at His right hand in the heavenly places, far above all principality and power and might and dominion" (Eph. 1:20–21). He describes our Master as "dwelling in unapproachable light" (1 Tim. 6:16). The man Christ Jesus has gone back to the place from where His Godhead came! You are the King of glory, O Christ! You are the eternal Son of the Father! You sit forever in the highest heaven, enthroned with all glory, clothed with all power, King of kings and Lord of lords! Unto your name we humbly present our hallelujahs, both now and forever.

We are in the highest glory in Christ as our representative, and by faith we are raised up together and made to sit together in the heavenlies, even in Him.

I. Now, concerning the text itself, which speaks of the ascent of our ever-blessed Lord, we will say, first, that *our Lord's triumph was set forth by His ascension.* He came here to fight the foes of God and man. It was a tremendous battle—not against flesh and blood—but against *spiritual* wickedness and evil powers. Our Lord fought against sin, death, hell, hate of God, and love of falsehood. He came to earth to be our champion. For you and for me, beloved, He entered the battle and wrestled till He sweat great drops of blood, and yes, "He poured out His soul unto death" (Isa. 53:12).

When He had ended the struggle He declared His victory by ascending to the Father's throne. *Now His descent is ended.* There was no need for Him to remain amid the men who despised Him. The shame, suffering, blasphemy, and rebuke are far beneath Him now. The sun has risen and the darkness of night has fled. He has gone up beyond the reach of sneering Sadducees and accusing Pharisees. The traitor cannot again kiss Him. Pilate cannot scourge Him. Herod cannot mock Him. He is far above the reach of priestly taunt and vulgar jest:

> *No more the cruel spear,*
> *The cross and nails no more;*
> *For hell itself shakes at His frown,*
> *And all the heavens adore.*

Now, also, our Lord's work is done. We are sure that the purpose of His love is secure or He would not have returned to His rest. The love that brought Him here would have kept Him here if all things necessary for our salvation had not been finished. Our Lord Jesus is no sudden enthusiast who rashly commences an enterprise of which He wearies before it is accomplished. He does not give up a work that He has once undertaken. Because He said, "I have finished the work which You have given Me to do" (John 17:4), and then ascended to the Father, I feel safe in asserting that all that was required of the Lord Christ for the overthrow of the powers of darkness is performed and endured; all that is needed for the salvation of His redeemed is fully done!

Whatever was the design of Christ's death, it will be accomplished to the fullest, for had He not secured its accomplishment, He would not have gone back. I do not believe in a defeated and disappointed Savior, or in a divine sacrifice that fails to effect its purpose. I do not believe in an atonement that is admirably wide but fatally ineffectual. I rejoice to hear my Lord say, "My Father...has given them to Me" (John 10:29). Whatever was the purpose of the Christ of God in the great transaction of the cross, it must be fully effected. To conceive a failure, even of a *partial* kind, is scarcely reverent.

Jesus has seen to it that in no point will His work be frustrated. Nothing is left undone of all His covenanted engagements. "It is finished" is a description of every item of the divine labor, and therefore has He ascended on high. There are no dropped stitches in the robe of Christ! I say again, the love that brought our Lord here would have kept Him here if He had not been absolutely sure that all His work and warfare for our salvation had been accomplished to the fullest.

Further, as we see here the ending of our Lord's descent and the accomplishment of His work, remember that *His ascent to the Father is representative*. Every believer rose with Him and grasped the inheritance. When He rose up, ascending on high, He taught our feet the way. At the last His people will be caught up together with the Lord in the air, and so will they be forever with the Lord. He has made a stairway for His saints to climb to their bliss, and He has traveled it Himself to assure us that the new and living way is available for us. In His ascension He bore all His people with Him.

As Levi was in the loins of Abraham when Melchizedek met him, so were all the saints in the loins of Christ when He ascended on high. Not one of the number will fail to come where the head has entered, else were Jesus the head of an imperfect and mutilated body! Though you have no other means of getting to glory but faith in Jesus, that way will bring you there without fail! Not only will He not be in glory and leave us behind, but He cannot be so since we are one with Him, and where He is His people must be. We are in the highest glory in Christ as our representative, and by faith we are raised up together and made to sit together in the heavenlies, even in Him.

Our Lord's ascent is to the highest heaven. I have noted this already, but let me remind you of it again, lest you miss an essential point. Our Lord Jesus is in no inferior place in the glory land. He was a servant here, but He is not so there. I know that He intercedes and thus carries on a form of service on our behalf, but no striving, vying, and tears are mingled with His present pleading. With authority He pleads. He is a priest upon His throne, blending with His plea the authority of His personal merit. He says, "All authority has been given to Me in heaven and on earth" (Matt. 28:18); therefore He is glorious in His prayers for us!

He is Lord of every place and of everything. He guides the wheels of providence and directs the flight of angels. His kingdom rules over all. He is exalted above every name that is named and all things are put under Him. Oh, what a Christ we have to trust in and to love! And on this account *we are called upon in the text to think much of His blessed person*. When we speak of what Christ has done, we must think much of the doing, but still more of the doer. We must not forget the benefactor in the benefits that come to us through Him. Note well how David puts it. To him the Lord is first and most prominent. He sees Him. He speaks to Him. "*You* have ascended on high. *You* have led captivity captive. *You* have received gifts for men."

Three times he addresses Him by that personal pronoun "you." Dwell on the fact that He, the Son of David, who for our sakes came down to earth and lay in the manger and hung upon a woman's breast, has gone up on high into glory! He who trod the weary ways of Palestine now reigns as a king in His palace. He who sighed, hungered, wept, bled, and died is now above all heavens! Behold your Lord upon the cross and mark the five ghastly wounds and all the shameful scourging and spitting that men have worked upon Him! See how that blessed body, prepared of the Holy Spirit for the indwelling of the second person of the adorable Trinity, was evilly treated! But there is an end to all this. "*You* have ascended on high." He who was earth's scorn is now heaven's wonder!

I saw you laid in the tomb, wrapped about with cerements and embalmed in spices, but you have ascended on high where death cannot touch you! The Christ who was buried here is now upon the throne! The heart that was broken here is palpitating in His bosom this minute, as full of love and condescension as when He dwelt among men! He has not forgotten us, for He has not forgotten Himself, and we are part and parcel of Him! He is still mindful of Calvary and Gethsemane. Even when you are dazzled by the superlative splendor of His exalted state, still believe that He is a brother born for adversity.

Let us rejoice in the ascent of Christ as being the ensign of His victory and the symbol of it! He has accomplished His work. If you had not led captivity captive, O Christ, you had never ascended on high. And if you had not won gifts of salvation for the sins of men, you had been here still suffering! You never would have relinquished your chosen task if you had not perfected it. You are so set on the salvation of men that for the joy that was set before you, you did endure the cross, despising the shame—and we know that all must have been achieved or you would still be working out your gracious enterprise. The voice of the ascension is *consummatum est*, "It is finished."

II. Having led your thoughts that way, I would, second, remind you that *the Lord's triumphal ascent demonstrated the defeat of all our foes.* "You have led captivity captive" is as certain as "You have ascended on high." Brethren, *we were once captives*—captives to tyrants who worked us woe and would soon have worked us death. We were captives to sin. We were captives to Satan and therefore captives under spiritual death. We were captives under many lusts and imaginations of our own hearts; we were captives to error, captives to deceit. But the Lord Jesus Christ has led captivity captive! *There* is our comfort!

Forget not that we were hopeless captives to all these. They were too strong for us and we could not escape from their cruel bondage. *The Lord Jesus, by His glorious victory here below, has subdued all our adversaries*, and in His going up on high, He has triumphed over them all, exhibiting them as trophies. The imagery may be illustrated by the triumph of Roman conquerors. They were known to pass along the Via Sacra and climb up to the capitol, dragging at their chariot wheels the vanquished princes with their hands bound behind their backs.

Christ has vanquished all those powers that held you captive. Whatever form your spiritual slavery took, you are fully delivered from it, for the Lord Christ has made captives those whose captives you were. "Sin shall not have dominion over you" (Rom. 6:14). Concerning Satan, our Lord has bruised his head beneath His heel. Death also is overcome and his sting is taken away. Death is no more the king of dread. "The sting of death is sin, and the strength of sin is the law. But thanks be to God, who gives us the victory through our Lord Jesus Christ" (1 Cor. 15:56–57). Whatever there was or is that can oppress our soul and hold it in bondage, the Lord Jesus has subdued and made it captive to Himself.

What then? Why, *from now on the power of all our adversaries is broken*. Courage, Christians! You can fight your way to heaven, for the foes that dispute your passage have been already beaten in the field! They bear upon them the proofs of the valor of your leader. True, the flock of the Lord is too feeble to force its way. But listen, "The one who breaks open will come up before them; they will break out, pass through the gate, and go out by it; their king will pass before them, with the LORD at their head" (Mic. 2:13). Easily may the sheep follow where the Shepherd leads the way! We have but to follow those heavenly feet that once were pierced and none of our steps will slide! Move on, O soldiers of Jesus, for your captain cries, "Follow me!"

Would He lead you into evil? Has He not said, "You shall tread upon the lion and the cobra, the young lion and the serpent you shall trample underfoot" (Ps. 91:13). Your Lord has set His foot on the necks of your enemies. You wage war with vanquished foes! What encouragement this glorious ascension of Christ should give to every tried believer! Remember, again, that the victory of our Lord Christ is the victory of all who are in Him. The seed of the woman will bruise the serpent's head (Gen. 3:15). Now, the seed of the woman is, first of all, the Lord Jesus, but also it is all who are in union with Him. There are still two seeds in the world: the seed of the serpent that cannot enter into this rest, and the seed of the woman who are born, not of blood, nor of the will of man, nor of the will of the flesh, but of God.

In these last is the living and incorruptible seed that lives and abides forever. Jesus, our Lord, represents them in all that He does because they died in Him, were buried in Him, are raised in Him, and in the day when He triumphed, they led captivity captive in Him. Looking at the great battle now raging in the world, I gaze with joyful confidence. We are fighting now with popery, with Mohammedanism, with idolatry in the foulest forms, but the battle is, in effect, won! We are struggling with the terrible infidelity that has fixed itself like a cancer upon the church of God, and our spirit sinks as we survey the horrors of this almost civil war. How often we groan because the battle does not go as we would desire it!

Yet there is no reason for dismay. God is in no hurry as we are. He dwells in the leisure of eternity and is not the prey of fear as we are. We read concerning the multitude, when they needed to be fed, that Jesus asked Philip a question, but Jesus knew what He would do (John 6:5–6). So today the Lord may put many questions to His valiant ones, and "among the divisions of Reuben there were great resolves of heart" (Judg. 5:15), but He knows what He is going to do and we may lay our heads upon His bosom and rest quietly. If He does not tell us how He will effect His purpose, yet assuredly He will not fail. His cause is sure to win the victory. How can the *Lord* be defeated? A vanquished Christ? We have not yet learned to blaspheme, and so we put the notion far from us! No, brothers and sisters, by those bleeding hands and feet He has secured the struggle. By that side opened down to His heart, we feel that His heart is fixed in our cause.

Especially by His resurrection and by His climbing to the throne of God, He has made the victory of His truth, the victory of His church—the victory of Himself—most sure and certain!

III. Let us notice, third, that *our Lord's triumphant ascension was celebrated by gifts*. The custom of bestowing gifts after victory was practiced among the peoples of the east, according to the song of Deborah. Those to whom a triumph was decreed in old Rome scattered money among the populace. Sometimes it seemed as if his share of the spoils of vanquished princes made every man in the city rich.

Thus our Lord, when He ascended on high, received gifts for men and scattered largesse all around. The psalm says, "You have received gifts among men" (Ps. 68:18). The Hebrew has it, "You have received gifts in Adam." That is, in human nature. Our Lord Christ had everything as Lord, but as the man, the mediator, He has received gifts from the Father. The King eternal, immortal, and invisible has bestowed upon His triumphant general a portion with the great, and He has ordained that He will divide the spoil with the strong. This our Lord values, for He speaks of all that the Father has given Him with the resolve that He will possess it.

When Paul quotes the passage, he says, "He gave gifts to men." Did Paul quote incorrectly? I think not. He quoted, no doubt, from the Greek version. Is the Greek version, therefore, compatible with the Hebrew? Assuredly! Dr. Owen says that the word rendered "received" may be read "gave." And if not, for Christ to *receive* for men is the same thing as to *give to* men, for He never receives for Himself, but at once gives it to those who are *in* Him. Paul looks to the central meaning of the passage and gives us the heart and soul of its sense. He is not intending to quote it verbatim, but to give in brief its innermost teaching.

Our Lord Jesus Christ has *nothing* that He does not give to His church. He gave Himself for us and He continues, still, to give Himself *to* us. He receives the gifts, but He only acts as the conduit through which the grace of God flows to us. It pleased the Father that in Him should all fullness dwell, and of His fullness have we all received. What are these great ascension gifts? I answer that *the sum of them is the Holy Spirit*. I invite your adoring attention to the sacred Trinity manifested to us here. How delightful it is to see the Trinity working out in unity the salvation of men!

"You have ascended on high"—there is Christ Jesus. "You have received gifts among men"—there is the Father bestowing those gifts. The gift itself is the Holy Spirit. This is the great generosity of Christ's ascension that He bestowed on His church at Pentecost. Thus you have Father, Son, and Holy Spirit blessedly coworking for the benediction of men, the conquest of evil, the establishment of righteousness. O my soul, delight yourself in Father, Son, and Holy Spirit!

One of the sins of modern theology is keeping these divine persons in the background so that they are scarcely mentioned in their several workings and offices. The theology that can feed your souls must be full of the Godhead and yield to Father, Son, and Holy Spirit perpetual praise. Beloved, the gifts here spoken of are those brought by the Holy Spirit. "But the water that I shall give him," said Christ, "will become in him a fountain of water springing up into everlasting life" (John 4:14). He said again, "If anyone thirsts, let him come to Me and drink" (7:37). We read that He "spoke concerning the Spirit, whom those believing in Him would receive" (7:39). "If you then, being evil, know how to give good gifts to your children, how much more will your Father who is in heaven give good things to those who ask Him!" (Matt. 7:11). To conquer the world for Christ, we need nothing but the Holy Spirit, and Christ secured this gift for us in the hour of His personal victory. If the Holy Spirit is but given, we have in Him all the weapons of our holy war.

But observe, according to Paul, these gifts that our Lord gave are *embodied in men*, for the Holy Spirit comes upon men whom He has chosen and works through them according to His good pleasure. Therefore He gave some apostles, some evangelists, and some pastors and teachers. No one may be judged to be a gift of God to the church in any of these offices unless the Spirit dwells upon him. All are given of God upon whom the Holy Spirit rests, whatever their office may be. It is ours to accept with great joy the men who are chosen and anointed to speak in the name of the Lord, be they what they may.

Paul, Apollos, and Cephas are all the gifts of the risen Christ to His redeemed ones for their edifying and perfecting! The Holy Spirit, in proportion as He abides in these servants of God, makes them to be precious blessings of heaven to His people, and they become the champions by whom the world is subdued to the Lord Jesus Christ. These gifts, given in the form of men, are *given for men*. Churches do not exist for preachers, but preachers for churches. We have sometimes feared that certain brothers thought that the assemblies of believers were formed to provide situations for clerical persons—but indeed, it is not so.

My brothers and sisters in the church, we who are your pastors are your *servants* for Christ's sake. Our rule is not that of lordship, but of love. Every

God-sent minister, if he discharges his duty aright, waits upon the bride of Christ with loving diligence and delights greatly to hear the Bridegroom's voice. I wish that you who talk of my Lord's servants as if they were rival performers would cease, thus, to profane the gifts of the ascended King. The varying abilities of those by whom the Lord builds up His church are all arranged by infinite wisdom, and it should be ours to make the most we can of them.

Comparing and contrasting the Lord's gifts is unprofitable work. It is better to drink of the well of Elim than to grow hot and feverish in disputing as to whether it is better or worse than Beersheba or Sychar. One minister may be better for you than another, but another may be better for somebody else than the one you prefer. The least gifted may be essential to a certain class of mind—therefore despise no one. When God gives gifts, will you turn them away contemptuously and say, "I like this one but the other I do not"? Did the Father bestow these gifts upon His Son? And has the Holy Spirit put them into different earthen vessels that the excellence of the power might be of God? And will you begin judging them?

No, beloved, the Lord has sent me to preach His gospel, and I rejoice to feel that I am sent for your sake. I entreat you to profit as much as you can by me by frequent hearing, by abounding faith, by practical obedience to the Word. Use all God's servants as you are able to profit by them. Hear them prayerfully, not for the indulgence of your curiosity, nor for the pleasing of your ear with rhetoric, but that you, through the Word of God, may feel His Spirit working in our hearts all the purpose of His will. Our conversion, sanctification, comfort, instruction, and usefulness all come to us by the Holy Spirit, and that Spirit sends His powerful message by the men whom He has given to be His mouths to men.

See how wonderful, then, was that ascension of our Lord in which He scattered down mercies so rich and appropriate among the sons of men! From His glorious elevation above all heavens He sends forth pastors, preachers, and evangelists, through whom the Holy Spirit works mightily in those who believe. By them He gathers the redeemed together and builds them up as a church to His glory!

IV. I want the attention, now, of all who are unconverted, for I have glorious tidings for them. To them I speak under my fourth head: *Our Lord's triumph has a very special bearing.* "You have received gifts *among men*," not for angels, not for devils, but for men, poor fallen men. I read not that it is said "among bishops or ministers," but "among men." And yet there is a special character mentioned. Does the text particularly mention saints, or those who have not defiled their garments? No, I do not read of them here.

What a strange sovereignty there is about the grace of God! Truly He will have mercy on whom He will have mercy, for in this instance He selects for special mention those whom you and I would have passed over without a word! "Even from the rebellious." I must pause to brush my tears away! Where are you, you rebels? Where are those who have lived in rebellion against God all their lives? Alas, you have been in open revolt against Him—you have raged against Him in your hearts and spoken against Him with your tongues!

> *W*hen God gives gifts, will you turn them away contemptuously and say, "I like this one but the other I do not"? Did the Father bestow these gifts upon His Son? And has the Holy Spirit put them into different earthen vessels that the excellence of the power might be of God?

Some have sinned as drunkards. Others have broken the laws of purity, truth, and honesty. Many rebel against the light, violate conscience, and disobey the Word—these, also, are among the rebellious. So are the proud, the wrathful, the slothful, the profane, the unbelieving, the unjust. Hear, all of you, these words and carry them home! And if they do not break your hearts with tender gratitude, you are hard indeed. "Even among the rebellious." When our Lord rode home in triumph, He had a pitying heart toward the rebellious! When He entered the highest place to which He could ascend, He was still the *sinner's* friend! When all His pains and griefs were being rewarded with endless horror, He turned His eyes upon those who had crucified Him and bestowed gifts upon them! This description includes those who have rebelled against God, though once they professed to be His loyal subjects.

Perhaps I am addressing some who have so far backslidden that they have thrown up all religion and have gone back into the world and its sins. These are apostates from the profession that once they made. To these I would give a word of encouragement if they will turn to the Lord. Once upon a time John Bunyan was under great temptation from the devil. This trial he records in his *Grace Abounding*. He thought that God had given him up and that he was cast away forever, and yet he found hope in this text. I have copied out a little bit that refers to it:

> I feared, also, that this was the mark that the Lord set on Cain, even continual fear and trembling under the heavy load of guilt that He had charged him for the blood of his brother Abel.
>
> Then did I wind and twine and shrink under the burden that was upon me, which burden did also so oppress me that I could neither stand, nor go, nor lie, either at rest or quiet. Yet that saying would sometimes come into my mind, "He has received gifts from the rebellious." Rebellious, thought I, why surely they are such as once were under subjection to their prince, even those who, after they had sworn subjection to His government, have taken up arms against Him; and this, thought I, is *my* very condition! Once I loved Him, feared Him, served Him, but now I am a rebel and I have sold Him. I said, let Him go if He will, but yet He has gifts from rebels; *and then why not from me?*

Oh, that I could cause every despairing heart to reason in this way! Oh, that the Holy Spirit would put this argument into every troubled mind at this moment—"And then why not from me?" Come home, dear brothers and sisters, come home, for there are gifts from the rebellious *and why not from you?* I know you deserted the Lord's Table, but the Lord of the table has not deserted you! I know you have, as far as you could, forsworn the name of Christ and even wished you could be unbaptized, but that cannot be, nor can the Lord leave you to perish! I know you have eagerly done evil with both hands and perhaps now you are living in a known sin, and when you go home today you will see it before your eyes.

Nevertheless, I charge you, return to the Lord at once! Come to your Lord and Savior, who still prays, "Father, forgive them, for they do not know what they do" (Luke 23:34). O my soul, I charge you, on your own account, hang on to this most precious declaration, for you, too, have been a rebel!

Would God that this dear word would cheer all my brothers and sisters and take it home to themselves with a believing repentance and a holy hatred of sin! I would print the words in stars across the brow of night: "Even from the rebellious."

V. I am done when I have handled the fifth point: *Our Lord's triumphant ascension secures the consummation of His whole work.* What does it say? That the Lord God "may dwell among them" (Exod. 25:8). When our Lord Christ came here at the first, He was willing enough to dwell among us, but it could not be. "The Word became flesh and dwelt among us" (John 1:14), like a Bedouin in his tent, but not as a dweller at home. He could not dwell here on that occasion. He was but a *visitor* and badly treated at that.

There was no room for Him in the inn where everybody else was freely welcome. He came to His own people—surely they will lodge Him—but His own people did not receive Him. There was no room for Him in the temple, where He had to use the scourge. There was no room for Him in the open streets, for they took up stones to stone Him. Out of the synagogue they hurried him, to cast him down headlong from the brow of the hill (Luke 4:29). "Away with Him! Away with Him!" was the cry of the ribald crowd. This dear visitor who came here all unarmed, without sword or bow, they treated as though He had been a spy or an assassin who had stolen among them to do them ill.

And so they ran upon Him with a spear and He, quitting these inhospitable realms that knew Him not, took home with Him the marks of man's discourtesy. O earth, earth! How could you drive away your dearest friend and compel Him to be as a wayfaring man who tarries but for a night? No, worse than that, as a man astonished who meets with wounding in the house of his friends? After He had risen again, He went home so that from His throne He might direct a work by which earth should become a place where God could abide. Again is the temple of God to be with men, and He will dwell among them.

This world of ours has been sprinkled with the precious blood of the Lamb of God and it is no longer as an unclean thing. Jesus is the Lamb of God who so takes away the sin of the world that God can treat with men on terms of divine grace and publish free salvation. The Lord God Himself had long been a stranger in the land! Did not the holy man of old say, "I am a stranger with You, a sojourner, as all my fathers were" (Ps. 39:12)? But Jesus, the Ascended One, is pouring down such gifts upon this sin-polluted world that it will yet become a new earth wherein dwells righteousness and the God of righteousness! This promise is partly fulfilled before your own eyes this day, for the Holy Spirit came at Pentecost and He has never returned.

Jesus said, "He may abide with you forever" (John 14:16). The holy dove has often been greatly grieved, but He has never spread His wings to depart. This is still the dispensation of the Spirit. You hardly need to pray to have the Spirit poured out, for that has been done. What you need is a baptism of the Holy Spirit; to go down *personally* into that glorious flood that has been poured forth. Oh, to be immersed into the Holy Spirit and into fire—covered with His holy influence—plunged in the Godhead's deepest sea and lost in His immensity! Here is our life and power, for thus the Lord God does dwell among us!

Ever since the Ascension, the Holy Spirit has remained among men, though He has not been, at all seasons, equally active. All through the night of Romanism and the schoolmen He still tarried. There were humble hearts that rejoiced to be His temples even in those doleful days. Today He is still with His regenerated ones. In spite of impudent striving against the divine inspiration of His Holy Scripture, and notwithstanding the follies of ecclesiastical amusements, He is with His chosen. Lord, what is man that your Spirit should dwell with him? But so it is and this is why our Lord went up to heaven and received divine gifts, that by Him the Lord God might dwell among us.

But there comes a day when this will be carried out to the letter. I think I hear the angels say, "Men of Galilee, why do you stand gazing up into heaven? This same Jesus, who was taken up from you into heaven, will so come in like manner as you saw Him go into heaven" (Acts 1:11). Now, the words "in like manner" must mean in person. In person our Lord was taken up into heaven, and in person He will come again! And when He comes, the Lord God will indeed dwell among us! Oh, that the day would come! We wait and watch for His glorious appearing, for then will He dwell among men in a perfect fashion. What happy days will we have when Jesus is here!

What a millennium His presence will bring. There can be no such auspicious era without it any more than there can be summer without the sun! He must come first, and then will the golden age begin! The central glory of that period will be that the Lord is here. Then will be heard the song that will never end, earth's homage to the Lord who renewed the heavens and the earth, and has taken up His dwelling in them. "They shall neither hunger anymore nor thirst anymore; the sun shall not strike them, nor any heat; for the Lamb who is in the midst of the throne will shepherd them and lead them to living fountains of waters" (Rev. 7:16–17).

Up till now this work has been going on and as yet it is incomplete. The saying "Every prospect pleases and only man is vile" is still most sadly true. The rankness of sin destroys the sweet odors of this world so that the pure and holy God cannot abide in it. But since the Lord Jesus has sweetened it with His sacred merits and the Spirit is purifying it by His residence in men, the Lord smells a savor of rest, and He will not give up this poor fallen planet. Even now His angels come and go in heavenly traffic with the chosen.

Soon the little boat of this globe will be drawn nearer to the great ship, and earth will lie alongside heaven. Then will men praise God day and night in His temple. Heaven will find her choristers among the ransomed from among men. The whole world will be as a censer filled with incense for the Lord of hosts. All this will be because of those gifts received and bestowed by our Lord Jesus in the day when He returned to His glory, leading captivity captive! O Lord, hasten your coming! We are sure that your abiding presence and glorious reign will come in due season. Your coming down secured your going up. Your going up secures your coming down again. Therefore we bless and magnify you, O ascended Lord, with all our hearts, and rise after you as you draw us upward from groveling things. So be it! Amen.

For Further Thought

1. *What aspect of the work of Christ is proved by Luke 24:24?*
2. *Genesis 3:15 is the first verse in scripture that tells about our Lord's victory. What is another verse that tells of this?*
3. *Read Acts 1:11. This verse indicates the way in which the Lord will return. What is this?*

CHRIST EXALTED

But this Man, after He had offered one sacrifice for sins forever,
sat down at the right hand of God, from that time
waiting till His enemies are made His footstool.
HEBREWS 10:12–13

AT the Lord's Table we wish to have no subject for contemplation but our blessed Lord Jesus Christ, and we have been accustomed generally to consider Him as the Crucified One, "a Man of sorrows and acquainted with grief" (Isa. 53:3). We have had before us the emblems of His broken body and of His blood shed for many for the remission of sins, but I am not quite sure that the crucified Savior is the only appropriate theme, although, perhaps, the most so. It is well to remember how our Savior left us; by what road He traveled through the shadows of death. But I think it is quite as well to recollect what He is doing while He is away from us; to remember the high glories to which the crucified Savior has attained.

And it is, perhaps, as much calculated to cheer our spirits to behold Him on His throne as to consider Him on His cross. We have seen Him on His cross, in some sense; that is to say, the eyes of men on earth did see the crucified Savior. But we have no idea of what His glories are above. They surpass our highest thought. Yet faith can see the Savior exalted on His throne, and surely there is no subject that can keep our expectations alive, or cheer our drooping faith, better than to consider that while our Savior is absent, He is absent on His throne. Though He has left His church to sorrow for Him, He has not left us comfortless. He has promised to come to us, yet while He tarries He is reigning, and while He is absent, He is sitting high on His Father's throne.

The apostle shows here the superiority of Christ's sacrifice over that of every other priest. "And every priest stands ministering daily and offering repeatedly the same sacrifices, which can never take away sins" (Heb. 10:11). But this man, or priest, for the word *man* is not in the original, "after He had offered one sacrifice for sins forever, sat down at the right hand of God" (10:12). You see the superiority of Christ's sacrifice rests in this: that the priest offered continually, and after he had slaughtered one lamb, another was needed. After one scapegoat was driven into the wilderness, a scapegoat was needed the next year, "but this Man, after He had offered one sacrifice for sins," did what thousands of scapegoats never did and what hundreds of thousands of lambs never could effect. He perfected our salvation and worked out an entire atonement for the sins of all His chosen ones.

We will notice, in the first place this morning, *the completeness of the Savior's work of atonement*; He has done it. We will gather that from the context. Second is *the glory that the Savior has assumed*, and third, *the triumph that He expects*. We will dwell very briefly on each point and endeavor to pack our thoughts as closely together as we can.

I. We are taught here, in the first place, *the completeness of the Savior's work*. He has done all that was necessary to be done to make atonement and an end of sin. He has done so much that it will never be needful for Him again to be crucified. His side, once opened, has sent forth a deep stream, deep enough and precious enough to wash away all sin. He needs not again that His side should be opened, or that any more His hands should be nailed to the cross. I infer that His work is finished from the fact that He is described here as sitting down. Christ would not sit down in heaven if He had more work to do.

Sitting down is the posture of rest. Seldom did He sit down on earth. He said, "I must be about My Father's business" (Luke 2:49). Journey after journey, labor after labor, preaching after preaching followed each other in quick succession. His was a life of incessant toil. *Rest* was a word that Jesus never spelled. He may sit for a moment on the well. But even there He preaches to the woman of Samaria. He goes into the wilderness but not to sleep. He goes there to pray. His midnights are spent in labors as hard as those of the day—labors of agonizing prayer, wrestling with His Father for the souls of men.

His was a life of continual bodily, mental, and spiritual labor. His whole man was exercised. But now He rests. There is no more toil for Him now. There is no more sweat of blood, no more the weary foot, no more the aching head. No more has He to do. He sits still. But do you think my Savior would sit still if He had not done all His work? Oh no, beloved. He said once, "For Zion's sake I will not hold My peace, and for Jerusalem's sake I will not rest, until her righteousness goes forth as brightness, and her salvation as a lamp that burns" (Isa. 62:1). And I am sure He would not rest or be sitting still unless the great work of our atonement were fully accomplished.

> He has promised to come to us, yet while He tarries He is reigning, and while He is absent, He is sitting high on His Father's throne.

Sit still, blessed Jesus, while there is a fear of your people being lost? Sit still, while their salvation is at hazard? No! And your truthfulness and your compassion tell us that you would still labor if the work were still undone. Oh, if the last thread had not been woven in the great garment of our righteousness, He would be spinning it now. If the last particle of our debt had not been paid, He would be counting it down now. And if all were not finished and complete, He would never rest, until, like a wise builder, He had laid the topstone of the temple of our salvation. No. The very fact that He sits still, rests, and is at ease proves that His work is finished and is complete.

And then note again that His sitting at the right hand of God implies that *He enjoys pleasure.* For at God's right hand there are pleasures forevermore. Now I think the fact that Christ enjoys infinite pleasure has in it some degree of proof that He must have finished His work. It is true; He had pleasure with His Father before that work was begun. But I cannot conceive that if, after having been incarnate, His work was still unfinished, He would rest. He might rest before He began the work, but as soon as He had begun it, you will remember, He said He had a baptism wherewith He must be baptized, and He appeared to be hastening to receive the whole of the direful baptism of agony.

He never rested on earth till the whole work was finished. Scarcely a smile passed His brow till the whole work was done. He was "a Man of sorrows and acquainted with grief" (Isa. 53:3) until He could say, "It is finished" (John 19:30). And I could scarcely conceive the Savior happy on His throne if there were any more to do. Surely, living as He was on that great throne of His, there would be anxiety in His breast if He had not secured the meanest lamb of His fold and if He had not rendered the eternal salvation of every blood-bought one as sacred as His own throne. The highest pleasure of Christ is derived from the fact that He has become the "head over all things to the church" (Eph. 1:22) and has saved that church.

He has joys as God. But as the Man-God, His joys spring from the salvation of the souls of men. That is His joy, which is full in the thought that He has finished His work and has cut it short in righteousness. I think there is some degree of proof, although not perhaps positive proof there, that Jesus must have finished His work.

But now, something else: *The fact that it is said He has sat down forever proves that He must have done it.* Christ has undertaken to save all the souls of the elect. If He has not already saved them, He is bound to do something that will save them. Remember He has given solemn oath and promise to His Father that He will bring many souls to glory and that He will make them perfect through His own righteousness. He has promised to present our souls unblemished and complete "before the glory of His face with joys divinely great." Well, if He has not done enough to do that, then He must come again to do it. But the fact that He is to sit there *forever*, that He is to wear no more the crown of thorns, that He is never again to leave His throne or cease to be King anymore, that He is still to be girded by His grandeur and His glory and sit forever. There is proof that He has accomplished the great work of propitiation. It is certain that He must have done all from the fact that He is to sit there *forever*, to sit on His throne throughout all ages, more visibly in the ages to come, but never to leave it—again to suffer and again to die.

Yet the best proof is that *Christ sits at His Father's right hand* at all. For the very fact that Christ is in heaven, accepted by His Father, proves that His work must be done. Why, beloved, as long as an ambassador from our country is at a foreign court, there must be peace. And as long as Jesus Christ our Savior is at His Father's court, it shows that there is real peace between His people and His Father. Well, as He will be there forever, that shows that our peace must be continual and, like the waves of the sea, will never cease. But that peace could not have been continual unless the atonement had been wholly made, justice entirely satisfied, and therefore from that very fact it becomes certain that the work of Christ must be done.

What? Will Christ enter heaven; will Christ sit on His Father's right hand before all the guilt of His people is rolled away? Ah, no. He was the sinner's substitute. And unless He paid the sinner's debt and died the sinner's death, there was no heaven in view for me. He stood in the sinner's place, and the guilt of all His elect was imputed to Him. God accounted Him as a sinner, and as a sinner He could not enter heaven until He had washed all that sin away in a crimson flood of His own gore, unless His own righteousness had covered up the sins that He had taken on Himself, and unless His own atonement had taken away those sins that had become His by imputation.

The fact that the Father allowed Him to ascend up on high, that He gave Him leave, as it were, to enter heaven, and that He said, "Sit at My right hand" (Matt. 22:44), proves that He must have perfected His Father's work and that His Father must have accepted His sacrifice. But He could not have accepted it if it had been imperfect. Thus we prove that the work must have been finished, since God the Father accepted it. Oh, glorious doctrine! This man has done it. This man has finished it. This man has completed it. He was the author. He is the finisher. He was the Alpha. He is the Omega.

Salvation is finished, complete! Otherwise He would not have ascended up on high, nor would He also sit at the right hand of God. Christian, rejoice! Your salvation is a finished salvation—atonement is wholly made. Neither stick nor stone of yours is wanted. Not one stitch is required to that glorious garment of His—not one patch to that glorious robe that He has finished. 'Tis done; 'tis perfectly done. You are accepted perfectly in His righteousness. You are purged in His blood. "By one offering He has perfected forever those who are being sanctified" (Heb. 10:14).

II. And now, our second point—*the glory that He has assumed.* "After He had offered one sacrifice for sins forever, sat down on the right hand of God" (Heb. 10:12). Now, by this you are to understand the complex person of Christ. Christ, as God, always was on His Father's throne. He always was God. And even when He was on earth, He was still in heaven. The Son of God did not cease to be omnipotent and omnipresent when He came wrapped in the garments of clay. He was still on His Father's throne. He never left it, never came down from heaven in that sense.

He was still there, God-blessed forever. As He has said, He was the Son of man who came down from heaven, who also at that very moment was in heaven (John 3:13). But Jesus Christ, as the Man-God, has assumed glories and honors that once He had not. For as man He did not at one time sit on His Father's throne. He was a man, a suffering man, a man full of pains and groans, more than mortals have ever known. But as God-Man, He has assumed a dignity next to God. He sits at the right hand of God. At the right hand of the glorious Trinity—Father, Son, and Holy Spirit—sits the person of the man Jesus Christ, exalted at the right hand of the majesty on high.

> *Remember He has given solemn oath and promise to His Father that He will bring many souls to glory and that He will make them perfect through His own righteousness.*

From this we gather that the dignity that Christ now enjoys is surpassing dignity. There is no honor, there is no dignity to be compared to that of Christ. No angel flies higher than He does. Save only the great three-in-one God, there is none to be found in heaven who can be called superior to the person of the man Christ Jesus. He sits on the right hand of God, far above all angels, principalities, powers, and every name that is named. God "has highly exalted Him and given Him the name which is above every name, that at the name of Jesus every knee should bow, of those in heaven, and of those on earth, and of those under the earth" (Phil. 2:9–10).

No dignity can shine like His. The sons of righteousness who have turned many to God are but as stars compared with Him, the brightest of the suns there. As for angels, they are but flashes of His brightness, emanations from His own glorious self. He sits there, the great masterpiece of deity. "God, in the person of His Son, has all His mightiest works outdone." That glorious man, taken into union with deity, that mighty Man-God, surpasses everything in the glory of His majestic person. Christian! Remember your Master has unsurpassed dignity.

In the next place, Christ has *real* dignity. Some persons have mere empty titles that confer but little power and little authority. But the man Christ Jesus, while He has many crowns and many titles, has not one tinsel crown or one empty title. While He sits there, He sits not there *pro forma*. He does not sit there to have nominal honor done to Him. But He has real honor and real glory. That Man-Christ, who once walked the streets of Jerusalem, now sits in heaven and angels bow before Him. That Man-Christ, who once hung on Calvary and there expired in agonies the most acute, now on His Father's throne, exalted, sits and sways the scepter of heaven—nay, devils at

His presence tremble, the whole earth owns the sway of His providence, and on His shoulders the pillars of the universe rest.

He upholds all things by the word of His power (Heb. 1:3). He overrules all mortal things, making the evil work a good and the good produce a better and a better still, in infinite progression. The power of the God-Man Christ is infinite. You cannot tell how great it is. He is "able to save to the uttermost those who come to God through Him" (Heb. 7:25). He is able to keep us from falling and to present us spotless before His presence (Jude 24). He is able to make "all things work together for good" (Rom. 8:28). He is "able even to subdue all things to Himself" (Phil. 3:21). He is able to conquer even death, for He has the power of death and He has the power of Satan, who once had power over death.

> *Christ, who once hung on Calvary and there expired in agonies the most acute, now on His Father's throne, exalted, sits and sways the scepter of heaven. . .*

He is Lord over all things, for His Father has made Him so. The glorious dignity of our Savior! I cannot talk of it in words, beloved. All I can say to you must be simple repetition. I can only repeat the statements of scripture. There is no room for flights. We must just keep where we ever have been, telling out the story that His Father has exalted Him to real honors and real dignities.

And once more, this honor that Christ has now received (I mean the Man-God Christ, not the God-Christ, for He already had that and never lost it and therefore could never obtain it; He was Man-God and as such He was exalted) was *deserved* honor. That dignity that His Father gave Him He well deserved. I have sometimes thought if all the holy spirits in the universe had been asked what should be done for the man whom the King delights to honor, they would have said, "Christ must be the man whom God delights to honor, and He must sit on His Father's right hand." Why, if I might use such a phrase, I can almost suppose His mighty Father putting it to the vote of heaven as to whether Christ should be exalted and that they carried it by acclamation, "Worthy is the Lamb who was slain to receive power and riches and wisdom, and strength and honor and glory and blessing!" (Rev. 5:12).

His Father gave Him that. But still the prayers of all the saints and of all the holy angels said to it, "Amen." And this thing I am certain of, that every heart here—every Christian heart—says "amen" to it. Ah, beloved, we would exalt Him; we would crown Him, "crown Him Lord of all." Not only will His Father crown Him, but also we ourselves would exalt Him if we had the power. And when we will have power to do it, we will cast our crowns beneath His feet and crown Him Lord of all. It is deserved honor. No other being in heaven deserves to be there. Even the angels are kept there, and God charges His angels with folly.

And certainly none of His saints deserve it. They feel that hell was their desert. But Christ's exaltation was a deserved exaltation. His Father might say to Him, "Well done, my Son; well done. You have finished the work that I had given you to do. Sit forever first of all men, glorified by union with the person of the Son. My glorious coequal Son, sit on my right hand, till I make your enemies your footstool."

One more illustration and we are done with this. We must consider the exaltation of Christ in heaven as being in some degree a representative exaltation. Christ Jesus, exalted at the Father's right hand, though He has eminent glories in which the saints must not expect to share, is essentially the express image of the person of God. He is the brightness of His Father's glory, yet to a very great degree, the honors that Christ has in heaven He has as our representative there. Ah, brethren, it is sweet to reflect how blessedly Christ lives with His people. You all know that we were

> One, when He died, one, when He rose,
> One, when He triumphed o'er His foes;
> One, when in heaven He took His seat,
> And angels sang all hell's defeat.

Today you know that you are one with Him, now, in His presence. We are at this moment raised up together, and may afterward sit together in heavenly places, even in Him (Eph. 2:6). As I am represented in parliament and as you are, so is every child of God represented in heaven. But as we are not one with our parliamentary representatives, that figure fails to set forth the glorious representation of us that our forerunner, Christ, carries on in heaven, for we are actually one with Him. We are members of His body, of His flesh and of His bones. His exaltation is our exaltation. He will give us to sit upon His throne, just as He has overcome and is seated with His Father on His throne.

He has a crown, and He will not wear His crown unless He gives us crowns, too. He has a throne, but He is not content with having a throne to Himself. On His right hand there must be His bride in gold of Ophir. And He cannot be there without His bride. The Savior cannot be content to be in heaven unless He has His church with Him, which is the fullness of Him who fills all in all (Eph. 1:23). Beloved, look up to Christ now. Let the eyes of your faith catch sight of Him. Behold Him there with many crowns upon His head. Remember, as you see Him there, you will one day be like He is, when you will see Him as He is.

You will not be as great as He is, you will not be as glorious in degree, but still you shall, in a measure, share the same honors and enjoy the same happiness and the same dignity that He possesses. Be content to live unknown for a little while. Be content to bear the sneer, the jest, the joke, and the ribald song. Be content to walk your weary way through the fields of poverty, or up the hills of affliction. By and by you will reign with Christ, for He has "made us kings and priests to our God; and we shall reign on the earth" (Rev. 5:10).

By and by we will share the glories of the Head. The oil has been poured on His head. It has not trickled down to us yet, save only in that faithful fellowship that we have. But by and by that oil will flow to the very skirts of the garments (Ps. 133:2), and we, the meanest of His people, will share a part in the glories of His house by being made kings with Him, to sit on His throne even as He sits on His Father's throne.

III. And now, in the last place: *What are Christ's expectations?* We are told: *He expects that His enemies will be made His footstool.* In some sense, that is already done. The foes of Christ are, in some sense, His footstool now. What is the devil but the very slave of Christ? He does no more than he is permitted against God's children. What is the devil but the servant of Christ, to fetch His children to His loving arms? What are wicked men but the unwitting servants of God's providence? Christ has even now "authority over all flesh, that He should give eternal life to as many as [God has] given Him" (John 17:2), in order that the purposes of Christ might be carried out.

Christ died for all and all, are now Christ's property. There is not a man in this world who does not belong to Christ in that sense, for He is God over him and Lord over him. He is either Christ's brother or else Christ's slave, His unwilling vassal who must be dragged out in triumph, if He follows Him not willingly. In that sense all things are now Christ's.

But we expect greater things than these, beloved, at His coming, *when all enemies will be beneath Christ's feet upon earth*. We are therefore, many of us, "looking for the blessed hope and glorious appearing of our great God and Savior Jesus Christ" (Titus 2:13). Many of us are expecting that Christ will come. We cannot tell you when. We believe it to be folly to pretend to guess the time, but we are expecting that even in our lifetime the Son of God will appear. We know that when He will appear, He will tread His foes beneath His feet and reign from pole to pole and from the river even to the ends of the earth.

Not long will antichrist sit on her seven hills. Not long will the false prophet delude his millions. Not long will idol gods mock their worshippers with eyes that cannot see and hands that cannot handle and ears that cannot hear. "Lo! He comes, with clouds descending." In the winds I see His chariot wheels. I know that He approaches, and when He approaches, "He breaks the bow and cuts the spear in two; He burns the chariot in the fire" (Ps. 46:9). And Christ Jesus will then be King over the whole world. He is King now, virtually. But He is to have another kingdom.

I cannot see how it is to be a spiritual one, for that is come already. He is as much King spiritually now as He ever will be in His church, although His kingdom will assuredly be very extensive. But the kingdom that is to come, I take it, will be something even greater than the spiritual kingdom. It will be a *visible kingdom of Christ on earth*. Then kings must bow their necks before His feet. Then at His throne the tribes of earth will bend. Then the rich and mighty, the merchants of Tyre and the travelers where gold is found, will bring their spices and myrrh before Him and lay their gold and gems at His feet.

> *Jesus will reign wherever the sun*
> *Does his successive journeys run;*
> *His kingdom stretch from shore to shore,*
> *Till moons will wax and wane no more.*

Once more, beloved: *Christ will have all His enemies put beneath His feet in that great day of judgment.* Oh, that will be a terrible putting of His foes beneath His feet, when at that second resurrection the wicked dead will rise. Then the ungodly will stand before His throne and His voice will say, "Depart from Me, you cursed" (Matt. 25:41). O rebel, you who have despised Christ, it will be a horrible thing for you, that that man, that gibbeted, crucified man whom you have often despised, will have power enough to speak you into hell. That the man whom you have scoffed and laughed at and of whom you have virtually said, "If you are the Son of God, come down from the cross" (see Matt. 27:42), will have power enough, in two or three short words, to damn your soul to all eternity. "Depart from Me, you cursed, into the everlasting fire prepared for the devil and his angels" (25:41).

Oh, what a triumph that will be, when men, wicked men, persecutors and all those who opposed Christ, are all cast into the lake that burns! But, if possible, it will be a greater triumph when he who led men astray will be dragged forth—

> *Shall lift his brazen front,*
> *With thunder scarred,*
> *Receive the sentence*
> *And begin anew his hell.*

Oh, when Satan will be condemned and when the saints will judge angels and the fallen spirits will all be under the feet of Christ, "then shall be brought to pass the saying that is written: 'Death is swallowed up in victory'" (1 Cor. 15:54). And when death, too, will come forth and the death of death and hell's destructions will grind his iron limbs to powder, then will it be said, "Death is swallowed up in victory." For the great shout of "Victory, victory, victory," will drown the shrieks of the past—shall put out the sound of the howling of death. And hell will be swallowed up in victory.

He is exalted on high. He sat down by His Father's right hand, "from that time waiting till His enemies are made His footstool" (Heb. 10:13).

For Further Thought

1. *According to Hebrews 10:12–13, what is the difference between the sacrifice of Christ and the sacrifices of Jewish ritual?*
2. *What is the meaning of the Lord's last words (John 19:30)?*
3. *Read Philippians 2:5–11. What does this reveal about the present position of Jesus Christ?*

CHRIST PRECIOUS TO BELIEVERS

Therefore, to you who believe, He is precious.
1 PETER 2:7

HERE we have no far-fetched statement. It belongs to everyday life. Those now present who believe can verify it on the spot! As believers they can tell us whether the Lord Jesus is precious to them or not. We are not now about to consider an abstruse doctrine or lose ourselves in a profound mystery of the faith. We have before us an assertion that even a babe in Christ may put to the test. Yes, you who but last week confessed your faith in the Lord Jesus Christ can tell in your own souls whether He is precious to you or not! If you can personally verify this sentence, it says a great deal for yourself. You need never raise the question as to whether you have the faith of God's elect and are true believers in Jesus. If Christ is precious to you, that question is answered once and for all by this statement that covers the whole ground: "Therefore, to you who believe, He is precious."

The converse of the statement is equally true: You who find Christ precious have true faith in Him. It is important, while looking at these words of the apostle Peter, that we should lay our hands upon our hearts and ask, "Do I know what this means? Is Jesus more to me than gold or any other thing that can be desired? Can I truly say:

> *Yes, you are precious to my soul,*
> *My transport and my trust:*
> *Jewels to you are gaudy toys,*
> *And gold is sordid dust.*

If you can testify this, then you have proved your own possession of saving faith. Dear friends, if we can verify this statement, it is not only satisfactory to ourselves but glorifying to our Lord!

Certain men are best respected where they are least known. Many a

336

character needs distance to lend enchantment to the view, but our Lord is most precious to those who are best acquainted with Him. Those who are actually trusting Him and thus putting Him to the test are those who have the highest opinion of Him. If you would have the best estimate of the Lord Jesus, we refer you to those who have had transactions with Him on the largest scale—to those who cast all their care upon Him for time and eternity. Their proof of Him is so satisfactory that He is more and more esteemed every day. He is far more precious to them than when they first heard of Him, and every thought of Him makes Him dearer to their hearts. What a glorious friend is He who is most precious to those who receive most from Him! Usually men feel sadness at an increase of obligation, but in this case the more we are His debtors, the more we rejoice to be so. Thousands here this morning can say, "I believe in Him and He is precious to me beyond all compare."

O my unbelieving hearer, is there no weight in this testimony? If those who believe in Christ uniformly declare that He becomes more and more delightful to them, should it not persuade you to trust Him? If large numbers of Christians were met with who turned round, after a few years, and confessed that they had been deceived and that, when the novelty was worn off, there was really nothing precious about the Lord Jesus, then unbelievers would be justified in their unbelief! But if it is not so—if it is the very reverse—what will I say to you who will not consider the claims of Jesus? Why do you continue to refuse a Savior to whom so many bear witness?

I can truly say our witness is not forced. It is joyfully spontaneous and we are glad to bear it on all occasions and in any company. If we do so unanimously, and I am sure we do, you ought to be convinced of the truth of our statement! And if your judgment were not perverted by sin, you *would* be convinced so that you would resolve to believe in Jesus even as we believe. Do you despise our testimony, which is also the testimony, in many instances, of your own father and mother and friends? Surely you are not so ungenerous as to call us all liars or fools! I pray you, therefore, give practical weight to the evidence by believing in Jesus, and He will be to you as precious as He is to us! This is but common sense! May God give you grace enough to follow the dictates of ordinary prudence, for these would certainly lead you to do what others have found to be so great a blessing to them.

Coming at once to the text, we will consider what Christ is to His people.

According to our text, He is precious. Second, consider what it is in them that makes them so greatly value their Lord: "Therefore, to you who believe, He is precious." It is their *faith* that apprehends the preciousness of Christ, and without it Jesus would never be precious in their eyes. Third, consider what they receive from Him. This thought arises out of another translation of the text, more strictly accurate than the one we use: "Therefore, to you who believe, He is precious." The Lord Jesus sheds honor and glory upon those who believe in Him. May that honor be ours! Oh, for the aid of the Holy Spirit in this promising meditation!

I. First, consider *what Christ is to His people*. We read in our own version, "Therefore, to you who believe, He is precious," yet the word is not an adjective, but a *noun*. Hence the Revised Version translates the text, "For you therefore that believe is the preciousness." His very self is preciousness itself! He is the essence, the substance, and the sum of all preciousness! Every believer will subscribe to this. Many things are more or less precious, but the Lord Jesus is preciousness itself, outsoaring all degrees of comparison!

> *Y*ou need never raise the question as to whether you have the faith of God's elect and are true believers in Jesus. If Christ is precious to you, that question is answered once and for all. . . .

How do believers show that Christ is thus precious to them? They do so by trusting everything to Him. Every believer places his hope solely upon the work of Jesus. With regard to the past, the present, and the future, he finds rest in Christ. The Lord Jesus is the case into which we have put all our treasures, and we prize Him accordingly. All our affection flows toward Him as all our hope flows from Him. Within His sacred name and person all our expectation is contained. He is all our salvation and all our desire. Despite the homely proverb, we have put all our eggs into this one basket. All our supplies are in this one ship. We have no reserve. We have deposited with our Lord everything that concerns us, and we have no secondary trust wherewith to supplement His power or love. We have committed to Him our all, and we know that He is able to keep that which we have committed to Him till that day.

As the advocate who alone pleads the causes of our soul before the living God, our Lord is most precious to us. Our implicit faith in Him proves our high estimate of Him. To believers the Lord Jesus is evidently very precious, because they would give up all that they have sooner than lose Him. Martyrs and confessors have actually given up all for Jesus times without number—history bears this witness abundantly. Tens of thousands have renounced property, liberty, and *life* sooner than deny Christ! To this day we have among us those who dare to go forth into the fever country for His name's sake, not counting their lives dear to them that they might spread abroad His gospel!

I hope that *we* also could part with everything sooner than separate from our Lord. We would, like the holy children, if the choice lay between apostasy and the fiery furnace, reply, "We are not careful to answer you in this matter." Let all things go, but we must hold fast our Lord. Brothers and sisters, could you give up your Savior? Very dear to you are your children, your spouse, and your friends, but if it really came to the point to give these up or the Lord Jesus, I am sure you would not hesitate. It is a desirable thing to be esteemed and respected by one's fellows, but when it comes to this, that for the truth of God's sake one must be an outcast and become the butt of enmity, there must be no question. Popularity and friendship must at once be sacrificed. Believer, you would far sooner take up your cross and go with Jesus than take up your crown and go away from Him. Is it not so?

We must not speak too confidently and declare that we would never deny Him, but yet He knows all things and He knows that we love Him so truly that for His sake we would suffer the loss of all things and count them but dung, that we might win Christ and be found in Him. This proves that our Lord is precious, since all else may go to the bottom so long as we can keep our hold on our Well Beloved. Saints also find their all in Him. He is not *one* delight, but all manner of delights to them! All that they can need or wish or conceive, they find in Him. To the believer, Christ is all. Our desires go not beyond the landmarks of His all-sufficiency. When saints have outward goods, they enjoy Jesus in them, and when outward goods are gone, they find them in Him. That which to a man is all things is, in the most emphatic sense, precious, and Christ is that to every believing soul.

So precious is Jesus to believers that they cannot speak well enough of Him. Could you, at your very best, exalt the Lord Jesus so gloriously as to satisfy yourself? I make free confession that I never preached a sermon about my Lord that came anywhere near my ideal of His merits. I am always dissatisfied when I have done my very best. I have often wished that I could rush back to the pulpit and try to preach Him better, but I am kept back from such an attempt by the fear that probably I might fail even more conspicuously. He is so glorious as to be glory itself! Who can describe the sun? He is so sweet in our apprehension that we cannot convey that apprehension to another by such feeble expressions as words. Our thoughts of the Lord Jesus Christ are far, far below His worth, but even those thoughts we cannot communicate to another, for they break the backs of words.

Language staggers under the weight of holy emotion that comes upon us in connection with the Lord Jesus! We can never say enough of God's unspeakable gift! On any other subject there is danger of exaggeration, but it is impossible here. If you find honey, it is well to eat cautiously of it, for it may pall upon you. But when you find Christ, take in all you can and pray for an enlarged capacity, for He will never grow too sweet. When you begin to talk of what you have tasted and handled concerning Jesus, speak with an open mouth and give your tongue unbounded liberty. You need now no bridle for your lips! Rather let a live coal from off the altar burn every bond and set you free to speak at large of Him who is still as far beyond you as the heavens are above the earth!

Saints show that in their estimation Christ is precious, for they can never *do* enough for Him. It is not all talk; they are glad to labor for Him who died for them. Though they grow weary *in* His work, they never grow weary *of* it. Have we not heard them sigh for a thousand tongues that they might sing the dear Redeemer's praises as they should be sung? Do they not often wish that they had ten thousand hands, yes, ten thousand bodies, that they might be in a thousand places at once seeking to glorify their Well Beloved? If they could have their utmost wish as to His glory and lay down all at His feet, even then they would be dissatisfied and feel themselves to be infinite debtors to their loving Lord! Oh, that we could crown Him with infinite glory! Oh, that we could set Him on a gloriously high throne among men, where every soul could see Him, love Him, and adore Him!

What great things saints have tried to do for Christ! Yet never one of them has expressed any satisfaction with what he has done; all have mourned over their shortcomings and wished that they could devise a tribute more equal to His worth. Saints show how precious Christ is to them in that He is their heaven. Have you ever heard them, when dying, talk about their joy in the prospect of being with Christ? They have not so much rejoiced because they were escaping the woes of this mortal life, nor even because they would rest from their toils, but because they would behold the Lord! Often have we seen the eyes sparkle as the dying believer said, "I will see the King in His beauty before many hours have passed."

When saints quit the world, their last thought is that they will be with their Redeemer—and when they enter heaven, their first thought is to behold His glory! To believers Jesus *is* heaven. The Lamb is the light, the life, and the substance of heavenly bliss:

> *Not all the harps above*
> *Could make a heavenly place,*
> *If God His residence remove,*
> *Or but conceal His face.*

We long to be with Christ! Many of us could say with David, "Although my house is not so with God, yet He has made with me an everlasting covenant, ordered in all things and secure. For this is all my salvation and all my desire" (2 Sam. 23:5). Christ is to us the covenant, and in Him we find the foundation of our first hope and the topstone of our highest joy. Is He not indeed precious to us?

If you are not satisfied with these proofs that Christ is precious to believers, I would invite my dear brothers and sisters to add another themselves. Let every one of us do something fresh by which to prove the believer's love to Christ! Let us not be satisfied with proof already given. Let us invent a new love token! Let us sing to the Lord a new song! Let not this cold world dare to doubt that to believers Christ is precious! Let us force the scoffers to believe that we are in earnest!

In thinking Christ to be precious, the saints are forming a just estimate of Him. "He is precious." For a thing to be rightly called precious, it should have three qualities: It should be rare, it should have an intrinsic value of its own, and it should possess useful and important properties. All those three things meet in our adorable Lord and make Him precious to discerning minds. As for rarity—talk not of the rarity of gold or of gems—He is the *only* One! He is absolutely unique. Other foundation can no man lay than that which is laid. He is the one sacrifice for sin. Neither the infinite God nor all the wealth of heaven could supply another like He. As God and man, He alone combines the two natures in one person. There is "one Mediator between God and men, the Man Christ Jesus" (1 Tim. 2:5). If we can never find another like He, after searching all the ages through, we may well call Him precious!

It is also most clear that He is intrinsically valuable, so who will estimate His worth? I should darken counsel by words without knowledge if I were to attempt in detail to tell you what He is. Only dwell on the simple fact that while He is God over all and has thus the fullness of the Godhead, He is also man, true man of the substance of His mother, and so has all the adaptation of *perfect* manhood. Consider how great this man was. Not even heaven itself can be compared with Christ Jesus! He is incomparably, immeasurably, inconceivably precious! As for useful qualities, where else will we find such a variety of uses in one place? He is eyes to the blind, ears to the deaf, feet to the lame, healing to the sick, freedom to the slave, joy to the mourner, and life to the dead!

> *O*ur desires go not beyond the landmarks of His all-sufficiency. When saints have outward goods, they enjoy Jesus in them, and when outward goods are gone, they find them in Him.

Think of His life and how it gives life to the believer! Think of His death and how it redeems from hell all those who trust in Him! Think of His resurrection and how it justifies believers; of His second coming and how it delights our hearts! Think of our Lord in all His offices, as prophet, priest, and king! Think of Him in all His relationships as husband, brother, friend! Think of Him under all the types and figures with which scripture delights to set Him forth! Think of Him in all positions and conditions!

Think of Him as you will and as you can. In every one of these He has a blessed use for the supply of some terrible need that afflicts His redeemed! He is set for the removal of your condemnation, the pardon of your sin, the justification of your person, the changing of your nature, the presentation of your offerings, the preservation of your graces, the perfecting of your holiness, and for all other good and necessary purposes. All good things meet in Him and meet in Him in profusion, even to superabundance! Why, He is precious indeed!

The saints form their estimate of Him upon scriptural principles. They are not so fanatical as to be carried away by mere passion. They can be brought to the Bible and they can give a reason for their estimate. The text puts it, "Therefore, to you who believe, He is precious." We have a *therefore* for our valuation of Christ. We have reckoned and calculated and have reason on our side! Though we count Him to be the chief among ten thousand and altogether lovely, we can justify our highest estimate of our dear Lord and Savior.

Observe the run of the context. Our Lord Jesus is very precious to us as a living stone. As a foundation He is firm as a stone. But in addition, He has life, and this life He communicates so that we also become living stones and are joined to Him in living, loving, lasting union. A stone alive and imparting life to other stones that are built upon it is indeed a precious thing in a spiritual house that is to be inhabited of God! This gives a character to the whole structure. Our Lord is, in fact, the source of all the life that fits the church to be a temple for the living God. We see that Christ in the church is the center and crown of it. He is as precious to it as the head is to the body. Without Christ we are useless stones over which men stumble and dead stones without feeling or power. But in Him, being quickened with a heavenly life, we are built together into a habitation of God through the Spirit. Solomon's temple was a mere thing of earth as compared with the spiritual house that God constructs out of those who are made alive by contact with the living stone.

I may add that our Lord is all the more precious to us because He was "disallowed indeed of men" (1 Pet. 2:4 KJV). Never is Christ dearer to the believer than when he sees Him to be despised and rejected of men. We do not follow the fashion. We know not the broad road and its crowds, and hence the Lord Jesus is immeasurably glorious to us when we see that the world knew Him not. Did they call the Master of the house Beelzebub? Then the more heartily we salute Him as Lord and God! Did they charge Him with drunkenness and madness and with being a friend of publicans and sinners? We bow at His feet with all the lowlier reverence and love! Did they spit upon Him? Did they scourge Him? Did they blindfold Him and then mock Him? Ah, then He is to our souls all the worthier of adoration! Crown the Crucified! As the sun at noonday is He when nailed to the cross and reviled by the ribald crowd!

Now is He glorious in our eyes, while scribes and Pharisees make jests around Him and He dies in agony. Worship Him, all you glorified ones! We feel as if worship fit for Him upon the throne did not reach the height He deserved when we see Him on the accursed tree. Here would our reverence sink lower than ever and our praise would rise above angelic adoration! Precious is our Lord Christ as we see Him going up to the cross bearing our sins in His own body! Precious is He when forsaken of God and discharging all our debt by His dread sacrifice! Unto you that believe, He is all the more precious because He is still disallowed of men.

> *Solomon's temple was a mere thing of earth as compared with the spiritual house that God constructs out of those who are made alive by contact with the living stone.*

He becomes inconceivably precious to us when we read the next words and view Him as chosen of God. God has chosen the man Christ Jesus to be our Savior. Upon whom else could the divine election have fallen? But He says, "I have given help to one who is mighty; I have exalted one chosen from the people" (Ps. 89:19). The choice of Jehovah must be divinely wise. Infinitely prudent is the choice of Him whom He has exalted to be a prince and a Savior. O glorious Christ, chosen of God, well may You be chosen of us! If Your Father's heart is set on You, well may ours be! To us You are precious!

Note well that the apostle calls Him precious, that is, precious to God. We feel abundantly justified in our high esteem of our Lord since He is so dear to the Father. He never looks with such delight on any as He does upon His own Son. Three times He spoke it out in words: "This is My beloved Son, in whom I am well pleased" (Matt. 3:17). The Father finds full rest in His Only Begotten. God finds in Him union and communion, as in "one brought up with Him" who was "daily his delight, rejoicing always before him" (Prov. 8:30 KJV).

The Father loves the Son and has given all things into His hands. The Father finds infinite delight in His well-beloved Son, and will not we be directed by His wisdom to do the same? Since God accounts Him elect and precious, we too will choose Him and reckon Him to be most precious to our hearts.

Moreover, we prize our Lord Jesus as our foundation. Jehovah says, "Behold, I lay in Zion a stone for a foundation, a tried stone, a precious cornerstone, a sure foundation" (Isa. 28:16). This foundation is not of our inventing, but of God's laying. What a privilege to have a foundation of the Lord's own laying! It is and must be the best, the surest, the most abiding, the most precious foundation! We value, in a building, a sound basis, and therefore we count our Lord most precious because nothing that rests upon Him can fail or fall.

Thus have I shown you that we run on good lines when Christ is precious to us. We are not here acting upon our own independent judgment or following a freak of fancy. If Christ is precious to us, we have God Himself at the back of our judgment and we are sure we do not err. Besides, we have this witness of the Spirit, that since we are pleased with Jesus, the Father is pleased with us! The Father is not only well pleased with Christ but also well pleased in Christ, and therefore He is well pleased with all who are in Him. He is so sweet that He sweetens all who come to God by Him. Precious Christ! Precious Christ!

II. Second, consider *what it is in the saints that makes them prize Christ at this rate.* It is their faith. "Therefore, to you who believe, He is precious." To carnal sense and reason, Jesus is far from precious. To human wisdom, Christ is not precious. See how men tug and labor to get rid of His deity and to trample on His precious blood! What labored learning is brought forth to drain inspiration out of His Bible and steal satisfaction out of His blood! But "therefore, to you who believe, He is precious." Faith calls Him precious when others esteem Him "a root out of dry ground" (Isa. 53:2).

Note well that to faith the promises concerning Christ are made. If you will read Psalm 118, to which Peter refers, you will find that the psalmist who rejoiced to see Him, made the headstone of the corner was a believer, for he says, "I will praise You, for You have answered me, and have become my salvation" (118:21). The whole psalm runs in that way. As for the passage quoted from Isaiah 28:16, it finishes thus: "Whoever believes will not act hastily," or "shall not be confounded." In both cases the preciousness of Christ is connected in the scriptures with a *believing* people. The Bible never expects that without faith men will glorify Christ. For, dear brothers and sisters, *it is by faith that the value of Christ is perceived.*

You cannot see Christ by mere reason, for the natural man is blind to the things of the Spirit. You may study the evangelists themselves, but you will never get to see the real Christ who is precious to believers except by a personal act of faith in Him. The Holy Spirit has removed the scales from the eyes of the man who believes. If you trust the Savior as a sinner must trust Him, you know more of Him by that act of faith than all the schools could have taught you. An ounce of faith is better than a ton of learning! Better to be Christ's patient than a doctor of divinity—for His cure will teach you more than all your studies. More is to be learned in the closet by penitent faith than in the university by persevering research. If we look to Him whom God has lifted up, as Moses lifted up the serpent in the wilderness, we will know more of Him than if we closed our eyes and spent a century in meditation.

By faith, again, the Lord Jesus is appropriated, and in possession lies much of His preciousness. Is the Kohinoor a precious thing to me? Well, it is precious in itself, but I cannot say that it is precious to me for I do not even know where it is, nor do I give it more thought than if it were a bit of glass. When a thing belongs to you, it has a value to you and you make a full estimate of it. Now, no man possesses Christ unless he believes in Him. O unbeliever, you have nothing to do with Jesus if you will not trust in Him! Though He is a priceless gift, He is nothing to you if you do not rest in Him! What have you to do to speak about Him? You are without Christ if you are without faith. Faith is the hand that grasps Him, the mouth that feeds upon Him, and therefore by faith He is precious.

By faith the Lord Jesus is more and more tasted and proved and becomes more and more precious. In proportion as we taste our Lord, He will rise in our esteem. If you have tasted that the Lord is gracious, He is precious to you. And if you have more than tasted and have gone on to feed upon Him, you have found Him to be marrow and fatness to your soul—and He is more precious than ever to you. The more afflictions a believer endures, the more he discovers the sustaining power of Christ, and therefore the more precious Christ becomes to him. You who have been caught in a storm at sea and have seen Him come to you walking on the water and have heard Him rebuke the winds and the waves—you prize Him beyond all price! In the great deeps of tribulation we find many a pearl of the knowledge of Christ. To us our Lord is as gold tried in the fire. Our knowledge is neither theoretical nor traditional—we have seen Him ourselves and He is precious to us.

Our sense of Christ's preciousness, as I have said before, is a proof of our possessing the faith of God's elect—and this ought to be a great comfort to any of you who are in the habit of looking within. If you inquire within yourselves, *Is my faith worked in my soul by the Holy Spirit?* you may have a sure test. Does it magnify Christ? If it makes Christ inexpressibly dear to you, it is the faith of God's elect. May God grant you to have more of it! *Christ becomes growingly precious to us as our faith grows.* If you have faith in Christ but do not exercise it every day, He will not be very precious to you. But if your faith keeps its eyes fixed on Him, it will more and more clearly perceive His beauties. If your soul is driven to Jesus again and again—if your faith anchors in Him continually—then He will be, indeed, more and more precious to you.

Everything depends upon faith. If you doubt Christ, He has gone down 50 percent in your esteem. Every doubt is a Christ crucifier. Every time you give way to skepticism and critical questioning, you lose a sip of sweetness. The dog that barks loses the bone, and the Christian who disputes loses spiritual food. In proportion as you believe with a faith that is childlike, clear, simple, strong, unbroken—in that proportion will Christ be dearer and dearer to you! I recommend you keep the door of your mind on the chain in these days—for those tramps and vagrants called doubts are prowling about in every quarter, and they may knock at your door with vile intent. The first thing they say when they are at a good man's door is, "I am an *honest* doubt." That which so loudly calls itself honest has good need to fabricate for itself a character.

The most honest doubt is a great thief. Most doubts are as dishonest as common housebreakers. Keep doubt out of the soul, or you will make small progress in the discovery of the preciousness of Christ. Never entertain a thought that is derogatory to Christ's person or to His atoning sacrifice. Reckon any opinion to be your enemy that is the enemy of the cross of Christ. Do not suffer your faith to diminish even in the least degree. Believe in Christ heartily and unsuspectingly! If you have a doubt as to whether you are a saint—you can have no question that you are a sinner—come to Christ as a *sinner* and put your trust in Him as your Savior! It is wonderful how a renewed confidence in Christ's saving grace will bring back all your joy and delight in Him, and sometimes do it at once.

"Or ever I was aware, my soul made me like the chariots of Amminadib" (Song of Sol. 6:12 KJV). When I was dull and dead, all of a sudden I touched His garment by faith and my life was renewed in me, even to leaping and rejoicing! God grant you, dear brothers and sisters, by faith, to know the preciousness of Christ, for only to you who believe is He precious! To you who doubt, to you who mistrust, to you who suspect, to you who live in the land of hesitation, He is without form or comeliness, but to you who believe without doubt, He is precious beyond all price.

III. Now I come to the last point. Briefly consider *what believers receive from Him*. Take the exact translation: "Unto you that believe He is honor." Honor? Can honor ever belong to a sinner like me? Worthless, base, only fit to be cast away—can I have honor? Listen! "Since you were precious in My sight, you have been honored, and I have loved you; therefore I will give men for you, and people for your life" (Isa. 43:4).

A woman had been a harlot, but she believed in Jesus and she was so honorable that she was allowed to wash His feet with tears and wipe them with the hairs of her head! Thus was she a handmaid in the courts of our God. A man had been a thief, but he believed while dying, and lo, he was the *first* person Jesus received when He came into His kingdom—he was so honorable! The Lord changes the rank when He forgives the sin. You are dishonorable no longer if you believe in Jesus! You are *honorable* before God now that He has become your salvation! Yesterday you fed the swine; today you are joyfully welcomed to your Father's house! Listen to that music and dancing—it is all for you! See the fatted calf killed and roasting at the fire—it is for you! For you the shoes upon your feet and the ring that decks your finger. Your Father gives Himself to you by those fond kisses that He lavishes upon you. Oh yes, Christ is *honor* to His people—His redemption makes precious what seemed to have no value before.

Further, let me notice that *it is a high honor to be associated with the Lord Jesus*. When a valiant man has achieved a great victory, everybody likes to claim some connection with him. The few persons still alive who were at the Battle of Waterloo are proud of the fact. And no wonder! Though only a drummer boy at the time, the old man is proud to tell that he was there when his countrymen broke the tyrant's power. Men even carry to the extreme of folly any slight connection with the great—like the man who boasted that the king had spoken to him, when it turned out that all His Majesty said was, "Get out of the way!"

We have *real* honor in being associated with our Lord Christ in *any* capacity. It is an honor to have washed the feet of His servants or to have given a cup of cold water to one of His disciples. Simple trust and grateful service make a link more precious than gold. Did men laugh at you for

Christ's sake? That honors you with Him! Did you suffer reproach for Christ's truth? It is well—thus are you bound up in the bundle of life with Him whom you love! The day will come when it will be thought to be the highest honor that ever was to have been denounced as a bigot and cast out as a troublemaker for the sake of Christ and His gospel. How pleased was John the Baptist to be connected with Jesus though he said of Him, "whose sandal strap I am not worthy to loose" (John 1:27).

How glad was Paul to be subservient to His Lord! He calls himself Christ's bondservant. We read it "servant" in our softened version, but Paul was charmed to feel that he had been *bought* with Christ's blood and was therefore as much His *property* as a man thought a slave to be when he had paid his price. Oh, to be as the dust of our Lord's feet! Even this is honor! To be His menial servant is better than to rule all of Russia! Some of us bless the Lord that we are associated with His old-fashioned cross, His timeworn truth, His despised atonement, His antiquated Bible. I proclaim I bind this as a chaplet about my brow! Jesus, the substitute, is my honor, and the doctrines of grace are my glory!

Again, *it is a great honor to be built on Him as a sure foundation.* If you read the passage in Isaiah 28, you will see that those who made lies their refuge were trodden down, but not those who rested on the sure foundation, for of them it is written, "Whoever believes will not act hastily" (Isa. 28:16). Because he had built upon Christ, the builder enjoyed an honorable rest. I do not know how I should feel if I had had to think of a way of salvation for myself, but I find it happy work to accept what God has clearly revealed in His Word.

A minister once said to me, "It must be very easy for you to preach."

I said, "Do you think so? I do not look at it as a light affair."

"Yes," he said, "it is easy, because you hold a fixed and definite set of truths upon which you dwell from year to year."

I did not see how this made it easy to preach, but I did see how it made my heart easy and I said, "Yes, that is true. I keep to one fixed line of truth."

"That is not my case," said he. "I revise my creed from week to week. It is with me constant change and progress."

I did not say much, but I thought the more. If the foundation is constantly being altered, the building will be rather shaky. Surely if the basis is not settled, we shall, in our work, show a good deal of jerry-building!

It is a precious thing to my heart to feel sure about the truths of God, the revealed facts of scripture. Having once made Christ my foundation, I will take a leaf out of the book of the Puritans of Massachusetts. I have heard that in their early days their counselors agreed that the state of Massachusetts should be governed by the laws of God until they had time to make better ones. So will I rest on Christ alone till I can find a better resting place! When we find that God has laid another foundation, we will look at it. When we discover a foundation more suitable for sinners than the sinner's Savior, we will consider it, but not till then.

> *It is an honor to believe what the lips of Jesus taught. I would sooner be a fool with Christ than a wise man with the philosophers.*

Beloved, *it is an honor to believe the doctrines taught by Christ and His apostles.* It is an honor to be on the same lines of truth as the Holy Spirit. It is an honor to believe what the lips of Jesus taught. I would sooner be a fool with Christ than a wise man with the philosophers. The day will come when he who cleaves most to the gospel of God will be the most honored man. *It is an honor to do as Christ bade us in His precepts.* Holiness is the truest royalty. It is never a disgrace to any man to be baptized into His name or to come to His table and break bread in remembrance of Him. Mary's advice is sound: "Whatever He says to you, do it" (John 2:5). *Obedience* to Jesus is no discredit to any man. It is an honor to "follow the Lamb wherever He goes" (Rev. 14:4). Take this as a sure word: Sin is disgrace, but *holiness* is honor!

It will be our great honor to see our Lord glorified. Psalm 118 depicts the exultation of the saints in the day when Christ will appear in His glory. See how it runs. "I will praise You, for You have answered me, and have become my salvation. The stone which the builders rejected has become the chief cornerstone. This was the LORD's doing; it is marvelous in our eyes. This is the day which the LORD has made; we will rejoice and be glad in it" (118:21–24). It is a very jubilant psalm. All the adversaries of the believer have been destroyed like swarms of bees and burned up like heaps of thorns, but the believer is safe, and more, he is glorified as he sees his despised and rejected Lord made head over all things to His church!

What an honor to have been with Him in His humiliation! How glorious to rehearse the story! The Lord laid Christ as the foundation though the heathen raged. The walls have risen despite the foe. The cornerstone is in its place, though the builders refused it. Glory! Glory! He whom we love has come to His own although the kings stood up and the rulers took counsel together against Him! Now, it is no more, "Crucify Him! Crucify Him!" but "Crown Him! Crown Him!" Now He is no more the servant of servants, but King of kings and Lord of lords. Hallelujah! Like bursts of great artillery, the praises of men and angels break forth again and again for Him!

Hallelujah! Hallelujah! Hallelujah! He must reign! He must reign! The Father wills it and reign He shall—all enemies being put under His feet. In that day, to you who believe, He will be an honor! You will be His honored attendants when He mounts the throne! Surely the angels will set great store by every one of you who believed in Christ in the day of His scorning—they will carry you as trophies through the golden streets! Here is a man who believed in Jesus when the world despised Him! Though he was poor and obscure, he dared to own his Lord and stand up for His truth. Happy man to have been able to give such a proof of loyalty!

He was a common soldier in the barracks and he was the butt of many a coarse joke—but he believed in Jesus! Honor to him! She was a humble workwoman and all the girls in the warehouse ridiculed her for being a Christian. Honor to her! Honor to all who bore dishonor for Christ! Before you go away, I would beg you to consider how you stand in this matter. Do you believe in Jesus? If you do believe, be afraid of nothing! Come forward and confess that sacred name! Proclaim that you are a follower of the Lamb, and then, in the day when He distributes crowns and thrones, He will have a crown and a throne for you! You, at the resurrection, will wake up in Him to glory and immortality!

FOR FURTHER THOUGHT

1. *According to 1 Peter 2:7, what does it indicate if a person can say, "Jesus Christ is precious"?*
2. *First Peter 2:6 gives reasons why Jesus Christ is precious to us. What are these?*
3. *How should the words of Matthew 3:17 and Proverbs 8:30 affect our attitude toward Jesus Christ?*

The Ascension and the Second Advent Practically Considered

And while they looked steadfastly toward heaven as He went up,
behold, two men stood by them in white apparel, who also said, "Men
of Galilee, why do you stand gazing up into heaven? This same Jesus,
who was taken up from you into heaven, will so come
in like manner as you saw Him go into heaven."
ACTS 1:10–11

FOUR great events shine out brightly in our Savior's story. All Christian minds delight to dwell upon His birth, His death, His resurrection, and His ascension. These make four rungs in that ladder of light, the foot of which is upon the earth, but the top reaches to heaven. We could not afford to dispense with any one of these four events, nor would it be profitable for us to forget or to underestimate the value of any one of them. That the Son of God was born of a woman creates in us the intense delight of a brotherhood springing out of a common humanity. That Jesus once suffered to the death for our sins and thereby made a full atonement for us is the rest and life of our spirits. The manger and the cross together are divine seals of love. That the Lord Jesus rose again from the dead is the warrant of our justification and also a transcendently delightful assurance of the resurrection of all His people and of their eternal life in Him. Has He not said, "Because I live, you will live also" (John 14:19)? The resurrection of Christ is the morning star of our future glory! Equally delightful is the remembrance of His ascension. No song is sweeter than this: "You have ascended on high, You have led captivity captive; You have received gifts among men, even from the rebellious, that the LORD God might dwell there" (Ps. 68:18).

Each one of these four events points to another, and they all lead up to a fifth. The fifth link in the golden chain is our Lord's second and most glorious advent. Nothing is mentioned between His ascent and His descent. True, a rich history comes between, but it lies in a valley between two stupendous mountains—we step from alp to alp as we journey in meditation from the Ascension to the Second Advent. I say that each of the previous four events points to it. Had He not come a first time, in humiliation, born under the law, He could not come a second time in amazing glory "apart from sin, for salvation" (Heb. 9:28). Because He died once, we rejoice that He dies no more. Death has no more dominion over Him, and therefore He comes to destroy that last enemy whom He has already conquered.

It is our joy, as we think of our Redeemer as risen, to feel that in consequence of His rising, the trumpet of the archangel will assuredly sound for the awaking of all His slumbering people when the Lord Himself will descend from heaven with a shout. As for His ascension, He could not a second time descend if He had not first ascended! But having perfumed heaven with His presence and prepared a place for His people, we may fitly expect that He will come again and receive us to Himself, that where He is, there we may be also. I want you, therefore, as in contemplation you pass with joyful steps over these four grand events, as your faith leaps from His birth to His death, and from His resurrection to His ascension, to be looking forward and even hastening to this crowning fact of our Lord's history—for before long He will so come in like manner as He was seen going up into heaven.

This morning, in our meditation, we will start from the Ascension, and if I had sufficient imagination, I would like to picture our Lord and the eleven walking up the side of Olivet, communing as they went, a happy company with a solemn awe upon them, but with an intense joy in having fellowship with each other! Each disciple was glad to think that his dear Lord and Master who had been crucified was now among them, not only alive but surrounded with a mysterious safety and glory that none could disturb. The enemy was as still as a stone; not a dog moved his tongue; His bitterest foes made no sign during the days of our Lord's afterlife below! The company moved peacefully onward toward Bethany, the Bethany that they all knew and loved. The Savior seemed drawn there at the time of His ascension, even as men's minds return to old and well-loved scenes when they are about to depart out of this world. His happiest moments on earth had been spent beneath the roof where lived Mary and Martha and their brother, Lazarus. Perhaps it was best for the disciples that He should leave them at that place where He had been most hospitably entertained, to show that He departed in peace and not in anger. There they had seen Lazarus raised from the dead by Him who was now to be taken up from them. The memory of the triumphant past would help the tried faith of the present. There they had heard the voice saying, "Loose him, and let him go" (John 11:44), and there they might fitly see their Lord loosened from all bonds of earthly gravitation that He might go to His Father and their Father. The memories of the place might help to calm their minds and arouse their spirits to that fullness of joy that ought to attend the glorifying of their Lord.

> *Though we have known Christ after the flesh, now after the flesh we know Him no more.*

But they have come to a standstill, having reached the brow of the hill. The Savior stands conspicuously in the center of the group, and following upon most instructive discourse, He pronounces a blessing upon them. He lifts His pierced hands, and while He is lifting them and is pronouncing words of love, He begins to rise from the earth. He has risen above them all, to their astonishment! In a moment He has passed beyond the olive trees that seem, with their silvery sheen, to be lit up by His milder radiance. While the disciples are looking, the Lord has ascended into midair and speedily He has risen to the regions of the clouds. They stand spellbound with astonishment, and suddenly a bright cloud, like a chariot of God, bears Him away! That cloud conceals Him from mortal gaze. Though we have known Christ after the flesh, now after the flesh we know Him no more. They are riveted to the spot, very naturally so. They linger long in the place; they stand with streaming eyes, wonder-struck, still looking upward.

It is not the Lord's will that they should long remain inactive—their reverie is interrupted. They might have stood there till wonder saddened into fear. As it was, they remained long enough, for the angel's words may be accurately rendered, "Why do you stand gazing up into heaven?"

Their lengthened gaze needed to be interrupted, and therefore two shining ones, such as before met the women at the sepulchre, are sent to them. These messengers of God appear in human form that they may not alarm them—and in white raiment as if to remind them that all was bright and joyous—and so these white-robed ministers stood with them as if they would willingly join their company. As no one of the eleven would break silence, the men in white raiment commenced the discourse. Addressing them in the usual celestial style, they asked a question that contained its own answer, and then went on to tell their message. As they had once said to the women, "Why do you seek the living among the dead? He is not here, but is risen!" (Luke 24:5–6), so did they now say, "Men of Galilee, why do you stand gazing up into heaven? This same Jesus, who was taken up from you into heaven, will so come in like manner as you saw Him go into heaven."

The angels showed their knowledge of them by calling them "men of Galilee" and reminded them that they were yet upon earth by recalling their place of birth. Brought back to their senses, their reverie over, the apostles at once girded up their loins for active service. They do not need twice telling, but hasten to Jerusalem. The vision of angels has singularly enough brought them back into the world of actual life again, and they obey the command, "Tarry in the city of Jerusalem" (Luke 24:49). They seem to say, "The taking up of our Master is not a thing to weep about. He has gone to His throne and to His glory, and He said it was expedient for us that He should go away. He will now send us the promise of the Father; we scarcely know what it will be like, but let us, in obedience to His will, make the best of our way to the place where He bade us await the gift of power."

Can you not see them going down the side of Olivet, taking that Sabbath day's journey into the cruel and wicked city without a thought of fear; having no dread of the bloodthirsty crew who slew their Lord, but happy in the memory of their Lord's exaltation and in the expectation of a wonderful display of His power? They held fellowship of the most delightful kind with one another and soon entered into the upper room where, in protracted prayer and communion, they waited for the promise of the Father. You see I have no imagination— I have barely mentioned the incidents in the simplest language. Yet try to realize the scene, for it will be helpful to do so, since our Lord Jesus is to come in the same manner as the apostles saw Him go up into heaven.

My first business this morning will be to consider *the gentle chiding* administered by the shining ones: "Men of Galilee, why do you stand gazing up into heaven?" Second, *the cheering description* of our Lord that the white-robed messengers used: "This same Jesus." And then, third, *the practical truth* that they taught: "This same Jesus, who was taken up from you into heaven, will so come in like manner as you saw Him go into heaven."

I. First, then, here is *a gentle chiding*. It is not sharply uttered by men dressed in black who use harsh speech and severely upbraid the servants of God for what was rather a mistake than a fault. No, the language is strengthening, yet tender. The fashion of a question allows them, rather, to reprove themselves than to be reproved—and the tone is that of brotherly love and affectionate concern.

Notice that what these saintly men were doing seems, at first sight, to be very right. I think if Jesus were among us now, we would fix our eyes upon Him and never withdraw them! He is altogether lovely, and it would seem wicked to yield our eyesight to any inferior object so long as He was to be seen. When He ascended up into heaven, it was the duty of His friends to look upon Him. It can never be wrong to look up; we are often bid to do so, and it is even a holy saying of the psalmist: "My voice You shall hear in the morning, O LORD; in the morning I will direct it to You, and I will look up" (Ps. 5:3). And again, "I will lift up my eyes to the hills—from whence comes my help?" (121:1). If it is right to look up into heaven, it must be still more right to look up while Jesus rises to the place of His glory!

Surely it had been wrong if they had looked anywhere else—it was due to the Lamb of God that they should behold Him as long as eyes could follow Him. He is the Sun—where should eyes be turned but to His light? He is the King—where should courtiers within the palace gate turn their eyes but to their King as He ascends to His throne? The truth is, there was nothing wrong in their looking up into heaven. But they went a little further than looking—they stood gazing. A little excess in right may be faulty. It may be wise to look but foolish to gaze. There is a very thin partition, sometimes, between that which is commendable and that which is censurable. There is a golden mean that is not easy to keep. The exact path of right is often as narrow as a razor's edge, and he must be wise that does not err either on the right hand or on the left.

Look is always the right word. Why, it is "Look to Me, and be saved" (Isa. 45:22). Look, yes, look steadfastly and intently. Let your posture be that of one "looking unto Jesus" (Heb. 12:2) always throughout life! But there is a *gazing* that is not commendable. This is when the look becomes not that of reverent worship but of an overweening curiosity; when there mingles with the desire to know what should not be known, a prying into that which it is for God's glory to conceal. Brothers and sisters, it is of little use to look up into an empty heaven! If Christ Himself is not visible in heaven, then in vain do we gaze, since there is nothing for a saintly eye to see! When the person of Jesus was gone out of the blue vault above them and the cloud had effectually concealed Him, why should they continue to gaze when God Himself had drawn the curtain? If infinite wisdom had withdrawn the object upon which they desired to gaze, what would their gazing be but a sort of reflection upon the wisdom that had removed their Lord?

Yet it did seem very right. Thus certain things that you and I may do may appear right and yet we may need to be chided out of them into something better—they may be right in themselves but not appropriate for the occasion, not seasonable or expedient. They may be right up to a point and then may touch the boundary of excess. A steadfast gaze into heaven may be, to a devout soul, a high order of worship, but if this filled up much of our working time, it might become the idlest form of folly!

> he Lord allows us to do that which is innocently natural, but He will not have us carry it too far, for then it might foster an evil nature.

Yet I cannot help adding that *it was very natural*. I do not wonder that the whole eleven stood gazing up, for if I had been there, I am sure I would have done the same. How struck they must have been with the ascent of the Master out of their midst! You would be amazed if someone from among our own number began, right now, to ascend into heaven! Would you not? Our Lord did not gradually melt away from sight as a phantom or dissolve into thin air as a mere apparition. The Savior did not disappear in that way at all, but He *rose*, and they saw that it was His very self that was so rising! His own body, the materialism in which He had veiled Himself, actually, distinctly, and *literally* rose to heaven before their eyes! I repeat, the Lord did not dissolve and disappear like a vision of the night, but He evidently rose till the cloud intervened so that they could see Him no more.

I think I would have stood looking to the very place where His cloudy chariot had been. I know it would be idle to continue to do so, but our hearts often urge us on to acts that we could not logically justify. Hearts are not to be argued with. Sometimes you stand by a grave where one is buried whom you dearly loved—you go there often to weep. You cannot help it; the place is precious to you, yet you could not prove that you do any good by your visits. Perhaps you even injure yourself thereby and deserve to be gently chided with the question, "Why?" It may be the most natural thing in the world, and yet it may not be a wise thing. The Lord allows us to do that which is innocently natural, but He will not have us carry it too far, for then it might foster an evil nature.

Therefore He sends an interrupting messenger—not an angel with a sword or even a rod; He sends some man in white raiment. I mean one who is both cheerful and holy, and he, by his conduct or his words, suggests to us the question, "Why do you stand here gazing?" *Cui bono?* What will be the benefit? What will it avail? Our understanding thus being called into action, we, being men of thought, answer to ourselves, "This will not do. We must not stand gazing here forever." And therefore we arouse ourselves to get back to the Jerusalem of practical life where, in the power of God, we hope to do service for our Master.

Notice, then, that the apostles were doing that which seemed to be right and what was evidently very natural, but that it is very easy to carry the apparently right and the absolutely natural too far. Let us take heed to ourselves and often ask our hearts, "Why?" For, third, notice that what they did *was not, after all, justifiable upon strict reason.* While Christ was going up, it was proper that they should adoringly look at Him. He might almost have said, "If you see me, when I am taken up, a double portion of My spirit will rest upon you." They did well to look where He led the way. But when He was gone, still to remain gazing was an act that they could not exactly explain to themselves and could not justify to others. Put the question thus: "What purpose will be fulfilled by your continuing to gaze into the sky? He is gone; it is absolutely certain that He is gone. He is taken up and God Himself has manifestly concealed all trace of Him by bidding yonder cloud sail in between Him and you. Why do you still gaze? He told you, 'I go to My Father' (John 14:12). Why do you stand and gaze?"

We may, under the influence of great love, act unwisely. I remember well seeing the action of a woman whose only son was emigrating to a distant colony. I stood in the station and I noticed her many tears and her frequent embraces of her boy. But the train came up and he entered the carriage. After the train had passed beyond the station, she was foolish enough to break away from friends who sought to detain her. She ran along the platform, leaped down upon the railroad, and pursued the flying train. It was natural, but it had been better left undone. What was the use of it? We had better abstain from acts that serve no practical purpose, for in this life we have neither time nor strength to waste in fruitless action. The apostles would be wise to cease gazing, for nobody would be benefited by it, and they would not themselves be blessed. What is the use of gazing when there is nothing to see? Well, then, did the angels ask, "Why do you stand gazing up into heaven?"

Again, put another question: What precept were they obeying when they stood gazing up into heaven? If you have a command from God to do a certain thing, you need not inquire into the reason of the command. It is disobedient to begin to canvass God's will. But when there is no precept whatever, why persevere in an act that evidently does not promise to bring any blessing? Who bade them stand gazing up into heaven? If Christ had done so, then in Christ's name, let them stand like statues and never turn their heads! But as He had not bid them, why did they do what He had not commanded and leave undone what He *had* commanded? For He had strictly charged them that they should tarry at Jerusalem till they were "endued with power from on high" (Luke 24:49). So what they did was not justifiable.

Here is the practical point for us: *What they did we are very apt to imitate.* "Oh," you say, "I will never stand gazing up into heaven." I am not sure of that. Some Christians are very curious, but not obedient. Plain precepts are neglected, but difficult problems they seek to solve. I remember one who used to always be dwelling upon the bowls and seals and trumpets. He was great at apocalyptic symbols, but he had seven children and no family prayer. If he had left the bowls and trumpets and minded his boys and girls, it would have been a deal better! I have known men marvelously proficient upon the book of Daniel and specially instructed in Ezekiel but singularly forgetful of Exodus 20 and not very clear upon Romans 8. I do not speak with any blame of such folks for studying Daniel and Ezekiel, but quite the reverse. Yet I wish they had been more zealous for the conversion of the sinners in their neighborhoods and more careful to assist the poor saints!

I admit the value of the study of the feet of the image in Nebuchadnezzar's vision and the importance of knowing the kingdoms that make up the ten toes, but I do not see the propriety of allowing such studies to overlay practical godliness. If the time spent over obscure theological propositions were given to a mission in the dim alley near the good man's house, more benefit would come to man and more glory to God. I would have you understand all mysteries, brothers and sisters, if you can—but do not forget that our chief business here below is to cry, "Behold! The Lamb" (John 1:29). By all manner of means, read and search till you know all that the Lord has revealed concerning things to come, but *first of all* see to it that your children are brought to the Savior's feet and that you are workers, together with God, in the building up of His church! The dense mass of misery, ignorance, and sin that is all around us on every side demands all our powers. And if you do not respond to the call, though I am not a man in white apparel, I will venture to say, "You men of Christendom, why do you stand gazing up into the mysteries, when so much is to be done for Jesus, but you are leaving it undone?" O you who are curious but not obedient, I fear I speak to you in vain, but I have spoken. May the Holy Spirit also speak!

Others are contemplative but not active. Many are given to the study of scripture and to meditation but not zealous for good works. Contemplation is so scarce in these days that I could wish there were a thousand times as much of it! But in the case to which I refer, everything runs in the one channel of thought; all time is spent in reading, in enjoyment, in rapture, in pious leisure. Religion never ought to become the subject of selfishness, and yet I fear some treat it as if its chief end was spiritual gratification. When a man's religion all lies in his saving himself and in enjoying holy things for himself, there is a disease upon him! When his judgment of a sermon is based upon the one question, "Did it feed me?" it is a selfish judgment. There is such a thing as getting a selfish religion in which you are first, you are second, you are third, and you are to the utmost end. Did Jesus ever think or speak in that fashion? Contemplation of Christ Himself may be so carried out as to lead you away from Christ—the recluse meditates on Jesus, but he is as unlike the busy self-denying Jesus as well can be! Meditation, unattended with *active service* in the spreading of the gospel among men, well deserves the rebuke of the angel, "Men of Galilee, why do you stand gazing up into heaven?"

Moreover, some are careful, anxious, and deliriously impatient for some marvelous interposition. We get, at times, into a sad state of mind because we do not see the kingdom of Christ advancing as we desire. I suppose it is with you as it is with me. I begin to fret and I am deeply troubled, and I feel that there is good reason that I should be, for the truth of God is fallen in the streets and the days of blasphemy and rebuke are upon us! Then we pine, for the Master is away, and we cry, "When will He be back? Oh, why are His chariots so long in coming? Why does He tarry through the ages?" Our desires sour into impatience and we commence gazing up into heaven, looking for His coming with a restlessness that does not allow us to discharge our duty as we should. Whenever anybody gets into that state, this is the word of God: "Men of Galilee, why do you stand gazing up into heaven?"

In certain cases, this uneasiness has drawn to itself a wrong expectation of immediate wonders and an intense desire for seeing signs. Ah me, what fanaticisms come of this! In America, years ago, one came forward who declared that on such a day the Lord would come, and he led a great company to believe his crazy predictions. Many took their horses and fodder for two or three days and went out into the woods, expecting to be all the more likely to see all that was to be seen when once away from the crowded city. All over the States there were people who had made ascension dresses in which to soar into the air in proper costume! They waited and they waited, and I am sure that no text could have been more appropriate for them than this: "Men of America, why do you stand here gazing up into heaven?"

> *Whenever you meet with a man who sets up to be a prophet, keep out of his way in the future! And when you hear of signs and wonders, turn to your Lord, and in patience possess your souls.*

Nothing came of it, and yet there are thousands in England and America who only need a fanatical leader and they would run into the same folly! The desire to know the times and seasons is a craze with many poor bodies whose insanity runs in that particular groove. Every occurrence is a sign of the times; a sign, I may add, that they do not understand! An earthquake is a special favorite with them. "Now," they cry, "the Lord is coming!" as if there had not been earthquakes of the sort we have heard of lately hundreds of times since our Lord went up into heaven! When the prophetic earthquakes occur in different places, we will know of it without the warnings of these people!

What a number of persons have been infatuated by the number of the beast and have been ready to leap for joy because they have found the number 666 in some great one's name! Why, *everybody's* name will yield that number if you treat it judiciously and use the numerals of Greece, Rome, Egypt, China, or Timbuktu! I feel weary with the silly way in which some people make toys out of scripture and play with texts as with a pack of cards! Whenever you meet with a man who sets up to be a prophet, keep out of his way in the future! And when you hear of signs and wonders, turn to your Lord, and in patience possess your souls. "The just shall live by his faith" (Hab. 2:4). There is no other way of living among wild enthusiasts! Believe in God and ask not for miracles and marvels or the knowledge of times and seasons. To know when the Lord will restore the kingdom is not in your power!

Remember the verse that I read just now in your hearing: "It is not for you to know the times or the seasons" (Acts 1:7 KJV). If I were introduced into a room where a large number of parcels were stored and I was told that there was something good for me, I should begin to look for that which had my name upon it. And when I came upon a parcel and I saw in pretty big letters, "It is not for you," I would leave it alone. Here, then, is a package of knowledge marked, "It is not for you to know the times or the seasons, which the Father hath put in his own power." Cease to meddle with matters that are concealed and be satisfied to know the things that are clearly revealed!

II. Second, I want you to notice *the cheering description* that these bright spirits give concerning our Lord. They describe Him thus: "This same Jesus."

I appreciate the description all the more because *it came from those who knew Him.* He was "seen by angels" (1 Tim. 3:16). They had watched Him all His life long and they knew Him, and when they, having just seen Him rise to His Father and His God, said of Him, "This same Jesus," then I know, by an infallible testimony, that He was the same and that He *is* the same.

Jesus is gone, but He still exists. He has left us, but He is not dead! He has not dissolved into nothing like the mist of the morning. "This same Jesus" is gone up to His Father's throne, and He is there today as certainly as He once stood at Pilate's bar. As surely as He hung upon the cross, so surely does He, the same man, sit upon the throne of God and reign over creation! I like to think of the positive identity of the Christ in the seventh heaven with the Christ in the lowest depths of agony. The Christ they spat upon is now the Christ whose name the cherubim and seraphim are hymning day without night! The Christ they scourged is He before whom principalities and powers delight to cast their crowns! Think of it and be glad this morning—but do not stand gazing up into heaven after a myth or a dream! Jesus lives! Mind that you live also. Do not loiter as if you had nothing at all to do, or as if the kingdom of God had come to an end because Jesus is gone from the earth, as to His bodily presence. It is not all over! He still lives and He has given you a work to do till He comes. Therefore go and do it.

"This same Jesus." I love that word, for *Jesus* means "a Savior." Oh, you anxious sinners here present, the name of Him who has gone up into His glory is full of invitation to you! Will you not come to "this same Jesus"? This is He who opened the eyes of the blind and brought forth the prisoners out of the prisons! He is doing the same thing today! Oh, that your eyes may see His light! He who touched the lepers and who raised the dead is still the same Jesus, able to save to the uttermost. Oh, that you may look and live! You have only to come to Him by faith, as she did who touched the hem of His garment! You have but to cry to Him as the blind man did whose sight He restored! He is the same Jesus, bearing about with Him the same tender love for guilty men and the same readiness to receive and cleanse all who come to Him by faith.

"This same Jesus." Why, that must have meant that He who is in heaven is the same Christ who was on earth! And it must also mean that *He who is to come will be the same Jesus who went up into heaven*! There is no change in our blessed Master's nature, nor will there ever be! There *is* a great change in His *condition*:

> *The Lord will come, but not the same*
> *As once in lowliness He came—*
> *A humble man before His foes,*
> *A weary man and full of woes.*

He will be "the same Jesus" in nature though not in condition. He will possess the same tenderness when He comes to judge, the same gentleness of heart when all the glories of heaven and earth will gird His brow. More our eyes will see Him in that day, and we will recognize Him not only by the nail prints, but also by the very look of His countenance, by the character that gleams from that marvelous face! And we will say, " 'Tis He! 'Tis He! The same Christ who went up from the top of Olivet from the midst of His apostles." Go to Him with your troubles, as you would have done when He was here. Look forward to His second coming without dread! Look for Him with that joyous expectancy with which you would welcome Jesus of Bethany who loved Mary, Martha, and Lazarus!

On the back of that sweet title came this question, "Why do you stand gazing into heaven?"

They might have said, "We stay here because we do not know where to go. Our Master is gone." But oh, it is the same Jesus, and He is coming again, so go down to Jerusalem and get to work! Do not worry yourselves! No grave accident has occurred—it is not a disaster that Christ has gone, but an advance in His work! Despisers tell us nowadays, "Your cause is done for! Christianity is spun out! Your divine Christ is gone! We have not seen a trace of His miracle-working hands, nor of that voice that no man could rival." Here is our answer: We are not standing gazing up into heaven. We are not paralyzed because Jesus is away. He lives, the great Redeemer lives, and though it is our delight to lift up our eyes because we expect His coming, it is equally our delight to turn our heavenly gazing into an earthward watching and to go down into the city and there to tell that Jesus is risen, that men are to be saved by faith in Him, and that whoever believes in Him will have everlasting life!

> *Look forward to His second coming without dread! Look for Him with that joyous expectancy with which you would welcome Jesus of Bethany who loved Mary, Martha, and Lazarus!*

We are not defeated! Far from it—His ascension is not a retreat, but an advance! His tarrying is not for lack of power, but because of the abundance of His long-suffering. The victory is not questionable. All things work for it—all the hosts of God are mustering for the final charge. This same Jesus is mounting His white horse to lead forth the armies of heaven, conquering and to conquer!

III. Our third point is this: *the great practical truth.* This truth is not one that is to keep us gazing into heaven, but one that is to make each of us go to his house to render earnest *service.* What is it? Why, first, that *Jesus is gone into heaven.* Jesus is gone! Jesus is gone! It sounds like a knell. Jesus is taken up from you into heaven! That sounds like a marriage peal! He is gone, but He is gone up to the hills where He can survey the battle! Up to the throne of God from where He can send us succor. The reserve forces of the Omnipotent stood waiting till their captain came, and now that He is come into the center of the universe, He can send legions of angels, or He can raise up hosts of men for the help of His cause. I see every reason for going down into the world and getting to work, for He is gone up into heaven and "all authority has been given to Him in heaven and on earth" (see Matt. 28:18). Is not that a good argument? "Go therefore and make disciples of all the nations, baptizing them in the name of the Father and of the Son and of the Holy Spirit" (28:19).

Jesus will come again. That is another reason for girding our loins, because it is clear that He has not quit the fight nor deserted the field of battle. Our great captain is still heading the conflict! He has ridden into another part of the field, but He will be back again, perhaps in the twinkling of an eye. You do not say that a commander has given up the campaign because it is expedient that he should withdraw from your part of the field. Our Lord is doing the best thing for His kingdom in going away. It was in the highest degree expedient that He should go and that we should, each one, receive the Holy Spirit. There is a blessed unity between Christ the King and the most common soldier in the ranks. He has not taken His heart from us, nor His care from us, nor His interest from us—He is bound up heart and soul with His people and their holy warfare—and this is the evidence of it: "And behold, I am coming quickly, and My reward is with Me, to give to every one according to his work" (Rev. 22:12).

Then, moreover, we are told in the text—and this is a reason why we should get to our work—that *He is coming in the same manner as He departed.* Certain of the commentators do not seem to understand English at all. "He who was taken up from you into heaven, will so come in like manner as you saw Him go into heaven." This, they say, relates to His *spiritual* coming at Pentecost! Give anybody a grain of sense and do they not see that a *spiritual* coming is not a coming in the same manner in that He went up into heaven? There is an analogy but certainly not a likeness between the two things! Our Lord was taken up; they could see Him rise! He will come again and "every eye will see Him." He went up not in *spirit*, but in person! He will come down in person. "This same Jesus will so come in like manner." He went up as a matter of fact, not in poetic figure and spiritual symbol, but as a matter of fact. "This *same* Jesus" *literally* went up. "This same Jesus" will *literally* come again! He will descend in clouds even as He went up in clouds and "shall stand at the latter day upon the earth" (Job 19:25 KJV), even as He stood before! He went up to heaven unopposed! No high priests, nor scribes, nor Pharisees, nor even one of the rabble opposed His ascension. It is ridiculous to suppose that they could. And when He comes a second time, none will stand against Him! His adversaries will perish; as the fat of rams will they melt away in His presence. When He comes, He will break rebellious nations with a rod of iron, for His force will be irresistible in that day.

Brothers and sisters, do not let anybody spiritualize away all this from you! Jesus is coming as a matter of *fact*—therefore go down to your sphere of service as a matter of fact. Get to work and teach the ignorant, win the wayward, instruct the children, and everywhere proclaim the sweet name of Jesus! As a matter of fact, give of your substance and don't just talk about it. As a matter of fact, consecrate your daily life to the glory of God. As a matter of fact, live wholly for your Redeemer! Jesus is not coming in a sort of mythical, misty, hazy way. He is literally and actually coming—and He will literally and actually call upon you to give an account of your stewardship. Therefore now, today, *literally* not symbolically, *personally* and not by deputy, go out through that portion of the world that you can reach and preach the gospel to every creature according as you have opportunity, for this is what the men in white apparel meant—*be ready to meet your coming Lord.*

If you would meet Him with joy, serve Him with earnestness!

What is the way to be ready to meet Jesus? If it is the same Jesus who went away from us who is coming, then let us be doing what He was doing before He went away! If it is the same Jesus who is coming, we cannot possibly put ourselves into a posture of which He will better approve than by going about doing good! If you would meet Him with joy, serve Him with earnestness! If the Lord Jesus Christ were to come today, I would like Him to find me at my studying, praying, or preaching. Would you not like Him to find you in your Sunday school, in your class, or out there at the corner of the street preaching or doing whatever you have the privilege of doing in His name? Would you meet your Lord in idleness? Do not *think* of it!

I called one day on one of our members and she was whitening the front steps. She got up all in confusion. She said, "Oh dear, sir, I did not know you were coming today, or I would have been ready."

I replied, "Dear friend, you could not be in better trim than you are. You are doing your duty like a good housewife, and may God bless you." She had no money to spare for a servant and she was doing her duty by keeping the home tidy. I thought she looked more beautiful with her pail beside her than if she had been dressed according to the latest fashion. I said to her, "When the Lord Jesus Christ comes suddenly, I hope He will find me doing as you were doing, namely, fulfilling the duty of the hour." I want you all to get to your pails without being ashamed of them! Serve the Lord in some way or other! Serve Him always! Serve Him intensely! Serve Him more and more. Go tomorrow and serve the Lord at the counter, or in the workshop, or in the field. Go and serve the Lord by helping the poor and the needy, the widow and the fatherless. Serve Him by teaching the children, especially by endeavoring to train your own children. Go and hold a temperance meeting and show the drunk that there is hope for him in Christ. Or go to the midnight meeting and let the fallen woman know that Jesus can restore her! Do what Jesus has given you the power to do, and then, you men of Britain, you will not stand gazing up into heaven, but you will wait upon the Lord in prayer and you will receive the Spirit of God—and you will proclaim to all around the doctrine of *believe and live*. Then when He comes He will say to you, "Well done, good and faithful servant. . . . Enter into the joy of your lord" (Matt. 25:21). May His grace enable us to do this. Amen.

For Further Thought

1. *What are the four great events in the life of Jesus Christ mentioned in this sermon?*
2. *To which event in the Lord's life does Psalm 68:18 refer?*
3. *Why should Acts 1:11 encourage us regarding the future?*

THE UNCHANGEABLE CHRIST

Jesus Christ is the same yesterday, today, and forever.
HEBREWS 13:8

LET me read to you the verse that comes before our text. It is always a good habit to look at texts in their connection. It is wrong, I think, to lay hold of small portions of God's Word and take them out of their connection as you might pluck feathers from a bird. It is an injury to the Word of God, and sometimes a passage of scripture loses much of its beauty, its true teaching, and its real meaning by being taken from the context. Nobody would think of mutilating Milton's poems by taking a few lines out of "Paradise Lost" and then imagining that he could really get at the heart of the poet's power. So, always look at texts in the connection in that they stand. The verse before our text is this, "Remember those who rule over you, who have spoken the word of God to you, whose faith follow, considering the outcome of their conduct. Jesus Christ is the same yesterday, today, and forever" (Heb. 13:7–8).

Observe, then, that God's people are a thoughtful people. If they are what they ought to be, they do a great deal of remembering and considering. That is the gist of this verse. If they are to remember and to consider their earthly leaders, much more are they to remember that great leader, the Lord Jesus, and all those matchless truths that fell from His blessed lips. I wish, in these days, that professing Christians remembered and considered a great deal more, but we live in such a flurry, hurry, and worry, that we do not give time for thought. Our noble forefathers of the Puritan sort were men with backbone, men of solid tread, independent and self-contained men who could hold their own in the day of conflict. And the reason was because they took time to meditate, time to keep a diary of their daily experiences, time to commune with God in secret. Take the hint and try and do a little more *thinking* in this busy London, and in these trying days, remember and consider.

My next remark is that God's people are an imitative people, for we are told here that they are to remember them who are their leaders, those who have spoken to them the Word of God, "whose faith follow, considering the outcome of their conduct." There is an itching after originality nowadays, for striking out a path for yourself! When sheep do that, they are bad sheep. Sheep follow the shepherd, and in a measure, they follow one another when they are all together following the shepherd. Our great Master never aimed at originality—He said that He did not even speak His own words, but the words that He had heard of His Father. He was docile and teachable. As the Son of God and the servant of God, His ears were open to hear the instructions of the Father, and He could say, "I always do those things that please Him" (John 8:29).

Now that is the true path for a Christian to take, to follow Jesus and, in consequence, to follow all such true saints as may be worthy of being followed, imitating the godly so far as they imitate Christ! The apostle puts it, "whose faith follow." Many young Christians, if they were to pretend to strike out a path for themselves, must infallibly fall into many sorrows. Whereas, by taking some note of the way in that more experienced and more instructed Christians have gone, they will keep by the way of the footsteps of the flock and they will also follow the footprints of the Shepherd. God's people are a thoughtful people and they are an imitative and humble people, willing to be instructed and willing to follow holy and godly examples.

> Before the first star was kindled, before the first living creature began to sing the praise of its Creator, He loved His church with an everlasting love!

One good reason, however, for imitating saints is given in our text. It is because our Lord and His faith are always the same. "Jesus Christ is the same yesterday, today, and forever." You see, if the old foundation shifted, if our faith was always changing, then we could not follow any of the saints who have gone before us. If we have a religion especially for the nineteenth century, it is ridiculous for us to imitate the men of the first century, and Paul and the apostles are just old fogies who are left behind in the far distant ages. If we are to go on improving from century to century, I cannot point you to any of the reformers, or the confessors, or the saints in the brave days of old, and say to you, "Learn from their example," because if religion has altogether changed and improved, it is a curious thing to say, but we ought to set an example for our ancestors! Of course, they cannot follow it because they have gone from the earth. But as we know so much better than our fathers, we cannot think of learning anything from them! As we have left the apostles all behind and gone in for something quite new, it is a pity that we should forget what they did, what they suffered, and think that they were just a set of simpletons who acted up to their own light. But then they had not the light we have in this wonderful nineteenth century!

O beloved, it almost makes my lips blister to talk after the present evil fashion, for grosser falsehood never could be uttered than the insinuation that we have shifted the everlasting foundations of our faith! Verily, if these foundations were removed, we might ask in many senses, "What will the righteous do? Whom will they copy? Whom will they follow? The landmarks having gone, what remains to us of the holy treasury of example with which the Lord enriches those who follow Christ?"

I. Coming to our text, "Jesus Christ is the same yesterday, today, and forever," my first observation is that *Jesus Christ is always the same*. He is, was, and will always be the same! Changes of position and of circumstances there have been in our Lord, but He is always the same *in His great love to His people*, whom He loved before the earth was. Before the first star was kindled, before the first living creature began to sing the praise of its Creator, He loved His church with an everlasting love! He spied her in the glass of predestination, pictured her by His divine foreknowledge, and loved her with all His heart. And it was for this cause that He left His Father and became one with her, that He might redeem her. It was for this cause that He went with her through all this vale of tears, discharged her debts, and bore her sins in His own body on the cross. For her sake He slept in the tomb, and with the same love that brought Him down, He has gone up again, and with the same heart beating true to the same blessed betrothal, He has gone into glory, waiting for the marriage day when He will come again to receive His perfected spouse who will have made herself ready by His grace! Never for a moment, whether as God over all, blessed forever, or as God and man in one divine person, or as dead and buried, or as risen and ascended—never has He changed in the love He bears to His chosen! He is

Jesus Christ, "the same yesterday, today, and forever."

Therefore, beloved brothers and sisters, He has never changed *in His divine purpose toward His beloved church.* He resolved in eternity to become one with her, that she might become one with Him, and, having determined upon this, when the fullness of time had come, He was born of a woman and made under the law. He took upon Him the likeness of sinful flesh, "and being found in appearance as a man, He humbled Himself and became obedient to the point of death, even the death of the cross" (Phil. 2:8). Yet He never abandoned His purpose. He set His face like a flint to go up to Jerusalem, even when the bitter cup was put to His lips and He seemed to stagger for a moment. He returned to it with a strong resolve, saying to His Father, "Father, if it is Your will, take this cup away from Me; nevertheless not My will, but Yours, be done" (Luke 22:42). That purpose is strong upon Him now. For Zion's sake He will not hold His peace, and for Jerusalem's sake He will not rest until her righteousness goes forth as brightness and her salvation as a lamp that burns!

Jesus is still pressing on with His great work, and He will not fail or be discouraged in it. He will never be content till all whom He has bought with His blood will become glorified by His power. He will gather all His sheep in the heavenly fold, and they will pass again under the hands of Him who counts them—every one of them being brought there by the Great Shepherd who laid down His life for them! Beloved, He cannot turn from His purpose. It is not according to His nature that He should, for He is Jesus Christ, "the same yesterday, today, and forever."

He is also "the same yesterday, today, and forever" *in the holding of His offices* for the carrying out of His purpose and giving effect to His love. He is still a prophet. Men try to set Him on one side. Science, falsely so called, comes forward and bids Him hold His tongue, but "the sheep follow him, for they know his voice. Yet they will by no means follow a stranger, but will flee from him, for they do not know the voice of strangers" (John 10:4–5). The teachings of the New Testament are as sound and true today as they were eighteen hundred years ago. They have lost none of their value, none of their absolute certainty; they stand fast like the everlasting hills! Jesus Christ was a prophet, and He is "the same yesterday, today, and forever."

He is the same, too, as a priest. Some now sneer at His precious blood— alas, that it should be so! But to His elect, His blood is still their purchase price. By this they overcome. Through the blood of the Lamb they win the victory, and they know that they will praise it in heaven when they have washed their robes and made them white in the blood of the Lamb! They never turn away from this great priest of theirs and His wondrous sacrifice, once offered for the sins of men and perpetually efficacious for all the blood-bought race! They glory in His everlasting priesthood before the Father's throne. In this we rejoice, yes, and will rejoice, that Jesus Christ is our priest, "the same yesterday, today, and forever."

And as King He is always the same. He is supreme in the church. Before you, O Jesus, all your loyal subjects bow! All the sheaves make obeisance to your sheaf—the sun and moon and all the stars obey and serve you, King of kings and Lord of lords! You are head over all things to your church, which is your body. Beloved, if there is any other office that our Lord has assumed for the accomplishment of His divine purposes, we may say of Him, concerning every position, that He is "the same yesterday, today, and forever."

So also, once more, He is the same *in His relationship to all His people.* I like to think that, as Jesus was the husband of His church ages ago, He is still her husband, for He hates divorce. As He was the brother born for adversity to His first disciples, He is still *our* faithful brother. As He was a friend who sticks closer than a brother to those who were sorely tried in the medieval times, He is equally a friend to us upon whom the ends of the earth have come. There is no difference whatever in the relationship of the Lord Jesus Christ to His people at any time! He is just as ready to comfort us tonight as He was to comfort those with whom He dwelt when here below! Sister Mary, He is as willing to come down to your Bethany and help you in your sorrow about Lazarus as He was when He came to Martha and Mary whom He loved! Jesus Christ is just as ready to wash your feet, my brother, after another day's weary travel through the foul ways of this world. He is as willing to take the basin and the towel and to give us a loving cleansing as He was when He washed His disciples' feet! Just what He was to them, He is to us! Happy is it if you and I can truly say, "What He was to Peter, what He was to John, what He was to Magdalene, that is Jesus Christ to me—the same yesterday, today, and forever."

Beloved, I have seen men change—oh, how they change! A little frost turns the green forest to bronze and every leaf forsakes its hold and yields to winter's blast. So fade our friends, and the most attached adherents drop away from us in the time of trial. But Jesus is to us what He always was.

When we get old and gray-headed and others shut the door on men who have lost their former strength and can serve their turn no longer, then will He say, "Even to hoar hairs will I carry you: I have made, and I will bear; even I will carry, and will deliver you" (Isa. 46:4 KJV), for He is Jesus Christ, "the same yesterday, today, and forever." Thus, beloved, with regard to Jesus Himself, He is always the same!

II. Now let us go a step further. *Jesus Christ is always the same in His doctrine.* This text must refer to the doctrine of Christ, since it is connected with imitating the saints' faith. "Whose faith follow, considering the outcome of their conduct. Jesus Christ is the same yesterday, today, and forever. Do not be carried about with various and strange doctrines. For it is good that the heart be established by grace" (Heb. 13:7–9). From the connection it is evident that our text refers to the teaching of Christ, who is "the same yesterday, today, and forever." This is not according to the so-called development folly. Theology, like every other science, is to grow, watered by the splendid wisdom of this enlightened age, fostered by the superlative ability of the gentlemen of light and leading of the present time, so much superior to all who came before them!

We think not so, brothers and sisters, for *the Lord Jesus Christ was the perfect revelation of God.* He was the express image of the Father's person and the brightness of His glory. In previous ages, God had spoken to us by His prophets, but in these last days He has spoken to us by His Son. Now as to that which was a complete revelation, it is blasphemous to suppose that there can be any more revealed than has been made known in the person and work of Jesus Christ, the Son of God! He is God's *ultimatum*—last of all, He sends His Son. If you can conceive a brighter display of God than is to be seen in the Only Begotten, I thank God that I am unable to follow you in any such imagination! To me, He is the last, the highest, the grandest revelation of God! And as He shuts up the book that contains the written revelation, He bids you never dare to take from it, lest He should take your name out of the Book of Life! And never dare to add to it, lest He should add to you the plagues that are written in this book!

At this time, *the salvation of our Lord Jesus Christ is the same as it was in all ages.* Jesus Christ still saves sinners from the guilt, the power, the punishment, and the defilement of sin. Still, "there is no other name under heaven given among men by which we must be saved" (Acts 4:12). Jesus

Christ still makes all things new. He creates new hearts and right spirits in the sons of men and engraves His law upon the tablets that once were stone, but which He has turned into flesh. There is no new salvation! Some may talk as if there were, but there is not! Salvation means to you today just what it meant to Saul of Tarsus on the way to Damascus. If you think it has another meaning, you have missed it altogether!

> *J*esus Christ still makes all things new. He creates new hearts and right spirits in the sons of men and engraves His law upon the tablets that once were stone, but which He has turned into flesh.

And, again, *salvation by Jesus Christ comes to men in the same way as it always did.* They have to receive it now by *faith.* In Paul's day, men were saved by faith, and they are not now saved by works. They began in the Spirit in the apostolic age, and we are not now to begin in the flesh. There is no indication in the book, and there is no indication in the experience of God's children, that there is ever to be any alteration as to the way in which we receive Christ! All live by Him. "For by grace you have been saved through faith, and that not of yourselves; it is the gift of God" (Eph. 2:8). It is the gift of God today as much as it ever was, for "Jesus Christ is the same yesterday, today, and forever."

Once more, *this salvation is just the same as to the persons to whom it is sent.* It is to be preached now, as always, to every creature under heaven. But it appeals with a peculiar power to those who are guilty and who, by God's grace, confess their guilt. It appeals to hearts that are broken, to men who are weary and heavy laden. It is to these that the gospel comes with great sweetness. I have quoted to you before those strange words of Joseph Hart: "A sinner is a sacred thing; the Holy Spirit has made him so." The Savior is only for sinners! He did not come to save the righteous. He came to seek and to save the lost, and still "to you the word of this salvation has been sent" (Acts 13:26), and this declaration still stands true: "This Man receives sinners and eats with them" (Luke 15:2). There is no change in this statement: "The poor have the gospel preached to them" (Matt. 11:5), and it comes to those who are farthest off from God and hope and inspires them with divine power and energy!

Beloved, I can bear witness that *the gospel is the same in its effects upon the hearts of men.* Still it breaks and still it makes whole! Still it wounds and still it heals! Still it kills and still it quickens! Still it seems to hurl man down to hell in their terrible experience of the evil of sin, but still it lifts them up into an ecstatic joy till they are exalted almost to heaven when they lay hold upon it and feel its power in their souls! The gospel that was a gospel of births and deaths, of killing and making alive, in the days of John Bunyan, has the same effect upon our hearts to this day when it comes with the power that God has put into it by His Spirit! It produces the same results and has the same sanctifying influence as it ever had.

Looking beyond the narrow stream of death, we can say that *the eternal results produced by the gospel of the Lord Jesus Christ are the same as they always were.* The promise is this day fulfilled to those who receive Him as much as to any who went before. Life eternal is their inheritance. They will sit with Him upon His throne and, on the other hand, the threat is equally sure of fulfillment: "These will go away into everlasting punishment" (Matt. 25:46). Christ has made no change in His words of promise or of threat, nor will His followers dare to do so, for His doctrine is "the same yesterday, today, and forever."

If you were to try to think over this matter and imagine for a minute that the gospel really did shift and change with the times, it would be very extraordinary. Look, here is the gospel for the first century. Make a mark and note how far it goes. Then there is a gospel for the second century. Make another mark, but then remember that you must change the color to another shade! Either these people must have altered, or else a very different effect must have been produced in the same kind of minds. In eternity, when they all get to heaven by these nineteen gospels in the nineteen centuries, there will be nineteen sets of people and they will sing nineteen different songs, depend upon it, and their music will not blend! Some will sing of free grace and dying love, while others will sing of evolution. What a discord it would be, and what a heaven it would be, too! I should decline to be a candidate for such a place!

No, let me go where they praise Jesus Christ and Him alone, singing, "To Him who loved us and washed us from our sins in His own blood. . . to Him be glory and dominion forever and ever. Amen" (Rev. 1:5–6). That is what the first-century saints sing, and it is what the saints of *every* century will sing, without any exception! And there will be no change in this song forever. The same results will flow from the same gospel till heaven and earth will pass away, for "Jesus Christ is the same yesterday, today, and forever."

III. We may sound the same note again, for a moment, because *Jesus Christ is the same as to His modes of working*—"Jesus Christ is the same yesterday, today, and forever."

How did Jesus Christ save souls in olden times? By *the foolishness of preaching*. And if you will look down through church history, you will find that, wherever there has been a great revival of religion, it has been linked with the preaching of the gospel! When the Methodists began to do so much good, what did they call the men who made such a stir? Methodist preachers, did they not say? That was always the name: "Here comes a Methodist preacher." Ah, my dear friends, the world will never be saved by Methodist doctors, or by Baptist doctors, or anything of the sort! But multitudes will be saved, by God's grace, through preachers! It is the preacher to whom God has entrusted this great work! Jesus said, "Preach the gospel to every creature" (Mark 16:15).

But men are getting tired of the divine plan. They are going to be saved by the priest, going to be saved by the music, going to be saved by theatricals, and who knows what! Well, they may try these things as long as they like, but nothing can ever come of the whole thing but utter disappointment and confusion—God dishonored, the gospel travestied, hypocrites manufactured by thousands, and the church dragged down to the level of the world! Stand to your guns, brothers, and go on preaching and teaching nothing but the Word of God, for it still pleases God, by the foolishness of preaching, to save those who believe! And this test still stands true: "Jesus Christ is the same yesterday, today, and forever."

But remember that there must always be *the prayers of the saints* with the preaching of the gospel. You must have often noticed that passage in the Acts concerning the new converts on the day of Pentecost: "They continued steadfastly in the apostles' doctrine" (Acts 2:42). They thought a great deal about doctrine in those days. "And fellowship." They thought a good deal of being in church fellowship in those days. "And in the breaking of bread." They did not neglect the blessed ordinance of the Lord's Supper in those days. "In the breaking of bread." And then what follows? "And in prayers." Some say nowadays that prayer meetings are religious expedients pretty well worn out. Ah, dear me! What a religious expedient that was that brought about Pentecost, when they were all assembled with one accord in one place, and when the whole church prayed and suddenly the place was shaken, and they heard the sound as of a rushing mighty wind, which betokened the presence of the Holy Spirit!

Well, you may try to do without prayer meetings if you like, but my solemn conviction is that, as these decline, the Spirit of God will depart from you and the preaching of the gospel will be of small account. The Lord will have the prayers of His people to go with the proclamation of His gospel if it is to be the power of God to salvation—and there is no change in this matter since Paul's day! Jesus Christ is "the same yesterday, today, and forever." God is still to be inquired of by the house of Israel to do it for them, and He still grants blessings in answer to believing prayer.

> The Lord will have the prayers of His people to go with the proclamation of His gospel if it is to be the power of God to salvation. . . .

Remember, too, that the Lord Jesus Christ has always been inclined to work by *the spiritual power of His servants*. Nothing comes out of a man that is not first in him. You will not find God's servants doing great things for Him unless God works mightily in them, as well as by them. You must first be endued with power from on high, or else the power will not manifest itself in what you do. Beloved, we need our church members to be better men and better women. We need baby Christians to become grown-up Christians, and we need the grown-up Christians among us to be "strong in the Lord and in the power of His might" (Eph. 6:10). God will work by His servants when they are adapted to His service, and He will make His instruments fit for His work. It is not in themselves that they have any strength. Their weakness becomes the reason why His strength is seen in them! Still, there is an adaptation, there is a fitness for His service, there is a cleanness that God puts upon His instruments before He works mighty things by them, and "Jesus Christ is the same yesterday, today, and forever" in this matter, too.

The Holy Spirit works all the good that is ever done in the world, and as the Holy Spirit honors Jesus Christ, so He puts great honor upon the Holy Spirit. If you and I try, either as a church or as individuals, to do without the Holy Spirit, God will soon do without us. Unless we reverently worship

Him and believingly trust in Him, we will find that we will be like Samson when his locks were shorn. He shook himself as he had done before, but when the Philistines were upon him, he could do nothing against them. Our prayer must always be, "Holy Spirit, dwell with me! Holy Spirit, dwell with Your servants!" We know that we are utterly dependent upon Him. Such is the teaching of our Master, and "Jesus Christ is the same yesterday, today, and forever."

IV. I do not want to weary you, my dear brothers and sisters, but may I be helped, just for a few moments, to speak on a fourth point! *Jesus Christ has always the same resources*, for He is "the same yesterday, today, and forever."

I will repeat what I said: Jesus Christ has always the same resources. We sit down sometimes, very sorrowful, and we say, "The times are very dark." I do not think that we can very well exaggerate their darkness, and they are full of threatening omens. And I do not think that any of us can really exaggerate those omens, they are so terrible. But still is it true, "The LORD lives! Blessed be my Rock!" (2 Sam. 22:47).

Does the church feel her need of *faithful men*? The Lord can send us as many as ever! When the pope ruled everywhere, nobody thought, I should imagine, that the first man to speak out for the old faith would be a *monk*. They thought they had taken stock of all the men whom God had at His command, and they certainly did not think that He had one of the leaders of the Reformation in a monastery! But there was Martin Luther, the monk who shook the world, and though men dreamed not what he would do, God knew all about him. There was Calvin, also, writing that famous book of his Institutes. He was a man full of disease. I think he had sixty diseases at once in his body, and he suffered greatly. Look at his portrait—pale and wan. And as a young man he was very timid. He went to Geneva and he thought he was called to write books, but Farel said to him, "You are called to lead us in preaching the gospel here in Geneva."

"No," said Calvin, for he shrank from the task.

But Farel said, "The blast of the Almighty God will rest upon you unless you come out and take your proper place."

Beneath the threat of that brave old man, John Calvin took his place, prompt and sincere in the work of God, in life and in death never faltering! Then there was Zwingli over there at Zurich. He had come out, too, and Oecolampadius, and Melancthon, and their fellows. Who ever expected *them* to do what they did? Nobody! "The Lord gave the word; great was the company of those who proclaimed it" (Ps. 68:11). And so, today, He has only to give the word, and you will see starting up all over the world earnest preachers of the everlasting gospel, for He has the same resources as always! He is Jesus Christ, "the same yesterday, today, and forever."

He has also the same resources of grace. The Holy Spirit is quite as able to convert men, to quicken, enlighten, sanctify, and instruct. There is nothing that He has done that He cannot do again! The treasuries of God are as full and as running over now as they were in the beginning of the Christian age! If we do not see such great things, where lies the restraining force? It is in our *unbelief*. All things are possible to him who believes. Before this year has gone, God can make a wave of revival break over England, Scotland, and Ireland; from one end to the other! Yes, and He can deluge the whole world with the gospel if we will but cry to Him for it! And He wills to do it, for He is "the same yesterday, today, and forever" in the resources of His grace.

V. So I close my sermon with this fifth head, on which I will be very short indeed. *Jesus Christ is always the same to me*—"yesterday, today, and forever." I will not talk about myself except to help you to think about yourselves. How long have you known the Lord Jesus Christ? Perhaps it has been only a short time, or possibly many years. Do you remember when you first knew Him? Can you point out the spot of ground where Jesus met you? Now, what was He to you at first? I will tell you what He was to me.

Jesus was to me, at first, *my only trust*. I leaned on Him very hard then, for I had such a load to carry. I laid my load and myself down at His feet. He was all in all to me. I had not a shred of hope outside of Him, nor any trust beyond Himself, crucified and raised for me. Now, dear brothers and sisters, have you got any further than that? I hope not! I know that I have not. I have not a shadow of a shade of confidence anywhere but in Christ's blood and righteousness! I leaned on Him very hard at the first, but I lean harder now! Sometimes I faint away into His arms. I have died into His life. I am lost in His fullness! He is all my salvation and all my desire. I am speaking for myself, but I think that I am speaking for many of you, too, when I say that Jesus Christ is to me "the same yesterday, today, and forever." His cross, before my failing eyes, will be my dying comfort as it is my living strength.

What was Jesus Christ to me at the first? He was the object of my warmest love. Was it not so with you? Was He not chief among ten thousand

and altogether lovely? What charms, what beauties were there in that dear face of His! What freshness, what a novelty, what a delight that set all our passions on fire! It was so in those early days when we went after Him into the wilderness. Though the entire world around was barren, He was all in all to us. Very well, what is He today? He is fairer to us now than He ever was! He is the one gem that we possess. Our other jewels have all turned out to be but glass and we have flung them from the chest, but He is the Kohinoor that our soul delights in! He is every perfection joined together to make one absolute perfection! He is all the graces, which adorn Him and overflow to us! Is not that what we say of Him? "Jesus Christ is the same yesterday, today, and forever."

> The Lord Jesus Christ knows every key in our souls, and He can wake up our whole being to harmonies of music that will set the world ringing with His praises!

What was Jesus Christ to me at the first? Well, He was *my highest joy*. In my young days, how my heart did dance at the sound of His name! Was it not so with many of you? We may be huskier in voice, heavier in body, and slower in moving our limbs, but His name has as much charm for us as it ever had! There was a trumpet that nobody could blow but one who was the true heir, and there is nobody who can ever fetch the true music out of us but our Lord to whom we belong! When He sets me to His lips, you would think that I was one of the trumpets of the seven angels! And there is no one else who can make me sound like that! I cannot produce such music as that by myself, and there is no theme that can ravish my heart, there is no subject that can stir my soul until I get to Him! I think it is with me as it was with Rutherford when the Duke of Argyle called out, as he began to preach about Christ, "Now, man, you are on the right string; keep to that!" The Lord Jesus Christ knows every key in our souls, and He can wake up our whole being to harmonies of music that will set the world ringing with His praises! Yes, He is our joy, our everything, and "the same yesterday, today, and forever."

Let us go forward, then, to the unchanging Savior, through the changing things of time and sense, and we will meet Him soon in glory, and He will be unchanged even there, as compassionate and loving to us when we will get home to Him and see Him in His splendor as He was to His poor disciples when He had not where to lay His head and was a sufferer among them.

Oh, do you know Him? Do you know Him? Do you know Him? If not, may He, this night, reveal Himself to you, for His sweet mercy's sake! Amen.

FOR FURTHER THOUGHT

1. *Spurgeon encourages us to learn two lessons from Hebrews 13:7 so we can better understand verse 8. What are these lessons?*

2. *The four sections of this sermon tell of ways that Jesus is always the same. What are some of these?*

3. *The apostle Paul told the first-century believers that they had the gift of faith (Eph. 2:8). According to Spurgeon, what verse tells us that this is still true today?*

The Son Glorified by the Father and the Father Glorified by the Son

Jesus spoke these words, lifted up His eyes to heaven,
and said: "Father, the hour has come. Glorify Your Son,
that Your Son also may glorify You."
JOHN 17:1

THIS was a prayer after a sermon. These words Jesus spoke, and then He lifted up His eyes to heaven in supplication. No discourse should be unattended by prayer, for how can we expect a blessing on what we have heard or spoken unless we ask it of the Lord? The sower should water with many a supplication the seed that he has sown, and the hearer should diligently seek the favor of Him who gives bread to the eater as well as seed to the sower. *It was a prayer in connection with the Lord's Supper.* Surely above all things, prayer should mix with every part of our attendance at the sacred table. Dare we come to the sacred feast without prayer? Can we sit there without prayer? Can we retire without prayer? If so, let us not wonder if the ordinance should be a mere form and unrefreshing to our souls. With sermon and with sacrament let us mingle the salt of supplication without prescribing how much.

Observe *the attitude of the prayer.* The Savior, it appears, prayed with uplifted eyes. There is much in this outward manifestation of His devotion. We have not time to enter into it fully, but this may suffice: the uplifted eyes showed to whom He was speaking and bore testimony that He was not idly drawing the bow at a venture, but directing His prayer to God and looking up as the arrow ascended to His Father's throne. It showed, also, that He was looking away from and above His disciples and their sympathy, above all the world and its enmity, and even above Himself. His outlook was toward the invisible—this is for our instruction. He could have prayed with eyes closed if it had so pleased Him, but His were the opened eyes of faith and love that could look into the face of God and could yet look upon all things round without distraction, and therefore it was not necessary for Him to draw down the curtains of His eyelids, but He gazed into the opened heaven.

Notice *the commencement of His prayer*, for it furnishes our text. He began by saying "Father." He did not say "our Father," because "*our* Father" is for *us*, for we, in the filial relationship that we sustain, are many. But "Father" is for Him, for He is one and He is such a Son as, in some respects, we can never be. Into the mysterious doctrine of the eternal filiation it is not ours to enter, but we know it to be a truth of God. "Father" is a word appropriate to our Lord's lips alone in its highest conceivable sense, and how grandly it comes from Him! It shows His love to God, His confidence in God, His complete resignation to the divine will, and His sweet acquiescence in it. He is about to be broken in pieces with the iron rod of His Father's vengeance, but He calls Him "Father." He is about to drink that cup of wormwood and gall that would have been hell to us if He had not drained it dry, but He says, "Father."

And herein He sets us an example: In all times of tribulation let us fall back upon our sonship, our adoption, and the fatherhood of our great God! To our Father let us go, for to whom else should a child so naturally fly? Where else can we go but to our Father who knows what we have need of before we ask Him and who will never desert His own but, like a father pities his children, will pity those who fear Him? *The prayer itself—* the very *fact* of the prayer—shows us His manhood. Jesus pleads—He must be man. He lifts His eyes to heaven and He cries, "Father." He must be like us, a man.

But the prayer, in some respects, speaks of the Deity that it scarcely veils. As in some statues that you must often have looked upon with admiration, you seem to see the face of the figure through the marble veil, so it is here in the prayer of Christ that the God shines through the man. It is such a prayer as only He might offer, since He is God as well as man. Dare you say, "Father, glorify me, that I may glorify you?" That would be a presumptuous expression for creature lips to utter! Only He who counted it not robbery to be equal with God, though He made Himself of no reputation, might thus pray! Though He cries to God, "Father. . .glorify Your Son," yet may

He add and put no explanatory sentence with it, "that Your Son also may glorify You." He is able to return all the glory God may give and has the power as much to magnify the Father's name as the Father may magnify His name. Here I see the humanity, but I admire and adore the deity of our blessed Lord.

> *T*he Lord Jesus Christ knows every key in our souls, and He can wake up our whole being to harmonies of music that will set the world ringing with His praises!

The first sentence of His prayer reveals His foresight: "Father, the hour is come." This is the hour ordained in the eternal purpose. The hour prophesied of which Daniel sought to know. The hour toward which all hours had pointed. The central hour—the hour up to which men dated and from which they will date again if they read time right. The hinge, pivot, and turning point of all human history! The dark yet delivering hour! The hour of vengeance and of acceptance! "The hour [is] come." He knew it. His inward infallible foresight made Him know that now was the time for Him to offer up Himself a sacrifice for sin. His expression is, however, very choice. "*The hour* [is] come." His faith thinks it but an hour. The midnight of Gethsemane, the morning of the scourging, the day of the crucifixion—all are but an hour, a short space.

Now is He in trouble, for His time of travail is come. But He counts it as an hour for joy of that which will be born into the world by His grievous pangs! Thus His love and patience make Him despise the time of shame and reckon it but a brief interval. The foresight of which we have spoken makes Him look beyond the hour. You and I look into the hour of darkness, as a frequent rule, and see no further, for our eyes are dim through unbelief. But He goes on beyond the hour and His prayer is, "Glorify Your Son, that Your Son also may glorify You." He fixes His eyes upon the glory that was yet to be revealed and for joy of which He counts even His death to be but an hour—looking upon it as soon to be over and lost in the glory of His Father!

In all this, brothers and sisters, let us imitate our Lord and let us keep our eyes not on the present, but on the future; not on this light affliction, which is but for a moment, but on the far more exceeding and eternal weight of glory that will come of it. And let us with holy confidence, whenever our hour of darkness arrives, resort to our God in secret. The best preparation for the worst hour is prayer! The best remedy for a depressed spirit is nearness to God! In this, then, let us follow our Master, and may the Holy Spirit help us to do so. Let us now consider the essential words of the prayer. They are twofold, and in them we find first *a petition for Himself*—"Father, glorify Your Son." And, second, *the motive of that petition*—"that Your Son also may glorify You."

I. Begin, then, with *the petition for Himself*, and I invite you to observe it as an *answered* petition. More than eighteen hundred years have rolled away since those divine words fell from our blessed Master's lips, and they have been answered and are *still* being answered! We will not look upon them from the standpoint of the apostles, but from our own, and regard the prayer as one that is granted. And, first, *it was answered in and during His sufferings*. Some of the early fathers confined the sense of these words to the passion of our Lord, and I like their strong expressions when they say that His cross was His throne and Gethsemane was as glorious as Olivet, if not more so—for the glory of the cross would be a wonderful theme if man had mind and words enough to expound upon it.

Do we speak of ignominy? Doubtless He died a felon's death. Do we speak of shame? No doubt they spat upon Him and derided Him. Do we speak of weakness? No doubt He slept in a grave. But in His ignominy, shame, and weakness, Jesus is most honorable, adorable, and strong! Faith sees a moral and spiritual splendor about her crucified Lord that outshines all the previous glories of His eternal throne. I will not so confine the sense of the words, but yet that sense must be included. The Son of God was glorified while He was dying, and *it was one part of His glory that He should be able to bear the enormous load of human guilt*. As a race we lay crushed beneath it.

A thousand Samsons could not relieve us! Angels and archangels, cherubim and seraphim could never lift the stupendous mass! But this one man alone, with no help, in weakness of body and in death pangs, bore away the enormous load of human guilt! The chastisement of our peace was upon Him. The Lord laid on Him the iniquity of us all! What a load it was! And that He could bear it was, indeed, a display of His glory. The lost in hell cannot bear the wrath of God! An eternity of suffering will not have discharged the dreadful penalty, and yet He bore that burden in an hour!

Oh, marvelous strength of the incarnate God! Glorious are you indeed, O Christ, upon your cross! More glorious, even, than in that moment when, with a word, you will shake not only earth, but also heaven, for now the weight of angry heaven rests on you and you stand fast beneath it. Glorify Him, beloved, you for whom He bore that weight! Glorify Him that He was able to endure it!

He was glorified, also, in the manner in which He bore it, in which He sustained it without shrinking or starting back. There was no guilt or guile in Him, though questioned again and again before Caiaphas, Herod, and Pilate. There were no angry speeches when He was browbeaten, buffeted, blindfolded, and spit upon. He displayed nothing but gentleness, even when His enemies had pierced His hands and His feet—nothing but triumphant pity and almighty love even when they mocked His agonies. They could not anger Him with all their reviling, and when they cried, "Let Him. . .come down from the cross, and we will believe Him" (Matt. 27:42), yet He did not loosen a hand from the cruel tree to smite the scorners nor shake His feet free from the nail to spurn the blasphemers.

Think of His physical agonies, of His mental torture, of His spiritual darkness. Consider that all the powers of earth and hell were let loose upon Him. And, worst of all, remember that the Father's face was hidden from Him till He cried, "Why have You forsaken Me?" (Matt. 27:46). Consider that our champion, having begun the redeeming work, went through with it and never drew back His hands from the covenant that He had made, nor flinched under the strokes He bore. I say He was glorious in His passion and His prayer was heard! The Father *did* glorify His Son even on the tree! It was an hour of glory that might dazzle angels' eyes; that hour when He said, "It is finished!" (John 19:30) and gave up the ghost. What had He finished? He had finished that which saved His people! He had peopled heaven with immortal spirits who will delight in Him forever and had shaken the gates of hell! God indeed glorified His Son in enabling Him to bear, and bear so well, all the weight of sin and the penalty that was due to it.

And now today, beloved, we see that *God glorified His Son in His death because in dying He saved His people*. I do not believe for a single moment that the result of Christ's death ever was, or ever could be, uncertain. That which He intended to do by it will be done and has been so far done to the last jot and tittle up to this moment. His great object was the redemption of His chosen. "Christ also loved the church and gave Himself for her" (Eph.

5:25). It is that a certain company were "redeemed from among men" (Rev. 14:4). Now, when He died, He did not render the redemption of His people *possible*, but He ransomed them *completely*.

By His agonies and death He did not merely give a bare hope of the pardon of sin, but He hurled the sin of all His elect into the depths of the sea in that same moment! He did not merely make the salvation of men a *possibility* if they would, but He *saved* His people then and there! He finished the work that He came to do, in proof whereof it is written that "this Man, after He had offered one sacrifice for sins forever, sat down at the right hand of God" (Heb. 10:12). And He would not have sat there if His work had not been done! According to the words of the prophet, He had finished transgression, made an end of sin, and brought in everlasting righteousness, for He had offered an effectual atonement that none can deny. And so the Father glorified His Son, even when He died, since He accepted His redeeming blood on behalf of His people.

The Father glorified His Son by making Him, even in the hour of His passion, to be victorious over all His enemies. Those nailed feet bruised the serpent's head so that he could never resume his former power. Those nailed hands grasped the serpent of sin and strangled it! And that dying head, as it bowed itself, smote death with its own sword, as David smote Goliath, for He "death, by dying, slew." The powers of evil were tremendous. Think of sin, of Satan, and of death; but all their hosts were defeated in that one pitched battle of which the cross was the banner and the dying Redeemer the champion! O glorious Lord, you have led captivity captive, making a show of your adversaries openly even on your cross, and nailing to the accursed tree the handwriting of ordinances that was against us. Yes, the Father glorified you even *there* while yet you were in the agonies of death!

Besides this, *there were some outward signs of the glory of Christ even in His death* that we can scarcely stop to mention. Did not the temple rend her veil? Did not the sun conceal his face? Did not the rocks split and the dead arise? Was not all Jerusalem filled with tremor and did not the centurion cry, "Truly this was the Son of God!" (Matt. 27:54)? Yes, the Father glorified His Son even when it pleased Him to bruise Him and to put Him to grief! With one hand He smote and with the other hand He glorified! There was a power to crush, but there was also a power to sustain working at the same time. The Father glorified His Son.

And now, beloved, what will I say concerning the Father glorifying the

Son after His death and as the result of it? I will not attempt to expound on it, but I will simply say that the rending of the veil at the moment of His death was the glorifying of Christ, for now there is a way to the throne of God made manifest for us, which before had been closed. Then the opening of His pierced side was another glorifying of Him, for this day the double fountain is to believers the effectual cleansing of both the guilt and the power of sin! And thus the Savior's pierced heart glorified Him in its power to bless. Then that poor body lay in the grave—I call it poor, for so it seemed—wrapped in linen and the spices. But, beloved, the Father glorified even that dead body that men thought to be corruptible, for it saw no corruption!

During the three days and nights no worm could come near it, nor trace of decay. That crystal vase in which the rich ointment of the Savior's soul had dwelt must not be injured. "Not one of His bones shall be broken" (John 19:36). Beautified by those scars as when a skillful artist renders an image lovelier than before by marks of the engraver's tool, that body must be safely guarded by watching angels till the morning comes. It barely dawned. As yet the sun was rising, lo, the Sun of righteousness Himself arose! As a man arising from his couch puts on his garments, so did our Lord put on the vesture of the body that He had laid aside and came again into the world alive as to His body and His soul—a perfect man!

Oh, it was a grand glorifying of Christ when the Father raised Him from the dead and His disciples saw him once again! Death had no bands to hold Him. The sepulchre's ward could not confine the unequaled prisoner. Declared to be glorious by His resurrection from the dead, His prayer was heard! And before long, when a few weeks had passed over Him, there came another glory—for from the brow of Olivet He gently ascended, floating in the air from the company of His disciples, rising up in the midst of angels till a cloud received Him out of human sight.

> *They brought His chariot from on high*
> *To bear Him to His throne.*
> *They clapped their triumphant wings and cried,*
> *"The glorious work is done!"*

His Father glorified Him, and now He sits at the right hand of God! Words, you are dumb things because you cannot tell of His present glory!

Early the other morning there came to my bedside a brother to awaken me whose face seemed to beam with joy as he said, "In my sleep last night I thought I saw the Lord upon His throne! And oh, the glory that the Father put upon Him! I wish I could fall asleep again that I might continue to dream on." Tears were in his eyes as he said, "Oh, the glory of Christ! Oh, the glory of Christ!" I reminded him of how Mercy laughed in her sleep and Christiana asked her why, and when she told her dream, the matron said she might well laugh if she so dreamed! Happy are those who, sleeping or waking, living or dying, may but get a glimpse of His glory! Nothing ever ravishes my heart like the thought of my Lord's being glorified! Oh, if I could by some means help to honor Him! If only I may but be the earthen vessel in which His treasure should be stored, or the trumpet by which His name might be proclaimed! That would be joy enough for me!

> Those nailed feet bruised the serpent's head so that he could never resume his former power. Those nailed hands grasped the serpent of sin and strangled it!

And you all feel the same, you who love Him. You delight to think how high His throne is and how bright is His countenance and how resplendent are His courts. Have patience. You will see Him soon, for the Father will glorify Him in the Second Advent. He tarries; He tarries long, as we think. Yet He says, "Behold, I am coming quickly, and My reward is with Me" (Rev. 22:12). He is coming to be glorified, even among the sons of men! So will the prayer of the text be fulfilled in the golden ages yet to dawn and then throughout eternity!

II. We pause a moment and then we will briefly think of *the motive of His prayer.* "Father, glorify Your Son, *that Your Son also may glorify You.*" Do notice this. When you pray, it is a grand thing to pray with a clean heart, but selfishness is uncleanness. In our blessed Lord there was no selfishness. He said, "I do not seek My own glory" (John 8:50), and even in this prayer that word of His is true, for He only seeks glory that He may glorify the Father. Beloved, the desire of our Lord is granted, for God is glorified in Jesus Christ more than in any other way.

The glory of God in nature is inconceivable in this round world and in all that dwells therein. The open sea calmly mirrors the sky or is ruffled with tempests. The wondrous expanse of heaven is fleecy with clouds, blue beneath a torrid sun, or lit up with innumerable stars. Yon hills with all their forests. Yon laughing valleys with their lowing herds and bleating flocks. "These are your glorious works, parent of good, Almighty." You get glory from every flickering blade of grass or frond of fern, and every flitting insect and creeping worm mean your praise! There is nothing but that which glorifies you, from leviathan to a minnow. Yet all nature put together fails to reveal all your glorious attributes! The divine faithfulness, justice, and truth are scarcely manifest in nature, though traces of them may be seen. But in the face of Jesus, who is the express image of the Father, God is glorified to the fullest!

In the death of Christ, above all things, God is glorified, for there all the attributes of God are seen. There was the power that sustained Christ beneath His more than Herculean task. There is the love that surrendered the darling of its bosom that He might die instead of traitors. There is the justice that would not, *could not* forgive sin without satisfaction. There is the truth of God that had threatened to punish and *did* punish, that had promised to give a Savior and *did* give Him. There is the faithfulness to the covenant that kept that covenant at such a dread expense. There is the wisdom that planned the marvelous way! Oh, salvation by a substitute! No, let me put it all together: the wholeness, the holiness of God! Yes, all His attributes are seen, each one equally magnified in the death of Jesus Christ. He is glorious, and the triune God is glorified in Him.

> *Oh, if I could by some means help to honor Him! If only I may but be the earthen vessel in which His treasure should be stored, or the trumpet by which His name might be proclaimed!*

And now, beloved, God is glorified in the death of Christ by the love of all those whom Jesus saves; by the sacred awe and filial fear of all whom Jesus brings to the Father's feet; by the ardent, patient devotion of all who are consecrated in heart and feel the sacred flame of love to Christ setting their souls on fire! Up there in heaven, where the white-robed never cease to sing, and here below where martyrs were burned for their love of God; where confessors defied all adversaries to spread abroad the glory of His name; where humble Christians suffer in patience, or labor on with diligence or walk in holiness, the Father's name is glorified through the passion of the Christ of God!

We had many things to say, but time fails us, and therefore we close with these three observations that we want to leave upon your minds. The first is this: *Christ's motive should be ours.* When you ask a blessing from God, ask it that you may glorify God by it. Do you pine to have your health back again? Be sure that you want to spend it for Him. Do you desire temporal advancement? Desire it that you may promote His glory. Do you even long for growth in grace? Ask it only that you may glorify Him! If there is anything that you dare wish and pray for, put it so: "Father, bless your child that your child may, in return, bless you and serve you." Those are clean prayers that have such a motive. All others have the taint of *self* about them. God help you to do everything for His glory—to speak for His glory, to live for His glory, to die for His glory; and then you will rise again and live forever for His glory! Happy, happy is the man whose lot this will be! Let this be the desire that masters you, even that which moved your Lord!

Next, *Christ's theology should be ours.* What is that? Why, first that He is to be glorified, and second, that the Father is to be glorified! Error sometimes blows one way and sometimes another. In years gone by, the difficulty was to bring men to glorify the Lord Jesus. They would worship God, but not the Christ of God. And so there came the great Arian fight and afterward Socinian controversies, for they would not glorify Christ. Oh, you who have been saved by Him, I am not afraid of you on *that* point, but nowadays there appears to be, in some minds, a forgetfulness of the *Father*!

Christ is loved, for He died, but many seem to look upon the Father as having no share in the wondrous work of redemption! But, beloved, they are one in our salvation! Father, Son, and Spirit agree in one in our redemption, and it would be fatal indeed for us to set one person of the divine Trinity above the other two! Let all men honor the Son even as they honor the Father and honor the Father even as they honor the Son! It would be traitorous to Christ's inmost wish if we were to glorify the Son and fail to reverence and love the Father!

Lastly, *let every believer here see His security.* Is it not a most wonderful guarantee of the safety of everyone for whom Christ died, that the glory of Christ and the glory of the Father—and I may add the glory of the blessed Spirit—are all equally concerned in the salvation of the believing soul? Dare

I say it? It would be a blot upon the everlasting glory if one believing soul were ever lost! Then were God's truth no longer sure, His faithfulness no longer firm, and His love no more immutable! His power might be doubted. His *changeableness* would be proven. But, beloved, it cannot be! Christ will not lose a sheep of His flock nor will the Comforter lose a spirit whom He has once begun to indwell! You can rest in this!

Abide without doubt or fear in Christ, for the mountains will depart and the hills be removed, but the covenant of His love will not be removed from you, says the Lord who has mercy on you. Believe in the Lord Jesus Christ, dear hearers, and these divine privileges will be yours! And as I prayed just now, so I pray yet again, that these things may belong to every soul in this house without exception, through faith in Christ Jesus, by the work of the Holy Spirit. Amen. Amen!

For Further Thought

1. *The first few paragraphs of this sermon discuss Jesus Christ's use of the name Father. What does Spurgeon say we can learn from this example?*
2. *This sermon urges us to see that our light affliction is but for a moment and that a far more exceeding and eternal weight of glory will come of it. What was Jesus looking forward to when He prayed the words of John 17:1?*
3. *The last few paragraphs of this sermon tell of the motive for prayer as seen in John 17:1. What is this motive?*

THE GLORY OF GOD IN
THE FACE OF JESUS CHRIST

For it is the God who commanded light to shine out of darkness,
who has shone in our hearts to give the light of the knowledge
of the glory of God in the face of Jesus Christ.
2 CORINTHIANS 4:6

THE apostle is explaining the reason for his preaching Christ with so much earnestness. He had received divine light and he felt bound to spread it. One great motive power of a true ministry is trusteeship. The Lord has put us in trust with the gospel; He has filled us with a treasure with which we are to enrich the world. The text explains in full what it is with which the Lord has entrusted us—He has bestowed upon us the light of the knowledge of the glory of God in the face of Jesus Christ, and it is ours to reflect the light, to impart the knowledge, to manifest the glory, to point to the Savior's face, and to proclaim the name of Jesus Christ our Lord. Having such a work before us, we faint not, but press onward with our whole heart.

I. With no other preface than this we will ask your attention this morning, first, to the subject of *the knowledge* in which Paul delighted so much. What was this knowledge that, to his mind, was the chief of all and the most worthy to be spread? It was the knowledge *of God*—truly a most necessary and proper knowledge for all God's creatures! For a man not to know his Maker and Ruler is deplorable ignorance indeed! The proper study of mankind is God. Paul not only knew that there is a God, for he had known that before his conversion. None could have more surely believed in the Godhead than did Paul as a Jew.

Nor does he merely intend that he had learned somewhat of the character of God, for that he had known from the Old Testament scriptures before he

393

was met with on the way to Damascus. Now he had come to know God in a closer, clearer, and surer way, for he had *seen* Him incarnate in the person of the Lord Jesus Christ. The apostle had also received the knowledge of *the glory of God*. Never had the God of Abraham appeared so glorious as now! God in Christ Jesus had won the adoring wonder of the apostle's instructed mind. He had known Jehovah's glory as the one and only God. He had seen that glory in creation, declared by the heavens and displayed upon the earth. He had beheld that glory in the law that blazed from Sinai and shed its insufferable light upon the face of Moses.

> *H*e has bestowed upon us the light of the knowledge of the glory of God in the face of Jesus Christ, and it is ours to reflect the light, to impart the knowledge, to manifest the glory, to point to the Savior's face, and to proclaim the name of Jesus Christ our Lord.

But now, beyond all else, he had come to perceive *the glory of God in the face, or person, of Jesus Christ*, and *this* had won his soul! This special knowledge had been communicated to him at his conversion when Jesus spoke to him out of heaven. In this knowledge he had made great advances by experience and by new revelations, but he had not yet learned it to the fullest, for he was still seeking to know it perfectly by the teaching of the divine Spirit, and we find him saying, "That I may know Him and the power of His resurrection, and the fellowship of His sufferings, being conformed to His death" (Phil. 3:10).

Paul knew not merely God, but God in Christ Jesus! Not merely "the glory of God," but "the glory of God in the face of Jesus Christ" (2 Cor. 4:6). The knowledge dealt with God, but it was Christward knowledge! He pined not for a Christless theism but for God in Christ! This, beloved, is the one thing that you and I should aim to know. There are parts of the divine glory that will never be seen by us in this life, speculate as we may. Mysticism would desire to pry into the unknowable; you and I may leave dreamers and their dreams and follow the clear light that shines from the face of Jesus. What of God it is necessary and beneficial for us to know He has revealed in Christ! And whatever is not there, we may rest assured it is unfit and unnecessary for us to know.

Truly the revelation is by no means scant, for there is vastly more revealed in the person of Christ than we will be likely to learn in this mortal life, and even eternity will not be too long for the discovery of all the glory of God that shines forth in the person of the Word made flesh. Those who would supplement Christianity had better first add to the brilliance of the sun or the fullness of the sea! As for us, we are more than satisfied with the revelation of God in the person of our Lord Jesus, and we are persuaded of the truth of His words, "He who has seen Me has seen the Father" (John 14:9). Hope not, my brothers and sisters, that the preacher can grapple with such a subject! I am overcome by it!

In my meditations I have felt lost in its lengths and breadths. My joy is great in my theme, and yet I am conscious of a pressure upon brain and heart, for I am as a little child wandering among the mountains, or as a lone spirit that has lost its way among the stars. I stumble among sublimities. I sink with amazement. I can only point with my finger to that which I see but cannot describe it. May the Holy Spirit Himself take of the things of Christ and show them to you! We will, for a minute or two, consider this glory of God in the face of Jesus Christ *historically*.

In every incident of the life of Jesus of Nazareth, the Lord's anointed, there is much of God to be seen. What volumes upon volumes might be written to show God as revealed in every act of Christ from His birth to His death! I see Him as a baby at Bethlehem lying in a manger, and there I perceive a choice glory in the mind of God, for He evidently despises the pomp and glory of the world that little minds esteem so highly. He might have been born in marble halls and wrapped in imperial purple, but He scorns these things, and in the manger among the oxen, we see a glory that is independent of the trifles of luxury and parade.

The glory of God in the person of Jesus asks no aid from the splendor of courts and palaces. Yet even as a baby, He reigns and rules! Mark how the shepherds hasten to salute the newborn King, while the magi from the far-off East bring gold, frankincense, and myrrh and bow at His feet. When the Lord condescends to show Himself in little things, He is still royal and commands the homage of mankind. He is as majestic in the minute as in the magnificent and as royal in the baby at Bethlehem as in later days in the man who rode through Jerusalem with hosannas! See the holy child Jesus in the temple when He is but twelve years old, sitting in the midst of the doctors, astonishing them with His questions! What wisdom there was in that child!

Do you not see there an exhibition of the truth of God that "the foolishness of God is wiser than men" (1 Cor. 1:25)? Even when God reserves His wisdom and gives forth utterances fit for a child, He baffles the wisdom of age and thought. Watch that youth in the carpenter's shop. See Him planing and sawing, cutting and squaring, working according to His parent's commands, till He is thirty years of age. What do we learn here when we see the incarnate God tarrying at the workman's bench? See we not how God can wait? Is not this a masterly display of the leisure of the eternal? The Infinite is never driven out of His restful pace of conscious strength.

> The Godhead was concealed at Bethlehem and Nazareth from the eyes of carnal men, but it is revealed to those who have spiritual sight with which to behold the Lord.

Had it been you and I, we would have hastened to begin our lifework long before! We could not have refrained from preaching and teaching for so long a period! But God can wait, and in Christ we see how prudence tempered zeal and made Him share in that eternal leisure that arises out of confidence that His end is sure. The Godhead was concealed at Bethlehem and Nazareth from the eyes of carnal men, but it is revealed to those who have spiritual sight with which to behold the Lord. Even in those early days of our Lord, while He was yet preparing for His great mission, we behold the glory of God in His youthful face and we adore.

As for His public ministry, how clearly the Godhead is there! Behold Him, brothers and sisters, while He feeds five thousand with a few loaves and fishes, and you cannot fail to perceive therein the glory of God in the commissariat of the universe, for the Lord God opens His hands and supplies the need of every living thing! See Him cast out devils and you learn of the divine power over evil! Hear Him raise the dead and you must reverence the divine prerogative to kill and to make alive! See Him cure the sick and you think you hear Jehovah say, "I wound and I heal" (Deut. 32:39). Hear how He speaks and infallibly reveals the truth of God, and you will perceive the God of knowledge to whom the wise-hearted owe their instruction!

It is always the Lord's way to make His truth known to those of humble and truthful hearts, and so did Jesus teach the sincere and lowly among men. Observe how Jesus dwelt among men, wearing the common smock-frock of the peasant, entering their cottages and sharing their poverty! Mark how He even washed His disciples' feet! Herein we see the condescension of God who must stoop to view the skies and bow to see what angels do. And yet He does not disdain to visit the sons of men!

In wondrous grace He thinks of us and has pity upon our low estate. See, too, the Christ of God, my brothers and sisters, bearing every day with the taunts of the ungodly, enduring "such hostility from sinners against Himself" (Heb. 12:3), and you have a fair picture of the infinite patience and the marvelous long-suffering of God! And this is no small part of His glory. Note well how Jesus loved His own who were in the world, yes, loved them to the end! And with what tenderness and gentleness He bore with them as a nurse with her child, for here you see the tenderness and gentleness of God and the love of the great Father toward His erring children.

You read of Jesus receiving sinners and eating with them, and what is this but the Lord God, merciful and gracious, passing by transgression, iniquity, and sin? You see Jesus living as a physician among those diseased by sin, with the one aim of healing their sicknesses. And here you see the pardoning mercy of our God, His delight in salvation, and the joy that He has in mercy. Beloved, I cannot go through the whole life of Jesus Christ—it is impossible, for time would fail us—but if you will yourselves select any single incident in which Jesus appears, whether in the chamber of sickness or at the grave, whether in weakness or in power, you shall, in each case, behold the glory of God!

Throughout His ministry, which was mainly a period of humiliation, there gleams forth in the character, acts, and person of Jesus the glory of the everlasting Father. His acts compel us not only to admire but also to adore! He is not merely a man whom God favors; He is also God Himself! What will I say of His death? Oh, never did the love of God reveal itself so clearly as when He laid down His life for His sheep, nor did the justice of God ever flame forth so conspicuously as when He would suffer in Himself the curse for sin rather than sin should go unpunished and the law should be dishonored! Every attribute of God was focused at the cross, and he who has eyes to look through his tears and see the wounds of Jesus will behold more of God there than a whole eternity of providence or an infinity of creation will ever be able to reveal to Him. Well might the trembling centurion, as he watched the cross, exclaim, "Truly this was the Son of God!" (Matt. 27:54).

Do I need to remind you, too, of the glory of God in the person of

Christ Jesus in His resurrection, when He spoiled principalities and powers, led death captive, and rifled the tomb? That is indeed a Godlike speech: "I am He who lives, and was dead, and behold, I am alive forevermore. Amen. And I have the keys of Hades and of Death" (Rev. 1:18). His power, His immortality, His eternal majesty all shone forth as He left the shades of death!

I will not linger over His ascension when He returned to His own again. Then His Godhead was conspicuous, for He again put on the glory that He had with the Father before the world was. There, amid the acclamations of angels and redeemed spirits, the glory of the conquering Lord was seen. By His descent He had destroyed the powers of darkness, and then He ascended that He might fill all things as only God can do. I would only hint at His session at the right hand of God, for there you know how

> *Adoring saints around Him stand,*
> *And thrones and powers before Him fall.*
> *The God shines gracious through the man,*
> *And sheds sweet glories on them all.*

In heaven they never conceive of Jesus apart from the divine glory that perpetually surrounds Him. No one in heaven doubts His deity, for all fall prostrate before Him, or now and then all seize their harps and wake their strings to the praise of God and the Lamb!

The glory of God will most abundantly be seen in the Second Advent of our Lord. Whatever of splendor we may expect at the Advent, whatever of glory will surround that reign of a thousand years, or the end when He will deliver up the kingdom to God, even the Father—in every transaction that prophecy leads us to expect—God in Christ Jesus will be conspicuous and angelic eyes will look on with adoring admiration as they see the eternal Father glorious in the person of His Son!

These are great themes. We do but mention them and leave them to your quiet thought. It is enough to point to a table if men have appetites for food. But now I will ask you to think of the glory of God in the face of Jesus Christ, in the same line of thought, only putting it in another fashion. Treat it *by way of observation*. When you look upon the material universe, you can see, if your eyes are opened, somewhat of the glory of God. The reverent mind perceives enough to constrain the heart to worship, and yet, after a while, it pines for more.

I have often heard the earth spoken of as the mirror of God's image. But when I was traveling among the Alps and saw many of the grandest phenomena of creation such as glaciers, avalanches, and tempests, I was so impressed with the narrowness of visible things in comparison with God that I wrote such lines as these:

> The mirror of the creatures lacks space
> To bear the image of the Infinite.
> 'Tis true the Lord has fairly writ His name,
> And set His seal upon creation's brow.
>
> But as the skillful potter much excels
> The vessel that he fashions on the wheel,
> E'en so, but in proportion greater far,
> Jehovah's self transcends His noblest works.
>
> Earth's ponderous wheels would break, her axles snap,
> If freighted with the load of deity.
> Space is too narrow for the Eternal's rest,
> And time too short a footstool for His throne.

If your mind has ever entered into communion with God, you will become conscious of the dwarfing of all visible things in His presence. Even when your thought sweeps round the stars and circumnavigates space, you feel that heaven, even the heaven of heavens, cannot contain Him. Everything conceivable falls short of the inconceivable glory of God!

When you come, however, to gaze upon the face of Christ Jesus, how different is the feeling! Now you have a mirror equal to the reflection of the eternal Face, for "in Him dwells all the fullness of the Godhead bodily" (Col. 2:9). His name is "Wonderful, Counselor, Mighty God" (Isa. 9:6). He is the image of God, "the brightness of His glory and the express image of His person" (Heb. 1:3). If your conception of Christ is truthful, it will coincide with the true idea of God and you will exclaim, "This is the true God and eternal life" (1 John 5:20). Like Thomas, you will salute the wounded Savior with the cry, "My Lord and my God!" (John 20:28).

Truly, "God was manifested in the flesh" (1 Tim. 3:16); not a part of

Him, but God in *perfection*. In the visible creation we see God's works, but in Christ Jesus we have God Himself, Immanuel, "God with us." The glory of God in the face of Jesus Christ is most sweetly conspicuous because you are conscious that not only are God's attributes there, but God Himself is there! In the person of Jesus we see the glory of God in *the veiling of His splendor*. The Lord is not eager to display Himself. "You are God, who hide Yourself" (Isa. 45:15), said the prophet of old. The world seems to be created rather to hide God than to manifest Him; at least it is certain that even in the grandest displays of His power we may say with the prophet, "There His power was hidden" (Hab. 3:4).

Though His light is brightness itself, yet it is only the robe that conceals Him. "Who cover Yourself with light as with a garment" (Ps. 104:2). If thus God's glory is seen in the field of creation as a light veiled and shaded to suit the human eye, we certainly see the same in the face of Jesus Christ, where everything is mild and gentle, full of grace as well as truth. How softly breaks the divine glory through the human life of Jesus; a babe in grace may gaze upon this brightness without fear! When Moses' face shone, the people could not look at him, but when Jesus came from His transfiguration, the people ran to Him and saluted Him! Everything is attractive in God in Christ Jesus! In Him we see God to the fullest, but the Deity so mildly beams through the medium of human flesh that mortal man may draw near and look and live.

This glory in the face of Jesus Christ is assuredly the glory of God, even though veiled, for thus in every other instance does God, in measure, shine forth. In providence and in nature such a thing as an unveiled God is not to be seen, and the revelation of God in Christ is after the same divine manner. In our Lord Jesus we see the glory of God *in the wondrous blending of the attributes*. Behold His mercy, for He dies for sinners! But see His justice, for He sits as judge of the quick and the dead. Observe His immutability, for He is the same yesterday, today, and forever! And see His power, for His voice shakes not only earth but also heaven. See how infinite is His love, for He espouses His chosen, but how terrible His wrath, for He consumes His adversaries. All the attributes of deity are in Him—power that can lull the tempest, and tenderness that can embrace little children. The character of Christ is a wonderful combination of all perfection making up one perfection. And so we see the glory of God in the face of Jesus Christ, for this *is* God's glory, that in Him nothing is excessive and nothing is deficient.

He is all that is good and great. In Him is light and no darkness at all.

Say, is it not so seen in Jesus our Lord? When I think of God, I am led to see His glory *in the outgoing of His great heart*, for He is altogether unselfish and unsparingly communicative. We may conceive a period when the Eternal dwelt alone and had not begun to create. He must have been inconceivably blessed, but He was not content to be enwrapped within Himself and to enjoy perfect bliss alone. He began to create and probably formed innumerable beings long before this world came into existence—and He did this that He might multiply beings capable of happiness. He delighted to indulge His heart by deeds of beneficence, manifesting the inherent goodness of His nature. In whatever God is doing, He is consulting the happiness of His creatures. Being in Himself independent of all, He loves to bless others.

He is living—we speak with awe in His presence—He is living, even He, not to Himself, but living in the lives of others, rejoicing in the joy of His creatures! This is His glory, and is it not to be seen most evidently in Christ Jesus, who saved others but could not save Himself (see Matt. 27:42)? Do you not see the great unselfish glory of God in Christ Jesus? When did He ever live to Himself? What single act of His had a selfish purpose? What word He spoke ever sought His honor? In what deed did He consult His own aggrandizement? Neither in life nor in death did Christ live within Himself. He lived for His people and died for them! See the glory of God in this!

There are two things I have noticed in the glory of God whenever my soul has been saturated with it, and these I have seen in Jesus. I have sat upon a lofty hill and looked abroad upon the landscape and seen hill, dale, woods, fields, and I have felt as if God had gone forth and spread His presence over all. I have felt *the outflow of deity*. There was not a pleasant tree nor a silvery stream nor a cornfield ripening for the harvest nor mountain shaggy with pines nor heath purple with heather but seemed aglow with God! Even as the sun pours itself over all things, so does God—and in the hum of an insect, as well as in the crash of a thunderbolt, we hear a voice saying, "God is here." God has gone forth out of Himself into the creation and filled all things! Is not this the feeling of the heart in the presence of Christ?

When we come near Him, He is the all-pervading Spirit. In any of the scenes in which Jesus appears, He is omnipresent. Who but He is at Bethlehem or at Nazareth or at Jerusalem? Who but He is in the world?

Is not He everybody to us, the one and only person of His age? I cannot think of Caesar or Rome or all the myriads that dwell on the face of the earth as being anything more than small figures in the background of the picture when Jesus is before me! He is to my mind most clearly the fullness, filling all in all. All the accessories of any scene in which He appears are submerged in the flood of glory that flows from His all-subduing presence. Truly the outgoing glory of God was in Christ.

> *I cannot think of Caesar or Rome or all the myriads that dwell on the face of the earth as being anything more than small figures in the background of the picture when Jesus is before me!*

But you must have had another thought when you have felt the glory of God in nature. You must have felt *the in-drawing of all things toward God.* You have felt created things rising to God as steps to His throne. As you have gazed with rapture on the landscape, every tree and hill has seemed to drift toward God, to tend toward Him, to return, in fact, to Him from whom it came! Is it not just so in the life of Christ? He seems to be drawing all things to Himself, gathering together all things in one in His own personality. Some of these things will not move, but yet His attraction has fallen on them, while others fly with alacrity to Him, according to His Word: "And I, if I am lifted up from the earth, will draw all peoples to Myself" (John 12:32).

Thus those observations of the glory of God that have been suggested to us by nature are also abundantly verified in Christ, and we are sure that the glory is the same. I cannot express my own thoughts to you so clearly and vividly as I would, but this I know, if you ever get a vision of the glory of God in nature and if you then turn your thoughts toward the Lord's Christ, you will see that the same God is in Him as in the visible universe and that the same glory shines in Him, only more clearly. There is one God, and that one God is gloriously manifested in Christ Jesus. "No one has seen God at any time. The only begotten Son, who is in the bosom of the Father, He has declared Him" (John 1:18).

Let us now treat this thought of the glory of God in the person of Christ by way of experience. Have you ever heard Christ's doctrine in your soul? If so, you have felt it to be divine, for your heart has perceived its moral and spiritual glory and you have concluded that God is in it for sure. Has your heart heard the voice of Christ speaking peace and pardon through the blood? If so, you have known Him to be Lord of all! Did you ever see the fullness of His atonement? Then you have felt that God Himself was there reconciling the world to Himself.

You have understood the union of the two titles "God, our Savior." Beloved, you have often felt your Lord's presence and you have been admitted into intimate communion with Him. Then I know that a profound awe has crept over you that has made you fall at His feet, and in the lowliest reverence of your spirit you have acknowledged Him to be Lord and God. But when He has bent over you in love and said, "Fear not," when He has opened His heart to you and shown you how dear you are to Him, then the rapture you have felt has been so divine that you have, beyond all question, known Him to be God!

There are times when the elevating influence of the presence of Christ has put His Godhead beyond the possibility of question—when we have felt that all the truths of God we ever heard before had no effect upon us compared with the truth that is in Him—that all the spirits in the world were ineffectual to stir us till His Spirit came into contact with our spirit! In this manner His omnipotent, all-subduing, elevating love has proved Him to be none other than very God of very God. Thus have we spoken of the supremely precious object of Christian knowledge.

II. Second, let us say a few words in noticing *the nature of His knowledge.* How and in what respects do we know the glory of God in the face of Jesus Christ? Briefly, first, we know it *by faith.* Upon the testimony of the infallible Word, we believe and are sure that God is in Christ Jesus. The Lord has spoken and said, "This is My beloved Son. Hear Him!" (Mark 9:7). We accept as a settled fact the Godhead of the Lord Jesus, and our soul never permits a question upon it. We know that the Son of God has come. We know that He has given us an understanding that we may know Him who is true and that we are in Him who is true, even in His Son, Jesus Christ. This is the true God and eternal life.

Knowing our Lord's divinity by faith, we next have used our perceptive faculty and, *by consideration and meditation,* we perceive that His life furnishes abundant evidence that He was God, for God's glory shines in that life. The more carefully we pay attention to the details given us by the four evangelists, the more is our understanding persuaded that no mere man stands before us. If, my brothers and sisters, your spiritual nature was set at the task to try to describe how God would act if He were here—what God would be if He became incarnate and dwelt among men—I am sure you would not have been able to imagine the life of Christ. But if someone had brought to you the description given by the evangelists, you would have said, "My task is done! This is indeed a noble conception of God manifest in the flesh."

I do not say that the wise men of this world would suppose God to have thus behaved, for their suppositions are sure to be the reverse of the simple, unaffected, openhearted conduct of Jesus! But this I do say, that the pure in heart will at once see that the acts of Christ are like the doings of God! He has done exactly what a pure intelligence might suppose God would have done! The more we have studied, the more we have seen the glory of God in Christ. And now we have come further than this, for we feel an inward consciousness that the deity is in Christ Jesus. It is not merely that we have believed it and that we somewhat perceive it by observation, but we have come into contact with Christ and have known therefore that He is God.

We love Him and we also love God. And we perceive that these two are one, and the more we love truth and holiness and love, which are great traits in the character of God, the more we see of these in Christ Jesus. It is by the *heart* that we know God and Christ, and as our affections are purified, we become sensible of God's presence in Christ. Oftentimes when our soul is in rapt fellowship with Jesus, we laugh to scorn the very thought that our Beloved can be less than divine! Moreover, there is one other thing that has happened to us while we have been looking at our Lord. Blessed be His name, we begin to grow like He! Our beholding Him has purified the eyes that have gazed on His purity. His brightness has helped our eyesight so that we see much already and will yet see more.

The light of the sun blinds us, but the light of Jesus Christ strengthens the eyes. We expect that as we grow in grace we will behold more and more of God's glory. But we will see it best in the Well Beloved, even in Christ Jesus our Lord! What a sight of God we will enjoy in heaven! We are heading that way, and as we get nearer and nearer, our sight and vision of the glory of God in Christ are every day increased! We know it, then! We know it! We believe it! We are conscious of it! We are affected by it! We are transformed by it! And thus at this day we have "the light of the knowledge of the glory of God in the face of Jesus Christ" (2 Cor. 4:6).

III. Third, let us gratefully review *the means of this knowledge*. How have we come at it? That brings us to read the text again: "God who commanded light to shine out of darkness, who has shone in our hearts to give the light of the knowledge of the glory of God in the face of Jesus Christ." Why did not *everybody* see the glory of God in Jesus Christ when He was here? It was conspicuous enough. Answer: It matters not how brightly the sun shines among *blind men*.

Now, the human heart is blind; it refuses to see God in creation except after a dim fashion. It utterly refuses to discern God in Christ. Therefore He is despised and rejected of men. Moreover, there is a god of this world, the prince of darkness, and since he hates the light, he deepens and confirms the natural darkness of the human mind, lest the light should reach the heart. He blinds men's minds with error and falsehood and foul imaginations, blocking up the windows of the soul either with unclean desires or with dense ignorance. We, at one time, did not perceive the glory of God in Christ because we were blind by nature and were darkened by the evil one. As only the pure in heart can see God, we, being impure in heart, could not see God in Christ.

What, then, has happened to us? To eternal grace be endless praise! God Himself has shined into our hearts. That same God who said, "Light be," and light was, has shined into our hearts! You know creation's story, how all things lay in black darkness? God might have gone on to make a world in darkness if He had pleased, but if He had done so, it would have been to us as though it had never been, for we could not have perceived it. Therefore He early said, "Let there be light." Now, God's glory in the face of Jesus Christ might have been all there and we should never have discerned it. As far as we are concerned, it would have been as though it had never been if the Lord had not entered into us and the thick darkness and said, "Let there be light."

Then burst in the everlasting morning; the light shined in the darkness and the darkness fled before it. Do you recollect the incoming of that illumination? If you do, then I know the first sight you saw by the new light was the glory of God in Jesus Christ! In fact, that light had come on purpose that you might see it, and at this present moment that is the main delight of your soul, the choice subject of your thoughts! In the light of God you have seen the light of the glory of God, as it is written, "In Your light we see light" (Ps. 36:9). One thing I want to say to comfort all who believe: Beloved, do you see the glory of God in Christ Jesus? Then let that sight be evidence to you of your salvation.

When our Lord asked His disciples, "Who do men say that I, the Son of Man, am?" Simon Peter answered, "You are the Christ, the Son of the living God" (Matt. 16:13, 16). Now note the reply of the Lord Jesus to that confession: "Blessed are you, Simon Bar-Jonah, for flesh and blood has not revealed this to you, but My Father who is in heaven" (16:17). If you can delight in God in Christ Jesus, then remember, no man can say that Jesus is the Christ but by the Holy Spirit, and you have said it! And this morning you are saying it! And therefore the Holy Spirit has come upon you.

> *We*, at one time, did not perceive the glory of God in Christ because we were blind by nature and were darkened by the evil one.

"Whoever believes that Jesus is the Christ is born of God" (1 John 5:1). You believe this, and therefore you are born of the Father. "Whoever denies the Son does not have the Father either; he who acknowledges the Son has the Father also" (1 John 2:23). You love God and you are His—the Spirit of God has opened your eyes and you are saved. While I have been preaching this morning, a number of my hearers have been saying, "We care nothing about Jesus Christ. His name is a most respectable one in our religion. We call ourselves Christians, but as to seeing the glory of God in Him when He was a baby and when He was despised and rejected of men, we know nothing of it. No doubt He is exalted now in heaven and we worship Him, though we hardly know why. But we see no special glory in Him."

Others of you have been saying, "Yes, God was in Christ Jesus reconciling the world to Himself, and He has reconciled me to Himself. I never loved God till I saw Him in Christ. I could never have any familiarity with God till I saw His familiarity with me in the person of His Son. I never understood how I could be God's son till I understood how God's Son became a man. I never saw how I could be a partaker of the divine nature till I saw how His Son became a partaker of the *human* nature and took me up to Himself that

He might take me up to His Father."

Oh, beloved, do you delight in Jesus Christ? Is He all your salvation and all your desire? Do you adore Him? Do you consecrate yourself to His honor? Do you wish to live for Him and to die for Him? Then be sure that you belong to Him, for it is the mark of the children of God that they love God in Christ Jesus!

IV. So I finish by mentioning, in the fourth place, *the responsibilities of this knowledge.* There have been considerable debates among the interpreters as to the precise meaning of this text, and some of them think it means that Paul is giving a reason why he preached the gospel. This makes the verse run thus: "For it is the God who commanded light to shine out of darkness, who has shone in our hearts to give the light of the knowledge of the glory of God in the face of Jesus Christ" (2 Cor. 4:6). God gave light to the apostles that they might show forth the light of the knowledge of God in the face of Jesus Christ to the nations.

I do not know whether this is the exact run of the text, but I know it is true. Never is a gleam of light given to any man to hide away. And to spiritual men, the great object of their lives, after they have received light, is to reflect that light in all its purity. You must not hoard up the light within yourself—it will not be light to you if you do. Only think of a person when his room is full of sunlight saying to his servant, "Quick, now! Close the shutters and let us keep this precious light to ourselves." Your room will be in the dark, my friend! So when a child of God gets the light from Christ's face, he must not say, "I will keep this to myself," for that very desire would shut it out. No, let the light shine through you! Let it shine everywhere!

You have the light that you may reflect it. An object that absorbs light is dark, and we call it black. But hang up a reflector in its place when the sun is shining, and it will not appear black—it will be so bright that you will hardly be able to look at it! An object is itself bright in proportion as it sends back the light that it receives. So you will find as a Christian that if you absorb light into yourself, you will be black, but if you scatter it abroad, you will be brilliant. You will be changed into the very image of the light that you have received. You will become a second sun!

I noticed last Sabbath evening, when I came into this pulpit, that at the angle of the building before me, on the left hand the sun seemed to be setting. And I saw the brightness of his round face and yet I knew it to be the wrong quarter of the heavens for the sun to be setting there. Perhaps you will observe that there is a peculiar window on the other side of the street, and it was reflecting the sun so well that I thought it was the sun himself, and I could hardly bear the light! It was not the sun—it was only a window—and yet the radiance was dazzling. And so a man of God, when he receives the light of Christ, can become so perfect a reflector that to common eyes, at any rate, he is brightness itself! He has become transformed from glory to glory as by the image of the Lord!

Brothers and sisters, if you have learned the truth of God, manifest it and make it plain to others! Proclaim *the gospel*, not your own thoughts, for it is *Christ* whom you are to make manifest! Teach not your own judgments, conclusions, and opinions, but the glory of God in the face of Jesus Christ! Let Jesus manifest Himself in His own light. Do not cast a light on Him or attempt to show the sun with a candle. Do not aim at converting men to your views, but let the light shine for itself and work its own way. Do not color it by being like a painted window to it, but let the clear white light shine through you that others may behold your Lord.

> *Proclaim the gospel, not your own thoughts, for it is Christ whom you are to make manifest! Teach not your own judgments, conclusions, and opinions, but the glory of God in the face of Jesus Christ!*

Scatter your light in all unselfishness. Wish to shine, not that others may say, "How bright he is," but that they, getting the light, may rejoice in the Source from which it came to you and to them. Be willing to make every sacrifice to spread this light that you have received! Consecrate your entire being to making known among the sons of men the glory of Christ. Oh, I wish we had swift messengers to run the world over to tell the story that God has come down among us! I wish we had fluent tongues to tell in every language the story that, coming down among us, God was arrayed in flesh like our own and that He took our sins and carried our sorrows.

Oh, that we had trumpet tongues to make the message peal through heaven and earth that God has come among men, and cries, "Come to Me, all you who labor and are heavy laden, and I will give you rest" (Matt. 11:28). Oh, for a voice of thunder to speak it or a lightning pen to write it across the heavens that God has reconciled the world to Himself by the death of

His Son, not imputing their trespasses to them, and that whoever believes in Christ Jesus has everlasting life! I cannot command thunder or lightning, but here are your tongues—go and tell it this afternoon! Here is my tongue and I have tried to tell it, and may it be silent in the dust of death before it ceases to declare that one blessed message, that God in Christ Jesus receives the sons of men in boundless love!

Tell it, brothers, with broken accents, if you cannot speak it more powerfully. Whisper it, sisters, gently whisper, if to none other, yet to your little children, and make the name of Immanuel, God with us, to be sweet in your infant's ears. You are growing in strength and talent, young man, so come, consecrate yourself to this. And you, gray-beard, before you lie down on your last bed to breathe out your spirit, tell the love of Jesus to your sons that they may tell it to *their* sons and hand it down to coming generations, that mankind may never forget that "the Word became flesh and dwelt among us, and we beheld His glory, the glory as of the only begotten of the Father, full of grace and truth" (John 1:14). God bless you. Amen.

For Further Thought

1. Second Corinthians 4:6 says, "God who commanded light to shine out of darkness." When did God first do this?
2. Second Corinthians 4:6 also says that God "has shone in our hearts." When did God first shine in your heart?
3. According to 2 Corinthians 4:6, where can we find the knowledge of the glory of God?

SERMONS RELATING TO THE HOLY SPIRIT

THE HOLY SPIRIT: THE GREAT TEACHER

"However, when He, the Spirit of truth, has come, He will guide you into all truth; for He will not speak on His own authority, but whatever He hears He will speak; and He will tell you things to come."
JOHN 16:13

THIS generation has gradually, and almost imperceptibly, become to a great extent a godless generation. One of the diseases of the present generation of mankind is the secret but deep-seated godlessness by which they have so far departed from the knowledge of God. Science has discovered to us second causes. And hence, many have too much forgotten the first great Cause, the author of all. They have been able so far to pry into secrets that the great axiom of the existence of a God has been too much neglected. Even among professing Christians, while there is a great amount of religion, there is too little godliness. While there is much external formalism but too little inward acknowledgment of God, there is too little living on God, living with God, and relying upon God.

Hence arises the sad fact that when you enter many of our places of worship, you will certainly hear the name of God mentioned, but except in the benediction, you would scarcely know there was a Trinity. In many places dedicated to Jehovah, the name of Jesus is too often kept in the background. The Holy Spirit is almost entirely neglected. And very little is said concerning His sacred influence. Even religious men have become to a large degree godless in this age. We sadly require more preaching regarding God; more preaching of those things that look not so much at the creature to be saved as at God the Great One to be extolled.

> *In many places dedicated to Jehovah, the name of Jesus is too often kept in the background. The Holy Spirit is almost entirely neglected. And very little is said concerning His sacred influence. Even religious men have become to a large degree godless in this age.*

My firm conviction is that in proportion as we have more regard for the sacred Godhead, the wondrous Trinity in unity, will we see a greater display of God's power and a more glorious manifestation of His might in our churches. May God send us a Christ-exalting, Spirit-loving ministry—men who will proclaim God the Holy Spirit in all His offices and will extol God the Savior as the author and finisher of our faith, who will not neglect that great God, the Father of His people, who, before all worlds, elected us in Christ His Son, justified us through His righteousness, and will inevitably preserve us and gather us together in one in the consummation of all things at the last great day.

Our text has regard to God the Holy Spirit. Of Him we will speak and Him only, if His sweet influence will rest upon us.

The disciples had been instructed concerning certain elementary doctrines by Christ, but He did not teach His disciples more than what we should call the ABCs of religion. He gives His reasons for this in the twelfth verse: "I still have many things to say to you, but you cannot bear them now." His disciples were not possessors of the Spirit. They had the Spirit so far as the work of conversion was concerned, but not as to the matters of bright illumination, profound instruction, prophecy, and inspiration. Jesus says, "I am now about to depart, and when I go from you, I will send the Comforter to you. You cannot bear these things now. Howbeit, when He, the Spirit of truth, is come, He will guide you into all truth."

The same promise that He made to His apostles stands good to all His children. And in reviewing it, we will take it as our portion and heritage and will not consider ourselves intruders upon the manor of the apostles or upon their exclusive rights and prerogatives. For we conceive that Jesus says even to us, "When He, the Spirit of truth, has come, He will guide you into all truth."

Dwelling exclusively upon our text, we have five things to say. First of all, here is *an attainment mentioned*—a knowledge of all truth. Second, here is *a difficulty suggested,* which is that we need guidance into all truth. Third, here is *a person provided*—"When He, the Spirit of truth, has come, He will guide you into all truth." Fourth, here is *a manner hinted at:* "He will guide you into all truth." Fifth, here is *a sign given as to the working of the Spirit*—we may know whether He works by His guiding us into *all truth*—into all of one thing. Not *truths*, but truth.

I. Here is *an attainment mentioned* that is knowledge of all truth. We know that some conceive doctrinal knowledge to be of very little importance and of no practical use. We do not think so. We believe the science of Christ crucified and a judgment of the teachings of scripture to be exceedingly valuable. We think it is right that the Christian ministry should be not only arousing but instructing, not merely awakening but enlightening, that it should appeal not only to the passions but to the understanding. We are far from thinking doctrinal knowledge to be of secondary importance. We believe it to be one of the first things in the Christian life, to know the truth and then to practice it. We scarcely need this morning tell you how desirable it is for us to be well taught in things of the kingdom.

First of all, *nature itself* (when it has been sanctified by grace), *gives us a strong desire to know all truth.* The natural man separates himself and intermeddles with all knowledge. God has put an instinct in him by which he is rendered unsatisfied if he cannot probe mystery to its bottom. He can never be content until he can solve secrets. What we call curiosity is something given us of God impelling us to search into the knowledge of natural things. That curiosity, sanctified by the Spirit, is also brought to bear in matters of heavenly science and celestial wisdom. "Bless the LORD," said David, "O my soul; and *all that is within me*, bless His holy name!" (Ps. 103:1, emphasis added).

If there is a curiosity within us, it ought to be employed and developed in a search after truth. "All that is within me," sanctified by the Spirit, should be developed, and, verily, the Christian man feels an intense longing to bury his ignorance and receive wisdom. If he, when in his natural estate, panted for terrestrial knowledge, how much more ardent is the wish to unravel, if possible, the sacred mysteries of God's Word? A true Christian is always intently reading and searching the scriptures that he may be able to certify himself as to its main and cardinal truths.

I do not think much of that man who does not wish to understand doctrines. I cannot conceive him to be in a right position when he thinks it is no matter whether he believes a lie or truth, whether he is heretic or orthodox, whether he received the Word of God as it is written or as it is diluted and misconstrued by man. God's Word will ever be to a Christian a source of great anxiety. A sacred instinct within will lead him to pry into it. He will seek to understand it. Oh! There are some who forget this—men who purposely abstain from mentioning what are called high doctrines because they think if they should mention high doctrines they would be dangerous. So they keep them back.

> *A* true Christian is always intently reading and searching the scriptures that he may be able to certify himself as to its main and cardinal truths.

Foolish men! They do not know anything of human nature. For if they did understand a grain's worth of humanity, they would know that the hiding of these things impels men to search them out. From the fact that they do not mention them, they drive men to places where these and these only are preached. They say, "If I preach election and predestination and these dark things, people will all go straightaway and become Antinomians." I am not so sure if they were to be called Antinomians it would hurt them much, but hear me, O you ministers who conceal these truths, that is the way to make them Antinomians, by silencing these doctrines.

Curiosity is strong. If you tell them they must not pluck the truth, they will be sure to do it. But if you give it to them as you find it in God's Word, they will not seek to wrest it. Enlightened men *will* have the truth, and if they see election in scripture, they will say, "*It is there*, and I will find it out. If I cannot get it in one place, I will get it in another." The true Christian has an inward longing and anxiety after it. He is hungry and thirsty after the word of righteousness, and he must and will feed on this bread of heaven, or at all hazards he will leave the husks that unsound divines would offer him.

Not only is this attainment to be desired because nature teaches us so, but knowledge of all truth is *very essential for our comfort*. I do believe that many persons have been distressed half their lives from the fact that they had not clear views of truth. Many poor souls, for instance, under conviction, abide three or four times as long in sorrow of mind as they would require to do if they had someone to instruct them in the great matter of justification.

Depend on this: The more you know of God's truth, all things else being equal, the more comfortable you will be as a Christian.

So there are believers who are often troubling themselves about falling away. But if they knew in their soul the great consolation that we are kept by the grace of God through faith to salvation, they would be no more troubled about it. So have I found some distressed about the unpardonable sin. But God instructs us in that doctrine and shows us that no conscience that is really awakened ever can commit that sin. He shows us that we need never fear or tremble. All that distress is for nothing. Depend on this: The more you know of God's truth, all things else being equal, the more comfortable you will be as a Christian.

Nothing can give a greater light on your path than a clear understanding of divine things. It is a mingle-mangled gospel too commonly preached that causes the downcast faces of Christians. Give me the congregation whose faces are bright with joy, let their eyes glisten at the sound of the gospel, then will I believe that it is God's own words they are receiving. Instead thereof you will often see melancholy congregations whose visages are not much different from the bitter countenance of poor creatures swallowing medicine, because the Word spoken terrifies them by its legality instead of comforting them by its grace. We love a cheerful gospel, and we think "all the truth" will tend to comfort the Christian.

"Comfort again?" says another. "Always comfort." Ah, but there is another reason why we prize truth, because we believe that a true knowledge of all the truth *will keep us very much out of danger*. No doctrine is so calculated to preserve a man from sin as the doctrine of the grace of God. Those who have called it a licentious doctrine did not know anything at all about it. Poor ignorant things, they little knew that their own vile stuff was the most licentious doctrine under heaven. If they knew the grace of God in truth, they would soon see that there was no preservative from lying like a knowledge that we are elect of God from the foundation of the world.

There is nothing like a belief in my eternal perseverance and the immutability of my Father's affection that can keep me near to Him from a motive of simple gratitude. Nothing makes a man so virtuous as belief of truth. A lying doctrine will soon beget a lying practice. A man cannot have an erroneous belief without by and by having an erroneous life. I believe the one thing naturally begets the other. Keep near God's truth. Keep near His Word. Keep the head right and especially keep your *heart* right with regard to truth, and your feet will not go far astray.

Again, I hold also that this attainment to the knowledge of all truth is very desirable for *the usefulness that it will give us in the world at large*. We should not be selfish; we should always consider whether a thing will be beneficial to others. Knowledge of all truth will make us very serviceable in this world. We will be skillful physicians who know how to take the poor distressed soul aside, to put the finger on his eye and take the scale off for him that heaven's light may comfort him. There will be no character, however perplexing may be its peculiar phase, but we will be able to speak to it and comfort it. He who holds the truth is usually the most useful man.

> Those who hold God's Word never need add something untrue in speaking to men. The sturdy truth of God touches every chord in every man's heart.

As a good Presbyterian brother said to me the other day, "I know God has blessed you exceedingly in gathering in souls, but it is an extraordinary fact that nearly all the men I know, with scarcely an exception, who have been made useful in gathering in souls, have held the great doctrines of the grace of God." Almost every man whom God has blessed to the building up of the church in prosperity and around whom the people have rallied has been a man who has held firmly to free grace from first to last, through the finished salvation of Christ. Do you not think you need to have errors in your doctrine to make you useful? We have some who preach Calvinism all the first part of the sermon and finish up with Arminianism because they think that will make them useful.

Useful? Nonsense is all it is! A man, if he cannot be useful with the truth, cannot be useful with an error. There is enough in the pure doctrine of God without introducing heresies to preach to sinners. As far as I know, I never felt hampered or cramped in addressing the ungodly in my life. I can speak with as much fervency and yet not in the same style as those who hold the contrary views of God's truth. Those who hold God's Word never need add something untrue in speaking to men. The sturdy truth of God touches every chord in every man's heart. If we can, by God's grace, put our hand inside a man's heart, we want nothing but that whole truth to move him thoroughly and to stir him up. There is nothing like the real truth and the whole truth to make a man useful.

II. Now again, here is *a difficulty suggested*, and that is that we require a guide to conduct us into all truth. The difficulty is that truth is not so easy to discover. There is no man born in this world by nature who has the truth in his heart. There is no creature who ever was fashioned since the Fall who has knowledge of truth innate and natural. Many philosophers have disputed whether there are such things as innate ideas at all. But it is of no use disputing as to whether there are any innate ideas of truth. There are none such. There are ideas of everything that is wrong and evil. But in us—that is, our flesh—there dwells no good thing.

We are born in sin and shaped in iniquity. In sin did our mother conceive us. There is nothing in us good and no tendency to righteousness. Then since we are not born with the truth, we have the task of searching for it. If we are to be blessed by being eminently useful as Christian men, we must be well instructed in matters of revelation. But here is the difficulty, that we cannot follow without a guide the winding paths of truth. Why is this?

First, because of *the very great intricacy of truth itself*. Truth itself is no easy thing to discover. Those who fancy they know everything and constantly dogmatize with the spirit of "We are the men, and wisdom will die with us" of course see no difficulties whatever in the system they hold. But I believe the most earnest student of scripture will find things in the Bible that puzzle him. However earnestly he reads it, he will see some mysteries too deep for him to understand. He will cry out, "Truth! I cannot find you. I know not where you are. You are beyond me. I cannot fully view you." Truth is a path that is so narrow that two can scarce walk together in it. We usually tread the narrow way in single file; two men can seldom walk arm in arm in the truth.

We believe the same truth in the main, but we cannot walk together in the path; it is too narrow. The way of truth is very difficult. If you step an inch aside on the right, you are in a dangerous error. If you swerve a little to the left, you are equally in the mire. On the one hand there is a huge precipice and on the other a deep morass. Unless you keep to the true line, to the breadth of a hair, you will go astray. Truth is a narrow path indeed. It is a path the eagle's eye has not seen and a depth the diver has not visited.

It is like the veins of metal in a mine; it is often of excessive thinness, and moreover it runs not in one continued layer. Lose it once and you may dig for miles and not discover it again. The eye must watch perpetually the direction of the lode. Grains of truth are like the grains of gold in the rivers of Australia; they must be shaken by the hand of patience and washed in the stream of honesty, or the fine gold will be mingled with sand. Truth is often mingled with error, and it is hard to distinguish it. But we bless God it is said, "When...the Spirit of truth, has come, He will guide you into all truth."

Another reason why we need a guide is *the invidiousness of error.* It busily steals upon us and if I may so describe our position, we are often like we were on Thursday night in that tremendous fog. Most of us were feeling for ourselves and wondering where on earth we were. We could scarcely see an inch before us. We came to a place where there were three turnings. We thought we knew the old spot. There was the lamppost, and now we must take a sharp turn to the left. But that was not so. We ought to have gone a little to the right. We have been so often to the same place that we think we know every flagstone and there's our friend's shop over the way.

It is dark, but we think we must be quite right, and all the while we are quite wrong and find ourselves half a mile out of the way. So it is with matters of truth. We think, *Surely this is the right path.* And the voice of the evil one whispers, "That is the way; walk in it." You do so and you find to your great dismay that instead of the path of truth, you have been walking in the paths of unrighteousness and erroneous doctrines. The way of life is a labyrinth. The grassiest paths and the most bewitching are the farthest away from right. The most enticing are those that are garnished with wrested truths. I believe there is not a counterfeit coin in the world so much like a genuine one as some errors are like the truth. One is base metal and the other is true gold. Still, in externals, they differ very little.

We also need a guide because *we are so prone to go astray.* Why, if the path of heaven were as straight as Bunyan pictures it, with no turning to the right hand or left—and no doubt it is—still, we are so prone to go astray that we should go to the right to the Mountains of Destruction or to the left in the dark Wood of Desolation. David says, "I have gone astray like a lost sheep" (Ps. 119:176). That means very often, for if a sheep is put into a field twenty times, if it does not get out twenty-one times, it will be because it cannot find a hole in the hedge. If grace did not guide a man, he would go astray though there were hand-posts all the way to heaven.

Let it be written, "Miklat, Miklat, the way to refuge." He would turn aside and the avenger of blood would overtake him if some guide did not, like the angels in Sodom, put his hand on his shoulder and cry, "Escape, escape for your life! Look not behind you! Stay not in all the plain." These, then, are the reasons why we need a guide.

III. In the third place, here is *a person provided*. This is none other than God, and this God is none other than a person. This person is "He, the Spirit," the "Spirit of truth." Not an influence or an emanation but actually a person. "When. . .the Spirit of truth, has come, He will guide you into all truth." Now, we wish you to look at this guide to consider how adapted He is to us.

In the first place, He is *infallible*. He knows everything and cannot lead us astray. If I pin my sleeve to another man's coat, he may lead me part of the way rightly, but by and by he will go wrong himself and I will be led astray with him. But if I give myself to the Holy Spirit and ask His guidance, there is no fear of my wandering.

Again, we rejoice in this Spirit because He is *ever-present*. We fall into a difficulty sometimes. We say, "Oh, if I could take this to my minister, he would explain it. But I live so far off and am not able to see him." That perplexes us and we turn the text round and round and cannot make anything out of it. We look at the commentators. We take down pious Thomas Scott, and as usual, he says nothing about it, if it is a dark passage. Then we go to holy Matthew Henry, and if it is an easy scripture, he is sure to explain it. But if it is a text hard to be understood, it is likely enough, of course, left in its own gloom. And even Dr. Gill himself, the most consistent of commentators, when he comes to a hard passage, manifestly avoids it in some degree.

But when we have no commentator or minister, we have still the Holy Spirit. And let me tell you a little secret. Whenever you cannot understand a text, open your Bible, bend your knee, and pray over that text. And if it does not split into atoms and open itself, try again. If prayer does not explain it, it is one of the things God did not intend you to know and you may be content to be ignorant of it. Prayer is the key that opens the cabinets of mystery. Prayer and faith are sacred picklocks that can open secrets and obtain great treasures. There is no college for holy education like that of the blessed Spirit, for He is an ever-present tutor to whom we have only to bend the knee and He is at our side, the great expositor of truth.

But there is one thing about the suitability of this guide that is remarkable. I do not know whether it has struck you that the Holy Spirit can "guide [us] *into* [a] truth." Now, man can guide us *to* a truth, but it is only the Holy Spirit who can guide us *into* a truth. "When He, the Spirit of truth, has come, He will guide you *into*"—mark that word—"all truth." Now, for instance, it is a long while before you can lead some people to election. But when you have made them see its correctness, you have not led them into it. You may show them that it is plainly stated in scripture, but they will turn away and hate it.

You take them to another great truth, but they have been brought up in a different fashion, and though they cannot answer your arguments, they say, "The man is right, perhaps," and they whisper (but so low that conscience itself cannot hear), "But it is so contrary to my prejudices that I cannot receive it." After you have led them *to* the truth and they see it is true, how hard it is to lead them *into* it! There are many of my hearers who are brought *to* the truth of their depravity but they are not brought *into* it and made to feel it. Some of you are brought to know the truth that God keeps us from day to day. But you rarely get into it, so as to live in continual dependence upon God the Holy Spirit and draw fresh supplies from Him.

The thing is to get inside it. A Christian should do with truth as a snail does with his shell—live inside it as well as carry it on his back and bear it perpetually about with him. The Holy Spirit, it is said, will lead us into all truth. You may be brought to a chamber where there is an abundance of gold and silver, but you will be no richer unless you effect an entrance. It is the Spirit's work to unbar the two-leaved gates and bring us into a truth so that we may get inside it and, as dear old Rowland Hill said, "not only hold the truth, but have the truth hold us."

IV. Fourth, here is *a method suggested*: "He will guide you into all truth." Now I must have an illustration. I must compare truth to some cave or grotto that you have heard of, with wondrous stalactites hanging from the roof and others starting from the floor—a cavern, glittering with spar and abounding in marvels. Before entering the cavern you inquire for a guide, who comes with his lighted flambeau. He conducts you down to a considerable depth and you find yourself in the midst of the cave. He leads you through different chambers. Here he points to a little stream rushing from amid the rocks and indicates its rise and progress.

> *Prayer is the key that opens the cabinets of mystery. Prayer and faith are sacred picklocks that can open secrets and obtain great treasures.*

There he points to some peculiar rock and tells you its name. Then he takes you into a large natural hall, tells you how many persons once feasted in it, and so on. Truth is a grand series of caverns. It is our glory to have so great and wise a Conductor. Imagine that we are coming to the darkness of it. He is a light shining in the midst of us to guide us. And by the light He shows us wondrous things. In three ways the Holy Spirit teaches us—by suggestion, direction, and illumination.

First, He guides us into all truth by *suggestion*. There are thoughts that dwell in our minds that were not born there but that were exotics brought from heaven and put there by the Spirit. It is not a fancy that angels whisper into our ears and that devils do the same. Both good and evil spirits hold converse with men. And some of us have known it. We have had strange thoughts that were not the offspring of our souls but that came from angelic visitors. And direct temptations and evil insinuations have we had that were not brewed in our own souls but that came from the pestilential cauldron of hell.

So the Spirit does speak in men's ears, sometimes in the darkness of the night. In ages gone by He spoke in dreams and visions, but now He speaks by His Word. Have you not at times had unaccountably in the middle of your business a thought concerning God and heavenly things and could not tell from where it came? Have you not been reading or studying the scriptures but a text came across your mind and you could not help it? Though you even put it down, it was like cork in water and would swim up again to the top of your mind. Well, the Spirit put that good thought there.

He often guides His people into all truth by suggesting, just as the guide in the grotto does with his flambeau. He does not say a word, perhaps, but He walks into a passage Himself and you follow Him. So the Spirit suggests a thought and your heart follows it up. Well can I remember the manner in which I learned the doctrines of grace in a single instant. Born, as all of us are by nature, an Arminian, I still believed the old things I had heard continually from the pulpit and did not see the grace of God. I remember sitting one day in the house of God and hearing a sermon as dry as possible and as worthless as all such sermons are, when a thought struck my mind: *How came I to be converted?*

I prayed, thought I. Then I thought, *How came I to pray?* I was induced to pray by reading the scriptures. How came I to read the scriptures? Why did I read them, and what led me to that? And then, in a moment, I saw that God was at the bottom of all and that He was the author of faith. And then the whole doctrine opened up to me, from which, by God's grace, I have not departed.

But sometimes He leads us by *direction.* The guide points and says, "There, gentlemen, go along that particular path; that is the way." So the Spirit gives a direction and tendency to our thoughts. Not suggesting a new one but letting a particular thought, when it starts, take such and such a direction. Not so much putting a boat on the stream as steering it when it is there. When our thoughts are considering sacred things, He leads us into a more excellent channel from that in which we started. Time after time have you commenced a meditation on a certain doctrine and, unaccountably, you were gradually led away into another. And then you saw how one doctrine leaned on another, as is the case with the stones in the arch of a bridge hanging on the keystone of Jesus Christ crucified. You were brought to see these things not by a new idea suggested but by direction given to your thoughts.

> *The Holy Spirit leads us into all truth by suggesting ideas, by directing our thoughts, and by illuminating the scriptures when we read them.*

But perhaps the best way in which the Holy Spirit leads us into all truth is by *illumination.* He illuminates the Bible. Now, have any of you an illuminated Bible at home? "No," says one, "I have a Morocco Bible. I have a Polyglot Bible. I have a Marginal Reference Bible." Ah! That is all very well, but have you an *illuminated* Bible? "Yes, I have a large family Bible with pictures in it." There is a picture of John the Baptist baptizing Christ by pouring water on His head and many other nonsensical things. But that is not what I mean. Have you an illuminated Bible?

"Yes, I have a Bible with splendid engravings in it." Yes. I know you may have. But have you an illuminated Bible? "I don't understand what you mean by an 'illuminated Bible.'" Well, it is the Christian man who has an illuminated Bible. He does not buy it illuminated originally, but when he reads it—

A glory gilds the sacred page,
Majestic like the sun
Which gives a light to every age;
It gives, but burrows none.

There is nothing like reading an illuminated Bible! Beloved, you may read to all eternity and never learn anything by it, unless the Holy Spirit illuminates it, and then the words shine forth like stars. The book seems made of goldleaf. Every single letter glitters like a diamond. Oh, it is a blessed thing to read an illuminated Bible lit up by the radiance of the Holy Spirit! Have you read the Bible and studied it, my brother, and yet have your eyes been unenlightened? Go and say, "O Lord, gild the Bible for me. I want an expounded Bible. Illuminate it. Shine upon it. For I cannot read it to profit unless you enlighten me." Blind men may read the Bible with their fingers, but blind souls cannot. We want a light to read the Bible by; there is no reading it in the dark. Thus the Holy Spirit leads us into all truth by suggesting ideas, by directing our thoughts, and by illuminating the scriptures when we read them.

V. The last thing is *an evidence*. The question arises: How may I know whether I am enlightened by the Spirit's influence and led into all truth? First, you may know the Spirit's influence by its *unity*. He guides us into all truth. Second, by its *universality*. He guides us into *all truth*.

If you are judging a minister, whether he has the Holy Spirit in him or not, you may know him in the first place by *the constant unity of his testimony*. A man who preaches yes and no cannot be enlightened by the Holy Spirit. The Spirit never says one thing at one time and another thing at another time. There are indeed many good men who say both yes and no, but still their contrary testimonies are not both from God the Spirit, for God the Spirit cannot witness to black and white, to a falsehood and truth. It has been always held as a first principle that truth is one thing.

But some persons say, "I find one thing in one part of the Bible and another thing in another, and though it contradicts itself, must I believe it?" That is all quite right, brother, *if it actually did contradict itself.* But the fault is not in the wood but in the carpenter. Just as many carpenters do not understand dovetailing, so there are many preachers who do not understand dovetailing. It is very nice work and it is not easily learned. It takes some apprenticeship to make all doctrines square together. Some preachers preach very good Calvinism for half an hour and the next quarter of an hour Arminianism. If they are Calvinists, let them stick to it. If they are Arminians, let them stick to it. Let their preaching be all of a piece.

Don't let them pile up things only to kick them all down again. Let us have one thing woven from the top throughout, and let us not rend it. How did Solomon know the true mother of the child? "Cut it in halves," said he. The woman who was not the mother did not care so long as the other did not get the whole, and she consented. "Ah," said the true mother, "give her the living child. Let her have it rather than cut it in halves." So the true child of God would say, "I give it up; let my opponent conquer. I do not want to have the truth cut in halves. I would rather be all wrong than have the Word altered to my taste."

We do not want to have a divided Bible. No, we claim the whole living child or none at all. We may rest assured that until we get rid of our linsey-woolsey doctrine and cease to sow mingled seed, we will not have a blessing. An enlightened mind cannot believe a gospel that denies itself. It must be one thing or the other. One thing cannot contradict another and yet it and its opposite be equally true. You may know the Spirit's influence, then, by the unity of its testimony.

And you may know it by its *universality.* The true child of God will not be led into *some* truth but into *all* truth. When first he starts he will not know half the truth. He will believe it but not understand it. He will have the germ of it but not the sum total in all its breadth and length. There is nothing like learning by experience. A man cannot set up for a theologian in a week. Certain doctrines take years to develop themselves. Like the aloe that takes a hundred years to be dressed, there are some truths that must lie long in the heart before they really come out and make themselves appear so that we can speak of them as that which we do know and testify of that which we have seen.

The Spirit will gradually lead us "into all truth." For instance, if it is true that Jesus Christ is to reign upon the earth personally for a thousand years, as I am inclined to believe it is, if I be under the Spirit, that will be more and more opened to me until I with confidence declare it. Some men begin very timidly. A man says at first, "I know we are justified by faith and have peace with God. But so many have cried out against eternal justification that I am afraid of it." But he is gradually enlightened and led to see that in the same hour when all his debts were paid, a full discharge was given. That in the moment when his sin was canceled, every elect soul was justified in God's mind, though they were not justified in their own minds till afterward. The Spirit will lead you into all truth.

Now, what are the practical inferences from this great doctrine? The first is with reference to the Christian who is afraid of his own ignorance. How many are there who are just enlightened and have tasted of heavenly things, who are afraid they are too ignorant to be saved? Beloved, God the Holy Spirit can teach anyone, however illiterate, however uninstructed. I have known some men who were almost idiots before conversion, but they afterward had their faculties wonderfully developed. Some time ago there was a man who was so ignorant that he could not read, and he never spoke anything like grammar in his life, unless by mistake.

And moreover, he was considered to be what the people in his neighborhood called daft. But when he was converted, the first thing he did was to pray. He stammered out a few words, and in a little time his powers of speaking began to develop. Then he thought he would like to read the scriptures, and after long, long months of labor, he learned to read. And what was the next thing? He thought he could preach. And he did preach a little in his own homely way, in his house. Then he thought, *I must read a few more books.* And so his mind expanded until, I believe, he is at the present day a useful minister, settled in a country village, laboring for God.

It needs but little intellect to be taught of God. If you feel your ignorance, do not despair. Go to the Spirit, the great teacher, ask His sacred influence, and it will come to pass that He "will guide you into all truth."

Another inference is this: Whenever any of our brethren do not understand the truth, let us take a hint as to the best way of dealing with them. Do not let us controvert with them. I have heard many controversies but never heard of any good from one of them. We have had controversies with certain men called Secularists, and very strong arguments have been brought against them. But I believe that the Day of Judgment will declare that contending with these men never did a very small amount of good. Better let them alone. Where there is no fuel, the fire goes out. And he who debates with them puts wood upon the fire.

So it is with regard to baptism. It is of no avail to quarrel with our paedobaptist friends. If we simply pray for them that the God of truth may lead them to see the true doctrine, they will come to it far more easily than by discussions. Few men are taught by controversy, for "a man convinced against his will is of the same opinion still." Pray for them that the Spirit of truth may lead them "into all truth." Do not be angry with your brother, but pray for him. Cry, "Lord! Open his eyes that he may behold 'wondrous things from Your law'" (Ps. 119:18).

> Go to the Spirit, the great teacher, ask His sacred influence, and it will come to pass that He "will guide you into all truth."

Lastly, we speak to some of you who know nothing about the Spirit of truth or about the truth itself. It may be that some of you are saying, "We care not much which of you is right; we are happily indifferent to it." Ah! But, poor sinner, if you knew the gift of God and who it was who spoke the truth, you would not say, "I care not for it." If you knew how essential the truth is to your salvation, you would not talk so. If you knew that the truth of God is that you are a worthless sinner but that God from all eternity, apart from all your merits, loved you; if you knew that He bought you with the Redeemer's blood and justified you in the forum of heaven and will by and by justify you in the forum of your conscience through the Holy Spirit by faith; if you knew that there is a heaven for you beyond the chance of a failure, a crown for you, the luster of which can never be dimmed, *then* you would say, "Indeed the truth is precious to my soul!" Why, my ungodly hearers, these men of error want to take away the truth that alone can save you, the only gospel that can deliver you from hell. They deny the great truths of free grace, those fundamental doctrines that alone can snatch a sinner from hell. And even though you do not feel interest in them now, I still would say you ought to desire to see them promoted.

May God give you grace to know the truth in your hearts! May the

Spirit "guide you into all truth"! For if you do not know the truth here, recollect there will be a sorrowful learning of it in the dark chambers of the pit where the only light will be the flames of hell! May you here know the truth! And the truth will make you free, and if the Son will make you free, you will be free indeed, for He says, "I am the way, the truth, the life."

Believe on Jesus, you chief of sinners! Trust His love and mercy and you are saved, for God the Spirit gives faith and eternal life.

For Further Thought

1. *John 16:13 tells of the Spirit as a guide. Into what does the Spirit guide us?*
2. *Spurgeon gives several reasons why we need the Spirit to guide us into the truth. What are some of these?*
3. *According to John 16:13, the Spirit of truth speaks. What does He speak?*

THE HOLY SPIRIT COMPARED
TO THE WIND

*"The wind blows where it wishes, and you hear the sound of it,
but cannot tell where it comes from and where it goes.
So is everyone who is born of the Spirit."*
JOHN 3:8

AT the present moment, I am not able to enter fully into the subject of the new birth. I am very weary, both in body and mind, and cannot attempt that great and mysterious theme. To everything there is a season and a time for every purpose under heaven, and it is not the time to preach upon regeneration when the head is aching, or to discourse upon the new nature when the mind is distracted. I selected my text with the intention of fixing upon one great illustration that strikes me just now as being greatly suggestive, and with divine assistance I may be able to work it out with profit to you and ease to myself.

I will endeavor to bring before you the parallel that our Savior here draws between the wind and the Holy Spirit. It is a remarkable fact, known, I daresay, to most of you, that in both the Hebrew and Greek languages the same word is used for *spirit* and for *wind*, so that our Savior, as it were, rode upon the wings of the wind while he was instructing the seeking rabbi in the deep things of God. He caught at the very name of the wind as a means of fastening a spiritual truth upon the memory of the inquirer, hinting to us that language should be watched by the teacher that he may find out suitable words and employ those that will best assist the disciple to comprehend and to retain his teaching. "The wind," said He, "blows," and the very same word would have been employed if He had meant to say, "The Spirit blows where He wishes."

There was intended, doubtless, to be a very close and intimate parallel between the Spirit of God and the wind, or otherwise the great ruler of providence who invisibly controlled the confusion of Babel would not have fashioned human language so that the same word should stand for both. Language, as well as nature, illustrates the wisdom of God! It is only in His light that we see light. May the Holy Spirit be graciously pleased to reveal Himself in His divine operations to all our waiting minds.

We are taught in God's Word that the Holy Spirit comes upon the sons of men and makes them new creatures. Until He enters them, they are dead in trespasses and sins. They cannot discern the things of God because divine truths of God are spiritual and spiritually discerned. Unrenewed men are carnal and possess not the power to search out the deep things of God. The Spirit of God creates a new heart in the children of God, and then in their newborn spirituality they discover and come to understand spiritual things, but not before. And therefore, my beloved hearers, unless you possess the Spirit, no metaphors, however simple, can reveal Him to you.

> *The Spirit of God creates a new heart in the children of God, and then in their newborn spirituality they discover and come to understand spiritual things, but not before.*

Let us not mention the name of the Holy Spirit without due honor. Forever blessed are You, most glorious Spirit, coequal and coeternal with the Father and with the Son! Let all the angels of God worship You! May You be held in honor world without end!

I. We will consider *in what sense the Holy Spirit may be compared to the wind.* The Spirit of God, to help the spiritually minded in their study of His character and nature, condescends to compare Himself to dew, fire, oil, water, and other suggestive types. And among the rest, our Savior uses the metaphor of wind. What is the first thought here but that of mystery? It was the objection on the score of mystery that our Lord was trying to remove from the mind of Nicodemus. Nicodemus, in effect, said, "I cannot understand it. How can it be? A man born again when he is old, created over again, and that by an invisible agency from above? How can these things be?"

Jesus at once directed his attention to the wind, which is nonetheless real and operative regardless of its mysterious origin and operation. You cannot tell from where the wind comes. You know it blows from the north or from the west, but at what particular place does that wind start on its journey? Where will it pause in its onward flight? You see that it is blowing to the east or to the west, but where is it going? From where did these particles of air originate that rush so rapidly past? Where are they going? By what laws are they guided in their course, and where will their journey end?

The gale may be blowing due east here, but it may be driving west a hundred miles away. In one district the wind may be rushing from the north, and yet not far from it there may be a strong current from the south. Those who ascend in balloons tell us that they meet with crosscurrents one wind blowing in this direction and another layer of air moving toward an opposite quarter. How is this? If you have watched the skies, you must occasionally have noticed a stream of clouds hurrying to the right, while higher up, another company is sailing to the left! It is a question whether thunder and lightning may not be produced by the friction of two currents of air traveling in different directions. But why is it that this current takes it into its head to go this way while another steers for quite another port? Will they meet across each other's path in regions far away?

All the true operations of the Spirit are due in no sense whatever to man, but always to God and to His sovereign will.

Are there whirlpools in the air as in the water? Are there eddies, currents, rivers of air, lakes of air? Is the whole atmosphere like the sea, only composed of less dense matter? If so, what is it that stirs up that great deep of air and bids it howl in the hurricane and then constrains it to subside into the calm? The philosopher may scheme some conjecture to prove that the trade winds blow at certain intervals because of the sun crossing the equator at those periods and that there must necessarily be a current of air going toward the equator because of the rarefaction. But he cannot tell you why the weathercock on yonder church steeple turned this morning from southwest to due east.

He cannot tell me why it is that the sailor finds that his sails are at one time filled with wind and in a few minutes they fall loosely about so that he must steer upon another tack if he would make headway. The various motions of the air remain a mystery to all but the infinite Jehovah. My brethren, the like mystery is observed in the work of the Spirit of God. His person and work are not to be comprehended by the mind of man. He may be here tonight, but you cannot see Him. He speaks to one heart, but others cannot hear His voice. He is not recognizable by the unrefined senses of the unregenerate.

The spiritual man discerns Him, feels Him, hears Him, and delights in Him, but neither wit nor learning can lead a man into the secret. The believer is often bowed down with the weight of the Spirit's glory, or lifted up upon the wings of His majesty. But even he knows not how these feelings are worked in him. The fire of holy life is at seasons gently fanned with the soft breath of divine comfort, or the deep sea of spiritual existence stirred with the mighty blast of the Spirit's rebuke. But still it is forevermore a mystery how the eternal God comes into contact with the finite mind of His creature, man. God is filling all heaven, meanwhile, and yet dwelling in a human body as in a temple; occupying all space and yet operating upon the will, the judgment, the mind of the poor insignificant creature called man.

We may inquire, but who can answer us? We may search, but who will lead us into the hidden things of the Most High? He brooded over chaos and produced order, but who will tell us after what fashion He worked? He overshadowed the Virgin and prepared a body for the Son of God, but into this secret who will dare pry? His is the anointing, sealing, comforting, and sanctifying of the saints, but how does He work all these things? He makes intercession for us according to the will of God. He dwells in us and leads us into all the truths of God, but who among us can explain to his fellow man the order of the divine working?

Though veiled from human eye like the glory that shone between the cherubim, we believe in the Holy Spirit and therefore see Him. But if our faith needed to sustain it, we should never believe at all. Mystery is far from being all that the Savior would teach by this simile. Surely He meant to show us that the operations of the Spirit are like the wind for divinity. Who can create a wind? The most ambitious of human princes would scarcely attempt to turn, much less to send forth, the wind! These steeds of the storm know neither bit nor bridle; neither will they come at any man's bidding. Let our senators do what they will; they will scarcely have the madness to legislate the winds!

Old Boreas, as the heathens called him, is not to be bound with chains and welded on an earthly anvil or in a Vulcanian forge. The wind blows where it wishes, and it does so because God directs it and suffers it neither to stay for man nor to tarry for the sons of men. So it is with the Spirit of God. All the true operations of the Spirit are due in no sense whatever to man but always to God and to His sovereign will. Revivalists may get up excitement with the best intentions and may warm people's hearts till they begin to cry out, but all this ends in nothing unless it is divine work. Have I not said scores of times from this pulpit, all that is of nature's spinning must be unraveled?

Every particle that nature puts upon the foundation will turn out to be but wood, hay, and stubble and will be consumed. It is only the gold, the silver, and the precious stones of God's building that will stand the fiery test. You must be born again from above, for *human* regenerations are lies. You may blow with your mouth and produce some trifling effects upon trifles as light as air. Man in his zeal may set the windmills of silly minds in motion. But truly to stir men's hearts with substantial and eternal truths of God needs a celestial breeze such as the Lord alone can send!

Did not our Lord also intend to hint at the sovereignty of the Spirit's work? For what other reason did He say, "The wind blows where it wishes"? There is arbitrariness about the wind. It does just as it pleases, and the laws that regulate its changes are unknown to man. "Free as the wind," we say, "the wild winds." So is the mighty working of God! It is a very solemn thought and one that should tend to make us humble before the Lord: that we are, as to the matter of salvation, entirely in His hands! If I have a moth in my hand tonight, I can bruise its wings, or I can crush it at my will, and by no attempts of its own can it escape from me. And every sinner is absolutely in the hands of God, and let him remember he is in the hand of an angry God, too.

The only comfort is that he is in the hand of a God who, for Jesus' sake, delights to have mercy upon even the vilest of the vile. Sinner, God can give you the Holy Spirit if He wills. But if He should say concerning you, "Let him alone," your fate is sealed; your damnation is sure! It is a thought that some would say is "enough to freeze all energy." Beloved, I would to God it would freeze the energy of the flesh and make the flesh dead in the sense of powerlessness, for God never truly begins to show His might till we have seen an end of all human power. I tell you, sinner, you are as dead

431

concerning spiritual things as the corpse that is laid in its coffin—as the corpse that is rotting in its grave and has become, like Lazarus in the tomb, stinking and offensive.

There is a voice that can call you forth out of your sepulchre, but if that voice comes not, remember where you are—justly damned, justly ruined, justly cut off forever from all hope. What do you say? Do you tremble at this? Do you cry, "O God! Have pity upon me"? He will hear your cry, sinner, for there never yet was a sincere cry that went up to heaven, though it were ever so feeble, but what it had an answer of peace. When one of the old saints was dying, he could only say, "O Lord, I trust you *languida fide*"; that is, "with a languid faith." It is poor work that, but oh, it is *safe* work. You can only trust Christ with a feeble faith. If it is such a poor trembling faith that it does not grip Him but only *touches* the hem of His garment, it nevertheless saves you!

If you can *look* at Him, though only from a great way off, yet it saves you. And oh, what a comfort this is, that you are still on pleading terms with Him and in a place of hope! "Whoever believes is not condemned." But oh, do not trifle with the day of divine grace, lest having frequently heard the warning and hardened your neck just as often, you should "suddenly be destroyed, and that without remedy" (Prov. 29:1). If He shuts you out, none can bid you come in! If He does but close the iron bar, you are shut out in the darkness of obstinacy, obduracy, and despair forever—the victim of your own delusions!

Sinner, if God saves you, He will have all the glory, for He has a right to do as He wills. "I will have mercy on whomever I will have mercy, and I will have compassion on whomever I will have compassion" (Rom. 9:15). But still, I think I have not yet brought out what is in the text. Do you not think that the text was intended to show the varied methods in which the Spirit of God works in the conversion and regeneration of men? "The wind blows where it wishes." Now observe the different force of the wind. This afternoon the wind seemed as if it would tear up every tree, and doubtless, had they been in leaf, many of those noble princes of the forest must have stretched themselves prone upon the earth. But God takes care that in these times of boisterous gales there should be no leaf, and therefore the wind gets but little purchase with which to drag up a tree.

But the wind does not always blow as it did this afternoon. On a summer's evening there is such a gentle zephyr that even the gnats who have been arranging a dance among themselves are not disturbed, but keep to their proper places. Yes, the aspen seems as if it could be quiet, though you know it keeps forever quivering, according to the old legend that it was the tree on which the Savior hung and therefore trembles still as though through fear of the sin that came upon it. It is but a legend. There are times when all is still and calm, when everything is quiet and you can scarcely detect the wind at all.

Now just so it is with the Spirit of God. To some of us He came like a rushing mighty wind. Oh, what tearing of soul there was then! My spirit was like a sea tossed up into tremendous waves, made, as Job says, to "boil like a pot" (41:31), till one would think the deep were hoary. Oh, how that wind came crashing through my soul and every hope I had was bowed as the trees of the wood in the tempest! Read the story of John Bunyan's conversion; it was just the same. Turn to Martin Luther; you find his conversion of the same sort. So might I mention hundreds of biographies in which the Spirit of God came like a tornado sweeping everything before it and the men could not but feel that God was in the whirlwind. To others He comes so gently they cannot tell when first the Spirit of God came. They recollect that night when Mother prayed so with brothers and sisters and when they could not sleep for hours because the big tears stood in their eyes on account of sin. They recollect the Sunday school and the teacher there. They remember that earnest minister. They cannot say exactly when they gave their hearts to God and they cannot tell about any violent convictions. They are often comforted by that text, "One thing I know: that though I was blind, now I see" (John 9:25). But they cannot get any further, though they sometimes wish they could.

> he Spirit of God, as a sovereign, will always choose His own way of operation. And if it is but the wind of the Holy Spirit, remember it is as saving in its gentleness as in its terror. . . .

Well, they need not wish it, for the Spirit of God, as a sovereign, will always choose His own way of operation. And if it is but the wind of the Holy Spirit, remember it is as saving in its gentleness as in its terror and is as efficient to make us new creatures when it comes with the zephyr's breath as when it comes with the hurricane's force. Do not quarrel with God's way of saving you! If you are brought to the cross, be thankful for it. Christ will not mind how you got there if you can say, "He is 'all my salvation and all my desire'" (2 Sam. 23:5). You never came to that without the Spirit of God bringing you to it. Do not therefore think you came the wrong way, for that is impossible!

Again, the wind not only differs in force, but it differs in direction. We have been saying several times the wind is always shifting. Perhaps there never were two winds that did blow exactly in the same direction. I mean that if we had power to detect the minute points of the compass, there would be found some deviation in every current, although, of course, for all practical purposes it blows from certain distinct points that the mariner marks out.

Now, the Spirit of God comes from different directions. You know very well, dear friends, that sometimes the Spirit of God will blow with mighty force from one denomination of Christians. Then suddenly they seem to be left, and God will raise up another body of Christians, fill them with Himself, and qualify them for usefulness. In the days of Wesley and Whitefield, there was very little of the divine Spirit anywhere except among the Methodists. I am sure they have not a monopoly of Him now. The divine Spirit blows also from other quarters. Sometimes He uses one man, sometimes another. We hear of a revival in the north of Ireland. By and by it is in the south of Scotland. It comes just as God wills, for direction.

And you know, too, dear friends, it comes through different instrumentalities in the same church. Sometimes the wind blows from this pulpit and God blesses me to your conversion. Another time it is from my good sister Mrs. Bartlett's class. On a third occasion it is the Sunday school. Again, it may be another class, or the preaching of the young men, or from the individual exertion of private believers. God causes the wind to blow just that way He wills. He works, also, through different texts of scripture. You were converted and blessed under one text; it was quite another that was made useful to me.

Some of you were brought to Christ by terrors, others of you by love, by sweet wooing words. The wind blows as God directs. Now, dear friends, whenever you take up a religious biography, do not sit down and say, "Now I will see whether I am just like this person." Nonsense! God never repeats Himself. Men make steel pens—thousands of grosses of them—all alike, but I will be bound to say that in quills from the common, there are no two of them precisely the same. If you look, you will soon discover that they differ in a variety of ways. Certain gardeners cut their trees into the shape of cheeses and a number of unnatural forms, but God's trees do not grow that way. They grow just any way—gnarl their roots and twist their branches.

Great painters do not continually paint the same picture again and again and again, and my divine Master never puts His pencil on the canvas to produce the same picture twice. Every Christian is a distinct work of divine grace on God's part that has in it some originality, some portion distinct from all others. I do not believe in trying to make all history uniform. It is said that Richard III had a humpback. Whether he really was deformed or whether history gave him the humpback, I cannot tell. But it is said that all his courtiers thought it was the most beautiful humpback that ever was seen, and they all began to grow humpbacks, too!

> *Great painters do not continually paint the same picture again and again and again, and my divine Master never puts His pencil on the canvas to produce the same picture twice.*

And I have known ministers who had some peculiar idiosyncrasy of experience that was nothing better than a spiritual humpback, but their people all began to have humpbacks, too—to think and talk all in the same way and to have the same doubts and fears. Now that will not do! It is not the way in which the Most High acts with regard to the wind, and if He chooses to take all the points of the compass and make use of them all, let us bless and glorify His name! Are not the different winds various in their qualities? Few of us like an east wind. Most of us are very glad when the wind blows from the south. Vegetation seems to love much the southwest.

A stiff northeaster is enough to make us perish. And long continuance of the north may well freeze the whole earth! While from the west the wind seems to come laden with health from the deep blue sea. And though sometimes too strong for the sick, yet it is never a bad time when the west wind blows. The ancients all had their different opinions about wind. Some were dry, and some were rainy. Some affected this disease, some touched this part of men, some the other. Certain it is that God's Holy Spirit has different qualities. In the canticles He blows softly with the sweet breath of love. Look further and you get that same Spirit blowing fiercely with threats and denunciation.

Sometimes you find Him convicting the world "of sin, and of righteousness, and of judgment" (John 16:8). That is the north wind. At other times He opens up Christ to the sinner and gives him joy and comfort. That is, the south wind blows softly and gives balminess in that poor troubled heart. And yet in all these works the same Spirit. Indeed, my subject is all but endless, and therefore I must stop. But even in the matter of duration you know how the wind will sometimes blow six weeks in this direction and, again, continue in another direction. And the Spirit of God does not always work with us. He does as He pleases; He comes and He goes. We may be in a happy hallowed frame at one time, and at another we may have to cry, "Come from the four winds, O breath" (Ezek. 37:9)!

II. We will consider, in the second place, *the parallel between the Holy Spirit and the effects of the wind.* "You hear the sound of it." Ah, that we do! The wind sometimes wails as if you could hear the cry of mariners far out at sea or the moans of the widows who must weep for them. And oh, the Spirit of God sets men wailing with an exceedingly bitter cry for sin, as one who is in sorrow for his firstborn.

"You hear the sound of it." Oh, it is a blessed sound, that wailing! Angels rejoice over one sinner who repents. Then comes the wind at another time with a triumphant sound, and if there is an aeolian harp in the window, how it swells, sweeps, descends, and then rises again! It gives all the tones of music and makes the air glad with its jubilant notes. So with the Holy Spirit. Sometimes He gives us faith, makes us bold, other times full of assurance, confidence, joy, and peace in believing. "You hear the sound" of a full diapason of the Holy Spirit's mighty melody within the soul of man filling him with peace and joy and rest and love.

Sometimes the wind comes, too, with another sound as though it were contending. You heard it, perhaps, this afternoon. We who are a little in the country hear it more than you do—it is as though giants were struggling in the sky together. It seems as if two seas of air, both lashed to fury, met and dashed against some unseen cliffs with terrible uproar. The Spirit of God comes into the soul sometimes and makes great contention with the flesh. Oh, what a stern striving there is against unbelief, against lust, against pride, against every evil thing.

"You hear the sound of it." You who know what divine experience means, you know when to go forth to fight your sins. When you can hear "the sound of marching in the tops of the mulberry trees" (2 Sam. 5:24), then you bestir yourself to destroy your sins. Sometimes the wind comes with a sweep as though it were going on forever. It comes past and dashes through the trees, sweeping away the rotten branches. Then away it goes across the Alps, dashing down an avalanche in its course, still onward. And as it flies, it blows away everything that is frail and weak. And on, on, on it speeds its way to some unknown goal.

And thus it is sometimes the Spirit of God will come right through us, as if He were bearing us away to that spiritual heritage that is our sure future destiny, bearing away coldness, barrenness, everything before it. We do not lament then that we do not pray. We do not believe that we *cannot* pray. "I can do everything" is our joyful shout as we are carried on the wings of the wind. "You hear the sound of it." I hope you have heard it sometimes in all its powerful, overwhelming, mighty influence till your soul has been blown away.

"You hear the sound of it." But then the wind does something more than make a sound. And so does the Holy Spirit. It *works* and produces manifest results. Just think what the wind is doing tonight. I cannot tell at what pitch it may be now. It is just possible that in some part of the ocean a vessel scuds along almost under bare poles. The mariners do their best to reef the sails. Away she goes; now the mast is gone. They do their best to bear up, but they find that in the teeth of the gale they cannot stand. The ship dashes on the rocks and she is wrecked. And oh, the Spirit of God is a great wrecker of false hopes and carnal confidences! I have seen the Spirit of God come to a sinner like a storm to a ship at sea. He had to take down the top gallants of the sinner's pride. Then every thread of carnal confidence had to be reefed, and then his hope itself had to be cut away. And on, on the vessel went, until she struck a rock and down she went. The man from that time never dared trust in his merits, for he had seen his merits wrecked and broken in pieces by the wind.

The wind, too, remember, is a great leveler. It always aims at everything that is high. If you are down low in the street, you escape its fury. But climb to the top of the Monument, or St. Paul's, and see whether you do not feel it! Get into the valley. It is all right. The lower branches of the trees are scarcely moved, but the top branches are rocked to and fro by it. It is a great leveler! So is the Holy Spirit. He never sees a man high but He brings him down. He makes every high thought bow before the majesty of His might.

And if you have any high thoughts tonight, rest assured that when the Spirit of God comes, He will lay them low, even with the ground. Now do not let this make you fear the Holy Spirit. It is a blessed thing to be rocked so as to have our hopes tested, and it is a precious thing to have our carnal confidences shaken. And how blessedly the wind purifies the atmosphere! In the Swiss valleys there is heaviness in the air that makes the inhabitants unhealthy. They take quinine and you see them going about with big swellings in their necks.

> The wind, too, remember, is a great leveler. It always aims at everything that is high. If you are down low in the street, you escape its fury.

From Martigny to Bretagne, there is a great valley in which you will see hundreds of persons diseased. The reason is that the air does not circulate. They are breathing the same air, or some of it, that their fathers breathed before them. There seems to be no ventilation between the two parts of the giant Alps, and the air never circulates. But if they have a great storm that sweeps through the valleys, it is a great blessing to the people. And so the Spirit of God comes and cleanses out our evil thoughts and vain imaginations, and though we do not like the hurricane, yet it brings spiritual health to our soul.

Again, the wind is a great trier of the nature of things. Here comes a great rushing up the street. It sweeps over the heaps of rubbish lying in the road. Away go all the light chaff, paper, and other things that have no weight in them! They cannot stand the brunt of its whirling power. But see, the pieces of iron, the stones, and all weighty things are left unmoved. In the country you will often see the farmer severing the chaff from the wheat by throwing it up into a current of air, and the light husks all blow away, while the heavy wheat sinks on the heap, cleansed and purified. So is the Holy Spirit the great testing power, and the result of His operations will be to show men what they are.

Here is a hypocrite; he has passed muster up to now and reckons himself to be a true and genuine man. But there comes a blast from heaven's mighty Spirit and he finds himself to be lighter than vanity. He has no weight in him; he is driven on and has no rest. He can find no peace. He hurries from one refuge of lies to another. " 'There is no peace,' says the LORD, 'for the wicked' " (Isa. 48:22). Thus also we try the doctrines of men; we bring the breath of inspiration to bear upon them. Do they abide the test? Or are they driven away? Can you hold that truth in the presence of God? Can you cling to it and find it stable in the hour of trial?

Is it a nice pleasant speculation for a sunny day when all is calm and bright, or will it bear the rough rude blast of adversity when God's Holy Spirit is purifying you with His healthful influence? True Christians and sound doctrines have ballast and weight in them; they are not moved nor driven away. But empty professors and hollow dogmas are scattered like chaff before the wind when the Lord will blow upon them with the breath of His Spirit. Therefore examine yourselves; try the doctrines and see if they are of God. What is the chaff to the wheat?

> *You are inundated with sin; a flood of iniquity comes in and you can never bail out the torrent. But with the help of God's Spirit it can be done!*

Have root in yourselves; then you will not wither in the hot blast nor be driven away in the tempestuous day. Is not the Spirit moreover like the wind in its developing of character? See, the dust is lying all over the picture; you cannot see the fair features of the beauteous sketch beneath. Blow off the dust, and the fine colors will be seen and once more the skill of the painter will be admired. Have you ever noticed some piece of fine mosaic, or perhaps some well-cut engraving on metal, all hidden and the fine lines filled up with dust?

You have blown off the accumulation and then you could admire the work. So does the Spirit of God. Men get all covered with dust in the hot dusty roadside of life till they are nearly the color of the earth itself. But they come to the hilltop of Calvary and here they stand till the wind of heaven has cleansed them from all the dust that has gathered around their garments. Oh, there is nothing like communion with the Spirit of God to counteract the earthly tendencies of a business life! There are some men who get covered with a yellow dust till they are almost hidden by it. They can talk of nothing else but money. Gold, gold, gold is getting to occupy nearly every thought.

Now, I have no quarrel with money in its right place, but I do not like to see men live in it. I always try to drive away that mean and groveling spirit that lives for nothing else but to accumulate money, but I cannot always succeed. Now, the Spirit of God will make a man see his folly and put his money into its right position and place the graces of the Christian character where men can see them and glorify God in them. Never let your business character or professional skill dim and hide your Christianity. If you do, God's Spirit will come to brighten you up, and He will have no mercy on these but will, in love to your soul, cleanse and give luster to God's work that is worked in you.

I have also noticed how helpful the wind is to all who choose to avail themselves of it. In Lincolnshire, where the country is flat and below the level of the sea, they are obliged to drain the land by means of windmills, and hundreds of them may be seen pumping up the water so as to relieve the land of the excess moisture. In many parts of the country, nearly all the wheat and corn is ground by means of the wind. If it were not for the wind, the inhabitants would be put to great inconvenience.

The Spirit of God is thus also a mighty helper to all who will avail themselves of His influences. You are inundated with sin; a flood of iniquity comes in and you can never bail out the torrent. But with the help of God's Spirit it can be done! He will so assist that you will see the flood gradually descending and your heart once more purified. You need always to ask His help. Fresh sin, like falling showers, will be poured into you by every passing day, and you will need a continuous power to cast it out. You may have it in God's Spirit! He will, with ceaseless energy, help you to combat sin and make you more than a conqueror!

Or, on the other hand, if you need some power to break up and prepare your spiritual food for you, you will find no better help than what God's Spirit can give. In Eastern countries they grind corn by hand, two sitting at a small stone mill. But it is a poor affair at best. So are our own vain attempts to prepare the bread of heaven for ourselves. We will only get a little and that little badly ground. Commentators are good in their way, but give me the teaching of the Holy Spirit. He makes the passage clear and gives me to eat of the finest wheat. How often we have found our utter inability to understand some part of divine truth. We asked some of God's people and they helped us a little, but after all, we were not satisfied till we took it to the throne of heavenly grace and implored the teachings of the blessed Spirit!

Then how sweetly it was opened to us! We could eat of it spiritually. It was no longer husk and shell, hard to be understood. It was as bread to us and we could eat to the full. Brethren, we must make more use of the wisdom that comes from above, for the Spirit, like the wind, is open to us all to employ for our own personal benefit. I see also here a thought as to the cooperation of man and the Spirit in all Christian work. It has pleased God to make us coworkers with Him—fellow laborers—both in the matter of our own salvation and also in the effort to benefit others. Look for a moment at yon stately boat. She moves not *because* of her sails, but she would not reach the desired haven without them.

It is the *wind* that propels her forward, but the wind would not act upon her as it does unless she had the rigging all fixed with her masts standing and her sails all bent so as to catch the passing breeze. But now that human seamanship has done its best, see how she flies! She will soon reach her haven with such a favoring gale as that. You have only to stand still and see how the wind bears her on like a thing of life. And so it is with the human heart. When the Spirit comes to the soul that is ready to receive such influences, then He helps you on to Christian grace and Christian work and makes you bear up through all opposition till you come to the port of peace and can anchor safely there. Without Him we can do nothing. Without us He will not work.

We are to preach the gospel to every creature, and while one plants and another waters, God adds the increase. We are to work out our own salvation—He works in us to will and to do of His own good pleasure. We must go up to possess the goodly land with our own spear and sword, but the hornet goes before us to drive out the foe. Jericho will be captured by a divine and miraculous interference, but even there, rams' horns will find a work to do and must be employed. The host of Midian will be slain, but our cry is, "The sword of the LORD and of Gideon!" (Judg. 7:18). We give God all the glory; nevertheless we use the means.

The water of Jordan must be sought out and used by all who desire a cleansing like Naaman the Syrian. A lump of figs must be used if other Hezekiahs are to be healed. But the Spirit is, after all, the great cleanser and healer of His people Israel. The lesson is clear to all: The wind turns mills that men make. It fills sails that human hands have spread. And the Spirit blesses human effort, crowns with success our labors, establishes the work of our hands upon us, and teaches all through that "the hand of the diligent makes rich" (Prov. 10:4). And "if anyone will not work, neither shall he eat" (2 Thess. 3:10).

Another thought suggests itself to my mind in connection with the wind and human effort. It is this: How completely dependent men are upon the wind as to what it will do for them. They are entirely at its mercy as to its time of blowing, its strength, and the direction it will take. I have already dwelt upon this thought of the sovereignty of the wind, but it comes up here in a more practical form. The steamer now can steer almost anywhere it pleases, and at all times it will proceed on its voyage.

> Brethren, let us do our part faithfully, spread every sail, make all as perfect as human skill and wisdom can direct, and then in patient continuance in well-doing, await the Spirit's propitious gales. . . .

But the sailing ship must tack according to the wind and when becalmed must wait for the breeze to spring up. The watermill and steam mill can be worked night and day, but the mill that depends upon the wind must abide by the wind's times of blowing and must turn round its sails so as to suit the direction of the current of air. In like manner we are compelled to wait on the pleasure of the Spirit. There is no reservoir of water that we can turn on when we will and work as we please. We would forget God far more than we do now if that were the case. The sailor who is depending on the wind anxiously looks up to the masthead to see how the breeze is shifting and turning round the vane. And he scans the heavens to see what weather he is likely to have.

He would not need to care nearly so much as he does now that he is absolutely dependent on the wind if he had steam power so as to sail in the very teeth of the storm if he so willed. God, then, keeps us looking up to heaven by making us to be completely at His mercy as to the times and ways of giving us His helping power. It is a blessed thing to wait on God, watching for His hand and in quiet contentment leaving all to Him. Brethren, let us do our part faithfully, spread every sail, make all as perfect as human skill and wisdom can direct, and then in patient continuance in well-doing await the Spirit's propitious gales, neither murmuring because He tarries nor being taken unawares when He comes upon us in His sovereign pleasure to do that which seems good in His sight.

Now tonight I have only given you some hints on this subject. You can work it out for yourselves. As you hear the wind, you may get more sermons out of it than I can give you just now. The thing is perfectly inexhaustible. And I think the business of the minister is not to say all that can be said about the subject. Somebody remarked concerning a certain minister that he was a most unfair preacher because he always exhausted the subject and left nothing for anybody else to say.

> *Do you know the Spirit of God? If you have not the Spirit, you are none of His. "You must be born again."*

That will never be said of me, and I would rather that it should not. A minister should suggest germs of thought, open up new ways, and present, if possible, the truth of God in such a method as to lead men to understand that the half is not told them. And now, my dear hearer, whether you listen often to my voice or have now stepped in for the first time, I would like to ring this in your ear. Do you know the Spirit of God? If you have not the Spirit, you are none of His. "You must be born again" (John 3:7). "What, Lord, '*must*'? Do you not mean 'may'?" No, you *must*. "Does it not mean, 'You can be'?" No, you must. When a man says "must," it all depends upon who he is. When God says "must," there it stands and it cannot be questioned.

There are the flames of hell. Would you escape from them? You must be born again. There are heaven's glories sparkling in their own light. Would you enjoy them? You must be born again! There is the peace and joy of a believer. Would you have it? You must be born again. What, not a crumb from off the table without this? No, not one. Not a drop of water to cool your burning tongues except you are born again. This is the one condition that never changes. God never alters it and never will.

You must, must, must. Which will it be? Shall your will stand or God's will? Oh, let God's "must" ride right over you and bow yourselves down and say, "Lord, I must! Then I will! Ah, and it has come to this: I must *tonight*. Give me Christ, or else I die. I have hold of the knocker of the door of your mercy and I must, I *will* get that door open. I will never let you go except you bless me! You say 'must,' Lord, and I say 'must,' too."

You must, "you must be born again." God fulfill the "must" in each of your cases, for Jesus Christ's sake. Amen.

For Further Thought

1. *To whom was Jesus speaking when He compared the Spirit to the wind in John 3:8?*

2. *In John 3:8, the Lord compares the wind of the Spirit to what kind of people?*

3. *Acts 2:2 compares the Spirit to the wind. What was the effect of the blowing wind of the Spirit at that time?*

THE HOLY SPIRIT'S INTERCESSION

Likewise the Spirit also helps in our weaknesses.
For we do not know what we should pray for as we ought,
but the Spirit Himself makes intercession for us with groanings
which cannot be uttered. Now He who searches the hearts
knows what the mind of the Spirit is, because He makes
intercession for the saints according to the will of God.
ROMANS 8:26–27

THE apostle Paul was writing to a tried and afflicted people, and one of his objectives was to remind them of the rivers of comfort that were flowing near at hand. He first of all stirred up their pure minds by way of remembrance as to their sonship, for he says, "As many as are led by the Spirit of God, these are sons of God" (Rom. 8:14). They were therefore encouraged to take part and lot with Christ, the Elder Brother, with whom they had become joint heirs. And they were exhorted to suffer with Him that they might afterward be glorified with Him. All that they endured came from a Father's hand, and this should comfort them. A thousand sources of joy are opened in that one blessing of *adoption*. Blessed is the God and Father of our Lord Jesus Christ, by whom we have been begotten into the family of grace!

When Paul had alluded to that consoling subject, he turned to the next ground of comfort, namely, that we are to be sustained under present trial by *hope*. There is an amazing glory in reserve for us, and though as yet we cannot enter upon it, but in harmony with the whole creation must continue to groan and travail, yet the hope itself should minister strength to us and enable us to bear patiently the light afflictions that are but for a moment. This also is a truth of God full of sacred refreshment: Hope sees a crown in reserve, mansions in readiness, and Jesus Himself preparing a place for us. By the rapturous sight hope sustains the soul under the sorrows of the hour! Hope is the grand anchor by whose means we ride out the present storm.

The apostle then turns to a third source of comfort, namely, the abiding of the Holy Spirit in and with the Lord's people. He uses the word "likewise" to intimate that in the same manner as hope sustains the soul, so does the Holy Spirit strengthen us under trial. Hope operates spiritually upon our spiritual faculties, and so does the Holy Spirit, in some mysterious way, divinely operate upon the newborn faculties of the believer so that he is sustained under his infirmities. In His light will we see light. I pray, therefore, that we may be helped of the Spirit while we consider His mysterious operations, that we may not fall into error or miss precious truths of God through blindness of heart.

The text speaks of our infirmities, or as many translators put it in the singular, our infirmity. By this is intended our affliction and the weakness that trouble discovers in us. The Holy Spirit helps us to bear the infirmity of our body and of our mind. He helps us to bear our cross, whether it is physical pain, mental depression, spiritual conflict, slander, poverty, or persecution. He helps our infirmity, and with a helper so divinely strong, we need not fear for the result! God's grace will be sufficient for us! His strength will be made perfect in weakness! I think, dear friends, you will all admit that if a man can pray, his trouble is at once lightened. When we feel that we have power with God and can obtain anything we ask for at His hands, then our difficulties cease to oppress us.

> *He* helps our infirmity, and with a helper so divinely strong, we need not fear for the result! God's grace will be sufficient for us! His strength will be made perfect in weakness!

We take our burden to our heavenly Father and tell Him in the accents of childlike confidence, and we come away quite content to bear whatever His holy will may lay upon us. Prayer is a great outlet for grief; it draws up the sluices and abates the swelling flood that otherwise might be too strong for us. We bathe our wounds in the lotion of prayer and the pain is lulled; the fever is removed. But the worst of it is that in certain conditions of heart we *cannot* pray. We may be brought into such perturbation of mind and perplexity of heart that we do not know *how* to pray. We see the mercy seat and we perceive that God will hear us. We have no doubt about that, for we know that we are His favored children and yet we hardly know what to desire.

We fall into such heaviness of spirit and entanglement of thought that the one remedy of prayer, which we have always found to be unfailing, appears to be taken from us. Here, then, in the nick of time, as a very present help in time of trouble, comes in the Holy Spirit! He draws near to teach us how to pray, and in this way He helps our infirmity, relieves our suffering, and enables us to bear the heavy burden without fainting under the load. At this time our subjects for consideration will be, first, *the help that the Holy Spirit gives*. Second, *the prayers that He inspires*. And third, *the success that such prayers are certain to obtain*.

I. First, then, let us consider *the help that the Holy Spirit gives*. The help that the Holy Spirit renders to us meets the weakness that we deplore. As I have already said, if in time of trouble a man can pray, his burden loses its weight. If the believer can take anything and everything to God, then he learns to glory in infirmity and to rejoice in tribulation. But sometimes we are in such confusion of mind that we know not for what we should pray as we ought to. In a measure, through our ignorance, we *never* know what we should pray for until we are taught of the Spirit of God, but there *are* times when this beclouding of the soul is dense indeed, and we do not even know what would help us out of our trouble if we could obtain it.

We see the disease, but the name of the medicine is not known to us. We look over the many things that we might ask for of the Lord and we feel that each of them would be helpful, but none of them would precisely meet our case. For spiritual blessings that we know to be according to the divine will, we could ask with confidence, but perhaps these would not meet our peculiar circumstances. There are other things for which we are allowed to ask, but we scarcely know whether, if we had them, they would really serve our turn, and we also feel diffidence as to praying for them. In praying for temporal things, we plead with measured voices, always referring our petition for revision to the will of the Lord.

Moses prayed that he might enter Canaan, but God denied him. The man who was healed asked our Lord that he might be with Him, but he received the answer, "Go home to your friends" (Mark 5:19). We pray on such matters with this reserve: "Nevertheless, not as I will, but as You will" (Matt. 26:39). At times this very spirit of resignation appears to increase our mental difficulty, for we do not wish to ask for anything that would be contrary to the mind of God and yet we must ask for *something*! We are reduced to such straits that we must pray, but what will be the particular subject of prayer we cannot, for a while, make out. Even when ignorance and perplexity are removed, we know not what we should pray for as we ought.

When we know the *matter* of prayer, we yet fail to pray in a right *manner*. We ask, but we are afraid that we will not have, because we do not exercise the thought or the faith that we judge to be essential to prayer. We cannot, at times, command even the *earnestness* that is the life of supplication. Torpor steals over us, our heart is chilled, our hands are numbed, and we cannot wrestle with the angel. We know what to pray for as to objects, but we do not know what to pray for as we ought. It is the *manner* of the prayer that perplexes us, even when the matter is decided upon! How can I pray? My mind wanders. I chatter like a crane. I roar like a beast in pain. I moan in the brokenness of my heart, but oh, my God, I know not what it is my inmost spirit *needs*, or if I know it, I know not how to frame my petition aright before you! I know not how to open my lips in Your majestic presence. I am so troubled that I cannot speak! My spiritual distress robs me of the power to pour out my heart before my God!

> We poor trembling sons of men dare take that word into our mouth that first came out of God's mouth and then come with it as an argument and plead it before the throne of the heavenly grace.

Now, beloved, it is in such a plight as this that the Holy Spirit aids us with His divine help, and hence He is a very present help in time of trouble. Coming to our aid in our bewilderment, He instructs us. This is one of His frequent operations upon the mind of the believer: "He will teach you all things." He instructs us as to our need and as to the promises of God that refer to that need. He shows us where our deficiencies are—what our sins are and what our necessities are. He sheds a light upon our condition and makes us feel our helplessness, sinfulness, and dire poverty very deeply. And then He casts the same light upon the promises of the Word and lays home to our heart that very text that was intended to meet the occasion, the *precise promise* that was framed with foresight of our present distress!

In that light He makes the promise shine in all its truthfulness, certainty, sweetness, and suitability so that we poor trembling sons of men dare take that word into our mouth that first came out of God's mouth and then come with it as an argument and plead it before the throne of the heavenly grace. Our prevalence in prayer lies in the plea, "Lord, 'do as You have said'" (1 Chron. 17:23). How greatly we ought to value the Holy Spirit, because when we are in the dark, He gives us light! And when our perplexed spirit is so befogged and beclouded that it cannot see its own need and cannot find out the appropriate promise in the scriptures, the Spirit of God comes in and teaches us all things and brings all things to our remembrance whatever our Lord has told us. He guides us in prayer and thus He helps our infirmity.

But the blessed Spirit does more than this! He will often direct the mind to the special subject of prayer. He dwells within us as a counselor and points out to us what it is we should seek at the hands of God. We do not know why it is so, but we sometimes find our minds carried as by a strong undercurrent into a particular line of prayer for some definite objective. It is not merely that our judgment leads us in that direction, though usually the Spirit of God acts upon us by enlightening our judgment, but we often feel an unaccountable and irresistible desire rising again and again within our heart, and this so presses upon us that we not only utter the desire before God at our ordinary times for prayer, but we feel it crying in our hearts all day long, almost to the supplanting of all other considerations.

At such times we should thank God for direction and give our desire a clear road. The Holy Spirit is granting us inward direction as to how we should order our petitions before the throne of grace, and we may now reckon upon good success in our pleading. Such guidance will the Spirit give to each of you if you will ask Him to illuminate you. He will guide you both negatively and positively. Negatively, He will forbid you to pray for such and such a thing, even as Paul essayed to go into Bithynia, but the Spirit would not allow him. And, on the other hand, He will cause you to hear a cry within your soul that will guide your petitions, even as He made Paul hear the cry from Macedonia, saying, "Come over to Macedonia and help us" (Acts 16:9). The Spirit teaches wisely, as no other teacher can. Those who obey His prompting will not walk in darkness. He leads the spiritual eyes to take good and steady aim at the very center of the target, and thus we hit the mark in our pleading.

Nor is this all, for the Spirit of God is not sent merely to guide and help our devotion, but He Himself makes intercession for us "according to the will of God." By this expression it cannot be meant that the Holy Spirit ever groans or personally prays, but that He excites intense desire and creates unutterable groans *in us* and these are ascribed to Him. Even as Solomon built the temple because he superintended and ordained all, yet I know not that he ever fashioned a timber or prepared a stone, so does the Holy Spirit pray and plead within us by *leading* us to pray and plead. This He does by awakening our desires. The Holy Spirit has a wonderful power over renewed hearts, as much power as the skillful minstrel has over the strings among which he lays his accustomed hand.

The influences of the Holy Spirit, at times, pass through the soul like winds through an Aeolian harp, creating and inspiring sweet notes of gratitude and tones of desire to which we should have been strangers if it had not been for His divine visitation. He knows how to create in our spirit hunger and thirst for good things. He can awaken us from our spiritual lethargy. He can warm us out of our lukewarmness. He can enable us, when we are on our knees, to rise above the ordinary routine of prayer into that victorious importunity against which nothing can stand! He can lay certain desires so pressingly upon our hearts that we can never rest till they are fulfilled! He can make the zeal for God's house to eat us up and the passion for God's glory to be like a fire within our bones. This is one part of that process by which, in inspiring our prayers, He helps our infirmity. He is a true advocate and most effectual comforter. Blessed be His name!

The Holy Spirit also divinely operates in the strengthening of the faith of believers. That faith is at first of His creating, and afterward it is of His sustaining and increasing. And oh, brothers and sisters, have you not often felt your faith rise in proportion to your trials? Have you not, like Noah's ark, mounted toward heaven as the flood deepened around you? You have felt as sure about the promise as you felt about the trial! The affliction was, as it were, in your very bones, but the promise was also in your very *heart*. You could not doubt the affliction, for you smarted under it, but you might almost as soon have doubted that you were afflicted as have doubted the divine help, for your confidence was firm and unmoved! The greatest faith is only what God has a right to expect from us, yet we never exhibit it except as the Holy Spirit strengthens our confidence and opens up before us the covenant with all its seals and securities.

He it is who leads our soul to cry, "Although my house is not so with God, yet He has made with me an everlasting covenant, ordered in all things and secure" (2 Sam. 23:5). Blessed be the divine Spirit, then, that since faith is essential to prevailing prayer, He helps us in supplication by increasing our faith! Without faith, prayer cannot go anywhere, for he who wavers is like a wave of the sea driven and tossed by the wind, and such a one may not expect anything of the Lord! Happy are we when the Holy Spirit removes our wavering and enables us, like Abraham, to *believe* without staggering, knowing full well that He who has promised is able, also, to perform!

> *Happy are we when the Holy Spirit removes our wavering and enables us, like Abraham, to believe without staggering, knowing full well that He who has promised is able, also, to perform!*

By three figures I will endeavor to describe the work of the Spirit of God in this matter, though they all fall short; and indeed, all that I can say must fall infinitely short of the glory of His work. The actual mode of His working upon the mind we may not attempt to explain. It remains a mystery, and it would be an unholy intrusion to attempt to remove the veil. There is no difficulty in our believing that as one human mind operates upon another mind, so does the Holy Spirit influence our spirits. We are forced to use words if we would influence our fellow men, but the Spirit of God can operate upon the human mind more directly and communicate with it in *silence*. Into that matter, however, we will not dive, lest we intrude where our knowledge would be drowned by our presumption.

My illustrations do not touch the mystery but set forth the grace. The Holy Spirit acts to His people somewhat as a prompter to a reciter. A man has to deliver a piece that he has learned, but his memory is treacherous, and therefore somewhere out of sight there is a prompter so that when the speaker is at a loss and might use a wrong word, a whisper is heard that suggests the right one. When the speaker has almost lost the thread of his discourse, he turns his ear and the prompter gives him the catchword and aids his memory. If I may be allowed the simile, I would say that this represents, in part, the work of the Spirit of God in us, suggesting to us the right desire and bringing all things to our remembrance whatever Christ has told us.

In prayer we should often come to a dead stand, but He incites, suggests, and inspires, and so we go onward. In prayer we might grow weary, but the Comforter encourages and refreshes us with cheering thoughts. When indeed we are, in our bewilderment, almost driven to give up prayer, the whisper of His love drops a live coal from off the altar into our souls, and our hearts glow with greater ardor than before! Regard the Holy Spirit as your prompter and let your ears be opened to His voice. But He is much more than this. Let me attempt a second simile: He is as an advocate to one in peril at law. Suppose that a poor man had a great lawsuit touching his whole estate and he was forced, personally, to go into court and plead his own cause and speak up for his rights. If he were an uneducated man, he would be in a poor plight. An adversary in the court might plead against him and overthrow him, for he could not answer him. This poor man knows very little about the law and is quite unable to meet his cunning opponent.

Now, suppose one who was perfect in the law should take up his cause warmly and come and live with him and use all his knowledge so as to prepare his case for him, draw up his petitions for him, and fill his mouth with arguments. Would not that be a grand relief? This counselor would suggest the line of pleading, arrange the arguments, and put them into right courtly language. When the poor man was baffled by a question asked in court, he would run home and ask his adviser and he would tell him exactly how to meet the objector. Suppose, too, that when he had to plead with the judge, this advocate at home should teach him how to behave and what to urge and encourage him to hope that he would prevail. Would not this be a great gift?

Who would be the pleader in such a case? The poor client would plead, but still, when he won the suit, he would trace it all to the advocate who lived at home and gave him counsel. Indeed, it would be the advocate pleading for him, even while he pleaded himself! This is an instructive emblem of a great fact. Within this narrow house of my body, this tenement of clay, if I am a true believer, there dwells the Holy Spirit, and when I desire to pray, I may ask Him what I should pray for as I ought and He will help me! He will write the prayers that I ought to offer upon the tablets of my heart, and I will see them there and so I will be taught how to plead! It will be the Spirit's own self pleading *in* me and *by* me and *through* me before the throne of grace! What a happy man, in his lawsuit, would such a poor man be! And how happy are you and I that we have the Holy Spirit to be our counselor!

Yet one more illustration: It is that of a father aiding his boy. Suppose it to be a time of war, centuries back. Bowmen, to a great extent, then conducted old English warfare. Here is a youth who is to be initiated in the art of archery, and therefore he carries a bow. It is a strong bow and therefore very hard to draw. Indeed, it requires more strength than the urchin can summon to bend it. See how his father teaches him. "Put your right hand here, my boy, and place your left hand so. Now pull." And as the youth pulls, his father's hands are on his hands and the bow is drawn! The lad draws the bow, yes, but it is quite as much his father, too.

We cannot draw the bow of *prayer* alone. Sometimes our hands do not break a bow of steel, for we cannot even bend it. And then the Holy Spirit puts His mighty hand over ours and covers our weakness so that we draw, and lo, what splendid drawing of the bow it then is! The bow bends so easily we wonder how! Away flies the arrow and it pierces the very center of the target, for He who gives the strength directs the aim! We rejoice to think that we have won the day, but it was His secret might that made us strong and to Him be the glory of it! Thus have I tried to set forth the cheering fact that the Spirit helps the people of God.

II. Our second subject is *the prayer that the Holy Spirit inspires*, or that part of prayer that is especially and peculiarly the work of the Spirit of God. The text says, "The Spirit Himself makes intercession for us with groanings which cannot be uttered." It is not the Spirit who groans, but *we* who groan, but as I have shown you, the Spirit excites the emotion that causes us to groan. It is clear then that the prayers that are incited in us by the Spirit of God are those that arise from our inmost soul. A man's heart is moved when he groans. A groan is a matter about which there is no hypocrisy. A groan comes not from the lips, but from the heart. A groan, then, is a part of prayer that we owe to the Holy Spirit, and the same is true of all the prayer that wells up from the deep fountains of our inner life.

The prophet cried, "O my soul, my soul! I am pained in my very heart! My heart makes a noise in me" (Jer. 4:19). This deep groundswell of desire, this tidal motion of the life-floods, is caused by the Holy Spirit. His work is never superficial but always deep and inward. Such prayers will rise within us when the mind is far too troubled to let us speak. We know not what we should pray for as we ought, and then it is that we groan or utter some other inarticulate sound. Isaiah said, "Like a crane or a swallow, so I chattered" (Isa. 38:14). The psalmist said, "I am so troubled that I cannot speak" (Ps. 77:4). In another place he said, "I am feeble and severely broken; I groan because of the turmoil of my heart." But he added, "Lord, all my desire is before You; and my sighing is not hidden from You" (Ps. 38:8–9).

The sighs of the prisoner surely come up into the ears of the Lord. There is real prayer in these groans that cannot be uttered. It is the power of the Holy Spirit in us that creates all real prayer, even that which takes the form of a groan because the mind is incapable, by reason of its bewilderment and grief, of clothing its emotion in words. I pray you never think lightly of the supplications of your anguish. Rather judge that such prayers are like Jabez, of whom it is written, "Jabez was more honorable than his brothers, and his mother called his name Jabez, saying, 'Because I bore him in pain'" (1 Chron. 4:9). That which is thrown up from the depth of the soul, when it is stirred with a terrible tempest, is more precious than pearl or coral, for it is the intercession of the Holy Spirit!

> *We know not what we should pray for as we ought, and then it is that we groan or utter some other inarticulate sound.*

These prayers are sometimes "groanings which cannot be uttered" because they concern such great things that they cannot be spoken. I *need*, my Lord! I need, I need; I cannot tell you *what* I need, but I seem to need all things! If it were some little thing, my narrow capacity could comprehend and describe it, but I need all covenant blessings! You know what I have need of before I ask you, and though I cannot go into each item of my need, I know it to be very great and such as I myself can never estimate. I groan, for I can do no more! Prayers that are the offspring of great desires, sublime aspirations, and elevated designs are surely the work of the Holy Spirit, and their power within a man is frequently so great that he cannot find expression for them! Words fail and even the sighs that try to embody them cannot be uttered.

But it may be, beloved, that we groan because we are conscious of the littleness of our desires and the narrowness of our faith. The trial, too, may seem too mean to pray about. I have known what it is to feel as if I could not pray about a certain matter, and yet I have been obliged to groan about it. A thorn in the flesh may be as painful a thing as a sword in the bones, and yet we may go and beseech the Lord thrice about it, and, getting no answer, we may feel that we know not what to pray for as we ought, and so it makes us groan. Yes, and with that natural groan there may go up an unutterable groaning of the Holy Spirit!

Beloved, what a different view of prayer God has from that which men think to be the correct one! You may have seen very beautiful prayers in print and you may have heard very charming compositions from the pulpit, but I trust you have not fallen in love with them. Judge these things rightly. I pray you never think well of fine prayers, for before the thrice-holy God it ill becomes a sinful suppliant to play the orator! We heard of a certain clergyman who was said to have given forth "the finest prayer ever offered to a Boston audience." Just so! The Boston audience *received* the prayer and there it ended! We need the mind of the Spirit in prayer and not the mind of the flesh! The tail feathers of pride should be pulled out of our prayers, for they need only the wing feathers of faith. The peacock feathers of poetical expression are out of place before the throne of God.

"Dear me, what remarkably beautiful language he uses in prayer!"

"What an intellectual treat his prayers are!" Yes, yes. But God looks at the *heart*. To Him fine language is as sounding brass or a tinkling cymbal, while a groan has music in it! We do not like groans. Our ears are much too delicate to tolerate such dreary sounds. But not so the great Father of spirits. A Methodist brother cries, "Amen," and you say, "I cannot bear such Methodist noise!" No, but if it comes from the man's heart, *God* can bear it! When you get upstairs into your chamber this evening to pray and find you cannot pray but have to moan, "Lord, I am too full of anguish and too perplexed to pray. Hear the voice of my roaring," though you reach to nothing else, you will be really praying!

When, like David, we can say, "I opened my mouth and panted" (Ps. 119:131), we are by no means in an ill state of mind. All fine language in prayer and especially all intoning or performing of prayers must be abhorrent to God! It is little short of profanity to offer solemn supplication to God after the manner called "intoning." The sighing of a true heart is infinitely more acceptable, for it is the work of the Spirit of God! We may say of the prayers that the Holy Spirit works in us that they are prayers of *knowledge*. Notice our difficulty is that we know not what we should pray for—but the Holy Spirit knows, and therefore He helps us by enabling us to pray intelligently, knowing what we are asking for, so far as this knowledge is necessary to valid prayer.

The text speaks of the "mind of the Spirit." What a mind that must be! The mind of that Spirit who arranged all the order that now pervades this earth! There was once chaos and confusion, but the Holy Spirit brooded over all, and His mind is the originator of that beautiful arrangement that we so admire in the visible creation! What a mind His must be! The Holy Spirit's mind is seen in our intercessions when, under His sacred influence, we order our case before the Lord and plead with holy wisdom for things convenient and necessary. What wise and admirable desires must those be that the Spirit of wisdom Himself works in us!

He works with us and enables us to pray after His mind and according to the will of God! His intercession is not in or for the unregenerate.

Moreover, the Holy Spirit's intercession creates prayers offered in a proper manner. I showed you that the difficulty is that we know not what we should pray for "as we ought," and the Spirit meets that difficulty by making intercession for us in a right manner. The Holy Spirit works in us humility, earnestness, intensity, importunity, faith, resignation, and all else that is acceptable to God in our supplications. We know not how to mingle these sacred spices in the incense of prayer. We, if left to ourselves, at our very best get too much of one ingredient or another and spoil the sacred compound. But the Holy Spirit's intercessions have in them such a blessed blending of all that is good that they come up as a sweet perfume before the Lord!

Spirit-taught prayers are offered as they ought to be. They are His own intercession in some respects, for we read that the Holy Spirit not only helps us to intercede, but also "makes intercession." It is twice over declared in our text that He makes intercession for us, and the meaning of this I tried to show when I described a father as putting his hands upon his child's hands. This is something more than helping us to pray, something more than encouraging us or directing us—but I venture no further except to say that He puts such force of His own mind into our poor weak thoughts and desires and hopes that He Himself makes intercession for us, working in us to will and to pray according to His good pleasure!

I want you to notice, however, that these intercessions of the Holy Spirit are only in the saints. He "makes intercession for us," and "He makes intercession for the saints." Does He do nothing for sinners, then? Yes, He *quickens* sinners into spiritual life and He strives with them to overcome their sinfulness and turn them into the right way. But in the saints He works *with* us and enables us to pray after *His mind* and according to the will of God! His intercession is not *in* or *for* the unregenerate. O unbelievers, you must first be made saints or you cannot feel the Spirit's intercession within you! What need we have to go to Christ for the blessing of the Holy Spirit that is peculiar to the children of God and can only be ours by faith in Christ Jesus!

"As many as received Him, to them He gave the right to become children of God" (John 1:12). And to the sons of God alone comes the Spirit of adoption and all His helping grace. Unless we are the sons of God, the Holy Spirit's indwelling will not be ours—we are shut out from the intercession of the Holy Spirit. Yes, and from the intercession of Jesus, too, for He has said, "I do not pray for the world but for those whom You have given Me, for they are Yours" (John 17:9). Thus I have tried to show you the kind of prayer that the Spirit inspires.

III. Our third and last point is *the sure success of all such prayers.* All the prayers that the Spirit of God inspires in us must succeed, because, first, there is a meaning in them that God reads and approves. When the Spirit of God writes a prayer upon a man's heart, the man himself may be in such a state of mind that he does not altogether know what it is! His interpretation of it is a groan and that is all. Perhaps he does not even get so far as that in expressing the mind of the Spirit, but he feels groans that he cannot utter. He cannot find a door of utterance for his inward grief.

Yet our heavenly Father, who looks immediately upon the heart, reads what the Spirit of God has indited there and does not need even our groans to explain the meaning! He reads the heart itself. He "knows," says the text, "what the mind of the Spirit is." The Spirit is one with the Father and the Father knows what the Spirit means! The desires that the Spirit prompts may be too spiritual for such babes in grace as we are actually to describe or to express, and yet they are *within* us. We feel desires for things that we should never have thought of if He had not made us long for them. We have aspirations for blessings that as to the understanding of them are still above us, yet the Spirit writes the desire on the renewed mind and the Father sees it!

Now that which God reads in the heart and approves of—for the word for "to know" in this case includes approval as well as the mere act of omniscience—what God sees and approves of in the heart must succeed.

Did not Jesus say, "Your Father knows the things you have need of before you ask Him" (Matt. 6:8)? Did He not tell us this as an encouragement to believe that we will receive all necessary blessings? So it is with those prayers that are all broken up, wet with tears, and discordant with sighs and inarticulate expressions and heaving of the bosom and sobbing of the heart and anguish and bitterness of spirit. Our gracious Lord reads them as a man reads a book, and they are written in a character that He fully understands!

To give a simple example, if I were to come into your house, I might find there a little child who cannot yet speak plainly. He cries for something and he makes very odd and objectionable noises, combined with signs and movements that are almost meaningless to a stranger. But his mother understands him and attends to his little pleas. A mother can translate baby talk. She comprehends incomprehensible noises! Even so does our Father in heaven know all about our poor baby talk, for our prayers are not much better. He knows and comprehends the cries and moans and sighs and chattering of His bewildered children! Yes, a tender mother knows her child's needs before the child knows what he needs. Perhaps the little one stutters, stammers, and cannot get his words out, but the mother senses what he would say and understands the meaning. Even so we know that our great Father "knows the thoughts we mean to speak before from our opening lips they break." Rejoice in this because the prayers of the Spirit are known and understood of God, and therefore they will be sure to reach Him!

The next argument for making us sure that they will reach Him is this: They are "the mind of the Spirit." God the ever-blessed is one, and there can be no division between the Father, the Son, and the Holy Spirit. These divine persons always work together and there is a common desire for the glory of each blessed person of the divine unity; and therefore it cannot be conceived, without profanity, that anything could be the mind of the Holy Spirit and not be the mind of the Father and the mind of the Son! The mind of God is one and harmonious! If, therefore, the Holy Spirit dwells in you and He moves you to any desire, then His mind is in your prayer and it is not possible that the eternal Father should reject your petitions. The prayer that *came* from heaven will certainly go back to heaven! If the Holy Spirit prompts it, the Father must and will accept it, for it is not possible that He should put a slight upon the ever-blessed and adorable Spirit.

But one more word and that closes the argument, namely, that the work of the Spirit in the heart is not only the *mind* of the Spirit that God knows, but it is also according to the will or mind of *God*, for He never makes intercession in us other than is consistent with the divine will. Now, the divine will or mind may be viewed two ways. First, there is the will declared in the proclamations of holiness by the Ten Commandments. The Spirit of God never prompts us to ask for anything that is unholy or inconsistent with the precepts of the Lord. Then second, there is the secret mind of God, the will of His eternal predestination and decree of which we know nothing. But we do know this: that the Spirit of God never prompts us to ask anything that is contrary to the eternal purpose of God.

Reflect for a moment—the Holy Spirit knows all the purposes of God, and when they are about to be fulfilled, He moves the children of God to pray about them and so their prayers keep touch and tally with the divine decrees. Oh, would you not pray confidently if you knew that your prayer corresponded with the sealed book of destiny? We may safely entreat the Lord to do what He has *ordained* to do! A carnal man draws the inference that if God has ordained an event, we need not pray about it. But faith obediently draws the inference that the God who secretly ordained to give the blessing has openly commanded that we *should* pray for it, and therefore faith obediently prays!

> he work of the Spirit in the heart is not only the mind of the Spirit that God knows, but it is also according to the will or mind of God. . . .

Coming events cast their shadows before them, and when God is about to bless His people, His coming favor casts the shadow of prayer over the church. When He is about to favor an individual, He casts the shadow of hopeful expectation over his soul! Our prayers—let men laugh at them as they will and say there is no power in them—are the indicators of the movement of the wheels of providence! Believing supplications are forecasts of the future! He who prays in faith is like the seer of old—he sees that which is yet to be. His holy expectancy, like a telescope, brings distant objects near to him, and things not seen as yet are visible to him! He is bold to declare that he has the petition that he has asked of God, and he therefore begins to rejoice and to praise God before the blessing has actually arrived! So it is, prayer prompted by the Holy Spirit is the footfall of the divine decree.

I conclude by saying, my dear hearers, see the absolute necessity of the Holy Spirit, for if the saints know not what they should pray for as they ought—if consecrated men and women, with Christ suffering in them, still feel their need of the instruction of the Holy Spirit—how much more do you who are *not* saints and have never given yourselves up to God require divine teaching! Oh, that you would know and feel your dependence upon the Holy Spirit that He may prompt you this day to look to Jesus Christ for salvation! It is through the once crucified but now ascended Redeemer that this gift of the Spirit, this promise of the Father, is shed abroad upon men! May He who comes from Jesus lead you to Jesus.

> *O you people of God, let this last thought abide with you— what condescension is this that this divine person should dwell in you forever and that He should be with you to help your prayers!*

And then, O you people of God, let this last thought abide with you: What condescension is this that this divine person should dwell in you forever and that He should be with you to help your prayers! Listen to me for a moment. If I read in the scriptures that in the most heroic acts of faith, God the Holy Spirit helps His people, I can understand it. If I read that in the sweetest music of their songs, when they worship best and chant their loftiest strains before the Most High God, the Spirit helps them, I can understand it. And even if I hear that in their wrestling prayers and prevalent intercessions, God the Holy Spirit helps them, I can understand it. But I bow with reverent amazement—my heart sinking into the dust with adoration—when I reflect that God the Holy Spirit helps us when we cannot speak but only groan!

Yes, and when we cannot even utter our groans, He not only helps us but claims as His own particular creation the "groanings which cannot be uttered"! This is condescension indeed! In deigning to help us in the grief that cannot even vent itself in groans, He proves Himself to be a true comforter! O God, my God! You have not forsaken me! You are not far from me nor from the voice of my roaring. You did, for a while, leave your Firstborn when He was made a curse for us, so that He cried in agony, "Why have You forsaken Me?" (Matt. 27:46). But you will not leave one of the many brethren for whom He died. Your Spirit will be with them, and when they cannot so much as groan, He will make intercession for them with groans that cannot be uttered!

God bless you, my beloved brothers and sisters, and may you feel the Spirit of the Lord thus working in you and with you. Amen and amen.

FOR FURTHER THOUGHT

1. *According to Romans 8:26, what is the activity in which the Spirit helps our weakness?*

2. *Read Acts 16:6–8. How did the Spirit assist the apostles in this case?*

3. *Does God expect a believer to be able to eloquently express his or her desires in prayer (see Rom. 8:26)?*

HONEY IN THE MOUTH!

*"He will glorify Me, for He will take of what is Mine and
declare it to you. All things that the Father has are Mine.
Therefore I said that He will take of Mine and declare it to you."*
JOHN 16:14–15

BELOVED friends, here you have the Trinity, and there is no salvation apart from the Trinity! It must be the Father, the Son, and the Holy Spirit. "All things that the Father has are Mine," says Christ, and the Father has all things. They were always His, they are still His, they always will be His, and they cannot become ours till they change ownership, till Christ can say, "All things that the Father has are Mine," for it is by virtue of the representative character of Christ standing as the surety of the covenant that the "all things" of the Father are passed over to the Son, that they might be passed over to us. It pleased the Father that in Him all fullness should dwell and that we all have received of His fullness. But yet we are so dull that though the conduit pipe is laid onto the great fountain, we cannot get at it. We are lame. We cannot reach it, but in comes the third person of the divine unity, even the Holy Spirit, and He receives of the things of Christ and then delivers them over to us! So we actually receive, through Jesus Christ, by the Spirit, what is in the Father!

Ralph Erskine, in his preface to a sermon upon the fifteenth verse, has a notable piece. He speaks of grace as honey for the cheering of the saints, for the sweetening of their mouths and hearts. But he says that in the Father, "the honey is in the flower, which is at such a distance from us that we could never extract it." In the Son, "the honey is in the comb, prepared for us." In our Immanuel, the God-Man, the Redeemer, the Word was made flesh, saying, "'All things that the Father has are Mine,' and Mine for your use and benefit—it is in the comb. But then we have honey in the mouth. That is the Spirit taking all things and making application of them, by showing them to us and making us to eat and drink with Christ and share of these things. Yes, eat not only the honey, but the honeycomb with the honey; not only His benefits, but Himself."

There never will be any more honey than there is in the flower. There it is. But how will you and I get it? We have not wisdom to extract the sweetness. We are not as the bees that are able to find it out. It is bee honey, not man honey. Yet you see in Christ it becomes the honey in the honeycomb, and therefore He is sweet to our taste as honey dropping from the comb. Sometimes we are so faint that we cannot reach out a hand to grasp that honeycomb, and alas, there was a time when our palates were so depraved that we preferred bitter things and even thought them sweet! But now that the Holy Spirit has come, we have got the honey in the mouth and the taste that enjoys it! Yes, we have now so long enjoyed it that the honey of grace has entered into our constitution and we have become sweet to God, His sweetness having been conveyed by this strange method to us.

> *If the full work of salvation requires a Trinity, so does that very breath by which we live. You cannot draw near to the Father except through the Son and by the Holy Spirit.*

Beloved friends, I scarcely need say to you, keep the existence of the Trinity prominent in your ministry! Remember, you cannot pray without the Trinity. If the full work of salvation requires a Trinity, so does that very breath by which we live. You cannot draw near to the Father except through the Son and by the Holy Spirit. There is undoubtedly a Trinity in nature. There certainly constantly turns up the need of a Trinity in the realm of grace, and when we get to heaven we will understand, perhaps, more fully what is meant by the Trinity in unity. But if that is a thing never to be understood, we will at least apprehend it more lovingly, and we will rejoice more completely as the three tones of our music will rise up in perfect harmony to Him who is one and indivisible and yet is three, forever blessed, Father, Son, and Holy Spirit, one God!

Now for the point that I am to open up to you this morning, though *I* cannot do it, but *He* must do it. We must sit here and have the text acted out upon us. "He will glorify Me, for He will take of what is Mine and declare it to you." May it be so just now!

First, *what the Holy Spirit does*: "He will take of what is Mine and declare it to you." Second, *what the Holy Spirit aims at and really effects*: "He will glorify Me." And third: *In doing both these things, He is the Comforter*. It is the Comforter who does this, and we will find our richest, surest comfort in this work of the Holy Spirit, who will take of the things of Christ and show them to us.

I. First, *what the Holy Spirit does*. It is clear, beloved friends, that the Holy Spirit *deals with the things of Christ*. As our brother Archibald Brown said when expounding the chapter just now, He does not aim at any originality. He deals with the things of Christ. All things that Christ had heard from His Father He made known to us. He kept to them. And now the Spirit takes of the things of Christ and of nothing else. Do not let us strain at anything new. The Holy Spirit could deal with anything in heaven above or in the earth beneath—the story of the ages past, the story of the ages to come, the inward secrets of the earth, the evolution of all things, if there is an evolution. He could do it all! Like the Master, He could handle any topic He chose, but He confines Himself to the things of Christ and therein finds unutterable liberty and boundless freedom.

Do you think, dear friend, that you can be wiser than the Holy Spirit? And if His choice must be a wise one, will yours be a wise one if you begin to take of the things of something or somebody else? You will have the Holy Spirit near you when you are receiving the things of Christ. But as the Holy Spirit is said never to receive anything else, when you are handling other things on the Sabbath, you will be handling them alone, and the pulpit is a dreary solitude, even in the midst of a crowd, if the Holy Spirit is not with you there. You may, if you please, think through a theology out of your own vast brain, but the Holy Spirit is not with you there. And mark you, there are some of us who are resolved to tarry with the things of Christ and keep on dealing with them as far as He enables us to do so! And we feel that we are in such blessed company with the divine Spirit that we do not envy you that wider range of thought, if you prefer it.

The Holy Spirit still exists, works, and teaches in the church. And we have a test by which to know whether what people claim to be revelation is revelation or not. That is: "He will take. . .what is Mine." The Holy Spirit will never go further than the cross and the coming of the Lord. He will go no further than that which concerns Christ. "He will take. . .what is Mine." When, therefore, anybody whispers in my ear that there has been revealed to him this or that, which I do not find in the teaching of Christ and His apostles, I tell him that we must be taught by the Holy Spirit. His one vocation is to deal with the things of Christ! If we do not remember this, we may be carried away by quirks, as many have been. Those who will have to do with other things, let them, but as for us, we will be satisfied to confine our thoughts and our teaching within these limitless limits: "He will take of what is Mine and declare it to you."

I like to think of the Holy Spirit handling such things. They seem so worthy of Him. Now He has gotten among the hills. Now is His mighty mind among the infinities when He has to deal with Christ, for Christ is the infinite veiled in the finite. Why, He seems something more than infinite when He gets into the finite, and the Christ of Bethlehem is less to be understood than the Christ of the Father's bosom! He seems, if it were possible, to have out-infinited the infinite, and the Spirit of God has themes here worthy of His vast nature!

When you have been the whole Sunday morning whittling away a text to the small end of nothing, what have you done? A king spent a day in trying to make a portrait on a cherrystone—a king who was ruling empires! And here is a minister who professes to have been called of the Holy Spirit to the employ of taking of the things of Christ, who spent a whole morning with precious souls who were dying while he spoke to them on a theme concerning which it did not signify the turn of a hair whether it was so or not! Oh, imitate the Holy Spirit! If you profess to have Him dwelling in you, be moved by Him! Let it be said of you, in your measure, as of the Holy Spirit without measure, "He will take of what is Mine and declare it to you."

But next, what does the Holy Spirit do? Why, *He deals with feeble men.* Yes, He dwells with us poor creatures! I can understand the Holy Spirit taking of the things of Christ and rejoicing therein, but the marvel is that He should glorify Christ by coming and showing these things to us! And yet, brothers, it is among us that Christ is to get His glory. Our eyes must see Him! An unseen Christ is little glorious. And the things of Christ unknown, the things of Christ untasted and unloved, seem to have lost their brilliance to a high degree. The Holy Spirit, therefore, feeling that to show a sinner the salvation of Christ glorifies Him, spends His time and has been spending these centuries in taking of the things of Christ and showing them to us. Ah, it is a great condescension on His part to show them to us. And it is a miracle, too. If it were reported that suddenly stones had life, hills had eyes, and trees had ears, it would be a strange thing. But for us who were dead and blind and deaf in an awful sense—for the spiritual is more emphatic than the natural—for us to be so far gone and for the Holy Spirit to be able to show the things of Christ to us is to His honor! And He does it. He comes from heaven to dwell with us. Let us honor and bless His name.

> *The incarnation of Christ is marvelous—that He should dwell in human nature. But observe, the Holy Spirit dwells in human nature in its sinfulness; not in perfect human nature, but in imperfect human nature!*

I never could make up my mind which to admire most as an act of condescension: the incarnation of Christ or the indwelling of the Holy Spirit. The incarnation of Christ is marvelous—that He should dwell in human nature. But observe, the Holy Spirit dwells in human nature in its *sinfulness*; not in perfect human nature, but in *imperfect* human nature! And He continues to dwell, not in one body that was fashioned strangely for Himself and was pure and without taint, but He dwells in *our* bodies! Know you not that they are the temples of the Holy Spirit, which were defiled by nature and in which a measure of defilement still remains, despite His indwelling? And this He has done these multitudes of years, not in one instance, nor in thousands of instances, but in a number that no man can number! He continues to come into contact with sinful humanity! Not to the angels nor to the seraphim nor to the cherubim nor to the host who have washed their robes and made them white in the blood of the Lamb does He show the things of Christ, but He will show them to *us*!

I suppose that it means this: that *He takes of the words of our Lord,* those that He spoke personally and by His apostles. Let us never allow anybody to divide between the word of the apostles and the word of Christ! Our Savior has joined them together. "I do not pray for these alone, but also for those who will believe in Me through their word" (John 17:20). And if any begin rejecting the apostolic word, they will be outside the number for whom Christ prays. They shut themselves out by that very fact! I wish that they would solemnly remember that the word of the apostles is the word of Christ. He tarried not long enough, after He had risen from the dead, to give us a further exposition of His mind and will. And He could not have given it before His death, because it would have been unsuitable. "I still have many things to say to you, but you cannot bear them now" (John 16:12). After the descent of the Holy Spirit, the disciples were prepared to receive that which Christ spoke by His servants, Paul and Peter and James and John.

Certain doctrines that we are sometimes taunted about as being not revealed by Christ but by His apostles were all revealed by Christ, every one of them! They can all be found in His teaching, but they are very much in the parabolic form. It is after He has gone up into glory and has prepared a people, by His Spirit, to understand the truths of God more fully that He sends His apostles and says, "Go forth, and open up to those whom I have chosen out of the world the meaning of all I said." The meaning is all there, just as all the New Testament is in the Old! And sometimes I have thought that, instead of the Old being less inspired than the New, it is more inspired! Things are packed away more tightly in the Old Testament than in the New, if possible. There are worlds of meaning in one pregnant line in the Old Testament, and in Christ's words it is just so. He is the Old Testament to which the Epistles come in as a kind of New Testament, but they are all one and indivisible. They cannot be separated.

Well, now, the words of the Lord Jesus and the words of His apostles are to be *expounded* to us by the Holy Spirit. We will never get at the center of their meaning apart from His teaching. We will never get at their meaning at all if we begin disputing about the words, saying, "I cannot accept the words." If you will not have the shell, you will never have the chick! It is impossible. "The words are not inspired," they say. Here is a man in the witness box and he has sworn to speak the truth and he says that he has. And now he is cross-examined and he says, "Now, I have spoken the truth, but I do not stand by my words." The cross-examining lawyer has got hold of a certain statement of his. The witness says, "Oh, I do not swear to the words, you know." The question is asked, "What, then, do you swear to? There is nothing else. We do not know anything about your meaning. All that you have sworn to must be your words." But what the fellow means is this: He is a liar. He is a perjurer. Well, I say no more than common sense would suggest to you if you were sitting in a court. Now, if a man says, "I have spoken the truth, but still I do not swear to the words," what is left? If we have no inspiration in the words of God, we have got an impalpable inspiration that oozes away between our fingers and leaves nothing behind!

Well, take the words and never dispute over them! Still, into their soulfulness of meaning you cannot come until the Holy Spirit will lead you into them. Those who wrote them for you did not fully understand what they wrote in many instances. There were some of them who inquired and searched diligently to know what manner of things those were that the Holy Spirit had spoken to them and of which He had made them speak. And you to whom the words come will have to do the same. You must go and say, "Great Master, we thank you for the book with all our hearts. And we thank you for putting the book into words. But now, good Master, we will not quibble over the letter, as did the Jews and the rabbis and the scribes of old, and so miss your meaning. Open wide the door of the words, that we may enter into the secret closet of their meaning. Teach us this, we pray you. You have the key. Lead us in."

Dear friends, whenever you want to understand a text of scripture, try to read the original. Consult anybody who has studied what the original means, but remember that the quickest way into a text is praying in the Holy Spirit. Pray the chapter over! I do not hesitate to say that if a chapter is read upon one's knees, looking up at every word to Him who gave it, the meaning will come to you with infinitely more light than by any other method of studying it. "He will glorify Me, for He will take of what is Mine and declare it to you." He will redeliver the Master's message to you in the fullness of its meaning!

But I do not think that is all that the text means. "He will take of what is Mine." In the next verse the Lord goes on to say, "All things that the Father has are Mine." I think that it means, therefore, that *the Holy Spirit will show us the things of Christ.* Here is a text for us: "the things of Christ." Christ speaks as if He had not any things, just then, that were specially His own, for He had not yet died. He had not yet risen. He was not pleading, then, as the great intercessor in heaven, all that was to come. But still, He says, "All things that the Father has are Mine." That is, all His attributes, all His glory, all His rest, all His happiness, all His blessedness, *all of that* is Mine, and the Holy Spirit will show that to you.

But I might almost read my text in another light, for He *has* died, risen, and gone on high, and lo, He comes! His chariots are on the way! Now, there are certain things that the Father has and that Jesus Christ has that are truly the things of Christ, *emphatically* the things of Christ. And my prayer is that you and I, preachers of the gospel, might have this text fulfilled in us: "He will take of Mine," that is, *my things*, and will show them to you.

Suppose, dear brothers, that we are going to preach the Word, and the Holy Spirit shows to us our Master in His Godhead. Oh, how we will preach Him as divine. How surely He can bless our congregation! How certainly He must be able to subdue all things to Himself, seeing that He is very God of very God! It is equally sweet to see Him as man. Oh, to have the Spirit's view of Christ's manhood, distinctly to recognize that He is bone of my bone and flesh of my flesh and that in His infinite tenderness He will be compassionate to me and deal with my poor people and with the troubled consciences that are round me! I have still to go to them and tell them of One who is touched with the feeling of their infirmities, having been tempted in all points as they still are! Oh, my brothers, if we once, no, if *every time* before we preach we get a view of Christ in His divine and human natures and come down fresh from that vision to speak about Him, what glorious preaching it would be for our people!

> *The fact is that Christ cannot get hold of us anywhere except by our sin. The point of contact between the sick one and the physician is the disease.*

It is a glorious thing to get a view of the offices of Christ by the Holy Spirit, but especially of His office as a Savior! I have often said to Him, "You must save my people. It is no business of mine. I never set up in that line or put over my door that I was a savior, but you have been apprenticed to this trade! You have learned it by experience and you claim it as your own honor. You are exalted on high to be a prince and a Savior. Do your own work, my Lord." I took this text and used it with sinners the other Sunday night, and I know that God blessed it when I said to them, "May the Holy Spirit show you that Christ is a Savior! A physician does not expect you to make any apologies when you call upon him because you are ill, for he is a physician and he needs you in order that he may prove his skill. So Christ is a Savior and you need not apologize for going to Him! He cannot be a Savior if there is not somebody to be saved!" The fact is that Christ cannot get hold of us anywhere except by our sin. The point of contact between the sick one and the physician is the disease. Our *sin* is the point of contact between Christ and us. Oh, that the Spirit of God would take of Christ's divine offices, especially that of a Savior, and show them to us!

Did the Holy Spirit ever show you these things of Christ, namely, His covenant engagements? When He struck hands with the Father, it was that He would bring many sons to glory—that of those whom the Father gave Him, He would lose none, but that they should be saved, for He is under bonds to His Father to bring His elect home. When the sheep have to pass, again, under the hands of Him who counts them, they will go under the rod, one by one, each one having the blood-mark, and He will never rest till the number in the heavenly fold will tally with the number in the book.

So I believe and it has seemed delightful to me to have this shown to me when I have gone to preach. It is a dull, dreary, wet, foggy morning. There are only a few present. Yes, but they are picked people whom God has ordained to be there—and there will be the right number there! I will preach and there will be some saved. We do not go at a chance, but, guided by the blessed Spirit of God, we go with a living certainty, knowing that God has a people that Christ is bound to bring home, and bring them home He will! And while He will see of the travail of His soul, His Father will delight in every one of them! If you get a clear view of that, it will give you backbone and make you strong. "He will take of Mine" and will show you my covenant engagements, and when you see them, you will be comforted.

But, beloved, the Holy Spirit favors you by taking what is peculiarly Christ's, namely, His love, and showing that to you. We have seen it, seen it at times more vividly than at other times. But if the full blaze of the Holy Spirit were to be concentrated upon the love of Christ and our eyesight was enlarged to its utmost capacity, it would be such a vision that heaven could not excel it! We should sit with our Bible before us in our study and feel, "I know a man in Christ who fourteen years ago—whether in the body I do not know, or whether out of the body I do not know, God knows—such a one was caught up to the third heaven" (2 Cor. 12:2). Oh, to see the love of Christ in the light of the Holy Spirit! When it is so revealed to us, it is not merely the surface that we see, but the love of Christ itself! You know that you never saw anything yet, strictly speaking. You only see the *appearance* of the thing—the light reflected by it; that is all you see. But the Holy Spirit shows us the naked truth of God, the *essence* of the love of Christ! And what that essence is, that love without beginning, without change, without limit, without end—that love set upon His people simply from motives within Himself. And from no motive *ab extra*. What that must be, what tongue can tell? Oh, it is a ravishing sight!

I think that if there could be one sight more wonderful than the love of Christ, it would be the blood of Christ:

> *Much we talk of Jesus' blood,*
> *But how little's understood.*

It is the climax of God! I do not know of anything more divine. It seems to me as if all the eternal purposes worked up to the blood of the cross and then worked from the blood of the cross toward the sublime consummation of all things. Oh, to think that He should become man! God has made spirit, pure spirit, embodied spirit—and then materialism—and somehow, as if He would take all up into one, the Godhead links Himself with the material and He wears dust about Him even as we wear it! And taking it all up, He then goes and, in that fashion, redeems His people from all the evil of their soul, their spirit, and their body by the pouring out of a life that, while it was human, was so in connection with the divine that we speak correctly of the blood of God.

Turn to the twentieth chapter of Acts and read how the apostle Paul puts it: "Shepherd the church of God which He purchased with His own blood" (20:28). I believe that Dr. Watts is not wrong when he tells of "God who loved and died." It is an incorrect accuracy, a strictly absolute accuracy of incorrectness! So it must be ever when the finite talks of the infinite. It was a wonderful sacrifice that could absolutely obliterate, annihilate, and extinguish sin and all the traces that could possibly remain of it, for He has finished the transgression, made an end of sins, made reconciliation for iniquity, and brought in everlasting righteousness (see Dan. 9:24). Ah, dear friends, you have seen this, have you not? But you have yet to see more of it. And when we get to heaven, we will then know what that blood means. And then with what vigor will we sing, "To Him who loved us and washed us from our sins in His own blood" (Rev. 1:5)!

Will anybody be there to say, "Is not that the religion of the shambles?" as they blasphemously call it. Ah, my friends, they will find themselves where they will wish they had believed "the religion of the shambles"! And I think that it will burn like coals of juniper into the soul of any man who has ever dared to talk like that; he did despite the blood of God and so, by his own willful deeds, will be cast away forever.

May the Holy Spirit show to you Gethsemane, Gabbatha, and Golgotha! And then may it please Him to give you a sight of what our Lord is now doing! Oh, how it would cheer you up at any time when you were depressed, only to see Him standing and pleading for you! Do you not think that if your wife were ill, your child were sick, and there was hardly any food in the cupboard; if you were to go out the back door and see Him with the breastplate on and all the stones glittering and your name there and Him pleading for you, don't you think you would go in and say, "There, Wife, it is all right. He is praying for us"? Oh, it would be a comfort if the Holy Spirit showed you a pleading Christ! And then to think that He is *reigning* as well as pleading! He is at the right hand of God, even the Father, who has put all things under His feet. And He waits till the last enemy will lie there. Now, you are not afraid, are you, of those who have been snubbing you and opposing you? Remember, He has said, "All authority has been given to Me in heaven and on earth. Go therefore and make disciples of all the nations, baptizing them in the name of the Father and of the Son and of the Holy Spirit, teaching them to observe all things that I have commanded you; and lo, I am with you always, even to the end of the age" (Matt. 28:18–20).

> *he darker the night grows and the fiercer the storm becomes, the better will we remember that He of the lake of Galilee came to them upon the waves in the night when the storm was wildest.*

Next, and best of all, may the Holy Spirit give you a clear view of His coming. This is our most brilliant hope: "Lo, He comes!" The more the adversary waxes bold and the less of faith there is, and when zeal seems almost extinct, these are the tokens of His coming. The Lord always said that He would not come unless there was first a falling away. And so the darker the night grows and the fiercer the storm becomes, the better will we remember that He of the lake of Galilee came to them upon the waves in the night when the storm was wildest. Oh, what will His enemies say when He comes? When they behold the nail prints of the Glorified and the man with the crown of thorns; when they see Him really come, they who have despised His Word and His ever-blessed blood, how will they flee before that face of injured love! And we, on the contrary, through His infinite mercy, will say, "This is what the Holy Spirit showed us and now we behold it literally! We thank Him for the foresights that He gave us of the beatific vision."

I am not yet done on the first head, because there is one point that I want you to remember. When the Holy Spirit takes of the things of Christ and shows them to us, He has a purpose in so doing. You will not laugh, I hope, when I remind you of what the little boys sometimes do at school with one another. I have seen a boy take out of his pocket an apple and say to his schoolmate, "Do you see that apple?"

"Yes," says the other.

"Then you may see me eat it," he says.

But the Holy Spirit is no Tantalus, taking of the things of Christ and holding them up to mock us! No. He says, "Do you see these things? If you can see them, you may *have* them." Did not Christ Himself say, "Look to Me, and be saved, all you ends of the earth" (Isa. 45:22)? *Looking* gives you a claim, and if you can see Him, He is yours! It is with you, with regard to the Spirit showing you things, as it was with Jacob. You know Jacob lay down and went to sleep. And the Lord said to him, "The land on which you lie I will give to you" (Gen. 28:13). Now, wherever you go, throughout the whole of scripture, if you can find a place where you can lie down, that is yours! If you can sleep on a promise, that promise is yours! "Lift your eyes now," said God to Abraham, "and look from the place where you are—northward, southward, eastward, and westward; for all the land which you see I give to you and your descendants forever" (Gen. 13:14–15).

May the Lord increase our holy vision of delighted faith, for there is nothing we see but we may also enjoy. All that is in Christ is there for us!

II. Now, second, *what the Holy Spirit aims at and what He really accomplishes*. "He will glorify Me."

Ah, brothers, the Holy Spirit never comes to glorify *us*, or to glorify a denomination, or, I think, even to glorify a systematic arrangement of doctrines! He comes to glorify Christ! If we want to be in accord with Him, we must preach in order to glorify Christ. May we never have this thought: *I will put that bit in. It will sound well. The friends will feel that oratory is not quite extinct, that Demosthenes lives again in this village.* No, no!

I would say, "Brother, though it is a very delightful piece, strike that out, because if you have had a thought of that kind about it, you had better not put yourself in the way of temptation by using it."

"Yes, that is a magnificent sentence! I do not know where I met with it or whether it is my own. I am afraid that most of our friends will not understand it, but then it will give them an impression that they have a deep thinker in their pulpit."

Well then, it may be very admirable, and further, it might be a very right thing to give them that precious piece; but if you have that thought about it, strike it out! Strike it out ruthlessly! Say, "No, no, no! If it is not distinctly my aim to glorify Christ, I am not in accord with the aim of the Holy Spirit and I cannot expect His help! We will not be pulling the same way, and therefore I will have nothing of that I cannot say that I am saying it simply, sincerely, and only that I may glorify Christ."

> *If you want to praise the Lord Jesus Christ, tell the people about Him. Take of the things of Christ and show them to the people and you will glorify Christ.*

How then does the Holy Spirit glorify Christ? It is very beautiful to think that He glorifies Christ *by showing Christ's things.* If you wanted to do honor to a man, you would, perhaps, take him a present to decorate his house. But here, if you want to glorify Christ, you must go and take the things *out of Christ's house* "the things of Christ." Whenever we have to praise God, what do we do? We simply say what He is! "You are this and you are that." There is no other praise. We cannot fetch anything from anywhere else and bring it to God. The praises of God are simply the facts about Himself! If you want to praise the Lord Jesus Christ, tell the people about Him. Take of the things of Christ and show them to the people and you will glorify Christ.

Alas, I know what you will do. You will weave words together and you will form and fashion them in a marvelous manner till you have produced a charming piece of literature. When you have carefully done that, put it in the fire under the oven and let it burn! Possibly you may help to bake some bread with it. Brethren, it is better for us to tell what Christ is than to invent ten thousand fine words of praise in reference to Him. "He will glorify Me, for He will take of what is Mine and declare it to you."

Again, I think that the blessed Spirit glorifies Christ by showing us the things of Christ *as Christ's*. Oh, to be pardoned! Yes, it is a great thing, but to find that pardon in His wounds, that is a greater thing! Oh, to get peace! Yes, but to find that peace in the blood of His cross! Brothers, have the blood-mark very visibly on all your mercies! They are all marked with the blood of the cross, but sometimes we think so much of the sweetness of the bread or of the coolness of the waters that we forget from *where* these came and *how* they came; then they lack their choicest flavor. That it came from Christ is the best thing about the best thing that ever came from Christ! That He saves me is, somehow, better than my being saved! It is a blessed thing to go to heaven, but I do not know that it is not a better thing to be in Christ and so, as the result of it, to get into heaven. It is He and that which comes of Himself that becomes best of all because it comes of Himself! So the Holy Spirit will glorify Christ by making us see that these things of Christ are indeed of Christ and completely of Christ and still are in connection with Christ, and we only enjoy them because we are in connection with Christ.

> hat ever such a wretch as I, who can understand everything but what I ought to understand, should be made to comprehend the heights and depths and to know, with all saints, the love of Christ that passes knowledge!

Then it is said in the text, "He will glorify Me, for He will take of what is Mine and declare it to *you* (emphasis added)." Yes, it does glorify Christ for the Holy Spirit to show Christ to us. How often I have wished that men of great minds might be converted! I have wished that we could have a few Miltons and such men to sing of the love of Christ, a few mighty men who teach politics and the like to consecrate their talents to the preaching of the gospel. Why is it not so? Well, because the Holy Spirit does not seem to think that that would be the way to supremely glorify Christ, and He prefers, as a better way, to take us commonplace sort of persons and to take the things of Christ and to show them to *us*. He does glorify Christ, and blessed be His name that ever my bleary eyes should look upon His infinite loveliness! That ever such a wretch as I, who can understand everything but what I ought to understand, should be made to comprehend the heights and depths and to know, with all saints, the love of Christ that passes knowledge!

You see, in a school, that clever boy. Well, it is not much for the master to have made a scholar of *him*. But here is one who shines as a scholar and his mother says that he was the greatest dolt in the family! All his school fellows say, "Why, he was the butt of all our jokes! He seemed to have no brains, but our master, somehow, got some brains into him and made him know something that he appeared at one time incapable of knowing." Somehow it does seem to be as if our very folly, impotence, and spiritual death—if the Holy Spirit shows to us the things of Christ—will go toward the increase of that great *glorifying of Christ* at which the Holy Spirit aims!

Then, beloved brothers, since it is for the honor of Christ for His things to be shown to men, He will show them to us, *that we may go and show them to other people*. This we cannot do, except as He is with us to make the others to see. But He will be with us while we tell forth what He has taught us, and so the Holy Spirit will really be showing to others while He is showing to us! A secondary influence will flow from this service, for we will be helped to *use the right means* to make others see the things of Christ.

III. Our time is almost gone, but in the third place I must just point out to you *how He is, in both of these things, our Comforter*. He is so, first, for this reason: *There is no comfort in the world like a sight of Christ*. He shows to us the things of Christ. Oh, brothers, if you are poor and if the Holy Spirit shows you that Christ had not where to lay His head, what a sight for you! And if you are sick and if the Holy Spirit shows you what sufferings Christ endured, what comfort comes to you! If you are made to see the things of Christ, each thing according to the condition that you are in, how speedily you are delivered out of your sorrow!

And then, if the Holy Spirit glorifies Christ, *this is the cure for every kind of sorrow*. He is the Comforter. I may have told you before, but I cannot help telling you again, that many years ago, after the terrible tragedy in the Surrey Gardens, I had to go away into the country and keep quite still. The very sight of the Bible made me cry. I could only keep alone in the garden and I was heavy and sad, for people had been killed and there I was, half dead myself.

And I remember how I got back my comfort and I preached on the Sabbath after I recovered. I had been walking round the garden and I was standing under a tree. If it is there now, I should know it and I remember these words: "Him God has exalted to His right hand to be Prince and Savior" (Acts 5:31).

Oh, I thought to myself, *I am only a common soldier. If I die in a ditch, I do not care. The King is honored. He wins the victory.* And I was like those French soldiers in the old times who loved the emperor. You know how, when they were dying, if he rode by, the wounded man would raise himself up on his elbow and cry once more, *"Vive l' Emperor!"* for the emperor was engraved on his heart! And so, I am sure, it is with every one of you, my brothers, in this holy war! If our Lord and King is exalted, then let other things go which way they like. If He is exalted, never mind what becomes of us. We are a set of pygmies; it is all right if *He* is exalted! God's truth is safe. We are perfectly willing to be forgotten, derided, slandered, or anything else that men please. The cause is safe and the King is on the throne. Hallelujah! Blessed be His name! Amen.

For Further Thought

1. *What does the Spirit of truth declare in John 16:14?*
2. *Consider John 16:15, and describe Christ's possessions.*
3. *To whom does the Spirit make His declaration?*

The Pentecostal
Wind and Fire

And suddenly there came a sound from heaven,
as of a rushing mighty wind, and it filled the whole house where they
were sitting. Then there appeared to them divided tongues, as of fire,
and one sat upon each of them. And they were all filled with
the Holy Spirit and began to speak with other tongues,
as the Spirit gave them utterance.
ACTS 2:2–4

FROM the descent of the Holy Spirit at the beginning we may learn something concerning His operations at the present time. Remember at the outset that whatever the Holy Spirit was at the first, He is that now, for as God, He remains forever the same. Whatever He did then He is able to do still, for His power is by no means diminished. As says the prophet Micah, "You who are named the house of Jacob: 'Is the Spirit of the LORD restricted?'" (Acts 2:7).

We would greatly grieve the Holy Spirit if we supposed that His might was less today than in the beginning. Although we may not expect and need not desire the miracles that came with the gift of the Holy Spirit, so far as they were *physical*, yet we may both desire and expect that which was intended and *symbolized* by them, and we may reckon to see the same *spiritual* wonders performed among us at this day.

Pentecost, according to the belief of the Jews, was the time of the giving of the law, and if when the law was given there was a marvelous display of power on Sinai, it was to be expected that when the gospel was given, whose ministration is far more glorious, there should be some special unveiling of the divine presence. If at the commencement of the gospel we behold the Holy Spirit working great signs and wonders, may we not expect a continuance of and, if anything, *increased* displays of His power as the ages roll on? The law vanished away, but the gospel will never vanish. It shines more and more to the perfect millennial day, and therefore I reckon that with the sole exception of physical miracles, whatever was worked by the Holy Spirit at the first, we may look to be worked continually while the dispensation lasts.

It ought not to be forgotten that Pentecost was the feast of firstfruits. It was the time when the first ears of ripe corn were offered to God. If, then, at the commencement of the gospel harvest we see so plainly the power of the Holy Spirit, may we not most properly expect infinitely *more* as the harvest advances and, most of all, when the most numerous sheaves will be gathered? May we not conclude that if the Pentecost was thus marvelous, the actual harvest will be still more wonderful? This morning my objective is not to talk of the descent of the Holy Spirit as a piece of history, but to view it as a fact bearing upon us at this hour, even upon us who are called in these latter days to bear our testimony for the truth of God.

> *he gift of the Comforter was not temporary and the display of His power was not to be once seen and no more. The Holy Spirit is here and we ought to expect His divine working among us.*

The Father has sent us the Comforter that He may dwell in us till the coming of the Lord. The Holy Spirit has never returned, for He came in accordance with the Savior's prayer to abide with us forever. The gift of the Comforter was not temporary and the display of His power was not to be once seen and no more. The Holy Spirit is here and we ought to expect His divine working among us. If He does not so work, we should search ourselves to see what it is that hinders Him and whether there may not be something in ourselves that vexes Him so that He restrains His sacred energy and does not work among us as He did before.

May God grant that the meditation of this morning will increase our faith in the Holy Spirit and inflame our desires toward Him so that we may look to see Him fulfilling His mission among men as at the beginning.

I. First, I will call your attention to *the instructive symbols* of the Holy Spirit that were made prominent at Pentecost. They were two. There was a *sound* as of a rushing mighty wind, and there were cloven tongues, as it were, of fire. Take the symbols separately. The first is wind, which is an emblem of deity and therefore a proper symbol of the Holy Spirit. Often in the Old Testament, God revealed Himself under the emblem of breath or wind. Indeed, as most of you know, the Hebrew word for *wind* and *spirit* is the same. So, with the Greek word, when Christ talked to Nicodemus, it is not very easy for translators to tell us when He said "spirit" and when He said "wind." Indeed, some most correctly render the original all the way through by the word *wind*, while others, with much reason, have also used the word *spirit* in their translation.

The original word signified either the one or the other, or both. Wind is, of all material things, one of the most spiritual in appearance. It is invisible, ethereal, mysterious, and therefore men have fixed upon it as being nearest akin to spirit. In Ezekiel's famous vision, when he saw the valley full of dry bones, we all know that the Spirit of God was indicated by that vivifying wind that came when the prophet prophesied and blew upon the withered relics till they were quickened into life. "The LORD has His way in the whirlwind" (Nah. 1:3); thus He displays Himself when He works. "The LORD answered Job out of the whirlwind" (Job 38:1); thus He reveals Himself when He teaches His servants.

Observe that this wind on the day of Pentecost was accompanied with a sound—a sound as of a mighty rushing wind, for although the Spirit of God can work in silence, yet in saving operations He frequently uses sound. I would be the last to depreciate meetings in which there is nothing but holy silence, for I could wish that we had more reverence for silence, and it is in *stillness* that the inner life is nourished. Yet the Holy Spirit does not work for the advancement of the kingdom of God by silence alone, for faith comes by *hearing*. There is a sound as of a mighty rushing wind when the Word of God is sounded forth throughout whole nations by the publishing of the gospel. If the Lord had not given men ears or tongues, silent worship would have been not only appropriate but also necessary. But inasmuch as we have ears, the Lord must have intended us to hear something, and as we have tongues, He must have meant us to speak.

Some of us would be glad to be quiet, but where the gospel has free course there is sure to be a measure of noise and stir. The sound came on this occasion, no doubt, to call the attention of the assembly to what was about to occur—to awaken them and to fill them with awe! There is something indescribably solemn about the rush of a rising tempest. It bows the soul before the sublime mystery of divine power. What more fitting as an attendant upon divine working than the deeply solemn rush of a mighty wind? With this awe-inspiring sound as of a mighty wind, there was clear indication of its coming from heaven. Ordinary winds blow from this or that quarter of the skies, but this descended from heaven itself. It was distinctly like a downdraft from above.

This sets forth the fact that the true Spirit, the Spirit of God, comes from neither this place nor that, neither can His power be controlled or directed by human authority. His working is always from above, from God Himself! The work of the Holy Spirit is, so to speak, the breath of God, and His power is always, in a special sense, the immediate power of God. Coming downward, therefore, this mysterious wind passed into the chamber where the disciples were assembled and filled the room. An ordinary rushing mighty wind would have been felt *outside* the room and would probably have destroyed the house or injured the inhabitants if it had been aimed at any one building, but this heavenly gust filled yet did not destroy the room. It blessed but did not overthrow the waiting company!

The meaning of the symbol is that just as wind, as breath and air, is the very life of man, so is the Spirit of God the life of the *spiritual* man! He quickens us at the first. He keeps us alive afterward. By Him is the inner life nurtured, increased, and perfected. The breath of the nostrils of the man of God is the Spirit of God. This holy breath was intended not only to quicken them but to invigorate them! What a blessing would a breeze be, just now, to us who sit in this heavy atmosphere! How gladly would we hail a gust from the breezy down or a gale from the open sea! If the winds of earth are so refreshing, what must a wind from heaven be?

That rushing mighty wind soon cleared away all earth. It engendered damps and vapors. It awakened the disciples and left them braced up for the further work of the Lord. They took in great drafts of heavenly life! They felt animated, awakened, and bestirred. A sacred enthusiasm came upon them because they were filled with the Holy Spirit! And, girded with that strength, they rose into a nobler form of life than they had known before. No doubt this wind was intended to show the irresistible power of the Holy Spirit, for simple as the air is, and mobile and apparently feeble, yet set it in motion and you feel that a thing of life is among you! Make that motion more rapid and who knows the power of the restless giant who has been awakened!

Look, it becomes a storm, a tempest, a hurricane, a tornado, a cyclone!

Nothing can be more potent than the wind when it is thoroughly roused, and so, though the Spirit of God is despised among men so much so that they do not even believe in His existence, yet let Him work with the fullness of His power and you will see what He can do! He comes softly, breathing like a gentle zephyr that fans the flowers but does not dislodge the insect of most transparent wings, and our hearts are comforted. He comes like a stirring breeze and we are quickened to a livelier diligence. Our sails are hoisted and we fly before the gale! He comes with yet greater strength and we prostrate ourselves in the dust as we hear the thunder of His power bringing down, with a crash, false confidences and refuges of lies! How the firm reliances of carnal men, which seemed to stand like rocks, are utterly cast down! How men's hopes, which appeared to be rooted like oaks, are torn up by the roots before the breath of the convicting Spirit! What can stand against Him? Oh, that we did but see in these latter days something of that mighty rushing wind that breaks the cedars of Lebanon and sweeps before it all things that would resist its power!

> *Our God is a consuming fire; hence the symbol of fire is a fit emblem of God the Holy Spirit. Let us adore and worship Him!*

The second Pentecostal symbol was fire. Fire, again, is a frequent symbol of deity. Abraham saw a burning lamp and Moses beheld a burning bush. When Solomon had built his holy and beautiful house, its consecration lay in the fire of God descending upon the sacrifice to mark that the Lord was there, for when the Lord had dwelt before in the tabernacle, which was superseded by the temple, He revealed Himself in a pillar of cloud by day and a pillar of fire by night. Our God is a consuming fire; hence the symbol of fire is a fit emblem of God the Holy Spirit. Let us adore and worship Him! Tongues of flame sitting on each man's head symbolized a personal visitation to the mind and heart of each one of the chosen company.

The fires came not to consume them, for the flaming tongue injured no one. To men whom the Lord has prepared for His approach, there is no danger in His visitations. They see God and their lives are preserved. They feel His fires and are not consumed. This is the privilege of only those who have been prepared and purified for such fellowship with God. The intention of the symbol was to show them that the Holy Spirit would illuminate them as fire gives light. "He will guide you into all truth" (John 16:13). From then on they were not to be untrained children, but to be teachers in Israel, instructors of the nations whom they were to disciple to Christ, and therefore the Spirit of the light of God was upon them!

But fire does more than give light; it inflames, and the flames that sat upon each showed them that they were to be ablaze with love, intense with zeal, burning with self-sacrifice, and that they were to go forth among men to speak not with the chill tongue of deliberate logic, but with burning tongues of passionate pleading, persuading, and entreating men to come to Christ that they might live! The fire signified inspiration. God was about to make them speak under a divine influence, to speak as the Spirit of God should give them utterance. Oh, blessed symbol! Would God that all of us experienced its meaning to the fullest and that the tongue of fire sat upon every servant of the Lord! May a fire burn steadily within to destroy our sin, a holy sacrificial flame to make us whole burnt offerings to God, a never-dying flame of zeal for God and devotion to the cross!

Note that the emblem was not only fire, but also a *tongue* of fire, for God meant to have a *speaking* church, not a church that would fight with the sword, with which weapon we have nothing to do, but a church that should have a sword proceeding out of its mouth, whose one weapon should be the proclamation of the gospel of Jesus Christ! I think, from what I know of some preachers, that when they had *their* Pentecost, the influence put upon them was in the form of tongues of *flowers*. But the apostolic Pentecost knew not flowers, but flames! What fine preaching we have nowadays! What new thoughts and poetical turns! This is not the style of the Holy Spirit!

Soft and gentle is the flow of smooth speech that tells of the dignity of man, the grandeur of the century, the toning down of all punishment for sin, and the probable restoration of all lost spirits, including the archfiend himself. This is the satanic ministry, subtle as the serpent, bland as his seducing words to Eve. The Holy Spirit calls us not to this mode of speech! Fire, intensity, zeal, passion as much as you will, but as for aiming at effect by polished phrases and brilliant periods, these are fitter for those who would deceive men than for those who would tell them the message of the Most High! The style of the Holy Spirit is one that conveys the truth of God to the mind in the most forcible manner. It is plain but flaming, simple but consuming! The Holy Spirit has never written a cold period throughout the whole Bible, and never did He speak by a man a lifeless word. He always gives and blesses the tongue of fire.

These, then, are the two symbols, and I should like you to carefully observe how the Holy Spirit teaches us by them. When He came from the Father to His Son, Jesus, it was as a dove. Let peace rest on that dear Sufferer's soul through all His days of labor and through the passion that would close them. His anointing is that of peace. He needed no tongue of flame, for He was already all on fire with love. When the Holy Spirit was bestowed by the Son of God upon His disciples, it was as breath: "He breathed on them, and said to them, 'Receive the Holy Spirit' " (John 20:22). To have life more abundantly is a chief necessity of servants of the Lord Jesus; therefore the Holy Spirit visits us.

Now that we have the Holy Spirit from Christ as our inner life and quickening, He also comes upon us with the intent to use us in blessing others, and this is the manner of His visitation. He comes as the wind that wafts the words we speak and as fire that burns a way for the truths of God we utter. Our words are now full of life and flame! They are borne by the breath of the Spirit and they fall like sparks and set the souls of men blazing with desire after God. If the Holy Spirit will rest upon me or upon you or upon any of us to qualify us for service, it will be after this fashion, not merely of life for ourselves, but of fiery energy in dealing with others! Come on us even now, O rushing mighty wind and tongue of fire, for the world has great need! It lies stagnant in the malaria of sin and needs a healing wind! It is shrouded in dreadful night and needs the flaming torch of the truth of God! There is neither health nor light for it but from you, O blessed Spirit! Come, then, upon it through your people!

Now put these two symbols together, only mind what you are doing. Wind and fire together! I have kept them separate in my discourse up to now and you have seen power in each one. What are they together? A rushing mighty wind alone is terrible! Who will stand against it? See how the gallant ships dash together and the monarchs of the forest bow their heads. And fire alone! Who will stand against it when it devours its prey? But set wind and fire to work in hearty union! Remember the old city of London? When first the flames began, it was utterly impossible to quench them because the wind fanned the flame and the buildings gave way before the torrent! Set the prairie on fire. If a rain shower falls and the air is still, the grass may, perhaps, cease to burn. But let the wind encourage the flame and see how the devourer sweeps along while the tall grass is licked up by tongues of fire!

We have lately read of forests on fire. What a sight! Hear how the mighty trees are crashing in the flame! What can stand against it! The fire sets the mountains on a blaze. What a smoke blackens the skies. It grows dark at noon! As hill after hill offers up its sacrifice, the timid imagine that the great day of the Lord has come. If we could see a spiritual conflagration of equal grandeur, it were a consummation devoutly to be wished! O God, send us your Holy Spirit in this fashion; give us both the breath of spiritual life and the fire of unconquerable zeal till nation after nation will yield to the sway of Jesus!

O you who are our God, answer us by fire, we pray! Answer us both by wind and fire and then will we see you to be God indeed. The kingdom comes not and the work is flagging. Oh, that you would send the wind and the fire! You will do this when we are all of one accord: all believing, all expecting, and all prepared by prayer. Lord, bring us to this waiting state!

II. Second, my brothers and sisters, follow me while I call your attention to *the immediate effects* of this descent of the Holy Spirit, for these symbols were not sent in vain. There were two immediate effects: The first was filling and the second was the gift of utterance. I call special attention to the first, namely, *filling*: "It filled the whole house where they were sitting." But it did not merely fill the house, but the men. "They were all filled with the Holy Spirit." When they stood up to speak, even the ribald mockers in the crowd noticed this, for they said, "They are full," and though they added, "of new wine," yet they evidently detected a singular fullness about them (Acts 2:13).

We are poor, empty things by nature, and useless while we remain so. We need to be filled with the Holy Spirit. Some people seem to believe in the Spirit of God giving utterance only, and they look upon instruction in divine things as of secondary importance. Dear, dear me! What trouble comes when we act upon that theory! How the empty vessels clatter, rattle, and sound! Men in such case utter a wonderful amount of nothing, and even when that nothing is set on fire it does not come to much. I dread a revival of that sort, where the first thing and the last thing is everlasting talk. Those who set up for teachers ought to be themselves taught of the Lord. How can they communicate that which they have not received? Where the Spirit of God is truly at work, He first *fills* and *then* gives utterance—that is His way.

Oh, that you and I were at this moment filled with the Holy Spirit!

Full! Then they were not cold, dead, and empty of life as we sometimes are. Full. Then there was no room for anything else in any one of them! They were too completely occupied by the heavenly power to have room for the desires of the flesh! Fear was banished; every minor motive was expelled! The Spirit of God, as it flooded their very beings, drove out of them everything that was extraneous. They had many faults and many infirmities before, but that day, when they were filled with the Spirit of God, faults and infirmities were no more perceptible! They became different men from what they had ever been before. Men full of God are the reverse of men full of self!

> *We are poor, empty things by nature, and useless while we remain so. We need to be filled with the Holy Spirit.*

The difference between an empty man and a full man is something very wonderful. Let a thirsty person have an empty vessel handed to him. There may be much noise in the handing, but what a mockery it is as it touches his lips. But fill it with refreshing water and perhaps there may be all the more silence in the passing of it, for a full cup needs careful handling, but oh, what a blessing when it reaches the man's lips! Out of a full vessel he may drink his full. Out of a full church the world will receive salvation, but never out of an empty one! The first thing we need, as a church, is to be filled with the Holy Spirit! The gift of utterance will then come as a matter of course.

They ask me, "May the sisters speak anywhere? If not in the assembly, may they not speak in smaller meetings?" I answer, yes, if they are full of the Holy Spirit. Shall this brother or that be allowed to speak? Certainly, if he is filled, he may flow. May a layman preach? I know nothing about laymen except that I am no cleric myself. Let all speak who are full of the Holy Spirit! "Spring up, O well!" (Num. 21:17). If it is a fountain of living water, who can restrain it? Who *could* restrain it? Let him overflow who is full, but mind he does not set up to pour out when there is nothing in him. For if he counts it his official duty to go pouring out, pouring out, pouring out at unreasonable length and yet nothing comes of it, I am sure he acts not by the Holy Spirit, but according to his own vanity.

The next Pentecostal symbol was *utterance*. As soon as the Spirit of God filled them, they began to speak at once. It seems to me that they began to speak before the people had come together. They could not help it—the inner forces demanded expression and they must speak! So when the Spirit of God really comes upon a man, he does not wait till he has gathered an audience of the size that he desires, but he seizes the next opportunity! He speaks to one person. He speaks to two. He speaks to three—to anybody. He must speak, for he is full and must have vent! When the Spirit of God fills a man, he speaks so as to be understood. The crowd spoke different languages and these Spirit-taught men spoke to them in the language of the country in which they were born. This is one of the signs of the Spirit's utterance.

If my friend over yonder talks in a Latinized style to a company of fruit sellers, I will guarantee you the Holy Spirit has nothing to do with him! If a learned brother fires over the heads of his congregation with a grand oration, he may trace his elocution, if he likes, to Cicero and Demosthenes. But do not let him ascribe it to the Holy Spirit, for that is not after His manner! The Spirit of God speaks so that His words may be understood, and if there is any obscurity, it lies in the language used by the Lord Himself.

The crowd not only understood, but they *felt*. There were lancets in this Pentecostal preaching, and the hearers "were pricked in their heart" (Acts 2:37 KJV). The truth of God wounded men and the slain of the Lord were many, for the wounds were in the most vital part. They could not understand it. They had heard speakers before, but this was quite a different thing. The men spoke fire flakes and one hearer cried to his fellow, "What is this?" The preachers were speaking flame and the fire dropped into the hearts of men till they were amazed and confused! Those are the two effects of the Holy Spirit—a fullness of the Spirit in the ministry and the church, and next, a fire ministry and a church on fire, speaking so as to be felt and understood by those around!

Causes produce effects like themselves, and this wind and fire ministry soon did its work. We read that this "was noised abroad" (Acts 2:6 KJV). Of course it was, because there had been a noise as of a rushing mighty wind. Next to that we read that all the people came together and were confounded. There was naturally a stir, for a great wind from heaven was rushing! All were amazed and astonished, and while some inquired believingly, others began to mock. Of course they did. There was a fire burning, and fire is a dividing thing. This fire began to separate between the precious and the vile as it always will when it comes into operation.

We may expect, at the beginning of a true revival, to observe a movement among the people; a noise and a stir. These things are not done in a corner. Cities will know of the presence of God and crowds will be attracted by the event. This was the immediate effect of the Pentecostal marvel, and I will now ask you to follow me to my third point, which is this:

III. The Holy Spirit being thus at work, what was *the most prominent subject* that these full men began to preach about with words of fire? Suppose that the Holy Spirit should work mightily in the church. What would *our* ministers preach about? We should have a revival, should we not, of the old discussions about predestination and free agency? I do not think so! These are happily ended, for they tend toward bitterness, and, for the most part, the disputants are not equal to their task. We should hear a great deal about the premillennial and the postmillennial advent, should we not? I do not think so! I never saw much of the Spirit of God in discussions or dreams upon times and seasons that are not clearly revealed. Should we not hear learned essays upon advanced theology? No, sir. When the *devil* inspires the church, we have modern theology—but when the Spirit of God is among us, that rubbish is shot out with loathing!

What *did* these men preach about? Their hearers said, "We hear them speaking in our own tongues the wonderful works of God" (Acts 2:11). Their subject was the wonderful works of God! Oh, that this might be, to my dying day, my sole and only topic: "the wonderful works of God." For, first, they spoke of redemption, that wonderful work of God! Peter's sermon was a specimen of how they spoke of it. He told the people that Jesus was the Son of God, that they had crucified and slain Him, but that He had come to redeem men and that there was salvation through His precious blood. He preached redemption! Oh, how this land will echo again and again with "Redemption, redemption, redemption, redemption by the precious blood!" when the Holy Spirit is with us! This is fit fuel for the tongue of flame. This is something worthy to be blown by the divine wind: "God was in Christ reconciling the world to Himself, not imputing their trespasses to them" (2 Cor. 5:19).

"The blood of Jesus Christ His Son cleanses us from all sin" (1 John 1:7). This is one of the wonderful works of God that we can never too frequently mention. They certainly spoke of the next wonderful work of God, namely, regeneration. There was no concealing of the work of the Holy Spirit in that primitive ministry! It was brought to the front. Peter said, "You shall receive the gift of the Holy Spirit" (Acts 2:38). The preachers of Pentecost told of the Spirit's work by the Spirit's power. Conversion, repentance, renewal, faith, holiness, and such things were freely spoken of and ascribed to their real author, the divine Spirit. If the Spirit of God will give us, once again, a full and fiery ministry, we will hear it clearly proclaimed, "You must be born again" (John 3:7), and we will see a people forthcoming who are born not of blood nor of the will of the flesh, but of the will of God and by the energy that comes from heaven! A Holy Spirit ministry cannot be silent about the Holy Spirit and His sacred operations upon the heart!

> *The* preachers of Pentecost told of the Spirit's work by the Spirit's power. Conversion, repentance, renewal, faith, holiness, and such things were freely spoken of and ascribed to their real author, the divine Spirit.

And very plainly they spoke on a third wonderful work of God, namely, remission of sins. This was the point that Peter pushed home to them—that on repentance they should receive remission of sins. What a blessed message is this: pardon for crimes of deepest dye—a pardon bought with Jesus' blood! Free pardon, full pardon, irreversible pardon given to the vilest of the vile when they ground their weapons of rebellion and bow at the feet that once were nailed to the cross! If we would prove ourselves to be under divine influence, we must keep to the divine message of fatherly forgiveness to returning prodigals. What happier word can we deliver?

These are the doctrines that the Holy Spirit will revive in the midst of the land when He works mightily—redemption, regeneration, and remission. If you would have the Spirit of God resting on your labors, dear brothers and sisters, keep these three things always to the front and make all men hear in their own tongue the wonderful works of God!

IV. I will close by noticing, in the fourth place, what were *the glorious results* of all this. Have patience with me if you find the details somewhat long. The result of the Spirit coming as wind and fire, filling and giving utterance, was, first, in the hearers' deep feeling. There was never in the world, perhaps, such a feeling excited by the language of mortal man as that which was awakened in the crowds in Jerusalem on that day! You might have seen a group here and a group there, all listening to the same story of the wondrous works of God and all stirred and affected, for the heavenly wind and fire went with the preaching and they could not help feeling its power.

We are told that they were pricked in the heart. They had painful emotions. They felt wounds that killed their enmity. The Word of God struck at the center of their being—it pierced the vital point. Alas, people come into our places of worship nowadays to hear the preacher, and their friends ask them on their return, "How did you like him?" Was that your errand, to see how you liked him? What practical benefit is there in such a mode of using the servants of God? Are we sent among you to give opportunities for criticism? Yet the mass of men seem to think that we are nothing better than fiddlers or actors who come upon the stage to help you while away an hour!

O my hearers, if we are true to our God and true to you, ours is a more solemn business than most men dream! The objective of all true preaching is the *heart*—we aim at divorcing the heart from sin and wedding it to Christ! Our ministry has failed and has not the divine seal set upon it unless it makes men tremble, makes them sad, and then soon brings them to Christ and causes them to rejoice! Sermons are to be heard by the thousands, and yet how little comes of them all because the heart is not aimed at, or else the archers miss the mark! Alas, our hearers do not present their hearts as our target but leave them at home and bring us only their ears or their heads! Here we need divine aid. Pray mightily that the Spirit of God may rest upon all who speak in God's name, for then they will create deep feeling in their hearers!

Then followed an earnest inquiry. "They were cut to the heart, and said to Peter and the rest of the apostles, 'Men and brethren, what shall we do?'" (Acts 2:37). Emotion is, of itself, but a poor result unless it leads to practical action. To make men feel is well enough, but it must be a feeling that impels them to immediate movement, or at least to earnest inquiry as to what they should do. O Spirit of God, if you will rest on me, even me, men will not hear and go their way and forget what they have heard! They will arise and seek the Father and taste His love! If you would rest on all the brotherhood that publish your Word, men would not merely weep while they hear and be affected while the discourse lasts, but they would go their way to ask, "What must we do to be saved?" (see Acts 16:30).

This is what we need! We do not require new preachers, but we need a new anointing of the Spirit. We do not require novel forms of service, but we need the fire Spirit, the wind Spirit to work by us till everywhere men cry, "What must we do to be saved?" Then came a grand reception of the Word. We are told that they gladly received the Word of God, and they received it in two senses. First, Peter bade them repent and they did. They were pricked to the heart from compunction on account of what they had done to Jesus, and they sorrowed after a godly sort and quit their sins. They also believed in Him whom they had slain and accepted Him as their Savior, then and there, without hesitancy. They trusted in Him whom God had set forth to be a propitiation, and thus they fully received the Word of God. Repentance and faith make up a complete reception of Christ, and they had both of these. Why should we not see this divine result today? We will see it in proportion to our faith.

> *If the Holy Spirit were fully with us, we should never have to complain that many believers never confess their faith, for they would be eager to confess the Savior's name in His own appointed way!*

But what next? Why, they were baptized directly! Having repented and believed, the next step was to make confession of their faith, and they did not postpone that act for a single day—why should they? Willing hands were there! The whole company of the faithful was glad to engage in the holy service, and that same day they were baptized in the name of the Father and of the Son and of the Holy Spirit! If the Holy Spirit were fully with us, we should never have to complain that many believers never confess their faith, for they would be eager to confess the Savior's name in His own appointed way! Delay to be baptized comes too often of fear of persecution, indecision, love of ease, pride, or disobedience. But all these vanish when the heavenly wind and fire are doing their sacred work! Sinful diffidence soon disappears! Sinful shame of Jesus is no more seen! Hesitancy and delay are banished forever when the Holy Spirit works with power!

Furthermore, there was not merely this immediate confession, but as a result of the Spirit of God, there was great steadfastness. "They continued steadfastly in the apostles' doctrine" (Acts 2:42). We have had plenty of revivals of the human sort and their results have been sadly disappointing. Under excitement, nominal converts have been multiplied. But where are they after a little testing? I am sadly compelled to admit that, so far as I can observe, there has been much sown and very little reaped that was worth reaping, from much of that which has been called revival. Our hopes were flattering as a dream, but the apparent result has vanished like a vision of the night! But where the Spirit of God is really at work the converts stand— they are well rooted and grounded, and therefore they are not carried about by every wind of doctrine! They continue steadfast in the apostolic truths of God!

We see next that there was abundant worship of God, for they were steadfast not only in the doctrine, but also in breaking of bread, in prayer, and in fellowship. There was no difficulty in getting a prayer meeting then! There was no difficulty in maintaining daily communion and holy fellowship then, for the Spirit of God was among them and the ordinances were precious in their eyes. "Oh," say some, "if we could get this minister or that evangelist, we should do well." Brothers and sisters, if you had the Holy Spirit, you would have everything else growing out of His presence, for all good things are summed up in Him!

Next to this there came striking generosity. Funds were not hard to raise. Liberality overflowed its banks, for believers poured all that they had into the common fund. Then was it indeed seen to be true that the silver and the gold are the Lord's! When the Spirit of God operates powerfully, there is little need to issue telling appeals for widows and orphans, or to go down on your knees and plead for missionary fields that cannot be occupied for need of money. At this moment our village churches can scarcely support their pastors at a starvation rate. But I believe that if the Spirit of God will visit all the churches, means will be forthcoming to keep all going right vigorously! If this does not happen, I tremble for our Nonconformist churches, for the means of their existence will be absent—as to both spiritual and temporal supplies they will utterly fail.

There will be no lack of money when there is no lack of grace. When the Spirit of God comes, those who have substance yield it to their Lord! And those who have but little grow rich by giving of that little! And those who are already rich become happy by consecrating what they have! There is no need to rattle the box when the rushing mighty wind is heard and the fire is dissolving all hearts in love! Then came continual gladness. "They ate their food with gladness" (Acts 2:46). They were not merely glad at prayer meetings and sermons, but glad at breakfast and at supper! Whatever they had to eat, they were for singing over it. Jerusalem was the happiest city that ever was when the Spirit of God was there! The disciples were singing from morning to night, and I have no doubt the outsiders asked, "What is it all about?"

The temple was never so frequented as then. There was never such singing before. The very streets of Jerusalem and the hill of Zion rang with the songs of the once-despised Galileans! They were full of gladness, and that gladness showed itself in praising God. I have no doubt they broke out, now and then, in the services with shouts of "Glory! Hallelujah!" I should not wonder but what all propriety was scattered to the winds. They were so glad, so exhilarated, that they were ready to leap for joy! Of course we never say, "Amen," or "Glory!" now. We have grown to be so frozenly proper that we never interrupt a service in any way, because, to tell the truth, we are not so particularly glad, we are not so especially full of praise, that we want to do anything of the sort! Alas, we have lost very much of the Spirit of God and much of the joy and gladness that attend His presence, and so we have settled into a decorous apathy! We gather the links of propriety instead of the palm branches of praise.

> There will be no lack of money when there is no lack of grace. When the Spirit of God comes, those who have substance yield it to their Lord! And those who have but little grow rich by giving of that little! And those who are already rich become happy by consecrating what they have!

May God send us a season of glorious disorder! Oh, for a sweep of wind that will set the seas in motion and make our ironclad brethren now lying so quietly at anchor to roll from stem to stern! As for us, who are as the little ships, we will fly before the gale if it will but speed us to our desired haven! Oh, for fire to fall again—fire that will affect the most stolid! This is a sure remedy for indifference. When a flake of fire falls into a man's bosom, he knows it. And when the Word of God comes home to a man's soul, he knows it, too. Oh, that such fire might first sit upon the disciples and then fall on all around!

And, to close, there was then a daily increase of the church: "The Lord added to the church daily those who were being saved" (2:47). Conversion was going on perpetually! Additions to the church were not events that happened once a year, but they were everyday matters, "so mightily grew the word of God and prevailed" (Acts 19:20 KJV). O Spirit of God, you are ready to work with us today even as you did then! Delay not, we beseech you, but work at once! Break down every barrier that hinders the incomings of your might! Overturn, overturn, O sacred wind! Consume all obstacles, O heavenly fire, and give us now both hearts of flame and tongues of fire to preach your reconciling Word for Jesus' sake. Amen.

For Further Thought

1. *What are the two symbols of the Holy Spirit seen in Acts 2:2–3?*
2. *What are the four effects of the Holy Spirit seen in Acts 2:2–4?*
3. *According to Acts 2:11, what did the disciples speak about on the day of Pentecost?*

SERMONS RELATING TO SALVATION

GRACE FOR GRACE

*Now we have received, not the spirit of the world, but the
Spirit who is from God, that we might know the things
that have been freely given to us by God.*
1 CORINTHIANS 2:12

THE course of our fallen race has been a succession of failures. Whenever there has been an apparent rise, it has been followed by a real fall. Into ever-increasing darkness the human mind seems resolved to plunge itself in its struggles after a false light. When men have been fools, they have danced in a delirium of sin. When they have been sober, they have given themselves up to a phantom wisdom of their own that has revealed their folly more than ever. It is a sad story, the story of mankind! Read it in the light of God's Word and it will bring tears from your very heart.

The only hope for man was that God should interpose. And He has interposed, as though He began a new creation or worked a resurrection out of the kingdom of death. God has come into human history and here the bright lights begin. Where God is at work in divine grace, abounding sin is conquered, hope begins, and good becomes perceptible. This better state is always markedly the effect of a break in the natural course of things, a supernatural product that would never have been seen in this poor world had it been let alone. See yonder avalanche rushing down the steep mountainside? Such is humanity left to itself.

Lo, God in Christ Jesus throws Himself in the way. He so interposes as to be crushed beneath the descending rocks. But beloved, He rises from the dreadful burial. He stops the avalanche in its terrible path. He hurls back the tremendous mass and changes the whole aspect of history. In this divine interposition, of which the Bible gives us the best record to which, I trust, our experience has added a happy appendix, we behold and adore the almighty grace of God. In the interposition of omnipotent grace, we note that the Lord so works as to preserve His own glory. He takes care that no flesh will glory in His presence.

He might have used the power of the great, but He has not. He might have instructed man by man's own wisdom, but He has not. He might have declared His gospel with the excellence of human speech, but He has not. He has taken for His tools not the armor of a king but the song of a shepherd. And He has placed His treasure of truth, not in the golden vase of talent, but in the earthen vessels of lowly minds. He has not made men speak for Him under the spell of genius but as they have been moved by His Holy Spirit. The Lord of hosts will save men, but He will not give men a yard of space for boasting. He will grant them a salvation that will humble them in the dust and lead them to know that He is God and beside Him there is none else. "The LORD of hosts hath purposed it, to stain the pride of all glory, and to bring into contempt all the honourable of the earth" (Isa. 23:9 KJV). God's gracious interposition reveals His sovereignty, His wisdom, His power, His love, and His grace. But it reveals *nothing* in men that can admit a boastful thought.

> *W*here God is at work in divine grace, abounding sin is conquered, hope begins, and good becomes perceptible.

The Lord our God has worked in a way parallel with His central interposition, which is seen at the cross where Jesus unveiled Jehovah's way of revealing power in weakness. It is in such a connection that Paul says, "I determined not to know anything among you except Jesus Christ and Him crucified" (1 Cor. 2:2). He knew that there was nothing else to know. The plan of the cross is to conquer death by death, to remove sin by the endurance of the penalty, to work mightily by suffering terribly, and to glorify Him by shame. The gibbet whereon Christ died was the abyss of reproach and the climax of suffering. But it was also the focus of God's interposing grace. He there glorified Himself in connection, not with honor and power, but with shame and death.

The great self-sacrifice of God is the great victory of divine grace.

Beloved, it is most sweet to think that all the ways of God to men are in harmony with this way of the cross and that the cross is the pattern of the Lord's constant method of accomplishing His designs of grace by weakness rather than by strength, by suffering rather than by the splendor of His majesty. Let me also add that this way that God has taken, by which He saves men and glorifies Himself, is entirely suitable to the condition of those whom He saves. If salvation had been by human excellence, I could never have been saved. If the plan of salvation had required that in which a man might rightly glory, how could it have come to sinners without strength or goodness?

Such a gospel would have been no gospel to us, for it would have been far out of our reach. God's plans are workable plans, suitable to the weakness of our fallen race. In Christ He comes to the wounded man where he is and does not ask him, in his fainting condition, to come a certain part of the way. Grace does not begin halfway down the alphabet, but it is the alpha of our hope.

It is my delightful task, though in much weakness, to set forth the exceeding freeness of the grace of God and thus to set before you an open door, that you who have never entered may boldly do so, and that you who have already entered may sit within and sing to the praise of the glory of His grace wherein He has made you accepted in the Beloved. My text speaks of the gifts of God freely given to us and of the way by which we may receive them and come to know their excellence and value. In all these three things it shows us that everything is of divine grace. It is given of grace, it is received through grace, it is understood by grace. Grace reigns, and grace alone.

This morning I will speak first of *the things that are freely given to us by God*. Second, of *the power to receive them*, which is also given, since it is spoken of as received. And third, of *the knowledge of them*, which is also given through the Spirit. When we have set forth these three things, we will have ranged through a wide domain of sovereign grace.

I. First, then, *the things of God are freely given*. All the blessings of salvation are a gift. All the inheritance of the covenant is a gift. All that which comes by our Lord Jesus to save and sanctify men is a gift. A gift is not a return for purchase money. We are not asked, in any sense, to bring a price to God in order to purchase pardon, justification, or eternal life. Where the notion of purchase is for an instant hinted at, it is only to show more plainly how free is the blessing: "Come. . .buy wine and milk without money and without price" (Isa. 55:1). God freely gives His grace, expecting nothing in return but that we do as freely receive as He does freely bestow.

And even that free reception is a part of the gift that He bestows upon us. Be not feeling in your purse; money is useless as to purchasing salvation. Be not searching in your character or in your resolutions to find some little recommendation; neither the coins of the merchant nor of the self-righteous are good here. The free grace of God would be insulted by being put up for auction or set forth for sale.

> *O*ur heavenly heritage is not held on lease, upon terms of annual payment. It is an unencumbered freehold to every man who has by faith put his foot upon it.

"The gift of God is eternal life in Christ Jesus our Lord" (Rom. 6:23). It is a gift and not a prize. There are heavenly prizes to be run for, to be fought for, and to be obtained by divine help. There is a recompense of reward to which we are to look and a crown for which we are to strive, but the divine grace that forgives sin and works faith is no prize for exertion but rather a gift for those without strength. "It is not of him who wills, nor of him who runs, but of God who shows mercy" (Rom 9:16). Jehovah will have mercy on whom He will have mercy, and He will have compassion on whom He will have compassion according to the good pleasure of His own will. Salvation is not granted to men as the result of anything they are or do or resolve to be. It is the undeserved gift of heaven. If it were of works, it would not be of divine grace. But it is of *faith* that it might be of divine grace alone.

The blessings of salvation are freely given us of God; therefore they are not a loan, handed to us for a time and to be one day recalled. Our heavenly heritage is not held on lease, upon terms of annual payment. It is an unencumbered freehold to every man who has by faith put his foot upon it. To give a thing and take a thing is for little children in their play. And even among *them* it is the subject of ridicule. But the gifts and calling of God are without repentance on His part. When He has given it, the deed is done outright and can never be reversed. O believer, if your sin is blotted out, it can never be written in again! God has declared that He has forgiven our transgressions. And then He adds, "Their sins and iniquities will I remember no more" (Heb. 10:17 KJV).

There is no playing fast and loose in connection with the everlasting love of God and its glorious acts. If you have God, you have Him by an eternal holding of which none can deprive you. God is our God forever and ever. The better part that Jesus gives to His beloved will not be taken away from us. The things of God are all of them free gifts, with no legal condition appended to them that would make their tenure one of payment rather than of absolute gift. We may not say that the blessings of salvation, such as pardon, justification, and eternal life, are gifts with an *if* in the core of them, rendering them uncertain. No, the gift of God is not temporary life, but eternal life.

We will dwell for a minute upon the fact that saving blessings are the gifts of God. Some despise the work of salvation and the blessings that accompany it. But surely they know not what they despise. Every part of salvation, from its alpha to its omega, is to the highest degree precious, for it is of God. It is the gift of the heavenly King, the gift of the almighty Sovereign whose hand makes the gift priceless. If the Lord Himself has given you this or that blessing, you should prize the gift as coming from such a hand! That which your father gave you, preserve, for there is sanctity in the gift of love. That which your choice friend has given you, wear it, and for his sake value it as the token of friendship. But that which your *God* has given you, prize above all things else—His touch has perfumed it with unutterable fragrance.

Value every part of the work of divine grace because it came from God and leads to God. God's gifts are always worthy of the Giver. God gives not trinkets and counterfeits. His gifts are solid gold and lasting treasure. The gifts of divine grace have a quality of divinity about them—they are all Godlike. The Lord gives upon a Godlike style. His grace is like the rest of His nature. How you are blessed if you are divinely pardoned and divinely justified! "It is God who justifies. Who is he who condemns?" (Rom. 8:33–34). Jehovah is your strength and your song. He also has become your salvation.

I like to think of every blessing of divine grace that I have received as coming from God, because each mercy then becomes prophetic of more. God is unchangeable, and therefore what He has given He will give again. "Still there's more to follow" is a popular way of putting a great truth. The stream that has begun to flow will never cease flowing. The more the Lord gives, the more we may expect. Every blessing is not only in itself a mercy, but it is a note for more mercies. When we get the most of God's mercy that we can hold, we are, by its greatness, enlarged to receive still more. Realization begets expectation, and expectation increases realization. Each mercy, as it comes, makes room for another larger than itself, even as the narrow end of the wedge opens the way for its wider portion.

Every mercy bears a thousand mercies in its heart. John Bunyan said that God's flowers bloom double. Not only do they bloom double, they bloom sevenfold. And out of every one of those flowers there comes a seed that will yield seventy times seven. Therefore be encouraged. The least of the things that are freely given to us by God draws behind it an endless chain of more than golden links of love. The seed of salvation, glory, and eternal life is small as a grain of mustard seed. But he who has it has received what neither earth nor heaven can fully contain. What a mercy is a single mercy! I cannot talk to you about the gifts of God. You must think over the subject. That which comes from God's own hand should be much on our mind.

I am going to dwell for a minute or two upon that word *freely*. "The things that [are] freely given to us by God." Hearken, you who have never found divine grace yet. Sing while you listen, you who have found it and are now enjoying it. "Freely given."

"Well," you say, "the word *given* is enough to express the meaning, is it not?" Yes, it would be enough, if men were willing to understand. But the additional word *freely* is meant to make the meaning doubly plain. When we say "grace," there is no need to say "*free* grace," is there? Yet there are some people who will be conveniently deaf, if they can. We wish to speak so that they not only can understand us but also cannot *misunderstand*, even if they try. The text is very expressive: "Freely given to us by God."

How is salvation freely given? It comes from God without compulsion. If a man is stopped on the road with, "Your money or your life," he gives his money. But it is not *freely* given. Now, none can force mercy from God, blessed be His name—there is no need to think of such a thing. God gives freely, that is, even without persuasion. God was never persuaded to be gracious. He is ready to pardon and His grace persuades us to accept mercy. Our praying does not turn the heart of God to love us but proves that we are turning to love Him. It is because He is gracious that He sets us praying. You have not, poor sinner, to convert an unwilling God to be willing to forgive. The conversion is in *your* will, not in His.

"He delights in mercy" (Mic. 7:18).

He persuades Japheth to dwell in the tents of Shem, but Japheth does not need to persuade Jehovah to receive him. The fountain of divine love pours forth its streams of grace at all seasons without pressure. There is no need to tread the grapes of mercy to force forth their cheering juice. The paths of the Lord drop fatness, distilling spontaneously as the dew and the rain.

Yes, the grace of God is so free in its gifts that they come without suggestion. A man may be generous of heart and yet he may need a hint to put it into his mind to relieve the needy. Mention a charity to him and inform him that it is in need, and his guineas are forthcoming. But he needs a prompter. No one has prompted the grace of God. No one ever suggested any deed of bounty to God. Out of His own heart the thought has come of itself. The gifts of His grace were in His eternal purpose from of old and were there of His own good pleasure. He freely instructs us how to pray for those gifts that He has of old purposed to bestow. Our prayer does not instruct the Lord. It only shows that He has, in a measure, instructed us.

> *No one has prompted the grace of God. No one ever suggested any deed of bounty to God. Out of His own heart the thought has come of itself.*

He gives freely in the sense of absolute spontaneity. He also gives without grudging. We have known men to say, "Well, I suppose I must give *something*. But these claims come terribly often. My purse is always being drawn upon. But I suppose I cannot get out of it without a subscription." He gives as if he were parting with his blood. His fingers tremble and linger long over the shilling that has to be extracted as forcibly as if it were a tooth. One wonders that the Queen's image is left upon it when it has been held with such pressure.

But the Lord gives out of the greatness of His heart, without so much as a trace of unwillingness. Even when the gift was His own Son, He freely delivered Him up. There is never a grudge in the Lord's mind toward those who draw upon Him the most largely or the most frequently. He does not upbraid. Many people who give make it an opportunity to upbraid, saying, "I do not think you ought to have been in this plight. You must have been wasteful and not so industrious as you ought to have been, or you would not be drawing upon me," and so on, until they have taken full compensation for their shilling out of the poor creature who feels bound to endure the chastisement.

God gives liberally and adds no sorrow to those who humbly seek wisdom at His hands. Oh, the splendor of the generosity of God! He is ready to save—waiting to deliver. It delights Him to bestow His goodness. The cost was paid long ago on Calvary's cross, and that is over. Since the great sacrifice has been presented, God freely gives all the blessings of divine grace to us with a willingness that shows that His heart goes with them.

Once more, you know that we use the word *freely* in the sense of bountifully. We say of such and such a person, "His banquet was spread with a free hand," or we say, "He helps his poor neighbors very freely." That is to say, his gifts are without stint. The benefits bestowed by some are like the provisions of a workhouse, weighed out by ounces. But free grace does not limit itself by calculations, nor does it bind the applicant by estimates. As a freehanded housekeeper makes liberal provision, so does the Lord provide more than need demands. The mere crumbs from the Lord's table would suffice to feed multitudes. The Lord gives not His Spirit by narrow measure—we are not straitened in Him. Come along with you, you needy saint or sinner. The more you can take in, the better pleased will the Lord be with you. And if, sitting at His table, you feel as if you could eat all that is upon it, hesitate not to make the trial, for you will be heartily welcome.

Your capacity will fail long before the provision. The Lord desires you to open your mouth wide and He will fill it—it is easier for Him to give than for you to open your mouth. He encourages and requests you to bring large petitions with you when you come before His mercy seat. Come and receive the things that are freely given to us by God.

I do not know whether I have made my intent quite so plain as I wanted to do. But this I would set before you: God gives His grace freely in the most emphatic sense. His sovereign grace is of Himself. "It is not of him who wills, nor of him who runs, but of God who shows mercy" (Rom. 9:16). He is not compelled to be gracious by the force of our importunity, but He often gives to those who have never asked of Him, as it is written, "I was found by those who did not seek Me" (Isa. 65:1). He calls by His divine power those who before were unwilling to come to Him. A good example is Saul of Tarsus, who received light and divine grace when he was in the act of persecuting the saints!

God gives His grace as freely as the sun, which, as soon as it rises from its chambers in the east, sows the earth with orient pearl. See how freely it visits the tiny flower that holds up its cup to have it filled with sunshine! How it peers into the glade of the forest, where, by the brook, the fern loves the shade. Whether the lark flies up to meet it or the mole burrows in the earth to escape its light, the sun shines all the same. It fills the heavens and floods the earth with the brilliance that is its nature to diffuse. The Lord comes by promise to those who seek Him. But He comes also in sovereign grace to those who seek Him not.

He is coming this morning to some of you who look not for Him. For He is like the dew that waits not for man, neither tarries for the sons of man. You came from the country and you said that you would go and hear Spurgeon this morning. But you did not know that the Lord was about to save you. Give yourself up to the writ of divine grace of which I am the officer this morning. Surrender your hearts to almighty love. And when you do so, you will perceive many of "the things that have been freely given to us by God."

Now, let us talk about what these things are. They are altogether immeasurable, these "things that have been freely given to us by God." Shall I tell you what they are in one word? *God.* God gives us God. God the Father gives Himself to the unworthy sons of men. He becomes their Father and their friend. He gives them His wisdom, His power, His love, His immutability. He gives Himself to men to be their possession forever. In adoption He gives His fatherhood and grants them sonship, so that they may cry, "Our Father who is in heaven." He gives them pardon and acceptance. He grants them answers to their prayers in ten thousand ways. He gives them His providence to guide and lead them. He gives them all they need for this life, and then He gives them an inheritance with Himself forever in the world to come. He who gave us Jesus, with Him also freely gives us all things. Beloved, the Son of God also gives Himself: He "loved me and gave Himself for me" (Gal. 2:20).

"Who Himself bore our sins in His own body on the tree" (1 Pet. 2:24). Jesus gives His people His blood to wash out their sins, His righteousness to cover them with beauty, His intercession to plead their cause, and His enthronement to secure their victory. He gives His loving care to prepare a place for them in the sky. He gives His resurrection to bring them up from the grave and His union with them to preserve them through the perils of life. We are married to Him, and so He freely gives His heart's love to us.

Even His crown, His throne, and His heaven He freely gives to His chosen. Oh, what a gift of grace this is that is freely given to us by God! "God so loved the world that He gave His only begotten Son" (John 3:16). He is God's unspeakable gift. Nobody can speak it, for nobody can compass it within the range of thought.

> *J*esus gives His people His blood to wash out their sins, His righteousness to cover them with beauty, His intercession to plead their cause, and His enthronement to secure their victory.

The Holy Spirit also freely gives Himself to us. He is the free Spirit, and never freer than when He gives Himself to enlighten, quicken, convert, comfort, and sanctify His people. He leads us to repentance and to faith. He conducts us to knowledge and holiness. He preserves and perfectly conforms us to the image of Christ. Thus see a summary of the things that are freely given to us by God, the Father, the Son, and the Holy Spirit.

All things are yours, the free gifts of God. Now if Paul, when he was writing as an apostle, spoke of these things not as what he had *won* or *deserved* but as *free gifts* to him, you and I, poor sinners that we are, may well be glad to accept these priceless gifts on the same terms. We are happy to think that these gifts are laid at our door, with nothing to pay and nothing to do but simply accept them as "the things that have been freely given to us by God." I have used simple language, but my theme is sublime. The Lord blesses it!

II. Our second head is this: *The power to receive these gifts is also freely given.* Some of you are saying, "I see very clearly that salvation is the gift of God, but how can I get it? How can I apprehend these blessings and make them my own?" Dear friend, the text says we have received the Spirit who is of God. The power with that we receive the gifts that God freely gives is the power of the Holy Spirit. And this also we do not purchase or deserve, but we freely receive it.

The power to grasp Christ does not lie in our nature—in its own strength or goodness. Our state is that of death, and death cannot grasp life. God the Holy Spirit must breathe life into us before we can rise from the grave of our natural depravity and lay hold upon Christ, who is our life. It is not in unrenowned human nature even to *see* the kingdom of God, much less to enter it. "The natural man does not receive the things of the Spirit of God" (1 Cor. 2:14). The power to receive the things of God lies not in high gifts or attainments. We should not think that a Homer or a Socrates or a Plato would be able to obtain the things of God more readily than common men. Genius is no help toward divine grace.

Indeed, great talent and great learning often miss the way where lowliness travels with ease. Do not sit down and say, "I am a poor stupid and cannot be taught of God." Or, "I am a humble countryman, or a poor woman keeping house for others. I cannot know these precious things." It is not so. Read the words of Paul in the first chapter of this Epistle: "For you see your calling, brethren, that not many wise according to the flesh, not many mighty, not many noble, are called" (1 Cor. 1:26). The power to receive the blessings of God does not lie in *talent* at all, but it lies in the *Spirit of God*.

> *C*ome then, dear hearts, you who feel so dull and dead and so void of strength that you cannot do anything. Remember right confidently that the Holy Spirit can enable you to receive all the gifts of God.

You think that if you had a long hand you could reach the grace of God? No. But if you have a withered hand, that divine grace can reach you. You suppose that if you had a clear eye you could see the Lord? Yes. But if you have no eye but a blind one, the Lord can open it and give you sight. Grace is not tied to the rare gifts of genius, nor to the precious acquirements of experience, nor to the high attainments of learning. No young child may say, "I cannot receive the things of God, for I am too young." Out of the mouth of babes and children He has perfected praise. Persons who have had a long and instructive experience are often as far from divine grace as if they had never suffered anything. Persons who have taken degrees at the university may be still as ignorant as Hottentots concerning heavenly things.

The power to *receive* is still of the Holy Spirit, and the Holy Spirit does not find good in us but *brings it to us*. "Well," says one, "but surely we must pass through a period of great anguish and distress before we can receive the things of God." Very often men do suffer greatly from a sense of guilt and the fear of punishment before they lay hold on Christ. But they do not lay hold on Christ by this *experience*. His pains do not restore the wounded man. The famishing man is not fed by his hunger. The power to lay hold on Christ is a *spiritual power*, which must be *given* from above. It lies not concealed within but is implanted by the Lord from without. No process of discipline or education or evolution can enable a man to lay hold on the things of God. He must be born again from above and his heart must be opened to receive the grace of God. A man can receive nothing unless it is *given* him to receive it, and that gift is the Holy Spirit.

The receptive power is not bestowed by human excitement or by the oratorical power of the preacher to whom the man listens. Possibly some have thought, *If I could hear So-and-So preach, I should then be able to believe.* Put that thought away. You will believe in Jesus Christ when the Holy Spirit leads you to see how worthy your Savior is of your confidence. You will never believe in Him if you are looking to yourself for the power to believe, rather than to the truth itself and to that Spirit who can make the truth clear to you and work in you to will and to do God's good pleasure.

Come then, dear hearts, you who feel so dull and dead and so void of strength that you cannot do anything. Remember right confidently that the Holy Spirit can enable you to receive all the gifts of God. May He at this time bless the truth to you, and you will feel the soft, sweet influence of repentance melting you to tears on account of sin. You will feel something telling you that in Christ there is just what you want, and you will feel a resolve forming in your heart, "I will have it if it may be had." Then you will come to a solemn decision for the present hour: "I will have it now. I will even now rest in Jesus, who died for the ungodly. Once and for all I will turn my eyes to the cross and look to Him who did hang upon it and trust my soul's weight on Him."

That is how the work is done. You may not know at the time that the moving power is the Spirit of God, but no one else works us to this thing but the Holy Spirit. We do not see the Spirit or hear His voice or recognize His person at the time. But being emptied of self, by the grace of God, and led to accept the things that are freely given to us by God, we are *spiritually enriched* and then we perceive that it was all of divine grace by the free gift of the Spirit of God.

One thing I should like to say before leaving this point. Remember there are two spirits: There is the Spirit of God and the spirit of the world. This last is everywhere active and believers feel it to be their foe—it works evil and only evil. Only the Spirit of God can save you. The spirit of the world will ruin all who yield to it. I warn you against the spirit of this age—the spirit of the world. Do not lay yourselves under the influence of the spirit of the world. For even if you are truly saved, its pestilential influence will injure you.

Are you seeking salvation? Keep clear of the spirit of the world as much as possible. And you will have no easy task, for its contagion will be found in men professing religion but cunningly undermining it. And it is prevalent in books that pretend to reverence our Lord while they betray Him. The religious world is more dangerous, by far, than the sensual world. It wears the sheepskin but it has all the fierceness of the wolf. You cannot expect the Spirit of God to bless you if you yield to the spirit of the world. Do not meddle with that which is doubtful. There are works of fiction nowadays in abundance whose tendency is polluting. The world is drenched with them. Avoid them as you would a bath of acid.

If you would find eternal life, go where the Spirit of God works. Search the scriptures and hear the truth of God through which the Spirit of God usually operates. And associate with those in whom the Spirit of God dwells. Hear that preaching that comes from God, for that alone will lead you to Him. You can soon tell what sort the preaching is. I do not think you need stay ten minutes before you will find out whether it is according to the spirit of the world or is in the power of the Spirit of God. Those two opposite spirits are waging a fierce battle at this hour. And I grieve to say it: Many who profess godliness are tainted with the spirit of the world. Take heed that you follow the right Spirit, for in so doing you will find the things that are freely given us of God and with them glory and immortality and eternal life.

Now, I have done what I wanted to do if I have made you feel how free salvation is. I would have you know that not only are the gifts of divine grace most free, but the very hand with which we take the gift is nerved to do so by God's grace. Undeserved bounty bestows not only the money but also the purse in which we carry it home. God gives not only the blessing to the heart but the heart to receive the blessing. Hallelujah!

III. My last head is this: *The knowledge of these gifts is freely given.* This is so in the lowest and most ordinary sense, since the revelation contained in the inspired scriptures communicates knowledge of the things freely given of God to our minds. These sacred writings are open to all, and all are invited to search them. Read the Word of God and you will know to the letter what are the free gifts of God to men. But this form of knowledge suffices not. We cannot know the things of God by mere reading; neither can a book teach them to us. The head learns by nature, but the heart must learn by divine grace. The way to know the things of God is for that which is written *in* the Word of God to be also written *upon* the heart by the same Spirit who wrote the book.

I heard about repentance, but I never knew repentance until I repented. I heard of faith, but I never knew faith until I believed. I heard of pardon, but I never knew pardon until I was washed in the blood of the Lamb. I read about justification by faith, but I was never justified till, by faith, I received the Lord Jesus to be my righteousness. Appropriation by faith gives an apprehension by the understanding—experimental enjoyment creates true acquaintance. Beloved, go to the Holy Spirit and ask Him to enable you to take the things that God freely gives, and when you possess them, you will know them.

If you still desire to know more of the infinite preciousness of the gifts of God, it is a wise ambition, and the Holy Spirit will fully and freely satisfy it. Resort to Him, for He is the great teacher. There is no instructor like He is. His knowledge surpasses that of all others, for He knows the mind of God. No man can communicate to you what he does not know, and no man knows the mind of God but the Spirit of God. The Holy Spirit knows the infinite and the unsearchable. And therefore He is able to teach you what you cannot learn elsewhere. The Spirit can unfold to you the mind and meaning of God in every gift of grace. There is no being taught effectually except the Spirit of God teaches you. All other teaching is superficial and therefore temporary and vain. But the Holy Spirit speaks to the soul and writes the lines of truth on the fleshy tablets of the heart so that they can never be erased. If you would know the things freely given us of God, the Holy Spirit must lead you into the inner secret of the sacred treasure-house.

By the same divine aid you must be enabled to feed upon these choice things and have a full enjoyment of them. The things of God, as I have said before, are best known by a personal enjoyment of them. Who can know meat and drink except by living upon them? When you can feed upon a scripture, when you can suck out the marrow of a doctrine, when you can extract the juice from a divine promise, when you are made fat and flourishing by inspired teaching, *then* has the Lord made you freely to know the blessings of His covenant. Oh, that the Holy Spirit may be to you as the seven-branched lamp gladdening your eyes with His light and as the loaves of the showbread nourishing your heart! And then may He lead you within the veil and make you to see the mercy seat and all the glory of the Lord your God!

Oh, to realize that blessing, "All your children shall be taught by the LORD" (Isa. 54:13)! May actual enjoyment and heavenly communion teach us so that we may come into holy familiarity with the choice things that are freely given to us by God. I do not know that I want to hear any lecture on bread. I know all that I want to know about that form of food, because I eat it every day. Even so, we need little talk about covenant blessings, because they are the continual portions of our souls, our strength in every stage of our heavenward pilgrimage and our song in anticipation of the eternal rest.

My dear brothers and sisters, go to this university of heaven. The terms are "nothing to pay," though the education is beyond all other. Blessed school, wherein sinners are made saints and saints are made to grow into the likeness of Jesus! Everything is as free in this university as in the first school of humble faith where the sinner learns repentance and ventures to trust His Savior. Eternal life is the gift of God in its first breathing. And it is still the gift of God in its highest development. When you stand before the throne of the Most High, you will stand there through divine grace alone. All along, from sin's pit to heaven's gate, without a break, the whole road is paved with divine grace.

We do not begin with grace and then go on to trust in works. We do not at first receive freely and then afterward have to live upon a hard-earned wage. No! Still, still, still He works in us to will and to do, and we lovingly work under His divine guidance as we are strengthened by His divine power. Grace lays the foundation:

> *Grace all the work will crown,*
> *Through everlasting days;*
> *It lays in heaven the topmost stone,*
> *And well deserves the praise.*

What of all this? Listen to me for a very few minutes more. I speak to those of you who know the things that are freely given to you by God.

Learn from these things to be humble. If you know anything, you have been taught it. If you possess anything, it has been given to you. You are a charity child. The clothes on your back are furnished by the Lord's favor. The bread in your mouth is the provision of His love. A proud saint is a contradiction in terms. "What do you have that you did not receive?" (1 Cor. 4:7).

In the next place, be generous. I cannot believe in a stingy saint. Here again there is a contradiction in terms. All things are freely given you; are you going to hoard them? "Freely you have received, freely give" (Matt. 10:8). He who turns over the coin in his pocket to make it as small as ever he can before he gives it is a poor creature. He gets the smallest change on Saturday that he may give it on Sunday. He is a saint, is he? Let those who can believe in his saintship. The child of God should be freehearted. He should give *himself* away because Jesus gave Himself for us. You should be of a large heart, for you serve a largehearted Christ who has given you all things freely to enjoy.

Next, be ready to impart what you know. If the Spirit of God has made you to know the things freely given of God, try to tell somebody else. Don't act as if you had a patent, or a monopoly, and wanted divine grace to be a secret. You have not the gift of God yourself if you have no desire that others should have it. The first instinct of a converted man is to try to convert others. If you have no wish to bring others to heaven, you are not going there yourself.

Try to impart this knowledge in the way in which you received it. You received it by the Holy Spirit. Then go and teach it—not in the words that man's wisdom teaches, but in the power of the Spirit of God. Last night I felt so sickly that I thought I should not be able to preach today. But I cheered myself with this reflection: If you cannot give wealth of illustration, if you can display no beauty of style, never mind—you can tell out the soul-saving truth of God in plain words and God will own it. Holy Spirit, bless my feeble words this morning! You can do it and you will have all the praise.

Go to your Sunday school class this afternoon, dear friends, and say, "Lord, put words into my mouth and teach me, that I may teach others. Enable me to labor, not in the power of *my* knowledge, eloquence, or experience, but under the guidance of your Spirit." Better five words in the Spirit than a long oration in your own power.

Lastly, if the Lord has given us all these things freely, let us praise Him.

I did not mind hearing our brother over there cry out, "Amen." He may do it again, if he likes. Sometimes it is well to let the living water of praise to God burst the pipes and flood the streets. What a dumb set we are! The Lord has to pull hard at the rope before our bell speaks at all. Let us praise Him for what He has done for us and make this vow this morning:

> *I will praise Him in life,*
> *I will praise Him in death,*
> *And praise Him as long*
> *as he lends me breath;*
> *And say, when the death-claw*
> *lies cold on my brow,*
> *"If ever I loved you,*
> *my Jesus, 'tis now."*

The Lord Himself bless you all, according to the riches of His grace. Amen.

FOR FURTHER THOUGHT

1. *According to 1 Corinthians 2:12, why have we been given the Spirit of God?*
2. *Read Romans 3:24. What aspect of our salvation does this verse say has been freely given to us?*
3. *Second Corinthians 4:6 says God has shone in our hearts. What does this verse say God has freely given us by this shining?*

ADOPTION

*Having predestined us to adoption as sons by Jesus Christ to Himself,
according to the good pleasure of His will. . .*
EPHESIANS 1:5

IT is at once a doctrine of scripture and of common sense that whatever God does in time, He predestined to do in eternity. Some men find fault with divine predestination and challenge the *justice* of eternal decrees. Now, if they remember that predestination is the counterfoil of history as an architectural plan, that is, the carrying out of what we read in the facts that happen, they may perhaps obtain a slight clue to the unreasonableness of their hostility.

I never heard anyone among professors wantonly and willfully find fault with God's dealings, yet I have heard some who would even dare to call into question the equity of His counsels. If the thing itself is right, it must be right that God intended to do the thing. If you find no fault with facts as you see them in providence, you have no ground to complain of decrees as you find them in predestination, for the decrees and the facts are just the counterparts one of the other. Have you any reason to find fault with God that He has been pleased to save you and save me? Then why should you find fault because scripture says He predetermined that He would save us?

I cannot see, if the fact itself is agreeable, why the decree should be objectionable. I can see no reason why you should find fault with God's foreordination if you do not find fault with what does actually happen as the effect of it. Let a man but agree to acknowledge an act of providence and I want to know how he can, except he runs in the very teeth of providence, find any fault with the predestination or intention that God made concerning that providence.

Will you blame me for preaching this morning? Suppose you answer, "No." Then can you blame me that I formed a resolution last night that I would preach? Will you blame me for preaching on this particular subject?

Do, if you please, then, and find me guilty for intending to do so. But if you say I am perfectly right in selecting such a subject, how can you say I was not perfectly right in intending to preach upon it? Assuredly you cannot find fault with God's predestination if you do not find fault with the effects that immediately spring from it.

> *Assuredly you cannot find fault with God's predestination if you do not find fault with the effects that immediately spring from it.*

Now we are taught in scripture, I affirm again, that all things that God chose to do in time were most certainly intended by Him to be done in eternity, and He predestined such things should be done. If I am called, I believe God intended before all worlds that I should be called. If in His mercy He has regenerated me, I believe that from all eternity He intended to regenerate me. And if in His loving-kindness He will at last perfect me and carry me to heaven, I believe it always was His intention to do so. If you cannot find fault with the thing itself that God does in the name of reason, common sense, and scripture, how dare you find fault with God's intention to do it?

But there are one or two acts of God that, while they certainly are decreed as much as other things, yet they bear such a special relation to God's predestination that it is rather difficult to say whether they were done in eternity or whether they were done in time. Election is one of those things that was done absolutely in eternity. All who were elect were elect as much in eternity as they are in time. But you may say, does the like affirmation apply to *adoption* or justification? My late eminent and now glorified predecessor Dr. Gill, diligently studying these doctrines, said that adoption was the act of God in eternity and that as all believers were elect in eternity, so beyond a doubt they were adopted in eternity.

He further stated that included the doctrine of justification, and he said that inasmuch as Jesus Christ was before all worlds justified by His Father and accepted by Him as our representative, therefore all the elect must have been justified in Christ from before all worlds. Now I believe there is a great deal of truth in what he said, though there was a considerable outcry raised against him at the time he first uttered it. However, that being a high and mysterious point, we would have you accept the doctrine that all those who are saved at last were elect in eternity when the means as well as the end were determined.

With regard to adoption, I believe we were predestined hereunto in eternity, but I do think there are some points with regard to adoption that will not allow me to consider the act of adoption to have been completed in eternity. For instance, the positive translation of my soul from a state of nature into a state of grace is a part of adoption, or at least it is an effect of it and so close an effect that it really seems to be a part of adoption itself. I believe that this was designed and in fact that it was virtually carried out in God's everlasting covenant. I think that it was then actually brought to pass in all its fullness.

So with regard to justification, I must hold that in the moment when Jesus Christ paid my debts, my debts were canceled. In the hour when He worked out for me a perfect righteousness, it was imputed to me, and therefore I may as a believer say I was complete in Christ before I was born—accepted in Jesus, even as Levi was blessed in the loins of Abraham by Melchizedek. But I know likewise that justification is described in the scriptures as passing upon me at the time I believe. "Having been justified by faith," I am told, "I have peace with God through Jesus Christ" (see Rom. 5:1). I think, therefore, that adoption and justification, while they have a very great alliance with eternity and were virtually done then, yet have both of them such a near relation to us in time and such a bearing upon our own personal standing and character that they have also a part and parcel of themselves actually carried out and performed in time in the heart of every believer.

I may be wrong in this exposition. It requires much more time to study this subject than I have been able yet to give to it, seeing that my years are not yet many. I will no doubt by degrees come to the knowledge more fully of such high and mysterious points of gospel doctrine. But nevertheless, while I find the majority of sound divines holding that the works of justification and adoption are due in our lives, I see, on the other hand, in scripture, much to lead me to believe that both of them were done in eternity.

And I think the fairest view of the case is that while they were virtually done in eternity, yet both adoption and justification are actually passed upon us in our proper persons, consciences, and experiences in time—so that both the Westminster Confession and the idea of Dr. Gill can be proved to be scriptural. We may hold them both without any prejudice the one to the other.

Well now, beloved, leaving then the predestination, let us come to as full a consideration as the hour will enable us to give of the doctrine of "the adoption of children by Jesus Christ to Himself, according to the good pleasure of His will" (see Eph. 1:5).

First, then, adoption and *the grace of God displayed in it*. Second, adoption and *the privileges that it brings*. Third, adoption and *the duties that it necessarily places upon every adopted child*.

I. First, *adoption, the grace of it*. Adoption is that act of God whereby men who were by nature the children of wrath, even as others, and were of the lost and ruined family of Adam, are from no reason in themselves, but entirely of the pure grace of God, translated out of the evil and black family of Satan and brought actually and virtually into the family of God. They take His name, share the privileges of sorts, and they are for all intents and purposes the actual offspring and children of God.

> *L*et us give all thanks to the free grace that overlooked the hole of the pit from where we were dug, and passed over the quarry from where we were hewn, and put us among the chosen people of the living God.

This is an act of pure grace. No man can ever have a right in himself to become adopted. If I had, then I should receive the inheritance in my own right. But inasmuch as I have no right whatever to be a child of God and can by no possibility claim so high a privilege in and of myself, adoption is the pure gratuitous effect of divine grace and of that alone. I could suppose that justification might be by works under the old covenant, but I could not suppose adoption to be under the old covenant at all. I could imagine a man keeping the law perfectly and being justified by it, if Adam had not fallen. But even upon such a supposition, Adam himself would have had no right to adoption—he would still have been only a servant and not a son.

Above all contradiction and controversy, that great and glorious act whereby God makes us of His family and unites us to Jesus Christ as our covenant head so we may be His children is an act of pure grace. It would have been an act of sovereign grace if God had adopted someone out of the best of families. But in this case He has adopted one who was a child and a rebel. We are by nature the children of one who was convicted of high treason. We are all the heirs and are born into the world the natural heirs of one who sinned against his Maker, who was a rebel against his Lord. Yet mark this: Notwithstanding the evil of our parentage, born of a thief who stole the fruit from his master's garden—born of a proud traitor who dared to rebel against his God—notwithstanding all this, God has put us into the family. We can well conceive that when God considered our vile original, He might have said within Himself, "How can I put you among the children?" With what gratitude should we remember that though we were of the very lowest original, grace has put us into the number of the Savior's family? Let us give all thanks to the free grace that overlooked the hole of the pit from where we were dug, and passed over the quarry from where we were hewn, and put us among the chosen people of the living God.

If a king should adopt any into his family it would likely be the son of one of his lords—at any rate some child of respectable parentage. He would not take the son of some common felon, or some gypsy child, to adopt him into his family. But God in this case has taken the very worst to be His children. The sons of God all confess that they are the last persons they should ever have dreamed He would have chosen. They say of themselves:

> *What was there in us that could merit esteem,*
> *Or give the Creator delight?*
> *'Twas "Even so, Father," we ever must sing,*
> *"Because it seemed good in your sight."*

Again, let us think not only of our original lineage but also of our personal character. He who knows himself will never think that he had much to recommend him to God. In other cases of adoption there usually is some recommendation. A man, when he adopts a child, sometimes is moved thereto by her extraordinary beauty, or at other times by her intelligent manners and winning disposition. But, beloved, when God passed by the field in which we were lying, He saw no tears in our eyes till He put them there Himself. He saw no contrition in us until He had given us repentance. There was no beauty in us that could induce Him to adopt us. On the contrary, we were everything that was repulsive.

And if He had said, when He passed by, "You are cursed; be lost forever," it would have been nothing but what we might have expected from a God who had been so long provoked and whose majesty had been so terribly insulted. But no, He found a rebellious child, a filthy, frightful, ugly child. He took him to His bosom and said, "Black though you are, you are comely in my eyes through my Son, Jesus. Unworthy though you are, yet I cover you with His robe, and in your Brother's garments I accept you." And taking us, all unholy and unclean, just as we were, He took us to be His—His children—His forever.

I was passing lately by the seat of a nobleman, and someone in the railway carriage observed that he had no children and he would give any price in the world if he could find someone who would renounce all claim to any son he might have. The child was never to speak to his parents anymore, or to be acknowledged, and this lord would adopt him as his son and leave him the whole of his estates. But he had found great difficulty in procuring any parents who would forswear their relationship and entirely give up their child.

Whether this was correct or not, I cannot tell. But certainly this was not the case with God. His only begotten and well-beloved Son was quite enough for Him. And if He had needed a family, there were the angels, and His own omnipotence was adequate enough to have created a race of beings far superior to us. He stood in no need whatever of any to be His darlings. It was, then, an act of simple, pure, gratuitous grace—and of nothing else—because He will have mercy on whom He will have mercy and because He delights to show the marvelous character of His condescension.

Did you ever think what a high honor it is to be called a son of God? Suppose a judge of the land should have before him some traitor who was about to be condemned to die. Suppose that equity and law demanded that the wretch should shed his blood by some terrible punishment. But suppose it were possible for the judge to step from his throne and to say, "Rebel, you are guilty, but I have found out a way whereby I can forgive your rebellions. Man, you are pardoned!" There is a flush of joy upon his cheek. "Man, you are made rich! See, there is wealth!"

Another smile passes over the countenance. "Man, you are made so strong that you will be able to resist all your enemies!" He rejoices again. "Man," says the judge at last, "you are made a prince! You are adopted into the royal family and you will one day wear a crown. You are now as much the son of God as you are the son of your own father." You can conceive the poor creature fainting with joy at such a thought, that he whose neck was just ready for the halter should have his head now ready for a crown, that he who expected to be clothed in the felon's garb and taken away to death is now to be exalted and clothed in robes of honor.

So, Christian, think what you did deserve—robes of shame and infamy—but you are to have those of glory. Are you in God's family now? Well said the poet, "It does not yet appear how great we must be made." We do not know the greatness of adoption yet. Yes, I believe that even in eternity we will scarce be able to measure the infinite depth of the love of God in that one blessing of "adoption. . .by Jesus Christ to Himself, according to the good pleasure of His will." Still, I think there is someone here who says, "I believe, sir, that men are adopted because God foresees that they will be holy, righteous, and faithful, and therefore, doubtless, God adopted them on the foresight of that."

> *The fact is, we are by nature utterly lost and ruined, and there is not a saint in heaven who would not have been damned and who did not deserve to be damned in the common doom of sinners.*

That is an objection I often have to reply to. Suppose, my friends, you and I should take a journey into the country one day and should meet with a person and should say to him, "Sir, can you tell me why the sails of yonder windmill go round?" He would of course reply, "It is the wind." But suppose you were to ask him, "What makes the wind?" and he were to reply, "The sails of the windmill." Would you not just think that he was an idiot? In the first place, he told you that the wind caused the revolution of the sails, and then, afterward, he tells you that the sails make the wind, that an effect can be the parent of that which is its own cause!

Now, any man you may ask will say that faith is the gift of God and that good works are God's workmanship. Well then, what is the cause of good works in a Christian? "Why, grace," they say. Then how can good works be the cause of grace? By all that is rational, where are your heads? It is too foolish a supposition for any man to reply to without making you laugh, and that I do not choose to do. And therefore I leave it. I say again, beloved, if the root causes the fruits upon a Christian, how can the fruit, in any degree, be the cause of the root? If the good works of any man are given him by grace, how can they, by any pretense whatever, be argued as the reason why God gives him grace?

The fact is, we are by nature utterly lost and ruined, and there is not a saint in heaven who would not have been damned and who did not deserve to be damned in the common doom of sinners. The reason why God has made a distinction is a secret to Him. He had a right to make that distinction if He pleased and He has done it. He has chosen some to eternal life, to the praise of His glorious grace. He has left others to be punished for their sins, to the praise of His glorious justice. And in one as in the other, He has acted quite rightly, for He has a right to do as He wills with His own creatures. Seeing they all deserved to be punished, He has a right to punish them all.

So, too, as He has reconciled justice with mercy or mated it with judgment, He has a right to forgive and pardon some and to leave the others to be unwashed, unforgiven, and unsaved, to willfully follow the error of their ways, to reject Christ, despise His gospel, and ruin their own souls. He who does not agree with that agrees not with scripture. I have not to prove it, I have only to preach it. He who quarrels with that quarrels with God. Let him fight his quarrel out himself.

II. The second thing is *the privileges that come to us through adoption.*

For the convenience of my young people—members of the church—I shall, just for a moment, give you a list of the privileges of adoption as they are to be found in our old *Confession of Faith*. I know many of you have this book and I am sure most of you will study at home this afternoon if you have opportunity, looking up all the passages. It is the Twelfth Article, upon adoption, where we read:

> All those that are justified, God vouchsafed, in and for
> the sake of His only Son Jesus Christ, to make partakers
> of the grace of adoption, by which they are taken into the
> number and enjoy the liberties and privileges of children
> of God, have His name put upon them, receive the spirit
> of adoption, have access to the throne of grace with
> boldness, are enabled to cry, "Abba, Father," are pitied,
> protected, provided for, and chastened by Him as a Father,
> yet never cast off, but sealed to the day of redemption and
> inherit the promises as heirs of everlasting salvation.

I will commence, then, with the privileges of adoption. There is one privilege not mentioned in the Confession that ought to be there. It is this:

When a man is adopted into a family and comes thereby under the regime of his new father, he has nothing whatever to do with the old family he has left behind and he is released from subjection to those whom he has left. And so, the moment I am taken out of the family of Satan, the prince of this world has nothing to do with me as my father and he is no more my father. I am not a son of Satan; I am not a child of wrath. The moment I am taken out of the legal family, I have nothing whatever to do with Hagar.

If Hagar comes to meddle with me, I tell her, "Sarah is my mother, Abraham is my father, and, Hagar, you are my servant and I am not yours. You are a bondwoman and I will not be your bond slave, for you are mine." When the law comes to a Christian with all its terrible threats and horrible denunciations, the Christian says, "Law! Why do you threaten me? I have nothing to do with you. I follow you as my rule, but I will not have you to be my ruler. I take you to be my pattern and mold, because I cannot find a better code of morality and of life, but I am not under you as my condemning curse.

"Sit in your judgment seat, O law, and condemn me. I smile on you, for you are not my judge; I am not under your jurisdiction. You have no right to condemn me." If, as the old divines say, the king of Spain were to condemn an inhabitant of Scotland, what would he say? He would say, "Very well, condemn me if you like, but I am not under your jurisdiction." So when the law condemns a saint, the saint says, "If my Father condemns me and chastens me, I bow to Him with filial submission for I have offended Him, but, O law, I am not under you any longer. I am delivered from you; I will not hear your sentence nor care about your thunders.

"All you can do against me, go and do it upon Christ. Or, rather, you have done it. If you demand punishment for my sin, look, there stands my substitute. You are not to seek it at my hands. You charge me with guilt. It is true, I am guilty, but it is equally true my guilt is put upon the Scapegoat's head. I tell you, I am not of your family. I am not to be chastened by you. I will not have a legal chastisement, a legal punishment. I am under the gospel dispensation now. I am not under you. I am a child of God, not your servant. We have a commandment to obey the Father whom we now have. But as to the family with which we were connected, we have nothing to do with it any longer." That is no small privilege. Oh, that we could rightly understand it and appreciate it and walk in the liberty wherewith Christ has made us free!

But now, as the Confession has it, one of the great blessings that God gives us is that we have His name put upon us. He will give to us a new name, as is the promise in the book of the Revelation. We are to be called after the name of God. Oh, remember, brothers and sisters, we are men and women, but we are God's men and women now. We are no longer mere mortals. We are so in ourselves. But by divine grace we are chosen immortals, God's sons, taken to Him. Remember, Christian, you bear the name of God upon you.

> *Oh, remember, brothers and sisters, we are men and women, but we are God's men and women now. We are no longer mere mortals.*

Mark another thing. We have the spirit of children as well as the name of children. Now, if one man adopts another child into his family, he cannot give it his own nature as his own child would have had. And if that child whom he will adopt should have been a fool, it may still remain so. He cannot make it a child worthy of him. But our heavenly Father, when He comes to carry out adoption, gives us not only the name of children, but the nature of children, too. He gives us a nature like His well-beloved Son, Jesus Christ. We had once a nature like our father Adam after he had sinned. He takes that away and gives us a nature like Himself, as it were, in the image of God.

He overcomes the old nature and He puts in us the nature of children. "God has sent forth the Spirit of His Son into your hearts, crying out, 'Abba, Father!'" (Gal. 4:6). And He gives us the nature and the character of children, so that we are as much by grace partakers of the spirit of children of God as we should have been if we had been His legitimately born children and had not been adopted into His family. Brethren, adoption secures to us regeneration. And regeneration secures to us the nature of children whereby we not only are made children but are made partakers of the grace of God, so that we are in ourselves made to God by our new nature as living children, actually and really like Himself.

The next blessing is that being adopted we have access to the throne. When we come to God's throne, one thing we ought always to plead is our adoption. The angel who keeps the mercy seat might stop us on the road, saying, "What is your claim to come here? Do you come as a subject or a servant? If you do, you have no right to come. But if you come as a son, come and welcome." Can you say you are a son in your prayers, Christian? Then never be afraid to pray. So long as you know your sonship, you will be sure to get all you want, for you can say, "Father, I ask not as a servant. If I were a servant, I should expect your wages, and knowing that as a servant I have been rebellious, I should expect wages of eternal wrath.

"But I am your son. Though as a servant I have often violated your rules and may expect your rod, yet, O Father, sinner though I be in and of myself, I am your son by adoption and grace. Spurn me not away. Put me not from your knee. I am your own child. I plead it. The Spirit bears witness with my Spirit that I am born of God. Father, will you deny your son?" What? Will He drive away His son? No, beloved, He will not. He will turn again, He will hear our prayer, and He will have mercy upon us. If we are His children, we may have access with boldness to the grace wherein we stand and access with confidence to the throne of the heavenly grace.

> *A*nother blessing is that God pities us. Think of that, children, in all your sufferings and sorrows. "As a father pities his children, so the Lord pities those who fear Him" (Ps. 103:13).

Another blessing is that God pities us. Think of that, children, in all your sufferings and sorrows. "As a father pities his children, so the Lord pities those who fear Him" (Ps. 103:13). Do you lie sick? The Lord stands by your bedside, pitying you. Are you tempted of Satan? Christ is looking down upon you, feeling in His heart your sighs and your groans. Did you come here this morning with a heavy heart, a desponding spirit? Remember, the loving heart of God sympathizes with you. In His measure, Christ feels afresh what every member bears. He pities you, and that pity of God is one of the efforts that flows into your heart by your adoption.

In the next place, He protects you. Just as a hen protects her brood under her feathers from birds of prey that seek their life, so the Lord makes His own loving arms encircle His children. No father will allow his son to die without making some attempt to resist the adversary who would slay him. God will never allow His children to perish while His omnipotence is able to guard them. If once that everlasting arm can be palsied, if once that everlasting hand can become less than almighty, then you may die. But while your Father lives, your Father's shield will be your preserver and His strong arm will be your effectual protection.

Once again, there is provision as well as protection. Every father will take care to the utmost of his ability to provide for his children. So will God. If you are adopted, being predestinated thereunto, most surely will He provide for you.

> *All needful grace will God bestow,*
> *And crown that grace with glory, too;*
> *He gives us all things and withholds*
> *No real good from upright souls.*

Mercies temporal, mercies spiritual you will have, and all because you are God's son, His redeemed child, made so by the blood of Jesus Christ.

And then you will likewise have education. God will educate all His children till He makes them perfect men in Christ Jesus. He will teach you doctrine after doctrine. He will lead you into all truth until at last, perfected in all heavenly wisdom, you will be made fit to join with your fellow commoners of the great heaven above.

There is also one thing, perhaps, you sometimes forget that you are sure to have in the course of discipline if you are God's sons, and that is God's rod. That is another fruit of adoption. Unless we have the rod we may tremble, fearing that we are not the children of God. God is no foolish father; if He adopts a child, He adopts him that He may be a kind and wise Father. He does not afflict willingly nor grieve the children of men for nothing, though when His strokes are felt, they are fewer than our crimes and lighter than our guilt. At the same time, He never spares the rod. He knows He would ruin His children if He did; therefore He lays it on with no very sparing hand and makes them cry out and groan while they think that He is turned to be their enemy.

But as the Confession beautifully has it, exactly in keeping with scripture, "Though chastened by God as by a father, yet never cast off, but sealed to the day of redemption, they inherit the promises, as heirs of salvation." It is one great doctrine of scripture that God cannot, as well as will not, cast off His children. I have often wondered how any persons can see any consistency in scripture phraseology when they talk about God's people being children of God one day and children of Satan the next. Now, it would startle me not a little if I should step into a lecture room and hear the lecturer asserting that my children might be my children today and his children the next. I should look at him and say, "I don't see that. If they are really mine, they are mine. If they are not mine, they are not mine, but I do not see how they can be mine today and yours tomorrow."

The fact is that those who preach thus *do* believe in salvation by works, though they mask and cover it with specious qualifications as much as they may. There is as much need for a Luther to come out against them as there was for him to come out against the Romanists. Ah, beloved, it is well to know that our standing is not of that character, but if we are children of God, nothing can unchild us. Though we be beaten and afflicted as children, we never will be punished by being cast out of the family and ceasing to be children. God knows how to keep His own children from sin. He will never give them liberty to do as they please. He will say to them, "I will not kill you—that is an act I could not do. But this rod will smite you." And you will be made to groan and cry under the rod so that you will hate sin and you will cleave to Him and walk in holiness even to the end.

> *I* have often wondered how any persons can see any consistency in scripture phraseology when they talk about God's people being children of God one day and children of Satan the next.

It is not a licentious doctrine, because there is the rod. If there were no rod of chastisement, then it would be a daring thing to say that God's children will go unpunished. They shall, so far as legal penalty is concerned. No judge will condemn them. But as far as paternal chastisement is concerned, they will not escape. "You only have I known of all the families of the earth," says God; "therefore I will punish you for all your iniquities" (Amos 3:2).

Lastly, as sure as we are the children of God by adoption, we must inherit the promise that pertains to it. "If children, then heirs—heirs of God and joint heirs with Christ, if indeed we suffer with Him, that we may also be glorified together" (Rom. 8:17).

III. And now the final point: There are *some duties that are connected with adoption*. When the believer is adopted into the Lord's family there are many relationships that are broken off. The relationship with old Adam and the law ceases at once. But then he is under a new law, the law of grace, and under new rules and under a new covenant. And now I beg to admonish you of duties, children of God. Because you are God's children, it has then become your duty to obey God. A servile spirit you have nothing to do with. You are a child. But inasmuch as you are a child, you are bound to obey your Father's faintest wish—the least intimation of His will.

What does He say to you? Does He bid you fulfill such and such an ordinance? It is at your peril if you neglect it. Then you are disobeying your Father who tells you to do so. Does He command you to seek the image of Jesus? Seek it. Does He tell you, "You shall be perfect, just as your Father in heaven is perfect" (Matt. 5:48)? Then not because the law says so, but because your Father says so, seek after it. Seek to be perfect in love and in holiness. Does He tell you to love one another? Love one another. Not because the law says, "Love your God," but because Christ says, "A new commandment I give to you, that you love one another; as I have loved you, that you also love one another" (John 13:34).

> *Are the cattle upon a thousand hills His and will He let you lack a meal? Is the earth the Lord's and the fullness thereof and will He let you go away empty and poor and miserable? Oh, surely not!*

Are you told to distribute to the poor and minister to the necessity of saints? Do it not because you think you are bound by the law to do it, but do it because Christ says so, because He is your Elder Brother—He is the Master of the household, and you think yourself most sweetly bound to obey. Does it say, "Love God with all your heart"? Look at the commandment and say, "Ah, commandment, I will seek to fulfill you. Christ has fulfilled you already. I have no need, therefore, to fulfill you for my salvation, but I will strive to do it because He is my Father now and He has a new claim upon me."

Does He say, "Remember the Sabbath day to keep it holy"? I will remember what Jesus said, "The Sabbath was made for man, and not man for the Sabbath" (Mark 2:27), and therefore I will not be the Sabbath's slave. But inasmuch as my Father rested on the seventh day, so also will I from all my works, and I will have no works of legality to defile His *rest*. I will do as many acts of mercy as ever I can. I will seek and strive to serve Him with filial homage. Because my Father rested, so will I in the finished work of Christ.

And so it is with each of the Ten Commandments. Take them out of the law, put them in the gospel, and then obey them. Do not obey them simply as being the law graven on tables of stone; obey them as gospel written on fleshy tables of the heart, "because we are not under law but under grace" (Rom. 6:15).

There is another duty, believer. It is this: If God is your Father and you are His son, you are bound to trust Him. Oh, if He were only your Master and you ever so poor a servant, you would be bound to trust Him. But when you know that He is your Father, will you ever doubt Him? I may doubt any man in this world. But I do not doubt my father. If he says a thing, if he promises a thing, I know if it is in his power, he will do it. And if he states a fact to me, I cannot doubt his word. And yet, O child of God, how often do you mistrust your *heavenly* Father? Do so no more. Let Him be true. Let every man be a liar—still doubt not your Father. What? Could He tell you an untruth? Would He cheat you?

No, your Father, when He speaks, means what He says. Can you not trust His love? What? Will He let you sink while He is able to keep you afloat? Will He let you starve while His granaries are full? Will He let you die of thirst when His presses burst with new wine? Are the cattle upon a thousand hills His and will He let you lack a meal? Is the earth the Lord's and the fullness thereof and will He let you go away empty and poor and miserable? Oh, surely not! Is all grace His and will He keep it back from you? No. He says to us today, "Son, you are ever with me, and all that I have is yours. Take what you will; it is all your own. But trust to your Father:

> *Leave to His sovereign will*
> *To choose and to command.*
> *With wonder filled, you then will own*
> *How wise, how strong His hand.*

Now go away, heirs of heaven, with light feet and with joy in your countenances. You know that you are His children and that He loves you and will not cast you away. Believe that to His bosom He now presses you—that His heart is full of love to you. Believe that He will provide for you, protect you, and sustain you and that He will at last bring you to a glad inheritance when you will have perfected the years of your pilgrimage and will be ripe for bliss. For He has "predestined us to adoption as sons by Jesus Christ to

Himself, according to the good pleasure of His will" (Eph. 1:5).

I need not this morning delay you any longer in personally addressing unconverted persons. Their welfare I always seek. I have sought, while speaking to the saints this morning, so to speak that every sinner may learn at least this one fact—salvation is of God alone—and that he may be brought into this state of mind to feel that if he is saved, God must save him or else he cannot be saved at all. If any of you acknowledge that truth, then in God's name I now bid you believe in Jesus. For as surely as ever you can feel that God has a right to save or to destroy you, grace must have made you feel that, and therefore you have a right now to come and believe in Jesus. If you know that, you know all that will make you feel empty, and therefore you have enough to make you cast your entire hope upon that fullness that is in Jesus Christ.

The Lord bless you and save you! Amen.

FOR FURTHER THOUGHT

1. *According to Ephesians 1:5, did God predestine you according to the number of things you might do for Him?*
2. *Ephesians 1:5 says we were predestined to adoption. By whom are we adopted?*
3. *Read Romans 8:15 and Galatians 4:6. Both these verses mention the Spirit of adoption. By that Spirit, what do we call God?*

FAITH

But without faith it is impossible to please Him.
HEBREWS 11:6

THE old assembly's catechism asks, "What is the chief end of man?" and its answer is, "To glorify God and to enjoy Him forever." The answer is exceedingly correct. But it might have been equally truthful if it had been shorter. The chief end of man is to please God, for in so doing (we need not say it, because it is an undoubted feat) He will please Himself. The chief end of man, we believe, in this life and in the next, is to please God his Maker. If any man pleases God, he does that which conduces most to his own temporal and eternal welfare. Man cannot please God without bringing to himself a great amount of happiness, for if any man pleases God, it is because God accepts him as His child.

It is because He gives him the blessings of adoption, pours upon him the bounties of His grace, makes him a blessed man in this life, and ensures him a crown of everlasting life, which he will wear and which will shine with unfading luster when the wreaths of earth's glory have all been melted away. While, on the other hand, if a man does *not* please God, he inevitably brings upon himself sorrow and suffering in this life. He puts a worm and rottenness in the eve of all his joys. He fills his death pillow with thorns and he supplies the eternal fire with firewood of flames that will forever consume him.

He who pleases God, is, through divine grace, journeying onward to the ultimate reward of all those who love and fear God. But he who is ill pleasing to God must, for scripture has declared it, be banished from the presence of God and consequently from the enjoyment of happiness. If, then, we are right in saying that to please God is to be happy, the one important question is, how can I please God? And there is something very solemn in the utterance of our text: "But without faith it is impossible to please Him" (Heb. 11:6).

That is to say, do what you may, strive as earnestly as you can, live as excellently as you please, make what sacrifices you choose, be as eminent as you can for everything that is lovely and of good repute—yet none of these things can be pleasing to God unless they are mixed with faith. As the Lord said to the Jews, "Every sacrifice will be seasoned with salt" (Mark 9:49). So He says to us, "With all your doings you must bring faith, or else without faith, it is impossible to please God."

This is an old law. It is as old as the first man. No sooner were Cain and Abel born into this world and no sooner had they attained to manhood than God gave a practical proclamation of this law, that "without faith it is impossible to please Him." Cain and Abel, one bright day, erected altars side by side with each other. Cain fetched of the fruits of the trees and of the abundance of the soil and placed them upon his altar. Abel brought of the firstlings of the flock and laid it upon his altar. It was to be decided which God would accept.

Cain had brought his best, but he brought it without faith. Abel brought his sacrifice, but he brought it with faith in Christ. Now, then, which will best succeed? The offerings are equal in value; so far as they themselves are concerned, they are alike good. Upon which will the heavenly fire descend? Which will the Lord God consume with the fire of His pleasure? Oh, I see Abel's offering burning and Cain's countenance has fallen, for to Abel and to his offering the Lord had respect, but to Cain and his offering the Lord had no respect.

It will be the same till the last man will be gathered into heaven. There will never be an acceptable offering that has not been seasoned with faith. Good though it may be, as apparently good in itself as that which has faith, yet, unless faith is with it, God never can and never will accept it, for He here declares, "Without faith it is impossible to please Him."

I will endeavor to pack my thoughts closely this morning and be as brief as I can, consistently with a full explanation of the theme. I will first have an *exposition* of what faith is. Second, I will have an *argument*, that without faith it is impossible to be saved. And third, I will ask a *question*: Have you that faith that pleases God? We will have, then, an exposition, an argument, and a question.

I. You will notice that the books that were written about two hundred years ago by the old Puritans have more sense in one line than there is in a page of our new books, and more in a page than there is in a whole volume of our modern divinity. The old writers tell you that faith is made up of three things: first, knowledge; then assent; and then what they call affiance, or the laying hold of the knowledge to which we give assent and making it our own by trusting in it.

Let us begin, then, at the beginning. The first thing in faith is knowledge. A man cannot believe what he does not know. That is a clear, self-evident axiom. If I have never heard of a thing in all my life and do not know it, I cannot believe it. And yet there are some persons who have a faith like that of the coal miner, who, when he was asked what he believed, said, "I believe what the church believes."

"What does the church believe?"

"The church believes what I believe."

"And pray, what do you and the church believe?"

"Why, we both believe the same thing."

Now this man believed nothing except that the church was right, but in *what* he could not tell. It is idle for a man to say, "I am a believer," and yet not to know what he believes. But I have seen some persons in this position. A violent sermon has been preached that has stirred up their blood. The minister has cried, "Believe! Believe! Believe!" And the people on a sudden have got it into their heads that they were believers and have walked out of their place of worship and said, "I am a believer."

> I hold no man's faith to be sure faith unless he knows what he believes. If he says, "I believe," and does not know what he believes, how can that be true faith?

And if they were asked, "Pray, what do you believe?" they could not give a reason for the hope that was in them. They believe they intend to go to chapel next Sunday. They intend to join that class of people. They intend to be very violent in their singing and very wonderful in their rant. Therefore they believe they will be saved. But what they believe they cannot tell. Now, I hold no man's faith to be sure faith unless he knows what he believes. If he says, "I believe," and does not know what he believes, how can that be true faith? The apostle has said, "How then shall they call on Him in whom they have not believed? And how shall they believe in Him of whom they have not heard? And how shall they hear without a preacher?" (Rom. 10:14).

It is necessary, then, to true faith, that a man should know something of the Bible. Believe me, this is an age when the Bible is not so much thought of as it used to be. Some hundred years ago the world was covered with bigotry, cruelty, and superstition. We always run to extremes and we have just gone to the other extreme now. It was then said, "One faith is right—down with all others by the rack and by the sword." Now it is said, "However contradictory our creeds may be, they are *all* right."

If we did but use our common sense, we should know that it is not so. But some reply, "Such and such a doctrine need not be preached and need not be believed." Then, sir, if it need not be preached, it need not be revealed. You impugn the wisdom of God when you say a doctrine is unnecessary—for you do as much as say that God has revealed something that was not necessary—and He would be as unwise to do more than was necessary as if He had done less than was necessary. We believe that every doctrine of God's Word ought to be studied by men and that their faith should lay hold of the whole matter of the sacred scriptures and more especially upon all that part of scripture that concerns the person of our all-blessed Redeemer.

There must be some degree of knowledge before there can be faith. "You search the scriptures," He says, "for in them you think you have eternal life; and these are they which testify of Me" (John 5:39). And by searching and reading comes knowledge, and by knowledge comes *faith*, and through faith comes salvation.

But a man may know a thing and yet not have faith. I may know a thing and yet not believe it. Therefore assent must go with faith. That is to say, what we know we must also agree unto as being most certainly the verity of God. Now, in order to have faith, it is necessary not only that I should read the scriptures and understand them but that I should receive them in my soul as being the very truth of the living God. And I should devoutly with my whole heart receive the whole of scripture as being inspired of the Most High and the whole of the doctrine that He requires me to believe to my salvation.

You are not allowed to halve the scriptures and to believe what you please. You are not allowed to believe the scriptures with halfheartedness, for if you do this willfully, you have not the faith that looks alone to Christ. True faith gives its full assent to the scriptures. It takes a page and says, "No matter what is in the page, I believe it." It turns over the next chapter and says, "Herein are some things hard to be understood, which they who are unlearned and unstable do wrest, as they do also the other scriptures, to their destruction. But hard though it be, I believe it."

It sees the Trinity. It cannot understand the Trinity in unity, but it believes it. It sees an atoning sacrifice. There is something difficult in the thought, but it believes it. And whatever it is that it sees in revelation, it devoutly puts his lips to the book and says, "I love it all. I give my full, free, and hearty assent to every word of it whether it is the threat or the promise, the proverb, the precept, or the blessing. I believe that since it is all the Word of God, it is all most assuredly true." Whosoever would be saved must know the scriptures and must give full assent to them.

But a man may have all this and yet not possess true faith, because the chief part of faith is found in the last point, namely, in an *engagement* to the truth. That is, not believing it merely, but taking hold of it as being ours and resting on it for salvation. *Recumbence* on the truth was the word that the old preachers used. You will understand that word. It means "leaning" on it, saying, "This is truth; I trust my salvation on it." Now true faith in its very essence rests in this: a *leaning* upon Christ. It will not save me to know that Christ is a Savior. But it will save me to trust Him to *be* my Savior.

> A man who has not faith proves that he cannot stoop. He has not faith for this reason: He is too proud to believe. He declares he will not yield his intellect; he will not become a child and believe meekly what God tells him to believe.

I will not be delivered from the wrath to come by believing that His atonement is sufficient, but I will be saved by making that atonement my trust, my refuge, and my all. The essence, the *essence* of faith lies in this: a casting of oneself on the promise. It is not the life buoy on board the ship that saves the man when he is drowning, nor is it his belief that it is an excellent and successful invention. No! He must have it around his loins or his hand upon it, or else he will sink.

To use an old and trite illustration, suppose a fire in the upper room of a house and the people gathered in the street. A child is in the upper story. How is he to escape? He cannot leap down—he would be dashed to pieces. A strong man comes beneath and cries, "Drop into my arms." It is a part of faith to know that the man is there; it is another part of faith to believe that the man is strong. But the essence of faith lies in the dropping down into the man's arms. That is the *proof* of faith and the real essence of it.

So, sinner, you are to know that Christ died for sin. You are also to understand that Christ is able to save, and you are to believe that, but you are not saved unless in addition to that, you put your trust in Him to be your Savior and to be yours forever. As Hart says in his hymn, which really expresses the gospel:

> *Venture on Him, venture wholly,*
> *Let no other trust intrude.*
> *None but Jesus*
> *Can do helpless sinners good.*

This is the faith that saves. And however unholy may have been your life up to this hour, this faith, if given to you at this moment, will blot out all your sins, change your nature, and make you a new man in Christ Jesus. It will lead you to live a holy life and make your eternal salvation as secure as if an angel should take you on his bright wings this morning and carry you immediately to heaven. Have you that faith? That is the one all-important question, for while with faith men are saved, without it men are damned.

As Brooks has said in one of his admirable works, "He who believes on the Lord Jesus Christ will be saved, be his sins ever so many. But he who believes not in the Lord Jesus must be damned, be his sins ever so few." Have you faith? For the text declares, "Without faith it is impossible to please God."

II. And now we come to the *argument* as to why without faith we cannot be saved. Now there are some gentlemen present who are saying, "Now we will see whether Mr. Spurgeon has any logic in him." No, you won't, sirs, because I never pretended to exercise it. I hope I have the logic that can appeal to men's hearts, but I am not very prone to use the less powerful logic of the head when I can win the heart in another manner. But if it were needful, I should not be afraid to prove that I know more of logic and of many other things than the little men who undertake to censure me. It would be well if they knew how to hold their tongues, which is at least a fine part of rhetoric.

My argument will be such as I trust will appeal to the heart and conscience, although it may not exactly please those who are always so fond of syllogistic demonstration: "Who could a hair divide between the west and northwest side."

1. "Without faith it is impossible to please God." And I gather it from the fact that there never has been the case of a man recorded in scripture who did please God without faith. The eleventh chapter of Hebrews is the chapter of the men who pleased God. Listen to their names: By faith Abel offered to God a more excellent sacrifice; by faith Enoch was translated; by faith Noah built an ark; by faith Abraham went out into a place that he should afterward receive; by faith he sojourned in the land of promise; by faith Sarah bore Isaac; by faith Abraham offered up Isaac; by faith Moses gave up the wealth of Egypt; by faith Isaac blessed Jacob; by faith Jacob blessed the sons of Joseph; by faith Joseph, when he died, made mention of the departure of the children of Israel; by faith the Red Sea was dried up; by faith the walls of Jericho fell down; by faith the harlot Rahab was saved. "And what more shall I say? For the time would fail me to tell of Gideon and Barak and Samson and Jephthah, also of David and Samuel and the prophets" (Heb. 11:32).

All these were men of faith. Others mentioned in scripture have done something. But God did not accept them. Men have humbled themselves, and yet God has not saved them. Ahab did and yet his sins were never forgiven. Men have repented and yet have not been saved, because theirs was the wrong repentance. Judas repented and went and hanged himself and was not saved. Men have confessed their sins and have not been saved. Saul did it. He said to David, "I have sinned. Return, my son David" (1 Sam. 26:21). And yet he went on as he did before.

Multitudes have confessed the name of Christ and have done many marvelous things, and yet they have never been pleasing to God for this simple reason: They had not faith. And if there is not one mentioned in scripture, which is the history of some four thousand years, it is not likely that in the other two thousand years of the world's history there would have been one, when there was not one during the first four thousand.

2. But the next argument is that faith is the stooping grace, and nothing can make a man stoop without faith. Now unless man does stoop, his sacrifice cannot be accepted. The angels know this. When they praise God, they do it veiling their faces with their wings. The redeemed know it. When

they praise God, they cast their sorrows before His feet. Now a man who has not faith proves that he cannot stoop. He has not faith for this reason: He is too proud to believe. He declares he will not yield his intellect; he will not become a child and believe meekly what God tells him to believe.

He is too proud and he cannot enter heaven, because the door of heaven is so low that no one can enter in by it unless they will bow their heads. There never was a man who could walk into salvation erect. We must go to Christ on our bended knees. For though He is a door big enough for the greatest sinner to come in, He is a door so low that men must stoop if they would be saved. Therefore it is that faith is necessary, because a want of faith is certain evidence of the absence of humility.

3. But now for other reasons. Faith is necessary to salvation because we are told in scripture that *works cannot save*. To tell a very familiar story, and even the poorest may not misunderstand what I say, a minister was one day going to preach. He climbed a hill on his road. Beneath him lay the villages, sleeping in their beauty, with the cornfields motionless in the sunshine. But he did not look at them, for his attention was arrested by a woman standing at her door and who, upon seeing him, came up to him with the greatest anxiety and said, "O sir, have you any keys about you? I have broken the key of my cabinet and there are some things that I must get directly."

Said he, "I have no keys." She was disappointed, expecting that everyone would have some keys. "But suppose," he said, "I had some keys; they might not fit your lock, and therefore you could not get the articles you want. But do not distress yourself; wait till someone else comes up. But," said he, wishing to improve the occasion, "have you ever heard of the key of heaven?"

"Ah, yes," she said, "I have lived long enough and I have gone to church long enough to know that if we work hard, if we get our bread by the sweat of our brow and act well toward our neighbors, if we behave, as the Catechism says, lowly and reverently to all our betters, and if we do our duty in that station of life in which it has pleased God to place us and say our prayers regularly, we will be saved."

"Ah," said he, "my good woman, that is a broken key, for you have broken the commandments; you have not fulfilled all your duties. It is a good key, but you have broken it."

"Pray, sir," said she, believing that he understood the matter and looking frightened, "what have I left out?"

"Why," said he, "the all-important thing: the blood of Jesus Christ. Don't you know it is said the key of heaven is at His girdle? He opens and no man shuts. He shuts and no man opens." And explaining it more fully to her, he said, "It is Christ and Christ alone who can open heaven to you, and not your good works."

"What? Minister," she said, "are our good works useless, then?"

"No," he said, "not *after* faith. If you believe first, you may have as many good works as you please. But if you believe, you will never trust in them. For if you trust in *them*, you have spent them and they are not good works any longer. Have as many good works as you please, but still put your trust wholly in the Lord Jesus Christ. If you do not, your key will never unlock heaven's gate."

So then, my hearers, we must have true faith, because the old key of works is so broken by us all that we never will enter paradise by it. If any of you pretend that you have no sins, to be very plain with you, you deceive yourselves and the truth is not in you. If you conceive that by your good works you will enter heaven, never was there a more fell delusion. You will find at the last great day that your hopes were worthless and that, like sere leaves from the autumn trees, your noble doings will be blown away or kindled into a flame within, and you yourselves must suffer forever. Take heed of your good works! Get them *after* faith, but remember the way to be saved is simply to believe in Jesus Christ.

4. Without faith it is impossible to be saved and to please God, because without faith there is no union to Christ. Now, union to Christ is indispensable to our salvation. If I come before God's throne with my prayers, I will never get them answered unless I bring Christ with me. The Molossians of old, when they could not get a favor from their king, adopted a singular expedient. They took the king's only son in their arms, and falling on their knees, cried, "O King, for your son's sake, grant our request."

He smiled and said, "I deny nothing to those who plead my son's name." It is so with God. He will deny nothing to the man who comes having Christ at his elbow. But if he comes alone, he must be cast away. Union to Christ is, after all, the great point in salvation. Let me tell you a story to illustrate this: The stupendous falls of Niagara have been spoken of in every part of the world. But while they are marvelous to hear of and wonderful as a spectacle, they have been very destructive to human life, when by accident any have been carried down them.

Some years ago, two men were being carried so swiftly down the current that they must both inevitably be borne down and dashed to pieces. Persons on the shore saw them but were unable to do much for their rescue. At last, however, one man was saved when a rope was floated to him and he grasped it. The same instant that the rope came into his hand, a log floated by the other man. The thoughtless and confused bargeman, instead of seizing the rope, laid hold on the log. It was a fatal mistake. They were both in imminent peril, but the one was drawn to shore because he had a connection with the people on the land, while the other, clinging to the log, was borne irresistibly along and never heard of afterward.

Do you not see that here is a practical illustration? Faith is a connection with Christ. Christ is on the shore, so to speak, holding the rope of faith, and if we lay hold of it with the hand of our confidence, He pulls us to shore. But our good works, having no connection with Christ, are drifted along down the gulf of fell despair. Grapple them as tightly as we may, even with hooks of steel, they cannot avail us in the least degree. You will see, I am sure, what I wish to show to you. Some object to anecdotes. I will use them till they are done objecting to them.

The truth is never more powerfully set forth to men than by telling them, as Christ did, a story of a certain man with two sons, or a certain householder who went on a journey, who divided his substance and gave to some ten talents to another one. Faith, then, is a union with Christ. Take care you have it. For if not, cling to your works and there you go floating down the stream! Cling to your works and there you go dashing down the gulf! Lost because your works have no hold on Christ and no connection with the blessed Redeemer!

But you, poor sinner, with all your sin about you, if the rope is round your loins and Christ has a hold of it, fear not:

> *His honor is engaged to save*
> *The mean of His sheep.*
> *All that His heavenly Father gave*
> *His hands securely keep.*

5. Just one more argument and then I have done with it. "Without faith it is impossible to please God," because *it is impossible to persevere in holiness without faith*. What a multitude of fair-weather Christians we have in this

age! Many Christians resemble the nautilus, which in fine smooth weather swims on the surface of the sea in a splendid little squadron, like the mighty ships. But the moment the first breath of wind ruffles the waves, they take in their sails and sink into the depths.

Many Christians are the same. In good company, in evangelical drawing rooms, in pious parlors, in chapels and vestries, they are tremendously religious. But if they are exposed to a little ridicule, if some should smile at them and call them Methodist, or Presbyterian, or some name of reproach, it is all over with their religion till the next fine day. Then when it is fine weather and religion will answer their purpose, up go the sails again and they are as pious as before.

> *Faith is a connection with Christ. Christ is on the shore, so to speak, holding the rope of faith, and if we lay hold of it with the hand of our confidence, He pulls us to shore.*

Believe me, that kind of religion is worse than irreligion. I do like a man to be thoroughly what he is—a downright man. And if a man does not love God, do not let him say he does. But if he is a true Christian, a follower of Jesus, let him say it and stand up for it. There is nothing to be ashamed of in it. The only thing to be ashamed of is to be hypocritical. Let us be honest to our profession and it will be our glory. Ah, what would you do without faith in times of persecution? You good and pious people who have no faith, what would you do if the stake were again erected in Smithfield and if once more the fires consumed the saints to ashes?

What would you do if the Lollard's Tower was again opened? If the rack were again piled, or in the event stocks were used, as they have been used by a Protestant church as witness to the persecution of my predecessor, Benjamin Keach, who was once set in the stocks at Aylesbury for writing a book against infant baptism? If even the mildest form of persecution were revived, how would the people be scattered abroad! And some of the shepherds would be leaving their flocks.

Another anecdote now, and I hope it will lead you to see the necessity of faith, while it may lead me on insensibly to the last part of my discourse. A slaveholding American, on one occasion buying a slave, said to the person from whom he was purchasing him, "Tell me honestly what are his faults."

Said the seller, "He has no faults that I am aware of but one, and that one is, he will pray."

"Ah," said the purchaser, "I don't like that. I know something that will cure him of it pretty soon."

So the next night Cuffey was surprised by his master in the plantation, while in earnest prayer, praying for his new master and his master's wife and family. The man stood and listened but said nothing at that time. But the next morning he called Cuffey and said, "I do not want to quarrel with you, my man, but I'll have no praying on my premises, so you just drop it."

"Massa," said he, "me canna leave off praying. Me must pray."

"I'll teach you to pray, if you are going to keep on at it."

"Massa, me must keep on."

"Well then, I'll give you five and twenty lashes a day till you leave off."

"Massa, if you give me fifty, I must pray."

"If that's the way you are saucy to your master, you will have it directly." So tying him up, he gave him five and twenty lashes and asked him if he would pray again.

"Yes, Massa, me must pray always; me canna leave off." The master looked astonished. He could not understand how a poor saint could keep on praying when it seemed to do no good but only brought persecution upon him. He told his wife of it.

His wife said, "Why can't you let the poor man pray? He does his work very well. You and I do not care about praying, but there's no harm in letting him pray if he gets on with his work."

"But I don't like it," said the master. "He almost frightened me to death. You should see how he looked at me!"

"Was he angry?"

"No, I should not have minded that. But after I had beaten him, he looked at me with tears in his eyes and as if he pitied me more than himself."

That night the master could not sleep. He tossed to and fro on his bed. His sins were brought to his remembrance.

He remembered he had persecuted a saint of God. Rising in his bed, he said, "Wife, will you pray for me?"

"I never prayed in my life," said she. "I cannot pray for you."

"I am lost," he said, "if somebody does not pray for me. I cannot pray for myself."

"I don't know anyone on the estate who knows how to pray, except

Cuffey," said his wife.

The bell was rung and Cuffey was brought in. Taking hold of his black servant's hand, the master said, "Cuffey, can you pray for your master?"

"Massa," said he, "me been praying for you ever since you flogged me, and me mean to pray always for you."

Down went Cuffey on his knees and poured out his soul in tears, and both husband and wife were converted. That Negro could not have done this without faith. Without faith, he would have gone away directly and said, "Massa, me leave off praying. Me no like de white man's whip." But because he persevered through his faith, the Lord honored him and gave him his master's soul for his hire.

III. And now in conclusion, *the question*, the vital question. Dear hearer, have you faith? Do you believe on the Lord Jesus Christ with all your heart? If so, you may hope to be saved. Yes, you may conclude with absolute certainty that you will never see perdition. Have you faith? Shall I help you to answer that question? I will give you three tests, as briefly as ever I can, not to weary you and then bid you farewell this morning.

He who has faith has renounced his own righteousness. If you put one atom of trust in yourself, you have no faith. If you place even a particle of reliance upon anything else but what Christ did, you have no faith. If you trust in your works, then your works are anti-Christ, and Christ and anti-Christ can never go together. Christ will have all or nothing. He must be a whole Savior or none at all. If, then, you have faith, you can say:

> *Nothing in my hands I bring,*
> *Simply to the cross I cling.*

Then true faith may be known by this: It begets a great esteem for the person of Christ. Do you love Christ? Could you die for Him? Do you seek to serve Him? Do you love His people? Can you say:

> *Jesus, I love Your charming name,*
> *'Tis music to my ear.*

Oh, if you do not love Christ, you do not believe in Him, for to believe in Christ begets love. And yet more—he who has true faith will have true *obedience.* If a man says he has faith and has no works, he lies. If any man declares that he believes in Christ and yet does not lead a holy life, he lies.

While we do not trust in good works, we know that faith always begets good works. Faith is the father of holiness, and he has not the parent who loves not the child. God's blessings are blessings with both His hands. In the one hand He gives pardon. But in the other hand He always gives holiness. And no man can have the one unless he has the other.

> *If you place even a particle of reliance upon anything else but what Christ did, you have no faith. If you trust in your works, then your works are anti-Christ, and Christ and anti-Christ can never go together.*

And now, dear hearers, will I get down upon my knees and entreat you for Christ's sake to answer this question in your own silent chamber: Have you faith? Oh, answer it—yes or no? Leave off saying, "I do not know," or "I do not care." Ah, you will care, one day, when the earth is reeling and the world is tossing to and fro. You will care when God will summon you to judgment and when He will condemn the faithless and the unbelieving. Oh, that you were wise—that you would care now and if any of you feel your need of Christ, let me beg of you, for Christ's sake now to seek faith in Him who is exalted on high to give repentance and remission and who, if He has given you repentance, will give you remission, too.

O sinners who know your sins! "Believe on the Lord Jesus Christ, and you will be saved" (Acts 16:31). Cast yourselves upon His love and blood, His doing and His dying, His miseries and His merits. And if you do this you will never fall, but you will be saved now and saved in that great day when not to be saved will be horrible indeed.

"Turn, turn from your evil ways! For why should you die, O house of Israel?" (Ezek. 33:11). Lay hold on Him, touch the hem of His garment, and you will be healed. May God help you to so do, for Christ's sake. Amen and amen.

For Further Thought

1. *According to Hebrews 11:5, what was it about Enoch that pleased God?*
2. *Romans 10:14 mentions one thing that is vital if a person is going to believe. What is that thing?*
3. *Galatians 2:16 says that we are justified by faith. What does this verse say does not justify us before God?*

God Alone the Salvation
of His People

He alone is my rock and my salvation.
PSALM 62:2

HOW noble a title; it is so sublime, suggestive, and overpowering. "My rock." It is a figure so divine that to God alone will it ever be applied. Look on yon rocks and wonder at their antiquity, for from their summits a thousand ages look down upon us. When this gigantic city was as yet unfounded, they were gray with age. When our humanity had not yet breathed the air, 'tis said that these were ancient things. They are the children of departed ages. With awe we look upon these aged rocks, for they are among nature's firstborn. You discover embedded in their bowels the remnants of unknown worlds, of which the wise may *guess*, but which nevertheless, they must fail to *know* unless God Himself should teach them what has been before them.

You regard the rock with reverence, for you remember what stories it might tell if it had a voice, of how through igneous and aqueous agency it has been tortured into the shape it now assumes. Even so is our God preeminently ancient. His head and His hair are white like wool, as white as snow, for He is "the Ancient of Days" (Dan. 7:9), and we are always taught in scripture to remember that He is without "beginning of days" (Heb. 7:3). Long before creation was begotten, "from everlasting to everlasting" He is God (Ps. 90:2).

"My rock!" What a history the rock might give you of the storms to which it has been exposed, of the tempests that have raged in the ocean at its base, and of the thunders that have disturbed the skies above its head while it has stood unscathed by tempests and unmoved by the buffeting of storms. So it is with our God. How firm has He stood, how steadfast has He been, though the nations have reviled Him and the kings of the earth have taken counsel together (see Ps. 2:2). By merely standing still He has broken the ranks of the enemy without even stretching forth His hand!

With motionless grandeur like a rock He has broken the waves and scattered the armies of His enemies, driving them back in confusion. Look at the rock again—see how firm and unmoved it stands! It does not stray from place to place, but it abides fast forever. Other things have changed, islands have been drowned beneath the sea, and continents have been shaken, but see, the rock stands as steadfast as if it were the very foundation of the whole world and could not move till the wreck of creation or the loosening of the bands of nature. So with God—how faithful He is in His promises! How unalterable in His decrees! How unswerving! How unchanging!

> *he mighty God is such a rock. We stand on Him and look down on the world, counting it to be a little thing.*

The rock is immutable; nothing has been worn from it. Yon old granite peak has gleamed in the sun or worn the white veil of winter snow. It has sometimes worshipped God with bare uncovered head, and at other times the clouds furnished it with veiling wings that like a cherub it might adore its Maker. But yet it itself has stood unchanged. The frosts of winter have not destroyed it nor have the heats of summer melted it. It is the same with God. Lo, He is my rock. He is the same and His kingdom will have no end. Unchangeable He is in His being, firm in His own sufficiency. He keeps Himself immutably the same. And "therefore you are not consumed, O sons of Jacob" (Mal. 3:6).

The ten thousand uses of the rock, moreover, are full of ideas as to what God is. You see the fortress standing on a high rock. The clouds can scarcely climb up those precipices upon which the assault cannot be carried. The armed cannot travel, for the besieged laugh at them from their eminence. So is our God a sure defense, and we will not be moved if He has set our feet upon a rock and established our goings (see Ps. 40:2). Many a giant rock is a source of admiration from its elevation. On its summit we can see the world outspread below, like some small map. We mark the river or broadly spreading stream as if it were a vein of silver inlaid in emerald.

We discover the nations beneath our feet, like drops in a bucket, and the islands are little things in the distance, while the sea itself seems but a basin of water, held in the hand of a mighty giant. The mighty God is such a rock. We stand on Him and look down on the world, counting it to be a little thing. We have climbed to Pisgah's top, from the summit of which we can race across this world of storms and troubles to the bright land of spirits; that world unknown to ear or eye, but in which God's truth is revealed to us by the Holy Spirit.

> *I* believe man to be utterly powerless in the first work of his salvation. He cannot break his chains, for though they are not chains of iron, they are chains of his own flesh and blood.

This mighty rock is our refuge and our high observatory from which we see the unseen and have the evidence of things that as yet we have not enjoyed. I need not, however, stop to tell you all about a rock—we might preach for a week upon it—but we give you that for your meditation during the week. "He is my rock." How glorious a thought! How safe am I and how secure and how may I rejoice in the fact that when I wade through Jordan's stream He will be my rock! I will not walk upon a slippery foundation, but I will tread on Him who cannot betray my feet. And I may sing when I am dying, "He is my rock, and there is no unrighteousness in Him" (Ps. 92:15).

We now leave the thought of the rock and proceed to the subject of our discourse, that is, God alone is the salvation of His people. "He only is my rock and my salvation." We will notice, first, *the great doctrine*, that God only is our salvation. Second, *the great experience*, to know and to learn that "He alone is my rock and my salvation." And third, *the great duty*, which you may guess is to give all the glory and the entire honor and place all our faith on Him who alone is our rock and our salvation.

I. The first thing is *the great doctrine* that God alone is our rock and our salvation. If anyone should ask us what we would choose for our motto, as preachers of the gospel, we think we should reply, "God only is our salvation." The late lamented Mr. Denham has put at the foot of his portrait a most admirable text, "Salvation is of the Lord." Now that is just an epitome of Calvinism. It is the sum and the substance of it. If anyone should ask you what you mean by a Calvinist, you may reply, "He is one who says salvation is of the Lord." I cannot find in scripture any other doctrine than this. It is the essence of the Bible. "He alone is my rock and my salvation."

Tell me anything that departs from this and it will be a heresy. Tell me a heresy and I will find its essence in that it has departed from this great, this fundamental, this rocky truth: God is my rock and my salvation. What is the heresy of Rome but the addition of something to the perfect merits of Jesus Christ, the bringing in of the works of the flesh to assist in our justification? And what is that heresy of Arminianism but the secret addition of something to the complete work of the Redeemer? You will find that every heresy, if brought to the touchstone, will discover itself here. It departs from this: "He alone is my rock and my salvation."

Let us now explain this doctrine fully. By the term *salvation* I understand not simply regeneration and conversion, but something more. I do not reckon that is salvation that regenerates me and then puts me in such a position that I may fall out of the covenant and be lost. I cannot call that a bridge that only goes halfway over the stream. I cannot call that salvation that does not carry me all the way to heaven, wash me perfectly clean, and put me among the glorified who sing constant hosannas around the throne. By salvation, then, if I may divide it into parts, I understand deliverance, preservation continually through life, sustenance, and the gathering up of the whole in the perfecting of the saints in the person of Jesus Christ at last.

1. By salvation, I understand *deliverance* from the house of bondage, wherein by nature I am born, and being brought out into the liberty wherewith Christ makes us free, together with a putting us on a rock and establishing our goings. This I understand to be wholly of God. And I think I am right in that conclusion because I find in scripture that man is dead. And how can a dead man assist in his own resurrection? I find that man is utterly depraved and hates the divine change. How can a man, then, work that change that he himself hates? I find man to be ignorant of what it is to be born again and, like Nicodemus, asking the foolish question, "Can [a man] enter a second time into his mother's womb and be born?" (John 3:4).

I cannot conceive that a man can do that which he does not understand, and if he does not know what it is to be born again, he cannot make himself to be born again. No, I believe man to be utterly powerless in the first work of his salvation. He cannot break his chains, for though they are not chains of iron, they are chains of his own flesh and blood. He must first break his own heart before he can break the fetters that bind him. And how should man break his own heart? What hammer is that which I can use upon my own soul to break it, or what fire can I kindle that can dissolve it? No, deliverance is of God alone. The doctrine is affirmed continually in scripture. And he who does not believe it does not receive God's truth. Deliverance is of God alone. "Salvation is of the Lord."

2. And if we are delivered and made alive in Christ, still *preservation* is of the Lord alone. If I am prayerful, God makes me prayerful. If I have graces, God gives me graces. If I have fruits, God gives me fruits. If I hold on in a consistent life, God holds me on in a consistent life. I do nothing whatever toward my own preservation except what God Himself first does in me. Whatever I have, all my goodness is of the Lord alone. Wherein I sin, *that* is my own, but wherein I act rightly, that is of God, wholly and completely. If I have repulsed an enemy, His strength nerved my arm. Did I strike a foe to the ground? God's strength sharpened my sword and gave me courage to strike the blow.

Do I preach His Word? It is not I, but grace that is in me. Do I live to God a holy life? It is not I, but Christ who lives in me. Am I sanctified? I did not sanctify myself. God's Holy Spirit sanctifies me. Am I weaned from the world? I am weaned by God's chastisements. Do I grow in knowledge? The great Instructor teaches me. I find in God all I want. But I find in myself nothing. "He alone is my rock and my salvation."

3. And again, *sustenance* also is absolutely requisite. We need sustenance in providence for our bodies and sustenance in grace for our souls. Providential mercies are wholly from the Lord. It is true the rain falls from heaven and waters the earth and "make[s] it bring forth and bud, that it may give seed to the sower and bread to the eater" (Isa. 55:10). But out of whose hand comes the rain and from whose fingers do the dewdrops distill? It is true, the sun shines and makes the plants grow and bud and bring forth the blossom and its heat ripens the fruit upon the tree. But who gives the sun its light and who scatters the genial heat from it? It is true, I work and toil, and this brow sweats. These hands are weary. I cast myself upon my bed and there I rest, but I do not ascribe my preservation to my own might. Who makes these sinews strong? Who makes these lungs like iron and who makes these nerves of steel? "He alone is my rock and my salvation."

He alone is the salvation of my body and the salvation of my soul. Do I feed on the Word? That Word would be no food for me unless the Lord made it food for my soul and helped me to feed upon it. Do I live on the manna that comes down from heaven? What is that manna but Jesus Christ incarnate, whose body and whose blood I eat and drink? Am I continually receiving fresh increase of might? Where do I gather my might? My salvation is of Him. Without Him I can do nothing. As a branch cannot bring forth fruit except it abide in the vine, no more can I except I abide in Him.

4. Then if we gather the three thoughts in one, the *perfection* we will soon have when we will stand yonder, near God's throne, will be wholly of the Lord. That bright crown that will sparkle on our brow like a constellation of brilliant stars will have been fashioned only by our God. I go to a land, but it is a land that the plow of earth has never upturned, though it is greener than earth's best pastures. And though it is richer than all her harvests ever saw, I go to a building of more gorgeous architecture than man has built. It is not of mortal architecture. It is "a house not made with hands, eternal in the heavens" (2 Cor. 5:1). The Lord will give all I will know in heaven. And I will say when at last I appear before Him:

> Grace all the work will crown
> Through everlasting days;
> It lays in heaven the topmost stone,
> And well deserves the praise.

II. And now, beloved, we come to *the great experience*. The greatest of all experience, I take it, is to know that "He alone is my rock and my salvation." We have been insisting upon a doctrine. But doctrine is nothing unless proved in our experience. Most of God's doctrines are only to be learned by practice—by taking them out into the world and letting them bear the wear and tear of life. If I ask any Christian in this place whether this doctrine is true, if he has had any deep experience, he will reply, "True I say, that it is. Not one word in God's Bible is truer than that, for indeed salvation is of God alone." "He [only] is my rock and my salvation."

But, beloved, it is very hard to have such an experimental knowledge of the doctrine that we never depart from it. It is very hard to believe that salvation is of the Lord. There are times when we put our confidence in something else but God, and we sin by linking hand in hand with God something besides Him. Let me now dwell a little upon the experience that will bring us to know that salvation is of God alone.

The true Christian will confess that salvation is of God alone *effectively*, that is, that God works in him to will and to do of His own pleasure. Looking back on my past life, I can see that the dawning of it all was of God and of God effectively. I took no torch with which to light the sun, but the sun did light me. I did not commence my spiritual life. No, I rather kicked and struggled against the things of the Spirit. When He drew me, for a time I did not run after Him. There was a natural hatred in my soul of everything holy and good. Wooing was lost upon me. Warnings were cast to the wind. Thunders were despised.

And as for the whispers of His love, they were rejected as being less than nothing and vanity. But sure I am, I can say now, speaking on behalf of myself and of all who know the Lord, "He alone is my salvation and your salvation, too." It was He who turned your heart and brought you down on your knees. You can say in very deed, then:

> *Grace taught my soul to pray,*
> *Grace made my eyes overflow.*

And coming to this moment, you can say:

> *'Tis grace has kept me to this day,*
> *And will not let me go.*

I remember when I was coming to the Lord. I thought I was doing it all myself, and though I sought the Lord earnestly, I had no idea the Lord was seeking me. I do not think the young convert is at first aware of this. One day when I was sitting in the house of God, I was not thinking much about the man's sermon, for I did not believe it. The thought struck me, *How did you come to be a Christian?* I sought the Lord. *But how did you come to seek the Lord?* The thought flashed across my mind in a moment, *I would not have sought Him unless there had been some previous influence in my mind to make me seek Him.*

I am sure you will not be many weeks a Christian, certainly not many months, before you will say, "I ascribe my change wholly to God." I desire to make this my constant confession. I know there are some who preach one gospel in the morning and another at night, who preach a good sound gospel in the morning because they are preaching to saints, but preach falsehood in the evening because they are preaching to sinners. But there is no necessity to preach truth at one time and falsehood at another. "The law of the LORD is perfect, converting the soul" (Ps. 19:7).

There is no need to put anything else in it in order to bring sinners to the Savior. But, my brothers and sisters, you must confess, "Salvation is of the Lord." When you turn back to the past, you must say, "My Lord, whatever I have, you gave it to me. Have I the wings of faith? I was a wingless creature once. Have I the eyes of faith? I was a blind creature once. I was dead till you made me alive, blind till you opened my eyes. My heart was a loathsome dunghill, but you put pearls there, if pearls there are, for pearls are not the produce of dunghills. You have given me all I have."

And so, if you look at the present, if your experience is that of a child of God, you will trace all to Him. Not only all you have had in the past, but all you have now. Here you are, sitting in your pew this morning. I just want you to review where you stand. Beloved, do you think you would be where you are now if it were not for divine grace? Only think what a strong temptation you had yesterday. They did consult to cast you down from your excellence (see Ps. 62:4). Perhaps you were served like I am sometimes. The devil sometimes seems to drag me right to the edge of a precipice of sin by a kind of enchantment, making me forget the danger by the sweetness that surrounds it.

And just when he would push me down, I see beneath me the yawning gulf and some strong hand put out; and I hear a voice saying, "Deliver him from going down to the Pit; I have found a ransom" (Job 33:24). Do you not feel that before this sun goes down you will be damned if grace does not keep you? Have you anything good in your heart that grace did not give you? If I thought I had a grace that did not come from God, I would trample it beneath my feet, as not being a godly virtue. I would guess it to be but a counterfeit, for it could not be right if it did not come from the mint of glory. It may look ever so much like the right thing, but it is certainly bad unless it came from God. Christian, can you say of all things past and present, "He alone is my rock and my salvation"?

And now look forward to the future. Man! Think how many enemies you have. How many rivers you have to cross, how many mountains to climb, how many dragons to fight, how many lions' teeth to escape, how many fires to pass through, how many floods to wade. What do you think, man? Can your salvation be of anything except of God? Oh, if I had not that everlasting arm to lean upon, I would cry, "Death! Hurl me anywhere!

Anywhere out of the world." If I had not that one hope, that one trust, bury me ten thousand fathoms deep beneath creation where my being might be forgotten! Oh, put me far away, for I am miserable if I have not God to help me all through my journey.

Are you strong enough to fight with one of your enemies without your God? I think not. A little silly maid may cast a Peter down and cast you down, too, if God does not keep you. I beseech you, remember this. I hope you know it by experience in the past, but try to remember it in the future—wherever you go, "salvation is of the Lord." Do not get to looking at your heart; do not get to examining to see whether you have anything to recommend you; just remember, salvation is of the Lord. "He alone is my rock and my salvation."

Effectively, it all comes of God. And I am sure we must add *meritoriously*. We have experienced that salvation is wholly of Him. What merits have I? If I were to scrape together all I ever had and then come to you and beg all you have got, I should not collect the value of a farthing among you all. We have heard of some Catholic who said that there was a balance struck in his favor between his good works and his bad ones and therefore he felt he deserved heaven. But there is nothing of the sort here.

I have seen many people, many kinds of Christians and many odd Christians, but I never yet met with one who said he had any merits of his own when he came to close quarters. We have heard of perfect men and we have heard of men perfectly foolish. And we have thought the characters perfectly alike. Have we any merits of our own? I am sure we have not if we have been taught of God. Once we thought we had. But there came a man called Conviction into our house one night and took away our glorying. Ah, we are vile still. I don't know whether Cowper said quite right when he said:

> *Since the dear hour that brought me to your foot*
> *And cut up all my follies by the root,*
> *I never trusted in an arm but yours,*
> *Nor hoped but in your righteousness divine!*

I think he made a mistake, for most Christians get trusting in self at times, but we are forced to own that salvation is of the Lord if we consider it meritoriously.

My dear friends, have you experienced this in your own hearts? Can you say "amen" to that as it goes round? Can you say, "I know that God is my helper?" I daresay you can, most of you. But you will not say it so well as you will by and by, if God teaches you. We *believe* it when we commence the Christian life, and we *know* it afterward. And the longer we live, the more we find it to be the truth: "Cursed is the man who trusts in man and makes flesh his strength, whose heart departs from the LORD" (Jer. 17:5). In fact, the crown of Christian experience is to be delivered from all trust in self or man and to be brought to rely wholly and simply on Jesus Christ.

> *If your experience is that of a child of God, you will trace all to Him. Not only all you have had in the past, but all you have now.*

I say, Christian, your highest and noblest experience is not to be groaning about your corruption, is not to be crying about your wanderings, but is to say, "With all my sin and care and woe, His Spirit will not let me go." "Lord, I believe; help my unbelief!" (Mark 9:24). I like what Luther says: "I would run into Christ's arms if He had a drawn sword in His hands." That is called venturesome believing. But as an old divine says, there is no such thing as venturesome believing. We cannot venture on Christ because it is no venture at all; there is no haphazard in the least degree.

It is a holy and heavenly experience when we can go to Christ amid the storm and say, "Oh, Jesus, I believe I am covered by your blood"—when we can feel ourselves to be all over rags and yet can say, "Lord, I believe that through Christ Jesus, ragged though I am, I am fully absolved." A saint's faith is little faith when he believes as a saint, but a sinner's faith is true faith when he believes as a sinner. The faith not of a sinless being but of a sinful creature, that is the faith that delights God. Go then, Christian. Ask that this may be your experience, to learn each day, "He alone is my rock and my salvation."

III. And now, in the third place, we speak of *the great duty*. We have had the great experience; now we must have the great duty.

The great duty is this: If God only is our rock and we know it, are we not bound to put all our trust in God, to give all our love to God, to set all our hope *upon* God, to spend all our life *for* God, and to devote our whole being to God? If God is all I have, surely all I have will be God's. If God alone is my hope, surely I will put all my hope upon God. If the love of God is alone that which saves, surely He will have my love alone. Come, let me talk to you for a little while, Christian. I want to warn you not to have two Gods, two Christs, two friends, two husbands, and two great fathers. Do not have two fountains, two rivers, two suns, or two heavens, but have only one. I want to bid you now, as God has put all salvation in Himself, to bring all yourself to God. Come, let me talk to you!

In the first place, Christian, *never join anything with Christ.* Would you stitch your old rags into the new garment He gives? Would you put new wine into old bottles? Would you put Christ and self together? You might as well yoke an elephant and an ant. They could never plow together. What? Would you put an archangel in the same harness with a worm and hope that they would drag you through the sky? How inconsistent! How foolish! What? You and Christ? Surely Christ would smile. No, Christ would *weep* to think of such a thing! Christ and man together? Christ and company? No, it never will be. He will have nothing of the sort!

He must be all. Note how inconsistent it would be to put anything else with Him. And note, again, how *wrong* it would be. Christ will never bear to have anything else placed with Him. He calls them adulterers and fornicators who love anything else but Him. He will have your whole heart to trust in Him, your whole soul to love Him, and your whole life to honor Him. He will not come into your house till you put all the keys at His feet. He will not come till you give Him attic, parlor, drawing room, and cellar, too. He will make you sing:

> *Yet if I might make some reserve,*
> *And duty did not call,*
> *I love my God with zeal so great*
> *That I should give Him all.*

Mark you, Christian, it is a sin to keep anything from God. Remember, *Christ is very grieved* if you do it. Assuredly you do not desire to grieve Him who shed His blood for you? Surely there is not one child of God here who would like to vex his blessed Elder Brother? There cannot be one soul redeemed by blood who would like to see those sweet blessed eyes of our

Best Beloved bedewed with tears. I know you will not grieve your Lord, will you? But I tell you, you will vex His noble spirit if you love anything but Him. He is so fond of you that He is jealous of your love. It is said concerning His Father that He is a jealous God, and He is a jealous Christ you have to deal with. Therefore put not your trust in chariots, stay not yourselves in horses, but say, "He alone is my rock and my salvation."

> *A saint's faith is little faith when he believes as a saint, but a sinner's faith is true faith when he believes as a sinner. The faith not of a sinless being but of a sinful creature, that is the faith that delights God.*

I beg you, mark also one reason why you should not look at anything else, and that is if you look at anything else, *you cannot see Christ so well.* "Oh," you say, "I can see Christ in His mercies." But you cannot see Him so well there as if you viewed His person. No man can look at two objects at the same time and see both distinctly. You may afford a wink for the world and a wink for Christ. But you cannot give Christ a whole look and a whole eye and the world half an eye, too. I beseech you, brothers and sisters, do not try it. If you look on the world, it will be a speck in your eye. If you trust in anything but Christ, between two stools you will come to the ground, and a fearful fall will you have. Therefore, Christian, look only on Him. "He alone is my rock and my salvation."

Mark you again Christian, I would bid you never put anything else with Christ. For as sure as ever you do, *you will have the whip for it.* There never was a child of God who harbored one of the Lord's traitors in his heart but he always had a charge laid against him. God has sent out a search warrant against all of us—and do you know what He has told His officers to search for? He has told them to search for all our lovers, all our treasures, and all our helpers. God cares less about our sins as sins than He does about our sins, or even our virtues, as usurpers of His throne. I tell you there is nothing in the world you set your heart upon that will not be hung upon a gallows higher than Haman's.

If you love anything but Christ, He will make you regret it. If you love your house better than Christ, He will make it a prison for you. If you love your child better than Christ, He will make it an adder in your breast to sting you. If you love your daily provisions better than Christ, He will make your drink bitter and your food like gravel in your mouth. Till you come to live wholly in Him, there is nothing that you have that He cannot turn into a rod if you love it better than Him.

And, mark once again, if you look at anything except God, *you will soon fall into sin.* There was never a man who kept his eye on anything save Christ who did not go wrong. If the mariner will steer by the pole star, he will go to the north. But if he steers sometimes by the pole star and sometimes by another constellation, he knows not where he will go. If you do not keep your eye wholly on Christ, you will soon be wrong. If you ever do give up the secret of your strength, namely, your trust in Christ; if you ever dally with the Delilah of the world and love yourself more than Christ, the Philistines will be upon you and shear your locks and take you out to grind at the mill. And you will surely grind till your God gives you deliverance by means of your hair growing once more and bringing you to trust wholly in the Savior.

> *I*f the mariner will steer by the pole star, he will go to the north. But if he steers sometimes by the pole star and sometimes by another constellation, he knows not where he will go. If you do not keep your eye wholly on Christ, you will soon be wrong.

Keep your eye, then, fixed on Jesus. For if you do turn away from Him, how ill will you fare! I bid you, Christian, beware of your graces. Beware of your virtues. Beware of your experience. Beware of your prayers. Beware of your hope. Beware of your humility. There is not one of your graces that may not damn you if they are left alone to themselves. Old Brooks says when a woman has a husband and that husband gives to her some choice rings, she puts them on her fingers. And if she should be so foolish as to love the rings better than her husband, if she should care only for the jewels and forget him who gave them, how angry would the husband be and how foolish she would be herself! Christian! I warn you, beware of your graces, for they may prove more dangerous to you than your sins.

I warn you of everything in this world. For everything has this tendency, especially a high estate. If we have a comfortable maintenance, we are most likely not to look so much to God. Ah, Christian with an independent fortune, take care of your money; beware of your gold and silver. It will curse you if it comes between you and your God. Always keep your eyes out to the cloud and not to the rain, to the river and not to the ship that floats on its bosom. Look not to the sunbeam but to the sun. Trace your mercies to God and say perpetually, "He alone is my rock and my salvation."

Lastly, I bid you once more to keep your eyes wholly on God and on nothing in yourself, because what are you now and what were you ever but a poor damned sinner if you were out of Christ? I had been preaching the other day all the former part of the sermon as a minister. Presently I thought I was a poor sinner, and then how differently I began to speak! The best sermons I ever preach are those I preach not in my ministerial capacity, but as a poor sinner preaching to sinners. I find there is nothing like a minister remembering that he is nothing but a poor sinner, after all. It is said of the peacock that although he has fine feathers, he is ashamed of his black feet. I am sure that we ought to be ashamed of ours.

However bright our feathers may appear at times, we ought to think of what we should be if grace did not help us. Oh, Christian, keep your eye on Christ, for out of Him you are no better than the damned in hell. There is not a demon in the pit but might put you to the blush if you are out of Christ. Oh, that you would be humble! Remember what an evil heart you have within you, even when grace is there. You have grace. God loves you, but remember, you have a foul cancer in your heart still. God has removed much of your sin, but still the corruption remains. We feel that though the old man is somewhat choked and the fire somewhat dampened by the sweet waters of the Holy Spirit's influence, yet it would blaze up worse than before if God did not keep it under.

Let us not glory in ourselves, then. The slave need not be proud of his descent; he has the brand-mark upon his hand. Out with pride! Away with it! Let us rest wholly and solely upon Jesus Christ.

Now, just one word to the ungodly—you who do not know Christ—you have heard what I have told you, that salvation is of Christ alone. Is not that a good doctrine for you? For you have not got anything, have you? You are a poor, lost, ruined sinner. Hear this, then, sinner: You have nothing and you do not want anything, for Christ has all. "Oh," you say, "I am a bond slave." Ah, but He has got the redemption. "No," you say, "I am black with sin." Yes, but He has got the bath that can wash you white. You say, "I am leprous!" Yes, but the Great Physician can take your leprosy away. You say, "I am condemned." Yes, but He has got the acquittal warrant signed and sealed, if you believe in Him.

You say, "But I am dead!" Yes, but Christ has life and He can give you life. You want nothing of your own—nothing to rely on but Christ. And if there is a man, woman, or child here who is prepared to say solemnly after me, with his or her heart, "I take Christ to be my Savior, with no powers and no merits of my own to trust in. I see my sins, but I see that Christ is higher than my sins. I see my guilt, but I believe that Christ is mightier than my guilt," I say, if any one of you can say that, you may go away and rejoice, for you are heirs of the kingdom of heaven.

> *Here, Lord, I believe in Jesus Christ. I have brought no money to pay for my soul, for there is the ticket; the money has been paid long ago. This is written in your Word: 'The blood of Christ cleans from all sin.'"*

I must tell you a singular story that was related at our church meeting, because there may be some very poor people here who may understand the way of salvation by it. One of the friends had been to see a person who was about to join the church. And he said to him, "Can you tell me what you would say to a poor sinner who came to ask you the way of salvation?"

"Well," said he, "I do not know. I think I can hardly tell you. But it so happened that a case of this sort did occur yesterday. A poor woman came into my shop and I told her the way. But it was in such a homely manner that I don't like to repeat it."

"Oh, tell me. I should like to hear it."

"Well, she is a poor woman who is always pawning her things, and by and by she redeems them again. I did not know how to tell her better than this. I said to her, 'Look here. Your soul is in pawn to the devil. Christ has paid the redemption money. You take faith for your ticket and so you will get your soul out of pawn.'"

Now, that was the simplest but the most excellent way of imparting a knowledge of salvation to this woman. It is true our souls were pawned to almighty vengeance. We were poor and could not pay the redemption money. But Christ came and paid it all, and faith is the ticket that we use to get our souls out of pawn.

We need not take a single penny with us. We have only to say, "Here, Lord, I believe in Jesus Christ. I have brought no money to pay for my soul, for there is the ticket; the money has been paid long ago. This is written in your Word: 'The blood of Christ cleans from all sin.'" If you take that ticket, you will get your soul out of pawn. And you will then say, "I'm forgiven, I'm forgiven, I'm a miracle of grace." May God bless you, my friends, for Christ's sake. Amen.

For Further Thought

1. *According to 2 Timothy 2:10, where is salvation found?*
2. *Second Corinthians 5:18 mentions our reconciliation with God. It gives the reason why this has happened. What is this reason?*
3. *Since only God is our salvation, what does 1 Corinthians 15:28 say is the end of God's purpose?*

Human Depravity
and Divine Mercy

And the LORD smelled a soothing aroma. Then the LORD said in His heart, "I will never again curse the ground for man's sake, although the imagination of man's heart is evil from his youth; nor will I again destroy every living thing as I have done."
GENESIS 8:21

PETER tells us that Noah's ark and baptism are figures of salvation. He puts the two together as pictures of the way by which we are saved. Noah was not saved by the world's being gradually reformed and restored to its primitive innocence, but a sentence of condemnation was pronounced, and death, burial, and resurrection ensued. Noah must go into the ark and become dead to the world. The floods must descend from heaven and rise upward from their secret fountains beneath the earth. The ark must be submerged with many waters—here was burial. And then after a time Noah and his family must come out into a totally new world of resurrection life.

It is the same in the figure of baptism. The person baptized, if he is already dead with Christ, is buried, not purified and improved, but buried beneath the waves. And when he rises he professes that he enjoys newness of life. Baptism is setting forth just what Noah's ark set forth, that salvation is by death and burial. You must be dead to the world. The flesh must be dead with Christ, buried with Christ; not improved, not made better, but utterly put aside as unimprovable, as worthless, dead, a thing to be buried and to be forgotten.

And we must come forth in resurrection life, feeling that above us there is a new heaven and beneath us a new earth where righteousness dwells, seeing that we are new creatures in Christ Jesus. It would be very instructive to dwell upon each point of the resemblance between Noah's deliverance and the salvation of every elect soul. Noah enters into the ark—there is a time when we distinctly enter into Christ and become one with Him. Noah was shut in the ark so that he could never come out again till God should open the door. There is a time when every child of God is shut in, when faith and full assurance give him evidence that he is indissolubly one with Christ Jesus. He is grasped in Christ's hand so that none can pluck him out. He is hidden in Christ's loins so that none can separate him from the love of God.

Then comes the flood, a season in the Christian's experience when he discovers his own depravity. He is saved. He is in the ark. He is, however, still a sinner, still the subject of inbred lusts. Suddenly all these corruptions break up! They beat upon his ark, they assail his faith, and they endeavor, if possible, to drown his soul in sin. But they do not destroy him, for by the grace of God he is where other men are not. He is where he cannot be drowned by sin. He is in Christ Jesus! He mounts as the floods deepen. The more he feels the depth of his depravity, the more he admires the fullness of the atoning sacrifice! The more terrible the temptation, the more joyous is his consolation in Christ Jesus.

> Noah was not saved by the world's being gradually reformed and restored to its primitive innocence, but a sentence of condemnation was pronounced, and death, burial, and resurrection ensued.

And so he rises in holy communion toward his God. Then comes the wind, typical of the breath of the sacred Spirit, by which the floods of corruption are calmed, and peace reigns within and the soul sings, "Therefore, having been justified by faith, we have peace with God through our Lord Jesus Christ" (Rom. 5:1). Then the tops of the mountains appear; sanctification takes place upon a part of the man. There are some bright graces that glisten out of the general flood of corruption. There are some points of his newborn nature that delight him with their beauty. His ark has grounded and settled. He no longer floats, so to speak, tossed about with a struggling faith and contending unbelief. He feels that as Christ Jesus is forever seated firmly at the right hand of God, so he, in Christ Jesus, has entered into rest.

The ark grounded on the top of Ararat. So does the believer's experience come to a settled condition. He is no more moved about with fears and questions but rejoices in the hope of the glory of God. He sends forth his thoughts in search after evidence of his complete salvation, and probably he sends out some of his own ignorant carnal expectations, just as Noah sent out the raven. These ignorant imaginations of what the work of the Spirit is go forth and never return because no unclean child of the old Adam can be a discerner of the new world. Then he sends out the dove; holy desires, earnest prayers go to and fro. By and by they come back with a token for good, some choice mercy from the hand of God—an olive branch of assured peace—and the believer surely knows not only that he is in Christ, not only that he is grounded in Christ, but that all the waters are calmed, all sin is gone, all danger removed, all death destroyed!

Then occurs a period when God opens the door. Christ had been as a sort of prison to the Christian up till then. The cross had been a burden. He did not rejoice in liberty. But God the Father now comes with the blessed Spirit and opens the door, and the believer is fully at liberty in the new world. The saved soul's first act is, like Noah's, to build an altar to God and, as a priest, to offer a sacrifice that, as it rises to heaven, is accepted because it is a memorial of Christ. The Lord smells a sweat savor, and though the believing man is still full of sin and from his youth up has an evil imagination, yet he hears the covenant voice that says, "I will no more curse. I will no more destroy."

He hears the covenant promise that confirms forever the faithfulness of God, and he rejoices to inherit, like Noah, a new world where righteousness dwells. I do not lay any stress upon these interpretations, but I know the apostle says concerning Hagar and Sarah, "Which things are an allegory" (Gal. 4:24 KJV). I believe that the book of Genesis is a book of dispensational truth, and if it were rightly read, not by the eye of curiosity, but by the heart of the student who has been made wise to see the deep things of God, very much of divine and holy teaching would be discovered in it.

But now I come to the text itself. We have here, first, *a very sad and painful fact*: "The imagination of man's heart is evil from his youth." We have, second, *God's most extraordinary reasoning*: "I will never again curse the ground for man's sake, although the imagination of man's heart is evil." Then, third, we have *some inferences less extraordinary* but practical to ourselves from the text.

I. To begin, then, with the text, we have here *a most painful fact* that man's nature is incurable. "The imagination of man's heart is evil from his youth."

You will remember, *before* the flood, in the fifth verse of the sixth chapter, it is written, "Then the LORD saw that the wickedness of man was great in the earth, and that every intent of the thoughts of his heart was only evil continually" (Gen. 6:5). After the flood it is just the same. The description in the sixth chapter belonged to the entire antediluvian race.

You might have hoped that after so terrible a judgment, when only a picked and peculiar few, that is, eight, were saved by water, that man began anew with a better stock, the old branches that were sere and rotten being cut away so the nature of man would be improved. It is not one whit so. The same God who, looking at man, declared that his imagination was evil before the flood, pronounces the very same verdict upon them afterward. O God! How hopeless is human nature! How impossible is it that the carnal mind should be reconciled to God! How needful is it that You should give us new hearts and right spirits, seeing that the old nature is so evil that even the floods of your judgments cannot cure it of its evil imaginations!

> *The sons of God saw the daughters of men, that they were fair, and the two races became mingled so as to produce monsters of iniquity.*

I would have you studiously notice the words used in both these passages, the antediluvian and the postdiluvian verdict of God. Look at the fifth verse of the sixth chapter. God saw not only outward sin that was great and multiplied and cried to Him for vengeance, He saw sin in the sons of men, the descendants of Cain. Worse still, He saw treachery and departure from God in the sons of the chosen ones; the sons of Seth had gone astray also. The sons of God saw the daughters of men, that they were fair, and the two races became mingled so as to produce monsters of iniquity. But worse than that, He saw that the thoughts of men's hearts were evil—man could not think without being evil.

No, more! The substratum that underlies actual thought is unformed, unfashioned thought—the eggs, the embryos of thought that are here called the imagination of the thought, the first conception, the infant motions of the soul—all these God found to be evil. But observe, He says they were "only evil." Not one trace of good! No gold amidst the dross, no light amidst the darkness—they were "only evil." And then He adds that word *continually.* What? Never any repentance? Never any yearning toward the right? No pure drops of holiness now and then? No, never!

"Every imagination"—notice that word. The whole verse is most clear, a broom that sweeps man clean of all boasted good. "Every imagination"— when he was at his best, when he stood at God's altar, when he tried to be right—even then his thoughts had evil in them! Dr. Dick says, "All man's thoughts, all his desires, all his purposes are evil, expressly or by implication, because the subject of them is avowedly sinful, or because they do not proceed from a holy principle and are not directed to a proper end. It is not *occasionally* that the human soul is thus under the influence of depravity. This is its habit and state. It seems impossible to construct a sentence that should more distinctly express its total corruption than this."

Look at this other passage that is our text. You will see it gives a different phase of the same evil, but it does not abate one jot or tittle of it. It is still "the imagination of man's heart." It is still the inward character, the core, the pith, and the marrow of mankind that God is dealing with. It is not the stream that comes from man that is foul, but the fountain of man, the innermost source of the fountain! The imagination of his heart is evil, and we are told here what we are not told in the other text, that his thoughts are evil from his youth, that is to say, from his earliest childhood.

And it would not be evil from his childhood in every case if there were not certain seeds of evil sown *before* that, and therefore we can go further and in the words of Holy Scripture we can confess with sorrowful truthfulness, "Behold, I was brought forth in iniquity, and in sin my mother conceived me" (Ps. 51:5). From the very earliest imaginable period in which human nature exists, it is a defiled, tainted thing and only worthy of God's utter abhorrence! And were it not that He smells a sweet savor in the sacrifice of Christ, He would say, as He did say in the sixth chapter, "I will destroy man whom I have created from the face of the earth, both man and beast, creeping thing and birds of the air, for I am sorry that I have made them" (Gen. 6:7).

I have thus brought out this painful fact distinctly, I hope, before you. It is true both before and after the flood. If you want any proof of its being true now, turn to the scores of passages of scripture that all prove it. I think, however, if our time were limited, as it is this morning, I should prefer to mention the third chapter of Paul's Epistle to the Romans. It is the most sweeping description of the universality of human depravity that could possibly have been penned. I will read from the ninth to the nineteenth verse:

> What then? Are we better than they? Not at all. For we
> have previously charged both Jews and Greeks that they
> are all under sin. As it is written:
> "There is none righteous, no, not one;
> There is none who understands;
> There is none who seeks after God.
> They have all turned aside;
> They have together become unprofitable;
> There is none who does good, no, not one."
> "Their throat is an open tomb;
> With their tongues they have practiced deceit";
> "The poison of asps is under their lips";
> "Whose mouth is full of cursing and bitterness."
> "Their feet are swift to shed blood;
> Destruction and misery are in their ways;
> And the way of peace they have not known."
> "There is no fear of God before their eyes."
>
> Now we know that whatever the law says, it says to those
> who are under the law, that every mouth may be stopped,
> and all the world may become guilty before God.

Jonathan Edwards says upon this passage:

> If the words that the apostle uses here [Rom. 3:10–19] do
> not most fully and determinately signify a universality, no
> words ever used in the Bible, or elsewhere, are sufficient
> to do it. I might challenge any man to produce any one
> paragraph in the scripture, from the beginning to the end,
> where there is such a repetition and accumulation of terms
> so strongly and emphatically and carefully formulated to
> express the most perfect and absolutely universality, or
> any place to be compared to it. What instance is there
> in the scripture, or indeed any other writing, when the
> meaning is only the much greater part? Where is meaning

is signified in such a manner by repeating such expressions as "they are all," "they are all together," "every one," "all the world" joined to multiplied negative terms to show the universality to be without exception? Saying, "There is no flesh. . .there is none, there is none, there is none, there is none," four times over besides the addition of "no, not one," "no, not one," once and again so that if this matter of universal depravity is not here set forth plainly, expressly, and fully, it must be because no words can do it and it is not in the power of language or any manner of terms and phrases, however contrived and heaped one upon another, determinately to let us remember the confessions of God's people.

You never heard a saint on his knees yet tell the Lord that he had a good nature, that he did not need renewing. Saints, as they grow in divine grace, are made to feel more and more acutely the evil of their old nature. You will find that those who are most like Christ have the deepest knowledge of their own depravity and are humblest while they confess their sinfulness. Those men who know not their own hearts may be able to boast, but that is simple ignorance, for if you will take down the biographies of any persons esteemed among us for holiness and for knowledge in the things of God, you will find them frequently crying out under a sense of inward carnality and sin.

If I may return to scripture, I cannot help quoting David: "I was brought forth in iniquity, and in sin my mother conceived me" (Ps. 51:5). It is a most villainous thing that some persons try to slander David's mother and suppose that there was something irregular about his birth that made him speak as he has done, whereas there cannot be the slightest imputation upon that admirable woman. David himself speaks of her with intense respect and says, "Save the son of your handmaid," as though he felt it no discredit to be the son of such a woman.

She was, doubtless, one of the excellent of the earth, and yet, excellent as she was, it could not but be otherwise that in sin her son was conceived. Let us not at all attempt to escape from the force of what David says. He is using no exaggerated expressions. There is no indication of hyperbole throughout the whole psalm. He is a brokenhearted man on his knees. He is confessing his own sin with Bathsheba and is not likely either to bring any accusation against his own mother or to use exaggerated terms! Beloved, it is so. We, all of us, the best of us, still have to bear about with us the marks of the unclean thing from which we sprang.

Take Paul again: Was there ever a man who knew more of what sanctity of nature means, or who was brought nearer to the image of Christ? Yet he cries out, "O wretched man that I am! Who will deliver me from this body of death?" (Rom. 7:24). He finds no joy until he can say, "I thank God through Jesus Christ our Lord." Still I think we have another proof, namely, our own observation. We have lived long enough to observe with our own eyes and by our reading that sin is the universal disease of manhood. Is it not certain, according to observation, that man's heart is evil? They used to tell pretty tales about the charming innocence of men dwelling in the wooded bowers of primeval forests, untainted by the vices of civilization, unpolluted by the inventions of commerce and art.

> *We have lived long enough to observe with our own eyes and by our reading that sin is the universal disease of manhood.*

The woods of America were searched and no such sweet babes of grace were discovered. The ferocity and cruelty of the Indians justify my saying that they were hateful and hating one another. The blood-red tomahawk might have been emblazoned as the Redman's coat of arms, and his eyes glaring with revenge might be taken as the true index of his character. Travelers have penetrated of late into the center of Africa, where we may expect to see nature in its primitive excellence, and what is the report that is brought back to us? Why, it is nature in its primitive devilry. That is all!

Let such abominable tyrants as messengers Grant and Speke describe to us indicate to us what man is when he is left in his primeval state, untainted by civilization. He is simply a greater devil. He is naked and he is not ashamed! In this, only, is he like our unfallen parents. Again, try the mildest races. There is the mild Hindu. You look into his gentle face and you cannot suppose him capable of cruelty. Trust well that mild Hindu, subdued by British arms so speedily and so cheerfully bowing his neck to the yoke. But you may as well trust the sleek and cunning tiger from his jungle. Let the story of the Sepoy Rebellion of a few years ago show us the gentleness of the mild Hindu!

Live among the mild Hindu, and if you dare read the first chapter of Paul's Epistle to the Romans, remember that it is a decent account of what, in ordinary life, is practiced among the Hindu but what could not be more clearly described, because the mouth of modesty would refuse to speak it, and the ears of modesty would tingle at the hearing of it. The life of the most respectable Hindu is tainted with vices too vile to mention. "Yes, but still," says one, "we must look at children, because sin may enter into us through education. Let us look at children."

Very well, I am willing to look at children, and I am unwilling that anybody should say a word that is harsh or severe against children's nature. But I will say that any man who declares children to be born perfect never was a father! If he would only watch his own child, not merely when that child has its toys around it and is pleased and happy, but when its little temper is ruffled, he would soon perceive evil nestling there. Is your child without evil? If you will look and listen, you will soon discover, if no other fault, this one: "The wicked are estranged from the womb; they go astray as soon as they are born, speaking lies" (Ps. 58:3).

One of the earliest vices of children that needs to be corrected with most constant and wise rigor is the tendency toward falsehood. It is all very pretty for people to talk about the innocence of children. But I would like them to have to keep one of the nursery schools like those at Manchester, where the children are left while the mothers are at work in the mills! They would soon discover in their pulling one another's hair and scratching at one another's eyes and such like pretty little diversions and innocent freaks that they are not altogether the sweet babes of innocence they are supposed to be!

"Well," says one, "still, human nature may have some spiritual good in it. Look at the men who make illustrious the page of history. Look at Socrates, for instance. Religion did nothing for Socrates, but yet what a fine character he was." Who told you that? I will venture to say that the philosopher's character would not bear description in a decent assembly. We know from undoubted authority that the purest philosophers at times indulged in bestiality and filth. Solon and Socrates were no exceptions. When infidels hold up these sages as being such patterns of what human nature might become, they have history dead against them. "The whole head is sick, and the whole heart faints" (Isa. 1:5).

And this, be it remembered, is without an exception in the long history of humanity, say six thousand years. There is not one who has escaped contamination, not one who has come into the world clean, not one who dares go before his Maker's bar and say, "Great God, I have never sinned but have kept your law from my youth up."

II. Now I want you to notice, in the second place, a most extraordinary thing: When I noticed it yesterday I was surprised and overwhelmed with grateful admiration. That is, *God's extraordinary reasoning.* Good reasoning, but most extraordinary. He says, "I will never again curse the ground for man's sake, although the imagination of man's heart is evil from his youth." Strange logic! In the sixth chapter He said man was evil and therefore He destroyed him. In the eighth chapter He says man is evil from his youth and therefore He will *not* destroy him!

Strange reasoning! Strange reasoning to be accounted for by the little circumstance in the beginning of the verse: The Lord smelled a sweet savor. There was a *sacrifice* there. That makes all the difference! When God looks on sin apart from sacrifice, justice says, "Destroy! Destroy! Smite! Curse! Destroy!" But when there is a *sacrifice*, God looks on sin with eyes of mercy, and though justice says, "Destroy," He says, "No, I have punished my dear Son. I have punished Him and will spare the sinner." Mercy looks to see if she cannot find some loophole, something that she can make into an excuse why she may spare mankind.

Is, then, natural depravity an excuse for sin? Does God use it as such? No, beloved, that our heart is vile is rather an aggravation of the vileness of our action than any *excuse* for it. Yet there is this one thing: We are born sinners, and God sees there, I will say, a sort of loophole. Rightly, upon the terms of justice, there is no conceivable reason why He should have mercy upon us. But divine grace makes and invents a reason. Oh, may I be helped while I try to show you where I think the ground of mercy lies! Devils fell separately. We have every reason to believe that every fallen angel sinned on his own account and fell. And it is very likely that on this account there was no possibility, as we know of, of their restoration. Every separate fallen spirit was given up forever to chains and darkness and flames of fire.

But men! Men did not fall separately and individually. Our case is a somewhat different one from that of fallen angels. We, all of us, fell without our own consent, without having, in fact, any finger in it, actually. We fell *federally* in our covenant head. It is in consequence of our falling in Adam that our heart becomes evil from our youth. Now it looks to me as if God's mercy caught that. He seemed to say, "These My creatures have, according to My arrangement of federation, fallen representatively. Then I can *save* them representatively. They perished in one, Adam. I will save them in another. They fell not by their own overt act, though indeed their own overt acts have added to this and deserve My wrath, but their first fall was not through themselves. They are sinful from their very infancy." Therefore He says, "I will deliver them by another as they fell by another."

> *W*e, all of us, fell without our own consent, without having, in fact, any finger in it, actually. We fell *federally* in our covenant head.

I do not know whether I can make it clear. I do not think that this was any reason before the bar of justice why God should save us, for I believe that He might justly have condemned the whole race of Adam on account of Adam's sin and their own guilt. But I do think that this was a blessed loophole through which His mercy could, as it were, come fairly to the sons of men. "There," He says, "I made them not distinct individuals but a race. They fell as a race; they will rise as an elect race. 'For as in Adam all die, even so in Christ all shall be made alive' (1 Cor. 15:22). And 'For as by one man's disobedience many were made sinners, so also by one Man's obedience many will be made righteous' (Rom. 5:19)."

I think you see the drift of it, then. Man's being sinful is, in the logic of justice, a reason for punishment. Man's being sinful from his youth by inheritance from his federal head becomes, through mercy, a reason why sovereign grace should light upon men while fallen angels are left to perish forever. Oh, I bless God that I did not fall first of all myself. I do bless the day, now, that I fell in Adam, for it may be if I had never fallen in Adam, I should have fallen in myself, and then I must have been, like fallen angels, shut out forever from the presence of God and in the flames of hell! One of the old divines used to say of Adam's sin, *beata culpa*, "happy fault"!

I dare not say that, but in one sense I will say, Blessed fall that renders it possible for me to rise! Blessed way of ruin that renders it possible for the blessed way of salvation to be brought about—salvation by substitution! Salvation by sacrifice! Salvation by a new covenant head, who for us is offered up that God may smell a sweet savor and may deliver us! I hope nobody will misconstrue what I have said and make out that I teach that human depravity is an *excuse* for sin—God forbid! It is only in the eyes of divine grace that it becomes the door of mercy.

You know if your child has offended you, you do not want to chastise him and yet you feel he deserves it. How you do try, if you are a loving parent, to find some reason why you may let him go. There is no reason—you know that. If you deal with him in terms of justice, there is no reason why having sinned he should not smart for it. But you keep casting about for an excuse—perhaps it is his mother's birthday and you let him off for that. Or else there was some little circumstance that softened the offense for which you may have him excused.

> Blessed fall that renders it possible for me to rise! Blessed way of ruin that renders it possible for the blessed way of salvation to be brought about—salvation by substitution! Salvation by sacrifice!

I do not know whether the story is true, but it is said of Queen Victoria when she was just queen, just a girl, that she was asked to sign a death warrant for a person who, by court martial, had been condemned to die. It is told that she said to the duke, "Cannot you find any reason why this man should be pardoned?"

The duke said, "No, it was a very great offense; he ought to be punished."

"But was he a good soldier?"

The duke said he was a shamefully bad soldier, had always been noted as a bad soldier.

"Well, cannot you invent for me any reason?"

"Well," he said, "I have every reason to believe from testimony that he was a good man as a man, although a bad soldier."

"That will do," she said, and she wrote across the warrant, "Pardoned," not because the man deserved it but because she wanted a reason for having mercy.

So my God seems to look upon man, and after He has looked him through and through and cannot see anything, at last He says, "He is evil from his youth," and He writes, "Pardoned." He smells the sweet savor first and His heart is turned toward the poor rebel. Then He turns to him with mercy and blesses him.

III. But now, third, by your leave and patience, I will have to lead you to a few inferences from the doctrine of the depravity of man. If the heart is so evil, then it is impossible for us to enter heaven as we are. We cannot suppose that those holy gates will enclose those whose imaginations and thoughts are evil, and evil continually. No, if that is the place into which nothing will enter that defiles, then no man being what he was in his first birth can ever stand there!

Another step. Then it is quite clear that if I am to enter heaven, no *outward* reform will ever do, for if I wash my face, that does not change my *heart*. And if I give up all my outward sins and become outwardly what I ought to be, yet still, if it is true that my heart is the villainous thing that scripture says it is, then my outward reformation cannot touch *that* and I am still shut out of heaven. If inside that cup and platter there is all this filthiness, I may cleanse the outside, but I have not touched that which will shut me out of heaven.

> *My* first birth makes me a creature; my second birth makes me a *new* creature, and I become what I never was before."

I go, then, a little farther and I observe that I must have a new *nature*— not new practice only, but a new nature—not new thoughts or new words, but a new nature so as to become a totally new man. And when I draw the inference, I have scripture to back me at once, for what does Jesus say to Nicodemus? "You must be born again" (John 3:7). But what is to be born again? To my first birth, I owe all I am by nature. I must get a *second* birth to which I am to owe all I am as I enter heaven. Multitudes of persons have been saying, "What is regeneration?" Here they have been writing hundreds of pamphlets and no two of them agree upon what regeneration is except that they say that a man may be regenerated and not converted.

Here is an extraordinary thing! An unconverted man who is regenerated? One who is an enemy to God and yet he has in himself a new nature? He has been born again and yet is not converted to God? What? Is there a regeneration that does not convert; a regeneration, in fact, that leaves men just where they were before? But to every babe in Christ, the word *regenerate* is as plain as possible; he wants no definition, no description. "To be born again? Why," he says, "I comprehend that it is to be made over again, a new creature in Christ Jesus! My first birth makes me a creature; my second birth makes me a *new* creature, and I become what I never was before."

> *A* simple faith in Jesus is the great, sure mark of a work of the Holy Spirit in your soul by which you are made to be a partaker of the inheritance of the saints in light. "Whoever believes that Jesus is the Christ is born of God"

I must remember that what is needed in me is not to bring out and develop what is good in me, for, according to God's Word in the sixth chapter of Genesis, there is *nothing* good; it is only evil. Grace does not enter to educate the germs of holiness within me, for there is no germ of good in man at all—he is "evil continually," and every imagination is "only evil." I must, then, die to sin! My old nature must be slain; it cannot be mended! It is too bad, too rotten to be patched up. It must die. By the death of Jesus it must be destroyed. It must be buried with Christ and I must rise in resurrection life to conformity with my Lord Jesus.

Well then, advancing one step further: It is clear if I must be this before I can enter heaven that I cannot give myself a new nature. A crab tree cannot transform itself into an apple tree! If I am a wolf, I cannot make myself a sheep. Water can rise to its own proper level, but it cannot go beyond it without pressure. I must have, then, something worked in me more than I can work in myself, and this indeed is good scriptural doctrine. "That which is born of the flesh"—what is it? When the flesh has done its very best, what is it? "That which is born of the flesh is flesh." It is filthy to begin with and filth comes of it. However, "that which is born of the Spirit is spirit. Do not marvel that I said to you, 'You must be born again'" (John 3:6–7).

My soul must come under the hand of the Spirit. Just as a piece of clay is on the potter's wheel and is made to revolve and is touched by the fingers of the potter and molded into what he wishes it to be, so must I lie passively in the hands of the Spirit of God and He must work in me to will and to do of His own good pleasure. And then I will begin to work out my own salvation with fear and trembling, but never, never till then. I must have more than nature can give me, more than my mother gave me, more than my father gave me, and more than flesh and blood can produce under the most favorable circumstances. I must have the Spirit of God from heaven.

Then comes this inquiry, "Have I received it? What is the best evidence of it?" The best evidence of it is this: Am I resting upon Christ Jesus alone for salvation? You generally find on potters' vessels that there is a certain mark so that you can know who made them. I want to know whether I am a vessel fit for the Master's use, molded by His hands and fashioned by His Spirit. Now, every single vessel that comes out of God's hands has a cross on it. Have you the cross on you? Are you resting upon Christ's bloody atonement made on Calvary? Is He to your soul your one rock of refuge—your one and only hope? Can you say this morning:

> Nothing in my hands I bring,
> Simply to your cross I cling.
> Naked, come to you for dress;
> Helpless, look to you for grace.
> Black, I to the fountain fly,
> Wash me, Savior, or I die!

Then, my brothers and sisters, you have a new heart and a right spirit! You are a new creature in Christ Jesus, for simple faith in Christ is what the old Adam never could attain! A simple faith in Jesus is the great, sure mark of a work of the Holy Spirit in your soul by which you are made to be a partaker of the inheritance of the saints in light. "Whoever believes that Jesus is the Christ is born of God" (1 John 5:1). Do you believe that Jesus is the Christ? Do you take Him to be God's anointed to you? Do you trust yourself to Him to plead for you, to work for you, to fulfill the law for you, to offer atonement for you?

If so, if Jesus is the Christ to you, you are born of God. The Spirit who is in you now will drive out the old nature, slay it utterly, cut it up root and branch, and you will one day bear the image of the heavenly, even as you have till now borne the image of the earthly. May God bless these words of mine to your souls' good.

> *Eternal Spirit, we confess*
> *And sing the wonders of your grace!*
> *Your power conveys our blessings down*
> *From God the Father and the Son.*
> *Enlightened by your heavenly ray,*
> *Our shades and darkness turn to day.*
> *Your inward teachings make us know*
> *Our danger and our refuge, too.*
> *Your power and glory work within,*
> *And break the chains of reigning sin,*
> *Does our imperious lusts subdue,*
> *And forms our wretched hearts anew.*
> *The troubled conscience knows your voice,*
> *Your cheering words awake our joys;*
> *Your words allay the stormy wind,*
> *And calm the surges of the mind.*

For Further Thought

1. *Romans 6:4 says we are buried in baptism. Where does this verse say our baptism puts us?*
2. *Compare Genesis 6:5 with 8:21. What do these verses tell you about the human condition before and after the flood?*
3. *Read 1 Corinthians 15:22. According to this verse, what happens in Adam? What happens in Christ?*

Justification by Faith—Illustrated by Abram's Righteousness

And he believed in the LORD,
and He accounted it to him for righteousness.
GENESIS 15:6

YOU will remember that last Lord's Day morning we spoke upon the *calling* of Abram and the faith by which he was enabled to enter upon that separated life at the bidding of the Most High. We will today pass from the consideration of his calling to that of his *justification*, that being most remarkably next in order in his history, as it is in point of theology in the New Testament, for "whom He called, these He also justified" (Rom. 8:30).

Referring to the chapter before us for a preface to our subject, note that after Abram's calling his faith proved to be of the most practical kind. Being called to separate himself from his kindred and from his country, he did not therefore become a recluse, a man of ascetic habits, or a sentimentalist unfit for the battles of ordinary life. No, but in the noblest style of true manliness, he showed himself able to endure the household trouble and the public trial that awaited him.

Lot's herdsmen quarreled with the servants of Abram, and Abram, with great disinterestedness, gave his younger and far inferior relative the choice of pasturage. He gave up the well-watered plain of Sodom, which was the best of the land. A little while after, the grand old man who trusted in his God showed that he could play the soldier and fight right gloriously against terrible odds. He gathered together his own household servants and accepted the help of his neighbors, pursued the conquering hosts of the allied kings, and smote them with as heavy a hand as if from his youth up he had been a military man.

Brothers and sisters, this everyday life faith is the faith of God's elect! There are persons who imagine saving faith to be a barren conviction of the truth of certain abstract propositions, leading only to a quiet contemplation upon certain delightful topics, or separating ourselves from all sympathy with our fellow creatures. But it is not so! Faith, restricted merely to religious exercise, is not Christian faith. It must show itself in *everything*. A merely religious faith may be the choice of men whose heads are softer than their hearts or more fit for cloisters than markets. But the manly faith that God would have us cultivate is a grand practical principle adapted for every day in the week, helping us to rule our household in the fear of God and to enter upon life's rough conflicts in the warehouse, the farm, or the exchange.

> *The manly faith that God would have us cultivate is a grand practical principle adapted for every day in the week, helping us to rule our household in the fear of God. . . .*

I mention this at the commencement of this discourse because as this is the faith that came of Abram's *calling*, so also does it shine in his *justification* and is indeed that which God counted to him for righteousness. Yet the first verse shows us that even such a believer as Abram needed comfort. The Lord said to him, "Fear not" (Gen. 15:1 KJV). Why did Abram fear? It was partly because of the reaction that is always caused by excitement when it is over. He had fought boldly and conquered gloriously, and now he fears.

Cowards tremble *before* the fight, and brave men *after* the victory. Elijah slew the priests of Baal without fear, but after all was over, his spirit sank and he fled from the face of Jezebel. Abram's fear originated in an overwhelming awe in the presence of God. The word of Jehovah came to him with power and he felt that same prostration of spirit that made the beloved John fall at the feet of his Lord in the Isle of Patmos, and made Daniel feel, on the banks of the Hiddekel, that there was no strength in him. "Fear not," said the Lord to the patriarch. His spirit was too deeply bowed. God would uplift His beloved servant into the power of exercising sacred familiarity.

Ah, brothers and sisters, this is a blessed fear. Let us cultivate it, for until it will be cast out by perfect love, which is better still, we may be content to let this good thing rule our hearts. Should not a man, conscious of great infirmities, sink low in his own esteem in proportion as he is honored with communion with the glorious Lord? When he was comforted, Abram received an open declaration of his justification. I take it, beloved friends, that our text does *not* intend to teach us that Abram was *not* justified before this time. Faith *always* justifies whenever it exists, and as soon as it is exercised, its result follows immediately.

The moment a man truly trusts his God he is justified. Yet many are justified who do not know their happy condition; many to whom, as yet, the blessing of justification has not been opened up in its excellence and abundance of privilege. There may be some of you here today who have been called by divine grace from darkness into marvelous light. You have been led to look to Jesus and you believe you have received pardon of your sin, and yet, for lack of knowledge, you know little of the sweet meaning of such words as these: "accepted in the Beloved" (Eph. 1:6); "perfect in Christ Jesus" (Col. 1:28); "complete in Him" (Col. 2:10). You *are* doubtless justified, though you scarcely *understand* what justification means. And you are accepted, though you have not realized your acceptance. And you are complete in Jesus Christ, though you have, today, a far deeper sense of your personal incompleteness than of the all-sufficiency of Jesus.

A man may be entitled to property though he cannot read the title deeds or has not, as yet, heard of their existence. The law recognizes right and fact, not our apprehension. But there will come a time, beloved, when you who are called will clearly realize your justification and will rejoice in it! It will be intelligently understood by you and will become a matter of transporting delight—lifting you to a higher platform of experience and enabling you to walk with a firmer step, sing with a merrier voice, and triumph with an enlarged heart!

I intend now, as God may help me, first to note *the means of Abram's justification*, second, *the object of the faith that justified him*, and third, *the attendants of his justification*.

I. First, brethren, *how was Abram justified?* We see in the text the great truth of God that Paul so clearly brings out in the fourth chapter of his Epistle to the Romans, that Abram was *not justified by his works*. Many had been the good works of Abram. It was a good work to leave his country and his father's house at God's bidding. It was a good work to separate from Lot in so noble a spirit. It was a good work to follow after the robber-kings with undaunted courage. It was a grand work to refuse to take the spoils of

Sodom and to lift up his hand to God that he would not take a thread even to a shoelace. It was a holy work to give to Melchizedek tithes of all that he possessed and to worship the Most High God.

Yet *none* of these are mentioned in the text, nor is there a hint given of any other sacred duties as the ground or cause, or part cause, of his justification before God. No, it is said, "And he believed in the LORD, and He accounted it to him for righteousness" (Gen. 15:6).

Surely, brothers and sisters, if Abram, after years of holy living, is not justified by his *works*, but is accepted before God on account of his *faith*, much more must this be the case with the ungodly sinner who, having lived in unrighteousness, yet believes on Jesus and is saved! If there is salvation for the dying thief and others like him, it cannot be of debt, but of grace, seeing they have no good works! If Abram, when full of good works, is not justified by them, but by his *faith*, how much more we, being full of imperfections, must come to the throne of the heavenly grace and ask that we may be justified by faith that is in Christ Jesus and saved by the free mercy of God!

Further, this justification came to Abram *not by obedience to the ceremonial law* any more than by conformity to the moral law. As the apostle has so plainly pointed out to us, Abram was justified *before* he was circumcised. The initiatory step into the outward and visible covenant, so far as it was ceremonial, had not yet been taken, and yet the man was perfectly justified! All that follows after cannot contribute to a thing that is already perfect. Abram, being already justified, cannot owe that justification to his subsequent circumcision; this is clear enough. And so, beloved, at this moment, if you and I are to be justified, these two things are certain: It cannot be by the works of the *moral* law and it cannot be by obedience to any *ceremonial* law, be it what it may, whether the sacred ritual given to Aaron or the superstitious ritual that claims to have been ordained by gradual tradition in the Christian church.

If we are indeed the children of faithful Abram, and are to be justified in Abram's way, it cannot be by submission to rites or ceremonies of any kind! Hearken to this carefully, you who would be justified before God: Baptism is, in itself, an excellent ordinance, but it cannot justify nor help to justify us! Confirmation is a mere figment of men and could not, even if commanded by God, assist in justification! And the Lord's Supper, albeit that it is a divine institution, cannot in any respect whatever minister to your acceptance or to your righteousness before God!

Abram had no ceremonies in which to rest. He was righteous through his *faith*, and righteous *only* through his faith. And so must you and I be if we are ever to stand as righteous before God at all. Faith, in Abram's case, was the only and unsupported cause of his being accounted righteous! Note, although in other cases Abram's faith produced works, and although in every case where faith is genuine it *produces* good works, yet the particular instance of faith recorded in this chapter was unattended by any works.

> *A*bram had no ceremonies in which to rest. He was righteous through his *faith*, and righteous *only* through his faith. And so must you and I be if we are ever to stand as righteous before God at all.

God brought him forth under the starlit heavens and bade him look up. "So shall your descendants be" (Gen. 15:5), said the sacred voice. Abram did what? *Believed the promise*, that was all. It was before he had offered sacrifice. Before he had said a holy word or performed a single action of any kind that the words immediately and instantly went forth, "He believed in the LORD, and He accounted it to him for righteousness." Always distinguish between the truth of God that living faith always produces works, and the lie that faith and works cooperate to justify the soul. We are made righteous *only* by an act of faith in the work of Jesus Christ. That faith, if true, always produces holiness of life. But our being righteous before God is not *because* of our holiness in life in any degree or respect, but simply because of our faith in the divine promise.

Thus says the inspired apostle: Abram's faith "'was accounted to him for righteousness.' Now it was not written for his sake alone that it was imputed to him, but also for us. It shall be imputed to us who believe in Him who raised up Jesus our Lord from the dead, who was delivered up because of our offenses, and was raised because of our justification" (Rom. 4:22–25).

I would have you note that *the faith that justified Abram was still an imperfect faith*, although it perfectly justified him. It was imperfect beforehand, for he had prevaricated as to his wife and bid Sarai, "Say you are my sister" (Gen. 12:13).

It was imperfect *after* it had justified him, for in the next chapter we find him taking Hagar, his wife's handmaid, in order to effect the divine purpose, and so showing a lack of confidence in the working of the Lord. It is a blessing for you and for me that we do not need perfect faith to save us! "If you have faith as a mustard seed, you will say to this mountain, 'Move from here to there,' and it will move; and nothing will be impossible for you" (Matt. 17:20). If you have but the faith of a little child, it will save you. Though your faith is not always at the same pitch as the patriarch's when he staggered not at the promise through unbelief, yet if it is simple and true, if it confides alone in the promise of God, it is an unhappy thing that it is no stronger, and you ought daily to pray, "Lord, increase my faith," but still it will justify you through Christ Jesus! A trembling hand may grasp the cup that bears a healing draught to the lip, but the weakness of the hand will not lessen the power of the medicine.

So far, then, all is clear: Works did not justify Abram, nor did ceremonies, nor partly by works and partly by faith, nor by the *perfection* of his faith—he is counted righteous simply because of his faith in the divine promise. I must confess that looking more closely into it, this text is too deep for me, and therefore I decline, at this present moment, to enter into the controversy that rages around it. But one thing is clear to me: If faith is, as we are told, accounted to us for righteousness, it is not because faith in itself has merit that may make it a fitting substitute for perfect obedience to the law of God. Nor can it be viewed as a substitute for such obedience. For, brothers and sisters, all good acts are a duty—to trust God is our *duty*—and he who has believed to his utmost has done no more than it was his duty to have done!

He who should believe without imperfection, if this were possible, would even then have only given to God a part of the obedience due. And if he should have failed in love or reverence or anything besides, his faith, as a virtue and a work, could not stand him in any prestige. In fact, according to the great principle of the New Testament, even faith, as a work, does not justify the soul! We are not saved by works at all or in any sense, but by divine grace alone, and the way in which faith saves us is not by itself as a work, but in some other way directly opposite. Faith cannot be its own righteousness, for it is of the very nature of faith to look out of self to Christ.

If any man should say, "My faith is my righteousness," then it is evident that he is confiding in his faith, and this is just the thing of all others that it would be unsafe to do, for we must look altogether away from ourselves to Christ alone or we have no true faith at all. Faith must look to the atonement and work of Jesus or else it is not the faith of scripture. Therefore to say that faith in and of itself becomes our righteousness, it seems to me, tears out the very heart of the gospel and to deny the faith that has been once delivered to the saints.

Paul declares, contrary to certain sectaries that rail against imputed righteousness, that we are justified and made righteous by the righteousness of Christ. On this he is plain and positive. He tells us, "As by one man's disobedience many were made sinners, so also by one Man's obedience many will be made righteous" (Rom. 5:19). The Old Testament verse before us as a text this morning gives us but, as it were, the *outward* aspect of justification; it is brought to us by faith, and the fact that a man has faith entitles him to be set down as a righteous man. In this sense God accounts faith to a man as righteousness. But the underlying and secret truth of God that the Old Testament does not so clearly give us is found in the New Testament declaration that we are accepted in the beloved and justified because of the *obedience of Christ*.

Faith justifies, but not in and by itself, but because it grasps the *obedience of Christ*. "As through one man's offense judgment came to all men, resulting in condemnation, even so through one Man's righteous act the free gift came to all men, resulting in justification of life" (Rom. 5:18). To the same effect is 2 Peter 1:1, which runs in our version as follows: "Simon Peter, a servant and an apostle of Jesus Christ, to them that have obtained like precious faith with us through the righteousness of God and our Savior Jesus Christ" (KJV). Now, everybody who is at all familiar with the original knows that the correct translation is "through the righteousness of our God and Savior Jesus Christ."

The righteousness that belongs to the Christian is the righteousness of our God and Savior, who "of God is made unto us righteousness" (see 1 Cor. 1:30). Hence the beauty of the old prophetic title of the Messiah, "the Lord our righteousness." I do not wish to enter into controversy as to *imputed righteousness* this morning. We may discuss that doctrine another time. But we feel confident that this text cannot mean that faith in itself, as a divine grace or a virtue, becomes the righteousness of any man. The fact is that faith is accounted to us for righteousness because it has Christ in its hand. It comes to God resting upon what Christ has done, depending alone upon the propitiation that God has set forth, and God therefore writes down every believing man as being a righteous man, not because of what he is in himself, but for what he is in *Christ*.

He may have a thousand sins, yet will he be righteous if he has faith. He may painfully transgress like Samson. He may be as much in the dark as Jephthah. He may fall as David, he may slip like Noah, but for all that, if he has a true and living faith, he is written down among the justified, and God accepts him! While there are some who gloat over the faults of believers, God spies out the pure gem of faith gleaming on their breast. He takes them for what they want to be, for what they are in heart, for what they would be if they could. And covering their sins with the atoning blood, and adorning their persons with the righteousness of the Beloved, He accepts them, seeing He beholds in them the faith that is the mark of the righteous man wherever it may be.

II. Let us pass on to consider *the promise upon which his faith relied* when Abram was justified. Abram's faith, like ours, rested upon *a promise received directly from God*. " 'This one shall not be your heir, but one who will come from your own body shall be your heir.' Then He brought him outside and said, 'Look now toward heaven, and count the stars if you are able to number them.' And He said to him, 'So shall your descendants be' " (Gen. 15:4–5).

> *The righteousness that belongs to the Christian is the righteousness of our God and Savior, who "of God is made unto us righteousness."*

Had any other spoken this promise, it would have been a subject of ridicule to the patriarch. But taking it as from the lips of God, he accepts it and relies upon it. Now, brothers and sisters, if you and I have true faith, we accept the promise "He who believes and is baptized will be saved" (Mark 16:16) as being altogether divine. If such a declaration were made to us by the priests of Rome, or by any human being on his own authority, we would not think it true. But inasmuch as it comes to us written in the sacred Word of God as having been spoken by Jesus Christ Himself, we lean upon it as not the word of man, but the Word of God.

Beloved, it may be a very simple remark to make, but after all, it is necessary that we must be careful that our faith in the truth of God is fixed upon the fact that God has declared it to be true, and not upon the oratory or persuasion of any of our most honored ministers or most respected acquaintances. If your faith stands in the wisdom of man, it is probably a faith *in* man. Remember it is only the faith that believes the promise because God spoke it that is *real* faith in God. Note that and test your faith thereby.

In the next place, Abram's faith was *faith in a promise concerning the seed.* It was told him before that he should have a seed in whom all the nations of the earth should be blessed. He recognized in this the same promise that was made to Eve at the gates of paradise, "I will put enmity between you and the woman, and between your seed and her Seed" (Gen. 3:15). "Abraham rejoiced to see My day," says our Lord, "and he saw it and was glad" (John 8:56). In this promise Abram saw the one Seed, as says the apostle in Galatians 3:16, "He does not say, 'And to seeds,' as of many, but as of one, 'And to your Seed,' who is Christ." He saw Christ by the eye of faith, and then he saw the multitude that should believe in Him, the seed of the father of the faithful.

The faith that justifies the soul concerns itself about Christ and not mere abstract truths. If your faith simply believes this dogma and that, it saves you not. But when your faith believes that God was in Christ reconciling the world to Himself, not imputing to them their trespasses; when your faith turns to God in human flesh and rests in Him with its entire confidence, then it justifies you, for it is the faith of Abram.

> *C*an you believe that you, a *sinner,* are nevertheless a *child,* a son, an heir, an heir of God and joint heir with Christ Jesus?

Dear hearer, have you such a faith as this? Is it faith in the promise of God? Is it faith that deals with Christ and looks alone to Him? Abram had faith in *a promise that seemed impossible to ever be fulfilled.* A child was to be born of his own loins, but he was nearly one hundred years old, and Sarai also was said to be barren years before! His own body was now dead, as it were, and Sarai, so far as childbearing was concerned, was equally so. The birth of a son could not happen unless the laws of nature were reversed.

But he considered not these things. He put them all aside. He saw death written on the creature, but he accepted the power of life in the Creator, and he believed without hesitation. Now, beloved, the faith that justifies us must be of the same kind. It seems impossible that I should ever be saved. I cannot save *myself.* I see absolute death written upon the best hopes that spring of my holiest resolutions. In my flesh, there dwells no good thing. I can do nothing. I am slain under the law. I am corrupt through my natural depravity. Yet for all this I believe that through the life of Jesus I will live and inherit the promised blessing!

It is small faith to believe that God will save you when divine graces flourish in your heart and evidences of salvation abound. But it is a grand faith to trust in Jesus in the teeth of all your sins, notwithstanding the accusations of conscience; to believe in Him who justifies not merely the godly but "the ungodly" (Rom. 4:5). To believe not in the Savior of saints, but in the Savior of *sinners*, and to believe that if any man sins we have an advocate with the Father, Jesus Christ, the righteous—this is precious and is counted to us for righteousness.

This justifying faith was faith that dealt with *a wonderful promise, base and sublime.* I imagine the patriarch, standing beneath the starry sky, looking up to those innumerable orbs and realizing he cannot count them! To his outward eye, long accustomed in the land of the Chileans to midnight observation, the stars appeared more numerous than they would to an ordinary observer. He looked and looked again with elevated gaze, and the voice said, "So shall your descendants be." Now he did not say, "Lord, if I may be the father of a clan, the progenitor of a tribe, I will be well content. But it is not credible that countless hosts can ever come of my barren body."

No, he *believed* the promise! He believed it just as it stood. I do not hear him saying, "It is too good to be true." No. God has said it, and nothing is too good for God to do. The greater the grace of the promise, the more likely it is to have come from Him, for good and perfect gifts come from the Father of lights. Beloved, does your faith take the promise as it stands in its vastness, in its height and depth and length and breadth? Can you believe that you, a *sinner*, are nevertheless a *child*, a son, an heir, an heir of God and joint heir with Christ Jesus? Can you believe that heaven is yours, with all its ecstasies of joy? Eternity is yours with its infinity of bliss, as is God with all His attributes of glory. Oh, this is the faith that justifies, far-reaching, wide-grasping faith that diminishes not the word of promise, but accepts it as it stands! May we have more and more of this large-handed faith!

Once more, Abram showed faith in *the promise as made to him.* Out of his own body a seed should come, and it was in him and in his seed that the whole world should be blessed! I can believe all the promises in regard to *other* people. I find faith in regard to my dear friends to be a very easy matter.

But oh, when it comes to close grips, and to laying hold for yourself, here is the difficulty! I could see a friend in ten troubles and believe that the Lord would not forsake him. I could read a saintly biography, and finding that the Lord never failed His servant when he went through fire and through water, I do not wonder at it. But when it comes to one's own self, the wonder begins!

Our heart cries, "What is this to me? What am I, and what is my father's house, that such mercy should be *mine*? *I* washed in blood and made whiter than snow today! Is it so? Can it be? *I* made righteous through my faith in Jesus Christ—perfectly righteous! Oh, can it be? What? For me the everlasting love of God, streaming from its perennial fountain? For me the protection of a special providence in this life, and the provision of a prepared heaven in the life to come? For me a harp, a crown, a palm branch, a throne! For me the bliss of forever beholding the face of Jesus and being made like He is and reigning with Him! It seems impossible!

And yet this is the faith that we must have, the faith that lays hold on Christ Jesus for itself, saying with the apostle, [He] loved me and gave Himself for me" (Gal. 2:20). This is the faith that justifies! Let us seek more and more of it, and God will have glory through it.

III. In the third place, let us notice *the attendants of Abram's justification*. With your Bibles open, kindly observe that after it is written his faith was accounted to him for righteousness, it is recorded that the Lord said to him, "I am the LORD, who brought you out of Ur of the Chaldeans, to give you this land to inherit it" (Gen. 15:7). When the soul is graciously enabled to perceive its complete justification by faith, then *it more distinctly discerns its calling*.

Then the believer perceives his privileged separation and discerns why he was convicted of sin, why he was led away from self-righteousness and the pleasures of this world to live the life of faith. Now he sees his high calling and the prize of it, and from the one blessing of justification he argues the blessedness of all the inheritance to which he is called. The clearer a man is about his justification, the more will he prize his calling, and the more earnestly will he seek to make it sure by perfecting his separation from the world and his conformity to his Lord.

Am I a justified man? Then I will not go back to that bondage in which I once was held. Am I now accepted of God through faith? Then I will live no longer by sight as I once did as a carnal man, when I understood not the power of trusting in the unseen God. One Christian grace helps another, and one act of divine grace casts a reflection upon another. Calling gleams with double glory side by side with the twin star of *justification*. Justifying faith receives more vividly the promises. "I have brought you," said the Lord, "into this land to inherit it." Abram was reminded again of the promise God made to him years before.

Beloved, no man reads the promises of God with such delight and with such a clear understanding as the man who is justified by faith in Christ Jesus. "For now," he says, "this promise is *mine*, and made to me. I have the pledge of its fulfillment in the fact that I walk in the favor of God. I am no longer obnoxious to His wrath. None can lay anything to my charge, for I am absolved through Jesus Christ, and therefore, if when I was a sinner He justified me, much more, being justified, will He keep His promise to me. If when I was a condemned rebel, He nevertheless in His eternal mercy called me and brought me into this state of acceptance, much more will He preserve me from all my enemies and give me the heritage that He has promised by His covenant of grace." A clear view of justification helps you much in grasping the promises of God; therefore seek it earnestly for your soul's comfort.

Abram, after being justified by faith, was led more distinctly to behold the power of sacrifice. By God's command he killed three bullocks, three goats, three sheep, with turtledoves and pigeons, being all the creatures ordained for sacrifice. The patriarch's hands are stained with blood. He handles the butcher's knife—he divides the beasts, he kills the birds and places them in an order revealed to him by God's Spirit at the time. There they are. Abram learns that there is no meeting with God except through *sacrifice*. God has shut every door except that over which the blood is sprinkled. All acceptable approaches to God must be through an atoning sacrifice, and Abram understood this.

While the promise is still in his ears and while the ink is yet wet in the pen of the Holy Spirit, writing him down as justified, he must see a *sacrifice*, and see it, too, in emblems that comprehend all the revelation of sacrifice made to Aaron. So, brothers and sisters, it is a blessed thing when your faith justifies you if it helps you to obtain more complete and vivid views of the atoning sacrifice of Jesus Christ! The purest and most bracing air for faith to breathe is on Calvary. I do not wonder that your faith grows weak when you fail to consider well the tremendous sacrifice that Jesus made for His people! Turn to the annals of the Redeemer's sufferings given us in the evangelists. Bow yourself in prayer before the Lamb of God—blush to think you should have forgotten His death that is the center of all history!

Contemplate the wondrous transaction of substitution once again, and you will find your faith revived! It is not the study of *theology*. It is not reading books upon points of controversy. It is not searching into mysterious prophecy that will bless your soul. It is looking to Jesus crucified! That is the essential nutrition of the life of faith, and mind that you keep to it. As a man already justified, Abram looked at the sacrifice all day long and till the sun went down, chasing away the birds of prey as you must drive off all disturbing thoughts. So must you also study the Lord Jesus and view Him in all His characters and offices. Be not satisfied unless you grow in divine grace and in the knowledge of your Lord and Savior Jesus Christ.

> *It is not reading books upon points of controversy. It is not searching into mysterious prophecy that will bless your soul. It is looking to Jesus crucified!*

Perhaps even more important was the next lesson that Abram had to learn. He was led to behold *the covenant*. I suppose that these pieces of the bullock, the lamb, the ram, and the goat were so placed that Abram stood in the midst with a part on this side and a part on that. So he stood as a worshipper all through the day, and toward nightfall, when a horror of great darkness came over him, he fell into a deep sleep. Who would not feel a horror passing over him as he sees the great sacrifice for sin and sees himself involved? There, in the midst of the sacrifice he saw, moving with solemn motion, a smoking furnace and a burning lamp answering to the pillar of cloud and fire that manifested the presence of God in later days to Israel in the wilderness.

In these emblems the Lord passed between the pieces of the sacrifice to meet His servant and enter into covenant with him. This has always been the most solemn of all modes of covenanting and has even been adopted in heathen nations on occasions of unusual solemnity. The sacrifice is divided and the covenanting parties meet between the divided pieces. The profane interpretation was that they imprecated upon each other the curse that if they broke the covenant they might be cut in pieces as these beasts had been. But this is not the interpretation that our hearts delight in! It is this: It is only in the midst of the sacrifice that God can enter into a covenant relationship with sinful man. God comes in His glory like a flame of fire, but subdued and tempered to us as with a cloud of smoke in the person of Jesus Christ. And He comes through the bloody sacrifice that has been offered once and for all through Jesus Christ on the tree. Man meets with God in the midst of the sacrifice of Christ!

Now, beloved, you who are justified, try this morning to reach this privilege that particularly belongs to you at this juncture of your spiritual history. Know and understand that God is in covenant bonds with you. He has made a covenant of grace with you that never can be broken. The sure mercies of David are your portion. After this sort does that covenant run: "I will give you a new heart and put a new spirit within you" (Ezek. 36:26). That covenant is made with you over the slaughtered body of the Son of God!

God and you cross hands over Him who sweats, as it were, great drops of blood falling to the ground. The Lord accepts us and we enter with Him into sacred league and amity over the Victim whose wounds and death ratify the compact. Can God forget a covenant with such sanctions? Can such a federal bond so solemnly sealed be ever broken? Impossible! Man is sometimes faithful to his oath, but God is *always* so. And when that oath is confirmed for the strengthening of our faith by the blood of the Only Begotten, to doubt is treason and blasphemy! God help us, being justified, to have faith in the covenant that is sealed and ratified with blood!

Immediately after, God made to Abram (and here the analogy still holds) *a discovery*, that the entire blessing that was promised, though it was surely his, would not come without an interval of trouble. "Your descendants will be strangers in a land that is not theirs, and will serve them, and they will afflict them four hundred years" (Gen. 15:13). When a man is first of all brought to Christ, he often is so ignorant as to think, *Now my troubles are all over. I have come to Christ and I am saved. From this day forward I will have nothing to do but to sing the praises of God.*

Alas, a conflict remains! We must understand, for sure, that the battle *now* begins! How often does it happen that the Lord, in order to educate His child for future trouble, makes the occasion when his justification is clearest to him the season of informing him that he may expect to meet with trouble? I was struck with that fact when I was reading for my own comfort, the other night, the fifth chapter of Romans. It runs thus: "Therefore, having been justified by faith, we have peace with God through our Lord Jesus Christ" (Rom. 5:1).

See how softly it flows. A justification sheds the oil of joy upon the believer's head. But what is the next verse? "And not only that, but we also glory in tribulations, knowing that tribulation produces perseverance," and so on (5:3). Justification ensures tribulation. Oh yes, the covenant is yours. You will possess the goodly land and Lebanon. But like all the seed of Abraham, you must go down into Egypt and groan, being burdened. All the saints must smart before they sing. They must carry the cross before they wear the crown. You are justified men and women, but you are not freed from trouble! Your sins were laid on Christ, but you still have Christ's cross to carry. The Lord has exempted you from the *curse*, but He has not exempted you from the *chastisement*. Learn that you enter upon the children's discipline on the very day in which you enter upon their accepted condition.

> *L*et us make it the first point of our care to be justified with Abraham's seed, and then whether we sojourn in Egypt or enjoy the peace of Canaan, it little matters.

To close the whole, the Lord gave to Abram *an assurance of ultimate success.* He would bring his seed into the Promised Land, and the people who had oppressed them He would judge. So let it come as a sweet revelation to every believing man this morning, that at the end he will triumph, and those evils that now oppress him will be cast beneath his feet! The Lord will bruise Satan under our feet shortly. We may be slaves in Egypt for a while, but we will come up out of it with great abundance of true riches that are better than silver or gold! We will be prospered by our tribulations and enriched by our trials!

Therefore let us be of good cheer. If sin is pardoned, we may well bear affliction. "Strike, Lord," said Luther, "now my sins are gone. Strike as hard as you will if transgression is covered." These light afflictions that are but for a moment are not worthy to be compared with the glory that will be revealed in us. Let us make it the first point of our care to be justified with

Abram's seed, and then whether we sojourn in Egypt or enjoy the peace of Canaan, it little matters. We are all safe if we are only justified by faith that is in Christ Jesus.

Dear friends, this last word, and I send you home. Have you believed in God? Have you trusted Christ? Oh, that you would do so today! To believe that God speaks truth ought not to be difficult, and if we were not very wicked, this would never need to be urged upon us—we should do it naturally. To believe that Christ is able to save us seems to me to be easy enough, and it *would be* if our hearts were not so hard. Believe your God, and think it no little thing to do so!

May the Holy Spirit lead you to a true trust. This is the work of God: that you believe on Jesus Christ whom He has sent. Believe that the Son of God can save, and confide yourself alone in Him, and He will save you. He asks nothing but faith, and even this He gives you! And if you have it, all your doubts and sins, your trials and troubles put together will not shut you out of heaven! God will fulfill His promise and surely bring you in to possess the land that flows with milk and honey.

For Further Thought

1. *According to Romans 5:18, what brings righteousness to the human race?*
2. *Read Romans 4:5. Does God justify godly or ungodly people by faith?*
3. *Romans 5:1 assures us that we are justified by faith. What does it say is the result of this justification?*

SALVATION TO THE UTTERMOST

*Therefore He is also able to save to the uttermost those
who come to God through Him, since He always
lives to make intercession for them.*

HEBREWS 7:25

SALVATION is a doctrine peculiar to revelation. Revelation affords us a complete history of it, but nowhere else can we find any trace thereof. God has written many books, but only one book has had for its aim the teaching of the ways of mercy. He has written the great book of creation, which it is our duty and our pleasure to read. It is a volume embellished on its surface with starry gems and rainbow colors and containing in its inner leaves marvels at which the wise may wonder for ages and yet find a fresh theme for their conjectures.

Nature is the spelling book of man in which he may learn his Maker's name. He has studded it with embroidery, with gold, with gems. There are doctrines of truth in the mighty stars and there are lessons written on the green earth and in the flowers upspringing from the sod. We read the books of God when we see the storm and tempest, for all things speak as God would have them. And if our ears are open, we may hear the voice of God in the rippling of every rill, in the roll of every thunder, in the brightness of every lightning bolt, in the twinkling of every star, in the budding of every flower.

God has written the great book of creation to teach us what He is; how great, how mighty. But I read nothing of salvation in creation. The rocks tell me, "Salvation is not in us." The winds howl, but they howl not salvation. The waves rush upon the shore, but among the wrecks that they wash up, they reveal no trace of salvation. The fathomless overhangs of oceans bear pearls, but they bear no pearls of grace. The starry heavens have their flashing meteors, but they have no voices of salvation. I find salvation written nowhere, till in this volume of my Father's grace I find His blessed

591

love unfolded toward the great human family, teaching them that they are lost but that He can save them, and that in saving them He can be just and yet the justifier of the ungodly.

Salvation, then, is to be found in the scriptures and in the scriptures only. We can read nothing of it elsewhere. And while it is to be found only in scripture, I hold that the peculiar doctrine of revelation is salvation. I believe that the Bible was sent not to teach me history but to teach me grace. Not to give me a system of philosophy but to give me a system of divinity. Not to teach worldly wisdom but spiritual wisdom. Hence I hold all preaching of philosophy and science in the pulpit to be altogether out of place. I would check no man's liberty in this matter, for God only is the judge of man's conscience. But it is my firm opinion that if we profess to be Christians, we are bound to keep to Christianity.

If we profess to be Christian ministers, we drivel away the Sabbath day, we fool our hearers, and we insult God if we deliver lectures upon botany or geology instead of delivering sermons on salvation. He who does not always preach the gospel ought not to be accounted as a truly called minister of God.

Well then, it is salvation I desire to preach to you. We have, in our text, two or three things. In the first place, we are told *who they are who will be saved*: those who come to God by Jesus Christ. In the second place we are told *the extent of the Savior's ability to save*: "He is. . .able to save to the uttermost." And in the third place, we have *the reason given why He can save*, "since He always lives to make intercession for them."

I. First, we are told *the people who are to be saved*. And the people who are to be saved are those who come to God by Jesus Christ. There is no limitation here of sect or denomination. It does not say the Baptist, the Independent, or the Episcopalian who comes to God by Jesus Christ. It simply says "them," by which I understand men of all creeds, men of all ranks, men of all classes who do but come to Jesus Christ. They will be saved, whatever their apparent position before men, or whatever may be the denomination to which they have linked themselves.

1. Now, I must have you notice, in the first place, *where these people come to*. They "come to God." By coming to God we are not to understand the mere formality of devotion, since this may be but a solemn means of sinning.

What a splendid general confession is that in the Church of England prayer book: "We have erred and strayed from your ways like lost sheep. We have done those things that we ought not to have done and we have left undone those things that we ought to have done and there is no health in us."

There is not to be found a finer confession in the English language. And yet how often, my dear friends, have the best of us mocked God by repeating such expressions verbally and thinking we have done our duty! How many of you go to chapel and must confess your own absence of mind while you have bowed your knee in prayer or uttered a song of praise! My friends, it is one thing to go to church or chapel. It is quite another thing to go to *God*. There are many people who can pray right eloquently and who do so. They have learned a form of prayer by heart, or perhaps use an extemporary form of words of their own composing, but who, instead of going to God, are all the while going *from* God.

Let me persuade you all not to be content with mere formality. There will be many damned who never broke the Sabbath as they thought, but who all their lives were Sabbath breakers. It is as much possible to break the Sabbath in a church as it is to break the Sabbath in the park. It is as easy to break it here in this solemn assembly as in your own houses. Every one of you virtually breaks the Sabbath when you merely go through a round of duties, and having done, you retire to your chambers, fully content with yourself, and fancy that all is over, that you have done your day's work, whereas you have never come to God at all but have merely come to the outward ordinance and to the visible means that is quite another thing from coming to God Himself.

> *My friends, it is one thing to go to church or chapel. It is quite another thing to go to God.*

And let me tell you again that coming to God is not what some of you suppose, that is, now and then sincerely performing an act of devotion but giving to the world the greater part of your life. You think that if sometimes you are sincere, if now and then you put up an earnest cry to heaven, God will accept you. And though your life may be still worldly and your desires still carnal, you suppose that for the sake of this occasional devotion God will be pleased, in His infinite mercy, to blot out your sins. I tell you, sinners, there is no such thing as bringing half of yourselves to God and leaving the other half away. If a man has come here, I suppose he has brought his whole self with him. And so, if a man comes to God, he cannot half of him come and half of him stay away.

Our whole being must be surrendered to the service of our Maker. We must come to Him with an entire dedication of ourselves, giving up all we are and all we ever will be—to be thoroughly devoted to His service. Otherwise we have never come to God aright. I am astonished to see how people in these days try to love the world and love Christ, too. According to the old proverb, they "hold with the hare and run with the hounds." They are real good Christians, sometimes, when they think they ought to be religious. But they are right bad fellows at other seasons, when they think that religion would be a little loss to them. Let me warn you all, it is of no earthly use for you to pretend to be on two sides of the question. "If God is God, serve Him. If Baal is God, serve him."

I like an out-and-out man of any sort. Give me a man who is a sinner. I have some hope for him when I see him sincere in his vices and open in acknowledging his own character. But if you give me a man who is half-hearted, who is not quite bold enough to be all for the devil nor quite sincere enough to be all for Christ, I tell you, I despair of such a man as that. The man who wants to link the two together is in an extremely hopeless case. Do you think, sinners, you will be able to serve two masters, when Christ has said you cannot? Do you fancy you can walk with God and walk with mammon, too? Will you take God on one arm and the devil on the other?

Do you suppose you can be allowed to drink the cup of the Lord and the cup of Satan at the same time? I tell you, you will depart a cursed and miserable hypocrite if you come to God that way. God will have the whole of you, or else you will not come at all. The whole man must seek after the Lord. The whole soul must be poured out before Him; otherwise it is no acceptable coming to God at all. Oh, those of you haltering between two opinions, remember this and tremble.

I think I hear one say, "Well then, tell us what it is to come to God." I answer, coming to God implies *leaving something else*. If a man comes to God, he must leave his sins. He must leave his righteousness. He must leave both his bad works and his good ones and come to God, leaving them entirely. Again, coming to God implies that *there is no aversion toward Him,* for a man will not come to God while he hates God. He will be sure to keep away. Coming to God signifies having some love to God. Again, coming to God signifies desiring God, desiring to be near to Him. And above all, it signifies praying to God and putting faith in Him. That is coming to God—and those that have come to God in that fashion are among the saved. They come to God—that is the place to which their eager spirits hasten.

2. But notice, next, *how they come.* They "come to God" *by Jesus Christ.* We have known many persons who call themselves natural religionists. They worship the God of nature and they think that they can approach God apart from Jesus Christ. There are some men we know of who despise the mediation of the Savior and who, if they were in an hour of peril, would put up their prayer at once to God, without faith in the Mediator. Do such of you fancy that you will be heard and saved by the great God your Creator, apart from the merits of His Son? Let me solemnly assure you, in God's most holy name, there never was a prayer answered for salvation by God the Creator, since Adam fell, without Jesus Christ the Mediator.

> *C*oming to God signifies desiring God, desiring to be near to Him. And above all, it signifies praying to God and putting faith in Him.

No man can come to God but by Jesus Christ, and if any one of you denies the divinity of Christ and if any soul among you does not come to God through the merits of a Savior, bold fidelity obliges me to pronounce you condemned persons! However amiable you may be, you cannot be right in the rest unless you think rightly of Him. I tell you, you may offer all the prayers that ever may be prayed, but you will be damned unless you put them up through Christ. It is all in vain for you to take your prayers and carry them yourself to the throne. "Get you hence, sinner; get you hence," says God. "I never knew you. Why did you not put your prayer into the hands of a mediator? It would have been sure of an answer. But as you presented it yourself, see what I will do with it!"

And He reads your petitions and casts them to the four winds of heaven and you go away unheard, unsaved. The Father will never save a man apart from Christ. There is not one soul now in heaven who was not saved by Jesus Christ. There is not one who ever came to God aright who did not come through Jesus Christ. If you would be at peace with God, you must come to Him through Christ as the way, the truth, and the life, making mention of His righteousness and of His only.

3. But when these people come, *what do they come for?* There are some who think they come to God but who do not come for the right thing. Many a young student cries to God to help him in his studies. Many a merchant comes to God that he may be guided through a dilemma in his business. They are accustomed, in any difficultly, to put up some kind of prayer, which if they knew its value, they might cease from offering, for "the sacrifice of the wicked is an abomination to the LORD" (Prov. 15:8). But the poor *sinner*, in coming to Christ, has only one objective. If the entire world were offered to him, he would not think it worth his acceptance if he could not have Jesus Christ.

There is a poor man, condemned to die, locked up in the condemned cell. The bell is tolling. He will soon be taken off to die on the gallows. There, man, I have brought you a fine robe. What? No smile? Look! It is stiff with silver! Can't you see how it is bedizened with jewels? Such a robe as that cost many and many a pound, and much fine workmanship was expended on it. Contemptuously he smiles at it! See here, man, I present you something else. Here is a glorious estate for you, with broad acres, fine mansions, parker, and lawns—take that title deed, 'tis yours. What? No smile, sir? Had I given that estate to any man who walked the street, less poor than you are, he would have danced for very joy. And will you not afford a smile when I make you rich and clothe you with gold?

Then let me try once more. There is Caesar's purple for you. Put it on your shoulders—there is his crown. It will sit on no other head but yours. It is the crown of empires that knows no limit. I'll make you a king. You will have a kingdom upon which the sun will never set. You will reign from pole to pole. Stand up and call yourself Caesar. You are emperor. What? No smile? What do you want? "Take away that bauble," says he of the crown. "Rend up that worthless parchment. Take away that robe. Yes, cast it to the winds. Give it to the kings of the earth who live.

"But I have to die, and of what use are these to me? Give me a pardon and I will not care to be a Caesar. Let me live a beggar rather than die a prince." So is it with the sinner when he comes to God. He comes for salvation. He says:

Wealth and honor I disdain;
Earthly comforts, Lord, are vain.
These will never satisfy,
Give me Christ, or else I die.

Mercy is his sole request. O my friends, if you have ever come to God, crying out for salvation and for salvation only, then you have come to God aright. It is useless then to mock you. You cry for bread—should I give you stones? You would but hurl them at me. Should I offer you wealth? It would be little. We must preach to the sinner who comes to Christ the gift for which he asks—the gift of salvation by Jesus Christ the Lord—as being his own by faith.

4. One more thought upon this coming to Christ. *In what style do these persons come?* I will try to give you a description of certain persons, all coming to the gate of mercy, as they think, for salvation. There comes one, a fine fellow in a coach and six! See how hard he drives and how rapidly he travels? He is a fine fellow; he has men in livery and his horses are richly caparisoned. He is rich, exceedingly rich. He drives up to the gate and says, "Knock at that gate for me. I am rich enough, but still I daresay it would be as well to be on the safe side. I am a very respectable gentleman. I have enough of my own good works and my own merits, and this chariot, I daresay, would carry me across the river death and land me safe on the other side. But still, it is fashionable to be religious, so I will approach the gate. Porter! Undo the gates and let me in. See what an honorable man I am."

You will never find the gates undone for that man. He does not approach in the right manner. There comes another. He has not quite so much merit, but still he has some. He comes walking along, and having leisurely marched up, he cries, "Angel! Open the gate to me. I am come to Christ. I think I should like to be saved. I do not feel that I very much require salvation; I have always been a very honest, upright, moral man. I do not know myself to have been much of a sinner. I have robes of my own. But I would not mind putting Christ's robes on. It would not hurt me. I may as well have the wedding garment. Then I can have my own, too."

Ah, the gates are still hard and fast and there is no opening of them. But let me show you the right man. There he comes, sighing and groaning, crying and weeping all the way. He has a rope on his neck, for he thinks he deserves to be condemned. He has rags on him. He comes to the heavenly throne, and when he approaches mercy's gate, he is almost afraid to knock. He lifts up his eyes and he sees it written, "Knock, and it will be opened to you" (Matt. 7:7). But he fears lest he should profane the gate by his poor touch. He gives at first a gentle rap, and if mercy's gate opens not, he is a poor dying creature. So he gives another rap, then another and another, and although he raps times without number, no answer comes.

> *O my friends, if you have ever come to God, crying out for salvation and for salvation only, then you have come to God aright.*

Still he is a sinful man and he knows himself to be unworthy, but he keeps rapping still. And at last the good angel, smiling from the gate, says, "Ah, this gate was built for beggars, not for princes. Heaven's gate was made for spiritual paupers, not for rich men. Christ died for sinners, not for those who are good and excellent. He came into the world to save the vile: "Not the righteous—sinners, Jesus came to call." Come in, poor man! Come in. Thrice welcome!" And the angels sing, "Thrice welcome!"

How many of you, dear friends, have come to God by Jesus Christ in that fashion? Not with the pompous pride of the Pharisee, not with the cant of the good man who thinks he deserves salvation. But with the sincere cry of a penitent, with the earnest desire of a thirsty soul after living water, panting as the thirsty hart in the wilderness after the water brooks, desiring Christ as they who look for the morning. I say, more than they who look for the morning. As my God who sits in heaven lives, if you have not come to God in this fashion, you have not come to God at all. But if you have thus come to God, here is the glorious word for you: "He is able to save to the uttermost those who come to God through Him."

II. Thus we have disposed of the first point, the coming to God. And now, second, *what is the measure of the Savior's ability?* This is a question as important as if it were for life or death—a question as to the ability of Jesus Christ. How far can salvation go? What are its limits and its boundaries?

Christ is a Savior. How far is He able to save? He is a Physician. To what extent will His skill reach to heal diseases? What a noble answer the text gives! "He is able to save to the uttermost." Now, I will certainly affirm, and no one can deny it, that no one here knows how far the uttermost is.

David said if he took the wings of the morning to fly to the uttermost parts of the sea, even there should God reach him. But who knows where the uttermost is? Borrow the angel's wings and fly far, far beyond the remotest star. Go where wing has never flapped before and where the undisturbed ether is as serene and quiet as the breast of deity itself. You will not come to the uttermost. Go on still, mounted on a morning ray; fly on still, beyond the bounds of creation, where space itself fails and where chaos takes up its reign. You will not come to the uttermost. It is too far for mortal intellect to conceive of. It is beyond the range of reason or of thought. Now, our text tells us that Christ is "able to save to the uttermost."

1. Sinner, I will address you first. Saints of God, I will address you afterward. Sinner, Christ is "able to save to the uttermost," by which we understand that *the uttermost extent of guilt* is not beyond the power of the Savior. Can anyone tell what is the uttermost amount to which a man might sin? Some of us conceive that Palmer has gone almost to the uttermost of human depravity. We fancy that no heart could be much viler than that which conceived a murder so deliberate and contemplated a crime so protracted. But I can conceive it possible that there might be even worse men than he and that if his life were spared and he were set at large, he might become even a worse man than he is now.

Yes, supposing he was to commit another murder and then another and another, would he have gone to the uttermost? Could not a man be yet guiltier? As long as ever he lives, he may become guiltier than he was the day before. But yet my text says Christ is "able to save to the uttermost." I may imagine a person has crept in here who thinks himself to be the most loathsome of all beings, the most condemned of all creatures. "Surely," says he, "I have gone to the utmost extremity of sin. None could outstrip me in vice."

My dear friend, suppose you *had* gone to the uttermost—remember that even then you would not have gone beyond the reach of divine mercy. For He is able to save to the uttermost, and it is possible that you yourself might go a little further and therefore you have not gone to the uttermost yet. However far you may have gone, if you have gone to the very arctic regions of vice where the sun of mercy seems to scatter but a few oblique rays, there can the light of salvation reach you. If I should see a sinner staggering on in his progress to hell, I would not give him up, even when he had advanced to the last stage of iniquity. Though his foot hung trembling over the very verge of perdition, I would not cease to pray for him. And though he should in his poor drunken wickedness go staggering on till one foot was over hell and he was ready to perish, I would not despair of him. Till the pit had shut its mouth upon him I would believe it still possible that divine grace might save him. See there! He is just upon the edge of the pit, ready to fall. But before he falls, free grace bids, "Stop that man!" Down mercy comes, catches him on her broad wings, and he is saved—a trophy of redeeming love.

> *If I should see a sinner staggering on in his progress to hell, I would not give him up, even when he had advanced to the last stage of iniquity.*

If there are any such in this vast assembly; if there are any here of the outcast of society, the vilest of the vile, the scum of this poor world, O you chief of sinners, Christ is "able to save to the uttermost." Tell that everywhere in every garret, in every cellar, in every haunt of vice, in every kennel of sin; tell it everywhere! "To the uttermost! He is able also to save them to the uttermost."

2. Yet again, not only to the uttermost of crime, but to *the uttermost of rejection*. I must explain what I mean by this. There are many of you here who have heard the gospel from your youth up. I see some here who like myself are children of pious parents. There are some of you upon whose infant forehead the pure heavenly drops of a mother's tears continually fell. There are many of you here who were trained up by one whose knee, whenever it was bent, was ever bent for you. She never rested in her bed at night till she had prayed for you, her firstborn son. Your mother has gone to heaven, it may be, and all the prayers she ever prayed for you are as yet unanswered.

Sometimes you wept. You remember well how she grasped your hand and said to you, "Ah, John, you will break my heart by this your sin, if you continue running on in those ways of iniquity—oh, if you did but know how your mother's heart yearns for your salvation, surely your soul would melt and you would fly to Christ." Do you not remember that time? The hot sweat stood upon your brow and you said—for you could not break her heart—"Mother, I will think of it." And you did think of it. But you met your companion outside and it was all gone; your mother's expostulation was brushed away, like the thin cobwebs of the gossamer, blown by the swift north wind—not a trace of it was left.

> *uppose it should come to this: that you had not a rag left, nor a crust, nor a drop of water. Still He would be able to save you, for He is "able to save to the uttermost."*

Since then you have often stepped in to hear the minister. Not long ago you heard a powerful sermon. The minister spoke as though he were a man just started from his grave, with as much earnestness as if he had been a sheeted ghost come back from the realms of despair. He told you of his own awful fate and warned you of it. You remember how the tears rolled down your cheeks while he told you of sin, of righteousness, and of judgment to come. You remember how he preached to you Jesus and salvation by the cross and you rose up from your seat in that chapel and you said, "Praise God. I am spared another day. I will turn to Him with full purpose of heart."

And there you are, still unchanged, perhaps worse than you were. And you have spent your Sunday afternoon the angel knows where. And your mother's spirit knows where you have spent it, too, and could she weep, she would weep over you who have this day despised God's Sabbath and trampled on His Holy Word. But do you feel in your heart tonight the tender motions of the Holy Spirit? Do you feel something say to you, "Sinner, come to Christ now"? Do you hear conscience whispering to you, telling you of your past transgression? And is there some sweet angel voice, saying, "Come to Jesus, come to Jesus. He will save you yet"?

I tell you, sinner, you may have rejected Christ to the very uttermost. But He is still able to save you. There are a thousand prayers on which you have trampled. There are a hundred sermons all wasted on you. There are thousands of Sabbaths that you have thrown away. You have rejected Christ—you have despised His Spirit. Still He ceases not to cry, "Return, return!" He is "able to save you to the uttermost," if you come to God by Him.

3. There is another case that demands my particular attention tonight. It is that of the man who has gone to *the uttermost of despair*. There are some poor creatures in this world who from a course of crime have become hardened. And when, by God's grace, they are at last aroused by remorse and the pricking of conscience, there is an evil spirit that broods over them. It tells them it is hopeless for such as they are to seek salvation. We have met with some who have gone so far that they have thought that even devils might be saved rather than they could. They have given themselves up for lost and signed their own death warrant. And in such a state of mind they have positively taken the halter in their hand, to end their unhappy lives.

Despair has brought many a man to a premature death. It has sharpened many a knife and mingled many a cup of poison. Have I a despairing person here? I know him by his somber face and downcast looks. He wishes he were dead, for he thinks that hell itself could be scarce worse torment than to be here expecting it. Let me whisper to him words of consolation. Despairing, soul! There is hope for you yet, for Christ is "able to save to the uttermost." And though you are put in the lowest dungeon of the Castle of Despair, though key after key has been turned upon you and this iron grating of your window forbids all filing, and the height of your prison wall is so awful that you could not expect to escape, yet let me tell you, there is One at the gate who can break every bolt and undo every lock.

There is One who can lead you out to God's free air and save you yet, for though the worst may come to the worst, He is "able to save you to the uttermost."

4. And now a word to the saint, to comfort him, for this text is his also. Beloved brothers and sisters in the gospel! Christ is able to save you to the uttermost. Are you brought very low by *distress*? Have you lost house and home, friend and property? Remember, you have not come to the uttermost yet. Bad off as you are, you might be worse. He is able to save you. Suppose it should come to this: that you had not a rag left, nor a crust, nor a drop of water. Still He would be able to save you, for He is "able to save to the uttermost."

So it is with temptation. If you should have the sharpest *temptation* with which mortal was ever tried, He is able to save you. If you should be brought into such a predicament that the foot of the devil should be upon your neck and the fiend should say, "Now I will make an end of you," God would be able to save you then. Yes, and in the uttermost *infirmity* should you live for many a year, till you are leaning on your staff and tottering along your weary life. If you should outlive Methuselah, you could not live beyond the uttermost—and He would save you then. Yes, and when your little boat is launched by *death* upon the unknown sea of eternity, He will be with you. And though thick vapors of gloomy darkness gather round you and you cannot see into the dim future, though your thoughts tell you that you will be destroyed, yet God will be "able to save you to the uttermost."

Then, my friends, if Christ is able to save a Christian to the uttermost, do you suppose He will ever let a Christian perish? Wherever I go, I hope always to bear my hearty protest against the most accursed doctrine of a saint's falling away and perishing. There are some ministers who preach that a man may be a child of God (now, angels, do not hear what I am about to say! Listen to me, you who are down below in hell, for it may suit you)—that a man may be a child of God today and a child of the devil tomorrow. That God may acquit a man and yet condemn him—save him by grace and then let him perish—suffer a man to be taken out of Christ's hands, though He has said such a thing will never take place.

How will you explain this? It certainly is no lack of *power*. You must accuse Him of a want of love, and do you dare to do that? He is full of love. And since He has also the power, He will never suffer one of His people to perish. It is true and ever will be true that He will save them to the very uttermost.

III. Now, in the last place, *why is it that Jesus Christ is "able to save to the uttermost"?* The answer is that He "always lives to make intercession for them." This implies that *He died*, which is indeed the great source of His saving power. Oh, how sweet it is to reflect upon the great and wondrous works that Christ has done whereby He has become "[the] High Priest of our confession" (Heb. 3:1), able to save us! It is pleasant to look back to Calvary's hill and to behold that bleeding form expiring on the tree. It is sweet, amazingly sweet, to pry with eyes of love between those thick olives and hear the groans of the man who sweat great drops of blood.

Sinner, if you ask me how Christ can save you, I tell you this: He can save you because He did not save Himself. He can save you because He took your guilt and endured your punishment. There is no way of salvation apart from the satisfaction of divine justice. Either the sinner must die, or else someone must die for him. Sinner, Christ can save you because if you come to God by Him, then He died for you. God has a debt against us, and He never remits that debt. He will have it paid. Christ pays it and then the poor sinner goes free.

And we are told another reason why He is able to save—not only because He died, but because *He lives to make intercession for us.* That man who once died on the cross is alive. That Jesus who was buried in the tomb is alive. If you ask me what He is doing, I bid you listen. Listen, if you have ears! Did you not hear Him, poor penitent sinner? Did you not hear His voice, sweeter than harpers playing on their harps? Did you not hear a charming voice? Listen! What did it say? "Father, forgive them" (Luke 23:34). Why, He mentioned your own name! "O my Father, forgive him. He knew not what he did. It is true he sinned against light, knowledge, and warnings. He sinned willfully and woefully. But, Father, forgive him!" Penitent, if you can listen, you will hear Him praying for you. And that is why He is able to save.

A warning and a question and I have done. First, a warning: Remember, *there is a limit to God's mercy.* I have told you from the scriptures that He is "able to save to the uttermost." But there is a limit to His purpose to save. If I read the Bible rightly, there is one sin that can never be forgiven. It is the sin against the Holy Spirit. Tremble, unpardoned sinners, lest you should commit that. If I may tell you what I think the sin against the Holy Spirit is, I must say that I believe it can be different in different people. But in many persons, the sin against the Holy Spirit consists in stifling their convictions.

Tremble, my hearers, lest tonight's sermon should be the last you hear. Go away and scorn the preacher, if you like. But do not neglect his warning. Perhaps the very next time you laugh over a sermon or mock a prayer or despise a text—after the very next oath you swear, God may say, "He is given to idols. Let him alone; my Spirit will no more strive with that man. I will never speak to him again." That is the warning.

And now, lastly, the question: *Christ has done so much for you—what have you ever done for Him?* Ah, poor sinner, if you knew that Christ died for you—and I know that He did if you repent—if you knew that one day you will be His, would you spit upon Him now? Would you scoff at God's day if you knew that one day it would be your day? Would you despise Christ if you knew that He loves you now and will display that love by and by? Oh, there are some of you who will loathe yourselves when you know Christ because you did not treat Him better.

He will come to you one of these bright mornings and He will say, "Poor sinner, I forgive you."

You will look up in His face and say, "What? Lord, forgive me? I used to curse you, I laughed at your people, and I despised everything that had to do with religion. Forgive me?"

"Yes," says Christ, "give me your hand. I loved you when you hated me. Come here!" And surely there is nothing that will break a heart half so much as thinking of the way in which you sinned against one who loved you so much.

Oh, beloved, hear again the text: "He is also able to save to the uttermost those who come to God through Him." I am no orator. I have no eloquence. But if I were the one and had the other, I would preach to you with all my soul. As it is, I only talk right on and tell you what I do know. I can only say once more:

> He is able. He is willing. Doubt no more.
> Come you thirsty, come and welcome,
> God's free bounty glorify.
> True belief and true repentance,
> Every grace that brings us near;
> Without money come to Jesus Christ and buy.

For "He is also able to save to the uttermost those who come to God through Him."

O Lord! Make sinners come! Spirit of God! Make them come! Compel them to come to Christ by sweet constraint, and let not our words be in vain or our labor lost. For Jesus Christ's sake! Amen.

FOR FURTHER THOUGHT

1. *According to Hebrews 7:25, what kind of person is Jesus able to save to the uttermost?*
2. *How do the people who are saved come to God?*
3. *What does this verse say is the extent of believers' salvation?*

Sovereignty and Salvation

"Look to Me, and be saved, all you ends of the earth!
For I am God, and there is no other."
Isaiah 45:22

Six years ago today, as near as possible at this very hour of the day, I was in the gall of bitterness and in the bonds of iniquity, but had yet, by divine grace, been led to feel the bitterness of that bondage and to cry out by reason of the soreness of its slavery. Seeking rest and finding none, I stepped within the house of God and sat there, afraid to look upward lest I should be utterly cut off and lest His fierce wrath should consume me. The minister rose in his pulpit, as I have done this morning, and read this text: "Look to Me, and be saved, all you ends of the earth! For I am God, and there is no other."

I looked that moment. The grace of faith was vouchsafed to me in the self-same instant, and now I think I can say with truth:

Ever since by faith I saw the stream
His flowing wounds supply,
Redeeming love has been my theme,
And will be till I die.

I will never forget that day while memory holds its places, nor can I help repeating this text whenever I remember that hour when first I knew the Lord. How strangely gracious! How wonderfully and marvelously kind, that he who heard these words so little time ago for his own soul's profit should now address you this morning, as his hearers, from the same text. It is my full and confident hope that some poor sinner within these walls may hear the glad tidings of salvation for himself also and may today, on this sixth of January, be turned from darkness to light and from the power of Satan to God.

If it were within the range of human capacity to conceive a time when

God dwelt alone, without His creatures, we should then have one of the grandest and most stupendous ideas of God. There was a season when as yet the sun had never run his race nor commenced flinging his golden rays across space to gladden the earth. There was an era when no stars sparkled in the firmament, for there was no sea of azure in which they might float. There was a time when all that we now behold of God's great universe was yet unborn, slumbering within the mind of God, as yet uncreated and nonexistent.

But there was God and He was over all, blessed forever. Though no seraphs hymned His praises, though no strong-winged cherubs flashed like lightning to do His high behests, though He was without a retinue, yet He sat as a king on His throne, the mighty God, forever to be worshipped, the dread supreme, in solemn silence dwelling by Himself in vast immensity, making of the placid clouds His canopy and the light from His own countenance forming the brightness of His glory. God was and God is.

From the beginning God was God. Before worlds had beginning, He was from everlasting to everlasting. Now when it pleased Him to create His creatures, does it not strike you how infinitely those creatures must have been below Him? If you are potters and you fashion upon the wheel a vessel, will that piece of clay arrogate to itself equality with you? No, at what distance will it be from you because you have been in part its Creator! So when the almighty formed His creatures, was it not consummate impudence that they should venture for a moment to compare themselves with Him?

Yet that archtraitor, that leader of rebels, Satan, sought to climb to the high throne of God, soon to find his aim too high and hell itself not low enough wherein to escape divine vengeance. He knows that God is God alone. Since the world was created, man has imitated Satan, the creature of a day, the ephemera of an hour, and has sought to match himself with the Eternal. Hence it has ever been one of the objects of the great Jehovah to teach mankind that He is God and beside Him there is none else.

This is the lesson He has been teaching the world since it went astray from Him. He has been busying Himself in breaking down the high places, in exalting the valleys, in casting down imaginations and lofty looks, that all the world might "know that the Lord is God alone; He can create and He destroy." This morning we will attempt to show you, in the first place, *how God has been teaching this great lesson to the world*: that He is God and beside

Him there is none else. And then, second, *the special way in which He designs to teach it in the matter of salvation*: "Look to Me, and be saved, all you ends of the earth! For I am God, and there is no other."

I. First, then, *how has God been teaching this lesson to mankind?* We reply He has taught it first of all *to false gods and to the idolaters who have bowed before them.* Man, in his wickedness and sin, has set up a block of wood and stone to be his maker and has bowed before it. He has fashioned for himself out of a goodly tree an image made to the likeness of mortal man, or of the fishes of the sea, or of creeping things of the earth; and he has prostrated his body and his soul, too, before that creature of his own hands, calling it God while it had neither eyes to see nor hands to handle nor ears to hear!

> *S*ince the world was created, man has imitated Satan, the creature of a day, the ephemera of an hour, and has sought to match himself with the Eternal.

But how has God poured contempt on the ancient gods of the heathen! Where are they now? Are they so much as known? Where are those false deities before whom the multitudes of Nineveh prostrated themselves? Ask the moles and the bats whose companions they are, or ask the mounds beneath which they are buried. Or go where the idle gazer walks through the museum to see them there as curiosities and smile to think that men should ever bow before such gods as these. And where are the gods of Persia? Where are they? The fires are quenched and the fire worshipper has almost ceased out of the earth.

Where are the gods of Greece? Those gods adorned with poetry and hymned in the most sublime odes? Where are they? They are gone. Who talks of them now, but as things that were of yore? Jupiter—does anyone bow before him? And who is he who adores Saturn? They are passed away and they are forgotten. And where are the gods of Rome? Does Janus now command the temple? Or do the vestal virgins now feed their perpetual fires? Are there any now who bow before these gods? No, they have lost their thrones.

And where are the gods of the South Sea Islands, those bloody demons before whom wretched creatures prostrated their bodies? They have well near become extinct. Ask the inhabitants of China and Polynesia where are the gods before which they bowed. Ask and echo says ask and ask again. They are cast down from their thrones. They are hurled from their pedestals, their chariots are broken, their scepters are burned in the fire, and their glories are departed. God has gotten to Himself the victory over false gods and taught their worshippers that He is God and that beside Him there is none else.

Are there gods still worshipped or idols before which the nations bow themselves? Wait but a little while and you will see them fall. Cruel Juggernaut, whose ear still crushes in its motion the foolish ones who throw themselves before it, will yet be the object of derision. And the most noted idols, such as Buddha and Brahma and Vishnu, will yet stoop themselves to the earth and men will tread them down as mire in the streets. For God will teach all men that He is God and that there is none else.

> When kings die and in funeral pomp are carried to the grave, we are taught the lesson: "I am God, and there is no other."

Mark you, yet again, how God has taught this truth *to empires*. Empires have risen up and have been the gods of the era. Their kings and princes have taken to themselves high titles and have been worshipped by the multitude. But ask the empires whether there is any besides God. Do you not think you hear the boasting soliloquy of Babylon: "I sit as queen, and am no widow, and will not see sorrow" (Rev. 18:7)? And think you not now, if you walk over ruined Babylon, that you will meet nothing save the solemn spirit of the Bible, standing like a prophet gray with age and telling you that there is one God and that beside Him there is none else?

Go to Babylon, covered with its sand, the sand of its own ruins. Stand on the mounds of Nineveh and let the voice come up: "There is one God, and empires sink before Him. There is only one Potentate, and the princes and kings of the earth with their dynasties and thrones are shaken by the trampling of His foot." Go, seat yourselves in the temple of Greece. Mark you there what proud words Alexander once did speak, but now where is he, and where is his empire, too? Sit on the ruined arches of the bridge of Carthage. Or walk through the desolated theaters of Rome, and you will hear a voice in the wild wind amid those ruins, "I am God, and there is no other."

"O city, you did call yourself eternal. I have made you melt away like dew. You said, 'I sit on seven hills and I will last forever.' I have made you crumble and you are now a miserable and contemptible place, compared with what you were. You were once stone; you made yourself marble. I have made you stone again and brought you low." Oh, how God has taught monarchs and empires that have set themselves up like new kingdoms of heaven that He is God and that there is none else!

Again, how He has taught this great truth to *monarchs*! There are some who have been most proud who have had to learn it in a way harder than others. Take, for instance, Nebuchadnezzar. His crown is on his head; his purple robe is over his shoulders. He walks through proud Babylon and says, "Is not this great Babylon, that I have built?" (Dan. 4:30). Do you see that creature in the field there? It is a man. "A man?" you say. Its hair has grown like an eagle's feathers and its nails like a bird's claws. It walks on all fours and eats grass like an ox. It is driven out from men. That is the monarch who said, "Is not this great Babylon that I have built?"

And now he is restored to Babylon's palace, that he may say, "I, Nebuchadnezzar, praise and extol and honor the King of heaven, all of whose works are truth, and His ways justice. And those who walk in pride He is able to put down" (Dan. 4:37). I remember another monarch. Look at Herod. He sits in the midst of his people and he speaks. Hear you the impious shout? It is "the voice of a god," they cry, "and not of a man!" (Acts 12:22). The proud monarch gives not God the glory. He accepts the title of the god and seems to shake the spheres, imagining himself divine. There is a worm that creeps into his body. And yet another and another, and before that sun has set, he is eaten up of worms. Ah, monarch! You thought of being a god and worms have eaten you! You have thought of being more than man. And what are you? Less than man, for worms consume you and you are the prey of corruption.

Thus God humbles the proud; thus He abases the mighty. We might give you instances from modern history, but the death of a king is all-sufficient to teach this one lesson, if men would but learn it. When kings die and in funeral pomp are carried to the grave, we are taught the lesson: "I am God, and there is no other." When we hear of revolutions and the shaking of empires, when we see old dynasties tremble and gray-haired monarchs driven from their thrones, then it is that Jehovah seems to put His foot upon land and sea and with His hand uplifted cries, "Hear, you inhabitants of the earth! You are but as grasshoppers! I am God, and there is no other."

Again, our God has had much to do to teach this lesson *to the wise men of this world*. For as rank, pomp, and power have set themselves up in the place of God, so has wisdom. And one of the greatest enemies of deity has always been the wisdom of man. The wisdom of man will not see God. Professing themselves to be wise, wise men have become fools. But have you not noticed, in reading history, how God has abased the pride of wisdom? In ages long gone by, He sent mighty minds into the world that devised systems of philosophy. "These systems," they said, "will last forever."

Their pupils thought them infallible and therefore wrote their sayings on enduring parchment, saying, "This book will last forever. Succeeding generations of men will read it, and to the last man that book will be handed down as the epitome of wisdom."

"Ah, but," said God, "that book of yours will be seen to be folly before another hundred years have rolled away." And so the mighty thoughts of Socrates and the wisdom of Solon are utterly forgotten now. And could we hear them speak, the very child in our school would laugh to think that he understands more of philosophy than they.

But when man has found the vanity of one system, his eyes have sparkled at another. If Aristotle will not suffice, here is Bacon. "Now I will know everything," and he sets to work and says that this new philosophy is to last forever. He lays his stones with fair colors and he thinks that every truth he piles up is a precious imperishable truth. But alas! Another century comes, it is found to be wood, hay, and stubble, and a new sect of philosophers rise up who refute their predecessors.

So, too, we have wise men in this day—wise secularists and so on, who fancy they have obtained the truth. But within another fifty years—mark that word—this hair will not be silvered over with gray before the last of that race will have perished and that man will be thought a fool who was ever connected with such a race. Systems of infidelity pass away like a dewdrop before the sun. For God says, "I am God, and there is no other."

This Bible is the stone that will break philosophy into powder. This is the mighty battering ram that will dash all systems of philosophy in pieces. This is the stone that a woman may yet hurl upon the head of every Abimelech, and he will be utterly destroyed. O church of God! Fear not! You will do wonders. Wise men will be confounded, and you will know and they, too, that He is God and that beside Him there is none else.

"Surely," says one, "the church of God does not need to be taught this." Yes, we answer, she does. For of all beings, those whom God has made the objects of His grace are perhaps the most apt to forget this cardinal truth, that He is God and that beside Him there is none else. How the church in Canaan forgot it when they bowed before other gods. He brought against them mighty kings and princes and afflicted them sorely. How did Israel forget it! And He carried them away captive into Babylon. And what Israel did in Canaan and in Babylon, that we do now. We, too, too often forget that He is God and beside Him there is none else.

> *God teaches His people every day by sickness, by affliction, by depression of spirits, by the forsaking of God, by the loss of the Spirit for a season, by the lacking of the joys of His countenance, that He is God, and that beside Him there is no other.*

Does not the Christian know what I mean when I tell him this great fact? For has he not done it himself? In certain times prosperity has come upon him; soft gales have blown his boat along just where his wild will wished to steer. And he has said within himself, *Now I have peace. Now I have happiness. Now the object I wished for is within my grasp. Now I will say, "Sit down, my soul, and take your rest. Eat, drink, and be merry. These things will well content you. Make these your god. Be blessed and happy."*

But have we not seen our God dash the goblet to the earth, spill the sweet wine, and instead thereof fill it with gall? And as He has given it to us, He has said, "Drink it, drink it. You have thought to find a God on earth, but drain the cup and know its bitterness." When we have drunk it, nauseous the draught was and we have cried, "Ah, God, I will drink no more from these things. You are God, and there is no other." And ah, how often, too, have we devised schemes for the future without asking God's permission. Men have said, like those foolish ones whom James mentioned, "Today or tomorrow we will go to such and such a city, spend a year there, buy and sell, and make a profit" (James 4:13). Whereas they knew not what was to be on the morrow, for long before the morrow came, they were unable to buy and sell because death had claimed them, and a small span of earth held all their frame. God teaches His people every day by sickness, by affliction, by depression of spirits, by the forsaking of God, by the loss of the Spirit for a season, by the lacking of the joys of His countenance, that He is God, and that beside Him there is no other.

And we must not forget that there are some special servants of God raised up to do great works, who in a peculiar manner have to learn this lesson. Let a man for instance be called to the great work of preaching the gospel. He is successful. God helps him, thousands wait at his feet, and multitudes hang upon his lips. As truly as that man is a man, he will have a tendency to be exalted above measure, and too much will he begin to look to himself and too little to his God. Let men speak who know and what they know let them speak, and they will say, "It is true; it is most true."

If God gives us a special mission, we generally begin to take some honor and glory to ourselves. But in the review of the eminent saints of God, have you ever observed how God has made them feel that He was God and beside Him there was none else? Poor Paul might have thought himself a god. He easily could have been puffed up above measure by reason of the greatness of his revelation. But Paul could feel that he was not a god, for he had a thorn in the flesh and gods *could not* have thorns in their flesh.

Sometimes God teaches the minister by denying him help on special occasions. We come up into our pulpits and say, "Oh, I wish I could have a good day today!" We begin to labor. We have been just as earnest in prayer and just as indefatigable. But it is like a blind horse turning round a mill, or like Samson with Delilah—we shake our vain limbs with vast surprise, make feeble flight, and win no victories. We are made to see that the Lord is God and that beside Him there is none else. Very frequently God teaches this to the minister by leading him to see his own sinful nature. He will have such an insight into his own wicked and abominable heart that he will feel as he comes up the pulpit stairs that he does not deserve so much as to sit in his pew, much less to preach to his fellows.

Although we feel always joy in the declaration of God's Word, yet we have known what it is to totter on the pulpit steps under a sense that the chief of sinners should scarcely be allowed to preach to others. Ah, beloved, I do not think he will be very successful as a minister who is not taken into the depths and blackness of his own soul and made to exclaim, "To me, who am less than the least of all the saints, this grace was given, that I should preach among the Gentiles the unsearchable riches of Christ" (Eph. 3:8).

There is another antidote that God applies in the case of ministers. If He does not deal with them personally, He raises up a host of enemies that it may be seen that He is God and God alone. What? Will a man subject himself to the calumnies of the multitude? Will he toil and work day after day unnecessarily? Will he stand up Sabbath after Sabbath and preach the gospel and have his name maligned and slandered if he has not the grace of God in him?

For myself, I can say that were it not that the love of Christ constrained me, this hour might be the last that I should preach, so far as the case of the thing is concerned. "Necessity is laid upon me; yes, woe is me if I do not preach the gospel!" (1 Cor. 9:16). But that opposition through which God carries His servants leads them to see at once that He is God and that there is none else. If everyone applauded, if all were gratified, we should think ourselves God, but when they hiss and hoot, we turn to our God and cry:

> *If on my face, for your dear name,*
> *Shame and reproach should be,*
> *I'll hail reproach and welcome shame*
> *If you'll remember me.*

II. This brings us to the second portion of our discourse. Salvation is God's greatest work, and therefore in His greatest work, He specially teaches us this lesson: He is God, and there is no other. Our text tells us *how He teaches it*. He says, "Look to Me, and be saved, all you ends of the earth!" He shows us that He is God and that beside Him there is none else in three ways. First, by the person to whom He directs us: "Look to Me, and be saved." Second, by the means He tells us to use to obtain mercy: "Look," simply "Look." And third, by the persons whom He calls to look: "Look to Me, and be saved, *all you ends of the earth!*"

1. First, *to whom does God tell us to look for salvation?* Oh, does it not lower the pride of man when we hear the Lord say, "Look to Me, and be saved, all you ends of the earth"? It is not "Look to your priest and be saved." If you did, there would be another God, and beside Him there would be someone else. It is not "Look to yourself." If so, then there would be a being who might arrogate some of the praise of salvation. But it is "Look to Me." How frequently you who are coming to Christ look to yourselves. "Oh!" you say. "I do not repent enough." That is looking to yourself. "I do not believe enough." That is looking to yourself. "I am too unworthy." That is looking to yourself.

"I cannot discover," says another, "that I have any righteousness." It is quite right to say that you have not any righteousness. But it is quite wrong to look for any. It is "Look to Me." God will have you turn your eye off yourself and look to Him. The hardest thing in the world is to turn a man's eye off himself. As long as he lives, he always has a predilection to turn his eye inside and look at himself, whereas God says, "Look to Me." The cry comes from the cross of Calvary, where the bleeding hands of Jesus drop mercy; from the Garden of Gethsemane, where the bleeding pores of the Savior sweat pardons: "Look to Me, and be saved, all you ends of the earth!"

From Calvary's summit, where Jesus cries, "It is finished," I hear a shout, "Look and be saved." But there comes a vile cry from our soul, "No, look to yourself! Look to yourself!" Ah, my hearer, look to yourself and you will be damned. That certainly will come of it. As long as you look to yourself, there is no hope for you. It is not a consideration of what *you are* but a consideration of what *God is* and what *Christ is* that can save you. It is looking from yourself to Jesus. Oh, there are men who quite misunderstand the gospel. They think that righteousness qualifies them to come to Christ, whereas *sin* is the only qualification for a man to come to Jesus.

> he viler a man is, the more eagerly I invite him to believe in Jesus. A sense of sin is all we have to look for as ministers. We preach to sinners.

Good old Crisp says, "Righteousness keeps me from Christ. The whole have no need of a physician, only they that are sick. Sin makes me come to Jesus when sin is felt. And in coming to Christ, the more sin I have, the more cause I have to hope for mercy." David said and it was a strange thing, too, "Have mercy upon me, O God. . . . Wash me thoroughly from my iniquity" (Ps. 51:1–2). But, David, why did you not say that it was little? Because David knew that the bigger his sins were, the better reason for asking for mercy. The viler a man is, the more eagerly I invite him to believe in Jesus. A sense of sin is all we have to look for as ministers. We preach to sinners. And let us know that a man will take the title of sinner to himself, and we then say to him, "Look to Christ and you will be saved."

"Look." This is all He demands of you, and even this He gives you. If you look to yourself, you are damned. You are a vile miscreant, filled with loathsomeness, corrupt and corrupting others. But look here! Do you see that man hanging on the cross? Do you behold His agonized head drooping meekly down upon His breast? Do you see that crown of thorns causing drops of blood to trickle down His cheeks? Do you see His hands pierced and rent and His blessed feet, supporting the weight of His own frame, rent well near in two with the cruel nails? Sinner! Do you hear Him shriek, "Eloi, Eloi, lama sabacthani?" (Mark 15:34). Do you hear Him cry, "It is finished!" (John 19:30)?

Do you see His head hang down in death? Do you see that side pierced with the spear and the body taken from the cross? Oh, look here! Those hands were nailed for you! Those feet gushed gore for you. That side was opened wide for you. And if you want to know how you can find mercy, there it is! "Look! Look to Me!" Look no longer to Moses. Look no longer to Sinai. Come here and look to Calvary, to Calvary's Victim and to Joseph's grave. And look yonder to the man who near the throne sits with His Father, crowned with light and immortality. "Look, sinner," He says this morning to you. "Look to Me, and be saved." It is in this way God teaches that there is none beside Him, because He makes us look entirely to Him and utterly away from ourselves.

2. But the second thought is *the means of salvation*. It is "Look to Me, and be saved." You have often observed, I am sure, that many people are fond of an intricate worship, an involved religion, one they can hardly understand. They cannot endure worship so simple as ours. They must have a man dressed in white and a man dressed in black. They must have what they call an altar and a chancel. After a little while, this will not suffice, and they must have flowerpots and candles. The clergyman then becomes a priest and he must have a variegated dress with a cross on it.

So it goes. What is simply a plate becomes a paten. And what was once a cup becomes a chalice. And the more complicated the ceremonies are, the better they like them. They like their minister to stand like a superior being. The world likes a religion they cannot comprehend! But have you ever noticed how gloriously simple the Bible is? It will not have any of your nonsense! It speaks plain and nothing but plain things. *"Look!"* There is not an unconverted man who likes this: "Look to Christ, and be saved." No, he comes to Christ like Naaman to Elijah.

And when it is said, "Go, wash in the Jordan!" he replies, "I verily thought he would come and put his hand on the place and call on the name of his

God, but the idea of telling me to wash in the Jordan; what a ridiculous thing. Anybody could do that!" (see 2 Kings 5:9–11). If the prophet had bid him do some great thing, would he not have done it? Ah, certainly he would. And if, this morning, I could preach that anyone who walked from here to Bath without his shoes and stockings, or did some other impossible thing, should be saved, you would start off tomorrow morning before breakfast.

If it would take me seven years to describe the way of salvation, I am sure you would all long to hear it. If only one learned doctor could tell the way to heaven, how would he be run after! And if it were in hard words with a few scraps of Latin and Greek, it would be all the better. But it is a simple gospel that we have to preach. It is only, "Look!"

"Ah," you say, "is that the gospel? I will not pay any attention to that." Why has God ordered you to do such a simple thing? Simply to take down your pride and to show you that He is God and that beside Him there is none else.

Oh, mark how simple the way of salvation is. It is, "Look, look, look!" Four letters and two of them alike! "*Look to Me, and be saved*, all you ends of the earth!" Some divines want a week to tell you what you are to do to be saved, but God the Holy Spirit only wants four letters to do it. "Look to Me, and be saved, all you ends of the earth!" How simple is that way of salvation! And oh, how instantaneous! It takes us some time to move our hand, but a *look* does not require a moment. So a sinner believes in a moment, and in the moment the sinner believes and trusts in his crucified God for pardon, he at once receives salvation in full through His blood.

There may be one who came in here this morning unjustified in his conscience who will go out justified rather than others. There may be some here, filthy sinners one moment, pardoned the next. It is done in an instant. "Look! Look! Look!" And how universal it is! Because wherever I am, however far off, it just says, "Look!" It does not say I am to see. It only says, "Look!" If we look on a thing in the dark we cannot see it, but we have done what we were told. So if a sinner only looks to Jesus, Jesus will save him. For Jesus in the dark is as good as Jesus in the light—and Jesus when you cannot see Him is as good as Jesus when you can. It is only, "Look!"

"Ah," says one, "I have been trying to see Jesus this year, but I have not seen Him." It does not say *see* Him, but *look* to Him! And it says that they who looked were lightened. If there is an obstacle before you and you only look in the right direction, it is sufficient. "Look to Me!" It is not seeing Christ so much as looking after Him. The will after Christ, the wish after Christ, the desire after Christ, the trusting in Christ, the hanging on Christ—that is what is wanted. "Look! Look! Look!" Ah, if the man bitten by the serpent had turned his sightless eyeballs toward the brazen serpent, though he had not seen it, he would still have had his life restored. It is *looking*, not seeing, that saves the sinner.

> *Some divines want a week to tell you what you are to do to be saved, but God the Holy Spirit only wants four letters to do it.*

We say again, how this *humbles* the man! There is a gentleman who says, "Well if it had been a thousand pounds that would have saved me, I would have thought nothing of it." But your gold and silver are cankered. They are good for nothing. "Then am I to be saved just the same as my servant Betty?" Yes, just the same; there is no other way of salvation for you. That is to show man that Jehovah is God and that beside Him there is none else. The wise man says, "If it had been to work the most wonderful problem, or to solve the greatest mystery, I would have done it. May I not have some mysterious gospel? May I not believe in some mysterious religion?"

No, it is, "Look!"

"What? Am I to be saved just like that ragged schoolboy who can't read his letters?" Yes, you must, or you will not be saved at all.

Another says, "I have been very moral and upright. I have observed all the laws of the land, and if there is anything else to do, I will do it. I will eat only fish on Fridays and keep all the fasts of the church if that will save me." No sir, that will not save you. Your good works are good for nothing. "What! Must I be saved in the same way as a harlot or a drunkard?" Yes, sir, there is only one way of salvation for all.

"For God has committed them all to disobedience, that He might have mercy on all" (Rom. 11:32). He has passed a sentence of condemnation on all so that the free grace of God might come upon many to salvation. "Look! Look! Look!" This is the simple method of salvation. "Look to Me, and be saved, all you ends of the earth!"

But lastly, mark how God has cut down the pride of man and has exalted Himself *by the persons whom He has called to look.* "Look to Me, and be saved, all you ends of the earth!" When the Jew heard Isaiah say that, "Ah," he exclaimed, "you ought to have said, 'Look to Me, O Jerusalem and be saved.' That would have been right. But those Gentiles—the dogs—are *they* to look and be saved?"

"Yes," says God, "I will show you, Jews, that though I have given you many privileges, I will exalt others above you. I can do as I will with my own."

Now, who are the ends of the earth? Why, there are poor heathen nations now that are very few degrees removed from brutes, uncivilized and untaught. If I might go and tread the desert and find the Bushman in his kraal, or go to the South Seas and find a cannibal, I would say to the cannibal or the Bushman, "Look to Jesus and be saved, all you ends of the earth." They are some of "the ends of the earth," and the gospel is sent as much to them as to the polite Grecians, the refined Romans, or the educated Britons.

> In all your troubles through this year, look to God and be saved. In all your trials and afflictions, look to Christ and find deliverance.

But I think "the ends of the earth" implies those who have gone the farthest away from Christ. I say, drunkard, this means you! You have been staggering back till you have got right to the ends of the earth. You have almost had *delirium tremens*; you cannot be much worse. There is not a man breathing worse than you. Is there? Ah, but God, in order to humble your pride, says to you, "Look to Me, and be saved." There is another who lived a life of infamy and sin until she has ruined herself, and even Satan seems to sweep her out at the back door. But God says, "Look to Me, and be saved, all you ends of the earth!"

I think I see one trembling here and saying, "Ah, I have not been one of these, sir, but I have been something worse, for I have attended the house of God and I have stifled convictions and put off all thoughts of Jesus. And now I think He will never have mercy on me." You are one of them. "Ends of the earth!" So long as I find any who feel like that, I can tell them that they are "the ends of the earth."

"But," says another, "I am so peculiar. If I did not feel as I do, it would be all very well. But I feel that my case is a peculiar one." That is all right. They are a peculiar people. You will do.

But another one says, "There is nobody in the world like me. I do not think you will find a being under the sun who has had so many calls and put them all away and so many sins on his head. Besides, I have guilt that I should not like to confess to any living creature." This one is one of "the ends of the earth." Therefore, all I have to do is to cry out, in the Master's name, "Look to Me, and be saved, all you ends of the earth! For I am God, and there is no other."

But you say sin will not let you look. I tell you, sin will be removed the moment you do look. "But I dare not. He will condemn me. I fear to look." He will condemn you more if you do not look. Fear, then, and look. But do not let your fearing keep you from looking. "But He will cast me out." Try Him. "But I cannot see Him." I tell you, it is not *seeing*, but *looking*. "But my eyes are so fixed on the earth, so earthly, so worldly." Ah, but, poor soul, He gives power to look and live. He says, "Look to Me, and be saved, all you ends of the earth!"

Take this, dear friends, for a New Year's text, both you who love the Lord and you who are only looking for the first time. Christian! In all your troubles through this year, look to God and be saved. In all your trials and afflictions, look to Christ and find deliverance. In all your agony, poor soul, in all your repentance for your guilt, look to Christ and find pardon. This year remember to put your eye heavenward and your heart heavenward, too.

Look to Christ; fear not. There is no stumbling when a man walks with his eyes up to Jesus. He who looked at the stars fell into the ditch. But he who looks at Christ walks safely. Keep your eyes up all year long. Look to *Him*, and be saved, and remember that *He* is God and beside *Him* there is none else. And you poor trembler, what do you say? Will you begin the year by looking to Him? You know how sinful you are this morning. You know how filthy you are, and yet it is possible that before you open your pew door and get into the aisle, you will be as justified as the apostles before the throne of God.

It is possible that before your foot treads the threshold of your door, you will have lost the burden that has been on your back and you will go on your way singing, "I am forgiven, I am forgiven. I am a miracle of grace. This day is my spiritual birthday." Oh, that it might be such to many of you, that at last I might say, "Here am I and the children you have given me." Hear this, convicted sinner! "This poor man cried and the Lord delivered him out of his distresses." Oh, taste and see that the Lord is good!

Now believe on Him. Now cast your guilty soul upon His righteousness. Now plunge your black soul into the bath of His blood. Now put your naked soul at the door of the wardrobe of His righteousness. Now seat your famished soul at the feast of plenty! Now "Look!" How simple does it seem! And yet it is the hardest thing in the world to bring men to. They never will do it, till constraining grace makes them. Yet there it is, "Look!" Go away with that thought. "Look to Me, and be saved, all you ends of the earth! For I am God, and there is no other." Amen.

FOR FURTHER THOUGHT

1. *Romans 1:21 describes the failure of the human response to God. What is that response?*
2. *Second Corinthians 12:1–5 describes some of Paul's great revelations. In verse 7, why did God send the apostle a thorn in the flesh?*
3. *Isaiah 45:22 begins with the word "look." Who is told to look? Where are they to look? Why are they to look?*

THE BLESSING OF
FULL ASSURANCE

*These are written that you may believe that Jesus is
the Christ, the Son of God, and that believing
you may have life in His name.*
JOHN 20:31

JOHN wrote to believers, "These things I have written to you who believe in the name of the Son of God" (1 John 5:13). It is worthy of note that all the Epistles are so written. They are not letters to everybody; they are letters to those who are called to be saints. It ought to strike some of you with awe when you open the Bible and think how large a part of it is not directed at you. You may read it and God's Holy Spirit may graciously bless it to you, but it is not directed to you. You are reading another man's letter. Thank God that you are permitted to read it, but long to be numbered with those to whom it is directed.

Thank God much more if any part of it should be used of the Holy Spirit for your salvation. The fact that the Holy Spirit speaks to the churches and to believers in Christ should make you bow the knee and cry to God to put you among the children, that this book may become your book from beginning to end, that you may read its precious promises as made to you. This solemn thought may not have struck some of you—let it impress you now.

We do not wonder that certain men do not receive the Epistles, for they were not written to them. Why should they quibble at words that are addressed to men of another sort from themselves? Yet we do not marvel, for we knew it would be so. Here is a will and you begin to read it. But you do not find it interesting. It is full of words and terms that you do not take the trouble to understand because they have no relation to yourself. But should you, in reading that will, come upon a clause in which an estate is left to you, I guarantee you that the nature of the whole document will seem changed to you.

You will be anxious now to understand the terms and to make sure of the clauses, and you will even wish to remember every word of the clause that refers to yourself. O dear friends, may you read the testament of our Lord Jesus Christ as a testament of love to yourselves, and then you will prize it beyond all the writings of the sages.

This leads me to make the second remark, that as these things are written to believers, believers ought especially to make themselves acquainted with them and to search into their meaning and intent. John says, "These are written that you may believe that Jesus is the Christ, the Son of God, and that believing you may have life in His name" (John 20:31). Do not, I beseech you, neglect to read what the Holy Spirit has taken care to write to you. It is not merely John who writes. John is inspired of the Lord, and the Spirit of God writes these things to you. Give earnest heed to every single word of what God has sent as His epistle to your hearts.

Value the scriptures. Luther said that "he would not be in paradise, if he might, without the Word of the Lord. But with the Word he could live in hell itself." He said at another time that "he would not take all the world for one leaf of the Bible." The scriptures are everything to the Christian, his meat and his drink. The saint can say, "Oh, how I love Your law!" (Ps. 119:97). If we cannot say so, something is wrong with us. If we have lost our relish for Holy Scripture, we are out of condition and need to pray for spiritual health.

This much is the porch of my sermon; let us now enter more fully into our subject, noticing, first, that John wrote *with a special purpose*, and then going on to assert, second, that *this purpose we ought to follow up*.

I. First, *John wrote with a special purpose*. Men do not write well unless they have some end in writing. To sit down with paper and ink before you and so much space to fill up will ensure very poor writing. John knew what he was doing. His intent and aim were clear to his own mind, and he tells us what they were.

According to the text, the beloved apostle had one clear purpose that branched out into three. To begin with, John wrote that we might enjoy the full assurance of our salvation. "These are written that you may believe that

Jesus is the Christ, the Son of God, and that believing you may have life in His name." Many who believe on the name of Jesus are not sure that they have eternal life. They only hope so. Occasionally they have assurance, but the joy is not abiding. They are like a minister I have heard of, who said he felt assured of his salvation, "except when the wind was in the east." It is a wretched thing to be so subject to circumstances as many are.

What is true when the wind is in the soft south or the reviving west is equally true when the wind is good for neither man nor beast. John would not have our assurance vary with the weatherglass, nor turn with the vane. He says, "These things have I written to you, that you may know that you have eternal life." He would have us certain that we are partakers of the new life and so know it as to reap the golden fruit of such knowledge and be filled with joy and peace through believing.

> The fact that the Holy Spirit speaks to the churches and to believers in Christ should make you bow the knee and cry to God to put you among the children, that this book may become your book from beginning to end, that you may read its precious promises as made to you.

I speak affectionately to the weaker ones who cannot yet say that they know they have believed. I speak not to your condemnation but to your consolation. Full assurance is not essential to salvation, but it is essential to *satisfaction*. May you get it at once. At any rate may you never be satisfied to live without it. You may have full assurance. You may have it without personal revelations; the Word of God works it in us. These things are written that you may have it. And we may be sure that the means used by the Spirit are equal to the effect that He desires.

Under the guidance of the Spirit of God, John so wrote as to attain his end in writing. What, then, has he written with the design of making us know that we have eternal life? Go through the whole epistle and you will see that it all presses in that direction. But we will not at this present time have more than a glance through this chapter.

He begins thus: "Whoever believes that Jesus is the Christ is born of God" (1 John 5:1). Do you believe that Jesus is the anointed of God? Is He so to you? Is He anointed as your Prophet, Priest, and King? Have you realized His anointing so as to put your trust in Him? Do you receive

Jesus as appointed of God to be the mediator, the propitiation for sin, the Savior of men? If so, you are born of God. "How may I know this?" Brethren, our evidence is the witness of God Himself as here recorded. We need no other witness.

Suppose an angel were to tell you that you are born of God—would that be a surer testimony than the infallible scripture? If you believe that Jesus is the Christ, you are born of God. John has thus positively declared the truth of God, that you may know that you have eternal life. Can anything be clearer than this?

Do you love God? Do you love His only begotten Son? You can answer those two questions surely. I knew a dear Christian woman who would sometimes say, "I know that I love Jesus. But my fear is that He does not love me." Her doubt used to make me smile, for it never could have occurred to me. If I love Him, I know it is because He first loved me. Love to God in us is always the work of God's love toward us. Jesus loved us and gave Himself for us, and therefore we love Him in return. Love to Jesus is an effect that proves the existence of its cause.

> *If you believe that Jesus is the Christ, you are born of God. John has thus positively declared the truth of God, that you may know that you have eternal life. Can anything be clearer than this?*

Do you love Jesus? Do you feel a delight in Him? Is His name as music to your ear and honey to your mouth? Do you love to hear Him extolled? Ah, dear friends! I know that to many of you a sermon full of His dear name is as a royal banquet. And if there is no Christ in a discourse, it is empty and vain and void to you. Is it not so? If you do indeed love Him who begat, and Him who is begotten of Him, then this is one of the things that is written: "That you may know that you have eternal life."

John goes on to give another evidence: "By this we know that we love the children of God, when we love God and keep His commandments" (1 John 5:2). Do you love God? And do you love His children? Listen to another word from the same apostle: "We know that we have passed from death to life, because we love the brethren" (1 John 3:14). That may appear to be very small evidence. But I can assure you it has often been a great comfort to my soul. I know I love the brethren. I can say to my

Lord, "Is there a lamb among your flock I would disdain to feed?" I would gladly cheer and comfort the least of His people. Well then, if I love the brethren, I love the Elder Brother. If I love the babes, I love the Father. And I know that I have passed from death to life. Brethren, take this evidence home in all its force. It is conclusive. John has said, "We know that we have passed from death to life, because we love the brethren." And he would not have spoken so positively if it had not been even so. Brethren, never be content with sentimental comforts. Set your feet firmly upon the rock of fact and truth. True Christian assurance is not a matter of guesswork but of mathematical precision. It is capable of logical proof and is no rhapsody or poetical fiction.

The Holy Spirit tells us that if we love the brethren, we have passed from death to life. You can tell whether you love the brethren, as such, for their Master's sake and for the truth's sake that is in them. And if you can truly say that you thus love them, then you may know that you have eternal life.

Our apostle gives us this further evidence: "This is the love of God, that we keep His commandments. And His commandments are not burdensome" (1 John 5:3). Obedience is the grand test of love. If you are living after your own will and pay no homage to God, you are none of His. If you never think of the Lord Jesus as your Master and never recognize the claims of God and never wish to be obedient to His will, you are not in possession of eternal life. If you desire to be obedient and prove that desire by your actions, then you have the divine life within you. Judge yourselves. Is the tenor of your life obedience or disobedience? By the fruit you can test the root and the sap.

But note that this obedience must be cheerful and willing. No doubt some, for a while, obey the commands of God unwillingly. They do not like them, though they bow to them. They fret and grizzle because of the restraints of piety. And this proves that they are hypocrites. What you wish to do, you are doing in the sight of God. If there could be such a thing as holiness forced upon a man, it would be unholiness. O my hearer, it may be that you cannot fall into a certain line of sin. But if you could, you would—your desires show what you really are. I have heard of Christian people, so called, going to sinful amusements just, as they say, to enjoy a little pleasure.

Ah, well, we see where you are! Where your pleasure is, your heart is. If you enjoy the pleasures of the world, you are of the world, and with the world you will be condemned. If to you God's commands are burdensome, then you are a rebel at heart. Loyal subjects delight in the royal law. His commandments are not burdensome. I said to one who came to join the church the other day, "I suppose you are not perfect?"

The reply was, "No, sir, I wish I might be."

I said, "And suppose you were?"

"Oh, then," she said, "that would be heaven to me." So it would be to me. We delight in the law of God after the inward man.

Oh, that we could perfectly obey in thought and word and deed! This is our view of heaven. Thus we sing of it:

There will we see His face,
And never, never sin;
There from the rivers of His grace
Drink endless pleasures in.

We would scarce ask to be rid of sorrow, if we might be rid of sin. We would bear any burden cheerfully if we could live without spot. We will also be without grief. His commandments are not burdensome but are ways of pleasantness and peace to us. Do you feel that you love the ways of God, that you desire holiness and follow after it joyfully? Then, dear friends, you have eternal life and these are the sure evidences of it. Obedience, holiness, delight in God, never came into a human heart except from a heavenly hand. Wherever they are found they prove that the Lord has implanted eternal life—for they are much too precious to be buried away in a dead soul.

John then proceeds to mention three witnesses. Now, dear hearers, do you know anything about these three witnesses? "There are three [who] bear witness in heaven: the Father, the Word, and the Holy Spirit; and these three are one" (1 John 5:7). Do you know "the Spirit"? Has the Spirit of God quickened you, changed you, illuminated you, and sanctified you? Does the Spirit of God dwell in you? Do you feel His sacred impulses? Is He the essence of the new life within you? Do you know Him as clothing you with His light and power? If so, you are alive to God.

Next, do you know "the water," the purifying power of the death of Christ? Does the crucified Lord crucify your sins? Is the water applied to you to remove the power of sin? Do you now long for perfect holiness in the fear of God? This proves that you have eternal life.

Do you also know "the blood"? This is a wretched age, in which men think little of the precious blood. My heart has well near been broken and my very flesh has been enfeebled as I have thought upon the horrible things that have been spoken of late about the precious blood by men called Christian ministers.

"O my soul, come you not into their secret! Unto their assembly, my honor, be you not united." Beloved friends, do you know the power of the blood to take away sin, the power of the blood to speak peace to the conscience, the power of the blood to give access to the throne of grace? Do you know the quickening, restoring, cheering power of the precious blood of Christ that is set forth in the Lord's Supper by the fruit of the vine? Then in the mouth of these three witnesses will the fact of your having eternal life be fully established. If the Spirit of God is in you, He is the earnest of your eternal inheritance. If the water has washed you, then you are the Lord's. Jesus said to Peter, "If I do not wash you, you have no part with Me" (John 13:8).

But you are washed, and therefore the Lord's. If the precious blood has cleansed you from the guilt of sin, you know that it has also purchased you from death and it is to you the guarantee of eternal life. I pray that you may, from this moment, enjoy the combined light of these three lamps of God: "the Spirit, the water, and the blood," and so have full assurance of faith.

Obedience, holiness, delight in God, never came into a human heart except from a heavenly hand. Wherever they are found they prove that the Lord has implanted eternal life. . . .

One thing more I would notice. Read the ninth verse. The apostle puts our faith and assurance on the ground that we receive "the witness of God." If I believe that I am saved because of this, that, and the other, I may be mistaken—the only sure ground is "the witness of God." The inmost heart of Christian faith is that we take God at His Word. And we must accept that Word, not because of the probabilities of its statements, nor because of the confirmatory evidence of science and philosophy, but simply and alone because the Lord has spoken it. Many professing Christians fall sadly short of this point. They dare to judge the Word instead of bowing before it. They do not sit at the Master's feet but become doctors themselves. I thank God that I believe everything that God has spoken, whether I am able to see its reason or not.

To me the fact that the mouth of God has spoken it stands in the place of all argument, either for or against. If Jehovah says so, so it is. Do you accept the witness of God? If not, you have made Him a liar and the truth is not in you. But if you have received "the witnesses of God," then this is His witness: that "God has given us eternal life, and this life is in His Son" (1 John 5:11). I say again, if your faith stands in the wisdom of men and is based upon the cleverness of a preacher, it will fail you. But if it stands on the sure Word of the Lord, it will stand forever, and this may be to you a special token that you have eternal life. I have said enough upon this subject. Oh, that God may bless it to you! May we be enabled, from what John has written, to gather beyond doubt that we have the life of God within our souls.

Furthermore, John wrote that we might know our spiritual life to be eternal. Please notice this, for there are some of God's children who have not yet learned this cheering lesson. The life of God in the soul is not transient but abiding. Not temporary but eternal. Some think that the life of God in the believer's soul may die out. But how then could it be eternal? If it dies, it is not eternal life. If it is eternal life, it cannot die. I know that modern deceivers deny that eternal means eternal, but you and I have not learned their way of pumping the meanings out of the words that the Holy Spirit uses. We believe that *eternal* means "endless," and that if I have eternal life, I will live eternally. Brethren, the Lord would have us know that we have eternal life.

Learn, then, the doctrine of the eternality of life given in the new birth. It must be eternal life, because it is "the life of God." We are born again of the Spirit of God by a living and incorruptible seed, which lives and abides forever. We are said to have been made "partakers of the divine nature" (2 Pet. 1:4). Surely this means, among other things, that we receive an undying life. For immortality is of the essence of the life of God. His name is "I Am Who I Am." He has life in Himself and the Son has life in Himself, and of this life we are the receivers. This was His purpose concerning His Son, that He might give eternal life to as many as the Father had given Him. If it is the life of God that is in a believer, and certainly it is, for He has begotten us again, then that life must be eternal. As children of God, we partake of His life, and as heirs of God, we inherit His eternity. "And this is eternal life, that they may know You, the only true God, and Jesus Christ whom You have sent" (John 17:3).

Beloved, our Lord Jesus Christ calls the life of His people *eternal life*. How often do I quote this text! It seems to lie on the tip of my tongue: "And I give them eternal life, and they shall never perish; neither shall anyone snatch them out of My hand" (John 10:28). And again, "He who believes in the Son has everlasting life" (John 3:36). It is not temporary life, not life that at a certain period must grow old and die, but *everlasting life*. "But the water that I shall give him will become in him a fountain of water springing up into everlasting life" (John 4:14). This is the life of Christ within the soul. "For you died, and your life is hidden with Christ in God." And, "I live; yet not I, but Christ liveth in me" (Gal. 2:20 KJV). Yet again, "When Christ who is our life appears, then you also will appear with Him in glory" (Col. 3:4). If our life is Christ's life, we will not die until Christ dies. If our life is hidden in Him, it will never be discovered and destroyed until Christ Himself is destroyed. Let us rest in this.

> *H*old fast to eternal salvation through the eternal covenant carried out by eternal love to eternal life.

Mark again how our Lord has put it: "Because I live, you will live also" (John 14:19). As long, then, as Jesus lives, His people must live, for the argument will always be the same: "Because I live, you will live also." We are so one with Christ that while the head lives, the members cannot die. We are so one with Christ that the challenge is given, "Who shall bring a charge against God's elect?" (Rom. 8:33). A list is added of things that may be supposed to separate, but we are told that they cannot do so, for "in all these things we are more than conquerors through Him who loved us" (8:37). Is it not clear, then, that we are quickened with a life so heavenly and divine that we can never die?

John tells us in this very chapter, "Whoever has been born of God does not sin" (1 John 3:9). He does not go back to his old sin; he does not again come under the dominion of sin. But "we know that whoever is born of God does not sin; but he who has been born of God keeps himself, and the wicked one does not touch him" (1 John 5:18).

Beloved, I entreat you to keep a hard and firm grip on this blessed doctrine of the perseverance of the saints. How earnestly do I long that you may know that you have eternal life! Away with your doctrine of being alive in Christ today and dead tomorrow! Poor, miserable doctrine that is! Hold fast to eternal salvation through the eternal covenant carried out by eternal love to eternal life. For the Spirit of God has written these things to you who believe on the name of the Son of God, that you may know that you have eternal life.

Once more, according to the authorized text, though not according to the Revised Version, John desired the increase and confirmation of their faith. He says, "That you may believe that Jesus is the Christ, the Son of God." John wrote to those who believed that they might believe in a more emphatic sense. As our Savior has come not only that we may have life but also that we may have it more abundantly, so does John write that having faith, we may have more of it. Come, beloved; listen for a moment to this! You have the milk of faith, but God wills that you should have this cream of assurance! He would increase your faith. May you believe more extensively.

Perhaps you do not believe all the truth of God because you have not yet perceived it. There were members of the Corinthian church who had not believed in the resurrection of the dead, and there were Galatians who were very cloudy upon justification by faith. Many a Christian man is narrow in the range of his faith from ignorance of the Lord's mind. Like certain tribes of Israel, they have conquered a scanty territory as yet, though all the land is theirs from Dan to Beersheba. John would have us push out our fences and increase the enclosure of our faith. Let us believe all that God has revealed, for every truth of God is precious and practically useful.

Perhaps your doctrinal belief has been poor and thin. Oh, that the Lord would turn the water into wine! Many of you live upon milk, and yet your years qualify you to feed on meat. Why keep the babes' diet? You who believe are exhorted to "go in and out and find pasture" (John 10:9). Range throughout the whole revelation of God. It will be well for you if your faith also increases intensively. Oh, that you may more fully believe what you do believe! We need deeper insight and firmer conviction. We do not *half* believe, as yet, any of us. Many of you only skim the pools of the truth of God. Blessed is the wing that brushes the surface of the river of life. But infinitely more blessed is it to plunge into the depths of it. This is John's desire for you: that you would believe with all your heart and soul and strength.

He would have you believe more constantly, so that you may say, "My heart is steadfast, O God, my heart is steadfast; I will sing and give praise" (Ps. 57:7). It is not always so with us. We are at times chicken-hearted. We play the man today and the mouse tomorrow. Lord, have mercy upon us. We are an inconsistent people, fickle as the wind. The Lord would have us abide always in Him with strong and mighty confidence, being rooted and built up in Him.

He would have us trust courageously. Some can believe in a small way about small things. Oh, for a boundless trust in the infinite God! We need more of a venturesome faith, the faith to do and dare. Often we see the way of power but have not the faith that would be equal to it. See Peter walking on the sea! I do not advise any of you to try it; neither did our Lord advise Peter to do so. We do well enough if we walk uprightly on land. But when Peter had once taken a few steps on the sea, he ought to have known that His Lord could help him all the rest of the way.

But alas, his faith failed and he began to sink. He could have walked all the way to Jesus if he had believed right on. So it is with us. Our faith is good enough for a spurt, but it lacks staying power. Oh, may God give us to believe so that we may not only trip over a wave or two but also walk on the water to the end! If the Lord bids you, you may go through fire and not be burned, through the floods and not be drowned. Such a fearless, careless, conquering faith may the Lord work in us!

We need also to have our faith increased in the sense of its becoming more practical. Some people have a fine new faith, as pretty as the bright poker in the parlor and as useless. We want an everyday faith, not to look at, but to use. Brothers and sisters, we need faith for the kitchen and the pantry, as well as for the drawing room and the conservatory. We need workshop faith, as well as prayer-meeting faith. We need faith as to the common things of life and the trying things of death. We could do with less paint if we had more power. We need less varnish and more verity. God give to you that you may believe on the name of the Son of God with a sound, commonsense faith that will be found wearable and washable and workable throughout life.

We need to believe more joyfully. Oh, what a blessed thing it is when you reach the rest and joy of faith! If we would truly believe the promise of God and rest in the Lord's certain fulfillment of it, we might be as happy as the angels. I notice how very early in the morning the birds begin to sing—

before the sun is up or even the first gray tints of morning light are visible, the little songsters are awake and singing. Too often we refuse to sing until the sun is more than up and noon is near. Shame on us! Will we never trust our God? Will we never praise Him for favors to come? Oh, for a faith that can sing through the night and through the winter! Faith that can live on a promise is the faith of God's elect. You will never enjoy heaven below until you believe without wavering. May the Lord give you such faith.

II. Thus I have gone through my first head and taken nearly all the time. I must now come to push of pike, as the old soldiers used to say. We must drive our teaching home. *The purpose that John had in his mind, we ought to follow up.* If he wished us to know that we have eternal life, brothers and sisters, let us try to know it. The Word of God was written for this purpose. Let us use it for its proper end. The whole of these scriptures was written that we might believe that Jesus is the Christ "and that believing [we] may have life in His name."

This book is written to you who believe, that you may know that you believe. Will you suffer your Bibles to be a failure to you? Will you live in perpetual questioning and doubt? If so, the book has missed its mark for you. The Bible is sent that you may have full assurance of your possession of eternal life—do not, therefore, dream that it will be presumptuous on your part to aspire to it. Our conscience tells us that we ought to seek full assurance of salvation. It cannot be right for us to be children of God and not to know our own Father.

How can we kneel down and say, "Our Father in heaven," when we do not know whether He is our Father or not? Will not a life of doubt tend to be a life of falsehood? May we not be using language that is not true to our consciousness? Can you sing joyful hymns that you fear are not true of you? Will you join in worship when your heart does not know that God is your God? Until the spirit of adoption enables you to cry, "Abba, Father," where is your love to God? Can you rest? Dare you rest while it is a question whether you are saved or not?

Can you go home to your dinner today and enjoy your meal while there is a question about your soul's eternal life? Oh, be not so foolhardy as to run risks on that matter! I pray you, make sure work for eternity. If you leave anything in uncertainty, let it concern your body or your estate but not your soul. Conscience bids you seek to know that you have eternal life, for without this knowledge many duties will be impossible of performance. Many scriptures, which I cannot quote this morning, stir you up to this duty.

Are you not bid to make your calling and election sure? Are you not a thousand times over exhorted to rejoice in the Lord and to give thanks continually? But how can you rejoice if the dark suspicion haunts you that perhaps, after all, you have not the life of God? You must get this question settled or you cannot rest in the Lord and wait patiently for Him. Come, brothers and sisters, I beseech you—as you would follow scripture and obey the Lord's precepts, get the assurance without which you cannot obey them.

Listen, as I close, to the reasons why each believer should seek to know that he has eternal life. Here they are. Assurance of your salvation will bring you "the peace of God, which surpasses all understanding" (Phil. 4:7). If you know that you are saved, you can sit down in poverty or in sickness or under slander and feel perfectly content. Full assurance is the Kohinoor among the jewels with which the heavenly bridegroom adorns His spouse. Assurance is a mountain of spices, a land that flows with milk and honey. To be the assured possessor of eternal life is to find a paradise beneath the stars, where the mountains and the hills break forth before you into singing.

> *Our conscience tells us that we ought to seek full assurance of salvation. It cannot be right for us to be children of God and not to know our own Father.*

Full assurance will sometimes overflow in waterfalls of delight. Peace flows like a river, and here and there it leaps in cascades of ecstatic joy. There are seasons when the plant of peace is in flower and then it sheds a perfume as of myrrh and cassia. Oh, the blessedness of the man who knows that he has eternal life! Sometimes in our room alone, when we have been enjoying this assurance, we have laughed outright, for we could not help it. If anybody had wondered why a man was laughing by himself alone, we could have explained that it was nothing ridiculous that had touched us, but our mouth was filled with laughter because the Lord had done great things for us, whereof we were glad!

That religion that sets no sweetmeats on the table is a stingy housekeeper.

I do not wonder that some people give up their starveling religion—it is hardly worth the keeping. The child of God who knows that he has eternal life goes to school, but he has many a holiday. And he anticipates that day of going home when he will see the face of his Beloved forever.

Brethren, full assurance will give us the full result of the gospel. The gospel ought to make us holy. And so it will, when we are in full possession of it. The gospel ought to make us separate from the world. The gospel ought to make us lead a heavenly life here below. And so it will, if we drink deep draughts of it. But if we take only a sip of it now and again, we give it no chance of working out its design in us. Do not paddle about the margin of the water of life, but first wade in up to your knees and then hasten to plunge into the waters to swim. Beware of contentment with shallow grace. Prove what the grace of God can do for you by giving yourself up to its power.

Full assurance gives a man a grateful zeal for the God he loves. These are the people who will go to the Congo for Jesus, for they know they are His. These are the people who will lay down their all for Christ, for Christ is theirs. These are the people who will bear scorn and shame and misrepresentation for the truth's sake, for they know that they have eternal life. These are they who will keep on preaching and teaching, spending and working, for theirs is the kingdom of heaven and they know it. Men will do little for what they doubt and much for what they believe. If you have lost your title deeds and you do not know whether your house is your own or not, you are not going to spend much in repairs and enlargements. When you know that heaven is yours, you are anxious to get ready for it. Full assurance finds fuel for zeal to feed upon.

This also creates and sustains patience. When we know that we have eternal life, we do not fret about the trials of this passing life. I could point to the brethren here this morning and I could mention sisters at home who amaze me by their endurance of pain and weakness. This I know concerning them, that they never have a doubt about their interest in Christ. And for this cause they are able to surrender themselves into those dear hands that were pierced for them. They know that they are the Lord's, and so they say, "Let Him do what seems good to Him" (1 Sam. 3:18).

A blind child was in his father's arms and a stranger came into the room and took him right away from his father. Yet he did not cry or complain. His father said to him, "Johnny, are you afraid? You do not know the person who has got hold of you."

"No, Father," he said, "I do not know who he is, but you do."

When pain gives us an awkward nip and we do not know whether we will live or die; when we are called to undergo a dangerous operation and pass into unconsciousness, then we can say, "I do not know where I am, but my Father knows and I leave all with Him." Assurance makes us strong to suffer.

This, dear friends, will give you constant firmness in your confession of divine truth. You who do not know whether you are saved or not, I hope the Lord will keep you from denying the faith. But those who have a firm grip of it, these are the men who will never forsake it.

A caviler in an omnibus said to a Christian man one day, "Why, you have nothing, after all, to rest upon. I can prove to you that your scriptures are not authentic."

The humble Christian man replied, "Sir, I am not a learned man and I cannot answer your questions. But I believe in the Lord Jesus Christ and I have experienced such a change in character, and I feel such a joy and peace through believing, that I wish you knew my Savior, too."

The answer he received was a very unexpected one. The unbeliever said, "You have got me there. I cannot answer that."

Just sow; you have got them there. If we know what has been worked in us by divine grace, they cannot overcome us. The full-assurance man baffles the very devil. Satan is cunning enough, but those who know and are persuaded are birds that he cannot take in the snares of hell. When you know that your Lord is able to keep that which you have committed to Him until that day, then you are firm as a rock. God make you so.

Dear brethren, this is the kind of thing that will enable you to bear a telling testimony for your Lord. It is of no use to stand up and preach things that may or may not be true. I am charged with being a dreadful dogmatist and I am not anxious to excuse myself. When a man is not quite sure of a thing, he grows very liberal—anybody can be a liberal with money that he cannot claim to be his own. The broad-school man says, "I am not sure, and I do not suppose that you are sure, for indeed nothing is sure." Does this sandy foundation suit you? I prefer rock.

The things that I have spoken to you from my youth up have been such as I have tried and proved and to me they wear an absolute certainty, confirmed by my personal experience. I have tried these things—they have saved me and I cannot doubt them. I am a lost man if the gospel I have preached to you is not true. And I am content to bide the issue of the Day of Judgment. I do not preach doubtingly, for I do not live doubtingly. I know what I have told you to be true. Why should I speak as if I were not sure? If you want to make your own testimony credible in such a day as this, you must have something to say that you are sure about. And until you are sure about it, I would advise you to hold your tongue. We do not require any more questionings. The market is overstocked. We need no more doubt, honest or dishonest.

Brethren, if you know that you have eternal life, you are prepared to live and equally prepared to die. How frequently do I stand at the bedside of our dying members! I am every now and then saying to myself, "I will certainly meet with some fainthearted one. Surely I will come across some child of God who is dying in the dark." But I have not met with any such. Brethren, a child of God may die in the dark.

One said to old Mr. Dodd, the quaint old Puritan, "How sad that our brother should have passed away in the darkness! Do you doubt his safety?"

"No," said old Mr. Dodd, "no more than I doubt the safety of Him who said, when He was dying, "My God, my God, why have you forsaken Me?"

Full assurance, as we have said before, is not of the essence of salvation. Still, I beg of you to note that all along through these many years, in each case, when I have gone to visit any of our brothers and sisters at death, I have always found them departing in sure and certain hope of seeing the face of their Lord in glory. I have often marveled that this should be without exception, and I glory in it. Often have they said to me, "We have fed on such good food that we may well be strong in the Lord."

God grant that you may have this assurance, all of you! May sinners begin to believe in Jesus and saints believe more firmly, for Christ's sake! Amen.

For Further Thought

1. *According to John 20:31, why did John write his gospel?*
2. *What did John say will be the result of a person's belief in Jesus Christ?*
3. *Read 1 John 3:14. How do we know that we have passed from death to life?*

IF THERE IS
NO RESURRECTION

Now if Christ is preached that He has been raised from the dead, how do some among you say that there is no resurrection of the dead? But if there is no resurrection of the dead, then Christ is not risen. And if Christ is not risen, then our preaching is empty and your faith is also empty. Yes, and we are found false witnesses of God, because we have testified of God that He raised up Christ, whom He did not raise up—if in fact the dead do not rise. For if the dead do not rise, then Christ is not risen. And if Christ is not risen, your faith is futile; you are still in your sins! Then also those who have fallen asleep in Christ have perished. If in this life only we have hope in Christ, we are of all men the most pitiable.

1 CORINTHIANS 15:12–19

OUR religion is not based upon opinions, but upon facts. We hear persons sometimes saying, "Those are your views, and these are ours." Whatever your views may be is a small matter; what are the *facts* of the case? We must, after all, if we want a firm foundation, come down to matters of *fact*. Now, the great facts of the gospel are that God was incarnate in Christ Jesus, that He lived here a life of holiness and love, that He died upon the cross for our sins, that He was buried in the tomb of Joseph, that the third day He rose again from the dead, that after a while He ascended to His Father's throne where He now sits—and that He will come, by and by, to be our judge, and in that day the dead in Christ will rise by virtue of their union with Him.

Now, very soon, within the church of God, there rose up persons who began to dispute the fundamental principles of the faith, and it is so even now. When those outside the church deny that Christ is the Son of God, deny His atoning sacrifice, and deny His resurrection, we are not at all astonished. They are unbelievers, and they are acting out their own profession. But when men *inside* the church of God call themselves Christians and yet deny the resurrection of the dead, then is our soul stirred within us, for it is a most solemn and serious evil to doubt those holy truths of God. They know not what they do; they cannot see all the result of their unbelief! If they could, one would think that they would start back with horror and let the truth of God stand where it ought to stand, where God has put it.

The resurrection of the dead has been assailed and is still assailed by those who are called Christians, even by those who are called Christian *ministers*, but who, nevertheless, spirit away the very idea of the resurrection of the dead, so that we are today in the same condition, to some extent, as the Corinthian church was when, in its very midst, there rose up men professing to be followers of Christ who said that there was no resurrection of the dead! The apostle Paul, having borne his witness and recapitulated the testimony about the resurrection of Christ, goes on to show the horrible consequences that must follow if there is no resurrection of the dead and if Christ is not raised. He showed this to be a foundational truth of God, and if it were taken away, much more was gone than they supposed—indeed, *everything* was gone—as Paul went on to prove.

> he meeting of objections is an endless work. When you have killed one regiment of them, there is another regiment coming on, and when you have put to the sword whole legions of doubts, doubters still swarm upon you like the frogs of Egypt!

Beloved friends, let us never tamper with the truth of God. I find it as much as I can do to enjoy the comfort of the truth and to learn the spiritual lessons of God's Word without setting up to be a critic upon it. And I find it immeasurably more profitable to my own soul to believingly adore than unbelievingly to invent objections, or even industriously to try to meet them. The meeting of objections is an endless work. When you have killed one regiment of them, there is another regiment coming on, and when you have put to the sword whole legions of doubts, doubters still swarm upon you like the frogs of Egypt! It is a poor business. It answers no practical end. It is far better to firmly believe what you profess to believe and to follow out to all the blessed consequences all of the truths of God that, in your own heart and soul, you have received of the Lord.

One of the truths most surely believed among us is that there will be a resurrection of all those who sleep in Christ. There will be a resurrection of the ungodly as well as of the godly. Our Lord Jesus said to the Jews,

> "Most assuredly, I say to you, he who hears My word and believes in Him who sent Me has everlasting life, and shall not come into judgment, but has passed from death into life. Most assuredly, I say to you, the hour is coming, and now is, when the dead will hear the voice of the Son of God; and those who hear will live. For as the Father has life in Himself, so He has granted the Son to have life in Himself, and has given Him authority to execute judgment also, because He is the Son of man. Do not marvel at this; for the hour is coming in which all who are in the graves will hear His voice and come forth—those who have done good, to the resurrection of life, and those who have done evil, to the resurrection of condemnation." (John 5:24–29)

Paul declared before Felix the doctrine of "a resurrection of the dead, both of the just and the unjust" (Acts 24:15), but his argument with the Corinthians specially referred to believers who will rise from the dead and stand with Christ in the day of His appearing, quickened with the life that quickened Him and raised up to share the glory that the Father has given to Him.

I. Paul's argument begins here, and this will be our first head: *If there is no resurrection, Christ is not raised.*

If the resurrection of the dead is impossible, Christ cannot have risen from the dead. Now, *the apostles bore witness that Christ had risen from the dead.* They had met Him, they had been with Him, and they had seen Him eat a piece of a broiled fish and of a honeycomb on one occasion. They had seen Him perform acts that could not be performed by a spirit, but which needed that He should be flesh and bones. Indeed, He said, "A spirit does not have flesh and bones as you see I have" (Luke 24:39). One of them put his finger into the print of the nails and was invited to thrust his hand into

Christ's side. He was known by two of them in the breaking of bread, a familiar token by which they recognized Him better than by anything else. They heard Him speak, they knew the tones of His voice, they were not deceived. On one occasion, five hundred of them saw Him at once, or, if there was any possibility of a mistake when they were all together, they were not deceived when they saw Him one by one and entered into very close personal communion with Him, each one after a different sort. "Now," says Paul, "if there is no resurrection of the dead, if that is impossible, then of course Christ did not rise, and yet we all assure you that we saw Him, and that we were with Him, and you must think that we are all liars, and that the Christian religion is a lie, or else you must believe that there is a resurrection of the dead."

"But," says one, "Christ might rise and yet not His people." Not so! According to our faith and firm belief, Christ is one with His people. When Adam sinned, the whole human race fell in him, for they were one with him—in Adam, all died. Even those who have not sinned after the similitude of Adam's transgression have, nevertheless, died. Even upon infants, the death sentence has taken effect because they were one with Adam. There is no separating Adam from his posterity. Now, Christ is the second Adam, and He has a posterity. All believers are one with Him and none can separate themselves from Him. If *they* do not live, then *He* did not live. And if He did not rise, then they will not rise—whatever happened to Him must also happen to them. They are so welded together, the head and the members, that there is no dividing them! If He had slept an eternal sleep, then every righteous soul would have done the same. If He rose again, they must rise again, for He has taken them to Himself to be part and parcel of His very being! He died that they might live. Because He lives, they will live also, and in His eternal life they must forever be partakers.

This is Paul's first argument, then, for the resurrection of the righteous: that, inasmuch as Christ rose, they must rise, for they are identified with Him.

II. Now he proceeds with his subject, arguing not so much upon the resurrection of others as upon the resurrection of Christ. And his next argument is that *if there is no resurrection, apostolic preaching fails*. "If Christ is not risen, then our preaching is empty" (see the fourteenth verse). "Yes, and we are found false witnesses of God, because we have testified of God that He raised up Christ, whom He did not raise up—if in fact the dead do not rise" (1 Cor. 15:15).

If Christ was not raised, the apostles were false witnesses. When a man bears false witness, he usually has a motive for doing so. What motive had these men? What did they gain by bearing false witness to Christ's resurrection? It was all loss and no profit to them if He had not risen. They declared in Jerusalem that He had risen from the dead, and straightway men began to haul them to prison and to put them to death! Those of them who survived bore the same testimony. They were so full of the conviction of it that they went into distant countries to tell the story of Jesus and His resurrection from the dead. Some went to Rome, some to Spain—probably some came even to this remote island of Britain. Wherever they went, they testified that Christ had risen from the dead and that they had seen Him alive—and that He was the Savior of all who trusted in Him!

Thus they always preached, and what became of them? I may say, with Paul, that "they were stoned, they were sawn in two, were tempted, were slain with the sword. They wandered about in sheepskins and goatskins, being destitute, afflicted, tormented" (Heb. 11:37). They were brought before the Roman emperor again and again, and before the proconsuls, and threatened with the most painful of deaths, but not one of them ever withdrew his testimony concerning Christ's resurrection! They still stood to it, that they had known Him in life, many of them had been near Him in death, and they had all communed with Him after His resurrection. They declared that Jesus of Nazareth was the Son of God, that He died and was buried, that He rose again, and that there was salvation for all who believed in Him!

Were these men false witnesses? If so, they were the most extraordinary false witnesses who ever lived! What were their morals? What kind of men were they? Were they drunkards? Were they adulterers? Were they thieves? No, they were the purest and best of mankind! Their adversaries could bring no charge against their moral conduct. They were eminently honest and they spoke with the accent of conviction. As I have already said, they suffered for their testimony. Now, under the law, the witness of two men was to be received, but what will we say of the witness of five hundred men? If it was true when they first declared that Jesus Christ rose from the dead, it is equally true now. It does not matter, though the event happened nearly nineteen hundred years ago, it is just as true now! The apostles bore witness that could not be denied, and so it still stands. We cannot assume that all these apostolic men were false witnesses of God.

If we even suppose that they were mistaken about this matter, we must suspect their witness about everything else. And the only logical result is to give up the New Testament altogether. If they were mistaken as to Christ having risen from the dead, they are not credible witnesses upon anything else! And if they are discredited, the whole of our religion falls with them— the Christian faith and especially all that the apostles built on Christ's resurrection must be turned out of doors as altogether a delusion! They taught that Christ's rising from the dead was the evidence that His sacrifice was accepted, that He rose again for our justification, that His rising again was the hope of believers in this life and the assurance of the resurrection of their bodies in the life to come. You must give up all your hope of salvation the moment you doubt the Lord's rising from the dead!

> *You* must give up all your hope of salvation the moment you doubt the Lord's rising from the dead!

Paul puts himself with the rest of the apostles and says, "And if Christ is not risen, then our preaching is empty and your faith is also empty. Yes, and we are found false witnesses of God" (1 Cor. 15:14–15). I venture to bring him forward as a solitary witness of the most convincing kind. I need not remind you how he was, at first, opposed to Christ. He was a Pharisee of the Pharisees, one of the most intolerant members of the sect that hated the very *name* of Christ! He had a righteousness that surpassed that of the men of his times. He was a religious leader and persecutor, and yet he was so convinced of the appearance of Christ to him on the way to Damascus that from that time he was completely turned round and he preached with burning zeal the faith that once he blasphemed! There is an honesty about Paul that convinces at once—and if he had not seen the Savior risen from the dead, he would not have been the man to say that he did.

Dear brothers and sisters, you may rest assured that Jesus Christ *did* rise from the dead! You cannot put down these good men as impostors. You cannot reckon the apostle Paul among those readily deceived, or among the deceivers of others. So you may be sure that Jesus Christ did rise from the dead, according to the Scriptures.

III. Once more, Paul's argument is that *if there is no resurrection, faith becomes a delusion.* As we have to give up the apostles and all their teaching *if Christ did not rise from the dead,* so we must conclude that *their hearers believed a lie:* "Your faith is also empty." Beloved, I speak to you who have believed in the Lord Jesus Christ and who are resting in Him with great comfort and peace of mind, yes, who have experienced a great change of heart and a great change in your lives through faith in Christ. Now, if He did not rise from the dead, you believe a lie! Take this home to yourselves: If he did not *literally* rise from the dead on the third day, this faith of yours that gives you comfort—this faith that has renewed you in heart and life, this faith that you believe is leading you home to heaven—must be abandoned as a sheer delusion! Your faith is fixed on a lie. Oh, dreadful inference! But the inference is clearly true that if Christ is not raised, you are risking your soul on a lie if Christ did not rise from the dead. This is a solemn statement. I said last Sabbath, and I repeat it:

> *Upon a life I did not live,*
> *Upon a death I did not die*
> *I risk my whole eternity.*

It is so. If Jesus Christ did not die for me and did not rise again for me, I am lost. I have not a ray of comfort from any other direction. I have no dependence on anything else but Jesus crucified and risen—and if that sheet anchor fails, everything fails with it, in my case—and so it must in yours.

> If Christ did not rise, do not trust Him, for such faith is in vain! But if you believe that He did die for you and did rise again for you, then believe in Him, joyously confident that such a fact as this affords a solid basis for your belief!

"Your faith is also empty," wrote Paul to the Corinthians, for if Christ is not risen, the trial will be too great for faith to endure, since it has for the very keystone of the arch the resurrection of Christ from the dead. If He did not rise, your faith rests on what never happened and is not true! And certainly your faith will not bear that or any other trial. There comes to the believer, every now and then, a time of great testing. Did you ever lie, as I have done several times, upon the brink of eternity, full of pain, almost over the border of this world, fronting eternity, looking into the dread abyss? There, unless you are sure about the foundation of your faith, you are in an evil case indeed! Unless you have a solid rock beneath you *then*, your hope will shrink away to nothing and your confidence will depart!

When you are sure that the Lord is raised, then you feel that there is something beneath your feet that does not stir. If Jesus died for you and Jesus rose for you, then, my dear brothers and sisters, you are not afraid even of that tremendous day when the earth will be burned up and the elements will melt with fervent heat! You feel a confidence that will bear even that test. If Christ did not rise from the dead and you are resting your soul on the belief that He did, what a failure it will be for you in another world! What disappointment when you do not wake up in His likeness! What dismay if there should be no pardon of sin, no salvation through the precious blood! If Christ is not raised, your faith is in vain. If it is in vain, give it up! Do not hold on to a thing that is not true! I would sooner plunge into the water and swim or wade through the river than I would trust myself to a rotten bridge that would break down in the middle. If Christ did not rise, do not trust Him, for such faith is in vain! But if you believe that He *did* die for you and *did* rise again for you, then believe in Him, joyously confident that such a fact as this affords a solid basis for your belief!

IV. Now I am going to advance a little further. Paul says next that *if there is no resurrection, they remained in their sins*. "If Christ is not risen, your faith is futile; you are still in your sins!" Ah, can you bear that thought, my beloved in Christ, that you are still in your sins? I think that the bare suggestion takes hold upon you, terrifies you, and chills your blood! A little while ago you were in your sins, dead in them, covered with them as with a crimson robe—you were condemned, lost. But now you believe that Christ has brought you out of your sins and washed you and made you white in His precious blood. Yes, and has so changed you that sin will not have dominion over you, for now you are, by grace, a child of God! Well, but if Christ did not rise again, you are still in your sins.

Observe that *for then there is no atonement made*, at least no satisfactory atonement. If the atonement of Christ for sin had been unsatisfactory, He would have remained in the grave. He went there on our behalf, a hostage for us, and if what He did upon the tree had not satisfied the justice of God, then He would never have come out of the grave again! Think for a minute what our position would be if I stood here to preach only a dead and buried Christ! He died nearly nineteen hundred years ago, but suppose He had never been heard of since? If He had not risen from the dead, could you have confidence in Him? You would say, "How do we know that His sacrifice was accepted?" We sing right truly:

> *If Jesus ne'er had paid the debt,*
> *He ne'er had been at freedom set.*

The Surety would have been under bonds unless He had discharged all His liability. But He has done so, and He has risen from the dead—

> *And now both the surety and sinner are free.*

Understand clearly what I am saying. The Lord Jesus Christ, the Son of God, took upon Himself the sum total of the guilt of all His people. "The LORD has laid on Him the iniquity of us all" (Isa. 53:6). He died and by His death obtained the full discharge of all our obligations. But His rising again was, so to speak, the receipt in full, the token that He had discharged the whole of the dread liabilities that He had taken upon Himself. And now, since Christ is raised, you who believe in Him are not in your sins. But if He had not risen, then it would have been true, "You are still in your sins."

It would have been true, also, in another sense. The life by which true believers live is the resurrection life of Him who said, "Because I live, you will live also" (John 14:19). But if Christ is not raised, there is no life for those who are in Him. If He were still slumbering in the grave, where would have been the life that now makes us joyful and makes us aspire after heavenly things? There would have been no life for you if there had not first been life for Him. Now Christ is raised from the dead, and in Him you rise into newness of life. But if He did not rise, you are still dead, still under sin, still without the divine life, still without the life immortal and eternal that is to be your life in heaven throughout eternity!

So you see once more the consequences that follow. "If Christ is not risen, your faith is futile; you are still in your sins!"

V. Now follows, if possible, a still more terrible consequence! *If there is no resurrection, all the pious dead have perished.* "Then also those who have fallen asleep in Christ have perished." Perished, by which is not meant *annihilated*—they are in a worse condition than that!

One phrase must be explained by another that went before it: If Jesus Christ is not risen, they are yet in their sins. They died, and they told us that they were blood-washed and forgiven and that they hoped to see the face of God with joy. But if Christ rose not from the dead, there is no sinner who has gone to heaven, there is no saint who ever died who has had any real hope. He has died under a delusion, and he has perished!

> *I*f we consider the mirth of the worldling to be no better than the husks of swine and there is no bread for us in the fact that Christ rose from the dead, then we are hungry indeed.

If Jesus Christ is not raised, the godly dead are yet in their sins, and *they can never rise*, for if Christ did not rise from the dead, they cannot rise from the dead! Only through His resurrection is there resurrection for the saints. The ungodly will rise to shame and everlasting contempt, but believers will rise into eternal life and felicity because of their oneness with Christ. But if He did not rise, they cannot rise. If He is dead, they must be dead, for they must share with Him. They are, they always must be, one with Him—and all the saints who ever died, died under a mistake if Christ did not rise! We cast away the thought with abhorrence! Many of us have had beloved parents and friends who have died in the Lord, and we know that the full assurance of their faith was no mistake. We have seen dear children die in sure and certain hope of a glorious resurrection! And we know that it was no error on their part. I have stood by many deathbeds of believers, many triumphant, and many more peaceful and calm than a sweet summer evening. They were not mistaken. No, dear sirs. Believing in Christ who lived and died and rose again, they had confidence in the midst of pain, and joy in the hour of their departure! We cannot believe that they were mistaken, and therefore we are confident that Jesus Christ *did* rise from the dead!

VI. Once more, *if there is no resurrection, our source of joy is gone.* If Jesus did not rise from the dead, we who believe that He did are, of all men, the most pitiable. "If in this life only we have hope in Christ," and we certainly have no hope of any other life apart from Christ, "we are of all men the most pitiable."

What does Paul mean? That Christian men are more miserable than others if they are mistaken? No, he does not mean *that*, for even the mistake, if it is a mistake, gives them joy. The error, if it is an error, yields them a present confidence and peace. But supposing they are sure that they are under an error, that they have made a mistake—then their comfort is gone and they are, of all men, the most pitiable!

Believers have given up sensuous joys. They have sedulously given them up. They find no comfort in them. There are a thousand things in which worldlings find a kind of joy, all of which the Christian loathes. Well, if you have given up the brown bread and cannot eat the white, then are you starved. If we consider the mirth of the worldling to be no better than the husks of swine, and there is no bread for us in the fact that Christ rose from the dead, then we are hungry indeed.

And more than that, *we have now learned superior things.* We have learned to love holiness and we seek after it. We have learned to love communion with God and it has become our heaven to talk with our Father and our Savior. We now look after things that are *spiritual.* And we try to handle carnal things as they should be handled, as things to be used but not abused. Now if, after having tasted these superior joys, they all turn out to be nothing—and they must turn out to be nothing if Jesus did not rise from the dead—then we are indeed of all men the most pitiable!

More than that, we have had high hopes, hopes that have made our hearts leap for joy. We have been ready, sometimes, to go straightaway out of the body, with high delights and raptures, in the expectation of being with Christ, which is far better. We have said, "And though after my skin worms destroy this body, yet in my flesh shall I see God: whom I shall see for myself, and mine eyes shall behold, and not another" (Job 19:26–27 KJV). We have been transported with the full conviction that our eyes "will see the King in His beauty; they will see the land that is very far off" (Isa. 33:17). And if that is not sure, if it can be proved that our hopes are in vain, then are we, of all men, the most pitiable!

You will wonder why I have been so long in bringing out these points, and what I am driving at. Well, what I am driving at is this. After all, everything hinges upon a fact, an ancient fact, and if that fact is *not* a fact, it is over with us. If Jesus Christ did *not* rise from the dead, then His gospel is all exploded. What I want you to notice is this: that there must be a basis of *fact* in our religion. These things must be facts or else nothing can give us consolation.

Our eternal hopes do not depend upon our moral condition, for, observe, these men in Corinth would not have been better or worse if Christ had not risen from the dead. Their character was just the same. It had been fashioned, it is true, by a belief that He *did* rise from the dead, but whether He did or did not, they were the same men, so that their hope did not depend upon their good moral condition. The apostle does not say, "If you are or are not in such and such a moral condition," but "If Christ is not risen, your faith is futile; you are still in your sins." So, my beloved, the reason of your being safe will be that Christ died for you and that He rose again. It is not the result of what you *are*, but of what He *did*. The hinge of it all is not in you—it is in Him—and you are to place your reliance, not upon what you are or hope to be, but wholly and entirely upon a great fact that transpired nearly nineteen hundred years ago. If He did not rise from the dead, you are still in your sins, be you as good as you may. But if He did rise from the dead and you are one with Him, you are not in your sins—they are all put away and you are accepted in the Beloved.

> The more true science, the better, but when science comes in to tell me that it has discovered anything about the way to heaven, then I have a deaf ear to it!

Now I go a step further. The great hope you have does not hinge even upon your spiritual state. You must be born again. You must have a new heart and a right spirit, or else you cannot lay hold of Christ and He is not yours. But still, your ultimate hope is not in what you are spiritually, but in what He is. When darkness comes over your soul and you say, "I am afraid I am not converted," still believe in Him who rose from the dead and when, after you have had a sight of yourself, you are drifting away to dark despair, still cling to Him who loved you and gave Himself for you and rose again from the dead for you! If you believe that Christ is risen from the dead, and if this is the foundation of your hope of heaven, that hope stands just as sure whether you are bright or whether you are dull, whether you can sing or whether you are forced to sigh, whether you can run or whether you are a broken-legged cripple only able to lie at Christ's feet.

If He died for you and rose again for you, that is the groundwork of your confidence, and I pray you keep to it. Do you see how Paul insists upon this? If Christ is not raised, your faith is in vain and you are still in your sins. The inference is that if Christ is raised and you have faith in Him, your faith is not in vain and you are not in your sins. You are saved! Your hope must not be here in what your hands can do, but there, on yonder cross, in *what He did*, and there, on yonder throne, in Him who has risen again for your justification.

The hardest thing in the world seems to be to keep people to this truth, for I have noticed that much of the modern-thought doctrine is nothing but old self-righteousness tricked out again. It is still bidding men to trust in *themselves*, to trust in their *moral character*, to trust in their *spiritual aspirations*, or something or other. I stand here tonight to say to you that the basis of your hope is not even your own *faith*, much less your own *good works*. It is what Christ has done once and for all, for "you are complete in Him" (Col. 2:10), and you can never be complete in any other way!

Here again, I would have you notice that Paul does not say that your being forgiven and saved depends upon your sincerity and your earnestness. You must be sincere and earnest—Christ is not yours if you are not—but still, you may be very sincere and very earnest, and yet be wrong all the while. And the more sincere and earnest you are in a wrong way, the further you will go astray. The self-righteous man may be very sincere as he goes about to establish a righteousness of his own, but the more he does it, the more he ruins himself. But here is the mark for you to aim at—not at your sincerity, though there must be that—but if Christ was raised and that is where you are resting your hopes, then you are not in your sins, but you are accepted in Christ and justified in Him.

This is where I stand, and I pray every believer to stand here. There are many new discoveries made in science. We are pleased to hear it. I hope that we will be able to travel more quickly and pay less for it. I hope that we will have better light and that it will not be so expensive. The more true science, the better, but when science comes in to tell me that it has discovered anything about the way to heaven, then I have a deaf ear to it! "If Christ is not risen, then our preaching is empty, and your faith is also empty. . . . You are still in your sins!" But if Christ is raised, then I know where I am. If it is really so that He is God in human flesh, if He took my sin and bore the consequences of it and made a clear sweep of it from before the judgment seat of the Most High, and if His rising again is God's testimony that the work is done and that Christ, who stood as substitute for me, is accepted for me, oh, hallelujah, hallelujah! What more do I need but to praise and bless the name of Him who has saved me with an effectual salvation? Now will I work for Him! Now will I spend and be spent in His service! Now will I hate every false way and every sin, and seek after purity and holiness, but not, in any sense, as the groundwork of my confidence. My one hope for time and eternity is *Jesus*, only *Jesus*! Jesus crucified and risen from the dead.

I do not know any passage of scripture that, more thoroughly than this one, throws the stress where the stress must be—not on man, but on Christ alone: "If there is no resurrection of the dead, then Christ is not risen. And if Christ is not risen, then our preaching is empty and your faith is also empty." O dear hearer, if you would be saved, your salvation does not lie with yourself, but with Him who left His Father's bosom and came down to earth a babe at Bethlehem and hung upon a woman's breast—upon Him who lived here, for thirty-three years, a life of suffering and of toil and who then took all the sin of His people upon Himself, carried it up to the tree and there bore all the consequences of it in His own body—

> *Bore all that Almighty God could bear,*
> *With strength enough, but none to spare.*

Jesus Christ bore that which has made God's pardon an act of justice and vindicated His forgiveness of sin so that none can say that He is unjust when He passes by transgression! Christ did all that and then, dying, was laid in the tomb, but the third day His Father raised Him from the dead in token that He spoke the truth when He said, on the cross, "It is finished!" (John 19:30).

The debt is now paid! Then, O sinner, leave your prison, for your debt is paid! Are you shut up in despair on account of your debt of sin? It is all discharged if you have believed in Him who was raised from the dead He has taken all your sin and you are free. That handwriting of ordinances that was against you is nailed to His cross. Go your way and sing, "The Lord is risen indeed," and be as happy as all the birds in the air, till you are, by and by, as happy as the angels in heaven through Jesus Christ our Lord. Amen.

For Further Thought

1. *Read 1 Corinthians 15:17. Where are we now, if Christ is not resurrected?*
2. *According to 1 Corinthians 15:18, if Christ is not resurrected, what has become of believers who have died?*
3. *If we do not hope in the resurrection but only look for blessings in this life, what kind of people are we? (See 1 Corinthians 15:19.)*

Sermons Relating to the Church

The Glory, Unity, and Triumph of the Church

"And the glory which You gave Me I have given them, that they may
be one just as We are one: I in them, and You in Me; that they may
be made perfect in one, and that the world may know that
You have sent Me, and have loved them as You have loved Me."
John 17:22–23

SOME words serve many uses and have many meanings. We are very apt to make mistakes if we give the same sense in all places to the same word. The word *world* throughout scripture is used with a very remarkable variety of meaning, and one had need to have his wits about him and to read carefully in order to know what is the precise force of the term in each place where it occurs. In the text before us, it is evident that Christ had a view to the world. He desired that the world might know that the Father had sent Him and might know, also, that God had loved His people even as He had loved His Son. From the somewhat altered expression in the twenty-first verse, we feel convinced that our Lord did not limit His desires for the world to its having a bare knowledge of these facts, but wished that it should also *believe* them, for thus runs the verse: "That the world may *know* that You have sent Me."

He wished, then, that this world might do exactly what He elsewhere says His own disciples had already done: "O righteous Father! The world has not known You, but I have known You; and these have known that You sent Me" (John 17:25). Certainly there is a world for which Jesus did not pray, for He said, "I pray for them. I do not pray for the world" (John 17:9), yet here there is a world for which, if He does not actually pray, He yet prays that certain gracious events may occur in order that certain results may be produced upon the world.

I say again, the word *world*, therefore, has many shades of meaning ranging from that jet black meaning in which the world lies in the wicked one—"Love not the world, neither the things that are in the world" (1 John 2:15 KJV)—upward to the milder sense in John 1:10, "He was in the world, and the world was made through Him, and the world did not know Him." And yet higher to the brighter meaning, "The kingdoms of this world have become the kingdoms of our Lord and of His Christ" (Rev. 11:15). It is not in the worst sense that our text speaks of the world, but in the same manner as we find it used in such passages as these: "The Lamb of God who takes away the sin of the world!" (John 1:29). "God was in Christ reconciling the world to Himself, not imputing their trespasses to them" (2 Cor. 5:19). And again in 1 John 2:2, "And He Himself is the propitiation for our sins, and not for ours only but also for the whole world."

> *H*e desired that the world might know that the Father had sent Him and might know, also, that God had loved His people even as He had loved His Son.

It is certain that "God so loved the world that He gave His only begotten Son, that whoever believes in Him should not perish but have everlasting life" (John 3:16), and we cannot suppose that the great Redeemer would refuse to pray for those for whom He was given. I understand in this particular place by the word *world* the whole mass of mankind upon the face of the earth who are not as yet converted. Among them there is an elect part, for our Lord speaks of some men who will yet believe on Him through the word of His servants, but these, at this present moment, are undistinguished from the rest. I understand here the word *world* to mean all as yet unrenewed out of the whole living family of man. On account of *these* our Lord would have His believing people brought into that admirable condition that we will now attempt to describe.

For the sake of the world, He would have the church in a high state of holy beauty and strength. May His gracious prayer be answered in all of us by the working of the Holy Spirit! I trust that I may say of all of you, my beloved in Christ, that you are living with this objective. At any rate, I know that you desire to live for the glory of our Lord Jesus and the salvation of men. We would make all men see what is the fellowship of this mystery, for we would have all men to be saved and come to the knowledge of the truth of God. Our wish is to bring multitudes to the Savior and to conquer province after province of this revolted world for King Jesus. "Let the whole earth be filled with His glory" (Ps. 72:19) is a prayer that we *cannot*, *dare* not, *would* not fail to pray!

> *H*e appeared on earth as the Son of man, the Son of God, but even in that condescending capacity He was surrounded with a glory of which John speaks in his first chapter.

Half the world would be a poor reward for the Redeemer's travail. Even here, where He was despised and rejected of men, our Lord must reign with fullness of glory, having dominion from sea to sea and from the river even to the ends of the earth! This is the consummation toward which we are tending, by the grace of God. We are striving earnestly for it, according to His working, which works in us mightily. Daily we labor to bring others into subjection to that blessed sovereignty under which we delight to dwell!

In this place our Lord tells us that this desirable end is to be brought about by a marvelous unity that, described in our text, is a unity of men with Christ, a unity of these men in Christ with one another, and the unity of Christ Himself with the eternal Father. "I in them, and You in Me; that they may be made perfect in one" (John 17:23). Let us speak about this unity this morning, always keeping in mind the drift, end, and objective of it, namely, that the world may believe that God has sent the Lord Jesus.

First, let us think upon *the great means of that unity*; then, second, upon *the unity itself*. Lastly, let us more fully consider *the effect to be produced by it*.

I. First, then, let us reflect upon *the great means of the unity* that Christ proposes here. It lies, in a nutshell, here: "The glory which You gave Me I have given them," with this objective, "that they may be one just as We are one." Here our blessed Lord does not speak of what He will give to His disciples, though there is a glory that is laid up for them that the faithful will receive at the last—but He mentions a glory that He has *already* given them. This could not be the incommunicable glory of His Godhead, for that was His by nature and not by the Father's gift. He speaks throughout the whole of His prayer in the capacity of the mediator who is both God and man in one person, and the glory that He says He had given to His people is a glory that the Father had given to Him in His complex person as incarnate God.

We are to regard, therefore, our Lord Jesus Christ as speaking here as Immanuel, God with us, who, though He counted it no robbery to be equal with God, had made Himself of no reputation and taken upon Himself the form of a servant. He appeared on earth as the Son of man, the Son of God, but even in that condescending capacity He was surrounded with a glory of which John speaks in his first chapter: "And the Word became flesh and dwelt among us, and we beheld His glory, the glory as of the only begotten of the Father, full of grace and truth" (John 1:14). As the Word made flesh, the Father has given our Lord exceeding glory. The explanations of the words before us are as many as the words themselves, and I suppose there is a measure of truth in each of them. I do not think it possible in one sermon, perhaps not in a hundred, nor even in a thousand, to bring out all that is intended here! Therefore I will not attempt any such a task, but will only follow one narrow track of practical thought, even as one passes through a field of corn along a narrow pathway gathering a few ears as he moves along.

It seems to me that a main part of the glory of our Lord, when on earth, lay in the moral and spiritual glory of His character. He was indeed glorious in holiness, and this is evidently the glory that He transfers to us. See the second epistle to the Corinthians, the third chapter and eighteenth verse: "But we all, with unveiled face, beholding as in a mirror the glory of the Lord, are being transformed into the same image from glory to glory, just as by the Spirit of the Lord." To the same effect are Peter's words in his first epistle: "If you are reproached for the name of Christ, blessed are you, for the Spirit of glory and of God rests upon you" (1 Pet. 4:14). The essence and cause of the glory that the Father gave the Son was, first of all, that He endowed Him with the Holy Spirit. "God does not give the Spirit by measure. The Father loves the Son, and has given all things into His hand" (John 3:34–35).

The Holy Spirit descended upon our Lord in His baptism and abode upon Him so that in the power of the indwelling Spirit He lived, spoke, acted, and in all that He did, the Spirit of God was manifest. In Him was fulfilled the word of the Lord by the prophet Isaiah: "There shall come forth a Rod from the stem of Jesse, and a Branch shall grow out of his roots. The Spirit of the LORD shall rest upon Him" (Isa. 11:1–2). In this Spirit there is glory, for the prophet further says, "His resting place shall be glorious" (11:10).

Now this glory, our Lord Jesus has given to all His disciples. Upon each true disciple, the Spirit of God rests according to his measure. If we have not the anointing to the fullest, it is either from lack of capacity or by reason of our own sin, for the Spirit of God is given to the saints—He dwells with us and will be in us always. My brothers and sisters, I would to God we realized this, that the glory of the Holy Spirit that was given to Christ is also given to us, so that it is ours to think, to feel, to speak, to act under His guiding influence and supernatural power! What are we apart from the Holy Spirit? How can we hope to convince even one man, much less the *world*, that God has sent His Son unless the Holy Spirit is with us?

But if He will come—and I trust He *has* come upon many of us—if He will take possession of every faculty and rule and reign in us in all the splendor of His holiness, then we shall indeed become a power for the conversion of mankind! Behold, the Lord Jesus has given us this Spirit, and in that power let us forever live. Owing to this endowment of the Holy Spirit, there rested upon Jesus Christ a wondrous glory in many respects. One of His first glories was that as man He knew the name and character of God. He knew what no man knows unless the Holy Spirit reveals it to him, namely, the nature, attributes, and mind of God. The pure in heart will see God, and those pure eyes of His had seen God to the fullest!

Has He not given us that same vision of the Father? Yes, for He tells us, "He who has seen Me has seen the Father" (John 14:9). And again in the sixth verse, "I have manifested Your name to the men whom You have given Me out of the world" (John 17:6). Our eyes have been opened by the blessed Spirit of God to see the invisible and our understandings have been strengthened to know the incomprehensible! Now, according to the language of the apostle, "we are well known to God" (2 Cor. 5:11). "No one has seen God at any time. The only begotten Son, who is in the bosom of the Father, He has declared Him" (John 1:18). Not to the fullest have we beheld the Father, but still, according as we have received this glory that rested upon Christ we have been made to know the Father! And now we have access to the heavenly; we are familiar with the divine; we speak with the Most High and delight ourselves in the Lord!

As we gaze into the unspeakable glory, we discern something of the holiness, the justice, and the wisdom of Jehovah and we behold yet more of His great mercy and abounding love. We were once blinded, but now it is our glory that we see and know the Lord our God! Henceforth we become like our Lord in another beam of His glory, for we also begin to manifest the divine name to the sons of men who dwell around us! The church, like the moon, reflects the glory of the great Father of lights and so is glorious with the borrowed splendor that her Lord puts upon her. Christ's knowledge of the Father is given to us and we endeavor to make it known to others. If men would see God, let them look at Jesus, for there is He to be seen! And with bated breath we add—let them look at Christ's *people*, for there also is God revealed! It is the glory of the saints that they are the mirrors of the divine character! And when they wear the glory that Jesus has given them, they manifest the eternal name to those whom the Lord has ordained to bless by their means!

The glory of our Lord consisted, next, in the power of the Spirit in His receiving, keeping, and giving forth the Word of God. Our Lord Jesus was a full revelation of the mind of God. "For the law was given through Moses, but grace and truth came through Jesus Christ" (John 1:17). He knew the plan of God—that blessed method of infinite love—and He imparted it to His followers. The depository of the divine Word was Christ, and this was greatly to His glory. Is not the Logos, "the Word," one of the brightest of His titles? But now, this day, He has given to *us* the Word, speaking it into our souls, and from now on we are to hold forth the Word of life in the midst of a crooked and perverse generation.

Would you know the mind of God? It is not merely in a book—it is still incarnated in men in whom the Spirit of the Lord is present! Still does the Lord make known His mind and will by the earnest, fervent teaching, pleading, and lives of those in whom the Spirit of God dwells! Do you think this to be a small glory? Why, my beloved, the glory of possessing the Spirit of God; the glory of knowing the eternal God; the glory of having received His Word is such as distinguishes the *chosen man* above his fellows infinitely more than all the crowns, titles, and decorations that monarchs can bestow! Tell me not of your stars and garters, your ribbons and your crosses. To be made partakers of the Holy Spirit and guardians of the truth of God is a greater glory than the princes of this world can so much as imagine.

This glory of the Lord Jesus also lay in the sanctification of His blessed person. He said, "For their sakes I sanctify Myself" (John 17:19). Look at how consecrated to God He was from His childhood till He said, "It is finished!" (John 19:30). What holiness shone upon His very brow where a guileless soul unveiled itself in brave sincerity! You could not have been with Him at a funeral or at a marriage banquet, in a sick chamber or in the midst of a crowd, in the presence of carping adversaries or in the bosom of His family of twelve without being charmed by that divine holiness that hedged Him all around! There was about Him a sweetness of unspeakable affection and majesty of unsullied purity that made Him glorious above all the sons of men! His enemies spat upon Him, but that very spit was the unconscious homage that malignant evil pays to conquering goodness.

> *Tell me not of your stars and garters, your ribbons and your crosses. To be made partakers of the Holy Spirit and guardians of the truth of God is a greater glory than the princes of this world can so much as imagine.*

The ungodly crucified Him, but even in that very act there was a sort of confession that they were baffled and confused and could not stand before Him! They cried, "Crucify Him, crucify Him!" (Luke 23:21), because His perfect purity rendered their own wickedness inexcusable and lashed their conscience with reflections that could not be borne. Our Lord's moral glory was great, for He was the pattern and paragon of everything that is lovely and of good repute—and He was wholly sanctified to God! This is the glory that He gives to us! His prayer is "Sanctify them by Your truth. Your word is truth" (John 17:17).

His disciples live to holiness and are known as a people zealous of good works. I have to speak as I find matters laid down in the Word of God, and if you do not find them to be so in yourselves, my brothers and sisters, then you must judge yourselves by the Word of God so that you are not judged at the last and condemned! So it is that those who have truly received Christ become a special, marked, and separated people. They are as much consecrated to God as the priests were under the old dispensation, and therefore they live for God, they live to God, and their whole being is subjected to the mind of God! This is a high state of grace, but nothing less than this ought to content any Christian!

Well then, our great Master gives us, next, the glory of His own mission. "As You sent Me into the world, I also have sent them into the world" (John 17:18). It is the glory of Jesus that He is the Messiah, the sent one, and now He sends all His servants to be messiahs or *missionaries* to mankind! Christ Jesus was sent to reveal the Father, sent to reclaim the wandering souls of men, sent to seek and to save the lost. And this is exactly what every true Christian is sent into the world to do. He is commissioned to reveal God in his every act and word. He is commissioned to win back rebellious hearts. He is commissioned to save the sons of men and bring them up out of the horrible pit into which their sins have cast them.

This is a glory indeed, for they who turn many to righteousness will shine as the stars forever and ever. What a promise is this: "And saviours shall come up on mount Zion to judge the mount of Esau; and the kingdom shall be the Lord's" (Obad. 21 kjv). Every Christian man, according to his measure, becomes among his race what Jesus was when He was here below, the friend of men, the seeker of the lost. Again, I trust your glad hearts appreciate this glory, for let me say it is such a glory that if it involves much strict living and much self-denial, if it involves much disgrace, misrepresentation, reproach, and even should it involve death by martyrdom, blessed is the man upon whom all these things come because the spirit of glory and of Christ rests upon him!

The true glory of any man is the man himself, the character he bears and not the estate that he possesses. My brothers and sisters, can I hope that you have a resplendent spiritual character? Dare I hope to win the same myself? Let us look again at this glory of the Son of God! Christ Jesus was the man of men, the model man, the manliest man in all respects, and yet He was, of all men, the most fully subordinated to the divine law and the most obedient in all things to the Father's will! See your calling, my brethren! You, too, are not to be common men, nor to belong to the herd that run foolishly after their own lusts, but you are to be model men, manly and brave yet always submissive to the great Father of your spirits. We are to be such men that those who look upon us may wish that there were such as we are.

Jesus was especially a model in His perfect self-abnegation. What did He seek for Himself? A kingdom? Yes, but a kingdom whose crown was made of thorns—a kingdom of *suffering* love. What did He live for? That He might be glorified? Yes, but that He might be glorified by saving others while refusing to save Himself. His crowning glory is that He humbled Himself and made Himself of no reputation and became obedient to death, even the death of the cross. Such will you and I be if we have the glory of Christ resting upon us—we will give up, forever, all self-seeking, all desire to shine, all wish to be great, all craving to be rich, and we will live not to ourselves, but to Him who died for us.

We are to live for God's glory and for Christ's purpose in the conviction of the world, and if we do, the Spirit of glory will be resting upon us. The matchless man of Nazareth had this glory: that He was one with God. The objectives, aims, and thoughts of God were His objectives, aims, and thoughts. His life ran parallel with the path of the Most High. This man was accepted of God, the love of God ever rested upon Him. He had access to God. He could speak with the Father when He would, and answers out of the excellent glory were vouchsafed Him. He was prevalent with God, for His prayers brought down, and *still* bring down, countless blessings upon the sons of men! He was the Son of God, and He overcame the world in the power of His sonship.

Now, this glory that the Father gave Him, He has given us, that we, too, may be accepted; that we, too, may have access; that we, too, may have prevalence in prayer; that we, too, may have the Spirit of adoption; and that we, too, may trample upon sin and overcome the hosts of darkness. This is the glory that rests upon *all* the faithful! Mark well that wherever this glory is seen, true unity is developed. Suppose I were to find a man living in the likeness of Christ with this spiritual glory conspicuous upon him. It may be that he is poor and illiterate, but what of that? Suppose he is a coal heaver—the glory of his character will be, nonetheless, more conspicuous than the dust. Then let us find another man on whom the same spiritual glory rests, and we will suppose that he is an earl, a supposition that, thank God, is not an impossible one.

The glory will be none the more dim because of the good man's honors. There, then, are the two—coal heaver and coroneted. And does it need half an eye to see that the glory of each is one? The holy consecration in each case is the same, and the degrees of rank do not affect the essential beauty of either. Is it not the same *life* that dwells in all saintly bosoms and the same *love* that prompts each holy deed? In a princess or in a dairyman's daughter, in a scholar or in a peasant, the glory of a high character is one. If you found among a savage tribe a single convert, truly consecrated to Christ and living to God according to the measure of his light, his manners might be rude and his knowledge slender, but there would be upon him the same kind of glory that you would mark as adorning a polished, educated Christian lady who, in the midst of her circle, spends a lovely life for Jesus.

> he matchless man of Nazareth had this glory: that He was one with God. The objectives, aims, and thoughts of God were His objectives, aims, and thoughts. His life ran parallel with the path of the Most High.

Should the untutored convert die by the spear of the savage whose soul he sought to bless, he is written in the same roll of martyrs as that which bears the names of bishops and apostles. Holiness is everywhere most precious! Unselfishness is in *any* instance beyond all price! Let us see love to God and love to men, and they are everywhere alike and reveal a oneness of inward life. In fact, oneness with Him who is the true life of men. If you bring a company of common Christians together and they begin discoursing and discussing, I daresay they will jangle and debate world without end. But if you could select a number of those upon whom the glory rests that the Father gave to His Son, I will guarantee you this, that within a short time they will be all on their knees together or singing together or engaged in some form of loving fellowship.

The people who are not one with each other are those who are not one with Christ. But once filled with His Spirit, we are one of necessity. You cannot help it; it is scarcely a matter of duty—it becomes a matter of necessity that you who have the love of Christ within you should love the brothers and sisters. Spiritual men are so essentially one, like two drops that close together, that they have an increasing tendency to unite. Spiritual men may wear different denominational names and may differ in their conscientious convictions on some matters, but these things do not hinder *union*—they rather give a zest to it. If the glory that the Father gave to Christ is resting upon these, they have discerned the mystical unity that encompasses them all, and they are delighted to acknowledge it by deeds of brotherly love rendered with spontaneous cheerfulness, blessing him who performs them and those who receive the benefits.

Beloved, those in whom Christ lives are *not uniform, but one*. Uniformity may be found in death, but this unity is life. Those who are quite uniform may yet have no love to each other, while those who differ widely may still be truly and intensely one. Our children are not uniform, but they make one family. Sons born at the same birth may exhibit a remarkable difference of character, and yet the father may be seen in both and they may be equally one in the family circle and in all the love that makes home the abode of happiness. So it is with all believers—born of the same everlasting Father, they are one in spirit, one in character, one in objective, one in aim, yes, one in the fullest sense.

At this moment, despite apparent differences, the whole host of the spiritual are one, and they press forward as with the tramp of one man against the common foe. I speak not of *professors*. I speak not of the *external* church. I speak not of the mixed multitude that come up out of Egypt and debase the character of our Israel! I speak of those of whom Christ could say to His Father, "The glory which You gave Me I have given them." *These* are one as the Father and the Son are one, but mere *professors* are not!

II. Time flies too rapidly, alas, and therefore we must, with great brevity, think upon the second point, namely, *the unity itself*. As I have remarked, it is *not* uniformity. Of this our Lord says nothing. Though we *are* one body in Him, yet all the members have not the same office. The eye is very different from the ear, and the foot has not the same form as the hand. Neither does He speak of any formal organization by which unity is to be secured. How many have tried to create a mechanical union and have made confusion worse confusion! Their eagerness for unity has threatened to dash everything to shivers! The very first step toward a visible unity of the church is, with most men, that *they* will fix a standard of what the church ought to be and cut off everybody who will not conform to their idea!

See how certain brothers, to show how they hate sectarianism, invent a new sect and diligently earn from their fellow believers the character of being more bitter and bigoted than any other professors! The oddities of nonsectarians are the scandal of the age! They have talked of union and scattered the saints right and left. Let us follow practical methods, and we will find them in the unity that the text describes.

First, it is written, "I in them." Christ lives in His people, and we are to act so, in the power of the Holy Spirit, that onlookers will say, "Surely Christ lives again in that man, for he acts out the precepts of Jesus. Did you notice how he bore the insult? Did you notice how he laid himself out to oblige and to serve? Did you observe how, without introducing religious talk, he gradually steered the conversation toward that which is to edification? Do you see how, if he stays in a hotel or if he sojourns in a family or if he sits in a workroom, his presence is soon felt by the pleasure that he diffuses, the confidence that he inspires?" He is everyone's friend when he is needed, the servant of all, the example of all. His voice is always for peace, and if he does, now and then, speak upbraidingly, men's consciences admit that he is just. Such a man honors his Lord by reminding men of Him.

> *The very first step toward a visible unity of the church is, with most men, that they will fix a standard of what the church ought to be and cut off everybody who will not conform to their idea!*

Our first consideration should not be, "Now I am here, how can I be comfortable?" but "I am here, how can I please others for their good? How can I relieve the distressed, help the weary, or cheer the sad?" It is a grand thing to do good in little ways. It is a glory to be the sweetener of life at home, the self-forgetting friend of all around. The world, before long, confesses that Christ is in such a man! The true Christian is Jesus come to life! His name implies this. How is he a Christian who is not like Christ? We commonly say that the oil upon the head runs down to the skirts of the garment—is it so? Is the love of Jesus, the generosity of Jesus, the zeal of Jesus, the gentleness of Jesus, the consecration of Jesus to be seen in us? If so, the glory of Jesus rests on us! But if not, we have need to begin again and do our first works.

The next point of the union is "You in Me." That is, God is in Christ. This is manifestly true, for you cannot read the life of Christ without seeing God in Him. "Come now," said one to an unbeliever, "what do you think of the life of Christ?"

"I am free to confess," said the other, "that it seems to me to be a very marvelous life and in every way worthy of praise."

"You do not, however, think Jesus Christ to be God?"

"No, I do not."

"But suppose," said the Christian, "that God had been here among men in human form—could He have acted more purely or more benevolently?"

"No," said the other. "If I admit the possibility of such a thing, I am not able to conceive of anything more divinely good."

"Why then," said the Christian, "do you not see that in very deed God was in Christ Jesus and He was one with God?"

So we believe and we rejoice greatly to hear our Lord say, "I and my Father are one." See, then, the unity of Christ in us and of God in Christ Jesus!

This brings about the union of believers with the Father—being one with Christ and Christ being one with the Father. The point is reached for which our Lord prayed: "That they may be one just as We are one: I in them, and You in Me; that they may be made perfect in one, and that the world may know that You have sent Me." Couple this with believers being one with each other and you get the being made "perfect in one" of which our text speaks. If you and I are one in Christ and one *with* Christ, then we are one with God, seeing Christ is one with God, and thus not in some few characteristics are we alike and one in name, but in life, in aim, and in desire!

Brothers and sisters, if you and I are living for the same design that our Lord lived for, and if the very life that quickens us is the life of Jesus, then, since Jesus lives always for the same thing that God purposes and works out, surely there is a grand unity, the likes of which are not found in the universe! This has great depths in it, grounded upon a mystical, spiritual union, but I leave the depths of doctrine, just now, to speak upon the experimental and practical truths of God that grow out of the matter of fact.

Moved by the same love of holiness, inspired by the same spirit of love, tenderness, and kindness, the eternal Father's will is the will of the Son, and the Spirit works in us to will and to do according to the good pleasure of the Lord. According to the measure of grace, the members of the body feel and move in union with the head, who also is in union with the Father. "Your kingdom come" is God's will thrilling through all the members of the body of Christ. Death to sin, destruction of strife, the end of injustice, the chasing away of every form of error—these are the common objectives of the Father and of all those whom He has begotten. The propagation of the truth of God, the increase of love, the reign of gentleness and peace among men—these are the mind of God, the mind of Christ, and the mind of all the saints, and so are we one with each other by ties spiritual and divine.

III. I could not enlarge upon that subject though I wished to do so, for I must now notice *the effect that this produces* according to our Lord's prophecy and prayer. First, it will convict the world of the truth of Christ's mission—"that the world may know that You have sent Me." How will they know it? Why, when they see such characters as I have so feebly tried to paint! When they see men who are no longer selfish, hard, and ungenerous—when they see men no longer governed by their passions, no longer earthbound—when they see loving men, men who desire that which is holy, just, and good! When they see men living for God, the world will say, "Their Master must have been sent of God."

Such men as these, alas, are so uncommon. And they are so precious when we find them that if the Lord Jesus has created such by His teaching and His Spirit, by their fruits we may know them, even as we know His people and He is manifestly sent of God. And then, brothers and sisters, not only will their characters convince the world, but their unity will convince it because the ungodly world will say, "We see the glory of Christianity in the poor man and we see the same in the rich man. We see a glory about a Christian prince and we see the same glory about a Christian needlewoman! And we observe that when these people meet each other, there is a divine union among them, for they are one. Surely their Master must be sent of God."

Christian people have things to talk about that others do not understand, and they pursue one common objective that others disregard. Whether they have little or much, they yield their all to one common cause and objective. Whether possessed of little ability or great ability, they are alike consecrated. One spirit breathes in them. See how they love one another! Even the world can see that while its great ones are always contending, these dwell in love. The world can easily see that while common men emulate each other and strive as to who will be the greatest, these only strive to serve the common cause, to help each other, and to stoop for their fellows' good. The world cannot help perceiving the divinity of the mission of Christ that has produced this perfect love and union among His followers. Then do they say,

"Assuredly God must have sent their leader, Christ Jesus, or He could not have produced such results."

Do you ask me where we see this? I reply that it is far too little seen, but when we will see it in the whole church, then will the world be convinced! Oh, my brethren, only fancy a church of the size of this, put down in this south of London, made up of holy men and holy women like Christ, who, with all their imperfections, as to the general bent and current of their lives are living to God and for the glory of Christ and for the good of their fellow men. Picture such a church in perfect unity, and I tell you it would present an argument for Christianity that would infinitely surpass all the books of analogy and evidence that have ever been written. This would be a nut that the adversary could not crack! It would baffle all his criticisms and syllogisms.

Christian people have things to talk about that others do not understand, and they pursue one common objective that others disregard. Whether they have little or much, they yield their all to one common cause and objective.

One individual Christian has often presented to the most desperate unbeliever a difficulty that has staggered him. "I could be altogether an atheist," said one, "if it were not for my aged mother. While I see her peace of mind, her holy living, her gentle, quiet temper, I cannot but believe that there is a power in religion that I cannot understand." If we would convince the world, my brothers and sisters, it must be by the glory that God has given to His Son resting upon each and all of us and so compacting us together, fusing us into one mass of living union. Only in the foundation of unity in Christ can the battle be won!

But the world is also to be convinced of the Father's *love* to us—"and have loved them as You have loved Me." Shall we ever convince them of that? Yes, when the world sees bodies of truly consecrated men and women living together in holy love, then they will also see much joy, much peace, much mutual consolation—and they will perceive that the very stars in heaven fight for them, that the providence of God makes all things work together for their good—and that the Lord has a special care over them as a shepherd has over his flock. Then they will say, "These are the people God has blessed. Look how He loves them!" They perceive, however, that they have to suffer and that they are afflicted and despised, and so they come to say, "God seems to love them just as He loved His Son, whom He did not spare from suffering, pain, and grief, but whom He upheld under all," and so they learn that God has the same special regard for those Christlike ones that He has for their Master and Lord. They will be made to see this! It will be forced upon them!

Moreover, as these men and women grow more and more like Jesus, the world will conclude that since God loved Jesus, He must love those who are like Christ. Why, do not even the ungodly, though they would be loath to confess it, take a kind of delight in a high and noble character? They have an admiration for it and their conscience tells them that God admires those in whom His Christ has produced it. They cannot avoid the feeling that God loves holy and loving people—and that it is great love on His part to make them what they are. So far the world becomes convinced.

But somebody may say, "What does our Lord mean by the world's knowing and believing this?" I answer that, doubtless, a part of the world will be convinced that Christ was sent of God. And part will be convinced that God loves His people. And yet they will stand out in obstinacy against God, for to the end even the gospel itself will be a savor of death to death to some.

Well, you and I have answered the purpose of God even upon such characters when it comes to pass that they are without excuse. But it is evident from this chapter that there is another part of the world who will not only know and believe historically, but will do this *spiritually*. This is the part of the world comprehended in our Lord's Prayer: "Neither pray I for these alone, but for them also which shall believe on me through their word" (John 17:20 KJV). And I take it, brothers and sisters, that when the day will come that Christians are Christians, then we will see great masses of the world convinced of the truth of Christianity and large numbers of the world suppliant at Jesus' feet!

Of the Christianity that is presented to the public gaze I would not be unduly censorious, but I fear it is often a Christianity that the world does well to despise. When the Jew went to Rome and asked for Christianity, he saw the Christians, so called, worshipping the virgin Mary and images of saints and relics and bones and I know not what. And he justly said, "Hear, O Israel: The LORD our God is one LORD" (Deut. 6:4 KJV). On the strength of such revelation the Jew rejected the Christianity of Rome and he did well. Don't you agree?

Now, here comes another Christianity that has lately displayed itself to many heathen nations. It comes with the Bible in its knapsack and the Martini-Henry rifle in its hand. Is not this a fine combination for conversion? Jesus comes before the Zulu riding upon a Gatling gun! Of course, these poor heathen know nothing about our political combinations, but if they suppose that Christians are invading their land, will they therefore love Christ?

> *Let us not be discouraged, for by grace we are on the way and we will not rest till we reach the goal! Oh, for grace so to live to God in Christ Jesus that the world will never be able to answer the argument of our lives!*

Missionaries, here is a difficulty for you to explain—how will you deal with it? You come from a Christian nation, a nation that enjoys the unspeakable privilege of a national church, a nation that salutes the savages in Christ's name with shot and shell. Will they receive Christianity coming in such guise? If they do not, small blame can we pour upon them. They will be only acting according to the light of reason and common sense. If there will ever come a Christianity that suffers long, is kind, does no evil, but seeks good to its neighbor, that teaches love to God and love to man, that seeks not its own but lays itself out for others, then I do not say that an ungodly world will be enamored of it if left to itself, but I do believe that the Spirit of God will go forth with it and will convict men of sin and of righteousness and of judgment, and then will the scattered family of Adam accept the one true faith and enter into a league of amity with each other, and there will be glory to God in the highest, on earth peace, goodwill toward men. Love conquers all. Love is the logic that convinces!

Notice two passages of Scripture with which I finish. One thing you want the world to know is that you are the disciples of Christ. "By this all will know that you are My disciples, if you have love for one another" (John 13:35). Does our Lord wish the world to be convinced? How does He Himself act? Hear Him! "But that the world may know that I love the Father, and as the Father gave Me commandment, so I do. Arise, let us go from here" (John 14:31). Love, you see again, proves the unity of the Son with the Father! And here again, in this second text, it is the love of the

Father to the chosen that is to be the sign to the world. Therefore let love abound. Let it be all the weapons of our war!

I know I have preached very feebly to you this morning upon such a theme. The subject is a great deal too much for my limited capacity, but it is good for us to feel how little we are, how low we are. It is good to look above our struggling selves to something much beyond our present attainments. I lie prostrate on my face before the Lord and confess that I have not yet attained all that I have set forth to you, and I suspect that your confession is very like my own. Let us not be discouraged, for by grace we are on the way and we will not rest till we reach the goal! Oh, for grace so to live to God in Christ Jesus that the world will never be able to answer the argument of our lives! Help us, O Spirit of the Lord! Amen.

For Further Thought

1. *What is the way we can be in unity that is mentioned in John 17:22?*
2. *According to John 17:23, why does the Son pray that the disciples be made perfect in one?*
3. *What are the three aspects of unity in John 17:22–23?*

THE CHURCH OF CHRIST

"I will make them and the places all around My hill a blessing;
and I will cause showers to come down in their season;
there shall be showers of blessing."

EZEKIEL 34:26

THE chapter [Ezek. 34] that I read at the commencement of the service is a prophetical one. I understand its meaning to refer not to the condition of the Jews during the captivity and their subsequent happiness when they should return to their land, but to a state into which they should fall after they had been restored to their country under Nehemiah and Ezra, and in which state they still continue to the present day. The prophet tells us that the shepherds then, instead of feeding the flock, fed themselves. They trod the grass instead of allowing the sheep to eat it, and they fouled the waters with their feet.

This is an exact description of the state of Judea after the captivity. For then there arose the scribes and Pharisees who took the key of knowledge and would not enter themselves nor allow others to enter. They laid heavy burdens on men's shoulders and would not touch them with one of their fingers. They made religion to consist entirely in sacrifices and ceremonies and imposed such a burden on the people that they cried out, "What a weariness is it!" (Mal. 1:13 KJV). That same evil has continued with the poor Jews to the present day. Should you read the nonsense of the Talmud and the Gemara and see the burdens they laid upon them, you would say, "They have 'shepherds that cannot understand'" (Isa. 56:11 KJV).

They give the sheep no food. They trouble them with fanciful superstitions and silly views, and instead of telling them that the Messiah is already come, they delude them with the idea that there is a messiah yet to come who will restore Judea and raise it to its glory. The Lord pronounces a curse upon these Pharisees and rabbis, those evil shepherds who will not suffer the sheep to lie down, neither will feed them with good pasture. But after having described this state, he prophesies better times for the poor Jew. The day is coming when the careless shepherds will be as nothing.

Then the power of the rabbis will cease. Then the traditions of the Mishna and the Talmud will be cast aside. The hour is approaching when the tribes will go up to their own country, when Judea, so long a howling wilderness, will once more blossom like the rose. Then, if the temple itself is not restored, yet on Zion's hill will be raised some Christian building where the chants of solemn praise will be heard, as of old the psalms of David were sung in the tabernacle. Not long will it be before they will come—shall come from distant lands, wherever they rest or roam.

And she who has been the offscouring of all things, whose name has been a proverb and a byword, will become the glory of all lands. Dejected Zion will raise her head, shaking herself from dust, darkness, and the dead. Then will the Lord feed His people and make them and the places all around His hill a blessing. I think we do not attach sufficient importance to the restoration of the Jews. We do not think enough of it. But certainly, if there is anything promised in the Bible, it is this. I imagine that you cannot read the Bible without seeing clearly that there is to be an actual restoration of the children of Israel.

May that happy day soon come! For when the Jews are restored, then the fullness of the Gentiles will be gathered in. And as soon as they return, then Jesus will come upon Mount Zion to reign with His ancients gloriously and the halcyon days of the millennium will then dawn. We will then know every man to be a brother and a friend. Christ will rule with universal sway.

This, then, is the meaning of the text: God would make Jerusalem and the places all around His hill a blessing. I will not, however, use it so this morning. I will use it in a more confined sense, or perhaps in a more enlarged sense, as it applies to the church of Jesus Christ and to this particular church with which you and I stand connected. "I will make them and the places all around My hill a blessing; and I will cause showers to come down in their season; there shall be showers of blessing."

There are two things here spoken of. First, *Christ's church is to be a blessing.* Second, *Christ's church is to be blessed.* These two things you will find in the different sentences of the text.

I. First, *Christ's church is to be a blessing.* "I will make them and the places all around My hill a blessing." The object of God in choosing a people was not only to save that people, but through them to confer essential benefits upon the whole human race. When He chose Abraham, He did not elect him simply to be God's friend and the recipient of peculiar privileges. But He chose him to make him, as it were, the conservator of truth. He was to be the ark in which the truth should be hid. He was to be the keeper of the covenant in behalf of the whole world.

And when God chooses any men by His sovereign electing grace and makes them Christ's, He does it not only for their own sake, that they may be saved, but also for the world's sake. For know you not that "you are the salt of the earth. . . . You are the light of the world. A city that is set on a hill cannot be hidden" (Matt. 5:13–14)? And when God makes you salt, it is not only that you may have salt in yourselves, but also that like salt you may preserve the whole mass. If He makes you leaven, it is that like the little leaven you may leaven the whole lump. Salvation is not a selfish thing. God does not give it for us to keep to ourselves, but that we may thereby be made the means of blessing to others.

> *W*hen God chooses any men by His sovereign electing grace and makes them Christ's, He does it not only for their own sake, that they may be saved, but also for the world's sake.

And the great day will declare that there is not a man living on the surface of the earth but has received a blessing in some way or other through God's gift of the gospel. The very keeping of the wicked in life and granting of the reprieve were purchased with the death of Jesus. Through His sufferings and death, the temporal blessings that both they and we enjoy are bestowed on us. The gospel was sent that it might first bless those who embrace it and then expand, so as to make them a blessing to the whole human race.

In thus speaking of the church as a blessing, we will notice three things. First, here is *divinity*: "*I* will make them a blessing." Second, here is *personality of religion*: "I will make *them* a blessing." And, third, here is *the development of religion*: "and the *places* all around My hill."

1. First, with regard to this blessing that God will cause His church to

be, here is *divinity*. It is God the everlasting Jehovah speaking. He says, "I will make them a blessing." None of us can bless others unless God has first blessed us. We need divine workmanship. "I will make them a blessing by helping them and by constraining them." God makes His people a blessing by helping them. What can we do without God's help? I stand and preach to thousands, or it may be hundreds. What have I done, unless a greater than man has been in the pulpit with me?

I work in the Sabbath schools; what can I do, unless the Master is there, teaching the children with me? We want God's aid in every position. And once He gives us that assistance, there is no telling with how little labor we may become a blessing, Ah, a few words sometimes will be more of a blessing than a whole sermon. You take some little prattler on your knee, and some few words that you say to him he remembers and makes use of in after years. I knew a gray-headed old man who was in the habit of doing this. He once took a boy to a certain tree and said, "Now, John, you kneel down at that tree and I will kneel down with you."

He knelt down and prayed and asked God to convert him and save his soul. "Now," said he, "perhaps you will come to this tree again, and if you are not converted, you will remember that I asked under this tree that God would save your soul." That young man went away and forgot the old man's prayer. But it chanced, as God would have it, that he walked down that field again and saw a tree. It seemed as if the old man's name was cut in the bark. He recollected what he prayed for, but the prayer was not fulfilled. But he dared not pass the tree without kneeling down to pray himself, and there was his spiritual birthplace. The simplest observation of the Christian will be made a blessing, if God helps him. "His leaf also shall not wither" (Ps. 1:3 kjv). The simplest word he speaks will be treasured up. And whatsoever he does will prosper.

But there is *constraint* here. "I will *make* them a blessing." I will give them to be a blessing. I will constrain them to be a blessing. I can say myself that I never did anything that was a blessing to my fellow creatures without feeling compelled to do it. I thought of going to a Sabbath school to teach. On a certain day, someone called, asked me, begged me, and prayed me to take his class. I could not refuse to go. And there I was held hand and foot by the superintendent and was compelled to go on. I was asked to address the children. I thought I could not, but no one else was there to do it, so I stood up and stammered out a few words.

And I recollect the first occasion on which I attempted to preach to the people. I am sure I had no wish to do it, but there was no one else in the place. And should the congregation go away without a single word of warning or address? How could I suffer it? I felt forced to address them. And so it has been with whatever I have laid my hand to. I have always felt a kind of impulse that I could not resist, but moreover felt placed by providence in such a position that I had no wish to avoid the duty and, if I had desired it, could not have helped myself.

And so it is with God's people. As they go through their lives, wherever they have been made a blessing, they will find that God seems to have thrust them into the vineyard. Such and such a man was once rich. What good was he in the world? He did but loll in his carriage. He did but little good and was of little service to his fellow creatures. Says God, "I will make him a blessing," so He strips away his riches and brings him into low circumstances. He is then brought into association with the poor, and his superior education and intellect make him a blessing to them. God makes him a blessing.

Another man was naturally very timid. He would not pray at the prayer meeting; he would hardly like to join the church. Soon he gets into a position in which he cannot help himself. "I will *make* him a blessing." And as sure as ever you are a servant of God; He will *make you* a blessing. He will have none of His gold in the lump. He will hammer it out and make it a blessing. I verily believe there are some in my congregation to whom God has given power to preach His name. They do not know it, perhaps, but God will make it known by and by. I would have every man look and see whether God is making him do a certain thing.

And when once he feels the impulse, let him by no means ever check it. I am somewhat of a believer in the doctrine of the Quakers as to the impulses of the Spirit, and I fear lest I should check one of them. If a thought crosses my mind, *Go to such a person's house,* I always like to do it, because I do not know but what it may be from the Spirit. I understand this verse to mean something like that. "I will make them a blessing. I will force them to do good. If I cannot make a sweet scent come from them in any other way, I will pound them in the mortar of affliction.

"If they have seed and the seed cannot be scattered in any other way, I will send a rough wind to blow the downy seed everywhere." That is, "I will *make* them a blessing." If you have never been *made* a blessing to anyone, depend upon it, you are not a child of God. For Jehovah says, "I *will* make them a blessing."

2. But notice, next, the *personality* of the blessing. "I will make *them* a blessing." That is, "I will make each member of the church a blessing." Many people come up to the house of prayer where the church assembles and you say, "Well, what are you doing at such and such a place where you attend?"

"Well, *we* are doing so-and-so."

"How do you spell *we*?"

"It is a plain monosyllable," say you.

"Yes, but do you put *I* in *we*?"

"No."

There are a great many people who could easily spell *we* without an *I* in it. For though they say, "We have been doing so-and-so," they do not say, "How much have I done? Did I do anything in it? Yes. This chapel has been enlarged. What did I subscribe? Two pence!"

Of course it is done. Those who paid the money have done it. "We preach the gospel." Do we indeed? Yes, we sit in our pew and listen a little and do not pray for a blessing. "We have got such a large Sunday school." Did you ever teach in it? "We have got a very good working society." Did you ever go to work in it? That is not the way to spell *we*. It is "I will make *them* a blessing." When Jerusalem was built, every man began nearest his own house. That is where you must begin to build, or to do something. Do not let us tell a lie about it. If we do not have some share in the building, if we handle neither the trowel nor the spear, let us not talk about *our church*. For the text says, "I will make *them* a blessing," every one of them.

"But, sir, what can I do? I am nothing but a father at home. I am so full of business, I can only see my children a little." But in your business, do you ever have any servants? "No, I am a servant myself." Do you have fellow servants? "No, I work alone." Do you work alone, then, and live alone, like a monk in a cell? I don't believe that. But you have fellow servants at work; cannot you say a word to their conscience? "I don't like to intrude religion into business." Quite right, too, so say I. When I am at business, let it be business. When you are at religion, let it be religion. But do you ever have an opportunity? Why, you cannot go into an omnibus, or a railway carriage, but what you can say something for Jesus Christ.

I have found it so, and I don't believe I am different from other people. *Cannot do anything?* Cannot you put a tract in your hat and drop it where you go? Cannot you speak a word to a child? Where does this man come from who cannot do anything? There is a spider on the wall. He takes hold on kings' palaces and spins his web to rid the world of noxious flies. There is a nettle in the corner of the churchyard. The physician tells me it has its virtues. There is a tiny star in the sky. That is noted in the chart and the mariner looks at it. There is an insect underwater. It builds a rock. God made all these things for something!

But here is a man whom God made and gave him nothing at all to do! I do not believe it. God never makes useless things. He has no superfluous workmanship. I care not what you are. You have something to do. Oh, may God show you what it is and then make you do it, by the wondrous compulsion of His providence and His grace.

3. But we have to notice, in the third place, the *development* of gospel blessing. "I will make them a blessing," but it does not end there—"and the places all around My hill." Religion is an expansive thing. When it begins in the heart, at first it is like a tiny grain of mustard seed. But it gradually increases and becomes a great tree, so that the birds of the air lodge in its branches. A man cannot be religious to himself. "For none of us lives to himself, and no one dies to himself" (Rom. 14:7). You have heard, a score of times, that if you do but drop a pebble in a brook, it causes a small ring at first, then another outside of that, and then another, and another, till the influence of the pebble is perceptible over the entire bosom of the water.

So it is when God makes His people a blessing. "I will make a minister a blessing to one or two. I will then make him a blessing to a hundred. I will then make him a blessing to thousands. And then I will make those thousands a blessing. I will make each one individually a blessing—and when I have done that, I will make the places all around a blessing. I will make them a blessing." I hope we will never be satisfied, as members of Park Street, until we are a blessing not only to ourselves but also to the places all around our hill. What are the places all around our hill? I think they are, first, our agencies, second, our neighborhood, and third, the churches adjacent to us.

First, there are our agencies. There is our Sabbath school; how near is that to our hill? I speak a great deal about this, because I want it to be brought into notice. I intend to preach a practical sermon this morning, to move some of you to come and teach in the Sabbath school, for there we require some suitable men to "come to the help of the LORD, to the help of the LORD against the mighty" (Judg. 5:23). Therefore I mention the Sabbath school as a place very near to the hill. It ought to be just at the very foot of it. Yes, it ought to be so near the hill that very many may pass from it to the church.

> *care not what you are. You have something to do. Oh, may God show you what it is and then make you do it, by the wondrous compulsion of His providence and His grace.*

Then there is our Visiting and Christian Instruction Society that we have for the visiting of this neighborhood. I trust that has been made a blessing. God has sent among us a man who labors zealously and earnestly in visiting the sick. I have, as the superintendent of my beloved brother the missionary, a regular account of his labors. His report has most highly gratified me and I am able to bear testimony to the fact that he is very efficiently laboring around us. I want that society to have all your sympathy and strength. I consider him as a Joshua, with whom you are to go forth by hundreds to those who live in the neighborhood.

Do you not know what dark places there are? Walk down a street a little to the right. See the shops open on a Sunday. Some, thank God, which used to open them, now come and worship with us. We will have more yet. For "the earth is the LORD's, and all its fullness" (1 Cor. 10:26), and why should not we have it? My brethren, as you visit the sick or distribute tracts from door to door, make this your prayer: that this society, being one of the places all around our hill, may be made a blessing! Let me not forget any agency connected with this church. There are several more that are places all around our hill, and the Lord has just put it into my heart to fashion other societies that will be made a blessing to this hill, and in a little while you will hear of them.

We have several brothers in this congregation to whom God has given a mouth of utterance. These are about to form themselves into a society for proclaiming the Word of God. Where God has so blessed His church and made us to be so noted and named among the people, why should we not keep on? We have been brought up to a great pitch of fervency and love. Now is the time for doing something. While the iron is hot, why not strike and fashion it? I believe we have the materials not only for making a church here that will be the glory of the Baptist churches in London but for making churches everywhere throughout the metropolis.

> believe we have the materials not only for making a church here that will be the glory of the Baptist churches in London but for making churches everywhere throughout the metropolis.

And we have more schemes on hand, that matured by sober judgment and backed by prudence will yet make this metropolis more honored than it has been by the sound of the pure gospel and the proclamation of the pure Word of God. May God make all our agencies—the places all around our hill—a blessing.

But next, there is the neighborhood. I am paralyzed sometimes when I think that we are of so little service to the neighborhood, though this is a green oasis in the midst of a great spiritual desert. Just at the back of us we could find you hundreds of Roman Catholics and men of the very worst character. And it is sad to think that we cannot make this place a blessing to them. It is made a great blessing to you, my hearers. But you do not come from this district. You come from anywhere and nowhere, some of you, I suppose. People say, "There is something doing in that chapel. Look at the crowd. But we cannot get in!"

This one thing I ask: Never come here to gratify your curiosity. You who are members of other congregations, just consider it your duty to stay at home. There are many stray sheep about. I would rather have them than you. Keep to your own place. I do not want to rob other ministers. Do not come here from charity. We are much obliged to you for your kindly intentions. But we would rather have your seat than your company if you are members of other churches. We want *sinners* to come; sinners of every sort. But do not let us have that sort of men whose ears are everlastingly itching for some new preacher, who are saying, "I want something else; I want something else." Oh, I beseech you, for God's sake, be of some good.

And if you are running about from one place to another, you can never expect to be. Do you know what is said of rolling stones? Ah, you have heard of that. They "gather no moss." Now, don't be rolling stones, but keep at home. God help to make us a blessing to the neighborhood! I long to see something done for the people around here. We must open our arms to them. We must go out into the open air to them. We must and will preach God's gospel to them. Let, then, the people around listen to the word of the gospel. And may it be said, "That place is the cathedral of Southwark!" So it is now. Out of it goes a blessing—God is pouring out a blessing upon it.

What else do we mean by the places all around our hill? We mean the churches adjacent. I cannot but rejoice in the prosperity of many churches around us. But as our beloved brother Mr. Sherman said last Thursday morning, "It is not invidious to say that there are very few churches that are in a prosperous state, but taking the churches at large, they are in a deplorable condition. It is only here and there," said he, "that God is pouring out His Spirit. But most of the churches are lying like barges at Black Friars Bridge when the tide is down—right in the mud—and all the king's horses and all the king's men cannot pull them off, till the tide comes and sets them afloat."

Who can tell, then, what good this church may do? If there is a light in this candlestick, let others come and light their candles by it. If there is a flame here, let the flame spread until all the neighboring churches will be lit up with the glory. Then indeed will we be made the rejoicing of the earth, for there is never a revival in one spot but it will affect others. Who will tell, then, where it will end?

> *Fly abroad, you mighty gospel.*
> *Win and conquer, never cease.*

And it never will cease when God once makes the places all around His hill a blessing.

II. The second point is that God's people are not only to be a blessing, but *they are to be blessed.* For read the second part of the verse. "And I will cause showers to come down in their season; there shall be showers of blessing." It is somewhat singular, as a prediction of the showers of blessings we hope to receive here, that God sent us showers on the first day of opening. If I were a believer in omens, I should pray that as it rained the first day so might it rain every day since. When it stops, may the chapel be shut up. For we only want it open so long as showers of grace continue to descend.

> *N*ow is the season to ask for showers. It is nighttime. Now the dew falls. The dew does not fall in the day; it falls in the night, the night of affliction, trial, and trouble.

First, here is *sovereign mercy*. Listen to these words: "I will cause showers to come down in their season." Is it not sovereign, divine mercy, for who can say, "I will cause showers," except God? Can the false prophet who walks among the benighted Hottentots? He says he is a rainmaker and can give them showers. But can he do it? Is there an imperial monarch, or the most learned man on earth, who can say, "I will give them the showers in their season?" No. There is only one. There is only one hand in which all the channels of the mighty ocean above the firmament are contained. There is only one voice that can speak to the clouds and bid them beget the rain.

"From whose womb comes the ice? And the frost of heaven, who gives it birth?" (Job 38:29). Who sends down the rain upon the earth? Who scatters the showers upon the green herb? Does not the Lord? Who else could do it? Is not rain in God's power? And who could send it except Him? We know that Catholics pretend that they can get grace without getting it from God directly. For they believe that God puts all His grace into the pope and then that runs down into smaller pipes, called cardinals and bishops, through which it runs into the priests. And by turning the tap with a shilling, you can get as much grace as you like.

But it is not so with God's grace. He says, "I will give them showers." Grace is the gift of God and is not to be created by man. Notice next, it is *needed grace*. "I will give them showers." What would the ground do without showers? You may break the clods, you may sow your seeds, but what can you do without the rain? Ah, you may prepare your barn and sharpen your sickles. But your sickles will be rusted before you have any wheat, unless there are showers. They are needed. So is the divine blessing.

> *In vain Apollos sows the seed,*
> *And Paul may plant in vain.*

In vain you come here, in vain you labor, in vain you give your money—

> *Till God the plenteous shower bestows,*
> *And sends salvation down.*

Then, next, it is *plenteous grace*. "I will send them showers." It does not say, "I will send them drops," but "I will send them showers." Remember the saying, "It seldom rains but it pours." So it is with grace. If God gives a blessing, He usually gives it in such a measure that there is not room enough to receive it. Where are we going to hold God's blessing that we have obtained already? I told the people on Thursday that God had promised us that if we brought the tithes into the storehouse, He would send us such a blessing that we would not have room to hold it. We have tried it. And the promise has been fulfilled, as it always will be as long as we rely upon it. Plenteous grace!

Ah, we will want plenteous grace, my friends. Plenteous grace to keep us humble, plenteous grace to make us prayerful, plenteous grace to make us holy, plenteous grace to make us zealous, plenteous grace to make us truthful, plenteous grace to preserve us through this life and at last to land us in heaven. We cannot do without showers of grace. How many are there here who have been dry in a shower of grace? Why, there is a shower of grace here. But how is it that it does not fall to some of the people?

It is because they put up the umbrella of their prejudice. And though they sit here, even as God's people sit, even when it rains they have such a prejudice against God's Word that they do not want to hear it. They do not want to love it and it runs off their prejudices. Nevertheless, the showers are there—and we will thank God for them where they do fall.

Again, it is *seasonable grace*. "I will give them the shower in its season." There is nothing like seasonable grace. There are fruits, you know, that are best in their season, and they are not good at any other time. And there are graces that are good in their season, but we do not always require them. A person vexes and irritates me. I want grace just at that moment to be patient. I have not got it and I get angry. Ten minutes after I am ever so patient. But I have not had grace in its season. The promise is "I will give them the shower in its season." Ah, poor waiting soul, what is your season this morning? Is it the season of drought? Then that is the season for showers. Is it a season of great heaviness and black clouds? Then that is the season for showers.

What is your season this morning, businessman? Lost money all the week, have you? Now is the season to ask for showers. It is nighttime. Now the dew falls. The dew does not fall in the day; it falls in the night, the night of affliction, trial, and trouble. There stands the promise—only go and plead it. "I will give them the shower in its season." We have one thought more and then we have done. Here is a varied blessing. "I will give you *showers* of blessing." The word is in the *plural*. All kinds of blessings God will send. The rain is all of one kind when it comes. But grace is not all of one kind, or it does not produce the same effect.

When God sends rain upon His church, He sends showers of blessing. There are some ministers who think that if there is a shower on their church, God will send a shower of work. Yes, but if He does, He will send a shower of comfort. Others think that God will send a shower of gospel truth. Yes, but if He sends that, He will send a shower of gospel holiness. For all God's blessings go together. They are like the sweet sister graces that danced hand in hand. God sends showers of blessing.

If He gives comforting grace, He also gives converting grace. If He makes the trumpet blow for the bankrupt sinner, He will also make it sound a shout of joy for the sinner who is pardoned and forgiven. He will send "showers of blessing."

Now then, there is a promise in that Bible. We have tried to explain and enlarge upon it. What will we do with it?

> In that book there lies hidden
> A pearl of price unknown.

Well, we have examined this rich promise. We as a church are looking at it. We are saying, "Is that ours?" I think most of the members will say,

"It is, for God has poured out upon us showers of blessing in their season."
Well then, if the promise is ours, the precept is ours as much as the promise.
Ought we not to ask God to continue to make us a blessing? Some say I did
so-and-so when I was a young man. But supposing you are fifty, you are not
an old man now. Is there not something you can do? It is all very well to talk
about what you *have* done. But what are you doing *now*?

> lenteous grace to keep us humble, plenteous grace to make us
> prayerful, plenteous grace to make us holy, plenteous grace to make
> us zealous, plenteous grace to make us truthful, plenteous grace to
> preserve us through this life and at last to land us in heaven.

I know what it is with some of you. You shined brightly once, but your
candle has not been trimmed lately and so it does not shine so well. May
God take away some of the worldly cares and trim the candles a little! You
know there were scissors and scissors trays provided in the temple for all
the candles, but no extinguishers. And if there should be a poor candle here
this morning with a wick that has not given light for a long while, you will
have no extinguisher from me—but I hope you will always have a trimming.
I thought the first time when I came to the lamps this morning it would
be to trim them. That has been the intention of my sermon—to trim you a
little—to set you to work for Jesus Christ.

O Zion, shake yourself from the dust! O Christian, raise yourself from
your slumbers! Warrior, put on your armor! Soldier, grasp your sword! The
captain sounds the alarm of war! O sluggard, why do you sleep? O heir of
heaven, has not Jesus done so much for you that you should live to Him?
O beloved brethren, purchased with redeeming mercies, girded about with
loving-kindness and with tenderness, "now for a shout of sacred joy," and
after that to the battle! The little seed has grown to this: Who knows what it
will be? Only let us together strive, without variance. Let us labor for Jesus.
Never did men have so fair an opportunity, for the last hundred years, "there
is a tide that, taken at the flood, leads on to fortune."

Shall you take it at the flood? Over the bar, at the harbor's mouth! O
ship of heaven, let your sails be out. Let not your canvas be furled. And
the wind will blow us across the sea of difficulty that lies before us. Oh,
that the latter day might have its dawning even in this despised habitation!

O my God! From this place cause the first wave to spring that will move another and then another, till the last great wave will sweep over the sands of time and dash against the rocks of eternity, echoing as it falls, "Hallelujah! Hallelujah! Hallelujah! The Lord God Omnipotent reigns!"

FOR FURTHER THOUGHT

1. *Spurgeon uses Ezekiel 34:26 as an allegory for the church. With this in view, how does the church become a blessing?*
2. *Ezekiel 34:26 assures us that there will be showers of blessing. When does it say that these blessings will come?*
3. *"Plenteous" is the word Spurgeon uses to describe God's grace in this sermon. How does 2 Corinthians 9:14 describe grace?*

FARM LABORERS

*I planted, Apollos watered, but God gave the increase. So then
neither he who plants is anything, nor he who waters, but God who
gives the increase. Now he who plants and he who waters are one,
and each one will receive his own reward according to
his own labor. For we are God's fellow workers;
you are God's field, you are God's building.*
1 CORINTHIANS 3:6–9

IN all ages since the fall there has been a tendency in the human heart to forget God and get away from Him. Idolatry has been the sin of all nations, including God's favored people, the Jews, and including certain persons who call themselves Christians who still make idols out of crosses and images. This vicious principle of ignoring God and setting up something between our minds and our Creator crops up everywhere and in every department of thought. When men study the works of God in nature, they often hang up a veil to hide the great Worker. Because God acts in a certain way, they call His method of action a law and straightway they speak of these laws as if they were forces and powers in and of themselves, and thus God is banished out of His own universe and His place is taken up in the scientific world by idols called "natural laws."

Take the region of providence and here you find persons, instead of seeing the hand of God everywhere, looking to second causes. They are seeking *causes* of prosperity and becoming very despondent if they do not appear to exist; or viewing the agents of affliction and becoming angry against them, instead of bowing before the God who has used them for correction. It is easy to make idols out of second causes and to forget the God who is everywhere present, causing all things to work together for good. That this evil principle should intrude into the church is very sad and yet it is with difficulty excluded.

You may bar all your doors as fast as you please, but the idol makers will come in with their shrines. In the instance of the church at Corinth, Paul found the brethren forgetting their God and Savior in their high esteem for certain preachers. Instead of all saying, "We are Christ's disciples," and uniting together to promote the common cause, they established parties and one said, "Paul, who founded this church, is to be had in the greatest reverence, and we are of Paul." Others replied, "But Apollos is more eloquent than the apostle Paul, and by him we have been edified till we have gone beyond Paul, and therefore we are of Apollos." But a third party declared that they were of no sect whatever, for they were "brethren" and were "of Christ."

These last, I suspect, either ignored or denounced the other two parties and would not commune with them, in order to testify against their sectarianism and to promote unity. I only surmise this from the conduct of those "brethren" who in our day take the Corinthians to be their model and cut off everybody else, being more exclusive than any other sect in Christendom! The apostle warns the saints in Corinth against this; he brings the Lord before their minds and bids them remember that if Paul plants and Apollos waters, still it is *God* who gives the increase. Since they think so highly of men, he will have it that "neither he who plants is anything, nor he who waters," but *God* who gives the increase is *everything*.

> This vicious principle of ignoring God and setting up something between our minds and our Creator crops up everywhere and in every department of thought.

See to it, dear friends, that you set the Lord always before you in this church and in all your churches! Know those who labor among you and esteem them highly in love for their work's sake, but do not make them your dependence. Remember that the ablest ministers, the most successful evangelists, the most profound teachers are, after all, nothing but laborers together with God. Let your mind be set upon the Master and not upon the servants! Do not say, "We are for this man because he plants," or "We are for the other because he waters," or "We are a third party for nobody at all." But let us join in ascribing all honor and praise to God, who works all our works in us, since every good gift and every perfect gift is from above and comes down from the Father of lights, to whom be glory world without end!

I will begin at the end of my text because I find it to be the easiest way of mapping out my discourse. We will first remark that *the church is God's farm*: "Ye are God's husbandry" (1 Cor. 3:9 KJV). In the margin of the Revised Version, we read, "Ye are God's tilled ground," and that is the very expression for me. "You are God's tilled ground," or farm. After we have spoken of the farm, we will next say a little upon the fact that He employs *laborers on the farm*. And when we have looked at the laborers—such poor fellows as they are—we will remember that God Himself is *the great worker*: "We are labourers together with God" (3:9 KJV).

I. We begin by considering that *the church is God's farm*. The Lord has made the church of His sovereign choice to be His own by *purchase*, having paid an immense price for it. "For the LORD's portion is his people; Jacob is the lot of his inheritance" (Deut. 32:9 KJV). Because the Lord's portion was under mortgage, therefore the only begotten Son laid down His life as the purchase price and redeemed His people to be the Lord's portion forever and ever. Henceforth it is said to all believers, "You are not your own. For you were bought at a price" (1 Cor. 6:19–20). Every acre of God's farm cost the Savior bloody sweat, yes, the blood of His heart! He loved us and gave Himself for us; that is the price He paid!

What a ransom! The death of Jesus has sometimes almost seemed too high a price to pay for such poor land as we are, but the Lord, having set His eyes and heart upon His people, would not draw back, but completed the redemption of the purchased possession! Therefore the church is God's freehold, and He has the title deeds of it, yes, of you and of me, for we belong only to Him, and we are glad to acknowledge the fact that "I am my beloved's, and my beloved is mine" (Song of Sol. 6:3). The church is God's farm by choice and purchase.

And now He has made it His by enclosure. It lay exposed, for a time, as part of an open common, bare and barren, covered with thorns and thistles and the haunt of every wild beast, for we were "by nature children of wrath, just as the others" (Eph. 2:3). We were part of the dreary desert till divine foreknowledge surveyed the waste and electing love marked out its portion with a full line of grace and thus set us apart to be the Lord's own estate forever. In due time *effectual* grace came forth with power and separated us from the rest of mankind, as fields are hedged and ditched to part them from the open heath.

Has not the Lord declared that He has chosen His vineyard and fenced it? Has He not said, "I will be a wall of fire all around her, and I will be the glory in her midst" (Zech. 2:5)?

> *We are a garden walled around,*
> *Chosen and made peculiar ground.*
> *A little spot, enclosed by grace*
> *Out of the world's wide wilderness.*

The Lord has also made this farm evidently His own by cultivation. What more could He have done for His farm? He has totally changed the nature of the soil—from being barren, He has made it a fruitful land! He has plowed it, dug it, fattened it, watered it, and planted it with all manner of flowers and fruits. It has already brought forth to Him many a pleasant fruit, and there are brighter times to come when angels will shout the harvest home and Christ "shall see the labor of His soul, and be satisfied" (Isa. 53:11).

This farm is *kept* what it is, as well as *made* what it is, by God's continual protection. Not only did He enclose it and work upon it by His miraculous power to make it His own farm, but also He continually maintains possession of it. "I, the LORD, keep it, I water it every moment; lest any hurt it, I keep it night and day" (Isa. 27:3). If it were not for God's continual power, her hedges would soon be thrown down and wild beasts would devour her fields. Wicked hands are always trying to break down her walls and lay her waste, again, so that there should be no true church in the world, but the Lord is jealous for His land and will not allow it to be destroyed. If God were to leave the church, she would become a howling wilderness, but she will not come to such an end.

A church would not long remain a church if God did not preserve it to Himself. What if God should say, "I will take away the hedge thereof, and it shall be eaten up; and break down the wall thereof, and it shall be trodden down: And I will lay it waste: it shall not be pruned, nor digged; but there shall come up briers and thorns: I will also command the clouds that they rain no rain upon it" (Isa. 5:5–6 KJV)? What a wilderness it would become! What does He say? "But go ye now unto my place which was in Shiloh, where I set my name at the first, and see what I did to it for the wickedness of my people Israel" (Jer. 7:12 KJV). Go to Jerusalem, where of old were the city of His glory and the shrine of His dwelling, and what is left there today? Go to Rome, where once Paul preached the gospel with power. What is it now but the center of idolatry?

The Lord may remove the candlestick and leave a place that was bright as day to become black as darkness itself! But God's farm remains a farm because He is always in it to prevent its returning to its former wildness. Omnipotent power is as necessary to keep the fields of the church under cultivation as to reclaim them at the first.

Inasmuch as the church is God's own farm, He expects to receive a harvest from it. He comes to us looking for sheaves where He has sowed so plentifully. The world is a wasteland and He looks for nothing from it, but *we* are tilled land, and therefore a harvest is due from us!

Barrenness suits the moorland, but to a farm it would be a great discredit. Love looks for returns of love. Divine grace given demands gracious fruit. Watered with the drops of the Savior's bloody sweat, will we not bring forth a hundredfold to His praise? Kept by the eternal Spirit of God, will there not be produced in us fruits to His glory? The Lord's husbandry upon us has shown a great expenditure of cost, labor, and thought. Ought there not to be a proportionate return? Ought not the Lord to have a harvest of obedience, a harvest of holiness, a harvest of usefulness, a harvest of praise? Shall it not be so?

God's farm remains a farm because He is always in it to prevent its returning to its former wildness. Omnipotent power is as necessary to keep the fields of the church under cultivation as to reclaim them at the first.

I think some churches forget that an increase is expected from every field of the Lord's farm, for they never have a harvest or even look for one. The people come together and take their seats on Sunday and listen to sermons—that is, when they do not go to sleep. The sacraments are celebrated, a little money is contributed, a few poor folk are relieved, and affairs crawl along at a snail's pace. As to affecting the whole village, or endeavoring to bring the surrounding population to Christ, I do not think it has occurred to some churches to attempt it, and when certain warmer spirits seek to bring sinners to Jesus, the older and more prudent folks fetch wet blankets and use them with very great effect so that every sign of enthusiasm is damped down.

Brethren, such things ought not to be! I conceive that if there were no Christians in England but the members of our baptized churches, these would suffice for God's great designs of mercy if they were once awakened to real labor. Alas, the loiterers are many, but the laborers are few. Look, my brethren, at the number of nonconforming churches in this land and at the earnest ministers remaining in the establishment. If these were more fully quickened into spiritual life, would there not be workmen enough on the home farm? If all churches felt that they did not exist for mere existence's sake, or mere enjoyment's sake, would they not act differently?

> God might plow and sow His chosen farm, the church, by miracle, or by angels, but it is a great instance of His condescension toward His church that He blesses her through her own sons and daughters.

Farmers do not plow their lands or sow their fields for amusement. They mean business and plow and sow because they desire a harvest! If this fact could but enter into the heads of some professors, surely they would look at things in a different light! But of late it has seemed as if we thought that God's church was not expected to produce anything, but existed for her own comfort and personal benefit. Brothers and sisters, it must not be so! The Great Husbandman must have some reward for His husbandry! Every field must yield its increase and the whole estate must bring forth to His praise! We join with the bride in the Song in saying, "My own vineyard is before me. You, O Solomon, may have a thousand, and those who tend its fruit two hundred" (Song of Sol. 8:12).

But I come back to the place from which I started. This farm is, by choice, by purchase, by enclosure, by cultivation, by preservation, entirely the Lord's. See, then, the injustice of allowing any of the laborers to call even a *part* of the estate his own! When a great man has a large farm of his own, what would he think if Hodge, the plowman, should say, "Look here, I plow this farm, and therefore it is mine! I will call this field Hodge's Acres"?

"And," says Hobbs, "I reaped *that* land last harvest, and therefore it is mine, and I will call it Hobbs's Field."

What if all the other laborers became Hodgeites and Hobbsites and so parceled out the farm among them? I think the landlord would soon eject the lot of them! The farm belongs to its owner, and let it be called by *His* name. It is absurd to call it by the names of the bumpkins who labor upon it. Is that a disrespectful title to apply to laborers? Why, I meant it for anybody and everybody whose name is used as the head of a party in the church!

I meant Luther, Calvin, Wesley, and other great men, for at their best, as compared with their Master, they are only farm laborers, and we ought not to call parts of the farm by their names! Who then is Paul, and who is Apollos? Is Christ divided? The entire church belongs to Him who has *chosen* it in His sovereignty, *bought* it with His blood, *fenced* it by His grace, *cultivated* it by His wisdom, and *preserved* it by His power! There is still but one church on the face of the earth, and those who love the Lord should keep this truth of God in mind.

Paul is a laborer, Apollos is a laborer, Cephas is a laborer, but not so much as a foot of the farm is Paul's, nor does a single parcel of land belong to Apollos, or the smallest allotment to Cephas. "You are Christ's, and Christ is God's" (1 Cor. 3:23). The fact is that in this case the laborers belong to the land and not the land to the laborers, "for all things are yours: whether Paul or Apollos or Cephas" (3:21–22). We preach not ourselves, but Christ Jesus the Lord, and ourselves your servants for Jesus' sake!

II. We now have to notice, as our second head, that *the Great Husbandman employs laborers.* By human agency God ordinarily works out His designs. He can, if He pleases, by His Holy Spirit, get directly at the hearts of men, but that is His business and not ours. We have to do with such words as these: "It pleased God by the foolishness of preaching to save them that believe" (1 Cor. 1:21 KJV). The Master's commission is not "Sit still and see the Spirit of God convert the nations," but "Go into all the world and preach the gospel to every creature" (Mark 16:15). This is God's method in supplying the race with food.

In answer to the prayer, "Give us this day our daily bread" (Matt. 6:11), He might have bid the clouds drop manna, morning by morning, at each man's door, but He sees that it is for our good to work, and so He uses the hands of the plowman and the sower for our supply. God might plow and sow His chosen farm, the church, by miracle, or by angels, but it is a great instance of His condescension toward His church that He blesses her through her own sons and daughters. He employs us for our own good, for we who are laborers in His fields receive much more good for ourselves than we bestow. Labor develops our spiritual muscle and keeps us in health. "To me," says Paul, "who am less than the least of all the saints, this grace was given, that I should preach among the Gentiles the unsearchable riches of Christ" (Eph. 3:8).

It is a divine grace, then. We find it to be a means of grace to our souls to preach the gospel. I have heard it said, and I believe there is some truth in it, that those who have to preach are under the temptation of getting so familiar with sacred things that they cease to feel their power. If this is true, it is an awful proof of our total depravity, for the more familiar we are with holy things, the more we ought to be affected by them. And this I know, it has been the greatest means of grace to me to be bound by my office to study the scriptures and wait upon God for help in expounding them.

Some of you who do not grow in grace by hearing other people might possibly get on better if you were, yourselves, to try to preach. At any rate, you might not be quite so faultfinding with other folks! When I hear a person say, "I cannot hear my minister," I suggest to him to buy a horn.

"Oh," he says, "I do not mean *that*. I mean that I cannot enjoy his preaching."

Then I say to him, "Preach yourself."

"I cannot do that."

"Then do not find fault with those who are doing their best." Instead of blaming the plowman, just try a turn in the furrow yourself. Why grumble at the weeds? Take a hoe and work at them like a man.

Do you think the hedges untidy? Put on the leather gloves and help us trim them! Our great Master means that every laborer on His farm should receive some benefit from it, for He never muzzles the ox that treads out the corn. The laborer's daily bread comes out of the soil. Though he works not for himself but for his Master, yet he still has his portion of food. In the Lord's granary there is seed for the sower, but there is also bread for the eater. However disinterestedly we may serve God in the husbandry of His church, we are, ourselves, partakers of the fruit. It is a great condescension on God's part that He uses us at all, for we are poor tools, at the best, and more hindrance than help.

The laborers employed by God are all occupied upon necessary work. Notice, "I planted, Apollos watered." Who beat the big drum or blew his own trumpet? Nobody! On God's farm none are kept for ornamental purposes. I have read some sermons that could only have been meant for show, for there was not a grain of gospel in them. They were plows with the share left out, drills with no wheat in the box, clod-crushers made of butter! I do not believe that our God will ever pay wages to men who only walk about His grounds to show themselves. Fine orators who display their eloquence are more like gypsies who stray on the farm to pick up chickens than honest laborers who work to bring forth a crop for their master.

Why, many of the members of our churches live as if their only business on the farm was to pluck blackberries or gather wildflowers! They are great at finding fault with other people's plowing and mowing, but not a hand's turn will they do themselves. Come on, my good fellows! Why do you stand all the day idle? The harvest is plenteous and the laborers are few. You who think yourselves more cultivated than ordinary people, if you are indeed Christians, must not strut about and despise those who are hard at work. If you do, I will say, "That person has mistaken his master. He may probably be in the employ of some gentleman farmer who cares more for show than profit, but our great Lord is practical—and on His estate His laborers attend to necessary labor."

When you and I preach or teach, it will be well if we say to ourselves, "What will be the use of what I am going to do? I am about to teach a difficult subject—will it do any good? I have chosen an abstruse point of theology—will it serve any purpose?" Brothers, a laborer may work very hard at a whim of his own and waste his labor, but this is folly! Some discourses do little more than show the difference between a Tweedledum and a Tweedledee, and what is the use of that? Suppose we sow the fields with sawdust, or sprinkle them with rose water, what of that? Will God bless our moral essays and fine compositions and pretty passages?

Brothers, we must aim at *usefulness*. We must, as laborers together with God, be occupied with something that is worth doing. "I," says one, "have planted." It is well, for planting must be done. "I," answers another, "have watered." That is also good and necessary. See to it that you can each bring in a solid report, but let no man be content with the mere child's play of oratory, or the getting up of entertainments and such like! On the Lord's farm there is a division of labor. Even Paul did not say, "I have planted *and* watered." No, Paul planted. And Apollos certainly could not say, "I have planted as well as watered." No, it was enough for him to attend to the watering. No one man has all gifts. How foolish, then, are they who say, "I enjoy So-and-So's ministry because he edifies the saints in doctrine, but when he was away the other Sunday, I could not profit by the preacher because he was all for the conversion of sinners."

Yes, he was planting! You have been planted a good while and do not need planting again, but you ought to be thankful that others were made partakers of the benefit! One sows and another reaps, and therefore, instead of grumbling at the honest plowman because he did not bring a sickle with him, you ought to have prayed for him that he might have strength to plow deep and break up hard hearts. Let us do all that we can and try to do more, for the more work we can turn our hands to, the better. "You must not have too many irons in the fire," said somebody. But I say, "Put all your irons into the fire, and if you have not fire enough, cry to God till you have! Set your whole soul on fire and keep all your irons hot." Yet you may find it wise to direct your strength into one line of things that you understand so that, by practice, you may come to be skillful in it. Each man should find out his own work and do it with all his might.

Observe that on God's farm, there is unity of purpose among the laborers. Read the text. "Now he who plants and he who waters are one." The Master has employed them, and though He may send them out at different times and to different parts of the farm, yet they are all one in being used for one end, to work for one harvest. In England we do not understand what watering means, because the farmer could not water his entire farm. But in the East a farmer waters almost every inch of ground. He would have no crop if he did not use all means for irrigating the fields. If you have ever been in Italy, Egypt, or Palestine, you will have seen a complete system of wells, pumps, wheels, buckets, channels, little streamlets, pipes, and so on, by which the water is carried all over the garden to every plant—otherwise in the extreme heat of the sun it would be dried up.

Planting needs wisdom and watering needs quite as much, and the piecing of these two works together requires that the laborers should be of one mind. It is a bad thing when laborers are at cross-purposes and work against each other. And this evil is worse in the church than anywhere else. How can I plant with success if my helper will not water what I have planted? Or what is the use of my watering if nothing is planted? Farming is spoiled when foolish people undertake it and quarrel over it, for from sowing to reaping the work is one, and all must be done to one end. Oh, for unity! Let as pull together all our days, even as we have done in this church to now.

We are called upon to notice in our text that all the laborers put together are *nothing*. "Neither he who plants is anything, nor he who waters" (1 Cor. 3:7). The workmen are nothing at all without their master! All the laborers on a farm could not manage it if they had no one at their head, and all the preachers and Christian workers in the world can do nothing unless God is with them! Remember that every laborer on God's farm has derived all his qualifications from God. No man knows how to plant or water souls unless God teaches him from day to day. All these holy gifts are the grants of free grace. All the laborers work under God's direction and arrangement, or they work in vain. They would not know when or how to do their work if their Master did not guide them by His Spirit, without whose help they cannot even think a good thought.

> Farming is spoiled when foolish people undertake it and quarrel over it, for from sowing to reaping the work is one, and all must be done to one end.

All God's laborers must go to Him for their seed, or else they will scatter tares. All good seed comes out of God's granary. If we preach, it must be the true Word of God or nothing can come of it. More than that, the heavenly Master gives all the strength in the laborer's arms that sow the heavenly seed. We cannot preach unless God is with us. A sermon is vain talk and dreary word spinning unless the Holy Spirit enlivens it. He must give us both the preparation of the heart and the answer of the tongue, or we will be as men who sow the wind. When the good seed is sown, the whole success of it rests with God. If He withholds the dew and the rain, the seed will never rise from the ground—and unless He will shine upon it, the green ear will never ripen.

The human heart will remain barren, even though Paul himself should preach, unless God the Holy Spirit will work with Paul and bless the Word to those who hear it. Therefore, since the increase is of God alone, put the laborers into their place. Do not make too much of us, for when we have done, we are all unprofitable servants. Yet, though inspiration calls the laborers *nothing*, it makes a great deal of them, for it says, "Each one will receive his own reward according to his own labor" (1 Cor. 3:8). They are nothing and yet they will be rewarded as if they were something! God works our good works in us and then rewards us for them!

Here we have mention of a personal service and a personal reward: "Each one will receive his own reward according to his own labor." The reward is proportionate, not to the success, but to the *labor*! Many discouraged workers may be comforted with that expression. You are not to be paid by results, but by *endeavors*. You may have a stiff bit of clay to plow or a dreary plot of land to sow where stones, birds, thorns, travelers, and a burning sun may all be leagued against the seed, but you are not accountable for these things. Your reward will be according to your labor. Some put a great deal of labor into a little field and make much out of it. Others use a great deal of labor throughout a long life and yet they see but small results, for it is written, "One sows and another reaps, but the reaping man will not get all the reward. The sowing man will receive his portion of the joy." The laborers are nobodies, but they will enter into the joy of their Lord!

> When Paul plants and Apollos waters, God does *give* the increase. We do not labor in vain! There would be no increase without God, but then we are not without God.

United, according to the text, the workers have been successful, and that is a great part of their reward. "I planted, Apollos watered, but God gave the increase." Frequently brethren say in their prayers, "A Paul may plant, an Apollos may water, but it is all in vain unless God gives the increase." This is quite true, but another truth of God is too much overlooked, namely, that when Paul plants and Apollos waters, God *does* give the increase. We do not labor in vain! There would be no increase without God, but then we are not without God. When such men as Paul and Apollos plant and water, there is sure to be an increase. They are the right kind of laborers. They work in a right spirit and God is certain to bless them.

This is a great part of the laborers' wages. I am rich, I am increased in goods, I have need of nothing when I see souls converted—my heart leaps for joy, my spirit is glad, and I am ready to sing, "My soul doth magnify the Lord" (Luke 1:46 KJV), but if it were ever to come to this, that I stood here Sunday after Sunday and saw no conversions but the church rather going down than increasing, I should take it as an intimation that I had better take my plow somewhere else and scatter the seed on other soil. I would break my heart over non-success, or cry to God to break it, for he who works and gets no fruit is disheartened in his labor.

What would you farmers do? You are half inclined to give up now because you have had two or three bad years. But what would you do if you never saw a harvest at all? Why, you would clear out and be off to the western prairies or to the bush of the southern continent to see if the soil somewhere else would repay your labor! Do the same, brother ministers! If you have been at work in one spot for years and have not led souls to Jesus, pack up your traps and go somewhere else! Do not forever break your plow upon rocks. It is a big world and there is plenty of good ground somewhere—let us seek it! If they persecute you in one city, flee to another and let the Word of God be published all the more widely by your moving about!

III. So much upon the laborers. Now for the main point again. *God Himself is the great worker.* He may use what laborers He pleases, but the increase comes only from Him. Brothers, you know it is so in natural things—the most skillful farmer cannot make the wheat germinate, grow, and ripen. He cannot even preserve a single field till harvesttime, for the farmer's enemies are many and mighty. In farming there's many a slip 'twixt the cup and the lip, and when the farmer thinks he will reap his crop, often there are blights and mildews lingering about to rob him of his gains. God must give the increase. If any man is dependent on God, it is the farmer, and as he, we are, all of us, dependent upon God from year to year for the food by which we live. Even the king must live by the increase of the field.

God gives the increase in the barn and the hayrack—and in the *spiritual* farm it is even more so, for what can man do in this business? If any of you think that it is an easy thing to win a soul, I would like you to try. Suppose that without divine aid you should try to save a soul—you might as well attempt to make a world! Why, you cannot create a fly! How can you create a new heart and a right spirit? Regeneration is a great mystery—it is out of your reach. "The wind blows where it wishes, and you hear the sound of it, but cannot tell where it comes from and where it goes. So is everyone who is born of the Spirit" (John 3:8).

What can you and I do in this matter? It is out of our pale and beyond our line. We can tell out the truth of God, but to apply that truth to the heart and conscience is quite another thing. I have stood here and preached

Jesus Christ—preached my whole heart out—and yet I know that I have never produced any saving effect upon a single unregenerate man unless the Spirit of God has taken the truth of God and opened the heart and placed the living seed within it! Experience teaches us this. Equally is it the Lord's work to keep the seed alive when it springs up. We think we have converts, but it is not long before we are disappointed in them. Many are like blossoms on our fruit trees—they are fair to look upon, but they do not come to anything! And others are like the many little fruits that fall off long before they have come to any size—a cold night or a blight will come and away go our hopes of a crop—it is just so with hopeful converts.

He who presides over a great church and feels an agony for the souls of men will soon be convinced that if God does not work, there will be no work done. We will see no conversion, no sanctification, no final perseverance, no glory brought to God, no satisfaction for the passion of the Savior unless He gives the increase! Well said our Lord, "Without Me you can do nothing" (John 15:5). What is the effect of all this upon your minds? Briefly I would draw certain practical lessons out of this important truth of God. The first is, if the whole farm of the church belongs exclusively to the great Master Worker and the laborers are worth nothing without Him, let this promote unity among all whom He employs!

If we are all under one Master, do not let us quarrel. It is a great pity when ministers harshly criticize one another and when Sunday school teachers do the same. It is a miserable business when we cannot bear to see good being done by those of a different denomination who work in ways of their own. If a new laborer comes on the farm and he wears a coat of a new cut and uses a hoe of a new shape, will I become his enemy? If he does his work better than I do mine, will I be jealous? Do you not remember reading in the Scriptures that upon one occasion the disciples could not cast out a devil? This ought to have made them humble, but to our surprise we read a few verses further on that John and others saw one casting out devils in Christ's name and John said, "We forbade him because he does not follow with us" (Luke 9:49).

They could not cast out the devil themselves, and they forbade those who could! A certain band of people is going about winning souls, but because they are not doing it in *our* fashion, we do not like it. It is true they use all sorts of strange devices and wild excitements, but they *do* save souls and that is the main point. Yet there are gentlemen who never converted half a soul in their lives who cry, "This is fanaticism!" Go and do better before you find fault! Instead of caviling, let us encourage all on Christ's side. Wisdom is justified of her children. The laborers ought to be satisfied with the new plowman if his Master is. Brother, if the great Lord has employed you, it is no business of mine to question His right. I do not like the looks of you and cannot think how He can have such a fellow upon the farm, but as He has employed you, I have no right to judge you, for I daresay I look as odd in your eyes as you do in mine!

> *I know that I have never produced any saving effect upon a single unregenerate man unless the Spirit of God has taken the truth of God and opened the heart and placed the living seed within it!*

Can I lend you a hand? Can I show you how to work better? Or can you tell me something so that I may do my work better? May not the Master employ whom He pleases? If a new hoe or a new rake comes out and you who have been doing work steadily for years open your eyes and say, "I will not use *that* newfangled thing," are you wise? Do not use the new invention if you have not tried it and can work better in your own way, but let the other man use it who finds it a handier tool. If new methods of getting a hearing for the gospel are invented by the ingenuity of earnestness, let the brothers use them. And if we cannot imitate them, let us at least feel that we are still one, because "one is your Master, even Christ" (Matt. 23:10 KJV).

This truth of God, however, ought to keep all the laborers very dependent. Are you going to preach, young man? "Yes, I am going to do a great deal of good." Are you? Have you forgotten that you are *nothing*? "Neither he who plants is anything." A great preacher is coming full of the gospel to comfort the saints. If he is not coming in strict dependence upon God, he, too, is nothing. "Nor he who waters is anything." Power belongs to God! Man is vanity and his words are wind. To God alone belongs power and wisdom. If we keep our places in all lowliness, our Lord will use us. But when we exalt ourselves, He will leave us to our nothingness.

Next, notice that this fact ennobles everybody who labors in God's husbandry. This passage makes my heart leap as I read it! My very soul is lifted up with joy when I mark these words, "We are God's fellow workers"!

We are God's fellow workers—mere laborers on His farm—but laborers *with* Him! Does the Lord work with us? Yes. "And they went forth, and preached every where, the Lord working with them, and confirming the word with signs following" (Mark 16:20 KJV) is language for all the sons of God as well as for the great Firstborn! God is with you, brother! God is with you, sister, when you are serving Him with all your heart. Speaking to your class concerning Jesus, it is God who speaks through you! Picking up that stranger on the way and telling him of salvation by faith, Christ is speaking with you even as He spoke with the woman at the well!

Addressing the rough crowd in the open air, young man, if you are preaching of pardon through the atoning blood, it is the God of Peter who is testifying of His Son even as He did on the day of Pentecost! O brother laborers, ours is a high honor, since the Father is with us and works by us! As Mr. Wesley said, "The best of all is, God is with us." The Lord of hosts is with us, and therefore we cannot fail! If we could, in working with God, be defeated, then God's own honor would be compromised, and that cannot be!

But lastly, how this should drive us to our knees! Since we are nothing without God, let us cry mightily to Him for help in this, our holy service! Let both sower and reaper pray together, or they will never rejoice together. As a church, God has blessed us so richly that in generations to come it will be spoken of as a wonder that God should so greatly favor a congregation for so many years—but it has been wholly and only in answer to prayer. So far from supposing that our union and prosperity are in any measure due to me, I declare that the only cause of all the soul winning that has been done in this place is to be found in the prayers of the saints! God in great mercy has given the spirit of prayer to you and to others who love me, and therefore I am highly favored. I am terribly afraid lest this prayerfulness should be dampened. I am jealous lest you should begin to think the preacher is something and so should fail to pray for him!

There is a thinner congregation when I am away, and therefore I am afraid that you have some reliance upon me and do not expect a blessing if I am absent. Is it so? Having begun in the Spirit, are you now made perfect in the flesh? Have you begun to be of Spurgeon? This will never do! Brothers and sisters, this will never do! We must get rid of the tendency before it grows upon us! God can bless one man as well as another. I do not know that He always does so, but He can and, perhaps if you expected Him to do so, He would do so. If you came up to this house with the same prayerfulness for others as you apportion me, you would get the same blessing! I am weakest of the weak apart from God—therefore pray for me—but others are weak, too, and therefore pray for them also.

> *Since we are nothing without God, let us cry mightily to Him for help in this, our holy service! Let both sower and reaper pray together, or they will never rejoice together.*

Do let us pray mightily for a blessing! Pray always! Pray in your bedchambers, at your family altars, at your work, in your leisure, and also in this place. Come in larger numbers to pray for a blessing. We have many appointed prayer meetings—keep them all flourishing. The windows of heaven are easily opened if our mouths and hearts are opened in prayer. If the blessing is withheld, it is because we do not cry for it and *expect* it! O brother laborers, come to the mercy seat and you will see God's farm watered from on high and tilled with divine skill—and the reapers will soon return from the folds bringing their sheaves with them, though perhaps they went forth weeping to the sowing. To our Father, who is the Husbandman, be all glory forever and ever! Amen.

For Further Thought

1. *According to 1 Corinthians 3:6, who deserves the credit for church growth?*
2. *The above verse mentions the labor of Paul and Apollos. Read Ephesians 3:8 and compare it with 1 Corinthians 3:10. What was given to these men to work like this?*
3. *What is the relationship between church workers as seen in 1 Corinthians 3:8?*

The Church's Love to Her Loving Lord

Tell me, O you whom I love, where you feed your flock,
where you make it rest at noon. For why should I be as
one who veils herself by the flocks of your companions?
Song of Solomon 1:7

WE will need to lift up our hearts to God and ask to be quickened in divine grace, or the precious truths in our text will not prove to us as honey out of the rock. We cannot appreciate the spirituality of this book unless God's Spirit will help us. Many read these words and only see a proof of the imaginative power of an eastern mind. Some read to scoff and blaspheme, and others, even good people, neglect to read this book altogether, being unable to drink in its spirit because of their need of that higher life of communion with the Beloved that is here so beautifully laid open to our view.

Now I am persuaded of better things of you, beloved. I am sure that you believe that every word of God is precious, and most certainly we say of this book, it is "more to be desired. . .than gold, yea, than much fine gold; sweeter also than honey and the honeycomb" (Ps. 19:10). This book of the canticles is most precious to us. It is the inner court of the temple of truth. It seems to us to belong to the secret place of the tabernacle of the Most High. We see our Savior's face in almost every page of the Bible, but here we see His heart and feel His love to us. We will hope this morning to speak of our own experience, as well as of the church that is here speaking.

You will perceive that she begins with a title, she expresses a desire, and she enforces it with an argument: "Tell me, O you whom I love, where you feed your flock, where you make it rest at noon. For why should I be as one who veils herself by the flocks of your companions?"

I. We commence with the title "O you whom I love." It is well to be able to call the Lord Jesus Christ by this name without an "if" or a "but." A very large proportion of Christian people can only say of Christ that they *hope* they love Him. They *trust* they love Him, but this is a very poor and shallow experience to be content to stay here. It seems to me that no one ought to give any rest to his spirit till he feels quite sure about a matter of such vital importance. We are not content to have a *hope* of the love of our parents, or of our spouse, or of our children! We feel we must be certain there.

> *T*he efficient cause of our love is the Holy Spirit of God. We should never have had a spark of love to Jesus if the divine Worker had not bestowed it upon us.

And we ought not to be satisfied with a hope that Christ loves us and with a bare trust that we love Him. The old saints did not generally speak with buts and ifs and hopes and trusts; they spoke positively and plainly. "I know whom I have believed," says Paul (2 Tim. 1:12 KJV). "I know that my redeemer liveth," says Job (19:25 KJV). "You whom I love," says Solomon in the song as we have it here. Learn, dear friends, to get that positive knowledge of your love to Jesus, and be not satisfied till you can talk about your interest in Him as a *reality* that you have made infallibly sure by having received the witness of the Holy Spirit and His seal upon your soul by faith that you are born of God and belong to Christ.

Speaking, then, of this title that rings the great bell of love to Jesus, let us notice first the cause and second the effect of that love. If we can look into the face of Him who once sweat great drops of blood and call Him "You whom I love," it is interesting to consider what is the *cause* of our love. And here our reply is very quick. The efficient cause of our love is the Holy Spirit of God. We should never have had a spark of love to Jesus if the divine Worker had not bestowed it upon us.

Well said John, "Love is of God" (1 John 4:7). Certainly it is so. Our love to Christ is one beam from Himself, like the sun. Certainly a man can no more naturally love Christ than a horse can fly. I grant you there is no physical disability, but there is a moral and spiritual disability that effectually disqualifies him from the high and lofty emotion of love to Jesus. Into that dead corpse the living spirit must be breathed—those who are dead in trespasses and sins cannot love Christ. That heart of stone must be transformed into a heart of flesh, for stones may be hurled at the Savior, but they can never love Him.

That lion must become a lamb, or it can never claim Christ as its shepherd. That raven must be turned into a dove, or it will never fly to Christ as its ark. Except a man is born again, we may say, he cannot see this precious sparkling jewel of the kingdom of God, which is love to Christ. Search yourselves, then, brethren. Do you love Him or not? If you love Him, you have been born again! And if you do not love Him, then you are still in darkness and are not His.

Can you pronounce His charming name,
His acts of kindness tell?
And while you dwell upon the theme,
No sweet emotion feel?

I think some of us would have to answer:

A very wretch, Lord, I should prove,
Had I no love to You.
Sooner than not my Savior love,
Oh, may I cease to be!

This, then, is the *efficient* cause—the Holy Spirit. The *rational* cause, the logical reason why we love Jesus, lies in Himself, in His looks, in His present working, and in His person, besides many other little fountains that all tend to swell the river, the growing, deepening river of our love to Him. Why do we love Jesus? We have the best of answers: because He first loved us! Hearken, you strangers who inquire why we should love the Savior so. We will give you such reasons that we will satisfy you and set your mouths watering to be partakers of the same reasons, that you may come to love Him, too!

Why do we love Him? Because before this round earth was fashioned between the palms of the great Creator, before He had painted the rainbow or hung out the lights of the sun and moon, Christ's delights were with *us*. He foresaw us through the glass of His prescience. He knew what we should be—looked into the book in which all His members were written, who in continuance were fashioned, when as yet there were none of them. And as He looked upon us, the glance was *love*. He delighted to sit upon the throne of glory and to remember His dear ones who were yet to be born! It was the great prospect that His mighty and infinite Spirit had a joy that was set before Him that He should see a multitude that no man could number who should be His beloved forever.

> *Loved of my Christ, for Him again*
> *With love intense I'll burn.*
> *Chosen of You before time began,*
> *I choose You in return.*

Oh, could you know that Jesus has loved you from before all worlds, then you *must* love Him! At least you will grant there cannot be a better reason for love than love. Love demands—no, it does not demand—it takes by almighty force, by irresistible energy, that heart captive upon whom it thus sets itself! This Jesus loved us for no reason whatever in ourselves. We were black as the tents of Kedar. We had much deformity but no beauty, and yet He loved us! And our deformity was of such a kind that it might meritoriously have made Him hate us. We kicked against Him and despised Him! Our language naturally was "We will not have this man to reign over us" (Luke 19:14), and when we heard of His loving us, we sneered at it.

He was despised and rejected of men. We hid, as it were, our faces from Him. He was despised and we esteemed Him not. We thought His love an empty tale, a paltry trifle, and yet He loved us. No, we were His enemies! We slew Him! We confess with sorrow that we were the murderers of the Prince of life and glory. Our hands were stained with His gore and our garments dyed with His blood—and yet He saw all this and still loved us! Shall we not love Him? Surely our heart is harder than adamant because we do not love Him more! But it would be hell-hardened steel if it did not love at all.

Our Savior so loved us that He stripped Himself of His robes of radiance. Listen, you children of God, it is the old story over again, but it is always new to you. He stripped Himself of His bright array. He laid aside His scepter and His crown and became an infant in Bethlehem's manger among the horned oxen. Thirty years of poverty and shame the King of heaven spent among the sons of men, and all out of love to us. Jesus the heavenly lover, panting to redeem His people, was content to abide here without a place to rest His head that He might rescue us!

Do you see Him yonder in the garden in His agony? His soul is exceedingly sorrowful even to death! His forehead, no, His head, His hair, and His garments are red with bloody sweat. Do you see Him giving His back to the smiters and His cheeks to them who pluck off His hair? See Him, as He hides not His face from shame and spitting, dumb like a sheep before her shearers and like a lamb that is brought to the slaughter! He opened not His mouth but patiently bore it all on our behalf. See Him with the cross upon His mangled shoulders, staggering through Jerusalem's streets, unwept for and unpitied, except by poor feeble women!

> *Jesus the heavenly lover, panting to redeem His people, was content to abide here without a place to rest His head that He might rescue us!*

See Him, you who love Him, and love Him more as He stretches out His hands to the nails and gives His feet to the iron. See Him, as with power to deliver Himself He is made captive. Behold Him as they lift up the cross with Him upon it and dash it down into its place and dislocate His bones. Hear that cry, "I am poured out like water, and all My bones are out of joint" (Ps. 22:14). Stand, if you can, and view that face so full of grief. Look till a sword will go through your own heart as it went through His mother's very soul. Oh, see Him as He thirsts and has that thirst mocked with vinegar!

Hear Him as He prays and has that prayer parodied, "Look, He is calling for Elijah! . . . Let us see if Elijah will come to take Him down" (Mark 15:35–36). See Him as they who love Him come and kiss His feet and bathe them with their tears. Will you not love Him who did all that friend could do for friend? He who gave His life for us? Beloved, here are a thousand crimson cords that tie us to the Savior, and I hope we feel their constraining power. It is His vast love, the old eternal bond, the love that redeemed, that suffered in our place, the love that pleaded our cause before the eternal throne; it is this that we give as a sufficient reason why we should love the Savior, if necessary, even to death!

Moreover, we have another reason. I trust many here can say that they love the Savior because of His present dealings toward them. What has He not done for us this very day? Some of you came here this morning heavy and you went away rejoicing! Perhaps you have had answers to prayer this very week. You have passed through the furnace and not a smell of fire has passed upon you. You have had many sins this week, but you have felt the efficacy of His blood again and again. Some of us have known what it is during the past six days to have the ravishing delights of private communion with Him. He has made us glad! Our spirits have leaped for very joy, for He has turned again the captivity of our soul.

You have drunk of Him as of "the brook by the wayside" (Ps. 110:7), and you have therefore lifted up your head. Beloved, if there were nothing else that Christ had done for my soul, that which I have tasted and handled of Him within the last few months would make me love Him forever, and I know that you can say the same! Nor is this all. We love the Savior because of the excellence of His person. We are not blind to excellence anywhere, but still we can see no excellence like His:

> *Jesus, You fairest, dearest one,*
> *What beauties You adorn*
> *Far brighter than the noonday sun,*
> *Or star that gilds the morn.*
>
> *Here let me fix my wandering eyes,*
> *And all Your glories trace;*
> *Till in the world of endless joys,*
> *I rise to Your embrace.*

Tigranes and his wife were both taken prisoners by Cyrus. Then Cyrus said to Tigranes, "What will you give for the liberation of your wife?"

And the king answered, "I love my wife so that I would cheerfully give up my life if she might be delivered from servitude."

Whereupon Cyrus said that if there was such love as that between them, they might both go free. So when they were away and many were talking about the beauty and generosity of Cyrus and especially about the beauty of his person, Tigranes, turning to his wife, asked her what *she* thought of Cyrus, and she answered that she saw nothing anywhere but in the face of the man who had said that he would die if she might only be released from servitude.

"The beauty of that man," she said, "makes me forget all others." And verily we would say the same of Jesus! We would not decry the angels, nor think ill of the saints, but the beauties of that man who gave His life for us are so great that they have eclipsed all others, and our soul only wishes to see Him and none other! As the stars hide their heads in the presence of the sun, so may your all be gone—your delights, your excellencies—when Christ Jesus, the chief delight, the chief excellency, makes His appearance. Dr. Watts says:

> His worth, if all the nations knew,
> Surely the whole earth would love Him, too.

And so it seems to us. Could you see Him, you must love Him. It was said of Henry VIII that if all the portraits of tyrants and murderers and thieves were out of existence, they might all be painted from the one face of Henry VIII. And turning that round another way, we will say that if all the excellencies, beauties, and perfections of the human race were blotted out, they might all be painted again from the face of the Lord Jesus:

> All over glorious is my Lord.
> He must be beloved and yet adored.

These are some of the reasons why our hearts love Jesus. Before I leave those reasons, I should like to put a few questions round among this great crowd. O friends, would you not love Jesus if you knew something of this love as shed abroad in your hearts—something of this love as being *yours*? Now, remember, there is a very great promise that Christ has made, and it is this: "Him that cometh to me I will in no wise cast out" (John 6:37 KJV). Now what does that refer to? Why, to anyone in the entire world who comes to Christ! Whoever you may be, if you come to Jesus—and you know that means just trusting Him, leaning upon Him—if you come to Him, He will not cast you out. And when He has received you to His bosom, you will then know (but you cannot know till then) how much He loves you! And then I think you will say with us, "Yes, His name is 'You whom I love.'"

I will now, for a short time, speak on the effects of this love, as we have dwelt on the cause of it. When a man has true love to Christ, it is sure to lead him to dedication. There is a natural desire to give something to the person whom we love, and true love to Jesus compels us to give ourselves to Him. One of the earliest acts of the Christian's life is to take ourselves and lay body, soul, and spirit upon the altar of consecration, saying, "Here I am. I give myself to you." When the pupils of Socrates had nearly all of them given him a present, there was one of the best scholars who was extremely poor, and he said to Socrates, "I have none of these things that the others have presented to you. But, O Socrates, I give you myself." Whereupon Socrates said it was the best present he had had that day. "My son, give Me your heart," is what Jesus asks. If you love Him, you must give Him this.

True love next shows itself in *obedience*. If I love Jesus, I will do as He bids me. He is my husband, my Lord. I call Him "Master." "If you love Me," He says, "keep My commandments" (John 14:15). This is His chosen proof of my love, and I am sure, if I love Him, I will keep His commandments. And yet there are some who profess to love Christ who very seldom think of keeping any of His commandments. "Do this in remembrance of me" (1 Cor. 11:24), He says, and yet some of you never come to His table. May I gently ask you how you make this disobedience consort with genuine affection for Him? "If you love Me, keep My commandments."

> 'Tis love that makes our willing feet
> In swift obedience move.

We can do anything for those we love, and if we love Jesus, no burden will be heavy, no difficulty will be great. We should rather wish to do more than He asks of us and only desire that He was a little more exacting that we might have a better opportunity of showing forth our affection.

True love, again, is always considerate and afraid lest it should give offense. It walks very daintily. If I love Jesus, I will watch my eyes, my heart, my tongue, my hands—being so fearful lest I should wake my Beloved—or make Him stir until He please. And I will be sure not to take in those bad guests, those ill-favored guests of pride and sloth and love of the world. I will tell them to be packing, for I have a dear one within who will not tarry long if He sees me giving glances to these wicked ones. My heart will be wholly His. He will sit at the head of the table. He will have the best dishes there—no, I will send all others away that I may have Him all to myself and that He may have my whole heart—all that I am and all that I have.

Again, true love to Christ will make us very jealous of His honor. As Queen Eleanor went down upon her knees to suck the poison from her husband's wound, so we will put our lips to the wound of Christ when He has been stabbed with the dagger of calumny or inconsistency. We will be willing sooner to take the poison ourselves and to be ourselves diseased and despised than that His name, His cross should suffer ill! Oh, what matters it what becomes of us if the King reigns? I will go home to my bed and die in peace if the King sits on the throne. Let me see King David once again installed in Zion's sacred halls, and my soul, in poverty and shame, will still rejoice if the banished King Jesus will once again come back and have His own and take His scepter and wear His crown!

> *I*f we love Christ, again, we will desire to promote His cause and we will desire to promote it ourselves. We will wish to see the strength of the mighty turned at the gate, that King Jesus may return triumphant!

Beloved, I trust we can say we would not mind if Christ would make a doormat of us, if He would wipe His church's filthy sandals on us, if we might but help to make her pure! We would hold the stirrup for Him to mount any day, yes, and be His horsing-block that He might mount His glorious charger and ride forth conquering and to conquer. Say, what matters it *what* we are, or *where* we are, if the King has His own? If we love Christ, again, we will desire to promote His cause and we will desire to promote it ourselves. We will wish to see the strength of the mighty turned at the gate, that King Jesus may return triumphant!

We will not wish to sit still while our brethren go to war, but we will want to take our portion in the fray, that like soldiers who love their monarch, we may prove by our wounds and by our sufferings that our love is real. The apostle says, "Let us not love in word or in tongue, but in deed and in truth" (1 John 3:18). Actions speak louder than words, and we will always be anxious to tell our love in deeds as well as by our lips. The true disciple asks continually, "Lord, what do You want me to do?" (Acts 9:6). He esteems it his highest honor to serve the Lord. "I would rather be a doorkeeper in the house of my God than dwell in the tents of wickedness" (Ps. 84:10).

> *There's not a lamb in all the flock,*
> *I would disdain to feed.*
> *There's not a foe before whose face*
> *I fear Your cause to plead.*
>
> *Would not my ardent spirit vie*
> *With angels round Your throne,*
> *To execute Your sacred will*
> *And make Your glory known?*

Yes, indeed, we thus can sing and mean, I trust, every word! Yes, we will go forth into the whole world and preach the gospel to every creature. We will tell of this love to all and labor to win for the Master's honor a multitude that no man can number out of every nation and kindred and tribe and tongue and people! I believe in an active love that has hands to labor and feet to run as well as a heart to feel, eyes to glance, and ears to listen. A mother's love is of the purest and most intense sort in the world, and it is the most practical. It shows itself in deeds of untiring devotion both night and day. So also should it be with us. We should let our affections prompt us to lifelong labor.

The love of Christ should constrain us to live and, if necessary, die to serve Him. Heaven is the place of purest, holiest attachment to Christ. Then we will understand most about His love to us and of all He has done to prove it, and the consequence will be that His servants will serve Him day and night in His holy temple. We are expecting a home in glory not of idleness, but of continual activity, and we are taught to pray now that we may do His will on earth as it is done in heaven.

Let us therefore, each one, be busily engaged in the great harvest. The harvest is great and the laborers are few. There is room for all and each man's place is waiting to receive him. If we truly love our Lord, we will at once press to the front and begin the work of faith and labor of love. Has not the Master been known to show His love to us in deeds? Look to Bethlehem, to Gabbatha, to Gethsemane, and to Golgotha. Yes, look to His whole life as He went about doing good, and see if all this will not stir you up to service! Listen to the life story of the Lord, and you will hear a voice from each one of His deeds of love saying to you, "Go and do likewise" (Luke 10:37).

And, once again, if we love Jesus, we will be willing to suffer for Him. Pain will become light. We will sing with Madame Guyon:

> *To me 'tis equal whether love*
> *Ordain my life or death,*
> *Appoint me ease, or pain.*

It is a high attainment to come to, but love can make us think ourselves of so small import that if Christ can serve Himself of us, we will make no choice as to what or where we may be. We can sing once more:

> *Would not my heart pour forth its blood*
> *In honor of Your name,*
> *And challenge the cold hand of death*
> *To dampen this immortal flame?*

Our hearts are, I trust, so full of real devotion to Christ that we can give Him everything and endure all things for His sake. Cannot we say:

> *For Him I count as gain each loss,*
> *Disgrace for Him renown,*
> *Well may I glory in His cross,*
> *While He prepares my crown?*

Darkness is light about us if we can serve Him there. The bitter is sweet if the cup is put to our lips in order that we may share in His sufferings and prove ourselves to be His followers. When Ignatius was led to his martyrdom, as he contemplated the nearness of his death and suffering, he said, "Now I begin to be a Christian." He felt that all that he had done and suffered before was not enough to entitle him to be called a follower of Christ. But as the Master's bloody baptism was before him, he realized the truth so dear to every right-minded Christian: that he was to be like to his

Lord. Here we can all prove our love! We can suffer His will calmly if we are not able to do it publicly.

> *Weak as I am, yet through Your love,*
> *I all things can perform.*
> *And, smiling, triumph in Your name*
> *Amid the raging storm.*

I pray God we may have such a love that thirsts after Jesus and cannot be satisfied without present communion with Him.

II. This brings me to the thought that I will only touch upon as the swallow skims the brook with his wings and then up and away, lest I weary you. The second point of consideration is *the desire of the church after Christ Jesus our Lord.* Having called Him by His title, she now expresses her longing to be with Him. "Tell me, O you whom I love, where you feed your flock, where you make it rest at noon." The desire of a renewed soul is to find Christ and to be with Him.

Stale meats left over from yesterday are very well when there is nothing else, but who does not like hot food fresh from the fire? And past communion with Christ is very well: "Therefore will I remember thee from the land of Jordan, and of the Hermonites, from the hill Mizar" (Ps. 42:6 kjv). But these are only stale meats, and a loving soul wants fresh food every day from the table of Christ. And you who have once had the kisses of His mouth, though you remember the past kisses with delight, yet want daily fresh tokens of His love. He who drinks of this water will never thirst again; it is true, except for *this water*! And then he will so thirst for it that he will be like Samuel Rutherford who began to be out of heart with the buckets; he wanted to get right to the wellhead that he might lie down and drink, and then, if he could have his fill, he would drink the well quite dry.

But there is no hope of that, or rather no fear of it. The well can never be empty, for it rises as we drink! A true loving soul, then, wants present communion with Christ. So the question is, "Tell me where You feed. Where do You get Your comfort from, O Jesus? I will go there. Where do Your thoughts go? To Your cross? Do You look back to that? Then I will go there. Where You feed, there will I feed."

Or does this mean actively, instead of being in the passive or the neuter?

Where do You feed Your flock? In Your house? I will go there, if I may find You there. In private prayer? Then I will not be slack in that. In the Word? Then I will read it night and day. Tell me where You feed; for wherever You stand as the shepherd, there will I be, for I want You. I cannot be satisfied to be apart from You. My soul hungers and thirsts to be with You.

She puts it again, "Where do you make your flock rest at noon?" for there is only rest in one place: where you cause your flock to rest at noon. That must be a God-given rest and only to be found in some one chosen place. Where is the shadow of that rock? It is very hot just now here in the middle of summer when the sun is pouring down his glorious rays like bright but sharp arrows upon us. And we who are condemned to live in this great wilderness of brown bricks and mortar often recollect those glades where the woods grow thick and where the waters leap from crag to crag down the hillside and where the birds are singing among the trees.

We delight to think of those leafy bowers where the sun cannot dart his rays, where, on some mossy bank, we may stretch ourselves to rest or have our weary limbs in some limpid stream. And this is just what the spouse is after. She feels the heat of the world's sun and she longs to be away from its cares and troubles that have furrowed and made her face brown till she looked as if she had been a busy keeper of the vineyards. She wants to get away to hold quiet communion with her Lord, for He is the brook where the weary may lay their wearied limbs! He is that sheltered nook, that shadow of the great rock in the weary land where His people may lie down and be at peace.

> *Jesus, the very thought of You*
> *With sweetness fills my breast.*
> *But sweeter far Your face to see*
> *And in Your presence rest.*
>
> *For those who find You find a bliss,*
> *No tongue, nor pen can show.*
> *The love of Jesus, what it is,*
> *None but His loved ones know.*

Now do you not want this tonight? Does not your soul want Christ tonight? My brothers, my sisters, there is something wrong with us if we can do without Christ. If we love Him, we must want Him. Our hearts ever say:

> *Abide with me from morn till eve,*
> *For without You I cannot live!*
> *Abide with me when night is near,*
> *For without You I dare not die.*

No, we cannot do without Christ. We must have Him. "Give me Christ, or else I die," is the cry of our souls. No wonder Mary Magdalene wept when she thought they had taken away her Lord and she knew not where they had laid Him! As the body suffers without food, so should we without Christ. As the fish perishes out of water, so should we apart from Christ. I must quote another verse of a hymn, for really the sweet songsters of Israel have lavished all their best prose, and very rightly so, to tell for us our love tale concerning our Beloved. I am sure that our heart's inner voice can set to sweetest music the words:

> *Oh, that I could forever sit*
> *With Mary at the Master's feet—*
> *Be this my happy choice.*
> *My only care, delight, and bliss,*
> *My joy, my heaven on earth be this,*
> *To hear the Bridegroom's voice.*

Yes! To be with Jesus is heaven anywhere on earth or in the skies. All else is wilderness and desert. It is paradise to be with Him. And heaven without Christ would be no heaven to me. My heart cannot rest away from Him. To have no Christ would be a punishment greater than I could bear! I should wander, like another Cain, over the earth, a fugitive and a vagabond. Verily there would be no peace for my soul. I am sure that the true wife, if her husband is called to go upon a journey, longs ardently for his return. If he is gone to the wars, she dreads lest he should fall. How each letter comes perfumed to her when it tells of his love and constancy, and how she watches for the day when she will clasp him in her arms once more.

Oh, you know that when you were children, if you were sent to school, how you counted till the holidays came on. I had a little almanac and marked out every day the night before and so counted one day less till the time I should get home again, and so may you.

> *May not a captive long*
> *His own dear land to see?*
> *May not the prisoner seek*
> *Release from bondage to be free?*

Of course he may. And so may you, beloved, pant and sigh as the hart pants for the water brooks—for the comfortable enjoyment of the Lord Jesus Christ's presence.

III. *The argument used by the church.* Here is the desire. Now, to close, she backs that up with an argument. She says, "Why should I be as one who veils herself by the flocks of your companions?" You have plenty of companions. Why should I not be one? Let us talk it over. Why should I lose my Lord's presence? But the devil tells me I am a great sinner. Ah, but it is all washed away and gone forever. That cannot separate me, for it does not exist. My sin is buried—

> *Plunged as in a shoreless sea—*
> *Lost as in immensity.*

The devil tells me I am unworthy, and that *is* a reason. But I was *always* unworthy and yet it was no reason why He should not love me at first, and therefore cannot be a reason why I should not have fellowship with Him now. Why should I be left out? Now I am going to speak for the poorest here: I do not know where he is. I want to speak for you who have got the least faith, you who think yourselves the smallest in all Israel. You are Mephibosheths who are lame in your feet and yet sit at the king's table. You are poor despised Mordecais who sit at the king's gate yet cannot get inside the palace.

I have this to say to you: Why should you be left there? Just try to reason. Why should I, Jesus, be left out in the cold when the night comes on? No, there is a cot for the little one, as well as a bed for his bigger brother. Why should I be turned aside? I am equally bought with a price. I cost Him in order to save me as much as the noblest of the saints. He bought *them* with blood; He could not buy me with less. I must have been loved as much, or else, seeing that I am of so little worth, I should not have been redeemed at all! If there is any difference, perhaps I am loved somewhat better! Is there not greater, better love shown in the choice of me than of some who are worthier than I am?

> *ell me where You feed; for wherever You stand as the shepherd, there will I be, for I want You. I cannot be satisfied to be apart from You. My soul hungers and thirsts to be with You.*

Why then should I be left out? I know if I have a child who is deformed, I love him all the more; it seems as if I had a more tender care for him. Then why should my heavenly Father be less kind to me than I should be to my offspring? Why should I be turned aside? He chose me. He cannot change His mind! Why then should He cast me off? He knew what I was when He chose me. He cannot therefore find out any fresh reason for turning me aside. He foresaw I should misbehave myself and yet He selected me. Well then, there cannot be a reason why I should be left to fall away.

Again, I ask, why should I turn aside? I am a member of His body, of His flesh and of His bones, and though I am less than the least of all His saints, He has said, "I will never leave you nor forsake you" (Heb. 13:5). Why should I turn aside? I have a promise all to myself. Has He not said, "A bruised reed He will not break, and smoking flax He will not quench" (Matt. 12:20)? Has He not said, "The LORD takes pleasure in those who fear Him, in those who hope in His mercy" (Ps. 147:11)? If I cannot do more, I can do that! I *do* hope in His mercy. Then why should I be turned aside? If any should think of doing so, it should not be me, for I want to be near Him! I am such a poor plant that I ought to be kept in the sun; I will never do in the shade.

My big brother, perhaps, may manage for a little time without comfort, but I cannot, for I am one of the Ready-to-Halts. I recollect how the shepherds of Mount Clear said, "Come in, Mr. Little-Faith! Come in, Mr. Feeble-Mind! Come in, Mr. Ready-to-Halt! Come in, Mary!" But they did not say, "Come in, Father Faithful. Come in, Matthew. Come in, Valiant-for-Truth." [These are characters in John Bunyan's *Pilgrim's Progress—Ed.*] No, they said these might do as they liked. They were quite sure to take their own part, but they looked first to the feeblest! Then why should I be turned aside? I am the feeblest and want His person most. I may use my very feebleness and proneness to fall as the reason why I should come to Him! Why should I be turned aside?

I may fall into sin. My heart may grow cold without His glorious presence—and then, what if I should perish! Why, here, let me think. If I am the meanest lamb in His flock, I cannot perish without doing the God of heaven damage. Let me say it again with reverence. If I, the least of His children, perish, I will do His Son dishonor, for what will the archfiend say? "Aha," says he, "You surety of the covenant, You could keep the *strong*, but You could not keep the *weak*. I have this lamb here in the pit that You could not preserve! Here is one of Your crown jewels," he says, "and though he is none of the brightest, though he is not the most sparkling ruby in Your coronet, yet he is one of Your jewels and I have him here in hell! You have no perfect regalia because I have a part of it here."

> *He knew what I was when He chose me. He cannot therefore find out any fresh reason for turning me aside. He foresaw I should misbehave myself and yet He selected me.*

Shall that ever be, after Christ has said, "They shall never perish; neither shall anyone snatch them out of My hand" (John 10:28)? Shall this be, when the strong arm of God is engaged for my succor and He has said to me, "The eternal God is your refuge, and underneath are the everlasting arms" (Deut. 33:27)? Jesus, turn me not aside, lest by my fall I grieve Your Spirit and lest by my fall I bring disgrace upon Your name!

Why should I turn aside? There is no reason why I should. Come, my soul, there are a thousand reasons why you should not! Jesus beckons you to come. You wounded saints, you who have slipped to your falling, you who are grieved, sorrowing and distressed, come to His cross! Come to His throne again! Backsliders, if you have been such, return! Return! Return! A husband's heart has no door to keep out his spouse, and Jesus' heart has no power to keep out His people!

Return! Return! There is no divorce sued out against you, for the Lord, the God of Jacob, says He hates putting away. Return! Return! Let us get to our chambers; let us seek renewed fellowship. And oh, you who have never had it and have never seen Christ, may you thirst after Him tonight, and if you do, remember the text I gave you: "The one who comes to Me I will by no means cast out" (John 6:37). Whoever you may be, if you will come to Jesus, He will not cast you out.

Come and welcome, sinner, come,
God bring you for Jesus' sake. Amen.

For Further Thought

1. *Solomon wrote of love for God (Song of Sol. 1:7). What does Ephesians 6:24 say will be the possession of those who love the Lord?*
2. *According to 1 John 4:19, why do we love God?*
3. *The one who loves God in Song of Solomon 1:7 desires to know two things. What are they?*

THE GREAT HOUSE AND THE VESSELS IN IT

But in a great house there are not only vessels of gold and silver,
but also of wood and clay, some for honor and some for dishonor.
Therefore if anyone cleanses himself from the latter, he will be
a vessel for honor, sanctified and useful for the Master,
prepared for every good work.

2 TIMOTHY 2:20–21

ONE of the most serious calamities that can befall a church is to have her own ministers teaching heresy. Yet this is no new thing, it has happened from the beginning. Paul and Peter and James and John, in their epistles, had to speak of seducers in the churches, even in those primitive days, and ever since then there have arisen in the very midst of the house of God those who have subverted the faith of many and led them away from the fundamental truths of God into errors of their own inventing.

The apostle compares this to gangrene, one of the most dangerous and deadly mischiefs that can occur to the body. It is *within* the body, eats deeper and deeper into the flesh, festering and putrefying, and if it is not stopped, it will continue its ravages till life is extinguished by "black mortification." False doctrine and an unchristian spirit in the midst of the church must be regarded as gangrene, a silent wolf ravenously gnawing at the heart, the vulture of Prometheus devouring the vitals. No external opposition is one-half so much to be dreaded!

Yet here is our comfort when distressed at the evils of the present age, among which this is one of the chief, that the truth of God abides forever the same! "The solid foundation of God stands" (2 Tim. 2:19). There is no moving that. Whether ten thousand oppose it or promulgate it, the truth of God is still the same in every jot and tittle. Even as the sun shines evermore, as well when clouds conceal its brightness as when, from a clear sky, it pours abroad a flood of glory, the lovers of profane and vain babblings have not taken away from us, nor can they take from us, the eternal truths of God!

The Lord lives, though they have said, "There is no God." The precious blood of Jesus has not lost its efficacy, though divines have beclouded the atonement. The Spirit of God is not less mighty to quicken and to console, though men have denied His personality. The resurrection is as sure as if Hymenaeus and Philetus had never said that it is passed already. And the eternal covenant of grace abides forever unbroken, though Pharisees and Sadducees unite to revile it! The foundation of God stands sure and moreover the foundation of the church remains sure, for "the Lord knows those who are His" (2 Tim. 2:19).

All that God has built upon the foundation that He Himself has laid keeps its place. Not one living stone that He ever laid upon the foundation has been lifted from its resting place. Earthquakes of error may test the stability of the building and cause great searching of heart, but sooner will the mountains that are all around Jerusalem start from their seats than the work or Word of the Lord be frustrated! The things that cannot be shaken remain unaltered in the very worst times. "After all," says the apostle, in effect, though in fewer words, "it is not such a very great wonder that there should be persons in the church who are not of the sterling metal of sincerity, nor of the gold and silver of truth that endures the fire. You must not look at Hymenaeus and Philetus as if they were prodigies. There have been many like they are, and there will be many more. These ill weeds grow in all ages, and they multiply and increase."

> *False doctrine and an unchristian spirit in the midst of the church must be regarded as gangrene, a silent wolf ravenously gnawing at the heart, the vulture of Prometheus devouring the vitals.*

Where, dear brothers and sisters, beneath the skies will we find absolute purity in any community? The very first family had a Cain in it, and there was a wicked Ham even in the select few within the ark. In the household of the father of the faithful, there was an Ishmael. Isaac, with his quiet walk with God, must be troubled with an Esau. And you know how, in the house of Jacob, there were many sons who walked not as they should. You know how Korah, Dathan, and Abiram and many other troublers in Israel were there when the church of God was in the wilderness and had a barrier of desert between it and the outer world!

Yes, even amidst the most select part of the visible church of God, in the *priesthood*, there were found those who dishonored it. Nadab and Abihu were slain with fire before the Lord, and Hophni and Phineas died in battle because they had made themselves vile, though God's anointed priests. Even when our divine Master had formed for Himself "a little garden, walled around, chosen, and made peculiar ground," there were but twelve choice trees, yet one of them bore evil fruit. "I have chosen you twelve, and one of you is a devil" (see John 6:70). In the great field that Christ has sown, tares will spring up among the wheat, for the enemy takes pains to sow them. Neither is it possible for us to root them up. In the King's garden, briars will grow; thorns and thistles will the most sacred soil yield us.

> The church is a great house belonging to a great person, for the church is the house of God, according to the promise: "I will dwell in them and walk among them"

Even the lilies of Christ grow among thorns. You cannot keep the best of churches altogether pure, for though the Lord Himself has prepared a vineyard and made a winepress and built a wall about it, yet the foxes come and spoil the vines. And though our great Lord has an orchard that yields rare fruit, yet when He comes to visit it, He finds a barren fig tree, dug about and fed, it is true, but still barren! Look to Christ's fold on earth and behold, there are wolves in sheep's clothing there! Look to the net that His servants draw to shore, and there are both good and bad fish in it. Yes, lift your eyes to the skies, and though there are myriads of stars, yet you will mark wandering stars among them—and meteors that are and are not—and are quenched in the blackness of darkness forever. Until we will come to the heaven of the Most High, we must expect to find chaff mixed with the wheat, dross with the gold, goats with the sheep, and dead flies in the ointment. Only let us see to it that *we* are not of that ill character, but are precious in the sight of the Lord.

Coming to the text, the apostle suggests the encouragement I have already given, under a certain metaphor. He says that in a great house there will naturally be varieties of furniture. And there will be vessels and utensils of many kinds—some of them will be of wood and of earthenware, for meaner purposes; but others of gold and silver, for state occasions, when the honor and glory of the great proprietor are to be displayed. There are vessels of precious metal in a great house, and these are its honor, decking the tables on high festivals when the Master is at home. But there are others of baser stuff kept in the background, never displayed at times of rejoicing, but meant for common drudgery.

There are cups and flagons of solid silver prized as perpetual heirlooms of the family that are carefully preserved. And there are plates and pots that are soon worn out and are only of temporary use. There are many sets of them being broken up in the lifetime of a family. The same is true in the church of God, which, being in the world, has its common side and its common vessels. But being, also, a heavenly house, the church has its nobler furniture, far more precious than gold that perishes though it is tried with fire.

For our instruction, may the Holy Spirit help us while we look first at *the great house*, second at *the meaner vessels*, peeping into the kitchen, and third at *the nobler vessels*, going into the china cabinet to look at the silver and gold. And then, fourth, before we leave the house, let us ask for an interview with the Master Himself.

I. First, let us consider *the great house*. The apostle compares the church to a great house. We feel sure he is not speaking of the world. It did not occur to him to speak about the world, and it would have been altogether superfluous to tell us that in the world there are all sorts of people—everybody knows that! The church is a great house belonging to a great person, for the church is the house of God, according to the promise: "I will dwell in them and walk among them" (2 Cor. 6:16).

The church is the temple in which the Lord is worshipped and the palace in which He rules. It is His castle and place of defense for His truth. It is the armory out of which He supplies His people with weapons. The church is God's mansion in which He abides: "This is my rest for ever: here will I dwell; for I have desired it" (Ps. 132:14 KJV). There He rests in His love and, in infinite condescension, manifests Himself as He does not to the world. King Solomon built a house for himself of the forest of Lebanon. And behold, the Lord has, of living stones, built for Himself a far more glorious house where He may abide! It is a great house because it is the house of the great God! Who can be so great as He? It is a great house because it is planned and designed upon a great scale.

I fear that some who live in the house have no idea how great it is. They have a very faint notion of its length and breadth. The great thoughts of God are far beyond their most elevated conception, so that He might say to them as He has said to others, "For My thoughts are not your thoughts, nor are your ways My ways" (Isa. 55:8). The palace of the King of kings is exceedingly magnificent, and for spaciousness far excels all the abodes of earthly princes. We read of the golden palace of Nero, that it reached from hill to hill and enclosed lakes and streams and gardens beneath its wondrous roof. But behold, the Lord has stretched the line of His electing grace over nations and kindreds even to the ends of the earth!

His house takes in a mighty sweep of humanity. Many are the rooms in the house, and there are dwellers in one room who have never yet seen any part of the great house but the little chamber in which they were born! They have never walked through the marvelous corridors, or moved in the vast halls that God has built with cedar pillars and cedar beams and carved work of heavenly workmanship. Some good men hardly care to see the long rows of polished columns, quarried by grace from the rough mass of nature that now shine resplendent as monuments of divine love and wisdom! Colossal is the plan of the Eternal—the church of God is worthy of the infinite mind!

Angels and principalities delight to study the stupendous plan, and well they may as the great architect unrolls His drawings, piece by piece, to let them see the various sections of the complete design. They are struck with admiration and exclaim, "Oh, the depth of the riches both of the wisdom and knowledge of God! How unsearchable are His judgments and His ways past finding out!" (Rom. 11:33). The church is no narrow cottage wherein a few may luxuriate in bigotry, but it is a great house, worthy of the infinite heart of Jehovah, worthy of the blood of Jesus, the incarnate God, and worthy of the power of the ever-blessed Spirit!

It is a great house because it has been erected at great cost and with great labor. Who can tell the cost of this mansion? It is a price beyond price, for God has given His only begotten Son—He had but one, and heaven could not match Him—that He might redeem to Himself a people who should be His dwelling place forever. Solomon's temple, now that they have laid bare a part of the foundations, even though it is in utter ruin, astonishes all beholders as they mark the enormous size and accurate adjustment of the stones—what must it have been in its glory? What cost was lavished on that glorious house!

But think of the labor and the skill, the divine art and engineering with which Jehovah has hewn out of the rock of sinful nature the stones with which He builds up His spiritual house! What energy has the Holy Spirit displayed! What resurrection power! Harder than any granite we were by nature, yet has He cut us away from the rock of which we formed a part and fashioned and squared us—and made us to be built together for a habitation of God through the Spirit. Tell it to the praise of the glory of His grace, that the Lord's omnipotent power and boundless wealth of love are revealed in His church!

When our eyes will see the church of God, at last, in all her beauty descending out of heaven from God, having the glory of God and her light like a stone most precious, even like a jasper stone; when we will see, I say, that the length and the breadth and the height of it are equal; when we will see its deep foundations laid in the eternal purpose and its walls built up with lofty pinnacles of glory, high as the divine person of her Lord; and when we will mark its wondrous compass, broad enough to hold the glory and honor of the nations, then will we shout for joy as we behold the riches and the power and the splendor of the great King of kings who has built for Himself this great house!

It is a great house, again, because its household arrangements are conducted on a great scale. You know how country people, when there is some rich lord living in the village, speak always of his mansion as the great house. It is for the great house that those bullocks are being fattened, and those sheep and lambs will be consumed at the great house. For there are many in the family and none are allowed to go hungry. Solomon kept a great house. When you read the account of the daily provision for his table, you see that it was a great house indeed, a vast and truly royal establishment!

Yes, but neither for quality nor quantity could Solomon's palace match the great house of God in its plenty. Speak of fine flour—behold, He has given us angels' food! Speak of royal dainties—behold, the Lord has given us fat things full of marrow, wines on the lees well refined! What a perpetual feast does the Lord Jesus keep up for all His followers! If any of them hunger, it is not because their rations are stinted. If there are any complaints, it is not because the Master's oxen and fatlings are not freely provided! Ah, no, to every man there is a good piece of meat and a flagon of wine dealt out, even as David dealt it out in the day when he removed the ark to the hill of Zion.

Glory be to God! He has said, "Eat, O friends; drink, yea, drink abundantly, O beloved" (Song of Sol. 5:1 KJV). In this mountain the hand of the Lord will rest, and He will make to all nations a feast of fat things. Behold, His oxen and fatlings are killed. All things are ready. It is a great house, where great sinners are fed on great dainties and filled with the great goodness of the Lord! It is a great house for the number of its inhabitants. How many have lived beneath that rooftree for ages. God is the home of His people, and His church is the home of God!

> In this mountain the hand of the Lord will rest, and He will make to all nations a feast of fat things. Behold, His oxen and fatlings are killed. All things are ready. It is a great house, where great sinners are fed on great dainties and filled with the great goodness of the Lord!

And what multitudes are dwelling there now! Not only the companies that we know of, with whom it is our delight to meet for solemn worship, but all over the world the Lord has a people who dwell in the midst of His church! And though men have disfigured their Master's house by chalking up odd signs over some of the rooms and calling them by other names than those of the owner, yet the Lord's people are all one church, and to whatever part or party they may seem to belong, if Christ is in them, they belong to Him of whom the whole family in heaven and earth is named, and they make up but one spiritual house. What a swarm there is of the Lord's children, and yet not one of the family remains unfed. The church is a great house wherein thousands dwell, yes, a number that no man can number!

Once more, it is a great house because of its importance. People speak of the great house in our remote counties because to the whole neighborhood it bears a special relationship, being connected with some of its most vital interests such as county politics and police. Dignity and wealth find their center at the great house. The church is a great house because it is God's hospice where He distributes bread and wine to refresh the weary and entertains wayfarers who otherwise had been lost in the storm. It is God's hospital into which He takes the sick, and there He nourishes them till they renew their youth like the eagle.

It is God's great lighthouse with its lantern flashing forth a directing ray so that wanderers far away may be directed to the haven of peace. "Out of Zion, the perfection of beauty, God will shine forth" (Ps. 50:2). It is the seat of God's magistracy, for there are set thrones of judgment, the thrones of the house of David. Behold, the Lord has set His King upon His holy hill of Zion, and therefore will the power of His scepter go forth to the ends of the earth! The great house of the church is the university for teaching all nations! It is the library wherein the sacred oracles are preserved! It is the treasury wherein His truth is deposited and the registry of newborn heirs of heaven!

It is important to heaven as well as to earth, for its topmost towers reach into glory and there is in it a ladder, the foot of which rests on earth, but the top reaches to heaven—up and down that the angels come and go continually. Said I not well that the apostle had wisely chosen the figure when he called the church a great house?

II. We will now go inside the great house, and we at once observe that it is well furnished. Our text, however, invites us to note that it contains a number of *meaner vessels*, articles of the coarser kind for ordinary and common uses. Here are plates, wooden buckets, pitchers and pots, and various vessels of coarse pottery. Some have thought that this figure of vessels to dishonor relates to Christians of a lower grade, persons of small grace and of less sanctified conversation. Now, although believers may, from some points of view, be comparable to earthen vessels, yet I dare not look upon *any* child of God, however low in grace, as a vessel to dishonor!

Moreover, the word "these" refers to the earthen and wooden vessels. Surely they cannot represent saints, or we should never be told to purge ourselves from them! If a man is God's child, into whatever state and condition he may fall, it is our business to look after him and endeavor to restore him, remembering ourselves also, lest we be tempted. But it cannot be right to purge ourselves from even the least of our believing brothers and sisters! Besides, that is not the run of the chapter at all.

The real meaning is that in the church of God there are unworthy persons serving inferior and temporary purposes who are vessels to dishonor. They are in the church, but they are like vessels of wood and vessels of earth. They are not the treasure of the mansion. They are not brought out on state occasions and are not set much store by, for they are *not* precious in the sight of the Lord. The apostle does not tell us how they came there, for it was not his intent to do so and no parable or metaphor could teach everything. Neither will I stay to describe how some professors have come into the church of God—some by distinct falsehood and by making professions that they knew were untrue, others through ignorance, others by being self-deceived and carried away with excitement.

The parable does not say how they got there, but they are there. Yet they are only vessels of wood and vessels of earth. It is no credit to them that they are where they are, for they are not vessels to honor, though in an honorable place. It is no honor to any man to be a member of a Christian church if he is, in himself, intrinsically worthless though they make a minister of him or elect him deacon. It is no honor to him to be in office if the metal he is made of does not fit him for so honorable a purpose. He is an intruder in an honorable position, and it is a dishonor to him to be where he is. It is no honor to a weed to grow in the best part of the garden. It is no honor to a barren fig tree to cumber the finest ground in the vineyard.

Ah, dear friend, if you are in the church of God, but not truly one of the Lord's people, it is a *dishonorable* thing of you to have come there! And it is equally dishonorable for you to remain there without fulfilling that great requisite that is demanded of everyone who names the name of Jesus—that he departs from all iniquity! The vessels in the great house are, however, of some use, even though they are made of wood and earth. And so there are persons in the church of God whom the Lord Jesus will not acknowledge as His treasure, but He nevertheless turns them to some temporary purpose. Some are useful as the scaffold to a house, or the dogshores to a ship, or the hedges to a field. I believe that some unworthy members of the church are useful in the way of watchdogs to keep others awake, or knives to let blood, or burdens to try strength. Some quarrelsome members of the church help to scour the other vessels lest they should rust through being peaceful.

The church is made up of men who are yet in the body, and it has to deal with the outside world. And sometimes the worldly men who are in her serve some purpose in connection with this, her lowest need. Judas made a good treasurer, for his economy saved more than he stole. Joab was a good warrior for David, though he was by no means a saint. False professors do not make the gospel untrue, and sometimes, when they have spoken it, God has blessed it. You may see, if you go down the Kennington Park Road today, a row of young trees planted by the road. How are they kept up while yet they are slender? Why, small posts of dead timber hold them up! And even so, a dead Sunday school teacher may yet be useful to a genuine Christian child, and a dead deacon may be the financial support of a living church! Yes, and there are dead preachers, too, who nevertheless serve to fill up a space, but what vessels to dishonor they are!

It is a dreadful thing, however, for those who are like the posts I just mentioned, because the quicker the young tree grows, the sooner will the post be taken away, having no share in the life that it helped to support. You see, then, that our great Master turns the base professors who get into the church to some good for His church. The servants of the great house can use the woodenware and the earthenware for a while, for rough everyday purposes, even as mere formalists can be employed in some scullery work or another.

> *Ah, dear friend, if you are in the church of God, but not truly one of the Lord's people, it is a dishonorable thing of you to have come there!*

There is one thing noticeable—the wooden and earthen vessels are not for the Master's use. When He holds high festival, His cups are all of precious metal! "All King Solomon's drinking vessels were gold" (1 Kings 10:21). Would you have the King of kings set an earthen pot upon His royal table? Shall the guests at His table eat from wooden bowls? False professors are only useful to the *servants*, not to the Master—they serve base purposes and are not to be seen on those great days when He manifests His glory. The great Master overrules all things, being the Master of the servants, and as far as that which answers the purpose of His servants and is serviceable to Him. But personally, between the King at His table and the wooden vessel, there is no congruity—it would be an insult to hand Him wine in any but a sumptuous cup of precious metal, or to bring Him butter in any but a lordly dish!

How sad it is that many Christians are useful to the church in various ways, but as for *personal* service rendered to the Lord Jesus Christ Himself, they have no share whatever and never can have till grace changes them from wood to silver, or from earth to gold. Note that in these vessels of which the apostle speaks the substance is base. They are wood, or they are earth, nothing more. So are we all, by nature, of base material. Grace must make us into silver or into golden vessels, or the Master cannot Himself use us, nor can our use in the church ever be to honor. The wooden vessels in the church are very easily hacked and carved and spoiled—if a man is inclined to mischief, he can put his knife to them and can cut great notches in them. He can ruin their character and render them worthless. Cunning teachers can soon take away from merely nominal Christians what they professed to believe, for they are very readily cut and hacked by those who play at such games.

As for the earthen vessels, how soon they are broken! Outside of any great house there are the remains of many broken pots that fell to the ground and shattered to pieces. And, I am sorry to say, we also can find enough of such relics to sadden us all. There were some in this house, once, who were comely to look upon. But there came a temptation and brushed them from the table—and they were shattered in a moment! Others of precious metal have endured far more shocks and tests of a severer kind. But those being only of earth were broken at once. Heaps of crockery accumulate outside every great house and certainly outside the great house of Christ. These vessels to dishonor, though turned to some account, require a great deal of care on the part of the servants.

True Christians are the glory of Christ, but false professors bring, at their very best, only dishonor. Better the smallest silver vessel than the largest earthen one!

When our forefathers used to eat from wooden plates, the time the good wives used to spend in scalding and cleaning them to keep them at all sweet to eat upon was something terrible! And there are members of the church who take a world of time from pastors and elders to keep them at all decent—we are continually trying to set them right, or keep them right in the common relationships of life. There are quarrels in their families that must be settled lest they become scandals—and these occupy the careful thought of their fellow Christians who have to watch for their good. Or they get lax in their doctrines or foolish in their habits or loose in their business transactions, and we have to be scouring and cleaning them times without number!

Certain sorts of earthen vessels you have to be very particular in handling.

Like eggshell china, you may hardly look at them. Thank God I have not many in this church—perhaps none of that sort as far as *my* handling is concerned—but other people's touches, though quite as wise, are not so welcome. Certain earthen vessels get dreadfully chipped unless they have dainty handling. If a brother does not take his hat off to them in very lowly style and behave very reverently, they are ready to take offense! They feel themselves hurt and slighted when no such thing was intended. They stand upon their dignity and expect the fullest recognition of it. These are real earthen pots, very apt to be chipped, perhaps a little cracked already and needing a great deal of care and trouble on the part of the Lord's servants, lest they should go to pieces and spill everything that is put into them.

There are such in all great houses, and in the Master's great house there are, I fear, not just a few. They are useful up to a certain point, but they bring no honor to the house because there are plenty as good as they in other houses—every cottage can have common earthen pitchers in it. They are vessels in which is no pleasure. They are not peculiar or precious. Nobody ever sounds abroad the Master's fame because He has so many thousands of wooden bowls or earthen pots. No, the King's honor comes from the plates—the gold and silver vessels, the peculiar treasure of kings. People speak about these rich goods and say, "You should see the sideboards loaded down with the massive services of gold and silver! You should see how the tables groan beneath the splendor of the royal feast when the king brings forth his treasures."

True Christians are the glory of Christ, but false professors bring, at their very best, only dishonor. Better the smallest silver vessel than the largest earthen one! Better the least of all the saints than the greatest of vain professors! So much for the vessels of dishonor.

III. We are now going into the treasury, or plate room, and will think of *the nobler vessels*. These are, first of all, of solid metal—vessels of silver and vessels of gold. They are not all equally valuable, but they are all precious. Here is weight for you—here is something that is worth treasuring, something that will last for ages and at any time will endure the fire. Now, in real Christians, those who really love the Lord, there is something substantial and weighty. When you get hold of them, you know the difference between them and the wooden professor. Even those who do not like them—strange taste, that which does not appreciate silver and gold—are nevertheless compelled to say, "That is a genuine article, worth a great deal, weighty and substantial."

Now, we shall, none of us, ever be vessels of silver and gold unless the Lord makes us so by divine grace. Vessels of earth are things of *nature*—any potter can make them. Vessels of wood are common enough. Copper soon produces a pail. But a vessel of silver or of gold is a rarer thing! It costs mining and searching, furnace work and fashioning, toil and skill. On each vessel to honor, Jesus Himself has put His hand to mold and fashion it and to cause it to be prepared for glory. Did you ever hear how vessels come to be golden? Listen to this, and you will know. One very dear to me has put the story into rhyme:

> "Oh, that I were a cup, a golden cup
> Meet for the Master's use!
> Brimming and trembling with that draught of joy
> Which fills His heart with gladness."
>
> So spoke a poor, vile, broken, earthy thing,
> A worthless castaway.
> The Master heard, and when He passed that way,
> He touched it with His wounded hand.
>
> Then lo! Its baseness vanished, and instead
> There stood a golden chalice wondrous fair,
> Overflowing with deep love for Him!
> He raised it to His gracious lips, and quaffed
> The wine that makes glad the heart of God,
> Then took the cup to heaven.

On the vessels of honor, you can see the hallmark. What is the hallmark that denotes the purity of the Lord's golden vessels? Well, He has only one stamp for everything. When He laid the foundation, what was the seal He put upon it? "The Lord knoweth them that are his. And, let every one that nameth the name of Christ depart from iniquity" (2 Tim. 2:19 KJV). That was God's seal! That was the impress of the great King upon the foundation stone. Do we find it here? Yes, we do. "If a man therefore purge himself from these, he shall be a vessel unto honour" (2 Tim. 2:21 KJV). You see, then, that the man who is the golden or silver vessel departs from all iniquity, and *that* is the token of his genuine character.

The man who is truly the Lord's seeks to be cleansed not only from the open sin of the world but also from the common sin of professing Christians. He labors to be purged from that which the wooden vessel and the earthen vessel would delight in. He wants to be pure within and without. He desires perfection. He labors daily to conquer every sin and strives with all his might to serve his Lord. He is not content to have a fair appearance, as wood and earth may have, he wishes to be solid, substantial metal, purged and purified to the utmost possible degree and fit for the highest purposes. Now, this seeking after purity is the hallmark of the King's vessels of gold and silver.

Notice, however, that they are *purged*, for the Lord will not use filthy vessels no matter what they may be. He will only use those that are clean. And He would have His true people purged, as I have said before, not only from gross sin, but also from doctrinal error and from association with the perverse-minded. We are to be purged from Hymenaeus and Philetus *and* from the vain babblings of which the apostle has been speaking in the previous part of the chapter. I fear that Christian men do a great deal of mischief by their complicity with those who are teaching what is downright falsehood. If we are to serve the Lord in the matter of advancing His truth, we must be true to the truth of God ourselves. If we join hand in hand with others and so form a confederacy when rude hands are pulling down the very pillars of the temple, it may be we will be partakers of other men's sins. We must be clean-handed in this matter!

And then notice that these gold and silver vessels are reserved as well as purged. They are made meet for the Master's use. Nobody is to drink out of them but the King Himself. This is the blessedness of the child of God when he comes to be what he should be, that he can sing as we did just now:

> *I am Yours and Yours alone,*
> *This I gladly, fully own!*
> *And in all my works and ways,*
> *Only now would seek your praise.*

As Joseph had a cup out of which he alone drank, so the Lord takes His people to be His peculiar treasure, vessels for His personal use. Brethren, I count it an honor to be useful to the meanest child of God, but I confess that the honor lies mainly in the fact that I am thereby serving the Master Himself. Oh, to be used by God! This is to answer the end of our being. If you can feel that God has used you, then may you rejoice indeed!

There are some Christians whom the Lord cannot much use because, first of all, they are not cleansed from selfishness. They have an eye to their own honor or aggrandizement. The Lord will not be in complicity with selfish aims! Some men are self-confident—there is too much of the "I" about them, and our Master will not use them. He will have our weakness but not our strength! And if we are great somebodies, He will pass us by and take some little nobody and make use of him. The Lord cannot use other men because they are too apt to be proud. If He were to give them a little success, it would be dangerous to their Christian existence! Their poor brains would begin to swim and they would think the Lord could hardly do without them! Indeed, when they meet with a little encouragement, they swell into such wonderful people that they expect everybody to fall down and worship them!

> *A man may work his heart out in the ministry or the Sunday school, but if he is practicing some secret sin, he cannot prosper. It is not possible that God should honor him!*

God will not use them, neither will He set upon His table vessels that are in any way defiled. There must be purity! A man may work his heart out in the ministry or the Sunday school, but if he is practicing some secret sin, he cannot prosper. It is not possible that God should honor him! There may be a measure of apparent success for a time, and in God's sovereignty, He may use His truth itself in spite of the man, but the man himself will not be useful to the Master. Littleness of grace and contentedness with which spiritual poverty also put many a man aside. We must be full if God is to pour out of us to the thirsty! We must be full of His light if we are to illuminate the darkness of others! We cannot reveal to the world what the Lord has not revealed to us.

Oh, for a holy character and holy communion with God! Then we will be golden vessels fit for the Master's use, and so, according to the text, we will be ready for every good work—ready for the work when it comes and ready at the work when it has come—because we will be completely consecrated to God and subject to His hand. In this readiness for whatever comes, we will be honored. Men may despise us, as they will, but what does it matter if *God* honors us? This height of grace may cost us a sharp experience, but must not gold be tried with fire? As thieves are most anxious to steal not the pots and wooden vessels, but the gold and the silver, so we may expect to be exposed to greater temptations and greater persecutions than others.

More grace involves more trials, but then we will have the delight of glorifying God more. Oh, to be vessels to honor! Beloved members of this church, aspire to this! You have acknowledged in your names that you are Christians! You have been baptized into the sacred name of the divine Trinity! You have borne, up to now, a consistent moral character. But oh, see to it that the inner substance is the real metal, the gold and silver! See to it that you are reserved for the Lord's own special use! Be as consecrated to Him as were the bowls before the altar. Never let the world drink out of you, as Belshazzar did out of the vessels taken at Jerusalem. May the Lord grant that you may never be defiled, but may be kept, by His grace, pure and consecrated to Him.

IV. Fourth, for a moment we must speak about *the Master*. He is introduced here, you see, as having certain vessels meet for His use, and this shows that He is *in* the house. There would be no need to reserve vessels for His use if He were not there. He is in the midst of His church by His indwelling Spirit. How this ought to make us wish to be purged, sanctified, and ready for Him! Your Master is not far away. His presence in the church is promised: "Lo, I am with you always, even to the end of the age" (Matt. 28:20). What manner of persons, therefore, ought you to be?

Second, the Master knows all about the house and knows the quality of all the vessels. There is no deceiving Him with the wooden plate—He knows it is not gold. And as for that earthen cup, though it may be gilded all over, He knows it is not gold. He reads the heart of everyone here present—wood or earth, silver or gold—the Master understands us. And then reflect that the Master will use us all as far as we are fit to be used. We are in God's house, and if we are wood, He will put us to wooden use.

There are many wooden preachers. If we are earth and earthly minded,

He may put us to earthly uses, as He did Judas, who carried the bag but had no grace. If you are silver, He will give you silver use. And if you are gold, He will give you golden service in which you will be happy, honored, and blessed. What comes of this, then, lastly? Why, brothers and sisters, let us bestir ourselves that we be purged, for the text says, "If a man therefore purge himself." It throws this business upon each one of us *personally*. A man must purge *himself* from ill company! And when we have confessed the responsibility, let us turn to God in prayer and feel that thorough purging is a work that we cannot achieve, and therefore we cry, "Cleanse me, O God! Sanctify me! Make me meet for Your service and prepared for every good work."

Beloved, finish with earnest prayer: Pray God that you may not be hypocrites! Beseech the Lord to search you and try you, that you not be found deceivers. And when you are sure that you are His, then ask Him to make you not merely silver, for it is very apt to tarnish, but rather the precious gold that, when exposed to the worst influences, scarcely shows a trace of dullness. Pure unalloyed gold may we be! And then may the Master, both in secret and in public, use us to His own joy. May He refresh Himself with our love and faith, yes, may His joy be fulfilled in us, that our joy may be full. God grant it may be so, for Christ's sake.

For Further Thought

1. Second Timothy 2:17 mentions teachings that spread like cancer or gangrene. What is the example of this given in verse 18?
2. What is the definition of the house of God in 1 Timothy 3:15?
3. Sometimes it is hard to tell who is a believer and who is not. What does 2 Timothy 2:19 say about this?

SERMONS RELATING TO BELIEVERS

CHRISTIANS KEPT IN TIME
AND GLORIFIED IN ETERNITY

Now to Him who is able to keep you from stumbling,
and to present you faultless before the presence of His glory with
exceeding joy, to God our Savior, who alone is wise, be glory and
majesty, dominion and power, both now and forever. Amen.
JUDE 24–25

OMITTING all preface, it will be well to observe in what state of mind Jude was when he penned this doxology, what had been his previous meditations, and when we have done so, we will endeavor to come directly to the text and observe what mercies he sums up in it and what praise is due from us to Him of whom he thus speaks.

I. Then, *under what influence was Jude's mind when he penned this doxology?* Our first observation is that in writing this very short but very full epistle, he had been led to consider the grievous falls of many others, and in contemplating those failures, he could not resist the impulse of penning these words, "To him who is able to keep you from stumbling." You observe in reading that he mentions the Israelites who came out of Egypt. That was a glorious day in that the whole host met at Succoth, having just escaped from the thralldom of Egypt, and now found themselves delivered from the whips and the lashes of the taskmasters and were no longer compelled to make bricks without straw and to build up palaces and tombs for the oppressors.

That was, if possible, a more glorious day than when God divided the Red Sea to make a way for His people. The depths stood upright in a heap when the elect multitude walked through. Do you not see them, as with songs and praises they are led all that night through the deep as on dry ground? They are all landed on the other side, and then their leader lifts up his rod and immediately there comes a wind and the waters return to their place. The infatuated Egyptian king, who with his hosts had followed them into the depths of the sea, is utterly destroyed. The depths have covered them.

They sank as lead in the mighty waters! There is not one of them left. "Then sang Moses and the children of Israel this song unto the LORD, and spake, saying, I will sing unto the LORD, for he hath triumphed gloriously: the horse and his rider hath he thrown into the sea" (Exod. 15:1 KJV). Is it credible, is it not too sadly incredible that this very people who stood by the Red Sea and marked the overthrow of God's enemies, within a few days were clamoring to go back into Egypt? And before many months had passed were for taking to themselves a leader that they might force their way back into the place of their bondage? Yes, and they who saw Jehovah's work and all His plagues in Zoan made to themselves a calf and bowed down before it and said, "These be thy gods, O Israel, which brought thee up out of the land of Egypt" (Exod. 32:4 KJV).

> Now to Him who is able to keep you from stumbling, and to present you faultless before the presence of His glory with exceeding joy, to God our Savior, who alone is wise, be glory and majesty, dominion and power, both now and forever. Amen.

With tears in your eyes, look at the many griefs that studded the pathway of their forty years' wandering, and with many fears reflect that out of all that multitude that came out of Egypt, there were but *two* who lived to cross the Jordan! Aaron must put off the breastplate, for he has sinned against God. And even Moses, the meekest of men, must go to the top of Nebo and is only permitted to gaze upon the prospect of that land that he must never actually enjoy! Except for Caleb and Joshua, there were none found faithful among all the tribes, and these alone will enter into the goodly land that flows with milk and honey.

Now when Jude thought of this, I do not wonder that he began to consider the case of himself and of his fellow believers united with him in church fellowship at Jerusalem and elsewhere. And knowing that all of them who were truly brought up out of Egypt by Jesus will surely enter into the promised rest, he cannot, he does not desire to resist the impulse of singing, "Now to Him who is able to keep you from stumbling, and to present you faultless before the presence of His glory with exceeding joy, to God our Savior, who alone is wise, be glory and majesty, dominion and power, both now and forever. Amen."

> *S*atan is allowed to go about the world. Still he wears his chains, and he has a tether, and the Lord knows how to pull him in, both by providence and direct acts of power.

If you read on to the next verse, you perceive that Jude had another example in his mind's eye: the angels that kept not their first estate. We do not know much of angels, but from what we gather in Holy Scripture—perhaps tinged in our reading with some of the half-inspired ideas of Milton—we believe that angels are spirits vastly superior to ourselves. In intelligence they may well be so, even if they had been created upon a par, for they have had many years in which to learn and gather experience, whereas man's existence is but a handbreadth. We regard an angel with intense respect, and while never paying any worship to those noble beings, we cannot but feel how little we are when compared with them.

One of these angels appears to have been named Lucifer, son of the morning. Perhaps he was a leader in the heavenly host and first among the princes of heaven. He, together with multitudes of others, fell from their allegiance to God. We know not how. We have no idea if they were tempted, unless one of them tempted the other, but they kept not their first estate. They were driven out of heaven. They were expelled from their starry thrones, and therefore they are reserved in chains of darkness until the great day of account.

Now, my brethren, can you think of the fall of angels without trembling? Can you think of the morning stars put out in blackness? Of the cherub, whose head did wear a crown, cast into the mire and his crown rolled into the dust? Can you think of these bright spirits transformed into the hideous fiends that devils are? Their hearts, once temples for God, now become the haunt of every unclean thing—themselves the most unclean? Can you think of that without feeling a tremor of fear lest you, too, should fall from your first estate? And without another, and a higher thrill of joy, when you think of Him who is "able to keep you from stumbling, and to present you faultless before the presence of His glory with exceeding joy"?

When any turn from Zion's way,
(Alas, what numbers do!),
I think I hear my Savior say,
"Will You forsake Me, too?"

Ah, Lord! With such a heart as mine,
Unless you hold me fast,
I feel I must, I will decline,
And prove like them at last.

But we can also sing right joyously:

The soul that on Jesus has leaned for repose,
He will not, He will not, desert to its foes.
He'll never, no never, no never forsake that soul,
Though all hell should endeavor to shake it.

We might continue to follow Jude, but we will not do so. We prefer to add something that Jude has not put in his epistle. Our first parent, Adam, lived in the midst of happiness and peace in the garden. Unlike ourselves he had no depravity, no bias toward evil. God made him upright. He was perfectly pure, and it was in his own will whether he should sin or not. The balance hung evenly in his hands.

But you have not forgotten how on that sad day he took of the forbidden fruit and ate and thereby cursed himself and all of us! My brethren, as you think of Adam, driven out of the Garden of Eden, sent out to till the ground from where he was taken, and compelled in the sweat of his face to eat bread; when you recollect the paradise he left, the happiness and peace that have forever passed away through his sin, do you not hear the voice that says to you, as a depraved and fallen creature, "Therefore let him who thinks he stands take heed lest he fall" (1 Cor. 10:12)? Conscious of your own weakness as compared with your parent Adam, you are ready to cry out, "O God, how can I stand where Adam falls?"

But here comes the joyous thought that Christ, who has begun with you, will never cease till He has perfected you! Can you help singing with Jude, "Now to Him who is able to keep us from stumbling?" It strikes me that every time we mark an apostate and see the fall of a sinner or of a fellow professor, we should go down on our knees and cry, "Hold you me up and I will be safe," and then rise up and sing:

> *To our redeemer God*
> *Eternal power belongs,*
> *Immortal crowns of majesty,*
> *And everlasting songs.*
>
> *He will present our souls*
> *Unblemished and complete*
> *Before the glory of His face,*
> *With joys divinely great.*

This partly accounts for the text before us. But on a further reference to the epistle, we get another part of the thoughts that had exercised the apostle's mind. Observe, dear friends, that the apostle had a very vivid and distinct sense of the nature of the place into which those fell and of their utter ruin and destruction. Notice, concerning the children of Israel, he says that God destroyed those who did not believe (Jude 5). What is it to be destroyed? Destroyed! This does not end with the white skeleton and the bleached bones that lay in the wilderness, a horror to the passerby! He means something more than even that!

Brought out of Egypt and yet destroyed! Take heed, professor! You may be brought into something like gospel liberty and yet may perish! Take heed, you carnal professor, I say! You may fancy you have escaped the bondage of the law, but yet you will never enter into the rest that remains for the people of God—you will be destroyed! Let that word *destroyed* ring in your ears, and it will make you bless God, who is able to keep you from stumbling, if it will lead you to flee to Him for help!

Next he says of the fallen angels that they are "reserved in everlasting chains under darkness for the judgment of the great day" (Jude 6). What that may be, we can but roughly guess. Satan is allowed to go about the world. Still he wears his chains, and he has a tether, and the Lord knows how to pull him in, both by providence and direct acts of power. We believe that these spirits are under darkness. A gloom, a thick darkness that may be felt, hangs perpetually over their minds. Wherever they may be, they are waiting till Christ will come to summon them as rebellious creatures before His bar that they may receive their sentence and begin afresh their dreadful hell.

And remember, dear brothers and sisters, unless eternal love will prevent it, this case must be ours! We, too, must enter into places reserved in darkness, wearing everlasting chains, to endure eternal fire. We should do so, we *must* do so, if it were not for Him "who is able to keep you from stumbling, and to present you faultless before the presence of His glory with exceeding joy." Nor is this all, for if you will patiently read the next verse, you will see that Jude has, if possible, introduced a more graphic picture.

The cities of Sodom and Gomorrah are bright as the sun goes down. The inhabitants are merry with boisterous laughter. There is plenty in the barn. There is luxury in the hall, for the plain of Sodom was well watered and lacked for nothing. Down went that sun upon a disastrous evening, never to rise upon most of those who were in that doomed city. At daybreak, just as the sun is beginning to shine upon the earth, angels hasten Lot and his family out of the city—and no sooner do they reach the little city of Zoar than straightway the heaven is red with supernatural flame and down descends a terrific rain, as if God had poured hell out of heaven! He rained fire and brimstone upon the cities, and the smoke of their torment went up so that Abraham, far away to the west, could see the rolling cloud and the terrible brightness of the fire, even at midday.

And as men go to the Dead Sea, they see to this day where death has reigned. There are masses of asphalt still floating upon the surface of that sea where there is nothing that lives. No fish swim in its turbid streams. There are indubitable evidences there of some dread judgment of God. And as Jude thought of this, he seemed to say, "O God, preserve us from such a doom, for this is the doom of all apostates, either in this world or in that which is to come, thus to be consumed with fire." And as he remembered that God would keep His people, he blessed that protecting hand that covers every saint, and he wrote down, "Now to Him who is able to keep you from stumbling."

I have a thought in my mind. I cannot, of course, tell whether it is right or not, but it strikes me just now that the author's name is Jude—Judas. Did he recollect Judas, his namesake that was called Iscariot, as he penned these words? He had known him, probably had respected him as the others had done. He had marked him that night when he sat at the table and like others said, "Is it I?" Probably Jude was very surprised when he saw Iscariot take the sop and dip in the dish with the Savior. And when he went out, he could scarcely believe his own ears when the Savior said that he who betrayed Him had gone forth!

He must have known how Judas kissed the Son of man and sold Him for thirty pieces of silver. He could not but be aware how in remorse he hanged himself and how his bowels gushed out. And I think the shadow of the doom of Judas fell upon this better Judas while he penned these words, which he seems to say with greater emphasis: "Now to Him who is able to keep you from stumbling. . .to God our Savior. . .be glory and majesty, dominion and power, both now and forever." Thus you see, dear friends, we are getting into the track, I think, of Jude's thoughts. He thought about the failures of others and the terrible way in which they had fallen.

Yet again, by your leave, Jude had a very clear view of the greatness of the sins into which apostates fall. Probably there is not in the whole compass of holy writ a more fearful picture of the sin of backsliders and apostates than in the epistle of Jude. I remember preaching to you one evening from that text, "Raging waves of the sea, foaming up their own shame; wandering stars for whom is reserved the blackness of darkness forever" (Jude 13).

I remember how you trembled, myself trembling most with such a terrible message to deliver! Where could such a text or simile be found but in the book of Jude? The sins of apostates are tremendous. They are usually not content with the average of human guilt. They must make themselves giants in iniquity. None make such devils as those who were once angels and none make such reprobates as those who once seemed to bid fair for the kingdom of heaven! These go into filthy dreams, into sensuality. They give "themselves over to sexual immorality and. . .after strange flesh," as he has put it.

In fact, where can we set the bounds to which a man will go, when he crucifies the Lord that bought him and puts Him to an open shame? Oh, beloved, as I think of the sin into which these apostates have gone, I cannot but feel that you must bless God with Jude, that there is one "who is able to keep you from stumbling, and to present you faultless before the presence of His glory with exceeding joy."

II. I might continue in this strain, but perhaps I had better not. I would rather turn to *the blessings of which Jude speaks*. He seems to ascribe in this doxology three blessings, at least, to the power of the Lord Jesus. The first is ability to keep you from stumbling, and for this, I am sure, the highest praise is due when you consider for a moment the dangerous way. In some respects, the path to heaven is very safe. It is so as God made it. But in other respects, there is no road as dangerous as the road to eternal life. It is beset with difficulties.

In some of our mountain climbing we have gone along narrow pathways where there was but a step between us and death—for deep down beneath us was a gaping precipice—perhaps a mile in perpendicular descent. One's brain reels at the thought of it now, yet we passed along quite safely. The road to heaven is much like that. One false step (and how easy it is to take that if divine grace is absent), and down we go!

What a slippery path is that which some of us have to tread. You know that there are a million opportunities in a single week for your foot to slip and for your soul to be ruined. There are some spots, I believe, upon some of the more difficult Swiss mountains where no man ought to go at all, and where, if any must go, they should be only such as have become most accomplished mountaineers through years of practice—for one has to cling to the side of the rock—to hold on, perhaps, by bushes or stones that may be there, with nothing for the feet to rest upon except, perhaps, an inch of projecting crag!

And so we go creeping on with our backs to the danger, for to look down upon it would be to make the brain reel and cause us to fall. And the result of falling, of course, would be the end of life—the body would be dashed into a thousand pieces. Such is truly the way to heaven. You must all have passed some such difficult places, and, in looking back, I can only, myself, say, "Unto Him that has kept me from falling, when my feet had well near gone and my steps had almost slipped. Unto Him be glory forever and ever!"

But next you have to think of the weakness of the person. Some men may travel roads that would not be safe for others, and what are you, my brother pilgrim, but a little babe? It is unsafe to trust you along the pathway to glory. In the best roads you are soon tripped up. Those feeble knees of yours can scarcely support your tottering weight. A straw might throw you and a pebble could wound you. Oh, if you will be kept, how must you bless the patient power that watches over you day by day! Reflect upon your tendency to sin; upon the giddiness of that poor brain, the silliness of that deceitful heart. Think how apt you are to choose danger, how the tendency is to cast yourselves down, how you rather are inclined to fall than to stand, and I am sure you will sing more sweetly than you have ever done, "Glory be to Him who is able to keep me from falling."

> *A straw might throw you and a pebble could wound you. Oh, if you will be kept, how must you bless the patient power that watches over you day by day!*

Then you have to notice further the many foes that try to push you down. The road is rough enough. The child is weak enough. But here and there is an enemy who is in ambush who comes out when we least expect him and labors to trip us up or hurl us down a precipice. I suppose you never did see a man fall from a precipice. Some of you may have been fools enough to go and see a man walk on a rope. In that case, I believe, you have incurred the guilt of murder, because, if the man does not kill himself, you encourage him to put himself where he probably might do so. But if you have ever really seen a man fall over a precipice, your hair must surely have stood on end, your flesh creeping on your bones, as you saw the poor human form falling off the edge never to stand in mortal life again! Surely as you left the place where you stood and fled away from the edge of the precipice, you cried, "O bless Him that made me stand and kept my feet from falling!"

How alarmed you would be if you were in such a position and had seen one fall and that same monster that had pushed him over should come to hurl you over also! And especially if you felt that you were as weak as water and could not resist the gigantic demon! Now just such is your case! You cannot stand against Satan! A little maid made Peter deny his Master, and a little maid may make the strongest among us tremble sometimes. Oh, if we are preserved in spite of such mighty enemies who are ever waiting to destroy us, we will have great cause to sing praises "to Him who is able to keep us from stumbling." Only Christ has the power to take us into heaven.

You may keep a man from starving, but you cannot take him into the king's palace and present him at court. Suppose that a man had been a rebel. You might hide him from the pursuers and aid in his escape, but you could not take him into the presence of the king and cause him to live in the royal castle of the land. But you see that Christ preserves His people though they have offended God and daily provoke His justice. And He does more, for He presents them to the King of kings in the high court of heaven itself! This it is that makes the other blessing so great. We are not anxious to always live in this world. We find ourselves in a strange land here and would be glad to fly away and be at rest. This is to us a wilderness state, and we rejoice to know that Canaan lies beyond.

Our heavenly Joshua can lead us into it! He can fight for us against Amalek, slay all our foes, and preserve us from falling. But better still, He can and He will take us into the Promised Land and give us to see the better country, even the heavenly, and to there will He conduct all the host so that not one will perish or be left behind! Christ gives preservation, but He adds *glorification*, and that is better still! Here then, my brothers and sisters, is a thought of incomparable sweetness! We are safe while in this world— "Happier, but not more secure are the glorified spirits in heaven." And we, too, will be, before long, as happy as they are, because He will present us with them before the presence of His glory with exceeding joy!

We cannot, however, enlarge on this point, though there is much, very much, that ought to be said. We proceed to notice the condition in which the saints are to be when presented—they are to be faultless—for our Lord never stops short of perfection in His work of love. That Savior who means to keep His people to the end will not present them at last just alive, all black and foul as when He helped them out of the miry places. He will not bring them in, as gallant men have to bring those whom they have rescued from drowning, with just the vital spark within them. No, our Savior will carry His people through this life, safe from falling, and He will present them, how?—faultless!

Oh, that is a wondrous word, *faultless*! We are a long way off from it now.

Faulty, yes; we are now faulty through and through. But Jesus Christ will never be content till we are *faultless*. And this He will make us in three ways: He will wash us till there is not a spot left, for the chief of sinners will be as white and fair as God's purest angel. The eyes of justice will look, and God will say, "No spot of sin remains in you."

You may have been a drunkard, a thief, an adulterer, and whatnot—but if Christ, in mercy, undertakes your case, He will wash you in His blood so thoroughly that you will be faultless at last! You will be without spot or wrinkle or any such thing. Now we are defiled and covered with sin as if we had "sat by the pots" (Exod. 16:3). We have reveled in uncleanness till we are as if we had been plunged into the pit (Job 9:31). Our own flesh must abhor us if we could but see how defiled we are by nature and by practice.

Now all this will be completely removed and we will be whiter than snow! You remember that when the disciples looked at Jesus on the Mount of Transfiguration, they saw that His garments were white and glistening, whiter than any fuller could make them. And so will we be hereafter, whiter and fairer than any earthly art can attain to. The sea of glass, clear as crystal, will not be whiter or purer than we will be when washed in the blood of the Lamb. But that is only one way.

If a man had no faults, it would still be necessary for him to have some virtues. A man cannot enter heaven simply because transgression is put away. The law must be kept! There must be a positive obedience to divine precepts. Religion is no negation, an absence of things merely evil. It is the presence of the good, the true, and the pure. But since even when we do our best we will be unprofitable servants, we need something higher than we can ever produce by these, our feeble and sinful powers! Therefore, the Lord our God imputes to us the perfect righteousness of His Son Christ Jesus, for

> *Lest the shadow of a spot*
> *Should on my soul be found,*
> *He took the robe the Savior worked,*
> *And cast it all around.*

The righteousness of Jesus Christ will make the saint who wears it so fair that he will be positively faultless! Yes, perfect in the sight of God! There is fullness in this that it delights my soul to dwell upon. A man may be faultless in *my* sight, but not in the sight of those who know him intimately.

A Christian may be so holy as to escape the censure of all just men. But ministering spirits who read the heart and deal with the inner man can speak of evil that has not come to light before human eyes. And we know that God sees even more clearly than angelic spirits, for He charges them with folly.

Now, God is to see no iniquity in us, no shortcoming. We will be tried in His scales and set in the light of His countenance and be pronounced faultless. God's law will not only have no charge against us, but it will be magnified in us and honored by us. We will have imputed to us that righteousness that belongs to Him who has done all this for us that He might "present us faultless before the presence of His glory."

> *You may have been a drunkard, a thief, an adulterer, and whatnot—but if Christ, in mercy, undertakes your case, He will wash you in His blood so thoroughly that you will be faultless at last!*

Fourth and best, perhaps, the Spirit of God will make new creatures of us. He has begun the work, and He will finish it. He will make us so perfectly holy that we will have no tendency to sin anymore. The day will come when we will feel that Adam in the garden was not purer than we are. You will have no taint of evil in you. Judgment, memory, will—every human power and passion shall be emancipated from the thralldom of evil. You will be holy even as God is holy, and in His presence you will dwell forever!

How altered we will be! Look within and see if your experience is not like the apostle Paul's, who found a potent law in his members so that when he would do good, evil was present with him, and when he desired to escape some evil, he did at times the very thing he allowed not but would most heartily condemn! So it is with us. We would be holy, but we are like a ball that has a bias in it. We cannot go in a straight and direct line. We try to hit the mark, but we are prone to start on one side like a deceitful bow. There is a black drop in our hearts that taints all the streams, and none of them can be pure.

But it will all be changed one day—we will be remade and all the evil gone, gone forever! How joyous must have been the entrance of Naaman, the Assyrian, into his house after he had washed in Jordan's stream and found his flesh restored to him as the flesh of a little child! I think I see him as the watchman on the tower has given notice of his approach in the distance. The whole household is at the gate to meet him and to see if he comes back in health. His wife, if Eastern customs would not permit her going forth in public, would look from her easement to catch a glimpse of his face—to see if the dread spots were gone.

How joyful the shout, "He is cured and clean!" But this is nothing compared with the rapture of that hour when the everlasting doors will be lifted up and we, made meet for the inheritance of the saints in light, will enter into the joy of our Lord! Or take another illustration from scripture and try and realize the happiness that reigned in the family of the maniac out of whom the legion of devils had departed. Perhaps he had been home before when under the evil influence of the foul fiends. How terrified they doubtless were with the mad frenzy of the poor, unhappy wretch as he cut himself with stones and broke all bonds put on him in tenderness and love in order to restrain his self-imposed misery and wounds.

And now, as he comes once more to his house, they see him approach and the old terror seizes them because they know not that he is a changed man, but suppose him still to be the demented being of days gone by. But he enters the door as calm and composed as if he had returned from a long journey and was only anxious to relate the incidents of the pilgrimage and greet loved friends once more! With no fierce frenzy rolling in his eyes, no loud discordant shrieks rending the air, all is the demeanor of a well-regulated, joyful, yet chastened mind! As his friends realize all this, they hear what great things the Lord has done for him! What joy must have been in that family circle! I should like to have seen it. I am sure it was a choice exhibition of real human bliss such as earth only witnesses now and then.

It must have been a beam of purest radiance lighting up the scene, like the splendor that Saul of Tarsus saw on the road to Damascus as it lit up the day when he was made a new creature in Christ Jesus. Here, also, we can most truthfully say that the joy, though great, was not comparable to the joy that will be ours when we are changed into new creatures—when we will be clothed and in our right mind—no longer prone to wander among the black mountains of iniquity and no more tempted to abide among those dead in trespasses and sins. Then we will be ever holy and always living to God and made like He! Oh, this is joy indeed! Not only will He keep us from falling, but also He will present us faultless!

My brothers and sisters, at the thought of this, I think you must join with Jude and say, "Now to Him who is able to do all this, be glory and majesty, dominion and power, both now and ever." I cannot speak to you as I would wish upon such a theme as this. Who could? But when we get to heaven, our song will be sweeter and louder, because we will understand better the dangers from that we have escaped and how very much we owe to Him who has kept us and brought us safely through all the vicissitudes of life to the place He has prepared for us. Meanwhile, never let us be forgetful of that mighty goodness that holds us fast and will not let us go.

III. Still I have not done with the text. I have already forestalled my next thought, but I think it requires a special notice. Observe, the apostle adds, "To present us faultless before His presence, *with exceeding great joy.*" Who will have the joy? My brothers and sisters, you will have it! Have you ever mused upon the parable of the prodigal son? I know you have! No one can have diligently read the Bible without staying to think over, again and again, of that most tender and instructive of our Lord's parables.

> *W*hen safely brought through all the weary pilgrimage from the far-off country, we will tread the golden streets and be safe inside the pearly gates and have the past all gone forever among the things we never will meet again.

Now, I ask, who was happy at that feast? Don't you think it was the prodigal? What was the character of those thoughts filling his heart and making it heave as if it would burst? How overjoyed he must have been! How utterly crushed down with his father's love and all the unexpected marks of kindness and affection! He had had his days of feasting and sinful merriment, but no songs could ever have been so sweet as those that rung round the old rooftree to welcome him home! No viands had ever tasted so delicious as that fatted calf! And no voice of any companion or witching charmer at his guilty feasts had ever sounded such melodious notes in his ears as those words of his father, "Let us eat and be merry" (Luke 15:23).

So will it be with us when we have been restored to ourselves—when wearied of the world and hungering and thirsting after righteousness we will have been led to the Father's house by the cords of love that the Spirit will cast around us. When safely brought through all the weary pilgrimage from the far-off country, we will tread the golden streets and be safe inside the pearly gates and have the past all gone forever among the things we never will meet again. What rapture will be ours! This will be heaven indeed, when sin will be gone, Satan shut out, temptation gone forever! You will have a joy of which you cannot now conceive. Rivers of pleasure will flow into your soul! You will drink such draughts of bliss as your soul has never known this side of the grave.

Oh, be joyful now with a respite of the joy that is to be revealed! And afterward you will have the fullness of divine bliss forever and ever! Who will be happy? Why, the minister will be happy! What pleasure was there in the heart of the shepherd youth, David, the son of Jesse, when he had gone forth to do battle with the lion and bear in order to rescue the lamb out of their jaws when God had delivered him and made him successful in his attempt! How gladly he must have watched the little lamb run to the side of its dam, and in the mutual pleasure of these poor dumb animals, I am sure he found a joy.

And so all the shepherds in heaven, all who have been faithful pastors who have cared for and tended their flocks, shall find a bliss unspeakable in welcoming to glory those darling ones preserved from the power of the devil who "walks about like a roaring lion, seeking whom he may devour" (1 Peter 5:8). Yes, ministers will be sharers in this happiness! I think we will have a special joy in bringing our sheaves with us. If it may please God to keep me from falling, if I just get inside the door of heaven with some of the many thousands that God has given to me as my spiritual children, I will fall prostrate before His feet the greatest debtor to His mercy that ever lived and one that has more cause than any other of His creatures to thank Him and ascribe to Him glory and honor, dominion and power, forever and ever!

Here I am, and the children whom you have given me! Unto you be praise! And what will be the joy of angels, too? How exceedingly great their bliss will be! If there is joy among the angels over one sinner who repents, what will there be over ten thousands times ten thousands, not of repenting, but of *perfected* sinners, cleansed from every stain, set free from every flaw? Oh, you cherubim and seraphim, how loud will be your music! How you will tune your harps anew! How every string will wake up to the sweetest music in praise of God! "Let the sea roar, and all its fullness" (1 Chron.

16:32) at the thought of the glorious joy at God's right hand!

Who will have joy, I ask again? Why, Christ will have the most joy of all! Angels and ministers and you, yourselves, will scarcely know such joy as He will have—all His sheep safely folded, every stone of the building placed in its proper position. All the blood-bought and blood-washed ones, all whom the Father gave Him, delivered out of the jaw of the lion! All whom He covenanted to redeem effectually saved, His counsel all fulfilled, His stipulations all carried out, the covenant not only ratified but also fulfilled in all its jots and tittles! Verily, none will be so happy as the great Surety in that day!

As the bridegroom rejoices over the bride, so will Christ rejoice over you. You know it is written that "Jesus...who for the joy that was set before Him endured the cross, despising the shame" (Heb. 12:2). And also, "He shall see the labor of His soul, and be satisfied" (Isa. 53:11). Now this satisfaction and joy will be our Lord's when the whole church is faultless and complete in the presence of His glory, but not till then. In that hour, when all His jewels are reckoned up and none found missing, He will rejoice anew in spirit and will thank God with yet more joy than He did when here on earth and thought of this day in prospect and by that thought nerved Himself for cruel suffering and a death of shame. Yes, Christ will be glad!

Our head will have His share of joy with all the members! And happily He will be able to bear more, as He most certainly deserves, and will have more. Who will have joy? Why, God Himself will have joy! It is no blasphemy to say that the joy of God on that occasion will be infinite. It is always infinite! But it will be then infinitely displayed before His creation's gaze. Listen to these words—you cannot fathom them, but you may look at them. It is written, "The LORD your God. . .will rejoice over you with gladness. . . . He will rejoice over you with singing" (Zeph. 3:17). As I have said on this platform before, I think that is the most wonderful text in the Bible in some respects—God Himself singing!

I can imagine, when the world was made, the morning stars shouting for joy. But God did not sing. He said it was very good, and that was all. There was no song. But oh, to think of it, that when the entire chosen race will meet around the throne, the joy of the eternal Father will swell so high that God, who fills all in all, will burst out into an infinite, godlike song! I will only put in this one more thought, that all this, beloved, is about you. All this you have a share in, the least in the church, the poorest in the family, the humblest believer—this is all true of you—He will keep you from stumbling and present you spotless before His presence with exceedingly great joy.

Oh, cannot you join the song and sing with me, "To God our Savior, who alone is wise, be glory and majesty, dominion and power, both now and forever. Amen"? For my part I feel like that good old saint who said that if she got to heaven, Jesus Christ should never hear the last of it. Truly He never shall.

> *I'll praise my Savior with my breath;*
> *And when my voice is at last in death,*
> *Praise will employ my nobler powers.*
>
> *My days of praise will ne'er be past,*
> *While life and thought and being last,*
> *Or immortality endures.*

I want you to go away with a sense of your own weakness and yet a belief in your own safety. I want you to know that you cannot stand a minute, that you will be damned within another second unless divine grace keeps you out of hell. But I want you to feel that since you are in the hands of Christ you cannot perish—neither can any pluck you out of His hands! And, poor sinners, my heart's desire is that you may be put into the hands of Christ tonight. That you may be done trusting yourselves. You can ruin, but you cannot save yourselves.

"O Israel, you are destroyed, but your help is from Me" (Hosea 13:9). Christ alone can save you! Oh, look out of self to Christ! Trust yourselves in His hands! He is "able to keep you from stumbling." You cannot even stand upright yourselves, and if He should set you upright, you cannot keep so for a minute without His protecting care. If saints need to be kept, how much more need have you to seek the shelter of the Savior's wounded side? Flee there as the dove to the cleft of the rock! If holy men of God cry daily for pardon and profess to have no right of themselves to heaven, how much more urgent is your case? You must perish if you die as you are! You can never make yourself faultless, but Christ can.

He wants to do it. He has opened a fountain for sin and for uncleanness. Wash and be clean! Again, I say, look to Jesus! Away with self and cling to

Christ! Down with self-confidence and up with simple faith in Christ Jesus! I will not let you go, dear friends, without singing one verse that I think will express the feeling of each one of us:

Let me among Your saints be found
Whenever the archangel's trump will sound,
To see Your smiling face.

Then loudest of the crowd I'll sing,
While heaven's resounding mansions ring
With shouts of sovereign grace.

FOR FURTHER THOUGHT

1. *Compare Jude 24 with 2 Timothy 1:12. Who is able to keep us in the faith?*
2. *Compare Jude 24 with Colossians 2:10. What is a believer's condition before God?*
3. *Compare Jude 25 with 1 Thessalonians 2:19. What emotion will we feel in the presence of the Lord at His coming?*

CONSECRATION TO GOD ILLUSTRATED BY ABRAHAM'S CIRCUMCISION

When Abram was ninety-nine years old,
the LORD appeared to Abram, and said to him, "I am Almighty God;
walk before Me and be blameless. And I will make My covenant
between Me and you, and will multiply you exceedingly.
GENESIS 17:1–2

W E commenced our exposition of the life of Abram with his calling, when he was brought out of Ur of the Chaldeans and separated to the Lord in Canaan. We then passed on to his justification, when he believed God and it was accounted to him for righteousness. And now you will bear with us if we continue in the same subject to a further stage and attempt to describe the fuller development of Abram's vital godliness in the open and clear revelation of his consecration to God.

In the chapter before us, we see his sanctification to the Lord, his ordination to service and purification as a vessel fitted for the master's use. All the called are justified, and all the justified are, by a work of the Holy Spirit, sanctified and made meet to be afterward glorified with Christ Jesus. Let me remind you of the order in which these blessings come. If we should speak of sanctification or consecration, it is not as a *first* thing, but as an elevation to be reached only by preceding stepping-stones.

In vain do men pretend to be consecrated to God before they are called of God's Spirit. Such have yet to be taught that no strength of nature can suffice to serve the Lord aright. They must learn, you must be born again, for assuredly until men are brought into *spiritual* life by effectual calling of the Holy Spirit, all their talk about serving God may be answered in the words of Joshua, "Ye cannot serve the LORD" (24:19 KJV). I speak of *consecration*, but it is not as a *first* thing, nor even as a *second* thing, for a man must be justified by faith in Christ Jesus or he will not possess the divine grace that is the root of all true sanctity.

Sanctification grows out of faith in Jesus Christ. Remember, holiness is a flower, not a root. It is not sanctification that saves but salvation that *sanctifies*. A man is not saved by his holiness. He becomes holy because he is already saved. Being justified by faith, and having peace with God, he walks no longer after the flesh but after the Spirit. And in the power of the blessing that he has received by grace, he dedicates himself to the service of his gracious God. Note, then, the due order of heavenly benefits: Consecration to God *follows* calling and justification.

Recalling your minds to Abram's history let me remind you that thirteen years had elapsed after the time in which God had said that Abram's faith was counted to him for righteousness. And those thirteen years, as far as we can gather from scripture, were not at all so full of brave faith and noble deeds as we might have expected them to be. How sure is that truth that the best of men are but men at the best, for which every man who had accepted God's promise and had not staggered at it through unbelief, within a few months afterward, or perhaps a few days, was taken with a fit of unbelief! And at the instigation of his wife, Abram adopted means that were not justifiable in order that he might obtain the promised heir.

A man must be justified by faith in Christ Jesus or he will not possess the divine grace that is the root of all true sanctity.

He used means that may not be so vicious to him as they would be in men of modern times, but that were suggested by an unbelieving policy and were fraught with evil. He takes Hagar to wife. He could not leave it to God to give him the promised seed. He could not leave it with God to fulfill His promise in His own time but justifies himself in turning aside from the narrow path of faith to accomplish, by doubtful methods, the end that God Himself had promised and undertaken to accomplish! How shorn of splendor is Abram seen when we read, "And Abram heeded the voice of Sarai" (Gen. 16:2). That business of Hagar is to the patriarch's deep discredit and reflects no honor at all upon either him or his faith.

Look at the consequences of his unbelieving! Misery soon followed. Hagar despises her mistress. Sarai throws all the blame on her husband. The poor bondwoman is so harshly dealt with that she flees from the household. How much of real cruelty may be meant by the term "dealing harshly," I cannot tell, but one marvels that such a man as Abram allowed one who had been brought into such a relationship with him to be heedlessly chased from his house while in a condition requiring care and kindness!

We admire the truthfulness of the Holy Spirit that He has been pleased to record the faults of the saints without extenuating them. Biographies of good men in scripture are written with unflinching integrity—their evil recorded as well as their good. These faults are not written that we may say, "Abraham did so-and-so; therefore we may do it." No, brothers and sisters, the lives of these good men are *warnings* to us as well as examples, and we are to judge them as we should judge ourselves—by the laws of right and wrong.

Abram did wrong both in taking Hagar to wife and in allowing her to be so badly used. In the years that followed, the child of the bondwoman mocked the child of the free woman, and an expulsion of both mother and child was necessary. There was deep sorrow in Abram's heart, a bitterness not to be told. Polygamy, though tolerated under the Old Testament, was *never* approved. It was only endured because of the hardness of men's hearts. It is evil, only evil, and that continually! In the family relationship there can be opened no more abundant and fruitful source of misery to the sons of men than lack of chastity to the marriage bond made with one wife, disguise that unchastity by what name you will.

All these thirteen years, so far as scripture informs us, Abram had not a single visit from his God. We do not find any record of his either doing anything memorable or having so much as a single audience with the Most High. Learn from this that if we once forsake the track of simple faith, once cease to walk according to the purity that faith approves, we strew our path with thorns, cause God to withhold the light of His countenance from us, and pierce ourselves through with many sorrows.

But mark, beloved, the exceeding grace of God: The way to recover Abram from his backsliding was that the Lord should appear to him, and consequently, we read in our text that at ninety-nine years of age, Abram was favored with a further visit from the Most High. This brings to my remembrance the words in the book of Revelation concerning the church in Laodicea: "You are neither cold nor hot. I could wish you were cold or hot. So then, because you are lukewarm, and neither cold nor hot, I will vomit you out of My mouth" (Rev. 3:15–16)—a very solemn declaration. But what follows? "Behold, I stand at the door and knock. If anyone hears My voice and opens the door, I will come in to him and dine with him, and he with Me" (Rev. 3:20). That means just this: For recovery out of a horrible state of languishing and lukewarmness there is no remedy but the coming of Jesus Christ to the soul in near and dear communion!

Truly it was so with Abram. The Lord would bring him out of his state of distrust and distance into one of high dignity and sanctity, and He would do it by manifesting Himself to Abram, for the Lord talked with him.

> *Midst darkest shades, if He appears,*
> *My dawning is begun.*
> *He is my soul's bright morning star,*
> *And He my rising sun.*

Breathe a prayer, my brothers and sisters: "Lord, reveal yourself to my poor backsliding, languishing spirit. Revive me, O Lord, for one smile from You can make my wilderness blossom as the rose." On the occasion of this gracious manifestation, God was pleased to do for Abram what I think is to us an admirable and instructive illustration of the consecration of our redeemed spirits entirely to His service.

I shall, this morning, as God may help me, first lead you to observe *the model of the consecrated life*, second, *the nature of the higher life*, and third, *its results*.

I. First, then, let us notice in the words of God to Abram *the model of the sanctified or consecrated life*. Here it is: "I am the Almighty God; walk before me, and be thou perfect" (Gen. 17:1 KJV). For a man to be thoroughly sanctified to the master's service, he must first realize the almightiness, all-sufficiency, and glory of God. Brethren, the God whom we serve fills all things and has all power and all riches. If we think little of Him, we will render little trust to Him and consequently little obedience. But if we have grand conceptions of the glory of God, we will learn to confide in Him most thoroughly. We will receive mercies from Him most plentifully, and we will be moved to serve Him most consistently.

Sin, at the bottom of it, very frequently has its origin in low thoughts of God. Take Abram's sin. He could not see how God could make him the father of many nations when Sarai was old and barren, hence his error with Hagar. But if he had remembered what God now brings to his recollection, that God is El Shaddai, the All-Sufficient One, he would have said, "No, I will remain true to Sarai, for God can effect His own purposes without my taking tortuous means to accomplish them. He is all-sufficient in Himself and not dependent upon creature strength. I will patiently hope and quietly wait to see the fulfillment of the master's promises."

Now, as it was with Abram, so it is with you, my brothers and sisters. When a man is in business difficulties, if he believes that God is all-sufficient to carry him through them, he will not practice any of the common tricks of trade nor degenerate into that shiftiness that is so usual among commercial men. If a man believes, being poor, that God is sufficient portion for him, he will not grow envious of the rich or discontented with his condition. The man who feels that God is an all-sufficient portion for his spirit will not look for pleasure in the pursuits of vanity. He will not go with the giddy multitude after their vain mirth. "No," says he, "God has appeared to me as God all-sufficient for my comfort and my joy. I am content so long as God is mine. Let others drink from broken cisterns if they will. I dwell by the overflowing fountain and am perfectly content."

> *When a man is in business difficulties, if he believes that God is all-sufficient to carry him through them, he will not practice any of the common tricks of trade nor degenerate into that shiftiness that is so usual among commercial men.*

O beloved, what glorious names our Lord deservedly wears! Whichever of His names you choose to dwell upon for a moment, what a mine of wealth and meaning it opens up to you! Here is this name: *El Shaddai. El,* that is, "the strong one," for infinite power dwells in Jehovah. How readily may we who are weak become mighty if we draw upon Him! And then, *Shaddai,* "the unchangeable and the invincible." What a God we have, then, who knows no variableness, neither shadow of turning, against whom none can stand! *El,* strong. *Shaddai,* unchangeable in His strength, therefore always strong in every time of need, ready to defend His people and able to preserve them from all their foes.

Come, Christian, with such a God as this, why need you abase yourself to win the good word of the wicked man? Why gad about to find earthly pleasures where the roses are always mixed with thorns? Why need you to put your confidence in gold and silver or in the strength of your body or in anything that is beneath the moon? You have El Shaddai to be yours! Your power to be holy will much depend upon your grasping with all the intensity of your faith the cheering fact that this God is your God forever and ever! He is your daily portion, your all-sufficient consolation. You dare not, cannot, will not wander into the ways of sin when you know that such a God is your shepherd and guide!

Following up this model of the consecrated life, notice the next words, "Walk before me." This is the style of life that characterizes true holiness. It is a walking before God. Ah! Brethren, Abram had walked before Sarai; he had paid undue respect to her views and wishes. He had walked, too, in the sight of his own eyes and the inclinations of his own heart when he was allied to Hagar. But now the Lord gently rebukes him with the exhortation, "Walk before me." It is remarkable that on the former divine visit to the patriarch, the Lord's message was, "Fear not."

Abram was then, as it were, but a child in spiritual things, and the Lord gave him comfort, for he needed it. He is now grown into a man, and the exhortation is practical and full of activity: a walk. The Christian man is to put out and use the strength and grace that he has *received*. The gist of the exhortation lies in the last words, "*Walk before me,*" by which I understand a habitual sense of the presence of God, or doing the right thing and shunning the wrong out of respect to the will of God; a consideration of God in all actions, public and private. Brethren, I deeply regret when I see Christian men, even in religious societies, in their calculations leaving out the greatest item in the whole calculation, namely, the divine element, the divine power and faithfulness.

Of the most of mankind I may say, without being censorious, that if there were no God, their course of action would not be different from what it is, for they do not feel themselves either restrained or constrained by any sense of the divine presence. "The transgression of the wicked saith within my heart, that there is no fear of God before his eyes" (Ps. 36:1 KJV). But this is the mark of the truly sanctified man of God: that he lives in every place as standing in the presence chamber of the divine majesty. He acts as knowing that the eyes that never sleep are always fixed on him. His heart's desire is that he may never do the wrong thing, not because he has respect to worldly greatness, and may never forget the right thing, not because he is in evil company, but because God, being everywhere, he is always in company where it would be impudent rebellion to sin. The saint feels that he must not and dare not transgress, because he is before the very face of God! This is the model of the sanctified character: for a man to realize what the Lord is, and then to act as in the immediate presence of a holy and jealous God.

The next words are "and be thou perfect." Brethren, does this mean *absolute* perfection? I will not controvert the belief of some that we may be absolutely perfect on earth. Freely do I admit that the model of sanctification is perfection. It was inconsistent with the character of God for Him to give us any other than a perfect command and a perfect standard. No law but that of *absolute* perfection could come from a perfect God to give us a model. God sets before His servants no rule of "Be as good as you can," but this: "Therefore you shall be perfect, just as your Father in heaven is perfect" (Matt. 5:48).

Has any man ever attained to it? Truly we have not, but for all that, every Christian man aims at it. I would far rather my child had a perfect copy to write by, though he might never write equal to it, than that he should have an imperfect copy set before him, because then he would never make a good writer at all. Our heavenly Father has given us the perfect image of Christ to be our example! He has given His perfect law to be our rule, and it is for us to aim at this perfection in the power of the Holy Spirit, and, like Abram, to fall upon our faces in shame and confusion of face when we remember how far we have come short of it. Perfection is what we wish for, pant after, and will at the last obtain.

We do not want to have the law toned down to our weakness. Blessed be God, we delight in the perfection of that law. We say with Paul, "The law is holy, and the commandment holy and just and good. . .but I am carnal, sold under sin" (Rom. 7:12, 14). The will of God is that to which we would be conformed, and if we who are believers had but one wish, and it could be granted to us at once, it should be this: to make us perfect in every good work to do His will, working in us that which is well-pleasing in His sight.

However, the word, *perfect*, as I have said, bears commonly the meaning of "upright," or "sincere." No double-dealing must the Christian man have. No playing fast and loose with God or man. No hypocritical professions or false principles. He must be as transparent as glass. He must be a man in whom there is no guile. He must be a man who has cast aside deceit in every shape, who hates and loathes it. He must walk before God, who sees all things, with absolute sincerity, earnestly desiring in all things, both great and small, to commend himself to the conscience of others as in the sight of the Most High.

Brothers and sisters, here is the model of the consecrated life! Do you long to attain it? I am sure every soul that is moved by God's grace does. But if your feeling about it is like mine, it will be just like that of Abram in the text, "Abram fell on his face" (Gen. 17:3). For oh, how far short we have come of this! We have not always thought of God as all-sufficient. We have been unbelieving. We have doubted Him here and doubted Him there. We have not gone to work in this world as if we believed the promise, "I will not leave you nor forsake you" (Josh. 1:5). We have not been satisfied to suffer or to be poor, and we have not been content to do His will without asking questions.

Brethren, we have not always walked before the Lord! If one may speak for the rest, we do not always feel the presence of God as a check to us. There are angry words, perhaps, at the table. There is wrongdoing in the place of business. There are carelessness, worldliness, pride, and I know not what beside of evil to mar the day's labor. And when we come back at night we have to confess, "I have gone astray like a lost sheep. I have forgotten my Shepherd's presence. I have not always spoken and acted as if I felt that You were always looking upon me."

> No double-dealing must the Christian man have. No playing fast and loose with God or man. No hypocritical professions or false principles. He must be as transparent as glass.

Thus it has come to pass that we have not been perfect. I feel ready to laugh, not the laugh of Abram, but that of thorough ridicule when I hear people talk about their being absolutely perfect. They must be of very different flesh and blood from us, or rather they must be great fools full of conceit and utterly ignorant of themselves, for if they did but look at a single action, they would find specks in it. And if they examined but one single day, they would perceive something in which they fell short if there were nothing in which they had transgressed.

You see your model, brethren. Study it in the life of Christ and then press forward to it with the zeal of the apostle who said, "Not that I have already attained, or am already perfected; but I press on, that I may lay hold of that for which Christ Jesus has also laid hold of me. Brethren, I do not count myself to have apprehended; but one thing I do, forgetting those things which are behind and reaching forward to those things which are ahead, I press toward the goal for the prize of the upward call of God in Christ Jesus" (Phil. 3:12–14).

II. Second, *the nature of his consecration* as illustrated in this chapter. On each point briefly: Genuine spiritual consecration begins with communion with God. Note the third verse: "Abram fell on his face, and God talked with him." By looking at Christ Jesus, His image is photographed upon our mind, and we are changed from glory to glory, as by the presence of the Lord. Distance from God's presence always means *sin*. Holy familiarity with God engenders holiness. The more you think of God, the more you meditate on His works, the more you praise Him, the more you pray to Him, the more constantly you talk with Him and He with you by the Holy Spirit, the more surely are you on the road to thorough consecration to His cause!

The next point in the nature of this consecration is that it is fostered by enlarged views of the covenant of grace. Read on: "As for me, behold, my covenant is with thee, and thou shalt be a father of many nations" (Gen. 17:4 KJV). This is said to help Abram to walk before God and to be perfect. From that we conclude that to grow in sanctification a man should increase in knowledge and also in the tenacity of the faith that grasps the covenant that God has made with Christ for His people that is ordered in all things and sure.

With your Bibles open, notice attentively that Abram was refreshed as to his own personal interest in the covenant. Note the second personal pronoun, how it is repeated. Take the sixth verse, "I will make thee exceeding fruitful, and I will make nations of thee, and kings shall come out of thee. . . . And I will give unto thee, and to thy seed after thee, the land wherein thou art a stranger, all the land of Canaan, for an everlasting possession; and I will be their God" (17:6, 8 KJV).

Thus Abram has the covenant brought home to himself. He is made to feel that he has a part and a lot therein. If you are ever to be sanctified to God's service, you must get a full assurance of your interest in all the covenant provisions! Doubts are like wild boars of the forest that tear up the flowers of sanctification in the garden of the heart. But when you have in your soul a God-given *assurance* of your interest in the precious blood of Jesus Christ, then will the foxes that spoil the vines be hunted to death and your tender grapes will give a good smell. Cry to God, beloved brothers and sisters, for strong faith to "read your title clear to mansions in the skies." Great holiness must spring from great faith! Faith is the root and obedience the branch, and if the root decays, the branch cannot flourish.

Ask to know that Christ is yours, and that you are His, for here you will find a fountain to water your consecration and make it yield fruit to Christ's service. Some professors act as if this were not the case. They foment their doubts and fears in order to perfect holiness. I have known Christians, when they are conscious that they have not lived as they ought to live, begin to doubt their interest in Christ, and, as they say, humble themselves in order to reach after fuller sanctification of life. That is to say, they starve themselves in order to grow strong! They throw their gold out of the window in order to become rich! They pull up the very foundation of their house to make it stand secure!

Beloved believer, sinner as you are, backslider as you are, believe in Jesus. Let not a sense of sin weaken your faith in Him. He died for *sinners*. "In due time Christ died for the ungodly" (Rom. 5:6). Cling to that cross. The more furious the storm the more need of the life buoy. Never leave it, but make your hold firmer! Confide alone in the virtue of that precious blood, for thus only will you slay your sins and advance in holiness. If you say within your heart, "Jesus cannot save such a one as I am. If I had marks and evidences of being God's child, I could then trust in the reward," you have cast away your shield, and the darts of the tempter will wound you terribly!

Cling to Jesus even when it is a question of whether you have a grain of divine grace in your hearts! Believe that He died for you, not because you are consecrated or sanctified, but died for you as *sinners* and saves you as *sinners*. Never lose your simple trust in the Crucified, for only by the blood of the Lamb can you overcome sin and be made fit for the Lord's work.

While reading these words, note how this covenant is revealed to Abram peculiarly as a work of divine power. Note the run of the passage, "I will make my covenant between Me and you." "I will make you exceedingly fruitful." "I will establish My covenant." "I will give to you." "I will be your God," and so on. Oh, those glorious "wills." Brethren, you cannot serve the

Lord with a perfect heart until first your faith gets a grip of the divine "will." If my salvation rests upon this poor, puny arm, upon my resolves, my integrity, and my faithfulness, it is shipwrecked forever!

But if my eternal salvation rests upon the great arm that bears up the universe, if my soul's safety is altogether in the hands that wheel the stars along, then blessed be His name, it is safe and well. And now, out of love to such a Savior, I will serve Him with all my heart! I will spend and be spent for Him who has thus graciously undertaken for me. Mark this, brothers and sisters. Be very clear about it, and ask to have the divine working made apparent to your soul, for that will help you to be consecrated to God.

> *A*sk to know that Christ is yours, and that you are His, for here you will find a fountain to water your consecration and make it yield fruit to Christ's service.

Further, Abraham had a view of the covenant in its everlastingness. I do not remember that the word *everlasting* had been used before in reference to that covenant, but in this chapter we have it over and over again. "I will establish my covenant for an everlasting covenant" (17:7, 13, 19). Here is one of those grand truths of God that many of the babes in grace have not as yet learned—namely, that the blessings of grace are not given today to be taken back tomorrow, but are *eternal* blessings. The salvation that is in Christ Jesus is not a salvation that will belong to us for a few hours while we are faithful to it and will then be taken away so that we will be left to perish. God forbid! "God is not a man, that He should lie, nor a son of man, that He should repent" (Num. 23:19). "I am the LORD," says He, "I do not change; therefore you are not consumed, O sons of Jacob" (Mal. 3:6).

When we put ourselves into the hands of Christ, we do not confide in a Savior who might suffer us to be destroyed, but we rest in one who has said, "I give them eternal life, and they shall never perish; neither shall anyone snatch them out of My hand" (John 10:28). Instead of the doctrine of the security of the saints leading to negligence of life, you will find that, on the contrary, where it is thoroughly well received in the heart by the power of the Holy Spirit, it begets such a holy confidence in God, such a flaming gratitude to Him, that it is one of the best incentives to consecration! Treasure up these thoughts, dear brothers and sisters, and if you would grow in divine grace and in conformity to Christ, endeavor to perceive your personal interest in the covenant, the divine power that guarantees its fulfillment, and the everlastingness of its character.

In considering the nature of this consecration, I would observe, next, that they who are consecrated to God are regarded as new men. The new manhood is indicated by the change of name. He is called no longer Abram, but Abraham, and his wife is no longer Sarai, but Sarah. You, beloved, are new creatures in Christ Jesus. The root and source of all consecration to God lies in *regeneration*. We are born again. A new and incorruptible seed is placed within us that lives and abides forever. The name of Christ is named upon us. We are no longer called sinners and unjust, but we become the children of God by faith that is in Christ Jesus.

Note further that the nature of this consecration was set forth to Abraham by the rite of *circumcision*. It would not be at all fitting or decorous for us to enter into any detail as to that mysterious rite, but it will suffice to say that the rite of circumcision signified the taking away of the filthiness of the flesh. We have the apostle Paul's own interpretation of circumcision in the verses that we read just now in his epistle to the Colossians. Circumcision indicated to the seed of Abraham that there was a defilement of the flesh in man that must forever be taken away or man would remain impure and out of covenant with God.

> *L*et me urge every believer here to see to it that in his own soul he realizes the spiritual meaning both of circumcision and baptism, and then consider the outward rites, for the thing signified is vastly more important than the sign.

Now, beloved, there must be, in order to secure our sanctification to Christ, a giving up, a painful relinquishing of things as dear to us as right eyes and right hands. There must be a denying of the flesh with its affections and lusts. We must mortify our members. There must be self-denial if we are to enter into the service of God. The Holy Spirit must pass sentence of death and cutting away upon the passions and tendencies of corrupt humanity. Much must perish that nature would cherish, but die it must because divine grace abhors it. Notice, with regard to circumcision, that it was peremptorily ordained that it should be practiced on every male of the race of Abraham, and if it were neglected, death followed. So, the giving up of sin, the giving up of the body, of the filth of the flesh, is necessary to every believer. Without holiness, no man will see the Lord.

Even the babe in Christ is as much to see death written upon the body of the filth of the flesh as a man who, like Abraham, has reached advanced years and come to maturity in spiritual things. There is no distinction, here, between the one and the other. Without holiness no man will see the Lord (Heb. 12:14). And where a supposed grace does not take away from us a love of sin, it is not the grace of God at all, but the presumptuous conceit of our own vain natures. It is often said that the ordinance of baptism is analogous to the ordinance of circumcision. I will not controvert that point, although the statement may be questioned.

But supposing it to be, let me urge every believer here to see to it that in his own soul he realizes the spiritual meaning both of circumcision and baptism, and then consider the outward rites, for the thing *signified* is vastly more important than the sign. Baptism sets forth far more than circumcision! Circumcision is putting away of the filth of the flesh, but baptism is the burial of the flesh altogether! Baptism does not say, "Here is something to be taken away," but *everything is dead* and must be buried with Christ in His tomb, and the man must rise anew with Christ. Baptism teaches us that by death we pass into the new life. As Noah's ark, passing through the death of the old world, emerged into a new world, even so, by a like figure, baptism sets forth our salvation by the resurrection of Christ, a baptism of which Peter says, it is "not the putting away of the filth of the flesh, but the answer of a good conscience toward God" (1 Pet. 3:21 KJV).

In baptism the man avows to himself and others that he comes by death into newness of life according to the words of the Holy Spirit, "Buried with him in baptism, wherein also ye are risen with him through the faith of the operation of God, who hath raised him from the dead" (Col. 2:12 KJV). The most valuable point is the *spiritual* meaning, and on that we experience what it is to be dead to the world, to be dead and buried with Christ and then to be raised with Him! Still, brethren, Abraham was not allowed to say, "If I get the *spiritual* meaning, I can do without the outward rite." He might have objected to that rite on a thousand grounds a great deal more strongly than any that the hesitating have urged against baptism, but he first accepted the *rite*, as well as the thing that it intended, and straightaway was circumcised.

And so I exhort you, brothers and sisters, to be obedient to the precept upon baptism, as well as attentive to the truth of God that it signifies. If you are indeed buried with Christ and risen with Him, despise not the outward and instructive sign by which this is set forth.

"Well," says one, "a difficulty suggests itself as to your views," for an argument is often drawn from this chapter, "that inasmuch as Abraham must circumcise all his seed, we ought to baptize all our children." Now, observe the *type* and interpret it not according to *prejudice*, but according to scripture. In the *type* the seed of Abraham are circumcised. You draw the inference that all typified by the seed of Abraham ought to be baptized, and I do not quibble at the conclusion. But I ask you, who are the true seed of Abraham? Paul answers in Romans 9:8—"They which are the children of the flesh, these are not the children of God: but the children of the promise are counted for the seed" (KJV).

As many as *believe* in the Lord Jesus Christ, whether they are Jews or Gentiles, are Abraham's seed. Whether eight days old in divine grace, or more or less, every one of Abraham's seed has a right to baptism. But I deny that the unregenerate, whether children or adults, are of the spiritual seed of Abraham. The Lord will, we trust, call many of them by His grace, but as yet they are "children of wrath, even as others" (Eph. 2:3 KJV). At such time as the Spirit of God will sow the good seed in their hearts, they are of Abraham's believing seed, but they are not so while they live in ungodliness and unbelief, or are as yet incapable of faith or repentance.

The answering person in *type* to the seed of Abraham is, by the confession of everybody, the believer. And the believer ought, seeing he is buried with Christ *spiritually*, to prove that fact by his *public* baptism in water, according to the Savior's own precept and example. "Thus," said Christ, "it is fitting for us to fulfill all righteousness" (Matt. 3:15), as He went down to the river Jordan. At the Jordan, was He sprinkled? Why go down to a river to be *sprinkled*? Why went He down into the water to be *sprinkled*? "Us." Did He mean babes? Was He a babe? Was not He, when He said "us," speaking of the faithful who are in Him? "Thus it is fitting for us to fulfill all righteousness." That is, all His saints.

But how does baptism fulfill all righteousness? Typically, thus: It is the picture of the whole work of Christ. There is His immersion in suffering. There is His death and burial. There is His coming up out of the water representing His resurrection. His coming up the banks of Jordan represents His ascension. It is a typical representation of how He fulfilled all righteousness and how the saints fulfilled it in Him.

But, brothers and sisters, I did not intend to go so far into the outward sign, because my soul's deepest desire is this: As Abraham, by the outward sign, was taught that there was a putting away of the filth of flesh that must be or death must follow, so are we taught by baptism that there is an actual death to the world and a resurrection with Christ that must be to every believer, however old or however young—or he has no part or lot in the matter of consecration to God or, indeed, in salvation itself!

III. I have a third head, but my time is gone, and therefore just these hints: *the results of such a consecration.* Immediately after God's appearing to Abraham, his consecration was manifest. First, in his prayer for his family: "Oh, that Ishmael might live before You!" (Gen. 17:18). Men of God, if you are indeed the Lord's and feel that you are His, begin now to intercede for all who belong to you. Never be satisfied unless they are saved, too! And if you have a son, an Ishmael, concerning whom you have many fears and much anxiety; as you are saved yourself, never cease to groan out that cry, "Oh, that Ishmael might live before you!"

The next result of Abraham's consecration was that he was most hospitable to his fellow men. Look at the next chapter. He sits at the tent door and three men come to him. The Christian is the best servant of humanity in a spiritual sense. I mean that for his master's sake he endeavors to do good to the sons of men. He is, of all men, the first to feed the hungry and to clothe the naked, and as much as lies in him to do good to all men, especially to such as are of the household of faith. The third result was that Abraham entertained the Lord Himself, for among those three angels who came to his house was the King of kings, the Infinite One!

Every believer who serves his God does, as it were, give refreshment to the divine mind. I mean this: God took an infinite delight in the work of His dear Son. He said, "This is my beloved Son, in whom I am well pleased" (Matt. 3:17), and He takes a delight, also, in the holiness of all His people. Jesus sees the travail of His soul and is satisfied by the works of the faithful. And you, brothers and sisters, as Abraham entertained the Lord, entertain the Lord Jesus with your patience and your faith—with your love and your zeal when you are thoroughly consecrated to Him. Once more, Abraham became the great *intercessor* for others.

The next chapter is full of his pleadings for Sodom. He had not been able to plead before, but after circumcision, after consecration, he becomes the king's remembrancer. He is installed into the office of a priest, and he stands there crying, "Will you not save the city? Will you destroy the righteous with the wicked?" O beloved, if we do but become consecrated to God, thoroughly so, as I have attempted feebly to describe, we will become mighty with God in our pleadings. I believe one holy man is a greater blessing to a nation than a whole regiment of soldiers. Did not they fear, more, the prayers of John Knox than the arms of ten thousand men?

A man who lives habitually near to God is like a great cloud forever dropping with fertilizing showers. This is the man who can say, "The earth and all its inhabitants are dissolved; I set up its pillars firmly" (Ps. 75:3). France would never have seen such a bloody revolution if there had been men of prayer to preserve her. England, amid the commotions that make her rock to and fro, is held fast because prayer is put up incessantly by the faithful. The flag of old England is nailed to her mast, not by the hands of her sailors, but by the prayers of the people of God! These, as they intercede day and night, and as they go about their spiritual ministry, these are they for whom God spares nations, for whom He permits the earth to still exist!

And when their time is over and they are taken away, the salt being taken from the earth, then will the elements dissolve with fervent heat, the earth also, and the works that are therein will be burnt up, but not until He has caught away the saints with Christ into the air will this world pass away. He will spare it for the righteous's sake. Seek after the highest degree of sanctity, my dear brothers and sisters, seek for it, labor for it! And while you rest in faith alone for justification, be not slack concerning growth in divine grace, that the highest attainments are your ambition, and God grant them to you for His Son's sake. Amen.

For Further Thought

1. *In Genesis 17:1, God told Abram to be perfect. In verse 3, what was Abram's response?*
2. *In Philippians 3:12, Paul considers the idea of being perfect. In verses 12–14, what are three things he does in response?*
3. *Romans 6:3 says that we were baptized into Christ's death. According to verse 4, how does that affect our walk before God?*

FAITH VERSUS SIGHT

For we walk by faith, not by sight.
2 CORINTHIANS 5:7

I think the apostle is explaining here how it was he could say that while he was at home in the body, he was absent from the Lord, and the reason this was not the state in which he wished to be forever. Having been possessed and actuated and moved by the principle of faith, he was not content to tabernacle in a body that could only be dwelt in satisfactorily through the influence of the faculty of sight. The apostle, however, mentions here a great general principle: "We walk by *faith*, not by sight." In talking upon this text this evening, we shall, without pretending to go into it fully, speak first of all upon *the posture mentioned*. Then upon *the two principles contrasted*, and finally upon *a certain caution that is here implied*.

I. First, a word or two about *the posture mentioned*. Paul, speaking of believers, says, "We walk by faith, not by sight." Walking is, of course, a posture that implies the possession of life. You can make a dead man sit in a certain position, or even stand in a chosen attitude, but to *walk* necessitates the possession of inward *life*. It becomes with us, therefore, a question in the first place of whether we have the life of God within us.

In the sense the term *walk* is here used, the ungodly man does not walk at all. He hastens after his own lusts, and he treads in the way of the flesh. But in a spiritual sense he is, and always must be, a stranger to walking until God has quickened him. When we see corpses walking along our roads and pass them at eventide in our streets, then will we expect to see Christian feelings, Christian emotions, and Christian character exhibited by unconverted men, but not till then! There must first be an *inward life* before there can be the *outward sign* of it.

Walking is a position that also signifies activity. You would suppose, from the way some Christians deport themselves, that their whole life was spent in meditation. It is a blessed thing to sit "with Mary at the Master's feet." But we walk as well as sit. We do not merely learn, but we practice what we know. We are not simply scholars, but, having been taught as scholars, we go on to show our scholarship by working in the vineyard or wherever else the Master may be pleased to place us. The quietists and mystics are a class of people who have a peculiar attraction for my mind, and I suppose the mention of such a name as that of Madame Guyon, who, among females, stands at the very head of the school, will awaken in many of you many sweet remembrances of times enjoyed in reading her blessed hymns and of her sweet and admirable life.

But, after all, it is not the highest style of Christian living to be a mystic or a quietist. We walk. Some Christians seem as if they always sit, but we walk. You would gather indeed from what others say, that the whole life of a Christian is to be spent in prayer. Prayer, it is true, is the vitality of the secret parts of Christian life, but we are not always on our knees! We are not constantly engaged in seeking blessings from heaven. We do continue in prayer, but we are also engaged in showing forth to others the blessings that we have received and in exhibiting in our daily actions the fruits that we have gathered on the mountaintop of communion with God. We walk, and this implies activity.

> There is a progress to be made in every Christian grace, and he who carefully marks the terms used about Christian graces will discover that there are degrees in all of them.

Oh, I would that some Christians would pay a little attention to their legs instead of paying it all to their heads! When children's heads grow too fast, it is a sign of disease, and they get the rickets or water on the brain. And there are some very sound brethren who seem to me to have got some kind of disease, and when they try to walk, they straightway make a tumble of it because they have paid so much attention to perplexing doctrinal views instead of looking, as they ought to have done, to the practical part of Christianity.

By all means, let us have doctrine! But by all means, let us have precepts, too. By all means, let us have inward experience, but by all means, let us also have outward holiness, without which no man can see the Lord. "We walk." This is more than some can say. They can affirm, "We talk. We think. We experience. We feel." But true Christians can say with the apostle Paul, "We walk." Oh, that we may ever be able to say it, too! Here, then, is the activity of the Christian life.

In the posture of walking, there is also implied *progress*. A man does not walk unless he makes some headway. We are not always practicing the goose step. We are not always lifting our foot and then putting it down in the same place. This may do very well for the beginners in the awkward squad at drill, and I am afraid that a great many of us are still in that squad—but the Christian who has got through his childhood and has grown somewhat makes progress. There are some who will tell you that they do not know that they have made any progress, or, if they do not say this, you can see that they have made none.

They are as bad-tempered as when they first joined the church. They are as changing, as narrow-minded, and as critical, as easily carried about with every wind of doctrine as they were at first. Such persons give some cause for suspicion as to whether they know much about the divine life at all, because they who have the divine life truly in them can say, "We walk." They go from strength to strength. Every one of them appears in Zion before God. They are not satisfied with *being* in the way; they desire also to *walk* in the way. God does not say to us, "This is the way," and then stop. He says, "This is the way, *walk* in it."

We are always to be making advances. We are to be going from faith in its beginnings to faith in its perfections, from faith to assurance, from assurance to full assurance. And from there, we are to go to the full assurance of hope to the full assurance of understanding, always forward, waxing stronger and stronger. There is a progress to be made in every Christian grace, and he who carefully marks the terms used about Christian graces will discover that there are degrees in all of them, while each of them are degrees one above the other. Walking implies progress, and the genuine Christian, when he is in a healthy state, may truthfully say, "We walk."

Walking also implies perseverance. When a man goes along a step or two and then stops or returns, we do not call that walking. The motion of the planets as seen by the eye have been described by the poet as "progressive, retrograde, and standing still." I am afraid there are many people of whom this would be a true description, but the true Christian keeps on. And though there may often appear to be times when he stops and seasons when he goes back, yet the scripture is not broken where it says that "the path of the just is as the shining light, that shineth more and more unto the perfect day" (Prov. 4:18 KJV).

The Christian's motto is "Upward and onward." Not as though he has already attained, either is already perfect, he presses forward to the mark for the prize of his high calling in Christ Jesus. We are not true Christians if we stop or start or turn aside. As an arrow from a bow that is drawn by some mighty archer speeds straightway toward its goal, such is the Christian life as it is and such is it as it always should be. We make progress, and we persevere in so doing.

I think, however, that by the term *walk*, the apostle meant to signify that, in the ordinary and customary actions of life, we are actuated by faith. You know walking is the common way of moving. You do not often talk of a child's walking. You do speak of it, of course, but you generally say, "There are the little ones running about the house." You do not say that they are "walking about the house," because the way of moving with the young is generally running, inasmuch as they have a great deal of extra energy and have not yet got into the wear and tear of life.

You do not find lambs walking at all in the ordinary way that sheep do. Now, it is very easy, in the beginning of the Christian life, to run in the ways of the Lord with rejoicing—but running, after all, is not the most manly form of progress—it is not that which can be kept up for long! Running fatigues and tires you—*walking* is that kind of progress in which a man continues hour after hour. And after his night's rest, he rises again to walk on as before until he reaches his goal.

In scripture, we often read of men who, by faith, did great exploits. "By thee I have run through a troop; and by my God have I leaped over a wall" (Ps. 18:29 KJV). Now this is a very great thing to do, and some Christians are always fixing their eyes upon exploits of faith. The apostle Paul cut through troops and did leap over walls, but in this place he speaks of the common actions of life. It is as if he said—"I not only leap walls by faith, but I walk by faith! I not only break through troops by faith, but I go and do my business by faith."

That man has not yet learned the true spirit of Christianity who is always saying, "I can preach a sermon by faith." Yes, sir, but can you make a coat by faith? "I can distribute tracts and visit the district by faith." Can you cook a dinner by faith? I mean this: Can you perform the common actions of the household and the daily duties that fall to your lot in the spirit of faith? This is what the apostle means. He does not speak about running or jumping or fighting, but about walking—and he means to tell you that the ordinary life of a Christian is different from the life of another man—that he has learned to introduce faith into *everything* he does. It was not a bad saying of one who said that he, "did eat and drink and sleep eternal life." We want not a homespun religion, but a religion that was spun in heaven and that will do to wear at home and about the house. "We walk by faith."

> *W*e must wear our piety, not as some holiday garment, but as our everyday dress, and then it is that we get into the spirit of true religion.

The Mohammedan worships his god at the holy hour. The true Christian calls all hours holy and worships always. Some set apart the seventh day of the week and therein do well, but in setting apart *all* the seven days, and *living* to God, and entering into rest throughout them all, we do better still. Our souls should not keep our religion for the tabernacle and the pew and the closet and the open Bible and the bended knee. Our religion must become the *atmosphere* in which we live, the element in which our souls breathe! Our God must dwell in us and we dwell in Him. We must feed upon Christ, not as a special dainty, but as the bread of heaven, and drink of Him, not as a luxury, but as the water of life. We must wear our piety, not as some holiday garment, but as our everyday dress, and then it is that we get into the spirit of true religion.

Summing up all, then, the whole of the Christian life, that is implied in the term *walk*, is here spoken of, and it is influenced by the principle of faith that we are now about to speak.

II. And now, second, in the text we have *two principles contrasted*. There is walking by *faith*, and there is walking by *sight*. The most of men, all men indeed, naturally walk by sight. They have a proverb that says, "Seeing is believing," and they are wise men, for they trust people as far as they can see them, and no further. The world thinks itself uncommonly knowing in always depending upon its own sight.

The highest degree of worldly wisdom seems to be just this: See everything for yourself and do not be taken in. Do not be led by the nose by anybody, but follow your own understanding. This is the text that the world's Solomons always preach from: "self-made men." That is the title of their book! Self-reliance is the name of their principle, and according to the world, the best and grandest thing that a man can do is have faith in himself. Their maxim is "Know things for yourself. Look after the main chance. Make money, make it honestly if you can, and honorably if possible, but if not, make it anyhow, by hook or by crook."

"Take care of number one" is the world's learned dictum.

Now the Christian is the very opposite of this. He says, "I do not care about looking after the things that are seen and are temporal. They are like dissolving views or the scenes from a child's magic lantern. There is nothing in them. They are but phantoms and shadows. The things that are not seen influence me because they are *eternal*. They endure, remain, and abide, and therefore they affect a creature that has learned that it has not mortality alone, but *immortality*, and who, expecting to live forever, therefore seeks for things that will be like his own existence."

Now, since the world thinks itself so very wise for holding everything it can, and thinks the Christian such a great fool for giving up what he can see for what he cannot see, in contradiction to the world's proverb "A bird in the hand is worth two in the bush," let us see where the wisdom of this matter is and where it is not. In the first place, we notice that walking by sight is a very childish thing. Any child can walk by sight, and so can any fool, too. We know how a child feels when she looks at a mountain, and we have all felt the same when we have gone to Switzerland and other places.

I had a friend with me who said of a certain mountain, "I will undertake to be at the top in half an hour." It took us five and a half hours steady toiling, and we did not go slowly either! Of course my friend judged by his *sight*, not being accustomed to mountains, and not knowing that sight is a very different thing when it comes to dealing with different landscapes, not knowing that a judgment that would be pretty accurate in England would be totally wrong in the mountains of Wales and still more erroneous in Switzerland. Not knowing all this, I daresay he would be startled at eventide, expecting to find himself at the top before the sun went down, whereas he would not have reached it till the middle of the night!

A child always judges everything by what he sees. You give him a number of coins. They are all counterfeit, but he is so pleased with them that he does not care about having real sovereigns. He is just as glad to have those he has, for they look quite as good. You offer him sixpence, and when he is yet a youngster, he will give you your sixpence back for a penny because the penny is the larger of the two. In that way, he judges by sight. That, you see, is a childish principle altogether. When a man grows up, he no longer judges so much by sight. He has learned a great many things in this world, and he has discovered that his eyes may be very greatly mistaken at times.

The child says, "How quickly these stars move! How fast the moon hastens through the clouds!" The man says, "No, no. It is the clouds that are moving." The child says that the sun rises in the morning and sets in the evening, and admires its motion. But the man knows that the sun does not move at all and that it is the earth that is moving. He believes this, and thus in a certain degree he has faith, because he cannot see the world move. Hodge once said he would not believe the world moved at all, because he found that his house still stood in the same place, and Hodge proved himself to have been thus only a big child. But it is a very manly thing to believe something that you cannot see. Even in common philosophy it is so.

The children all sat at home in England and in Spain and in France, and they said, "Oh, this is all the world there is." And they had their Mediterranean Sea in the middle of the earth. But there was a man among them who said he did not believe it but thought the world was round, and that there was another half to it.

"You are a fool," they said.

"Fool or not," he replied, "I believe it."

And Columbus stood up, head and shoulders taller than the rest of his fellows, got a few to go with him, and started—a company of fools they were called. They could not see anything!

They sailed on and on and on, for many weary days, and the unbelievers said they had better go back. There were several pieces of seaweed floating about that looked as if they came from some other shore or had been washed down some not far distant river. Columbus did not care much for these seaweeds because he believed, and believed firmly, that there was another half of the globe. And when the land birds came and lighted on his ship, though they gladdened his heart, yet they did not make him believe any the more. And when he saw America, and stood on the strand of the land of gold, he still only had to keep on as he had done. He had walked by faith before, and he could continue in the same course now. When he came back, everybody said, "What a wonderful man is Columbus!" Just fifty, and all the rest were children. He was the only true man among them.

Now the Christian is a man! I mean to say he is a man in the scriptural sense of the term. He has become a full-grown man in Christ Jesus. The worldling says, "This is all the world. Let us eat and drink, for tomorrow we die. Let us make money and spend it and enjoy ourselves, for this is the end of the world." The Christian says, "No, there must be another half to the world! I am sure there must be another land beyond the sea, so I will loose my anchor and turn my helm, and try to find it. I will leave this world to you children and will seek another and a more heavenly one."

> We thank Him that we believed in God and were actuated by a noble principle of faith. Compared with that the world's wisdom is but the folly of the child.

So we sail away, and by and by we see the bits of seaweed. And when at last the angelic messengers come like birds of paradise and light upon the masts of our vessels, we thank God that we were ever enabled, with true manly courage, to loose our anchor, to set out upon our voyage, and to turn our helm toward the sea! We thank Him that we believed in God and were actuated by a noble principle of faith. Compared with that the world's wisdom is but the folly of the child. This, then, is the first thing we have to say about these two principles—that the one is childish while the other is manly.

Again, the one is groveling while the other is noble. I think the world must be pretty well ashamed of itself if it still considers this poor earth to be all that a soul has to live for. I feel as if I could not talk upon the matter. Solomon tried everything there was in this world—riches, power, pleasure—every sort of delicacy and delight he had, beyond the point of satisfaction. And what was his verdict upon it all? "Vanity of vanities, all is vanity" (Eccles. 1:2). A man earning his bread all day long, what is he? Is he better than the donkey that I saw a little while ago at Carisbrook Castle, pumping up water and always going round? What more is he than that?

"Well, but he makes money and acquires houses and land." Yes, and there is only so much more probate tax to be paid when he dies, and I suppose the worms know no difference between a man who died worth three hundred thousand pounds and a poor wretch who was buried by the parish! It does not come to anything more than that! The children go to the seaside with their little wooden spades and build up a pier of sand, but the tide comes and washes it away. And this is just what men do. They build with heavier stuff that gives them more care and not half as much merriment in piling up as the youngsters have in digging up their sand, but the end is just the same!

Only the children live to build again, while these big children, these grovelers, are washed out to sea with all their works and perish everlastingly. You have walked upon the beach, I daresay, when the sea has gone down. I do not mean the beach at Ramsgate where everybody goes, but a long way out in some quiet spot. If you have, you will have seen what hundreds of little mounds there are all over the beach, where the worms have come up and made a number of small heaps. That is all we do, and it is all that the world is, just a big place covered all over with little heaps of dirt that we have all piled up.

But where have we gone? If there is not another world to live for, I must say that this life is a most unutterably empty kind of thing! It is not worthy of a man! But oh, to believe what God tells me: that there is a God; that God became flesh to bear me up to Himself! To believe that I am God's *son*, that I have an immortality within myself that will outlast the stars, that I will one day see His face and sing His praise forever with cherubim and seraphim! Why, there is something here! The man who believes this feels as if he begins to grow! He bursts the poor engrossments of his flesh and expands into something worthy of a man who is made in the image of the Most High!

The principle of seeing everything, and of liking only to get what I can see and touch and handle is the poor instinct of beasts and birds, but the principle of living upon what I *cannot* see and upon something that I can believe is one worthy of a man. As much as man is higher than the beast, so much and yet more a thousandfold is the life of faith superior to that of mere sight and feeling.

Again, there is something exceedingly ignorant about believing only what I can see. What, then, will I believe? Even in common life the man who walks by sight must necessarily be a fool—I say "necessarily," because nine out of ten things in the world that are the most wonderful and potent cannot be seen, at least not by the eyes. A man who will not believe in electricity, well, what can you make of him in these days? Such a man will believe in the vapor that puffs from the steam engine, but since nobody ever did or could see steam, inasmuch as it is an invisible agent, he cannot ever believe in that!

He lives in the midst of a great world, and he cannot account for most things in it because he will not believe in anything beyond what he sees. If he carries this principle out, the marvels of other countries and the wonders of other ages are all shut out from his poor dull mind. And this is most decidedly the case with regard to spiritual things. If you walk only by sight and believe only what you see, what do you believe? You believe that while you are living here, it is a good thing to make the best you can of it. And that then you will die and be buried, and that will be the end of you! What a poor, miserable, ignorant belief this is!

But when you believe in what God reveals and come to walk by faith, how your information expands! Now riddles are all solved, and the inexplicable is understood! Now you begin to comprehend things in a way that you never could have done had you walked only by sight. Now you can understand those trials and troubles that come to you! Now you can understand the complexity of your nature and the conflicts that you feel within you. You never could have done this on the principle of sight, but believing what God says, you have got into a state in which you will be educated and taught till you become wise and able to have fellowship with the only wise God!

Let me say, again, that walking by sight is such a very deceptive way of walking. After all, the eyes do not see anything. It is the *mind* that sees *through* the eyes. The eyes in every man have some sort of defect in them. They need to be educated for a long time before they tell the truth! And even then there are a thousand things about which they do not always speak truly. The man who walks by his eyes will be deceived in many ways. The angler baits his hook and casts his fly upon the water, and the silly fish, which jumps by sight, has the hook in its jaws in a moment. You can evermore, if you will, go from bad to worse in unseen danger if you judge according to the sight of the eyes.

The world is wise enough to say that "honesty is the best policy." The world was not quite itself when it said that, for mostly it is present gain that Satan sets before us, and present pleasure. "Snatch the hour as it passes," says Satan. "These things are sure—you do not know what may come afterward." And so the poor soul is deceived by judging according to what he *thinks* he sees. Whereas the man who has a God to go to and to believe in, is never deceived. The promise to him always stands fast. The person of Christ is always his sure refuge, and God Himself is his perpetual inheritance.

> *Walking by sight is just this: "I believe in myself." Whereas walking by faith is, "I believe in God."*

Let me add, again, that the principle of sight is a very changeable one. You can see well enough, you know, in the day, but what will you do in the night when you cannot see? It is well enough to talk of walking by sight in the light, but what will you do when the darkness comes on? It is very well to talk about living on time present while you are here, but when you go upstairs and lie on your deathbed, what about the principle of living for the present then? When you cannot stay here any longer, when, notwithstanding all the ties that held you to earth, death begins to drag you away and you cry to him, "Stop! I cannot leave wife and children and business just yet!" And when death remorselessly tears you away from all that is dear to you, how about the principle of sight then? It is a strange principle to die with, but let me say, on the other hand, that the principle of faith does best in the dark.

He who walks by faith can walk in the sunlight as well as you can, for he walks with God. He has enlightened eyes, but he can walk in the dark as you cannot, for his light is still shining upon him. He trusts in the unseen and in the invisible, and his soul rejoices when present things are passing away. We will not tarry longer upon this point except to say one thing: namely, that those who walk by sight walk alone. Walking by sight is just this: "I believe in myself." Whereas walking by faith is, "I believe in God." If I walk by sight, I walk by myself. If I walk by faith, then there are two of us, and the second one—ah, how great, how glorious, how mighty is He!

He is the great All-in-All! He is God all-sufficient! Sight goes to war at its own charges and becomes bankrupt and is defeated. Faith goes to war at the charges of the king's exchequer, and there is no fear that faith's bank will ever be broken. Sight builds the house from its own quarry and on its own foundation, but it begins to build and is never able to finish. And what it does build rests on sand and falls. But faith builds on the foundation laid in eternity—in the fair colors of the Savior's blood—in the covenant of grace! It goes to God for every stone to be used in the building and brings forth the top-stone with shouts of "Grace, divine grace to it."

Beloved, when you say, "I will do so-and-so," you may be very proud. But when you can say, "God will do so-and-so, and I believe it," then you will be humble and yet you may glory and boast as much as you will because there are two of you together. It is not the sword of Gideon, but "the sword of the LORD and of Gideon" (Judg. 7:18), and Jehovah cannot be defeated. "The life that I live I live not, but Christ hides in me," and this is the grand advantage. In living by sight, you have to get your own wisdom, your own judgment, and your own strength to guide you. And when you get into trouble, you must be your own deliverer, your own comforter, and your own helper, or else you must run to somebody as weak as yourselves who will only send you deeper down into the mire.

But when you walk by faith, should there seem to be a mistake, you have not made it. Should anything seem to go wrong, you did not steer the ship. And if the ship should run aground, you are not answerable and will not be blamed. It is yours to be watchful and careful and to believe that all things work together for the good of those who love God and are the called according to His purpose. But besides this we know that nothing can go wrong while God is in the vessel! Blessed be God, when Christ is on Lake Gennesaret there may come a stormy night, but every vessel gets safely to port, and we can always sing:

Be gone unbelief, my Savior is near,
And for my relief will surely appear.
By faith let me wrestle, and He will perform,
With Christ in the vessel, I smile at the storm.

III. And now, having contrasted the two principles, I am about to close by noticing *the caution implied* in the text. The apostle says positively, "We walk by faith," and then he adds negatively, "not by sight." The caution is

Never mix the two principles. Some of you will not know what I am talking about, but I will try to make you understand it. Some of you are actuated in what you do by something that you can *see*. You can see your children, and you will work for them. You can see money; you will strive for that. You can see such-and-such temporal good; you will seek after that.

But the Christian believes in God, and he lives to God. He lives as if there were a God, but you live as if there were no God. He believes in a hereafter—you say you do, too—but you live as if there were no hereafter, while the Christian lives as if there was one. He believes in sin, and you say you do, yet you never weep about it, while the Christian lives as if sin were a real disease and he could not bear it. You say you believe in Christ the Savior, but you live as if you do not believe in Him. The Christian lives upon his belief that there is a Savior. All that he does is affected and acted upon not by what he sees, but by what he does not see and yet believes! He walks according to that faith.

Now, the thing that neither you nor I can understand is this: How is it that the man who has once learned to walk by faith can be so stupid as ever to mix the two principles together? You may go on a journey by land, or you may go by water, but to try to swim and walk at the same time would be rather stupid. A drunken man tries to walk on both sides of the street at once; there is a sort of intoxication that sometimes seizes upon Christians that makes them also try to walk by two principles. They cannot do it! It is like trying to go due east and due west at the same time. The principles themselves are antagonistic to one another, yet there are some Christians who attempt it.

Shall I show you what I mean by this? You say, "I believe God loves me. I have prospered in business ever since I have been a Christian." Yes, the first part of that is faith, but the second part of it is sight. Suppose you had not prospered in business, what then? Why, according to your way of reasoning, you would have said, "I do not believe that God loves me, for I have not prospered in business since I have been a Christian." So, you see, you would really be walking by *sight*.

Genuine Christian reasoning is this: "I have trusted in the Lord Jesus Christ. He says that as many as receive Him are the sons of God. I have received Him, and I am therefore a son of God. Now, whether my Father kisses me or flogs me, I know that I am His son. I am not going to be guided by my state and condition, but by my faith as to the promise of the Word.

He says that if I have received Christ, I have the privilege of being a child of God. Then, whether I am rich or poor, whether I am sick or healthy, all these are matters of sight. I do not bring them into the calculation. I take the naked Word of God as it stands—that I am God's child. If He slays me, I am His child. If He lets me go to prison, if He should suffer me to rot in a dungeon or to burn at the stake, I am still His child! I do not look upon circumstances as at all affecting my position."

> *Whether my Father kisses me or flogs me, I know that I am His son. I am not going to be guided by my state and condition, but by my faith as to the promise of the Word.*

Oh, beloved, if you once begin calculating your position before God according to your *temporal* circumstances, where will you be? Do not talk any more of believing—you have given it up—and you are really walking by sight. Perhaps many of you do not make precisely this mistake, but there is another way of doing it. "Now," says one, "I have believed in Jesus Christ, but I am afraid I am not saved, for I feel tonight so depressed in spirits and so unhappy."

"Oh," says another, "you need not tell me that I have trusted in Jesus Christ, for I am sure I am saved, because I feel so happy."

Now you are both wrong, as wrong as wrong can be! When you said you trusted in Christ—so far, so good. But when you said you were afraid you were not saved because you were so unhappy, or, on the other hand, that you were sure you were saved because you were so happy—that is walking by sight! You are mixing up two principles that will no more go together than fire and water. If I have believed in Jesus Christ, I may at this moment, through disease of body or some other present temporal affliction, be very heavy in spirit, but I am saved notwithstanding. "He that believes on Him is not condemned."

I may be very troubled. I may see a great deal in myself that may make me distressed—but if I believe, I am not condemned and cannot be. Or, if I have strong faith and am possessed of great joy, this is no proof of my being saved. It is my *believing* that is the proof of that. I do not hang upon my feelings—I rely simply upon Christ! I must learn the difference between feeling and believing, or else I will always be blundering and making mistakes. The Lord sometimes takes you to the mountaintop and you have such sweet communion with Him! And then you say, "My mountain stands firm, I will never be moved."

Ah, poor simpleton, you do not know what you are saying, for in a short time you may go down into the depths and cry, "All thy waves and thy billows are gone over me" (Ps. 42:7 KJV). You think that God has forgotten to be gracious, and you begin to write bitter things against yourself—whereas that is the very time to have faith in God.

> *When we in darkness walk,*
> *Nor feel the heavenly flame,*
> *Then is the time to trust the Lord,*
> *And wait upon His name.*

You think that you will use your candle in the daytime, but candles were made for the night. Faith is not meant for sweet frames and feelings only. It is meant for dark frames and horrible feelings. Do you think that the minister has no changes? If he had no changes, within he would know himself to be a Moabite and not an Israelite, for Moab is settled on his lees!

What, then, is the way to maintain peace when there are changes within the soul? How can we be peaceful when we are sometimes taken up to heaven and are another time cast down? Why, the only way is never to be unduly elated by prosperity without or within and never to be unduly depressed by adversity or by doubts and fears! We must learn to live neither upon things without nor upon things within, but upon things *above*, which are the true food for a newborn spirit. What is your title for heaven, Christian? Every evidence will one day be taken from you except that which is comprised in these three words: "It is written."

The genuine foundation upon which I may rest for salvation is this: "God has said it." It is not "I have *experienced* it," for there will often be times when I will be afraid that my experience is a delusion. But if "God has said it," we can never be afraid! On the oath and covenant of the Most High we must, every one of us, come and build! If we do that, all will be well with us. But this is a work so far above human nature that human nature does not even understand it, and though I have tried to speak very plainly, I am conscious that I have spoken in riddles to many of you. God Himself must open the eyes to understand what living faith means, and then He must give that living faith and perpetuate it, or else, as Israel went back in their hearts to Egypt, so will we go back to the garlic and onions of the things that are seen and have but little of the manna that comes from an unseen heaven.

And now, in closing, I would affectionately bid you take heed of one thing. You must be sure, if you walk by faith, that you walk by the *right* faith. I mean you must be sure that it is faith in Jesus Christ. If you put faith in your dreams, as some of you still do, or in anything you thought you saw when you were walking, or in a voice you thought you heard from the clouds, or in texts of scripture coming to your mind—if you put faith in anything else but Christ—I do not care how good it may be or how bad it may be—you must beware, for such a faith as that will give way. You may have a very strong faith in everything else but Christ and perish!

> *I*f you take that Word as it stands, and rest upon it, and act upon it with all your heart and soul, the worst storm that ever blew will never shake your rock and refuge, nor you, either!

There was an architect who had a plan for building a lighthouse on the Eddystone rock. He was quite satisfied, and as he sat by the fire looking at his plans, he was quite sure that no storm that ever came could shake the building. He applied for the contract to build the lighthouse and did build it—and a very singular-looking place it was. There were a great many flags about it and ornaments, and it looked very promising. Some shook their heads a little, but he was very, very firm and said he should like to be in it himself in the worst wind that ever blew. He was in it at the time he wanted to be, and he was never heard of again, nor was anything more ever seen of his lighthouse. The whole thing was swept away. He was a man of great faith, only it happened to be founded on mistaken principles.

Now sometimes, because there is a way of talking that looks very much like assurance, you may say, "I am not afraid. I never had a doubt or a fear. I know it is all right with my soul. I am not afraid of the test of the Day of Judgment." Well, whether you wish it or not, that test for the labor of your lighthouse will come, and if it should prove that you built it yourself, it will be swept away, and you with it. But if your soul takes God's Word, and reading that Word, believes it and is willing to be taught its inward meaning—if you take that Word as it stands, and rest upon it and act upon it with all your heart and soul, the worst storm that ever blew will never shake your rock and refuge, nor you, either! And you will be safe when earth's old columns bow and all her wheels will go to wreck and confusion.

Rest in the Lord Jehovah! Depend on the blood and righteousness of the Lord Jesus Christ for all that you need. Rest wholly in Him with the whole weight of your soul and spirit, and then there will be no fear that what you will see is God's face with acceptance. May God teach us faith on the right principle, and may we walk by it and not by sight—and then the Lord will give us that reward that is given to those who walk by faith in the living God.

For Further Thought

1. *In Romans 5:1–2, what are two things that we have by faith that people who walk by sight cannot see?*
2. *Hebrews 11:1 describes faith in two ways. What are they?*
3. *Read Galatians 3:22. What gift is given to those who believe, and how do they receive it?*

Forgiveness Made Easy

Forgiving one another, even as God for
Christ's sake hath forgiven you.
Ephesians 4:32 KJV

THE heathen moralists, when they wished to teach virtue, could not point to the example of their gods, for, according to their mythologists, the gods were a compound of every imaginable and, I had almost said, unimaginable vice! Many of the classic deities surpassed the worst of men in their crimes—they were as much greater in iniquity as they were supposed to be superior in power. It is an ill day for a people when their gods are worse than themselves! The blessed purity of our holy faith is conspicuous, not only in its precepts, but in the character of the God whom it reveals. There is no excellence that we can propose, but we can see it brightly shining in the Lord our God! There is no line of conduct in which a believer should excel, but we can point to Christ Jesus our Lord and Master as the pattern of it! In the highest places of the Christian faith, you have the highest virtue, and to God our Father and the Lord Jesus be the highest praise.

We can urge you to the tenderest spirit of forgiveness by pointing to God who, for Christ's sake, has forgiven you. What nobler motive can you require for forgiving one another? With such high examples, brothers and sisters, what manner of people ought we to be? We have sometimes heard of men who were better than their religion, but that is quite impossible with *us*. We can never, in spirit or in act, rise to the sublime elevation of our divine religion. We should constantly be rising above ourselves and above the most gracious of our fellow Christians, and yet above us we would still behold our God and Savior. We may go from strength to strength in thoughts of goodness and duties of piety, but Jesus is higher still, and evermore we must be looking up to Him as we climb the sacred hill of grace.

At this time, we wish to speak a little concerning the duties of love and forgiveness, and here we note, at once, that the apostle sets before us the example of God Himself. Upon that bright example we will spend most of our time, but I hope not quite so much as to forget the practical part that is so much needed in these days by certain unforgiving spirits who nevertheless assume the Christian name. The theme of God's forgiving love is so fascinating that we may linger awhile—and a long while, too—upon that bright example of forgiveness that God has set before us, but from it all I hope we will be gathering grace by which to forgive others even to seventy times seven. We will take the text, phrase by phrase, and so we will obtain the clearest divisions.

I. The first phrase to think about is *"for Christ's sake."* We use these words very often, but probably we have never thought of their force. And even at this time we cannot bring forth the whole of their meaning. Let us touch thereon with thoughtfulness, praying the good Spirit to instruct us. "For Christ's sake." All the good things that God has bestowed upon us have come to us "for Christ's sake." But *especially* the forgiveness of our sins has come "for Christ's sake." This is the plain assertion of the text. What does it mean? It means, surely, first for the sake of the great atonement that Christ has offered.

The great God can, as a just lawgiver and king, readily pass by our offenses because of the expiation for sin that Christ has offered. If sin were merely a personal affront toward God, we have abundant evidence that He would be ready enough to pass it by without exacting vengeance, but it is a great deal more than that. Those who view it as a mere personal affront against God are but very shallow thinkers. Sin is an attack upon the moral government of God. It undermines the foundations of society, and were it permitted to have its way, it would reduce everything to anarchy and even destroy the governing power and ruler himself.

God has a great realm to govern, not merely of men that dwell on the face of the earth, but beneath His sway there are angels, principalities, powers, and untold worlds of intelligent beings! It would certainly be a monstrous thing to suppose that God has made yonder myriads of worlds that we see sparkling in the sky at night without having placed some living creatures in them. It is far more reasonable to suppose that this earth is an altogether insignificant speck in the divine dominion, a mere province in the boundless empire of the King of kings.

Now, this world, having rebelled against God high-handedly, as it has done, unless there were a satisfaction demanded for its rebellion, would be a tolerated assault upon the dominion of the great judge of all and a lowering of His royal influence over all His domain. If sin in man's case were left unpunished, it would soon be known throughout myriads of worlds and, in fact, by ten thousand times ten thousand races of creatures, that they might sin with impunity, because if one race had done so, why not all the rest? This would be a proclamation of universal license to rebel. It would probably be the worst calamity that could happen—that any sin should go unpunished by the supreme judge. Sometimes in a state, unless the lawgiver executes the law against the murderer, life will be in peril and everything will become insecure and, therefore, it becomes mercy to write the death warrant.

So is it with God in reference to this world of sinners. It is His very love as well as His holiness and His justice that, if I may use such a term, compels Him to severity of judgment so that sin cannot and must not be blotted out till atonement has been presented. There must, first of all, be a sacrifice for sin, that, mark you, the great Father, to show His love, supplies, for it is His own Son who is given to die! And so the Father Himself supplies the ransom through His Son, that Son is one with Himself by bonds of essential unity, mysterious but most intense. If God demands the penalty in justice, He Himself supplies it in love. It is a wondrous mystery, this mystery of the way of salvation by an atoning sacrifice, but this much is clear, that God, for Christ's sake, has forgiven us, because satisfaction has been made to the injured honor of the divine government and justice is satisfied.

I want you to consider, for a moment, how readily God may now blot out sin since Christ has died. The blotting out of sin seems hard till we see the cross, and then it appears easy enough. I have looked at sin till it seemed to blind me with its horror and I said to myself, "This damned spot can never be washed out. No fuller's soap can change its hue. Sooner might the Ethiopian change his skin or the leopard his spots. O sin, you deep, eternal evil, what can remove you?" And then I have seen the Son of God dying on the cross and read the anguish of His soul and heard the cries that showed the torment of His spirit when God, His Father, had forsaken Him, and it has seemed to me as if the blotting out of sin were the easiest thing under heaven!

When I have seen Jesus die, I have not been able to understand how any sin could be difficult to remove. Let a man stand on Calvary and look on Him whom he has pierced and believe and accept the atonement made, and it becomes the simplest thing possible that his debt should be discharged now that it is paid, that his freedom should be given now that the ransom is found and that he should be no longer under condemnation, since the guilt that condemned him has been carried away by his great substitute and Lord. It is because of what Jesus Christ has suffered in our place that God, for Christ's sake, has forgiven us.

The second rendering of the text would be this: that God has forgiven us because of the representative character of Christ. It should never be forgotten that we originally fell by a representative. Adam stood for us, and he was our federal head. We did not fall personally at the first, but in our representative. Had he kept the conditions of the covenant, we would have stood through him, but inasmuch as he fell, we fell in him. I pray you do not quibble at the arrangement, because there lies the hope of our race! The angels probably fell individually, one by one, and hence they fell irretrievably and there was no restoring them.

> It is His very love as well as His holiness and His justice that, if I may use such a term, compels Him to severity of judgment so that sin cannot and must not be blotted out till atonement has been presented.

But as we fell in *one* Adam, there remained the possibility of our rising in *another* Adam, and therefore, in the fullness of time, God sent forth His Son Jesus Christ, born of a woman, made under the law to become the second Adam! He undertook to remove our burdens and to fulfill the conditions of our restoration. According to the covenant, He must appear in our nature and that nature, in the fullness of time, He assumed. He must bear the penalty, which He has done in His personal suffering and death. He must obey the law, which He has done to the utmost. And now Christ Jesus, having borne the penalty and fulfilled the law, is Himself justified before God and stands forth before God as the representative of all that are in Him.

God, for Christ's sake, has accepted us in Him, has forgiven us in Him, and looks upon us with infinite love, changeless in Him. This is how all our blessings come to us, in and through Christ Jesus. And if we are indeed in

Him, the Lord does not only *forgive* us our sins, but He bestows upon us the boundless riches of His grace in Him. In fact, He treats us as He would treat His Son. He deals with us as He would deal with Jesus! Oh, how pleasant to think that when the just God looks upon us, it is through the reconciling medium—He views us through the mediator. We sometimes sing a hymn that says, "Him and then the sinner see, look through Jesus' wounds on me," and this is just what the Lord does. He counts us just for the sake of our Savior's atonement and because of His representative character.

> *Remember that our Lord Jesus has been obedient to His Father's will—obedient to death, even to the death of the cross. Therefore God has highly exalted Him and given Him a name that is above every name.*

Now go a little further. When we read, "for Christ's sake," it surely means for the deep love that the Father bears Him. My brothers and sisters, can you guess, even, a little of the love that the Father has toward the only begotten? We cannot pry into the wondrous mystery of the eternal filiation of the Son of God lest we are blinded by excess of light, but this we know, that they are *one* God—Father, Son, and Holy Spirit—and the union that exists between them is intense beyond conception. "The Father loves the Son" was always true and is true now. But how deeply, how intensely He loves the Son, no mind can conceive!

Now, brethren, the Lord will do great things for the sake of a Son whom He loves as He loves Jesus, for in addition to the fact of His eternally loving Him, as being one with Him by nature and essence, there is now the super-added cause of love arising out of what the Lord Jesus has done as the servant of the Father. Remember that our Lord Jesus has been obedient to His Father's will—obedient to death, even to the death of the cross. Therefore God has highly exalted Him and given Him a name that is above every name. One of the sweetest thoughts, to my mind, that I sometimes suck at when I am alone is that God the Father will do anything for Christ. Here is also another piece of a honeycomb: When I can plead Christ's name, I am sure to win my suit because of Him. "For Christ's sake" is a plea that always touches the heart of the great God.

Prove that for you to receive such and such a blessing will glorify Christ, and the Father cannot withhold it, for it is His delight to honor Jesus. We speak after the manner of men, of course, and on such a theme as this we must be careful, but still, we can only speak as men, being only men. It is the joy of the Father to express His love to His Son. Throughout all ages they have had fellowship, one with another. They have always been one in all their designs—they have never differed on any point and cannot differ! And you notice when our Lord says, "Father. . .glorify Your Son" (John 17:1), He is so knit with the Father that He adds, "that Your Son also may glorify You." Their mutual love is inconceivably great. Therefore, brothers and sisters, God will do anything for Jesus.

God will forgive us for Christ's sake. Yes, He has done so in the case of thousands around me. And you, big evil sinner, if you will go to God at this moment and say, "Lord, I cannot ask You to forgive me for my own sake, but do it out of love for Your dear Son," He will do it, for He will do anything for the sake of Jesus. If you are, at this time, conscious of sin so as to despair of yourself, it is well that you should be so, for self-despair is only common sense, since there is nothing in yourself upon which you can rely. But do catch at this hope—it is not a straw, it is a good substantial life buoy: If you can ask forgiveness for the sake of Jesus, God will do anything for Jesus, and so He will do anything for you for His dear sake!

So we read our text once more in the light of a truth of God that grows out of the love of God—namely, that God forgives sin for the sake of glorifying Christ. Christ took the shame that He might magnify His Father, and now His Father delights to magnify Him by blotting out the sin. If you can prove that any gift to you would reflect glory upon Christ, you may depend upon it, you will have it! If there were anything under heaven that would make Christ more illustrious, the Father would not spare it for a moment! If you see that for you to have your sin forgiven would raise the fame of the Savior, go and plead that argument with God and you will surely prevail. Will it not make Christ glad if He saves such a sinner as you are? Then go with this argument in your mouth, "Father, glorify your Son by exalting Him as a glorious Savior in saving me."

I find this often a great lever at a dead lift, to say to the Lord, "Lord, You know the straits I am in. You know how undeserving I am. You know what a poor, undone creature I am before You. But if Your dear Son will help and save me, the very angels will stand and wonder at His mighty grace! And so it will bring glory to Him and, therefore, I entreat You to be gracious to me." You can be certain to prevail if you can plead that it will glorify Christ, and surely you would not wish to have a thing that would not glorify Him! Your prayer will always be prevalent if your heart is in such a state that you are willing to have or *not* to have according as it will honor your Lord. If it will not glorify Christ, be more than content to do without the choicest earthly good. But be you doubly grateful when the gift that is granted tends to bring honor to the ever dear and worshipful name of Jesus. "For Christ's sake." It is a precious phrase. Dwell upon it, and then lay up this sentence in the archives of your memory: The Father will do anything for the sake of Jesus Christ His Son.

II. Second, we pass on to observe what it is that we are told in the text has been done *for* us and *to* us, for Christ's sake. "God for Christ's sake *has forgiven* you." First, notice that He has done this certainly. The apostle does not say he *hopes* so, but he says, "God for Christ's sake has forgiven you." Are you in the number of the forgiven, my dear hearer? Have you believed in the Lord Jesus Christ? Then, as sure as you have believed, God for Christ's sake has forgiven you. Have you put your trust in the atoning sacrifice? Then God for Christ's sake has forgiven you. You have not begun to be a Christian, I hope, with the idea that one day, at some future period, you may obtain forgiveness. No. "God for Christ's sake has forgiven you."

Pardon is not a prize to be run for, but a blessing *received* at the first step of the race. If you have believed in Jesus, your sins are all gone—all gone. All your sins have been erased from the records of the past, never to be mentioned against you forever! The moment a sinner looks to Christ, the burden of his sins rolls from off his shoulders never to return. If Christ has washed you (and He has if you have believed in Him), then you are clean every whit, and before the Lord you stand delivered from every trace of guilt. Pardon is not a matter of *hope*, but a matter of fact. Expectation looks for many a blessing, but *pardon* is a realized favor that faith holds in her hand even now.

If Christ took your load, your load cannot remain on your own back—if Christ paid your debts, then they do not stand in God's books against you. How can they? It stands to reason that if your Substitute has taken your sins and put them away, your sins lay no more on you. God for Christ's sake has forgiven you. Get hold of that grand truth of God and hold it, though all the devils in hell roar at you! Grasp it as with a hand of steel! Grip it as for life—"God for Christ's sake has forgiven me"—and may each one of us be able to say that. We will not feel the divine sweetness and force of the text unless we can make a personal matter of it by the Holy Spirit.

Then notice that God has forgiven us *continuously*. He not only forgave us, at the first, all our sins, but He continues daily to forgive, for the act of forgiveness is a continuous one. I have sometimes heard it said that we were so forgiven when we first believed that there is no need to ask for further forgiveness. I reply, we were so completely forgiven when we first believed that we ought *continually* to ask for the perpetuity of that one far-reaching act, that the Lord may continue to exert toward us that fullness of forgiving grace that absolved us perfectly at the first, that we may continue to walk before Him with a sense of that complete forgiveness, clear and unquestioned.

I know I was forgiven when I first believed in Christ. And I am equally sure of it now. The one absolution continues to ring in my ears like joyous bells that never cease. Pardon once given continues to be given. When, through doubt and anxiety, I was not sure of my pardon, yet it was still true, for he that believes on Him is not condemned, even though he may write bitter things against himself. Beloved friend, catch hold of that and do not let it go! Divine pardon is a continuous act, and this forgiveness on God's part was most free. We did nothing to obtain it by merit, and we brought nothing with that to purchase it. He forgave us for Christ's sake, not for anything that we had done.

True, we did repent and believe, but repentance and faith He gave us, so that He did not forgive us for the sake of them, but purely of His own dear love because He delights in mercy and is never more like Himself than when He passes by transgression, iniquity, and sin. Remember, also, that He forgave us *fully*. It was not here and there a sin that He blotted out, but the whole horrible list and catalog of our offenses He destroyed at once! The substitution of our Lord has finished that matter even to perfection.

> *Because the sinless Savior died,*
> *My sinful soul is counted free,*
> *For God, the just, is satisfied*
> *To look on Him and pardon me.*

All our transgressions are swept away at once, carried off as by a flood and so completely removed from us that no guilty trace of them remains.

They are all gone!

O you believers, think of this, for the "all" is no little thing. It includes sins against a holy God, sins against His loving Son, sins against gospel as well as against law, sins against man as well as against God, sins of the body as well as sins of the mind, sins as numerous as the sands on the seashore and as great as the sea itself, and all are removed from us as far as the east is from the west! All this evil was rolled into one great mass and laid upon Jesus, and having borne it all, He has made an end of it forever. When the Lord forgave us, He forgave us the whole debt. He did not take the bill and say, "I strike out this item and that," but the pen went through it all, writing, "Paid." It was a receipt in full of all demands. Jesus took the handwriting that was against us and nailed it to His cross to show before the entire universe that its power to condemn us had ceased forever. We have in Him a full forgiveness.

> *He not only forgave us, at the first, all our sins, but He continues daily to forgive, for the act of forgiveness is a continuous one.*

And let it be remembered that this forgiveness that God has given us for Christ's sake is an *eternal* forgiveness. He will never rake up our past offenses and impute them a second time. He will not find us on an evil day and say, "I have had great patience with you, but now I will deal with you after your sins." Far from it! He that believes in Jesus has *everlasting life* and will never come into condemnation! Irreversible is the pardon of heaven. "The gifts and calling of God are without repentance" (Rom. 11:29 KJV). He never repents what He has given or forgiven. 'Tis done; 'tis done forever. Jehovah absolves, and the sentence stands fast forever. "There is therefore now no condemnation to those who are in Christ Jesus. . . . Who shall bring a charge against God's elect? It is God who justifies. Who is he who condemns?" (Rom. 8:1, 33–34). Blessed be God for eternal pardon!

And since I could not find a word to finish with but this one, I will use it—He has divinely pardoned us! There is such a truth, reality, and emphasis in the pardon of God as you can never find in the pardon of man. Though a man should forgive all you have done against him, if you have treated him very badly, yet it is more than you could expect that he should quite forget it, but the Lord says, "their sins and their iniquities will I remember no more" (Heb. 8:12 KJV). If a man has played you false, although you have forgiven him, you are not likely to trust him again. It is an old proverb, "Never ride a broken-kneed horse." And it is not a bad proverb, either.

But see how the Lord deals with His people. When Peter was set on his legs again, he was a broken-kneed horse, yet see how gloriously the Lord rode that charger on the day of Pentecost! Did He not go forth conquering and to conquer? The Lord lets bygones be bygones so completely that He trusts pardoned souls with His secrets, for the secret of the Lord is with them that fear Him, and He entrusts some of us with His choicest treasures, for Paul said, "He counted me faithful, putting me into the ministry; who was before a blasphemer, and a persecutor, and injurious" (1 Tim. 1:12–13 KJV). He commits to our keeping that priceless case that encloses the best hope of men, namely, the gospel of Jesus! "We have this treasure in earthen vessels" (2 Cor. 4:7). This shows how perfect is our forgiveness—no, I must say it: How divine is the forgiveness that we have received!

Let us rejoice in that grand promise that comes to us by the mouth of Jeremiah of old, "'In those days and in that time,' says the LORD, 'The iniquity of Israel shall be sought, but there shall be none; and the sins of Judah, but they shall not be found; for I will pardon those whom I preserve'" (Jer. 50:20). Here is annihilation—the *only* annihilation I know of—the absolute annihilation of sin through the pardon that the Lord gives to His people. Let us sing it as though it were a choice hymn: "The iniquity of Israel shall be sought, but there shall be none!"

III. Now, if you have drunk into the spirit of our subject, you will be strengthened to hear what I have to say to you upon a point of practice. "*Forgiving one another*, even as God for Christ's sake has forgiven you." Let me say at the commencement that I do not know of anyone here present who has fallen out with anybody else and, therefore, I will make no personal allusions. If I did know of quarrels and bickering, it is very likely that I should talk about the same. But I do not happen to know of any, and if, therefore, my remarks should come home, I would earnestly beg each one so affected to believe that what I say *is intended* for him or her and to receive it as a pointed, personal message from God.

"Forgiving one another, even as God for Christ's sake has forgiven you."

Now observe how the apostle puts it. Does he say, "forgiving another"? No, that is not the text. If you look at it, it is "forgiving *one* another." One another! Ah, then that means that if you have to forgive today, it is very likely that you will, yourself, need to be forgiven tomorrow, for it is "forgiving one another." It is turn and turn about, a mutual operation, a cooperative service! In fact, it is a joint stock business of mutual forgiveness, and members of Christian churches should take large shares in this concern. "Forgiving one another." You forgive me, and I forgive you; and we forgive them, and they forgive us; and so a circle of unlimited forbearance and love goes round the world!

There is something wrong about me that needs to be forgiven by my brother, but there is also something wrong about my brother that needs to be forgiven by me, and this is what the apostle means—that we are, all of us mutually, to be exercising the sacred art and mystery of forgiving one another. If we always did this, we should not endure those who have a special faculty for spying out faults. There are some who, whatever church they are in, always bring an ill report of it. I have heard this sort of thing from many: "There is no love among Christians at all." I will tell you the character of the gentleman who makes that observation—he is both unloving and unlovely, and so he is out of the track of the pilgrims of love.

Another cries, "There is no sincerity in the world!" That man is a hypocrite—you can be quite sure of that! Judge a bird by its song and a man by his utterance. The censorious measure our corn, but they use their own bushels. You may know very well what a man is by what he says of others. Judging other men by their own judgment of their fellow men is a gauge of character that very seldom will deceive you. Their speech betrays their heart. Show me your tongue, sir! Now I know whether you are sick or well. He who speaks with an ill tongue of his neighbor has an ill heart—rest assured of that. Let us begin our Christian career with the full assurance that we will have a great deal to forgive in other people, but that there will be a great deal *more* to be forgiven in ourselves! And let us set our account upon having to exercise gentleness and needing its exercise from others, "forgiving one another, even as God for Christ's sake has forgiven you."

Note again: When we forgive, it is a poor and humble business compared with God's forgiving us, because we are only forgiving one another—that is, forgiving fellow servants. But when God forgives us, the judge of all the earth is forgiving, not His fellows, but His rebel subjects, guilty of treason against His majesty! For God to forgive is something great—for us to forgive, though some think it great—should be regarded as a very small matter. Then reflect on the matter to be forgiven. Our Lord in His parable tells us that the fellow servant owed a few pence, but the servant himself owed his master a fortune. What we owe God is infinite, but what our fellow creature owes us is a very small sum.

What did he do that has so much offended you? "He said a very shameful thing about me." It was very bad of him, no doubt. "Then he played me a very nasty trick and acted very ungracious! In fact, he behaved scandalously, and if you hear the story, you will be quite indignant." Well, I am indignant. He is a bad fellow, no doubt about it, but so are you! So were you certainly when you first came to God—bad as your friend is to you, you have been much worse to the Lord. I will guarantee that his blacks toward you are whites compared with your blacks in the presence of God! "Oh, but you would not believe how basely he acted." No, and I daresay I should hardly believe it if I heard how base you have been to the Lord. At any rate, it should make our eyes fill with tears to think how we have grieved our God and vexed His Spirit.

> *You forgive me, and I forgive you; and we forgive them, and they forgive us; and so a circle of unlimited forbearance and love goes round the world!*

Some of us have had so much manifest forgiveness, so much outward sin forgiven, that for us to forgive ought to be as *natural* as to open our hands! After such forgiveness as the Lord has bestowed on some of us, we would be wicked servants indeed if we were to take our brother by the throat and say, "Pay me what you owe." We would deserve to be given over to the tormentors by our angry Master if we did not count it joy to pass by a brother's fault! If anyone here who is a Christian finds a difficulty in forgiveness, I am going to give him three words that will help him wonderfully. I would put them into the good man's mouth. I gave them to you just now and prayed you to get the sweetness of them. Here they are again! "For Christ's sake."

Cannot you forgive an offender on that ground? Ah, the girl has acted very shamefully, and you, her father, have said some strong things, but I beg you to forgive her for Christ's sake. Cannot you do it with that motive? It is true your son has behaved very wrongly, and nothing hurts a father's heart more than the wicked conduct of a son. You said, in a fit of anger, a very stern thing and denied him your house forever. I entreat you to eat your words for Christ's sake. Sometimes when I have been pleading a case like that, the person I have been persuading has kindly said, "I will do it for you, sir." I have said, "I will thank you if you will do it at all, but I would rather you have said you would do it for my Master, for what a blessed Master He has been to you! Do it for His sake."

> *hough you leave all your substance to His cause, He will not accept a penny of it if you die in an unforgiving temper. There is no grace where there is no willingness to overlook faults.*

I may be speaking very plainly home to some of you. I hope I am. If there are any of you who have got into a bad state of heart and have said you will never forgive a rebellious son, do not say so again till you have looked at the matter for Christ's sake. Not for the boy's sake, not for your neighbor's sake who has offended you, not for any other reason do I urge you to be merciful, but for Christ's sake. Come, you two brothers who have fallen out, love each other for Christ's sake. Come, you two sisters, come you two friends who have been alienated—get together directly and end all your ill feeling for Christ's sake. For Christ's sake, you must not keep a drop of malice in your soul. Oh, charming words! How they melt us, and as they melt us, there seems to be no trace of anger left behind. For Christ's sake, our love suffers long and never fails!

I do not know how to put this next word I am going to say. It is a paradox. You must forgive or you cannot be saved. But at the same time, you must not do it from compulsion, you must do it freely. There is a way of carrying this into practice, though I cannot explain it in words. You must forgive, not because you are forced to, but because you heartily do it. Remember, it is of no use for you to put your money into that offering box as you go out unless you remember, first, to forgive your brother. God will not accept the gifts, prayers, or praises of an unrelenting heart. Though you leave all your substance to His cause, He will not accept a penny of it if you die in an unforgiving temper. There is no grace where there is no willingness to overlook faults.

John asks, "He who does not love his brother whom he has seen, how can he love God whom he has not seen?" (1 John 4:20). The very prayer that teaches you to ask for mercy bids you say, "And forgive us our debts, as we forgive our debtors" (Matt. 6:12). Unless you have forgiven others, you read your own death warrant when you repeat the Lord's Prayer! Finally, I want to say to you all that as brothers and sisters in Christ Jesus, if we are to forgive one another, there must be some other things that we ought to do. And the first is do not let us provoke each other to offend. If I know that a man does not like a certain thing, I will not thrust it in his way.

Do not say, "Well, but if he is short-tempered, I cannot help it! He should not be so ready to take offense. I cannot be always paying deference to his absurd sensitiveness!" No. But, brother, your friend is very ready to take offense, and you know that he is. Have respect, then, to his infirmity of temper such as you would have if he were afflicted in body. If you have rheumatism or gout, your friends do not go stamping across the room and saying, "He ought not to mind that! He ought not to feel it." Kindhearted people step across the floor with a light step for fear they should hurt the poor suffering limb. If a man has a diseased mind and is very irritable, treat him gently, pity his infirmity, and do not irritate him.

A friend wrote me, a short while ago, a letter of serious complaint against a brother who had been very angry with him and had spoken very sharply while excited to passion. I felt bound to hear the other side of the story, and I was obliged to say, "Now, you two brothers are both wrong. You, my brother, lost your temper, but you, my other brother, irritated him so that I do not wonder he lost his temper! And when you saw he had lost his temper, why did you not go away or do something to quiet him? No, but you remained to increase the wrath and then wrote to expose him." I blame the wood for burning, but what will I say of the bellows? It was wrong to blaze, but was it right to fan the flame? Very often when a man is angry he may not be the only one to blame. Therefore, brothers and sisters, if we are to forgive one another, do not let us provoke one another to offend!

In the next place, do not make offenses. Oftentimes a man has been offended at another for no reason at all. One person has said of another as he passed him in the street, "He will not even nod to me. He is too proud to acknowledge me because I am a poor man." Now, that beloved friend who was thus blamed could not see much further than his hand, for he was nearsighted! Another has been censured for not hearing, though he was deaf! And another for not shaking hands when his arm was crippled. Do not imagine offenses where they are not intended. Next, do not take offenses where they *are* intended. It is a splendid thing if you will not be offended. Nothing makes a man feel so small as when you accept what he intended for an insult as if it were a compliment and thank him for it! Can you master yourself to that point?

Remember, when you have conquered yourself, you have conquered the world. You have overcome everybody when you have so fully overcome your own spirit that you remain content with that which naturally would excite your wrath. Then, if you must be offended, dear brother, do not exaggerate an offense. Some good women, I was about to say, and men also, when they come as talebearers with a charge, make a great many flourishes and additions. They go a long way around, and they bring innumerable beliefs, suggestions, hints, and hearsays into the business until a sparrow's egg becomes as huge as ever were an egg laid by an ostrich.

> *Charity covers a multitude of sins. Not only one, two, three sins will charity cover, but she carries a cloak that covers a whole host of faults.*

I begin coolly to strip off the feathers and the paint, and I say, "Now, I do not see what that point had to do with it or what that remark has in it. All I can see when I come to look at the bare fact is such and such, and that was not much, was it?"

"Oh, but there was more intended." Do not believe that, dear brother, dear sister! If there must be something wrong, let it be as little as you can. If you have a telescope, look through the large hole and minify instead of magnifying, or, better still, do not look at it at all! A blind eye is often the best eye a man can have. And a deaf ear is better by far than one that hears too much.

"Do not malign a servant to his master," says Solomon, "lest he curse you, and you be found guilty" (Prov. 30:10). Something you have done may irritate a servant, and he may make remarks that are unbecoming and impertinent. Don't hear what he is muttering! Keep out of hearing. He will be sorry tomorrow, and if he thinks you did not hear him, he will continue in your service and be faithful to you. What would you do if your employer picked you up for every word and if he caught up every sentence you uttered? How would you live at all if he reckoned sharply with you? No, dear friends, as you have to forgive one another, do not take offense—and when offense is given, do not exaggerate it—and, if you can, do not even observe it!

Then, again, do not publish offenses. There has been something very offensive said. What then? Do not repeat it! Do not go first to one and then to another and say, "Now this is quite private, and mind you, keep it a secret: So-and-So has spoken shamefully." Better that you should let your heart break than go up and down with a firebrand in this fashion! If a brother has done wrong, why should you do wrong? You will be doing wrong if you publish his fault. Remember how the curse came upon Noah's son for exposing his father? And how much better it is for us all when something is wrong to go backward and cover it without even looking at it ourselves, if we can help it! Cover it up! Cover it up! Charity covers a multitude of sins. Not only one, two, three sins will charity cover, but she carries a cloak that covers a whole host of faults.

Above all, my brothers and sisters—and with this I close—never in any way, directly or indirectly, avenge yourselves. For any fault that is ever done to you, the Master says to you, "Resist not evil. In all things bend, bow, yield, and submit."

"If you tread on a worm it will turn," says somebody. And is a *worm* your example? Christ will be mine! It is a shocking thing when a Christian man forgets his Lord to find an excuse for himself among the poor creatures under his feet! But if it must be so, what does a worm do when it turns? When you have stepped on a worm, does it bite? Does the worm hurt anyone? Ah, no. It has turned, but it has turned in its agony and writhed before you, that is all. You may do that, too, if you must.

Brother, the most splendid vengeance you can ever have is to do good to them that do you evil and to speak well of them that speak ill of you. They will be ashamed to look at you. They will never hurt you again if they see that you cannot be provoked unless it is to greater love and larger kindness. This ought to be the mark of Christians! Not "I will have the law on you," or, "I will avenge myself." But "I will bear and forbear even to the end." Do not take that into your hand what God says belongs to Him, but as He, for Christ's sake, has forgiven you, so also forgive all those who do you wrong. "How long am I to do that?" asks one. "I would not mind doing it three or four times." There was one of old who would go the length of six or seven, but Jesus Christ said, "Up to seventy times seven" (Matt. 18:22). That is a very considerable number. You may count whether you have yet reached that amount, and if you have, you will now be glad to *begin again*, still forgiving, even as God for Christ's sake has forgiven you!

God help us to be patient to the end! Though I have not, just now, been preaching Christ Jesus as the object of the sinner's trust, yet remember that He must also be the object of our imitation. This is the kind of doctrine that Christ Himself preached and, therefore, since He preached continually this love to our neighbor and forgiveness of our enemies, we ought both to preach and to practice it. Go and believe in Him and be imitators of Him, remembering that He forgave His murderers upon the cross whereon He worked out our redemption! May His Spirit rest upon you always. Amen.

FOR FURTHER THOUGHT

1. *Compare Ephesians 4:32 with Colossians 3:13. Why should we forgive one another?*
2. *Romans 5:6 shows why God has forgiven us for Christ's sake. What is that reason?*
3. *Read Romans 8:38–39. Will there be any time when God does not forgive us for Christ's sake?*

The Believer Sinking
in the Mire

Deliver me out of the mire, and let me not sink.
Psalm 69:14

MANY rivers and especially the Nile have on their banks deep deposits of black mud. And when any person seeks to leap on shore, if he should ignorantly or through misfortune spring upon this soft mud, he would, unless speedily pulled out, be sucked under until he was utterly swallowed up and suffocated in the mire. Having no handhold or foothold, the more he labored to extricate himself from the thick adhesive mud, the deeper he would descend until he would be choked in the filth, unless someone was near to help him out and save him from destruction. True believers, beloved, are sometimes in deep mire and in fear of being swallowed up. This was the state and condition of the psalmist when he wrote this psalm. He felt that he was sinking and could not deliver himself, and therefore he cries to God for strength in the words of the text, "Deliver me out of the mire, and let me not sink."

Mr. Gadsby, in his *Wanderings*, narrates an incident that, with reflections of his own, I will read to you at the outset.

> Being brought to a stand as just mentioned, I hailed the captain to heave to and take me on board. One of the men was, therefore, sent in the small boat, but the river near the western side was so shallow that he could not get the boat within some distance of the bank. He consequently, as is usual in such cases, jumped overboard that he might carry me to the boat on his back.
>
> No sooner, however, had he sprung from the boat than I heard him scream. I turned to see what was the matter, and I

found him struggling in the mud. He was sinking as though in quicksand. And the more he struggled the faster and deeper he sank. His fellow boatmen were not slack—they quickly saw the dilemma he was in and two of them dashed in and swam to the small boat. I was almost choked with terror and I breathed, or rather gasped, with difficulty. "Can they reach the poor fellow?" I said to myself. "If not, he must inevitably be swallowed up alive!" Now they reach the boat! Now they are near him!

And now, praise the Lord, he grasps firmly hold—O that death-like grasp—of the side of the boat! But this was not until he had sunk up to his chest. Seeing him safe, I breathed more freely. And I feel that now, though only relating the circumstance, the excitement has caused an increased and painful action of the heart. How I thought of poor David! Had he really witnessed a similar scene to this, literally, when, speaking of the feelings of his soul spiritually, he said, "I sink in deep mire, where there is no standing; I am come into deep waters, where the floods overflow me" (Ps. 69:2)?

O what an agonizing state to be in! And yet many of my readers, I have no doubt, who never witnessed such a scene literally, know something about it spiritually, as David did, whether he had seen it with his bodily eyes or not. Well might he, in the struggling of his soul, exclaim, "Deliver me out of the mire, and let me not sink! (14). Let me grasp firmly hold of the ark and be pulled safely on board! Well! just at the right time, just before the poor fellow's arms (shall I say his arms of faith?) were disabled, swallowed up—deliverance came!"

The prayer of our text leads us to three reflections: First, that the true believer *may be in the mire* and very near sinking. Second, that the true believer *may be in such a condition that God alone can deliver him.* And third, that in whatever condition the believer may be, *prayer is forevermore his safe refuge.* If a man finds that his own strength fails, he can look up to Him who is an ever-present help in time of trouble and cry to Him, "Deliver me out of the mire and let me not sink."

I. We commence with the statement that *the true believer may be in the mire.* Let us consider for a moment three things: what kind of mire the believer may be brought into, why God suffers him to be brought there, and how we can prove that he is really and truly a believer even though God suffers him to be brought into the mire. The truest believer in the world may be brought into the deep mire of unbelief. Some of us who have preached the Word for years and have been the means of working faith in others and of establishing them in the knowledge of the fundamental doctrines of the Bible have, nevertheless, been the subjects of the most fearful and violent doubts as to the truth of God and the very gospel we have preached.

Times may have occurred to the best of God's servants when they have even doubted the existence of the God whom they have loved to serve, when even the deity and reality of the Lord Jesus who has rescued them from sin by His precious blood has been a matter of grievous and horrible questioning. Little do people know, who are ignorant of the private history of God's believing people, what struggles they have with their own base-born, wicked unbelief. It is not only Thomas who has said, "Unless I see in His hands the print of the nails, and put my finger into the print of the nails, and put my hand into His side, I will not believe" (John 20:25).

> *I*f a man finds that his own strength fails, he can look up to Him who is an ever-present help in time of trouble and cry to Him, "Deliver me out of the mire, and let me not sink."

There have been thousands of eminent saints who have been attacked by unbelief and have been in doubt as to things that they once received as certain truths of God and that still in their heart of hearts they know to be true. They could have died for those truths one day. They could have established them beyond all doubt and question the next day. And yet upon the third they might be compelled, through strong temptation, to sit down and with tears streaming from their eyes, cry bitterly to their helper, "Oh, God, save me from this accursed unbelief that robs me of every comfort and takes the foundations away and lays my glory in the dust! What can I do? If the foundations are removed, what can the righteous do? O settle my soul upon your Word and establish me in your truth, O you God of truth."

A man may be a true believer and yet feel that he is sinking fast into the mire and clay of unbelief, as some of us know to our lamentation and dismay. A believer may be quite settled in his belief of the gospel and may never doubt the inspiration of scripture, the atonement of Christ, and all those precious truths that are commonly received among us and yet, through sin or temptation, or some other cause, he may not have a full assurance of his own interest in those glorious and vital truths.

A true believer in Christ, in fact, may often suspect himself to be a hypocrite when he is most sincere; to be an apostate when he is most diligently following the Lord. And he may set himself down as the chief of sinners when the testimony of men and of God is that he is a perfect and an upright man, one who fears God and eschews evil. A believer may be in a state of high spiritual health and yet may think himself to be sick to death! He may be clothed in fair white linen and yet reckon himself to be naked, poor, and miserable. He may be rich with all the treasures of his heavenly Father's kingdom and yet may scarcely know where he can find a ready crust with which to supply his present pressing spiritual needs.

> *Pray, brother, the prayer of that good man who asked for neither poverty nor riches. Ask that you may have food convenient for you. Pray, "Give me this day my daily bread."*

There are such things as princes in rags. And there have been such things and probably are now, as princes of the blood-royal peers of God's own realm sitting on the dunghill. Many a justified and accepted saint has had to moan out under a deep sense of sin, just as the poor publican did, "God, be merciful to me a sinner" (Luke 18:13). I daresay many of you think that God's ministers never have any question about their interest in Jesus Christ. I wish they never had. Brethren, I wish sincerely *I* never had! It is seldom that I do, very seldom. But there are times when I would change my soul's place with the poorest believer out of heaven, when I should be content to sit behind the door of heaven, if only I might be numbered among God's people.

True believers sometimes droop into this state; whether they are God's people or not, they cannot tell. Whether their sins are forgiven or not is a matter of solemn enquiry with their souls. Whether they have ever passed from death to life or not is the great problem that they sit down and earnestly consider. And whether they are God's people or not is a question they have great difficulty in answering. This is deep mire indeed, for it is woe with another woe at its heels to lose the assurance of one's present salvation.

In addition to this, at times the Lord's chosen are brought into another kind of mire that will never swallow them up, but that may prove a matter of very severe trial to them while they are in it. I mean temporal trouble. When the soul is alarmed about spiritual things and bodily or pecuniary troubles come also, then the sea is boisterous indeed. It is ill when two seas meet; when Moab and Ammon come against Judah at the same time; when both upper and nether springs appear to be dried up; when God, with both hands, thrusts us into the deep mire.

Certain of my brethren are frequently in trouble. Their whole life is a floundering out of one slough of despond into another. You have had many losses in business—nothing but losses, perhaps. You have had many crosses, disappointments, bereavements—nothing prospers with you. Well, brother, there is this consolation: You are one of a very large family, for many of God's people pass though just such tribulation. It was said by Matthew Henry, I think, that "prosperity was the blessing of the Old Covenant, but that adversity is the peculiar blessing of the New."

I do not know whether that is true or not, but I do know this: Christ has said, "In the world you will have tribulation; but be of good cheer, I have overcome the world" (John 16:33). It is no sign, beloved, that you are not a child of God because you feel the rod. It is rather a token of your being one of the adopted that you are made to pass under the rod of the covenant and to utter the prayer of David: "Lord, deliver me out of the deep mire and let me not sink." You are allowed to plead against the thing you so much fear. You may cry, "Leave me not to become penniless! Leave me not to dishonor my character!" But remember that none of your trials can prove you to be a lost man. Pray, brother, the prayer of that good man who asked for neither poverty nor riches. Ask that you may have food convenient for you. Pray, "Give me this day my daily bread."

"Deliver me out of the mire, and let me not sink."

I have not come to the blackest mire yet. God's own people are, at seasons, suffered to sink in the mire of inward corruption. There are times when believers have such a sight of the little hell within their own hearts that they are ready to despair of the possibility of their being completely sanctified and made meet to be partakers of the inheritance of the saints in light. Our God, at seasons, permits the fountains of the great deep of human depravity to be broken up, and then what floods of sin come pouring forth! We little know what lies secreted in our deceitful hearts—envy, blasphemies, murders, lust. There is enough in the heart of any man to make a full-grown devil if restraining grace did not prevent it.

Today you may have had such enjoyments of the Lord's countenance that you have been ready to sing, "You have made my mountain stand strong. I will never be moved" (see Ps. 30:6–7). But tomorrow you may have such a sight of self that you may exclaim, "O wretched man that I am! Who will deliver me from this body of death?" (Rom. 7:24). Remember, if you have the nature of God in you, you have also the nature of the old Adam. You are one with Christ and, "as is the heavenly, such are they also that are heavenly." But you are also one with Adam and, "as is the earthy, such are they also that are earthy" (1 Cor. 15:48 kjv).

You are to *be* immortal, but you are reminded that you *are* mortal. You are one day to be raised in glory. But you must remember as long as you are here, the time of glory is not come. You drag about, to your shame, your weakness, your dishonor, and your misery—a body of sin and death. The best of God's children know this. And I think the holier they are, the more likely they are to feel the conflict within. It is the fashion in our country for men to wear black coats. I suppose it is because they do not show the dirt so much as a white garment—and if we wore white garments, the filth would reveal itself and we should have to change them very often.

So, my brethren, the more a Christian is like his master, the more clearly he sees his own faults. O Lord, grant us divine grace to see much of our sins through the tears of repentance and to see much of the Savior through the eyes of faith, for if we see little of Him we will get into the plight of David when he was in the deep mire and cried, "Lord, deliver me out of the mire, and let me not sink."

Beloved, it is painful to reflect that the best of God's people are allowed to fall into the mire of satanic temptations. There is no knowing what suggestion Satan may thrust into the ears and into the soul of the greatest believer that heaven ever made. God may whisper in your ears one day and Satan the next, yet you may be a child of God on both occasions. Oh, beloved, I dare scarcely say in the midst of this assembly what I know on this point. If I were only to reveal my own struggles and conflicts with Satan, I might stagger some of you! But this I know, that no Christian minister will ever be able to enter into the trials and experiences of God's people unless he has stood foot to foot with the arch fiend and wrestled with the prince of hell.

Martin Luther was right when he said that temptation and adversity were the two best books in his library. He had never written his commentary upon Galatians if he had not been one who was frequently tempted and tossed about by Satan. That fiery, vehement nature of his was like a great coal fire burning up the works of Satan and all that Satan could do only stirred up the flame and caused it to burn more brightly. Satan will suggest not merely little sins, but the worst and foulest of sins to the best of God's chosen people.

He will even venture in his baseness to urge the man of God to destroy himself when under depression of spirits. And although the saint hates the very thought, yet he may be driven to the verge of it by an influence that he feels that all his puny might is unable to resist. It is a fearful thing to fight with Apollyon. We will sing of it in heaven as one of the greatest and most marvelous mercies of God that He delivered us out of the mouth of our cruel adversary.

Why is it that believers are allowed to fall into it? The answer is that they sometimes get into it through their own sin. It is a chastisement upon them. They were not faithful enough when they walked in the light, and therefore they are put into the darkness. If they had minded their steps when they were going down the hill, they would not have been subject to such afflictions in the valley. Rest assured that a great many of our sorrows are the foul weeds that spring up from the seeds of our own sins.

If you had been a fruitful tree, the pruning knife would not have been so often used. The rod is never taken down from the shelf except when it is absolutely necessary. And we are made to smart bitterly under it because we so greatly require it. God does not punish in a penal sense, but He does chastise. And He generally does it by permitting us to be filled with our own ways. We have to drink the powder of the idol calf that we have ourselves set up. We had need to walk with holy jealousy, for we serve a jealous God.

Oh, for grace to serve Him well! Our heavenly Father sends these troubles, or permits them to come, to try our faith. If our faith is worth anything at all, it will stand the test.

Superficial brilliance is always afraid of fire, but gold is not. The paste gem dreads to be touched by the diamond, but the true diamond fears no test. People who have a kind of confectionery godliness will wish to be preserved from temptations, for they cannot endure them. But the Christian counts it all joy when he falls into different trials, knowing that "tribulation produces perseverance; and perseverance, character; and character, hope. Now hope does not disappoint, because the love of God has been poured out in our hearts by the Holy Spirit who was given to us" (Rom. 5:3–5).

> *People who have a kind of confectionery godliness will wish to be preserved from temptations, for they cannot endure them. But the Christian counts it all joy when he falls into different trials*

My dear friends, if your faith is only a sunshiny faith, get rid of it! For you may not have many bright days between this and heaven. If your godliness can only walk with Christ when He wears silver slippers, you had better give it up, for Christ very often walks barefoot. It is a poor faith that can only trust God when friends are true, the body full of health, and the business profitable. That is true faith that holds by the Lord's faithfulness when friends are gone, when the body is sick, when our spirits are depressed, when we are driven from the enjoyment of assurances into the desert land and cannot see the light of our Father's countenance.

A faith that can say in the midst of the direst trouble, "Though He slay me, yet will I trust in Him," is heaven-born faith indeed! I believe in my Lord because He is a God who cannot lie. He is faithful and true to His every word and, therefore, let the whole creation go to rack and ruin, my faith will not waver or give up its confidence. The Lord may also let His servants slip into the deep mire to glorify Himself, for He is never, perhaps, more glorified than in the faith of His own people.

When an architect has erected a bridge of whose enormous strength he is well satisfied, he has no objection that it will be put to any test. "No," he says, "let the heaviest train pass over it that has ever been dragged by a locomotive. Let the most terrible tempest come that has ever blown from the four winds! I have built my structure in a manner so substantial that the more it is tried and proved, the more you will admire its firmness and completeness. So our gracious God, beloved, glorifies Himself by permitting His people to be subjected to trials and by enabling them to endure the strain.

We would never know the music of the harp if the strings were left untouched. We would never enjoy the juice of the grape if it were never trod in the winepress. We would never discover the sweet perfume of cinnamon if it were not pressed and beaten. And we would never know the warmth of fire if the coals were not utterly consumed. The excellence of the Christian is brought out by the fire of trouble. The wisdom of the great Workman and the glory of His skill and power are discovered by the trials through which His vessels of mercy are permitted to pass.

Again, beloved, trials are permitted to show the natural weakness of the creature that no flesh may glory in the presence of God. Men of iron nerve are raised up to face all opposition and confront the powers of darkness. Their testimony never falters, their course is as true and bright as the sun in the heavens, and men rejoice in their light. With faith undaunted they beard the infernal lion in his den and in the day of battle seek the thickest of the fight. All the devils in hell cannot frighten them, and all the foes upon earth cannot stir them from their divine purpose. They win souls as many as the sands of the sea, and their spiritual children are for number, like gravel.

They revive the flame that lingers in the embers of the church. They set the world ablaze with heavenly fire. They comfort many and set free thousands of prisoners, yet suddenly, and it may be in the last hour, their joy departs, their assurance flees, and their confidence departs. May not this be necessary that men may not trace the champion's noble bearing to the strength of his natural constitution, but discern that the eternal God was the support of his faith? We might have dreamed that the successful warrior was something different from other men, but when he is brought low, we discern clearly that it was distinguishing grace rather than a distinguished man that is to be seen and wondered at. The man was but an earthen vessel in which God had put His precious treasure, and He makes the earthiness of the vessel manifest that all men may see that the excellence of the power is not of us, but of God!

There is, perhaps, another reason why God permits His people to sink for a time into deep depression, and that is to make heaven sweeter when they enter its pearly gates. There must be some shades in the picture to bring out the beauty of the lights. Could we be so supremely blessed in heaven if we had not known the curse of sin and the sorrow of earth? Rest, rest, rest! In whose ear does that sound sweetest? Not in the ears of the loiterers who scorn all knowledge of the word *toil*, but in the ears of those who are exhausted and fatigued by the labors of the day!

Peace! Is there a man in England who knows the blessedness of that word? Yes, there are some. The soldier knows it. He has heard the whiz of the bullet. He has seen the smoke of the battle and the garment stained with blood. And the din, the shrieks, and the death of the field of fight have stirred his heart. To him, peace is a peerless gift. Who will know the peace of heaven but those who have experienced the warfare of earth and have endured conflicts with sin and the prince of the power of the air?

Beloved, there must be the foil of sorrow to bring out the bright sparkling of the diamond of glory. The happiest moments of mere physical pleasure I can remember have been just after a long illness or some acute pain. When pain is lulled to sleep, how happy one is! I saw a brother the other day affected by the most painful of all bodily complaints. He was telling me of the sufferings he had endured, and he said, "I am so happy now it is all over." And I suppose, my beloved, that heaven will derive some of its excess of delights, its overflowing joy, from the contrast with the pain and misery and conflict and suffering that we have had to pass through here below.

> Spiritual life is the first requisite for spiritual grief and spiritual contrition. Depend upon it, beloved, that those who suffer as I have described are the children of God, for they show it.

There will be something better to talk about than *troubles* in heaven, but the recollection of them may afford a flavor to our happiness that it would have lacked without it. We shall, I doubt not, with transporting joys, recount the labors of our feet.

These are some of the reasons why God permits His people to sink for a while in the deep mire where there is no standing. But the question is raised,

"Are these men who are thus tossed about by doubts and vexed with the great depravity of their hearts, truly, at that time, God's people?" Certainly they are! If they were not God's people, the pain of the temptation that they endure could not have reached them. This spot is the spot of God's children, and none others are marked with it.

The man who lives in sin, as his element, never feels the weight of it. A fish may be deep in the sea with thousands of tons of water rolling over his head, but it does not feel the load. But if a man has only a bucketful of water to carry upon his head, he feels the weight of it and rejoices to lose his burden. The sinner whose element is sin laughs at the weight by which a believer is borne down. Conflicts and pains such as I have been speaking of are not possible to those destitute of spiritual life. Spiritual *life* is the first requisite for spiritual *grief* and spiritual *contrition*. Depend upon it, beloved, that those who suffer as I have described are the children of God, for they show it.

They show it by the way in which they bear their trials. In their worst times there is always a clear distinction that marks them as separate from other men. If they cannot shout, "Victory!" they bear patiently. If they cannot sing to God with their mouths, yet their hearts bless Him. There is a degree of light even in their worst darkness, but it never becomes Egyptian darkness. Some one star, at least, gilds the gloom. In the blackest night there is still a candle somewhere or other for the Lord's chosen.

If they get into the mire, they do not perish there. They cry for help when their woes surround them, and in the very nick of time, when everything appears to be lost, their heavenly Father hastens to their aid. It is well known to the students of Christian biography that the most eminent of God's saints have had to pass through trials similar to those that I have been describing. Luther was a man of the strongest faith and yet at times of the faintest hope. He was and he was not a firm believer. His faith never wavered as to the truth of the cause that he advocated, but his faith as to his own interest in Christ seldom, if ever, amounted to full assurance.

The force of Luther's faith spent itself in carrying on with fearful vigor the war against antichrist and error of all shapes. He believed the truth of God and held right manfully justification by faith. But he was at times very doubtful as to whether he himself was justified in Christ Jesus. He believed in salvation by the precious blood of Christ. But especially at the last, it became a very serious matter with him as to whether *he* had ever been washed in that precious blood. Roman Catholic biographers, who, of course, if they can, will slander him, say that he had doubts as to everything that he preached and that at the last he found his faith was not in accordance with truth.

Not so! No man stuck to his testimony with more tenacity than the great reformer! Yet I marvel not that they should say so. He never doubted the truth of the things that he preached, but he did doubt his own interest in them frequently. And when he came to die, his testimony, though amply sufficient, was nothing like so brilliant as that of many a poor old woman who has died in a humble cottage resting upon Jesus.

The poor peasant who knew no more than her Bible was true was utterly unknown to the Vatican, and fame's trumpet will never resound her name, yet she entered into eternal peace with far louder shouting of joy than Martin Luther, who shook the world with his thundering valor! "Here lies he that never feared the face of man" is a most proper epitaph for John Knox. And yet at the last, for some hours, he passed through fearful temptation. And what do you suppose it was? The temptation of self-righteousness! The devil could not charge him with sin, for Knox's life had been so straightforward and honest that no man could impugn his motives or deny his Christianity.

And, therefore, the devil came to him in another and craftier way. He whispered, "John Knox, you have deserved well of your master! You will get to heaven well enough through your own merits." It was as hard a struggle as the lionhearted soldier of the cross had ever encountered to hold to his simple faith in Jesus Christ in his hour of peril. Now no Christian man denies that Luther and Knox were men of faith. And yet they were men who had to pray, "Deliver me out of the mire."

I know as I look around on this congregation that some of you can heartily sympathize in the truth before us. But if there are no others here who can, I can by God's grace most thoroughly say, "I know whom I have believed and am persuaded that He is able to keep what I have committed to Him until that day" (2 Tim. 1:12). But I know also that the Christian life is one of stern conflict and battle. And though we do rejoice in the Lord always, there are times when it is as hard a work as we can possibly do. No, *harder* work than we can accomplish without the help of the eternal Spirit—to keep our faith alive at all—for our souls are brought almost to death's door.

I wished to enlarge on this matter for the comfort of those who are tossed to and fro by doubts and fears. I have been attempting to describe the case of those who, for the greater part of their lives have lived in the shade and seen but little of the light of God's countenance. Oh, may the sun shine on them yet with cheering rays!

II. I turn very briefly to the second point—*when believers are in such a state they know experimentally that no one can deliver them but their God.* The Word of God itself, if not laid home by the divine Spirit, cannot help them. You may possibly be in such a condition that every promise scowls at you as though it were transformed into a threat. When you turn over the pages of the book once so full of comfort to you, it seems withered into a howling wilderness.

Even those promises that you have been accustomed to offer to others in their time of need appear to shut their doors against you. "No admittance here," says one promise. Unbelief puts its burning finger right across another. Past sin accuses you and cries, "You cannot claim this Word, for your transgression has forfeited it." So you may look through the whole Bible and find nothing upon which your souls may rest. You have noticed strong posts by the sides of rivers to which ships may be safely moored. To get the rope fairly around one of the promises of God will yield good enough moorings for a Christian—but there are times when we have great difficulty in getting the rope around so as to hold fast.

> It is only by the effectual application of the Word to your heart by the Holy Spirit that you can be brought out of this deep mire. At such times other believers cannot aid you.

The fault is not in the *promise* but in us. At such seasons the preaching of the gospel is apparently without power. You say to yourselves, "I do not know how it is, but I do not profit by the ministry as I once did. It used to make me leap for joy when I heard of the precious things of God. But I come away uncomforted from that table that once furnished me a feast of consolation." It is not the fault of the minister. He still, as a good steward, brings forth things new and old. It is not the fault of the Word. It is still milk for babes and strong meat for full-grown men, but you painfully feel that you are changed. You lament in words like these: "I go where others go and find no comfort there."

This is a case in which the Holy Spirit must Himself exercise His comforting office. It is only by the effectual application of the Word to your heart by the Holy Spirit that you can be brought out of this deep mire. At such times other believers cannot aid you. Those about you can prove to you how foolish it is to be in such a state, and you can even see your folly for yourself, yet you lie there helpless to lift hand or foot. They tell you of the faithfulness of God. They remind you of the glorious future and point to the land beyond the skies. But you only sigh, "Oh, that I had wings like a dove! I would fly away and be at rest" (Ps. 55:6).

Human sympathy is at a nonplus, and all we can do is weep with you, for we cannot dry your tears. Why does our gracious God permit this? Perhaps it is because you have been living without Him, and now He is going to take away everything upon which you have been in the habit of depending. Another reason may be that He wishes to drive you to Himself. Oh, it is a blessed thing to live in the fountainhead! While our skin bottles are full, we are content like Hagar and Ishmael to go into the wilderness. But when those are dry, nothing will serve us but "You, God, see me" (Gen. 21:14–19).

We must then come to the well. We are like the prodigal. We love the swine troughs and forget our father's house. Remember, we can make swine troughs and husks even out of the forms of religion. Do not misunderstand me. They are blessed things, but we may put them in God's place and then they are of no value. Anything becomes an idol when it keeps us away from God! Even the bronze serpent is to be despised as Nehushtan, a mere piece of brass, if I worship *it* instead of *God* (2 Kings 18:4).

The prodigal was never safer than when he was driven to his father's bosom, because he could find sustenance nowhere else. And, brothers and sisters, I think our Lord favors us with a famine in the land that it may make us seek after the Savior more. The best position for a Christian is living wholly and directly on God's grace. The best position is still to be where he was at first, having nothing and yet possessing all things. Not building a wooden house on the rock, piling it higher and higher with our own wood, and then getting up to the top and saying, "How high I am!" but having no wood at all—just keeping down on the bare, solid rock—this is wisdom!

When the wind comes and the storm blows, we will see that the structures that we build will give way and fall to our own damage. But if we stand on the rock that never shakes, we cannot suffer loss. I pray God that you and I may never get beyond the fountain filled with blood. Stand there, brothers and sisters, and be happy! We pray to always feel ourselves to be sinners, blood-washed sinners pleading. Never for a moment think that our standing is in our sanctification, our mortification, our graces, or our feelings, but know that because Christ on Calvary offered a full, free, efficacious atonement forever, one that believes on Him is, therefore, saved.

We are complete in Him, having nothing of our own to trust but resting upon the merits of Him whose passion and whose life furnish for us the only sure ground of confidence. Beloved, when we are brought to this, then it is that God comes to help us. We are sure in our poverty to turn to Him afresh with new earnestness. Infants, when they are among strangers, are pleased with little toys and amusements. But when they become hungry, nothing will do for them but their mother's breast. So it is with a child of God. He may for a time be satisfied and find pleasure in the things of this world, but he only finds lasting and sure happiness in being embraced in his Father's arms.

When the boys walk out with us in fair weather, they will run in front of us ever so far, but as soon as they see any danger in the way, they quickly return to Father's side. So when everything goes well with us, we frequently run a long way from God, but as soon as we are overtaken by trouble or see a lion in the way, we fly to our heavenly Father. I bless God for the mire and for my sinking in it, when it makes me cry out, "Deliver me, O my God, out of the deep mire, and let me not sink."

III. In the last place, our text shows us that *prayer is the never-failing resort of the Christian* in any case and in every plight. When you cannot use your sword, you may take to the weapon of all prayer. Your powder may be damp, your bowstring may be relaxed, your sword may be rusty, and your spear may be bent—but the weapon of prayer is never out of order (Eph. 6:17–18). Men have to sharpen the sword and the spear, but prayer never rusts. There is this blessed thing about prayer: It is a door that none can shut.

Devils may surround you on all sides, but there is always one way open, and as long as that road is unobstructed, you will not fall into the enemy's hands. We can never be taken by blockade, escalade, mine, or storm so long as heavenly succor can come down to us by Jacob's ladder to relieve us in the times of our need. Prayer is never forbidden. Remember, Christian, it is never wrong for you to pray, for the gates of heaven are open day and night. Your prayer is heard in heaven in the dead of the night, in the midst of your business, in the heat of noonday, or in the shades of evening. You can be in poverty, sickness, obscurity, slander, doubt, or even sin, but it is still true that your God will welcome your prayer at any time and in every place.

Again, prayer is never futile. True prayer is, forevermore, true power. You may not always get what you ask for, but you will always have your real needs supplied. When God does not answer His children according to the letter, He does so according to the spirit. If you ask for silver, will you be angered because He gives you gold? If you seek bodily health, should you complain if instead He makes your sickness turn to the healing of spiritual maladies? Is it not better to have the cross be sanctified than to have the cross removed? Was not the apostle more enriched when God suffered him still to endure the thorn in the flesh and yet said to him, "My strength is sufficient for you" (2 Cor. 12:9)? Better to have all-sufficient grace than to have the thorn taken away.

What is your condition my brother, my sister? Let me entreat you not to cease from prayer. There may be spiritual life in you, and yet the devil may tempt you to say, "I cannot pray." But you *can* pray! You *do* pray! You *must* pray! If you have spiritual life, although you can scarcely bend your knees and are almost afraid to utter words once dear to you, yet your soul desires, pants, hungers, thirsts—and that is the essential of prayer, that is the very marrow and essence of prayer.

Sobs and looks are prayers. And though you say you cannot pray, you *must* pray. You cannot help praying if you are a Christian. "I cannot breathe"—this might be true in a certain sense. I cannot, perhaps, breathe under an asthmatic affection without great difficulty and much pain. But I must breathe if I live! And so with you; you must breathe if you live. And you do pray, *must* pray, if you are truly a child of God. At any rate, I pray by the power of God, the Holy Spirit, you may break through those evils, those nets of the devil that hold you in bondage and begin with your whole soul to pray. Never mind what form your prayer takes, but pray.

My dear brothers and sisters, everything depends now upon your prayer. If Satan can stop your prayer, he has stripped you of your last resort, your last hope! He will take you by storm if you leave off praying. Pray! If it costs you your life, pray! Go not to your ease and take not your rest until you have prayed. Give no sleep to your eyes till you have prayed. Slumber not until you have had dealings with God in prayer. Not pray? Are you willing to be damned? Not pray? Are you willing to make your bed in hell? Not pray? Shall devils be your companions? Shall heaven's gate be shut against you?

> *True prayer is, forevermore, true power. You may not always get what you ask for, but you will always have your real needs supplied.*

Not pray? Why, my brothers and sisters, you must pray now! Oh, send up the prayer from the very bottom of your heart: "O God, deliver me out of the deep mire, and let me not sink. Save me, O my God! God be merciful to me a sinner." May God the Holy Spirit sweetly compel you to pray! May He incline, guide, direct, and instruct you *how* to pray, that this very night you may offer up a prayer that God in His great goodness will hear and answer!

Pray: "Lord, my soul is besieged. I am shut up by my sins. Oh, God, raise the siege and deliver me from the enemy. Lord, help me with your Almighty arm. Make my extremity your opportunity. I am a foul beggar sitting on a dunghill. Lord, come and lift me up and put me among the princes and I will praise your name forever and ever." May the blessed virgin's song be yours. "He has put down the mighty from their thrones, and exalted the lowly. He has filled the hungry with good things, and the rich He has sent away empty" (Luke 1:52–53).

And may you find in the goodness and mercy and loving-kindness of God a speedy deliverance out of the deep mire, that you may not sink! May God give a blessing to these words to your comfort! I know some of you will say, "I am not in such a state." Thank God that you are not! Be grateful for your mercies lest you lose them. Be thankful for your full assurance and your comfortable hope lest those favors should become dim, like dying tapers and waning moons. Rejoice now, O Christian, as the young man does in his youth, and let your heart cheer you in your youthful joy!

But remember, if you are not careful how you walk in these flowery paths, if you become too confident in your own strength or goodness, God will bring you down and make you cry out as sharply and as sorrowfully as David—"Deliver me out of the mire, and let me not sink."

FOR FURTHER THOUGHT

1. *Paul breathed out "threats and murder against the disciples of the Lord" (Acts 9:1). According to 1 Timothy 1:13, why was God merciful to him?*
2. *Read Romans 5:1–5. According to verse 5, why can we glory in our tribulations?*
3. *In 2 Timothy 1:12, why does Paul say that he is not ashamed?*

THE DEATH OF THE CHRISTIAN

"You shall come to the grave at a full age,
as a sheaf of grain ripens in its season."
JOB 5:26

WE do not believe all that Job's friends said. They spoke very often as uninspired men, for we find them saying many things that are not true. And if we read the book of Job through, we might say with regard to them, "Miserable comforters are you all!" (Job 16:2), for they did not speak concerning God's servant Job the thing that was right. Nevertheless, they gave utterance to many holy and pious sentences that are well worthy of regard as having come from the lips of three men distinguished in their age for their learning, talent, and ability. Three gray-headed sires were able to speak what they knew from experience. Their mistakes are not to be wondered at, because they had not then that clear, bright, shining light that we enjoy in these modern times.

They had few opportunities to meet together. There were but few prophets in those days that taught them the things of the kingdom. We marvel that, without the light of the gospel revelation, they were able to discover so much of the truth as they did. However, I must make a remark concerning this chapter. These words are not so much the utterance of the man who here speaks—Eliphaz the Temanite—but are the very Word of God. They are not so much the simple saying of the unwise comforter who upbraided Job, as the speech of the great Comforter who consoles His people and who only utters the thing that is right.

The opinion is justified by the fact that this chapter is quoted by the apostle Paul. Eliphaz says in the thirteenth verse of chapter five, "He catches the wise in their own craftiness." And we find the apostle Paul, in 1 Corinthians 3:19, saying, "For it is written, 'He catches the wise in their own craftiness,'" thus giving sanction to this passage as having been inspired of God, at all events as being most certainly truthful. Most certainly, the experience of such a man as Eliphaz is worthy of much regard. And when he, speaking of the general condition of God's people—that they are hid from the scourge of the tongue, that they are not afraid of destruction when it comes (Job 5:21), that they laugh at destruction and famine and so on—we may accept his words as being proven by experience and authenticated by inspiration.

"You shall come to the grave at a full age, as a sheaf of grain ripens in its season." Here is a very beautiful comparison, the comparison of the aged Christian to a shock of corn. Go into the harvest field and you will see how much the wheat reminds you of the aged believer. How much anxiety has been expended on that field! When the seeds first sprang up, the farmer feared that worms would bite the tender shoots and the blades would be devoured. Or that some sharp frost would consume the infant plants and cause them to wither and die. And then, month after month, as the seasons came, he anxiously looked toward heaven and longed that the rains might come or that the genial sunshine might pour out its vivifying floods of light upon the field.

When it came somewhat to maturity, how greatly he feared lest the mildew and blast should shrivel up the precious ears. The grain stands in the fields now, and in some respects the farmer is freed from his anxiety. The months of his travail are over. He has waited patiently for the precious fruits of the soil, and now they are here. And so it is with the gray-headed man. How many years of anxiety have been expended upon him? In his youth, it seemed likely that he might be smitten down by death, yet he has passed safely through youth, manhood, and age. What varied accidents have been warded from him? How has the shield of the providential keeper been over his head to keep him from the shafts of the pestilence or from the heavy hand of accident that might have taken his life?

How many anxieties has he had himself? How many troubles has he passed through? Look upon the hoary-headed veteran! Mark the scars that troubles have inflicted upon his forehead! And see, deeply written in his breast, the dark mementos of the sharp struggles and trials he has endured! And now, his anxieties are somewhat over. He is come very nearly to the haven of rest. A few short years of trial and trouble will land him on fair Canaan's coast. We look upon him with the same pleasure that the farmer regards the wheat, because the anxiety is over and the time of rest is now approaching. Mark how weak the stem has become, how every wind shakes it to and fro. It is withered and dried! See how the head hangs down to earth, as if it were about to kiss the dust and show from where it had its origin!

So, mark the aged man: Tottering are his steps, the eyes that look out of the windows are darkened, the grinders cease because they are few, and the grasshopper has become a burden. Yet even in that weakness there is glory. It is not the weakness of the tender blade, it is the weakness of the full ripe corn. It is a weakness that shows its maturity. It is a weakness that gilds it with glory. Even as the color of the wheat is golden so that it looks more beauteous than when the greenness of its verdure is on it, so the gray-headed man has a crown of glory on his head. He is glorious in his weakness more than the young man in his strength or the maiden in her beauty.

> *Even as the color of the wheat is golden so that it looks more beauteous than when the greenness of its verdure is on it, so the gray-headed man has a crown of glory on his head.*

Is not a shock of corn a beautiful picture of the state of man, moreover, because very soon it must be taken home? The reaper is coming. Even now I hear the sickle sharpening. The reaper has well edged it, and he will soon cut down the corn. Look! He is coming across the field to reap his harvest. And then, by and by, it will be carried into the barn and safely housed, no more subject to blight or mildew or insect or disease. There it will be secured where no snow can fall upon it, no winds can molest it. It will be safe and secure. And joyful will be the time when harvest home will be proclaimed and the shock of corn, fully ripe, will be carried into the farmer's garner.

Such is the aged man. He, too, will soon be taken home. Death is even now sharpening his sickle, and the angels are getting ready their chariot of gold to bear him up to the skies. The barn is built. The house is provided. Soon the great Master will say, "First gather together the tares and bind them in bundles to burn them, but gather the wheat into my barn" (Matt. 13:30).

This morning we will consider *the death of Christians in general*. Not of the aged Christian merely, for we will show you that while this text does seem to bear upon the aged Christian, in reality it speaks with a loud voice to every man who is a believer. "You shall come to the grave at a full age, as a sheaf of grain ripens in its season."

We will mark four things in the text. First, we will consider that death is *inevitable*, because it says, "you shall come." Second, that death is *acceptable*, because it does not read, "I will make you go to your grave," but "You shall come there." Third, that death is always *timely*: "You shall come to your grave in full age." Fourth, that death to the Christian is always *honorable*, for the promise declares to him, "You shall come to the grave at a full age, as a sheaf of grain ripens in its season."

I. The first remark, namely, that death, even to the Christian, is *inevitable*, is very trite, simple, and common, and we need scarcely have made it. But we found it necessary, in order to introduce one or two remarks upon it. How familiar is the thought that all men must die and therefore, what can we say upon it? And yet we blush not to repeat it, for while it is a truth so well known, there is none so much forgotten. While we all believe it in theory and receive it in the brain, how seldom is it impressed on the heart? The sight of death makes us remember it. The tolling of the solemn bell speaks to us of it. We hear the deep-tongued voice of time as the bell tolls the hours and preaches our mortality. But very usually we forget it.

> The wicked man, when he dies, is driven to his grave, but the Christian comes to his grave.

Death is inevitable to all. But I wish to make an observation concerning death, and that is that while it is written, "It is appointed for men to die once" (Heb. 9:27), yet a time will come when some Christian men will not die at all. We know that had Adam never sinned, he would not have died, for death is the punishment of sin. And we know that Enoch and Elijah were translated to heaven without dying. Therefore, it does seem to follow that death is not absolutely necessary for a Christian. Moreover, we are told in scripture that there are some who will be "alive and remain," when Jesus Christ will come. And the apostle says, "I tell you a mystery: We shall not all sleep, but we shall all be changed—in a moment, in the twinkling of an eye, at the last trumpet" (1 Cor. 15:51–52).

There will be some who will be found living, of whom the apostle says,

"Then we who are alive and remain shall be caught up together with them in the clouds to meet the Lord in the air. And thus we shall always be with the Lord" (1 Thess. 4:17). We know that flesh and blood cannot inherit the kingdom. But it is possible that they will be refined by some spiritual process that will preclude the necessity of dissolution. Oh, I have thought of that idea very much, and I have wondered whether it should not be possible that some of us might be in that happy number who will not see death. Even if we are not, there is something very cheering in the thought that Christ did so conquer death that He not only delivers the lawful captive out of the prison, but He saves a band from the jaws of the monster and leads them by his den unharmed!

He not only resuscitates the dead and puts new life into those who are slain by the fell scythe, but some He actually takes to heaven by a byroad. He says to death, "Away, you monster! On these you will never put your hand! These are chosen men and women. And your cold fingers will never freeze the current of their soul. I am taking them straight to heaven without death. I will transport them in their bodies up to heaven without passing through your gloomy portals or having been captives in your dreary land of shades." How glorious is the thought that Christ has vanquished death, that some men will not die.

But you will say to me, "How can that be? For the body has mortality mingled with its very essence." We are told, it is true, by eminent men that there is a necessity in nature that there should be death, since one animal must prey upon another. And even could all animals be taught to give up their prey, they must feed upon plants and so devour certain minute insects that had hidden thereon. Death therefore seems to be the law of nature. Be it remembered that men have already lived far beyond the present allotted term, and it does seem most easy to conceive that the creature that can subsist a thousand years could exceed that period. But this objection is not valid, since the saints will not live forever in this world but will be removed to a habitation where laws of glory will supersede laws of nature.

II. And now comes a sweet thought that death to the Christian is always *acceptable.* "You shall *come* to your grave." Old Caryl makes this remark on this verse: "A willingness and a cheerfulness to die. You will *come*, you will not be dragged or hurried to your grave, as it is said of the foolish rich man in Luke twelve, 'This night your soul will be required of you' (v. 20). But you will come to your grave quietly and smilingly, as it were. You will go to your grave, as it were, upon your own feet and rather walk than be carried to your sepulcher." The wicked man, when he dies, is driven to his grave, but the Christian *comes* to his grave.

Let me tell you a parable. Behold, two men sat together in the same house when death came to each of them. He said to one, "You will die."

The man looked at him. Tears suffused his eyes, and tremblingly he said, "O death, I cannot! I will not die." He sought out a physician and said to him, "I am sick, for death has looked upon me. His eyes have paled my cheeks, and I fear I must depart. Physician, there is my wealth. Give me health and let me live." The physician took his wealth but gave him not his health with all his skill. The man changed his physician, tried another, and thought that perhaps he might spin out the thread of life a little longer.

But alas! Death came and said, "I have given you time to try your varied excuses. Come with me. You will die." And he bound him hand and foot and made him go to that dark land of Hades. As the man went, he clutched at every side post by the way, but death, with iron hands, still pulled him on. There was not a tree that grew along the way but he tried to grasp it. But death said, "Come on! You are my captive and you will die." And unwillingly as the laggard schoolboy who goes slowly to school, so did he trace the road with death. He did not *come* to his grave, but death fetched him to it; the grave came to him.

But death said to the other man, "I am come for you."

He smilingly replied, "Ah, death! I know you; I have seen you many a time. I have held communion with you. You are my Master's servant. You have come to fetch me home. Go and tell my Master I am ready, whenever He pleases. Death, I am ready to go with you." And together they went along the road and held sweet company.

Death said to him, "I have worn these skeleton bones to frighten wicked men. But I am not frightful. I will let you see myself. The hand that wrote upon Belshazzar's wall was terrible because no man saw anything but the hand. But," said death, "I will show you my whole body. Men have only seen my bony hand and have been terrified."

And as they went along, death ungirded himself to let the Christian see his body, and he smiled, for it was the body of an angel. He had wings of cherubs and a body glorious as Gabriel. The Christian said to him, "You are not what I thought you were. I will cheerfully go with you." At last death touched the believer with his hand. It was even as when the mother does in sport smite her child a moment. The child loves that loving pinch upon the arm, for it is a proof of affection. So did death put his finger on the man's pulse and stopped it for a moment, and the Christian found himself by death's kind finger changed into a spirit. Yes, found himself brother to the angels. His body had been etherealized, his soul purified, and he himself was in heaven.

You tell me this is only a parable. But let me give you some facts that will back it up. I will tell you some of the deathbed savings of dying saints and show you that, to them, death has been an agreeable visitant of whom they were not afraid. You will not disbelieve dying men. It was ill to act the hypocrite's part at such a time. When the play is over, men will take off the mask; and so with these men when they came to die, they stood out in solemn unclothed reality.

First, let me tell you what Dr. Owen, that celebrated prince of Calvinists, said. While his works are to be found, I am not afraid that men will lack arguments to defend the gospel of free grace. A friend called to tell Dr. Owen that he had put to press his *Meditations on the Glory of Christ*. There was a momentary gleam in his languid eye as he answered, "I am glad to hear it. Oh," said he, "the long wished-for time has come at last, in which I will see that glory in another manner than I have ever done or was capable of doing in this world."

> My work is done. I have done with all my friends. The entire world is now nothing to me. Oh, to be in heaven to praise and glorify God with His holy angels."

"But," you may say, "this man was a mere theologian, let us hear a poet speak." George Herbert, after some severe struggles and having requested his wife and nieces, who were weeping in extreme anguish, to leave the room, committed his will to Mr. Woodnott's care. Crying out, he said, "I am ready to die. Lord, forsake me not now, My strength fails. But grant me mercy for the merits of my Lord Jesus. And now, Lord, receive my soul." Then he laid himself back and breathed out his life to God. Thus the poet dies. That glorious fancy of his that might have pictured gloomy things if it had pleased was only shed with rapturous sight of angels. As he used to say himself, "I think I hear the church bells of heaven ringing." And I think he did hear them when he came near the river Jordan.

"But," you will say, "one was a theologian and the other a poet—it might have been all fancy." Now learn what an active man, a missionary, said. "I am almost in eternity. I long to be there. . . . My work is done. I have done with all my friends. The entire world is now nothing to me. Oh, to be in heaven to praise and glorify God with His holy angels." That is what Brainard said. He counted all things loss for the excellence of the knowledge of Jesus Christ and went among wild untutored Indians to preach the gospel.

But it is possible you will say, "These were men of ages gone by." Now you will have men of modern times. And first, hear what the great and eminent Scotch preacher, Haldane, said. He raised himself a little and distinctly repeated these words: "When Christ who is our life appears, then you also will appear with Him in glory" (Col. 3:4). He was then asked if he thought he was going home. He answered, "Perhaps not quite yet." Mrs. Haldane affectionately said, "Then you will not leave us very soon." He replied with a smile, "To depart and to be with Christ is far better." On being asked if he felt much peace and happiness, he twice repeated, "Exceeding great and precious promises." He then said, "But I must rise." Mrs. Haldane said, "You are not able to get up." He smiled and answered, "I will be satisfied when I awake with His likeness." She said, "Is that what rising up you meant?" He replied, "Yes, that is the rising I meant. I must rise!"

And now, what said Howard, the great philanthropist, the man who while possessing true religion and being the most eminent and distinguished of Christians, would from his plain commonsense mode of acting, never be suspected of being a fanatic and an enthusiast? A few days before his death, when the symptoms of his disease began to assume a most alarming appearance, he said to Admiral Priestman, "You endeavor to divert my mind from dwelling on death. But I entertain very different sentiments. Death has no terror for me. I always look forward to it with cheerfulness, if not with pleasure."

But perhaps you may say, "We never knew any of these people. We should like to hear of somebody whom we did know." Well, you will hear of one whom you have heard me affectionately mention. He was not of our denomination, but he was a very prince in Israel—I refer to Joseph Irons. Many of you heard the sweet and blessed things that proceeded out of his lips and will perhaps be able to verify what is said of him. At intervals he repeated short portions of scripture and select sentences, such as, "How long, Lord?" "Come, Lord Jesus!" "I long to go home to be at rest." Seeing his dear wife shedding tears, he said, "Do not weep for me. I am waiting for that far more exceeding and eternal weight of glory."

After a pause to recover his breath, he added, "He that has preserved me thus far will never leave or forsake me. Fear not—all is well. Christ is precious. I am going home, for I am a shock of corn fully ripe." Now that is a man you did know, many of you. And it proves the fact that I have asserted, that to a Christian death is acceptable come when it may. I am sure I can say, with many of my brethren here, that could I now have the greatest favor conferred on me that mortals could desire, I would ask that I might die. I never wish to have the choice given to me. But to die is the happiest thing man can have, because it is to lose anxiety, it is to slay care, and it is to have the peculiar sleep of the beloved. To the Christian, then, death must be acceptable.

A Christian has nothing to lose by death. You say he has to lose his friends. I am not so sure of that. Many of you have many more friends in heaven than on earth. Some Christians have more beloved and longed-for ones above than below. You often count your family circle, but do you do as that little girl of whom Wordsworth speaks, when she said, "Master, we are seven." Some of them were dead and gone to heaven, but she would have it that they were all brothers and sisters still. Oh, how many brothers and sisters we have upstairs in the upper room in our Father's house! How many dear ones linked with us in the ties of relationship, for they are as much our relations now as they were then! Though in the resurrection they neither marry nor are given in marriage. Yet, in that great world, who has said that the ties of affection will be severed so that we will not even there claim kindred with one another as well as kindred with Jesus Christ?

What have we to lose by death? Come when he may, should we not open the door for him? I would love to feel like that woman who said, when she was dying, "I feel like a door on the latch, ready to be opened to let my Lord in." Is not that a sweet state, to have the house ready, so that it will require no setting in order? When death comes to a wicked man, he finds him moored fast. He snaps his cable and drives his ship to sea. But when he comes to the Christian, he finds him winding up the anchor, and he says, "When you have done your work and shipped the anchor, I will take you home." With sweet breath, he blows on him and the ship is wafted gently to heaven. With no regrets for life, but with angels at the prow, spirits guiding the rudder, sweet songs coming through the cordage and canvass silvered over with light.

III. Then third, the Christian's death is always *timely*. "You shall come to your grave in a full age."

"Ah," says one, "that is not true. Good people do not live longer than others. The most pious man may die in the prime of his youth." But look at my text. It does not say you will come to your grave in old age, but in a "full age." Well, who knows what full age is? Full age is whenever God likes to take His children home. Some fruits, you know, are late in coming to perfection, and we do not think their flavor is good till Christmas, or till they have gone through the frost—while some are fit for table now. All fruits do not get ripe and mellow at the same season. So it is with Christians. They are at a "full age" when God chooses to take them home. They are at "full age" if they die at twenty-one.

They are not more if they live to be ninety. Some wines can be drunk very soon after the vintage. Others need to be kept. But what does this matter, if when the liquor is broached it is found to have its full flavor? God never broaches His cask till the wine has perfected itself. There are two mercies to a Christian. The first is that he will never die too soon. And the second is that he will never die too late.

First, he will never die *too soon*. Spencer, who blazed out so brilliantly some years ago, preached so wonderfully that many expected that a great light would shine steadily and that many would be guided to heaven. But then suddenly the light was quenched in darkness, and he drowned while yet in his youth. Men wept and said, "Ah, Spencer died too soon." So it has been sung of Kirk White, the poet, who worked so laboriously at his studies. Like the eagle that finds that the arrow that smote him was winged by a feather from his own body, so was his own study the means of his death. And the poets said he died too soon. It was untrue. He did not die too soon. No Christian ever does.

"But," say some, "how useful might they have been had they lived." Ah, but how damaging they might have been! And were it not better to die than to do something afterward that would disgrace them and bring disgrace to the Christian character? Were it not better for them to sleep while their work was going on than to break it down afterward? We have seen some sad instances of Christian men who have been very useful in God's cause but have afterward had sad falls and have dishonored Christ. Though they were saved and brought back at last, we could almost wish that they had died rather than lived.

You don't know what might have been the career of these men who were taken away so soon. Are you quite sure they would have done so much good? Might they not have done much evil? Could we have a dream of the future and see what they might have been, we should say, "Ah, Lord! Let it stop while it is well." Let him sleep while the music plays, there may be hideous sounds afterward. We long not to keep awake to hear the dreary notes. The Christian dies well. He does not die too soon.

> *So it is with Christians. They are at a "full age" when God chooses to take them home. They are at "full age" if they die at twenty-one.*

Again, the Christian never dies *too late*. That old lady there is eighty years old. She sits in a miserable room, shivering before a small fire. She is kept by charity. She is poor and miserable. "What's the good of her?" says everybody. "She has lived too long. A few years ago she might have been of some use. But now look at her! She can scarcely eat unless her food is put into her mouth. She cannot move. And what good can she be?" Do not you find fault with your Master's work? He is too good a husbandman to leave His wheat in the field too long and let it shale out. Go and see her and you will be reproved. Let her speak—she can tell you things you never knew in all your life. Or, if she does not speak at all, her silent unmurmuring serenity, her constant submission, teaches you how to bear suffering.

So there is something you can yet learn from her. Say not the old leaf hangs too long on the tree. An insect may yet twist itself therein and fashion it into its habitation. Say not the old sear leaf ought to have been blown off long ago. The time is coming when it will fall gently on the soil. But it remains to preach to unthinking men the frailty of their lives. Hear what God says to each of us: "You will come to the grave at a full age." Cholera! You may fly across the land and taint the air—I will die in a "full age." I may preach today and as many days as I please in the week, but I will die at a full age. However ardently I may labor, I will die at a full age.

Affliction may come to drain my very life's blood and dry up the very sap and marrow of my being. Ah, but affliction, you will not come too soon. I will die at a full age. And you waiting man and you tarrying woman, you are saying, "O Lord, how long? How long? Let me come home." You will not be kept from your beloved Jesus one hour more than is necessary. You will have heaven as soon as you are ready for it. Heaven is ready enough for you, and your Lord will say, "Come up higher!" when you have arrived at a full age—but never before or after.

IV. Now the last thing is that a Christian will die with *honor*. "You will come to the grave at a full age, as a sheaf of grain ripens in its season." You hear men speak against funeral honors, and I certainly do enter my protest against the awful extravagance with which many funerals are conducted and the absurdly stupid fashions that are often introduced. It would be a happy thing if some persons could break through them and if widows were not obliged to spend the money that they need so much themselves on a needless ceremony that makes death not honorable, but rather despicable.

But I think that while death should not be flaunted out with gaudy plumes, there is such a thing as an honorable funeral that every one of us may desire to have. We do not wish to be carried away just as a bundle of tares—we would prefer that devout men should carry us to the grave and make much lamentation over us. Some of us have seen funerals that were very like a "harvest home." I can remember the funeral of a sainted minister under whom I once sat. The pulpit was hung in black, and crowds of people came together. And when an aged veteran in the army of Christ rose up to deliver the funeral oration over his remains, there stood a weeping people lamenting that a prince had fallen that day in Israel.

Then, verily, I felt what Mr. Jay must have experienced when he preached the funeral sermon for Rowland Hill, "Wail, O cypress, for the cedar has fallen" (Zech. 11:2), there was such a melancholy grandeur there. And yet my soul seemed lit up with joy to think it possible that some of us might share in the same affection and that the same tears might be wept over us when we come to die. Ah, my brethren here, my brethren in office, my brethren in this church, it may somewhat cheer your hearts to know that when you depart your death will be to us a source of the deepest grief and most piercing sorrow. Your burial will not be that prophesied for Jehoiakim, the burial of an ass with none to weep over him. But devout men will assemble and say, "Here lies the deacon who for years served his master so faithfully." And, "Here lies the Sunday school teacher," will the child say, "who early taught me the Savior's name."

And if the minister should fall, I think a crowd of people following him to the tomb would well give him such a funeral as a "sheaf of grain ripens in its season." I believe we ought to pay great respect to the departed saints' bodies. "The memory of the just is blessed." And even you little saints in the church, don't think you will be forgotten when you die. You may have no gravestone. But the angels will know where you are as well without a gravestone as with it. Some will weep over you. You will not be hurried away but will be carried with tears to your grave.

But I think there are two funerals for every Christian: One is the funeral of the *body*, and the other of the soul. Funeral, did I say, of the soul? No, I meant not so. I meant not so. It is a *marriage* of the soul. For as soon as it leaves the body, the angel reapers stand ready to carry it away. They may not bring a fiery chariot as they had for Elijah. But they have their broad spreading wings. I rejoice to believe that angels will come as convoys to the soul across the ethereal plains. Lo! Angels at the head support the ascending saint, and lovingly they look upon his face as they bear him upward. And angels at the feet assist in wafting him up yonder through the skies, and as the husbandmen come out from their houses and cry, "A joyous harvest home," so will the angels come forth from the gates of heaven and say, "Harvest home! Harvest home! Here is another shock of corn fully ripe gathered into the garner."

I think the most honorable and glorious thing we will ever behold, next to Christ's entrance into heaven and His glory there, is the entrance of one of God's people into heaven. I can suppose it is made a holiday whenever a saint enters, and that is continually, so that they keep perpetual holiday. Oh, I think there is a shout that comes from heaven whenever a Christian enters it, louder than the noise of many waters. The thundering acclamations of a universe are drowned as if they were but a whisper in that great shout that all the ransomed raise when they cry, "Another and yet another comes." And the song is still swelled by increasing voices, as they chant, "Blessed husbandman, blessed husbandman, your wheat is coming home. Shocks of corn fully ripe are gathering into your garner."

Well, wait a little, beloved. In a few years more, you and I will be carried through the ether on the wings of angels. I think I die and the angels approach. I am on the wings of cherubs. Oh, how they bear me up, how swiftly and yet how deftly. I have left mortality with all its pains. Oh, how rapid is my flight! Just now I passed the morning star. Far behind me now the planets shine. Oh, how swiftly do I fly and how sweetly! Cherubs! What sweet flight is yours and what kind arms are these I lean upon! And on my way you kiss me with the kisses of love and affection. You call me brother. Cherubs, am I your brother? I who just now was captive in a tenement of clay, am I your brother? "Yes!" they say. Oh, hark! I hear music strangely harmonious!

> *I* think the most honorable and glorious thing we will ever behold, next to Christ's entrance into heaven and His glory there, is the entrance of one of God's people into heaven.

What sweet sounds come to my ears! I am nearing paradise. 'Tis even so. Do not spirits approach with songs of joy? "Yes!" they say. And before they can answer, behold they come—a glorious convoy! I catch a sight of them as they are holding a great review at the gates of paradise. And ah, there is the golden gate. I enter in. And I see my blessed Lord. I can tell you no more. All else were things unlawful for flesh to utter. My Lord! I am with you, plunged into you, lost in you just as a drop is swallowed in the ocean, as one single tint is lost in the glorious rainbow! Am I lost in you, glorious Jesus? And is my bliss consummated? Is the wedding day come at last?

Have I really put on the marriage garments? And am I yours? Yes! I am. There is nothing else now for me. In vain your harps, you angels. In vain all else. Leave me a little while. I will know your heaven by and by. Give me some years; yes, give me some ages to lean here on this sweet bosom of my Lord. Give me half an eternity and let me bask myself in the sunshine of that one smile. Yes, give me this. Did you speak, Jesus? "Yes, I have loved you with an everlasting love, and now you are mine! You are with me."

Is not this heaven? I want nothing else, and I tell you once again, you blessed spirits, I will see you by and by. But with my Lord I will now take my feast of loves. Oh, Jesus! Jesus! Jesus! You are heaven! I want nothing else. I am lost in you!

Beloved, is not this to go to "the grave in full age, like as a shock of corn," fully ripe? The sooner the day will come, the more we will rejoice. Oh, tardy wheels of time! Speed on your flight, O angels. From where do you come with haggard wings? Oh, fly through the ether and outstrip the lightning's flash! Why may I not die? Why do I tarry here? Impatient heart, be quiet a little while. You are not yet fit for heaven, else you would not be here. You have not done your work, else you would have your rest. Toil on a little longer. There is rest enough in the grave. You will have it there. On! On!

> *With my scrip on my back*
> *And my staff in my hand,*
> *I'll march on in haste*
> *Through an enemy's land.*
>
> *Though the way may be rough*
> *It cannot be long.*
> *So, I'll smooth it with hope*
> *And I'll cheer it with song.*

My dear friends, you who are not converted, I have no time to say anything to you this morning. I wish I had. But I pray that all I have said may be yours. Poor hearts, I am sorry I cannot tell you this is yours now. I would I could preach to every one of you and say that you all will be in heaven. But God knows there are some of you that are on the road to hell, and do not suppose you will enter heaven if you go hell's road. Nobody would expect, if he proceeded to the north, to arrive at the south. No. God must change your heart. By simple trust in Jesus, if you give yourself up to His mercy, even though the vilest of the vile, you will sing before His face.

And I think, poor sinner, you will say to me as a poor woman did last Wednesday, after I had been preaching, when I believe everybody had been crying, from the least to the greatest and even the preacher in the pulpit. As I went down, I said to one, "Are you chaff or wheat?"

And she said, "Ah, I trembled tonight, sir."

I said to another, "Well, sister, I hope we will be in paradise soon."

And she replied, "*You* may, sir."

And I came to another and said, "Well, do you think you will be gathered with the wheat?"

And she answered, "One thing I can say, if God ever lets me get into heaven, I will praise Him with all my might. I will sing myself away and will never think I can sing loud enough."

It reminded me of what an old disciple once said: "If the Lord Jesus does but save me, He will never hear the last of it." Let us praise God, then, eternally.

> *While life, or thought, or being lasts,*
> *Or immortality endures!*

FOR FURTHER THOUGHT

1. *What does 1 Thessalonians 4:17 say will happen to the dead believers at the time Christ returns?*
2. *What are Paul's three statements at the end of his life as recorded in 2 Timothy 4:7?*
3. *In 2 Timothy 4:8, Paul says he will receive a crown of righteousness in the day the Lord returns. According to this verse, who else will get such a crown?*

The Form of Godliness
without the Power

Having a form of godliness but denying its power.
And from such people turn away!
2 Timothy 3:5

PAUL warns us of certain characters that will appear in the last times. It is a terrible list. The like have appeared in other days, but we are led by his warning to apprehend that they will appear in greater numbers in the last days than in any previous age. "Lovers of themselves, lovers of money, boasters, proud, blasphemers, disobedient to parents, unthankful, unholy, unloving, unforgiving, slanderers, without self-control, brutal, despisers of good, traitors, headstrong, haughty, lovers of pleasure rather than lovers of God" (2 Tim. 3:2–4).

These will swarm like flies in the decaying years, and will make the times exceeding perilous. We are nearing that period at this very time. That these people would, some of them, be within the church is the most painful part of it. But they will be so, for they are comprehended in this last clause of the black catalog that we have taken for our text: "Having a form of godliness but denying its power."

Paul does not paint the future with rose-colored glasses. He is no smooth-tongued prophet of a golden age into which this dull earth may be imagined to be growing. There are sanguine brothers and sisters who are looking forward to everything growing better and better and better, until, at last, this present age ripens into a millennium. They will not be able to sustain their hopes, for scripture gives them no solid basis to rest upon. We who believe that there will be no millennial reign without the King, and who expect no rule of righteousness except from the appearing of the righteous Lord, are nearer the mark.

Apart from the second advent of our Lord, the world is more likely to sink into a pandemonium than to rise into a millennium. A divine interposition seems to me the hope set before us in scripture and indeed to be the only hope adequate to the occasion. We look to the darkening down of things. The state of mankind, however improved politically, may yet grow worse and worse *spiritually*. Certainly, we are assured in verse 13 that "evil men and impostors will grow worse and worse, deceiving and being deceived." There will spring up in the Christian church and all around it, a body of faithless men who profess to have faith, ungodly men who will unite with the saints, men having the form of godliness but denying the power.

> Paul does not paint the future with rose-colored glasses. He is no smooth-tongued prophet of a golden age into which this dull earth may be imagined to be growing.

We may call *these* hard times if we will, but we have hardly yet come to the border of those truly harder times when it will go hard with the church and she will need, even more than today, to cry mightily to the Lord to keep her alive. With this cloud upon our spirit, we come to the text itself. Let us consider it carefully, and may the Holy Spirit help us!

True religion is a spiritual thing, but it necessarily embodies itself in a *form*. Man is a spiritual creature, but the human spirit needs a *body* in which to enshrine it. And thus, by this need, we become allied to materialism. And if not "half dust, half deity," as one has said, we are certainly both matter and soul. In each of us there is the form or body and the soul or power. It is so with religion. It is essentially a *spiritual* thing, but it requires a form in which to embody and manifest itself.

Christian people fall into a certain outward method of procedure, a peculiar outward mode of uttering their faith that becomes to true godliness what the body is to the soul. The form is useful, the form is necessary, and the form ought to be vitalized just as the body is useful, necessary, and vitalized by the soul. If you get both the form, as modeled in the Word of God and the power, as bestowed by the Spirit of God, you do well and are living Christians. If you get the power alone, without the ordained form, you somewhat maim yourself. But if you get the form without the power, then you dwell in spiritual death.

The body without the spirit is dead. And what follows upon death with flesh? Why, corruption follows, corruption so horrible that even love itself has to cry, "Bury my dead out of my sight" (Gen. 23:4). So that if there is in any the body of religion without the *life* of religion, it leads to decay and thus to corruption—and that has a tendency to decompose the character. The raw material of a devil is an angel bereft of holiness. You cannot make a Judas except out of an apostle. The eminently good in outward *form*, when without inward *life*, decays into the foulest thing under heaven. You cannot wonder that these are called "perilous times," in which such characters abound.

One Judas is an awful weight for this poor globe to bear, but a tribe of them must be a peril indeed. Yet, if not of the very worst order, those are enough to be dreaded who have the shadow of religion without its substance. Of such I have to speak at this time. From such may God give you divine grace to turn away! May none of us ever be spots in our feasts of love or clouds without water carried about of winds. But this we will be if we have the *form* of godliness without the *power* thereof.

With great solemnity of soul I approach this subject, seeking from the Lord the aid of His Spirit, who makes the Word to be a discerner of the thoughts and intents of the heart. First, I will speak of *the men*, and second, of *their folly*. And when I am done with that, I will have some words of instruction to give by way of conclusion.

I. First, let us talk awhile of *the men*. They had the form of godliness but denied its power. Note what they had, and then observe what they had not. They had a *form* of godliness. What is a form of godliness? It is, first of all, attention to the ordinances of religion. These, so far as they are scriptural, are few and simple. There is baptism, wherein in figure the believer is buried with Christ that he may rise into newness of life. And there is the Lord's Supper, wherein, in type and emblem he feeds upon Christ and sustains the life that came to him by fellowship with Christ's death. Those who have obeyed the Lord in these two ordinances have exhibited in their own persons the form of godliness. That form is every way instructive to others and impressive to the man himself.

Every baptized person and every communicant at the Lord's Table should be godly and gracious. But neither baptism nor the Lord's Supper will secure this. Where there is not the life of God in the soul, neither holiness nor godliness follow upon the ordinances. And thus we may have around us baptized worldlings and men who go from the table of the Lord to drink the cup of devils. It is sad that it should be so. Such persons are guilty of presumption, falsehood, sacrilege, and blasphemy. Ah me, we sit beside such every Sabbath!

The form of godliness involves attendance with the assemblies of God's people. Those who have professed Christ are accustomed to come together at certain times for worship, and in their assemblies they join in common prayer and common praise. They listen to the testimony of God by His servants whom He calls to preach His Word with power. They also associate together in church fellowship for purposes of mutual help and discipline. This is a very proper form, full of blessing both to the church and to the world when it does not die down into mere form. A man may go to heaven alone, but he will do better if he travels there with Mr. Great-Heart and Father Honest and Christiana and the children. [These are characters from John Bunyan's *Pilgrim's Progress. Ed.*]

Christ's people are called sheep for one reason: They love to go in flocks. Dogs do very well separately, but sheep do best in company. The sheep of Christ love to be together in the same pasture and to follow in a flock the footsteps of the Good Shepherd. Those who constantly associate in worship, unite in church fellowship, and work together for sacred purposes have a form of godliness, and a very useful and proper form it is. Alas, it is of no value without the power of the Holy Spirit.

> *S*ome have a form of godliness upheld and published by religious activity. It is possible to be intensely active in the outside work of the church and yet to know nothing of spiritual power.

Some go further than public worship. They use a great deal of religious talk. They freely speak of the things of God in Christian company. They can defend the doctrines of scripture, they can plead for its precepts, and they can narrate the experience of a believer. They are fondest of talking of what is doing in the church; the tattle of the streets of Jerusalem is very pleasant to them. They flavor their speech with godly phrases when they are in company that will relish it. I do not censure them. On the contrary,

I wish there were more of holy talk among professors. I wish we could revive the old habit: "They that feared the LORD spake often one to another" (Malachi 3:16 KJV).

Holy conversation causes the heart to glow and gives us a foretaste of the fellowship of the glorified. But there may be a savor of religion about a man's conversation, yet it may be a borrowed flavor, like hot sauces used to disguise the staleness of ancient meat. That religion that comes from the lips outward but does not well up from the deep fountains of the *heart* is not that living water that will spring up to eternal life. Tongue godliness is an abomination if the heart is destitute of divine grace.

More than this, some have a form of godliness upheld and published by religious activity. It is possible to be intensely active in the outside work of the church and yet to know nothing of spiritual power. One may be an excellent Sunday school teacher after a fashion and yet have need to be taught what it is to be born again. One may be an eloquent preacher or a diligent officer in the church of God and yet know nothing of the mysterious power of the Spirit of truth upon the heart. It is well to be like Martha in service. But one thing is needful—to sit at the Master's feet and learn as Mary did.

When we have done all the work our position requires of us, we may only have displayed the form of godliness. Unless we hearken to our Lord and from His presence derive power, we will be as a sounding brass and a tinkling cymbal. Brethren, I speak to myself and to each one of you in solemn earnestness. If much speaking, generous giving, and constant occupation could win heaven, we might easily make sure of it. But more than these are needed. I speak to each one of you. And if I singled out anyone more than another to be the pointed object of my address, it would be the best among us, the one who is doing most for his master and who, in his inmost soul, is thinking, "That warning does not apply to me."

O my active and energetic brother, remember the word, "Therefore let him who thinks he stands take heed lest he fall" (1 Cor. 10:12). If any of you dislikes this searching sermon, your dislike proves how much you need it. He that is not willing to search himself should stand self-incriminated by that unwillingness to look at his affairs. If you are right, you will not object to being weighed in the balances. If you are indeed pure gold, you may still feel anxiety at the sight of the furnace, but you will not be driven to anger at the prospect of the fire. Your prayer will always be, "Search me, O God, and know my heart; try me, and know my anxieties; and see if there is any wicked way in me, and lead me in the way everlasting" (Ps. 139:23–24).

I need not enlarge further. You all know what a form of godliness is and most of us who are here present hold fast that form. May we never dishonor it! I trust we are anxious to make that form accurate according to scripture so that our form of godliness may be that into which the earliest saints were delivered. Let us be Christians of a high type, cast in our Lord's own mold. But do not become sticklers for the form and neglect the inner life. That will never do. Shall we fight about a man's clothes and allow the man himself to die?

But now, as these people had not the power of godliness, how did they come to hold the form of it? This needs several answers. Some come by the form of godliness in a hereditary way. Their ancestors were always godly people, and they almost naturally take up with the profession of their fathers. This is common, and where it is honest, it is most commendable. It is a great mercy when, instead of the fathers, will be the children. And we may hopefully anticipate that our children will follow us in the things of God if, by example, instruction, and prayer, we have sought it before the Lord.

We are unhappy if we do not see our children walking in God's truth. Yet the idea of birthright membership is an evil one and is as perilous as it is unscriptural. If children are taken into the church simply because of their earthly parentage, surely this is not consistent with that description of the sons of God that is found in the inspired scripture, "Who were born, not of blood, nor of the will of the flesh, nor of the will of man, but of God" (John 1:13). Not *generation* but *regeneration* makes the Christian. You are not Christians because you can trace a line of fleshly descent throughout twenty generations of children of God.

You must yourselves be born again. For except a man is born from above, he cannot see the kingdom of God. Many, no doubt, lay hold naturally on the form of godliness because of family ties—this is poor work. Ishmael is a sorry son of Abraham and Esau of Isaac and Absalom of David. Grace does not run in the blood. If you have no better foundation for your religion than your earthly parentage, you are in a wretched case.

Others have accepted the form of godliness by the force of authority and influence. They were as lads made apprentice to godly men. As girls they were under the guidance of pious teachers. And as they grew up, they came under the influence of persons of superior intelligence and character who were on the Lord's side. This accounts for their form of godliness.

Many persons are the creatures of their surroundings. Religion or irreligion is with them the result of circumstances. Such persons were led to make a profession of faith in Christ because others did so and friends encouraged them to do the same.

The deep searching of heart that they ought to have exhibited was slurred over, and they were found among the people of God without having to knock for entrance at the wicket gate. I do not wish anyone to condemn himself because godly friends guided him to the Savior; far from it. But there is danger lest we fail to have personal repentance and personal faith and are content to lean upon the opinions of others.

> *Do not suppose that all unconverted people are without religion. Much religiousness is found in the heathen, and there are races that have naturally more of reverence than others.*

I have seen the form of godliness taken up on account of friendships. Many a time courtship and marriage have led to a formal religiousness but a lacking heart. The future husband is induced to make a profession of religion for the sake of gaining one who was a sincere Christian and would not have broken her Lord's command to be unequally yoked together with an unbeliever. Godliness should never be put on in order that we may put a wedding ring upon the finger. This is a sad abuse of religious profession.

Other kinds of friendship, also, have led men and women to profess a faith they never had and to unite themselves visibly with the church, while in spirit and in truth they were never truly a part of it. I put these things to you that there may be a great searching of heart among us all and that we may candidly consider how we have come by our form of godliness. Certain persons assume the form of godliness from a natural religious disposition. Do not suppose that all unconverted people are without religion. Much religiousness is found in the heathen, and there are races that have naturally more of reverence than others.

The German, with his profound philosophy, is often free, not only from superstition but from reverence. The Russian is by race naturally religious, not to say superstitious. I am speaking after the manner of men. The usual Russian takes off his hat to holy places, pictures, and persons, and he is little inclined to disbelieve or scoff. We perceive like differences among our own acquaintances. Skeptics readily fool one man, while another is ready, with open mouth, to believe every word. One is naturally an infidel. Another is as naturally credulous.

I mean, then, that to some the form of godliness commends itself because they have a natural leaning that way. They could not be happy unless they were attending where God is worshipped or unless they were reckoned among the believers in Christ. They must play at religion even if they do not make it their life business. Let me remind you of the questionable value of that which springs out of fallen human nature. Assuredly, it brings no one into the spiritual kingdom, for "that which is born of the flesh is flesh." Only "that which is born of the Spirit is spirit" (John 3:6).

"You must be born again" (3:7). Beware of everything that springs up in the field without the sowing of the husbandman, for it will turn out to be a weed. O sirs, the day will come when God will try us as with fire, and that which comes of unregenerate nature will not stand the test but will be utterly consumed!

I do not doubt that, in these silken days, many have a form of godliness because of the respect it brings them. Time was when to be a Christian was to be reviled, if not to be imprisoned and perhaps burned at the stake. Hypocrites were fewer in those days, for a profession cost too much. Yet strange to say, some played the Judas even in those times. Today religion walks forth in her velvet slippers. And in certain classes and ranks, if men did not make some profession of religion, they would be looked upon with suspicion. Therefore men will take the name of Christian upon them and wear religion as a part of full dress.

The cross is at this day worn as a necklace. The cross as the instrument of our Savior's shame and death is forgotten, and instead thereof, it is made the badge of honor, a jewel wherewith ungodly men may adorn themselves. Is this indicative of the deceitfulness of the age? Beware of seeking respect by a hypocritical godliness. Honor gained by a heartless profession is, in God's sight, the greatest disgrace. The actor may strut in his mimic royalty, but he must take off his crown and robes when the play is over. And what will he then be?

From the days of Iscariot until now, some have taken up a form of godliness to gain thereby. To make gain of godliness is to imitate the son of perdition. This is a perilous road, yet many risk their souls for the lucre that they find therein. Apparent zeal for God may really be zeal for gold.

The emperor Maximilian showed great zeal against idolatry and published a decree that images of gold and silver should be melted down. He was extremely zealous about this. The images were all to be melted down and the metal forfeited to the emperor.

It was shrewdly suspected that this great iconoclast was not altogether swayed by unselfish motives. When a business brings grist to the mill, it is not hard to keep to it. Some love Christ because they carry His moneybag for Him. Beware of that kind of godliness that makes a man hesitate until he sees whether a duty will pay or not and then makes him eager because he sees it will answer his purpose.

Once more, I do not doubt that a form of godliness has come to many because it brings them ease of conscience and they are able, like the Pharisee, to thank God that they are not as other men are. Have they not been to church? Have they not paid for their pew? They can now go about their daily business without those stings of conscience that would come of neglecting the requirements of religion. These people profess to have been converted, and they are numbered with believers. But, alas, they are not of them.

> Many who have the form of godliness are strangers to its power and so are in religion worldly, in prayer mechanical, in public one thing, and in private another.

Of all people, these are the hardest to reach and the least likely to be saved. They hide behind the earthworks of a nominal religion. They are out of reach of the shot and shell of gospel rebukes. They fly among the sinners, and they have taken up their quarters among the saints. Sad is that man's plight who wears the name of life but has never been quickened by the Holy Spirit. Thus I have very feebly tried to show what these men had and why they had it.

Let us now remember what they did *not* have. They had the form of godliness. But they denied the power of it. What is that power? God Himself is the power of godliness. The Holy Spirit is the life and force of it. Godliness is the power that brings a man to God and binds him to Him. Godliness is that which creates repentance toward God and faith in Him. Godliness is the result of a great change of heart in reference to God and His character. Godliness looks toward God and mourns its distance from Him. Godliness hastens to draw near and rests not till it is at home with God.

Godliness makes a man like God. Godliness leads a man to love God and to serve God. It brings the fear of God before his eyes and the love of God into his heart. Godliness leads to consecration, to sanctification, to concentration. The godly man seeks first the kingdom of God and His righteousness and expects other things to be added to him. Godliness makes a man commune with God and gives him a partnership with God in His glorious designs. And so it prepares him to dwell with God forever.

Many who have the form of godliness are strangers to its power and so are in religion worldly, in prayer mechanical, in public one thing, and in private another. True godliness lies in *spiritual power*, and they who are without this are dead while they live.

What is the general history of those who have not this power? Well, dear friends, their course usually runs thus: They do not begin with denying the power, but they begin by trying to do without it. They would like to become members of the church, and as they fear that they are not fit for it, they look about for something that looks like conversion and the new birth. They try to persuade themselves that they have been changed. They accept *emotion* as regeneration and a belief of doctrine for belief in Christ.

It is rather hard at first to reckon brass as gold, but it grows easier as it is persisted in. Patching up a conversion and manufacturing regeneration, they venture forward. At the first they are a good deal suspicious of themselves, but they industriously kill every question by treating it as a needless doubt. Thus, by degrees, they believe a lie.

The next step is easy: They deceive themselves and come to believe that they are surely saved. All is now right for eternity, so they fancy, and they fold their arms in calm security. Meeting with godly people, they put on a bold front and speak up as bravely as if they were the true soldiers of King Jesus. Good people are charmed to meet with fresh brethren and at once take them into their confidence. Thus they deceive others and help to strengthen themselves in their false hope.

They use the choice phrases of earnest Christians. Mixing with them, they pick up their particular expressions and pronounce Shibboleth in the most approved fashion. At last they take the daring step of denying the power. Being without it themselves, they conceive that others are without it, also. Judging from their own case, they conclude that it is all an affair of words. They get on very well without any supernatural power, and others, no doubt, do the same, only they add a little cant to it to please the very godly folk.

They practically deny the power in their lives, so that those who see them and take them for Christians say, "There really is nothing in it. For these people are as we are. They have a touch of paint here and a little varnish there, but it is all the same wood." Practically, their actions assure the world that there is no power in Christianity. It is only a name. Very soon, privately, in their hearts they think it is so and they invent doctrines to match. Looking about them, they see inconsistent Christians and faulty believers, and they say to themselves, "There is not much in faith, after all. I am as good as any of these believers and perhaps better, though I am sure there is no work of the Spirit in me."

Thus, within their own hearts they believe, what, at first, they dare not speak. They count godliness an empty thing. By-and-by, in some cases, these people profanely deny the divine power of our holy faith, and then they become the greatest enemies of the cross of Christ. These traitors, nourished in the very house of God, are the worst foes of the truth of God and righteousness. They ridicule that which once they professed to reverence. They have measured Christ's corn with their own bushel. And because they never felt the powers of the world to come, they imagine that no one else has done so either.

Look at the church of the present day—the advanced school, I mean. In its midst we see preachers who have a form of godliness but deny the power thereof. They talk of the Lord Jesus, but they deny His Godhead, that is, His power. They speak of the Holy Spirit but deny His personality, wherein lies His very existence. They take away the substance and power from all the doctrines of revelation, though they pretend still to believe them. They talk of redemption, but they deny substitution, which is the essence of it.

They extol the scriptures but deny their infallibility, wherein lies their value. They use the phrases of orthodoxy and believe nothing in common with the orthodox. I know not which to loathe more, their teachings or their spirit. Surely they are worthy of each other. They burn the kernel and preserve the husk. They kill the truth and then pretend to reverence its sepulcher. "They say they are Jews and are not, but lie" (Rev. 3:9).

This is horrible, but the evil is widely spread, and in the presence of it the children of God are framing compromises, selling their Lord, and becoming partakers with the despisers of His truth. "Having a form of godliness but denying its power" is the sin of the age, the sin that is ruining the churches of our land.

II. In the second place, we are to observe *the wicked folly* of this hypocritical conduct. Those who rest in the mere show of godliness are acting in a shameless manner, and I will try to expose it.

First, they degrade the very name of Christ. Brethren, if there is no spiritual power in godliness, it is worth nothing. We want no clouds without rain. Of shams and mere pretenses we have more than enough. Those who have not the power of godliness show us a very damaging picture of religion. They make out our Lord's religion to be comparable to a show at a country fair, with fine pictures and loud drumming on the outside and nothing within worth a moment's consideration. The best of the show is on the outside.

Or if there is anything within, it is a masquerade in which all act borrowed parts but no one is what he seems to be. Gracious Lord, never suffer us so to act as to make the world think that our Redeemer is nothing more than the clever manager of a theater, where nothing is real but all is pantomime. Brothers and sisters, if you pray at all, pray God to make you real through and through. May you be made of true metal! It were better for you that you had never been born than that you should make Christ dishonorable among the sons of men by leading them to conclude that religion is all a piece of acting.

The folly of this is illustrated by the fact that there is no value in such a dead form. The form of godliness without the power is not worth the trouble it takes to put it together and keep it together. Imitation jewels are pretty and brilliant, but if you take them to the jeweler, he will give you nothing for them. There is a religion that is all paste gems—a godliness that glitters but is not gold. And in that day when you will want to realize something from it, you will be wretchedly disappointed.

A form of godliness joined to an unholy heart is of no value to God. I have read that the swan was not offered upon the altar of God because, although its feathers are as white as snow, yet its skin is black. God will not accept that external morality that conceals internal impurity. There must be a pure heart as well as a clean life. The power of godliness must work within, or else God will not accept our offering. There is no value to man or to God in a religion that is a dead form.

Next, there is no use in mere formality. If your religion is without spiritual life, what is the use of it? Could you ride home on a dead horse? Would you hunt with dead dogs? Would anyone like to go into battle with a pasteboard helmet? When the sword fell on it, what use would such a helmet be? What an outcry has been raised about bad swords! Is false religion any better? In the depth of winter, can you warm yourself before a painted fire? Could you dine off the picture of a feast when you are hungry?

> *The form of godliness without the power is not worth the trouble it takes to put it together and keep it together. Imitation jewels are pretty and brilliant, but if you take them to the jeweler, he will give you nothing for them.*

There must be vitality and substantiality—or else the form is utterly worthless and worse than worthless, for it may flatter you into deadly self-conceit. Moreover, there is no comfort in it. The form without the power has nothing in it to warm the heart, to raise the spirits, or to strengthen the mind against the day of sickness or the hour of death. O God, if my religion has been a mere form, what will I do in the swelling of Jordan? My fine profession will all disappear and nothing will come of it wherewith I may face the last enemy.

Peter called hypocrites "wells without water" (2 Pet. 2:17). You are thirsty and you gladly spy a well. It is well surrounded with a curb and provided with a windlass and bucket. You hasten to draw water. What? Does the bucket come up empty? You try again. How bitter is your disappointment! A well without water is a mockery. It is a mere pit of destruction, a deadly delusion. Are some of you possessors of a religion that never yields you a drop of comfort? Is it a bondage to you? Do you follow Christ as a slave follows his master? Away with such a religion!

The godliness that is worth having is a joy to a man; it is his choice, his treasure, and his all. When it does not yield him conscious joy, he prizes it as the only source from which to draw the joy that is expected of him. He follows Christ with love, out of his heart's desire after Him, and not from the force of fashion or the power of fear.

To have the form of godliness without the power of it is to lack constancy in your religion. You never saw a mirage, perhaps. But those who travel in the

East, when they come home, are sure to tell you about them. It is a very hot and thirsty day, and you are riding on a camel. Suddenly there rises before you a beautiful scene. Just a little from you are brooks of water flowing between beds of osiers and banks of reeds and rushes. Yonder are palm trees and orange groves, and a city rises on a hill, crowned with minarets and towers.

You are rejoiced and ask your guide to lead you nearer to the water that glistens in the sun. He grimly answers, "Take no notice, it is a mirage. There is nothing yonder but the burning sand." You can scarce believe him. It seems so real! But lo, it is all gone, like a dream of night. And so is the hope that is built upon the form of godliness without the power. The white ants will eat up all the substance of a box and yet leave it standing till a touch causes the whole fabric to fall in dust. Beware of a profession of which the substance has been eaten away. Believe in nothing that has not the stamp of eternity upon it.

Be careful, poor child. You may blow your bubble, and the sunlight may paint it with rainbows. But in an instant it is gone and not a trace of it remains. Your transient globe of beauty is for you and your fellow children and not for men.

> Regard the ill savor of false professors as a part of the cross that you will have to bear for your Lord. To be associated with some who are not true seems inevitable in this life however carefully we choose our company.

In reality this kind of religion is in opposition to Christ. It is Jannes and Jambres over again (2 Tim. 3:8). The magician of hypocrisy is trying to work miracles that belong to God only. In appearance he would produce the same marvels as the finger of God. But he fails. God grant that we may never be guilty of resisting the truth of God by a lying profession. False men do serious injury to true godliness. For, like Ehud, they come with a pretended message from God and with their dagger sharpened at both edges; they strike vital godliness in its very heart (Judg. 3:12–26). Nobody can do so much damage to the church of God as the man who is within its walls but not within its life.

This nominal godliness, which is devoid of power, is a shameful thing. I close with that. It is a shameful thing for this life, for the Lord Jesus loathes it. When He passed by the fig tree, which was so early with its leaves but so empty of fruit, He saw therein the likeness of the vainglorious professor who has no real holiness, and He said, "Let no fruit grow on you ever again" (Matt. 21:19). His Word withered it at once, and it stood as a terrible emblem of the end of a false profession.

How shameful will such a fruitless, lifeless professor be in eternity, when the secrets of all hearts will be revealed! What shame and everlasting contempt will await him when his falsehood will be detected and his baseness will fill all holy minds with horror! Oh, beware of the hell of the false professor!

I have done when I have added a few words of instruction. The form of godliness is most precious. Let those who feel the power of godliness honor it and use it. Do not despise it because others have damaged it. Come forth and make an open profession of religion. But see that you have the power of it. Cry to God that you may never wear a sleeve that is longer than your arm; you may never go beyond what is really and truly your own. It will be better for you to go to God as a lost soul and cry for mercy than to profess yourself saved when you are not.

Yet confess Christ without fail or fear. Do not be ashamed of Jesus because of the ill manners of His disciples. Regard the ill savor of false professors as a part of the cross that you will have to bear for your Lord. To be associated with some who are not true seems inevitable in this life however carefully we choose our company.

My next is a word of discrimination. Those to whom my text has nothing to say will be the first to take it home to themselves. When I discharge my heart with a faithful sermon, certain trembling souls whom I would gladly comfort are sure to think that I mean them. A poor woman in deep distress comes to me, crying, "Sir, I have no feeling." Dear heart, she has ten times too much feeling. Another moans out, "I am sure I am a hypocrite." I never met with a hypocrite who thought himself one. And I never shall.

"Oh," said another, "I feel condemned." He that feels himself condemned may hope for pardon. If you are afraid of yourselves, I am not afraid of you. If you tremble at God's Word, you have one of the surest marks of God's elect. Those who fear that they are mistaken are seldom mistaken. If you search yourselves and allow the Word of God to search you, it is well with you. The bankrupt trader fears to have his books examined. The sound man even pays an accountant to overhaul his affairs. Use discrimination and neither acquit nor condemn yourself without reason.

If the Spirit of God leads you to weep in secret for sin and to pray in secret for divine grace, if He leads you to seek after holiness, if He leads you to trust alone in Jesus, then you know the power of godliness, and you have never denied it. You who cry, "Oh, that I felt more of the power of the Holy Spirit, for I know that He could comfort and sanctify me and make me live the life of heaven on earth!" You are not the aim of either the text or the sermon for you have not denied the power. No, no, this text does not belong to you but to quite another class of people.

Let me give you a word of admonition. Learn from the text that there is something in godliness worth having. The form of godliness is not all. There is a blessed power. The Holy Spirit is that power, and He can work in you to will and to do of God's good pleasure. Come to Jesus Christ, dear souls. Do not come to the minister, or to the church, in the first place. But come to Jesus. Come and lay yourselves at His feet and say, "Lord, I will not be comforted unless you comfort me." Come and take everything at first hand from your crucified Lord. Then will you know the power of godliness.

Beware of secondhand religion; it is never worth carrying home. Get your godliness direct from heaven by the personal dealing of your own soul with your Savior. Profess only what you possess and rest only in that which has been given you from above. Your heavenly life, as yet, may be very feeble, but the grain of mustard seed will grow. You may be the least in Israel, but that is better than being the greatest in Babylon.

The Lord bless these words and apply them to each one in his own way by His Holy Spirit. You can make either a blister of them or a plaster of them, as conscience will direct. God guide you, for Jesus Christ's sake. Amen.

For Further Thought

1. *How does Jude 12 describe people who have only a form of godliness?*
2. *Two men are praying in Luke 18:9–13. Which one has a form of godliness but denies its power?*
3. *Second Peter 2:10–20 tells of people who have a form of godliness but deny its power. How does verse 17 describe them?*

THE GOSPEL'S POWER IN
A CHRISTIAN'S LIFE

Only let your conversation be as it becometh the gospel of Christ.
PHILIPPIANS 1:27 KJV

THE word *conversation* does not merely mean our talk with one another, but the whole course of our life and behavior in the world. The Greek word signifies the actions and the privileges of citizenship, and we are to let our whole citizenship, our actions as citizens of the New Jerusalem, be such as becomes the gospel of Christ. Observe, dear friends, the difference between the exhortations of the legalists and those of the gospel. He who would have you perfect in the flesh exhorts you to *work* that you may be saved, that you may accomplish a meritorious righteousness of your own and so may be accepted before God.

But he who teaches the doctrines of divine grace urges you to holiness for quite another reason. He teaches that you are saved because you believe in the Lord Jesus Christ, and he speaks to as many as are saved in Jesus and asks them to make their actions conformable to their position. He only seeks what he may reasonably expect to receive. "Let your conversation be such as becomes the gospel of Christ. You have been saved by it, you profess to glory in it, and you desire to extend it. Let then your conversation be such as becomes it."

The one, you perceive, bids you to *work* that you may enter heaven by your working. The other exhorts you to labor, because heaven is yours as the gift of divine grace, and he would have you act as one who is made meet to be a partaker of the inheritance of the saints in light. Some persons cannot hear an exhortation without at once crying out that we are legal. Such persons will always find this tabernacle the wrong place for them to feed in. We are delighted to preach good high doctrine and to insist that salvation is of grace alone! But we are equally delighted to preach good high *practice* and to insist that a grace that does not make a man better than his neighbors is a grace that will never take him to heaven nor render him acceptable before God!

I have already remarked that the exhortation is given in a form that is highly reasonable. The followers of any other religion, as a rule, are conformed to their religion. No nation has ever yet risen above the character of its so-called gods. Look at the disciples of Venus. Were they not sunk deep in licentiousness? Look at the worshippers of Bacchus. Let their Bacchanalian rebels tell how they entered into the character of their deity. The worshippers to this day of the goddess Kale, the goddess of thieves and murderers, known as the Thugs, enter most heartily into the spirit of the idol that they worship.

We do not marvel at the crimes of the ancients when we recollect the gods whom they adored: Moloch, who delighted in the blood of little children; Jupiter, Mercury, and the like, whose actions stored in the classical dictionary are enough to pollute the minds of youth. We marvel not that licentiousness abounded, for "like gods, like people."

"A people are never better than their religion," it has often been said, but in most cases they are rather worse. It is strictly in accordance with nature that a man's religion should season his conversation. Paul puts it, therefore, to you who profess to be saved by Jesus Christ, "Let your conversation be as it becomes the gospel of Christ."

To get at this we must meditate for two or three minutes upon what the gospel is, then take up the points in which our conversation ought to be like to the gospel. And finally, utter a few earnest words to press upon professors of religion the stern necessity of letting their conversation be such as becomes the gospel of Christ.

I. *The gospel of Christ, what is it?* We look at the last two words, "of Christ." Indeed, if you understand Christ, you understand the gospel. Christ is the author of it. He, in the council chamber of eternity, proposed to become the Surety for poor fallen man! He, in the fullness of time, worked out eternal redemption for as many as His Father had given Him. He is the author of it as its architect and builder. We see in Christ Jesus the alpha and the omega of the gospel. He has provided in the treasury of grace all that is necessary to make the gospel the gospel of our salvation.

And as He is the author of it, so He is the matter of it. It is impossible to preach the gospel without preaching the person, the work, the offices, and the character of Christ. If Christ is preached, the gospel is promulgated, and if Christ is put in the background, then there is no gospel declared. "I determined not to know anything among you," said the apostle, "except Jesus Christ and Him crucified" (1 Cor. 2:2). And so saying, he was carrying out his commission to preach the gospel both to Jews and to Gentiles. The sum total, the essential, the marrow—what the old Puritans would have called the *quintessence*—of the gospel is Christ Jesus! So that when we have done preaching the gospel, we may say, "Now of the things that we have spoken He is the sum," and we may point to Him in the manger, to Him on the cross, to Him risen, to Him coming in the second advent, to Him reigning as prince of the kings of the earth—yes, point to Him everywhere as the sum total of the gospel.

> We see in Christ Jesus the alpha and the omega of the gospel. He has provided in the treasury of grace all that is necessary to make the gospel the gospel of our salvation.

It is also called the gospel of Christ, because it is He who will be the finisher of it. He will put the finishing stroke to the work as He laid the foundation stone. The believer does not begin in Christ and then seek perfection in himself. No, as we run the heavenly race, we are still looking to Jesus! As His hand first tore away the sin that does so easily beset us and helped us to run the race with patience, so that same hand will hold out the olive branch of victory, will weave it into a chaplet of glory and put it about our brow. It is the gospel of Jesus Christ. It is His property. It glorifies His person. It is sweet with the savor of His name. It bears throughout the mark of His artistic fingers. If the heavens are the work of God's fingers and the moon and the stars are by His ordinance, so we may say the same of the whole plan of salvation. The whole of it, great Jesus, is your workmanship, and by your ordinance it stands fast!

It is the gospel of Jesus Christ, and though hundreds of times this has been explained, it will not be amiss to go over it again. It is the "good-spell," the good news of Jesus Christ, and it is good news emphatically, because it clears away sin, the worst evil on earth. Better still, it sweeps away death and hell! Christ came into the world to take sin upon His shoulders and to carry it away, hurling it into the red sea of His atoning blood. Christ, the scapegoat, took the sin of His people upon His own head and bore it all away into the wilderness of forgetfulness, where, if it is searched for, it will be found no more forever.

This is good news, for it tells that the cancer at the vitals of humanity has been cured! That the leprosy that rose even to the very brow of manhood has been taken away! Christ has filled a better stream than the river Jordan and now says to the sons of men, "Go, wash and be clean" (see 2 Kings 5:1–14). Besides removing the worst of ills, the gospel is good news because it brings the best of blessings. What does it do but give life to the dead? It opens dumb lips, unstops deaf ears, and unseals blind eyes! Does it not make earth the abode of peace? Has it not shut the doors of hell upon believers and opened the gates of heaven to all who have learned to trust in Jesus' name? Good news? Why, that word *good* has got a double meaning when it is applied to the gospel of Jesus Christ!

Well were angels employed to go and tell it, and happy are the men who spend and are spent in the proclamation of such glad tidings of great joy. "God is reconciled!" "Peace on earth!" "Glory to God in the highest!" "Goodwill toward men!" God is glorified in salvation, sinners are delivered from the wrath to come, and hell does not receive the multitudes of men, but heaven is filled with the countless host redeemed by blood. It is "good news," too, because it is a thing that could not have been invented by the human intellect. It was news to angels, and they have not ceased to wonder at it yet! They still stand looking upon the mercy seat, desiring to know more of it. It will be news in eternity! We shall

> *Sing with rapture and surprise,*
> *His loving kindness in the skies.*

The good news, put simply into a few words, is just this: "That God was in Christ reconciling the world to Himself, not imputing their trespasses to them" (2 Cor. 5:19); "God so loved the world, that He gave His only begotten Son, that whoever believes in Him should not perish but have everlasting life" (John 3:16); "This is a faithful saying and worthy of all acceptance, that Christ Jesus came into the world to save sinners" (1 Tim. 1:15). So much then for what the gospel is.

II. Now I am not going to speak to those who do not welcome the gospel; I will speak to them another time. I pray God helps them to believe it, but today I have especially to speak to believers. The text says we are to *let our conversation be such as becomes the gospel*. What sort of conversation, then, will we have? In the first place, the gospel is very simple. It is unadorned. No meretricious ornaments to clog the pile. It is simple and "not with persuasive words of human wisdom" (1 Cor. 2:4). It is grandly sublime in its simplicity. Let the Christian be such. It does not become the Christian minister to be arrayed in blue and scarlet and fine linen and vestments and robes. These belong to Antichrist and are described in the book of Revelation as the sure marks of the whore of Babylon.

It does not become the Christian man or the Christian woman to be guilty of spending hours in the adornment of his or her person. Our adornment should be "the incorruptible beauty of a gentle and quiet spirit" (1 Pet. 3:4). There should be about our manner, our speech, our dress, and our whole behavior that simplicity that is the very soul of beauty. Those who labor to make themselves admirable in appearance, by gaudy ornaments, miss the road. Beauty is its own adornment, and she is most adorned when unadorned the most.

The Christian man ought always to be simple in all respects. I think wherever you find him, you ought not to need a key to him. He should not be like certain books that you cannot make out without having somebody tell you the hard words. He should be a transparent man like Nathaniel, who was "an Israelite indeed, in whom is no deceit" (John 1:47). The man who catches the spirit of his Master is, like Christ, a child-man, a man-child. You know they called Him that holy child, Jesus. So let us be remembering that except we are converted and become as little children, who are eminently simple and childlike, we cannot enter into the kingdom of heaven.

In the next place, if our conversation is such as becomes the gospel, we will remember that the gospel is preeminently true. There is nothing in the gospel that is false, no admixture, nothing put in as an *argumentum ad hominem* to catch the popular ear. It tells the truth, the naked truth, and if men dislike it, the gospel cannot help it. It is gold without dross. It is pure water without admixture. Now such should the Christian be. He should make his conversation true. The saints are men of honor, but sometimes, brethren, I think that many of us talk too much to speak nothing but the truth of God.

I do not know how people could bring out broadsheets every morning with so much news if it were all true! I suppose there must be a little padding to fill it up, and some of that is very poor stuff. And people that keep on talking, talking, talking, cannot grind all meal. Surely it must be, some of it, rather coarse bran. And in the conversation of a good many professing Christians, how much is there that is scandal, if not slander, uttered against other Christians? How much uncharitableness, if not willful falsehood, is spoken by some professors? Too often a rebuke is taken up heedlessly and repeated without any care being taken to ascertain whether it is true or not.

The Christian's lips should speak truth when falsehood drops from the lips of all other men. A Christian man should never need to take an oath, because his word is as good as an oath. His *yes* should be yes, and his *no*, no. It is for him to so live and speak that he will be in good repute in all society—if not for the etiquette of his manners, certainly for the truthfulness of his utterances! Show me a man who is habitually or frequently a liar and you show me a man who will have his portion in the lake that burns with fire and brimstone!

I do not care to what denomination of Christians he may belong; if a man speaks the thing that is not, I am sure he is none of Christ's. And it is very sad to know that there are some in all fellowships who have this great and grievous fault that you cannot trust them in what they say. God deliver us from that! Let our conversation be such as becomes the gospel of Christ, and then it will be invariably truthful! Or, if there is error in it, it will always be through misadventure and never on purpose or from carelessness.

In the next place, the gospel of Jesus Christ is a very fearless gospel. It is the very reverse of that pretty thing called modern charity. The last created devil is modern charity. Modern charity goes cap in hand round to us all, and it says, "You are *all* right, every one of you! Do not quarrel any longer! Sectarianism is a horrid thing. Down with it! Down with it!" And so it tries to induce all sorts of persons to withhold a part of what they believe, to silence the testimony of all Christians upon points wherein

SERMONS RELATING TO BELIEVERS

they differ. I believe that thing called sectarianism nowadays is none other than true honesty.

Be a sectarian, my brother. Be profoundly a sectarian! I mean by that, hold everything that you see to be in God's Word with a tighter grasp, and do not give up even the little pieces of truth. At the same time, let that sectarianism that makes you hate another man because he does not agree with you be far from you! But never consent to that unholy league and covenant that seems to be rife throughout our country that would put a padlock on the mouth of every man and send us all about as if we were dumb, which says to me, "You must not speak against the errors of such and such a church." And to another, "You must not reply." We cannot but speak! If we did not, the stones in the street might cry out against us.

> *The saints are men of honor, but sometimes, brethren, I think that many of us talk too much to speak nothing but the truth of God.*

That kind of charity is unknown to the gospel. Now hear the Word of God! "He who believes and is baptized will be saved; but he who does not believe" will what? "Will get to heaven some other way?" No! "Will be *condemned*" (Mark 16:16). That is the gospel. You perceive how boldly it launches out its censure? It does not *pretend* "you may reject me and go by another road and at last get safely to your journey's end!" No, no, no! You will be condemned, it says! Do you not perceive how Christ puts it? Some teachers come into the world and say to all, "Yes, gentlemen, by your leave, you are all right. I have a point or two that you have not taught. Just make room for me; I will not turn you out. I can stand in the same temple as yourself."

But hear what Christ says: "All who ever came before Me are thieves and robbers, but the sheep did not hear them" (John 10:8). Hear what His servant Paul says, "But even if we, or an angel from heaven, preach any other gospel to you than what we have preached to you," what then? "Let him be excused for his mistake?" No! "Let him be accursed" (Gal. 1:8). Now this is strong language, but mark you, this is just how the Christian ought to live! As the gospel is very fearless in what it has to say, so let the Christian always be. It strikes me that a living that becomes the gospel of Christ is always a bold and fearless kind of living!

Some people go crawling through the world as if they asked some great man's permission to live. They do not know their own minds. They take their words out of their mouths, look at them, and ask the opinion of a friend or two. "What do you think of these words?" And when these friends censure them, they put them in again and will not say them. Like jellyfish, they have no backbone. Now God has made men upright, and it is a noble thing for a man to stand erect on his own feet. And it is a nobler thing still for a man to say that in Christ Jesus he has received that freedom that is freedom indeed, and therefore he will not be the slave of any man.

"O Lord," says David, "truly I am Your servant...You have loosed my bonds" (Ps. 116:16). Happy is he whose bonds are loosed! Let your eyes be like that of an eagle; yes, let them be brighter still! Let them never be dimmed by the eyes of any other man. Let your heart be like that of the lion, fearless! Say of yourself, "Careless, myself a dying man, of dying men's esteem," I must live as in the sight of God, as I believe I should live, and then let man say his best or say his worst, it will be no more than the chirping of a grasshopper when the sun goes down. Who are you that you should be afraid of a man who will die, or the son of man who is but a worm? (Job 25:6). Make yourselves like men! Be strong! Fear not! For only so will your conversation be such as becomes the gospel of Christ.

> *L*et there be such a gentleness about your carriage that the little children may not be afraid to come to you and the publican and harlot may not be driven away by your hostility, but invited to goodness by the gentleness of your words and acts.

But again, the gospel of Christ is very gentle. Hear it speak: "Come to Me, all you who labor and are heavy laden, and I will give you rest" (Matt. 11:28). Here is its spirit in its founder: "A bruised reed He will not break, and smoking flax He will not quench" (12:20). Moreover, bad temper, snapping off of people's heads, making men offenders for a word—all this is quite contrary to the gospel. Some people seem to have been nursed upon vinegar and their entire attitude far better suits Sinai than Zion. You might think that they had always come to the mount that might not be touched, that burns with fire, for they seem, *themselves*, to burn with fire. I may say to them that the best of them is sharper than a thorn hedge.

Now, dear friends, let it never be so with us. Be firm, be bold, be fearless, but be cautious! If you have a lion's heart, have a lady's hand. Let there be such a gentleness about your carriage that the little children may not be afraid to come to you and the publican and harlot may not be driven away by your hostility, but invited to goodness by the gentleness of your words and acts. Again, the gospel of Christ is very loving. It is the speech of the God of love to a lost and fallen race. It tells us, "God so loved the world that He gave His only begotten Son, that whoever believes in Him should not perish but have everlasting life" (John 3:16).

It proclaims in every word the divine grace of Him who loved us and gave Himself for us. "Greater love hath no man than this, that a man lay down his life for his friends" (John 15:13 kjv). This same mind that was in Christ Jesus should dwell richly in us. His last command to His disciples was "Love one another." He who loves is born of God, while without this grace, whatever we may think of ourselves or whatever others may think of us, we are really, in God's sight, nothing better than sounding brass and tinkling cymbals. Is not this an age in which we will do well to direct our attention to the flower of paradise? The atmosphere of the church should foster this heavenly plant to the highest perfection. The world ought to point to us and say, "See how these Christians love one another? Not in word only, but in deed and in truth!"

I care not for that love that calls me a beloved and longed-for brother, and then if I happen to differ in sentiment and practice, treats me as a schismatic and denies me the rights of the brotherhood, and if I do not choose to subscribe to an arbitrarily imposed contribution to its funds, seizes my goods and sells them in the name of the law, order, and church of Christ! From all such will our good Lord deliver us! But oh, for more real hearty union and love to all the saints, and for more of that realization of the fact that we are *one* in Christ Jesus.

At the same time pray for more love to *all* men. We ought to love all our hearers, and the gospel is to be preached by us to every creature. I hate sin everywhere, but I love and wish to love yet more and more every day the souls of the worst and vilest of men. Yes, the gospel speaks of love, and I must breathe it forth, too, in every act and deed. If our Lord was love incarnate, and we are His disciples, let all take knowledge of us that we have been with Jesus and learned of Him.

The gospel of Christ, again, is the gospel of mercy, and if any man would act as becomes the gospel, he must be a man of mercy. Do I see him? He is praying. He has been to the sacramental table, and he has been drinking the wine that betokens the Savior's blood—what a good man he is! See him on Monday—he has his hands on his brother's throat, saying, "Pay me what you owe!" Is that such as becomes the gospel of Christ? There he sits. He will give his subscription to a charity, but he will grind down the needlewoman! He will get fat on her blood and bones! He will take a grasp, if he can, of the poor and sell them and devour them as though they were bread, and yet at the same time, for a pretense he will make long prayers.

Is this such as becomes the gospel of Christ? I think not. The gospel of Christ is mercy, generosity, and liberality. It receives the beggar and hears his cry! It picks up even the vile and undeserving and scatters lavish blessings upon them, and it fills the bosom of the naked and of the hungry with good things. Let your conversation be such as becomes the gospel of Christ! You *miserly* and *stingy* people have not a conversation such as becomes the gospel of Christ! There might be plenty of money for God's treasury, for God's church, and for God's poor if there were not some who seem to live only to amass and to hoard!

Their life is diametrically opposed to the whole current and spirit of the gospel of Christ Jesus. Forgive all who offend you! Help all, as far as you are able to do it, live a life of unselfishness! Be prepared, as much as lies in you, to do good to all men and especially to the household of faith! And so will your conversation be such as becomes the gospel of Christ. I must not, however, omit to say that the gospel of Christ is *holy*. You cannot find it excusing sin. It pardons it, but not without an atonement so dreadful that sin never seems so exceedingly sinful as in the act of mercy that puts it away.

"Holy! Holy! Holy!" is the cry of the gospel—and such is the cry of cherubim and seraphim. Now, if our conversation is to be like the gospel, we must be holy, too. There are some things that the Christian must not even name, much less indulge in. The grosser vices are to him things to be hidden behind the curtain and totally unknown. The amusements and pleasures of the world, so far as they may be innocent, are his, as they are other men's. But wherein they become sinful or doubtful, he discards them with disgust, for he has secret sources of joy and needs not, therefore, to go and drink of that muddy river of which thirsty worldlings are so fond. He seeks to be holy as Christ is holy. And there is no conversation that becomes the gospel of Christ except that.

III. Dear friends, I might thus continue, for the subject is a very wide one. But I stop because, unhappily for me, though perhaps happily for your patience, my time has gone. Having just indicated what the Christian life ought to be, I must, in a few words, plead with you that by the power of God's Holy Spirit you will seek to make your lives such. I could mention many reasons, but I will only give you one or two.

The first is, if you do not live like this, you will make your fellow members who are innocent of your sin, suffer. This ought to be a very convincing motive. If a Christian man could dishonor himself and bear the blame alone, he might put up with it, but you cannot! I say, sir, if you are seen intoxicated, or if you are known to fall into some sin of the flesh, you will make the life of every poor girl in the church harder than it is. And every poor young man who has to put up with persecution will feel that you have put a sting into the arrows of the wicked that could not otherwise have been there. You sin against the congregation of God's people!

I know there are some of you here that have to suffer a good deal for Christ's sake. The jeer rings in your ears from morning to night, and you learn to put up with it manfully. But it is very hard when they can say to you, "Look at So-and-So, he is a church member! Look at what he did. You are *all* a parcel of hypocrites!" Now, my dear friends, you know that is not true! You know that there are many in our churches of whom the world is not worthy. They are the excellent, the devout, the Christlike. Do not sin, then, for their sakes, lest you make them to be grieved and sorely vexed.

Again, do you not see how you make your Lord to suffer, for they do not lay your sins at your door merely, but they say that springs from your *religion*. If they would impute the folly to the fool, I might not care! But they impute it to the wisdom that must have made that fool wise if he could have learned. They will lay it to my door. That does not matter much, I have long lost my character. But I cannot bear it should be laid at Christ's door—that is, at the door of the gospel.

When I said just now that I had lost my character, I meant just this: that the world loathes me and I would not have it do otherwise. So let it; I say there is no love lost between us. If the world hates Christ's minister, he can only say he desires that he may never inherit the curse of those who love the world in whom the love of the Father is not found. Yet it has ever been the lot of the true Christian minister to be the butt of slander and, nevertheless, to glory in the cross with all its shame.

But I know, dear friends, you would not, any of you, wish that I should bear the reproach of your sins, yet I have to do it very often. Not very often for many, but for some. There are those, of whom I might tell you even weeping, that they are the enemies of the cross of Christ, and some others whom we would pluck out of the fire, hating the garment spotted with the flesh. They bring sad dishonor upon us, upon the ministry, upon the gospel, and upon Christ Himself. You do not want to do that! At least, I hope you do not. Then let your conversation be such as becomes the gospel of Christ.

And then, remember, dear friends, unless your conversation is such, you will pull down all the witness that you have ever borne for Christ. How can your Sunday school children believe what you tell them when they see your actions contradict your teaching? How can your own children at home believe in your religion when they see the godlessness of your life? The men at the factory will not believe in your going to prayer meeting when they see you walking inconsistently among them. Oh, the great thing the church needs is more holiness! The worst enemies of the church are not the infidels. Really, one does not know who the infidels are nowadays. They are so small a fry and so few of them, that one would have to hunt to find them out.

> *here are those, of whom I might tell you even weeping, that they are the enemies of the cross of Christ, and some others whom we would pluck out of the fire, hating the garment spotted with the flesh.*

No, the worst enemies of the church are the hypocrites, the formalists, the mere professors, and the inconsistent walkers. You, if there are any such here, you pull down the walls of Jerusalem, you open the gates to her foes, and as much as lies in you, you serve the devil. May God forgive you! May Christ forgive you! May you be washed from this atrocious sin! May you be brought humbly to the foot of the cross to accept mercy, which until now you have rejected. It is shocking to think how persons dare to remain members of Christian churches and even to enter the pulpit when they are conscious that their private life is foul! Oh, how can they do it?

How is it that their hearts have grown so hard? What? Has the devil bewitched them? Has he turned them away from being men and made them as devilish as himself that they should dare to pray in public and to sit at the sacramental table and to administer ordinances while their hands are foul and their hearts unclean and their lives are full of sin? I charge you, if there are any of you whose lives are not consistent, give up your profession, or else make your lives what they should be!

May the eternal Spirit, who still winnows His church, blow away the chaff and heave only the good golden wheat upon the floor! And if you know yourselves to be living in any sin, may God help you to mourn over it, to loathe it, to go to Christ about it tonight—to take hold of Him, to wash His feet with your tears, to repent unfeignedly, and then to begin anew in His strength a life that will be such as becomes the gospel. I think I hear some ungodly person here saying, "Well, I do not make any profession. I am all right."

Now, listen, dear friend, listen! I have a word for you. A man is brought up before the magistrates, and he says, "Well, I never made any profession of being an honest man."

"Oh," says the magistrate, "there is six months for you then." You see, he is a villain outright!

And you that say, "Oh, I never made any profession," place yourselves among the condemned ones by putting yourself on that ground! But some people make a boast of it. "I never made a profession." Never made a profession of doing your duty to your Maker? Never made a profession of being obedient to the God in whose hands your breath is? Never made a profession of being obedient to the gospel?

Why, it will be very short work with you when you come to be tried at last. There will need to be no witnesses, for you never made a profession, you never pretended to be right. What would you think of a man who said, "Well, I never made a profession of speaking the truth"?

"Well," says another, "I never made a profession of being chaste."

"Why," you would say, "let us get out of this fellow's company, because evidently nothing but evil can come from him, for he is not good enough even to make a profession!"

Now I put that strongly that you may remember it! Will you go home and just meditate on this: "I never made a profession of being saved. I never made a profession of repenting of my sins, and therefore I am every day making a profession of being God's enemy, of being impenitent, of being unbelieving. And when the devil comes to look for his own, he will know me, for I make a profession of being one of his by not making a profession of being one of Christ's."

The fact is that I pray God to bring us all here first to be Christ's and then to make a profession of it. Oh, that your heart might be washed in Jesus' blood and then, having given it to Christ, give it to Christ's people! The Lord bless these words of mine for Jesus' sake. Amen.

FOR FURTHER THOUGHT

1. *Philippians 1:27 mentions three aspects of conduct that are appropriate for the gospel. What are they?*
2. *Titus 2:11–12 says that we should live "soberly, righteously, and godly in this present age." What do these verses say teaches this way of life?*
3. *Romans 6:4 uses a three-word phrase to describe our conduct, or walk, as a result of the death and resurrection of Christ. What is this phrase?*

THE SECRET OF
POWER IN PRAYER

*"If you abide in Me, and My words abide in you, you will
ask what you desire, and it shall be done for you."*
JOHN 15:7

BELIEVERS do not enjoy the gifts of divine grace all at once.
Coming to Christ, we are saved by a true union with Him. But it is by
abiding in that union that we further receive the purity, the joy, the power,
and the blessedness that are stored up in Him for His people. See how our
Lord states this when He speaks to the believing Jews in the eighth chapter
of this gospel, at the thirty-first and thirty-second verses: "Then Jesus said
to those Jews who believed Him, 'If you abide in My word, you are My
disciples indeed. And you shall know the truth, and the truth shall make you
free,'" We do not know all the truth of God at once; we learn it by *abiding*
in Jesus.

Perseverance in divine grace is an educational process by which we
learn the truth of God fully. The emancipating power of that truth is also
gradually perceived and enjoyed. The truth will make you free. One bond
after another snaps, and we are free indeed. You who are young beginners
in the divine life may be cheered to know that there is something better still
for you—you have not yet received the full recompense of your faith. As
our hymn puts it, "It is better than before." You will have happier views of
heavenly things as you climb the hill of spiritual experience. As you abide
in Christ, you will have firmer confidence, richer joy, greater stability, more
communion with Jesus, and greater delight in the Lord your God.

Infancy is beset with many evils from which manhood is exempt. It
is the same in the spiritual as in the natural world. There are degrees of
attainment among believers, and the Savior here incites us to reach a high
position by mentioning a certain privilege that is not for all who say that

they are in Christ but for only those who are *abiders* in Him. Every believer should be an abider, but many have hardly earned the name as yet. Jesus says, "If you abide in Me, and My words abide in you, you will ask what you desire, and it shall be done for you." You have to *live* with Christ to know Him, and the longer you live with Him, the more you will admire and adore Him, and the more you will receive from Him, even grace for grace.

> *P*erseverance in divine grace is an educational process by which we learn the truth of God fully. The emancipating power of that truth is also gradually perceived and enjoyed.

Truly He is a blessed Christ to one who is but a month old in divine grace. But these babes can hardly tell what a precious Jesus He is to those whose acquaintance with Him covers well-near half a century! Jesus, in the esteem of abiding believers, grows sweeter and dearer, fairer and lovelier each day. Not that He improves in Himself, for He is perfect. But as *we* increase in our knowledge of Him, we appreciate more thoroughly His matchless excellences. How glowingly do His old acquaintances exclaim, "Yes, He is altogether lovely!" Oh, that we may continue to grow up in Him in all things who is our head, that we thus may prize Him more and more!

I call your earnest attention to our text, begging you to consider with me three questions. First, *what is this special blessing?* "You will ask what you desire, and it shall be done for you." Second, *how is this special blessing obtained?* "If you abide in Me and My words abide in you." Then, third, *why is it obtained in this way?* There must be a reason for the conditions laid down as necessary to obtaining the promised power in prayer. Oh, that the anointing of the Holy Spirit that abides on us may now make this subject very profitable to us!

I. *What is this special blessing?* Let us read the verse again. Jesus says, "If you abide in Me, and My words abide in you, you will ask what you desire, and it shall be done for you."

Observe that our Lord had been warning us that severed from Him we can do nothing, and therefore we might naturally have expected that

He would now show us how we can do all spiritual acts. But the text does not run as we should have expected it to run. The Lord Jesus does not say, "Without Me you can do nothing, but if you abide in Me and My words abide in you, you will do all spiritual and gracious things." He does not now speak of what they *should* themselves be enabled to do but of what should be done for them.

He says not, "Strength will be given you sufficient for all those holy doings of which you are incapable apart from Me." That would have been true enough, and it is the truth of God that we looked for here. But our most wise Lord improves upon all parallelisms of speech and improves upon all expectancies of heart and says something better still. He does not say, "If you abide in Me, and My words abide in you, you will do spiritual things," but "*you will ask.*" By prayer you will be enabled to do. But before all attempts to do, you will ask. The choice privilege here given is a mighty prevailing *prayerfulness*. Power in prayer is very much the gauge of our spiritual condition. And when that is secured to us in a high degree, we are favored as to all other matters.

One of the first results, then, of our abiding union with Christ will be the certain exercise of prayer. You will ask. If others neither seek nor knock nor ask, you at any rate will do so. Those who keep away from Jesus do not pray. Those in whom communion with Christ is suspended feel as if they could not pray. But Jesus says, "If you abide in Me, and My words abide in you, you will ask." Prayer comes spontaneously from those who abide in Jesus, even as certain oriental trees, without pressure, shed their fragrant gums.

Prayer is the natural out-gushing of a soul in communion with Jesus. Just as the leaf and the fruit will come out of the vine without any conscious effort on the part of the branch but simply because of its living union with the stem, so prayer buds and blossoms and produces fruit out of souls abiding in Jesus. As stars shine, so do abiders pray. It is their use and their second nature. They do not say to themselves, "Now it is the time for us to get to our task and pray." No, they pray as wise men eat—namely, when the desire for it is upon them. They do not cry out as under bondage, "At this time I ought to be in prayer, but I do not feel like it. What a weariness it is!" No, they have a glad errand at the mercy seat, and they are rejoiced to go upon it.

Hearts abiding in Christ send forth supplications as fires send out flames and sparks. Souls abiding in Jesus open the day with prayer. Prayer surrounds them as an atmosphere all day long. At night they fall asleep praying. I have known them even to dream a prayer, and at any rate, they are able joyfully to say, "When I awake, I am still with You." Habitual asking comes out of abiding in Christ. You will not need urging to prayer when you are abiding with Jesus. He says, You will ask. And depend upon it, you will!

> *Hearts abiding in Christ send forth supplications as fires send out flames and sparks. Souls abiding in Jesus open the day with prayer. Prayer surrounds them as an atmosphere all day long.*

You will also feel most powerfully the *necessity* of prayer. Your great need of prayer will be vividly seen. Do I hear you say, "What? When we abide in Christ and His words abide in us, have we not already attained?" Far are we, then, from being satisfied with ourselves. It is *then* that we feel more than ever that we must ask for *more* divine grace. He who knows Christ best knows his own necessities best. He who is most conscious of life in Christ is also most convinced of his own death apart from Christ. He who most clearly discerns the perfect character of Jesus will be most urgent in prayer for divine grace to grow like Him. The more I seem to be in my Lord, the more I desire to obtain from Him, since I know that all that is in Him is put there on purpose that I may receive it.

"Of His fullness have we all received, and grace for grace" (John 1:16). It is just in proportion as we are linked to Christ's fullness that we feel the necessity of drawing from it by constant prayer. Nobody needs to prove to an abider in Christ the doctrine of prayer, for we enjoy the thing itself. Prayer is now as much a necessity of our spiritual life as breath is of our natural life—we cannot live without asking favors of the Lord! "If you abide in Me, and My words abide in you, you will ask"—and you will not wish to cease from asking. He has said, "Seek My face," and your heart will answer, "Your face, LORD, I will seek" (Ps. 27:8).

Note next that the fruit of our abiding is not only the exercise of prayer and a sense of the necessity of prayer, but it includes *liberty* in prayer. "You will ask what you desire." Have you not been on your knees at times without power to pray? Have you not felt that you could not plead as you desired? You wanted to pray, but the waters were frozen up and would not flow. You said mournfully, "I am shut up, and I cannot come forth" (Ps. 88:8 KJV). The will was present but not the freedom to present that will in prayer. Do you, then, desire liberty in prayer so that you may speak with God as a man speaks with his friend? Here is the way to it: "If you abide in Me, and My words abide in you, you will ask what you desire."

I do not mean that you will gain liberty as to mere fluency of utterance, for that is a very *inferior* gift. Fluency is a questionable endowment, especially when it is not attended with weight of thought and depth of feeling. Some brethren pray by the yard. But true prayer is measured by weight and not by length. A single groan before God may have more fullness of prayer in it than a fine oration of great length. He who dwells with God in Christ Jesus is the man whose steps are enlarged in intercession. He comes boldly because he abides at the throne. He sees the golden scepter stretched out and hears the King saying, "Ask what you will, and it will be done to you."

It is the man who abides in conscious union with his Lord who has freedom of access in prayer. Well may he come to Christ readily, for he is *in* Christ and *abides* in Him. Attempt not to seize this holy liberty by excitement or presumption—there is but one way of really gaining it, and here it is—"If you abide in Me, and My words abide in you, you will ask what you desire." By this means alone will you be enabled to open your mouth wide, that God may fill it. Thus will you become Israel's and as princes have power with God.

This is not all. The favored man has the privilege of *successful* prayer. "You will ask what you desire, and it shall be done for you." You may not do it, but it shall be done for you. You long to bear fruit. Ask and it shall be done for you. Look at the vine branch. It simply remains in the vine, and by remaining in the vine the fruit comes from it. It is done for it. Brothers and sisters in Christ, the purpose of your being, its one object and design, is to bring forth fruit to the glory of the Father. To gain this end you must abide in Christ, as the branch abides in the vine. This is the method by which your prayer for fruitfulness will become successful. "It shall be done for you."

Concerning this matter, "You will ask what you desire, and it shall be done for you." You will have wonderful prevalence with God in prayer, insomuch that before you call He will answer and while you are yet speaking, He will hear. "The desire of the righteous shall be granted" (Prov. 10:24 KJV). To the same effect is the other text: "Delight yourself also in the LORD, and He shall give you the desires of your heart" (Ps. 37:4). There is great breadth in this text: "You will ask what you desire, and it shall be done for you." The Lord gives the abider carte blanche. He puts into his hand a signed check and permits him to fill it up as he wills.

Does the text mean what it says? I never knew my Lord to say anything He did not mean. I am sure that He may sometimes mean more than we understand Him to say, but He never means less. Mind you, He does not say to all men, "I will give you whatever you ask." Oh no, that would be an unkind kindness, but He speaks to His disciples and says, "If you abide in Me, and My words abide in you, you will ask what you desire, and it shall be done for you." It is to a certain class of men who have already received great grace at His hands. It is to them He commits this marvelous power of prayer.

O my dear friends, if I may covet earnestly one thing above every other, it is that I may be able to ask what I will of the Lord and have it! The man who prevails in prayer is the man to preach successfully, for he may well prevail with man for God when he has already prevailed with God for men! This is the man to face the difficulties of business life. For what can baffle him when he can take all to God in prayer? One such man as this, or one such woman as this in a church is worth ten thousand of us common people. In these we find the peerage of the skies. In these are the men in whom is fulfilled God's purpose concerning man, whom He made to have dominion over all the works of His hands.

> *O my dear friends, if I may covet earnestly one thing above every other, it is that I may be able to ask what I will of the Lord and have it! The man who prevails in prayer is the man to preach successfully.*

The stamp of sovereignty is on the brows of these men. They shape the history of nations, they guide the current events through their power on high. We see Jesus with all things put under Him by the divine purpose and as we rise into that image. We also are clothed with dominion and are made kings and priests to God. Behold Elijah, with the keys of the rain swinging at his girdle, he shuts or opens the windows of heaven! There are such men still alive. Aspire to be such men and women, I beseech you, that to you the text may be fulfilled, "You will ask what you desire, and it shall be done for you."

The text seems to imply that if we reach this point of privilege, this gift will be a perpetuity. "You will ask." You will always ask; you will never get beyond asking, but you will ask successfully. "You will ask what you desire, and it shall be done for you." Here we have the gift of *continual* prayer. Not for the week of prayer, not during a month's conference, nor upon a few special occasions will you pray prevailingly. But you will possess this power with God so long as you abide in Christ and His words abide in you. God will put His omnipotence at your disposal. He will put forth His Godhead to fulfill the desires that His own Spirit has worked in you.

I wish I could make this jewel glitter before the eyes of all the saints till they cried out, "Oh, that we had it!" This power in prayer is like the sword of Goliath. Wisely may every David say, "There is none like it; give it to me" (1 Sam. 21:9). This weapon of all-prayer beats the enemy and at the same time enriches its possessor with all the wealth of God. How can he lack anything to whom the Lord has said, "Ask what you desire, and it shall be done for you"? Oh, come let us seek this promise. Listen and learn the way. Follow me while by the light of the text I point out the path. May the Lord lead us in it by His Holy Spirit!

II. How is this privilege of mighty prayerfulness *to be obtained*? The answer is, "If you abide in me and my words abide in you." Here are the two feet by which we climb to power with God in prayer.

Beloved, the first line tells us that we are to abide in Christ Jesus our Lord. It is taken for granted that we are already in Him. May it be taken for granted in your case, dear hearer? If so, you are to abide where you are. As believers we are to remain tenaciously clinging to Jesus, lovingly knit to Jesus. We are to abide in Him by always trusting Him, and Him only, with the same simple faith that joined us to Him at the first. We must never admit any other thing or person into our heart's confidence as our hope of salvation. We must rest alone in Jesus as we received Him at the first. His Godhead, His manhood, His life, His death, His resurrection, and His glory at the right hand of the Father—in a word, Himself—must be our heart's sole reliance. This is absolutely essential. A temporary faith will not save. An abiding faith is necessary.

But abiding in the Lord Jesus does not only mean *trusting* in Him. It includes our yielding ourselves up to Him to receive His life and to let that life work out its results in us. We live *in* Him, *by* Him, *for* Him, and *to*

Him when we abide in Him. We feel that all our separate life has gone, for "you died, and your life is hidden with Christ in God" (Col. 3:3). We are nothing if we get away from Jesus. Then we would be branches withered and only fit to be cast into the fire. We have no reason for existence except that which we find in Christ, and what a marvelous reason that is! The vine needs the branch as truly as the branch needs the vine. No vine ever bore any fruit except upon its branches. Truly it bears all the branches and so bears all the fruit.

But yet it is by the branch that the vine displays its fruitfulness. Thus are abiding believers necessary to the fulfillment of their Lord's design. Wonderful thing to say, that the saints are necessary to their Savior! The church is His body, the fullness of Him who fills all in all. I want you to recognize this: that you may see your blessed responsibility, your practical obligation to bring forth fruit that the Lord Jesus may be glorified in you. Abide in Him and never diminish your consecration to His honor and glory, never dream of being your own master. Be not the servant of men but abide in Christ. Let Him be the object, as well as the source, of your existence.

> When you see the work of the Spirit increasing in you, do not let the devil tempt. He will try to get you to boast that now you are somebody; you need not come to Jesus as a poor sinner and rest in His precious blood alone for salvation.

Oh, if you get there and stop there in perpetual communion with your Lord, you will soon realize a joy, a delight, a power in prayer such as you never knew before! There are times when we are conscious that we are in Christ and we know our fellowship with Him. And oh, the joy and the peace that we drink from this cup! Let us abide there. "Abide in Me," says Jesus. You are not to come and go, but to *abide*. Let that blessed sinking of yourself into His life, the spending of all your powers for Jesus, and the firm faith of your union with Him remain in you forever. Oh, that we might attain to this by the Holy Spirit!

As if to help us to understand this, our gracious Lord has given us a delightful parable. Let us look through this discourse of the vine and its branches. Jesus says, "Every branch in Me. . .that bears fruit He prunes"

(John 15:2). Take care that you abide in Christ when you are being purged. "Oh," says one, "I thought I was a Christian. But, alas! I have more troubles than ever. Men ridicule me, the devil tempts me, and my business affairs go wrong." Brother, if you are to have power in prayer, you must take care that you abide in Christ when the sharp knife is cutting everything away. Endure trial and never dream of giving up your faith because of it. Say, "Though He slay me, yet will I trust Him" (Job 13:15).

Your Lord warned you when you first came into the vine that you would have to be purged and cut closely. And if you are now feeling the purging process, you must not think that some strange thing has happened to you. Rebel not because of anything you may have to suffer from the dear hand of your heavenly Father who is the husbandman of the vineyard. Rather, cling to Jesus all the more closely. Say, "Cut, Lord, cut to the quick if You will! But I will cling to You. To whom should we go? You have the words of eternal life." Yes, cling to Jesus when the purging knife is in His hand, and so shall you "ask what you desire, and it shall be done for you."

Take care, also, that when the purging operation has been carried out you still cleave to your Lord. Notice the third and fourth verses in John 15: "You are already clean because of the word which I have spoken to you. Abide in Me, and I in you." Abide *after* cleansing where you were *before* cleansing. When you are *sanctified*, abide where you were when first *justified*. When you see the work of the Spirit increasing in you, do not let the devil tempt. He will try to get you to boast that now you are somebody; you need not come to Jesus as a poor sinner and rest in His precious blood alone for salvation. Abide still in Jesus. As you kept to Him when the knife cut you, keep to Him now that the tender grapes begin to form.

Do not say to yourself, "What a fruitful branch I am! How greatly I adorn the vine! Now I am full of vigor!" You are nothing and nobody. Only as you abide in Christ are you one whit better than the waste wood that is burned in the fire. "But do we not make progress?" Yes, we grow, but we abide. We never go an inch farther. We abide in Him. Or, if not, we are cast forth and are withered. Our whole hope lies in Jesus at our best times as well as at our worst. Jesus says, "You are already clean because of the word which I have spoken to you. Abide in Me, and I in you." Abide in Him as to all your fruitfulness. "As the branch cannot bear fruit of itself, unless it abides in the vine, neither can you, unless you abide in Me" (John 15:4).

"Here, then, I have something to do," cries one. Certainly you have, but not apart from Jesus. The branch has to bear fruit. But if the branch imagines that it is going to produce a cluster, or even a grape out of itself alone, it is utterly mistaken. The fruit of the branch must come forth of the stem. Your work for Christ must be Christ's work in you or else it will be good for nothing. I pray you, see to this. Your Sunday school teaching, your preaching, or whatever you do, must be done in Christ Jesus. Not by your natural talent can you win souls, nor by plans of your own inventing can you save men. Beware of homemade schemes. Do for Jesus what Jesus bids you do. Remember that our work for Christ, as we call it, must be Christ's work first if it is to be accepted of Him. Abide in Him as to your fruit bearing.

Yes, abide in Him as to your very *life*. Do not say, "I have been a Christian man now twenty or thirty years; I can do without continued dependence upon Christ." No, you could not do without Him if you were as old as Methuselah! Your very *being* as a Christian depends upon your still clinging, still trusting, still depending on your Master, and this He must give you, for it all comes from Him and Him alone. To sum it all up, if you want that splendid power in prayer of which I spoke just now, you must remain in loving, living, lasting, conscious, practical, abiding union with the Lord Jesus Christ. And if you get to that by divine *grace*, then you will ask what you desire and it will be done for you.

But there is a second qualification mentioned in the text, and you must not forget it: "and My words abide in you." How important, then, are Christ's words! He said in the fourth verse, "Abide in Me, and I in you," and now as a parallel to this it is, "If you abide in Me, and My words abide in you." What, then? Are Christ's words and Himself identical? Yes, practically so. Some talk about Christ being the Master, but as to doctrine they do not care what His Word declares. So long as their hearts are right toward His person, they claim liberty of thought. Yes, but this is a mere subterfuge.

We cannot separate Christ from the Word. For, in the first place, He *is* the Word. And in the next place, how dare we call Him Master and Lord and do not the things that He says and reject the truth of God that He teaches? We must obey His precepts or He will not accept us as disciples, especially that precept of love that is the essence of all His words. We must love God and our brethren—yes, we must cherish love to all men and seek their good. Anger and malice must be far from us. We must walk even as He walked. If Christ's words abide not in you, both as to belief and practice, you are not in Christ. Christ and His gospel and His commands are one.

If you will not have Christ and His words, neither will He have you nor your words, and you will ask in vain. You will by and by give up asking; you will become as a withered branch. Beloved, I am persuaded better things of you and things that accompany salvation, though I thus speak. Oh, for divine grace to pass through these two-leaved gates, these two golden doors! "If you abide in Me, and My words abide in you." Push through the two and enter into this large room: "You will ask what you desire, and it shall be done for you."

III. It is my last work to try to show *why this privilege should be so obtained*. Why is this extraordinary power of prayer given to those who abide in Christ? May what I have to say encourage you to make the glorious attempt to win this pearl of great price! Why is it, that by abiding in Christ and having His words abide in us, we get to this liberty and prevalence in prayer?

I answer, first, because of the fullness of Christ. You may very well ask what you desire when you abide in Christ, because whatever you may require is already lodged in Him. Good Bishop Hall worked out this thought in a famous passage. I will give you the substance of it. Do you desire the grace of the Spirit? Go to your Lord's anointing. Do you seek holiness? Go to His example. Do you desire pardon of sin? Look to His blood. Do you need mortification of sin? Look to His crucifixion. Do you need to be buried to the world? Go to His tomb. Do you want to feel the fullness of a heavenly life? Behold His resurrection. Would you rise above the world? Mark His ascension. Would you contemplate heavenly things? Remember His sitting at the right hand of God and know that He has "raised us up together, and made us sit together in the heavenly places in Christ Jesus" (Eph. 2:6).

I see clearly enough why the branch gets all it wants while it abides in the stem, since all it wants is already *in* the stem and is placed there for the sake of the branch. What does the branch want more than the stem can give it? If it did want more, it could not get it. For it has no other means of living but by sucking its life out of the stem. O my precious Lord, if I want anything that is not in you, I desire always to be without it. I desire to be denied a wish that wanders outside of you. But if the supply of my desire is already in you for me, why should I go elsewhere? You are my all, where else should I look? Beloved, "it pleased the Father that in Him all the fullness should dwell" (Col. 1:19), and the good pleasure of the Father is our good pleasure. We are glad to draw everything from Jesus. We feel sure that, ask what we will, we will have it, since He has it ready for us.

The next reason for this is the richness of the Word of God. Catch this thought: "If my words abide in you, you will ask what you desire, and it will be done to you." The best praying man is the man who is most believingly familiar with the promises of God. After all, prayer is nothing but taking God's promises to Him and saying to Him, "Do as you have said." Prayer is the promise utilized. A prayer that is not based on a promise has no true foundation. If I go to the bank without a check, I need not expect to get money. It is the order to pay that is my power inside the bank and my warrant for expecting to receive.

O my precious Lord, if I want anything that is not in you, I desire always to be without it. I desire to be denied a wish that wanders outside of you.

You who have Christ's words abiding in you are equipped with those things that the Lord regards with attention. If the Word of God abides in you, you are the man who can pray because you meet the great God with His own words and thus overcome omnipotence with omnipotence. You put your finger down upon the very lines and say, "Do as you have said." This is the best praying in the entire world! O beloved, be filled with God's Word. Study what Jesus has said, what the Holy Spirit has left on record in this divinely inspired book, and in proportion as you *feed* on the Word, are *filled* with the Word, *retain* the Word in your faith, and *obey* the Word in your life, you will be a master in the art of prayer!

You will acquire skill as a wrestler with the covenant angel in proportion as you can plead the promises of your faithful God. Be well instructed in the doctrines of divine grace and let the word of Christ dwell in you richly, that you may know how to prevail at the throne of grace. Abiding in Christ and His words abiding in you are like the right hand and the left hand of Moses that were held up in prayer so that Amalek was smitten, Israel was delivered, and God was glorified!

Let us go a little further. You still may say you do not quite see why a man who abides in Christ and in whom Christ's words abide should be allowed to ask whatever he wills and it will be done to him. I answer you again: It is so because in such a man as that there is a predominance of divine grace that causes him to have a renewed will that is according to the will of God. Suppose a man of God is in prayer and he thinks that such and such a thing is desirable, yet he remembers that he is nothing but a babe in the presence of his all-wise Father, and so he bows his will and asks as a favor to be taught what to will.

Though God bids him ask what he wills, he shrinks and cries, "My Lord, here is a request that I am not quite clear about. As far as I can judge, it is a desirable thing, and I will it. But, Lord, I am not fit to judge for myself, and therefore I pray You, give not as *I* will, but as You will." Do you not see that when we are in such a condition as this, *our* real will is *God's* will? Deep down in our hearts we will only desire that which the Lord Himself wills. And what is this but to ask what we will and it is done to us? It becomes safe for God to say to the sanctified soul, "Ask what you desire, and it shall be done for you." The heavenly instincts of *that* man lead him right. The divine grace that is within his soul thrusts down all covetous lusting and foul desires, and his will is the actual *shadow* of God's will.

The spiritual life is master in him, and so his aspirations are holy, heavenly, and Godlike. He has been made a partaker of the divine nature—and as a son is like his father, so now in desire and will he is one with his God. As the echo answers to the voice, so does the renewed heart echo the mind of the Lord. Our desires are reflected beams of the divine will—you will ask what you desire, and it will be even so.

You clearly see that the holy God cannot pick up a common man in the street and say to him, "I will give you whatever you will." What would he ask for? He would ask for a good drink or permission to enjoy himself in evil lust. It would be very unsafe to trust most men with this permit. But when the Lord has taken a man and has made him new—has quickened him into newness of life and has formed him in the image of His dear Son— then He can trust him! Behold, the great Father treats us in our measure as He treats His firstborn. Jesus could say, "I know that You always hear me" (John 11:42), and the Lord is educating us to the same assurance.

We can say with one of old, "My God will hear me." Do not your mouths water for this privilege of prevailing prayer? Do not your hearts long to get at this? It is by the way of holiness. It is by the way of union to Christ. It is by the way of a permanent abiding in Him and an obedient holding fast of His truths that you are to come to this privilege! Behold, the only safe and true way. When once that way is really trod, it is a most sure and effectual way of gaining substantial power in prayer.

I have not quite done. A man will succeed in prayer when his faith is strong. And this is the case with those who abide in Jesus. It is *faith* that prevails in prayer. The real eloquence of prayer is a believing desire. "All things are possible to him who believes" (Mark 9:23). A man abiding in Christ, with Christ's words abiding in him, is eminently a believer and consequently eminently successful in prayer. He has strong faith indeed, for his faith has brought him into vital contact with Christ, and he is, therefore, at the source of every blessing and may drink to his full at the well itself.

Such a man, once more, will also possess the indwelling of the Spirit of God. If we abide in Christ and His words abide in us, then the Holy Spirit has come and taken up His residence in us. And what better help in prayer can we have? Is it not a wonderful thing that the Holy Spirit Himself makes intercession in the saints according to the will of God? He makes "intercession for us with groanings which cannot be uttered" (Rom. 8:26). What man knows the mind of a man save the spirit of a man? The Spirit of God knows the mind of God, and He works in us to will what God wills, so that a believing man's prayer is God's purpose reflected in the soul as in a mirror.

The eternal decrees of God project their shadows over the hearts of godly men in the form of prayer. What God intends to do, He tells to His servants by inclining them to ask Him to do what He Himself is resolved to do. God says, "I will do this and that." But then He adds, "I will yet for this be inquired of by the house of Israel, to do it for them" (Ezek. 36:37 KJV). How clear it is that if we abide in Christ and His words abide in us, we may ask what we will! For we will only ask what the Spirit of God moves us to ask. And it is impossible that God the Holy Spirit and God the Father should be at cross-purposes with one another. What the one prompts us to ask, the other has assuredly determined to bestow.

I struck out a line just now to which I must return for a single moment. Beloved, do you not know that when we abide in Christ and His words abide in us, the Father looks upon us with the same eye with which He looks upon His dear Son? Christ is the vine, and the vine includes the branches. The branches are a part of the vine. God, therefore, looks upon us as *part* of Christ, members of His body, of His flesh and His bones. Such is the Father's love to Jesus that He denies Him nothing. He was obedient to death, even the death of the cross. Therefore does His Father love Him as the God-Man mediator, and He will grant Him all His petitions. And is it so that when you and I are in real union to Christ, the Lord God looks upon us in the same way as He looks on Jesus and says to us, "I will deny you nothing. You will ask what you desire, and it shall be done for you"? So do I understand the text.

> The eternal decrees of God project their shadows over the hearts of godly men in the form of prayer. What God intends to do, He tells to His servants by inclining them to ask Him to do what He Himself is resolved to do.

I call your attention to the fact that in that fifteenth chapter, the ninth verse, that I did not read this morning, runs thus: "As the Father loved Me, I also have loved you; abide in My love" (John 15:9). The same love that God gives to His Son, the Son gives to us! And therefore we are dwellers in the love of the Father *and* of the Son. How can our prayers be rejected? Will not Infinite Love have respect to our petitions? O dear brothers and sisters in Christ, if your prayers speed not to the throne, suspect that there is some sin that hinders them—your Father's love sees a necessity for chastening you this way.

If you do not abide in Christ, how can you hope to pray successfully? If you pick and choose His words and doubt this and doubt that, how can you hope to speed to the throne? If you are willfully disobedient to any of His words, will not this account for failure in prayer? But abide in Christ and take fast hold upon His words and be altogether His disciple—*then* will you be heard of Him. Sitting at Jesus' feet, hearing His words, you may lift up your eyes to His dear face and say, "My Lord, hear me now." And He will answer you graciously. He will say to you, "I have heard you in a time accepted, and in the day of salvation have I succored you. Ask what you will, and it will be done to you." Oh, for power at the mercy seat!

Beloved friends, do not hear this sermon and then go away and forget it. Try to reach this place of boundless influence. What a church we could be if you were all mighty in prayer! Dear children of God, do you want to be half starved? Beloved brethren, do you desire to be poor, little, puny, driveling children who will never grow into men? I pray you, aspire to be strong in the Lord and to enjoy this exceedingly high privilege. What an army would you be if you all had this power with God in prayer! It is within your reach, you children of God! Only abide in Christ and let His words abide in you, and then this special privilege will be yours! These are not irksome duties, but they are in themselves a joy. Go in for them with your whole heart, and then you will get this added to you—that you will ask what you desire and it shall be done for you.

Unhappily, to a portion of this congregation my text says nothing at all. For some of you are not even in Christ, and therefore you cannot abide in Him. O sirs, what will I say to you? You seem to me to miss a very heaven even now! If there were no hell hereafter, it is hell enough not to know Christ now, not to know what it is to prevail with God in prayer, not to know the choice privilege of abiding in Him and His words abiding in you. Your first matter is that you believe in Jesus Christ to the saving of your souls, yielding your *souls* to His cleansing, your *lives* to His government. God has sent Him forth as a Savior. Accept Him. Receive Him as your teacher. Yield yourself up to Him as your master. May His gracious Spirit come and do this work upon you now. And then, after this, but not before, you may aspire to this honor.

First of all, you must be born again. I cannot say to you, as you are now, "Grow," because you will only grow a bigger sinner. However much you may be developed, you will only develop what is in you, and that is the heir of wrath will become more and more the child of evil. You must be made anew in Christ—there must be an absolute change, a reversal of all the currents of nature, a making of you a new creature in Christ Jesus. And then you may aspire to abide in Christ and let His words abide in you, and the consequent prevalence with God in prayer will be yours.

Gracious Lord, help us this morning. Poor creatures as we are, we can only lie at Your feet. Come and uplift us to Yourself for Your mercy's sake! Amen.

FOR FURTHER THOUGHT

1. *John 15:7 tells of answered prayer. What does it say are the three things we must do as we pray?*
2. *The last phrase in John 15:5 expresses a secret of prayer. What is it?*
3. *Spurgeon says that John 15:9 gives the reason Christ answers our prayers. What is that reason?*

The Watchword for Today: "Stand Fast"

For our citizenship is in heaven, from which we also eagerly
wait for the Savior, the Lord Jesus Christ, who will transform our
lowly body that it may be conformed to His glorious body, according
to the working by which He is able even to subdue all things to
Himself. Therefore, my beloved and longed-for brethren,
my joy and crown, so stand fast in the Lord, beloved.
PHILIPPIANS 3:20–21; 4:1

EVERY doctrine of the Word of God has its practical bearing. As each tree bears seed after its kind, so does every truth of God bring forth practical virtues. Hence you find the apostle Paul very full of "therefores." His therefores are the conclusions drawn from certain statements of divine truth. I marvel that our excellent translators should have divided the argument from the conclusion by making a new chapter where there is least reason for it.

Last Lord's day I spoke with you concerning the most sure and certain resurrection of our Lord Jesus. Now there is a practical force in that truth of God that constitutes part of what is meant by the power of His resurrection. Since the Lord has risen and will surely come a second time, and will raise the bodies of His people at His coming, there is something to wait for and a grand reason for steadfastness while thus waiting. We are looking for the coming of our Lord and Savior Jesus Christ from heaven and for Him to "transform our lowly body that it may be conformed to His glorious body." Therefore let us stand fast in the position that will secure us this honor. Let us keep our posts until the coming of the Great Captain will release the sentinels. The glorious resurrection will abundantly repay us for all the toil and travail we may have to undergo in the battle for the Lord. The glory to be revealed even now casts a light upon our path and causes sunshine within our hearts! The hope of this happiness makes us even now strong in the

Lord and in the power of His might.

Paul was deeply anxious that those in whom he had been the means of kindling the heavenly hope might be preserved faithful until the coming of Christ. He trembled lest any of them should seem to draw back and prove traitors to their Lord. He dreaded lest he should lose what he hoped he had gained, by their turning aside from the faith. Hence he beseeches them to "stand fast." He expresses in the sixth verse of the first chapter his conviction that He who had begun a good work in them would perform it, but his intense love makes him exhort them, saying, "Stand fast in the Lord, beloved." By such exhortations, final perseverance is promoted and secured.

Paul has fought bravely and, in the case of the Philippian converts, he believes that he has secured the victory, but he fears lest it should yet be lost. He reminds me of the death of the British hero Wolfe who, on the heights of Quebec, received a mortal wound. At the moment when the enemy fled and when he knew that they were running, a smile was on his face, and he cried, "Hold me up. Let not my brave soldiers see me drop. The day is ours. Oh, do keep it!" His sole anxiety was to make the victory sure! Thus warriors die and thus Paul lived. His very soul seems to cry, "We have won the day. Oh, do keep it!"

> *Every doctrine of the Word of God has its practical bearing. As each tree bears seed after its kind, so does every truth of God bring forth practical virtues.*

O my beloved hearers, I believe that many of you are "in the Lord," but I entreat you to "stand fast in the Lord." In your case, also, the day is won, but oh, do keep it! There is the pith of all I have to say to you this morning—may God the Holy Spirit write it on your hearts! Since you have done all things well up to now, I entreat you to obey the injunction of Jude to "keep yourselves in the love of God" (Jude 21) and to join with me in adoring Him who alone is able to keep us from falling and to present us faultless before His presence with exceedingly great joy. Unto Him be glory forever! Amen.

In leading out your thoughts I will keep to the following order: First, it seems to me from the text that *the apostle perceived that these Philippian Christians were in their right place*: They were, "in the Lord" and in such a position that Paul could safely bid them "stand fast" in it. Second, *he longed for them that they should keep their right place*: "Stand fast in the Lord, beloved." And third, *he urged the best motives for keeping their place*. These motives are contained in the first two verses of our text, upon which we will enlarge further on.

I. Paul joyfully perceived that his beloved *converts were in their right place*. It is a very important thing indeed that we should begin well. The start is not everything, but it is a great deal. It has been said by the old proverb that "well begun is half done," and it is certainly so in the things of God. It is vitally important to enter in at the strait gate, to start on the heavenly journey from the right point. I have no doubt that many slips and falls and apostasies among professors are due to the fact that they were not right at first. The foundation was always upon the sand, and when the house came down, at last, it was no more than might have been expected. A flaw in the foundation is pretty sure to be followed by a crack in the superstructure! See to it that you lay a good foundation. It is better to have no repentance than a repentance that needs to be repented of! It is better to have no faith than a false faith! It is better to make no profession of religion than to make an untruthful one! God give us grace that we may not make a mistake in learning the alphabet of godliness, or else in all our learning we will blunder on and increase in error. We should learn early the difference between grace and merit, between the purpose of God and the will of man, between trust in God and confidence in the flesh. If we do not start aright, the further we go, the further we will be from our desired end and the more thoroughly in the wrong will we find ourselves. Yes, it is of prime importance that our new birth and our first love should be genuine beyond all question.

The only position, however, in which we can begin aright is to be in the Lord. This is to begin as we may safely go on. This is the essential point. It is a very good thing for Christians to be in the church, but if you are in the church before you are in the Lord, you are out of place! It is a good thing to be engaged in holy work, but if you are in holy work before you are in the Lord, you will have no heart for it; neither will the Lord accept it! It is not essential that you should be in this church or in that church, but it *is* essential that you should be "in the Lord"! It is not essential that you should be in the Sunday school, nor in the working meeting, nor in the Tract Society, but it *is* essential to the last degree that you should be in the Lord! The apostle rejoiced over those who were converted at Philippi because he knew they were in the Lord. They were where he wished them to remain, and therefore he said, "Stand fast in the Lord."

What is it to be in the Lord? Well, brothers and sisters, *we are in the Lord vitally and evidently when we fly to the Lord Jesus by repentance and faith* and make Him to be our refuge and hiding place. Is it so with you? Have you fled out of *self*? Are you trusting in the Lord *alone*? Have you come to Calvary and beheld your Savior? As the doves build their nests in the rocks, have you thus made your home in Jesus? There is no shelter for a guilty soul but in His wounded side! Have you come there? Are you in Him? Then stay there. You will never have a better refuge! In fact, there is no other. No other name is given under heaven among men whereby we must be saved. I cannot tell you to stand fast in the Lord unless you are there. Hence my first enquiry is, are you in Christ? Is He your only confidence? In His life, His death, and His resurrection, do you find the grounds of your hope? Is He Himself all your salvation and all your desire? If so, stand fast in Him.

> *It is a very good thing for Christians to be in the church, but if you are in the church before you are in the Lord, you are out of place!*

Next, these people, in addition to having fled to Christ for refuge, were now *in Christ as to their daily life*. They had heard Him say, "Abide in me," and therefore they remained in the daily enjoyment of Him, in reliance upon Him, in obedience to Him, and in the earnest copying of His example. They were Christians! That is to say, they were persons upon whom was named the name of Christ. They were endeavoring to realize the power of His death and resurrection as a sanctifying influence, killing their sins and fostering their virtues. They were laboring to reproduce His image in themselves so that they might bring glory to His name. Their lives were spent within the circle of their Savior's influence. Are you so, my dear friends? Then stand fast! You will never find a nobler example. You will never be saturated with a more divine spirit than that of Christ Jesus your Lord. Whether we eat or drink, or whatever we do, let us do all in the name of the Lord Jesus and so live in Him.

These Philippians had, moreover, realized that they were *in Christ by a real and vital union with Him.* They had come to feel, not like separated individualities copying a model, but as members of a body made like their head. By a living, loving, lasting union, they were joined to Christ as their covenant head. They could say, "Who shall separate us from the love of Christ?" (Rom. 8:35). Do you know what it is to feel that the life that is in you is first in Christ and still flows from Him, even as the life of the branch is mainly in the stem? "I live; yet not I, but Christ liveth in me" (Gal. 2:20 KJV). This is to be in Christ! Are you in Him in this sense? Forgive my pressing the question. If you answer me in the affirmative, I will then entreat you to "stand fast" in Him. It is in Him and in Him only that spiritual life is to be sustained, even as only *from* Him can it be received. To be engrafted into Christ is salvation, but to *abide in* Christ is the full enjoyment of it. True union to Christ is eternal life. Paul, therefore, rejoiced over these Philippians because they were joined to the Lord in one spirit.

This expression is very short but very full. "In Christ." Does it not mean that we are in Christ as the birds are in the air that buoys them up and enables them to fly? Are we not in Christ as the fish are in the sea? *Our Lord has become our element*—vital and all surrounding! In Him we live, move, and have our being. He is in us, and we are in Him. We are filled with all the fullness of God because all fullness dwells in Christ and we dwell in Him. Christ to us is all. He is in all and He is all-in-all! Jesus to us is everything in everything. Without Him we can *do* nothing and we *are* nothing! Thus are we emphatically *in* Him. If you have reached this point, "stand fast" in it! If you dwell in the secret place of the tabernacles of the Most High, abide under the shadow of the Almighty. Do you sit at His table and eat of His dainties? Then prolong the visit and think not of removal. Say in your soul:

> *Here would I find a settled rest,*
> *While others go and come;*
> *No more a stranger, or a guest,*
> *But like a child at home.*

Has Jesus brought you into His green pastures? Then lie down in them. Go no further, for you will never fare better. Stay with your Lord, however long the night, for only in Him have you hope of morning!

You see that these people were where they should be—in the Lord—and this was the reason why the apostle took such delight in them. Kindly read the first verse of the fourth chapter and see how he loves them and joys over them. He heaps up titles of love! Some dip their morsel in vinegar, but Paul's words were saturated with honey. Here we not only have sweet words, but they mean something, that his love was real and fervent! The very heart of Paul is written out large in this verse: "Therefore, my beloved and longed-for brethren, my joy and crown, so stand fast in the Lord, beloved."

> Because they were in Christ, first of all they were Paul's brothers
> and sisters. This was a new relationship, not earthly but heavenly.

Because they were in Christ, first of all they were Paul's brothers and sisters. This was a new relationship, not earthly but heavenly. What did this Jew from Tarsus know about the Philippians? Many of them were Gentiles. Time was when he would have called them dogs and despised them as the uncircumcised. But now he says, "My brethren." That poor word has become very hackneyed. We talk of brethren without particularly much of brotherly love, but true brothers and sisters have a love for one another that is very unselfish and admirable—and so there is between real Christians a brotherhood that they will neither disown, nor dissemble, nor forget! It is said of our Lord, "for which cause he is not ashamed to call them brethren" (Heb. 2:11 KJV). And surely they need never be ashamed to call one another brethren! Paul, at any rate, looks at the jailer, that jailer who had set his feet in the stocks, and he looks at the jailer's family, at Lydia, and at many others—in fact, at the whole company that he had gathered at Philippi—and he salutes them lovingly as "my brethren." Their names were written in the same family register because they were in Christ and therefore had one Father in heaven!

Next, the apostle calls them "my *beloved and longed-for*." The verse almost begins with this word, and it quite finishes with it. The repetition makes it mean "my *doubly* dear ones." Such is the love that every true servant of Christ will have for those who have been begotten to the faith of Christ by his means. Oh yes, if you are in Christ, His ministers *must* love you! How could there be a lack of affection in our hearts toward you since we have been the means of bringing you to Jesus? Without cant or display, we call you our "beloved and longed-for."

Then the apostle calls them his *"longed-for,"* that is, his most desired ones. He first desired to see them converted. After that he desired to see them baptized. Then he desired to see them exhibiting all the graces of Christians. When he saw holiness in them, he desired to visit them and commune with them. Their constant kindness created in him a strong desire to speak with them face-to-face. He loved them and desired their company because they were in Christ! So he speaks of them as those for whom he longs. His delight was in thinking of them and in hoping to visit them. Then he adds, "My joy and crown." Paul had been the means of their salvation, and when he thought of that blessed result, he never regretted all that he had suffered. His persecutions among the Gentiles seemed light indeed, since these priceless souls were his reward! Though he was nothing but a poor prisoner of Christ, he talks in right royal style: They are his *crown.*

They were his *stephanos,* or "crown," given as a reward for his life-race. This, among the Greeks, was usually a wreath of flowers placed around the victor's brow. Paul's crown would never fade. He writes as he feels the amaranth around his temples—even now he looks upon the Philippians as his chaplet of honor! They were his joy and his crown! He anticipated, I do not doubt, that throughout eternity it would be a part of his heaven to see them amid their blessedness and to know that he helped to bring them to that felicity by leading them to Christ! O beloved, it is indeed our highest joy that we have not run in vain, neither labored in vain. You who have been snatched as brands from the burning and are now living to the praise of our Lord Jesus Christ, you are our prize, our crown, our joy!

These converts were all this to Paul simply because they were "in Christ." They had begun well, they were where they should be, and he, therefore, rejoiced in them.

II. But second, it was for this reason that *he longed that they should stay there.* He entreated them to stand fast. "So stand fast in the Lord, my beloved and longed-for." The beginning of religion is not the whole of it. You must not suppose that the sum of godliness is contained within the experience of a day or two, or a week, or a few months, or even a few years. Precious are the feelings that attend conversion, but dream not that repentance, faith, and so forth are for a season and then all is done with! I am afraid there are some who secretly say, "Everything is now complete. I have experienced the necessary change; I have been to see the elders and the pastor. I have been baptized and received into the church. Now, all is right forever."

That is a false view of your condition! In conversion you have started in the race, but you must run to the end of the course. In your confession of Christ, you have carried your tools into the vineyard, but the day's work now begins. Remember, "He who endures to the end will be saved" (Matt. 10:22). Godliness is a lifelong business. The working out of the salvation that the Lord Himself works *in* you is not a matter of certain hours or of a limited period of life. Salvation is unfolded throughout our entire sojourn here. We continue to repent and to believe—and even the process of our conversion continues as we are changed more and more into the image of our Lord. Final perseverance is the necessary evidence of genuine conversion!

> *Godliness is a lifelong business. The working out of the salvation that the Lord Himself works in you is not a matter of certain hours or of a limited period of life.*

In proportion as we rejoice over converts, we feel an intense bitterness when any disappoint us and turn out to be merely temporary camp followers. We sigh over the seed that sprang up so speedily but that withers so soon because it has neither root nor depth of earth. We were ready to say, "Ring the bells of heaven," but the bells of heaven did not ring because these people talked about Christ and said they were in Christ, but it was all a delusion! After a while, for one reason or another, they went back. "They went out from us, but they were not of us; for if they had been of us, they would have continued with us; but they went out that they might be made manifest, that none of them were of us" (1 John 2:19). Our churches suffer most seriously from the great numbers who drop out of their ranks and either go back to the world or else must be pursuing a very secret and solitary path in their way to heaven, for we hear no more of them. Our joy is turned to disappointment, our crown of laurel becomes a circle of faded leaves, and we are weary at the remembrance of it. With earnestness, therefore, we say to you who are beginning the race, "Continue in your course. We beseech you turn not aside, neither slacken your running till you have won the prize!"

I heard an expression yesterday that pleased me much. I spoke about the difficulty of keeping on. "Yes," answered my friend, "and it is harder, still, to keep on keeping on." So it is. There is the pinch. I know lots of fellows who are wonders at the start. What a rush they make! But then there is no stay in them—they soon lose breath. The difference between the spurious and the real Christian lies in this staying power. The real Christian has a life within him that can never die—an incorruptible seed that lives and abides forever. The spurious Christian, however, begins after a fashion but ends almost as soon as he begins! He is esteemed a saint but turns out a hypocrite. He makes a fair show for a while, but soon he quits the way of holiness and makes his own damnation sure. God save you, dear friends, from anything that looks like apostasy! Hence I would, with all my might, press upon you these two most weighty words: "Stand fast."

I will put the exhortation thus: "Stand fast *doctrinally*." In this age all the ships in the waters are pulling up their anchors! They are drifting with the tide. They are driven about with every wind. It is your wisdom to put down more anchors. I have taken the precaution to cast four anchors out of the stern, as well as to see that the great bower anchor is in its proper place. I will not budge an inch from the old doctrine for any man! Now that the cyclone is triumphant over many a bowing wall and tottering fence, those who are built upon the one foundation must prove its value by standing fast. We will listen to no teaching but that of the Lord Jesus! If you see a truth to be in God's Word, grasp it by your faith, and if it is unpopular, grapple it to you as with hooks of steel. If you are despised as a fool for holding it, hold it the more. Like an oak, take deeper root, because the winds would tear you from your place. Defy reproach and ridicule and you have already vanquished it. Stand fast, like the British squares in the olden times. When fierce assaults were made upon them, every man seemed transformed to rock. We might have wandered from the ranks a little in more peaceful times to look after the fascinating flowers that grow on every side of our march. But now we know that the enemy surrounds us, so we keep strictly to the line of march and tolerate no roaming. The watchword of the host of God just now is, "Stand fast!" Hold to the faith once delivered to the saints.

Hold fast the form of sound words and deviate not one jot or tittle from them. Stand fast doctrinally!

Practically also, abide firm in the right, the true, the holy. This is of the utmost importance. The barriers are broken down—they would amalgamate church and world—yes, even church and *stage*. It is proposed to combine God and devil in one service! Christ and Belial are to perform on one stage! Surely now is the time when the lion will eat straw like the ox and very dirty straw, too. So they say. But I repeat to you this Word of God: "Come out from among them and be separate, says the Lord. Do not touch what is unclean" (2 Cor. 6:17). Write "Holiness to the Lord" (Exod. 28:36), not only on your altars, but also upon the bells of the horses. Let everything be done as before the living God. Do all things to holiness and edification. Strive together to maintain the purity of the disciples of Christ. Take up your cross and go outside the camp bearing His reproach. If you have already stood apart in your decision for the Lord, continue to do so. Stand fast! In nothing be moved by the laxity of the age. In nothing be affected by the current of modern opinion. Say to yourself, "I will do as Christ bids me to the utmost of my ability. I will follow the Lamb wherever He goes." In these times of worldliness, impurity, self-indulgence, and error, it becomes the Christian to gather up his skirts and keep his feet and his garments clean from the pollution that lies all around him. We must be more Puritan and precise than we have been. Oh, for grace to stand fast!

Mind also that you stand fast *experimentally*. Pray that your inward experience may be a close adhesion to your master. Do not go astray from His presence. Neither climb with those who dream of perfection in the flesh, nor grovel with those who doubt the possibility of present salvation. Take the Lord Jesus Christ to be your sole treasure, and let your heart be always with Him. Stand fast in faith in His atonement, in confidence in His divinity, in assurance of His second advent. I pine to know within my soul the power of His resurrection and to have unbroken fellowship with Him. In communion with the Father and the Son, let us stand fast! He will fare well whose heart and soul, affections and understanding are wrapped up in Christ Jesus and in no one else. Concerning your inward life, your secret prayer, your walk with God, here is the watchword of the day—"Stand fast."

To put it very plainly, "Stand fast *in the Lord*," without wishing for another trust. Do not desire to have any hope but that which is in Christ.

Do not entertain the proposition that you should unite another confidence to your confidence in the Lord. Have no hankering after any other fashion of faith except the faith of a sinner in his Savior. All hope but that which is set before us in the gospel and brought to us by the Lord Jesus is a poisoned delicacy, highly colored but by no means to be so much as *tasted* by those who have been fed upon the bread of heaven! What do we need more than Jesus? What way of salvation do we seek but that of grace? What security but the precious blood? Stand fast and wish for no other rock of salvation save the Lord Jesus!

Next, stand fast *without wavering in our trust*. Permit no doubt to worry you. Know that Jesus can save you, and what is more, know that He *has* saved you! So commit yourself to His hands that you are as sure of your salvation as of your existence! The blood of Jesus Christ cleans us from all sin this day—His righteousness covers us, and His life quickens us into newness of life. Tolerate no doubt, mistrust, suspicion, or misgiving. Believe in Christ up to the hilt! As for myself, I will yield to be lost forever if Jesus does not save me! I will have no other string to my bow, no second door of hope or way of retreat. I could risk a thousand souls on my Lord's Word and feel no risk. Stand fast without wishing for another trust and without wavering in the trust you have.

Moreover, stand fast *without wandering into sin*. You are tempted this way and that way—stand fast! Inward passions rise. Lusts of the flesh rebel. The devil hurls his fearful suggestions. The men of your own household tempt you. Stand fast! Only so will you be preserved from the torrents of iniquity. Keep close to the example and spirit of your Master, and having done all, still stand.

As I have said, stand fast without wandering, so next I must say stand fast *without wearying*. You are a little tired. Never mind. Take a little rest and brush up again. "Oh," you say, "this toil is so monotonous." Therefore, do it better, and that will be a change. Your Savior endured His life and labor without this complaint, for zeal had eaten Him up. "Alas," you cry, "I cannot see *results*!" Never mind. Wait for results, even as the farmer waits for the precious fruits of the earth. "Oh, sir, I plod along and make no progress." Never mind. You are a poor judge of your own success. Work on, for in due season you will reap if you faint not. Practice perseverance. Remember that if you have the work of faith and the labor of love, you must complete the trio by adding the patience of *hope*. You cannot do without this last.

"Therefore, my beloved brethren, be steadfast, immovable, always abounding in the work of the Lord, knowing that your labor is not in vain in the Lord" (1 Cor. 15:58).

I am reminded of Sir Christopher Wren, when he cleared away old St. Paul's to make room for his splendid pile. He was compelled to use battering rams upon the massive walls. The workmen kept on battering and battering. An enormous force was brought to bear upon the walls for days and nights, but it did not appear to have made the least impression upon the ancient masonry. Yet the great architect knew what he was doing. He bade them keep on incessantly, and the ram fell again and again upon the rocky wall until at length the whole mass was disintegrating and coming apart. And then each stroke began to tell. At a blow it reeled! At another it quivered! At another it moved visibly. At another it fell over amid clouds of dust! These last strokes did the work!

> *What do we need more than Jesus? What way of salvation do we seek but that of grace? What security but the precious blood? Stand fast and wish for no other rock of salvation save the Lord Jesus!*

Do you think so? No, it was the *combination of blows*, the first as truly as the last! Keep on with the battering ram. I hope to keep on until I die. And, mark you, I may die, and I may not see the errors of the hour totter to their fall, but I will be perfectly content to sleep in Christ, for I have a sure expectation that this work will succeed in the end! I will be happy to have done my share of the work, even if I personally see little apparent result. Lord, let your work appear to your servants, and we will be content that your glory should be reserved for our children. Stand fast, my brothers and sisters, in incessant labors, for the end is sure!

In addition to standing fast in that respect, stand fast *without warping*. Timber, when it is rather green, is apt to go this way or that. The spiritual weather is very bad. Just now, for green wood, it is one day damp with superstition, and another day it is parched with skepticism. Rationalism and ritualism are both at work. I pray that you may not warp! Keep straight. Keep to the truth of God, the whole truth of God, and nothing but the truth, for in the Master's name we bid you, "Stand fast in the Lord."

Stand fast, for there is great need. Many walk of whom I have told you often and now tell you even weeping, that they are the enemies of the cross of Christ!

Paul urged them to stand fast because even in his own case, spiritual life was a struggle. Even Paul said, "Not that I have already attained" (Phil. 3:12). He was pressing forward. He was straining his whole energy by the power of the Holy Spirit. He did not expect to be carried to heaven on a feather bed! He was warring and agonizing. You, beloved, must do the same. What a grand example of perseverance did Paul set to us all! Nothing enticed him from his steadfastness. "None of these things move me" he said, "nor do I count my life dear to myself" (Acts 20:24). He has entered into his rest because the Lord his God helped him to stand fast, even to the end. I wish I had power to put this more earnestly, but my very soul goes forth with it. "Stand fast in the Lord, my beloved and longed-for."

III. Third, *the apostle urged the best motives for their standing fast*. He says, "Stand fast *because of your citizenship*." Read the twentieth verse: "For our citizenship is in heaven." Now, if you are what you profess to be, if you are in Christ, you are citizens of the New Jerusalem. Men ought to behave themselves according to their citizenship and not dishonor their city. When a man was a citizen of Athens, in the olden time, he felt it incumbent upon him to be brave. Xerxes said, "These Athenians are not ruled by kings: How will they fight?"

"No," said one, "but every man respects the law and each man is ready to die for his country." Xerxes soon knew that the same obedience and respect of law ruled the Spartans and that these, because they were of Sparta, were all brave as lions.

He sends word to Leonidas and his little troop to give up their arms. "Come and take them," was the courageous reply! The Persian king had myriads of soldiers with him, while Leonidas had only three hundred Spartans at his side, yet they kept the pass and it cost the eastern despot many thousands of men to force a passage! The sons of Sparta died rather than desert their post! Every citizen of Sparta felt that he must stand fast—it was not for such a man as he to yield. I like the spirit of Bayard, that "knight without fear and without reproach." He knew not what fear meant. In his last battle, his spine was broken, and he said to those around him, "Place me up against a tree so that I may sit up and die with my face to the enemy."

Yes, if our backs were broken, if we could no more bear the shield or use the sword, it would be incumbent upon us, as citizens of the New Jerusalem, to die with our faces toward the enemy! We must not yield! We dare not yield if we are of the city of the great king! The martyrs cry to us to stand fast! The clouds of witnesses bending from their thrones above beseech us to stand fast! Yes, all the hosts of the shining ones cry to us, "Stand fast!" Stand fast for God, the truth, and holiness, and let no man take your crown.

The next argument that Paul used was *their outlook*. "For our citizenship is in heaven, from which we also eagerly wait for the Savior, the Lord Jesus Christ." Brethren, Jesus is coming! He is even now on the way. You have heard our tidings till you scarcely credit us, but the Word of God is true, and it will surely be fulfilled before long. The Lord is coming indeed! He promised to come to die, and He kept His Word. He now promises to come to reign, and you may be sure that He will keep His tryst with His people. He is coming! Ears of faith can hear the sound of His chariot wheels. Every moment of time, every event of providence is bringing Him nearer. Blessed are those servants who will not be sleeping when He comes, nor wandering from their posts of duty! Happy will they be whom their Lord will find faithfully watching and standing fast in that great day!

> *If you are what you profess to be, if you are in Christ, you are citizens of the New Jerusalem. Men ought to behave themselves according to their citizenship and not dishonor their city.*

To us, beloved, He is coming, not as judge and destroyer, but as Savior. We look for the Savior, the Lord Jesus Christ. Now, if we do look for Him, let us "stand fast." There must be no going into sin, no forsaking the fellowship of the church, no leaving the truth, no trying to play fast and loose with godliness, no running with the hare and hunting with the hounds. Let us stand so fast in singleness of heart that whenever Jesus comes, we will be able to say, "Welcome, welcome, Son of God!"

Sometimes I wait through the weary years with great comfort. There was a ship, some time ago, outside a certain harbor. A heavy sea made the ship roll fearfully. A dense fog blotted out all buoys and lights. The captain never left the wheel. He could not tell his way into the harbor, and no pilot could get out to him for a long time. Eager passengers urged him to be courageous and make a dash for the harbor. He said, "No. It is not my duty to run so great a risk. A pilot is required here, and I will wait for one if I wait a week." The truest courage is that which can bear to be charged with cowardice! To wait is much wiser than when you cannot hear the foghorn and have no pilot and steam on and wreck your vessel on the rocks. Our prudent captain waited his time and at last he spied the pilot's boat coming to him over the boiling sea. When the pilot was at his work, the captain's anxious waiting was over. The church is like that vessel—she is pitched to and fro in the storm and the dark—and the Pilot has not yet come. The weather is very threatening. All around, the darkness hangs like a pall. But Jesus will come walking on the water before long! He will bring us safely to the desired haven. Let us wait with patience. Stand fast! Stand fast! Jesus is coming, and in Him is our sure hope!

Further, there was another motive. *There was an expectation.* "He will change our lowly body," or rather, "body of our humiliation." Only think of it, dear friends! No more headaches or heartaches, no more feebleness and fainting, no more inward tumor or consumption. The Lord will transfigure this body of our humiliation into the likeness of the body of His glory. Our frame is now made up of decaying substances. It is of the earth, earthy. "So to the dust, return we must." This body groans, suffers, becomes diseased, and dies. Blessed be God, it will be wonderfully changed, and then there will be no more death, neither sorrow nor crying, neither will there be any more pain.

The natural appetites of this body engender sad tendencies to sin, and in this respect, it is a vile body. It will not always be so! The great change will deliver it from all that is gross and carnal. It will be pure as the Lord's body! Whatever the body of Christ is now, our body is to be like it. We spoke of it last Sunday, you know, when we heard Him say, "Handle Me" (Luke 24:39). We are to have a real, corporeal body as He had, for substance and reality! And like His body, it will be full of beauty, full of health and strength. It will enjoy peculiar immunities from evil and special adaptations for good. That is what is going to happen to me and to you. Therefore let us stand fast. Let us not willfully throw away our prospects of glory and immortality. What? Relinquish resurrection? Relinquish heaven? Relinquish likeness to the risen Lord? O God, save us from such a terrible piece of apostasy! Save us from such immeasurable folly! Suffer us not to turn our backs in the day of battle, since that would be to turn our backs from the crown of life that fades not away!

Lastly, the apostle urges us to stand fast because of *our resources*. Somebody may ask, "How can this body of ours be transformed and transfigured until it becomes like the body of Christ?" I cannot tell you anything about the process. It will all be accomplished in the twinkling of an eye, at the last trumpet. But I can tell you by what power it will be accomplished. The omnipotent Lord will lay bare His arm and exercise His might, "according to the working by which He is able even to subdue all things to Himself." O brothers and sisters, we may well stand fast since we have infinite power at our backs! The Lord is with us with all His energy, even with His all-conquering strength that will yet subdue all His foes! Do not let us imagine that any enemy can be too strong for Christ's arm. If He is able to subdue all things to Himself, He can certainly bear us through all opposition. One glance of His eyes may wither all opposers. Or, better still, one word from His lips may turn them into friends.

> *T*he Lord is with us with all His energy, even with His all-conquering strength that will yet subdue all His foes! Do not let us imagine that any enemy can be too strong for Christ's arm.

The army of the Lord is strong in reserves. These reserves have never yet been fully called out. We who are in the field are only a small squadron holding the fort. But our Lord has at His back ten thousand times ten thousands who will carry war into the enemy's camp. When the captain of our salvation comes to the front, He will bring His heavenly legions with Him. Our business is to watch until He appears on the scene, for when He comes, His infinite resources will be put in marching order.

I like that speech of Wellington (who was so calm amid the roar of Waterloo), when an officer sent word, "Tell the commander-in-chief that he must move me, I cannot hold my position any longer, my numbers are so thinned."

"Tell him," said the great general, "he *must* hold his place! Every Englishman today must die where he stands or else win the victory." The officer read the command to stand, and he did stand till the trumpet sounded victory! And so it is now. My brothers and sisters, we must die where we are rather than yield to the enemy. If Jesus tarries, we must not desert our posts. Wellington knew that the heads of the Prussian columns would soon be visible, coming in to ensure the victory, and so by faith we can perceive the legions of our Lord approaching. In serried ranks His angels fly through the opening heaven! The air is teeming with them. I hear their silver trumpets. Behold, He comes with clouds! When He comes, He will abundantly recompense all who stood fast amid the rage of battle.

Let us sing, "Hold the Fort, for I Am Coming!"

For Further Thought

1. *According to 1 Corinthians 15:54, what event will fulfill the saying, "Death is swallowed up in victory"?*
2. *What does Philippians 3:20–21 say our bodies will be like when Christ changes them?*
3. *The understanding of Christ's changing our body when He comes again will enable us to do what in this life (Phil. 4:1)?*

SERMONS RELATING TO THE WORD OF GOD

THE BIBLE TRIED AND PROVED

The words of the LORD are pure words,
like silver tried in a furnace of earth, purified seven times.
PSALM 12:6

IN this psalm, our text stands in contrast with the evil of the age. The psalmist complains, "The godly man ceases! For the faithful disappear from among the sons of men" (12:1). It was a great grief to him, and he found no consolation except in the words of the Lord. So what if men fail, the word of the Lord abides! What a comfort it is to quit the arena of controversy for the green pastures of revelation. One feels like Noah when shut within the ark. He saw no longer the death and desolation that reigned outside. Live in communion with the Word of God, and even in the absence of Christian friends, you will not lack for company.

Furthermore, the verse stands in fuller contrast still with the words of the ungodly when they rebel against God and oppress His people. They say, "With our tongue we will prevail; our lips are our own; who is lord over us" (12:4)? They boasted, they domineered, they threatened. The psalmist turned away from the voice of the boaster to the words of the Lord. He saw the promise, the precept, and the doctrine of pure truth, and these consoled him while others spoke every man vanity with his neighbor. He had not so many of the words of the Lord as we have, but what he had made his own by meditation, he prized above the finest gold.

In the good company of those who had spoken under divine direction, he was able to bear the threats of those who surrounded him. So, dear friends, if at any time your lot is cast where the truths you love so well are despised, get back to the prophets and apostles and hear through them what God the Lord will speak. The voices of earth are full of falsehood, but the word from heaven is very pure. There is a good practical lesson in the position of the text—learn it well. Make the Word of God your daily companion, and then whatever may grieve you in the false doctrine of the hour, you will not be too much cast down. For the words of the Lord will sustain your spirit.

Looking at the text, does it not strike you as a marvel of condescension that Jehovah, the infinite, should use *words*? He has arranged for us, in His wisdom, this way of communicating with one another. But as for Himself, He is pure spirit and boundless. Shall He contract His glorious thoughts into the narrow channel of sound and ear and nerve? Must the eternal mind use *human* words? The glorious Jehovah spoke *worlds*! The heavens and the earth were the utterances of His lips. To Him it seems more in accordance with His nature to speak tempests and thunders than to stoop to the humble vowels and consonants of a creature of the dust.

> *Our* condescending God is so well pleased to speak to us by words that He has even deigned to call His only-begotten Son, the Word. "The Word became flesh and dwelt among us" (John 1:14).

Will He in very deed communicate with man in man's own way? Yes, He stoops to speak to us by *words*. We bless the Lord for verbal inspiration. Of that we can say, "I have treasured the words of His mouth more than my necessary food" (Job 23:12). I do not know of any other inspiration; neither am I able to conceive of any that can be of true service to us. We need a plain revelation upon which we can exercise faith. If the Lord had spoken to us by a method in which His meaning was infallible but His words were questionable, we should have been rather puzzled than edified. For it is a task indeed to separate the true sense from the doubtful words. We would always be afraid that the prophet or apostle had not, after all, given us the divine sense. It is easy to hear and to repeat words. But it is not easy to convey the meaning of another into perfectly independent words of your own.

We believe that holy men of old, though using their own language, were led by the Spirit of God to use words that were also the words of God. The divine Spirit so operated upon the spirit of the inspired writer that he wrote the words of the Lord, and we, therefore, treasure up every one of them. To us every word of God is pure and full of soul nutriment. Man does not live by bread only, but by every word that proceeds out of the mouth of the Lord. So we can heartily declare with the psalmist, "You are my portion, O Lord; I have said that I would keep Your words" (Ps. 119:57).

Our condescending God is so well pleased to speak to us by words that He has even deigned to call His only-begotten Son, *the Word*. "The Word became flesh and dwelt among us" (John 1:14). The Lord uses words not with reluctance but with pleasure. And He would have us think highly of them, too, as He said to Israel by Moses, "Therefore you shall lay up these words of mine in your heart and in your soul" (Deut. 11:18).

We believe that we have the words of God preserved for us in the scriptures. We are exceedingly grateful that it is so. If we had not the words of the Lord thus recorded, we should have felt that we lived in an evil time, since neither voice nor oracle is heard today. I say we should have fallen upon evil days if the words that God spoke of old had not been recorded under His direction. With this book before us, the Lord now speaks what He spoke two thousand years ago, for He "will not call back His words" (Isa. 31:2). His Word abides forever. It was spoken, not for one occasion, but for all ages.

The Word of the Lord is so instinct with everlasting life and eternal freshness that it is as vocal and forceful in the heart of the saint today as it was to the ear of Abraham when he heard it in Canaan, or to the mind of Moses in the desert, or to David when he sang it on his harp. I thank God that many of us know what it is to hear the divine Word spoken again in our souls! By the Holy Spirit the words of scripture come to us with a *present* inspiration—not only has the book *been* inspired, it *is* inspired. This book is more than paper and ink. It talks with us. Was not that the promise, "When you awake, they will speak with you" (Prov. 6:22)?

We open the book with this prayer: "Speak, Lord, for Your servant hears" (1 Sam. 3:9). And we often close it with this feeling: "Here I am, for You called me" (3:5). As surely as if the promise had never been uttered before but had been spoken out of the excellent glory for the first time, the Lord has made Holy Scripture to be His direct word to our heart and conscience. I say not this of you all, but I can say it assuredly of many here present, may the Holy Spirit at this hour speak to you again!

In trying to handle my text, there will be three points to dwell upon. First, *the quality of the words of God*: "The words of the Lord are pure words." Second, *the trials of the words of God*: "As silver tried in a furnace of earth, purified seven times." And third, *the claims of these words* derived from their purity and the trials that they have undergone. Eternal Spirit, help me to speak correctly concerning your own Word, and help us to feel aright while we hear!

I. First, then, beloved friends, consider *the quality of the words of God*. "The words of the Lord are pure words." From this statement, I gather first the uniformity of their character. No exception is made to any of the words of God, but they are all described as "pure words." They are not all of the same character. Some are for teaching, others are for comfort, and others for rebuke. But they are so far of a uniform character that they are all "pure words." I conceive it to be an evil habit to make preferences in Holy Scripture. We must preserve this volume as a whole. Those sin against scripture who delight in doctrinal texts but omit the consideration of practical passages.

> Whether the Holy Spirit speaks by Isaiah or Jeremiah or John or James or Paul, the authority is still the same. Even concerning Jesus Christ our Lord, this is true.

If we preach doctrine, they cry, "How sweet!" They will hear of eternal love, free grace, and the divine purpose. And I am glad they will. To such I say, "Eat the fat and drink the sweet, and rejoice that there are fat things full of marrow in this book. But remember that men of God in old times took great delight in the commands of the Lord. They had respect to Jehovah's precepts, and they loved His law. If any turn on their heel and refuse to hear of duties and ordinances, I fear that they do not love God's Word at all. He that does not love it *all* loves it *not at all*.

On the other hand, they are equally mistaken who delight in the preaching of duties but care not for the doctrines of grace. They say, "That sermon was worth hearing, for it has to do with daily life." I am very glad that they are of this mind. But if at the same time they refuse other teaching of the Lord, they are greatly at fault. Jesus said, "He who is of God hears

God's words" (John 8:47). I fear you are not of God if you account a portion of the Lord's words to be unworthy of your consideration.

Beloved, we prize the whole range of the words of the Lord. We do not set aside the histories any more than the promises:

> I'll read the histories of Your love,
> And keep Your laws in sight,
> While through the promises I love
> With ever fresh delight.

Above all, do not drop into the semi-blasphemy of some who think the New Testament vastly superior to the Old. I would not err by saying that in the Old Testament you have more of the bullion of truth than in the New—for therein I should be falling into the evil that I condemn. But this I will say: They are of *equal authority*, and they cast such light upon each other that we could not spare either of them. "Therefore what God has joined together, let not man separate" (Matt. 19:6). In the whole book, from Genesis to Revelation, the words of Jehovah are found, and they are always pure words.

Neither is it right for any to say, "Thus spoke Christ Himself. But such and such a teaching is Pauline." No! It is not Pauline. If it is recorded here, it is of the Holy Spirit. Whether the Holy Spirit speaks by Isaiah or Jeremiah or John or James or Paul, the authority is still the same. Even concerning Jesus Christ our Lord, this is true. For He says of Himself, "The word which you hear is not Mine but the Father's who sent Me" (John 14:24). In this matter He puts Himself upon the level of others who were as the mouth of God.

We accept the words of the apostles as the words of the Lord, remembering what John said: "We are of God. He who knows God hears us; he who is not of God does not hear us. By this we know the spirit of truth and the spirit of error" (1 John 4:6). A solemn judgment is thus pronounced upon those who would set the Spirit of Jesus against the Spirit that dwelt in the apostles. The words of the Lord are not affected in their value by the medium through which they came. The revealed truth is all of the same quality even when the portions of it are not of the same weight of metal.

Abiding by the text, we observe next the purity of the words of the Lord: "The words of the Lord are pure words." In commerce there is silver and silver, as you all know—silver with alloy and silver free from baser metal. The Word of God is the silver without the dross. It is as silver that has been purified seven times in a crucible of earth in the furnace till every worthless particle has been removed—it is absolutely pure. David said truly, "The entirety of Your word is truth" (Ps. 119:160). It is truth in the form of goodness, without mixture of evil. The commandments of the Lord are just and right.

We have occasionally heard opponents carp at certain coarse expressions used in our translation of the Old Testament. But the coarseness of translators is not to be set to the account of the Holy Spirit, but to the fact that the force of the English language has changed and modes of expression that were current at one period become too gross for another. But I will assert this: I have never yet met with a single person to whom the words of God have of themselves suggested any evil thing. I have heard a great many horrible things said, but I have never met with a case in which any man has been led into sin by a passage of scripture.

Perversions are possible and probable, but the book itself is absolutely pure. Details are given of very gross acts of criminality, but they leave no injurious impression upon the mind. The saddest story of Holy Scripture is a beacon and never a lure. This is the cleanest, clearest, purest book extant among men. No, it is not to be mentioned in the same hour with the fabulous records that pass for holy books. It comes from God, and every Word is pure.

It is also a book pure in the sense of truth, being without mixture of error. I do not hesitate to say that I believe that there is no mistake whatever in the original Holy Scriptures from beginning to end. There may be, and there are mistakes of translation. For translators are not inspired—but even the *historical* facts are correct. Doubt has been cast upon them here and there and at times with great show of reason—doubt that it has been impossible to meet for a season. But only give space enough and search enough, and the stones buried in the earth cry out to confirm each letter of scripture!

Old manuscripts, coins, and inscriptions are on the side of the Bible, and against it there are nothing but theories and the fact that many an event in history has no other record but that which the Bible affords us. The book has been of late in the furnace of criticism. But much of that furnace has grown cold from the fact that the criticism is beneath contempt. "The words of the Lord are pure words"—there is not an error of any sort in the whole compass of them. These words come from Him who can make no mistake and who can have no wish to deceive His creatures.

If I did not believe in the infallibility of the Bible, I would rather be without it. If I am to judge the book, it is no judge of me. If I am to sift it, like the heap on the threshing floor, and lay this aside and only accept that, according to my own judgment, then I have no guidance whatever unless I have conceit enough to trust my own heart. The new theory denies infallibility to the words of God but practically imputes it to the judgments of men. At least this is all the infallibility that they can get at. I protest that I will rather risk my soul with a guide inspired from heaven than with the differing leaders who arise from the earth at the call of modern thought.

Again, this book is pure in the sense of reliability. It has in its promises no mixture of failure. Mark this: No prediction of scripture has failed. No promise that God has given will turn out to be mere verbiage. Take the promise as the Lord gave it and you will find Him faithful to every jot and tittle of it. Some of us are not yet entitled to be called "old and gray-headed," though the iron gray is pretty conspicuous upon our heads. But up to now we have believed the promises of God, tested, and tried them. And what is our verdict? I bear my solemn testimony that I have not found one Word of the Lord fall to the ground.

The fulfillment of a promise has been delayed sometimes beyond the period that my impatience would have desired. But to the right instant the promise has been kept—not to the ear only—but in deed and in truth. You may lean your whole weight upon any of the words of God and they will bear you up. In your darkest hour, you may have no candle but a single promise, yet that lone light will make high noon of your midnight. Glory be to His name! The words of the Lord are without evil, without error, and without failure.

Furthermore, on this first head the text not only speaks of the uniform character of God's words and of their purity but of their *preciousness*. David compares them to refined silver, and silver is a precious metal. In other places he has likened these words to pure gold. The words of the Lord might have seemed comparable to paper money, such as our own bank notes. But no, they are the metal itself. I remember the time when a friend of ours used to go into the western counties, from one farm to another, buying cheese, and he was in the habit of taking quite a weight of coin with him. He had found that the farmers of that period did not care for bank notes and would not look at checks. They were more ready to sell when they saw that they would be paid in metal, down on the nail.

In the words of God, you have the solid money of truth. It is not fiction, but the substance of truth. God's words are as bullion. When you have them in the grip of faith, you have the substance of things hoped for. Faith finds in the promise of God the reality of what she looks for. The promise of God is as good as the performance itself. God's words, whether of doctrine, of practice, or of comfort, are solid metal to the man of God who knows how to put them in the purse of personal faith. As we use silver in many articles within our houses, so do we use God's Word in daily life. It has a thousand uses. As silver is the current coin of the merchant, so are the promises of God a currency both for heaven and earth—we deal with God by His promises, and so He deals with us.

As men and women deck themselves with silver by way of ornament, so are the words of the Lord our jewels and our glory. The promises are things of beauty, which are a joy forever. When we love the Word of God and keep it, the beauty of holiness is upon us. This is the true ornament of character and life, and we receive it as a love-gift from the bridegroom of our souls.

Beloved, I need not enlarge in your presence upon the preciousness of the Word of God. You have, many of you, prized it long and have proved its value. I have read of a German Christian woman who was accustomed to mark her Bible whenever she met with a passage that was especially precious to her. But toward the end of her life, she ceased from the habit, for she said, "I find it unnecessary. For the whole of the scripture has now become most precious to me." To some of us the priceless volume is marked from beginning to end by our experience. It is all precious and altogether precious.

> No treasures so enrich the mind,
> Nor will Your Word be sold
> For loads of silver well refined,
> Nor heaps of choicest gold.

Furthermore, this text sets before us not only the purity and preciousness of the Lord's words, but the *permanence* of them. They are as silver that has passed through the hottest fires. Truly, the Word of God has for ages stood the fire—and fire applied in its fiercest heat—"tried in a furnace of earth," that is to say in that furnace that refiners regard as their last resort. If the devil could have destroyed the Bible, he would have brought up the hottest coals from the center of hell. He has not been able to destroy one single line! Fire, according to the text, was applied in a skillful way—silver is placed in a crucible of earth that the fire may get at it thoroughly.

The refiner is quite sure to employ his heat in the best manner known to him so as to melt away the dross—so have men with diabolical skill endeavored, by the cleverest criticism, to destroy the words of God. Their object is not purification—it is the *purity of scripture* that annoys them— they aim at consuming the divine testimony. Their labor is in vain. For the sacred book remains still what it always was—the pure words of the Lord.

> *T*he promise of God is as good as the performance itself. God's words, whether of doctrine, of practice, or of comfort, are solid metal to the man of God who knows how to put them in the purse of personal faith.

But some of our misconceptions of its meaning have happily perished in the fires. The words of the Lord have been tried frequently and they have been tried perfectly, "purified seven times." What more remains, I cannot guess, but assuredly the processes have already been many and severe. It abides unchanged. The comfort of our fathers is our comfort. The words that cheered our youth are our support in age. "The grass withers, the flower fades, but the word of our God stands forever" (Isa. 40:8).

These words of God are a firm foundation, and our eternal hopes are wisely built on them. We cannot permit anyone to deprive us of this basis of hope. In the olden time, men were burned rather than cease to read their Bibles. We endure less brutal oppositions, but they are far subtler and difficult to resist. Still let us always abide by the everlasting words, for they will always abide by us.

Unchanged, unchangeable are the words of the ever blessed. They are as silver without dross, which will continue from age to age. This we do believe, and in this we do rejoice. Nor is it a tax upon our faith to believe in the permanence of Holy Scripture, for he who is omniscient and knows everything spoke these words. Therefore, there can be in them no mistake.

He who is omnipotent and can do everything spoke them. And therefore His words will be carried out. Spoken by Him who is immutable, these words will never change. The words that God spoke thousands of years ago are true at this hour, for they come from Him who is the same yesterday, today, and forever.

He who spoke these words is infallible, and therefore *they* are infallible. When did He ever err? Could He err and yet be God? "Has He said, and will He not do? Or has He spoken, and will He not make it good?" (Num. 23:19)? Rest you sure of this: "The words of the LORD are pure words." But time hastens me on to the next point.

II. Second and carefully, let us consider *the trials of the words of God.* They are said to be as silver that has been tried in a furnace. The words of God have been tested by blasphemy, by ridicule, by persecution, by criticism, and by candid observation. I will not attempt an oratorical flight while describing the historical tests of the precious metal of divine revelation, but I will mention trials of a commonplace order that have come under my own notice and probably under yours also. This may be more homely, but it will be more edifying. The Lord help us!

In dealing with the sinner's obstinacy, we have tested the words of the Lord. There are men who cannot be convinced or persuaded. They doubt everything, and with closed teeth they resolve not to believe though a man declare it to them. They are encased in the armor of prejudice, and they cannot be wounded with the sharpest arrows of argument though they profess great openness to conviction. What is to be done with the numerous people who are related to Mr. Obstinate? You might as well argue with an express train as with Mr. Obstinate. He runs on and will not stop though a thousand should stand in his way.

Will the words of God convince him? There are some in this place today of whom I should have said—if I had known them before their conversion—that it was a vain task to preach the gospel to them. They so much loved sin and so utterly despised the things of God. Strangely enough, they were among the first to receive the Word of God when they came under the sound of it. It came to them in its native majesty, in the power of the Holy Spirit. It spoke with a commanding tone to their inmost heart. It threw open the doors that had long been shut up and rusted on their hinges, and

Jesus entered to save and reign!

These who had defiantly brandished their weapons threw them down and surrendered unconditionally to Almighty love, willing believers in the Lord Jesus. Brethren, we have only to have faith in God's Word and speak it out straight and we will see proud rebels yielding. No mind is so desperately set on mischief or so resolutely opposed to Christ that it cannot be made to bow before the power of the words of God. Oh, that we used more the naked sword of the Spirit! I am afraid we keep this two-edged sword in a scabbard and somewhat pride ourselves that the sheath is so elaborately adorned. What is the use of the sheath? The sword must be made bare, and we must fight with it without attempting to garnish it.

Tell forth the words of God. Omit neither the terrors of Sinai nor the love notes of Calvary. Proclaim the Word with all fidelity as you know it and cry for the *power of the Highest* and the most obstinate sinner out of hell can be laid low by its means. The Holy Spirit uses the Word of God. This is His one battering ram with which He casts down the strongholds of sin and self in those human hearts with which He effectually deals. The Word of God will bear the tests furnished by the hardness of the natural heart, and it will, by its operations, prove its divine origin.

> *The words of God have been tested by blasphemy, by ridicule, by persecution, by criticism, and by candid observation.*

Here begins another trial. When you have a man fairly broken down, he has but come part of the way. A new difficulty arises. Will the words of the Lord overcome the penitent's *despair*? The man is full of terror on account of sin, and hell has begun to burn within his bosom. You may talk to him lovingly, but his soul refuses to be comforted. Until you bring the words of the Lord to bear upon him, his soul abhors all manner of meat (Ps. 107:18). Tell him of a dying Savior. Dwell on free grace and full pardon. Speak of the reception of the prodigal son and of the Father's changeless love. Attended by the power of the Spirit, and only by the Holy Spirit, these truths will bring light to those who sit in darkness.

The worst forms of depression are cured when Holy Scripture is *believed*. Often have I been baffled when laboring with a soul convicted of sin and unable to see Jesus. But I have never had a doubt that in the end the words of the Lord would become a cup of consolation to the fainting heart. We may be baffled for a season, but with the words of the Lord as our weapons, despair will not defeat us. O you who are in bondage under fear of punishment, you will come forth to liberty yet—your chains will be broken if you will accept the words of God. My Master's Word is a great opener of prison doors—He has broken the gates of brass and cut the bars of iron asunder.

> *P*ersonally, when I have been in trouble, I have read the Bible until a text has seemed to stand out of the book and salute me, saying, "I was written especially for you."

That is a most wonderful Word, which, like a battle-ax, smashes in the helmet of presumption and at the same time, like the finger of love, touches the tender wound of the bleeding and heals it in an instant! The words of the Lord—for breaking down or lifting up—are equally effective. In certain instances, the words of God are tried by the seeker's singularity. How frequently have persons told us that they were sure there was *nobody* like themselves in the entire world! They were men up in a corner—strange fish, the like of which no sea could yield. Now, if these words are indeed of God, they—and nothing else—will be able to touch every case.

The words of God have been put to that test, and we are amazed at their universal adaptation. There is a text to meet every remarkable and out-of-the-way case. In certain instances we have heard of an odd text, concerning which we could not *before* see why it was written. Yet it has evidently a special fitness for a particular person to whom it has come with divine authority. The Bible may be compared to the locksmith's bunch of keys. You handle them one by one and say of one, "That is a strange key; surely it will fit no lock that ever was made!" But one of these days, the smith is sent to open a very peculiar lock. None of his keys open it. At last he selects that singular specimen. Look! It enters, shoots back the bolt, and gives access to the treasure!

The words of this book are proved to be the words of God because they have an infinite adaptation to the varied minds that the Lord has made. What a gathering of locks we have here this morning! I could not describe you all. Bramah and Chubb and all the rest of them could not have devised such a variety. Yet I am sure that there is a key in this inspired volume that is in every way suited to each lock. Personally, when I have been in trouble, I have read the Bible until a text has seemed to stand out of the book and salute me, saying, "I was written especially for you." It has looked to me as if the story must have been in the mind of the writer when he penned that passage.

And so it *was* in the mind of that divine author who is at the back of all these inspired pages. Thus have the words of the Lord stood the test of adaptation to the singularities of individual men. We frequently meet with people of God who have tested the words of God in time of sore trouble. I make here an appeal to the experience of the people of God. You have lost a dear child. Was there not a Word of the Lord to cheer you? You lost your property. Was there a passage in the scriptures to meet the disaster? You have been slandered, yet was there not a word to console you? You were very sick and depressed. Had not the Lord provided a comfort for you in that case?

I will not multiply questions. The fact is that you never were high but the Word of the Lord was up with you. And you never were low but what the scripture was down with you. No child of God was ever in any ditch, pit, cave, or abyss but the words of God found him out. How often do the gracious promises lie in ambush to surprise us with their loving-kindness! I adore the infinity of God's goodness as I see it mirrored in the glass of scripture.

Again the Word of God is tried and proved as a guide in perplexity. Have we not been forced, at times, to come to a pause and say, "I do not know what to think about this. What is the proper course?" This book is an oracle to the simple-hearted man in mental, moral, and spiritual perplexity. Oh, that we used it more! Rest assured that you will never be in a labyrinth so complicated that this book, blessed of the Spirit, will not help you through. This is the compass for all mariners upon the sea of life—by its use you will know where lies the pole. Abide by the words of the Lord, and your way will be clear.

Beloved, the words of God endure another test. They are our preservatives in times of temptation. You can write a book that may help a man when he is tempted in a certain direction. Will the same volume strengthen him when he is attracted in the opposite direction? Can you conceive a book that will be a complete fence encircling a man in all directions, keeping him from the abyss yonder and from the gulf on the other side? Yet such is the Bible. The devil himself cannot invent a temptation that is not met in these pages. And all the devils in hell together, if they were to hold parliament and to call in the aid of all evil men, could not invent a device that is not met by this matchless library of truth. It reaches the believer in every condition and position and preserves him from all evil. "How can a young man cleanse his way? By taking heed according to Your word" (Ps. 119:9).

Lastly on this point, here is a grand test of the book—it helps men to *die*. Believe me, it is no child's play to die! You and I will find ourselves in that solemn article before we know it, and then we will need strong consolation. Nothing upon earth ever gives me so much encouragement in the faith as to visit members of this church when they are about to die. It is very sad to see them wasting away or racked with pain, but the chief effect produced upon the visitor is gladsome rather than gloomy. I have this week seen a sister well known to many of you who has a cancer in her face and may, in all probability, soon be with her Lord.

> *O*h, for an intense belief of every Word that God has spoken! Do not hold it as a dead creed, but let it hold you as with an Almighty hand. Have no controversy with any of the Lord's words. Believe without a doubt.

It is a dread affliction, and one knows not what it may yet involve. But the gracious patient knows neither murmurs nor fears. No one in this place, though in the flush of health, could be calmer, more restful than our sister is! She spoke to me with full confidence that living or dying she is the Lord's, and she had bright anticipations of being forever with the Lord. The little she could say with her voice was supplemented by a great deal that she expressed with her eyes and with her whole demeanor. Here was no excitement, no fanaticism, and no action of drugs upon the brain, just a sweetly reasonable, quiet, and assured hope of eternal joy.

Brethren, it is not hard to pass out of this world when we are resting on that old and sure gospel that I have preached to you these many years. Personally, I can both live and die on the eternal truths that I have proclaimed to you. And this assurance makes me bold in preaching. Not long ago I sat by a brother who was near his end. I asked him, "You have no fear of death?"

He replied cheerfully, "I should be ashamed of myself if I had. After all that I have learned of the glorious gospel from your lips these many years, it is a joy to depart and to be with Christ. That is far better."

Now, if this inspired volume with its wonderful record of the words of God helps us in the trials of life—directs us in our daily paths and enables us to weather the last great storm—surely it is precious beyond description, "as silver tried in a furnace of earth purified seven times."

III. Now third, what are *the claims of these words of the Lord*? The claims of these words are many. First, they deserve to be studied. Beloved, may I urge upon you the constant searching of inspired scripture?

Here is the latest new novel! What will I do with it? Cast it to the ground. Here is another piece of fiction that has been very popular! What will I do with it? Throw it on one side or thrust it between the bars of the grate? This sacred volume is the freshest of novels. It would be, to some of you, an entirely new book. We have a society for providing the Bible for readers, but we greatly need *readers* of the Bible. I grieve that even to some who bear the Christian name, Holy Scripture is the least read book in their library.

One said of a preacher the other day, "How does he keep up the congregation? Does he always give the people something new?"

"Yes," said the other, "he gives them the gospel. And in these days that is the newest thing out." It is truly so. The old, old gospel is always new. The modern doctrine is only new in *name*. It is, after all, nothing but a hash of stale heresies and moldy speculations. If God has spoken, listen! If the Lord has recorded His words in a book, *search* its pages with a believing heart. If you do not accept it as God's inspired Word, I cannot invite you to pay any particular attention to it. But if you regard it as the book of God, I charge you, as I will meet you at the judgment seat of Christ—*study* the Bible *daily*. Treat not the eternal God with disrespect but delight in His Word.

Do you read it? Then believe it. Oh, for an intense belief of every Word that God has spoken! Do not hold it as a dead creed, but let it hold you as with an Almighty hand. Have no controversy with any of the Lord's words. Believe without a doubt. The brother of the famous Unitarian, Dr. Priestly, was permitted to preach for his brother in his chapel in Birmingham. But he was charged to take no controversial subject. He was obedient to the letter of his instructions but very rebellious against their spirit since he took for his text this verse: "And without controversy great is the mystery of godliness: God was manifested in the flesh" (1 Tim. 3:16). Assuredly, there is no controversy among *spiritual* men upon the glorious truth of the incarnation of our Lord Jesus.

So also, all the words of the Lord are out of the region of debate; they are to us *absolute certainties*. Until a doctrine becomes an absolute certainty to a man, he will never know its sweetness. The truth of God has little influence upon the soul till it is fully believed.

Brothers and sisters, obey the book! Do it freely. Do it heartily. Do it constantly. Err not from the commandment of God. May the Lord make you perfect in every good work, to do His will! "Whatever He says to you, do it" (John 2:5). You who are unconverted, may you obey that gospel word that says, "He who believes and is baptized will be saved" (Mark 16:16). Repentance and faith are at once the commands and the gifts of God. Neglect them not.

Furthermore, these words of God are to be preserved. Give up no line of God's revelation. You may not know the particular importance of the text assailed, but it is not for you to assess the proportionate value of God's words. If the Lord has spoken, be prepared to die for what He has said. I have often wondered whether, according to the notions of some people, there is any truth for which it would be worthwhile for a man to go to the stake. I should say not, for we are not sure of *anything*, according to the modern notion.

Would it be worthwhile dying for a doctrine that may not be true next week? Fresh discoveries may show that we have been the victims of an antiquated opinion. Had we not better wait and see what will turn up? It will be a pity to be burned too soon or to lie in prison for a dogma that will, in a few years, be superseded. Brethren, we cannot endure this shifty theology! May God send us a race of men who have backbones! Men who believe something and would die for what they believe. This book deserves the sacrifice of our all for the maintenance of every line of it.

Believing and defending the Word of God, let us *proclaim* it. Go out this afternoon on this first Sunday of summer and speak in the street the words of this book. Go to a cottage meeting or to a workhouse or to a lodging house and declare the divine words. "Truth is mighty and will prevail," they say. It will *not* prevail if it is not made known. The Bible itself works no wonders until its truths are published abroad. Tell it among the heathen that the Lord reigns from the tree. Tell it among the multitude that the Son of God has come to save the lost and that whosoever believes in Him will have eternal life!

Make *all* men know that "God so loved the world that He gave His only begotten Son, that whoever believes in Him should not perish but have everlasting life" (John 3:16). This thing was not done in a corner. Keep it not a secret. Go into the entire world and preach the gospel to every creature. And may God bless you! Amen.

For Further Thought

Using the three themes of this sermon:
1. *Name some of the qualities of the Word of God.*
2. *Describe some of the trials of God's Word.*
3. *What are the claims of the words of the Lord?*

The Infallibility of Scripture

The mouth of the LORD has spoken.
ISAIAH 1:20

WHAT Isaiah said was spoken by Jehovah. It was audibly the utterance of a man. But really it was the utterance of the Lord Himself. The lips that delivered the words were those of Isaiah, yet it was the very truth of God that "the mouth of the LORD has spoken." The mouth of God speaks all scripture, being inspired of the Spirit. However this sacred book may be treated nowadays, the Lord Jesus Christ, our Master and Lord, did not treat it contemptuously, negligently, or questioningly. It is noteworthy how He reverenced the written Word. The Spirit of God rested upon Him personally, without measure, and He could speak out of His own mind the revelation of God, yet He continually quoted the Law and the Prophets and the Psalms.

And always He treated the sacred writings with intense reverence, strongly in contrast with the irreverence of modern thought. I am sure, brethren, we cannot be wrong in imitating the example of our divine Lord in our reverence for that scripture that cannot be broken. I say, if He, the anointed of the Spirit and able to speak Himself as God's mouth, quoted the sacred writings and used the Holy Book in His teachings, how much more should we. We who have no spirit of prophecy resting upon us and are not able to speak new revelations must come back to the Law and to the testimony and value every single word that "the mouth of the LORD has spoken."

The like valuation of the Word of the Lord is seen in our Lord's apostles. They treated the ancient scriptures as supreme in authority and supported their statements with passages from holy writ. The writers of the New Testament pay the utmost degree of deference and homage to the Old Testament. We never find an apostle raising a question about the degree of inspiration in this book or that. No disciple of Jesus questions the authority of the books of Moses or of the prophets. If you want to make petty objections or cast suspect upon it, you find no sympathy in the teaching of Jesus or any of His apostles. The New Testament writers sit reverently down before the Old Testament and receive God's words as such without any question whatever.

You and I belong to a school that will continue to do the same, let others adopt what behavior they please. As for us and for our house, this priceless book will remain the standard of our faith and the ground of our hope so long as we live. Others may choose what gods they will and follow what authorities they prefer. But, as for us, the glorious Jehovah is our God, and we believe concerning each doctrine of the entire Bible that "the mouth of the Lord has spoken."

I. Coming closely, then, to our text, "The mouth of the Lord has spoken," our first head will be: *This is our warrant for teaching scriptural truth.* We preach because "the mouth of the Lord has spoken." It would not be worth our while to speak what Isaiah had spoken if in it there were nothing more than Isaiah's thoughts—neither should we care to meditate hour after hour upon the writings of Paul if there were nothing more than Paul in them. We feel no imperative call to expound and to enforce what men have spoken. But since "the mouth of the Lord has spoken," "woe to us if we preach not the gospel"! We come to you with "thus says the Lord," and we should have no justifiable motive for preaching our lives away if we have not this message.

> *L*et others adopt what behavior they please. As for us and for our house, this priceless book will remain the standard of our faith and the ground of our hope so long as we live.

The true preacher, the man whom God has commissioned, delivers his message with awe and trembling because "the mouth of the Lord has spoken." He bears the burden of the Lord and bows under it. Ours is no trifling theme but one that moves our whole soul. They called George Fox a Quaker because when he spoke he would quake exceedingly through the force of the truth of God that he so thoroughly apprehended. Perhaps if you and I had a clearer sight and a closer grip of God's Word and felt more of its majesty, we should quake also. Martin Luther, who never feared the face of man, yet declared that when he stood up to preach, he often felt his knees knock together under a sense of his great responsibility.

Woe to us if we dare to speak the Word of the Lord with less than our whole heart and soul and strength! Woe to us if we handle the Word as if it were an occasion for display! If it were our own word, we might be studious of the graces of oratory. But if it is God's Word, we cannot afford to think of ourselves. We are bound to speak it, "not with wisdom of words, lest the cross of Christ should be made of no effect" (1 Cor. 1:17). If we reverence the Word, it will not occur to us that we can improve upon it by our own skill in language. Oh, it were far better to break stones on the road than to be a preacher unless one had God's Holy Spirit to sustain him. Our charge is solemn and our burden is heavy.

The heart and soul of the man who speaks for God will know no ease, for he hears in his ears that warning admonition, "If the watchman sees the sword coming and does not blow the trumpet, and the people are not warned, and the sword comes and takes any person from among them, he is taken away in his iniquity; but his blood I will require at the watchman's hand" (Ezek. 33:6). If we were commissioned to repeat the language of a king, we should be bound to do it decorously lest the king suffer damage. But if we rehearse the revelation of God, a profound awe should take hold upon us and a godly fear lest we mar the message of God in the telling of it. No work is so important or honorable as the proclamation of the gospel of our Lord Jesus, and for that very reason it is weighted with a responsibility so solemn that none may venture upon it lightly or proceed in it without an overwhelming sense of his need of great divine grace to perform his office aright.

We who preach a gospel live under intense pressure, of that we can assuredly say, because "the mouth of the LORD has spoken" (Isa. 1:20). We live in eternity rather than in time. We speak to you as though we saw the great white throne and the divine judge before whom we must give an account of not only what we say but also how we say it.

Dear brethren, because the mouth of the Lord has spoken the truth of God, we therefore endeavor to preach it with absolute fidelity. We repeat the Word as a child repeats his lesson. It is not ours to correct the divine revelation but simply to echo it. I do not take it to be my office to bring you new and original thoughts of my own, but rather to say, "The word which ye hear is not mine, but the Father's which sent me" (John 14:24 KJV). Believing that "the mouth of the LORD has spoken," it is my duty to repeat God's Word to you as correctly as I can after having heard it and felt it in my own soul. It is not mine to amend or adapt the gospel. What? Shall we attempt to improve upon what God has revealed? Is the infinitely wise to be corrected by creatures of a day?

Is the infallible revelation of the infallible Jehovah to be shaped, moderated, and toned down to the fashions and fancies of the hour? God forgive us if we have ever altered His Word unwittingly. Wittingly we have not done so, nor, by His grace, will we. His children sit at His feet and receive His words, and then they rise up in the power of His Spirit to publish far and near the Word that the Lord has given. "He who has My Word, let him speak My Word faithfully," is the Lord's injunction to us. If we could abide with the Father according to our measure, after the manner of the Lord Jesus and then come forth from communion with Him to tell what He has taught us in His Word, we should be accepted of the Lord as preachers and accepted also of His living people far more than if we were to dive into the profound depths of science or rise to the loftiest flights of rhetoric.

What is the chaff to the wheat? What are man's discoveries to the teachings of the Lord? "The mouth of the LORD has spoken." Therefore, O man of God, add not to His words lest He add to you the plagues that are written in His book, and take not from them lest He take your name out of the Book of Life!

Again, dear friends, as "the mouth of the LORD has spoken," we speak the divine truth with courage and full assurance. Modesty is a virtue. But hesitancy when we are speaking for the Lord is a great fault. If an ambassador sent by a great king to represent his majesty at a foreign court should forget his office and think only of himself, he might be so humble as to lower the dignity of his prince, so timid as to betray his country's honor. He is bound to remember not so much what he is in himself but whom he represents. Therefore, he must speak boldly and with the dignity that beseems his office and the court he represents. It was the custom with certain oriental despots to require ambassadors of foreign powers to lie in the dust before them.

Some Europeans, for the sake of trade interests, submitted to the degrading ceremony. But when it was demanded of the representative of England, he scorned thus to lower his country. God forbid that he who speaks for God should dishonor the King of kings by a pliant subservience. We preach not the gospel by your leave. We do not ask tolerance nor court applause. We preach Christ crucified, and we speak boldly as we ought to speak because it is God's Word and not our own. We are accused of dogmatism, but we are bound to dogmatize when we repeat that which the mouth of the Lord has spoken. We cannot use *ifs*, for we are dealing with God's *shalls and wills*. If He says it is so, it is so. And there is the end of it. Controversy ceases when Jehovah speaks.

Those who fling aside our Master's authority may very well reject our testimony. We are content they should do so. But if we speak that which the mouth of the Lord has spoken, those who hear His Word and refuse it do so at their own peril. The wrong is done not to the ambassador but to the king. Not to *our* mouth but to the mouth of God, from whom the truth has proceeded.

We are urged to be charitable. We are charitable. But it is with our own money. We have no right to give away what is put into our trust and is not at our disposal. When we have to do with the truth of God, we are stewards and must deal with our Lord's treasury, not on the lines of charity to human opinions but by the rule of fidelity to the God of truth. We are bold to declare with full assurance that which the Lord reveals. That memorable Word of the Lord to Jeremiah is needed by the servants of the Lord in these days:

> *Thou therefore gird up thy loins, and arise, and speak unto them all that I command thee: be not dismayed at their faces, lest I confound thee before them. For, behold, I have made thee this day a defenced city, and an iron pillar, and brasen walls against the whole land, against the kings of Judah, against the princes thereof, against the priests thereof, and against the people of the land. And they shall fight against thee; but they shall not prevail against thee; for I am with thee, saith the* LORD, *to deliver thee. (Jer. 1:17–19 KJV)*

When we speak for the Lord against error, we do not soften our tones. But we speak thunderbolts. When we come across false science, we do not lower our flag. We give place by subjection not for an hour. One Word of God is worth more than libraries of human lore. "It is written," is the great gun that silences all the batteries of man's thought. They should speak courageously who speak in the name of Jehovah, the God of Israel.

I will also add under this head that because "the mouth of the LORD has spoken," therefore we feel bound to speak His Word with diligence as often as ever we can and with perseverance as long as ever we live. Surely it would be a blessed thing to die in the pulpit, spending one's last breath in acting as the Lord's mouth. Dumb Sabbaths are fierce trials to true preachers. Remember how John Newton, when he was quite unfit to preach and even wandered a bit by reason of his infirmities and age yet persisted in preaching. And when they dissuaded him, he answered with warmth, "What? Shall the old African blasphemer leave off preaching Jesus Christ while there is breath in his body?"

We do not ask tolerance nor court applause. We preach Christ crucified, and we speak boldly as we ought to speak because it is God's Word and not our own.

So they helped the old man into the pulpit again that he might once more speak of free grace and dying love. If we had common themes to speak about, we might leave the pulpit as a weary pleader quits the forum. But as "the mouth of the LORD has spoken," we feel His Word to be as fire in our bones and we grow wearier with refraining than with testifying. O my brethren, the Word of the Lord is so precious that we must in the morning sow this blessed seed, and in the evening we must not withhold our hands. It is a living seed and the seed of life, and therefore we must diligently scatter it. Brethren, if we get a right apprehension concerning gospel truth—that "the mouth of the LORD has spoken"—it will move us to proclaim with great ardor and zeal.

We will not drone the gospel to a slumbering handful. Many of you are not preachers, but you are teachers of the young, or in some other way you try to publish the Word of the Lord—do it, I pray you, with much fervor of Spirit. Enthusiasm should be conspicuous in every servant of the Lord. Let those who hear you know that you are all there—that you are not merely speaking from the lips outwardly—but that from the depths of your soul your very heart is welling up with a good matter when you speak of things that you have made, touching the King.

The everlasting gospel is worth preaching even if one stood on a burning pyre and addressed the crowd from a pulpit of flames. The truths of God revealed in scripture are worth living for and dying for. I count myself thrice happy to bear reproach for the sake of the old faith. It is an honor of which I feel myself to be unworthy. And yet most truly can I use the words of our hymn:

> *Shall I, to soothe the unholy throng,*
> *Soften Your truths and smooth my tongue?*
> *To gain earth's gilded toys, or flee*
> *The cross endured, my God, by You?*
>
> *The love of Christ does me constrain*
> *To seek the wandering souls of men;*
> *With cries, entreaties, tears, to save,*
> *To snatch them from the fiery wave.*
>
> *My life, my blood I here present,*
> *If for Your truth they may be spent—*
> *Fulfill Your sovereign counsel, Lord!*
> *Your will be done, Your name adored!*

I cannot speak out my whole heart upon this theme, which is so dear to me, but I would stir you all up to be instant in season and out of season in telling out the gospel message. Specially repeat such a word as this: "For God so loved the world that He gave His only begotten Son, that whoever believes in Him should not perish but have everlasting life" (John 3:16). And this: "The one who comes to me I will by no means cast out" (6:37). Proclaim boldly, proclaim in every place, proclaim to every creature, "for the mouth of the LORD has spoken." How can you keep back the heavenly news? Since "the mouth of the LORD has spoken," will not your mouth rejoice to repeat it?

Whisper it in the ear of the sick. Shout it on the street corners. Write it on your stationery. Send it forth from the press. But everywhere let this be your great motive and warrant: Preach the gospel because "the mouth of the

LORD has spoken." Let nothing be silent that has a voice when the Lord has given the Word by His own dear Son.

> *Float, float, you winds, His story,*
> *And you, you waters, roll,*
> *Till like a sea of glory*
> *It spreads from pole to pole.*

II. Let us now row in another direction for a moment or two. In the second place, "the mouth of the LORD has spoken." *This is the claim of God's Word upon your attention.*

Every word that God has given us in the Bible claims our attention because of the infinite majesty of Him who spoke it. I see before me a parliament of kings and princes, sages and senators. I hear one after another of the gifted Chrysostoms pour forth eloquence like the "golden-mouthed." They speak and they speak well. Suddenly there is a solemn hush. What a stillness; who is now to speak? They are silent because God the Lord is about to lift up His voice. Is it not right that they should be so? Does He not say, "Keep silence before me, O islands" (Isa. 41:1 KJV)? What voice is like His voice? "The voice of the LORD is powerful" (Ps. 29:4 KJV).

The voice of the Lord is full of majesty. The voice of the Lord breaks the cedars; yes, the Lord breaks the cedars of Lebanon. The voice of the Lord shakes the wilderness. The Lord shakes the wilderness of Kadesh. See that you refuse not Him who speaks. O my hearer, let it not be said of you that you went though this life, God speaking to you in His book, and you refusing to hear! It matters very little whether you listen to me or not. But it matters a very great deal whether you listen to God or not. It is He who made you. In His hands is your breath. And if He speaks, I implore you, open your ears and be not rebellious. There is an infinite majesty about every line of scripture, but especially about that part of scripture in which the Lord reveals Himself and His glorious plan of saving grace in the person of His dear Son Jesus Christ. The cross of Christ has a great claim upon you. Hear what Jesus preaches from the tree. He says, "Incline your ear, and come unto me: hear, and your soul shall live" (Isa. 55:3 KJV).

God's claim to be heard lies also in the condescension that has led Him to speak to us. It was something for God to have made the world and bid us look at the work of His hands. Creation is a picture book for children. But for God to speak in the language of mortal men is still more marvelous, if you think about it. I wonder that God spoke by the prophets. But I admire still more that He should have written down His Word in black and white, in unmistakable language that can be translated into all tongues, so that we may all see and read for ourselves what God the Lord has spoken to us. And what indeed He continues to speak.

For what He has spoken He still speaks to us, as freshly as if He spoke it for the first time. O glorious Jehovah, do you speak to mortal man? Can there be any that neglect to hear you? If you are so full of loving-kindness and tenderness that you will stoop out of heaven to converse with your sinful creatures, none but those who are more brutal than the ox and the ass will turn a deaf ear to you!

> *There is an infinite majesty about every line of scripture, but especially about that part of scripture in which the Lord reveals Himself and His glorious plan of saving grace in the person of His dear Son Jesus Christ.*

God's Word has a claim, then, upon your attention because of its majesty and its condescension. But, further, it should win your ear because of its intrinsic importance. "The mouth of the Lord has spoken," so it is no trifle. God never speaks vanity. No line of His writing treats of the frivolous themes of a day. That which may be forgotten in an hour is for mortal man and not for the eternal God. When the Lord speaks, His speech is Godlike, and its themes are worthy of one whose dwelling is infinity and eternity. God does not play with you, man, will you trifle with Him? Will you treat Him as if He were altogether such a one as yourself? God is in earnest when He speaks to you, will you not in earnest listen?

He speaks to you of great things that have to do with your soul and its destiny. It is not a vain thing for you, because it is your life. Your eternal existence, your happiness or your misery, hang on your treatment of that which the mouth of the Lord has spoken. Concerning eternal realities, He speaks to you. I pray you, be not so unwise as to turn away your ear. Act not as if the Lord and His truth were nothing to you. Treat not the Word of the Lord as a secondary thing that might wait your leisure and receive attention when no other work is before you. Put all else aside and hearken to your God.

Depend upon it: If "the mouth of the LORD has spoken," there is an urgent, pressing necessity. God does not break silence to say that which might as well have remained unsaid. His voice indicates great urgency. Today, if you will hear His voice, hear it, for He demands immediate attention. God does not speak without abundant reason. And, O my hearer, if He speaks to you by His Word, I beseech you to believe that there must be overwhelming cause for it! I know what Satan says. He tells you that you can do very well without listening to God's Word. I know what your carnal heart whispers. It says, "Listen to the voice of business and of pleasure. But listen not to God." But, oh, if the Holy Spirit will teach your reason to be reasonable and put your mind in mind of true wisdom, you will acknowledge that the first thing you have to do is to heed your Maker!

You can hear the voices of others another time. But your ear must hear God first since He is first, and that which He speaks must be of first importance. Without delay you must make haste to keep His commandments. Without reserve answer to His call and say, "Speak, LORD, for Your servant hears" (1 Sam. 3:9). When I stand in this pulpit to preach the gospel, I never feel that I may calmly invite you to attend to a subject that is one among many and may very properly be let alone for a time should your minds be already occupied. No. You may be dead before I again speak with you, and so I beg for immediate attention. I do not fear that I may be taking you off from other important business by entreating you to attend to that which the mouth of the Lord has spoken.

No business has any importance in it compared with this; this is the master theme of all. It is your soul, your own soul, your ever-existing soul that is concerned, and it is your God who is speaking to you. Do hear Him, I beseech you. I am not asking a favor of you when I request you to hear the Word of the Lord—it is a *debt* to your Maker that you are bound to pay. Yes, it is, moreover, kindness to your own self. Even from a selfish point of view I urge you to hear what the mouth of the Lord has spoken, for in His Word lies salvation. Hearken diligently to what your Maker, your Savior, your best Friend, has to say to you: "Do not harden your hearts, as in the rebellion" (Ps. 95:8), but "incline your ear, and come to Me. Hear, and your soul shall live" (Isa. 55:3). "Faith comes by hearing, and hearing by the word of God" (Rom. 10:17).

Thus I have handled my text in two ways—it is warrant and motive for the preacher. It is a demand upon the attention of the hearer.

III. And now, third, *this gives to God's Word a very special character.* When we open this sacred book and say of that which is here recorded, "The mouth of the Lord has spoken," it gives to the teaching a special character.

In the Word of God the teaching has unique dignity. This book is inspired as no other book is inspired, and it is time that all Christians avowed this conviction. I do not know whether you have read Mr. Smiles' life of our late friend George Moore. But in it we read that at a certain dinner party, a learned man remarked that it would not be easy to find a person of intelligence who believed in the inspiration of the Bible. In an instant George Moore's voice was heard across the table, saying boldly, "I do, for one."

Nothing more was said. My dear friend had a strong way of speaking, as I well remember. For we have upon occasions vied with each other in shouting when we were together at his Cumberland home. I think I can hear his emphatic way of putting it: "I do, for one." Let us not be backward to take the old-fashioned and unpopular side and say outright, "I do, for one." Where are we if our Bibles are gone? Where are we if we are taught to distrust them? If we are left in doubt as to which part is inspired and what is not, we are as badly off as if we had no Bible at all. I hold no *theory* of inspiration. I accept the inspiration of the scriptures as a *fact*.

Those who thus view the scriptures need not be ashamed of their company, for some of the best and most learned of men have been of the same mind. The great philosopher Locke spent the last fourteen years of his life in the study of the Bible, and when asked what was the shortest way for a young gentleman to understand the Christian religion, he bade him read the Bible, remarking, "Therein are contained the words of eternal life. It has God for its author, salvation for its end and truth, without any admixture of error for its matter." There are those on the side of God's Word whom you need not be ashamed of in the matter of intelligence and learning.

And if it were not so, it should not discourage you when you remember that the Lord has hidden these things from the wise and prudent and has revealed them to babes. We believe with the apostle that the foolishness of God is wiser than men. It is better to believe what comes out of God's mouth and be called a fool than to believe what comes out of the mouth of philosophers and be, therefore, esteemed a wise man. There is also about that which the mouth of the Lord has spoken an absolute certainty. What man has said is unsubstantial, even when true, is like grasping fog—there is nothing of it. But with God's Word you have something to grip, something to have and to hold. This is substance and reality.

But of human opinions we may say, "Vanity of vanities; all is vanity" (Eccles. 1:2 KJV). Though heaven and earth should pass away, yet not one jot or tittle of what God has spoken will fail. We know that and feel at rest. God cannot be mistaken. God cannot lie. These are postulates that no one can dispute. If "the mouth of the LORD has spoken," this is the judge that ends the strife where wit and reason fail. And henceforth we question no more.

Again, if "the mouth of the LORD has spoken," we have in this utterance the special character of immutable fixedness. Once spoken by God, not only is it so now, but also it is always so. The Lord of hosts has spoken, and who will disannul it? The rock of God's Word does not shift like the quicksand of modern scientific theology. One said to his minister, "My dear sir, surely you ought to adjust your beliefs to the progress of science."

"Yes," said he, "but I have not had time to do it today, for I have not yet read the morning papers." One would have need to read the morning papers and take in every new edition to know where scientific theology now stands, for it is always chopping and changing. The only thing that is certain about the false science of this age is that it will be soon disproved. Theories vaunted today will be scrapped tomorrow.

> Where are we if our Bibles are gone? Where are we if we are taught to distrust them? If we are left in doubt as to which part is inspired and what is not, we are as badly off as if we had no Bible at all.

The great scientists live by killing those who went before them. They know nothing for certain except that their predecessors were wrong. Even in one short life we have seen system after system—the mushrooms, or rather the toadstools, of thought—rise and perish. We cannot adapt our religious belief to that which is more changeful than the moon. Try it whoever will. As for me, if "the mouth of the LORD has spoken," it is the truth of God to me in this year of divine grace, 1888. And if I stand among you a gray-headed old man, Lord willing, somewhere in 1908, you will find me making no advance upon the divine ultimatum. If "the mouth of the LORD has spoken," we behold in His revelation a gospel that is without variableness, revealing "Jesus Christ the same yesterday, and to day, and for ever" (Heb. 13:8 KJV).

Brothers and sisters, we hope to be together forever before the eternal throne where bow the blazing seraphim, and even then we will not be ashamed to avow that same truth of God that this day we feed upon from the hand of our God.

> *For He's the Lord, supremely good,*
> *His mercy is forever sure;*
> *His truth, that always firmly stood,*
> *To endless ages will endure.*

Here let me add that there is something unique about God's Word because of the almighty power that attends it. "Where the word of a king is, there is power" (Eccles. 8:4 KJV). Where the Word of a God is, there is omnipotence. If we dealt more largely in God's own Word as "the mouth of the LORD has spoken," we should see far greater results from our preaching. It is God's Word, not our comment on God's Word, that saves souls. Souls are slain by the sword, not by the scabbard, nor by the tassels that adorn the hilt of it.

If God's Word is brought forward in its native simplicity, no one can stand against it. The adversaries of God must fail before the Word as chaff perishes in the fire. Oh, for wisdom to keep closer and closer to that which the mouth of the Lord has spoken! I will say no more on this point, although the theme is a very large and tempting one—especially if I were to dwell upon the depth, the height, the adaptation, the insight, and the self-proving power of that which "the mouth of the LORD has spoken."

IV. Fourth and very briefly, *this makes God's Word a ground of great alarm to many*. Shall I read you the whole verse? "But if ye refuse and rebel, ye shall be devoured with the sword: for the mouth of the LORD hath spoken it" (Isa. 1:20 KJV). Every threat that God has spoken, because He has spoken it, has a tremendous dread about it. Whether God threatens a man or a nation, or the whole class of the ungodly, if they are wise, they will feel a trembling take hold upon them because "the mouth of the LORD has spoken."

God has never yet spoken a threat that has fallen to the ground. When He told Pharaoh what He would do, He did it. The plagues came thick and heavy upon him. When the Lord at any time sent His prophets to denounce judgments on the nations, He carried out those judgments. Ask travelers concerning Babylon and Nineveh and Edom and Moab and Bashan. And they will tell you of the heaps of ruins that prove how the Lord carried out His warnings to the letter. One of the most awful things recorded in history is the siege of Jerusalem. You have read it, I do not doubt, in Josephus or elsewhere. It makes one's blood run cold to think of it. Yet the prophets foretold it all, and their prophecies were fulfilled to the bitter end.

You talk about God as being "love," and if you mean by this that He is not severe in the punishment of sin, I ask you what you make of the destruction of Jerusalem? Remember that the Jews were His chosen nation and that the city of Jerusalem was the place where His temple had been glorified with His presence. Brethren, if you roam from Edom to Zion and from Zion to Sidon and from Sidon to Moab, you will find, amid ruined cities, the tokens that God's words of judgment are sure. Depend on it, then, that when Jesus says, "These will go away into everlasting punishment" (Matt. 25:46), it will be so. When He says, "If you do not believe that I am He, you will die in your sins" (John 8:24), it will be so.

> *A*sk travelers concerning Babylon and Nineveh and Edom and Moab and Bashan. And they will tell you of the heaps of ruins that prove how the Lord carried out His warnings to the letter.

The Lord never plays at frightening men. His Word is not an exaggeration to scare men with imaginary bugbears. There is emphatic truth in what the Lord says. He has always carried out His threats to the letter and to the moment. And, depend upon it; He will continue to do so, "for the mouth of the LORD has spoken."

It is of no avail to sit down and draw inferences from the nature of God and to argue, "God is love, and therefore He will not execute the sentence upon the impenitent." He knows what He will do better than you can infer. He has not left us to inferences, for He has spoken pointedly and plainly. He says, "He that believeth not shall be damned" (Mark 16:16 KJV), and it will be so, "for the mouth of the LORD has spoken." Infer what you like from

His nature. But if you draw an inference contrary to what He has spoken, you have inferred a lie and you will find it so.

"Alas," says one, "I shudder at the severity of the divine sentence." Do you? It is well! I can heartily sympathize with you. What must he be that does not tremble when he sees the great Jehovah taking vengeance upon iniquity! The terrors of the Lord might well turn steel to wax. Let us remember that the gauge of the truth of God is not our pleasure or our terror. It is not my shuddering that can disprove what the mouth of the Lord has spoken. It may even be a proof of its truth. Did not all the prophets tremble at manifestations of God? Remember how one of them cried, "When I heard, my belly trembled; my lips quivered at the voice: rottenness entered into my bones" (Habakkuk 3:16 KJV).

> *When friends forsake me and foes belie me and my own spirit goes down below zero and I am depressed almost to despair, I am resolved to hang to the bare Word of the Lord and prove it to be in itself an all-sufficient stay and support.*

One of the last of the anointed seers fell at the Lord's feet as dead. Yet he did not use all the shrinking of his nature as an argument for doubt. O my unconverted and unbelieving hearers, do remember that if you refuse Christ and rush upon the keen edge of Jehovah's sword, your unbelief of eternal judgment will not alter it nor save you from it. I know why you do not believe in the terrible threats. It is because you want to be easy in your sins. A certain skeptical writer, when in prison, was visited by a Christian man who wished him well, but he refused to hear a word about religion.

Seeing a Bible in the hand of his visitor, he made this remark: "You do not expect me to believe in that book, do you? Why, if that book is true, I am lost forever." Just so. Therein lies the reason for half the infidelity in the world and all the infidelity in our congregations. How can you believe that which condemns you? Ah, my friends, if you would believe it to be true and act accordingly, you would also find in that which the mouth of the Lord has spoken a way of escape from the wrath to come! For the book is far more full of hope than of dread. This inspired volume flows with the milk of mercy and the honey of divine grace. It is not a doomsday book of wrath but a testament of grace.

Yet if you do not believe its loving warnings nor regard its just sentences, they are true all the same. If you dare its thunders, if you trample on its promises, and even if you burn it in your rage, the Holy Book still stands unaltered and unalterable. "The mouth of the LORD has spoken." Therefore, I pray you, treat the sacred scriptures with respect and remember that "these are written, that ye might believe that Jesus is the Christ, the Son of God; and that believing ye might have life through his name" (John 20:31 KJV).

V. And so, I must finish for time fails, when I notice in the fifth place, that *this makes the Word of the Lord the reason and rest of our faith.* "The mouth of the LORD has spoken" is the foundation of our confidence. Forgiveness is available, for God has said it. Look, friend, you are saying, "I cannot believe that my sins can be washed away; I feel so unworthy." Yes, but "the mouth of the LORD has spoken." Believe over the head of your unworthiness. "Ah," says one, "I feel so weak I can neither think nor pray nor do anything else as I should." Is it not written, "for when we were yet without strength, in due time Christ died for the ungodly" (Rom.5:6 KJV)? "The mouth of the LORD has spoken." Therefore, over the head of your inability, still believe it, for it must be so.

I think I hear some child of God saying, "God has said, 'I will never leave you nor forsake you,' but I am in great trouble. All the circumstances of my life seem to contradict the promise." Yet "the mouth of the LORD has spoken," and the promise must stand. "Trust in the LORD, and do good; so shalt thou dwell in the land, and verily thou shalt be fed" (Ps. 37:3 KJV). Believe God in the teeth of circumstances. If you cannot see a way of escape or a means of help, yet still believe in the unseen God and in the truth of His presence, "for the mouth of the LORD has spoken."

I think I have come to this pass with myself, at any rate for the time present, that when circumstances deny the promise, I believe it nonetheless. When friends forsake me and foes belie me and my own spirit goes down below zero and I am depressed almost to despair, I am resolved to hang to the bare Word of the Lord and prove it to be in itself an all-sufficient stay and support. I will believe God against all the devils in hell, God against Ahithophel and Judas and Demas and all the rest of the turncoats. Yes, and God against my own evil heart. His purpose will stand, "for the mouth of the LORD has spoken." Away, you that contradict it, ours is a well-grounded confidence, "for the mouth of the LORD has spoken."

By-and-by we will come to die. The death sweat will gather on our brow, and perhaps our tongue will scarcely serve us. Oh, that then, like the grand old German emperor, we may say, "My eyes have seen Your salvation" (Luke 2:30). When we pass through the rivers, God will be with us and the floods will not overflow us, "for the mouth of the LORD has spoken." When we walk through the valley of the shadow of death, we will fear no evil, for He will be with us, His rod and His staff will comfort us. "The mouth of the LORD has spoken." Ah, what will it be to break loose from these bonds and rise into glory? We will soon see the King in His beauty and be ourselves glorified in His glory, for "the mouth of the LORD has spoken." "He who hears My word and believes in Him who sent Me has everlasting life" (John 5:24). Therefore a glad eternity is ours.

Brethren, we have not followed cunningly devised fables. We are not wanton boys that swim on floats that will soon burst under us. But we are resting on firm ground. We abide where heaven and earth are resting, where the whole universe depends, where even eternal things have their foundation. We rest on God Himself. If God will fail us, we gloriously fail with the whole universe. But there is no fear. Therefore, let us trust and not be afraid. His promise must stand: "The mouth of the LORD has spoken." O Lord, it is enough! Glory be to your name, through Christ Jesus! Amen.

FOR FURTHER THOUGHT

According to the themes of three sections of this sermon:

1. *What is the minister's justification for preaching the Word of God?*
2. *Why should people pay attention to the Word of God?*
3. *Why is the Word of God the resting place for our faith?*

THE BIBLE

"I have written for him the great things of My law,
but they were considered a strange thing."
HOSEA 8:12

OUR text is God's complaint against Ephraim. It is no mean proof of His goodness that He stoops to rebuke His erring creatures. It is a great argument of His gracious disposition that He bows His head to notice terrestrial affairs. He might, if He pleased, wrap Himself with night as with a garment. He might put the stars around His wrist for bracelets and bind the sun around His brow for a coronet. He might dwell alone, far, far above this world, up in the seventh heaven, and look down with calm and silent indifference upon all the doings of His creatures. He might do as the heathens supposed their Jove did, sit in perpetual silence, sometimes nodding his awful head to make the Fates move as he pleased.

But Jove never thought of the little things of earth, disposing of them as beneath his notice, engrossed within his own being, swallowed up within himself. He lived alone and retired. And I, as one of Jove's creatures, might stand by night upon a mountaintop and look upon the silent stars and say, "You are the eyes of God, but you look not down on me. Your light is the gift of his omnipotence, but your rays are not smiles of love to me. God, the mighty Creator, has forgotten me; I am a despicable drop in the ocean of creation, a dry leaf in the forest of beings, an atom in the mountain of existence. He knows me not. I am alone, alone, alone."

But it is not so, beloved. *Our* God is of another order. He notices every one of us. There is not a sparrow or a worm but is found in His decrees. There is not a person upon whom His eye is not fixed. He knows our most secret acts. Whatsoever we do or bear or suffer, the eye of God still rests upon us and we are beneath His smile, for we are His people. Or beneath His frown—for we have erred from Him.

Oh, how ten-thousandfold merciful is God, that, looking down upon the race of man, He does not smile it out of existence. We see from our text that God looks upon man, for He says of Ephraim, "I have written for him the great things of My law, but they were considered a strange thing" (Hosea 8:12). But see how when He observes the sin of man He does not dash him away and spurn him with His foot? He does not shake him by the neck over the gulf of hell until his brain does reel and then drop him forever. But rather He comes down from heaven to plead with His creatures. He argues with them, He puts Himself, as it were, upon a level with the sinner, states His grievances, and pleads His claim.

O Ephraim, "I have written for him the great things of My law, but they were considered a strange thing"! I come here tonight in God's stead, my friends, to plead with you as God's ambassador, to charge many of you with a sin—to lay it to your hearts by the power of the Spirit so that you may be convinced of sin, of righteousness, and of a judgment to come. The crime I charge you with is the sin of our text. God has written to you the great things of His law, but they have been to you as a strange thing.

It is concerning this blessed book, the Bible, that I mean to speak tonight. Here lies my text: this Word of God. Here is the theme of my discourse, a theme that demands more eloquence than I possess, and a subject upon which a thousand orators might speak at once, a mighty, vast, incomprehensive theme that might engross all eloquence throughout eternity and still it would remain unexhausted.

Concerning the Bible, I have three things to say tonight, and they are all in my text. First, *its author*: "I have written." Second, *its subjects*: the great things of God's law. And third, *its common treatment*. It has been accounted by most men a strange thing.

I. First, then, concerning this book, who is *the author*? The text says that it is God. "I have written for him the great things of My law." Here lies my Bible. Who wrote it? I open it, and I find it consists of a series of tracts. A man called Moses wrote the first five tracts. I turn on, and I find others. Sometimes I see David is the penman, at other times, Solomon. Here I read Micah, then Amos, and then Hosea. As I turn further on, to the more luminous pages of the New Testament, I see Matthew, Mark, Luke, and John, Paul, Peter, James, and others. But when I shut up the book, I ask myself who is the author of it?

Do these men jointly claim the authorship? Are they the compositors of this massive volume? Do they between themselves divide the honor? Our holy religion answers, "No!" This volume is the writing of the living God. Each letter was penned with an Almighty finger. Each word in it dropped from the everlasting lips; each sentence was dictated by the Holy Spirit. Albeit that Moses was employed to write his histories with his fiery pen, God guided that pen. It may be that David touched his harp and let sweet psalms of melody drop from his fingers, but God moved his hands over the living strings of his golden harp.

> This volume is the writing of the living God. Each letter was penned with an Almighty finger. Each word in it dropped from the everlasting lips; each sentence was dictated by the Holy Spirit.

It may be that Solomon sang canticles of love or gave forth words of consummate wisdom, but God directed his lips and made the preacher eloquent. If I follow the thundering Nahum when his horses plow the waters or Habakkuk when he sees the tents of Cushan in affliction, if I read Malachi, when the earth is burning like an oven, if I turn to the smooth page of John, who tells of love, or the rugged, fiery chapters of Peter, who speaks of the fire devouring God's enemies, if I turn to Jude, who launches forth anathemas upon the foes of God, everywhere I find God speaking. It is God's voice, not man's. The words are God's words, the words of the Eternal, the Invisible, the Almighty, the Jehovah of this earth. This Bible is God's Bible. And when I see it, I seem to hear a voice springing up from it, saying, "I am the book of God. Man, read me. I am God's writing. Open my leaf, for God penned me. Read it, for He is my author, and you will see Him visible and manifest everywhere."

How do you know that God wrote the book? That is just what I will not try to prove to you. I could, if I pleased, do a demonstration, for there are arguments enough, there are reasons enough, if I cared to occupy your time tonight in bringing them before you, but I will do no such thing. I might tell you, if I pleased, that the grandeur of the style is above that of any mortal writing and that all the poets who have ever existed, could not, with all their works united, give us such sublime poetry and such mighty language as is to be found in the scriptures.

I might insist that the subjects it treats are beyond the human intellect, that man never could have invented the grand doctrines of a trinity in the Godhead. Man could not have told us anything of the creation of the universe. He could never have been the author of the majestic idea of providence, that all things are ordered according to the will of one great supreme being and work together for good. I might enlarge upon its honesty, since it tells the faults of its writers; its unity, since it never belies itself; its master simplicity, that he who runs may read it. And I might mention a hundred more things that would all demonstrate that the book is of God.

But I come not here to prove it. I am a Christian minister, and you are Christians, or profess to be so, and there is never any necessity for Christian ministers to make a point of bringing forth infidel arguments in order to answer them. It is the greatest folly in the world. Infidels, poor creatures, do not know their own arguments till we tell them and then they glean their blunted shafts to shoot them at the shield of truth again. It is folly to bring forward these firebrands of hell, even if we are well prepared to quench them. Let men of the world learn error of themselves. Do not let us be propagators of their falsehoods.

> If man wrote these words, we might reject them, but oh, let me think the solemn thought that this book is God's handwriting and that these words are God's.

True, there are some preachers who are short of stock and want them to fill up! But God's own chosen men need not do that. They are taught of God, and God supplies them with matter, with language, and with power. There may be someone here tonight who has come without faith, a man of reason, a freethinker. With him I have no argument at all. I profess not to stand here as a controversialist, but as a preacher of things that I know and feel. But I, too, have been like him. There was an evil hour when once I slipped the anchor of my faith; I cut the cable of my belief. I no longer moored myself hard by the coasts of revelation.

I allowed my vessel to drift before the wind. I said to reason, "Be you my captain." I said to my own brain, "Be you my rudder." And I started on my mad voyage. Thank God it is all over now, but I will tell you its brief history. It was one hurried sailing over the tempestuous ocean of free thought. I went on, and as I went, the skies began to darken. But to make up for that deficiency, the waters were brilliant with flashes of light. I saw sparks flying upward that pleased me, and I thought, "If this is free thought, it is a happy thing." My thoughts seemed gems, and I scattered stars with both my hands.

But soon, instead of these flashes of glory, I saw grim fiends fierce and horrible start up from the waters. And as I dashed on, they gnashed their teeth and grinned upon me. They seized the prow of my ship and dragged me on, while I, in part, gloried at the rapidity of my motion but yet shuddered at the terrific rate with which I passed the old landmarks of my faith. As I hurried forward with an awful speed, I began to doubt my very existence. I doubted that there was a world. I doubted that there was such a thing as myself.

I went to the very verge of the dreary realms of unbelief. I went to the very bottom of the sea of infidelity. I doubted everything. But here the devil foiled himself. For the very extravagance of the doubt proved its absurdity. Just when I saw the bottom of that sea, there came a voice that said, "And can this doubt be true?" At this very thought I awoke. I started from that death-dream, which God knows might have damned my soul and ruined my body if I had not awoke. When I arose, faith took the helm. From that moment, I doubted not.

Faith steered me back. Faith cried, "Away, away!" I cast my anchor on Calvary. I lifted my eye to God, and here I am alive and out of hell. Therefore, I speak what I know. I have sailed that perilous voyage. I have come safe to land. Ask me again to be an infidel! No, I have tried it. It was sweet at first but bitter afterward. Now, lashed to God's gospel more firmly than ever, standing as on a rock of adamant, I defy the arguments of hell to move me, for "I know whom I have believed and am persuaded that He is able to keep what I have committed to Him until that Day" (2 Tim. 1:12).

But I will neither plead nor argue this night. You profess to be Christian men and women, or else you would not be here. Your profession may be lies. What you *say you* are may be the very opposite of what you *really* are, but still I suppose you all admit that this is the Word of God. A thought or two then upon it: "I have written for him the great things of My law."

First, my friends, stand over this volume and *admire its authority*. This is no Solomon book. It is not the sayings of the sages of Greece. Here are not the utterances of philosophers of past ages. If man wrote these words, we might reject them, but oh, let me think the solemn thought that this book is God's handwriting and that these words are God's. Let me look at its date. It is dated from the hills of heaven. Let me look at its letters. They flash glory on my eyes. Let me read the chapters. They are big with meaning and mysteries unknown. Let me turn over the prophecies. They are pregnant with unthought-of orders.

Oh, book of books! And did my God write you? Then will I bow before you. Book of vast authority, you are a proclamation from the Emperor of heaven! Far be it from me to exercise my reason in contradicting you. Reason! Your place is to stand and find out what this volume means, not to tell what this book *ought* to say. Come my reason, my intellect, sit down and listen, for these words are the words of God. I do not know how to enlarge on this thought. Oh, if you could ever remember that this Bible was actually and really written by God!

Oh, if you had been let into the secret chambers of heaven, if you had beheld God grasping His pen and writing down these letters, then surely you would respect them. But they are just as much God's handwriting as if you had seen God write them. This Bible is a book of authority; it is an authorized book, for God has written it. Oh, tremble; tremble lest any of you despise it. Mark its authority, for it is the Word of God.

Then, since God wrote it, mark its *truthfulness*. If I had written it, there would be worms of critics who would at once swarm on it and would cover it with their evil spawn. Had I written it, there would be men who would pull it to pieces at once and perhaps quite right, too. But this is the Word of God. Come, search you critics and find a flaw. Examine it from its Genesis to its Revelation and find an error. This is a vein of pure gold, unalloyed by quartz or any earthy substance. This is a star without a speck, a sun without a blot, a light without darkness, a moon without its paleness, and a glory without dimness. O Bible! It cannot be said of any other book that it is perfect and pure, but of you we can declare all wisdom is gathered up in you, without a particle of folly.

This is the judge that ends the strife where wit and reason fail. This is the book untainted by any error—it is pure, unalloyed, perfect truth. Why? It is because God wrote it. Ah, charge God with error if you please. Tell Him that His book is not what it ought to be. I have heard men with prudish and mock modesty who would like to alter the Bible. And (I almost blush to say it) I have heard ministers alter God's Bible because they were afraid of it.

Gentlemen! Pull the velvet out of your mouths. Speak God's Word. We want none of your alterations. I have heard men in prayer, instead of saying, "Make your calling and *election* sure" (2 Pet. 1:10 KJV, emphasis added), say, "Make your calling and salvation sure." Pity they were not born when God lived, far-far back, that they might have taught God how to write. Oh, impudence beyond all bounds! Oh, full-blown self-conceit to attempt to dictate to the all-wise, to teach the omniscient and instruct the eternal. It is strange that there should be men so vile as to use the penknife of Jehoiachin to cut passages out of the Word because they are unpalatable.

Oh, you who dislike certain portions of the holy writ, rest assured that your taste is corrupt and that God will not stay for your little opinion. Your dislike is the very reason why God wrote it, because you ought not to be suited. You have no right to be pleased. God wrote what you do not like. He wrote the truth. Oh, let us bend in reverence before it, for God inspired it. It is pure truth. Here from this fountain gushes *aqua vitae*, "the water of life," without a single particle of earth. Here from this sun there come forth rays of radiance without the mixture of darkness.

Blessed Bible, you are all truth. Yet once more, before we leave this point, let us stop and consider *the merciful nature of God* in having written us a Bible at all. Ah, He might have left us without it, to grope our dark way, as blind men seek the wall. He might have suffered us to wander on with the star of reason as our only guide. I recollect a story of Mr. Hume, who so constantly affirmed that the light of reason is abundantly sufficient. Being at a good minister's house one evening, he had been discussing the question and declaring his firm belief in the sufficiency of the light of nature. On leaving, the minister offered to hold him a candle, to light him down the steps. He said, "No, the light of nature would be enough, the moon would do."

It so happened that the moon was covered with a cloud and he fell down the steps. "Ah," said the minister, "you had better have had a little light from above after all, Mr. Hume." So, supposing the light of nature to be sufficient, we had better have a little light from above, too, and then we will be sure to be right. Better, have two lights than only one. The light of creation is a bright light. God may be seen in the stars, His name is written in gilt letters on the brow of night. You may discover His glory in the ocean waves, yes, in the trees of the field.

But it is better to read it in two books than in one. You will find it here more clearly revealed, for He has written this book Himself and He has given you the key to understand it if you have the Holy Spirit. Ah, beloved, let us thank God for this Bible. Let us love it. Let us count it more precious than much fine gold.

But let me say one thing before I pass on to the second point. If this is the Word of God, what will become of some of you who have not read it for the last month? "Month, sir! I have not read it for this year." Yes, there are some of you who have not read it at all. Most people treat the Bible very politely. They have a small pocket volume, neatly bound. They put a white pocket handkerchief around it and carry it to their places of worship. When they get home, they lay it up in a drawer till next Sunday morning. Then it comes out again for a little bit of a treat and goes to chapel. That is all in the way of an airing the poor Bible gets.

That is your style of entertaining this heavenly messenger. There is dust enough on some of your Bibles to write *damnation* with your fingers. There are some of you who have not turned over your Bibles for a long, long, long while and what do you think? I tell you blunt words, but true words. What will God say at last? When you will come before Him, He will say, "Did you read my Bible?"

"No."

"I wrote you a letter of mercy. Did you read it?"

"No."

"Rebel! I have sent you a letter inviting you to me; did you ever read it?"

"Lord I never broke the seal. I kept it shut up."

"Wretch!" says God, "then you deserve hell. If I sent you a loving epistle and you would not even break the seal. What will I do with you?"

Oh, let it not be so with you. Be Bible readers. Be Bible searchers.

II. Our second point is *the subjects on which the Bible treats*. The words of the text are these: "I have written for him the great things of My law." The Bible treats of great things and of great things only. There is nothing in this Bible that is unimportant. Every verse in it has a solemn meaning, and if we have not found it out yet, we hope yet to do it. You have seen mummies wrapped round and round with folds of linen. Well, God's Bible is like that. It is a vast roll of white linen, woven in the loom of truth. You will have to continue unwinding it, roll after roll, before you get the real meaning of it from the very depth. When you have found, as you think, a part of the meaning, you will still need to keep on unwinding, unwinding, and all eternity you will be unwinding the words of this wondrous volume. Yet there is nothing in the Bible but great things. Let me divide so as to be briefer. First, all things in this Bible are great—but second, some things are the greatest of all.

All things in the Bible are great. Some people think it does not matter what doctrines you believe, that it is immaterial what church you attend, that all denominations are alike. Well, I dislike Mrs. Bigotry above almost all people in the world, and I never give her any compliment or praise, but there is another woman I hate equally as much, and that is Mrs. Latitudinarianism, a well-known character who has made the discovery that all of us are alike.

> *You have seen mummies wrapped round and round with folds of linen. Well, God's Bible is like that. It is a vast roll of white linen, woven in the loom of truth. You will have to continue unwinding it, roll after roll, before you get the real meaning of it from the very depth.*

Now, I believe that a man may be *saved* in any church. Some have been saved in the Church of Rome, a few blessed men, whose names I could mention here. Blessed be God, I know that multitudes are saved in the Church of England. She has a host of pious, praying men in her midst. I think that all sections of Protestant Christians have a remnant according to the election of grace, and they had need to have, some of them, a little salt, for otherwise they would go to corruption.

But when I say that, do you imagine that I think them all on a level? Are they all alike truthful? One set says infant baptism is right, another says it is wrong. Yet you say they are both right? I cannot see that. One teaches we are saved by free grace, another says that we are not but are saved by free will. And yet you believe they are both right? I do not understand that. One says that God loves His people and never leaves off loving them. Another says that He did not love His people before they loved Him, that He often loves them and then ceases to love them and turns them away.

They may both be right in the main. But can they both be right when one says yes and the other says no? I must have a pair of spectacles to enable me to look backward and forward at the same time before I can see that. It cannot be, sirs, that they both are right. But some say they differ upon nonessentials. This text says, "I have written for Him the *great* things of My law." There is nothing in God's Bible that is not great. Did ever any of you sit down to see that was the purest religion? "Oh," you say, "we never took the trouble. We went just where our father and mother went." Ah, that is a profound reason indeed. You went where your father and mother did. I thought you were sensible people. I didn't think you went where other people pulled you but went of your own selves. I love my parents above all that breathe, and the very thought that they believed a thing to be true helps me to think it is correct. But I have not followed them. I belong to a different denomination, and I thank God I do. I can receive them as Christian brothers and sisters, but I never thought that because they happened to be one thing, I was to be the same.

No such thing. God gave me brains, and I will use them. And if you have any intellect, use it, too. Never say it doesn't matter. It *does* matter. Whatever God has put here is of eminent importance—He would not have written a thing that was indifferent. Whatever is here is of some value. Therefore search all questions, try all by the Word of God. I am not afraid to have what I preach tried by this Bible. Only give me a fair field, no favor, and this Bible. If I say anything contrary to it, I will withdraw it the next Sabbath day. By this I stand, by this I fall. Search and see, but don't say, "It does not matter."

If God says a thing, it must always be of importance. But while all things in God's Word are important, *all are not equally important.* There are certain fundamental and vital truths that must be believed, or otherwise no man would be saved. If you want to know what you must believe if you would be saved, you will find the great things of God's law between these two covers—they are all contained here. As a sort of digest or summary of the great things of the law, I remember an old friend of mine once saying, "Ah, you preach the three Rs and God will always bless you."

I said, "What are the three Rs?"

He answered, "*Ruin, redemption*, and *regeneration*."

They contain the sum and substance of divinity and of ruin. We were all ruined in the Fall. We were all lost when Adam sinned, and we are all ruined by our own transgressions. Our own evil hearts and our own wicked wills ruin us all. And we all will be ruined unless grace saves us. Then there is a second R for redemption. We are ransomed by the blood of Christ, a lamb without blemish and without spot. We are rescued by His power. We are ransomed by His merits. We are redeemed by His strength.

Then there is R for regeneration. If we have been pardoned, we must also be regenerated, for no man can partake of redemption unless he is regenerate. Let him be as good as he pleases. Let him serve God as he imagines, as much as he likes—unless he is regenerate and has a new heart, a new birth, he will still be in the first R, that is, ruin. These things contain an epitome of the gospel. I believe there is a better epitome in the five points of Calvinism: election according to the foreknowledge of God, the natural depravity and sinfulness of man, particular redemption by the blood of Christ, effectual calling by the power of the Spirit [irresistible grace], and ultimate perseverance of the saints by the efforts of God's might.

I think all those need to be believed for salvation. But I should not like to write a creed like the Athanasian, beginning with, "Whosoever should be saved, before all things it is necessary that he should deny the Catholic faith, that faith is this. . ." When I got so far, I should stop, because I should not know what to write. I hold the catholic faith of the Bible, the whole Bible and nothing but the Bible. It is not for me to draw up creeds. But I ask you to search the scriptures, for this is the Word of life.

God says, "I have written for him the great things of My law." Do you doubt their greatness? Do you think they are not worth your attention? Reflect a moment, man. Where are you standing now?

> Lo, on a narrow neck of land
> 'Twixt two unbounded seas I stand;
> An inch of time, a moment's space,
> May lodge me in yon heavenly place,
> Or shut me up in hell.

I recollect standing on a seashore once, upon a narrow neck of land, thoughtless that the tide might come up. The tide kept continually washing up on either side. But wrapped in thoughts, I still stood there until at last there was the greatest difficulty in getting on shore. The waves had washed between the shore and me. You and I stand each day on a narrow neck, and there is one wave coming up there. See how near it is to your foot. Lo, another throws at every tick of the clock, "Our hearts, like muffled drums, are beating funeral marches to the tomb."

We are always tending downward to the grave each moment that we live. *This Bible* tells me that if I am converted, when I die there is a heaven of joy and love to receive me. It tells me that angels' pinions will be stretched, and I, borne by strong cherubic wings, will out-soar the lightning and mount beyond the stars, up to the throne of God, to dwell forever.

> *Far from a world of grief and sin*
> *With God eternally shut in.*

Oh, it makes the hot tear start from my eye; it makes my heart too big for this, my body and my brain whine at the thought of

> *Jerusalem, my happy home,*
> *Name ever dear to me.*

Oh, that sweet scene beyond the clouds. Sweet fields arrayed in living green and rivers of delight. Are not these great things? But then, poor unregenerate son! The Bible says if you are lost, you are lost forever. It tells you that if you die without Christ, without God, there is no hope for you, that there is a place without a gleam of hope where you will read in burning letters, "You knew your duty, but you did it not."

It tells you that you will be driven from His presence with a "Depart from Me, you cursed" (Matt. 25:41). Are not these great things? Yes, sirs, as heaven is desirable, as hell is terrible, as time is short, as eternity is infinite, as the soul is precious, as pains are to be shunned, as heaven is to be sought, as God is eternal, and as His words are sure. These are great things, things you ought to listen to.

III. Our last point is *the treatment that the poor Bible receives in this world.* It is accounted a strange thing. What does that mean—the Bible accounted a strange thing? In the first place, it means that it is very strange to some people because *they never read it.* I remember reading, on one occasion, the sacred story of David and Goliath, and there was a person present, positively grown up to years of maturity, who said to me, "Dear me! What an interesting story! What book is that in?"

And I recollect a person once coming to me in private. I spoke to her about her soul. She told me how deeply she felt, how she had a desire to serve God. But she found another law in her members. I turned to a passage in Romans and read to her, "The good that I would I do not: but the evil which I would not, that I do" (7:19 KJV). She said, "Is that in the Bible? I did not know it." I did not blame her, because she had no interest in the Bible till then. But I did wonder that there could be found persons who knew nothing about such a passage.

> *I* hold the catholic faith of the Bible, the whole Bible and nothing but the Bible. It is not for me to draw up creeds. But I ask you to search the scriptures, for this is the Word of life.

Ah, you know more about your ledgers than your Bible. You know more about your daybooks than what God has written. Many of you will read a novel from beginning to end, and what have you got? A mouthful of froth when you have done. But you cannot read the Bible—that solid, lasting, substantial, and satisfying food goes uneaten, locked up in the cupboard of neglect, while anything that man writes, as a catch of the day is greedily devoured. "I have written for him the great things of My law, *but* they were considered a strange thing"

You have never read it. I bring the broad charge against you. Perhaps you say I ought not to charge you with any such thing. I always think it better to have a worse opinion of you than too good a one. I charge you with this: You do not read your Bibles. Some of you never have read it through. I know I speak what your heart must say is honest truth. You are not Bible readers. You say you have the Bible in your houses. Do I think you are such heathens as not to have a Bible? But when did you last read it? How do you know that your spectacles, which you have lost, have not been there for the last three years?

Many people have not turned over its pages for a long time, and God might say to them, "I have written for him the great things of My law, but they were considered a strange thing"

There are others who read the Bible, but when they read it, they say it is so horribly dry. That young man over there says it is a "bore." That is the word he uses. He says, "My mother said to me, when you go up to town, read a chapter every day. Well, I thought I would please her, and I said I would. I am sure I wish I had not. I did not read a chapter yesterday or the day before. We were so busy. I could not help it."

"You do not love the Bible, do you?"

"No, there is nothing in it that is interesting."

Ah, I thought so. But a little while ago *I* could not see anything in it. Do you know why? Blind men cannot see, can they? But when the Spirit touches the scales of the eyes, they fall off. And when He puts eye salve on, then the Bible becomes precious. I remember a minister who went to see an old lady, and he thought he would give her some precious promises out of the Word of God. Turning to one, he saw written in the margin, "*P*," and he asked, "What does this mean?"

"That means precious, sir."

Further down He saw "*T* and *P*," and he asked what the letters meant.

"That," she said, "means tried and proved, for I have tried and proved it."

If you have tried God's Word and proved it, if it is precious to your souls, then you are Christians. But those persons who despise the Bible have neither part nor lot in the matter. If it is dry to you, you will be dry at last in hell. If you do not esteem it as better than your necessary food, there is no hope for you, for you lack the greatest evidence of your Christianity.

> *I* charge you with this: You do not read your Bibles. Some of you never have read it through. I know I speak what your heart must say is honest truth. You are not Bible readers.

Alas, alas, the worst case is to come. *There are some people who hate the Bible*, as well as despise it. Has such a one stepped in here? Some of you said, "Let us go and hear what the young preacher has to say to us." This is what he has to say to you: "Behold you despisers, marvel and perish" (Acts 13:41). This is what he has to say to you: "The wicked shall be turned into hell, and all the nations that forget God" (Ps. 9:17). And this again he has to say to you: "Behold, there will come in the last days, mockers like yourselves who 'walk according to their own ungodly lusts'" (Jude 18).

But more: He tells you tonight that if you are not saved, you must find salvation here. Therefore, despise not the Bible, but search it, read it, and come to it. Rest you well assured, O scorner, that your laughs cannot alter truth, your jests cannot avert your inevitable doom. Though in your hardihood you should make a league with death and sign a covenant with hell, yet swift justice will overtake you and strong vengeance strike you low. In vain do you jeer and mock, for eternal verities are mightier than your sophistries; nor can your smart sayings alter the divine truth of a single word of this volume of revelation.

Oh, why do you quarrel with your best friend and ill treat your only refuge? There yet remains hope even for the scorner. Hope in a Savior's veins. Hope in the Father's mercy. Hope in the Holy Spirit's omnipotent agency.

I have done when I have said one word. My friend, the philosopher says it may be very well for me to urge people to read the Bible. But he thinks there are a great many sciences far more interesting and useful than theology. *Extremely obliged to you for your opinion, sir.*

"What science do you mean? Is it the science of dissecting beetles and arranging butterflies?"

"No," you say, "certainly not."

"Is it the science, then, of arranging stones and telling us of the strata of the earth?"

"No, not exactly that."

"Which science, then?"

"Oh, all sciences," you say, "are better than the science of the Bible."

"Ah, sir, that is your opinion, and it is because you are far from God that you say so."

But the science of Jesus Christ is the most excellent of sciences. Let no one turn away from the Bible because it is not a book of learning and wisdom. It is. Would you know astronomy? It is here. It tells you of the Sun of righteousness and the star of Bethlehem. Would you know botany? It is here. It tells you of the plant of renown, the Lily of the Valley and the Rose of Sharon. Would you know geology and mineralogy? You will learn it here, for you may read of the rock of ages and the white stone with a name graven thereon, which no man knows.

Would you study history? Here is the most ancient of all the records of the history of the human race. Whatever your science is, come and bend over this book. Your science is here. Come and drink out of this fair fount of knowledge and wisdom, and you will find yourselves made wise to salvation. Wise and foolish, babes and men, gray-headed sires, youths and maidens—I speak to you, I plead with you, I beg of you respect your Bibles and search them out, for in them you think you have eternal life, and these are they that testify of Christ.

I have done. Let us go home and practice what we have heard. I have heard of a woman, who, when she was asked what she remembered of the minister's sermon, said, "I don't recollect anything of it. It was about short weights and bad measures, and I didn't recollect anything but to go home and burn the bushel." So, if you will remember to go home and burn the bushel, that is, if you will recollect going home and reading your Bibles, I will have said enough.

And may God, in His infinite mercy, when you read your Bibles, pour into your soul the illuminating rays of the sun of righteousness by the agency of the ever-adorable Spirit. Then you will by God's grace read to your profit and to your soul's salvation.

We may say of the Bible:

God's cabinet of revealed counsel 'tis!
Where weal and woe are ordered so
That every man may know what will be his.
Unless his own mistake, false application make,
It is the index to eternity.
He cannot miss of endless bliss
That takes this chart to steer by;
Nor can he be mistook, that speaks by this book.
It is the book of God.
What if I should say, good of books,
Let him that looks
Angry at that expression, as too bold,
His thoughts in silence smother,
Till he find such another.

For Further Thought

1. *Spurgeon says that Hosea 8:12 describes a certain sin. What is it?*
2. *What are the three Rs?*
3. *Do you know a Bible verse that describes the importance of the Holy Scripture? If so, what is that verse?*

Blessed Discipline

Blessed is the man whom thou chastenest, O L ORD,
and teachest him out of thy law; that thou mayest give him rest
from the days of adversity, until the pit be digged for the wicked.
For the L ORD will not cast off his people, neither will he forsake his
inheritance. But judgment shall return unto righteousness:
and all the upright in heart shall follow it.
PSALM 94:12–15 KJV

THERE are times when the wicked seem to have things all their own way. This earth is not the realm of final justice. We are not yet standing before the Lord's great judgment seat. God permits many things to be for a while in confusion. They who are highest with Him are often lowest with men, and those for whom He has no regard seem to heap up the treasures of the world till their eyes stand out with fatness and they have more than heart can wish! Let no child of God be astonished at this arrangement. It has often been so in the past, and it has been the great enigma that has puzzled the world. The children of God have also sat down and looked into it, but it has been, even to them, a great deep that they could not fathom. They have sighed over it, but their sighs have not altered the facts. It is still true that often the wicked triumph and the servants of iniquity delight themselves in the high places of the earth. The righteous need not wonder that they suffer now, for that has been the lot of God's people all along, and there have been certain times in human history when God has seemed to be altogether deaf to the cries of His suffering people. Remember the martyr age and the days of the covenanters, who were hunted upon the mountains like the partridge. You must not wonder if the easy places of the earth are not yours and if the sentinel's stern duties should fall to your lot. It is so, and so it must be, for God has so ordained it.

To comfort any of the Lord's children who have begun to worry themselves because things do not go with them as they desire, I have selected this text, and I pray the Lord to bless it to them.

I. First, I will ask you to notice that *God's children are under instruction.* Other children may run about and take holiday. They may wander into the woods, gather the flowers, and do very much what they like, but God's own children have to go to school. This is a great privilege for them, although they do not always think so. Children are not often good judges of what is best for themselves. No doubt we should like to play the truant. We should be very glad to put away our schoolbags, quit the schoolhouse, go out by ourselves, and wander at our own sweet will, but our heavenly Father loves us too much to let it be so with us, because we are His children. Therefore He will have us trained and prepared for that high destiny that awaits us by and by.

> *God's own children have to go to school. This is a great privilege for them, although they do not always think so. Children are not often good judges of what is best for themselves*

Note how this tuition is described in our text. The very first word concerning it is "chasten." "Blessed is the man whom thou chastenest, O Lord, and teachest him out of thy law" (Ps. 94:12 KJV), as if the chastening were the primary part of the teaching, as if it occupied so large a share of it that it was put first. In God's schoolhouse the rod is still extant because *with the Lord, chastening is teaching.* He does not spoil His children but chastens them, yes, even to scourging, as the apostle puts it. His chastening is severest with those whom He loves best. "For whom the Lord loves He chastens, and scourges every son whom He receives" (Heb. 12:6). Some of us know what it is to have this teaching by chastening. I have often told you that I am afraid I have never learned anything of God except by the rod, and in looking back, I am afraid that I must confirm that statement. I have forgotten some of the gentle lessons, but when they have been whipped into me, I have remembered them.

I met with a friend the other day who said that it was the very reverse with him. He could not remember any benefit that he had ever gained by chastening, and he thought that all the good he had received from the Lord had come to him by tenderness and prosperity. I did not argue with him about the matter, for the experiences of God's people may differ, but this I know, dear friends, that some of us have learned much from the Lord's chastening rod!

For instance, we have learned the evil of sin. "Before I was afflicted I went astray, but now I keep Your Word" (Ps. 119:67). There are some sorrows that evidently come as the result of our own folly. We have to reap the harvest of the seed that we sow, and by this process we are made to see that it is an exceedingly evil and bitter thing to sin against God. This is an important lesson. I wish that more had thoroughly learned it. I wish that some Christian professors had anything like a true idea of the exceeding sinfulness of sin, but I believe that instruction upon this point often comes from the chastening hand of God.

Our chastening teaches us the unsatisfactory nature of worldly things. We can easily become attached to the things that we possess. It is a very difficult thing to handle gold without allowing it to adhere to your fingers and, when it gets into your purse, you need much grace to prevent it getting into your heart. Even our children can soon grow into idols—and our health and our comfort may make us forget God. I never knew affliction and trial to make us do that, but when the gourds are taken away, then the sun shines on us. How often has God shaken all the leaves off our trees, and *then* we have seen the heavens that we never saw when all the leaves were green! By losing this and losing that, we are made to feel that all the things that we possess perish in the using and are such temporary joys that we cannot hope to fill our hearts with them.

Do we not also learn by affliction our own frailty and our own impatience? We are wonderfully patient when we have nothing to suffer, as we are all great heroes and very courageous when there is no fighting to be done. We sometimes say to one another, "What a mass of faith that brother has! What a vast mountain of faith that sister possesses!" We are almost inclined to envy them, but we remember the fable of the stag that had such magnificent antlers that he said to himself as he looked at his fine figure in the water, "It is most absurd for us stags to be afraid of dogs. The next time I hear a dog bark, I will just toss him on my horns and there will soon be an end of him." Yes, so he thought, but just then the baying of a hound was heard in the distance, and the boastful stag took to his heels and ran as fast as the rest of the herd did! So it is often with those who seem to have great faith when they do not need it, but when they do need it, where is it? Stretch some men upon a bed of sickness for a week or two and see whether they will be able to swagger at the rate they now do! They would sing another song, I guarantee you, if once they had such a twist of pain as some of us have had to endure and the beads of perspiration stood on their brow while they tried to bear it. Ah yes, we find how great our weakness is when first one thing is taken away and then another, and the chastening hand of God makes the blows to fall thick and heavy upon us!

Do we not, then, learn also, the value of prayer? I said to this friend to whom I have referred, "Did you not pray much more under your affliction than you did before?"

"Oh yes!" he replied. "I grant you that trials give new life to prayer."

Do we ever pray in such dead earnest as when everything seems to be sinking from under our feet and our sweetest cups are full of bitterness? Then we turn to God and say, "Show me why You contend with me" (Job 10:2). I do not think that we ever pray with such fervor of supplication in our prosperity as we do in our adversity.

And then how precious the promises become! As we only see the stars when the shadows gather at night, so the promises shine out like newly kindled stars when we get into the night of affliction! I am sure that there are passages of scripture that are full of consolation, the depths of which we do not even imagine—and we will never know all that is in them till we get into the depths of soul trouble that correspond with them. There are points of view from which scenery is to be beheld at its best, and until we find out those points of view, we may be missing the sight of some of the most beautiful objects in nature! God leads us one way and another by our chastisements to understand and prize His promises.

And, oh, dear friends, how should we ever know the faithfulness of God if it were not for affliction? We might talk about it and theoretically understand it, but to try to prove the greatness of Jehovah's love and the absolute certainty of His eternal faithfulness—this comes not except by the way of affliction and trial!

I might talk on forever about the sweet uses of adversity and not exhaust the subject. You experienced people of God know even more than I do about this matter, for some of you have done business in deeper waters than my boat has yet plowed, and yet I think my keel has passed over the deep places of the sea of trouble, and there may be deeper depths before me still. I have probably said enough to prove to you that chastening is a divine way of instructing us. You will find that if you want the most Christlike saints and the most deeply experimental believers, and the Christians who are best acquainted with the Word of God, you must look for them among those who are the most intimately acquainted with the fiery furnace and its burning heat.

If you read the text through, dear friends, you will notice that the rod is not without the Word. I call your special attention to this: "Blessed is the man whom thou chastenest, O Lord, and teachest him out of thy law." The rod and the book go together! The rod drives us to the book, and the book explains the meaning of the rod! We must have them both if we would be fully instructed in the things of God. The Word of God is our schoolbook. At first it is our primer, and when we get furthest advanced in grace, it will be our most profound classic! And all along the way it will supply us with our choicest poetry and everything else that we desire.

> *The rod and the book go together! The rod drives us to the book, and the book explains the meaning of the rod! We must have them both if we would be fully instructed in the things of God.*

We look to the Bible for comfort when we are chastened. We turn over its pages and seek to find a passage that fits our case and ministers relief to our necessity. Have you not often done so? Why, this book is something like the locksmith's bunch of keys! Perhaps you have lost the key of your drawer and you cannot get at your things. You send for the smith, and he keeps on trying different keys till at last he finds one that exactly fits the wards of your lock. So, if you keep on fingering away at the promises, you will come, at last, upon one that was made on purpose for your case! Perhaps your lock is one with very peculiar wards—you could never make out why it was shaped just as it is—but now that you have found the key that opens it, you understand that both lock and key were made to fit each other.

The Word of God is not only used at such times for comfort, but also for direction. How frequently you have been unable to see your way! You have wished that there were some prophet of God with the Urim and Thummim that he might tell you what to do. The great guiding principles of God's truth, His law and His gospel, faith in Him and in His providential care, have furnished you with a direction quite as clear as if some prophet had plainly told you what to do. You have sought the direction of the Word of the Lord when you have gone to enquire in His temple. He has answered you out of the secret place of thunder, and you have known without a doubt the way that you should take.

That, then, is the second use of the Word, first for comfort, and next for direction.

At such times, too, we have proved, dear friends, the *power* of the Word of God. When your vessel is sailing along very smoothly, the Word of God may grow to be a dead letter with you, but when the waves are rolling mountains high and dashing over you, and you are soaked through and through and fear that the deep will swallow you up, then you begin to test the promises and to prove the power of the Word of God! When its inexpressible sweetness reaches your heart, then you can indeed feel that you have been taught out of God's Word. You see how the two things go together: "Blessed is the man whom thou chastenest, O LORD, and teachest him out of thy law." O Lord, still use the rod if You see that it is necessary. But go on teaching us out of Your Word! We are slow to learn and poor scholars at best, but You may yet make something of us.

That leads me to say that, according to our text, *God Himself is our teacher*. He is not satisfied with giving us a book and smiting us when we are inattentive to its teachings, but He Himself teaches us. Was there ever a teacher so full of wisdom, a teacher who understood His pupils so well, a teacher so altogether a master of the whole art of teaching? Was there ever a teacher so patient, so able to apply His lessons to the heart itself, so full of power to give understanding as well as to make the thing clear to the understanding when it is given? Happy are the people who have God as their tutor! Happy pupils, even though, when the school bell rings, you have half a mind to stay away and play with yonder children who do not belong to your school! Yet happy are you if you are truly God's scholars. Even if every now and then your days are spent in weeping and your lessons are so badly done that they bring the rod upon you, yet are you happy children. "Blessed is the man whom thou chastenest, O LORD, and teachest him out of thy law."

So much, then, for our first heading.

II. Now, on our second point I will say a little, and only a little. We have had God's children under instruction. Now let us think of *God's children educated.* The Lord has chastened and taught His child for this purpose: "That You may give him rest from the days of adversity, until the pit is dug for the wicked" (Ps. 94:13).

"What," you ask, "chastened to give us *rest?* It is usual for chastening to *break* our rest." Yes, I know that it is so with other chastening, but in very deed this is the way in which God gives rest to His people.

First, *we learn to rest in the will of God.* Our will is naturally very stubborn, and when we are chastened, at first we fight back, like a bullock unaccustomed to the yoke, but by degrees we feel that we must bear the yoke. We then go a little further and we feel that we *ought* to bear it, even though God should lay upon us anything He pleases and we should feel it very galling. By-and-by the yoke begins to fit our neck and we come even to *love* it. I do not suppose that many of us will ever get like Samuel Rutherford when he said that he began to wonder what he loved better—Christ or his cross—for his cross had brought him so much blessing that he was quite in love with it. No, we have not reached that point yet that we love our cross. Still, we can say this: that we have learned that it is "sweet to lie passive in His hands and know no will but His." If we struggle against God's will, we only increase our sorrow. Our self-will usually lies at the root of our greatest griefs. Give way and you have won! Yield to God and you have obtained the blessing you desire. The bitterness is gone out of your grief when you consent to be grieved if God will have it so.

We make advances in our spiritual education when *we learn to rest after our afflictions.* When any trouble is over, great delights often come to us. It is with us as it was with our Master. He had been with the wild beasts. Worse still, He had been tempted of the devil. But angels came and ministered to Him. There is sometimes to a believer a wonderfully clear shining after the rain. Perhaps there is no happier period of life than the state of convalescence, when the sick man is gradually recovering his former strength after a long illness. So God gives surprising peace to His people when He takes away their troubles, but He also gives them a great measure of peace *in* their troubles. Thus, for another lesson, *we learn to rest in adversity.* The Lord chastens us in order that we may learn how to stand fast and bear up bravely while the trouble is yet upon us.

I have often had to notice the singularity of my Lord's loving-kindness and tenderness to myself in the time of need. I do not say that it is singularity for *Him,* for He is often doing it, but the singularity lies in the fact that the Lord does it when nobody else could or would do it. He gives us comfort when nobody else is either willing or able to render any comfort to us. My gracious God sends this very afternoon a remarkable instance of how good cheer is sent to me just when I most need it. I was heavy and sad at heart, and there came to my door to see me a foreign gentleman, an officer of considerable rank in the Italian army. He spoke to me in very good English, but I cannot tell you all what he said to me, though it was most cheering and kind. I asked him why he should come so far to see me.

> *God gives surprising peace to His people when He takes away their troubles, but He also gives them a great measure of peace in their troubles.*

He spoke of me as though I were a great man, and I assured him that he was quite mistaken, for I was nothing of the kind. As we walked along and talked, he said, "But you are the greatest man in all the world to me."

"Why is that?" I asked.

And He answered, "I was a Catholic, and a bad Catholic, too. I did not rightly know anything about the Lord Jesus Christ, and I was fast becoming an infidel. But I met with a sermon of yours in Italian and, by reading it, I was brought into the light and liberty of the gospel. I found the Savior, and I felt that I must come and tell you about it." Then he further cheered and encouraged my heart by letting me see how much he knew of our Lord Jesus, and he had learned it all from nothing but the Bible itself, which he had read after being guided to it by a stray sermon of mine.

"Well," I thought, "my Master sends this man all the way from the south of Italy to come just at this particular time when I was sorely needing just such a comforting message." Why should He do so? Only that He likes, when His children have to take bitter medicine, to give them a piece of sugar after it! Therefore, my brothers and sisters, be willing to take your medicine; otherwise there may come a sharp chastening with it. Oh, for grace so to suffer and so to endure, that we may give ourselves up into the hands of the Ever-blessed One, and thus He will perfect in us the instruction of His wonderful Word! Then will it be true that the Lord has taught us to rest even in the days of our adversity.

Much more might be said upon this part of my subject, especially about learning to look beyond this present life, but I have not the time or the strength to say it.

III. I must now go on to the third point, that *God's children are still dear to Him.* We have thought of them at school, chastened and instructed, and we have seen them learning a few lessons. Now let us notice how dear they are to their Lord at all times, for the text says, "The LORD will not cast off His people, nor will He forsake His inheritance" (Ps. 94:14).

First, then, *the Lord will not cast off His people.* Sometimes you are cast down, but you are never cast *off.* Sometimes others cast you off, but the Lord will not cast off His people! Sometimes you are cast into the furnace. Yes, it may be so, but in the furnace, you are not cast off. Metal put into the furnace is not thrown away. Had it been worthless, it might have been left on the heap with the slag. But it is put into the furnace because it is of value. When you are put into the furnace and into the greatest heat that can be obtained, it is that the Lord may take away your dross and purify you for His service.

> *In the furnace God may prove you.*
> *There to bring you forth more bright.*
> *But can never cease to love you—*
> *You are precious in His sight!*
> *God is with you,*
> *God, your everlasting light.*

"The LORD will not cast off His people." Lay hold of that precious assurance! Even if Satan should come and whisper to you, "The Lord has cast you off," do not believe it! It cannot be. The devil has *his* castoffs, but God has no castoffs. Sometimes He takes the devil's castaways and makes them to be the trophies of His mighty grace—and when He has done so, they are His people, concerning whom the psalmist says, "The LORD will not cast off His people."

Then, further, *the Lord will not forsake His people,* for it is added, "Nor will He forsake His inheritance." He chose them to be His inheritance. He has bought them as His inheritance, and He will never forsake them! Still will you be supported by the Lord, but never forsaken by Him! Still will you be owned by Him, but never forsaken. Still will you be kept, defended against all comers, and preserved to be the Lord's own people, for He will not forsake His inheritance!

I do not feel as if I need to say much more upon this theme, but it is enough for me, I think, just to remind you of those precious words of our great and gracious Father that are many times repeated in His Word, "I will never leave you nor forsake you" (Heb. 13:5), and leave them with you, His children. Take them and feed upon them! God give you to know the full comfort of them!

IV. So I will close with this fourth point: *God's people will be righted in the end.* "Judgment will return to righteousness, and all the upright in heart will follow it" (Ps. 94:15).

> *The* Lord will not cast off His people." Lay hold of that precious assurance! Even if Satan should come and whisper to you, "The Lord has cast you off," do not believe it! It cannot be.

Just now, judgment has gone away. It has gone up to its own land. Judgment is within the veil, but there are reasons for its absence from us. Judgment has gone away, perhaps, that it may try the faith of God's people. The Lord does not today strike down the profane nor slay the hypocrite as He might if He dealt with them in strict justice. Judgment has gone out of the world for a while, though it watches and records all things. It is gone, partly, for our trial and testing, that we may learn to trust an absent God and Savior. Judgment is also gone away in order that mercy may be extended to the ungodly, that they may live and that they may turn to God, for He wills not the death of any, but that they may turn to Him and live. Judgment has gone up to the throne for a while until the wicked will have completed the full measure of their sin, "until the pit is dug for the wicked." Not yet is the iniquity of the Amorites full, and judgment has gone away and will stay away until it is.

Do not be in a hurry, child of God! The Lord has timed His absence. Listen to this next word: *"Judgment will return to righteousness."* You will soon hear the trumpet. You will hear the sound of that blast, "the loudest and the last," telling you that the day of the great assize has come and that the judge has arrived to right all wrongs, to punish all iniquity, and to reward all virtue, all true, faithful service! "Judgment will return." We cannot tell how long it will linger, but it will return. Christ will come again! As surely as He ascended into heaven, He will so come in like manner as He went up. He will judge the earth in righteousness and His people with His truth. Behold, He comes! And when He comes, judgment will return to righteousness.

> *God's people will be righted in the end. "Judgment will return to righteousness, and all the upright in heart will follow it"*

And what then? Judgment *will be welcomed by the godly.* When it comes, "All the upright in heart will follow it." The chariot of righteousness will lead the way, and all the people of God will follow it in a glorious procession. Then will they receive their Lord's commendation, "Well done, good and faithful servant" (Matt. 25:23 KJV). They will follow it as they wear their golden crowns, no, as they cast them at the foot of the throne of God, saying, "You are worthy, O Lord, to receive glory and honor and power" (Rev. 4:11). Saints will follow the chariot of judgment coming forth from their concealment and shining as the sun in the kingdom of their Father! They will come from the places where slander has banished them and show themselves again, and God will be glorified in them! Now, you who love the Lord, be not in a hurry to have all this fulfilled. Leave your cases in the dear hands of Him who will before long judge all righteously.

I have done when I have reminded you that He is accursed who has never felt the chastening hand of God or sat at His feet to learn of Him. But he is blessed indeed who yields himself entirely up to the discipline of the Lord. May it be so with every one of you, for our Lord Jesus Christ's sake! Amen.

FOR FURTHER THOUGHT

1. *When life chastens a believer, how does God's Word give instruction?*
2. *According to Psalm 94:13, what does God's chastening bring to a believer?*
3. *What two qualities does Spurgeon say are the marks of the righteous?*

HOLY LONGINGS

My soul breaks with longing for
Your judgments at all times.
PSALM 119:20

ONE of the best tests of a man's character will be found in his deepest and heartiest longings. You cannot always judge a man by what he is doing at any one time, for he may be under constraints that compel him to act contrary to his true self, or he may be under an impulse from which he will soon be free. He may, for a while, back off from that which is evil, yet he may be radically bad. Or he may be constrained by force of temptation to that which is wrong, yet his real self may rejoice in righteousness. A man may not be pronounced to be good because, for the moment, what he is doing may be condemned as evil because, under certain constraints, he may be committing sin. A man's longings are more inward and more near to his real self than his outward acts—they are more natural in that they are entirely free and beyond compulsion or restraint.

As a man longs in his heart, so is he. I mean not every idle wish, as I now speak, but strong desires of the heart. These are the true life of a man's nature. You will know whether you yourself are evil by answering this question: To what have you the greatest desire? Do you long continually after selfish pleasures? Then you are evil beyond all question! Do you sigh to be, feel, and do that which is good? Is this the great aim of your life? Then in the core of your being, there is some good thing toward the Lord God of Israel. So then, dear hearers, your heart longings may furnish you with helps for self-examination, and I beg you to apply them, as things of the heart touch the root of the matter. Unbelievers are people who err in their heart, and men truly find the Lord when they seek Him with their whole heart. So the heart is all-important, and its longings are among the surest marks of its condition.

Moreover, heart longings are prophecies of what a man will be. It is not always capacity, if we could ascertain it, that will certify us as to what a man will do, for many men of large abilities achieve nothing for lack of inclination. Their talents lie hidden in the earth and, although they might have succeeded marvelously well in certain pursuits, they do nothing at all remarkable because they have no tendencies in that direction. An individual may have the means to relieve the poor and yet never perform a charitable act from lack of generosity. Or he may have great mental powers yet never produce a line of useful literature because he is eaten up with idleness. But other things being equal, the longings of a man are a pretty sure index of what he will be. They cannot create capacity, but they develop it. They lead to the use of means for its increase, and they make the mind keen to seize opportunities.

By some means or other, a man usually becomes what he intensely longs to be, especially if those desires are formed in early youth while yet the world is all before him where to choose. Hence our proverb: "The child is father to the man." Even in little children, tastes and pursuits have been prophetic. The young artist sketches his sister in the cradle; the youthful engineer is busy with his boyish inventions. If his longings deepen, strengthen, and become vehement with the increase of his years, the young man's character is being molded from within, and this is often a greater force than that of circumstances acting from without.

> *Unbelievers are people who err in their heart, and men truly find the Lord when they seek Him with their whole heart. So the heart is all-important, and its longings are among the surest marks of its condition.*

Thus it is in spiritual things—we may form forecasts as to what we will be from our burning and pressing desires. Desires are the buds out of which words and deeds will ultimately be developed. Spiritual desires are the shadows of coming blessings. What God intends to give us, He first sets us longing for. Therefore, prayer is wonderfully effective because it is the embodiment of a longing that is inspired by God because He intends to bestow the blessing prayed for! What are your longings, then, my hearer? Do you long to be holy? The Lord will make you holy! Do you long to conquer sin? You will overcome it by faith in Jesus! Are you pining after fellowship with Christ? He will come and make His abode with you! Does your soul thirst, yes, even pant after God as the hart for the water brooks? Then you will be filled with all His fullness, for all these longings are prophetic of that which is to be, even as the snowdrop and crocus and anemone foretell the approach of spring.

I say not that it is so with all human wishes, for "the sluggard desires and has nothing" and many a man has such evil cravings within his heart that it were contrary to the purity of God for Him to grant them. But where there are intense, heartbreaking yearnings of a holy order, depend upon it, they are tokens of good things to come! Where the grace of God reigns in the soul, it makes a man become a stranger among his fellows, and it breeds in him peculiar affections and novel desires. The verse that precedes my text runs thus: "I am a stranger in the earth" (Ps. 119:19). He was a king surrounded by courtiers and friends, yet he was not at home but like one banished from his native land. And being thus a stranger in the earth, he had a remarkable desire that worldlings could not understand, and that singular craving he here expresses: "My soul breaks with longing for your judgments at all times."

Worldly men care nothing for the judgments of God. No, they care nothing for God Himself! But when a man becomes born anew, a citizen of heaven, there grows up within his spirit a spiritual appetite of which he had felt nothing before—and he longs after God and His Holy Word. See to it, brothers and sisters, whether your souls cry out for God, for the living God, for again I say, by your longings you may test yourselves—by your heart's desires you may forecast your future—and by your hungering and thirsting you may judge whether you are men of this world or citizens of the world to come. With such aids to self-judgment, no man ought to remain in doubt as to his spiritual condition and eternal prospects.

In order that we may be helped to the right use of this text, we will handle it thus—first, we will notice *the saint's absorbing object*: "your judgments." Second, we will reflect upon *the saint's ardent longing*: "My soul breaks with longing for your judgments." And, third, we will mention *the saint's cheering reflections*, that he may readily draw from the fact that he does experience such inward heartbreak. Of these we will speak as the divine Spirit will enable us, for without Him we know nothing.

I. First, then, let us think of *the saints' absorbing objective*. They long after God's judgments. The word *judgments* is here used as synonymous with the

"Word of God." It does not mean those judgments of God with which He smites sinners and executes the sentence of His law, but it refers to the revealed will or declared judgments of God. All through this long psalm, the writer is speaking of the Word of God, the law of God, the testimonies, and the precepts, the statutes of God—and here the word *judgments* is used in the same sense. Perhaps I will give you the meaning pretty readily if I remind you that the commandments and doctrines of the Word are God's judgments about moral and spiritual things, His decisions as to what is right and what is wrong, and His solutions of the great problems of the universe.

God's revealed plan of salvation is God's decision upon man's destiny, God's judgment of condemnation against human sin, and yet His judgment of justification on behalf of believing sinners whom He regards as righteous through faith in Jesus Christ. The Bible may be rightly regarded as the book of divine judgments, the recorded sentences of the high court of heaven, the infallible decision of perfect holiness upon questions that concern our souls.

> *This is the judge that ends the strife*
> *Where wit and reason fail.*
> *Our guide through devious paths of life,*
> *Our shield when doubts assail.*

You may come to the scriptures as men came to the throne of Solomon, where hard cases were at once met. But a greater than Solomon is here! Search God's Word and you will have before your eyes the ultimate judgment of unerring truth, the last decree from the supreme authority from which there is no appeal! The Bible contains the verdicts of the judge of all the earth, the judgments of God who cannot lie and cannot err.

Thus, God's Word is rightly called His "judgments." It is a book not to be judged by us, but to be our judge—not a word of it may be altered or questioned. But to it we may constantly refer as to a court of appeal whose sentence is decisive. David in our text tells us how he desired the Lord's judgments, or His Word, by which we understand, first, that he greatly reverenced the Word of God. He was not among those who regard the Bible as only a very important portion of human literature, but as being no more inspired than the works of Shakespeare or Bacon. Little as David had of the scriptures, he had a solemn reverence for what he had and stood in awe of it. I have no objection to honest criticism of the keenest kind, but I am shocked at certain divines who cut and carve the blessed Word of God as if it were some vile carcass given over to their butchery.

When learned men handle the words of this book, let them not forget whose book it is and whose words they are that they are examining! There is a near approach to blasphemy against God Himself in irreverence to His Word. There is no book like this for authority and majesty. It is hedged about with solemn sanctions so that it has both a wall of fire all around it and a glory in its midst to make it distinct from all other writings. All other books might be heaped together in one pile and burned, as the Muslims burned the Alexandrian Library, with less loss to the world than would be occasioned by the total obliteration of a single page of the sacred volume! All other books are at the best but as gold leaf, whereof it takes acres to make an ounce of the precious metal. But this book is solid gold! It contains ingots, masses, mines, yes, and whole worlds of priceless treasure. Its contents cannot be exchanged for pearls, rubies, or the "terrible crystal" itself.

Even in the mental wealth of the wisest men, there are no jewels like the truths of revelation. Oh, sirs, the thoughts of men are vanity, the conceptions of men are low and groveling at their best—and He who has given us this book has said, "For My thoughts are not your thoughts, nor are your ways My ways,' says the LORD. 'For as the heavens are higher than the earth, so are My ways higher than your ways, and My thoughts than your thoughts'" (Isa. 55:8–9). Let it be to you and to me a settled matter that the Word of the Lord will be honored in our minds and enshrined in our hearts! Let others speak as they may, "our soul breaks with longing for the Lord's judgments." We could sooner part with all that is sublime and beautiful, cheering or profitable in human literature than lose a single syllable from the mouth of God.

But more: inasmuch as the psalmist greatly reverenced God's Word, he intensely desired to know its contents. He had not much of it, probably only the five books of Moses, but the Pentateuch was enough to fill his whole soul with delight. Never depreciate, I pray you, the Old Testament! Remember that the great things that are said in the Psalms about the Word of God were not spoken concerning the New Testament—that was not then written—although they may most fitly be applied by us to the entire series of inspired books. They were originally spoken only concerning the first five of them, so that the first part of the Bible, according to the Holy Spirit's own testimony, is to be valued beyond all price.

Indeed, the substance of the New Testament is in the books of Genesis, Exodus, Leviticus, Numbers, and Deuteronomy—there shut up like Noah in the ark or hidden like Moses in his mother's house. The lovely form of queenly truth is there, only her veil conceals her countenance. The clearer shining of the New Testament is not a different light, nor perhaps is it, in itself, brighter—it shines through a thinner medium and therefore more fully enlightens us. If I might venture to compare one part of God's Word with another, I have even thought that the first books are the deepest and that if we had but skill to find it out, we should discover within them a more condensed mass of revelation than even in the New Testament! I will not defend the opinion, but usually the lower strata, though most hidden, are the densest, and certainly that which is most easy to be understood is not, therefore, of necessity the fullest of meaning, but the reverse.

> *When learned men handle the words of this book, let them not forget whose book it is and whose words they are that they are examining. There is a near approach to blasphemy against God Himself in irreverence to His Word.*

The various books of scripture do not increase in real value; they only advance in their adaptation to us. The light is the same, but the lantern is clearer and we see more. The treasure of the gospel is contained in the mines of the books of Moses, and I do not wonder, therefore, that David, instinctively knowing it to be there, but not being able to reach it, felt a great longing after it. He was not so well able to get at the truths of God as we are since he had not the life of Christ to explain the types, nor apostolic explanations to open up the symbols of the law, and therefore, he sighed inwardly and felt a killing heartbreak of desire to reach that which he knew was laid up in store for him. He saw the jewelry box but could not find the key!

If he had not been sure that the treasure was there, he would not have cried, "Open my eyes, that I may see wondrous things from Your law" (Ps. 119:18). But he was like a voyager on the verge of a discovery who, nevertheless, cannot quite reach it. He was like Columbus out at sea with the fruits of an unknown continent floating beneath his keel but the wind not favoring his reaching the shore. He was like a miner whose pick has struck upon a lump of metal, and he is sure that gold is there, but he cannot get it away from the quartz in which it is embedded. The more certain he is that it is there and the harder it is to reach, the more insatiable does his desire become to possess the treasure! Hence, I see the reasonableness of the psalmist's vehement passion and I marvel not that he cried, "My soul breaks with longing for your judgments at all times."

But I am sure that David did not merely want to know as a matter of intellectual pleasure, but wished to feed upon God's Word; and what a very different thing that is, that feeding upon the Word of God, from the bare knowledge of it! You can teach a child many chapters out of the Bible, yet he may not have fed on a word of it. I have known persons to be so foolish as to set it as a punishment for a child to learn a portion of scripture. I call this foolish, and surely it is also wicked to make the Word of God into a punishment, as well as turn the temple into a prison! Undoubtedly many know the history, the doctrine, and the letter of God's Word as well as others know their Homer or their Virgil and, so far, so good. But oh, to feed upon the Word of God is quite another thing!

> *Our judgment must be daily more and more conformed to the judgments of God that are laid down in scripture. And there must be in our spirit a longing after holiness until we delight in the law of the Lord*

An oven full of bread is well enough, but for nourishment, a loaf on the table is better and a morsel in the mouth is better still! And if the mouthfuls are well digested and taken up into the system, they are then best of all! In like manner, truths of God in a sermon are to be valued, but the truth of God, attentively heard, comes nearer to practical benefit, and truth of God believed is better still! And truths of God absorbed into the spiritual system are best of all! Alas, I fear we are not so absorbent as we ought to be. I like to see men who can be spiritual sponges of God's truth suck it right up and take it into themselves! It would be well, however, that they would not be so far like sponges as to part with the truth when the hands of the world attempt to wring it out of them!

I say we are not receptive enough, brothers and sisters, because our hearts are not in tune with God. Do we not feel, at times, that certain doctrines of the Word are hard? We do not quite agree with the divine judgments on this or that. Though we dare not question their rightness, we rather wish they were different. Friends, this must not be so any longer! All that kind of feeling must be gone! We must agree with God in all that He has spoken and let our belief run side by side with the teaching of the Lord. It is high time that we were altogether agreed with God. "Do you not know that we shall judge angels?" (1 Cor. 6:3). We will sit, at the last great day, as assessors with Christ in the great assize to judge the fallen spirits! Does it not become us to be of the same mind with our Lord? Should we not delight in His Word even now, that we may the more heartily say, "Amen," to His verdict from the great white throne?

Our judgment must be daily more and more conformed to the judgments of God that are laid down in scripture. And there must be in our spirit a longing after holiness until we delight in the law of the Lord and meditate therein both day and night. We will grow to the likeness of that which we feed upon, heavenly food will make us heavenly minded! The Word of God received into the heart changes us into its own nature and, by rejoicing in the decisions of the Lord, we learn to judge after His judgment and to delight ourselves in that which pleases Him. This sense, I think, comes nearer to the explanation of David's intense longing. Doubtless, he longed to obey God's Word—he wished in everything to do the will of God without fault either of omission or of commission.

Do you, my hearer, long after perfection in that same fashion? All that truly know God must have a mighty yearning to run in the way of the Lord's commandments. He does not live before God who does not crave to live like God. There is no regeneration where there are no aspirations after holiness. The actual practice of obedience is necessary as a proof of the possession of true grace, for the rule is invariable, "By their fruits ye shall know them" (Matt. 7:20 KJV). No man knows the Word of God till he obeys it. "If any man will do his will, he shall know of the doctrine" (John 7:17 KJV).

The psalmist also longed to feel the power of God's judgments in his own heart. You know something about this, my friend, if the Spirit of God has had dealings with you. Have you not felt the Lord judging you in the chamber of your conscience? The Spirit comes by the Word of God and sets our iniquities before us, our secret sins in the light of His countenance. You had forgotten the wrong, or at least you hardly remembered it as a sin, but suddenly you saw it all. As I have looked upon a landscape under a cloudy sky, a gleam of sunlight has suddenly fallen upon one portion of it and made it stand out brilliantly from the midst of the surrounding gloom, so has the Holy Spirit poured a clear light upon some one act or set of acts of my life and I have seen it as I never saw it before.

That inner light has judged us and led us to seek fresh cleansing—the judgments of God have come into our souls and led us anew to cry for mercy. I have found it so, have you? The sins of our youth and our former transgressions have been judged of the Lord within us. I do not think that David fully recognized all the sins of his youth till he had become an old man and, alas, many who have sinned in ways in which he never erred have failed to know the evil of their transgressions till in their bones and in their flesh they have felt its terrible effects years afterward. The Lord will judge His people and make sin bitter to them. Ought we to wish for this? I say, yes! Every true man should feel a longing in his soul to have every sin within him exposed, condemned, and executed. He should wish to hide nothing, but that it would be revealed and he be humbled by the sight.

There are two judgments, one of which we must undergo—either judgment in the forum of the conscience, or else judgment before the great white throne at last. You must either condemn yourself or be condemned! A court of arraigns must be held in your heart, and you must be tried, cast, and condemned in your own soul, or else you will not fully know the judgments of the Lord or truly seek pardon at His hands. God justifies the men who condemn themselves, and none but these will ever obtain the righteousness that is of God by faith. Therefore we may long for stripping judgments that we may obtain the robe of righteousness. We may cry to be emptied that grace may fill us. David desires that God's Word would come right into him, hold its court and judge, and try him—and he came to feel this process to be so necessary and so salutary that his soul broke with the longing that he had to be dealt with by God after this fashion.

This is wisdom and prudence when a man so desires sanctification that he is straitened till painful processes are being carried on by which his purity is to be produced. It is a wise child who will, for the sake of health, even long to take the appointed medicine! God's children are not far from being well when they have reached such a point of sacred judgment. This is the wish of all true believers: to be perfectly conformed to the Word of God. Some of us can honestly say that we would not have a second wish for ourselves if our heavenly Father would grant us this one: that we might be perfect even as He is. We would leave all other matters with Him as to wealth or poverty, health or sickness, honor or shame, life or death if He would but give us complete conformity to His will. This is the objective of the craving, yearning, and sighing of our souls. We hunger to be holy!

Here I must correct myself as to our one desire, for surely, if the Lord would make us holy, we should then desire that all other men would be the same. Oh, that the world was converted to God! Oh, that the truth of God would go forth like the brightness of the morning! Would God that every error and superstition might be chased away like bats and owls before the rising of the sun! O God, Your servants long for this! We ask for nothing except these two things: first reign, O Lord, in the triple kingdom of our nature, and then reign over *all* nature! Let the whole earth be filled with Your glory and our prayers are ended. I hope that in this sense our soul breaks for the longing that it has toward God's judgments.

II. And now. Second, let us think of *the saints' ardent longings*. First, let me say of these longings that they constitute a living experience, for dead things have no aspirations or cravings. You will visit the graveyard and exhume all the bodies you please, but you will find neither desire nor craving. Longing lingers not within a lifeless corpse. Where the heart is breaking with desire, there is life. This may comfort some of you since you have not attained, as yet, to the holiness you desire. But you long for it. Ah, then, you are a living soul; the life of God is in you. You have not yet come to be conformed to the precept, but oh, how you wish you were. That wish proves that a spark of the divine life is in your soul.

The stronger that longing becomes, the stronger is the life from which it springs. A feeble life has feeble desires. A vigorous life has vehement desires, burning like coals of juniper! Are you earnestly longing this morning? Can you say that your heart pines for God as the watcher through the midnight sighs for the dawn, or as the traveler over burning sand longs for the shadow of a great rock? Oh, then, though I would not have you rest in longings; indeed, I know you never can. Yet they are a proof that you are spiritually alive! Heart longings are far better tests than attendance at sacraments, for men who are dead in sin have dared to come both to baptism and the Lord's Supper. Eager desires prove spiritual life much better than supposed attainments, for these supposed attainments may all be imaginary. But a heart breaking for the longing that it has for God's Word is no fancy. It is a fact too painful to be denied!

Next, remember that the expression used in our text represents a humble sense of imperfection. David had not yet come to be completely conformed to God's words, nor yet to know them perfectly, or else he would not have said that he longed for them. So it is with us. We have not reached perfection, but do not let us, therefore, be discouraged, for the apostle of the Gentiles said, "Not as though I had already attained, either were already perfect" (Phil. 3:12 KJV). And the man after God's own heart, even David, when he was at his best—and I think he was so when he was writing this blessed psalm—says not so much that he had obtained anything as that he longed after it, not so much that he had yet grasped it, but sighed for it. "My soul breaks for the longing."

I do not envy those who have no more longings, who have reached so divine a height that they can climb no higher. I heard of one who said his will was so perfectly resigned to the will of God that in fact he had no will, and so he had given up prayer, having nothing to seek. This is stupid talk! When a man gets so full of life that he no longer breathes, I should say that he is dead. Prayer is the breath of the soul, and he that can do without it is dead in sin. When a man thinks himself so good that he cannot be better, he is probably so bad that he could not be worse. That is the judgment that caution will pronounce upon him, for all good men long to be better, and better men desire to be best of all that they may dwell in heaven. The more grace the saints have, the more they desire. Sacred greed is begotten by the possession of the love of God. "My soul breaks with longing for your judgments."

Furthermore, the expression of the text indicates an advanced experience. Augustine dwells upon this idea, for he rightly says that at first there is an aversion in the heart to God's Word and desire after it is a matter of growth. After aversion is removed, there often comes indifference in the heart—it is no longer opposed to godliness, but it does not care to possess it. Then, through divine grace, there springs up in the soul a sense of the beauty of God's Word and will and an admiration of holiness. This leads on to a measure of desire after the good thing and a degree of appetite for it. But it shows a considerable growth in grace when we ardently long after it and a still larger growth when the soul breaks because of these longings! It is a blessed thing when the soul is so stretched with desire that it is ready to snap, or when, like a vessel full of fermenting liquor, the working within threatens to break up the vessel altogether.

The text represents the agonizing of an earnest soul. Such a state of things shows a considerable advancement in the divine life, but when a believer has those desires at all times, he is not far from being a full-grown Christian. "Oh," you say, "he thinks so little of what he has that he is crushed under the burden of desire for more." Yes, and he is the very man who has most of spiritual wealth! Those desires are mysterious entries in the account book of his heart, and rightly read they prove his wealth, for in the divine life, the more a man desires, the more he has already obtained! You may make tallies of your desires, and as you reckon by those tallies, they will tell you to a penny what your spiritual wealth is. The fuller a man is of grace, the more he hungers for grace! Strange it is to say so, but the paradox is true—the more he drinks and the more he is satisfied and ceases to thirst in one sense, the more he is devoured with thirst after the living God!

> *Heart longings are far better tests than attendance at sacraments, for men who are dead in sin have dared to come both to baptism and the Lord's Supper. Eager desires prove spiritual life much better than supposed attainments.*

It is an advanced experience, then, and it is an experience that I cannot quite describe to you except by saying that it is a bitter sweet or, rather, a sweet bitter, if the adjective is to be stronger than the noun! There is bitterness about being crushed with desire. It is inevitable that there should be, but the aroma of this bitter herb is inexpressibly sweet—no perfume can excel it! After all, a bruised heart knows more peace and rest than a heart filled with the world's delights. How safe such a soul is. "Oh," said one, "I cannot go to hell. It is impossible, because I love Jesus Christ and long after Him. It is not possible for Him to forbid me the privilege of loving Him; and to love Him and long for Him is happiness!" Better to feel a heavenly hunger than a worldly fullness! Heartbreak for God is a sweeter thing than content in sinful pleasures! There is an inexpressible sweetness, a dawning of heaven, in longing after God and yet, because you feel you have not yet attained what you desire, there is a bitter mixed with it.

I think the only thing that honey needs to improve it is just a touch of bitter or acid in it. When you eat much honey, it begins to taste bad because it is all sweet, but just a taste of lemon or a dash of quassia might strengthen the taste and enable it to take in a fresh freight of sweetness. It is surely so with true religious experience. Pangs of strong desire increase our overflowing pleasures, and the longings and hungering make attaining and enjoying to be all the more delightful. May the Lord send us more of this lamb with bitter herbs, this mingled experience in that we are "sorrowful, yet always rejoicing" (2 Cor. 6:10).

Still, that longing after God's Word may become very wearing to a man's soul. The sense of our text in the Hebrew is that of attrition or wearing down. Keble reads it:

> My soul is worn and wasted quite,
> Your laws desiring day and night.

They wear out the man when they become so fervent as those confessed in the text. I believe that some of the Lord's holy ones have been worn down to sickness and depression by the passion of their hearts after God. Their souls have become like sharp swords that cut through their scabbards, for they have destroyed the body by intense inner desires. At times holy men draw so near to God and pine so greatly after His glory that for half a word they would pass the frontier and enter into heaven! They are so fully in accord with God that the shell that shuts in their soul is almost broken and the newborn spirit is ready for its fullest life and liberty. How blessed to shake off the last fragment of that which holds us back from the freedom of an immortal life in perfect agreement with God! Oh, to attain to this!

One saint cried, "Let me see the face of God."

Another answered, "You cannot see God's face and live!"

To that he replied, "Then let me see my God and die."

So do we feel that our soul comes near to dying with its longings after its God. Little would we tremble, even if we knew that the joy of realization would be killing and would pass us over the border into Immanuel's land where we will see the King in His beauty! But I must not linger though there is much to tempt me to speak on. Are you searching yourselves, brothers and sisters, to see whether you have such longings? If so, do you have them at all times? We are not to long for God's Word and will by fits and starts. We are not to have desires awakened by novelty or by excitement. Nor are we to long for divine things, because for a while temporal things fail us and we are sick and sorry and weary of the world and so in disgust turn to God.

Brethren, I trust you long after God when all is bright in providence and that you love His Word when all is pleasant in family affairs. It is well to desire the Lord's will when He is permitting you to have your own will as well as when He is thwarting you. God is always to be our delight. He is our defense in war, but He is also our joy in peace. Do not use Him as sailors use those harbors of refuge for which they are not bound, into which they only run into in time of storm, but if it is fair, they stand far out to sea! The Lord's will is to be the path of our feet and the element of our life. This it is to be a true child of God: to always have a yearning soul toward God's Word, to be eager after His commandments at all times. May the Holy Spirit keep us ever hungering and thirsting after God and His truth.

III. And now I am going to close with a few cheering reflections. I think this morning some heart has been saying, "There are comforting thoughts for me in all this. I am a poor thing. I have not grown much. I have not done much. I wish I had, but I do have strong longings. I am very dissatisfied, and I am almost ready to die with desire for Christ." My dear soul, listen. Let this encourage you! First, God is at work in your soul. Never did a longing after God's Word grow up in the soul of itself. Weeds come up of themselves, but the rarest kind of plants, I guarantee you, will never be found where there has been no sowing! And this flower, called love-lies-bleeding—this plant of intense eagerness after God—never sprang up in the human breast of itself! God has placed it there!

Friend, there was a time when you had no such longings. Ah, and if you were left to yourself, you would never have such longings again! You would decline till you became as content with the world as others are. You know you would! Come, then, beloved, God is at work in your soul. Let this comfort you. The great potter has you upon the wheel, He has not cast you away as worthless, His work may pain you, but it is honorable and glorious. Your heart may swell with unutterable longings, and it may be torn by throes of desire, but life thus proves its presence and reaches forth to something yet beyond. These pains of desire are the Lord's doings, and they should be perceived with gratitude.

The result of God's work is very precious. Though it is only a gracious desire, thank God for it. Though you can get no further than holy longing, be grateful for that longing. I would have you strive for the highest gifts, but I would not have you despise what God has already given you! I have known times when I thought myself in a very strange case and I judged ill of myself. Yet a month or two afterward, I have looked back upon that condition that I condemned and I have wished that I could return to it! Has it not been so with you? You have been racked with sighs, groans, cravings, and other forms of unrest, and you have said, "O God, deliver me from this sore travail!" But when, within a week, you have had to lament insensibility and lukewarmness, you have cried, "Lord, put me back into my state of desire! Lord, set me hungering and thirsting again. A fierce appetite is better than this deadness."

Oh, you who are longing, be thankful that you are, for you have a rich promise to cheer you, since it is written, "He will fulfill the desire of those who fear Him" (Ps. 145:19). The more wretched and unhappy you are under a sense of sin, the more grateful you ought to be for tenderness of heart. And the more you are longing to lay on Christ and to become like Christ, the more you should thank God that He has worked this longing in you. How sweet is that Word of God, "Lord, You have heard the desire of the humble; You will prepare their heart; You will cause Your ear to hear" (Ps. 10:17). Listen once again: Not only is the desire precious, but it is leading on to something more precious! Hear that which is written: "The desire of the righteous will be granted" (Prov. 10:24).

> *This it is to be a true child of God: to always have a yearning soul toward God's Word, to be eager after His commandments at all times.*

What do you say to such words as these: "When the poor and needy seek water, and there is none, and their tongue faileth for thirst, I the LORD will hear them, I the God of Israel will not forsake them" (Isa. 41:17 KJV)? Do you think that God prompts us to desire a thing that He does not mean to bestow upon us? Is that the way you treat your children? I know you will play with the little ones, sometimes, and hold a nut or a penny in your closed hand and bid them open your fingers for themselves. But you give them their treat before long. You would not hold a sweetmeat before a poor child, promise it to him, excite his desires for it, and then refuse him a taste of it. That would be a cruel pastime! God is not unkind. If He makes you hunger, for that hunger He has made ready the bread of heaven! If He makes you thirst, for that thirst He has already filled the river of the water of life! If the desire comes from God, the supply of that desire will as certainly come from God! Rest you sure of that and cry mightily to Him with strong faith in His goodness.

> *We see all God's decisions against sin and for righteousness embodied in our Savior. We see that if we can get Christ we have then found the wisdom of God and the power of God and, in fact, the all-sufficiency of God!*

Meanwhile, the desire itself is doing you good. It is driving you out of yourself. It is making you feel what a poor creature you are, for you can dig no well in your own nature and find no supplies within your own spirit. It is compelling you to look only to God. Do not need much compelling. Come readily to your Lord! Be one of those vessels that can sail with a capful of wind. Come by faith to Jesus, even though you fear that your desires are by no means so vivid and intense as those of my text. Believe and you will be established. Rest assured of this, that there is in God whatever your soul needs. In Christ Jesus dwells all the fullness of the Godhead bodily, and in that divine fullness there must of necessity be more than a creature can require. In Christ Jesus there is exactly what your soul is panting for.

Yes, I mean you weakest ones of the flock! You feeblest of the saints! You who dare not put your names down among God's people at all! If there is a sacred longing in your spirit, there is that in Christ that is adapted to you in spite of your feebleness and unworthiness. God is ready to give you whatever you are ready to receive. Only come and trust Him for it and look to His dear Son, for in Jesus you have all things. Oh, this is the blessedness of this longing after God's judgments: that it makes Christ precious! And with that remark, I have done.

We see all God's Word in Christ. We see all God's decisions against sin and for righteousness embodied in our Savior. We see that if we can get

Christ we have then found the wisdom of God and the power of God and, in fact, the all-sufficiency of God. If we can become like Christ, we will be like God Himself. This, I say, makes Christ so precious and makes us long to more fully know Him and call Him ours! Come, you longing ones, come to my Lord Jesus even now! Come, you who are bursting with wishes and desires, come and trust the Savior and rest in Him now! And may this be the hour in which you will find how true it is, "Blessed are they which do hunger and thirst after righteousness: for they shall be filled" (Matt. 5:6 KJV). May you yet sing the virgin's song, "He has filled the hungry with good things, and the rich He has sent away empty" (Luke 1:53).

For Further Thought

1. *In general terms, what does Spurgeon consider our "absorbing objective" to be?*
2. *What are some things that Spurgeon calls a believer's "ardent longings"?*
3. *Why should a believer who deeply desires the Lord, yet feels that he or she is not growing in faith, be encouraged?*

Sermons Relating to the TULIP Concept (Total depravity, Unconditional election, Limited atonement, Irresistible grace, Perseverance of the saints)

Human Inability
(Total Depravity of Man)

"No one can come to Me unless the Father who sent Me draws him; and I will raise him up at the last day."
John 6:44

"Coming to Christ" is a very common phrase in Holy Scripture. It is used to express those acts of the soul wherein leaving at once our self-righteousness and our sins, we fly to the Lord Jesus Christ and receive His righteousness to be our covering and His blood to be our atonement. Coming to Christ, then, embraces in it repentance, self-negation, and faith in the Lord Jesus Christ. It sums within itself all those things that are the necessary attendants of these great states of heart, such as the belief of the truth, earnestness of prayer to God, the submission of the soul to the precepts of God's gospel, and all those things that accompany the dawn of salvation in the soul.

Coming to Christ is just the one essential thing for a sinner's salvation. He who comes not to Christ, do what he may, or think what he may, is yet in "the gall of bitterness, and in the bond of iniquity" (Acts 8:23 KJV). Coming to Christ is the very first effect of regeneration. No sooner is the soul quickened than it at once discovers its lost estate, is horrified thereat, looks out for a refuge and believing Christ to be a suitable one, flies to Him, and reposes in Him.

Where there is not this coming to Christ, it is certain that there is as yet no quickening. Where there is no quickening, the soul is dead in trespasses and sins, and being dead it cannot enter into the kingdom of heaven. We have before us now an announcement very startling, some say very obnoxious. Coming to Christ, though described by some people as being the very easiest thing in the entire world, is in our text declared to be a thing utterly and entirely impossible to any man unless the Father will draw him to Christ.

It will be our business, then, to enlarge upon this declaration. We doubt not that it will always be offensive to carnal nature, but nevertheless, the offending of human nature is sometimes the first step toward bringing it to bow itself before God. And if this is the effect of a painful process, we can forget the pain and rejoice in the glorious consequences.

I will endeavor this morning, first of all, to notice *man's inability*, wherein it consists. Second, *the Father's drawings*—what these are and how they are exerted upon the soul. And then I will conclude by noticing *a sweet consolation* that may be derived from this seemingly barren and terrible text.

I. First, then, *man's inability*. The text says, "No man can come to me, except the Father which hath sent me draw him" (John 6:44 KJV). Wherein does this inability lie?

First, it does not lie in any *physical* defect. If in coming to Christ, moving the body or walking with the feet should be of any assistance, certainly man has all physical power to come to Christ in that sense. I remember to have heard a very foolish Antinomian declare that he did not believe any man had the power to walk to the house of God unless the Father drew him. Now the man was plainly foolish, because he must have seen that as long as a man was alive and had legs, it was as easy for him to walk to the house of God as to the house of Satan.

If coming to Christ includes the utterance of a prayer, man has no physical defect in that respect. If he is not dumb, he can say a prayer as easily as he can utter blasphemy. It is as easy for a man to sing one of the songs of Zion as to sing a profane and libidinous song. There is no lack of physical power in coming to Christ that can be wanted with regard to the bodily strength man most assuredly has. And any part of salvation that consists in that is totally and entirely in the power of man without any assistance from the Spirit of God.

Nor, again, does this inability lie in any mental lack. I can believe this Bible to be true just as easily as I can believe any other book to be true. So far as believing on Christ is an act of the mind, I am just as able to believe on Christ as I am able to believe on anybody else. Let his statement be but true, it is idle to tell me I cannot believe it. I can believe the statement that Christ makes as well as I can believe the statement of any other person. There is no deficiency of faculty in the mind—it is as capable of appreciating as a mere mental act the guilt of sin, as it is of appreciating the guilt of assassination. It is just as possible for me to exercise the mental idea of seeking God as it is to exercise the thought of ambition.

> *C*oming to Christ, though described by some people as being the very easiest thing in the entire world, is entirely impossible to any man unless the Father will draw him to Christ.

I have all the mental strength and power that can possibly be needed, so far as mental power is needed in salvation at all. No, there is not any man so ignorant that he can plead a lack of intellect as an excuse for rejecting the gospel. The defect, then, does not lie either in the body, or, what we are bound to call, speaking theologically, the mind. It is not any lack or deficiency there, although it is the vitiation of the mind, the corruption or the ruin of it, which after all is the very essence of man's inability.

Permit me to show you wherein this inability of man really does lie. It lies deep *in his nature*. Through the Fall and through our own sin, the nature of man has become so debased, depraved, and corrupt, that it is impossible for him to come to Christ without the assistance of God the Holy Spirit. Now, in trying to exhibit how the nature of man thus renders him unable to come to Christ, you must allow me just to take this figure. You see a sheep—how willingly it feeds upon the herbage! You never knew a sheep to seek after carrion. It could not live on lion's food.

Now bring me a wolf, and you ask me whether a wolf cannot eat grass, whether it cannot be just as docile and as domesticated as the sheep. I answer, "No," because its nature is contrary to it. You say, "Well, it has ears and legs. Can it not hear the shepherd's voice and follow him wherever he leads it?" I answer, "Certainly." There is no physical cause why it cannot do so, but its nature forbids it, and therefore I say it *cannot* do so. Can it not be tamed? Cannot its ferocity be removed?

Probably it may so far be subdued that it may become apparently tame, but there will always be a marked distinction between it and the sheep because there is a distinction in nature. Now, the reason why man cannot come to Christ is not because he cannot come, so far as his body or his mere power of mind is concerned. Man *cannot* come to Christ, because his nature is so corrupt that he has neither the will nor the power to come to Christ unless drawn by the Spirit.

But let me give you a better illustration. You see a mother with her babe in her arms. You put a knife into her hand and tell her to stab that babe in the heart. She replies and very truthfully, "I cannot." Now, so far as her bodily power is concerned, she can if she pleases. There is the knife and there is the child. The child cannot resist, and she has quite sufficient strength in her hand immediately to stab it. But she is quite correct when she says she cannot do it. As a mere act of the mind, it is quite possible she might think of such a thing as killing the child, yet she says she cannot think of such a thing. And she does not say falsely, for her nature as a mother forbids her doing a thing from which her soul revolts.

Simply because she is that child's parent, she feels she cannot kill it. It is even so with a sinner. Coming to Christ is so obnoxious to human nature that although, so far as physical and mental forces are concerned (and these have but a very narrow sphere in salvation), men could come if they would. It is strictly correct to say that they cannot and will not unless the Father who has sent Christ does draw them. Let us enter a little more deeply into the subject and try to show you wherein this inability of man consists, in its more minute particulars.

1. First, it lies in the *obstinacy of the human will*. "Oh," says the Arminian, "men may be saved if they will." We reply, "My dear sir, we all believe that. But it is the 'if they will' that is the difficulty. We assert that no man will come to Christ unless he is drawn. No, we do not assert it, but Christ Himself declares it: 'You will not come to Me that you might

have life.' And as long as that 'you will not come' stands on record in Holy Scripture, Christ will not be brought to believe in any doctrine of the freedom of the human will."

It is strange how people, when talking about free will, talk of things that they do not at all understand. "Now" says one, "I believe men can be saved if they will." My dear sir, that is not the question at all. The question is this: Are men ever found naturally willing to submit to the humbling terms of the gospel of Christ? We declare, upon scriptural authority, that the human will is so desperately set on mischief, so depraved, so inclined to everything that is evil, and so disinclined to everything that is good, that without the powerful, supernatural, and irresistible influence of the Holy Spirit, no human will can ever be constrained toward Christ.

> Man cannot come to Christ, because his nature is so corrupt that he has neither the will nor the power to come to Christ unless drawn by the Spirit.

You reply that men sometimes are willing, without the help of the Holy Spirit. I answer, did you ever meet with any person who was? Scores and hundreds, no, thousands of Christians have I conversed with, of different opinions, young and old, but it has never been my lot to meet with one who could affirm that he came to Christ of himself without being drawn. The universal confession of all true believers is this: "I know that unless Jesus Christ had sought me when a stranger wandering from the fold of God, I would to this very hour have been wandering far from Him, at a distance from Him, and loving that distance well." With common consent, all believers affirm the truth that men will not come to Christ till the Father who has sent Christ does draw them.

2. Again, not only is the will obstinate, but the *understanding is darkened*. Of that we have abundant scriptural proof. I am not now making mere assertions, but stating doctrines authoritatively taught in the Holy Scriptures and known in the conscience of every Christian, that the understanding of man is so dark that he cannot by any means understand the things of God until his understanding has been opened. Man is by nature blind within. The cross of Christ, so laden with glories and glittering with attractions, never attracts him, because he is blind and cannot

see its beauties. Talk to him of the wonders of the creation. Show to him the many-colored arch that spans the sky. Let him behold the glories of a landscape. He is well able to see all these things. But talk to him of the wonders of the covenant of grace, speak to him of the security of the believer in Christ, tell him of the beauties of the person of the Redeemer, and he is quite deaf to all your description. You are as one who plays a goodly tune, it is true, but he regards not, he is deaf, and he has no comprehension. Or, to return to the verse that we so specially marked in our reading, "The natural man receiveth not the things of the Spirit of God: for they are foolishness unto him: neither can he know them, because they are spiritually discerned" (1 Cor. 2:14 KJV), and inasmuch as he is a *natural* man, it is not in his power to discern the things of God. "Well," says one, "I think I have arrived at a very tolerable judgment in matters of theology. I think I understand almost every point."

My brethren, when man fell in the garden, manhood fell entirely. There was not one single pillar in the temple of manhood that stood erect.

True, that you may do in the *letter* of it. But the *spirit* of it, the true reception thereof into the soul, and the actual understanding of it, is impossible for you to have attained unless the Spirit has drawn you. For as long as the scripture stands true that carnal men cannot receive spiritual things, it must be true that you have not received them unless you have been renewed and made a spiritual man in Christ Jesus. The will, then, and the understanding, are two great doors, both blocked up against our coming to Christ. And until these are opened by the sweet influences of the divine Spirit, they must be forever closed to anything like coming to Christ.

3. Again, *the affections*, which constitute a very great part of man, are depraved. Man, as he is, before he receives the grace of God, loves anything and everything above spiritual things. If you want proof of this, look around you. There needs no monument to the depravity of the human affections. Cast your eyes everywhere—there is not a street, nor a house, no, nor a heart, that does not bear upon it sad evidence of this dreadful truth. Why is it that men are not found on the Sabbath day universally flocking

to the house of God? Why are we not more constantly found reading our Bibles? How is it that prayer is a duty almost universally neglected? Why is it that Christ Jesus is so little loved? Why are even His professed followers so cold in their affections to Him?

From where do these things arise? Assuredly, dear brethren, we can trace them to no other source than the corruption and vitiation of the affections. We love that which we ought to hate, and we hate that which we ought to love. It is but human nature, fallen human nature, that man should love this present life better than the life to come. It is but the effect of the Fall that man should love sin better than righteousness and the ways of this world better than the ways of God. And again, we repeat it, until these affections are renewed and turned into a fresh channel by the gracious drawings of the Father, it is not possible for any man to love the Lord Jesus Christ.

4. Yet once more, *conscience*, too, has been overpowered by the Fall. I believe there is no more egregious mistake made by divines than when they tell people that conscience is the deputy of God within the soul and that it is one of those powers that retains its ancient dignity and stands erect amid the fall of its compeers. My brethren, when man fell in the garden, manhood fell entirely. There was not one single pillar in the temple of manhood that stood erect. It is true that conscience was not *destroyed*. The pillar was not shattered. It fell, and it fell in one piece, and here it lies alone, the mightiest remnant of God's once perfect work in man.

But that conscience is fallen, I am sure. Look at men. Who among them is the possessor of a good conscience toward God but the regenerated man? Do you imagine that if men's consciences always spoke loudly and clearly to them, they would live in the daily commission of acts that are as opposed to the right as darkness to light? No, beloved—conscience can tell me that I am a sinner, but conscience cannot make me *feel* that I am one. Conscience may tell me that such and such a thing is wrong, but how wrong it is, conscience itself does not know.

Did any man's conscience, unenlightened by the Spirit, ever tell him that his sins deserved damnation? Or if conscience did do that, did it ever lead any man to feel an abhorrence of sin as sin? In fact, did conscience ever bring a man to such a self-renunciation that he did totally abhor himself and all his works and come to Christ? No, conscience, although it is not dead, is ruined. Its power is impaired; it has not that clearness of eye, that strength of hand, and that thunder of voice that it had before the Fall. It has ceased, to a great degree, to exert its supremacy in man's soul. Then beloved, it becomes necessary, because conscience is depraved, that the Holy Spirit should step in to show us our need of a Savior and draw us to the Lord Jesus Christ.

"Still," says one, "as far as you have so far gone, it appears to me that you consider that the reason why men do not come to Christ is that they *will* not, rather than they *cannot*." True, most true. I believe the greatest reason for man's inability is the obstinacy of his will. That once overcome, I think the great stone is rolled away from the sepulcher and the hardest part of the battle is already won. But allow me to go a little further. My text does not say, "No man *will* come," but it says, "No man *can* come." Now, many interpreters believe that the *can* here is but a strong expression conveying no more meaning than the word *will*. I feel assured that this is not correct.

> It is true the Spirit gave me the will to do it, but still I did it myself, and therein will I glory. For if I did these things myself without assistance from on high, I will not cast my crown at His feet. It is my own crown, I earned it, and I will keep it.

There is in man not only unwillingness to be saved, but there is a spiritual powerlessness to come to Christ. And this I will prove to every Christian at any rate. Beloved, I speak to you who have already been quickened by divine grace. Does not your experience teach you that there are times when you have a will to serve God and yet have not the power? Have you not sometimes been obliged to say that you have wished to believe but you have had to pray, "Lord, help my unbelief?" Because, although willing enough to receive God's testimony, your own carnal nature was too strong for you and you felt you needed supernatural help.

Are you able to go into your room at any hour you choose and fall upon your knees and say, "Now, it is my will that I should be very earnest in prayer and that I should draw near to God?" I ask this: Do you find your power equal to your will? You could say, even at the bar of God Himself, that you are sure you are not mistaken in your willingness. You are willing to be wrapped up in devotion. It is your will that your soul should not wander from a pure contemplation of the Lord Jesus Christ, but you find that you cannot do that, even when you are willing, without the help of the Spirit.

Now, if the quickened child of God finds a spiritual inability, how much more the sinner who is dead in trespasses and sin? If even the advanced Christian, after thirty or forty years, finds himself sometimes willing and yet powerless—if such is his experience—does it not seem more than likely that the poor sinner who has not yet believed should find a need of strength as well as a want of will?

But, again, there is another argument. If the sinner has strength to come to Christ, I should like to know how we are to understand those continual descriptions of the sinner's state that we meet with in God's Holy Word. Now, a sinner is said to be *dead* in trespasses and sins. Will you affirm that death implies nothing more than the absence of a will? Surely a corpse is quite as *unable* as *unwilling*. Or again, do not all men see that there is a distinction between will and power? Might not that corpse be sufficiently quickened to get a will and yet be so powerless that it could not lift as much as its hand or foot? Have we ever seen cases in which persons have been just sufficiently reanimated to give evidence of life, and have yet been so near death that they could not have performed the slightest action?

Is there not a clear difference between the giving of the will and the giving of power? It is quite certain, however, that where the will is given, the power will follow. Make a man willing and he will be made powerful, for when God gives the will, He does not tantalize man by giving him to wish for that which he is unable to do. Nevertheless, He makes such a division between the will and the power that it will be seen that both things are quite distinct gifts of the Lord God.

Then I must ask one more question. If that were all that were needed to make a man willing, do you not at once degrade the Holy Spirit? Are we not in the habit of giving all the glory of salvation wrought in us to God the Spirit? But now, if all that God the Spirit does for me is to make me *willing* to do these things for myself, am I not in a great measure a sharer with the Holy Spirit in the glory? And may I not boldly stand up and say, "It is true the Spirit gave me the will to do it, but still I did it myself, and therein will I glory. For if I did these things myself without assistance from on high, I will not cast my crown at His feet. It is my own crown, I earned it, and I will keep it."

Inasmuch as the Holy Spirit is evermore in Holy Scripture set forth as the person who works in us to will and to do of His own good pleasure, we hold it to be a legitimate inference that He must do something more for us than the mere making of us *willing*. Therefore, there must be another thing besides want of will in a sinner. There must be absolute and actual want of *power*.

Now, before I leave this statement, let me address myself to you for a moment. I am often charged with preaching doctrines that may do a great deal of hurt. Well, I will not deny the charge, for I am not careful to answer in this matter. I have my witnesses here present to prove that the things that I have preached have done a great deal of hurt, but they have not done hurt either to morality or to God's church. The hurt has been on the side of Satan. There are not ones or twos but many hundreds who this morning rejoice that they have been brought near to God. From having been profane Sabbath-breakers, drunkards, or worldly persons, they have been brought to know and love the Lord Jesus Christ. And if this is any hurt, may God of His infinite mercy send us a thousand times as much.

But further, what truth is there in the world that will not hurt a man who chooses to make hurt of it? You who preach general redemption are very fond of proclaiming the great truth of God's mercy to the last moment. But how dare you preach that? Many people make hurt of it by putting off the day of grace and thinking that the last hour may do as well as the first. Why, if we ever preached anything that man could misuse and abuse, we must hold our tongues forever. Still says one, "Well then, if I cannot save myself and cannot come to Christ, I must sit still and do nothing."

If men do say so, on their own heads will be their doom. We have very plainly told you that there are many things you can do. To be found continually in the house of God is in your power. To study the Word of God with diligence is in your power. To renounce your outward sin, to forsake the vices in which you indulge, to make your life honest, sober, and righteous is in your power. For this you need no help from the Holy Spirit. All this you can do yourself. But to come to Christ *truly* is not in your power until the Holy Spirit renews you. But mark you, your want of power is no excuse, seeing that you have no desire to come and are living in willful rebellion against God. Your want of power lies mainly in the obstinacy of your nature.

Suppose a liar says that it is not in his power to speak the truth, that he has been a liar so long that he cannot leave it off. Is that an excuse for him? Suppose a man who has long indulged in lust should tell you that he finds his lusts have so girt about him like a great iron net that he cannot get rid of them. Would you take that as an excuse? Truly it is none at all. If a drunkard has become so foully a drunkard that he finds it impossible to pass a public bar without stepping in, do you therefore excuse him? No, because his inability to reform lies in his *nature*—which he has no desire to restrain or conquer.

The thing that is done and the thing that causes the thing that is done, being both from the root of sin, are two evils that cannot excuse each other. It is because you have learned to do evil that you cannot now learn to do well, and instead, therefore, of letting you sit down to excuse yourselves, let me put a thunderbolt beneath the seat of your sloth that you may be startled by it and aroused.

Remember, that to sit still is to be damned to all eternity. Oh, that God the Holy Spirit might make use of this truth in a very different manner! Before I am done, I trust I will be enabled to show you how it is that this truth, which apparently condemns men and shuts them out, is, after all, the great truth that has been blessed to the conversion of men.

II. Our second point is *the Father's drawings*. "No man can come to me, except the Father which hath sent me draw him." How, then, does the Father draw men? Arminian ministers generally say that God draws men by the preaching of the gospel. Very true, the preaching of the gospel is the instrument of drawing men, but there must be something more than this. Let me ask to whom did Christ address these words? Why, to the people of Capernaum, where he had often preached, where he had uttered mournfully and plaintively the woes of the law and the invitations of the gospel. In that city He had done many mighty works and worked many miracles.

In fact, such teaching and such miraculous attestation had He given to them, that He declared that Tyre and Sidon would have repented long ago in sackcloth and ashes if they had been blessed with such privileges. Now, if the preaching of Christ Himself did not avail to the enabling of these men to come to Christ, it cannot be possible that all that was intended by the drawing of the Father was simply preaching. No, brethren, you must note again, He does not say no man can come except the *minister* draw him, but except the *Father* draw him.

Now there is such a thing as being drawn by the gospel and drawn by the minister without being drawn by God. Clearly it is a divine drawing that is meant, a drawing by the Most High God, the first person of the most glorious Trinity sending out the third person, the Holy Spirit, to induce men to come to Christ. Another person turns round and asks with a sneer, "Then do you think that Christ drags men to Himself, seeing that they are unwilling?" I remember meeting once with a man who said to me, "Sir, you preach that Christ takes people by the hair of their heads and drags them to Himself." I asked him whether he could refer to the date of the sermon wherein I preached that extraordinary doctrine, for if he could, I should be very much obliged. However, he could not.

> *C*hrist never compelled any man to come to Him against his will. If a man is unwilling to be saved, Christ does not save him against his will. How, then, does the Holy Spirit draw him? Why, by making him willing.

But said I, while Christ does not drag people to Himself by the hair of their heads, I believe that He draws them by the *heart* quite as powerfully as your caricature would suggest. Mark that in the Father's drawing there is no compulsion whatever. Christ never compelled any man to come to Him against his will. If a man is unwilling to be saved, Christ does not save him against his will. How, then, does the Holy Spirit draw him? Why, by *making him willing*. It is true He does not use moral persuasion. He knows a nearer method of reaching the heart. He goes to the secret fountain of the heart, and he knows how, by some mysterious operation, to turn the will in an opposite direction, so that, as Ralph Erskine paradoxically puts it, the man is saved "with full consent against his will." That is, against his *old* will he is saved.

But he is saved with full consent, for he is made willing in the day of God's power. Do not imagine that any man will go to heaven kicking and struggling all the way against the hand that draws him. Do not conceive that any man will be plunged in the bath of a Savior's blood while he is striving to run away from the Savior. Oh, no! It is quite true that first of all man is unwilling to be saved. When the Holy Spirit has put His influence into the heart, the text is fulfilled: "Draw me, we will run after thee" (Song of Sol. 1:4 KJV). We follow on while He draws us, glad to obey the voice that once we had despised. But the gist of the matter lies in the *turning* of the will.

How that is done no flesh knows. It is one of those mysteries that are clearly perceived as a fact, but the cause of that no tongue can tell and no heart can guess. The apparent way, however, in which the Holy Spirit operates, we can tell you. The first thing the Holy Spirit does when He comes into a man's heart is this: He finds him with a very good opinion of himself. And there is nothing that prevents a man coming to Christ like a good opinion of himself. "Why," says man, "I don't want to come to Christ. I have as good righteousness as anybody can desire. I feel I can walk into heaven on my own rights."

The Holy Spirit lays bare his heart, lets him see the loathsome cancer that is there eating away his life, and uncovers to him all the blackness and defilement of that sink of hell, the human heart. Then the man stands aghast: "I never thought I was like this. Oh, those sins I thought were little have swelled out to an immense stature. What I thought was a molehill has grown into a mountain. It was but the hyssop on the wall before, but now it has become a cedar of Lebanon."

"Oh," says the man within himself, "I will try and reform. I will do good deeds enough to wash these black deeds out."

Then comes the Holy Spirit and shows him that he cannot do this, takes away all his fancied power and strength, so that the man falls down on his knees in agony and cries, "Oh, once I thought I could save myself by my good works, but now I find that

> *Could my tears forever flow,*
> *Could my zeal no respite know,*
> *All for sin could not atone,*
> *You must save and You alone.*

Then the heart thinks and the man is ready to despair. And says he, "I never can be saved. Nothing can save me." Then comes the Holy Spirit and shows the sinner the cross of Christ, gives him eyes anointed with heavenly eye salve, and says, "Look to yonder cross. That man died to save sinners. You feel that you are a sinner. He died to save you." And He enables the heart to believe and to come to Christ. And when it comes to Christ, by this sweet drawing of the Spirit, it finds a peace with God that passes all understanding, which keeps his heart and mind through Jesus Christ our Lord. Now, you will plainly perceive that all this may be done without any compulsion. Man is as much drawn willingly, as if he were not drawn at all. And he comes to Christ with full consent, with as full a consent as if no secret influence had ever been exercised in his heart. But that influence *must* be exercised, or else there never has been and there never will be any man who either can or will come to the Lord Jesus Christ.

III. And now we gather up our ends and conclude by trying to make a practical application of the doctrine. And we trust a comfortable one. "Well," says one, "if what this man preaches is true, what is to become of my religion? For do you know I have been a long while trying and I do not like to hear you say a man cannot save himself. I believe he can, and I mean to persevere. But if I am to believe what you say, I must give it all up and begin again." My dear friends, it will be a very happy thing if you do. Do not think that I will be at all alarmed if you do so.

Remember, what you are doing is building your house upon the sand, and it is but an act of charity if I can shake it a little for you. Let me assure you, in God's name, if your religion has no better foundation than your own strength, it will not stand at the bar of God. Nothing will last to eternity but that which came from eternity. Unless the everlasting God has done a good work in your heart, all you may have done must be unraveled at the last day of account. It is all in vain for you to be a churchgoer or chapelgoer, a good keeper of the Sabbath, and an observer of your prayers. It is all in vain for you to be honest to your neighbors and reputable in your conversation. If you hope to be saved by these things, it is all in vain for you to trust in them.

Go on and be as honest as you like. Keep the Sabbath perpetually. Be as holy as you can. I would not dissuade you from these things. God forbid. Grow in them, but oh, do not *trust* in them. For if you rely upon these things, you will find they will fail you when most you need them.

And if there is anything else that you have found yourself able to do unassisted by divine grace, the sooner you can get rid of the hope that has been engendered by it, the better for you, because it is a foul delusion to rely upon anything that flesh can do.

Spiritual men must inhabit a spiritual heaven, and preparation for it must be the work of the Spirit of God. "Well," cries another, "I have been sitting under a ministry where I have been told that I could, at my own option, repent and believe, and the consequence is that I have been putting it off from day to day. I thought I could come one day as well as another. That I had only to say, 'Lord, have mercy upon me,' and believe, and then I should be saved. Now you have taken all this hope away for me, sir. I feel amazement and horror taking hold upon me." Again, I say, "My dear friend, I am very glad of it. This was the effect that I hoped to produce by God's grace. I pray that you may feel this a great deal more. When you have no hope of saving yourself, I will have hope that God has begun to save you.

> He who has got a will, though he has not power, has grace begun in his heart, and God will not leave him until the work is finished.

As soon as you say, "Oh, I cannot come to Christ. Lord, draw me, help me," I will rejoice over you. He who has got a will, though he has not power, has grace begun in his heart, and God will not leave him until the work is finished. But, careless sinner, learn that your salvation now hangs in God's hand. Oh, remember that you are entirely in the hand of God. You have sinned against Him, and if He wills to damn you, damned you are. You cannot resist His will nor thwart His purpose. You have deserved His wrath, and if He chooses to pour the full shower of that wrath upon your head, you can do nothing to reverse it.

If, on the other hand, He chooses to save you, He is able to save you to the very uttermost. But you lie as much in His hand as the summer's moth beneath your own finger. He is the God whom you are grieving every day. Does it not make you tremble to think that your eternal destiny now hangs upon the will of Him whom you have angered and incensed? Does not this make your knees knock together and your blood curdle? If it does so, I rejoice inasmuch as this may be the first effect of the Spirit's drawing in your soul. Oh, tremble to think that the God whom you have angered is the God upon whom your salvation or your condemnation entirely depends. Tremble and "kiss the Son, lest He be angry, and you perish in the way, when His wrath is kindled but a little" (Ps. 2:12).

Now, the comfortable reflection is this: Some of you this morning are conscious that you are coming to Christ. Have you not begun to weep the penitential tear? Did not your closet witness your prayerful preparation for the hearing of the Word of God? And during the service this morning, has not your heart said within you, "Lord, save me, or I perish, for save myself I cannot?" And could you not now stand up in your seat and sing this song?

> *Oh, sovereign grace my heart subdue;*
> *I would be led in triumph, too,*
> *A willing captive of my Lord,*
> *To sing the triumph of His Word.*

And have I not myself heard you say in your heart, "Jesus, Jesus, my whole trust is in You. I know that no righteousness of my own can save me, but only You. O Christ, sink or swim, I cast myself on You"? Oh, my brothers and sisters, you are drawn by the Father, for you could not have come unless He had drawn you. Sweet thought! And if He has drawn you, do you know what is the delightful inference? Let me repeat just one text, and may that comfort you. "The LORD has appeared of old to me, saying: 'Yes, I have loved you with an everlasting love; therefore with lovingkindness I have drawn you'" (Jer. 31:3).

Yes, my poor weeping brothers and sisters, inasmuch as you are now coming to Christ, God has drawn you. And inasmuch as He has drawn you, it is a proof that He has loved you from before the foundation of the world. Let your heart leap within you. You are one of His! Your name was written on the Savior's hands when they were nailed to the accursed tree. Your name glitters on the breastplate of the great High Priest today. And it was there before the daystar knew its place or planets ran their round. Rejoice in the Lord, you who have come to Christ, and shout for joy all you who have been drawn of the Father. For this is your proof, your solemn testimony, that you from among men have been chosen in eternal election and that you will be kept by the power of God, through faith, to the salvation that is ready to be revealed.

For Further Thought

1. *According to 1 Corinthians 2:14, why can't the natural man understand the things of the Spirit of God?*
2. *Read Ephesians 1:1–5. What do verses 4 and 5 say happens to sons of disobedience?*
3. *In Colossians 1:12–13, how do we get from the power of darkness into the kingdom of God's beloved Son?*

ELECTION
(UNCONDITIONAL ELECTION)

But we are bound to give thanks to God always for you,
brethren beloved by the Lord, because God from the beginning
chose you for salvation through sanctification by the Spirit
and belief in the truth, to which He called you by our gospel,
for the obtaining of the glory of our Lord Jesus Christ.
2 THESSALONIANS 2:13–14

IF there were no other text in the sacred Word except this one, I think we should all be bound to receive and acknowledge the truthfulness of the great and glorious doctrine of God's ancient choice of His family. But there seems to be an inveterate prejudice in the human mind against this doctrine, and although most other doctrines will be received by professing Christians, some with caution, others with pleasure, this one seems to be most frequently disregarded and discarded. In many of our pulpits, it would be reckoned a high sin and treason to preach a sermon upon *election*, because they could not make it what they call a practical discourse.

I believe they have erred from the truth. Whatever God has revealed He has revealed for a purpose. There is nothing in scripture that may not, under the influence of God's Spirit, be turned into a practical discourse, "All Scripture is given by inspiration of God, and is profitable" for some purpose of spiritual usefulness (2 Tim. 3:16). It is true, it may not be turned into a freewill discourse—that we know right well—but it can be turned into a practical free *grace* discourse. And free grace practice is the best practice when the true doctrines of God's immutable love are brought to bear upon the hearts of saints and sinners. Now, I trust that some of you who are startled at the very sound of this word will say, "I will give it a fair hearing. I will lay aside my prejudices. I will just hear what this man has to say."

Do not shut your ears and say at once, "It is high doctrine." Who has authorized you to call it high or low? Why should you oppose yourself to God's doctrine? Remember what became of the children who found fault with God's prophet and exclaimed, "Go up, you baldhead! Go up, you baldhead!" (2 Kings 2:23). Say nothing against God's doctrines, lest haply some evil beast should come out of the forest and devour you, also. There are other woes besides the open judgment of heaven; take heed that these fall not on your head. Lay aside your prejudices, listen calmly, listen dispassionately—hear what scripture says.

And when you receive the truth, if God should be pleased to reveal and manifest it to your souls, do not be ashamed to confess it. To confess you were wrong yesterday is only to acknowledge that you are a little wiser today. Instead of being a reflection on yourself, it is an honor to your judgment and shows that you are improving in the knowledge of the truth of God. Do not be ashamed to learn and to cast aside your old doctrines and views. But take up that which you may more plainly see to be in the Word of God. And if you do not see it to be here in the Bible—whatever I may say, or whatever authorities I may plead—I beseech you, as you love your souls, reject it. And if from this pulpit you ever hear things contrary to this sacred Word, remember that the Bible must be first and God's minister must lie underneath it.

We must not stand on the Bible to preach; we must preach with the Bible above our heads. After all we have preached, we are well aware that the mountain of truth is higher than our eyes can discern. Clouds and darkness are all around its summit, and we cannot discern its topmost pinnacle. Yet we will try to preach it as well as we can. But since we are mortal and liable to err, exercise your judgment; "Test the spirits, whether they are of God" (1 John 4:1), and if on mature reflection on your bended knees you are led to disregard election, a thing that I consider to be utterly impossible, then forsake it. Do not hear it preached, but believe and confess whatever you see to be God's Word. I can say no more than that by way of introduction.

First I will speak a little concerning the *truthfulness* of this doctrine: "God from the beginning chose you for salvation." Second, I will try to prove that this election is *absolute*: "He has from the beginning chosen you for salvation," not for sanctification, but "*through sanctification* by the Spirit and belief in the truth." Third, this election is *eternal* because the text says,

"God has from *the beginning* chosen you." Fourth, it is *personal*: "*He* has chosen you."

Then we will look at the *effects* of the doctrine and see what it does. Lastly, as God may enable us, we will try and look at its *tendencies* and see whether it is indeed a terrible and licentious doctrine. We will take the flower and, like true bees, see whether there is any honey whatever in it, whether any good can come *of* it—or whether it is an unmixed, undiluted evil.

I. First, I must try and prove that the doctrine is *true*. And let me begin with an *argumentum ad hominem*. I will speak to you according to your different positions and stations. There are some of *you* who belong to the Church of England, and I am happy to see so many of you here. Though now and then I certainly say some very hard things about church and state, yet I love the old church, for she has in her communion many godly ministers and eminent saints. Now I know you are great believers in what the Articles declare to be sound doctrine. I will give you a specimen of what they utter concerning election, so that if you believe them, you cannot avoid receiving election. I will read a portion of the Seventeenth Article upon Predestination and Election:

> *Predestination to life is the everlasting purpose of God,*
> *whereby (before the foundations of the world were laid) He*
> *has continually decreed by His counsel secret to us, to deliver*
> *from curse and damnation those whom He has chosen in Christ*
> *out of mankind and to bring them by Christ to everlasting*
> *salvation, as vessels made to honor. Wherefore they that are*
> *endued with so excellent a benefit of God are called according*
> *to God's purpose by His Spirit working in due season; they*
> *through grace obey the calling; they are justified freely; they are*
> *made sons of God by adoption; they are made like the image*
> *of His only-begotten Son Jesus Christ; they walk religiously*
> *in good works and at length, by God's mercy, they attain to*
> *everlasting felicity.*

Now, I think any churchman, if he is a sincere and honest believer in mother church, must be a thorough believer in election. True, if he turns to certain other portions of the prayer book, he will find things contrary to the doctrines of free grace and altogether apart from scriptural teaching. But if he looks at the articles, he must see that God has chosen His people to eternal life. I am not so desperately enamored, however, of that book as you may be, and I have only used this article to show you that if you belong to the establishment of England, you should at least offer no objection to this doctrine of predestination.

Another human authority whereby I would confirm the doctrine of election is the old Waldensian Creed. If you read the creed of the old Waldenses, which emanated from them in the midst of the burning heat of persecution, you will see that these renowned professors and confessors of the Christian faith did most firmly receive and embrace this doctrine as being a portion of the truth of God. I have copied from an old book one of the Articles of their faith: "That God saves from corruption and damnation those whom He has chosen from the foundations of the world, not for any disposition, faith, or holiness that before saw in them, but of His mere mercy in Christ Jesus His Son, passing by all the rest according to the irreprehensible reason of His own free will and justice."

> *I love to proclaim these strong old doctrines that are called by nickname Calvinism but that are surely and verily the revealed truth of God as it is in Christ Jesus.*

It is no novelty, then, that I am preaching no new doctrine. I love to proclaim these strong old doctrines that are called by nickname Calvinism but that are surely and verily the revealed truth of God as it is in Christ Jesus. By this truth I make a pilgrimage into the past, and as I go I see father after father, confessor after confessor, martyr after martyr, standing up to shake hands with me. Were I a Pelagian, or a believer in the doctrine of free will, I should have to walk for centuries all alone. Here and there a heretic of no very honorable character might rise up and call me brother. But taking these things to be the standard of my faith, I see the land of the ancients peopled with my brothers and sisters—I behold multitudes who confess the same as I do and acknowledge that this is the religion of God's own church.

I also give you an extract from the old Baptist Confession. We are Baptists in this congregation—the greater part of us at any rate—and we like to see what our own forefathers wrote. Some two hundred years ago the Baptists assembled together and published their articles of faith to put an end to certain reports against their orthodoxy that had gone forth to the world. I turn to this old book that I have just published, *The Baptist Confession of Faith*, and I find the following as the Third Article:

> *By the decree of God for the manifestation of His glory some men and angels are predestinated, or foreordained, to eternal life through Jesus Christ to the praise of His glorious grace. Others being left to act in their sin to their just condemnation to the praise of His glorious justice. These angels and men thus predestinated and foreordained, are particularly and unchangeably designed and their number so certain and definite that it cannot be either increased or diminished. Those of mankind that are predestinated to life, God, before the foundation of the world was laid, according to His eternal and immutable purpose and the secret counsel and good pleasure of His will, has chosen in Christ to everlasting glory out of His mere free grace and love, without any other thing in the creature as condition or cause moving Him hereunto.*

As for these human authorities, I care not one rush for all three of them. I care not what they say, pro or con, as to this doctrine. I have only used them as a kind of confirmation to your faith, to show you that while I may be railed upon as a heretic and as a hyper-Calvinist, after all, I am backed up by antiquity. All the past stands by me. I do not care for the present. Give me the past and I will hope for the future. Let the present rise up in my teeth; I will not care. Though a host of the churches of London may have forsaken the great cardinal doctrines of God, it matters not. If a handful of us stand alone in an unflinching maintenance of the sovereignty of our God, if we are beset by enemies, yes, and even by our own brothers and sisters who ought to be our friends and helpers, it matters not—if we can but count upon the past—the noble army of martyrs, the glorious host of confessors. They are our friends. They are the witnesses of truth, and they stand by us. With these for us, we will not say that we stand alone, but we may exclaim, "Lo, God has reserved to Himself 'seven thousand in Israel, all whose knees have not bowed to Baal'" (1 Kings 19:18). But the best of all is, *God* is with us!

The great truth of God is always the Bible and the Bible alone. My hearers, you do not believe in any other book than the Bible, do you? If I could prove this from all the books in Christendom—if I could fetch back the Alexandrian library and prove it there—you would not believe it any more. But you surely will believe what is in God's Word. I have selected a few texts to read to you. I love to give you a whole volley of texts when I am afraid you will distrust a truth so that you may be too astonished to doubt, if you do not in reality believe. Just let me run through a catalog of passages where the people of God are called "elect." Of course, if the people are called "elect," there must be *election*. If Jesus Christ and His apostles were accustomed to call believers by the title of elect, we must certainly believe that they were so; otherwise the term does not mean anything.

Jesus Christ says, "Unless the Lord had shortened those days, no flesh would be saved; but for the elect's sake, whom He chose, He shortened the days." And, "For false christs and false prophets will rise and show signs and wonders to deceive, if possible, even the elect." And, "Then will He send His angels, and gather together His elect from the four winds, from the farthest part of earth to the farthest part of heaven" (Mark 13:20, 22, 27). "And shall God not avenge His own elect who cry out day and night to Him, though He bears long with them?" (Luke 18:7). These and many other passages might be selected, wherein the word *elect*, or *chosen*, or *foreordained*, or *appointed* is mentioned—or the phrase *my sheep*, or some similar designation, showing that Christ's people are distinguished from the rest of mankind.

But you have concordances, and I will not trouble you with texts. Throughout the Epistles the saints are constantly called "the elect." They were not ashamed of the word in *those* days. They were not afraid to talk about it. Nowadays the word has been dressed up with diversities of meaning and persons have mutilated and marred the doctrine so that they have made it a very doctrine of devils. I do confess that many who call themselves believers have gone to rank Antinomianism. But not withstanding this, why should I be ashamed of it if men wrest it? We love God's truth on the rack as well as when it is walking upright. If there were a martyr whom we loved before he came on the rack we should love him more still when he was stretched there.

When God's truth is stretched on the rack, we do not call it falsehood. We love not to see it racked, but we love it even when racked because we can discern what its proper proportions ought to have been if it had not been racked and tortured by the cruelty and inventions of men. If you will read many of the epistles of the ancient fathers, you will find them always writing to the people of God as the elect. Indeed the common conversational term used among many of the churches by the primitive Christians to one another was that of the *elect*. They would often use the term with one another, showing that it was generally believed that all God's people were manifestly "elect."

> *When the Gentiles heard this, they were glad, and glorified the word of the Lord; and as many as were ordained to eternal life believed.*

But now for the verses that will positively prove the doctrine. Open your Bibles and turn to John 15:16, and there you will see that Jesus Christ has chosen His people, for He says, "You did not choose Me, but I chose you and appointed you that you should go and bear fruit, and that your fruit should remain, that whatever you ask the Father in My name He may give you." Then in the nineteenth verse, "If you were of the world, the world would love its own. Yet because you are not of the world, but I chose you out of the world, therefore the world hates you." Then in the seventeenth chapter and the eighth and ninth verses, "For I have given to them the words which You have given Me; and they have received them, and have known surely that I came forth from You; and they have believed that You sent Me. I pray for them. I do not pray for the world but for those whom You have given Me, for they are Yours."

Turn to Acts 13:48: "And when the Gentiles heard this, they were glad, and glorified the word of the Lord; and as many as were ordained to eternal life believed" (KJV). They may try to split that passage into hairs if they like—but it says, "ordained to eternal life" in the original as plainly as it possibly can. And we do not care about all the different commentaries thereupon. You scarcely need to be reminded of Romans 8, because I trust you are all well acquainted with that chapter and understand it by this time. In the twenty-ninth and following verses, it says:

Whom he did foreknow, he also did predestinate to be conformed to the image of his Son, that he might be the firstborn among many brethren. Moreover whom he did predestinate, them he also called: and whom he called, them he also justified: and whom he justified, them he also glorified. What shall we then say to these things? If God be for us, who can be against us? He that spared not his own Son, but delivered him up for us all, how shall he not with him also freely give us all things? Who shall lay any thing to the charge of God's elect? (8:29–33 KJV)

It would also be unnecessary to repeat the whole of the ninth chapter of Romans. As long as that remains in the Bible, no man will be able to prove Arminianism. So long as that is written there, not the most violent contortions of the passage will ever be able to exterminate the doctrine of election from the scriptures. Let us read such verses as these: "For the children being not yet born, neither having done any good or evil, that the purpose of God according to election might stand, not of works, but of Him that calleth; it was said unto her, The elder shall serve the younger" (9:11–12 KJV). Then read the twenty-second verse: "What if God, willing to shew his wrath, and to make his power known, endured with much longsuffering the vessels of wrath fitted to destruction: and that he might make known the riches of his glory on the vessels of mercy, which he had afore prepared unto glory. . . ?" (9:22–23 KJV).

Then go on to Romans 11:7. "What then? Israel hath not obtained that which he seeketh for; but the election hath obtained it, and the rest were blinded" (KJV). In the fifth verse of the same chapter, we read, "Even so then at this present time also there is a remnant according to the election of grace" (KJV). You, no doubt, all recollect the passage in 1 Corinthians 1:26–29:

For ye see your calling, brethren, how that not many wise men after the flesh, not many mighty, not many noble, are called: but God hath chosen the foolish things of the world to confound the wise; and God hath chosen the weak things of the world to confound the things which are mighty; and base things of the world, and things which are despised, hath

God chosen, yea, and things which are not, to bring to nought things that are: that no flesh should glory in his presence (KJV).

Again, remember the passage in 1 Thessalonians 5:9: "God hath not appointed us to wrath, but to obtain salvation by our Lord Jesus Christ" (KJV), and then you have my text, which I think would be quite enough. But if you need any more, you can find them at your leisure if we have not quite removed your suspicions as to the doctrine not being true. I think, my friends, that this overwhelming mass of scripture testimony must stagger those who dare to laugh at this doctrine. What will we say of those who have so often despised it and denied its divinity? What will we say to those who have railed at its justice and dared to defy God and call Him an almighty tyrant, when they have heard of His having elected so many to eternal life? Can you, O rejecter, cast it out of the Bible? Can you take the penknife of Jehudi and cut it out of the Word of God?

Would you be like the women at the feet of Solomon and have the child rent in halves that you might have your half? Is it not here in scripture? And is it not your duty to bow before it and meekly acknowledge what you understand not, to receive it as the truth even though you could not understand its meaning? I will not attempt to prove the justice of God in having thus elected some and left others. It is not for me to vindicate my Master. He will speak for Himself, and He does so. "Nay but, O man, who art thou that repliest against God? Shall the thing formed say to him that formed it, Why hast thou made me thus? Hath not the potter power over the clay, of the same lump to make one vessel unto honour, and another unto dishonour" (Rom. 9:20–21 KJV)? "Woe unto him that saith unto his father, What begettest thou? or to the woman, What hast thou brought forth?" (Isa. 45:10 KJV). "I form the light, and create darkness: I make peace, and create evil: I the LORD do all these things" (Isa. 45:7 KJV).

But there are some who say, "It is hard for God to choose some and leave others." Now, I will ask you one question: Is there any of you here this morning who wishes to be holy, who wishes to be regenerate, to leave off sin and walk in holiness? "Yes, there is," says someone, "I do." Then God has elected you. But another says, "No. I don't want to be holy. I don't want to give up my lusts and my vices." Why should you grumble, then, that God has not elected you? For if you were elected, you would not like it, according to your own confession. If God this morning had chosen you to holiness, you say you would not care for it. Do you not acknowledge that you prefer drunkenness to sobriety, dishonesty to honesty? You love this world's pleasures better than religion—then why should you grumble that God has not chosen you to religion?

If you love religion, He has chosen you to it. If you desire it, He has chosen you to it. If you do not, what right have you to say that God ought to have given you what you do not wish for? Supposing I had in my hand something that you do not value, and I said I will give it to such and such a person, you would have no right to grumble that I did not give it to you. You could not be so foolish as to grumble that the other has got what you do not care about. According to your own confession, many of you do not want religion, do not want a new heart and a right spirit, do not want the forgiveness of sins. You do not want sanctification. You do not want to be elected to these things; then why should you grumble?

> *I*f God this morning had chosen you to holiness, you say you would not care for it. Do you not acknowledge that you prefer drunkenness to sobriety, dishonesty to honesty?

You count these things but as husks, and why should you complain of God who has given them to those whom He has chosen? If you believe them to be good and desire them, they are there for you. God gives liberally to all those who desire. But first of all *He* makes them desire; otherwise they never would. If you love these things, He has elected you to them and you may have them. But if you do not, who are you that you should find fault with God when it is your own desperate will that keeps you from loving these things? Suppose a man in the street should say, "What a shame it is I cannot have a seat in the chapel to hear what this man has to say." And suppose he says, "I hate the preacher. I can't bear his doctrine. But still it's a shame I have not a seat."

Would you expect a man to say so? No, you would at once say, "That man does not care for it. Why should he trouble himself about other people having what they value and he despises?" You do not like holiness; you do not like righteousness. If God has elected me to these things, has He hurt you by it? "Ah, but," say some, "I thought it meant that God elected some to heaven and some to hell." That is a very different matter from the gospel doctrine. He has elected men to holiness and to righteousness and through that to heaven. You must not say that He has elected these simply to heaven and others only to hell. He has elected you to *holiness* if you love holiness. If any of you love to be saved by Jesus Christ—Jesus Christ elected you to be saved. If any of you desire to have salvation, you are elected to have it—if you desire it sincerely and earnestly. But if you don't desire it, why on earth should you be so preposterously foolish as to grumble because God gives what you do not like to other people?

II. Thus I have tried to say something with regard to the truth of the doctrine of election. And now, briefly, let me say that election is absolute, that is, it does not depend upon what we are. The text says, "God from the beginning chose you for salvation." But our opponents say that God chooses people because they are good—that He chooses them on account of sundry works that they have done. Now, we ask in reply to this, what works are those on account of which God elects His people? Are they what we commonly call "works of law," which are works of obedience that the creature can render? If so, we reply to you, if the works of the law cannot justify men, it seems to us pretty clear that the works of the law cannot elect them. If they cannot be justified by their good deeds, they cannot save them.

Then the decree of election could not have been formed upon good works. "But," say others, "God elected them on the foresight of their faith." Now God *gives* faith; therefore He could not have elected them on *account* of faith that He foresaw. There will be twenty beggars in the street, and I determine to give one of them a shilling. Will anyone say that I determined to give that one a shilling—that I elected him to have the shilling—because I foresaw that he would have it? That would be talking nonsense.

In like manner, to say that God elected men because He foresaw they would have faith—which is salvation in the germ—would be too absurd for us to listen to for a moment. Faith is the gift of God. Every virtue comes from Him. Therefore it cannot have caused Him to elect men, because it is His gift. Election, we are sure, is absolute and altogether apart from the virtues that the saints have afterward. What if a saint should be as holy and devout as Paul? What if he should be as bold as Peter or as loving as John? Still he could claim nothing but what he received from his Maker.

I never knew a saint yet of any denomination that thought that God saved him because He foresaw that he would have these virtues and merits.

Now, my brethren, the best jewels that the saint ever wears, if they are jewels of our own fashioning, are not of the first water. There is something of earth mixed with them. The highest grace we ever possess has something of earthliness about it. We feel this when we are most refined, when we are most sanctified, and our language must always be:

> *I the chief of sinners am;*
> *Jesus died for me.*

Our only hope, our only plea, still hangs on grace as exhibited in the person of Jesus Christ. And I am sure we must utterly reject and disregard all thought that our graces, which are gifts of our Lord, which are His right hand planting, could have ever caused His love. And we ever must sing:

> *What was there in us that could merit esteem?*
> *Or give the Creator delight?*
> *It was even so, Father, we ever must sing,*
> *Because it seemed good in Your sight.*

He will have mercy on whom He will have mercy. He saves because He will save. And if you ask me why He saves me, I can only say because He would do it. Is there anything in me that should recommend me to God? No. I lay aside everything. I had nothing to recommend me. When God saved me I was the most abject, lost, and ruined of the race. I lay before Him as an infant in my blood. Verily, I had no power to help myself. O how wretched did I feel and know myself to be! It you had something to recommend you to God, I never had. I will be content to be saved by grace—unalloyed, pure grace. I can boast of no merits. If you can do so, still I cannot. I must sing:

> *Free grace alone*
> *From the first to the last*
> *Has won my affection*
> *And held my soul fast.*

III. Then, third, this election is *eternal*. God from the beginning chose you for eternal life. Can any man tell me when the beginning was? Years ago we thought the beginning of this world was when Adam came upon it. But we have discovered that thousands of years before that God was preparing chaotic matter to make it a fit abode for man, putting races of creatures upon it who might die and leave behind the marks of His handiwork and marvelous skill before He tried His hand on man. But that was not the beginning, for revelation points us to a period long before this world was fashioned—to the days when the morning stars were begotten—when, like drops of dew, from the fingers of the morning stars and constellations fell trickling from the hand of God; when, by His own lips, He launched forth ponderous orbs; when with His own hand He sent comets, like thunderbolts, wandering through the sky to find one day their proper sphere.

We go back to years gone by, when worlds were made and systems fashioned, but we have not even approached the beginning yet. Until we go to the time when all the universe slept in the mind of God as yet unborn; until we enter the eternity where God the Creator lived alone, everything sleeping within Him, all creation resting in His mighty gigantic thought, we have not guessed the beginning. We may go back, back, back, ages upon ages. We may go back, if we might use such strange words, whole eternities and yet never arrive at the beginning. Our wings might be tired and our imagination would die away. Could it outstrip the lightnings flashing in majesty, power, and rapidity, it would soon weary itself before it could get to the beginning.

But God from the *beginning* chose His people. When the unnavigated ether was yet unfanned by the wing of a single angel, when space was shoreless or unborn, when universal silence reigned and not a voice or whisper shocked the solemnity of silence. When there was no being and no motion, no time and nothing but God Himself, alone in His eternity; when, without the song of an angel, without the attendance of even the cherubim, long before the living creatures were born or the wheels of the chariot of Jehovah were fashioned, in the beginning was the Word, in the beginning God's people were one with the Word, in the beginning He chose them for eternal life.

Our election, then, is eternal. I will not stop to prove it; I only just run over these thoughts for the benefit of young beginners that they may understand what we mean by eternal, absolute election.

IV. And, next, the election is *personal*. Here again, our opponents have tried to overthrow election by telling us that it is an election of nations and not of people. But here the apostle says, "God from the beginning chose you." It is the most pitiable shift on earth to make out that God has not chosen persons but nations, because the very same objection that lies against the choice of persons lies against the choice of a nation. If it were not just to choose a person, it would be far more unjust to choose a nation, since nations are but the union of multitudes of persons. To choose a nation seems to be a more gigantic crime—if election is a crime—than to choose one person.

Surely to choose ten thousand would be reckoned to be worse than choosing one—to distinguish a whole nation from the rest of mankind seems to be a greater extravaganza in the acts of divine sovereignty than the election of one poor mortal and leaving out another. But what are nations but men? What are whole peoples but combinations of different units? A nation is made up of that individual, and that, and that. And if you tell me that God chose the Jews, I say then, He chose that Jew and that Jew and that Jew. And if you say He chooses Britain, then I say He chooses that British man and that British man and that British man.

So that it is the same thing after all, election then is personal—it must be so. Everyone who reads this text and others like it will see that scripture continually speaks of God's people one by one and speaks of them as having been the special subjects of election.

Sons we are through God's election,
Who in Jesus Christ believe;
By eternal destination
Sovereign grace we here receive.

We know it is personal election.

V. The other thought is—for my time flies too swiftly to enable me to dwell at length upon these points—that election produces *good results.* "God from the beginning chose you for salvation through sanctification by the Spirit and belief in the truth." How many men mistake the doctrine of election altogether! And how my soul burns and boils at the recollection of the terrible evils that have accrued from the spoiling and the wresting of that glorious portion of God's glorious truth!

How many are there who have said to themselves, "I am elect," and have sat down in sloth and worse than that! They have said, "I am the elect of God," and with both hands they have done wickedness. They have swiftly run to every unclean thing because they have said, "I am the chosen child of God, irrespective of my works; therefore I may live as I like and do what I like." Oh, beloved! Let me solemnly warn every one of you not to carry the truth too far—or, rather not to turn the truth into error, for we cannot carry it too far. We may overstep the truth—we can make that which was meant to be sweet for our comfort a terrible mixture for our destruction.

> *L*ong before the living creatures were born or the wheels of the chariot of Jehovah were fashioned, in the beginning was the Word, in the beginning God's people were one with the Word, in the beginning He chose them for eternal life.

I tell you there have been thousands of men who have been ruined by misunderstanding election—who have said, "God has elected me to heaven and to eternal life"—but they have forgotten that it is written, God has elected them "through sanctification by the Spirit and belief in the truth." This is God's election—election to *sanctification* and to *faith*. God chooses His people to be holy and to be believers. How many of you here, then, are believers? How many of my congregation can put their hands upon their hearts and say, "I trust in God that I am sanctified"? Is there one of you who says, "I am elect"?

One of you says, "I trust I am elect," but I jog your memory about some vicious act that you committed during the last six days. Another of you says, "I am elect," but I would look you in the face and say, "*Elect?* You are a most cursed hypocrite, and that is all you are." Others would say, "I am elect," but I would remind them that they neglect the mercy seat and do not pray. Oh, beloved! Never think you are elect unless you are *holy*. You may come to Christ as a sinner, but you may not come to Christ as an elect person until you can see your holiness. Do not misconstrue what I say: Do not say, "I am elect," and yet think you can be living in sin. That is impossible.

The elect of God are holy. They are not pure, they are not perfect, they are not spotless; but taking their life as a whole, they are holy persons. They are marked and distinct from others, and no man has a right to conclude himself elect except in his holiness. He may be elect and yet lying in darkness, but he has no right to believe it. No one can say it, if there is no evidence of it. The man may live one day, but he is dead at present. If you are walking in the fear of God, trying to please Him and to obey His commandments, doubt not that your name has been written in the Lamb's Book of Life from before the foundation of the world.

And, lest this should be too high for you, note the other mark of election—that is, faith, which is belief of the truth of God. Whoever believes God's truth and believes on Jesus Christ is elect. I frequently meet with poor souls who are fretting and worrying themselves about this thought: "What if I should not be elect?"

"Oh, sir," they say, "I know I put my trust in Jesus. I know I believe in His name and trust in His blood. But what if I should not be elect?" Poor dear creature! You do not know much about the gospel or you would never talk so, for *he that believes is elect.* Those who are elect are elect to sanctification and to faith. If you have faith, you are one of God's elect. You may know it and ought to know it, for it is an absolute certainty.

> The elect of God are holy. They are not pure, they are not perfect, they are not spotless; but taking their life as a whole, they are holy persons. They are marked and distinct from others.

If you, as a sinner, look to Jesus Christ this morning and say, "Nothing in my hands I bring; simply to Your cross I cling," you are elect. I am not afraid of election frightening poor saints or sinners. There are many divines who tell the enquirer, "Election has nothing to do with you." That is very bad, because the poor soul is not to be silenced like that. If you could silence him so it might be well—but he will think of it, he can't help it. Say to him then, if you believe on the Lord Jesus Christ you are elect. If you will cast yourself on Jesus, you are elect. I tell you, the chief of sinners—I tell you in His name—if you will come to God without any works of your own, cast yourself on the blood and righteousness of Jesus Christ; if you will come now and trust in Him, you are elect. You were loved of God from before the foundation of the world, for you could not do that unless God had given you the power and had chosen you to do it.

Now you are safe and secure if you do but come and cast yourself on Jesus Christ and wish to be saved and to be loved by Him. But think not that any man will be saved without faith and without holiness. Do not conceive, my hearers, that some decree passed in the dark ages of eternity will save your souls, unless you believe in Christ. Do not sit down and fancy that you are to be saved without faith and holiness. That is a most abominable and accursed heresy and has ruined thousands.

Lay not election as a pillow for you to sleep on, or you may be ruined. God forbid that I should be sewing pillows under armholes that you may rest comfortably in your sins. Sinner! There is nothing in the Bible to palliate your sins. But if you are condemned, O man; if you are lost, O woman, you will not find in this Bible one drop to cool your tongue or one doctrine to palliate your guilt. Your damnation will be entirely your own fault, and your sin will richly merit it—because you believe not, you are condemned. "You believe not because you are not of My sheep. You will not come to Me that you might have life."

Do not fancy that election excuses sin—do not dream of it—do not rock yourself in sweet complacency in the thought of your irresponsibility. You are responsible. We must give you both things. We must have divine sovereignty, and we must have man's responsibility. We must have election, but we must ply your hearts; we must send God's truth at you.

VI. Now, lastly, what are the true and legitimate tendencies of right conceptions concerning the doctrine of election? First, I will tell you what the doctrine of election will make saints do under the blessing of God. And second, what it will do for sinners if God blesses it to them.

First, I think election, to a saint, is one of the most *stripping* doctrines in the entire world—to take away all trust in the flesh or all reliance upon anything except Jesus Christ. How often do we wrap ourselves up in our own righteousness and array ourselves with the false pearls and gems of our own works and doings? We begin to say, "Now I will be saved, because I have this and that evidence." Instead of that, it is naked faith that saves—faith and that alone unites to the Lamb irrespective of works, although it is productive of them.

How often do we lean on some work other than that of our own beloved Jesus and trust in some might other than that which comes from on High?

Now if we would have this might taken from us, we must consider election. Pause, my soul, and consider this. God loved you before you had a being. He loved you when you were dead in trespasses and sins and sent His Son to die for you. He purchased you with His precious blood before you could say His name. Can you then be proud?

I know nothing, nothing again, that is more *humbling* for us than this doctrine of election. I have sometimes fallen prostrate before it when endeavoring to understand it. I have stretched my wings, and eaglelike, I have soared toward the sun. Steady has been my eye and true my wing for a season. But when I came near it and the one thought possessed me, "God from the beginning chose you for salvation," I was lost in its luster. I was staggered with the mighty thought—and from the dizzy elevation down came my soul, prostrate and broken, saying, "Lord, I am nothing, I am less than nothing. Why me? Why me?"

> *Election in the Christian should make him very fearless and very bold. No man will be so bold as he who believes that he is elect of God. What cares he for man if he is chosen of his Maker?*

Friends, if you want to be humbled, study election, for it will make you humble under the influence of God's Spirit. He who is proud of his election is not elect, and he who is humbled under a sense of it may believe that he is. He has every reason to believe that he is, for it is one of the most blessed effects of election that it helps us to humble ourselves before God.

Once again, election in the Christian should make him very *fearless* and very *bold*. No man will be so bold as he who believes that he is elect of God. What cares he for man if he is chosen of his Maker? What will he care for the pitiful chirpings of some tiny sparrows when he knows that he is an eagle of a royal race? Will he care when the beggar points at him, when the blood royal of heaven runs in his veins? Will he fear if the entire world stands against him? If earth were all in arms abroad, he dwells in perfect peace, for he is in the secret place of the tabernacle of the Most High, in the great pavilion of the Almighty.

"I am God's," he says, "I am distinct from other men. They are of an inferior race. Am I not noble? Am I not one of the aristocrats of heaven? Is not my name written in God's book?" Does he care for the world? No. Like the lion that cares not for the barking of the dog, he smiles at all his enemies, and when they come too near him, he moves himself and dashes them to pieces. What cares he for them? He walks about them like a colossus—while little men walk under him and understand him not.

His brow is made of iron. His heart is of flint. What does he care for man? No—if one universal hiss came up from the wide world, he would smile at it, for he would say:

> *He that has made his refuge God,*
> *Shall find a most secure abode.*

I am one of His elect. I am chosen of God and precious—and though the world cast me out, I fear not. Ah, you time-serving professors, some of you will bend like the willows. There are few oaken Christians nowadays who can stand the storm, and I will tell you the reason. It is because you do not believe yourselves to be elected. The man who knows he is elected will be too proud to sin. He will not humble himself to commit the acts of common people.

The believer in God's truth will say, "*I* compromise my principles? *I* change my doctrines? *I* lay aside my views? *I* hide what I believe to be true? No! Since I know I am one of God's elect, in the very teeth of all men I will speak God's truth, whatever man may say." Nothing makes a man so truly bold as to feel that he is among God's elect. He will not quiver, he will not shake, who knows that God has chosen him.

Moreover, election will make us *holy*. Nothing under the gracious influence of the Holy Spirit can make a Christian holier than the thought that he is chosen. "Shall I sin," he says, "after God has chosen me? Shall I transgress after such love? Shall I go astray after so much loving kindness and tender mercy? No, my God, since you have chosen me, I will love You. I will live to You 'since You, the everlasting God, my Father are become.' I will give myself to You to be Yours forever, by election and by redemption, casting myself on You and solemnly consecrating myself to Your service."

Last, to the ungodly: What says election to you? First, you ungodly ones, I will excuse you for a moment. There are many of you who do not like election, and I cannot blame you for it, for I have heard those preach election that have sat down and said, "I have not one word to say to the sinner." Now, I say you *ought* to dislike such preaching as that, and I do not blame you for it. But, I say, take courage. Take hope, O you sinner, that there is election!

So far from dispiriting and discouraging you, it is a very hopeful and joyous thing that there is election. What if I told you perhaps none can be saved, none are ordained to eternal life? Would you not tremble and fold your hands in hopelessness and say, "Then how can I be saved, since none are elect?" But, I say, there is a multitude of elect, beyond all counting—a host that no mortal can number. Therefore, take heart, poor sinner! Cast away your despondency. May you not be elect as well as any other? For there is a host innumerable chosen! There is joy and comfort for you!

Then, not only take heart, but also go and try the Master. Remember, if you were not elect, you would lose nothing by it. O sinner! Come to the throne of electing mercy! You may die where you are. Go to God and, even supposing He should spurn you, suppose His uplifted hand should drive you away (a thing impossible), yet you will not lose anything. You will not be more damned for that. Besides, supposing you are damned, you would have the satisfaction at least of being able to lift up your eyes in hell and say, "God, I asked mercy of You and You would not grant it. I sought it, but You did refuse it."

That you will never say, O sinner! If you go to Him and ask Him, you will receive, for He never has spurned one yet! Is not that hope for you? Though there is an allotted number, yet it is true that all who seek belong to that number. Go and seek, and if you should be the first one to go to hell, tell the devils that you did perish thus; tell the demons that you are a castaway after having come as a guilty sinner to Jesus. I tell you it would disgrace the eternal—with reverence to His name—and He would not allow such a thing. He is jealous of His honor, and He could not allow a sinner to say that.

But ah, poor soul! Do not think thus, that you can lose anything by coming. There is yet one more thought: Do you love the thought of election this morning? Are you willing to admit its justice? Do you say, "I feel that I am lost? I deserve it, and if my brother is saved I cannot murmur. If God destroys me, I deserve it, but if He saves the person sitting beside me, He has a right to do what He will with His own and I have lost nothing by it."

Can you say that honestly from your heart? If so, then the doctrine of election has had its right effect on your spirit and you are not far from the kingdom of heaven. You are brought where you ought to be, where the Spirit wants you to be. And, being so this morning, depart in peace! God has forgiven your sins. You would not feel that if you were not pardoned; you would not feel that if the Spirit of God were not working in you. Rejoice, then, in this! Let your hope rest on the cross of Christ. Think not on election, but on Christ Jesus. Rest on Jesus—Jesus first, last, and without end.

For Further Thought

1. *Romans 8:29–30 describes the five steps in a believer's progress from beginning to end. What are these five steps?*
2. *According to Ephesians 1:4, when and why did God choose us?*
3. *Read Ephesians 1:11. According to what are we predestined?*

Particular Redemption
(Limited Atonement)

"The Son of Man did not come to be served, but to serve,
and to give His life a ransom for many."
Matthew 20:28

WHEN first it was my duty to occupy this pulpit and preach in this hall, my congregation assumed the appearance of an irregular mass of persons collected from all the streets of this city to listen to the Word. I was then simply an evangelist, preaching to many who had not heard the gospel before. By the grace of God, the most blessed change has taken place, and now, instead of having an irregular multitude gathered together, my congregation is as fixed as that of any minister in the whole city of London. I can from this pulpit observe the countenances of my friends who have occupied the same places, as nearly as possible, for these many months. And I have the privilege and the pleasure of knowing that a very large proportion, certainly three-fourths of the persons who meet together here are not persons who stray here from curiosity, but are my regular and constant hearers.

And observe that my character also has been changed. From being an evangelist, it is now my business to become your pastor. You were once a motley group assembled to listen to me, but now we are bound together by the ties of love. Through association we have grown to love and respect each other, and now you have become the sheep of my pasture and members of my flock. And I have now the privilege of assuming the position of a pastor in this place, as well as in the chapel where I labor in the evening. I think, then, it will strike the judgment of every person that as both the congregation and the office have now changed, the teaching itself should in some measure suffer a difference.

It has been my desire to address you from the simple truths of the gospel. I have very seldom, in this place, attempted to dive into the deep things of God. A text that I have thought suitable for my congregation in the evening, I should not have made the subject of discussion in this place in the morning. There are many high and mysterious doctrines that I have often taken the opportunity of handling in my own place that I have not taken the liberty of introducing here, regarding you as a company of people casually gathered together to hear the Word.

But now, since the circumstances are changed, the teaching will be changed also. I will not now simply confine myself to the doctrine of the faith or the teaching of believer's baptism. I will not stay upon the surface of matters, but will venture, as God will guide me, to enter into those things that lie at the basis of the religion that we hold so dear. I will not blush to preach before you the doctrine of God's divine sovereignty. I will not stagger to preach in the most unreserved and unguarded manner the doctrine of election. I will not be afraid to propound the great truth of the final perseverance of the saints. I will not withhold that undoubted truth of scripture the effectual calling of God's elect. I will endeavor, as God will help me to keep back nothing from you who have become my flock. Seeing that many of you have now tasted that the Lord is gracious, we will endeavor to go through the whole system of the doctrines of grace that saints may be edified and built up in their most holy faith.

> We hold that Christ, when He died, had an object in view, and that object will most assuredly and beyond a doubt, be accomplished.

I begin this morning with the doctrine of redemption. Jesus gave His life a ransom for many (Matt. 20:28). The doctrine of redemption is one of the most important doctrines of the system of faith. A mistake on this point will inevitably lead to a mistake through the entire system of our belief.

Now, you are aware that there are different theories of redemption. All Christians hold that Christ died to redeem, but all Christians do not teach the same redemption. We differ as to the nature of atonement and as to the design of redemption. For instance, the Arminian holds that Christ, when He died, did not die with an intent to save any particular person. And they teach that Christ's death does not in itself secure, beyond doubt, the salvation of any man living. They believe that Christ died to make the salvation of all men possible, or that by the doing of something else, any man who pleases may attain to eternal life. Consequently, they are obliged to hold that if man's will would not give way and voluntarily surrender to grace, then Christ's atonement would be worthless.

They hold that there was no particularity and specialty in the death of Christ. Christ died, according to them, as much for Judas in hell as for Peter who mounted to heaven. They believe that for those who are consigned to eternal fire, there was made as true and real a redemption as for those who now stand before the throne of the Most High. Now we believe no such thing. We hold that Christ, when He died, had an object in view, and that object will most assuredly and beyond a doubt, be accomplished. We measure the design of Christ's death by the *effect* of it. If anyone asks us, "What did Christ design to do by His death?" we answer that question by asking him another: "What *has* Christ done, or what *will* Christ do by His death?"

For we declare that the measure of the effect of Christ's love is the measure of the design of it. We cannot so belie our reason as to think that the intention of Almighty God could be frustrated, or that the design of so great a thing as the atonement can by any way whatever be missed of. We hold (we are not afraid to say what we believe) that Christ came into this world with the intention of saving a multitude that no man can number. And we believe that as the result of this, every person for whom He died must, beyond the shadow of a doubt, be cleansed from sin and stand, washed in His blood, before the Father's throne. We do not believe that Christ made any effectual atonement for those who are forever damned. We dare not think that the blood of Christ was ever shed with the intention of saving those whom God foreknew never would be saved and some of whom were even in hell when Christ, according to some men's account, died to save them.

I have thus just stated our theory of redemption and hinted at the differences that exist between two great parties in the professing church. It will be now my endeavor to show the greatness of the redemption of Christ Jesus. And by so doing, I hope to be enabled by God's Spirit to bring out the whole of the great system of redemption so that it may be understood by us all, even if all of us cannot receive it. For you must bear in mind that some of you, perhaps, may be ready to dispute things that I assert. But you will remember that this is nothing to me. I will at all times teach those things that I hold to be true without let or hindrance from any man breathing. You have the like liberty to do the same in your own places and to preach your own views in your own assemblies, as I claim the right to preach mine, fully and without hesitation.

Christ Jesus "gave His life a ransom for many." And by that ransom He wrought out for us a great redemption. I will endeavor to show the greatness of this redemption, measuring it in five ways. We will note its greatness, first of all, *from the heinousness of our own guilt*, from which He has delivered us. Second, we will measure His redemption *by the sternness of divine justice*. Third, we will measure it *by the price He paid*—the pangs He endured. Then we will endeavor to magnify it, by noting *the deliverance that He actually worked out*. And we will close by noticing *the vast number for whom this redemption is made*, who in our text are described as "many."

I. First, then, we will see that the redemption of Christ was no little thing, if we do but measure it, first, by our *own sins*. My brethren, for a moment look at the hole of the pit from where you were dug, and the quarry where you were hewn. You who have been washed, cleansed, and sanctified, pause for a moment and look back at the former state of your ignorance. The sins in which you indulged, the crimes into which you were hurried, the continual rebellion against God in which it was your habit to live. One sin can ruin a soul forever. It is not in the power of the human mind to grasp the infinity of evil that slumbers in the heart of one solitary sin. There is a very infinity of guilt couched in one transgression against the majesty of heaven. If, then, you and I had sinned but once, nothing but an atonement infinite in value could ever have washed away the sin and made satisfaction for it.

But has it been once that you and I have transgressed? No, my brethren, our iniquities are more in number than the hairs of our head. They have mightily prevailed against us. We might as well attempt to number the sands upon the seashore or count the drops that in their aggregate make the ocean as attempt to count the transgressions that have marked our lives. Let us go back to our childhood. How early we began to sin! How we disobeyed our parents and even then learned to make our mouth the house of lies! In our childhood how full of wantonness and waywardness we were! Headstrong and giddy, we preferred our own way and burst through all restraints that godly parents put upon us.

Nor did our youth sober us. Wildly we dashed, many of us, into the very midst of the dance of sin. We became leaders in iniquity. We not only sinned ourselves, but we taught others to sin. And as for your manhood, you who have entered upon the prime of life—you may be more outwardly sober, you may be somewhat free from the dissipation of your youth—but how little has the man become bettered! Unless the sovereign grace of God has renewed us, we are now no better than we were when we began. And even if it has operated, we have still sins to repent of, for we all lay our mouths in the dust and cast ashes on our head and cry, "Unclean! Unclean!"

> *O you lofty mountains! The home of the tempest, the birthplace of the storm! Man may climb your summits and stand wonderingly upon your snows. But you hills of sin! You tower higher than our thoughts.*

Oh! You who lean wearily on your staff, the support of your old age, have you not sins still clinging to your garments? Are your lives as white as the snowy hairs that crown your head? Do you not still feel that transgression besmears the skirts of your robe and mars its spotlessness? How often are you now plunged into the ditch, till your own clothes do abhor you! Cast your eyes over the sixty, the seventy, the eighty years during which God has spared your lives. And can you for a moment think it possible that you can number up your innumerable transgressions, or compute the weight of the crimes that you have committed? O you stars of heaven! The astronomer may measure your distance and tell your height, but O you sins of mankind! You surpass all thought! O you lofty mountains! The home of the tempest, the birthplace of the storm! Man may climb your summits and stand wonderingly upon your snows. But you hills of sin! You tower higher than our thoughts. You chasms of transgressions! You are deeper than our imagination dares to dive.

Do you accuse me of slandering human nature? It is because you know it not! If God had once manifested your heart to yourself, you would bear me witness that so far from exaggerating, my poor words fail to describe the desperateness of our evil. Oh, if we could each of us look into our hearts today, if our eyes could be turned within so as to see the iniquity that is graven as with the point of the diamond upon our stony hearts, we should then say to the minister that however he may depict the desperateness of guilt, yet can he not by any means surpass it. How great then, beloved, must be the ransom of Christ when He saved us from all these sins!

The men for whom Jesus died, however great their sin, when they believe, are sanctified from all their transgressions. Though they may have indulged in every vice and every lust that Satan could suggest and that human nature could perform, yet once believing, by God's grace, all their guilt is washed away. Year after year may have coated them with blackness, till their sin has become of double dye, but in one moment of faith, one triumphant moment of confidence in Christ, the great redemption takes away the guilt of numerous years. No, more. If it were possible for *all* the sins that men have done in thought or word or deed since worlds were made or time began to meet on *one* poor head, the great redemption is all-sufficient to take all these sins away and wash the sinner whiter than the driven snow!

Oh, who will measure the heights of the Savior's all-sufficiency? First, tell how high is sin and then remember that as Noah's flood prevailed over the tops of the earth's mountains, so the flood of Christ's redemption prevails over the tops of the mountains of our sins. In heaven's courts there are today men who once were murderers and thieves and drunkards and whoremongers and blasphemers and persecutors. But they have been washed, they have been sanctified. Ask them from where the brightness of their robes has come and where their purity has been achieved, and they, with united breath, will tell you that they have washed their robes and made them white in the blood of the Lamb. O you troubled consciences! O you weary and heavy-laden ones! O you who are groaning on account of sin! The great redemption now proclaimed to you is all-sufficient for your wants. And though your numerous sins exceed the stars that deck the sky, here is atonement made for them all, a river that can overflow the whole of them and carry them away from you forever.

This, then, is the first measure of the atonement: the greatness of our guilt.

II. Second, we must measure the great redemption *by the sternness of divine justice.* God is love, always loving, but my next proposition does not at all interfere with this assertion. *God is sternly just*, inflexibly severe in His dealings with mankind. The God of the Bible is not the God of some men's imagination, who thinks so little of sin that He passes it by without demanding any punishment for it. He is not the God of the men who imagine that our transgressions are such little things, such mere peccadilloes that the God of heaven winks at them and suffers them to die forgotten.

No. Jehovah, Israel's God, has declared concerning Himself, "The Lord your God is a jealous God" (Deut. 6:15). It is His declaration, I "will by no means clear the guilty" (see Exod. 34:7 kjv) and "The soul who sins shall die" (Ezek. 18:4). Teach, my friends, to look upon God as being as severe in His justice as if He were not loving—and yet as loving as if He were not severe. His love does not diminish His justice, nor does His justice, in the least degree, make warfare upon His love. The two things are sweetly linked together in the atonement of Christ. But mark this; we can never understand the fullness of the atonement till we have first grasped the scriptural truth of God's immense justice.

Oh, my brothers and sisters, can you think what must have been the greatness of the atonement that was the substitution for all this agony that God would have cast upon us if He had not poured it upon Christ?

There was never an ill word spoken, nor an ill thought conceived, nor an evil deed done for which God will not have punishment from someone or another. He will either have satisfaction from you or else from Christ. If you have no atonement to bring through Christ, you must forever lie paying the debt that you never can pay in eternal misery. For as surely as God is God, He will sooner lose His Godhead than suffer *one* sin to go unpunished or one particle of rebellion not revenged. You may say that this character of God is cold, stern, and severe. I cannot help what you say of it. It is nevertheless true. Such is the God of the Bible. And though we repeat it is true that He is love, it is no truer that He is love than that He is full of justice, for every good thing meets in God and is carried to perfection. While love reaches to consummate loveliness, justice reaches to the sternness of inflexibility in Him.

He has no bend, no warp in His character. No attribute so predominates as to cast a shadow upon the other. Love has its full sway, and justice has no narrower limit than His love. Oh, then, beloved, think how great must have been the substitution of Christ when it satisfied God for all the sins of His people. For man's sin God demands eternal punishment. And God has prepared a hell into which He casts those who die impenitent. Oh, my brothers and sisters, can you think what must have been the greatness of the atonement that was the substitution for all this agony that God would have cast upon us if He had not poured it upon Christ? Look! Look! Look with solemn eye through the shades that part us from the world of spirits and see that house of misery that men call hell! You cannot endure the spectacle!

Remember that in that place there are spirits forever paying their debt to divine justice, but though some of them have been there these six thousand years sweltering in the flame, they are no nearer a discharge than when they began. And when ten thousand times ten thousand years will have rolled away, they will no more have made satisfaction to God for their guilt than they have done up till now. And now can you grasp the thought of the greatness of your Savior's mediation when He paid your debt and paid it all at once so that there now remains not one farthing of debt owing from Christ's people to their God except a debt of love? To justice the believer owes nothing. Though he owed originally so much that eternity would not have been long enough to suffice for the paying of it, yet in one moment Christ did pay it all. The man who believes is entirely sanctified from all guilt and set free from all punishment through what Jesus has done. Think, then, how great His atonement if He has done all this.

I must just pause here and utter another sentence. There are times when God the Holy Spirit shows to men the sternness of justice in their own consciences. There is a man here today who has just been cut to the heart with a sense of sin. He was once a free man, a libertine, in bondage to none. But now the arrow of the Lord sticks fast in his heart and he has come under a bondage worse than that of Egypt. I see him today. He tells me that his guilt haunts him everywhere. The Negro slave, guided by the pole star, may escape the cruelties of his master and reach another land where he may be free. But this man feels that if he were to wander the whole world over he could not escape from guilt. He who has been bound by many irons cannot find a file that can unbind him and set him at liberty. This man tells you that he has tried prayers and tears and good works but cannot get the shackles from his wrists. He feels as a lost sinner still, and emancipation, do what he may, seems to him impossible.

The captive in the dungeon is sometimes free in thought, though not in body. Through his dungeon walls his spirit leaps and flies to the stars, free as the eagle that is no man's slave. But this man is a slave in his thoughts—he cannot think one bright, one happy thought. His soul is cast down within him. The iron has entered into his spirit, and he is sorely afflicted. The captive sometimes forgets his slavery in sleep, but this man cannot sleep. By night he dreams of hell; by day he seems to feel it. He bears a burning furnace of flame within his heart and, do what he may, he cannot quench it. He has been confirmed, he has been baptized, he takes the sacrament, he attends a church, or he frequents a chapel. He regards every rubric and obeys every canon—but the fire burns still.

> See the Savior's limbs, how they quiver! Every bone has been put out of joint by the dashing of the cross into that socket! How He weeps! How He sighs! How He sobs!

He gives his money to the poor; he is ready to give his body to be burned. He feeds the hungry, he visits the sick, he clothes the naked, but the fire burns still. Do what he may, he cannot quench it. O, you sons of weariness and woe! This that you feel is God's justice in full pursuit of you, and happy are you that you feel this, for now to you I preach this glorious gospel of the blessed God! You are the man for whom Jesus Christ has died. For you He has satisfied stern justice. And now all you have to do to obtain peace and conscience is just to say to your adversary who pursues you, "Look you there! Christ died for me. My good works would not stop you; my tears would not appease you. Look you there! There stands the cross; there hangs the bleeding God! Hark to His death-shriek! See Him die! Are you not satisfied now?" And when you have done that, you will have the peace of God that passes all understanding, that will keep your heart and mind through Jesus Christ your Lord, and then will you know the greatness of His atonement.

III. In the third place, we may measure the greatness of Christ's redemption by *the price he paid*. It is impossible for us to know how great were the pangs of our Savior, yet some glimpse of them will afford us a little idea of the greatness of the price that He paid for us. O Jesus, who will describe Your agony?

Come, all you springs,
Dwell in my head and eyes.
Come, clouds and rain!
My grief has need of all the watery things,
That nature has produced. Let every vein
Suck up a river to supply my eyes,
My weary weeping eyes too dry for me,
Unless they get new conduits, new supplies
To bear them out and with my state agree.

O Jesus! You were a sufferer from your birth, a Man of sorrows and grief's acquaintance. Your sufferings tell on you in one perpetual shower, until the last dread hour of darkness. Then not in a shower, but in a cloud, a torrent, a cataract of grief your agonies did dash upon you. See Him yonder! It is a night of frost and cold, but He is abroad. It is night. He sleeps not. He is in prayer. Hark to His groans! Did ever man wrestle as He wrestles? Go and look in His face! Was ever such suffering depicted upon mortal countenance as you can there behold? Hear His own words: "My soul is exceedingly sorrowful, even to death" (Matt. 26:38). He rises. He is seized by traitors and dragged away.

Let us step to the place where just now He was engaged in agony. O God! And what is this we see? What is this that stains the ground? It is blood! From where did it come? Had He some wound that oozed afresh through His dire struggle? Ah, no. "His sweat became like great drops of blood falling down to the ground" (Luke 22:44). O agonies that surpass the word by which we name you! O sufferings that cannot be compassed in language! What could you be that thus could work upon the Savior's blessed frame and force a bloody sweat to fall from His entire body?

This is the beginning, the opening of the tragedy. Follow Him mournfully, you sorrowing church, to witness the consummation of it. He is hurried through the streets. He is first to one bar and then to another. He is cast and condemned before the Sanhedrin. Herod mocks Him. Pilate tries Him. His sentence is pronounced: "Let Him be crucified!" (Matt. 27:22). And now the tragedy comes to its height. His back is bared. He is tied to the low

Roman column. The bloody scourge plows furrows on His back. And with one stream of blood His back is red, a crimson robe that proclaims Him emperor of misery. He is taken into the guardroom. His eyes are bound, and then they buffet Him and say, "Prophesy, who is it that smote thee?" (Luke 22:64 KJV).

They spit into His face. They plait a crown of thorns and press His temples with it. They array Him in a purple robe. They bow their knees and mock Him. All silently He stands. He answers not a word. When He was reviled, He reviled not again but committed Himself to Him whom He came to serve. And now they take Him, and with many a jeer and jibe they drive Him from the place and hurry Him through the streets. Emaciated by continual fasting and depressed with agony of spirit, He stumbles beneath His cross.

Daughters of Jerusalem! He faints in your streets. They raise Him up. They put His cross upon another's shoulders and urge Him on, perhaps with many a spear prick, till at last He reaches the mount of doom. Rough soldiers seize Him and hurl Him on His back. The transverse wood is laid beneath Him; His arms are stretched to reach the necessary distance. The nails are grasped. Four hammers at one moment drive four nails through the tenderest parts of His body. And there He lies upon His own place of execution dying on His cross. It is not done yet. The rough soldiers lift the cross. There is the socket prepared for it. It is dashed into its place. They fill up the place with earth. And there it stands.

But see the Savior's limbs, how they quiver! Every bone has been put out of joint by the dashing of the cross into that socket! How He weeps! How He sighs! How He sobs! No, more. Hark how at last He shrieks in agony, "My God, My God, why have You forsaken Me?" (Mark 15:34). O sun, no wonder you did shut your eye and look no longer upon a deed so cruel! O rocks! No wonder that you did melt and rend your hearts with sympathy when your Creator died! Never man suffered as this Man suffered. Even death itself relented, and many of those who had been in their graves arose and came into the city.

This however, is but the outward. Believe me, brethren, the inward was far worse. What our Savior suffered in His body was nothing compared to what He endured in His soul. You cannot guess, and I cannot help you to guess, what He endured within. Suppose for one moment—to repeat a sentence I have often used—suppose a man who has passed into hell—

suppose his eternal torment could all be brought into one hour, and then suppose it could be multiplied by the number of the saved, that is a number past all human enumeration. Can you now think what a vast aggregate of misery there would have been in the sufferings of all God's people if they had been punished through all eternity?

> *We* think that Calvin, after all, knew more about the gospel than almost any uninspired man who has ever lived.

And recollect that Christ had to suffer an equivalent for all the hells of all His redeemed. I can never express that thought better than by using those oft-repeated words, it seemed as if hell was put into His cup, He seized it, and "at one tremendous draught of love, He drank damnation dry." There was nothing left of all the pangs and miseries of hell for His people ever to endure. I say not that He suffered the same, but He did endure an equivalent for all this and gave God the satisfaction for all the sins of all His people, and consequently gave Him an equivalent for all their punishment. Now can you dream, can you *guess* the great redemption of our Lord Jesus Christ?

IV. I will be very brief upon the next head. The fourth way of measuring the Savior's agonies is this: We must compute them by *the glorious deliverance He has effected.*

Rise up, believer; stand up in your place and this day testify to the greatness of what the Lord has done for you! Let me tell it for you! I will tell your experience and mine in one breath. Once my soul was laden with sin. I had revolted against God and grievously transgressed. The terrors of the law got hold upon me. The pangs of conviction seized me. I saw myself guilty. I looked to heaven and I saw an angry God sworn to punish me. I looked beneath me and I saw a yawning hell ready to devour me. I sought by good works to satisfy my conscience, but all in vain. I endeavored, by attending to the ceremonies of religion, to appease the pangs that I felt within, but all without effect.

My soul was exceeding sorrowful almost to death. I could have said with the ancient mourner, "My soul chooses strangling and death rather than life." This was the great question that always perplexed me: "I have sinned.

God must punish me. How can He be just if He does not? Then, since He is just, what is to become of me?" At last my eyes turned to that sweet Word that says, "The blood of Jesus Christ His Son cleanses us from all sin" (1 John 1:7). I took that text to my chamber. I sat there and meditated. I saw one hanging on a cross. It was my Lord Jesus. There was the crown of thorns and there the emblems of unequaled and peerless misery.

"This is a faithful saying and worthy of all acceptance, that Christ Jesus came into the world to save sinners" (1 Tim. 1:15). Then said I within myself, "Did this man die for sinners? *I* am a sinner. Then He died for me. Those He died for He will save. He died for sinners. I am a sinner. He died for me. He will save me." *My* soul relied upon that truth. I looked to Him, and as I viewed the flowing of His soul-redeeming blood, *my* spirit rejoiced, for I could say:

> *Nothing in my hands I bring,*
> *Simply to His cross I cling.*
> *Naked I look to Him for dress,*
> *Helpless, I come to Him for grace!*
> *Black, I to this fountain fly—*
> *Wash me, Savior, or I die!*

And now, believer, you will tell the rest. The moment that you believed, your burden rolled from your shoulder and you became light as air. Instead of darkness, you had light. For the garments of heaviness you had the robes of praise. Who will tell of your joy since then? You have sung on earth hymns of heaven, and in your peaceful soul you have anticipated the eternal Sabbath of the redeemed. Because you have believed you have entered into rest. Yes, tell it to the whole world over that they who believe, by Jesus' death are justified from all things from which they could not be freed by the works of the law. Tell it in heaven that none can lay anything to the charge of God's elect. Tell it upon earth that God's redeemed are free from sin in Jehovah's sight. Tell it even in hell—God's elect can never go there, for Christ has died for His elect, and who is he who will condemn them?

V. I have hurried over that to come to the last point, which is the sweetest of all. Jesus Christ, we are told in our text, came into the world, "to give His life a ransom for many." The greatness of Christ's redemption may be measured by the *extent of its design*. He gave His life a ransom for many. I must now return to that controverted point again. We are often told (I mean those of us who are commonly nicknamed by the title of Calvinists. We are not very much ashamed of that. We think that Calvin, after all, knew more about the gospel than almost any uninspired man who has ever lived) that we limit the atonement of Christ because we say that Christ has not made a satisfaction for all men, or all men would be saved.

Now our reply to this is that, on the other hand, our opponents limit it though we do not. The Arminians say Christ died for all men. Ask them what they mean by it. Did Christ die so as to secure the salvation of all men? They say, "No, certainly not." We ask them the next question: Did Christ die so as to secure the salvation of any man in particular? They answer, "No." They are obliged to admit this if they are consistent. They say, "No, Christ has died that any man may be saved *if. . .*," and then follow certain conditions of salvation. We say, then, we will just go back to the old statement, Christ did not die so as beyond a doubt to secure the salvation of anybody, did he? You must say, "No." You are obliged to say so, for you believe that even after a man has been pardoned, he may yet fall from grace and perish.

Now, who is it who limits the death of Christ? Why, you. You say that Christ did not die so as to infallibly secure the salvation of anybody. We beg your pardon when you say *we* limit Christ's death. We say, "No, my dear sir, it is you that do it. We say Christ so died that He infallibly secured the salvation of a multitude that no man can number, which through Christ's death not only may be saved, but *are* saved, *must* be saved, and cannot by any possibility run the hazard of being anything *but* saved. You are welcome to your atonement. You may keep it. We will never renounce ours for the sake of it."

Now, beloved, when you hear anyone laughing or jeering at a limited atonement, you may tell him this: General atonement is like a great wide bridge with only half an arch. It does not go across the stream. It only professes to go halfway—it does not secure the salvation of anybody. Now, I would rather put my foot upon a bridge as narrow as Hungerford, which went all the way across, than on a bridge that was as wide as the world, if it did not go all the way across the stream. I am told it is my duty to say that *all* men have been redeemed, and I am told that there is a scriptural warrant for it: "Who gave Himself a ransom for all, to be testified in due time" (1 Tim. 2:6).

Now, that looks like a very great argument indeed on the other side of the question. For instance, look here: "The *world* is gone after him" (John 12:19 KJV). Did the entire *world* go after Christ? "Then all the land of Judea, and those from Jerusalem, went out to him and were all baptized by him in the Jordan River" (Mark 1:5). Was *all Judea*, or *all Jerusalem* baptized in Jordan? "We know that we are of God, and the whole world lies under the sway of the wicked one" (1 John 5:19). Does "the whole world" there mean everybody? If so, how was it, then, that there were some who were "of God"? The words *world* and *all* are used in some seven or eight senses in scripture. And it is very rarely that "all" means all persons taken individually. The words are generally used to signify that Christ has redeemed *some of all sorts*, some Jews, some Gentiles, some rich, and some poor, and has not restricted His redemption to either Jew or Gentile.

> *A*re you a sinner? That felt, that known, and that professed, you are now invited to believe that Jesus Christ died for you because you are a sinner.

Leaving controversy, however, I will now answer a question. Tell me then, sir, for whom did Christ die? Will you answer me a question or two, and I will tell you whether He died for you. Do you want a Savior? Do you feel that you need a Savior? Are you this morning conscious of sin? Has the Holy Spirit taught you that you are lost? Then Christ died for you, and you will be saved. Are you this morning conscious that you have no hope in the world but Christ? Do you feel that you of yourself cannot offer an atonement that can satisfy God's justice? Have you given up all confidence in yourselves? And can you say upon your bended knees, "Lord, save, or I perish?" Christ died for you.

If you are saying this morning, "I am as good as I ought to be. I can get to heaven by my own good works," then remember, the scripture says of Jesus, "I did not come to call the righteous, but sinners, to repentance" (Matt. 9:13). So long as you are in that state I have no atonement to preach to you. But if this morning you feel guilty, wretched, and conscious of your guilt and are ready to take Christ to be your only Savior, I cannot only say to you that you may be saved, but what is better still, that you *will* be saved.

When you are stripped of everything but hope in Christ. When you are prepared to come empty-handed and take Christ to be your all and to be yourself nothing at all—then you may look up to Christ and you may say, "You dear, you bleeding Lamb of God! Your griefs were endured for me. By your stripes I am healed, and by your sufferings I am pardoned." And then see what peace of mind you will have—for if Christ has died for you, you cannot be lost. God will not punish twice for one thing.

If God punished *Christ* for your sin, He will never punish you. "Payment, God's justice cannot twice demand, first, at the bleeding Surety's hand, and then again at mine." We can today, if we believe in Christ, march to the very throne of God, stand there, and if it is said, "Are you guilty?" we can say, "Yes, guilty." But if the question is put, "What have you to say why you should not be punished for your guilt?" we can answer, "Great God, Your justice and Your love are both our guarantees that You will not punish us for sin. For did You not punish Christ for sin for us? How can You, then, be just—how can You be God at all if You punish Christ the substitute and then punish man himself afterward?"

Your only question is, "Did Christ die for me?" And the only answer we can give is, "This is a faithful saying, and worthy of all acceptation, that Christ came into the world to save sinners." Can you write your name down among the sinners? Not among the complimentary sinners, but among those that feel it, bemoan it, lament it, and seek mercy on account of it? Are you a sinner? That felt, that known, and that professed, you are now invited to believe that Jesus Christ died for you because you are a sinner. And you are bidden to cast yourself upon this great immovable rock and find eternal security in the Lord Jesus Christ.

For Further Thought

1. *First Corinthians 6:9–11 tells about some of the believers in the church in Corinth. What sanctified them so that they could be called "saints" (1:2)?*
2. *Lamentations 1:12–14 describes Christ's crucifixion. What does verse 13 say God sent to our Lord while He gave His life as a ransom?*
3. *According to John 1:29, how much sin did Jesus Christ take away when He died on the cross?*

EFFECTUAL CALLING (IRRESISTIBLE GRACE)

And when Jesus came to the place, He looked up and saw him,
and said to him, "Zacchaeus, make haste and come down,
for today I must stay at your house."
LUKE 19:5

NOTWITHSTANDING our firm belief that you are, for the most part, well instructed in the doctrines of the everlasting gospel, we are continually reminded in our conversation with young converts how absolutely necessary it is to repeat our former lessons and repeatedly assert and prove over and over again those doctrines that lie at the basis of our holy religion. Our friends, therefore, who have many years ago been taught the great doctrine of effectual calling will believe that while I preach very simply this morning, the sermon is intended for those who are young in the fear of the Lord, that they may better understand this great starting point of God in the heart, the effectual calling of men by the Holy Spirit.

I will use the case of Zacchaeus as a great illustration of the doctrine of effectual calling. You remember the story. Zacchaeus had a curiosity to see the wonderful man, Jesus Christ, who was turning the world upside down and causing an immense excitement in the minds of men. We sometimes find fault with curiosity and say it is sinful to come to the house of God from that motive. I am not quite sure that we should hazard such an assertion. The motive is not sinful, though certainly it is not virtuous. Yet it has often been proved that curiosity is one of the best allies of grace. Zacchaeus, moved by this motive, desired to see Christ. But there were two obstacles in the way. First, there was such a crowd of people that he could not get near the Savior. Second, he was so exceedingly short in stature that there was no hope of his reaching over people's heads to catch a glimpse of Him.

What did he do? He did as the boys were doing, for the boys of old times were no doubt just like the boys of the present age; they were perched up in the boughs of the tree to look at Jesus as He passed along. Elderly man though he is, Zacchaeus jumps up, and there he sits among the children. The boys are too much afraid of that stern old publican, whom their fathers dreaded, to push him down or cause him any inconvenience. Look at him there. With what anxiety he is peeping down to see Christ—for the Savior had no pompous distinction. No one is walking before Him with a silver mace. He does not hold a golden staff in His hand, and He has no pontifical dress. In fact, He is dressed like those around Him. He has a coat like that of a common peasant, made of one piece from top to bottom. Zacchaeus could scarcely distinguish Him. However, before he has caught sight of Christ, Christ has fixed His eye upon him. Standing under the tree, He looks up and says, "Zacchaeus, make haste and come down; for today I must stay at your house." Down comes Zacchaeus. Christ goes to his house. Zacchaeus becomes Christ's follower and enters into the kingdom of heaven.

I. Now, first, effectual calling is *a very gracious truth of God*. You may guess this from the fact that Zacchaeus was a character that we should suppose the last to be saved. He belonged to a bad city, Jericho, a city that had been cursed, and no one would suspect that anyone would come out of Jericho to be saved. It was near Jericho that the man fell among thieves. We trust Zacchaeus had no hand in it, but there are some who, while they are publicans, can be thieves also. We might as well expect converts from St. Giles's, or the lowest parts of London, from the worst and vilest dens of infamy, as from Jericho in those days.

> For God to look down on His creatures is mercy, but for Christ so to humble Himself that He has to look up to one of His own creatures, that becomes mercy indeed!

Ah, my brethren, it matters not where you come from. You may come from one of the dirtiest streets, one of the worst back slums in London, but if effectual grace calls you, it is an effectual call that knows no distinction of place. Zacchaeus also was of an exceedingly bad trade and probably cheated the people in order to enrich himself. Indeed, when Christ went into his house, there was a universal murmur that He had gone to be a guest with a man who was a sinner. But, my brethren, grace knows no distinction. It is no respecter of persons. God calls whom He wills, and He called this worst of publicans, in the worst of cities, from the worst of trades. Besides, Zacchaeus was one who was least likely to be saved, because he was rich. It is true, rich and poor are welcome, and no one has the least excuse for despair because of his condition, yet it is a fact that not many great men after the flesh are called, but God has chosen the poor of this world to be rich in faith.

But even here grace knows no distinction. The *rich* Zacchaeus is called from the tree. Down he comes and he is saved. I have thought it one of the greatest instances of God's condescension that He can look *down* on man. But I will tell you there was a greater condescension than that when Christ looked *up* to see Zacchaeus. For God to look down on His creatures is mercy, but for Christ so to humble Himself that He has to look up to one of His own creatures, that becomes mercy indeed!

Ah, many of you have climbed up the tree of your own good works and perched yourselves in the branches of your holy actions and are trusting in the free will of the poor creature or resting in some worldly maxim. Nevertheless, Christ looks up even to proud sinners and calls them down. "Come down," says He, "today I must stay at your house." Had Zacchaeus been a humble-minded man, sitting by the wayside, or at the feet of Christ, we should then have admired Christ's mercy. But here he is lifted up and Christ looks up to him and bids him come down.

II. Next, it was a *personal* call. There were boys in the tree as well as Zacchaeus, but there was no mistake about the person who was called. It was, "*Zacchaeus*, make haste and come down." There are other calls mentioned in scripture. It is said especially, "Many are called, but few are chosen" (Matt. 22:14). Now that is not the effectual call that was intended by the apostle when he said, "Whom He called, these He also justified" (Rom. 8:30). That is a *general* call that many men, yes, all men reject, unless there comes after it the personal, particular call that makes us Christians. You will bear me witness that it was a personal call that brought you to the Savior. It was some sermon that led you to feel that you were, no doubt, the person intended.

The text, perhaps, was "You, God, see me." And perhaps the minister laid particular stress on the word "me," so that you thought God's eyes were fixed upon you. And before the sermon was concluded, you thought you saw God open the books to condemn you, and your heart whispered, " 'Can anyone hide himself in secret places, so I shall not see him?' says the LORD" (Jer. 23:24). You might have been perched in the window or stood packed in the aisle, but you had a solemn conviction that the sermon was preached to you and not to other people. God does not call His people in shoals but in units.

"Jesus saith unto her, Mary. She turned herself, and saith unto him, Rabboni; which is to say, Master" (John 20:16 KJV). Jesus saw Peter and John fishing by the lake, and He said to them, "Follow Me" (Matt. 4:19). He saw Matthew sitting at the table at the receipt of custom, and He said to him, "Follow Me," and Matthew did so (9:9). When the Holy Spirit comes home to a man, God's arrow goes into his heart. It does not graze his helmet or make some little mark upon his armor; it penetrates between the joints of the harness, entering the marrow of the soul. Have you felt, dear friends, that personal call? Do you remember when a voice said, "Arise, He calls you"? Can you look back to when you said, "My Lord, *my* God"; when you knew the Spirit was striving with you and you said, "Lord, I come to you, for I know that you call me"? *I* might call the whole of you throughout eternity, but if *God* call one, there will be more effect through His personal call of one than my general call of multitudes.

III. Third, it is a *hastening* call. "Zacchaeus, *make haste.*" The sinner, when the ordinary ministry calls him, replies, "Tomorrow." He hears a telling sermon, and he says, "I will turn to God by and by." The tears roll down his cheek, but they are wiped away. Some goodness appears, but like the cloud of the morning, the sun of temptation dissipates it. He says, "I solemnly vow from this time to be a reformed man. After I have once more indulged in my darling sin, I will renounce my lusts and decide for God." Ah, that is only a *minister's* call and is good for nothing. Hell, they say, is paved with good intentions. These good intentions are begotten by general calls.

The road to perdition is laid all over with branches of the trees whereon men are sitting, for they often pull down branches from the trees, but they do not come down themselves. The straw laid down before a sick man's door causes the wheels to roll more noiselessly. So there are some who strew their path with promises of repentance and so go more easily and noiselessly down to perdition. But God's call is not a call for tomorrow. "*Today,* if you will hear His voice: 'Do not harden your hearts, as in the rebellion, as in the day of trial in the wilderness'" (Ps. 95:7–8). God's grace always comes with

EFFECTUAL CALLING (IRRESISTIBLE GRACE)

dispatch, and if God draws you, you will run after God and not be talking about delays. Tomorrow is not written in the almanac of time.

Tomorrow is in Satan's calendar and nowhere else. Tomorrow is a rock whitened by the bones of mariners who have been wrecked upon it. Tomorrow is the wrecker's light gleaming on the shore, luring poor ships to destruction. Tomorrow is the idiot's cup that he lays at the foot of the rainbow but that none has ever found. Tomorrow is the floating island of Loch Lomond that none has ever seen. Tomorrow is a dream. Tomorrow is a delusion. Tomorrow, yes, tomorrow you may lift up your eyes in hell, being in torment. Yonder clock says, "Today." Your pulse whispers, "Today." I hear my heart speak as it beats, and it says, "Today." Everything cries, "Today." And the Holy Spirit is in union with these things and says, "*Today* if you will hear His voice, 'Do not harden not your hearts.'" Sinners, are you inclined now to seek the Savior? Are you breathing a prayer now? Are you saying, "Now or never; I must be saved now"? If you are, then I hope it is an *effectual call*, for Christ, when He gives an effectual call, says, "Zacchaeus, make haste."

IV. Next, it is a *humbling* call. "Zacchaeus, make haste and *come down*." Many a time has a minister called men to repentance with a call that has made them proud, exalted them in their own esteem, and led them to say, "I can turn to God when I like. I can do so without the influence of the Holy Spirit." They have been called to *go up* and not to *come down*. God always humbles a sinner. Can I not remember when God told me to come down? One of the first steps I had to take was to go right down from my good works. And oh, what a fall was that! Then I stood upon my own self-sufficiency, and Christ said, "Come down! I have pulled you down from your good works, and now I will pull you down from your self-sufficiency."

Well, I had another fall, and I felt sure I had gained the bottom, but Christ said, "Come down!" And He made me come down till I fell on some point at which I felt I was not savable. "Down, sir! Come down, yet." And down I came until I had to let go of every branch of the tree of my hopes in despair. Then I said, "I can do nothing. I am ruined." The waters were wrapped round my head, and I was shut out from the light of day and thought myself a stranger from the commonwealth of Israel.

"Come down lower yet, sir! You have too much pride to be saved." Then I was brought down to see my corruption, my wickedness, and my filthiness.

"Come down," says God, when He means to save. Now, proud sinners, it is of no use for you to be proud, to stick yourselves up in the trees—Christ will have you down. Oh, you that dwell with the eagle on the craggy rock, you will come down from your elevation; you will fall by grace or you will fall with a vengeance one day. "He hath put down the mighty from their seats, and exalted them of low degree" (Luke 1:52 KJV).

V. Fifth, it is an *affectionate* call. "Today I must stay at your *house.*" You can easily conceive how the faces of the multitude change! They thought Christ to be the holiest and best of men and were ready to make Him a king. But He says, "Today I must stay at your house." There was one poor Jew who had been inside Zacchaeus's house—he had "been on the carpet," as they say in country villages when they are taken before the justice—and he recollected what sort of a house it was. He remembered how he was taken in there and his conceptions of it were something like what a fly would have of a spider's den after he had once escaped.

There was another who had been restrained of nearly all his property. The idea he had of walking in there was like walking into a den of lions. "What?" said they, "Is this holy man going into such a den as that, where we poor wretches have been robbed and ill-treated? It was bad enough for Christ to speak to him up in the tree, but the idea of going into his house!" They all murmured at His going to be "a guest with a man who is a sinner" (Luke 19:7). Well, I know what some of His disciples thought: They thought it very imprudent. It might injure His character, and He might offend the people. They thought He might have gone to see this man at night, like Nicodemus, and given him an audience when nobody saw Him! To acknowledge such a man publicly was the most imprudent act He could commit.

Why did Christ do as He did? It was because He would give Zacchaeus an *affectionate* call. "I will not come and stand at your threshold or look in at your window, but I will come into your house; the same house where the cries of widows have come into your ears and you have disregarded them. I will come into your parlor, where the weeping of the orphan has never moved your compassion. I will come there, where you, like a ravenous lion have devoured your prey. I will come there, where you have blackened your house and made it infamous. I will come into the place where cries have risen to high heaven, wrung from the lips of those whom you have oppressed.

"I will come into your house and give you a blessing." Oh, what affection there was in that! Poor sinner, my Master is a very affectionate Master. He will come into your house. What kind of a house have you got? A house that you have made miserable with your drunkenness, a house you have defiled with your impurity, a house you have defiled with your cursing and swearing, a house where you are carrying on an illegal trade that you would be glad to get rid of? Christ says, "I will come into your house." And I know some houses now that once were dens of sin where Christ comes every morning. Husband and wife, who once could only quarrel and fight, bend their knees together in prayer. Christ comes there at dinnertime, when the workman comes home for his meals. Some of my hearers can scarce come for an hour to their meals, but they must have a word of prayer and reading of the scriptures.

> Oh, you that dwell with the eagle on the craggy rock, you will come down from your elevation; you will fall by grace or you will fall with a vengeance one day.

Christ comes to them. Where the walls were plastered up with the lascivious songs and idle pictures, there is a Christian almanac in one place. There is a Bible on the chest of drawers, and though it is only one room they live in, if an angel should come in and God should say, "What have you seen in that house?" he would say, "I have seen good furniture, for there is a Bible there—here and there a religious book—the filthy pictures are pulled down and burned. There are no cards in the man's cupboard now. Christ has come into his house." Oh, what a blessing that we have our household God as well as the Romans! Our God is a household God. He comes to live with His people! He loves the tents of Jacob.

Now, poor ragamuffin sinner, you who live in the filthiest den in London, if such a one is here, Jesus says to you, "Zacchaeus, make haste and come down, for today I must stay at your *house*."

VI. Again, it was not only an affectionate call, but it was an *abiding call*. Today I must stay at your house." A *common call* is like this: "Today I will walk into your house at one door and out at the other." The common call that is given by the gospel to all men is a call that operates upon them for a time, and then it is *all over*—but the saving call is an *abiding call*. When Christ speaks, He does not say, "Make haste, Zacchaeus, and come down, for I am just coming to look in." No. He says, "I must stay at your house. I am coming to sit down to eat and drink with you. I am coming to have a meal with you. Today I must stay at your house."

"Ah," says one, "you cannot tell how many times I have been impressed, sir. I have often had a series of solemn convictions and I thought I really was saved—but it all died away like a dream. When one awakes, all has vanished that he dreamed. So was it with me." Ah, but poor soul, do not despair. Do you feel the strivings of Almighty grace within your heart bidding you repent today? If you do, it will be an *abiding call*. If it is Jesus at work in your soul, He will come and tarry in your heart and consecrate you for His own forever. He says, "I will come and dwell with you and that forever. I will come and say:

> *Here I will make my settled rest,*
> *No more will go and come;*
> *No more a stranger or a guest,*
> *But Master of this home.*

"Oh," you say. "That is what I want. I want an *abiding* call, something that will last. I do not want a religion that will wash out, but a fast-color religion." Well, that is the kind of call Christ gives. His ministers cannot give it, but when Christ speaks, He speaks with power and says, "Zacchaeus, make haste and come down, for today I must stay at your house."

VII. There is one thing, however, I cannot forget, and that is that it was a *necessary* call. Just read it over again. "Zacchaeus, make haste and come down, for today I must stay at your house." It was not a thing that He might do or might not do; it was a necessary call. The salvation of a sinner is as much a matter of necessity with God as the fulfillment of His covenant that the rain will no more drown the world. The salvation of every blood-bought child of God is a necessary thing for three reasons: because it is God's *purpose*, because it is Christ's *purchase*, and because it is God's *promise*. It is necessary that the child of God should be saved. Some divines think it is very wrong to lay stress on the word *must*, especially in that passage where it is said, "He must go through Samaria."

"Why," they say, "He must needs go through Samaria because there was no other way He could go, and therefore He was forced to go that way." Yes, gentlemen, we reply, no doubt. But then there might have been another way. Providence made it so that He must go through Samaria and that Samaria should lie in the route He had chosen.

"He *must* needs go through Samaria" (John 4:4 kjv, emphasis added). Providence directed man to build Samaria directly in the road, and grace constrained the Savior to move in that direction. It was not, "Come down, Zacchaeus, because I *may* abide at your house," but "I *must*." The Savior felt a strong necessity—just as much a necessity as there is that man should die; as strong a necessity as there is that the sun should give us light by day and the moon by night; just as much a necessity is there that every blood-bought child of God will be saved.

> *The salvation of a sinner is as much a matter of necessity with God as the fulfillment of His covenant that the rain will no more drown the world. The salvation of every blood-bought child of God is a necessary thing.*

"Today I must stay at your house." And oh, when the Lord comes to this, that He *must*, then He *will*. What a thing it is with the poor sinner, then, at other times we ask, "Shall I let Him in at all? There is a stranger at the door. He is knocking now, and He has knocked before; will I let Him in?" But this time it is, "*I must stay at your* house." There was no knocking at the door, but smash went the door into atoms! And in He walked: "I must, I shall, I will—I care not for your protecting your vileness, your unbelief. I must, I will—I must stay at your house."

"Ah," says one, "I do not believe God would ever make me to believe as you believe or become a Christian at all." Ah, but if He will but say, "Today I must stay at your house," there will be no resistance in you. There are some of you who would scorn the very idea of being a canting Methodist. "What, sir? Do you suppose I would ever turn into one of your religious people?" No, my friend, I don't *suppose* it. I *know* it for a certainty. If God says, "I must," there is no standing against it. Let Him say, "Must," and it must be.

I will just tell you an anecdote proving this. A father was about sending his son to college, but as he knew the influence to which he would be exposed, he was not without a deep and anxious solicitude for the spiritual and eternal welfare of his favorite child. Fearing lest the principles of Christian faith that he had endeavored to instill into his mind would be rudely assailed, but trusting in the efficacy of that Word that is quick and powerful, he purchased, unknown to his son, an elegant copy of the Bible and deposited it at the bottom of his trunk.

The young man entered upon his college career. The restraints of a pious education were soon broken off, and he proceeded from speculation to doubts and from doubts to a denial of the reality of religion. After having become in his own estimation wiser than his father, he discovered one day while rummaging through his trunk, with great surprise and indignation, the sacred deposit. He took it out, and while deliberating on the manner in which he should treat it, he determined that he would use it as waste paper on which to wipe his razor while shaving. Accordingly, every time he went to shave, he tore out a leaf or two of the Holy Book and thus used it till nearly half the volume was destroyed.

But while he was committing this outrage upon the Sacred Book, a text now and then met his eye and was carried like a barbed arrow to his heart. At length he heard a sermon that discovered to him his own character and his exposure to the wrath of God. It riveted upon his mind the impression that he had received from the last torn leaf of the blessed yet insulted volume. Had worlds been at his disposal, he would freely have given them all, could they have availed, in enabling him to undo what he had done. At length he found forgiveness at the foot of the cross. The torn leaves of that sacred volume brought healing to his soul—for they led him to repose on the mercy of God, which is sufficient for the chief of sinners.

I tell you there is not a reprobate walking the streets and defiling the air with his blasphemies. There is not a creature abandoned so as to be well-nigh as bad as Satan himself—if he is a child of life—who is not within the reach of mercy. And if God says, "Today I must stay at your house," He then assuredly will.

Do you feel, my dear hearer, just now, something in your mind that seems to say you have held out against the gospel a long while, but today you can hold out no longer? Do you feel that a strong hand has got hold of you, and do you hear a voice saying, "Sinner, I must stay at your house. You have often scorned Me; you have often laughed at Me; you have often spit in the face of mercy and blasphemed me. But sinner, I must stay at your house. You banged the door yesterday in the missionary's face. You burned the tract; you laughed at the minister; you have cursed God's house; you have violated the Sabbath—but, sinner, I must stay at your house and I will"?

"What? Lord," you say, "abide at *my* house? Why, it is covered all over with iniquity. Abide in *my* house? Why, there is not a chair or a table but would cry out against me. Abide in *my* house? Why, the joists and beams and flooring would all rise up and tell You that I am not worthy to kiss the hem of Your garment. What? Lord, abide at *my* house?"

> *S*inner, we will know whether God calls you by this: If He calls, it will be an effectual call, not a call that you hear and then forget, but one that produces good works.

"Yes," says He, "I *must*. There is a strong necessity. My powerful love constrains Me, and whether you will let Me or not, I am determined to make you willing and you will let Me in."

Does not this surprise you, poor trembler, you who thought that mercy's day was gone and that the bell of your destruction had tolled your death knell? Oh, does not this surprise you, that Christ not only asks you to come to Him, but invites Himself to your table, and what is more, when you would put Him away, kindly says, "I must, I will come in?" Only think of Christ going after a sinner, crying after a sinner, begging a sinner to let Him save him—and that is just what Jesus does to His chosen ones.

The sinner runs away from Him, but free grace pursues him and says, "Sinner, come to Christ." And if our hearts are shut up, Christ puts His hand in at the door, and if we do not rise but repulse Him coldly, He says, "I must, I will come in." He weeps over us till His tears win us. He cries after us till His cries prevail and at last, in His own well-determined hour, He enters into our heart and there He dwells. "I must stay at your house," says Jesus.

VIII. And now, lastly, this call was an *effectual* one, for we see the fruits it brought forth. Open was Zacchaeus's door, spread was his table, generous was his heart, washed were his hands, unburdened was his conscience, joyful was his soul. "Here, Lord," says he, "the half of my goods I give to the poor. I daresay I have robbed them of half their property, and now I restore it. And if I have taken anything from anyone by false accusation, I will restore it to him fourfold." Away goes another portion of his property. Ah, Zacchaeus, you will go to bed tonight a great deal poorer than when you got up this morning, but infinitely richer, too! You may be poor, very poor, in this world's goods, compared with what you were when you first did climb that sycamore tree, but richer, infinitely richer, in heavenly treasure. Sinner, we will know whether God calls you by this: If *He* calls, it will be an *effectual* call, not a call that you hear and then forget, but one that produces good works. If God has called you this morning, down will go that drunken cup, up will go your prayers. If God has called you this morning, there will not be *one* shutter down today in your shop, but *all* and you will have a notice stuck up: "This house is closed on the Sabbath day and will not again on that day be opened."

Tomorrow there will be such and such worldly amusement—but if God has called you, you will not go. And if you have robbed anybody (and who knows but I may have a thief here), if God calls you, there will be a restoration of what you have stolen—you will give up all that you have—so that you will follow God with all your heart. We do not believe a man to be converted unless he does renounce the error of his ways—unless, practically, he is brought to know that Christ Himself is Master of his conscience and His law is his delight.

> *"Zacchaeus, make haste and come down, for today I must stay at your house."*
>
> *So he made haste and came down, and received Him joyfully. . . .*
>
> *Then Zacchaeus stood and said to the Lord, "Look, Lord, I give half of my goods to the poor; and if I have taken anything from anyone by false accusation, I restore fourfold."*
>
> *And Jesus said to him, "Today salvation has come to this house, because he also is a son of Abraham; for the Son of Man has come to seek and to save that which was lost." (Luke 19:5–10)*

Now, one or two lessons. *A lesson to the proud*: Come down, proud heart, come down! Mercy runs in valleys, but it goes not to the mountaintop. Come down, come down, lofty spirit! The lofty city—He lays it low even to the ground and then He builds it up. Again, a *lesson to the poor despairing soul*: I am glad to see you in God's house this morning—it is a good sign. I care not what you came for. You heard there was a strange kind of man that preached here, perhaps. Never mind about that. You are all quite as strange as he is. It is necessary that there should be strange men to gather in other strange men.

Now, I have a mass of people here. And if I might use a figure, I should compare you to a great heap of ashes. And mingled with that are a few steel filings. Now, my sermon, if it is attended with divine grace, will be a sort of magnet. It will not attract any of the ashes—they will keep just where they are—but it will draw out the steel filings. I have got a Zacchaeus there. There is a Mary up there. A John down there, a Sarah, or a William, or a Thomas there—God's chosen ones. They are steel filings in the congregation of ashes, and my gospel, the gospel of the blessed God, like a great magnet, draws them out of the heap.

There they come. There they come. Why? It is because there was a magnetic power between the gospel and their hearts. Ah, poor sinner, come to Jesus, believe His love, trust His mercy. If you have a *desire* to come, if you are forcing your way through the ashes to get to Christ, then it is because Christ is calling you. Oh, all of you who know yourselves to be sinners— every man, woman, and child of you—yes, you little children (for God has given me some of you to be my wages), do you feel yourselves sinners?

Then believe on Jesus and be saved. You have come here from curiosity, many of you. Oh, that you might be met with and saved. I am distressed for you lest you should sink into hell. Oh, listen to Christ while He speaks to you. Christ says, "Come down." This morning go home and humble yourselves in the sight of God. Go and confess your iniquities that you have sinned against Him. Go home and tell Him that you are a wretch, undone without His sovereign grace. Then look to Him, for rest assured He has first looked to you. You say, "Sir, oh, I am willing enough to be saved, but I am afraid He is not willing."

Stop! Stop! No more of that! Do you know that is part blasphemy? Not quite all. If you were not ignorant, I would tell you that it was full blasphemy. You cannot look to Christ before He has looked to you. If you are willing to be saved, He gave you that will. Believe on the Lord Jesus Christ and be baptized and you will be saved. I trust the Holy Spirit is calling you.

Young man up there, young man in the window, make haste! Come down! Old man sitting in these pews, come down! Merchant in yonder aisle, make haste. Matron and youth, not knowing Christ, oh, may He look at you! Old grandmother, hear the gracious call. And you, young lad, Christ may be looking at you. I trust He is, and saying to you, "Make haste and come down, for today I must stay at your house."

For Further Thought

1. *In Galatians 1:15, how was Paul called by God?*
2. *Read 2 Timothy 1:9. God's calling of His believers is according to what two things?*
3. *What did Peter and Andrew do when Jesus called them? What did James and John do? (See Matthew 4:18–22.)*

Final Perseverance
(Perseverance of the Saints)

For it is impossible for those who were once enlightened,
and have tasted the heavenly gift, and have become partakers
of the Holy Spirit, and have tasted the good word of God and
the powers of the age to come, if they fall away, to renew them
again to repentance, since they crucify again for themselves
the Son of God, and put Him to an open shame.
Hebrews 6:4–6

THERE are some spots in Europe that have been the scenes of frequent warfare, as, for instance, the kingdom of Belgium, which might be called the battlefield of Europe. War has raged over the whole of Europe, but in some unhappy spots, battle after battle has been fought. So there is scarce a passage of scripture that has not been disputed between the enemies of the truth of God and the upholders of it—but this passage with one or two others has been the special subject of attack. This is one of the texts that has been trod under the feet of controversy, and there are opinions upon it as adverse as the poles. Some assert that it means one thing and some declare that it means another. We think that some of them approach somewhat near the truth, but others of them desperately err from the mind of the Spirit.

We come to this passage ourselves with the intention to read it with the simplicity of a child and whatever we find therein to state it. And if it may not seem to agree with something we have up to now held, we are prepared to cast away every doctrine of our own rather than one passage of scripture. Looking at the scope of the whole passage, it appears to us that the apostle wished to push the disciples on. There is a tendency in the human mind to stop short of the heavenly mark. As soon as ever we have attained to the first principles of religion, have passed through baptism, and understand the resurrection of the dead, there is a tendency in us to sit still and to say, "I have passed from death to life. Here I may take my stand and rest."

The Christian life was intended not to be a sitting still, but a *race*, a perpetual *motion*. The apostle, therefore, endeavors to urge the disciples forward and make them run with diligence the heavenly race, looking to Jesus. He tells them that it is not enough to have on a certain day passed through a glorious change, to have experienced at a certain time a wonderful operation of the Spirit. Rather, he teaches them it is absolutely necessary that they should have the Spirit all their lives, that they should, as long as they live, be progressing in the truth of God. In order to make them persevere if possible, he shows them that if they do not, they must most certainly be lost, for there is no other salvation but that which God has already bestowed on them, and if that does not keep them, carry them forward, and present them spotless before God, there cannot be any other. He says it is impossible, if you are once enlightened and then fall away, that you should ever be renewed again to repentance.

We shall, this morning, answer one or two questions. The first question will be: Who are the people here spoken of? Are they true Christians or not? Second, what does "falling away" mean? And third, what is intended when it is asserted that it is impossible to renew them to repentance?

I. First, then, we answer the question, *Who are the people here spoken of?* If you read Dr. Gill, Dr. Owen, and almost all the eminent Calvinistic writers, they all assert that these persons are *not* Christians. They say that enough is said here to represent a man who is a Christian externally but not enough to give the portrait of a true believer. Now, it strikes me they would not have said this if they had not had some doctrine to uphold, for a child reading this passage would say that *the persons intended by it must be Christians*. If the Holy Spirit intended to describe Christians, I do not see that He could have used more explicit terms than there are here. How can a man be said to be enlightened, to taste of the heavenly gift, and to be made partaker of the Holy Spirit without being a child of God? With all deference to these learned doctors, and I admire and love them all, I humbly concede that they allowed their judgments to be a little warped when they said that.

And I think I will be able to show that none but true believers are here described. First, they are spoken of as having been once enlightened. This refers to the enlightening influence of God's Spirit, poured into the soul at the time of conviction, when man is enlightened with regard to his spiritual state. At this time he is made to see how evil and bitter a thing it is to sin against God, made to feel how utterly powerless he is to rise from the grave of his corruption—and is further enlightened to see, that by the deeds of the law will no flesh living be justified, and to behold Christ on the cross as the sinner's only hope.

The first work of grace is to enlighten the soul. By nature we are entirely dark. The Spirit, like a lamp, sheds light into the dark heart, revealing its corruption, displaying its sad state of destitution, and in due time, revealing also Jesus Christ, so that in His light we may see light. I cannot consider a man truly enlightened unless he is a child of God. Does not the term indicate a person taught of God? It is not the whole of Christian experience—but is it not a part?

> The Christian life was intended not to be a sitting still, but a race, a perpetual motion. The apostle, therefore, endeavors to urge the disciples forward and make them run with diligence the heavenly race, looking to Jesus.

Having enlightened us, as the text says, the next thing that God grants to us *is a taste of the heavenly gift*, by which we understand *the heavenly gift of salvation*, including the pardon of sin, justification by the imputed righteousness of Jesus Christ, regeneration by the Holy Spirit, and all those gifts and graces in which the earlier dawn of spiritual life conveys salvation. All true believers have tasted of the heavenly gift. It is not enough for a man to be enlightened. The light may glare upon his eyeballs, and yet he may die. He must *taste* as well as *see* that the Lord is good. It is not enough to see that I am corrupt; I must taste that Christ is able to remove my corruption. It is not enough for me to know that He is the only Savior; I must taste of His flesh and of His blood and have a vital union with Him.

We most certainly think that when a man has been enlightened and has had an experience of grace, he is a Christian. Whatever those great divines might hold, we cannot think that the Holy Spirit would describe an unregenerate man as having been enlightened and as having tasted of the heavenly gift. No, my brethren, if I have tasted of the heavenly gift, then that heavenly gift is mine. If I have had ever so short an experience of my

Savior's love, I am one of His. If He has brought me into the green pastures and made me taste of the still waters and the tender grass, I need not fear as to whether I am really a child of God.

I will venture to say there are some good Christian people here who have tasted the heavenly gift, who have never tasted the good Word of God.

Then the apostle gives a further description, a higher state of grace, which is *sanctification by participation of the Holy Spirit.* It is a peculiar privilege to believers, after their first tasting of the heavenly gift, to be made partakers of the Holy Spirit. He is an indwelling Spirit. He dwells in the hearts, souls, and minds of men. He makes this mortal flesh His home. He makes our soul His palace, and there He rests. We do assert (and we think on the authority of scripture), that no man can be a partaker of the Holy Spirit and yet be unregenerate. Where the Holy Spirit dwells, there must be life, and if I have participation with the Holy Spirit and fellowship with Him, then I may rest assured that the blood of the Savior has purchased my salvation. You need not fear, beloved—if you have the Holy Spirit, you have that which ensures your salvation. If you, by an inward communion, can participate in His Spirit, and if by a perpetual indwelling the Holy Spirit rests in you, you are not only a Christian, but also you have arrived at some maturity in and by grace. You have gone beyond mere enlightenment—you have passed from the bare taste—you have attained to a positive feast and a partaking of the Holy Spirit.

Lest there should be any mistake, however, about the persons being children of God, the apostle goes to a further stage of grace. They have *tasted the good Word of God.* Now I will venture to say there are some good Christian people here who have tasted the heavenly gift, who have never tasted the good Word of God. I mean by that, that they are really converted, have tasted the heavenly gift, but have not grown so strong in grace as to know the sweetness, the richness, and the fatness of the very Word that saved them. The Word has saved them, but they have not come yet to realize, love, and feed upon the Word as many others have.

It is one thing for God to work a work of grace in the soul; it is quite another thing for God to show us that work. It is one thing for the Word to work in us; it is another thing for us really and habitually to relish, taste, and rejoice in that Word. Some of my hearers are true Christians, but they have not got to that stage wherein they can love election and suck it down as a sweet morsel. They have not got wherein they can take the great doctrines of grace and feed upon them. But these people had. They had tasted the good Word of God as well as received the good gift—they had attained to such a state that they had loved the Word, had tasted and feasted upon it. It was the man of their right hand. They had counted it sweeter than honey, yes, sweeter than the droppings of the honeycomb. They had tasted the good Word of God. I say again, if these people are not believers, who are?

And they had gone further still. They had attained the summit of piety. They had received *"the powers of the age to come"*—not miraculous gifts that are denied us in these days, but all those powers with which the Holy Spirit endows a Christian. And what are they? Why, there is the power of *faith*, which commands even the heavens themselves to rain and they rain, or stop the bottles of heaven that they rain not. There is the power of *prayer*, which puts a ladder between earth and heaven and bids angels walk up and down, to convey our wants to God and bring down blessings from above. There is the *power* with which God girds His servant when he speaks by inspiration. This enables him to instruct others and lead them to Jesus. And whatever other powers there may be—the power of holding communion with God, or the power of patiently waiting for the Son of man—they were possessed by these individuals.

They were not simply children, but they were men. They were not merely alive, but they were entitled with power. They were men whose muscles were firmly set, whose bones were strong. They had become giants in grace and had received not only the light, but the power also of the world to come. These, we say, whatever the meaning of the text must have been, were beyond a doubt none other than true and real Christians.

II. And now we answer the second question: *What is meant by falling away?* We must remind our friends that there is a vast distinction between *falling away* and *falling*. It is nowhere said in scripture that if a man fall he cannot be renewed. On the contrary, "a righteous man may fall seven times and rise again" (Prov. 24:16). And however many times the child of God does fall, the Lord still holds the righteous. Yes, when our bones are broken, He binds up our bones again and sets us once more upon a rock. He says, "Return, O backsliding children, for I am married to you" (Jer. 3:14), and if the Christian does backslide ever so far, He still calls His children back again.

Falling is not *falling away*. Let me explain the difference. A man who falls may behave just like a man who falls away, and yet there is a great distinction between the two. I can use no better illustration than the distinction between fainting and dying. There lies a young creature. She can scarcely breathe. She cannot herself lift up her hand, and if lifted up by anyone else, it falls. She is cold and stiff; she is faint but not dead. There is another one, just as cold and stiff as she is, but there is this difference: She *is* dead. The Christian may faint and may fall down in a faint, too. And some may pick him up and say he is dead—but he is not. If he falls, God will lift him up again, but if he falls away, God Himself cannot save him. For it is impossible, if the righteous fall away, "to renew them again to repentance."

Moreover, to fall away is not to commit sin under a temporary surprise and temptation. Abraham goes to Egypt. He is afraid that his wife will be taken away from him, and he says, "She is my sister." That was a sin under a temporary surprise; a sin of which, by and by he repented and God forgave him. Now that is *falling*, but it is not *falling away*. Even Noah might commit a sin that has degraded his memory even till now and will disgrace it to the latest time. But, doubtless, Noah repented and was saved by sovereign grace. Noah *fell*, but Noah did not fall *away*. A Christian may go astray once and speedily return again—and though it is a sad, woeful, and evil thing to be surprised into a sin—yet there is a great difference between this and the sin that would be occasioned by a total falling away from grace.

> *Beloved, you may even have denied Christ by open profession, and yet if you repent, there is mercy for you. Christ has not cast you away. You will repent yet. You have not fallen away.*

Nor can a man who commits a sin that is not exactly a surprise be said to fall away. I believe that some Christian men (God forbid that we should say much of this! Let us cover the nakedness of our brother with a cloak) have, for a period of time, wandered into sin yet have not positively fallen away. There is that black case of David—a case that has puzzled thousands. Certainly for some months David lived without making a public confession of his sin, but doubtless he had achings of heart, for grace had not ceased its work. There was a spark among the ashes that Nathan stirred up that showed that David was not dead, or else the match that the prophet applied would not have caught light so readily. And so, beloved, you may have wandered into sin for a time and gone far from God, yet you are not the character here described, concerning whom it is said that it is impossible you should be saved. Wanderer though you are, you are your Father's son still, and mercy cries, "Repent, repent! Return to your first husband, for then it was better with you than it is now. Return, O wanderer, return."

Again, falling away is not even a giving up of profession. Some will say, "Now there is So-and-So. He used to make a profession of Christianity, and now he denies it; and what is worse, he dares to curse and swear and says that he never knew Christ at all. Surely *he* must be fallen away." My friend, he has fallen, fallen fearfully and fallen woefully, but I remember a case in scripture of a man who denied his Lord and Master before His own face! You remember his name. He is an old friend of yours, our friend Simon Peter! He denied Him with oaths and curses and said, "I do not know Him" (Luke 22:57). And yet Jesus looked on Simon. He had *fallen*, but he had not *fallen away*, because only two or three days after that, there was Peter at the tomb of his Master running there to meet his Lord, to be one of the first to find Him risen!

Beloved, you may even have denied Christ by open profession, and yet if you repent, there is mercy for you. Christ has not cast you away. You will repent yet. You have not fallen away. If you had, I might not preach to you, for it is impossible for those who have fallen away to be renewed again to repentance.

But someone says, "What is falling away?" Well, *there never has been a case of it yet*, and therefore I cannot describe it from observation. But I will tell you what I suppose it is. To fall away would be for the Holy Spirit entirely to go out of a man and for His grace entirely to *cease*. That is, to fall away would not mean to lie dormant, but to cease to be, so that God who had begun a good work would leave off doing it entirely, take His hand completely and entirely away, and say, "There, man! I have half saved you; now I will damn you." That is what falling away is.

It is not to sin temporarily. A child may sin against his father and still be alive. Falling away is like cutting the child's head off clean. Not falling merely, for then our Father could pick us up, but being dashed down a precipice where we are lost forever. Falling away would involve God's grace changing its living nature, God's immutability becoming variable, God's faithfulness becoming changeable, and God Himself being undeified. Falling away would necessitate all these things.

III. Now comes the third question. Suppose a child of God *could* fall away and grace could cease in a man's heart. Paul said *it is impossible for him to be renewed*. What did the apostle mean? One eminent commentator says he meant that it would be very hard. It would be very hard indeed for a man who fell away to be saved. But we reply, "My dear friend, it does not say anything about its being very hard; it says it is *impossible*; and we like to read our Bible just as a child would read it." It says it is impossible, and we say that it would be utterly *impossible*. If such a case as is supposed were to happen, *impossible* for man and also *impossible* for God, for God has purposed that He never will grant a second salvation to save those whom the first salvation has failed to deliver.

I think, however, I hear someone say, "It seems to me that it is possible for some such to fall away, because it says, 'It is impossible. . .if they fall away, to renew them again to repentance.'"

Well, my friend, I will grant you your theory for a moment. You are a good Christian this morning. Let us apply it to yourself and see how you will like it. You have believed in Christ and committed your soul to God, and you think that in some unlucky hour you may fall entirely away. Mark you, if you come to me and tell me that you have fallen away, how would you like me to say to you, "My friend, you are as much damned as the devil in hell! For it is impossible to renew you to repentance"?

"Oh, no, sir," you would say. "I will repent again and join the church." That is just the Arminian theory all over, but it is not in God's scripture. If you once fall away, you are as damned as any man who suffers in the gulf forever. And yet we have heard a man talk about people being converted three, four, and five times, and regenerated over and over again. I remember a good man (I suppose he was) pointing to a man who was walking along the street and saying, "That man has been born again three times, to my certain knowledge" (I could mention the name of the individual, but I refrain from doing so), "and I believe he will fall again," said he. "He is so much addicted to drinking that I do not believe the grace of God will do anything for him unless he becomes a teetotaler."

Now, such men cannot read the Bible, because in case their members do positively fall away, here it is stated as a positive fact that it is impossible to renew them again to repentance. But I ask my Arminian friend, does he not believe that as long as there is life there is hope? "Yes," he says:

While the lamp holds out to burn,
The vilest sinner may return.

Well, it is not very consistent to say this and in the very next breath say that there are some people who fall away and consequently fall into such a condition that they cannot be saved. I want to know how you make these two things fit each other. I want you to make these two doctrines agree, and until some enterprising individual will bring the north pole and set it on the top of the south, I cannot tell how you will accomplish it. The fact is that you are quite right in saying, "While there is life there is hope," but you are wrong in saying that any individual ever did fall into such a condition that it was impossible for him to be saved.

We come now to do two things: first, to prove the doctrine that if a Christian falls away, he cannot be saved, and second, to improve the doctrine or to show its use.

I. Now I am going to prove the doctrine that if a Christian *fall away*—not *fall*, for you understand how I have explained that—and ceases to be a child of God, and if grace dies out in his heart, he is then beyond the possibility of salvation and it is impossible for him ever to be renewed. Let me show you why. First, it is utterly impossible if you consider the work that has already broken down. When men have built bridges across streams, if they have been built of the strongest material and in the most excellent manner and yet the foundation has been found so bad that none will stand, what do they say? "Why, we have already tried the best that engineering or architecture has taught us; the best has already failed. We know nothing that can exceed what has been tried. And we do, therefore, feel that there remains no possibility of ever bridging that stream or ever running a line of railroad across this bog or this morass, for we have already tried what is acknowledged to be the best scheme."

As the apostle says, "These people have been once enlightened. They have had once the influence of the Holy Spirit revealing to them their sin. What now remains to be tried? They have been once convicted. Is there anything superior to conviction? Does the Bible promise that the poor sinner will have anything over and above the conviction of his sin to make him sensible of it? Is there anything more powerful than the sword of the Spirit? If it has not pierced the man's heart, is there anything else that will do it? Here is a man who has been under the hammer of God's law but who has not broken his heart. Can you find anything stronger? The lamp of God's Spirit has already lit up the caverns of his soul—if that is not sufficient, where will you borrow another?

Ask the sun—has he a lamp brighter than the illumination of the Spirit? Ask the stars—have they a light more brilliant than the light of the Holy Spirit? Creation answers no. If that fails, then there is nothing else. These people, moreover, had tasted the heavenly gift—and though they had been pardoned and justified, yet pardon through Christ and justification were not enough (on this supposition) to save them. How else can they be saved? God has cast them away. After He has failed in saving them by these, what else can deliver them? Already they have tasted of the heavenly gift; is there a greater mercy for them? Is there a brighter dress than the robe of Christ's righteousness? Is there a more efficacious bath than that "fountain filled with blood"? No. All the earth echoes, "No." If the one has failed, what else does there remain?

These persons, too, have been partakers of the Holy Spirit. If that fails, what more can we give them? If, my hearer, the Holy Spirit dwells in your soul and that Holy Spirit does not sanctify you and keep you to the end, what else can be tried? Ask the blasphemer whether he knows a being or dares to suppose a being superior to the Holy Spirit! Is there a being greater than omnipotence? Is there a might greater than that which dwells in the believer's newborn heart? And if already the Holy Spirit has failed, O Heaven, tell us where we can find anything that can excel His might.

If that is ineffectual, what next is to be tried? These people, who had "tasted the good word of life," had loved the doctrines of grace. Those doctrines had entered into their souls and they had fed upon them. What new doctrines will be preached to them? Prophet of ages! Where will you find another system of divinity? Who will we have? Shall we raise Moses from the tomb? Shall we fetch up all the ancient seers and bid them prophesy? If, then, there is only one doctrine that is true and if these people have fallen away after receiving that, how can they be saved?

Again, these people, according to the text, have had "the powers of the age to come." They have had power to conquer sin, power in faith, power in prayer, power of communion. With what greater power will they be endowed? This has already failed—what next can be done? O you angels! Answer, what next? What other means remain? What else can avail, if already the great things of salvation have been defeated? What else will now be attempted? He had been once saved, yet it is supposed that he is lost. How then can he *now* be saved? Is there a supplementary salvation? Is there something that will overtop Christ and be a Christ where Jesus is defeated?

> *Is there anything more powerful than the sword of the Spirit? If it has not pierced the man's heart, is there anything else that will do it?*

And then the apostle says that the greatness of their sin that they would incur, if they did fall away, would put them beyond the bounds of mercy. Christ died, and by His death He made atonement for His own murderers. He made atonement for those sins that crucified Him once, but do we read that Christ will ever die for those who crucify Him twice? But the apostle tells us that if believers do fall away, they will "crucify again for themselves the Son of God and put Him to an open shame." Where then would be an atonement for that? He has died for me. What? Though the sins of the entire world were on my shoulders, still they only crucified Him once, and that one crucifixion has taken all those sins away. But if I crucified Him again, where would I find pardon? Could heavens, could earth, could Christ Himself with His heart full of love point me to another Christ? Show to me a second Calvary? Give me a second Gethsemane? Ah, no! The very guilt itself would put us beyond the pale of hope if we were to fall *away*!

Again, beloved, *think what it would necessitate to save such a man.* Christ has died for him once, yet he has fallen away and is lost. The Spirit has regenerated him once, and that regenerating work has been of no use. God has given him a new heart (I am only speaking, of course, on the supposition of the apostle). He has put His law in that heart, yet He has departed from him contrary to the promise that He should not. He has made him like a shining light, but he did not shine to the perfect day. He shone only to blackness. What next? There must be a second incarnation, a second Calvary, a second Holy Spirit, a second regeneration, a second justification, although the first was finished and complete. In fact, I know not what. It would necessitate the upsetting of the whole kingdom of nature and grace, and it would indeed be a world turned upside down, if after the gracious Savior failed, He were to attempt the work again.

If you read the seventh and eighth verses, you will see that *the apostle calls nature in to his assistance.* He says, "For the earth which drinks in the rain that often comes upon it, and bears herbs useful for those by whom it is cultivated, receives blessing from God; but if it bears thorns and briers, it is rejected and near to being cursed, whose end is to be burned" (Heb. 6:7–8). Look! There is a field. The rain comes on it, and it brings forth good fruit. Well, then, there is God's blessing on it. But there is, according to your supposition, another field on that the same rain descends, that the same dew moistens. It has been plowed and harrowed as well as the other, and the farmer has exercised all his craft upon it and yet it is not fertile.

Well, if the rain of heaven did not fertilize it, what next? Already all the arts of agriculture have been tried, every implement has been worn out on its surface, and yet it has been of no avail. What next? There remains nothing but that it will be burned and cursed, given up like the desert of Sahara and resigned to destruction. So, my hearer, could it be possible that grace could work in you and then not affect your salvation? That the influence of divine grace could come down, like rain from heaven and yet return to God void? There could not be any hope for you, for you would be "near to being cursed," and your end would be "to be burned."

There is one idea that has occurred to us. It has struck us as a singular thing that our friends should hold that men can be converted, made into new creatures, then fall away and be converted again. I am an old creature by nature. God creates me into a new thing. He makes me a new creature. I cannot go back into an old creature, for I cannot be uncreated. But suppose that new creatureship of mine is not good enough to carry me to heaven. What is to come after that? Must there be something above a new creature, a new, new creature? Really, my friends, we have got into the country of Dreamland, but we were forced to follow our opponents into that region of absurdity, for we do not know how else to deal with them.

And one thought more. There is nothing in scripture that teaches us that there is any salvation, save the one salvation of Jesus Christ, that tells us of any other power surpassing the power of the Holy Spirit. These things have already been tried on the man, yet according to the supposition, they have failed, for he has fallen away. Now God has never revealed a supplementary salvation for men on whom one salvation has had no effect. And until we are pointed to one scripture that declares this, we will still maintain that the doctrine of the text is this: If grace is ineffectual, if grace does not keep a man, then there is nothing left but that he must be damned. And what is that but to say, only going a little all around, that grace *will do it*? So these words, instead of militating *against* the Calvinistic doctrine of final perseverance, form one of the firmest *proofs* of it that could be afforded.

And now, lastly, we come to *clarify this doctrine*. If Christians can fall away and cease to be Christians, they cannot be renewed again to repentance. "But," says one, "you say they cannot fall away. What is the use of putting this 'if' in like a bugbear to frighten children or like a ghost that can have no existence?" My learned friend, "Who are you to reply against God?" (Rom. 9:20). If God has put it in, He has put it in for wise reasons and for excellent purposes. Let me show you why.

> There is nothing in scripture that teaches us that there is any salvation, save the one salvation of Jesus Christ, that tells us of any other power surpassing the power of the Holy Spirit.

First, O Christian, it is put in to keep you from stumbling away. God preserves His children from falling away. But He keeps them by the use of means, and one of these is the *terror* of the law, showing them what would happen if they were to fall away. There is a deep precipice—what is the best way to keep anyone from going down there? Why, to tell him that if he did he would inevitably be dashed to pieces. In some old castle there is a deep cellar where there is a vast amount of fixed air and gas that would kill anybody who went down. What does the guide say?

"If you go down you will never come up alive." Who thinks of going down? The very fact of the guide telling us what the consequences would be, keeps us from it. Our friend puts away from us a cup of arsenic; he does not want us to drink it, but he says, "If you drink it, it will kill you." Does he suppose for a moment that we should drink it? No. He tells us the consequence, and he is sure we will not do it. So God says, "My child, if you fall over this precipice, you will be dashed to pieces." What does the child do? He says, "Father, keep me. Hold me up, and I will be safe." It leads the believer to greater dependence on God, to a holy fear and caution, because he knows that if he were to fall away, he could not be renewed. And he stands far away from that great gulf because he knows that if he were to fall into it, there would be no salvation for him.

It is calculated to excite *fear*, and this *holy fear* keeps the Christian from falling. If I thought as the Arminian thinks, that I might fall away and then return again, I should pretty often fall away. For sinful flesh and blood would think it very nice to fall away and be a sinner—go and see the play at the theater or get drunk—and then come back to the church and be received again as a dear brother who had fallen away for a little while. No doubt the minister would say, "Our brother Charles is a little unstable at times." A little unstable? He does not know anything about *grace*—for grace engenders a *holy caution*, because we feel that if we were not preserved by divine power, we should perish.

We tell our friend to put oil in his lamp that it may continue to burn! Does that imply that it will be allowed to go out? No, God will give him oil to pour into the lamp continually. Like John Bunyan's figure, there was a fire, and he saw a man pouring water upon it. "Now," says the Preacher, "don't you see that fire would go out, that water is calculated to put it out, and if it does, it will never be lighted again?" But God does not permit that! For there is a man *behind* the wall who is pouring oil on the fire—and we have cause for gratitude in the fact that if the oil were not put in by a heavenly hand, we should inevitably be driven to destruction. Take care then, Christian, for this is a caution.

II. Another reason for this "if" is that it is to excite our gratitude. Suppose you say to your little boy, "Don't you know, Tommy, that if I were not to give you your dinner and your supper you would die? There is nobody else to give you dinner and supper." What then? The child does not *think* that you are not going to give him his dinner and supper—he *knows* you will—and he is grateful to you for them. The chemist tells us that if there were no oxygen mixed with the air, animals would die. Do you suppose that there will be no oxygen and therefore we will die? No, he only teaches you the great wisdom of God, in having mixed the gases in their proper proportions.

Says one of the old astronomers, "There is great wisdom in God, that He has put the sun exactly at a right distance—not so far away that we should be frozen to death and not so near that we should be scorched." He says, "If the sun were a million miles nearer to us, we should be scorched to death." Does the man suppose that the sun will be a million miles nearer, and therefore, we will be scorched to death? He says, "If the sun were a million miles farther off, we should be frozen to death." Does he mean that the sun will be a million miles farther off, and therefore we will be frozen to death? Not at all. Yet it is quite a rational way of speaking to show us how grateful we should be to God. So says the apostle. Christian, if you should fall away and you could never be renewed to repentance, then it is by His grace that He keeps you.

> *See a stone that hangs in air,*
> *See a spark in ocean live:*
> *Kept alive with death so near,*
> *I to God the glory give.*

There is a cup of sin that would damn your soul, O Christian. Oh, what grace is that which holds your arm and will not let you drink it? There you are, at this hour, like the bird catcher of St. Kilda—you are being drawn to heaven by a single rope. If that hand that holds you lets you go, if that rope that grasps you breaks, you will be dashed on the rocks of damnation. Lift up your heart to God, then, and bless Him that His arm is not wearied and is never shortened that it cannot save. Lord Kenmure, when he was dying, said to Rutherford, "Man! My name is written on Christ's hand, and I see it! That is bold talk, man, but I see it!" Then, if that is the case, His hand must be severed from His body before my name can be taken from Him. And if it is engraved on His heart, His heart must be rent out before they can rend my name out.

Hold on, then, and trust, believer! You have an anchor of the soul both sure and steadfast that enters within the veil. The winds are bellowing, the tempests howling; should the cable slip or your anchor break, you are lost. See those rocks on which myriads are driving? You are wrecked there if grace leaves you. See those depths in which the skeletons of sailors sleep? You are there if that anchor fails you. It would be impossible to moor you again, if once that anchor broke, for there are no other anchors. There can be no other salvation—if that one fails you, it is impossible that you ever should be saved. Therefore thank God that you have an Anchor that cannot fail, and then loudly sing:

> *How can I sink with such a prop,*
> *As my eternal God*
> *Who bears the earth's huge pillars up,*
> *And spreads the heavens abroad?*
>
> *How can I die, when Jesus lives*
> *Who rose and left the dead?*
> *Pardon and grace my soul receives*
> *From my exalted head.*

FOR FURTHER THOUGHT

1. *What are four things listed in Hebrews 6:4–5 that God grants to us when we become believers?*
2. *First Corinthians 5:1 tells of a certain case of immorality in the church, and verse 5 tells of the discipline given to the immoral one. What does 2 Corinthians 2:6–8 say was the eventual outcome of this?*
3. *Second Corinthians 2:8 describes the church's attitude toward an immoral man. What is that attitude?*

SELECTIONS FROM JOHN PLOUGHMAN'S TALKS,
OR PLAIN ADVICE FOR PLAIN PEOPLE

CONTENTS

PREFACE

IN *John Ploughman's Talks*, I have written for plowmen and common people. Hence, refined taste and dainty words have been discarded for strong proverbial expressions and homely phrases. I have aimed my blows at the vices of the many and tried to inculcate those moral virtues without which men are degraded. Much that needs to be said to the toiling masses would not well suit the pulpit and the Sabbath; these lowly pages may teach thrift and industry all the days of the week in the cottage and the workshop; and if some learn these lessons, I shall not repent the adoption of a rustic style.

Ploughman is a name I may justly claim. Every minister has put his hand to the plow; and it is his business to break up the fallow ground. That I have written in a semi-humorous vein needs no apology, since thereby sound moral teaching has gained a hearing from at least three hundred thousand persons. There is no particular virtue in being seriously unreadable.

C. H. Spurgeon

1

To the Idle

IT is of no more use to give advice to the idle than to pour water into a sieve; and as to improving them, one might as well try to fatten a greyhound. Yet, as the Old Book tells us to cast our bread upon the waters, we will cast a hard crust or two upon these stagnant ponds, for there will be this comfort about it: If lazy fellows grow no better, we shall be none the worse for having warned them, for when we sow good sense, the basket gets none the emptier. We have a stiff bit of soil to plow when we chide with sluggards, and the crop will be of the smallest. But if none but good land were farmed, plowmen would be out of work, so we will put the plow into the furrow. Idle men are common enough and grow without planting, but the quantity of wit among seven acres of them would never pay for raking. Nothing is needed to prove this but their name and character; if they were not fools, they would be idlers; and though Solomon says, "The sluggard is wiser in his own conceit than seven men that can render a reason," yet in the eyes of everyone else, his folly is as plain as the sun in the sky. If I hit hard while speaking to them, it is because I know they can bear it; for if I had them down on the floor of the old barn, I might thresh many a day before I could get them out of the straw, and even the steam thresher could not do it. It would kill them first, for laziness is in some people's bones and will show itself in their idle flesh, do what you will with them.

Well, then, first and foremost, it strikes me that lazy people ought to have a large looking glass hung up, where they are bound to see themselves in it. For sure, if their eyes are at all like mine, they would never bear to look at themselves long or often. The ugliest sight in the world is one of those thoroughbred loafers who would hardly hold up his basin if it were to rain with porridge, and for certain would never hold up a bigger pot than he wanted filled for himself. Perhaps, if the shower should turn to beer, he might wake himself up a bit, but he would make up for it afterward.

This is the slothful man in the Proverbs who "buries his hand in the bowl; it wearies him to bring it back to his mouth" (26:15). I say that men the like of this ought to be served like the drones that the bees drive out of the hives. Every man ought to have patience and pity for poverty; but for laziness, a long whip or a turn at the treadmill might be better. This would be a healthy purgative for all sluggards, but there is no chance of some of them getting their full dose of this medicine, for they were born with silver spoons in their mouths and, like spoons, will scarce stir their own tea unless somebody lends them a hand. They are, as the old proverb says, "as lazy as Ludham's dog that leaned his head against the wall to bark," and like lazy sheep, it is too much trouble for them to carry their own wool. If they could see themselves, it might by chance do them a world of good, but perhaps it would be too much trouble for them to open their eyes even if the glass were hung for them.

> *he sluggard is wiser in his own conceit than seven men that can render a reason," yet in the eyes of everyone else, his folly is as plain as the sun in the sky.*

Everything in the world is of some use, but it would puzzle a doctor of divinity or a philosopher or the wisest owl in our steeple to tell the good of idleness. That seems to me to be an ill wind that blows nobody any good—a sort of mud that breeds no eels, a dirty ditch that would not feed a frog. Sift a sluggard grain by grain, and you'll find him all chaff. I have heard men say that it is better to do nothing than to do mischief, but I am not even sure of that. That saying glitters well, but I don't believe it's gold. I grudge laziness even that pinch of praise; I say it is bad and bad altogether. For look ye, a man doing mischief is a sparrow picking the corn, but a lazy man is a sparrow sitting on a nest full of eggs that will all turn to sparrows before long and do a world of hurt.

Don't tell me—I'm sure of it—that the rankest weeds on earth don't grow in the minds of those who are busy at wickedness but in foul concerns of idle men's imaginations, where the devil can hide away unseen like an old serpent as he is. I don't like our boys to be in mischief, but I would sooner see them up to their necks in the mud in their larks than sauntering about with nothing to do. If the evil of doing nothing seems to be less today, you will find it to be greater tomorrow. The devil is putting coals on the fire, and so the fire does not blaze; but depend upon it, it will be a bigger fire in the end. Idle people, you had need be your own trumpeters, for no one else can find any good in you to praise. I'd sooner see you through a telescope than anything else, for I suppose you would then be a long way off; but the biggest pair of spectacles in the parish could not see anything in you worth talking about. Moles and rats and weasels, there is something to be said for, though there's a pretty sight of them nailed up on our old barn; but as for you, you'll be of use in the grave and help to make a fat churchyard, but no better song can I sing in your favor than this verse, as the parish clerk said, "gall of my own composing":

> A good for nothing lazy lout,
> Wicked within and ragged without
> Who can bear to have him about?
> Turn him out! Turn him out!

"As vinegar to the teeth, and as smoke to the eyes," so is the sluggard to every man who is spending his sweat to earn an honest living, while these fellows let the grass grow up to their ankles and stand cluttering the ground, as the Bible says.

A man who wastes his time and his strength in sloth offers himself to be a target for the devil, who is a wonderfully good rifleman and will riddle the idler with his shots: In other words, idle men tempt the devil to tempt them. He who plays when he should work has an evil spirit to be his playmate; and he who neither works nor plays is a workshop for Satan. If the devil catches a man idling, he will set him to work, find him tools, and before long pay him wages. Is not this where the drunkenness comes from that fills our towns and villages with misery? Idleness is the key of beggary and the root of all evil. Fellows have two stomachs for eating and drinking when they have no stomach for work. That little hole just under the nose swallows up in idle hours the money that should put clothes on the children's backs and bread on the cottage table. We have God's word that "the drunkard and the glutton shall come to poverty"; and to show the connection between them, it is said in the same verse, "and drowsiness shall clothe a man with rags." I know it as well as I know that moss grows on old thatch and that drunken, loose habits grow out of lazy hours. I like leisure when I can get it, but that's quite another thing; that's cheese, and the other is chalk. Idle folks never know what leisure means; they are always in a hurry and a mess, and by neglecting to work in the proper time, they always have a lot to do. Lolling about hour after hour with nothing to do is just making holes in the hedge to let the pigs through; and they will come through—make no mistake—and the rooting they will do nobody knows except those who have to look after the garden. The Lord Jesus tells us Himself that while men slept the enemy sowed the tares. That hits the nail on the head, for it is by the door of sluggishness that evil enters the heart more often, it seems to me, than by any other. Our old minister used to say, "A sluggard is fine raw material for the devil; he can make anything he likes out of him, from a thief right up to a murderer." I'm not the only one who condemns the idle, for once when I was going to give our minister a pretty long list of the sins of one of our people that he was asking after, I began with "She's dreadfully lazy."

"That's enough," said the old gentleman. "All sorts of sins are in that one; that's the sign by which to know a full-fledged sinner."

> The Lord Jesus tells us Himself that while men slept the enemy sowed the tares. That hits the nail on the head, for it is by the door of sluggishness that evil enters the heart more often, it seems to me, than by any other.

My advice to my boys has been, "Get out of the sluggard's way, or you may catch his disease and never get rid of it." I am always afraid of their learning the ways of the idle and am very watchful to nip anything of the sort in the bud, for you know it is best to kill the lion while it is a cub. Sure enough our children have all our evil nature about them, for you can see it growing of itself like weeds in a garden. Who can bring a clean thing out of the unclean? A wild goose never lays a tame egg. Our boys will be off to the green with the ne'er-do-wells unless we make it greener still at home for them and train them up to hate the company of the slothful. Never let them go to the "Rose and Crown." Let them learn to earn a crown while they are young and grow the roses in their father's garden at home. Bring them up bees, and they will not be drones.

There is much talk about bad masters and mistresses nowadays. I daresay that there is a good deal in it, for there is bad of all sorts now as there always was. Another time, if I am allowed, I will have a say about that matter, but I am sure there is plenty of room for complaint against some among the working people, too, especially upon this matter of slothfulness. You know we are obliged to plow with such cattle as we have found for us, but when I am set to work with some men, I'd as soon drive a team of snails or go out rabbit hunting with a dead ferret. Why, you might sooner get blood out of a gatepost or juice out of a cork than work out of some of them, yet they are always talking about their rights. I wish they would give an eye to their own wrongs and not lean on the plow handles. Lazy lie-a-beds are not working men at all, any more than pigs are bullocks or thistles apple trees. All are not hunters who wear red coats, and all are not working men who call themselves so. I wonder sometimes that some of our employers keep so many cats that catch no mice. I would as soon drop my halfpence down a well as pay some people for pretending to work. It only irritates you and makes your flesh crawl to see them all day creeping over a cabbage leaf. Live and let live, say I, but I don't include sluggards in that license. "If anyone will not work, neither shall he eat" (2 Thess. 3:10).

Here, perhaps, is the proper place to say that some of the higher classes, as they are called, set a shamefully bad example in this respect: Our great folks are some of them quite as lazy as they are rich, and often more so; the big dormice sleep as long and as sound as the little ones. Many a parson buys or hires a sermon so that he may save himself the trouble of thinking. Is not this abominable laziness? They sneer at the ranters; but there is not a ranter in the kingdom who would not be ashamed to stand up and read somebody else's sermon as if it were his. Many of our squires have nothing to do but to part their hair in the middle; and many of the London grandees, ladies and gentlemen alike, as I am told, have no better work than killing time. Now, they say the higher a monkey climbs, the more his tail is seen; and so, the greater these people are, the more their idleness is noticed, and the more they ought to be ashamed of it. I don't say they ought to plow, but I do say they ought to do something for the state besides being like the caterpillars on the cabbage, eating up the good things; or like the butterflies, showing themselves off but making no honey. I cannot be angry with these people somehow, for I pity them when I think of the stupid rules of fashion they are forced to mind and the vanity in which they drag out their days. I'd sooner by half bend my back double with hard work than be a jack-a-dandy with nothing to do but to look in the mirror and see in it a fellow who never put a single potato into the nation's pot but took a good many out. Let me drop on these Surrey hills, worn out like my master's old brown mare, sooner than eat bread and cheese and never earn it; better to die an honorable death than live a good-for-nothing life. It would be better to get into my coffin than be dead but alive, a man whose life is a blank.

However, it is not much ease that lazy people get by all their scheming, for they always take the most pains in the end. They will not mend the thatch, and so they have to build a new cottage; they will not put the horse in the cart, and so they have to drag it themselves. If they were wise, they would do their work well, so as to save doing it twice, and tug hard while they are in harness, so as to get the work out of the way. My advice is, if you don't like hard work, just pitch into it, settle it off, and have your turn at rest.

> It is not much ease that lazy people get by all their scheming, for they always take the most pains in the end. They will not mend the thatch, and so they have to build a new cottage.

I wish all religious people would take this matter under their consideration, for some professors are amazingly lazy and make sad work for the tongues of the wicked. I think a godly plowman ought to be the best man in the field and let no team beat him. When we are at work, we ought to be at it and not stop the plow to talk, even though the talk may be about religion. For then we not only rob our employers of our own time, but of the time of the horses, too. I used to hear people say, "Never stop the plow to catch a mouse," and it's quite as silly to stop for idle chat; besides, the man who loiters when the master is away is an eye-server, which, I take it, is the very opposite of a Christian. If some of the members at our meeting were a little spryer with their arms and legs when they are at labor and a little quieter with their tongues, they would say more for religion than they now do. The world says the greatest rogue is the pious rogue, and I'm sorry to say one of the greatest sluggards I know of is a professing man of the "Mr. Talkative" kind. His garden is so overgrown with weeds that I often feel half a mind to weed it for him, to save our meeting the shame he brings upon it: if he were a young lad, I'd talk to him about it and try to teach him better, but who can be a schoolmaster to a child of sixty years old? He is a regular thorn to our good minister, who is quite grieved about it and sometimes says he will go somewhere else because he cannot bear such conduct; but I tell him that wherever a man lives, he is sure to have one thornbush near his door, and it is a mercy if there are not two. However, I do wish that all Christians would be industrious, for religion never was designed to make us idle. Jesus was a great worker, and His disciples must not be afraid of hard work.

> I believe that when Paul plants and Apollos waters, God gives the increase, and I have no patience with those who throw the blame on God when it belongs to themselves.

As to serving the Lord with cold hearts and drowsy souls, there has been too much of it, and it causes religion to wither. Men ride stallions when they hunt for gain but snails when they are on the road to heaven. Preachers go on seesawing, droning, and prosing; and the people fall to yawning and folding their arms then say that God is withholding the blessing. Every sluggard, when he finds himself enlisted in the ragged regiment, blames his luck; and some churches have learned the same wicked trick. I believe that when Paul plants and Apollos waters, God gives the increase, and I have no patience with those who throw the blame on God when it belongs to themselves.

Now I have come to the end of my tether. I am afraid I have been beating a dead horse, but I have done my best, and a king can do no more. An ant can never make honey if it works its heart out, and I shall never put my thoughts so prettily together as some do, book-fashion, but truth is truth even when dressed in homespun, and so there is an end of my rigmarole.

For Further Thought

1. *In 2 Thessalonians 3:10–13, Paul advises against slothfulness. In verses 7–9 he gives an example of a person who is not slothful. Who is that person?*

2. *Three workers are mentioned in 1 Corinthians 3:6. John Ploughman says that the work of the first two is necessary for that of the third. Who is the third worker in this verse?*

2

ON RELIGIOUS GRUMBLERS

WHEN a man has a particularly empty head, he generally sets up for a great judge, especially in religion. None is so wise as the man who knows nothing. His ignorance is the mother of his impudence and the nurse of his obstinacy; and though he does not know a bee from a bull's foot, he settles matters as if all wisdom were at his fingers' ends—the pope himself is not more infallible. Hear him talk after he has been at a meeting and heard a sermon, and you will know how to pull a good man to pieces if you never knew it before. He sees faults where there are none; and if there be a few things amiss, he makes every mouse into an elephant. Although you might put all his wit into an eggshell, he weighs the sermon in the balances of his conceit with all the airs of a born-and-bred Solomon. If it be up to his standard, he lays on his praise with a trowel; but if it be not to his taste, he growls and barks and snaps at it like a dog at a hedgehog. Wise men in this world are like trees in a hedge; there is only here and there one. When these rare men talk together upon a discourse, it is good for the ears to hear them; but the bragging wiseacres I am speaking of are vainly puffed up by their fleshly minds, and their quibbling is as senseless as the cackle of geese on a common. Nothing comes out of a sack but what was in it; and as their bag is empty, they shake nothing but wind out of it. It is very likely that neither ministers or their sermons are perfect—the best garden may have a few weeds in it, the cleanest corn may have some chaff—but cavaliers cavil at anything or nothing and find fault for the sake of showing off their deep knowledge. Sooner than let their tongues have a holiday, they would complain that the grass is not a nice shade of blue and say that the sky would have looked neater if it had been whitewashed.

One tribe of these Ishmaelites is made up of high-flying ignoramuses who are very mighty about the doctrine of a sermon: Here they are as decisive as sledgehammers and as certain as death. Those who know nothing are confident in everything; hence they are bullheaded beyond measure. Every clock and even the sundial must be set according to their watches. The slightest difference from their opinion proves a man to be rotten at heart. Venture to argue with them, and their little pots boil over in quick style; ask them for reason, and you might as well go to a sandpit for sugar. They have bottled up the sea of truth and carry it in their waistcoat pockets; they have measured heaven's line of grace and have tied a knot in a string at the exact length of electing love. As for the things that angels long to know, they have seen them all as boys see sights in a peep show at our fair. Having sold their modesty and become wiser than their teachers, they ride a very high horse and jump over all five-barred gates of Bible texts that teach doctrines contrary to their notions. When this mischief happens to good men, it is a great pity for such sweet pots of ointment to be spoiled by flies, yet one learns to bear with them just as I do with old Violet, for he is a rare horse, though he does set his ears back and throw out his legs at times. But there is a bragging lot about, who are all sting and no honey, all whip and no hay, all grunt and no bacon. These do nothing but rail from morning to night at all who cannot see through their spectacles. If they would but mix up a handful of good living with all their bushels of bounce, it would be more bearable; but no, they don't care for such legality. Men as sound as they are can't be expected to be good at anything else. They are the heavenly watchdogs to guard the house of the Lord from those thieves and robbers who don't preach sound doctrine; and if they do worry the sheep or steal a rabbit or two on the sly, who would have the heart to blame them? The Lord's dear people, as they call themselves, have enough to do to keep their doctrine sound; and if their manners are cracked, who can wonder? No man can see to everything at once. These are the moles that want catching in many of our pastures, not for their own sakes, for there is not a sweet mouthful in them, but for the sake of the meadows that they spoil. I would not find half a fault with their doctrine if it were not for their spirit, but vinegar is sweet next to it, and crabs are figs in comparison. It must be very high doctrine that is too high for me, but I must have high experience and high practice with it, or it turns my stomach. However, I have said my say and must leave the subject, or somebody will ask me, what have you to do with Don Quixote's windmill?

Sometimes it is the way the preacher speaks that is hauled over the coals. Here again is a dime field for faultfinding, for every bean has its black, and every man has his failing. I never knew a good horse that had not some odd habit or other, and I never yet saw a minister worth his salt who had not some quirk or oddity. Now, these are the bits of cheese that quibblers smell out and nibble at: This man is too slow and another too fast; the first is too flowery and the second is too dull. Dear me, if all God's creatures were judged in this way, we should wring the dove's neck for being too tame, shoot the robins for eating spiders, kill the cows for swinging their tails and the hens for not giving us milk. When a man wants to beat a clog, he can soon find a stick; and at this rate, any fool may have something to say against the best minister in England. As to a preacher's manner, if there be but plain speaking, none should cavil at it—because it lacks polish—for if a thing is good—and earnestly spoken, it cannot sound much amiss. No man should use bad language in the pulpit—and all language is bad which common people cannot make head or tail of—but godly, sober, decent, plain words none should carp at. A countryman is as warm in homespun as a king in velvet, and a truth is as comfortable in homely words as in fine speech. As to the way: Of dishing up the meat, hungry men leave that to the cook; only let the meat be sweet and substantial. If hearers were better, sermons would be better. When men say they can't hear, I recommend them to buy a horn and remember the old saying, "There's none so deaf as those who will not hear." When young speakers get downhearted because of hard, unkind remarks, I generally tell them of the old man and his boy and his ass and what came of trying to please everybody. No piper ever suited all ears. Where whims and fancies sit in the seat of judgment, a man's opinion is only so much wind; therefore take no more notice of it than of the wind whistling through a keyhole.

> *It is very likely that neither ministers or their sermons are perfect—the best garden may have a few weeds in it, the cleanest corn may have some chaff.*

I have heard men find fault with a discourse for what was not in it. No matter how well the subject in hand was brought out, there was another subject about which nothing was said, and so all was wrong. That is as reasonable as finding fault with my plowing because it does not dibble the holes for the beans or abusing a good cornfield because there are no turnips in it. Does any man look for every truth in one sermon? You might as well look for every dish at one meal, and rail at a joint of beef because there are neither bacon or veal or green peas or parsnips on the table. Suppose a sermon is not full of comfort to the saint; yet if it warns the sinner, shall we despise it? A handsaw would be a poor tool to shave with; shall we therefore throw it away? Where is the use of always trying to hunt out faults? I hate to see a man smelling about for things to rail at like a rat catcher's dog sniffing at rat holes. By all means let us cut down error, root and branch, but do let us save our pruning shears till there are brambles to chop, and not fall foul of our own mercies. Judging preachers is a poor trade, for it pays neither party concerned in it. At a plowing match they do give a prize to the best of us; but these judges of preachers are precious slow to give anything even to those whom they profess to think so much of. They pay in praise but give no pudding. They get the gospel for nothing, and if they do not grumble, they think that they have made an abundant return.

> *A countryman is as warm in homespun as a king in velvet, and a truth is as comfortable in homely words as in fine speech.*

Everybody thinks himself a judge of a sermon, but nine out of ten might as well pretend to weigh the moon. I believe that, at bottom, most people think it an uncommonly easy thing to preach, and that they could do it amazingly well themselves. Every donkey thinks itself worthy to stand with the king's horses; every girl thinks she could keep house better than her mother. But thoughts are not facts; for the sprat thought itself a herring, yet the fisherman knew better. I daresay that those who can whistle imagine that they can plow, but there's more than whistling in a good plowman. And let me tell you, there's more in good preaching than taking a text and saying, first, second, and third. I try my hand at preaching myself, and in my poor way I find it no very easy thing to give the folks something worth hearing. If the line critics, who reckon us up on their thumbs, would but try their own hands at it, they might be a little quieter. Dogs, however, always will bark; and what is worse, some of them will bite, too. But let decent people do all they can, if not to muzzle them, yet to prevent them from doing any great mischief. It is a dreadful thing to see a happy family of Christians broken up by talkative faultfinders, and all about nothing or less than nothing. Small is the edge of the wedge, but when the devil handles the beetle, churches are soon split to pieces, and men wonder why. The fact is, the worst wheel of the cart creaks most, and one fool makes many, and thus many a congregation is set at odds with a good and faithful minister who would have been a lasting blessing to them if they had not chased away their best friend. Those who are at the bottom of the mischief have generally no part or lot in the matter of true godliness, but like sparrows, fight over corn that is not their own, and, like jackdaws, pull to pieces what they never helped to build. From mad dog grumbling professors may we all be delivered, and may we never take the complaint from either of them. Faultfinding is dreadfully catching: One dog will set a whole kennel howling, and the wisest course is to keep out of the way of a man who has the complaint called the grumbles. The worst of it is that the foot and mouth disease go together, and he who bespatters others generally rolls in the mud himself before long. "The fruit of the Spirit is love," and this is a very different apple from the sour Siberian crab that some people bring forth. Good-bye, all ye sons of Grizzle, John Ploughman would sooner pick a bone in peace than fight over an ox roasted whole.

For Further Thought

1. *In 1 Corinthians 2:4, Paul says that, when speaking to the believers, he didn't use persuasive words of human wisdom. According to this verse, what did the apostle's speech demonstrate?*
2. *Romans 16:17 tells of people who cause division in the church. What does verse 18 say about their way of speaking?*

3

ON THE PREACHER'S APPEARANCE

A good horse cannot be a bad color, and a really good preacher can wear what he likes, and none will care much about it; but though you cannot know wine by the barrel, a good appearance is a letter of recommendation even to a plowman. Wise men neither fall in love or take a dislike at first sight, but still the first impression is always a great thing even with them; and as to those weaker brethren who are not wise, a good appearance is half the battle.

What is a good appearance? Well, it's not being pompous and starchy and making oneself high and mighty among the people, for proud looks lose hearts, and gentle words win them. It's not wearing fine clothes either, for foppish dress usually means a foul house within and the doorstep without fresh whitewash. Such dressing tells the world that the outside is the best part of the puppet. When a man is as proud as a peacock, all strut and show, he needs converting himself before he sets up to preach to others. The preacher who measures himself by his mirror may please a few silly girls, but neither God nor man will long put up with him. The man who owes his greatness to his tailor will find that needle and thread cannot long hold a fool in a pulpit. A gentleman should have more in his pocket than on his back, and a minister should have more in his inner man than on his outer man. I would say, if I might, to young ministers, do not preach in gloves, for cats in mittens catch no mice; don't curl and oil your hair like dandies, for nobody cares to hear a peacock's voice; don't have your own pretty self in your mind at all, or nobody else will mind you. Away with gold rings and chains and jewelry; why should the pulpit become a goldsmith's shop? Forever away with surplices and gowns and all those nursery doll dresses, men should put away childish things. A cross on the back is the sign of a devil in the heart; those who do as Rome does should go to Rome and show their colors. If priests suppose that they get the respect of honest men by their fine ornamental dresses, they are much mistaken, for it is commonly said, "Fine feathers make fine birds," and "An ape is never so like an ape as when he wears a popish cape."

> *What is a good appearance? Well, it's not being pompous and starchy and making oneself high and mighty among the people, for proud looks lose hearts, and gentle words win them.*

Among us dissenters the preacher claims no priestly powers and therefore should never wear a peculiar dress. Let fools wear fools' caps and fools' dresses, but men who make no claim to be fools should not put on fools' clothes. None but a very silly sheep would wear wolf's clothing. It is a singular taste that makes honest men covet the rags of thieves. Besides, where's the good of such finery? Except a duck in pattens, no creature looks more stupid than a dissenting preacher in a gown that is of no manner of use to him. I could laugh till I held my sides when I see our doctors in gowns and bands, puffed out with their silks, and touched up with their little bibs, for they put me so much in mind of our old turkey when his temper is up and he swells to his biggest. They must be weak folks indeed who want a man to dress like a woman before they can enjoy his sermon, and he who cannot preach without such milliner's tawdry finery may be a man among geese, but he is a goose among men. At the same time, the preacher should endeavor, according to his means, to dress himself respectably; and, as to neatness, he should be without spot, for kings should not have dirty footmen to wait at their table, and they who teach godliness should practice cleanliness. I should like white neckties better if they were always white, but dirty brown is neither here nor there. From a slovenly smoking, snuff-taking, beer-drinking parson may we be delivered. Some that I meet with may, perhaps, have very good manners, but they did not happen to have them about them at the time. Like the Dutch captain with his anchors, they had left them at home. This should never be the case, for, if there be a well-behaved man in the parish, it should be the minister. A worn coat is no discredit, but the poorest may be neat, and men should be scholars rather than teachers till they are so. You cannot judge a horse by its harness; but a modest, gentlemanly appearance, in which the dress is just such as nobody could make a remark upon, seems to me to be the right sort of thing.

This little bit of my mind is meant to warn you young striplings who have just started in the ministry; and if any of you get cross over it, I shall tell you that sore horses cannot bear to be combed, and again "those whom the shoe fits must wear it." John Ploughman, you will say, had better mend his own smock and let the parsons alone; but I take leave to look about me and speak my mind, for a cat may look at a king, and a fool may give wise men good advice. If I speak too plainly, please remember that an old dog cannot alter his way of barking, and he who has long been used to plow a straight furrow is very apt to speak in the same straightforward manner.

For Further Thought

1. *The New Testament is silent about men's attire. But 1 Timothy 2:8–10 speaks about women's. According to these verses, what is proper attire for godly women?*
2. *First Peter 3:3–4 similarly speaks of women's attire. What does verse 4 say a woman should wear?*

4

On Good Nature and Firmness

Do not be all sugar, or the world will suck you down; but do not be all vinegar, or the world will spit you out. There is a medium in all things; only blockheads go to extremes. We need not be all rock or all sand, all iron or all wax. We should neither fawn upon everybody like silly lapdogs nor fly at all persons like surly mastiffs. Blacks and whites go together to make up a world. Hence, on the point of temper, we have all sorts of people to deal with. Some are as easy as an old shoe, but they are hardly ever worth more than the other one of the pair; others take fire as fast as tinder at the smallest offense and are as dangerous as gunpowder. To have a fellow going about the farm as cross with everybody as a bear with a sore head, with a temper as sour as spoiled milk and as sharp as a razor, looking as surly as a butcher's dog, is a great nuisance; yet there may be some good points about the man, so that he may be a man for all that. But poor soft Tommy, as green as grass, and as ready to bend as a willow, is nobody's money and everybody's scorn. A man must have a backbone, or how is he to hold up his head? But that backbone must bend, or he will knock his brow against the beam.

There is a time to do as others wish and a time to refuse. If we make ourselves asses, then everybody will ride us, but if we would be respected, we must be our own masters and not let others saddle us as they think fit. If we try to please everybody, we shall be like a toad under a harrow and never have peace; and if we play lackey to all our neighbors, whether good or bad, we shall be thanked by no one, for we shall soon do as much harm as good. He that makes himself a sheep will find that the wolves are not all dead. He who lies on the ground must expect to be trodden on. He who makes himself a mouse the cats will eat. If you let your neighbors put the calf on your shoulder, they will soon clap on the cow. We are to please our neighbor for his good to edification, but this is quite another matter. There are old foxes about whose mouths are always watering for young geese, and if they can coax them to do just what they wish, they soon make their market out of them. What a jolly good fellow you will be called if you will make yourself a hack for your friends, and what a mess will they soon bring you into!

Out of that mess you will have to get all alone, for your friends will be sure to say to you, "Good-bye basket; I've carried all my apples," or they will give you their good wishes and nothing more, and you will find out that fair words won't feed a cat or butter your bread or fill your pocket. Those who make so very much of you either mean to cheat you or else are in need of you, though when they have sucked the orange, they will throw the peel away. Be wise, then, and look before you leap, lest a friend's advice should do you more mischief than an enemy's slander. "The simple believes every word, but the prudent considers well his steps" (Prov. 14:15). Go with your neighbor as far as good conscience will go with you, but part company where the shoe of conscience begins to pinch your foot. Begin with your friend as you mean to go on, and let him know very early that you are not a man made of putty, but one who has a judgment of his own and means to use it. Pull up the moment you find you are out of the road, and take the nearest way back at once. The way to avoid great faults is to beware of small ones. Therefore, pull up in time if your friend would not drag you into the ditch. Better offend your acquaintance than lose your character and hazard your soul. Don't be ashamed to walk down Turnagain Lane. Never mind being called a turncoat when you turn from bad courses: Better to turn in time than to burn in eternity. Do not be persuaded to ruin yourself—it is buying gold too dear to throw oneself away to please our company. Put your foot down where you mean to stand, and let no man move you from the right. Learn to say no, and it will be of more use to you than to be able to read Latin.

> *A man must have a backbone, or how is he to hold up his head? But that backbone must bend, or he will knock his brow against the beam.*

A friend to everybody is often a friend to nobody; or else in his simplicity he robs his family to help strangers and becomes brother to a beggar. There is wisdom in generosity as in everything else, and some had need to go to school to learn it. A kindhearted soul may be very cruel to his own children, while he takes the bread out of their mouths to give to those who call him a generous fellow but laugh at his folly. Very often he who lends his money loses both his gold and his friends, and he who is surety is never sure. Take John Ploughman's advice, and never be security for more than you are quite willing to lose. Remember, the Word of God says, "He who is surety for a stranger will suffer, but one who hates being surety is secure" (Prov. 11:15).

> ash vows are much better broken than kept. He who never changes, never mends; he who never yields, never conquers.

When we are injured, we are bound as Christians to bear it without malice; but we are not to pretend that we do not feel it, for this will but encourage our enemies to kick us again. He who is cheated twice by the same man is half as bad as the rogue; and it is very much so in other injuries. Unless we claim our rights, we are ourselves to blame if we do not get them. Paul was willing to bear stripes for his Master's sake, but he did not forget to tell the magistrates that he was Roman; and when those gentlemen wished to put him out of prison privately, he said, "No indeed! Let them come themselves and get us out" (Acts 16:37). A Christian is the gentlest of men, but then he is a man. A good many people don't need to be told this, for they are up in a moment if they think anybody is likely to ill treat them. Long before they know whether it is a thief in the farmyard or the old mare got loose, they are up with the window and firing off the old blunderbuss. Dangerous neighbors these; a man might as well make a seat out of a bull's forehead as expect to find comfort in their neighborhood.

"Make no friendship with an angry man, and with a furious man do not go" (Prov. 22:24). "He who is slow to wrath has great understanding, but he who is impulsive exalts folly" (Prov. 14:29). "Do you see a man hasty in his words? There is more hope for a fool than for him" (Prov. 29:20).

In my day I have seen a few downright obstinate men, whom neither sense nor reason could alter. There's a queer chap in our village who keeps a bulldog, and he tells me that when the creature once gives a bite at anything, he never lets go again, and if you want to get it out of his mouth, you must cut his head off. That's the sort of man that has fretted me many a time and almost made me mad. You might sooner argue a pitchfork into a threshing machine or persuade a brickbat to turn into marble, than to get the fellow to hear common sense. Getting spots out of leopards is nothing at all compared with trying to lead a downright obstinate man. Right or wrong, you might as easily make a hill walk to London as turn him when his mind is made up. When a man is right, this sticking to his text is a grand thing (our minister says, "it is the stuff that martyrs are made of"), but when an ignorant, wrongheaded fellow gets this hard grit into him, he makes martyrs of those who have to put up with him. Old Master Pighead swore he would drive a nail into an oak board with his fist and so lamed his hand for life; he could not sell his corn at his own price, and so he let the rats eat up the ricks. You cannot ride by his fields without noticing his obstinacy, for he vows, "He won't have none of these ever newfangled notions," and so he grows the worst crops in the parish. Worst of all, his daughter went among the Methodists, and in a towering rage, he turned her out of doors. Though I believe he is very sorry for it, he will not yield an inch, but stands to it that he will never speak to her so long as he lives. Meanwhile, the dear girl is dying through his unkindness. Rash vows are much better broken than kept. He who never changes, never mends; he who never yields, never conquers.

With children, you must mix gentleness with firmness; they must not always have their own way, but they must not always be thwarted. Give to a pig when it grunts and to a child when he cries, and you will have a fine pig and a spoiled child. A man who is learning to play on a trumpet and a petted child are two very disagreeable companions, even as next-door neighbors; but unless we look well to it, our children will be a nuisance to others and a torment to ourselves. "The rod and rebuke give wisdom, but a child left to himself brings shame to his mother" (Prov. 29:15). If we never have headaches through rebuking our little children, we shall have plenty of heartaches when they grow up. Strict truthfulness must rule all our dealings with the young. Our "yea must be yea, and our nay be nay," and that always. Never promise a child and then fail to perform whether you promise him a bun or a beating. Be obeyed at all costs. Disobedient children are unhappy children; for their own sakes, make them mind you. If you yield up your authority once, you will hardly ever get it again, for he who says A must say B, and so on. We must not provoke our children to anger, lest they be discouraged; but we must rule our household in the fear of the Lord, and in so doing we may expect a blessing.

Since John Ploughman has taken to writing, he has had a fine chance of showing his firmness and his gentleness, too, for he has received bushels of advice for which he begs to present his compliments, as the squire's lady says. He does not mind either returning the advice or some of his own instead, by way of showing his gratitude; for he is sure it is very kind of so many people to tell him so many different ways in which he might make an idiot of himself. He means to glean as many good hints as he can from the acres of his friends' stubble; and while sticking to his own style, because it suits his hand, he will touch himself up a bit if he can. Perhaps if the minister will lend him Cowper or Milton, he may even stick a sprig of poetry into his nosegay and come out as fine as the flowers in May. But he cannot promise, for the harvest is just on, and reaping leaves no time for rhyming. The worst of it is, the kind friends who are setting John to rights contradict one another: One says it is very poor stuff and all in an assumed name, for the style is not rough enough for a plowman; another says the matter is very well, but the expressions are so coarse that he is amazed the editor put it in the magazine. John means to pay his advisers all the attention they deserve, and as some of the mice have been bold enough to make a nest in the cat's ear, he means to be after them and write a paper upon giving advice gratis, in which they will be likely to get a flea in their ear in return for their instructions.

For Further Thought

1. *Second Corinthians 1:15–17 shows that Paul was accused of being changeable. But the apostle says that because the gospel doesn't change, neither does he (see verses 18–20). What does verse 20 say about the promises of God?*
2. *In Ephesians 4:25, why does Paul say that we should speak truth to our neighbor?*

5

ON PATIENCE

PATIENCE is better than wisdom: An ounce of patience is worth a pound of brains. All men praise patience, but few enough can practice it. It is a medicine that is good for all diseases: Therefore, every old woman recommends it, but it is not every garden that grows the herbs to make it with. When one's flesh and bones are full of aches and pains, it is as natural for us to murmur as for a horse to shake his head when the flies tease him, or a wheel to rattle when a spoke is loose. But nature should not be the rule with Christians, or what is their religion worth? If a soldier fights no better than a plowboy, off with his red coat. We expect more fruit from an apple tree than from a thorn, and we have a right to do so. The disciples of a patient Savior should be patient themselves. Grin and bear it is the old-fashioned advice, but sing and bear it is a great deal better. After all, we get very few cuts of the whip, considering what bad cattle we are; and when we do smart a little, it is soon over. Pain past is pleasure, and experience comes by it. We ought not to be afraid of going down into Egypt when we know we shall come out of it with jewels of silver and gold.

Impatient people water their miseries and plow up their comforts; sorrows are visitors that come without invitation, but complaining minds send a wagon to bring their troubles home in. Many people are born crying, live complaining, and die disappointed; they chew the bitter pill, which they would not even know to be bitter if they had the sense to swallow it whole in a cup of patience. They think every other man's burden to be light and their own feathers to be heavy as lead. They are hardly done by in their own opinion: No one's toes are so often trodden on by the black ox as theirs, the snow falls thickest round their door, and the hail rattles hardest on their windows. Yet, if the truth were known, it is their fancy rather than their fate that makes things go so hard with them. Many would be well off if they could but think so. A little sprig of the herb called content, if put into the poorest soup, will make it taste as rich as the Lord Mayor's turtle. John Ploughman grows the plant in his garden, but the late hard winter nipped it terribly, so that he cannot afford to give his neighbors a slip of it; they had better follow Matthew 25:9, and go to those who sell and buy for themselves. Grace is a good soil to grow it in, but it wants watering from the fountain of mercy. To be poor is not always pleasant, but worse things than that happen at sea. Small shoes are apt to pinch, but not if you have a small foot; if we have little means, it will be well to have little desires. Poverty is no shame, but being discontented with it is. In some things, the poor are better off than the rich; for if a poor man has to seek meat for his stomach, he is more likely to get what he is after than the rich man who seeks a stomach for his meat. A poor man's table is soon spread, and his labor spares his buying sauce. The best doctors are Dr. Diet, Dr. Quiet, and Dr. Merryman, and many a godly plowman has all these gentlemen to wait upon him. Plenty makes dainty, but hunger finds no fault with the cook. Hard work brings health, and an ounce of health is worth a sack of diamonds. It is not how much we have, but how much we enjoy, that makes happiness. There is more sweet in a spoonful of sugar than in a cask of vinegar. It is not the quantity of our goods, but the blessing of God on what we have that makes us truly rich. The parings of a pippin are better than a whole crab; a dinner of herbs with peace is better than a stalled ox and contention therewith. Better is little with the fear of the Lord than great treasure and trouble therewith. A little wood will heat my little oven; why, then, should I murmur because all the woods are not mine?

> *Many people are born crying, live complaining, and die disappointed; they chew the bitter pill, which they would not even know to be bitter if they had the sense to swallow it whole in a cup of patience.*

When troubles come, it is of no use to fly in the face of God by hard thoughts of providence. That is kicking against the pricks and hurting your feet. The trees bow in the wind, and so must we. Every time the sheep bleats, it loses a mouthful, and every time we complain, we miss a blessing. Grumbling is a bad trade and yields no profit, but patience has a golden hand. Our evils will soon be over. After rain comes clear shining;

black crows have wings; every winter turns to spring; every night breaks into morning.

> Blow the wind never so fast,
> It will lower at last.

If one door should be shut, God will open another; if the peas do not yield well, the beans may; if one hen leaves her eggs, another will bring out all her brood. There's a bright side to all things and a good God everywhere. Somewhere or other in the worst flood of trouble there always is a dry spot for contentment to get its foot on. If there were not, it would learn to swim.

Friends, let us take to patience and water gruel, as the old folks used to tell us, rather than catch the miserables and give others the disease by wickedly finding fault with God. The best remedy for affliction is submitting to providence. What can't be cured must be endured. If we cannot get bacon, let us bless God that there are still some cabbages in the garden. "Must" is a hard nut to crack, but it has a sweet kernel. "All things work together for good to those who love God" (Rom. 8:28). Whatever falls from the skies is, sooner or later, good for the land; whatever comes to us from God is worth having, even though it is a rod. We cannot, by nature, like trouble any more than a mouse can fall in love with a cat, yet Paul by grace came to glory in tribulations. Losses and crosses are heavy to bear, but when our hearts are right with God, it is wonderful how easy the yoke becomes. We must go to glory by the way of Weeping Cross; and as we were never promised that we should ride to heaven in a feather bed, we must not be disappointed when we see the road to be rough, as our fathers found it before us. All's well that ends well; and, therefore, let us plow the heaviest soil with our eye on the sheaves of harvest and learn to sing at our labor while others murmur.

For Further Thought

1. *Romans 5:1–3 says that believers can glory in tribulations. According to verses 3–5, what does tribulation produce?*
2. *Read 2 Timothy 3:10–12. What does verse 12 say will happen to people who "live godly in Christ Jesus"?*

6

On Gossips

IN Walton Church in our county, there is a scold's bridle, which was used in years gone by to keep women's tongues from troubling their husbands and their neighbors. They did queer things in those good old times. Was this bridle a proof of what our parson calls the wisdom of our ancestors, or was it a bit of needless cruelty?

"It is nothing; only a woman drowning," is a wicked and spiteful old saying, which like the bridle, came out of the common notion that women do a world of mischief with their tongues. Is it so or not? John Ploughman will leave somebody else to answer, for he admits that he cannot keep a secret himself and likes a dish of chat as well as anybody; only John does not care for cracking people's characters and hates the slander that is so sweet to some people's teeth. John puts the question to wiser men than himself: Are women much worse than men in this business? They say that silence is a fine jewel for a woman, but it is very little worn. Is it so? Is it true that a woman only conceals what she does not know? Are women's tongues like lambs' tails, always wagging? They say foxes are all tail, and women all tongue. Is this false or not? Was that old prayer a needful one: "From big guns and women's tongues deliver us?" John has a right good and quiet wife of his own, whose voice is so sweet that he cannot hear it too often, and, therefore, is not a fair judge. But he is half afraid that some other women would sooner preach than pray and would not require strong tea to set their clappers going. Still what is sauce for the goose is sauce for the gander, and some men are quite as bad blabs as the women.

What a pity that there is not a tax upon words: what an income the Queen would get from it. But, alas, talking pays no toll. If lies paid double, the government might pay off the national debt, but who could collect the money? Common fame is a common liar. Hearsay is half lies. A tale never loses in the telling. As a snowball grows by rolling, so does a story. They who talk much lie much. If men only said what was true, what a peaceable world we should see. Silence seldom makes mischief; but talking is a plague to the parish. Silence is wisdom; by this rule, wise men and wise women are scarce. Still waters are the deepest, but the shallowest brooks brawl the most. This shows how plentiful fools must be. An open mouth shows an empty head. If the chest had gold or silver in it, it would not always stand wide open. Talking comes by nature, but it needs a good deal of training to learn to be quiet; yet regard for truth should put a bit into every honest man's mouth and a bridle upon every good woman's tongue.

> Let us then be careful that we do not hurt our neighbor in so tender a point as his character, for it is hard to get dirt off if it is once thrown on.

If we must talk, at least let us be free from slander, but let us not blister our tongues with backbiting. Slander may be sport to talebearers, but it is death to those whom they abuse. We can commit murder with the tongue as well as with the hand. The worst evil you can do a man is to injure his character. As the Quaker said to his dog, "I'll not beat you or abuse you, but I'll give you an ill name." All are not thieves that dogs bark at, but they are generally treated as if they are. The world for the most part believes that where there is smoke there is fire, and what everybody says must be true. Let us then be careful that we do not hurt our neighbor in so tender a point as his character, for it is hard to get dirt off if it is once thrown on; and when a man is once in people's bad books, he is hardly ever quite out of them. If we would be sure not to speak amiss, it might be as well to speak as little as possible; for if all men's sins were divided into two bundles, half of them would be sins of the tongue. "If any man offend not in word, the same is a perfect man, and able also to bridle the whole body" (James 3:2 KJV).

Gossips of both genders, give up the shameful trade of talebearing, and don't be the devil's bellows any longer to blow up the fire of strife. Quit setting people by the ears. If you do not cut a bit off your tongues, at least season them with the salt of grace. Praise God more and blame neighbors less. Any goose can cackle, any fly can find out a sore place, any empty barrel can give forth sound, any briar can tear a man's flesh. The flies will not go down your throat if you keep your mouth shut, and no evil speaking will come out either. Think much, but say little; be quick at work and slow at talk; and above all, ask the great Lord to set a watch over your lips.

For Further Thought

1. *What is the exhortation for busybodies in 2 Thessalonians 3:11–12?*
2. *What does 1 Timothy 5:14 say will help the busybodies mentioned in verse 13?*

7

ON SEIZING OPPORTUNITIES

SOME men are never awake when the train starts but crawl into the station just in time to see that everybody is off and then sleepily say, "Dear me, is the train gone? My watch must have stopped in the night." They always come into town a day after the fair and open their wares an hour after the market is over. They make their hay when the sun has left off shining and cut their corn as soon as the fine weather is ended. They cry, "Hold hard!" after the shot has left the gun and lock the stable door when the steed is stolen. They are like a cow's tail, always behind; they take time by the heels and not by the forelock, if indeed they ever take him at all. They are of no more worth than an old almanac; their time has gone for lack of use. Unfortunately, you cannot throw them away as you would the almanac, for they are like the cross old lady who had an annuity left her and meant to take out the full value of it; they won't die, though they are of no use alive. Take-It-Easy and Live-Long are first cousins, they say, and the more's the pity. If they are immortal till their work is done, they will not die in a hurry, for they have not even begun to work yet. Shiftless people generally excuse their laziness by saying, "I am only a little behind"; but a little late is much too late, and a miss is as good as a mile. My neighbor Sykes covered up his well after his child was drowned in it and was very busy down at the old farm bringing up buckets of water after every stick of the house had been burnt; one of these days, he'll be making his will when he can't hold a pen, and he'll be trying to repent of his sins when his senses are going.

These slow coaches think that tomorrow is better than today and take for their rule an old proverb turned topsy-turvy: "Never do today what you can put off till tomorrow." They are forever waiting until their ship comes in and always dreaming about things looking up by and by, while grass grows in their furrows and the cows get through the gaps in their hedges. If the birds would but wait to have salt put on their tails, what a breakfast they would take home to their families! But while things move as fast they do, the youngsters at home will have to fill their mouths with empty spoons. "Never mind say they; there are better times coming. Wait a little longer." Their birds are all in the bush, and rare fat ones they are, according to their account; and so they had need to be, for they have had none in the hand yet, and wife and children are half-starved. "Something will turn up," they say. Why don't the idlers go and turn it up themselves? Time and tide wait for no man, yet these fellows loiter about as if they had a freehold of time, a lease of their lives, and a rabbit hutch full of opportunities. They will find out their mistake when want turns them out, and that will not be long with some in our village, for they are already a long way on the road to Needham. They who would not plow must not expect to eat; they who waste the spring will have a lean autumn. They would not strike when the iron was hot, and they will soon find the cold iron very hard.

He that will not when he may,
When he will he shall have nay.

Time is not tied to a post like a horse to a manger. It passes like the wind, and he who would grind his corn by it must set the mill sails. He who gapes till he be fed will gape till he be dead. Nothing is to be got without pains except poverty and dirt. In the old days, they said, "Jack gets on by his stupidity." Jack would find it very different nowadays, I think; but never in old times or any other times would Jack get on by foolishly letting present chances slip by him, for hares never run into the mouths of sleeping dogs. He who has time and looks for better time, time comes that he repents himself of time. There's no good in lying down and crying, "God help us!" God helps those who help themselves. When I see a man who declares that the times are bad and that he is always unlucky, I generally say to myself, "That old goose did not sit on the eggs till they were all addled, and now providence is to be blamed because they won't hatch." I never had any faith in luck at all, except that I believe good luck will carry a man over a ditch if he jumps well and will put a bit of bacon into his pot if he looks after his garden and keeps a pig. Luck generally comes to those who look after it, and my notion is that it taps at least once in a lifetime at everybody's door, but if industry does not open it, away it goes. Those who have lost the last coach and let every opportunity slip by them turn to abusing providence for setting everything against them: "If I were a hatter," says one, "men would be born without heads." "If I went to the sea for water," quotes another, "I should find it dried up." Every wind is foul for a crazy ship. Neither the wise or the wealthy can help him who has long refused to help himself.

> They who would not plow must not expect to eat; they who waste the spring will have a lean autumn. They would not strike when the iron was hot, and they will soon find the cold iron very hard.

John Ploughman, in the most genteel manner, sends his compliments to his friends; and now that harvest is over and the hops all picked, according to promise, he intends giving them a bit of poetry just to show that he is trying the polishing brushes. John asked the minister to lend him one of the poets, and he gave him the works of George Herbert—very good, no doubt, but rather tangled, like Harkaway Wood. Still, there's a good deal in the queer old verses, and every now and then one comes upon clusters of the sweetest nuts, but some of them are rather hard to crack. The following verse is somewhat near the subject now in hand and is plain enough in reason; though, begging the poet's pardon, John can't see a rhyme in it. However, as it is by the great Herbert, it must be good and will do well enough to ornament John's talk, like a flower stuck in a buttonhole of his Sunday coat.

Let your mind still be bent, still plotting where,
And when, and how your business may be done.
Slackness breeds worms; but the sure traveler,
though he alight sometimes, still goes on.
Acting and stirring spirits live alone:
Write on the others, here lies such a one.

FOR FURTHER THOUGHT

1. *Acts 20:33–35 pictures the apostle Paul as industrious, not idle. What are the two reasons for laboring like this that are given in verse 35?*
2. *What is the basic rule about work given in 2 Thessalonians 3:10?*

8

ON KEEPING ONE'S
EYES OPEN

To get through this world, a man must look about him and even sleep with one eye open; for there are many baits for fishes, many nets for birds, and many traps for men. While foxes are so common, we must not be geese. There is a very great difference in this matter among people of my acquaintance: Many see more with one eye than others with two, and many have fine eyes and cannot see a jot. All heads are not sense boxes. Some are so cunning that they suspect everybody and so live all their lives in miserable fear of their neighbors. Others are so simple that every knave takes them in and makes his penny out of them. One man tries to see through a brick wall and hurts his eyes, while another finds a hole in it and sees as far as he pleases. Some work at the mouth of a furnace and are never scorched, and others burn their hands at the fire when they only mean to warm them. Now, it is true that no one can give another experience, and we must all pick up wit for ourselves, yet I shall venture to give some of the homely cautions that have served my turn, and perhaps they may be of use to others as they have been to me.

> When you see a man with a great deal of religion displayed in his shop window, you may depend upon it that he keeps a very small stock of it within.

Nobody is more like an honest man than a thorough rogue. When you see a man with a great deal of religion displayed in his shop window, you may depend upon it that he keeps a very small stock of it within. Do not choose your friend by his looks: Handsome shoes often pinch the feet. Don't be fond of compliments. Remember, "Thank you, pussy, and thank you, pussy," killed the cat. Don't believe in the man who talks most, for mewing cats are seldom good mousers. By no means put yourself in another person's power: If you put your thumb between two grinders, they are very apt to bite. Drink nothing without seeing it. Sign nothing without reading it, and make sure that it means no more than it says. Don't go to law unless you have nothing to lose: Lawyers' houses are built on fools' heads. In any business, never wade into water where you cannot see the bottom. Put no dependence upon the label of a bag, and count money after your own kin. See the sack opened before you buy what is in it, for he who trades in the dark asks to be cheated. Keep clear of the man who does not value his own character. Beware of everyone who swears: He who would blaspheme his Maker would make no bones of lying or stealing. Beware of no man more than of yourself; we carry our worst enemies within us. When a new opinion or doctrine comes before you, do not bite till you know whether it is bread or a stone. Do not be sure that the gingerbread is good because of the gilt on it. Never shout, "Hello!" till you are quite out of the wood, and don't cry, "Fried fish!" till they are caught in the net. There's always time enough to boast—wait a little longer. Don't throw away dirty water till you have got clean. Keep on scraping the roads till you can get better work: The poorest pay is better than none, and the humblest office is better than being out of employment. Always give up the roads to bulls and madmen, and never fight with a coal heaver or contend with a base character, for they will be sure to blacken you.

> Neither trust or contend,
> Nor lay wagers, or lend,
> And you may depend—
> You'll have peace to your ends.

I cannot say quite so much as that old rhyme does, for there's more than that which is needed to give peace, but certainly it will help toward it. Never ride broken-kneed horses: The trader who has once been a fraudulent bankrupt is not the man for you to deal with. A rickety chair is a dangerous seat. Be shy of people who are overly polite, and don't be too fast with those who are forward and rough. When you suspect a design in anything, be on your guard: Set the trap as soon as you smell a rat, but mind that you don't catch your own fingers in it. Have very little to do with a boaster, for his beer is all froth; and though he brags that all his goods and even his copper kettles are gold and silver, you will soon find out that a boaster and a liar are first cousins. Commit all your secrets to no man; trust in God with all your heart, but let your confidence in friends be weighed in the balances of prudence, seeing that men are but men, and all men are frail. Trust not great weights to slender threads. Yet be not evermore suspicious, for suspicion is a cowardly virtue at best. Remember that men are not angels; but they are not devils, and it is too bad to think them so. One thing to be sure of: Never believe in any priest of any religion, for before a man could be bad enough to pretend to be a priest, he must have hardened his heart and blinded his conscience to the most horrible degree. Our governors imprison gypsies for telling fortunes, and yet they give fat pensions to those vagabonds who deceive the people in much weightier things. "Bad company" said the thief, as he went to the gallows between the hangman and a priest—a very honest speech and a very true word, though spoken in jest. It is the ignorance of fools that keeps the pot boiling for priests. May God clean this land from the plague of their presence and make men wise enough to see through their crafty devices. Lastly, my advice to all is this: Remember that good wisdom is that which will turn out to be wise in the end; seek it, friends, and seek it at the hands of the wisest of all teachers, the Lord Jesus. Trust Him, and He will never fail you; be guided by His word, and it will never mislead you; pray in His name, and your requests will be granted. Remember, he that leans on man will find him a broken reed, but he who builds on Christ has a firm foundation. You may follow Jesus with your eyes shut, if you please; but when others guide you, keep all your eyes open even if you have a dozen and all of them as powerful as telescopes.

For Further Thought

1. *Read 1 John 4:1–2. Why are we to test the spirits of those who teach the scriptures?*
2. *According to Romans 16:17–18 how are the hearts of the simple deceived?*

9

THOUGHTS ABOUT THOUGHT

VERY little of this paper is to be set down to the account of John Ploughman, for our minister, as I may say, found the horses and held the plow handles; the plowman only put in a smack of the whip every now and then, just to keep folks awake. "Two heads are better than one," said the woman when she took her dog with her to market. Begging his pardon, our minister is the woman, and the only sensible head in the whole affair. He is a man who is used to giving his people many things of a very different sort from anything a plowman is likely to turn out of his wallet; but I have, at his request, dropped in a few homely proverbs into his thoughts, as he says, "by way of salt," which is his very kind way of putting it. I only hope I have not spoiled his writing with my rough expressions. If he thinks well of it, I should like a few more of his pieces to tack my sayings to; and the public shall always be honestly told whether the remarks are to be considered as altogether "John Ploughman's Talk" or as the writing of two characters rolled into one.

There are not so many hours in a year as there may be thoughts in an hour. Thoughts fly in flocks, like starlings, and swarm like bees. Like the withered leaves in autumn, there is no counting them; and like links in a chain, one draws on another. What a restless being man is! His thoughts dance up and down like midges on a summer's evening. Like a clock full of wheels with the pendulum in full swing, his mind moves as fast as time flies. This makes thinking such an important business. Many littles make much; and so many light thoughts make a great weight of sin. A grain of sand is light enough, but Solomon tells us that a heap of sand is heavy. When there are so many children, the mother better look well after them. We ought to mind our thoughts, for if they turn to be our enemies, they will be too many for us and will drag us down to ruin. Thoughts from heaven, like birds in spring, will fill our souls with music; but thoughts of evil will sting us like vipers.

There is a notion abroad that thought is free; but I remember reading that, although thoughts are toll free, they are not hell free; and that saying quite agrees with the good Old Book. We cannot be summoned before an early court for thinking, but depend upon it, we shall have to be tried for it at the Last Judgment. Evil thoughts are the marrow of sin, the malt that sin is brewed from, the tinder that catches the sparks of the devil's temptations, the churn in which the milk of imagination is churned into purpose and plan, the nest in which all evil birds lay their eggs. Be certain, then, that as sure as fire burns brushwood as well as logs, God will punish thoughts of sin as well as deeds of sin.

Nurse sin on the knees of thought, and it will grow into a giant. Dip rope in naphtha, and how it will blaze when fire gets to it. Lay a man soaked in depraved thought, and he is ready to flame up into open sin as soon as the opportunity occurs.

Let no one suppose that thoughts are not known to the Lord, for He has a window into the closest closet of the soul, a window to which there are no shutters. As we watch bees in a glass hive, so does the eye of the Lord see us. The Bible says, "Hell and Destruction are before the LORD; so how much more the hearts of the sons of men" (Prov. 15:11). Man is all outside to God. With heaven there are no secrets. That which is done in the private chamber of the heart is as public as the streets before the all-seeing eye.

But some will say that they cannot help having bad thoughts. That may be, but the question is: Do they hate them or not? We cannot keep thieves from looking in at our windows, but if we open our doors to them and receive them joyfully, we are as bad as they. We cannot help the birds flying over our heads, but we may keep them from building their nests in our hair. Vain thoughts will knock at the door, but we must not open to them. Though sinful thoughts rise, they must not reign. He who turns a morsel over and over in his mouth does so because he likes the flavor, and he who meditates upon evil loves it and is ripe to commit it. Think of the devil, and he will appear; turn your thoughts toward sins and your hands will soon follow. Snails leave their slime behind them, and so do vain thoughts. An arrow may fly through the air and leave no trace; but an ill thought always leaves a trail like a serpent. Where there is much traffic of bad thinking, there will be much mire and dirt; every wave of wicked thought adds something to the corruption that rots upon the shore of life. It is dreadful to think that a vile imagination, once indulged, gets the key of our minds and can get in again very easily, whether we will it or not, and can so return as to bring seven other spirits with it more wicked than itself. What may follow, no one knows. Nurse sin on the knees of thought, and it will grow into a giant. Dip rope in naphtha, and how it will blaze when fire gets to it. Lay a man soaked in depraved thought, and he is ready to flame up into open sin as soon as the opportunity occurs. This shows us the wisdom of watching, every day, the thoughts and imaginations of our hearts. Good thoughts are blessed guests and should be heartily welcomed, well fed, and much sought.

For Further Thought

1. *Philippians 2:5 advises that we allow the mind of Christ to be in us. According to verses 6–8, what was on Christ's mind as He lived among us?*

2. *According to Colossians 3:3, why should we set our minds "on things above, not on things on the earth" (3:2)?*

10

FAULTS

HE who boasts of being perfect is perfect in folly. I have been a good deal up and down the world, and I never did see either a perfect horse or a perfect man, and I never shall till two Sundays come together. You cannot get white flour out of a coal sack or perfection out of human nature; he who looks for it had better look for sugar in the sea. The old saying is, "Lifeless is faultless." About dead men we should say nothing but good; but as for the living, they are all tarred more or less with the black brush, and half an eye can see it. Every head has a soft place in it, and every heart has its black drop. Every rose has its prickles, and every day its night. Even the sun shows spots, and the skies are darkened with clouds. Nobody is so wise but he has folly enough to stock a stall at Vanity Fair. Where I could not see the fool's cap, I have nevertheless heard the bells jingle. As there is no sunshine without some shadows, so is all human good mixed up with more or less of evil. Even poor law guardians have their little failings, and parish beadles are not wholly of heavenly nature. The best wine has its dregs. All men's faults are not written on their foreheads, and it's quite as well they are not, or hats would need very wide brims. Yet, as sure as eggs are eggs, faults of some sort nestle in every bosom. There is no telling when a man's sins may show themselves, for hares pop out of the ditch just when you are not looking for them. A horse that is weak in the legs may not stumble for a mile or two, but it is in him, and the rider had better hold him up well. The tabby cat is not lapping milk just now, but leave the dairy door open and we will see if she is not as bad a thief as the kitten. There's fire in the flint, cool as it looks: Wait till the steel gets a knock at it, and you will see. Everybody can read that riddle, but it is not everybody that will remember to keep his gunpowder out of the way of the candle.

If we would always recollect that we live among men who are imperfect, we should not be in such a fever when we find out our friends' failings.

What's rotten will rend, and cracked pots will leak. Blessed is he who expects nothing of poor flesh and blood, for he shall never be disappointed. The best of men are men at best, and the best wax will melt.

> It is a good horse that never stumbles,
> And a good wife that never grumbles.

But surely such horses and wives are found only in the fool's paradise, where dumplings grow on trees. In this wicked world the straightest timber has knots in it, and the cleanest field of wheat has its share of weeds. The most careful driver one day upsets the cart; the cleverest cook spills a little broth; and as I know to my sorrow, a very decent plowman will now and then break the plow and often make a crooked furrow. It is foolish to turn off a tried friend because of a failing or two, for you may get rid of a one-eyed nag and buy a blind one. Being all of us full of faults, we ought to keep two bears and learn to bear and forbear with one another. Since we all live in glass houses, we should none of us throw stones. Everybody laughs when the saucepan says to the kettle, "How black you are!" Other men's imperfections show us our imperfection, for one sheep is much like another; and if there's a speck in my neighbor's eye, there is no doubt one in mine. We ought to use our neighbors as mirrors to see our own faults in, and mend in ourselves what we see in them.

> If fault-finders would turn their dogs to hunt out the good points in other folks; the game would pay better, and nobody would stand with a pitchfork to keep the hunters off his farm.

I have no patience with those who poke their noses into every man's house to smell out his faults and put on magnifying glasses to discover their neighbors' flaws. Such folks had better look at home; they might see the devil where they little expected. What we wish to see, we shall see or think we see. Faults are always thick where love is thin. A white cow is all black if your eye chooses to make it so. If we sniff long enough at rose water, we shall find out that it has a bad smell. It would be a far more pleasant business, at least for other people, if fault-finders would turn their dogs to hunt out the good points in other folks; the game would pay better, and nobody would stand with a pitchfork to keep the hunters off his farm. As for our own faults, it would take a large slate to hold the account of them; but, thank God, we know where to take them and how to get the better of them. With all our faults, God loves us still if we are trusting in His Son. Therefore, let us not be downhearted, but hope to live and learn and do some good service before we die. Though the cart creaks, it will get home with its load, and the old horse, broken-kneed as he is, will do a sight of work yet. There is no use in lying down and doing nothing because we cannot do everything as we should like. Faults or no faults, plowing must be done; imperfect people must do it, too, or there will be no harvest next year. Bad plowman as John may be, the angels won't do his work for him, and so he is off to do it himself. Go along, Violet! Gee, whoa! Dapper!

For Further Thought

1. *Paul mentions his faults in 1 Timothy 1:13. Why was God merciful to him (1:14)?*
2. *Some of the believers in the church in Corinth came from faulty backgrounds (1 Cor. 6:9–10). What are the two things that washed, sanctified, and justified them (v. 11)?*

ALL OF GRACE

Contents

Where sin abounded, grace abounded much more.
Romans 5:20

1

To You

HE who spoke and wrote this message will be greatly disappointed if it does not lead many to the Lord Jesus. It is sent forth in childlike dependence upon the power of God the Holy Spirit, to use it in the conversion of millions, if so He pleases. No doubt many poor men and women will take up this little volume, and the Lord will visit them with grace. To answer this end, the very plainest language has been chosen, and many homely expressions have been used. But if those of wealth and rank should glance at this book, the Holy Spirit can impress them also, since that which can be understood by the unlettered is nonetheless attractive to the instructed. Oh, that some might read it who will become great winners of souls!

Who knows how many will find their way to peace by what they read here? A more important question to you, dear reader, is this: Will you be one of them?

A certain man placed a fountain by the wayside, and he hung up a cup near to it by a little chain. He was told sometime after that a great art critic had found much fault with its design. "But," said he, "do many thirsty persons drink at it?" Then they told him that thousands of poor people, men, women, and children, slaked their thirst at this fountain; and he smiled and said that he was little troubled by the critic's observation, only he hoped that on some sultry summer's day the critic himself might fill the cup and be refreshed and praise the name of the Lord.

Here is my fountain, and here is my cup. Find fault if you please; but do drink of the water of life. I only care for this. I would rather bless the soul of the poorest crossing sweeper or rag gatherer than please a prince of the blood and fail to convert him to God.

Reader, do you mean business in reading these pages? If so, we are agreed at the outset; but nothing short of your finding Christ and heaven is the business aimed at here. Oh, that we may seek this together! I do so by dedicating this little book with prayer. Won't you join me by looking up to God and asking Him to bless you while you read? Providence has put these pages in your way; you have a little spare time in which to read them; and you feel willing to give your attention to them. These are good signs. Who knows but the set time of blessing is come for you? At any rate, "Today, if you will hear His voice, do not harden your hearts" (Heb. 3:15).

For Further Thought

1. *Jesus Christ offers humanity spiritual water. What is the effect of drinking that water? (See John 4:14.)*
2. *In John 7:37 Jesus again offers spiritual water. According to verse 38, how does one drink that water?*

2

WHAT ARE WE AT?

I heard a story; I think it came from the north country: A minister called upon a poor woman, intending to give her help, for he knew that she was very poor. With his money in his hand, he knocked at the door, but she did not answer. He concluded she was not at home and went his way. A little after he met her at the church and told her that he had remembered her need: "I called at your house and knocked several times, and I supposed you were not at home, for I had no answer."

"At what hour did you call, sir?"

"It was about noon."

"Oh, dear," she said. "I heard you, sir, and I am so sorry I did not answer, but I thought it was the man calling for the rent."

Many a poor woman knows what this meant. Now, it is my desire to be heard, and therefore I want to say that I am not calling for the rent; indeed, it is not the object of this book to ask anything of you, but to tell you that salvation is all of grace, which means *free, gratis, for nothing.*

> The Lord Himself invites you to a conference concerning your immediate and endless happiness, and He would not have done this if He did not mean well toward you.

Oftentimes when we are anxious to win attention, our hearer thinks, "Ah! Now I am going to be told my duty. It is the man calling for that which is due to God, and I am sure I have nothing wherewith to pay. I will not be at home." No, this book does not come to make a demand upon you, but to bring you something. We are not going to talk about law, duty, and punishment, but about love, goodness, forgiveness, mercy, and eternal life. Do not, therefore, act as if you were not at home. Do not turn a deaf ear or a careless heart. I am asking nothing of you in the name of God or man. It is not my intent to make any requirement at your hands, but I come in God's name to bring you a free gift, which it shall be to your present and eternal joy to receive. Open the door and let my pleadings enter. "Come now, and let us reason together" (Isa. 1:18). The Lord Himself invites you to a conference concerning your immediate and endless happiness, and He would not have done this if He did not mean well toward you. Do not refuse the Lord Jesus who knocks at your door, for He knocks with a hand that was nailed to the tree for such as you are. Since His only and sole object is your good, incline your ear and come to Him. Hearken diligently, and let the good Word sink into your soul. It may be that the hour is come in which you shall enter upon that new life which is the beginning of heaven. Faith comes by hearing, and reading is a sort of hearing: Faith may come to you while you are reading this book. Why not? O blessed Spirit of all grace, make it so!

FOR FURTHER THOUGHT

1. *Revelation 3:20 pictures Jesus Christ knocking on a door. According to this verse, what will He do if someone opens the door?*
2. *Read Isaiah 1:18. What does it say will happen to a believer's sins?*

3

GOD JUSTIFIES THE UNGODLY

HIS message is for you. You will find the text in the epistle to the Romans, the fourth chapter and the fifth verse: *But to him who does not work but believes on Him who justifies the ungodly, his faith is accounted for righteousness.*

I call your attention to those words, "Him who justifies the ungodly." They seem to me to be very wonderful words.

Are you not surprised that there should be such an expression as that in the Bible, "Him who justifies the ungodly"? I have heard that men who hate the doctrines of the cross bring it as a charge against God, that He saves wicked men and receives to Himself the vilest of the vile. See how this scripture accepts the charge and plainly states it! By the mouth of His servant Paul, by the inspiration of the Holy Spirit, He takes to Himself the title of "Him who justifies the ungodly." He makes those just who are unjust, forgives those who deserve to be punished, and favors those who deserve no favor. You thought, did you not, that salvation was for the good? That God's grace was for the pure and holy, who are free from sin? It has fallen into your mind that, if you were excellent, then God would reward you; and you have thought that because you are not worthy, therefore there could be no way of your enjoying His favor. You must be somewhat surprised to read a text like this: "Him who justifies the ungodly." I do not wonder that you are surprised; for with all my familiarity with the great grace of God, I never cease to wonder at it. It does sound surprising, does it not, that it should be possible for a holy God to justify an unholy man? We, according to the natural legality of our hearts, are always talking about our own goodness and our own worthiness, and we stubbornly hold to it that there must be somewhat in us in order to win the notice of God. Now, God, who sees through all deceptions, knows that there is no goodness whatever in us. He says, "There is none righteous, no, not one" (Rom. 3:10). He knows that "all our righteousnesses are like filthy rags"

(Isa. 64:6), and therefore, the Lord Jesus did not come into the world to look after goodness and righteousness, and to bestow them upon persons who have none of them. He came, not because we are just, but to make us so: He justifies the ungodly.

When a counselor comes into court, if he is an honest man, he desires to plead the case of an innocent person and justify him before the court from the things that are falsely laid to his charge. It should be the lawyer's object to justify the innocent person, and he should not attempt to screen the guilty party. It lies not in man's right or in man's power truly to justify the guilty. This is a miracle reserved for the Lord alone. God, the infinitely just sovereign, knows that there is not a just man upon earth who does good and sins not, and therefore, in the infinite sovereignty of His divine nature and in the splendor of His ineffable love, He undertakes the task, not so much of justifying the just as of justifying the ungodly. God has devised ways and means of making the ungodly man to stand justly accepted before Him: He has set up a system by which with perfect justice He can treat the guilty as if he had been all his life free from offense. He can treat him as if he were wholly free from sin. He justifies the ungodly.

Jesus Christ came into the world to save sinners. It is a very surprising thing, a thing to be marveled at most of all by those who enjoy it. I know that it is to me even to this day the greatest wonder that I ever heard of that God should ever justify me. I feel myself to be a lump of unworthiness, a mass of corruption, and a heap of sin apart from His almighty love. I know by a full assurance that I am justified by faith that is in Christ Jesus, treated as if I had been perfectly just, and made an heir of God and a joint heir with Christ; and yet by nature I must take my place among the most sinful. I, who am altogether undeserving, am treated as if I am deserving. I am loved with as much love as if I had always been godly, whereas previously I was ungodly. Who can help being astonished at this? Gratitude for such favor stands dressed in robes of wonder.

Now, while this is very surprising, I want you to notice how available it makes the gospel to you and to me. If God justifies the ungodly, then, dear friend, He can justify you. Is not that the very kind of person that you are? If you are unconverted at this moment, it is a very proper description of you; you have lived without God, you have been the reverse of godly; in one word, you have been and are ungodly. Perhaps you have not even attended a place of worship on Sunday, but have lived in disregard of God's day and house and Word—this proves you to have been ungodly. Sadder still, it may be you have even tried to doubt God's existence and have gone the length of saying that you did so. You have lived on this fair earth, which is full of the tokens of God's presence, and all the while you have shut your eyes to the clear evidences of His power and Godhead. You have lived as if there were no God. Indeed, you would have been very pleased if you could have demonstrated to yourself to a certainty that there was no God whatever. Possibly you have lived a great many years in this way, so that you are now pretty well settled in your ways, yet God is not in any of them. If you were labeled *ungodly*, it would as well describe you as if the sea were to be labeled salt water. Would it not?

> *Jesus Christ came into the world to save sinners. It is a very surprising thing, a thing to be marveled at most of all by those who enjoy it.*

Possibly you are a person of another sort; you have regularly attended to all the outward forms of religion, yet you have had no heart in them at all, but have been really ungodly. Though meeting with the people of God, you have never met with God for yourself; you have been in the choir but have not praised the Lord with your heart. You have lived without any love for God in your heart or regard to His commands in your life. Well, you are just the kind of man to whom this gospel is sent—this gospel that says that God justifies the ungodly. It is very wonderful, but it is happily available for you. It just suits you. Does it not? How I wish that you would accept it! If you are a sensible man, you will see the remarkable grace of God in providing for such as you are, and you will say to yourself, "Justify the ungodly! Why, then, should not I be justified, and justified at once?"

Now, observe further, that it must be so, that the salvation of God is for those who do not deserve it and have no preparation for it. It is reasonable that the statement should be put in the Bible; for, dear friend, no others need justifying but those who have no justification of their own. If any of my readers are perfectly righteous, they want no justifying. You feel that you are doing your duty well and almost putting Heaven under an obligation to you. What do you want with a Savior or with mercy? What do you want with justification? You will be tired of my book by this time, for it will have no interest to you.

If any of you are giving yourselves such proud airs, listen to me for a little while. You will be lost as sure as you are alive. You righteous men, whose righteousness is all of your own working, are either deceivers or deceived; for the scripture cannot lie, and it says plainly, "There is none righteous, no, not one." In any case, I have no gospel to preach to the self-righteous, no, not a word of it. Jesus Christ Himself came not to call the righteous, and I am not going to do what He did not do. If I called you, you would not come. Therefore, I will not call you under that character. No, I bid you rather look at that righteousness of yours till you see what a delusion it is. It is not half so substantial as a cobweb. Have done with it! Flee from it! Oh, believe that the only persons that can need justification are those who are not in themselves just! They need that something should be done for them to make them just before the judgment seat of God. Depend upon it. The Lord only does that which is needful. Infinite wisdom never attempts that which is unnecessary. Jesus never undertakes that which is superfluous. To make him just who is just is no work for God—that were a labor for a fool. But to make him just who is unjust—that is work for infinite love and mercy. To justify the ungodly—this is a miracle worthy of a God. And for certain it is so.

> Dear friend, no others need justifying but those who have no justification of their own. If any of my readers are perfectly righteous, they want no justifying.

Now look. If there be anywhere in the world a physician who has discovered sure and precious remedies, to whom is that physician sent? Is it to those who are perfectly healthy? I think not. Put him down in a district where there are no sick persons, and he feels that he is not in his place. There is nothing for him to do. "Those who are well have no need of a physician, but those who are sick" (Matt. 9:12). Is it not equally clear that the great remedies of grace and redemption are for the sick in soul? They cannot be for the whole, for they cannot be of use to such. If you, dear friend, feel that you are spiritually sick, the Great Physician has come into the world for you. If you are altogether undone by reason of your sin, you are the very person aimed at in the plan of salvation. I say that the Lord of love had just such as you in His eye when He arranged the system of grace. Suppose a man of generous spirit were to resolve to forgive all those who were indebted to him; it is clear that this can only apply to those really in his debt. One person owes him a thousand pounds; another owes him fifty pounds; each one has but to have his bill receipted, and the liability is wiped out. But the most generous person cannot forgive the debts of those who do not owe him anything. It is out of the power of omnipotence to forgive where there is no sin. Pardon, therefore, cannot be for you who have no sin. Pardon must be for the guilty. Forgiveness must be for the sinful. It is absurd to talk of forgiving those who do not need forgiveness, pardoning those who have never offended.

Do you think that you must be lost because you are a sinner? This is the reason why you can be saved. Because you own yourself to be a sinner I would encourage you to believe that grace is ordained for such as you are. One of our hymn writers even dared to say:

> *A sinner is a sacred thing;*
> *The Holy Spirit has made him so.*

It is truly so, that Jesus seeks and saves that which is lost. He died and made a real atonement for real sinners. When men are not playing with words or calling themselves "miserable sinners" out of mere compliment, I feel overjoyed to meet with them. I would be glad to talk all night to bona fide sinners. The inn of mercy never closes its doors upon such, neither weekdays or Sunday. Our Lord Jesus did not die for imaginary sins, but His heart's blood was spilled to wash out deep crimson stains, which nothing else can remove.

He that is a black sinner is the kind of man that Jesus Christ came to make white. A gospel preacher on one occasion preached a sermon from, "Even now the ax is laid to the root of the trees" (Matt. 3:10), and he delivered such a sermon that one of his hearers said to him, "One would have thought that you had been preaching to criminals. Your sermon ought to have been delivered in the county jail."

"Oh no," said the good man, "if I were preaching in the county jail, I should not preach from that text; there I should preach, 'This is a faithful saying and worthy of all acceptance, that Christ Jesus came into the world to save sinners'" (1 Tim. 1:15).

Just so: The law is for the self-righteous, to humble their pride; the gospel is for the lost, to remove their despair.

If you are not lost, what do you want with a savior? Should the shepherd go after those who never went astray? Why should the woman sweep her house for the bits of money that were never out of her purse? No, the medicine is for the diseased; the quickening is for the dead; the pardon is for the guilty; liberation is for those who are bound; the opening of eyes is for those who are blind. How can the Savior, His death upon the cross, and the gospel of pardon be accounted for unless it be upon the supposition that men are guilty and worthy of condemnation? The sinner is the gospel's reason for existence. You my friend, to whom this word now comes, if you are undeserving, ill-deserving, and hell-deserving—you are the sort of man for whom the gospel is ordained, arranged, and proclaimed. God justifies the ungodly.

> If you, dear friend, feel that you are spiritually sick, the Great Physician has come into the world for you. If you are altogether undone by reason of your sin, you are the very person aimed at in the plan of salvation.

I would like to make this very plain. I hope that I have done so already; but still, plain as it is, it is only the Lord that can make a man see it. It does at first seem most amazing to an awakened man that salvation should really be for him as a lost and guilty one. He thinks that it must be for him as a penitent man, forgetting that his penitence is a part of his salvation. "Oh," says he, "but I must be this and that"—all of which is true, for he shall be this and that as the result of salvation; but salvation comes to him before he has any of the results of salvation. It comes to him, in fact, while he deserves only this bare, beggarly, base, and abominable description: "ungodly." That is all he is when God's gospel comes to justify him.

May I therefore urge upon any who have no good thing about them, who fear that they have not even a good feeling, or anything whatever that can recommend them to God, that they will firmly believe that our gracious God is able and willing to take them without anything to recommend them, and to forgive them spontaneously, not because they are good, but because He is good. Does He not make His sun to shine on the evil as well as on the good? Does He not give fruitful seasons and send the rain and the sunshine in their time upon the most ungodly nations? Aye, even Sodom had its sun and Gomorrah had its dew. Oh, friend, the great grace of God surpasses my conception and your conception, and I would have you think worthily of it! As high as the heavens are above the earth, so high are God's thoughts above our thoughts. He can abundantly pardon. Jesus Christ came into the world to save sinners. Forgiveness is for the guilty. Do not attempt to touch yourself up and make yourself something other than you really are, but come as you are to Him who justifies the ungodly.

A great artist some short time ago had painted a part of the corporation of the city in which he lived, and he wanted, for historic purposes, to include in his picture certain characters well known in the town. Everybody knew a crossing sweeper, unkempt, ragged, and filthy, and there was a suitable place for him in the picture. The artist said to this ragged and rugged individual, "I will pay you well if you will come down to my studio and let me take your likeness." He came round in the morning, but he was soon sent about his business, for he had washed his face, combed his hair, and donned a respectable suit of clothes. He was needed as a beggar and was not invited in any other capacity. Even so, the gospel will receive you into its halls if you come as a sinner, not otherwise. Wait not for reformation, but come at once for salvation. God justifies the ungodly, and that takes you up where you now are. It meets you in your worst estate.

> *God is able and willing to take them without anything to recommend them, and to forgive them spontaneously, not because they are good, but because He is good.*

Come in your disorder. I mean, come to your heavenly Father in all your sin and sinfulness. Come to Jesus just as you are—leprous, filthy, naked, neither fit to live or fit to die. Come, you who are the very sweepings of creation. Come, though you hardly dare to hope for anything but death. Come, though despair is brooding over you, pressing upon your bosom like a horrible nightmare. Come and ask the Lord to justify another ungodly one. Why should He not? Come, for this great mercy of God is meant for such as you are. I put it in the language of the text, and I cannot put it more strongly: The Lord God Himself takes to Himself this gracious title: "Him who justifies the ungodly." He makes just and causes to be treated as just those who by nature are ungodly. Is not that a wonderful word for you? Reader, do not delay till you have well considered this matter.

For Further Thought

1. *Romans 5:18 mentions Adam's disobedience resulting in condemnation to all. What does Christ's righteous act bring?*
2. *What was our condition when Christ died for the ungodly? (See Romans 5:6.)*

4

It Is God Who Justifies

Who shall bring a charge against God's elect?
It is God who justifies.
ROMANS 8:33

A wonderful thing it is, this being justified, or made just. If we had never broken the laws of God, we should not have needed it, for we should have been just in ourselves. He who has all his life done the things that he ought to have done, and has never done anything which he ought not to have done, is justified by the law. But you, dear reader, are not of that sort I am quite sure. You have too much honesty to pretend to be without sin, and therefore you need to be justified.

Now, if you justify yourself, you will simply be a self-deceiver. Therefore do not attempt it. It is never worthwhile.

If you ask your fellow mortals to justify you, what can they do? You can make some of them speak well of you for small favors, and others will backbite you for less. Their judgment is not worth much.

Our text says, "It is God who justifies," and this is a deal more to the point. It is an astonishing fact, and one that we ought to consider with care. Come and see.

In the first place, nobody else but God would ever have thought of justifying those who are guilty. They have lived in open rebellion; they have done evil with both hands; they have gone from bad to worse; they have turned back to sin even after they have smarted for it, and have therefore for a while been forced to leave it. They have broken the law and trampled on the gospel. They have refused proclamations of mercy and have persisted in ungodliness. How can they be forgiven and justified? Their fellowmen, despairing of them, say, "They are hopeless cases." Even Christians look upon them with sorrow rather than with hope, but not so their God. He, in the splendor of his electing grace, having chosen some of them before the foundation of the world, will not rest till He has justified them and made them to be accepted in the Beloved. Is it not written, "Whom He predestined, these He also called; whom He called, these He also justified; and whom He justified, these He also glorified" (Rom. 8:30)? Thus you see there are some whom the Lord resolves to justify. Why should not you and I be of the number?

None but God ever would have thought of justifying me. I am a wonder to myself. I doubt not that grace is equally seen in others. Look at Saul of Tarsus who foamed at the mouth against God's servants. Like a hungry wolf, he worried the lambs and the sheep right and left, yet God struck him down on the road to Damascus and changed his heart, and so fully justified him that before long, this man became the greatest preacher of justification by faith who ever lived. He must often have marveled that he was justified by faith in Christ Jesus, for he was once a determined stickler for salvation by the works of the law. None but God ever would have thought of justifying such a man as Saul the persecutor, but the Lord God is glorious in grace.

But even if anybody had thought of justifying the ungodly, none but God could have done it. It is quite impossible for any person to forgive offenses that have not been committed against him. A person has greatly injured you. You can forgive him, and I hope you will, but no third person can forgive him apart from you. If the wrong is done to you, the pardon must come from you. If we have sinned against God, it is in God's power to forgive, for the sin is against Him. That is why David says, in the fifty-first Psalm: "Against You, You only, have I sinned, and done this evil in Your sight" (v. 4), for then God, against whom the offense is committed, can put the offense away. That which we owe to God, our great Creator can remit if so it pleases Him, and if He remits it, it is remitted. None but the great God, against whom we have committed the sin, can blot out that sin; let us, therefore, see that we go to Him and seek mercy at His hands. Do not let us be led aside by those who would have us confess to them; they have no warrant in the Word of God for their pretensions. But even if they were ordained to pronounce absolution in God's name, it must still be better to go ourselves to the great Lord through Jesus Christ, the mediator, and seek and find pardon at His hand since we are sure that this is the right way. Proxy religion involves too great a risk. You had better see to your soul's matters yourself and leave them in no man's hands.

Only God can justify the ungodly, but He can do it to perfection. He casts our sins behind His back; He blots them out; He says that though they be sought for, they shall not be found. With no other reason for it but His own infinite goodness, He has prepared a glorious way by which He can make scarlet sins as white as snow and remove our transgressions from us as far as the east is from the west. He says, "I will not remember your sins" (Isa. 43:25). He goes the length of making an end of sin. One of old called out in amazement, "Who is a God like You, pardoning iniquity and passing over the transgression of the remnant of His heritage? He does not retain His anger forever, because He delights in mercy" (Mic. 7:18).

> *If* the wrong is done to you, the pardon must come from you. If we have sinned against God, it is in God's power to forgive, for the sin is against Him.

We are not now speaking of justice, or of God's dealing with men according to their deserts. If you profess to deal with the righteous Lord on law terms, everlasting wrath threatens you, for that is what you deserve. Blessed be His name, He has not dealt with us after our sins; but now He treats us according to the terms of free grace and infinite compassion, and He says, "I will love them freely" (Hosea 14:4). Believe it, for it is certainly true that the great God is able to treat the guilty with abundant mercy; yea, He is able to treat the ungodly as if they had been always godly. Read carefully the parable of the prodigal son, and see how the forgiving father received the returning wanderer with as much love as if he had never gone away and had never defiled himself with harlots. So far did he carry this that the elder brother began to grumble at it; but the father never withdrew his love. Oh, my brother, however guilty you may be, if you will only come back to your God and Father, He will treat you as if you had never done wrong! He will regard you as just and deal with you accordingly. What say you to this?

Do you not see—for I want to bring out clearly what a splendid thing it is—that as none but God would think of justifying the ungodly, and none but God could do it, yet the Lord can do it? See how the apostle puts the challenge, "Who shall bring a charge against God's elect? It is

God who justifies" (Rom. 8:33). If God has justified a man, it is well done, it is rightly done, it is justly done, and it is everlastingly done. I read a statement in a magazine that is full of venom against the gospel and those who preach it, that we hold some kind of theory by which we imagine that sin can be removed from men. We hold no theory. We publish a fact. The grandest fact under heaven is this: Christ by His precious blood does actually put away sin, and God, for Christ's sake, dealing with men on terms of divine mercy, forgives the guilty and justifies them, not according to anything that He sees in them or foresees will be in them, but according to the riches of His mercy that lie in His own heart. This we have preached, do preach, and will preach as long as we live. "It is God who justifies"—who justifies the ungodly. He is not ashamed of doing it, nor are we of preaching it.

The justification that comes from God Himself must be beyond question. If the judge acquits me, who can condemn me? If the highest court in the universe has pronounced me just, who shall lay anything to my charge? Justification from God is a sufficient answer to an awakened conscience. The Holy Spirit by His means breathes peace over our entire nature, and we are no longer afraid. With this justification we can answer all the roarings and railings of Satan and ungodly men. With this we shall be able to die: With this we shall boldly rise again and face the last great court session.

> Bold shall I stand in that great day,
> For who aught to my charge shall lay?
> While by my Lord absolved I am
> From sin's tremendous curse and blame.
> —Count Ludwig Von Zinzendorf

Friend, the Lord can blot out all your sins. I make no shot in the dark when I say this. "Every sin and blasphemy will be forgiven men" (Matt. 12:31). Though you are steeped up to your throat in crime, He can with a word remove the defilement and say, "I am willing; be cleansed" (Luke 5:13). The Lord is a great forgiver.

He can even at this hour pronounce the sentence, "Your sins are forgiven" (Luke 7:48), and if He do this, no power in heaven or earth or under the earth can put you under suspicion, much less under wrath. Do not doubt the power of almighty love. You could not forgive your fellow man had he offended you as you have offended God, but you must not measure God's corn with your bushel; His thoughts and ways are as much above yours as the heavens are high above the earth.

"Well," say you, "it would be a great miracle if the Lord were to pardon me." It is just so. It would be a supreme miracle, and therefore He is likely to do it, for He does "great things, and unsearchable" (Job 5:9) which we looked not for.

I was myself stricken down with a horrible sense of guilt, which made my life a misery to me, but when I heard the command, "Look to Me, and be saved, all you ends of the earth! For I am God, and there is no other" (Isa. 45:22), I looked, and in a moment the Lord justified me. Jesus Christ, made sin for me, was what I saw, and that sight gave me rest. When those who were bitten by the fiery serpents in the wilderness looked to the serpent of brass, they were healed at once; and so was I when I looked to the crucified Savior. The Holy Spirit, who enabled me to believe, gave me peace through believing. I felt as sure that I was forgiven as before I felt sure of condemnation. I had been certain of my condemnation because the Word of God declared it and my conscience bore witness to it, but when the Lord justified me, the same witnesses made me equally certain. The Word of the Lord in the scripture says, "He who believes in Him is not condemned" (John 3:18), and my conscience bears witness that I believed and that God in pardoning me is just. Thus I have the witness of the Holy Spirit and my own conscience, and these two agree in one. Oh, how I wish that my reader would receive the testimony of God upon this matter, and then full soon he would also have the witness in himself!

> *Do not doubt the power of almighty love. You could not forgive your fellow man had he offended you as you have offended God, but you must not measure God's corn with your bushel.*

I venture to say that a sinner justified by God stands on even a surer footing than a righteous man justified by his works, if such there were. We could never be surer that we had done enough works; conscience would always be uneasy lest, after all, we should come short, and we could only have the trembling verdict of a fallible judgment to rely upon. But when

God Himself justifies and the Holy Spirit bears witness thereto by giving us peace with God, why then we feel that the matter is sure and settled, and we enter into rest. No tongue can tell the depth of that calm that comes over the soul that has received the peace of God that passes all understanding.

For Further Thought

1. *Read Romans 8:35. What are seven things that cannot separate believers from the love of God?*
2. *Read Romans 8:38–39. What are ten more things that cannot separate believers from the love of God?*

5

JUST AND THE JUSTIFIER

WE have seen the ungodly justified and have considered the great truth that only God can justify any man. We now come a step further and make the inquiry, How can a just God justify guilty men? Here we are met with a full answer in the words of Paul in Romans 3:21–26. We will read six verses from the chapter so as to get the run of the passage:

> *But now the righteousness of God apart from the law is revealed, being witnessed by the Law and the Prophets, even the righteousness of God, through faith in Jesus Christ, to all and on all who believe. For there is no difference; for all have sinned and fall short of the glory of God, being justified freely by His grace through the redemption that is in Christ Jesus, whom God set forth as a propitiation by His blood, through faith, to demonstrate His righteousness, because in His forbearance God had passed over the sins that were previously committed, to demonstrate at the present time His righteousness, that He might be just and the justifier of the one who has faith in Jesus.*

Here suffer me to give you a bit of personal experience. When I was under the hand of the Holy Spirit, under conviction of sin, I had a clear and sharp sense of the justice of God. Sin, whatever it might be to other people, became to me an intolerable burden. It was not so much that I feared hell, but that I feared sin. I knew myself to be so horribly guilty that I remember feeling that if God did not punish me for sin, He ought to do so. I felt that the judge of all the earth ought to condemn such sin as mine. I sat on the judgment seat, and I condemned myself to perish, for I confessed that had I been God I could have done no other than send such a guilty creature as I was down to the lowest hell. All the while, I had upon my mind a deep concern for the honor of God's name and the integrity of His moral government. I felt that it would not satisfy my conscience if I could be forgiven unjustly. The sin I had committed must be punished. But then there was the question how God could be just and yet justify me who had been so guilty. I asked my heart, "How can He be just and yet the justifier?" I was worried and wearied with this question; neither could I see any answer to it. Certainly, I never could have invented an answer that would have satisfied my conscience.

The doctrine of the atonement is to my mind one of the surest proofs of the divine inspiration of Holy Scripture. Who would or could have thought of the just ruler dying for the unjust rebel? This is no teaching of human mythology or dream of poetical imagination. This method of expiation is only known among men because it is a fact; fiction could not have devised it. God Himself ordained it; it is not a matter that could have been imagined.

I had heard the plan of salvation by the sacrifice of Jesus from my youth up; but I did not know any more about it in my innermost soul than if I had been born and bred a Hottentot. The light was there, but I was blind; it was of necessity that the Lord Himself should make the matter plain to me. It came to me as a new revelation, as fresh as if I had never read in scripture that Jesus was declared to be the propitiation for sins that God might be just. I believe it will have to come as a revelation to every newborn child of God whenever he sees it; I mean that glorious doctrine of the substitution of the Lord Jesus. I came to understand that salvation was possible through vicarious sacrifice, and that provision had been made in the first constitution and arrangement of things for such a substitution. I was made to see that He who is the Son of God, coequal and coeternal with the Father, had of old been made the covenant head of a chosen people that He might in that capacity suffer for them and save them. Inasmuch as our fall was not at the first a personal one, for we fell in our federal representative, the first Adam, it became possible for us to be recovered by a second representative, even by Him who has undertaken to be the covenant head of His people, so as to be their second Adam. I saw that before I actually sinned, I had fallen by my first father's sin; and I rejoiced that therefore it became possible in point of law for me to rise by a second head and representative. The fall by Adam left a loophole of escape; another Adam can undo the ruin made by the first. When I was anxious about the possibility of a just God pardoning me, I understood and saw by faith that He who is the Son of God became man, and in His own blessed person bore my sin in His own body on the tree. I saw that the chastisement of my peace was laid on Him, and that with His stripes I was healed. Dear friend, have you ever seen that? Have you ever understood how God can be just to the full, not remitting penalty or blunting the edge of the sword, and yet can be infinitely merciful and can justify the ungodly that turn to Him? It was because the Son of God, who is supremely glorious in His matchless person, undertook to vindicate the law by bearing the sentence due to me, that God is able to pass by my sin. The law of God was more vindicated by the death of Christ than it would have been had all transgressors been sent to hell. For the Son of God to suffer for sin was a more glorious establishment of the government of God than for the whole race to suffer.

> *This is no teaching of human mythology or dream of poetical imagination. This method of expiation is only known among men because it is a fact; fiction could not have devised it.*

Jesus has borne the death penalty on our behalf. Behold the wonder! There He hangs upon the cross! This is the greatest sight you will ever see. Son of God and Son of Man, there He hangs, bearing pains unutterable, the just for the unjust, to bring us to God. Oh, the glory of that sight! The innocent punished! The Holy One condemned! The ever blessed made a curse! The infinitely glorious put to a shameful death! The more I look at the sufferings of the Son of God, the surer I am that they must meet my case. Why did He suffer, if not to turn aside the penalty from us? If, then, He turned it aside by His death, it is turned aside, and those who believe in Him need not fear it. It must be so, that since expiation is made, God is able to forgive without shaking the basis of His throne, or in the least degree blotting the statute book. Conscience gets a full answer to her tremendous question. The wrath of God against iniquity, whatever that may be, must be beyond all conception terrible. Well did Moses say, "Who knows the power of Your anger?" (Ps. 90:11). Yet when we hear the Lord of glory cry, "Why have You forsaken Me?" (Mark 15:34) and see Him yielding up His spirit, we feel that the justice of God has received abundant vindication by obedience so perfect and death so terrible, rendered by so divine a person. If God Himself bows before His own law, what more can be done? There is more in the atonement by way of merit than there is in all human sin by way of demerit.

The great gulf of Jesus' loving self-sacrifice can swallow up the mountains of our sins, all of them. For the sake of the infinite good of this one representative man, the Lord may well look with favor upon other men, however unworthy they may be in and of themselves. It was a miracle of miracles that the Lord Jesus Christ should stand in our stead and "bear that we might never bear His Father's righteous ire." But He has done so. "It is finished" (John 19:30). God will spare the sinner because He did not spare His Son. God can pass by your transgressions because He laid those transgressions upon His only begotten Son nearly two thousand years ago. He who was the scapegoat for His people carried your sins away.

What is it to believe in Him? It is not merely to say He is God and the Savior, but to trust Him wholly and entirely and take Him for all your salvation from this time forth and forever—your Lord, your Master, your all. If you will have Jesus, He has you already. If you believe on Him, I tell you that you cannot go to hell; for that were to make the sacrifice of Christ of none effect. It cannot be that a sacrifice should be accepted, and yet the soul should die for whom that sacrifice has been received. If the believing soul could be condemned, then why was there a sacrifice? If Jesus died in my stead, why should I die also? Every believer can claim that the sacrifice was actually made for him: By faith he has laid his hands on it and made it his own, and therefore he may rest assured that he can never perish. The Lord would not receive this offering on our behalf and then condemn us to die. The Lord cannot read our pardon written in the blood of His own Son and then smite us. That is impossible. Oh, that you may have grace given you at once to look away to Jesus and to begin at the beginning, even at Jesus, who is the fountainhead of mercy to guilty man!

"He justifies the ungodly," and it is God who justifies, therefore, and for that reason only it can be done, and He does it through the atoning sacrifice of His divine Son. Therefore it can be justly done—so justly done that none will ever question it, so thoroughly done that in the last tremendous day, when heaven and earth shall pass away, there shall be none who shall deny the validity of the justification. "Who shall bring a charge against God's elect? It is God who justifies. Who is he who condemns? It is Christ who died, and furthermore is also risen, who is even at the right hand of God, who also makes intercession for us" (Rom. 8:33–34).

Now, poor soul! Will you come into this lifeboat, just as you are? Here is safety from the wreck! Accept the sure deliverance. "I have nothing with me," say you. You are not asked to bring anything with you. Men who escape for their lives will leave even their clothes behind. Leap for it just as you are.

> *Every believer can claim that the sacrifice was actually made for him: By faith he has laid his hands on it and made it his own, and therefore he may rest assured that he can never perish.*

I will tell you this thing about myself to encourage you. My sole hope for heaven lies in the full atonement made upon Calvary's cross for the ungodly. On that I firmly rely. I have not the shadow of a hope anywhere else. You are in the same condition as I am, for we neither of us have anything of our own worth as a ground of trust. Let us join hands and stand together at the foot of the cross and trust our souls once for all to Him who shed His blood for the guilty. The one and the same Savior will save us. If you perish trusting Him, I must perish too. What can I do more to prove my own confidence in the gospel that I set before you?

FOR FURTHER THOUGHT

1. *According to Galatians 3:13, how did Christ redeem us from the curse of the law?*
2. *What does Galatians 3:14 say we receive when we believe?*

6

CONCERNING DELIVERANCE
FROM SINNING

IN this place I would say a plain word or two to those who understand the method of justification by faith in Christ Jesus but whose trouble is that they cannot cease from sin. We can never be happy, restful, or spiritually healthy till we become holy. We must be rid of sin. But how is that riddance to be worked? This is the life-or-death question of many. The old nature is very strong, and they have tried to curb and tame it; but it will not be subdued, and they find themselves, though anxious to be better, if anything, growing worse than before. The heart is so hard, the will is so obstinate, the passions are so furious, the thoughts are so volatile, the imagination is so ungovernable, the desires are so wild that the man feels that he has a den of wild beasts within him, which will eat him up sooner than be ruled by him. We may say of our fallen nature what the Lord said to Job concerning Leviathan: "Will you play with him as with a bird, or will you leash him for your maidens?" (41:5). A man might as well hope to hold the north wind in the hollow of his hand as expect to control by his own strength those boisterous powers that dwell within his fallen nature. This is a greater feat than any of the fabled labors of Hercules. God is wanted here.

"I could believe that Jesus would forgive sin," says one, "but then my trouble is that I sin again, and that I feel such awful tendencies to evil within me. As surely as a stone, if it is flung up into the air, soon comes down again to the ground, so do I, though I am sent up to heaven by earnest preaching, return again to my insensible state. Alas! I am easily fascinated with the dragon eyes of sin and am thus held as under a spell so that I cannot escape from my own folly."

Dear friend, salvation would be a sadly incomplete affair if it did not deal with this part of our ruined estate. We want to be purified as well as pardoned. Justification without sanctification would not be salvation at all. It would call the leper clean and leave him to die of his disease. It would forgive the rebellion and allow the rebel to remain an enemy to his king. It would remove the consequences but overlook the cause, and this would leave an endless and hopeless task before us. It would stop the stream for a time but leave an open fountain of defilement, which would sooner or later break forth with increased power. Remember that the Lord Jesus came to take away sin in three ways: He came to remove the penalty of sin, the power of sin, and, at last, the presence of sin. At once you may reach to the second part; the power of sin may immediately be broken; and so you will be on the road to the third, namely, the removal of the presence of sin. "You know that He was manifested to take away our sins" (1 John 3:5).

> *Justification without sanctification would not be salvation at all. It would call the leper clean and leave him to die of his disease. It would forgive the rebellion and allow the rebel to remain an enemy to his king.*

The angel said of our Lord, "You shall call His name JESUS, for He will save His people from their sins" (Matt. 1:21). Our Lord Jesus came to destroy in us the works of the devil. That which was said at our Lord's birth was also declared in His death, for when the soldier pierced His side, forthwith came there out blood and water to set forth the double cure by which we are delivered from the guilt and the defilement of sin.

If, however, you are troubled about the power of sin and about the tendencies of your nature, as you well may be, here is a promise for you. Have faith in it, for it stands in that covenant of grace, which is ordered in all things and sure. God, who cannot lie, has said in Ezekiel 36:26: "I will give you a new heart and put a new spirit within you; I will take the heart of stone out of your flesh and give you a heart of flesh."

You see, it is all "I will," and "I will." "I will give," and "I will take away." This is the royal style of the King of kings, who is able to accomplish all His will. No word of His shall ever fall to the ground.

The Lord knows right well that you cannot change your own heart and cannot cleanse your own nature; but He also knows that He can do both.

He can cause the Ethiopian to change his skin and the leopard his spots. Hear this, and be astonished: He can create you a second time; He can cause you to be born again. This is a miracle of grace, but the Holy Spirit will perform it. It would be a very wonderful thing if one could stand at the foot of Niagara Falls and could speak a word that would make the river Niagara begin to run upstream and leap up that great precipice over which it now rolls in stupendous force. Nothing but the power of God could achieve that marvel; but that would be more than a fit parallel to what would take place if the course of your nature were altogether reversed. All things are possible with God. He can reverse the direction of your desires and the current of your life, and instead of going downward from God, He can make your whole being tend upward toward God. That is, in fact, what the Lord has promised to do for all who are in the covenant; and we know from scripture that all believers are in the covenant. Let me read the words again: "Then I will give them one heart, and I will put a new spirit within them, and take the stony heart out of their flesh, and give them a heart of flesh" (Ezek. 11:19).

> When God puts a new heart into us, the new heart is there forever, and never will it harden into stone again. He who made it flesh will keep it so.

What a wonderful promise! And it is yea and amen in Christ Jesus to the glory of God by us. Let us lay hold of it, accept it as true, and appropriate it to us. Then shall it be fulfilled in us, and we shall have, in after days and years, to sing of that wondrous change the sovereign grace of God has wrought in us.

It is well worthy of consideration that when the Lord takes away the stony heart, that deed is done; and when that is once done, no known power can ever take away the new heart He gives and the right spirit He puts within us. "The gifts and calling of God are without repentance" (Rom. 11:29 KJV)—that is, without repentance on His part; He does not take away what He once has given. Let Him renew you and you will be renewed. Man's reformations and cleanings up soon come to an end, for the dog returns to his vomit, but when God puts a new heart into us, the new heart is there forever, and never will it harden into stone again. He who made it flesh will keep it so. Herein we may rejoice and be glad forever in that which God creates in the kingdom of His grace.

> *I* once heard a convert say, "*Either all the world is changed, or else I am.*" The new nature follows after right as naturally as the old nature wanders after wrong.

To put the matter very simply: Did you ever hear of Mr. Rowland Hill's illustration of the cat and the sow? I will give it in my own fashion to illustrate our Savior's expressive words, "Ye must be born again" (John 3:7 KJV). Do you see that cat? What a cleanly creature she is! How cleverly she washes herself with her tongue and her paws! It is quite a pretty sight! Did you ever see a sow do that? No, you never did. It is contrary to its nature. It prefers to wallow in the mire. Go and teach a sow to wash itself, and see how little success you would gain. It would be a great sanitary improvement if swine would be clean. Teach them to wash and clean themselves as the cat has been doing! Useless task. You may by force wash that sow, but it hastens to the mire and is soon as foul as ever. The only way in which you can get a sow to wash itself is to transform it into a cat; then it will wash and be clean, but not till then! Suppose that transformation to be accomplished, and then what was difficult or impossible is easy enough; the swine will henceforth be fit for your parlor and your hearth rug. So it is with an ungodly man: You cannot force him to do what a renewed man does most willingly; you may teach him and set him a good example, but he cannot learn the art of holiness, for he has no mind to it. His nature leads him another way. When the Lord makes a new man of him, then all things wear a different aspect. So great is this change that I once heard a convert say, "Either all the world is changed, or else I am." The new nature follows after right as naturally as the old nature wanders after wrong. What a blessing to receive such a nature! Only the Holy Spirit can give it.

Did it ever strike you what a wonderful thing it is for the Lord to give a new heart and a right spirit to a man? You have seen a lobster, perhaps, which has fought with another lobster and lost one of its claws, and a new claw has grown. That is a remarkable thing; but it is a much more astounding fact that a man should have a new heart given to him. This indeed is a miracle beyond the powers of nature. There is a tree. If you cut off one of its limbs, another one may grow in its place; but can you change the tree; can you sweeten sour sap; can you make the thorn bear figs? You can graft something better into it, and that is the analogy that nature gives us of the work of grace, but absolutely to change the vital sap of the tree would be a miracle indeed. Such a prodigy and mystery of power God works in all who believe in Jesus.

If you yield yourself up to the Lord's divine working, He will alter your nature. He will subdue the old nature and breathe new life into you. Put your trust in the Lord Jesus Christ, and He will take the stony heart out of your flesh and give you a heart of flesh. Where everything was hard, everything shall be tender; where everything was vicious, everything shall be virtuous; where everything tended downward, everything shall rise upward with impetuous force. The lion of anger shall give place to the lamb of meekness; the raven of uncleanness shall fly before the dove of purity; the vile serpent of deceit shall be trodden under the heel of truth.

I have seen with my own eyes such marvelous changes of moral and spiritual character that I despair of none. I could, if it were fitting, point out those who were once unchaste women who are now pure as the driven snow, and blaspheming men who now delight all around them by their intense devotion. Thieves are made honest, drunkards sober, liars truthful, and scoffers zealous. Wherever the grace of God has appeared to a man, it has trained him to deny ungodliness and worldly lusts and to live soberly, righteously, and godly in this present evil world. And, dear reader, it will do the same for you.

"I cannot make this change," says one. Who said you could? The scripture that we have quoted speaks not of what man will do, but of what God will do. It is God's promise, and it is for Him to fulfill His own engagements. Trust in Him to fulfill His Word to you, and it will be done.

"But how is it to be done?" What business is that of yours? Must the Lord explain His methods before you will believe Him? The Lord's working in this matter is a great mystery: The Holy Spirit performs it. He who made the promise has the responsibility of keeping the promise, and He is equal to the occasion. God, who promises this marvelous change, will assuredly carry it out in all who receive Jesus, for to all such He gives power to become the sons of God. Oh, that you would believe it! Oh, that you would do the gracious Lord the justice to believe that He can and will do this for you, great miracle though it will be! Oh, that you would believe that God cannot lie! Oh, that you would trust Him for a new heart and a right spirit, for He can give them to you! May the Lord give you faith in His promise, faith in His Son, faith in the Holy Spirit, and faith in Him, and to Him shall be praise and honor and glory forever and ever! Amen.

FOR FURTHER THOUGHT

1. *Titus 2:11 declares that the grace of God has appeared to all people. What do verses 12–14 say that this grace teaches us?*
2. *In Romans 7:24 there is the cry, "O wretched man that I am! Who will deliver me from this body of death?" What is the answer to this cry in Romans 8:2?*

7

By Grace through Faith

For by grace you have been saved through faith.
Ephesians 2:8

I think it well to turn a little to one side that I may ask my reader to observe adoringly the fountainhead of our salvation, which is the grace of God. "By grace you have been saved." Because God is gracious, therefore sinful men are forgiven, converted, purified, and saved. It is not because of anything in them, or that ever can be in them, that they are saved, but because of the boundless love, goodness, pity, compassion, mercy, and grace of God. Tarry a moment, then, at the wellhead. Behold the pure river of water of life as it proceeds out of the throne of God and of the Lamb!

What an abyss is the grace of God! Who can measure its breadth? Who can fathom its depth? Like all the rest of the divine attributes, it is infinite. God is full of love, for "God is love." God is full of goodness; the very name *God* is short for *good*. Unbounded goodness and love enter into the very essence of the Godhead. It is because His mercy endures forever that men are not destroyed, because His compassions fail not that sinners are brought to Him and forgiven.

Remember this, or you may fall into error by fixing your minds so much upon the faith that is the channel of salvation as to forget the grace that is the fountain and source even of faith itself. Faith is the work of God's grace in us. No man can say that Jesus is the Christ but by the Holy Spirit. "No one can come to Me," says Jesus, "unless the Father who sent Me draws him" (John 6:44). So that faith, which is coming to Christ, is the result of divine drawing. Grace is the first and last moving cause of salvation; and faith, essential as it is, is only an important part of the machinery that grace employs. We are saved through faith, but salvation is by grace. Sound forth those words as with the archangel's trumpet: "By grace you are saved." What glad tidings for the undeserving!

Faith occupies the position of a channel or conduit pipe. Grace is the fountain and the stream; faith is the aqueduct along which the flood of mercy flows down to refresh the thirsty sons of men. It is a great pity when the aqueduct is broken. It is a sad sight to see around Rome the many noble aqueducts that no longer convey water into the city because the arches are broken and the marvelous structures are in ruins. The aqueduct must be kept entire to convey the current; and, even so, faith must be true and sound, leading right up to God and coming right down to ourselves, that it may become a serviceable channel of mercy to our souls.

> *The righteousness of faith is not the moral excellence of faith, but the righteousness of Jesus Christ that faith grasps and appropriates.*

Still, I again remind you that faith is only the channel or aqueduct and not the fountainhead, and we must not look so much to it as to exalt it above the divine source of all blessing that lies in the grace of God. Never make a Christ out of your faith or think of it as if it were the independent source of your salvation. Our life is found in looking to Jesus, not in looking to our own faith. By faith all things become possible to us; yet the power is not in the faith, but in the God upon whom faith relies. Grace is the powerful engine, and faith is the chain by which the carriage of the soul is attached to that great motivating power. The righteousness of faith is not the moral excellence of faith, but the righteousness of Jesus Christ that faith grasps and appropriates. The peace within the soul is not derived from the contemplation of our own faith; it comes to us from Him who is our peace, the hem of whose garment faith touches, and virtue comes out of Him into the soul.

See then, dear friend, that the weakness of your faith will not destroy you. A trembling hand may receive a golden gift. The Lord's salvation can come to us though we have only faith as a grain of mustard seed. The power lies in the grace of God and not in our faith. Great messages can be sent along slender wires, and the peace-giving witness of the Holy Spirit can reach the heart by means of a threadlike faith that seems almost unable to sustain its own weight. Think more of Him to whom you look than of the look itself. You must look away even from your own looking and see nothing but Jesus and the grace of God revealed in Him.

For Further Thought

1. *Where does Ephesians 2:8 say that we get our faith?*
2. *In Acts 16:14, what happened to Lydia that caused her to believe?*

8

FAITH: WHAT IS IT?

WHAT is this faith concerning which it is said, "By grace you are saved, through faith?" There are many descriptions of faith; but almost all the definitions I have met with have made me understand it less than I did before I saw them. The Negro said, when he read the chapter, that he would confound it; and it is very likely that he did so, though he meant to expound it. We may explain faith till nobody understands it. I hope I shall not be guilty of that fault. Faith is the simplest of all things, and perhaps because of its simplicity, it is the more difficult to explain.

What is faith? It is made up of three things: knowledge, belief, and trust. Knowledge comes first. "How shall they believe in Him of whom they have not heard?" (Rom 10:14). I want to be informed of a fact before I can possibly believe it. "Faith comes by hearing" (10:17). We must first hear in order that we may know what is to be believed. A measure of knowledge is essential to faith; hence the importance of getting knowledge. "Incline Your ear to me, and hear my speech" (Ps. 17:6). Such was the word of the ancient psalmist, and it is the word of the gospel still. Search the scriptures and learn what the Holy Spirit teaches concerning Christ and His salvation. Seek to know God: "He who comes to God must believe that He is, and that He is a rewarder of those who diligently seek Him" (Heb. 11:6). May the Holy Spirit give you the spirit of knowledge and of the fear of the Lord! Know the gospel: Know what the good news is, how it talks of free forgiveness, of change of heart, of adoption into the family of God, and of countless other blessings. Know especially Christ Jesus the Son of God, the Savior of men, united to us by His human nature and yet one with God, and thus able to act as mediator between God and man, able to lay His hand upon both and to be the connecting link between the sinner and the judge of all the earth. Endeavor to know more and more of Christ Jesus. Endeavor especially to know the doctrine of the sacrifice of Christ; for the point upon which saving faith mainly fixes itself is this: "God was in Christ reconciling the world to Himself, not imputing their trespasses to them" (2 Cor. 5:19). Know that Jesus was made "a curse for us" (for it is written, "Cursed is everyone who hangs on a tree") (Gal. 3:13). Drink deep of the doctrine of the substitutionary work of Christ; for therein lies the sweetest possible comfort to the guilty sons of men, since God "made Him who knew no sin to be sin for us, that we might become the righteousness of God in Him" (2 Cor. 5:21). Faith begins with knowledge.

> The heart believes that Jesus is verily and in truth our God and Savior, the Redeemer of men, the Prophet, Priest, and King of His people.

The mind goes on to believe that these things are true. The soul believes that God is and that He hears the cries of sincere hearts; that the gospel is from God; that justification by faith is the grand truth that God has revealed in these last days by His Spirit more clearly than before. Then the heart believes that Jesus is verily and in truth our God and Savior, the Redeemer of men, the Prophet, Priest, and King of His people. All this is accepted as sure truth, not to be called in question. I pray that you may at once come to this. Get firmly to believe that "the blood of Jesus Christ His Son cleanses us from all sin" (1 John 1:7); that His sacrifice is complete and fully accepted of God on man's behalf, so that he who believes on Jesus is not condemned. Believe these truths as you believe any other statements; for the difference between common faith and saving faith lies mainly in the subjects upon which it is exercised. Believe the witness of God just as you believe the testimony of your own father or friend. "If we receive the witness of men, the witness of God is greater" (1 John 5:9).

So far you have made an advance toward faith; only one more ingredient is needed to complete it, which is trust. Commit yourself to the merciful God; rest your hope on the gracious gospel; trust your soul on the dying and living Savior; wash away your sins in the atoning blood; accept His perfect righteousness, and all is well. Trust is the lifeblood of faith; there is no saving faith without it. The Puritans were accustomed to explain faith by the word *recumbency*. It meant leaning upon a thing. Lean with all your weight upon

Christ. It would be a better illustration still if I said fall at full length and lie on the Rock of Ages. Cast yourself upon Jesus; rest in Him; commit yourself to Him. That done, you have exercised saving faith. Faith is not a blind thing, for faith begins with knowledge. It is not a speculative thing, for faith believes facts of which it is sure. It is not an unpractical, dreamy thing, for faith trusts and stakes its destiny upon the truth of revelation. That is one way of describing what faith is.

Let me try again. Faith is believing that Christ is what He is said to be and that He will do what He has promised to do, and then to expect this of Him. The scriptures speak of Jesus Christ as being God in human flesh; as being perfect in His character; as being made a sin offering on our behalf; as bearing our sins in His own body on the tree. The scripture speaks of Him as having finished transgression, made an end of sin, and brought in everlasting righteousness. The sacred records further tell us that He rose again from the dead, that He "always lives to make intercession" for us (Heb. 7:25), that He has gone up into the glory and has taken possession of heaven on the behalf of His people, and that He will shortly come again to judge the world in righteousness and "the peoples with equity" (Ps. 98:9). We are most firmly to believe that it is even so; for this is the testimony of God the Father when He said, "This is My beloved Son. Hear Him!" (Mark 9:7). God the Holy Spirit also testifies this; for the Spirit has borne witness to Christ, both in the inspired Word and by numerous miracles and by His working in the hearts of men. We are to believe this testimony to be true.

> *Faith is not a blind thing, for faith begins with knowledge. It is not a speculative thing, for faith believes facts of which it is sure. It is not an unpractical, dreamy thing, for faith trusts and stakes its destiny upon the truth of revelation.*

Faith also believes that Christ will do what He has promised. Since He has promised to cast out none who come to Him, it is certain that He will not cast us out if we come to Him. Faith believes that since Jesus said, "The water that I shall give him will become in him a fountain of water springing up into everlasting life" (John 4:14), it must be true; and if we get this living water from Christ, it will abide in us and will well up within us in streams of holy life. Whatever Christ has promised to do He will do, and we must believe this, so as to look for pardon, justification, preservation, and eternal glory from His hands, according as He has promised them to believers in Him.

Then comes the next necessary step. Jesus is what He is said to be, and Jesus will do what He says He will do. Therefore we must each one trust Him, saying, "He will be to me what He says He is, and He will do to me what He has promised to do. I leave myself in the hands of Him who is appointed to save, that He may save me. I rest upon His promise that He will do even as He has said." This is a saving faith, and he that has it has everlasting life. Whatever his dangers and difficulties, whatever his darkness and depression, whatever his infirmities and sins, he who believes thus on Christ Jesus is not condemned and shall never come into condemnation.

May that explanation be of some service! I trust it may be used by the Spirit of God to direct my reader into immediate peace. "Do not be afraid; only believe" (Mark 5:36). Trust and be at rest.

My fear is lest the reader should rest content with understanding what is to be done and yet never do it. Better the poorest real faith actually at work than the best ideal of it left in the region of speculation. The great matter is to believe on the Lord Jesus at once. Never mind distinctions and definitions. A hungry man eats though he does not understand the composition of his food, the anatomy of his mouth, or the process of digestion: He lives because he eats. Another far cleverer person understands thoroughly the science of nutrition; but if he does not eat, he will die with all his knowledge. There are no doubt many at this hour in hell who understood the doctrine of faith but did not believe. On the other hand, not one who has trusted in the Lord Jesus has ever been cast out, though he may never have been able intelligently to define his faith. Oh, dear reader, receive the Lord Jesus into your soul, and you shall live forever! "He who believes in the Son has everlasting life" (John 3:36).

FOR FURTHER THOUGHT

1. *What is the definition of faith given in Hebrews 11:1?*
2. *According to Galatians 5:6, how does faith work?*

9

HOW MAY FAITH
BE ILLUSTRATED?

TO make the matter of faith clearer still, I will give you a few illustrations. Though the Holy Spirit alone can make my reader see, it is my duty and my joy to furnish all the light I can, and to pray the divine Lord to open blind eyes. Oh, that my reader would pray the same prayer for himself!

The faith that saves has its analogies in the human frame.

It is the eye that looks. By the eye we bring into the mind that which is far away; we can bring the sun and the far-off stars into the mind by a glance of the eye. So by trust we bring the Lord Jesus near to us; and though He is far away in heaven, He enters into our hearts. Only look to Jesus, for the hymn is strictly true:

> *There is life in a look at the Crucified One,*
> *There is life at this moment for you.*

Faith is the hand that grasps. When our hand takes hold of anything for itself, it does precisely what faith does when it appropriates Christ and the blessings of His redemption. Faith says, "Jesus is mine." Faith hears of the pardoning blood and cries, "I accept it to pardon me." Faith calls the legacies of the dying Jesus hers; and they are hers, for faith is Christ's heir; He has given Himself and all that He has to faith. Take, O friend, that which grace has provided for you. You will not be a thief, for you have a divine permit: "Take the water of life freely." He who may have a treasure simply by his grasping it will be foolish indeed if he remains poor.

Faith is the mouth that feeds upon Christ. Before food can nourish us, it must be received into us. This is a simple matter, this eating and drinking. We willingly receive into the mouth that which is our food, and then we consent that it should pass down into our inward parts, wherein it is taken up and absorbed into our bodily frame. Paul says, in his epistle to the Romans, in the tenth chapter, "The word is near you, in your mouth" (v. 8). Now then, all that is to be done is to swallow it, to suffer it to go down into the soul. Oh, that men had an appetite! For he who is hungry and sees meat before him does not need to be taught how to eat. "Give me," said one, "a knife and a fork and a chance." He was fully prepared to do the rest. Truly, a heart that hungers and thirsts after Christ has but to know that He is freely given, and at once it will receive Him. If my reader is in such a case, let him not hesitate to receive Jesus, for he may be sure that he will never be blamed for doing so: For unto "as many as received Him, to them He gave the right to become children of God" (John 1:12). He never repulses one, but He authorizes all who come to remain sons forever.

> ruly, a heart that hungers and thirsts after Christ has but to know that He is freely given, and at once it will receive Him.

The pursuits of life illustrate faith in many ways. The farmer buries good seed in the earth and expects it not only to live but also to be multiplied. He has faith in the covenant arrangement, that seedtime and harvest shall not cease, and he is rewarded for his faith.

The merchant places his money in the care of a banker and trusts in the honesty and soundness of the bank. He entrusts his capital to another's hands and feels far more at ease than if he had the solid gold locked up in an iron safe.

The sailor trusts himself to the sea. When he swims he takes his foot from the bottom and rests upon the buoyant ocean. He could not swim if he did not wholly cast himself upon the water.

The goldsmith puts precious metal into the fire, which seems eager to consume it, but he receives it back again from the furnace purified by the heat.

You cannot turn anywhere in life without seeing faith in operation between man and man or between man and natural law. Now, just as we trust in daily life, even so are we to trust in God as He is revealed in Christ Jesus.

Faith exists in different persons in various degrees, according to the amount of their knowledge or growth in grace. Sometimes faith is little more than a simple clinging to Christ, a sense of dependence and a willingness so to depend. When you are down at the seaside, you will see limpets sticking to the rock. You walk with a soft tread up to the rock; you strike the mollusk a rapid blow with your walking stick, and off he comes. Try the next limpet in that way. You have given him warning; he heard the blow with which you struck his neighbor, and he clings with all his might. You will never get him off, not you! Strike and strike again, but you may as soon break the rock. Our little friend, the limpet, does not know much, but he clings. He is not acquainted with the geological formation of the rock, but he clings. He can cling, and he has found something to cling to: This is all his stock of knowledge, and he uses it for his security and salvation. It is the limpet's life to cling to the rock, and it is the sinner's life to cling to Jesus. Thousands of God's people have no more faith than this: They know enough to cling to Jesus with all their heart and soul, and this suffices for present peace and eternal safety. Jesus Christ is to them a Savior strong and mighty, a rock immovable and immutable; they cling to Him for dear life, and this clinging saves them. Reader, cannot you cling? Do so at once.

> Thousands of God's people have no more faith than this: They know enough to cling to Jesus with all their heart and soul, and this suffices for present peace and eternal safety.

Faith is seen when one man relies upon another, knowing the superiority of the other. This is a higher faith, the faith that knows the reason for its dependence and acts upon it. I do not think the limpet knows much about the rock, but as faith grows it becomes more and more intelligent. A blind man trusts himself with his guide because he knows that his friend can see, and trusting, he walks where his guide conducts him. If the poor man is born blind, he does not know what sight is; but he knows that there is such a thing as sight and that it is possessed by his friend. Therefore he freely puts his hand into the hand of the seeing one and follows his leadership. "We walk by faith, not by sight" (2 Cor. 5:7). "Blessed are those who have not seen and yet have believed" (John 20:29). This is as good an image of faith as well can be; we know that Jesus has about Him merit, power, and blessing that we do not possess, and therefore we gladly trust ourselves to Him to be to us what we cannot be to ourselves. We trust Him as the blind man trusts his guide. He never betrays our confidence; but He is made of God "unto us wisdom, and righteousness, and sanctification, and redemption" (1 Cor. 1:30 KJV).

Every boy who goes to school has to exert faith while learning. His schoolmaster teaches him geography and instructs him as to the form of the earth and the existence of certain great cities and empires. The boy does not himself know that these things are true, except that he believes his teacher and the books put into his hands. That is what you will have to do with Christ if you are to be saved; you must simply know because He tells you, believe because He assures you it is even so, and trust yourself with Him because He promises you that salvation will be the result. Almost all that you and I know has come to us by faith. A scientific discovery has been made, and we are sure of it. On what grounds do we believe it? On the authority of certain well-known men of learning whose reputations are established. We have never made or seen their experiments, but we believe their witness. You must do the like with regard to Jesus: Because He teaches you certain truths, you are to be His disciple and believe His words; because He has performed certain acts, you are to be His client and trust yourself with Him. He is infinitely superior to you and presents Himself to your confidence as your Master and Lord. If you will receive Him and His words, you shall be saved.

Another and a higher form of faith is that faith which grows out of love. Why does a boy trust his father? The reason why the child trusts his father is because he loves him. Blessed and happy are they who have a sweet faith in Jesus intertwined with deep affection for Him, for this is a restful confidence. These lovers of Jesus are charmed with His character and delighted with His mission. They are carried away by the lovingkindness that He has manifested, and therefore they cannot help trusting Him because they so much admire, revere, and love Him.

The way of loving trust in the Savior may thus be illustrated. A lady is the wife of the most eminent physician of the day. She is seized with a dangerous illness and is smitten down by its power, yet she is wonderfully calm and quiet, for her husband has made this disease his special study and has healed thousands who were similarly afflicted. She is not in the least troubled, for she feels perfectly safe in the hands of one so dear to her and in whom skill and love are blended in their highest forms. Her faith is reasonable and natural; her husband, from every point of view, deserves it of her. This is the kind of faith that the happiest of believers exercise toward Christ. There is no physician like Him; none can save as He can. We love Him, and He loves us, and therefore we put ourselves into His hands, accept whatever He prescribes, and do whatever He bids. We feel that nothing can be wrongly ordered while He is the director of our affairs, for He loves us too well to let us perish or suffer a single needless pang.

> *Faith that refuses to obey the commands of the Savior is a mere pretense and will never save the soul. We trust Jesus to save us; He gives us directions as to the way of salvation; we follow those directions and are saved.*

Faith is the root of obedience, and this may be clearly seen in the affairs of life. When a captain trusts a pilot to steer his vessel into port, he manages the vessel according to his direction. When a traveler trusts a guide to conduct him over a difficult pass, he follows the track that his guide points out. When a patient believes in a physician, he carefully follows his prescriptions and directions. Faith that refuses to obey the commands of the Savior is a mere pretense and will never save the soul. We trust Jesus to save us; He gives us directions as to the way of salvation; we follow those directions and are saved. Let not my reader forget this. Trust Jesus and prove your trust by doing whatever He bids you.

A notable form of faith arises out of assured knowledge; this comes of growth in grace and is the faith that believes Christ because it knows Him and trusts Him because it has proved Him to be infallibly faithful. An old Christian was in the habit of writing *T* and *P* in the margin of her Bible whenever she had tried and proved a promise. How easy it is to trust a tried and proved Savior! You cannot do this as yet, but you will do so. Everything must have a beginning. You will rise to strong faith in due time. This mature faith asks not for signs and tokens, but bravely believes. Look at the faith of the master mariner—I have often wondered at it. He looses his cable; he steams away from the land. For days, weeks, or even months, he never sees sail or shore, yet on he goes day and night without fear, till one morning he finds himself at the desired haven toward which he has been steering. How has he found his way over the trackless deep? He has trusted in his compass, his nautical almanac, his glass, and the heavenly bodies; and obeying their guidance, without sighting land, he has steered so accurately that he has not to change a point to enter into port. It is a wonderful thing—that sailing or steaming without sight. Spiritually it is a blessed thing to leave altogether the shores of sight and feeling and to say good-bye to inward feelings, cheering providences, signs, tokens, and so forth. It is glorious to be far out on the ocean of divine love, believing in God and steering for heaven straightaway by the direction of the Word of God. "Blessed are those who have not seen and yet have believed" (John 20:29). To them shall be administered an abundant entrance at the last and a safe voyage on the way. Will not my reader put his trust in God in Christ Jesus? There I rest with joyous confidence. Brother, come with me, and believe our Father and our Savior. Come at once.

For Further Thought

1. *What is the result of a believer's justification by faith? (See Romans 5:1.)*
2. *According to Romans 10:17, how does a person obtain faith?*

10

WHY ARE WE
SAVED BY FAITH?

WHY is faith selected as the channel of salvation? No doubt this inquiry is often made. "By grace you are saved through faith," is assuredly the doctrine of Holy Scripture and the ordinance of God, but why is it so? Why is faith selected rather than hope, love, or patience?

It becomes us to be modest in answering such a question, for God's ways are not always to be understood; nor are we allowed presumptuously to question them. Humbly we would reply that as far as we can tell, faith has been selected as the channel of grace because there is a natural adaptation in faith to be used as the receiver. Suppose that I am about to give a poor man alms: I put it into his hand. Why? Well, it would hardly be fitting to put it into his ear or to lay it upon his foot; the hand seems made on purpose to receive. So, in our mental frame, faith is created on purpose to be a receiver: It is the hand of the man, and there is fitness in receiving grace by its means.

Do let me put this very plainly. Faith that receives Christ is as simple an act as when your child receives an apple from you because you hold it out and promise to give him the apple if he comes for it. The belief and the receiving relate only to an apple, but they make up precisely the same act as the faith that deals with eternal salvation. What the child's hand is to the apple, your faith is to the perfect salvation of Christ. The child's hand does not make the apple or improve the apple or deserve the apple; it only takes it; and faith is chosen by God to be the receiver of salvation because it does not pretend to create salvation or to help in it, but it is content humbly to receive it. "Faith is the tongue that begs pardon, the hand that receives it, and the eye that sees it; but it is not the price that buys it." Faith never makes herself her own plea; she rests all her argument upon the blood of

Christ. She becomes a good servant to bring the riches of the Lord Jesus to the soul because she acknowledges whence she drew them and owns that grace alone entrusted her with them.

Faith, again, is doubtless selected because it gives all the glory to God. It is of faith that it might be by grace, and it is of grace that there might be no boasting, for God cannot endure pride. "The proud he knows afar off," and He has no wish to come nearer to them. He will not give salvation in a way that will suggest or foster pride. Paul says that we are saved, "not of works, lest anyone should boast" (Eph. 2:9). Now, faith excludes all boasting. The hand that receives charity does not say, "I am to be thanked for accepting the gift." That would be absurd. When the hand conveys bread to the mouth, it does not say to the body, "Thank me, for I feed you." It is a very simple thing that the hand does though a very necessary thing, and it never arrogates glory to itself for what it does. So God has selected faith to receive the unspeakable gift of His grace, because it cannot take to itself any credit but must adore the gracious God who is the giver of all good. Faith sets the crown upon the right head, and therefore the Lord Jesus was wont to put the crown upon the head of faith, saying, "Your faith has saved you. Go in peace" (Luke 7:50).

> *God has selected faith to receive the unspeakable gift of His grace, because it cannot take to itself any credit but must adore the gracious God who is the giver of all good.*

Next, God selects faith as the channel of salvation because it is a sure method, linking man with God. When man confides in God, there is a point of union between them, and that union guarantees blessing. Faith saves us because it makes us cling to God and so brings us into connection with Him. I have often used the following illustration, but I must repeat it because I cannot think of a better. I am told that years ago a boat was upset above the falls of Niagara, and two men were being carried down the current when persons on the shore managed to float a rope out to them, which rope was seized by them both. One of them held fast to it and was safely drawn to the bank; but the other, seeing a great log come floating by, unwisely let go of the rope and clung to the log, for it was the bigger thing of the two and apparently better to cling to. Alas! The log with the man on it went right over the vast abyss because there was no union between the log and the shore. The size of the log was no benefit to him who grasped it; it needed a connection with the shore to produce safety. So when a man trusts to his works, or to sacraments, or to anything of that sort, he will not be saved, because there is no junction between him and Christ. But faith, though it may seem to be like a slender cord, is in the hands of the great God on the shore; infinite power pulls in the connecting line and thus draws the man from destruction. Oh, the blessedness of faith, for it unites us to God!

> *Faith furnishes us with armor for this life and education for the life to come. It enables a man both to live and to die without fear; it prepares both for action and for suffering.*

Faith is chosen again because it touches the springs of action. Even in common things faith of a certain sort lies at the root of all. I wonder whether I shall be wrong if I say that we never do anything except through faith of some sort. If I walk across my study, it is because I believe my legs will carry me. A man eats because he believes in the necessity of food; he goes to business because he believes in the value of money; he accepts a check because he believes that the bank will honor it. Columbus discovered America because he believed that there was another continent beyond the ocean; and the Pilgrim fathers colonized it because they believed that God would be with them on those rocky shores. Most grand deeds have been born of faith. For good or for evil, faith works wonders by the man in whom it dwells. Faith in its natural form is an all-prevailing force, which enters into all manner of human actions. Possibly he who derides faith in God is the man who in an evil form has the most of faith; indeed, he usually falls into a credulity that would be ridiculous if it were not disgraceful. God gives salvation to faith, because by creating faith in us, He thus touches the real mainspring of our emotions and actions. He has, so to speak, taken possession of the battery, and now He can send the sacred current to every part of our nature. When we believe in Christ and the heart has come into the possession of God, we are saved from sin and are moved toward repentance, holiness, zeal, prayer, consecration, and every other gracious thing. "What oil is to the wheels, what weights are to a clock, what wings are to a bird, what sails are to a ship, faith is to all holy duties and services." Have faith, and all other graces will follow and continue to hold their course.

Faith, again, has the power of working by love; it influences the affections toward God and draws the heart after the best things. He who believes in God will beyond all question love God. Faith is an act of the understanding; but it also proceeds from the heart. "With the heart one believes unto righteousness" (Rom. 10:10), and hence God gives salvation to faith because it resides next door to the affections and is near akin to love; and love is the parent and the nurse of every holy feeling and act. Love to God is obedience. Love to God is holiness. To love God and to love man is to be conformed to the image of Christ, and this is salvation.

Moreover, faith creates peace and joy; he who has it rests and is tranquil, is glad and joyous, and this is a preparation for heaven. God gives all heavenly gifts to faith. For this reason among others, that faith works in us the life and spirit that are to be eternally manifested in the upper and better world. Faith furnishes us with armor for this life and education for the life to come. It enables a man both to live and to die without fear; it prepares both for action and for suffering; and hence the Lord selects it as a most convenient medium for conveying grace to us and thereby securing us for glory.

Certainly faith does for us what nothing else can do; it gives us joy and peace and causes us to enter into rest. Why do men attempt to gain salvation by other means? An old preacher says, "A silly servant who is bidden to open a door sets his shoulder to it and pushes with all his might, but the door stirs not, and he cannot enter, use what strength he may. Another comes with a key and easily unlocks the door and enters right readily. Those who would be saved by works are pushing at heaven's gate without result; but faith is the key that opens the gate at once." Reader, will you not use that key? The Lord commands you to believe in His dear Son; therefore you may do so; and doing so you shall live. Is not this the promise of the gospel: "He who believes and is baptized will be saved" (Mark 16:16)? What can be your objection to a way of salvation that commends itself to the mercy and the wisdom of our gracious God?

FOR FURTHER THOUGHT

1. *What is the means by which Christ dwells in our hearts? (See Ephesians 3:17.)*
2. *Galatians 2:20 says we have been crucified with Christ, and it is "no longer I who live." What does this verse say is the way we now live?*

11

ALAS!

I CAN DO NOTHING!

AFTER the anxious heart has accepted the doctrine of atonement and learned the great truth that salvation is by faith in the Lord Jesus, it is often sore troubled with a sense of inability toward that which is good. Many are groaning, "I can do nothing." They are not making this into an excuse, but they feel it as a daily burden. They would if they could. They can each one honestly say, "to will is present with me, but how to perform what is good I do not find" (Rom. 7:18).

This feeling seems to make the entire gospel null and void, for what is the use of food to a hungry man if he cannot get at it? Of what avail is the river of the water of life if one cannot drink? We recall the story of the doctor and the poor woman's child. The sage practitioner told the mother that her little one would soon be better under proper treatment, but it was absolutely needful that her boy should regularly drink the best wine and that he should spend a season at one of the German spas. This, to a widow who could hardly get bread to eat! Now, it sometimes seems to the troubled heart that the simple gospel of "Believe and live" is not, after all, so very simple, for it asks the poor sinner to do what he cannot do. To the really awakened but half instructed there appears to be a missing link; yonder is the salvation of Jesus, but how is it to be reached? The soul is without strength and knows not what to do. It lies within sight of the city of refuge and cannot enter its gate.

Is this want of strength provided for in the plan of salvation? It is. The work of the Lord is perfect. It begins where we are and asks nothing of us in order for its completion. When the Good Samaritan saw the traveler lying wounded and half dead, he did not bid him rise and come to him and mount the ass and ride off to the inn. No, he came to where he was and ministered to him and lifted him upon the beast and bore him to the inn. Thus doth the Lord Jesus deal with us in our low and wretched estate.

We have seen that God justifies, that He justifies the ungodly, and that He justifies them through faith in the precious blood of Jesus. We have now to see the condition these ungodly ones are in when Jesus works out their salvation. Many awakened persons are not only troubled about their sin, but about their moral weakness. They have no strength with which to escape from the mire into which they have fallen or to keep out of it in after days. They not only lament over what they have done, but over what they cannot do. They feel themselves to be powerless, helpless, and spiritually lifeless. It may sound odd to say that they feel dead, and yet it is even so. They are, in their own esteem, to all good incapable. They cannot travel the road to heaven, for their bones are broken. "None of the men of strength have found their hands"; in fact, they are without strength. Happily, it is written as the commendation of God's love to us: "When we were yet without strength, in due time Christ died for the ungodly" (Rom. 5:6 KJV).

> *The* one thing that the poor strengthless sinner has to fix his mind upon and firmly retain as his one ground of hope is the divine assurance that "in due time Christ died for the ungodly."

Here we see conscious helplessness succored—succored by the interposition of the Lord Jesus. Our helplessness is extreme. It is not written, "When we were comparatively weak Christ died for us" or "When we had only a little strength." Instead, the description is absolute and unrestricted: "When we were still without strength." We had no strength whatever that could aid in our salvation; our Lord's words were emphatically true: "Without me ye can do nothing" (John 15:5 KJV). I may go further than the text and remind you of the great love wherewith the Lord loved us, even when we "were dead in trespasses and sins" (Eph. 2:1 KJV). To be dead is even more than to be without strength.

The one thing that the poor strengthless sinner has to fix his mind upon and firmly retain as his one ground of hope is the divine assurance that "in due time Christ died for the ungodly." Believe this and all inability will disappear. As it is fabled of Midas that he turned everything into gold by his touch, so it is true of faith that it turns everything it touches into good. Our very needs and weaknesses become blessings when faith deals with them.

Let us dwell upon certain forms of this want of strength. To begin with, one man will say, "Sir, I do not seem to have strength to collect my thoughts and keep them fixed upon those solemn topics that concern my salvation; a short prayer is almost too much for me. It is so partly, perhaps, through natural weakness, partly because I have injured myself through dissipation, and partly also because I worry myself with worldly cares, so that I am not capable of those high thoughts that are necessary before a soul can be saved." This is a very common form of sinful weakness. Note this! You are without strength on this point; and there are many like you. They could not carry out a train of consecutive thought to save their lives. Many poor men and women are illiterate and untrained, and these would find deep thought to be very heavy work. Others are so light and trifling by nature that they could no more follow out a long process of argument and reasoning than they could fly. They could never attain to the knowledge of any profound mystery if they expended their whole life in the effort. You need not, therefore, despair: That which is necessary to salvation is not continuous thought, but a simple reliance upon Jesus. Hold on to this one fact: "In due time Christ died for the ungodly." This truth will not require from you any deep research, profound reasoning, or convincing argument. There it stands: "In due time Christ died for the ungodly." Fix your mind on that and rest there.

Let this one great, gracious, glorious fact lie in your spirit till it perfumes all your thoughts and makes you rejoice even though you are without strength, seeing the Lord Jesus has become your strength and your song, yea, He has become your salvation. According to the scriptures, it is a revealed fact that in due time Christ died for the ungodly when they were yet without strength. You have heard these words hundreds of times maybe, yet you have never before perceived their meaning. There is a cheering savor about them, is there not? Jesus did not die for our righteousness, but He died for our sins. He did not come to save us because we were worth the saving, but because we were utterly worthless, ruined, and undone. He came not to earth out of any reason that was in us, but solely and only out of reasons that He fetched from the depths of His own divine love. In due time He died for those whom He describes, not as godly, but as ungodly, applying to them as hopeless an adjective as He could well have selected. If you have but little mind, fasten it to this truth, which is fitted to the smallest capacity and is able to cheer the heaviest heart. Let this text lie under your tongue like a sweet morsel till it dissolves into your heart and flavors all your thoughts; and then it will little matter though those thoughts should be as scattered as autumn leaves. Persons who have never shone in science or displayed the least originality of mind have nevertheless been fully able to accept the doctrine of the cross and have been saved thereby. Why shouldn't you?

> *However pure our tears, there will always be some dirt in them. There will be something to be repented of even in our best repentance.*

I hear another man cry, "Oh, sir, my want of strength lies mainly in this, that I cannot repent sufficiently!" A curious idea that men have of what repentance is! Many fancy that so many tears are to be shed and so many groans are to be heaved and so much despair is to be endured. Whence comes this unreasonable notion? Unbelief and despair are sins, and therefore I do not see how they can be constituent elements of acceptable repentance. Yet there are many who regard them as necessary parts of true Christian experience. They are in great error. Still, I know what they mean, for in the days of my darkness, I used to feel the same way. I desired to repent, but I thought that I could not do it, yet all the while I was repenting. Odd as it may sound, I felt that I could not feel. I used to get into a corner and weep because I could not weep; and I fell into bitter sorrow because I could not sorrow for sin. What a jumble it all is when in our unbelieving state we begin to judge our own condition! It is like a blind man looking at his own eyes. My heart was melted within me for fear because I thought that my heart was as hard as an adamant stone. My heart was broken to think that it would not break. Now I can see that I was exhibiting the very thing that I thought I did not possess; but then I knew not where I was.

Oh, that I could help others into the light that I now enjoy! Fain would I say a word that might shorten the time of their bewilderment. I would say a few plain words and pray the Comforter to apply them to the heart.

Remember that the man who truly repents is never satisfied with his own repentance. We can no more repent perfectly than we can live perfectly. However pure our tears, there will always be some dirt in them. There will be something to be repented of even in our best repentance. But listen! To repent is to change your mind about sin and Christ and all the great things of God. There is sorrow implied in this, but the main point is the turning of the heart from sin to Christ. If there be this turning, you have the essence of true repentance even though no alarm and no despair should ever have cast their shadow upon your mind.

If you cannot repent as you would, it will greatly aid you to do so if you will firmly believe that "in due time Christ died for the ungodly." Think of this again and again. How can you continue to be hard-hearted when you know that out of supreme love "Christ died for the ungodly"? Let me persuade you to reason with yourself thus: *Ungodly as I am, though this heart of steel will not relent, though I smite in vain upon my breast, yet He died for such as I am, since He died for the ungodly. Oh, that I may believe this and feel the power of it upon my flinty heart!*

Blot out every other reflection from your soul, and sit down by the hour together and meditate deeply on this one resplendent display of unmerited, unexpected, unexampled love: "Christ died for the ungodly." Read over carefully the narrative of the Lord's death as you find it in the four evangelists. If anything can melt your stubborn heart, it will be a sight of the sufferings of Jesus and the consideration that He suffered all this for His enemies.

> *O Jesus! sweet the tears I shed,*
> *While at Your feet I kneel,*
> *Gaze on Your wounded, fainting head,*
> *And all Your sorrows feel.*
>
> *My heart dissolves to see You bleed,*
> *This heart so hard before;*
> *I hear You for the guilty plead,*
> *And grief o'erflows the more.*
>
> *'Twas for the sinful You didst die,*
> *And I a sinner stand:*
> *Convinc'd by Your expiring eye,*
> *Slain by Your pierced hand.*
> —Ray Palmer

Surely the cross is that wonder-working rod that can bring water out of a rock. If you understand the full meaning of the divine sacrifice of Jesus, you must repent of ever having been opposed to One who is so full of love. It is written, "They will look on Me whom they pierced. Yes, they will mourn for Him as one mourns for his only son, and grieve for Him as one grieves for a firstborn" (Zech. 12:10). Repentance will not make you see Christ; but to see Christ will give you repentance. You may not make a Christ out of your repentance, but you must look for repentance to Christ. The Holy Spirit, by turning us to Christ, turns us from sin. Look away, then, from the effect to the cause, from your own repenting to the Lord Jesus, who is exalted on high to give repentance.

I have heard another say, "I am tormented with horrible thoughts. Wherever I go, blasphemies steal in upon me. Frequently at my work a dreadful suggestion forces itself upon me, and even on my bed I am startled from my sleep by whispers of the evil one. I cannot get away from this horrible temptation." Friend, I know what you mean, for I have myself been hunted by this wolf. A man might as well hope to fight a swarm of flies with a sword as to master his own thoughts when they are set on by the devil. A poor tempted soul, assailed by satanic suggestions, is like a traveler I have read of, about whose head and ears and whole body there came a swarm of angry bees. He could not keep them off or escape from them. They stung him everywhere and threatened to be the death of him. I do not wonder you feel that you are without strength to stop these hideous and abominable thoughts that Satan pours into your soul, yet I would remind you of the scripture before us: "When we were still without strength, in due time Christ died for the ungodly." Jesus knew where we were and where we should be. He saw that we could not overcome the prince of the power of the air. He knew that we should be greatly worried by him. But even then, when He saw us in that condition, Christ died for the ungodly. Cast the anchor of your faith upon this. The devil himself cannot tell you that you are not ungodly; believe, then, that Jesus died even for such as you are. Remember Martin Luther's way of cutting the devil's head off with his own sword.

"Oh," said the devil to Martin Luther, "you are a sinner."

"Yes," said he, "Christ died to save sinners." Thus he smote him with his own sword.

Hide you in this refuge and keep there: "In due time Christ died for the ungodly." If you stand to that truth, the blasphemous thoughts that you have not the strength to drive away will go away of themselves, for Satan will see that he is answering no purpose by plaguing you with them.

These thoughts, if you hate them, are none of yours, but are injections of the devil for which he is responsible, not you. If you strive against them, they are no more yours than are the cursings and falsehoods of rioters in the street. It is by means of these thoughts that the devil would drive you to despair, or at least keep you from trusting Jesus. The poor diseased woman could not come to Jesus for the press, and you are in much the same condition because of the rush and throng of these dreadful thoughts. Still, she put forth her finger and touched the fringe of the Lord's garment, and she was healed. Do you the same.

Jesus died for those who are guilty of all manner of sin and blasphemy, and therefore I am sure He will not refuse those who are unwillingly the captives of evil thoughts. Cast yourself upon Him, thoughts and all, and see if He is not mighty to save. He can still those horrible whisperings of the fiend, or He can enable you to see them in their true light so that you may not be worried by them. In His own way, He can and will save you and at length give you perfect peace. Only trust Him for this and everything else.

Sadly perplexing is that form of inability that lies in a supposed want of power to believe. We are not strangers to the cry:

> *Oh, that I could believe,*
> *Then all would easy be;*
> *I would, but cannot; Lord, relieve,*
> *My help must come from You.*

Many remain in the dark for years because they have no power, as they say, to do that which is the giving up of all power and reposing in the power of another, even the Lord Jesus. Indeed, it is a very curious thing, this whole matter of believing, for people do not get much help by trying to believe. Believing does not come by trying. If a person were to make a statement of something that happened this day, I should not tell him that I would try to believe him. If I believed in the truthfulness of the man who told the incident to me and said that he saw it, I should accept the statement at once. If I did not think him a true man, I should, of course, disbelieve him, but there would be no trying in the matter. Now, when God declares that there is salvation in Christ Jesus, I must either believe Him at once or make Him a liar. Surely you will not hesitate as to which is the right path in this case; the witness of God must be true, and we are bound at once to believe in Jesus.

But possibly you have been trying to believe too much. Now do not aim at great things. Be satisfied to have a faith that can hold in its hand this one truth: "For when we were still without strength, in due time Christ died for the ungodly." He laid down His life for men while as yet they did not believe in Him or were able to believe in Him. He died for men, not as believers, but as sinners. He came to make these sinners into believers and saints. But when He died for them, He viewed them as utterly without strength. If you hold to the truth that Christ died for the ungodly and believe it, your faith will save you, and you may go in peace. If you will trust your soul with Jesus, who died for the ungodly, even though you cannot believe all things, or move mountains, or do any other wonderful works, yet you are saved. It is not great faith, but true faith, that saves; and the salvation lies not in the faith, but in the Christ in whom faith trusts. Faith as a grain of mustard seed will bring salvation. It is not the measure of faith, but the sincerity of faith that is the point to be considered. Surely a man can believe what he knows to be true; and as you know Jesus to be true, you, my friend, can believe in Him.

The cross that is the object of faith is also, by the power of the Holy Spirit, the cause of it. Sit down and watch the dying Savior till faith springs up spontaneously in your heart. There is no place like Calvary for creating confidence. The air of that sacred hill brings health to trembling faith. Many a watcher there has said:

> While I view You, wounded, grieving,
> Breathless on the cursed tree,
> Lord, I feel my heart believing
> That You suffer'dst thus for me.

"Alas!" cries another, "my want of strength lies in this direction, that I cannot quit my sin, and I know that I cannot go to heaven and carry my sin with me." I am glad that you know that, for it is quite true. You must be divorced from your sin or you cannot be married to Christ. Recollect the question that flashed into the mind of young Bunyan when at his sports on the green on Sunday: "Wilt thou have your sins and go to hell, or wilt thou quit your sins and go to heaven?" That brought him to a dead stand. That is a question that every man will have to answer, for there is no going on in sin and going to heaven. That cannot be. You must quit sin or quit hope. Do you reply as follows? "Yes, I am willing enough. To will is present with me, but how to perform that which I would I find not. Sin masters me, and I have no strength." Come, then, if you have no strength, this text is still true: "When we were still without strength, in due time Christ died for the ungodly." Can you believe that? Even if other things may seem to contradict it, will you believe it? God has said it, and it is a fact; therefore, hold on to it like grim death, for your only hope lies there. Believe this and trust Jesus, and you shall soon find power with which to slay your sin; but apart from Him, the strongman will hold you forever his bond slave. Personally, I could never have overcome my own sinfulness. I tried and failed. My evil propensities were too many for me, till, in the belief that Christ died for me, I cast my guilty soul on Him, and then I received a conquering principle by which I overcame my sinful self. The doctrine of the cross can be used to slay sin, even as the old warriors used their huge two-handed swords and mowed down their foes at every stroke. There is nothing like faith in the sinner's Friend: It overcomes all evil. If Christ has died for me, ungodly as I am, without strength as I am, then I cannot live in sin any longer but must arouse myself to love and serve Him who has redeemed me. I cannot trifle with the evil that slew my best Friend. I must be holy for His sake. How can I live in sin when He has died to save me from it?

> *Faith as a grain of mustard seed will bring salvation. It is not the measure of faith, but the sincerity of faith that is the point to be considered.*

See what a splendid help this is to you who are without strength, to know and believe that in due time Christ died for such ungodly ones as you are? Have you caught the idea yet? It is somehow so difficult for our darkened, prejudiced, and unbelieving minds to see the essence of the gospel. At times I have thought, when I have done preaching, that I have laid down the gospel so clearly that the nose on one's face could not be plainer, yet I perceive that even intelligent hearers have failed to understand what was meant by "Look unto me and be ye saved." Converts usually say that they did not know the gospel till such and such a day, yet they had heard it for years. The gospel is unknown, not from want of explanation, but from absence of personal revelation. This the Holy Spirit is ready to give and will give to those who ask Him. Yet when given, the sum total of the truth revealed all lies within these words: "Christ died for the ungodly."

> If Christ has died for me, ungodly as I am, without strength as I am, then I cannot live in sin any longer but must arouse myself to love and serve Him who has redeemed me.

I hear another bewailing himself thus: "Oh, sir, my weakness lies in this, that I do not seem to keep long in one mind! I hear the word on a Sunday, and I am impressed; but in the week I meet with an evil companion, and my good feelings are all gone. My fellow workmen do not believe in anything. They say such terrible things, and I do not know how to answer them, and so I find myself knocked over." I know this Plastic Pliable very well, and I tremble for him; but at the same time, if he is really sincere, his weakness can be met by divine grace. The Holy Spirit can cast out the evil spirit of the fear of man. He can make the coward brave. Remember, my poor vacillating friend, you must not remain in this state. It will never do to be mean and beggarly to yourself. Stand upright and look at yourself, and see if you were ever meant to be like a toad under a harrow, afraid for your life either to move or to stand still. Do have a mind of your own. This is not a spiritual matter only, but one that concerns ordinary manliness. I would do many things to please my friends, but to go to hell to please them is more than I would venture. It may be very well to do this and that for good fellowship, but it will never do to lose the friendship of God in order to keep on good terms with men. "I know that," says the man, "but still, though I know it, I cannot pluck up courage. I cannot show my colors. I cannot stand fast." Well, to you also I have the same text to bring: "When we were still without strength, in due time Christ died for the ungodly." If Peter were here, he would say, "The Lord Jesus died for me even when I was such a poor weak creature that the maid who kept the fire drove me to lie and to swear that I knew not the Lord." Yes, Jesus died for those who forsook Him and fled. Take a firm grip on this truth: "Christ died for the ungodly while they were still without strength." This is your way out of your cowardice. Get this wrought into your soul—"Christ died for me"—and you will soon be ready to die for Him. Believe it, that He suffered in your place and stead, and offered for you a full, true, and satisfactory expiation. If you believe that fact, you will be forced to feel, "I cannot be ashamed of Him who died for me." A full conviction that this is true will nerve you with a dauntless courage. Look at the saints in the martyr age. In the early days of Christianity, when this great thought of Christ's exceeding love was sparkling in all its freshness in the church, men were not only ready to die, but they grew ambitious to suffer and even presented themselves by hundreds at the judgment seats of the rulers, confessing the Christ. I do not say that they were wise to court a cruel death, but it proves my point that a sense of the love of Jesus lifts the mind above all fear of what man can do to us. Why should it not produce the same effect in you? Oh, that it might now inspire you with a brave resolve to come out upon the Lord's side and be His follower to the end!

May the Holy Spirit help us to come thus far by faith in the Lord Jesus, and it will be well!

For Further Thought

1. Read Romans 5:6–9. According to verse 8, what were we when Christ died for us?
2. According to verse 9, from what does Christ's death save us?

12

THE INCREASE OF FAITH

HOW can we obtain an increase of faith? This is a very earnest question for many. They say they want to believe but cannot. A great deal of nonsense is talked upon this subject. Let us be strictly practical in our dealing with it. Common sense is as much needed in religion as anywhere else. "What am I to do in order to believe?" One who was asked the best way to do a certain simple act replied that the best way to do it was to do it at once. We waste time in discussing methods when the action is simple. The shortest way to believe is to believe. If the Holy Spirit has made you candid, you will believe as soon as truth is set before you. You will believe it because it is true. The gospel command is clear; "Believe on the Lord Jesus Christ, and thou shalt be saved" (Acts 16:30 KJV). It is idle to evade this by questions and quibbles. The order is plain; let it be obeyed.

But still, if you have difficulty, take it before God in prayer. Tell the great Father exactly what it is that puzzles you, and beg Him by His Holy Spirit to solve the question. If I cannot believe a statement in a book, I am glad to inquire of the author what he means by it; and if he is a true man, his explanation will satisfy me. Much more will the divine explanation of the hard points of scripture satisfy the heart of the true seeker. The Lord is willing to make Himself known; go to Him and see if it is not so. Repair at once to your closet and cry, "O Holy Spirit, lead me into the truth! What I know not, teach You me."

Furthermore, if faith seems difficult, it is possible that God the Holy Spirit will enable you to believe if you hear very frequently and earnestly that which you are commanded to believe. We believe many things because we have heard them so often. Do you not find it so in common life, that if you hear a thing fifty times a day, at last you come to believe it? Some men have come to believe very unlikely statements by this process, and therefore I do not wonder that the good Spirit often blesses the method of often hearing the truth and uses it to work faith concerning that which is to be believed. It is written, "Faith comes by hearing." Therefore hear often. If I earnestly and attentively hear the gospel, one of these days I shall find myself believing that which I hear, through the blessed operation of the Spirit of God upon my mind. Only mind you hear the gospel, and do not distract your mind with either hearing or reading that which is designed to stagger you.

> *I*f I earnestly and attentively hear the gospel, one of these days I shall find myself believing that which I hear, through the blessed operation of the Spirit of God upon my mind.

If that, however, should seem poor advice, I would add next, consider the testimony of others. The Samaritans believed because of what the woman told them concerning Jesus. Many of our beliefs arise out of the testimony of others. I believe that there is such a country as Japan. I never saw it, yet I believe that there is such a place because others have been there. I believe that I shall die. I have never died, but a great many have done so whom I once knew, and therefore I have a conviction that I shall die also. The testimony of many convinces me of that fact. Listen, then, to those who tell you how they were saved, how they were pardoned, how they were changed in character. If you will look into the matter, you will find that somebody just like yourself has been saved. If you have been a thief, you will find that a thief rejoiced to wash away his sin in the fountain of Christ's blood. If unhappily you have been unchaste, you will find that men and women who have fallen in that way have been cleansed and changed. If you are in despair, you have only to get among God's people and inquire a little, and you will discover that some of the saints have been equally in despair at times, and they will be pleased to tell you how the Lord delivered them. As you listen to one after another of those who have tried the Word of God and proved it, the divine Spirit will lead you to believe. Have you not heard of the African who was told by the missionary that water sometimes became so hard that a man could walk on it? He declared that he believed a great many things the missionary had told him, but he would never believe that. When he came to England, it came to pass that one frosty day he saw the river frozen, but he would not venture on it. He knew that it was a deep river, and he felt certain that he would be drowned if he ventured upon it. He could not be induced to walk the frozen water till his friend and many others went upon it; then he was persuaded and trusted himself where others had safely ventured. So, while you see others believe in the Lamb of God and notice their joy and peace, you will yourself be gently led to believe. The experience of others is one of God's ways of helping us to faith. You have either to believe in Jesus or die; there is no hope for you but in Him.

A better plan is this: Note the authority upon which you are commanded to believe, and this will greatly help you to faith. The authority is not mine, or you might well reject it. But you are commanded to believe upon the authority of God Himself. He bids you believe in Jesus Christ, and you must not refuse to obey your Maker. The foreman of a certain works had often heard the gospel, but he was troubled with the fear that he might not come to Christ. His good master one day sent a card around to the works. It said, "Come to my house immediately after work." The foreman appeared at his master's door, and the master came out and said somewhat roughly, "What do you want, John, troubling me at this time? Work is done, what right have you here?"

"Sir," said he, "I had a card from you saying that I was to come after work."

"Do you mean to say that merely because you had a card from me you are to come up to my house and call me out after business hours?"

"Well, sir," replied the foreman, "I do not understand you, but it seems to me that, as you sent for me, I had a right to come."

"Come in, John," said his master, "I have another message that I want to read to you," and he sat down and read these words: "Come unto me, all ye that labour and are heavy laden, and I will give you rest" (Matt. 11:28 KJV).

"Do you think after such a message from Christ that you can be wrong in coming to Him?"

The poor man saw it all at once and believed in the Lord Jesus unto eternal life because he perceived that he had good warrant and authority for believing. So have you, poor soul! You have good authority for coming to Christ, for the Lord Himself bids you trust Him.

If that does not breed faith in you, think over what it is that you have to believe, which is that the Lord Jesus Christ suffered in the place and stead of sinners and is able to save all who trust Him. Why, this is the most blessed fact that ever men were told to believe; the most suitable, the most comforting, and the most divine truth that was ever set before mortal minds.

I advise you to think much upon it and search out the grace and love that it contains. Study the four evangelists, study Paul's epistles, and then see if the message is not such a credible one that you are forced to believe it.

If that does not do, then think upon the person of Jesus Christ. Think of who He is and what He did and where He is and what He is. How can you doubt Him? It is cruelty to distrust the ever-truthful Jesus. He has done nothing to deserve distrust. On the contrary, it should be easy to rely upon Him. Why crucify Him anew by unbelief? Is not this crowning Him with thorns again and spitting upon Him again? What! Is He not to be trusted? What worse insult did the soldiers pour upon Him than this? They made Him a martyr. But you make Him a liar—this is worse by far. Do not ask, "How can I believe?" But answer another question: How can you disbelieve?

If none of these things avail, then there is something wrong about you altogether, and my last word is: Submit yourself to God! Prejudice or pride is at the bottom of this unbelief. May the Spirit of God take away your enmity and make you yield. You are a rebel, a proud rebel, and that is why you do not believe your God. Give up your rebellion; throw down your weapons; yield at discretion; surrender to your King. I believe that never did a soul throw up his hands in self-despair and cry, "Lord, I yield," but what faith became easy to him before long. It is because you still have a quarrel with God and resolve to have your own will and your own way that you cannot believe. "How can ye believe, which receive honour one of another, and seek not the honour that cometh from God only?" (John 5:44 KJV). Proud self creates unbelief. Submit, O man. Yield to your God, and then shall you sweetly believe in your Savior. May the Holy Spirit now work secretly but effectually with you and bring you at this very moment to believe in the Lord Jesus! Amen.

FOR FURTHER THOUGHT

1. *In John 4:42, why did the people of the village believe in Jesus Christ?*
2. *Read John 6:29. What causes people to believe in Jesus Christ?*

13

REGENERATION AND
THE HOLY SPIRIT

"YOU must be born again." This word of our Lord Jesus has appeared to flame in the way of many, like the drawn sword of the cherub at the gate of paradise. They have despaired because this change is beyond their utmost effort. The new birth is from above, and therefore it is not in the creature's power. Now, it is far from my mind to deny, or even to conceal, a truth in order to create a false comfort. I freely admit that the new birth is supernatural and that the sinner's own self cannot work it. It would be a poor help to my reader if I were wicked enough to try to cheer him by persuading him to reject or forget what is unquestionably true.

But is it not remarkable that the very chapter in which our Lord makes this sweeping declaration also contains the most explicit statement as to salvation by faith? Read the third chapter of John's gospel, and do not dwell alone upon its earlier sentences. It is true that the third verse says: "Jesus answered and said unto him, Verily, verily, I say unto thee, Except a man be born again, he cannot see the kingdom of God" (KJV). But, then, the fourteenth and fifteenth verses speak: "And as Moses lifted up the serpent in the wilderness, even so must the Son of man be lifted up: that whosoever believeth in him should not perish, but have eternal life" (KJV). The eighteenth verse repeats the same doctrine in the broadest terms: "He that believeth on him is not condemned: but he that believeth not is condemned already, because he hath not believed in the name of the only begotten Son of God" (KJV). It is clear to every reader that these two statements must agree since they came from the same lips and are recorded on the same inspired page. Why should we make a difficulty where there can be none? If one statement assures us of the necessity to salvation of something only God can give, and if another assures us that the Lord will save us upon our believing in Jesus, then we may safely conclude that the Lord will give to those who believe all that is declared to be necessary to salvation. The Lord does, in fact, produce the new birth in all who believe in Jesus, and their believing is the surest evidence that they are born again.

We trust in Jesus for what we cannot do ourselves. If it were in our own power, what need would we have of looking to Him? It is ours to believe; it is the Lord's to create us anew. He will not believe for us; neither are we to do regenerating work for Him. It is enough for us to obey the gracious command; it is for the Lord to work the new birth in us. He who could go so far as to die on the cross for us, can and will give us all things that are needful for our eternal safety.

"But a saving change of heart is the work of the Holy Spirit." This also is most true, and let it be far from us to question it or to forget it. But the work of the Holy Spirit is secret and mysterious, and it can only be perceived by its results. There are mysteries about our natural birth into which it would be an unhallowed curiosity to pry. Still more is this the case with the sacred operations of the Spirit of God. "The wind blows where it wishes, and you hear the sound of it, but cannot tell where it comes from and where it goes. So is everyone who is born of the Spirit" (John 3:8). This much, however, we do know: The mysterious work of the Holy Spirit cannot be a reason for refusing to believe in Jesus to whom that same Spirit bears witness.

> The work of the Holy Spirit is secret and mysterious, and it can only be perceived by its results.

If a man were bidden to sow a field, he could not excuse his neglect by saying that it would be useless to sow unless God caused the seed to grow. He would not be justified in neglecting tillage because the secret energy of God alone can create a harvest. No one is hindered in the ordinary pursuits of life by the fact that unless the Lord build the house they labor in vain that build it. It is certain that no man who believes in Jesus will ever find that the Holy Spirit refuses to work in him. In fact, his believing is the proof that the Spirit is already at work in his heart.

God works in providence, but men do not therefore sit still. They could not move without the divine power giving them life and strength, and yet they proceed upon their way without question, the power being bestowed from day to day by Him in whose hand their breath is, and whose are all their ways. So is it in grace. We repent and believe, though we could do neither if the Lord did not enable us. We forsake sin and trust in Jesus, and then we perceive that the Lord has wrought in us to will and to do of His own good pleasure. It is idle to pretend that there is any real difficulty in the matter.

Some truths that are hard to explain in words are simple enough in actual experience. There is no discrepancy between the truth that the sinner believes and that the Holy Spirit works his faith in him. Only folly can lead men to puzzle themselves about plain matters while their souls are in danger. No man would refuse to enter a lifeboat because he did not know the specific gravity of bodies; neither would a starving man decline to eat till he understood the whole process of nutrition. If you, my reader, will not believe till you can understand all mysteries, you will never be saved at all; and if you allow self-invented difficulties to keep you from accepting pardon through your Lord and Savior, you will perish in a condemnation that will be richly deserved. Do not commit spiritual suicide through a passion for discussing metaphysical subtleties.

FOR FURTHER THOUGHT

1. *In John 3:8, to what does Jesus compare the blowing wind?*
2. *According to 1 Peter 1:23, what causes people to be born again?*

14

"My Redeemer Liveth"

CONTINUALLY have I spoken to the reader concerning Christ crucified, who is the great hope of the guilty; but it is our wisdom to remember that our Lord has risen from the dead and lives eternally.

You are not asked to trust in a dead Jesus, but in one who, though He died for our sins, has risen again for our justification. You may go to Jesus at once as to a living and present friend. He is not a mere memory, but a continually existent person who will hear your prayers and answer them. He lives on purpose to carry on the work for which He once laid down His life. He is interceding for sinners at the right hand of the Father, and for this reason He is able to save them to the uttermost that come unto God by Him. Come and try this living Savior if you have never done so before.

This living Jesus is also raised to an eminence of glory and power. He does not now sorrow as "a humble man before his foes," or labor as the carpenter's son; but He is exalted far above principalities and power and every name that is named. The Father has given Him all power in heaven and in earth, and He exercises this high endowment in carrying out His work of grace. Hear what Peter and the other apostles testified concerning Him before the high priest and the council: "The God of our fathers raised up Jesus whom you murdered by hanging on a tree. Him God has exalted to His right hand to be Prince and Savior, to give repentance to Israel and forgiveness of sins" (Acts 5:30–31).

The glory that surrounds the ascended Lord should breathe hope into every believer's breast. Jesus is no mean person; He is the crowned and enthroned Redeemer of men. The sovereign prerogative of life and death is vested in Him; the Father has put all men under the mediatorial government of the Son so that He can quicken whom He will. He opens, and no man shuts. At His word the soul that is bound by the cords of sin and condemnation can be unloosed in a moment. He stretches out the silver scepter, and whosoever touches it lives.

It is well for us that as sin lives and the flesh lives and the devil lives, so Jesus lives; and it is also well that whatever might these may have to ruin us, Jesus has still greater power to save us.

All His exaltation and ability are on our account. He is exalted "to be" and exalted "to give." He is exalted to be a Prince and a Savior that He may give all that is needed to accomplish the salvation of all who come under His rule. Jesus has nothing that He will not use for a sinner's salvation, and He is nothing that He will not display in the aboundings of His grace. He links His princedom with His saviorship, as if He would not have the one without the other; and He sets forth His exaltation as designed to bring blessings to men, as if this were the flower and crown of His glory. Could anything be more calculated to raise the hopes of seeking sinners who are looking Christward?

Jesus endured great humiliation, and therefore there was room for Him to be exalted. By that humiliation He accomplished and endured all the Father's will, and therefore He was rewarded by being raised to glory. He uses that exaltation on behalf of His people. Let my reader raise his eyes to these hills of glory, whence his help must come. Let him contemplate the high glories of the Prince and Savior. Is it not most hopeful for men that a Man is now on the throne of the universe? Is it not glorious that the Lord of all is the Savior of sinners? We have a friend at court; yea, a friend on the throne. He will use all His influence for those who entrust their affairs in His hands. Well does one of our poets sing:

> *He ever lives to intercede*
> *Before His Father's face;*
> *Give Him, my soul, your cause to plead,*
> *No doubt the Father's grace.*

Come, friend, and commit your cause and your case to those once pierced hands, which are now glorified with the signet rings of royal power and honor. No suit ever failed that was left with this great Advocate.

For Further Thought

1. *Job declared, "I know that my Redeemer lives" as recorded in Job 19:25. What is the further prophecy of this verse?*
2. *Read Acts 17:30–34. How did the people respond when they heard of the resurrection?*

15

REPENTANCE MUST GO
WITH FORGIVENESS

IT is clear from the text which we have lately quoted that repentance is bound up with the forgiveness of sins. In Acts 5:31 we read that Jesus is "exalted. . .to give repentance. . .and forgiveness of sins" (KJV). These two blessings come from that sacred hand which once was nailed to the tree but is now raised to glory. Repentance and forgiveness are riveted together by the eternal purpose of God. What God has joined together let no man put asunder.

Repentance must go with remission, and you will see that it is so if you think a little upon the matter. It cannot be that pardon of sin should be given to an impenitent sinner; this would confirm him in his evil ways and teach him to think little of evil. If the Lord were to say, "You love sin and live in it, and you are going on from bad to worse, but all the same, I forgive you," this would proclaim a horrible license for iniquity. The foundations of social order would be removed, and moral anarchy would follow. I cannot tell what innumerable mischiefs would certainly occur if you could divide repentance and forgiveness and pass by the sin while the sinner remained as fond of it as ever. In the very nature of things, if we believe in the holiness of God, it must be so, that if we continue in our sin and will not repent of it, we cannot be forgiven but must reap the consequence of our obstinacy. According to the infinite goodness of God, we are promised that if we will forsake our sins, confessing them, and will by faith accept the grace that is provided in Christ Jesus, God is faithful and just to forgive us our sins and to cleanse us from all unrighteousness. But so long as God lives, there can be no promise of mercy to those who continue in their evil ways and refuse to acknowledge their wrongdoing. Surely no rebel can expect the king to pardon his treason while he remains in open revolt. No one can be so foolish as to imagine that the judge of all the earth will put away our sins if we refuse to put them away ourselves.

Moreover, it must be so for the completeness of divine mercy. That mercy that could forgive the sin and yet let the sinner live in it would be scant and superficial mercy. It would be unequal and deformed mercy, lame upon one of its feet and withered as to one of its hands. Which, think you, is the greater privilege, cleansing from the guilt of sin or deliverance from the power of sin? I will not attempt to weigh in the scales two mercies so surpassing. Neither of them could have come to us apart from the precious blood of Jesus. But it seems to me that to be delivered from the dominion of sin, to be made holy, to be made like to God, must be reckoned the greater of the two if a comparison has to be drawn. To be forgiven is an immeasurable favor. We make this one of the first notes of our psalm of praise: "Who forgiveth all thine iniquities" (Psalm 103:3 kjv). But if we could be forgiven and then could be permitted to love sin, to riot in iniquity, and to wallow in lust, what would be the use of such forgiveness? Might it not turn out to be a poisoned sweet, which would most effectually destroy us? To be washed and yet to lie in the mire; to be pronounced clean and yet to have the leprosy white on one's brow, would be the veriest mockery of mercy. What is it to bring the man out of his sepulcher if you leave him dead? Why lead him into the light if he is still blind? We thank God that He who forgives our iniquities also heals our diseases. He who washes us from the stains of the past also uplifts us from the foul ways of the present and keeps us from failing in the future. We must joyfully accept both repentance and remission; they cannot be separated. The covenant heritage is one and indivisible and must not be parceled out. To divide the work of grace would be to cut the living child in halves, and those who would permit this have no interest in it.

> We thank God that He who forgives our iniquities also heals our diseases. He who washes us from the stains of the past also uplifts us from the foul ways of the present and keeps us from failing in the future.

I will ask you who are seeking the Lord whether you would be satisfied with one of these mercies alone? Would it content you, my reader, if

God would forgive you your sin and then allow you to be as worldly and wicked as before? Oh, no! The quickened spirit is more afraid of sin itself than of the penal results of it. The cry of your heart is not, "Who shall deliver me from punishment?" but "O wretched man that I am! Who shall deliver me from the body of this death? Who shall enable me to live above temptation and to become holy, even as God is holy?" Since the unity of repentance with remission agrees with gracious desire, and since it is necessary for the completeness of salvation and for holiness' sake, rest you sure that it abides.

Repentance and forgiveness are joined together in the experience of all believers. There never was a person yet who did unfeignedly repent of sin with believing repentance that was not forgiven; and on the other hand, there never was a person forgiven who had not repented of his sin. I do not hesitate to say that beneath the copes of heaven there never was, there is not, and there never will be any case of sin being washed away, unless at the same time the heart was led to repentance and faith in Christ. Hatred of sin and a sense of pardon come together into the soul, and abide together while we live.

These two things act and react upon each other: The man who is forgiven, therefore repents; and the man who repents is also most assuredly forgiven. Remember, first, that forgiveness leads to repentance. As we sing in Hart's words:

Law and terrors do but harden,
All the while they work alone;
But a sense of blood-bought pardon
Soon dissolves a heart of stone.

When we are sure that we are forgiven, then we abhor iniquity; and I suppose that when faith grows into full assurance, so that we are certain beyond a doubt that the blood of Jesus has washed us whiter than snow, it is then that repentance reaches to its greatest height. Repentance grows as faith grows. Do not make any mistake about it; repentance is not a thing of days and weeks, a temporary penance to be over as fast as possible! No, it is the grace of a lifetime, like faith itself. God's little children repent, and so do the young men and the fathers. Repentance is the inseparable companion of faith. All the while that we walk by faith and not by sight, the tear of repentance glitters in the eye of faith. That is not true repentance that does not come of faith in Jesus, and that is not true faith in Jesus that is not tinctured with repentance. Faith and repentance, like Siamese twins, are vitally joined together. In proportion as we believe in the forgiving love of Christ, in that proportion we repent; and in proportion as we repent of sin and hate evil, we rejoice in the fullness of the absolution Jesus is exalted to bestow. You will never value pardon unless you feel repentance, and you will never taste the deepest draught of repentance until you know that you are pardoned. It may seem a strange thing, but so it is—the bitterness of repentance and the sweetness of pardon blend in the flavor of every gracious life and make up an incomparable happiness.

These two covenant gifts are the mutual assurance of each other. If I know that I repent, I know that I am forgiven. How am I to know that I am forgiven except I know also that I am turned from my former sinful course? To be a believer is to be a penitent. Faith and repentance are but two spokes in the same wheel, two handles of the same plow. Repentance has been well described as a heart broken for sin and from sin; and it may equally well be spoken of as turning and returning. It is a change of mind of the most thorough and radical sort, and it is attended with sorrow for the past and a resolve of amendment in the future.

> Repentance is to leave
> The sins we loved before;
> And show that we in earnest grieve,
> By doing so no more.

Now, when that is the case, we may be certain that we are forgiven, for the Lord never made a heart to be broken for sin and broken from sin without pardoning it. If, on the other hand, we are enjoying pardon through the blood of Jesus, are justified by faith, and have peace with God through Jesus Christ our Lord, we know that our repentance and faith are of the right sort.

Do not regard your repentance as the cause of your remission, but as the companion of it. Do not expect to be able to repent until you see the grace of our Lord Jesus and His readiness to blot out your sin. Keep these blessed things in their places, and view them in their relation to each other.

They are the Jachin and Boaz of a saving experience; I mean that they are comparable to Solomon's two great pillars that stood in the forefront of the house of the Lord and formed a majestic entrance to the Holy Place. No man comes to God aright except he passes between the pillars of repentance and remission. Upon your heart the rainbow of covenant grace has been displayed in all its beauty when the light of full forgiveness has shined upon the teardrops of repentance. Repentance of sin and faith in divine pardon are the warp and woof of the fabric of real conversion. By these tokens shall you know an Israelite indeed.

> Faith and repentance are but two spokes in the same wheel, two handles of the same plow.

To come back to the scripture upon which we are meditating: both forgiveness and repentance flow from the same source and are given by the same Savior. The Lord Jesus in His glory bestows both upon the same persons. You are neither to find the remission or the repentance elsewhere. Jesus has both ready, and He is prepared to bestow them now, and to bestow them most freely on all who will accept them at His hands. Let it never be forgotten that Jesus gives all that is needful for our salvation. It is highly important that all seekers after mercy should remember this. Faith is as much the gift of God as is the Savior upon whom that faith relies. Repentance of sin is as truly the work of grace as the making of an atonement by which sin is blotted out. Salvation, from first to last, is of grace alone. You will not misunderstand me. It is not the Holy Spirit who repents. He has never done anything for which He should repent. If He could repent, it would not meet the case; we must ourselves repent of our own sin, or we are not saved from its power. It is not the Lord Jesus Christ who repents. What should He repent of? We ourselves repent with the full consent of every faculty of our mind. The will, the affections, and the emotions all work together most heartily in the blessed act of repentance for sin, yet at the back of all that is our personal act, there is a secret holy influence that melts the heart, gives contrition, and produces a complete change. The Spirit of God enlightens us to see what sin is and thus makes it loathsome in our eyes. The Spirit of God also turns us toward holiness, makes us heartily to appreciate, love, and desire it, and thus gives us the impetus by which we are led onward from stage to stage of sanctification. The Spirit of God works in us to will and to do according to God's good pleasure. To that good Spirit let us submit ourselves at once, that He may lead us to Jesus, who will freely give us the double benediction of repentance and remission, according to the riches of His grace.

"By grace you have been saved" (Eph. 2:8).

For Further Thought

1. *Read Acts 5:30–31. Why did God raise Jesus Christ from the dead and exalt Him?*
2. *According to Acts 26:17–18, why does God turn people from darkness to light?*

16

How Repentance
Is Given

To return to the grand text: "Him hath God exalted with his right hand to be a Prince and a Saviour, for to give repentance to Israel, and forgiveness of sins" (Acts 5:31 KJV). Our Lord Jesus Christ has gone up that grace may come down. His glory is employed to give greater currency to His grace. The Lord has not taken a step upward except with the design of bearing believing sinners upward with Him. He is exalted to give repentance, and this we shall see if we remember a few great truths.

The work that our Lord Jesus has done has made repentance possible, available, and acceptable. The law makes no mention of repentance, but says plainly, "The soul who sins shall die" (Ezek. 18:20). If the Lord Jesus had not died and risen again and gone unto the Father, what would your repenting or mine be worth? We might feel remorse with its horrors, but never repentance with its hopes. Repentance, as a natural feeling, is a common duty deserving no great praise. Indeed, it is so generally mingled with a selfish fear of punishment that the kindliest estimate makes but little of it. Had not Jesus interposed and wrought out a wealth of merit, our tears of repentance would have been so much water spilled upon the ground. Jesus is exalted on high, that through the virtue of His intercession repentance may have a place before God. In this respect He gives us repentance because He puts repentance into a position of acceptance, which otherwise it could never have occupied.

When Jesus was exalted on high, the Spirit of God was poured out to work in us all needful graces. The Holy Spirit creates repentance in us by supernaturally renewing our nature and taking away the heart of stone out of our flesh. Oh, sit not down straining those eyes of yours to fetch out impossible tears! Repentance comes not from unwilling nature, but from free and sovereign grace. Get not to your chamber to smite your breast in order to fetch from a heart of stone feelings that are not there. But go to Calvary and see how Jesus died. Look upward to the hills whence comes your help. The Holy Spirit has come on purpose that He may overshadow men's spirits and breed repentance within them, even as once He brooded over chaos and brought forth order. Breathe your prayer to Him, "Blessed Spirit, dwell with me. Make me tender and lowly of heart that I may hate sin and unfeignedly repent of it." He will hear your cry and answer you.

> If the Lord Jesus had not died and risen again and gone unto the Father, what would your repenting or mine be worth? We might feel remorse with its horrors, but never repentance with its hopes.

Remember, too, that when our Lord Jesus was exalted, He not only gave us repentance by sending forth the Holy Spirit, but by consecrating all the works of nature and of providence to the great ends of our salvation, so that any one of them may call us to repentance, whether it crow like Peter's cock or shake the prison like the jailer's earthquake. From the right hand of God, our Lord Jesus rules all things here below and makes them work together for the salvation of His redeemed. He uses both bitters and sweets, trials and joys, that He may produce in sinners a better mind toward their God. Be thankful for the providence that has made you poor or sick or sad; for by all this Jesus works the life of your spirit and turns you to Himself. The Lord's mercy often rides to the door of our hearts on the black horse of affliction. Jesus uses the whole range of our experience to wean us from earth and woo us to heaven. Christ is exalted to the throne of heaven and earth in order that, by all the processes of His providence, He may subdue hard hearts unto the gracious softening of repentance.

Besides, He is at work at this hour by all His whispers in the conscience, by His inspired book, by those of us who speak out of that book, and by praying friends and earnest hearts. He can send a word to you that shall strike your rocky heart as with the rod of Moses and cause streams of repentance to flow forth. He can bring to your mind some heartbreaking text out of Holy Scripture that shall conquer you right speedily. He can mysteriously soften you and cause a holy frame of mind to steal over you when you least look for it. Be sure of this, that He who is gone into His glory, raised into all the splendor and majesty of God, has abundant ways of working repentance in those to whom He grants forgiveness. He is even now waiting to give repentance to you. Ask Him for it at once.

Observe with much comfort that the Lord Jesus Christ gives this repentance to the most unlikely people in the world. He is exalted to give repentance to Israel. To Israel! In the days when the apostles thus spoke, Israel was the nation that had most grossly sinned against light and love, by daring to say, "His blood be on us and on our children" (Matt. 27:25). Yet Jesus is exalted to give them repentance! What a marvel of grace! If you have been brought up in the brightest of Christian light yet have rejected it, there is still hope. If you have sinned against conscience, against the Holy Spirit, and against the love of Jesus, there is yet space for repentance. Though you may be as hard as unbelieving Israel of old, softening may yet come to you, since Jesus is exalted and clothed with boundless power. For those who went the furthest in iniquity and sinned with special aggravation, the Lord Jesus is exalted to give to them repentance and forgiveness of sins. Happy am I to have so full a gospel to proclaim! Happy are you to be allowed to read it!

> *If you have sinned against conscience, against the Holy Spirit, and against the love of Jesus, there is yet space for repentance.*

The hearts of the children of Israel had grown hard as an adamant stone. Luther used to think it impossible to convert a Jew. We are far from agreeing with him, yet we must admit that the seed of Israel have been exceedingly obstinate in their rejection of the Savior during these many centuries. Truly did the Lord say, "Israel would have none of Me" (Ps. 81:11). Yet on behalf of Israel, our Lord Jesus is exalted for the giving of repentance and remission. Probably my reader is a Gentile, yet he may have a very stubborn heart, which has stood out against the Lord Jesus for many years. Nevertheless, in him our Lord can work repentance. It may be that you will yet feel compelled to write as William Hone did when he yielded to divine love. He was the author of those most entertaining volumes called the *Everyday Book*, but he was once a stouthearted infidel. When subdued by sovereign grace, he wrote:

> *The proudest heart that ever beat*
> *Hath been subdued in me;*
> *The wildest will that ever rose*
> *To scorn Your cause and aid Your foes*
> *Is quell'd my Lord, by You.*
>
> *Your will, and not my will be done,*
> *My heart be ever Yours;*
> *Confessing You the mighty Word,*
> *My Savior Christ, my God, my Lord,*
> *Your cross shall be my sign.*

The Lord can give repentance to the unlikeliest, turning lions into lambs and ravens into doves. Let us look to Him, that this great change may be wrought in us. Assuredly the contemplation of the death of Christ is one of the surest and speediest methods of gaining repentance. Do not sit down and try to pump up repentance from the dry well of corrupt nature. It is contrary to the laws of mind to suppose that you can force your soul into that gracious state. Take your heart in prayer to Him who understands it, and say, "Lord, cleanse it. Lord, renew it. Lord, work repentance in it." The more you try to produce penitent emotions in yourself, the more you will be disappointed; but if you believingly think of Jesus dying for you, repentance will burst forth. Meditate on the Lord's shedding His heart's blood out of love to you. Set before your mind's eye the agony and bloody sweat, the cross and passion; and, as you do this, He who was the bearer of all this grief will look at you, and with that look He will do for you what He did for Peter, so that you also will go out and weep bitterly. He who died for you can, by His gracious Spirit, make you die to sin; and He who has gone into glory on your behalf can draw your soul after Him, away from evil and toward holiness.

I shall be content if I leave this one thought with you; look not beneath the ice to find fire, neither hope in your own natural heart to find repentance. Look to the Living One for life. Look to Jesus for all you need between Hell

Gate and Heaven Gate. Never seek elsewhere for any part of that which Jesus loves to bestow; but remember, Christ is all.

For Further Thought

1. *To whom were the people speaking when they said, "His blood be on us and on our children"? (See Matthew 27:24–26.)*
2. *Colossians 3:11 says, "Christ is all and in all." Where do you place yourself among the various types of people listed in this verse?*

17

The Fear of Final Falling

A dark fear haunts the minds of many who are coming to Christ; they are afraid that they shall not persevere to the end. I have heard the seeker say: "If I were to cast my soul upon Jesus, yet peradventure I should after all draw back into perdition. I have had good feelings before now, and they have died away. My goodness has been as the morning cloud and as the early dew. It has come on a sudden, lasted for a season, promised much, and then vanished away."

I believe that this fear is often the father of the fact and that some who have been afraid to trust Christ for all time and for all eternity have failed because they had a temporary faith that never went far enough to save them. They set out trusting to Jesus in a measure but looking to themselves for continuance and perseverance in the heavenward way; and so they set out faultily, and as a natural consequence, turned back before long. If we trust to ourselves for our holding on, we shall not hold on. Even though we rest in Jesus for a part of our salvation, we shall fail if we trust to self for anything. No chain is stronger than its weakest link. If Jesus is our hope for everything except one thing, we shall utterly fail, because in that one point we shall come to naught. I have no doubt whatever that a mistake about the perseverance of the saints has prevented the perseverance of many who did run well. What did hinder them that they should not continue to run? They trusted to themselves for that running, and so they stopped short. Beware of mixing even a little of self with the mortar with which you build, or you will make it untempered mortar, and the stones will not hold together. If you look to Christ for your beginnings, beware of looking to yourself for your endings. He is Alpha. See to it that you make Him Omega also. If you begin in the Spirit, you must not hope to be made perfect by the flesh. Begin as you mean to go on, and go on as you began, and let the Lord be all in all to you. Oh, that God the Holy Spirit may give us a very clear idea of where the strength must come from by which we shall be preserved until the day of our Lord's appearing!

Here is what Paul once said upon this subject when he was writing to the Corinthians: "Our Lord Jesus Christ: who shall also confirm you unto the end, that ye may be blameless in the day of our Lord Jesus Christ. God is faithful, by whom ye were called unto the fellowship of his Son Jesus Christ our Lord" (1 Corinthians 1:7–9 KJV). This language silently admits a great need by telling us how it is provided for. Wherever the Lord makes a provision, we are quite sure that there was a need for it, since no superfluities encumber the covenant of grace. Golden shields hung in Solomon's courts that were never used, but there are none such in the armory of God. What God has provided, we shall surely need. Between this hour and the consummation of all things, every promise of God and every provision of the covenant of grace will be brought into requisition. The urgent need of the believing soul is confirmation, continuance, final perseverance, and preservation to the end. This is the great necessity of the most advanced believers, for Paul was writing to saints at Corinth who were men of a high order, of whom he could say, "I thank my God always on your behalf, for the grace of God which is given you by Jesus Christ" (1 Cor. 1:4 KJV). Such men are the very persons who most assuredly feel that they have daily need of new grace if they are to hold on and hold out and come off conquerors at the last. If you were not saints, you would have no grace, and you would feel no need of more grace; but because you are men of God, therefore you feel the daily demands of the spiritual life. The marble statue requires no food, but the living man hungers and thirsts, and he rejoices that his bread and his water are made sure to him, for else he would certainly faint by the way. The believer's personal wants make it inevitable that he should daily draw from the great source of all supplies, for what could he do if he could not resort to his God?

This is true of the most gifted of the saints—those men at Corinth who were enriched with all utterance and with all knowledge. They needed to be confirmed to the end, or else their gifts and attainments would prove their ruin. If we had the tongues of men and of angels, if we did not receive fresh grace, where should we be? If we had all experience till we were fathers in the church, if we had been taught of God so as to understand all mysteries, yet we could not live a single day without the divine life flowing into us from our covenant head? How could we hope to hold on for a single hour, to say nothing of a lifetime, unless the Lord should hold us on? He who began the good work in us must perform it unto the day of Christ, or it will prove a painful failure.

> *Beware of mixing even a little of self with the mortar with which you build, or you will make it untempered mortar, and the stones will not hold together.*

This great necessity arises very much from ourselves. In some there is a painful fear that they shall not persevere in grace because they know their own fickleness. Certain persons are constitutionally unstable. Some men are by nature conservative, not to say obstinate; but others are as naturally variable and volatile. Like butterflies they flit from flower to flower till they visit all the beauties of the garden and settle upon none of them. They are never long enough in one place to do any good, not even in their business or in their intellectual pursuits. Such persons may well be afraid that ten, twenty, thirty, forty, perhaps fifty years of continuous religious watchfulness will be a great deal too much for them. We see men joining first one church and then another till they box the compass. They are everything by turns and nothing long. Such have double need to pray that they may be divinely confirmed and may be made not only steadfast but also unmovable, or otherwise they will not be found "always abounding in the work of the Lord" (1 Cor. 15:58 KJV).

All of us, even if we have no constitutional temptation to fickleness, must feel our own weakness if we are really quickened of God. Dear reader, do you not find enough in any one single day to make you stumble? You who desire to walk in perfect holiness, as I trust you do; you who have set before you a high standard of what a Christian should be—do you not find that before the breakfast things are cleared away from the table, you have displayed enough folly to make you ashamed of yourselves? If we were to shut ourselves up in the lone cell of a hermit, temptation would follow us, for as long as we cannot escape from ourselves, we cannot escape from incitements to sin. There is that within our hearts that should make us watchful and humble before God. If He does not confirm us, we are so weak that we shall stumble and fall; not overturned by an enemy, but by our own carelessness. Lord, be our strength. We are weakness itself.

Besides that, there is the weariness that comes of a long life. When we begin our Christian profession, we mount up with wings as eagles; further on we run without weariness. But in our best and truest days, we walk without fainting. Our pace seems slower, but it is more serviceable and better sustained. I pray God that the energy of our youth may continue with us so far as it is the energy of the Spirit and not the mere fermentation of proud flesh. He who has long been on the road to heaven finds that there was good reason why it was promised that his shoes should be iron and brass, for the road is rough. He has discovered that there are Hills of Difficulty and Valleys of Humiliation, that there is a Vale of Deathshade, and, worse still, a Vanity Fair—and all these are to be traversed. If there be Delectable Mountains (and, thank God, there are), there are also Castles of Despair, the inside of which pilgrims have too often seen. Considering all things, those who hold out to the end in the way of holiness will be men wondered at.

> *You who have set before you a high standard of what a Christian should be—do you not find that before the breakfast things are cleared away from the table, you have displayed enough folly to make you ashamed of yourselves?*

"O world of wonders, I can say no less." The days of a Christian's life are like so many Kohinoors of mercy threaded upon the golden string of divine faithfulness. [In Spurgeon's day, the Kohinoor was the largest known diamond.] In heaven we shall tell to angels and principalities and powers the unsearchable riches of Christ that were spent upon us and enjoyed by us while we were here below. We have been kept alive on the brink of death. Our spiritual life has been a flame burning on in the midst of the sea, a stone that has remained suspended in the air. It will amaze the universe to see us enter the pearly gate, blameless in the day of our Lord Jesus Christ. We ought to be full of grateful wonder if kept for an hour; and I trust we are.

If this were all, there would be enough cause for anxiety, but there is far more. We have to think of what a place we live in. The world is a howling wilderness to many of God's people. Some of us are greatly indulged in the providence of God, but others have a stern fight of it. We begin our day with prayer, and we hear the voice of holy song full often in our houses; but many good people have scarcely risen from their knees in the morning before they are saluted with blasphemy. They go out to work, and all day long they are vexed with filthy conversation like righteous Lot in Sodom. Can you even walk the open streets without your ears being afflicted with foul language? The world is no friend to grace. The best we can do with this world is to get through it as quickly as we can, for we dwell in an enemy's country. A robber lurks in every bush. Everywhere we need to travel with a drawn sword in our hand, or at least with that weapon that is called "all prayer" ever at our side (Eph. 6:17–18), for we have to contend for every inch of our way. Make no mistake about this, or you will be rudely shaken out of your fond delusion. O God, help us and confirm us to the end, or where shall we be?

True religion is supernatural at its beginning, supernatural in its continuance, and supernatural in its close. It is the work of God from first to last. There is great need that the hand of the Lord should be stretched out still. That need my reader is feeling now, and I am glad that he should feel it; for now he will look for his own preservation to the Lord who alone is able to keep us from failing and glorify us with His Son.

For Further Thought

1. *Galatians 3:1 says the Galatian believers were foolish and bewitched. Verse 3 gives the reason why Paul says this. What is that reason?*
2. *In Philippians 1:3–6 the apostle prays about the believers' progress in the faith. In verse 6, who began this work, and who will complete it?*

18

CONFIRMATION

I want you to notice the security that Paul confidently expected for all the saints. He says, "Who shall also confirm you unto the end, that ye may be blameless in the day of our Lord Jesus Christ" (1 Cor. 1:8 KJV). This is the kind of confirmation that is above all things to be desired. You see it supposes that the persons are right, and it proposes to confirm them in the right. It would be an awful thing to confirm a man in ways of sin and error. Think of a confirmed drunkard or a confirmed thief or a confirmed liar. It would be a deplorable thing for a man to be confirmed in unbelief and ungodliness. Only those to whom the grace of God has been already manifested can enjoy divine confirmation. It is the work of the Holy Spirit. He who gives faith strengthens and establishes it. He who kindles love in us preserves it and increases its flame. What He makes us to know by His first teaching, the good Spirit causes us to know with greater clearness and certainty by still further instruction. Holy acts are confirmed till they become habits, and holy feelings are confirmed till they become abiding conditions. Experience and practice confirm our beliefs and our resolutions. Both our joys and our sorrows, our successes and our failures, are sanctified to the selfsame end, even as the tree is helped to root itself both by the soft showers and the rough winds. The mind is instructed, and in its growing knowledge it gathers reasons for persevering in the good way. The heart is comforted, and so it is made to cling more closely to the consoling truth. The grip grows tighter, and the tread grows firmer, and the man himself becomes more solid and substantial.

This is not a merely natural growth, but is as distinct a work of the Spirit as conversion. The Lord will surely give it to those who are relying upon Him for eternal life. By His inward working He will deliver us from being as unstable as water and cause us to be rooted and grounded. It is a part of the method by which He saves us—thus building us up into Christ Jesus and causing us to abide in Him. Dear reader, you may daily look for this, and you shall not be disappointed. He whom you trust will make you to be as a tree planted by the rivers of waters, so preserved that even your leaf shall not wither.

What a strength to a church is a confirmed Christian! He is a comfort to the sorrowful and a help to the weak. Would you not like to be such? Confirmed believers are pillars in the house of our God. These are not carried away by every wind of doctrine or overthrown by sudden temptation. They are a great stay to others and act as anchors in the time of church trouble. You who are beginning the holy life hardly dare to hope that you will become like them. But you need not fear; the good Lord will work in you as well as in them. One of these days you who are now a babe in Christ shall be a father in the church. Hope for this great thing; but hope for it as a gift of grace and not as the wages of work or as the product of your own energy.

> *Both our joys and our sorrows, our successes and our failures, are sanctified to the selfsame end, even as the tree is helped to root itself both by the soft showers and the rough winds.*

The inspired apostle Paul speaks of these people as to be confirmed unto the end. He expected the grace of God to preserve them personally to the end of their lives or till the Lord Jesus should come. Indeed, he expected that the whole church of God in every place and in all time would be kept to the end of the dispensation, till the Lord Jesus as the bridegroom should come to celebrate the wedding feast with his perfected bride. All who are in Christ will be confirmed in Him till that illustrious day. Has He not said, "Because I live, ye shall live also" (John 14:19 KJV)? He also said, "I give unto [my sheep] eternal life; and they shall never perish, neither shall any man pluck them out of my hand" (10:28 KJV). He who has begun a good work in you will confirm it unto the day of Christ. The work of grace in the soul is not a superficial reformation; the life implanted as the new birth comes of a living and incorruptible seed, which lives and abides forever. And the promises of God made to believers are not of a transient character, but involve for their fulfillment the believer's holding on his way till he comes to endless glory. We are kept by the power of God through faith unto salvation. "The righteous will hold to his way" (Job 17:9). Not as the result of our own merit or strength, but as a gift of free and undeserved favor, those who believe are preserved in Christ Jesus. Of the sheep of His fold Jesus will lose none; no member of His body shall die; no gem of His treasure shall be missing in the day when He makes up His jewels. Dear reader, the salvation that is received by faith is not a thing of months and years; for our Lord Jesus has obtained eternal salvation for us, and that which is eternal cannot come to an end.

Paul also declares his expectation that the Corinthian saints would be "confirmed to the end blameless." This blamelessness is a precious part of our keeping. To be kept holy is better than merely to be kept safe. It is a dreadful thing when you see religious people blundering out of one dishonor into another; they have not believed in the power of our Lord to make them blameless. The lives of some professing Christians are a series of stumbles; they are never quite down, yet they are seldom on their feet. This is not a fit thing for a believer; he is invited to walk with God, and by faith he can attain to steady perseverance in holiness; and he ought to do so. The Lord is able, not only to save us from hell, but to keep us from falling. We need not yield to temptation. Is it not written, "Sin shall not have dominion over you" (Rom. 6:14)? The Lord is able to keep the feet of His saints; and He will do it if we will trust Him to do so. We need not defile our garments; we may by His grace keep them unspotted from the world. We are bound to do this, for without holiness "no man shall see the Lord" (Heb. 12:14 kjv).

The Lord can give you an irreproachable character. Even though in your past life you may have gone far into sin, the Lord can altogether deliver you from the power of former habits and make you an example of virtue.

The apostle prophesied for these believers that which he would have us seek after—that we may be preserved, blameless unto the day of our Lord Jesus Christ. The Revised Version has "unreproveable" instead of "blameless." Possibly a better rendering would be "unimpeachable." God grant that in that last great day we may stand free from all charge, that none in the whole universe may dare to challenge our claim to be the redeemed of the Lord. We have sins and infirmities to mourn over, but these are not the kind of faults that would prove us to be out of Christ. We shall be clear of hypocrisy, deceit, hatred, and delight in sin, for these things would be fatal charges.

Despite our failings, the Holy Spirit can work in us a character spotless before men so that, like Daniel, we shall furnish no occasion for accusing tongues, except in the matter of our religion. Multitudes of godly men and women have exhibited lives so transparent, so consistent throughout, that none could gainsay them. The Lord will be able to say of many a believer, as He did of Job when Satan stood before Him, "Hast thou considered my servant Job...a perfect and an upright man, one that feareth God, and escheweth evil?" (Job 1:8 KJV). This is what my reader must look for at the Lord's hands. This is the triumph of the saints—to continue to follow the Lamb whithersoever He goes, maintaining our integrity as before the living God. May we never turn aside into crooked ways and give cause to the adversary to blaspheme. Of the true believer it is written, He "keeps himself, and the wicked one does not touch him" (1 John 5:18). May it be so written concerning us!

Friend just beginning in the divine life, the Lord can give you an irreproachable character. Even though in your past life you may have gone far into sin, the Lord can altogether deliver you from the power of former habits and make you an example of virtue. He cannot only make you moral, but He can make you abhor every false way and follow after all that is saintly. Do not doubt it. The chief of sinners need not be a whit behind the purest of the saints. Believe for this, and according to your faith shall it be unto you.

Oh, what a joy it will be to be found blameless in the Day of Judgment! We sing not amiss when we join in that charming hymn:

> Bold shall I stand in that great day,
> For who aught to my charge shall lay;
> While through Your blood absolved I am,
> From sin's tremendous curse and shame?

What bliss it will be to enjoy that dauntless courage, when heaven and earth shall flee away from the face of the judge of all! This bliss shall be the portion of everyone who looks alone to the grace of God in Christ Jesus and in that sacred might wages continual war with all sin.

FOR FURTHER THOUGHT

1. *Jude 24 says that God is able to keep you from stumbling. What is God's goal in this?*

2. *Romans 14 speaks of people who are weak in the faith (v. 1). According to verse 4, why are we not to judge such people? Who is able to make them stand?*

19

WHY SAINTS PERSEVERE

THE hope that filled the heart of Paul concerning the Corinthian brethren we have already seen to be full of comfort to those who trembled as to their future. But why was it that he believed that the brethren would be confirmed unto the end?

I want you to notice that he gives his reasons. Here they are: "God is faithful, by whom ye were called unto the fellowship of his Son Jesus Christ our Lord" (1 Cor. 1:9 KJV). The apostle does not say, "You are faithful." Alas! The faithfulness of man is a very unreliable affair; it is mere vanity. He does not say, "You have faithful ministers to lead and guide you, and therefore I trust you will be safe." Oh, no! If men keep us, we shall be but ill kept. He puts it, "God is faithful." If we are found faithful, it will be because God is faithful. On the faithfulness of our covenant God, the whole burden of our salvation must rest. On this glorious attribute of God the matter hinges. We are variable as the wind, frail as a spiderweb, weak as water. No dependence can be placed upon our natural qualities or our spiritual attainments, but God abides faithful. He is faithful in His love; He knows no variableness, neither shadow of turning. He is faithful to His purpose; He doth not begin a work and then leave it undone. He is faithful to His relationships; as a Father He will not renounce His children, as a friend He will not deny His people, as a Creator He will not forsake the work of His own hands. He is faithful to His promises and will never allow one of them to fail to a single believer. He is faithful to His covenant, which He has made with us in Christ Jesus and ratified with the blood of His sacrifice. He is faithful to His Son and will not allow His precious blood to be spilled in vain. He is faithful to His people to whom He has promised eternal life and from whom He will not turn away.

This faithfulness of God is the foundation and cornerstone of our hope of final perseverance. The saints shall persevere in holiness because God perseveres in grace. He perseveres to bless, and therefore believers persevere in being blessed. He continues to keep His people, and therefore they continue to keep His commandments. This is good solid ground to rest upon, and it is delightfully consistent with the title of this little book, *All of Grace*. Thus it is free favor and infinite mercy that ring in the dawn of salvation, and the same sweet bells sound melodiously through the whole day of grace.

You see that the only reasons for hoping that we shall be confirmed to the end and be found blameless at the last are found in our God; but in Him these reasons are exceedingly abundant.

> *O*ur destiny is linked with that of our Lord, and until He can be destroyed, it is not possible that we should perish.

They lie first in what God has done. He has gone so far in blessing us that it is not possible for Him to run back. Paul reminds us that He has "called [us] unto the fellowship of his Son Jesus Christ our Lord" (1 Cor. 1:9 KJV). Has he called us? Then the call cannot be reversed; for "the gifts and calling of God are without repentance" (Rom. 11:29 KJV). From the effectual call of His grace, the Lord never turns. "Whom he called, them he also justified: and whom he justified, them he also glorified" (Rom. 8:30 KJV). This is the invariable rule of the divine procedure. There is a common call, of which it is said, "Many are called, but few chosen" (Matt. 20:16), but this of which we are now thinking is another kind of call, which betokens special love and necessitates the possession of that to which we are called. In such a case it is with the called one even as with Abraham's seed, of whom the Lord said, "I have taken from the ends of the earth, and called from its farthest regions, and said to you, 'You are My servant, I have chosen you and have not cast you away'" (Isa. 41:9).

In what the Lord has done, we see strong reasons for our preservation and future glory, because the Lord has called us into the fellowship of His Son Jesus Christ. It means into partnership with Jesus Christ, and I would have you carefully consider what this means. If you are indeed called by divine grace, you have come into fellowship with the Lord Jesus Christ, so as to be joint owner with Him in all things. Henceforth you are one with

Him in the sight of the Most High. The Lord Jesus bare your sins in His own body on the tree, being made a curse for you; and at the same time, He has become your righteousness, so that you are justified in Him. You are Christ's and Christ is yours. As Adam stood for his descendants, so does Christ stand for all who are in Him. As husband and wife are one, so is Jesus one with all those who are united to Him by faith—one by a conjugal union that can never be broken. More than this, believers are members of the body of Christ, and thus are one with Him by a loving, living, lasting union. God has called us into this union, this fellowship, this partnership, and by this very fact He has given us the token and pledge of our being confirmed to the end. If we were considered apart from Christ, we should be poor perishable units, soon dissolved and borne away to destruction; but as one with Jesus we are made partakers of His nature and are endowed with His immortal life. Our destiny is linked with that of our Lord, and until He can be destroyed, it is not possible that we should perish.

Dwell much upon this partnership with the Son of God, unto which you have been called, for all your hope lies there. You can never be poor while Jesus is rich, since you are in one firm with Him. Want can never assail you, since you are joint proprietor with Him who is possessor of heaven and earth. You can never fail, for though one of the partners in the firm is as poor as a church mouse and in himself an utter bankrupt who could not pay even a small amount of his heavy debts, yet the other partner is inconceivably, inexhaustibly rich. In such partnership you are raised above the depression of the times, the changes of the future, and the shock of the end of all things. The Lord has called you into the fellowship of His Son Jesus Christ, and by that act and deed He has put you into the place of infallible safeguard.

If you are indeed a believer, you are one with Jesus, and therefore you are secure. Do you not see that it must be so? You must be confirmed to the end until the day of His appearing if you have indeed been made one with Jesus by the irrevocable act of God. Christ and the believing sinner are in the same boat: Unless Jesus sinks, the believer will never drown. Jesus has taken His redeemed into such connection with Himself, that He must first be smitten, overcome, and dishonored before the least of His purchased ones can be injured. His name is at the head of the firm, and until it can be dishonored, we are secure against all dread of failure.

So, then, with the utmost confidence, let us go forward into the unknown future, linked eternally with Jesus. If the men of the world should cry, "Who is this coming up from the wilderness, leaning upon her beloved?" (Song of Sol. 8:5), we will joyfully confess that we do lean on Jesus, and that we mean to lean on Him more and more. Our faithful God is an ever-flowing well of delight, and our fellowship with the Son of God is a full river of joy. Knowing these glorious things, we cannot be discouraged. Nay, rather we cry with the apostle, "Who shall separate us from the love of Christ?" (Rom. 8:35).

FOR FURTHER THOUGHT

1. *According to 1 Corinthians 10:13, why will we not be overtaken by temptation?*
2. *In Colossians 1:10, the apostle prays that the believers would walk worthy of the Lord. What is the way to do this given in verse 11?*

20

CLOSE

IF my reader has not followed me step-by-step as he has read my pages, I am truly sorry. Book reading is of small value unless the truths that pass before the mind are grasped, appropriated, and carried out to their practical issues. It is as if one saw plenty of food in a shop and yet remained hungry for want of personally eating some. It is all in vain, dear reader, that you and I have met, unless you have actually laid hold upon Christ Jesus my Lord. On my part there was a distinct desire to benefit you, and I have done my best to that end. It pains me that I have not been able to do you good, for I have longed to win that privilege. I was thinking of you when I wrote this page, and I laid down my pen and solemnly bowed my knee in prayer for everyone who should read it. It is my firm conviction that great numbers of readers will get a blessing, even though you refuse to be of the number. But why should you refuse? If you do not desire the choice blessing that I would have brought to you, at least do me the justice to admit that the blame of your final doom will not lie at my door. When we two meet before the great white throne, you will not be able to charge me with having idly used the attention which you were pleased to give me while you were reading my little book. God knows I wrote each line for your eternal good. I now in spirit take you by the hand. I give you a firm grip. Do you feel my brotherly grasp? The tears are in my eyes as I look at you and say, Why will you die? Will you not give your soul a thought? Will you perish through sheer carelessness? Oh, do not so; but weigh these solemn matters, and make sure work for eternity! Do not refuse Jesus, His love, His blood, His salvation. Why should you do so? Can you do it?

I beseech you, do not turn away from your Redeemer! If, on the other hand, my prayers are heard, and you, my reader, have been led to trust the Lord Jesus and receive from Him salvation by grace, then keep you ever to this doctrine and this way of living. Let Jesus Christ be your all in all, and let free grace be the one line in which you live and move. There is no life like that of one who lives in the favor of God. To receive all as a free gift preserves the mind from self-righteous pride and from self-accusing despair. It makes the heart grow warm with grateful love, and thus it creates a feeling in the soul that is infinitely more acceptable to God than anything that can possibly come of slavish fear. Those who hope to be saved by trying to do their best know nothing of that glowing fervor, that hallowed warmth, that devout joy in God, which come with salvation freely given according to the grace of God. The slavish spirit of self-salvation is no match for the joyous spirit of adoption. There is more real virtue in the least emotion of faith than in all the tuggings of legal bond slaves or all the weary machinery of devotees who would climb to heaven by rounds of ceremonies. Faith is spiritual, and God who is a spirit delights in it for that reason. Years of prayer-saying, churchgoing or chapelgoing, ceremonies, and performances may only be an abomination in the sight of Jehovah; but a glance from the eye of true faith is spiritual, and it is therefore dear to Him. Look you first to the inner man and to the spiritual, and the rest will then follow in due course.

> *Let Jesus Christ be your all in all, and let free grace be the one line in which you live and move. There is no life like that of one who lives in the favor of God.*

If you are saved yourself, be on the watch for the souls of others. Your own heart will not prosper unless it is filled with intense concern to bless your fellow men. The life of your soul lies in faith; its health lies in love. He who does not pine to lead others to Jesus has never been under the spell of love himself. Get to the work of the Lord, the work of love. Begin at home. Visit next your neighbors. Enlighten the village or the street in which you live. Scatter the word of the Lord wherever your hand can reach.

Reader, meet me in heaven! Do not go down to hell. There is no coming back again from that abode of misery. Why do you wish to enter the way of death when heaven's gate is open before you? Do not refuse the free pardon, the full salvation that Jesus grants to all who trust Him. Do not hesitate and delay. You have had enough of resolving; come to action. Believe in Jesus now, with full and immediate decision. Take with you words and come unto your Lord this day, even this day. Remember, O soul, it may be now or never with you. Let it be now; it would be horrible that it should be never.

Again I charge you, meet me in heaven.

FOR FURTHER THOUGHT

1. *In 2 Timothy 4:2, Paul urges Timothy to preach the Word. Verse 3 gives the reason. What is that reason?*
2. *Acts 26 tells of Paul preaching the gospel to King Agrippa. In the end, he is accused of being mad (v. 24). What are the apostle's final words to the royal gathering? (See v. 29.)*

SERMONS IN CANDLES: TWO LECTURES ON THE
ILLUSTRATIONS THAT MAY BE FOUND IN COMMON CANDLES

Contents

"The bright shining of a candle doth give thee light."
LUKE 11:36 KJV

LECTURE NUMBER ONE

LECTURING was once so common an exercise that I have heard it said that all society might be divided into "Lecturer and the Lectured," and the division was said to hold good both by night and by day, as Mr. and Mrs. Caudle could bear testimony.

Lectures are now "the light of other days." No longer is Exeter Hall crowded to hear a series of lectures by great divines; and in vain do minor institutions invite an audience to "a popular lecture." The magic spell has departed; the lectured ones are delivered. Who is responsible for the falling off in attendance at lectures? Did the talk become too dreary? Were the prelections too abstruse or too commonplace? Will mine be like them?

I am not adept at lecturing, and when I take to it under constraint, I either signally fail in it or else the successful production is a sermon in disguise. You cannot drive out nature by command; the old pulpit hand must preach even though you bid him do somewhat else. It would be no good sign if it were otherwise; for a man must keep to one thing and be absorbed in it or he will not do it well. I have preached now for so many years that use is second nature; and a lecture, a speech, an address, and I fear even a conversation all have a tendency to mold themselves sermon-fashion. It is just the old story over again of the artist who had been painting red lions all his life. The landlord of a public house in a certain street desired to have his establishment known as The Angel, and he commissioned the clever gentleman of the brush to produce one of those flaming spirits. The budding academician replied, "You had better have a red lion. I can paint red lions against any man, and they seem the right sign for publicans who do a roaring trade."

"But," said Boniface, "there are three of your red lions quite handy already, and we want a little variety. I have made up my mind to have an angel. Cannot you arrange it?"

"Well," said the artist, "I will see what I can do. You shall have your angel, but it will be awfully like a red lion."

So, when I am requested to "lecture," I reply, "I cannot manage it; my business is to preach." But if they press their suit, and I am weak enough to yield, I warn them that my lecture will be wonderfully like a sermon.

I suppose "a lecture" signifies a reading, but enough of my brethren use manuscripts, and I will not compete with them. If I cannot speak extemporaneously, I will hold my tongue; to read I am ashamed.

In a lecture one has the advantage of more freedom than in a sermon. One is permitted to take a wider range of subjects and to use an easier style than a theological discourse allows. I will use this freedom, but my aim will be the same as if I were preaching. I trust my lecture may possibly impress some minds to which a sermon would seem too dull a business. By calling this lecture "Sermons in Candles," I claim the right to mingle the severe with the lively, the grave with the gay. In due proportions, the mixture may be taken with good effect.

This is how the lecture came about in the first place. It has grown considerably since it was born, as all lively children do. In addressing my students in the college long ago, I was urging upon them the duty and necessity of using plenty of illustrations in their preaching, that they might be both interesting and instructive. I reminded them that the Savior had many "likes" in his discourses. He said over and over again, "The kingdom of heaven is *like*," "The kingdom of heaven is *like*." The common people heard him gladly, because he was full of emblem and simile. A sermon without illustrations is like a room without windows. One student remarked that the difficulty was to get illustrations in any great abundance. "Yes," I said, "if you do not wake up, but go through the world asleep, you cannot see illustrations; but if your minds were thoroughly aroused, yet you could see nothing else in the world but a single tallow candle, you might find enough illustrations in that luminary to last you for six months." Now, the young brethren in the college are too well behaved to say, "Oh!" or give a groan of unbelief, should I perchance say a strong thing; but they look, and they draw their breath, and they wait for an explanation. I understand what they mean and do not make too heavy a draft upon their faith by long delays in explaining myself. The men who were around me at that particular moment thought that I had made rather a sweeping assertion, and their countenances showed it. "Well," I said, "I will prove my words," and my attempt to prove them produced the rudiments of this lecture.

To the nucleus thus obtained, other things have been added as the address has been repeated. The lecture is a cairn, upon which stone after stone has been thrown, till it has become a heap—in fact, two heaps. To use a figure from the subject itself, my candles have been dipped again and again, and each time they have grown in bulk, till I now feel that they are ready to go from the makers to the consumers. The matter has been molded under my own hand, but at the same time the materials are so various that whether my candle is a dip, or a mold, or a composite, I leave to you to decide.

> he Savior had many "likes" in his discourses. He said over and over again, "The kingdom of heaven is like," "The kingdom of heaven is like." A sermon without illustrations is like a room without windows.

This lecture of mine has proved a boon to several other public instructors, who have largely used it—and possibly have improved upon the original. I am sure they have not been freer than welcome. As I have taken out no letters of patent, I have never called upon them for a royalty for the use of my invention. Still, if their consciences trouble them, I am like Matthew, "at the receipt of custom" (Matt. 9:9 KJV). I have now resolved to print my lecture; and I hope those gentlemen will not be angry with me for stopping their borrowing, but rather I trust they will think me generous for having refrained from publishing the lecture for so long a period as five-and-twenty years. These candles have now become ancient lights, but I do not propose to prevent anybody's building near the premises, for they will not block up my light. These symbols have light in themselves that cannot be hid. My friends can go on delivering their own versions all the same; and if they think fit, they may use the original text also. A man who would deliver the lecture and sell the book at the close might drive a good trade. In any case, the subject admits of further variations, and it can never be quite exhausted so long as lecturers have brains and lectured ones have eyes.

Candles were far more familiar objects in my boyhood than in these days of gas and electricity. Now fathers show their boys and girls how to make gas at the end of a tobacco pipe; but in my time the greatest of wonders was a Lucifer match. Our lights were so few that they justified the wit that declared that the word *luxury* was derived from *lux*, the Latin for "light." Assuredly, a good light is a high form of luxury. I can never forget the rushlight, which dimly illuminated the sitting room of the old house; or the dips, which were pretty fair when there were not too many of them to the pound; or the mold candles, which came out only when there was a party or some specific personage was expected. Short sixes were very respectable specimens of household lights. Composites have never seemed to me to be so good as the old sort, made of pure tallow; but I daresay I may be wrong. Nevertheless, I have no liking for composites in theology, but prefer the genuine article without compromise.

Once I thoughtlessly hung a pound of tallow candles on a clotheshorse. This construction was moved near the fire, and the result was a mass of fat on the floor and the cottons of the candles almost divested of tallow: a lesson to us all not to expose certain things to a great heat, lest we dissolve them. I fear that many a man's good resolutions only need the ordinary fire of daily life to make them melt away. So, too, with fine professions and the boastings of perfection that abound in this age of shams.

The candle with a rush wick was the poor man's friend. Thrifty laborers' wives made them themselves; and White, in his *Selborne*, has a letter that gives quite an elaborate account of this economical home manufacture. Good housewives saved the skimmings of the bacon pot, precipitated the salt, and then put a little wax from their beehives into the grease. The rushes were gathered in summer and steeped in water, the rinds removed, and the pith preserved entire. To dip the rushes in the scalding fat required great care; but when the work was done, the laborer's house could be cheered in a small way with candlelight for eight hundred hours for three shillings. He adds that the very poor, who are always the worst economists, buy a half-penny candle every evening and thus get only two hours' light for their money instead of eleven. Moral: There should be economy even in rushlights; how much more in consuming the light of life!

In those days it was a youthful joke to send a boy to the shop for a pound of cotton rushes. The grocer, if of an angry sort, was apt to make a rush at the lad, who thus appeared to mock him. It was in these times that we heard the story of the keeper of the chandler's shop, who told her customers candles "was riz."

"Riz?" said her neighbor. "Everything is riz except my wages. But why have they riz?"

"They tell me," said the other, "that tallow has gone up because of the war with Russia."

"Well," replied the customer, "that is a queer story. Have they begun to fight by candlelight?" That woman had some inkling of the law of supply and demand. She may never have read Adam Smith, but it is possible that she was a Smith herself.

Those were the days when a wit is represented as saying to his tradesman, "I hope these candles will be better than the last."

"I am sure I don't know, sir. Was anything the matter with those I sent you?"

"Matter enough," replied the wit; "they burned very well till they were about half gone, and then they would burn no longer." The catch is that, of course, they burned shorter.

We had practical fun with candles, too, for we would scoop out a turnip, cut eyes and a nose in the rind, and then put a candle inside. This could be judiciously used to amuse, but it might also be injudiciously turned to purposes of alarming youngsters and greenhorns, who ran away under the apprehension that a ghost was visible. Other things beside turnips can be used to frighten foolish people; but it is a shame to use the light of truth with such a design.

I do not think I ever saw the smoke of a candle employed as Swift suggests, when he says to servants in general, "Write your own names and your sweethearts' with the smoke of a candle, on the roof of the kitchen or servants' hall, to show your learning." But smudges caused by candlesnuffs were not unusual in slovenly rooms.

> *I fear that many a man's good resolutions only need the ordinary fire of daily life to make them melt away. So, too, with fine professions and the boastings of perfection that abound in this age of shams.*

No doubt the youths in my audience have found a candle helpful in astronomical observations, when they have smoked glass over a candle to use it in watching an eclipse. Many are the side uses of every useful article.

I have a distinct remembrance of a mission room where my father frequently preached, which was illuminated by candles in tin sconces that hung on the wall. These luminaries frequently went very dim for want of snuffing, and on one occasion an old man, who wanted to see his hymnbook, took the candle from its original place. Out of his hand he made a candlestick; his finger and thumb he used as a pair of snuffers; and, finding it needful to cough, he accidentally made use of his mouth as an extinguisher. Thus the furniture of a candle was all contained in his proper person.

That wild wit Dean Swift, in his advice to servants, says:

> There are several ways of putting out candles, and you ought to be instructed in them all: You may run the candle end against the wainscot, which puts the snuff out immediately; you may lay it on the ground and tread the snuff out with your foot; you may hold it upside down until it is choked with its own grease or cram it into the socket of the candlestick; you may whirl it round in your hand till it goes out; or you may spit on your finger and thumb and pinch the snuff till it goes out. The cook may rub the candle's nose into the meal tub, or the groom into a vessel of oats, a lock of hay, or a heap of litter. The housemaid may put out her candle by running it against the looking glass, which nothing cleans so well as candle snuff; but the quickest and best of all methods is to blow it out with your breath, which leaves the candle clean and readier to be lighted.

Some part or other of this advice must have been frequently followed, for an extinguisher was not always close at hand.

By the way, a candle blown out did not yield the most delicate of perfumes, neither was a street rendered delicious by having a candle factory in it. There used to be, in Paternoster Row, an establishment that was odiously odorous, but we were always assured that the smell was not unhealthy. Perhaps it was not, but we confess we should have preferred to avoid the experiment. In the formation of the best of things, there may be disagreeable processes. As to the smoke of a candle that is newly put out, we may remark upon it that the failure of a life that should have been a light is a very sickening calamity. If the light of professors of religion is blown out, the result is most unsavory. How well it is for us that we have to deal with one of whom it is written, "The smoking flax shall he not quench" (Isa. 42:3 KJV). Even when faith is so low that we are rather an offense than an illumination, He will not quench it, so tender is His love.

When preaching in a low-pitched building crowded with people, I have seen the candles burn low for want of air, a clear indication that we were killing ourselves by inhaling an atmosphere from which the vitalizing principle had almost all gone. I have been afraid of the lights going out, and have thought it better to let the congregation go out rather sooner than usual. To this day ventilation remains an unknown art. The various schemes that have been so much cried up are admirable upon paper, and there they had better remain. Oh, that we could have more oxygen in our places of worship! It would be next to the grace of God for value.

> Even when faith is so low that we are rather an offense than an illumination, He will not quench it, so tender is His love.

On one occasion, having a candle on each side of me in a small pulpit, I was somewhat vigorous and dashed one of my luminaries from its place. It fell upon the bald head of a friend below, who looked up with an expression that I can see at this moment, and it makes me smile still. I took no more notice of the accident than to weave it into what I was saying, and I believe most of my hearers considered it to have been a striking practical illustration of the remark that accompanied it: "How soon is the glory of life dashed down!"

Before my time the candles in places of worship offered a sad temptation to ungodly men and boys, who would bring sparrows in their pockets and let them fly during the evening service. The poor birds made at once for the lights, and no end of confusion was the consequence. German critics and their humble admirers play the part of these sparrows nowadays with the great lights of inspired scripture.

Outside some of the older meetinghouses there used to be a wooden stand near the graveyard gate, on which a lantern was placed with a candle within it, to light the way to the place where prayer was went to be made. The natural light was dim in those times; but I am old-fashioned enough to believe that the gospel light was in many a lowly sanctuary far more brilliant than it is today in mimic Gothic chapels. The blaze of "modern thought" that pleases lovers of novelty does not guide the perplexed to heaven or cheer the passage of the departing through the valley of the shadow of death.

In our time we have smeared our boots with a tallow candle to keep out the wet when we have had to tramp through the snow and the water; and we have also tallowed our nose when it has been running with a cold. Still, we cannot conscientiously recommend the old prescription (dated 1430?) that we find recorded in doggerel rhyme:

> *Put your feet in hot water*
> *As high as your thighs;*
> *Wrappe your head up in flanelle*
> *As low as your eyes;*
> *Take a quart of rum'd gruelle*
> *When in bed as a dose;*
> *With a number four dippe*
> *Well tallow your nose.*

I take the liberty of suggesting that if the rum were poured into the hot water provided for the feet, it would be more likely to be useful than when put into the gruel. The candle will be quite sufficient to make the nose to shine, without setting it on fire with ardent spirits.

I remember reading, when I went to school, a capital story illustrating presence of mind, and it comes to my remembrance after nearly fifty years. The anecdote is in *Chambers' Moral Classbook* and is much too good to be lost.

In Edinburgh, in the reign of George II, there was a grocer named George Dewar, who, besides teas, sugar, and other articles, now usually sold by grocers, dealt extensively in garden seeds. Underneath his shop he had a cellar, in which he kept a great quantity of his merchandise. One day he desired his servant maid to go down to the cellar with a candle to fetch him a supply of a particular kind of soap kept there. The girl went to do her master's bidding, but she imprudently did not provide herself with a candlestick, and therefore found it necessary, while filling her basket with pieces of soap, to stick the candle into what she thought a bag of black seed, which stood open by her side. In returning, both her hands were required to carry the basket, so that she had to leave the candle where it was. When Mr. Dewar saw her coming up the trap door without the candle, he asked her where she had left it. She replied that she had stuck it into some black seed near the place where the soap lay. He instantly recollected that this black seed was gunpowder, and he knew that a single spark falling from the candle would blow up the house. He also knew that the candle, if left where it was, would in a little time burn down to the powder. To fly, then, was to make the destruction of his house and property certain, while to go down and attempt to take away the candle, was to run the risk of being destroyed himself, for he could not tell that a spark was not to fall the next instant into the powder. He made up his mind in a moment and descended into the cellar. There he saw the candle burning brightly in the midst of the bag of gunpowder. He approached softly, lest, by putting the air in motion, he might cause the candle to sparkle. Then, stooping with the greatest deliberation over the sack, he formed his hands into a hollow, like the basin of a bedroom candlestick, and clasped the candle between his fingers. He thus had the chance of catching any spark which might fall: None, however, fell, and he bore away the candle in safety.

Bravo Mr. Dewar! But why did you leave your powder where your maid could run you into so great a risk? Presence of mind is greatly to be commended, but general carefulness may prevent the need of so great a demand upon courage as this case required.

I could multiply my reminiscences, but my business is not so much to lecture upon candles themselves as upon the sermons that lie within them. The Eskimos consider tallow candles a great luxury; and I have met with a missionary who assured me that in the far north of America he had learned greatly to prefer a candle to a piece of sugar or any other dainty. May not tastes be thus perverted in reference to spiritual things? Is it not often so?

I will not offer you a discussion upon the physical or chemical nature of candles. I will not feed you on candles, for you have not the educated taste of my friend from the Hudson's Bay Territory. No, I will give you candlelight, and not the candles themselves; but if you would know all about them, read a capital set of lectures entitled *Faraday on the Chemical History of a Candle* published by Chatto and Windus.

All this time I have been guilty of a terrible omission: I have not defined a candle; and how can a man know anything or teach anything if he is not very careful to describe the subject of his discourse in the most difficult manner conceivable? I regret that I cannot find a regular jaw-breaking definition in any of the dictionaries. They have treated the subject in too light a manner and have not by any means confounded and obfuscated the word *candle* as it deserves to be confounded and obfuscated. The *Century Dictionary* describes it as "a taper: a cylindrical body of tallow, wax, spermaceti, or other fatty material, formed on a wick composed of linen or cotton threads woven or twisted loosely, or (as formerly) of the pith of a rush, and used as a source of artificial light." This is all very well; but how much more we might have known if the lexicographer had called candles "nascent possibilities of illumination materialized in oleaginous cylindrical forms"! It is some comfort, that while certain great linguists derive the word from the Latin *candela*, which comes from *candere*, "to burn"; others take it from the Welsh, which I guess must be *llandyllyn*, "to blaze"; and a third party perceive its origin in the ancient Danish *kindil*, "to burn or kindle." Do you not all feel the better for these learned criticisms? Would you not feel safer still if I could assure you that luminous and voluminous scientists have had serious doubts as to whether candles were known to the ancients at all; and if so, whether indeed there are such things now extant? Alfred the Great is said to have invented lanterns to preserve his candles from the drafts that came into his hall through windows that were innocent of glass, but this is extremely doubtful. Only the fossilized believer accepts the popular belief. The learned critic sees things in another light, or rather does not see them at all. According to the learned Dr. Batseyes, there would seem to have been two Alfreds, one who allowed the cakes to burn, and another who went to battle with the Danes. There does not appear to be any justification for believing that either of these Alfreds could have cared about candles so much as to invent lanterns for their protection. A person who would allow cakes to burn would scarcely be careful of mere tallow candles, and a man who fought with the Danes was far more likely to put the fat into the fire than to preserve it from the wind. What think you of that? There is more in it than in most of the biblical criticisms that I have met with. I am rather pleased with my historic doubt. With a little effort, I fancy I could qualify myself to be a practicer of destructive criticism, but I conceive that the game would not be worth the candle, and I should only be doing more of that which is already overdone.

It would be too great a task for me to guide you into every corner in history or archaeology where the candle leads the way. But there are a few odds and ends that may be worth picking up. Candle ends must not be wasted, but put upon the save-all and used for a good purpose.

> *Presence of mind is greatly to be commended, but general carefulness may prevent the need of so great a demand upon courage as this case required.*

Diogenes with his lantern lives before us as he ranges through the city in the glare of the sun looking for an honest man. He could not dispense with his light even now if he went to some places in our land—I mean not exclusively the parliaments of politicians; there are religious assemblies where his lantern would not be unnecessary.

Alfred the Great, to whom we have already referred, is said to have measured time by the burning of candles, marking them, we suppose, so that so much candle meant an hour. No wonder that, to secure accuracy in his chronometer, he invented a shield in the form of a lantern to keep off the drafts that would cause his measurers of time to burn away in no time.

Our forefathers kept a festival known as Candlemas: It comes on February 2 and celebrates the purification of the Virgin and the presentation of the infant Christ in the temple. The feast takes its name from the custom, as old as the seventh century, of carrying lighted candles in procession, in memory of Simeon's words, "A light to lighten the Gentiles" (Luke 2:32 KJV).

On this day Roman Catholics consecrate the candles to be used in their churches throughout the year. The feast is retained in the Anglican and Lutheran churches. It is frequently called The Purification. In Scotland, Candlemas is one of the quarter days for paying and receiving rents, interest, school fees, etc. In former days the boy who brought his Dominie the largest present was made king of the school. Poor honors that could thus be bought! How like most of the glories of the world!

Christmas Eve has its candles to light up the Christmas tree. Our German friends observe this pretty ceremony with great care, to the great delight of the juniors of the family. Among the things in Luther's life that charm all hearts were his enjoyment of music and his delight in the children's Christmas tree.

In Chaucer's England one hears little of candles, but in the list of articles of a manor house of the time, we read of "an iron or lantern candlestick," meaning, we suppose, an iron candlestick covered with brass, or a brass candlestick. Ancient candlesticks, such as we are able to set before you, were more solid than elegant and look as if they might have been copied from an hourglass. After long research in olden history for some hints about candles, a friend who noticed our failure suggested that we should search through a history of Greece, but we did not give him a fig, much less a groat, for his puny wit. Of old, the Shunammitish woman, who had a prophet's chamber, had provided a candlestick for the man of God; but far nearer our own day, a domestic candlestick seems to have been a rare thing in this country. Until windows were supplied with glass, naked candles must have been too liable to be blown out to be used without lanterns. Moreover, we suspect that our fathers were not so apt to turn night into day as we are, but went to bed with the lamb and rose with the lark. They lost somewhat by this habit, but possibly they gained more. The curfew, which put out all lights at an early hour, has been represented as an instrument of tyranny; but in all probability, it was a needful social regulation to prevent the frequent fires that fell out in wooden houses, where the floor was covered with rushes and candles were apt to be carelessly used. On the whole, we do not weep very bitterly over "the good old times," when we sit at ease far into the night and read by the electric light.

> *Diogenes with his lantern lives before us as he ranges through the city in the glare of the sun looking for an honest man. He could not dispense with his light even now.*

The making of lanterns would seem to have been a flourishing trade in the olden time. Many were made of horn, but we have seen an engraving in which tin or thin iron would seem to be largely used.

Excommunications were pronounced by "bell, book, and candle." After the formula had been read and the book closed, the assistants cast the lighted candles they held in their hands to the ground so as to extinguish them, and the bells were clashed without order: The last two ceremonies symbolized the quenching of grace and the disorder in the souls of the persons excommunicated. Now we understand why

The Cardinal rose with a dignified look,
He call'd for his candle, his bell, and his book!
In holy anger and pious grief
He solemnly cursed that rascally thief!

There was a special warning form of the same terrible punishment wherein the sinner was allowed space for repentance so long as a candle continued to burn. If he expressed no regret till the light was out, he was cast off; but while the candle yet would burn, the vilest sinner might return.

While remembering the holy candles of the Church of Rome, one cannot forget the miracles connected with these humble household luminaries.

We quote from Hone's *Everyday Book*:

Several stories of the miraculous faculties of St. Genevieve, the patron saint of Paris, represent [candles] as very convenient in vexatious cases of ordinary occurrence; one of these will serve as a specimen. On a dark, wet night she was going to church with her maidens with a candle borne before her, which the wind and rain put out; the saint merely called for the candle, and as soon as she took it in her hand it was lighted again, without any fire of this world.

Other stories of her lighting candles in this way call to mind a candle, greatly venerated by E. Worsley in *A Discourse of Miracles Wrought in the Roman Catholic Church, or, a Full Refutation of Dr. Stillingfleet's Unjust Exceptions against Miracles* (8 vols., 1676). At page 64, he says, "that the miraculous wax candle yet seen at Arras, the chief city of Artois, may give the reader entertainment, being most certain, and never doubted by any. In 1105, that is, more than five hundred years ago (of so great antiquity the candle is), a merciless plague reigned in Arras. The whole city, ever devout to the Mother of God, experienced her, in this their necessity, to be a true mother of mercy. The manner was thus: The Virgin Mary appeared to two men and enjoined them to tell the Bishop of Arras that on the next Saturday, toward morning, she would appear in the great church and put into his hands a wax candle burning, from whence drops of wax should fall into a vessel of water prepared by the bishop. She said, moreover, that all the diseased that drank of this water should forthwith be cured. This, truly promised, truly happened. Our Blessed Lady appeared all beautiful, having in her hands a wax candle burning, which diffused light over the whole church; this she presented to the bishop; he, blessing it with the sign of the cross, set it in the urn of water, when drops of wax plentifully fell down into the vessel. The diseased drank of it, all were cured, the contagion ceased, and the candle, to this day preserved with great veneration, spends itself yet loses nothing, and therefore remains still of the same length and greatness it did five hundred years ago. A vast quantity of wax, made up of the many drops which fall into the water upon those festival days when the candle burns, may be justly called a standing, indeficient miracle.

This candle story, though gravely related by a Catholic writer, as "not doubted of by any," and as, therefore, not to be questioned, altogether failed in convincing the Protestant Stillingfleet that miracles wrought in the Roman Catholic Church ought to be believed. It fails with us also.

Even these lying wonders are more pleasant reading than the stories that relate to the use of candles in the conversion of Protestant heretics. They had their choice either to turn or burn, and judicious proselyters gave the obstinate a little taste of flame beforehand, to save them from the greater fire. Here are two precious stories from the famous *Acts and Monuments*.

Fox tells us concerning Thomas Tomkins, a weaver of Shoreditch who was burned at Smithfield, that Bishop Bonnet kept him in prison at Fulham half a year, "during which time the said bishop was so rigorous with him that he beat him bitterly about the face, whereby his face was swelled."

The rage of this bishop was not so great against him,

but the constancy of the sufferer was much greater with patience to bear it; who, although he had not the learning as others had, yet he was so endued with God's mighty Spirit, and so perfectly planted in the knowledge of God's truth, that by no means could he be removed from the confession of the truth. Whereupon Bonner the bishop, being greatly vexed against the poor man, when he saw that by no persuasions he could prevail against him, devised another practice not so strange as cruel, further to try his constancy; to the intent, that seeing he could not otherwise convince him by doctrine out of the scriptures, yet he might overthrow him by a fore-feeling and terror of death. So he calls for Thomas Tomkins, who, coming before the bishop, and standing as he was wont, in defense of his faith, the bishop having there a taper or wax candle of three or four wicks standing upon the table, took Tomkins by the fingers and held his hand directly over the flame, supposing that by the smart and pain of the fire being terrified, he would leave off the defense of his Protestant doctrine.

Tomkins, thinking no otherwise but there presently to die, began to commend himself unto the Lord, saying, "O Lord! Into your hands I commend my spirit!" In the time that his hand was in burning, the same Tomkins afterward reported to one James Hinse that "his spirit was so rapt that he felt no pain." In the which burning he never quailed, till the veins shrank and the sinews burst.

If a bishop acted thus, we do not wonder that the more brutal ones among the bigoted laity did the like. Here is another record from that Fox who spied out and laid bare the doings of Romish devotees.

On the second of August, 1557, five men and five women were burnt at Colchester for the testimony and witness of Christ Jesus and his glorious gospel. In the number was one William Mount, of Much Bentley, in Essex, husbandman, with Alice, his wife, and Rose Allin, maid, the daughter of the said Alice Mount.

At two o'clock on a Sunday morning in March, one master Edmund Tyrrel took with him the bailiff and two constables, with divers others, a great number. Going into the room where Father Mount and his wife lay, they bade them rise, for that they must go to Colchester Castle. Mother Mount, being very ill, asked that her daughter might fetch her some drink. This Tyrrel permitted. So Rose Mount took a stone jug in one hand and a candle in the other and went to draw drink for her mother; and as she came back again through the house, Tyrrel met her and willed her to give her father and mother good counsel and advise them to be better Catholic people.

ROSE: Sir, they have a better instructor than I; for the Holy Spirit doth teach them, I hope; and He, be ye sure, will not suffer them to err.

TYRREL: Why? Art thou still in that mind, thou naughty housewife? Marry, it is time to look upon such heretics indeed.

ROSE: Sir, with that which you call heresy, do I worship my Lord God; I tell you truth.

TYRREL: Then I perceive you will burn, gossip, with the rest, for company's sake.

ROSE: No, sir, not for company's sake, but for my Lord Jesus Christ's sake, if so I be compelled; and I hope in His mercies if He call me to it, He will enable me to bear it.

So he, turning to his company, said, "Sirs, this gossip will burn; do you not think it?" "Marry, sir," quoth one, "prove her, and ye shall see what she will do by and by."

Then the cruel Tyrrel, taking the candle from her, held her wrist and put the burning candle under her hand, burning cross-wise over the back thereof so long the very sinews cracked asunder." Yet the brave Rose endured the

pain like a true heroine and then went and fetched her
mother the drink.

How many of us, who preach with much confidence, could have endured
the like torture? Let us hope that if we were called to such pain, grace would
be given to sustain us under it.

One is soon weary of such quotations, and we will leave them when we
have reminded ourselves of the brave word of old Latimer. When standing
on the fagots, with his back to the stake, he turned round to his brother
bishop, Ridley, and said, "Be of good comfort, Master Ridley, and play the
man, and we shall this day light such a candle, by God's grace, in England,
as I trust shall never be put out."

And so say all of us.

In the city of London in olden times, the streets being unlighted by
public lamps and thieves being plentiful, a law was made for everybody
to put a candle out over his door. As the story comes to me, the law was
obeyed—a candle was exhibited, but it was not lighted. The letter of the law
was darkness, for the spirit of the law was absent.

The wise corporation had to meet and ordain a regulation that everybody
should light the candle that by law was to be over his door. So they did; but
after it had been lighted according to law, the wind blew it out, and again the
citizens saved their tallow. The city fathers made another alteration in their
edict and decreed that everybody should hang a lantern over his door. This
was soon accomplished, but the householders put no candle in the lantern.
The corporation has always been amazingly wise and is so still. You laugh,
but my reverence for all public bodies is so great that you cannot suppose
that I intended anything sarcastic. The council went over the old ground and
settled that the lantern should have a candle in it. Again, the good folks did
as they were bidden, but they did not light the candle. This called forth the
decree that in the lantern there should be a lighted candle. Canny citizens
put only a very small length of candle; and though it was soon burnt out,
they could not be charged with a breach of the law in that case made and
provided. The corporation specified the length of the candle to be lighted,
but I daresay clever people still dodged the law. It is never difficult to drive a
coach and four through the Acts of Parliaments and Corporations. There is
one way of doing a right thing, but there are dozens of ways of not doing it;

and people are very ingenious at avoiding rules that involve expense. Candles suggest save-alls, and economical minds need not that the hint be repeated. Misers have been known to go to bed to save candle for themselves; what would they not do to escape burning a candle for other people?

The watchmen of our city were in the old time the themes of constant jest. They had come to be venerable persons wrapped in capes of many folds and nightcaps of the warmest sort. Each one of these had his lantern, with which he emulated in the streets the glowworms of the country lanes. Stowe represents these guardians of the night as carrying and using bells to give warning to householders to put out fire and light candle. Nice helps to repose these old gentlemen must have been, especially if they conscientiously obeyed orders, and both knocked at doors and sounded their alarms to wake people out of their first sleep to look to their candles! All very pretty it sounds in the rhyme, but not quite so delightful if heard in the still of night.

> *A light here, maids, hang out your light,*
> *And see your horns be clean and bright,*
> *That so your candle clear may shine,*
> *Continuing from six till nine;*
> *That honest men that walk along*
> *May see to pass safe without wrong.*

In the days of Henry VIII, the citizens of London did little in the way of hanging out candles, and hence men cut purses in the dark with impunity. Harry's remedy was, "Hang up the thieves, and let honest men keep indoors." Very thoroughly did he practice his own rule, so that it is recorded that three score and twelve thousand petty thieves were hung up during his reign. Poor saving this, to spare the hanging out of candles and indulge in the hanging up of men! There can be no doubt that good light is the friend of honesty and the destruction of thieves. This is a parable that we need not wait to expound.

Many bequests have been left for the keeping up of lights, especially in places near the river Thames. I will give you a specimen. John Wardall, by will, dated 29 August, 1656, gave to the Grocers' Company a tenement called "The White Bear," in Walbrook, to the intent that they should yearly, within thirty days after Michaelmas, pay to the churchwardens of St. Botolph, Billingsgate, £4, to provide a good and sufficient iron and glass lantern, with a candle, for the direction of passengers to go with more security to and from the waterside all night long, to be fixed at the northeast corner of the parish church of St. Botolph, from the feast day of St. Bartholomew to Lady Day. Out of this sum £1 was to be paid to the sexton for taking care of the lantern. It is well in life and in death to minister light to this dark world.

It was a curious way of expressing his appreciation of a politician, when Mr. Alderman White, of Winchester, sent Wilkes, the author of the notorious Number 45, a present of forty-five dozen candles. Possibly the worthy Alderman had an eye to advertisement as well as to admiration. At any rate, he succeeded, for the wags, one of which signs himself Will Wickham, immortalized him in their verses.

> *What hero, what king,*
> *Sweet muse, wilt thou sing?*
> *What alderman venture to handle?*
> *No subject so bright*
> *As Alderman White,*
> *And his forty-five dozen of candle.*
>
> *From him the bright name*
> *Of freedom shall flame,*
> *And all who that cause understand ill*
> *May see wrong from right,*
> *By the true patriot light*
> *Of forty-five dozen of candle.*
>
> *On a theme so sublime,*
> *I forever would rhyme,*
> *But my muse I no longer shall dandle*
> *So I wish you goodnight,*
> *Mr. Alderman White;*
> *But beware of a thief in the candle.*

We must not fail to mention Hogarth's famous drawing of *The Politician*. That admirable publication, *The Penny Magazine* in the year 1834, had such an excellent exposition of the picture that I cannot forbear to quote it in full.

This piece of exquisite humor, is said to have been
suggested to Hogarth by a living and well-known
character in his day, a Mr. Tibson, laceman in the
Strand, who preferred politics to trade and the *Gazetteer*
newspaper to the ledger and day book. Never was a ruling
passion—an intentness on a favorite subject—more
happily portrayed than in the print before us. The mere
position or seat of the old quidnunc tells a story! From
the way in which he has squared himself in his chair, you
may see he is a man determined not to budge until he
has conned his dear paper through to the last line, word,
and syllable. His short, stout legs, with those broad bases
of high-quartered shoes, are set down on the floor like
pillars! It would require a dray horse to drag him from his
occupation!

To throw a full, clear light on his sheet (the only sheet,
we may be sure, he ever reads), he has taken his tallow
candle from its socket and, indifferent to the abomination
of grease, holds it in his right hand, whilst his left hand
grasps his journal—the Benjamin of his heart.

The ascending flame has set fire to his hat, has literally
burnt a hole through its broad brim. The candle has also
fearfully burnt down and has guttered; the red-hot wick
and the base of the flame are within the eighth of an inch
of his finger, and it is difficult to say which part of him
will be burnt first, his forehead, his nose, or his unflinching
hand. But what of that? He is rapt and altogether
unconscious of his danger, and on he will read until the fire
reaches him. Look at his countenance the while, with its
deep lines of thought, and the half acute and half solemn
compression of his lips! There is many a siege and blockade
in the dropping corner of that mouth, and a campaign or a
treaty in every wrinkle of that face!

Thanks to the introduction of narrow-brimmed hats,
there is now no danger of our quidnuncs setting fire to
their beavers. Their heads indeed are sometimes heated by
flaming paragraphs, but the heat is all inward. There are

political occasions on which the people have to think and
to act, as far as they can act legally; but the only way to
think and to act rightly is to be cool and not set their hats
or their heads on fire.

In the days of the great Napoleon the rage of English people against
Boney knew no bounds. Woodward designed a cartoon entitled *The Corsican
Moth*, which, flying toward the candle, is made to say, "It is a very fierce
flame; I am afraid I shall singe my wings!" Old George III, just below the
candlestick, is muttering, "You little contemptible insect, I shall see you
consumed by and by!" We are glad that no such irrational hate now stirs our
population with enmity to France. There is no need for me to moralize upon
the moth and the candle; yet it were well if some who have been already
injured by vicious courses could have the sense to shun those evils which
have already wrought them so much ill.

It brings us back to the Dark Ages, when we find that, so late as 1836,
His Majesty William IV was dependent upon wax candles for the due
delivery of his speech to Parliament. I will give you the passage:

A ROYAL SPEECH BY CANDLELIGHT

The opening day of the Session of Parliament in 1836
(February 4) was unusually gloomy, which added to an
imperfection in the sight of King William IV, and the
darkness of the House rendered it impossible for His
Majesty to read the royal speech with facility. Most
patiently and good-naturedly did he struggle with the
task, often hesitating, sometimes mistaking, and at others
correcting himself. On one occasion he stuck altogether,
and after two or three ineffectual efforts to make out the
word, he was obliged to give it up, when, turning to Lord
Melbourne, who stood on his right hand, and looking him
most significantly in the face, he said in a tone sufficiently
loud to be audible in all parts of the House, "Eh! What
is it?" Lord Melbourne, having whispered the obstructing
word, the King proceeded to toil through the speech;
but by the time he got to about the middle, the librarian

brought him two wax lights, on which he suddenly paused. Then raising his head and looking at the Lords and Commons, he addressed them on the spur of the moment in a perfectly distinct voice and without the least embarrassment or mistake of a single word, in these terms:

"My Lords and Gentlemen, I have hitherto not been able, from want of light, to read this speech in the way its importance deserves; but as lights are now brought me, I will read it again from the commencement, and in a way which, I trust, will command your attention."

The King, though evidently fatigued by the difficulty of reading in the first instance, began at the beginning and read through the speech in a manner that would have done credit to a professor of elocution!

Ladies and gentlemen, it would seem to be a wonder that a King should be able to read without fainting away! When he does his royal best, he seems to be nearly as good as "a professor of elocution." This is not saying much. People who try to flatter rulers generally succeed in making them ridiculous. Think of His Majesty's being able to deliver an extempore speech of one sentence! Wonders will never cease.

Let us get to our "Sermons in Candles" in real earnest. We will begin with the candlelight that we find in Holy Scripture.

The golden candlestick of the tabernacle and temple may hardly be mentioned in this place, for it was rather a seven-branched stand for oil lamps than for candles. Its representation on the arch of Titus at Rome is visible to all and stands as all enduring testimony to the truth of Holy Scripture.

Our Lord walks among the golden candlesticks of his churches; but these again are candelabra or lampstands. In a country where olive oil abounded so much as in Palestine, there was no need of the candle of our colder climate—the lamp being so readily supplied with the best of fuel. These lamps were of many forms; but what mattered it, so long as their light was good? Many are the methods of the churches, but the main thing is to shine with gospel light.

In the Word of God, we read of candles in different connections, but my previous remark applies to all the passages. The probability is that they all relate to lamps. That, however, shall not hinder me from speaking upon them. Candles are mentioned in relation to the character and condition of wicked men. Job 18:6 says, "The light shall be dark in his tabernacle, and his candle shall be put out with him" (KJV). His light never was that of the Sun of Righteousness, but he set up the candle of creature comfort that he might forget the night of his soul. Yet even this was but a temporary light, a mere candle that melted as it shone. God is against the ungodly man, and therefore, in due season, his very light will become darkness, and even his small joy will be gone like a candle that is blown out. In all cases a candle is doomed to cease its shining sooner or later. It comes to an end by gradual and natural consumption even if all goes well with it; but in the case mentioned in the text, it is quenched by violence, or "put out." How great is the darkness of the sinner in such a case! If the believer has his candlestick of earthly comfort removed out of its place, his God still abides with him; and therefore he rejoices in heavenly light and does not stumble; but when the ungodly lose their candle, they have lost all; and so Job adds, "The steps of his strength shall be straitened, and his own counsel shall cast him down" (18:7). When the lamp goes out in the Arab tent, all is gloomy and desolate; and hence the misery that is symbolized by the quenching of the candle is great.

> God is against the ungodly man, and therefore, in due season, his very light will become darkness, and even his small joy will be gone like a candle that is blown out.

In another place Job (21:17) says, "How oft is the candle of the wicked put out!" (KJV). Suddenly the glory, the prosperity, yea, the very life of the wicked may come to an end. It has been so in hundreds of cases. Some think the passage means "How seldom!" rather than "How often!" Assuredly, the righteous have often considered providence to be slack in its dealings with the ungodly. But is it not great long-suffering that spares the guilty, in the hope of their repentance? Why should we grudge them a little candlelight, when, alas! They will so soon dwell in the outer darkness?

Job does not restrict this metaphor to the sons of evil, but uses it in reference to his own condition. Hear how he sighs, "Oh that I were as in months past, as in the days when God preserved me; when his candle shined upon my head" (29:2–3 KJV). He had known prosperity, and that was gone! He had enjoyed heavenly fellowship, and that had been obscured. The candle of the Lord is a candle indeed. When that brightness is reflected from our faces, we are as happy as the angels in heaven; but when it is taken away, we sit in a darkness that may be felt. He who has once enjoyed fellowship with God will never again be happy without it. If we had remained in the blindness of nature, we should not have known the glory of divine love, or should we have been in distress when a conscious sense of it is withdrawn; but now that we are enlightened by divine grace, darkness brings woe to us. When we lose the candle of the Lord, we imitate Job in sighing for its return.

David, who knew full well the brightness of that candle, and also knew the miss of it, jubilantly cries out in Psalm 18:28 KJV, "Thou wilt light my candle." The Scotch version well rhymes it:

The Lord will light my candle so,
That it shall shine full bright:
The Lord my God will also make
My darkness to be light.

Believers shall not be left in the dark. If no servant comes to light our candle, the Lord Himself will do it. What a mass of meaning can be packed away in one figurative expression! Matthew Henry, without the least straining of the metaphor, reads the passage thus: "You wilt revive and comfort my sorrowful spirit and not leave me melancholy: Thou wilt recover me out of my troubles and restore me to peace and prosperity: Thou wilt make my honor bright, which is now eclipsed; Thou wilt guide my way and make it plain before me, that I may avoid the snares laid for me; Thou wilt light my candle to work by and give me an opportunity of serving You and the interests of Your kingdom among men."

Solomon spoke of a candle when he said, "The spirit of man is the candle of the LORD, searching all the inward parts of the belly" (Prov. 20:27 KJV). Did he not refer to conscience? Did he not mean that conscience is in some respects a divine light—"the candle of the LORD"—and in all respects a discovering light—searching all the inward parts? Take care that you never trifle with this candle. A loss of light in the conscience means decrease of light for our whole manhood. I am afraid that conscience in many persons has become no better than an unkindled candle, not giving light or even making darkness visible.

I have heard of a man who said, "Conscience! Conscience! I have plenty of conscience."

"Yes," said one, "and it is as good as new, for I have never known you to use it." In that case it was a candle unlighted, and the old rhyme has it:

> *A candle that affords no light,*
> *What profits it by day or night?*

An enlightened conscience is greatly to be prized, and it should be kept free from everything that might mar its brightness. Milton says:

> *He that has light within his own clear breast,*
> *May sit in the center and enjoy bright day.*

God grant that we may never do violence to our conscience even in the least degree, for this is to quench our own light!

Solomon mentions the candle in his graphic picture of the virtuous woman, who not only worked by day, but wrought far into the night. He says in Proverbs 31:18, "Her candle goeth not out by night" (KJV). Many would have their hours shortened as to work and lengthened as to sleep, but she did the very reverse. She lengthened her days by taking hours out of her nights. A wonderful example that woman was! I recollect hearing, when I was a boy, a minister preach about her from this text: "Who can find a virtuous woman? for her price is far above rubies." The opening of that memorable discourse was somewhat in this fashion:

" 'Who can find a virtuous woman?' Why, anyone who chooses to look for her; and the only reason why Solomon could not find her was because he looked in the wrong place. Virtuous women kept clear of a king who had such a multitude of wives. But," said the preacher, "if Solomon were here now and were made truly wise, he would not long ask, 'Who can find a virtuous woman?' He would join the church and find himself at once among a band of holy women, whose adornment is a meek and quiet spirit.

If he were permitted to look in upon the Dorcas meeting, he would see many of the sort of whom he once said, 'She stretches out her hand to the poor; yea, she reaches forth her hands to the needy.' If he would adjourn to the Sunday school, he would there meet with others of whom he would say, 'She opens her mouth with wisdom; and in her tongue is the law of kindness.' We, who serve the Lord Jesus, meet many a time with virtuous women, of each of whom we could say with the wise king, 'Her price is far above rubies.'"

> *A loss of light in the conscience means decrease of light for our whole manhood. I am afraid that conscience in many persons has become no better than an unkindled candle, not giving light or even making darkness visible.*

The preacher of whom I have spoken interested me by the remark, "Why 'above rubies'? Why not above diamonds? My brethren, the diamond is but a pale and sickly stone, which needs the glare of candlelight or gas to set it off; but the ruby is a ruddy, healthy gem, which is beautiful by daylight. Lovely is the woman whose face is full of the glow of activity in domestic life. That is the kind of woman who makes the housewife in whom the heart of her husband safely trusts." Whatever one may think of the correctness of the exposition, the sentiment of the preacher was sound and practical.

In scripture the candle is mentioned when the destruction of a city is described. "Moreover I will take from them the voice of mirth, and the voice of gladness, the voice of the bridegroom, and the voice of the bride, the sound of the millstones, and the light of the candle" (Jer. 25:10 KJV). When no longer there were days of joy—no festivals, no weddings—then was the city brought low; but when the sound of the grinding of the meal by the millstone altogether ceased in the morning, and the light of the candle was no more to be seen in the evening, then was the city deserted and left to be a desolation. If you passed a city on a hill and saw no candle shining from any window, then you knew that the inhabitants had ceased. The description is as graphic as it is pictorial. The fate of the spiritual Babylon, or apostate church, is set forth in the book of Revelation, in the most solemn and sweeping terms:

*And a mighty angel took up a stone like a great millstone, and
cast it into the sea, saying, Thus with violence shall that great
city Babylon be thrown down, and shall be found no more at
all. And the voice of harpers, and musicians, and of pipers,
and trumpeters, shall be heard no more at all in thee; and no
craftsman, of whatsoever craft he be, shall be found any more in
thee; and the sound of a millstone shall be heard no more at all
in thee; and the light of a candle shall shine no more at all in
thee. (18:21–23 KJV)*

Who, that has read with care the story of the apostate church, can do
other than rejoice with the holy apostles and prophets that God will thus
deal with her?

The prophet Zephaniah, in his first chapter, at the twelfth verse, mentions
candles in that memorable passage wherein he describes the overthrow of
Jerusalem by the Babylonians: "I will search Jerusalem with candles." The
same description might stand for the destruction of the city by the Romans,
for Josephus tells us that princes and priests and mighty men were dragged
even out of the sewers, pits, caves, and tombs in which they had hidden
themselves from fear of death. The imagery of the prophet well describes the
conduct of soldiers when sacking a city. They not only seize all that they can
see at once or with a slight search, but rightly judging that the people will
have hidden their treasures, they ransack their darkest cellars and closets,
and pry into their furniture; and so that they may see the better, they light
many candles and look into every corner and cranny so that nothing may
escape them. Now, when God comes to search His church, He will do it
Himself: "I will search Jerusalem"; and He will do it as minutely as spoilers
in the hour of sack. He will find out every hypocrite, "and punish the men
that are settled on their lees: that say in their heart, The LORD will not do
good, neither will he do evil" (Zeph. 1:12 KJV). Ah me! If the Lord thus
examines our churches; if He comes to close work with men's souls and
searches with candles to find out their condition; shall we be able to endure
an investigation so thorough, so minute, so all-discovering?

When we reach the New Testament, we remember our Savior's
words: "Neither do men light a candle, and put it under a bushel, but on a
candlestick; and it giveth light unto all that are in the house" (Matt. 5:15
KJV). Grace is meant to be seen; to conceal it is contrary to common sense.

Our Lord also speaks of a high degree of grace in Luke 11:36, "If then your whole body is full of light, having no part dark, the whole body will be full of light, as when the bright shining of a lamp gives you light." How blessed to have no part dark! To have the whole body full of light! This is no dim twinkling, but the bright shining of a candle, or rather of a lamp, whereby all in the room are made glad. What a beautiful condition of heart! But we ought all to possess it; for darkness is a work of the devil, and our Lord Jesus has come to destroy all the work of the devil. God grant that the whole of our being may be irradiated with the brightness of His grace! Then we shall have nothing to conceal, and nothing around us will lie in darkness. Our houses will be lit up with glory, and the bells on the horses, and the vessels of our dwellings will reflect the brightness of our consecrated lives. Alas, so many have a measure of divine knowledge and grace yet have some part of their nature still in the darkness! You cannot help noticing that their sanctification is partial. Perhaps it will be the wiser course to keep our eyes at home and pray the Lord to enlighten our darkness, that we may ourselves shine as lights in the world.

> will search Jerusalem"; and He will do it as minutely as spoilers in the hour of sack. He will find out every hypocrite, "and punish the men that are settled on their lees; that say in their heart, The Lord will not do good, neither will he do evil."

Remember, also, the remarkable parable of the woman who had lost her piece of money. The question is put in Luke 15:8, "What woman having ten pieces of silver, if she lose one piece, doth not light a candle, and sweep the house, and seek diligently till she find it?" (kjv). In this way must we look for lost souls, with the light of the gospel and the bosom of the law. You must be at some expense if you would find the lost! You must light a candle and let it be burnt up. You must make a little dust, too, for nothing worth doing will be accomplished without a stir. Yet dust making is not all. Certain people seem to think that you will find all the lost pieces of money by merely making dust enough and noise enough, but they are wrong. There must be more light than dust. Nothing can be done without the light of the candle. Instruction must be given, as well as excitement created. A little dust is a good sign, for it shows that the lethargic order is being disturbed and old things are passing away; but at the same time, we must not make so much dust that we cannot see by the light of our candle. Indeed, we must not be content either with the dust or the light; we may not rest till we spy out our lost treasure and place it in safety. Use the candle more than the broom. Be not negligent as to either, but keep your eye open to find the money.

There is even a connection between candles and heaven, though it is of a negative kind; for there "they need no candle, neither light of the sun" (Rev. 22:5 KJV). Here on earth creature comforts yield us their candlelight; but there the Creator Himself will fill us with His own presence, and we shall no more need these temporal blessings than a man requires a candle at noonday. How soon may we be privileged to know how bright is the place where "the Lord God gives them light"! Thus the scripture is not without its sermons in candles, as I have shown you.

One allusion I will venture to mention, though the word employed is *lamp*. David says, "Thy word is a lamp unto my feet, and a light unto my path" (Ps. 119:105). David drew his comparison from what is seen every night in an Oriental city. He who goes out into the street at night in Eastern towns is bound to carry a lantern with him. You would find it very necessary if you were there, if only because of the dogs who prowl about for their living. They are very fond of shinbones, and they do not like them any the less if they happen to be alive, with a little meat upon them. A light may keep them off. Besides that, there are open gutters and heaps of filth, and nobody knows the abominations of the unspeakable Turk and his cousins in the East. You must, therefore, when you go out at night, carry a lantern for your own protection; and the law also compels you to do so. If you are out without a lantern, the police put you down as an individual who is abroad with ill design. The very common lantern, with which children are so pleased, is a fair specimen of what are used at this day, and therefore it resembles what David used, for fixings in the East undergo little or no change. The proper use of such a lantern was to guide the feet, and this is the use of the Word of God. Certain brethren hold it up so as to see the stars, hoping to find out what is going to happen next week or next year. How great they are over seals and trumpets! One admires the depth and the darkness of their research. We may leave them to their discoveries: Time will show whether they are correct or not.

Others hold the heavenly light where its only use would be to minister warmth and comfort to the heart. These we do not blame, unless they forget other matters. David made a practical use of the sacred light: He held it where it would shine upon his way and enable him to keep out of foul places and walk in a clean path. The Bible is a blessing to us in many ways; but he is wisest who makes it his *Everyday Book* and rules his family life and his business life by its holy precepts. Read the prophecies, prize the promises, but fail not, by God's grace, to practice the precepts.

Many people use their Bibles like lights to be hung up at a Chinese feast of lanterns, for amusement or for show. Their theology is a brilliant advertisement of their information; their biblical studies make their conversation attractive; but bona fide practical godliness they fight shy of. They prefer the book of Revelation to the Sermon on the Mount. Very general is this unpractical treatment of Holy Scripture. Have you not heard of the Golden Rule? A wonderful precept is that Golden Rule, and I am sure you all admire it. I have been told that one day the Golden Rule wandered out of church into the Stock Exchange, got its hat knocked over its eyes, and was led out by the beadle, who asked, "What could have induced you to come here? What business have you out of church? You are neither a bull nor a bear." The jobbers and brokers could not do their business with this precious Golden Rule prying about, for its teaching did not allow latitude enough to either buyers or sellers. Perhaps I am mistaken. I am not sure that it was the Stock Exchange; on second thought, it may have been the Coal Exchange, or possibly Mark Lane. I am getting a little mixed. I wonder whether it was the Cattle Market, or Covent Garden, or Mincing Lane. Perhaps, after all, I am in error, and it was your shop. But this I do know, that the Golden Rule is always highly respected when it keeps itself to itself, but if it meddles with tradespeople, they say, "Business is business." To this I would reply, "And business has no business to be such business as it often is." The Golden Rule in business generally is, "Do others, or others will do you." But the Word of God speaks in nobler fashion. Scripture lays down bylaws that most of men treat with respectful negligence: They have no objection to the light and comfort of scripture in sickness, sorrow, or death; but they want it not in their everyday walks in the city. This is not as it should be. Use the light of God every day and all the day.

It is time to quit these scriptural allusions and come to the work of presenting emblems and illustrations. I will begin by borrowing. I dare-say you have seen a little, square, podgy book, as broad as it is long; very much like a smaller *Bradshaw's Railway Guide*. I refer to *Quarles' School of the Heart*. If ever you have been shut up in a remote farmhouse where there was nothing to read except the almanac for the year 1843, when you had read that through three times and had picked over *Buchan's Family Medicine*, you were driven at last to this quaint old book of uncouth cuts and rhymes. It is an immortal work, and despite the critics, it has true poetry in it, though its metaphors are often grotesque and strained. Toward the end you find certain emblems made from candles, and I have put seven of them together to set forth the "Seven Ages of Man." This first candle, long and slender, is the child, which, if spared, has quite a length of light and life before it.

> Many people use their Bibles like lights to be hung up at a Chinese feast of lanterns, for amusement or for show. Their theology is a brilliant advertisement of their information; their biblical studies make their conversation attractive.

When newly lighted, the flame is easily blown out, but there are large possibilities of continuance. So also at twenty we anticipate long years of life, yet it may end in one short hour. The other candles show us as thirty, forty, fifty, sixty, seventy years of age. Our figure goes no further, for "if by reason of strength they are eighty years, yet their boast is only labor and sorrow" (Ps. 90:10). Look at this shining emblem, and judge each one his own position as to his remainder of life. Mark how little is left to some of you! Pray God that you may use all that remains to the praise of God. I asked concerning a sick friend the other day, and the answer I received was a shake of the head and the remark, "I am sorry to say, he cannot last much longer. It is only a matter of time; his life hangs on a thread." I answered, "And that is exactly the case with me." Is it not true of everyone of us that we are mortal, and that our departure is only a matter of time? Our life is ended as easily as a candle is blown out.

Quarles has written many books, and he frequently brings in candlelight. Having introduced him, I leave you to make his further acquaintance as your taste directs.

Gotthold, wishing to seal a letter, called for a lighted candle. The maid obeyed his orders; but proceeding too hastily, the flame, which had not yet gathered sufficient strength, went out.

"Here," said Gotthold, "we have that which may well remind us of the gentleness and moderation to be observed in our comportment toward weak and erring brethren. Had this candle, when first lighted, been carried slowly, and shaded by the hand from the air, it would not have been extinguished, but would soon have burned with rigor. In like manner, many a weak brother might be set right if we only came to his help in the right way and with kindly advice. It is not by violent strokes that you reduce the dislocated limb. Christ Himself does not quench the smoking flax, but blows upon it with the gentle breath of the blessed words that proceed out of his mouth (Luke 4:22); and this was the reason why disconsolate sinners flocked around, and pressed upon Him, to hear what He said" (Luke 5:1; 15:1).

But you will soon be weary of me if I do not bring to an end this first part of my "Sermons in Candles." I will close with a short meditation, from quaint Bishop Hall, and a rhyme from Master John Bunyan. The bishop, whose wording I have a little altered, has contemplation under the heading of *On Occasion of the Lights Brought In.*

Well as we love the light, we are wont to salute it, at its first coming in, with winking or closed eyes; as not abiding to see that without which we cannot see. All sudden changes, though for the better, have a kind of trouble attending them. By how much more excellent any object is, by so much more is our weak sense misaffected in the first apprehending of it.

O Lord, if Thou shouldest manifest Your glorious presence to us here, we should be confounded at the sight of it. How wisely, how mercifully have Thou reserved that for our glorified estate; where no infirmity shall dazzle our eyes; where perfect righteousness shall give us perfect boldness both of sight and fruition!

Master Bunyan gives us a world of thought in the doggerel rhyme with which I end this first lesson.

Meditations upon a Candle

Man's like a candle in a candlestick,
Made up of tallow and a little wick;
And as the candle is before 'tis lighted,
Just such be they who are in sin benighted.
Nor can a man his soul with grace inspire,
More than can candles see themselves on fire.
Candles receive their light from what they are not;
Men, grace from Him, for whom at first they care not.
We manage candles when they take the fire;
God rules men when grace doth them inspire.
As biggest candles give the better light,
So grace on biggest sinners shines most bright.
The candle shines to make another see;
A saint unto his neighbor light should be.
The blinking candle we do much despise;
Saints dim of light are high in no man's eyes.
Again, though it may seem to some a riddle,
We used to light our candle at the middle.
True, light doth at the candle's end appear,
And grace the heart first reaches by the ear;
But 'tis the wick the fire doth kindle on,
As 'tis the heart that grace first works upon.
Thus both do fasten upon what's the main,
And so their life and vigor do maintain.
As candles in the wind are apt to flare,
So Christians in a tempest to despair.
We see the flame with smoke attended is;
And in our holy lives there's much amiss.
Sometimes a thief will candlelight annoy:
And lusts do seek our graces to destroy.
What brackish is will make a candle sputter;
'Twixt sin and grace there's oft a heavy clutter.
Sometimes the light burns dim, 'cause of the snuff,
And sometimes 'tis extinguish'd with a puff:
But watchfulness prevents both these evils,

Keeps candles light, and grace in spite of devils.
But let not snuffs or puffs make us to doubt;
Our candle may be lighted, though puff'd out.
The candle in the night doth all extol,
Nor sun, or moon or stars then shine so well:
So is the Christian in our hemisphere,
Whose light shows others how their course to steer.
When candles are put out, all's in confusion;
Where Christians are not, devils make intrusion.
They then are happy who such candles have;
All others dwell in darkness and the grave.
But candles that do blink within the socket,
And saints whose eyes are always in their pocket,
Are much alike; such candles make us fumble;
And at such saints, good men and bad do stumble.
Good candles don't offend, except sore eyes,
Nor hurt, unless it be the silly flies.
How good are shining candles in the night!
How sweet is holy living for delight!
But let us draw toward the candle's end.
The fire, you see, doth wick and tallow spend;
So wastes man's life, until his glass is run,
And so the candle and the man are done.
The man now lays him down upon his bed;
The wick yields up its fire, and so is dead.
The candle now extinct is, but the man
By grace mounts up to glory, there to stand.

LECTURE NUMBER TWO

I am afraid the science of emblems does not flourish so well among us as it did in a former age, when it constituted an important branch of learning. You might find a rare field of recreative study in emblem literature. So many have tried it that certain of the older emblem books have become too expensive for the ordinary reader to purchase. There has been a run upon them, and this has raised the price beyond their intrinsic value.

In almost every collection of emblems, I have found the candle, and perhaps most frequently of all, the candle and the fly. I am not cruel enough to wish to give you an actual example of the way in which flies, moths, and other insects are glamoured with the glare of a candle; but I may give you the facsimile of an old cut from Gilles Corrozet's *Hecatomgraphie*, a French work dated 1540. Under the motto "War is sweet only to the inexperienced," he gives, in illustration, a number of moths or butterflies fluttering toward a candle, said candle and moths being of gigantic size if compared with the room. Attached to the woodcuts are verses that signify that those alone seek the battlefield who know not its great dangers. This reminds me that the good Earl of Shaftesbury told me that when he was Lord Ashley, he once rode with the Duke of Wellington through the lovely villages off Berkshire, and for half an hour the warrior was silent. When at length he spoke, he said, "I daresay you wonder what has made me so quiet. I was thinking of the havoc which war would make of all this peace and beauty. If war should ever come here, it might be my duty to burn and destroy all these happy homes. Whether there follow upon it defeat or victory, war is a great calamity." The great soldier spoke the truth. May those nations that delight in war rest content with former burnings of their wings and let the flame alone.

Others have used the same emblem as a warning against the indulgence of sinful passions. The motto is "*Brevis et damnosa voluptas*," "short but ruinous pleasure." The sin promised to enlighten the eyes, but it burned into the very soul. Full often when we hear of young people ruined by unbridled appetites, we are apt to say with the world's great poet: "Thus has the candle singed the moth." Error has the same effect on certain restless minds. No sooner is a new theory started than they make a dash for it; and though it costs them comfort, fellowship, and holiness, they fly at it again. "O foolish Galatians, who hath bewitched you?" (Gal. 3:1 KJV). The fascination of novelty appears to be irresistible when minds are weak and conceited.

> *If war should ever come here, it might be my duty to burn and destroy all these happy homes. Whether there follow upon it defeat or victory, war is a great calamity.*

Here is a picture of a candle. In artistic circles the drawing of an object may cost far more than the object itself. The shah of Persia once asked the price of the painting of a donkey, and when he heard the amazing demand, he calculated how many real asses could have been purchased with the money. No doubt a well-painted picture of a candle would cost as much as would light us for many a month, yet it would never yield to our necessity a single beam of light. So the resemblance of true godliness costs a man far more care and trouble than the genuine article would involve, and yet it is nothing after all. One cannot light himself to bed by the picture of a candle, neither can he find comfort in the hour of death by the imitation of religion. There must be reality, and that reality involves flame and light; in our case a flame and light that none but God can give. If there be nothing of heavenly fire and spiritual truth about our piety, our profession is vain. The great distinction between living grace and its imitation can be seen by all spiritual minds. We are overdone with portraits, but men are by no means plentiful. We have as many paintings of candles as the church walls will hold, but we have few real lamps, or else this world would not remain so dark as it now is. Those candles that are not consumed by their own flame are giving no light, and those persons who are themselves unaffected in heart and life by their religion may fear that they are mocking themselves with the mere appearance of sacred things. You may sit a long time in front of a painted fire before you will be warmed, and you may long maintain formal religion yet never derive comfort from it. To look for a lost ring in a dark cellar by the help of the picture of a candle is not more unreasonable than to look for rest of heart in a godliness that is a mere pretense.

Our third emblem is not a candle, but a case for candles, a casket for those jewels of light. Look well at this curiosity, you dwellers in cities, for I do not suppose that any of you have such a piece of furniture in your houses.

It is a candle box, well fashioned and neatly japanned. Here at the back are two plates with holes in them by which to hang up the box against the wall. It closes very neatly, opens very readily, and keeps its contents out of harm's way. I can assure you that I have within it a number of the very best candles, from the most notable makers. Wax, stearine, palmatine, and so forth: There could not be a handsomer assortment than I now exhibit to you. Let no one despise this display. Here we have capacity, elegance, preparation, and plenty of each. But suppose that we were in this room without the gas and I were simply to exhibit the candle box and its contents and say, "Here is brilliance! You need no electric lighting; this box abundantly suffices for the enlightenment of this large assembly!"

> We could readily find communities of Christian people who are shut up to themselves and are without the living fire of the Spirit of God. What is the good of them?

You would reply, "But we see none the better for your boasted illumination. The candles are shut up in their box and yield no single beam of light." Herein detect a resemblance to many a church. We could readily find communities of Christian people who are shut up to themselves and are without the living fire of the Spirit of God. What is the good of them?

This is a very respectable candle box, is it not? It could hardly be more respectable. Even so, yonder is a highly respectable congregation! Very refined and select! The minister is a man of high culture and advanced thought. He can confound a text of scripture with any living man. He attracted at least five horses to his place of preaching last Sunday. They say it takes a great deal of ability to draw a horse to church! As for his hearers, they are all the cream of the cream. Don't you know that the doctor, the brewer, the lawyer, and the auctioneer all attend that most honored sanctuary? With an M.D., a D.D., and an F.R.S., two wealthy dowagers, a colonel, a county councilman, and a professor, it is worthwhile for a fellow to go to that chapel—I beg pardon—church, for the sake of the social distinction it will bestow upon him. The people are so very respectable that they do not know one another and never think of shaking hands. They are all so very select that they float about in distinguished isolation, like so many icebergs in the Atlantic. The families walk up the aisles with the most becoming dignity, and they walk down the aisles with the most proper decorum. They can do without warmth, brotherly love, sympathy, and cooperation, for their eminent "respectability" suffices for every need. Of course, they can do nothing more, for it costs them all their time, talent, thought, and spare cash to maintain their superior respectability. Like the gentleman with his well-brushed hat, no wonder that they look so superior, for they give their whole minds to it.

One asked a member of a certain respectable church whether he taught in a ragged school, and really he could hardly answer the fellow. The superior person champed the words *ragged school* as a donkey might a roll of oakum. Another, a portly deacon, was asked whether he would join in holding an open-air service, but he looked the intruder through and through as if he would like to open him. None of the ladies and gentlemen help the temperance work, for they are too respectable to go in with vulgar water drinkers; neither do they visit the lodging houses, for that would be too disreputable for their royal highnesses. All these make up an eminently respectable community, but why they are respected, this deponent says not.

> Fire is one of those things for which there is no accounting as to what may come of it. Its spread is not to be measured even by leagues when it once gets firm hold and the wind drives it on.

Here, take away this candle box! I want no more of it or its contents, for it gives no jot of light! That is what will happen to very respectable churches that do no work for God or man; they will be put away, and even their candlestick will be taken out of its place. If they do not mend their ways, not a few of our dissenting churches will die out and leave nothing behind them but a name to laugh at. A church that does nothing for those around it mocks the need of men, leaves the world in darkness, and grieves the Lord who designed His people to be the lights of the world.

As in a community, so with a single person, grace is essential to usefulness. All the candles in that box remain useless till the wick is lighted with a touch of fire; and this lone candle is equally so. See, I bring another candle in contact with it. They are tête-à-tête, or wick-à-wick, but the first has no influence upon the second. A thousand such interviews will produce no result. If there were a living flame here, you could soon set not only this one candle shining, but as many as you chose to bring; but without it nothing can be done. No man can communicate what he doesn't have; you cannot hope to save your fellow man till you know the salvation of God for yourself. To be a preacher or teacher before one has received the divine life is as foolish as for a candle to set up for a lighter of others before it has been lighted itself. How different the result when the living flame is there! See how the one sets the other ablaze at once!

I see before me quite an array of candles. Variety is charming, and number is cheering. The more the merrier, and especially of such reputable and notable light givers as these.

We may consider that we are having quite an illumination. With so many luminaries we need hardly regret the set of sun. But is it so? I, for one, am none the better for these promising lights; are you? I put on my spectacles. But there is no improvement. I can see nothing, yet there are candles enough and to spare! There is no mystery about it—the candles are not lighted, and until they are lighted they cannot remove our darkness. Grace is needed to make gifts available for the service of God.

Let us look more closely into our collection of lights. Here is one that I should suppose to be an archbishop at the least. This specimen is a doctor of divinity. These are gentry, and these are merchants, and those are cultured individuals; but without the light from on high, they are all equally unserviceable. A poor converted lad in a workshop will be of more spiritual use than a parliament of unregenerate men. I introduce to you a lighted rushlight, and there is more to be seen by this ignoble luminary than by all the rest. Little ability, set on fire by the life of God, may produce greater results than ten talents without the divine power. "A living dog is better than a dead lion"; a zealous but illiterate Christian may be worth twenty lifeless philosophers.

Herein is great encouragement, dear friends, that if you once get a light, it will spread from one to another without end. This one, lighted candle would suffice to set a hundred candles shining. It may light a much finer candle than itself. Fire is one of those things for which there is no accounting as to what may come of it. Its spread is not to be measured even by leagues when it once gets firm hold and the wind drives it on. Piety in a cottage may enlighten a nation. If the church of God were reduced to one person, it might, within an incredibly short time, become a great multitude.

There is a true apostolical succession in the kingdom of grace. Office has the pretense of it, but grace gives the reality. At Mr. Jay's Jubilee, Timothy East of Birmingham told how, by the youthful ministry of William Jay, a thoughtless youth was converted and became a minister. Under the preaching of that man, Timothy East himself was led to repentance, and then by a sermon from Timothy East, John Williams, who became the martyr of Erromanga and the apostle of the South Sea Islands, was savingly impressed. See how the light goes from Jay to another, from that other to East, from East to Williams, and from Williams to the savages of the southern seas!

A family tree of an equally interesting character has been traced with regard to books as surely as with living witnesses for God. A poor man lent a Puritan tract, old and torn, to Baxter's father. It was called *Bunny's Resolutions.* Through reading this little book, Richard Baxter, afterward the great preacher of Kidderminster, received a real change of heart. Baxter wrote *The Saint's Everlasting Rest,* which was blessed to the conversion of Doddridge. He wrote *The Rise and Progress,* which was the means of the conversion of Legh Richmond. And he wrote his *Dairyman's Daughter,* which has been translated into more than fifty languages and has led to the conversion of thousands of souls. How many of these converted ones have in their turn written books and tracts that have charmed others to Jesus, eternity alone will reveal. We can never see the issues of our acts. We may strike a match, and from that little flame a street may be lighted. Give a light to your next-door neighbor, and you may be taking the nearest way to instruct the twentieth century or to send the gospel to Chinese Tartary or to overthrow the popular science fetish of the hour. A spark from your kitchen candle may, in its natural progression from one to another, light the last generation of men so the word of the hour may be the light of the age by which men may come in multitudes to see their Savior and Lord. Let your light shine, and what will come of it thou shalt see hereafter.

Coming one Thursday in the late autumn from an engagement beyond Dulwich, my way lay up to the top of the Herne Hill Ridge. I came along the level out of which rises the steep hill I had to ascend. While I was on the lower ground, riding in a hansom cab, I saw a light before me, and when I came near the hill, I marked that light gradually go up the hill, leaving a train of stars behind it. This line of newborn stars remained in the form of one lamp, then another, and another. It reached from the foot of the hill to its summit. I did not see the lamplighter. I do not know his name, his age, or his residence, but I saw the lights that he had kindled, and these remained when he himself had gone his way. As I rode along, I thought to myself, "How earnestly do I wish that my life may be spent in lighting one soul after another with the sacred flame of eternal life! I would myself be as much as possible unseen while at my work and would vanish into the eternal brilliance above when my work is done." Will you, my brother, begin to light up some soul tonight? Speak of Jesus to some person who knows Him not. Who can tell but you may save a soul from death? Then carry the flame to another, and to another. Mark the years of your life by your continual diligence in spreading "the light of the knowledge of the glory of God in the face of Jesus Christ" (2 Cor. 4:6 KJV).

> *In the service of God, we find the greatest expansion of our being. It makes the dead man speak, and it also makes a single living man spread himself over a province.*

The taper that I hold in my hand is in itself a poor thing as an illuminator, but it has created quite a splendor in the room by the light which it has communicated to others. Andrew was not a very great personage, but he called his brother Peter and led him to Jesus, and Peter was a host in himself. Never mind how small a taper you may be; burn on, shine at your best, and God bless you. You may lead on to grand results despite your feebleness. He that called Dr. John Owen is forgotten; I might almost say was never known. He was a small taper—but what a candle he lighted! Those holy women who talked together as they sat in the sun at Bedford were a blessing to John Bunyan, but we know not the name of even one of them. Everywhere the hidden ones are used of the Lord as the means of lighting up those who shine as stars in the churches.

In the service of God, we find the greatest expansion of our being. It makes the dead man speak, and it also makes a single living man spread himself over a province. Our forefathers were fond of riddles. I cannot say that they were very witty ones, but there was solidity in them. Here is one: What is that of which twenty could be put into a tankard and yet one would fill a barn? Twenty candles unlighted would scarce fill a jug, but one when it is lighted will beneficially fill a barn with light or viciously fill it with fire and smoke. A man, what is he? A man of God, what is he not? Our influence may enlighten the world and shine far down the ages if the Holy Spirit's fire shall kindle us.

Here is a candle that has never given any light yet and never will as it now is. Hear its reason for not giving light! It is so unfortunate that it cannot find a proper candlestick in which to stand upright and fulfill the purpose for which it was made. Let us try to accommodate it. Here is a fine church candlestick, and we set our candle in the socket. Does it shine? No. Shall we try a lower place? It does not shine any better. We will put this candle in the most enviable position, in this real silver candlestick of the most elaborate workmanship. It does not shine one whit the more. Neither high nor low places will make a man what he is not.

I know persons who cannot get on anywhere; but according to their own belief, the fault is not in themselves but in their surroundings. I could sketch you a brother who is unable to do any good because all the churches are so faulty. He was once with us, but he came to know us too well and grew disgusted with our dogmatism and want of taste. He went to the Independents who have so much more culture, breadth, and liberality. He grew weary of what he called "cold dignity." He wanted more fire and therefore favored the Methodists with his patronage. Alas! He did not find them the flaming zealots he had supposed them to be and very soon outgrew both them and their doctrines, and joined our most excellent friends the Presbyterians. These proved to be by far too high and dry for him, and he became rather sweet upon the Swedenborgians, and would have joined them had not his wife led him among the Episcopalians. Here he might have enjoyed the *otium cum dignitate*, have taken it easy with admirable propriety, and have even grown into a churchwarden. But he was not content, and before long I heard that he was an Exclusive Brother! There I leave him, hoping that he may be better in his new line than he has ever been in the old ones. "The course of nature could no further go." If he has not fallen among a loving, united people now, where will he find them? Yet I expect that as Adam left paradise, so will he ultimately fall from his high estate. He reminds me of a very good man who changed his religious views so often, that I once asked him, "What are you now?" He told me, and I went on my way; but when I met him next, and made the same inquiry, he was something else. At our next meeting my reverend brother was grieved because I said to him the third time, "What are you now?" He reproved me for it; but when I somewhat impenitently repeated the query and pressed it home, I found that he really had entered another denomination since I had last seen him. What a pity that the churches should be so bad, that when a man has gone the complete round he finds none that quite comes up to his mark! If some of these brethren go on their way to heaven alone, they will increase the heaven below of those who are not forced to put up with them.

> *If some of these brethren go on their way to heaven alone, they will increase the heaven below of those who are not forced to put up with them.*

The same illustration suggests to me to ask you whether you know the young man who cannot serve God as an apprentice but is going to do wonders when he is out of his time. Yes, he only wants to be put into another candlestick. So he thinks. But we know better. When he is out of his time and has become a journeyman, he will postpone his grand plans of usefulness till he has started as a master on his own account. Alas! When he is a master, he will wait till he has made money and can retire from business. So, you see, the candle does not shine, but it imputes its failure to the candlesticks! The candlesticks are not to be blamed.

Poor Dick Miss-the-Mark believes that he ought to have been Oliver Cromwell, but as that character is hardly in season in this year of grace, Richard is unable to be Cromwell, and therefore he is not himself at all. That wart over the eye and other Cromwellian distinctions are a dead loss in his case. He cannot develop his genius for want of a King Charles and a Prince Rupert. The proper candlestick is not forthcoming, and so this fine candle cannot shine.

This is a very simple affair. It is a Field's Self-fitting Candle; but it is very handy. You see, owing to the shape of its lower end, the candle will fit into any candlestick, whether it be large or small. A man of this sort makes himself useful anywhere. In poverty he is content; in wealth he is humble. Put him in a village, and he instructs the ignorant; place him in a city, he seeks the fallen. If he can preach, he will do so; and if that is beyond his capacity, he will teach in the Sabbath school. Like the holy missionary Brainerd, if he cannot convert a tribe, he will, even on his dying bed, be willing to teach a poor child his letters. It is a great thing not only to be able to fit in to all kinds of work, but to cope with all sorts of people. The power of adaptation to high and low, learned and ignorant, sad and frivolous, is no mean gift. If, like Nelson, we can lay our vessel side by side with the enemy and come to close quarters without delay, we shall do considerable execution. Commend me to the man who can avail himself of any conversation and any topic, to drive home saving truth upon the conscience and heart. He who can ride a well-trained horse, properly saddled, does well; but the fellow who can leap upon the wild horse of the prairie and ride him barebacked is a genius indeed. "All things to all men," rightly interpreted, is a motto worthy of the great apostle of the Gentiles (1 Cor. 9:22) and of all who, like him, would win souls for Jesus.

> It is a great thing not only to be able to fit in to all kinds of work, but to cope with all sorts of people. The power of adaptation to high and low, learned and ignorant, sad and frivolous, is no mean gift.

It is a pity when a man is too big for his position—as some candles are too big to fit in certain candlesticks. Don't I know some Jacks-in-office who are worlds too great to be of the slightest use to anybody? Don't ask them a question unless you desire to be eaten up alive. On the other hand, it is not pretty to see a candle with paper round it to keep it in its place; nor is it nice to see a little man padded out to make him fill up an important office. Some men in prominent positions are like the small boy on the high horse; they need a deal of holding on. Be fit for your office or find one for which you are fit. It is not a very great invention to make a candle self-fitting, but the result is very pleasant. Though the expression "the right man in the right place" is said to be a tautology, I like it, and I like best of all to see it in actual life. Try to fit yourself to whatever comes in your way.

Hearty service, rendered from pure motives, is acceptable to God, even when persons of education and taste have just cause to find fault with its imperfections. If we cannot bear witness for the gospel in grammatical language, we may be thankful that we can do it at all, and we may be encouraged by the unquestionable fact that God blesses the most unpolished utterances. When you go to do a bit of carpentering in the shed and need a light, you are sometimes on the lookout for the means of setting up your bit of candle in a handy way. Here is the great invention in which your research usually ends. You see I have stuck a candle into a ginger beer bottle, and the light that comes from it is quite as clear as if I had a fine plated candlestick. Here is a popular implement, and it is both handy and cheap. Who would find any fault with it if he were in the dark and wanted to find something in a hurry? If you have no fitter candlestick, a ginger beer bottle does mightily well. How often our Lord has used men of scanty education or of none at all! How useful He has made the things that are despised! Yet, at the same time, if it were left to me to make my choice as to how I would have my candle set up, I should not object to have it in a more presentable stand. I would not quarrel even if the candle given to me to go to bed with were in a silver candlestick. For use I would sooner have a ginger beer bottle with a bright candle in it than a plated candlestick with a dead candle in it that I could not light. Who would object to be rid of the guttering and the hot dropping tallow, and to handle a concern that would not dirty his hands? A thing of beauty and of brightness is a joy forever. Grace shines nonetheless because the person and his speech are graceful. The world, with its board schools, is getting more and more educated, and the rage for ginger beer bottle lights is not so great as it was. We have now passed beyond the age in which vulgarity and power were supposed to be nearly related. As there is no sin that I know of in grammatical language and good taste, I hope we shall never set a fictitious value upon coarseness or go out of our way to marry godliness with slang. Our Lord and His cause should be served with our best. Even our best is not of itself worthy of His glory, but at least let us not give to Him the offal and the refuse of human speech. Young man, blaze away; but you need not be coarse. Bring us a light, but use a decent candlestick if you can.

Some excellent persons have very little talent indeed. It is not merely that there is a want of education, but there is a want of capacity. Now, when that happens to be the case, my next illustration may be a serviceable hint.

On this board we have fixed a number of very small candles, and as they are all well alight, the result is by no means unsatisfactory. As a company of illuminators, they make a pleasant and notable shining, and I note that the children present are greatly pleased with their brightness. Let us observe how a number of good little people, well lighted by grace, can by combination really give out a great deal more illumination than far greater persons who shine alone. If one of you cannot do much in a place by yourself, look up other friends, start a Sunday school, and all of you work together. You may do great things by earnest unity. Form a little army for preaching in the street. Band together to visit from house to house. Scatter tracts over the whole area by concerted action. Unity is light. Even children, youths, and maidens may make a great blaze by working together in the holy cause. But you must each one of you shine your quota, and no one must try to save his candle and take things easy. All at it and always at it, and you will not labor in vain. Yonder great ecclesiastical candle has never given a tenth of the light of these little instruments; or would he, I fear, if I were now to set him burning. The unanimous services of the lesser members of our churches might suffice to light up our country and the world itself by the blessing of God.

> *Hearty service, rendered from pure motives, is acceptable to God, even when persons of education and taste have just cause to find fault with its imperfections.*

Still, if we had an equal number of larger candles, we should have a brighter blaze. How often have I wished that men of great parts, position, and wealth were brought into the service of our Lord! Perhaps we do not pray sufficiently for them; or possibly, if we had them, we might place too much reliance upon them. Yet the soul of a gentleman of influence is as precious as that of a poor man; and we should know no difference of grades in our prayers. If any among my audience are endowed with ten talents, they have ten good reasons for yielding themselves to the service of God. How can they do better with themselves than by serving the purpose of their creation and redemption! May almighty grace bring in some who will be great lights in this dark age! We need men fitted to be leaders; may the Lord send them soon!

This candle hanging on the wall, all moldy and perishing, may serve as a striking likeness of those who have done nothing for their God or for their fellow men. It is better to be consumed in shining than to perish ignominiously in doing nothing. I need scarcely quote the old proverb, "It is better to wear out than to rust out." Idleness is a destroyer. For every evil brought upon us by excessive labor, ten will come to us by laziness. Our accidents happen in our holidays. When the pot is not boiling, the flies will come to it. Mice will not nibble a lighted candle, but when the fire is gone, they find tallow a rather toothsome article. Who cares to be eaten by mice? Who wishes to die of the miserables? Who would like to be eaten up with whims or nibbled away by crotchets? Since we have no such desire, let us accept that sacred fire that will cause us to yield up our whole being to the hallowed purpose of light-giving. For this reason we are kept in this dark world. We must be burning and shining lights, or we miss our vocation. Truly, he who saves his life loses it, and only he who spends his life for God shall find it unto life eternal.

Have you ever heard of a person who, in real earnest, did the very foolish thing that I am attempting in pretense! I have a candle here, and I want to light it. What shall I do?

Before me I see a candle burning very brightly, and I will take a light from it for this other candle. I have not succeeded. How is it that I have altogether failed? I am of a very persevering turn of mind; I will give it a fair trial. I cannot succeed in lighting my candle, and you are all laughing at me, and you whisper that I must be over-much stupid to try to light a candle while an extinguisher is upon it. I subside. Do you not think that very many persons go with an extinguisher on to hear a minister preach? Listen to yonder young lady: "Well, I will go to hear him, Mary Anne, because you press me, but I am sure I shall not like him." Is she not very like a candle covered with an extinguisher? Why our nameless friend does not like the preacher she has not told us, but probably her prejudice will be the more intense in proportion as she is unable to give a reason for it. Prejudice is a blind and deaf judge who decides a case before he has seen or heard the evidence. "Hang them first and try them afterward" is one of his sage observations. Remember the old lines about unreasonable dislikes:

I do not like you, Dr. Fell,
The reason why I cannot tell;
But this I know, and know full well,
I do not like you, Dr. Fell.

Just so. That is a very effective extinguisher.

Our young lady friend showed the prejudice of ignorance, but there is such a thing as the prejudice of learning, and this is a very effectual extinguisher. Dr. Taylor of Norwich once said that he had read the Bible through—I think it was ten times—and he could not anywhere find the deity of Christ in it. Honest John Newton observed, "Yes, and if I were to try ten times to light a candle with an extinguisher on it, I should not succeed." Once make up your mind to refuse a doctrine or a command, and you will not see it where God Himself has written it as with a sunbeam. Kick against a truth, and the arguments for it will seem to have no existence. Let prejudice of any sort wholly cover the candle of your mind, and whatever you do, there is no likelihood of your receiving the light. There are none so deaf as those who will not hear. The country people say that "some are like the hogs in harvest that can hear and won't." Of course, hogs are deaf when they are called out of a field where there is plenty to eat; and of course, sinners are deaf when we bid them quit the pleasures of sin. This prejudice makes men totally blind. How can we perceive anything lovable where we have resolved to hate? How can we see even the sun itself when a dark body comes between him and us? How can men believe in the Lord Jesus when they are such great believers in themselves?

> The soul of a gentleman of influence is as precious as that of a poor man; and we should know no difference of grades in our prayers.

The only case in which I am willing to bear with prejudice is when a dislike of me leads people to watch the more carefully what I have to say. If they will during a sermon be wide awake that they may find fault, I will forgive their object out of respect to their action. Of all devils the worst is the devil of slumber. He haunts places of worship, and it is not easy to chase him away, especially in warm weather. I greatly fear lest my people should become so used to me that, like the miller, they can go to sleep all the easier for the grinding of the wheels—I mean, all the quicker for the sound of my voice. I have read of an old Scotchwoman who always went to sleep when her own minister was discoursing; but whenever there was a probationer from the college, she was noticed to watch him as a cat would a rat. Her minister said to her, "Janet, you paid me a very poor compliment. You listened with opened ears and eyes to the young man last Sunday, but you went to sleep when I preached this morning." The canny old lady replied, "Dear sir, you do not understand the matter. You are so sound and solid that I feel all is safe when you have got it in hand, and so I may take my rest. As to those young fellows, I do not know where they may go, and so I am bound to keep awake and watch them." Be so kind as to be similarly suspicious of me, and watch me in the same way. You may find out my weak points, and it is not improbable that I may do the like for you. At any rate, I hope that more good may come of it than if you diverge into a snore, as some are reported to have done. This is the only case that I remember in which prejudice is likely to be of use to anyone.

Butchers, it seems, are accustomed to do their work with a candle fastened upon their foreheads in this fashion. As I am not one of those gentlemen "who kills his own," you will excuse me if I have not managed the affair in an orthodox manner. There is an old story of one who had lost his candle and traveled all round his premises searching for it by its own light. It is told as a jest, and it must have been a mirthful incident where it happened. I remember an old gentleman who could see very little without spectacles but went up and down the house searching for his glasses, looking through them all the time. The parable is this: A person full of doubts and fears about his personal condition before God is searching for grace within by the light of that very grace for which he is looking. He is fearfully anxious because he can see no trace of gracious anxiety in his mind. He feels sad because he cannot feel sad. He repents because he cannot repent. He has the candle on his forehead and is seeing by the light of it, yet he is searching for that very light, without which he could not search at all. Many a time a man laments that he does not feel, and all the while he is overwhelmed with pain through the impression that he does not feel pain as he should.

This bull's-eye lantern may be used as an illustration of how persons may have the best of light and fail to use it. See, I have shut it up, and no ray of light comes from it. I am told that, when the Bible Society first started, its agents were very diligent in calling round to see whether householders had Bibles or not. One of them called upon an aged person and said, "Please, madam, have you a Bible?" The excellent lady was astonished, not to say indignant, that persons should dare to come around insulting respectable Christian people and asking them whether they had a Bible. Of course she had a Bible. She would let the visitor see it with his own eyes, and then he would not think her a heathen any longer. "Mary, go upstairs and fetch the Bible from off the drawers, and let the gentleman see the large family Bible which my father left me." The volume was brought down and laid upon the table, and when it was put on its back, it opened itself naturally at a certain place. "Ah!" said the venerable lady, "Well, after all, I think there is a providence in your coming, for here are my spectacles, which I lost years ago, and I could not imagine where they were." If she had not possessed a Bible, she would have thought herself a heathen, but having a Bible and never reading it, she thought herself an exemplary Christian. Bibles that are never read are like lanterns that are never turned on. How shall we answer for our neglect at the last great day?

There is plenty of light in this lantern, but nobody sees anything of it; and here we have the portrait of many religious people who keep their knowledge to themselves. Oh no, they never mention it; its name is never heard; they are tongue-tied professors. They pride themselves upon having plenty of gospel light, but they never let out a ray; they never say a word for Jesus to the souls around them. Perhaps they think that their example is too valuable to need a word to be added to it, like the bell that was made of metal too precious to have a tongue put in it and so could never be made to ring. Some folks are quite sullen in keeping themselves to themselves. If we try to turn on their bull's-eye, as I sometimes do, they are just a little hot, as this lantern has become. We have to mind how we handle them, or we shall burn our fingers. One who was gently spoken to and urged to help a needy cause, replied crustily, "What I give is nothing to nobody." That was unconscious truth, no doubt, but said in a nasty way that made the receiver feel as if he had tumbled backward upon a circular saw. It is my business to attempt with members of the church to turn on the light that is now shut up, and I hope you will therefore bear with my personality and not give me a warmer reception than you can help. I refer to the kind of warmth that comes through a hot temper. Suffer me to exhort you. Is it not the Lord's will that you should shine? Is it not for your own comfort? May there not be souls waiting in the dark till you bring them the knowledge of the Savior? Will you not remember Heber's missionary hymn and practice its lesson?

> *Can we whose souls are lighted*
> *With wisdom from on high,*
> *Can we to men benighted,*
> *The lamp of life deny?*

Some seem to have a great capacity for denying light to their fellows. I have known persons to almost glory in their reticence with their own children. "I never spoke to him about religion" was the complacent confession of an old professor as to his son. Some of these hide away in the dark themselves, lest they should be called upon to work. A prospectus of a burial club began, "Whereas many persons find it difficult to bury themselves. . ." Alas! To my knowledge many persons bury themselves most easily, and one of my constant labors is to fetch them out of the sepulchre of their indolence. I wish they would respond to my call and not lie in their coffins and grumble at my disturbing them. Again, dark lantern, I must turn you on!

> *I am pleased to see Christian people like lanterns fully turned on. Should not our town and our age get all the light from us that we can possibly give?*

When we get the lantern pouring forth its brightness, or begin in earnest to study the Word of God, how cheering is the light! No man shall walk in darkness who uses the clear shining of revelation. By this he shall see treasures, detect enemies, and discern his way. I am pleased to see Christian people like lanterns fully turned on. Should not our town and our age get all the light from us that we can possibly give? A friend who sits in one of the best seats, is the owner of more than half a million of money, and puts a shilling into a collection wants turning on to the full. A lady yonder, who has a first-rate education and remarkable fluency of speech yet has no work in the Sunday school or in the Bible classes wants her light turned on also. And so does my friend, Mr. Candoit, who as yet has more capacity for work than experience in it. When I think of what he might be doing, I am inclined to turn on to him to turn him on. However, I remember how hot I found the bull's-eye lantern just now, and I will let him alone. I do not wish to drive anyone into a service so honorable. In all gracious work give me spontaneous combustion. Those who do not wish to give light will never do so. So good-bye, dark lanterns! Before I quite part with you, I bequeath you this motto, "Arise shine!"

Here is a common lantern. The wind may blow, but the candle is safe within. The groom can cross the stableyard in a shower of rain or in a fall of snow when his light is thus safeguarded. On board ship also, the lantern is of the utmost use, for even a gale of wind will not blow out the candle that is secure in a good lantern.

Surely God will preserve His own gospel, though popes and monks, men of "modern thought," and theoretical scientists blow at its candle with all the fury of fiends. Burn on O sacred light, that you may guide men to the haven of rest! Bright Pharos of the sea of time, thou cross of Christ, cast your splendor over stormy waves, and warn passing mariners to shun the ironbound coasts of error!

The providence of God is the great protector of our life and usefulness, and under the divine care we are perfectly safe from every danger.

> *Plagues and deaths around me fly;*
> *Till He please I cannot die:*
> *Not a single shaft can hit*
> *Till the God of love thinks fit.*

Yet we are apt to complain of the very providence that blesses us. Years ago a farmer returned from market with a golden burden, for he had sold his corn. He thought it hard that it should rain and spoil his best coat; but when he came to the lone place between the woods and perceived that a highwayman would have shot him if the rain had not damped his powder, he had a much more vivid idea of the wisdom of God.

Remember Bernard Gilpin, the apostle of the north. He was seized and taken to London to be tried as a heretic. On the road he fell from his horse and broke his leg. His persecutors knew that his wont was to say, "It is all for the best," so they taunted him with the enquiry, "Is this all for the best?" He meekly replied that he had no doubt it would turn out to be so. Gilpin was right. A delay was caused on the road, and he and his guard arrived in London just as Queen Mary died. They heard the bells ringing when they came to Highgate Hill and learned that Queen Elizabeth was on the throne. He was too late to be burned because he had broken his leg. He had escaped the flames. In some way or other the Lord will preserve His people from all evil even as the lantern preserves the light that is placed within it.

There is a still happier preservation. "Preserved in Christ Jesus" (Jude 1). What a precious word! A feeble life is secure when hidden away in Christ. He it is that guards us safe from every ill design. Not the world, the flesh, or the devil can blow out the flame that He has kindled, for He surrounds it with His own almighty grace. Even to eternity our light shall shine if we by faith are put into Christ.

But there are imitations of this security; there are confidences that are vain. A man may be so far a Christian as to be safe against the coarser vices, yet the tempter may find out a place where he lies open to attack. My assistant will play the part of the tempter and blow at this candle.

He has done no harm as yet, for the guardian lantern has covered the quarter upon which he has blown; but if he will try again, the result may be different. He may then hit upon the weak point. A man's religion may save him from certain sins, but not from others. He may not perish by drink, but he may be ruined by "covetousness, which is idolatry" (Col. 3:5 KJV). He may escape the pestilence of profanity and be carried off by the fever of pride. In vain are we guarded in head and feet if a poisoned arrow enters the breast. A candle in one of the old emblems is made to say, "I lie open only here," but it is just there that the wind enters and blows it out.

Where there is a weakness, the archenemy will find it out and bring his force to bear; and as he is the prince of the power of the air, he can blow with a vengeance, and the man's candle is put out because he had not found that perfect security whom none but the Lord Jesus Christ can give. Beware of trusting to good resolutions or outward religiousness: These are cracked lanterns. No man is safe out of Christ: He alone is the perfect protection of His people. You are complete in Him but in no one else.

I do not know whether I can manage so to blow out this candle as to light it again by the help of its own smoke and this taper. Yes, I have managed it, and it is a pretty experiment. See, the flame travels down the smoke and lights the wick again. When a man has been a real Christian, if his light seems blown out, he readily takes fire again if he has not been long in an ill condition. He who stays from the house of God can be easily brought back if looked after at once. He who has known how to pray is soon set praying again after an unhappy neglect if he be taken soon. Never leave backsliders long, but with holy carefulness bring the holy fire to bear upon them as speedily as you can. The force of his former habit will aid you in restoring to the wanderer the religious feeling that had almost left him. The Lord Jesus is very tender in such cases, for a smoking flax He will not quench. Let none of us be guilty of delays lest the destruction of precious souls be laid at our door.

The same symbol will apply, on the other hand, to all forms of evil fire. It is no wonder that seeming converts so often and so speedily go back to old habits. You think their sin extinguished, but it is only the flame that is gone. The smoke of desire remains and will soon catch fire again and burn as strongly as before if the flame of temptation is near. Oh, for grace to get that fire of hell snuffed out altogether! Let beginners in grace, in whom the flame of sin has been freshly blown out, beware of their old companions and haunts and habits lest, going near the fire, their natural smoke of inclination should invite the flame of open transgression again to kindle upon them.

Here is a candle that is in a lantern of a tolerably respectable sort; at least it was respectable long ago, and you might not now have noticed its forlorn condition if it had not been for the candle within. As soon as you place a light within, the imperfections of the lantern are shown up, and it is the same with human characters. Many a man would have seemed a decent sort of fellow if he had not professed to be a Christian. But his open confession of religion fixed many eyes upon him, and his imperfections were at once observed of all observers. He who unites with a church and takes upon himself the name of Christ claims a higher character than others, and if he is not true to his profession, his inconsistency is marked and very justly so. How often do we see that an unconverted man may steal a horse, but a Christian must not look over the hedge at it! That which is winked at in a man of the world is a grave fault in a Christian. It is no more than natural and just that great professors should be expected to be better than others. It is inevitable that the very light they have should reveal their faults and flaws.

Brethren, let us not exhibit our candle in a dirty lantern or our religion in a doubtful character. I have heard of a minister who was a capital preacher, but he bought a wig of one of his hearers and forgot to pay for it. A bad habit that! Not to pay at all is worst of all, but even to be long-winded is objectionable. When the barber came home from the meeting, he said, "That was a beautiful discourse, but his wig spoiled it. I like his deep expositions. But oh, that wig! Will he ever pay for that wig?" A friend who heard me tell this story remarked, "The wig stuck in the man's throat."

Let us pay for our wigs if we wear such inventions, and let us see to it that there is nothing else about our person or character that may bring the gospel into discredit. We have heard of a wonderful preacher, of whom they said that he preached so well and lived so badly, that when he was in the pulpit, they thought he ought never to come out of it. But when he was out of the pulpit, they changed their minds and sorrowfully concluded that he ought never to go into it again. Every man should be clean—it is a natural, sanitary duty; but there is a special precept that says, "Be ye clean, that bear the vessels of the LORD" (Isa. 52:11 KJV). And this relates to moral and spiritual character. An unholy minister is unclean with a vengeance. Prominent persons are looked at through microscopes. The more light you have, the more will your faults be shown up and observed.

In the case of this other lantern, little or no light would come from it if it were not for its cracks and rents. The light passes through the broken places. Do you not think that the sicknesses and infirmities of many godly people have been the making of them, and that the light divine has gleamed through the rifts in their tenements of clay? Do not light-givers sometimes shine the better for sickness? Some ministers preach the better for being afflicted. Do not wish your minister to be ill or to be tried, but I cannot doubt the fact that the trials of ministers are the best part of their education. One who was rather a critic in sermons used to ask, "Has the doctor been ill within the last six months? For he is not worth hearing else."

An old Scotchwoman found that when her minister lost his sight, he could not read his dry old manuscripts and was therefore forced to preach extemporaneously. Perhaps she was a little cruel when she said, "Praise be to God. It would have been well if he had lost his sight twenty years ago." To her mind the sermons were so much better when they came forth from his heart than when he read them from the sapless manuscript that to her the good man's loss of sight was a gain. If, in any way, you are able to tell out a sweeter experience and so afford greater comfort to others through your body being like a broken lantern, be thankful for it. Happy are we if our losses are the gains of others. So long as our soul shines out with holier radiance, we will glory in infirmities.

As adjuncts to a candle, we used to have tinderbox, flint, steel, and certain brimstone matches. I am almost afraid to employ these implements as illustrations, for they are almost as much out of date as the flint arrowheads of the prehistoric period. Few of you have ever struck a light with a flint in your lives, though I hope you will all strike a light in some better sense.

Shall I instruct you in the practical science of getting a light with flint and steel? The first thing is to make your tinder by burning, or rather scorching, a piece of rag. Toast it or char it till it is tenderly made into tinder. Neither do it too little or too much; cook your rags to a turn. Be very mindful to keep your tinder dry as a bone, for a spark will be of no service if it does not fall where it will be nourished, and the least damp will kill it. The sparks of temptation would be harmless if it were not for the tinder of corruption in our hearts. Good teaching is also lost unless it falls upon a mind prepared to receive it, so that the metaphor can be used either way.

Having secured your tinder, you had next to know how to strike your flint and steel so as to create sparks. Many a knock of the fingers would you get if you did not look alive. Possibly you would also bark your knuckles if you did know the art, if the weather was cold and your hands were half frozen. So is it in your dealing with men's consciences. You may give a hard knock and fetch fire out of them, or you may break your own knuckles by bringing upon yourself personal ill will.

If you were so skillful or so fortunate as to cause a spark to drop into the tinder, you had to blow upon it very gently, just as the first sign of grace in any heart needs encouraging with the fostering breath of sympathy. How often have I seen a servant go down on her knees to blow at a coal that seemed to have a little life in it! Let us do the like with those persons concerning whom we are somewhat hopeful.

When the spark had become fairly prosperous in the tinder, then you applied the point of your brimstone match. You do not quite know what I mean. Well, mind you do not make a brimstone match when you get married. The brimstone, at the sharpened point of the match, would take fire when it touched the spark, and then your labor approached its reward. When you had your match flaming and smelling, you lit your candle, and having done with your elaborate apparatus, you popped the flat lid of the box upon the tinder to put it all out. This last operation of damping down resembles the behavior of critics toward young preachers and writers if they see a spark or two of fire in them. I know this illustration by heart, for I had the lid popped upon myself when I was a young spark. The work was not done very effectually, but this was not due to any want of ill intent on the part of my critics. I owe them much for which I feel no gratitude, because they meant me no good.

I found it very difficult to procure this ancient relic in London. Indeed, I had to give up all idea of purchase, and this specimen was specially made to order. Be glad that now you have lucifers and vestas to flame forth in an instant, for on a cold winter's morning it was tedious work to use this complicated instrumentality when it was in perfect condition, and many things might happen to make that condition imperfect and render your labor fruitless. If you had the gout in your hand, you could not strike the sparks; if the tinder was damp, the sparks could not live; and if there happened to be no tinder because you forgot to make it, or if the matches were missing, you were done for. Three cheers for the good old times of tinderboxes; may they never come back!

Let me set before you an admirable illustration, which is not one of my own, but comes from the great master of assemblies. Here is a candle, and of course we have brought it with a view to its giving light, but the absurd action that I am bent upon is to cover it up with a bushel. It would be a very ridiculous thing to be at the pains of providing a lighted candle and then to hide it under a bushel. Yet I will do so to make the folly apparent to you all. I notice that you laugh, and well you may. You may use a bushel and use a candle, but by putting the candle under the bushel, you use neither of them but misuse both. I am sure none of you would be guilty of such an absurd action. And can it be that even a single person here would be so profane as to believe that the all-wise God would do that which we all condemn as folly? And yet when those of you who have grace in your hearts profess to believe that you are placed where you can do no good, you virtually charge the Lord with lighting a candle and putting it under a bushel. Yonder is my respected brother, a workingman. Hear what he has to say: "My dear, Mr. Spurgeon, you cannot expect me to be doing any work in the church, for my daily labor leaves me no time for anything else. I could call the larks up in the morning; I am often abroad before the world is properly aired. Moreover, I have to work much too late to leave me a spare hour. I am willing but quite unable to do a hand's turn for my Lord." Yes, yes; I see: You have to complain of a bushel that hides your light. God has lighted you and then has put you where your light is condemned to be unseen. Do you quite believe that it is so? Have you no suspicion that, after all, you could shine if you were exceedingly anxious to do so?

> When those of you who have grace in your hearts profess to believe that you are placed where you can do no good, you virtually charge the Lord with lighting a candle and putting it under a bushel.

"There!" cries another, "I have little patience with a man who talks in that fashion; but as for me, I have hundreds of men to look after, and a great going concern involving large capital, and this requires the whole of my energy both by day and by night. My cares are never over. Mine is brainwork of the most exhausting sort, and when I get away from the mill, I feel no soul for reading or prayer or working in the cause of God. If it were hand labor, I should like the change to mental work; but I cannot keep on forever thinking or I shall soon wear out my brain." Just so, my friend: God has given you the light of His grace and has then deliberately placed a great golden bushel over the top of you! Do you feel sure that it is so? Is there not a still small voice that whispers that there is something wrong?

But my friend Mrs. Fruitful over yonder says, "I quite agree with you, sir. These people are not tied to their homes as I am, for I have eleven children; and what can I do? I have a great deal more to do than you men dream of, and it is no fiction that a mother's work is never ended. If anyone can plead a good excuse from the Lord's work, I am sure I can." Good sister, I sympathize with you, far more than with those who have already spoken. You have your share of life's burden in your large little family. It is true, eleven is better than so very many, but I have no doubt they are a handful, a lapful, and a heartful. Yet, surely, it cannot be quite true that you are altogether denied the pleasure of shining for your Lord; else it would seem as if He had kindled you as His own candle and then had put you under the bushel of a large family to prevent your shining.

Yet there is the candle, and there is the bushel. We cannot imagine that the bushel is to be on the top of the candle. Still, they must be in some relation to each other. If we must not put the candle under the bushel, would it be amiss to put the bushel under the candle? See how well it looks! It is an admirable ideal. Let us carry out its principle! Cannot the working-man talk to his mates and be a witness for Jesus in the shop? Parsons are all very well, but holy artisans can carry the truth where we have no entrance! Cannot the great manufacturer see to the interests of those whom he employs and treat them not as "hands," but as souls? Might he not do a world of good among his mill people if he had but a mind? I think so. And you, good mother of those dozen children save one, surely you have a work ready at hand in your own house. What a splendid Sunday school you have at home! Your children could not have a better teacher; and from what little I know of them, I should say that you could not have much finer children to instruct. You will not be forced to walk weary miles to get to your class; nor will you be tempted to neglect your house. You can stay at home and train for God valuable church members, fine workers among the poor, and soul-winning missionaries for the home and foreign field. What nobler work can there be than that of a mother among her own little ones? See how, by being set upon the bushel, the candle stands in a place of vantage and obtains a worthy pedestal from which to spread its light far and wide! Wisely used, that which would hinder the idle will assist the diligent. This is one of the feats of faith, to turn difficulties into helps, to slay the lion and find honey in his carcass, and thus, on stepping-stones of growing victory, rise to complete triumphs.

If there be real light in a man, you cannot keep him under a bushel. You may try to repress a man of talent, but he finds his level in due time. You may endeavor to destroy real grace when you meet with it among men; but neither you nor the devil will succeed. If you manage to place the gracious soul under a sort of bushel, something will happen for which you were not looking. If there is the real life of God within the person who is despised and covered up, the flame will find out a way for the revelation of the light. Grace may be oppressed, but it cannot be suppressed. In fact, it may be said of persecuted believers as of Israel in Egypt that the more they afflicted them, the more they multiplied. See, the covered candle burns the bushel. No, it is not a bushel! It turns out to be a mere bandbox. The light must, and will, burn its own way and do its own work. That which is in a man will sooner or later come out. The genius that is in the man, and still more, the spiritual life that is in him, will shine forth to the praise and glory of God, and there is no stopping it. I have heard of a gentleman who said he had learned to conceal his religion, and he believed that you might live in his house for a twelvemonth and never discover what his religion was. This he boasted of till one told him that he had lived two years in a man's house and had never seen the color of his money, for he was too poor to have any.

This is not technically called a candle, but in effect it is one. A nightlight is a delightful invention for the sick. It has supplanted the rushlight, which would frequently be set in a huge sort of tower, which, to me, as a sick child at night, used to suggest dreadful things. With its light shining through the round holes at the side, like so many ghostly eyes, it looked at me staringly; and with its round ring on the ceiling, it made me think of Nebuchadnezzar's fiery furnace. The nightlight is so mild and quiet that it suits our weakness yet cheers our gloom. Blessed be the child who first thought of it! Does it not remind you of a good, tender nurse? I always say—as a fine specimen of what I mean—my wife. She tells me that I cannot say this of her now, as she is so great an invalid, but I can speak of what she has been and would be now if strength sufficed. She has been far more than a nightlight to me in hours of pain. She moves across the room like the ancient deities, who were said to float rather than to walk. What gentle grace and tenderness! What unwearied watchfulness all through the night!

Do you remember the old charwoman nurse? Was her name Sarah Gamp or Betsy Prig? One evening when you were supposed to be asleep, you saw her, in the glass, stirring your gruel, and she took a pinch of snuff right over the cup to regale her lovely nose. No, you did not take your gruel like a man; your stomach turned at the mess and at the creature who had stirred in the droppings of her snuff. Her voice was hoarse; she stamped with her two beetle crushers when she traversed the room; she made your pillow hard when she shook it up; and she seemed an ogre in your eyes. The only good point about her was that you got well all the quicker, that you might escape from her clutches.

Honored among women be the memory of Florence Nightingale! Her name and fame gave an impetus to the movement for trained nurses, which has been so fraught with comfort to thousands. Our young ladies who devote themselves to this sacred service deserve all the encouragement we can give them. God bless you, gentle nightlights!

Our nightlight is set in water to make it quite safe. We do well to guard ourselves against the personal dangers of our position. Even when doing good we must be on our watch lest we fall into temptation.

Nightlights are marked to burn just so many hours and no more, and so are we. Long may you each one shine and yield comfort to those around you, but whether your hours be few or many, may you burn steadily to the end! If we may but fulfill our mission, it will be enough. May none of us take fire in a wrong way, blaze into a shameful notoriety, fill the air with an ill savor, and then go out in darkness before half our work is done!

There is room for fresh forms of candle still, and we should not wonder if the article once more became the subject of advertising, as soap is at present. In other lands, as, for instance, on the northwest coast of America, candles have a singular originality about them; for there they burn a fish, a species of smelt, which grows nearly a foot long and is full of fat. We should rather think the smelt smells when they put a rush or a piece of bark down the center of him and make a natural candle of him. The light must be rather fishy, but so is everything else in that region, and therefore it does not matter much.

There is in China and the East Indies a candle fly; but though it bears the name, we do not suppose that it serves the purpose of a candle. We have heard of reading by the light of glowworms in our hedges, but we doubt whether ordinary type could thus be deciphered. Glowworms remind us of most expositors, of whom Young says:

> *The commentators each dark passage shun,*
> *And hold their failing candles to the sun.*

Fireflies might serve our turn better, for they are like living lamps. They had a great charm for us when we saw them for the first time by the Italian lakes. The nightlight is a sober night comforter. May it be long before any of you learn its value in long hours of suffering!

Here is a candle that is as good as a candle can well hope to be. The light is clear and pure. Speaking popularly, the candle is perfect and is giving forth a bright light. Yet if you knew it better, you would take another view of it. It is disseminating black smoke as well as clear light. Here is a sheet of bright tin plate. Just hold it over the candle, and you will see that it is yielding something other than light. Of course, there will be nothing on the bright tin but that which comes out of the candle.

> *May none of us take fire in a wrong way, blaze into a shameful notoriety, fill the air with an ill savor, and then go out in darkness before half our work is done!*

Will one of you be so good as to put his finger on this tin and then touch the tip of his nose and his forehead with it? I cannot persuade any of you to try the effect, but if you did so, you would prove to us all that the best of candles does not field unmingled light. I am told that a man may be perfect. No doubt we ought to be so, and in the biblical sense, I hope many are so. But if all possible tests were applied to them, a measure of imperfection would be found in the brightest of the saints. It is as old Master Trapp says, "We may be perfect, but not perfectly perfect." Grace makes us perfect after our kind, but only in glory will the last remains of sin be altogether removed.

I should not care to be like this sheet of tin, used to expose the faults of others, when it would be better to leave them unnoticed. Some Peeping Toms have the gift of detecting the imperfections of good men. I do not covet their talent. In the process, these prying folk, like this tin, grow very sooty themselves. Do not attempt to imitate them.

In the next similitude you have a simpler reminder of the imperfections to which men are liable. A candle needs snuffers, and men need chastisements, for both are subject to infirmity. In the temple of Solomon there were snuffers and snuff dishes, but they were all of gold. God's rebukes are in love, and so should ours be; holy reproofs in the spirit of affection are snuffers of gold. Never use any other, and use even these with discretion, lest you put out the flame that it is your aim to improve. Never reprove in anger. Do not deal with a small fault as if it were a great crime. If you see a fly on your boy's forehead, don't try to kill it with a sledgehammer, or you may kill the boy also. Do the needful but very difficult work of reproof in the kindest and wisest style, so that the good you aim at may be attained.

It was a shocking habit of bad boys to snuff the candle and then open the snuffers and let the smoke and the smell escape. The snuffers are made on purpose to remove the snuff, or consumed wick, and then to quench it by pressure and prevent any offensive smoke; but young urchins of a mischievous sort would set the snuffers wide and let the filthy smoke fill the room with its detestable odor. So do some who hear of a brother's faults make them known, and they seem to take pleasure in filling society with unsavory reports. I pray you, do not do so. If the candle has something wrong with it, touch it carefully, snuff it with discretion, and shut up the obnoxious matter very carefully. Let us be silent about things that are a discredit to Christian character. Keep an ill report secret, and do not be like the young lady who called in a dozen friends to help her keep a secret, and yet, strange to say, it got out. Remember, you may yourself deserve rebuke one of these days; and as you would like this to be done gently and privately, so keep your remarks about others within the happy circle of tender love. To rebuke in gentle love is difficult, but we must aim at it till we grow proficient. *Golden* snuffers, remember, only golden snuffers. Put away those old rusty things, those unkind sarcastic remarks. They will do more harm than good, and they are not fit things to be handled by servants of the Lord Jesus.

See how precious material runs to waste if the light is not trimmed! There is a thief in the candle, and so it takes to guttering and running away instead of fielding up its substance to be used for the light. It is sad when a Christian man has some ill habit or sinister aim. We have seen fine lives wasted through a love of wine. It never came to actual drunkenness, but it lowered the man and spoiled his influence. So is it with a hasty temper, a proud manner, or a tendency to find fault. How many would be grandly useful but for some wretched impediment! Worldliness runs away with many a man's energies; love of amusement makes great gutters in his time; or fondness for feasts and gilded society robs him of his space for service. With some, political heat runs away with the zeal that should have been spent on religion. And in other cases, sheer folly and extravagance cause a terrible waste of energy that belonged to the Lord. You see there is fire and there is light, but something extraneous and mischievous is at work, and it needs to be removed. If this is your case, you may well desire the Lord to snuff you, however painful the operation may be. Depend upon it, we have no life force to spare, and everything that lessens our consecrated energy is a robbery of God.

Here is a sputtering candle. (I can give a specimen of it in actual fact, but I do not know how to sketch the sputter on paper.) You can light the thing, but it seems to spit at you and crackle as if in a bad temper. Never mind. It is its pretty way, and it will get over it and burn comfortably by and by. We once had among us a good brother—it was years ago, and he is now beyond our censure—who would always give, and give liberally, too; but he took the money out in grumbling. He thought there were too many appeals; he thought the thing ought to be provided for in another way; he thought—in fact he seemed to be full of discontented thoughts—but he ended up by saying, "There's my share of it." It was a pity, for he was real good. If any of you have the sputtering habit, I would advise you not to spend many pains in cultivating it: It is not pretty and does not commend a man to those about him. When a candle has been so long in the cellar that it has become thoroughly damp, it is apt to spit and sputter a little; but there is no reason why you and I should keep in the cellar and be sick of the blues; let us abide in the sunnier side of the house, and then we shall burn and shine with a happy cheerfulness. I hope we are not cut-on-the-cross or born like Attila to be "the scourge of mankind." I suppose it needs all sorts of people to make up a world, but the fewer of the grizzling, complaining sort, the better for those who have to live with them. Our sputtering candle has now got over his weakness, for he has burned out his damp bit; and whenever you and I come to a cantankerous half hour, may we get through it as fast as possible and keep ourselves to ourselves all the time, that nobody may know that we have been in the sulks. Go into your growlery and get it over. Better still, go into your closet and get it under.

We have seen a courteous contrivance at some tobacco shops for giving a light to passersby. It may serve as a suggestion to us for far higher purposes. If we know the divine truth, let us be ready to communicate it and by our winning manner constantly say, "Take a light." Let us be approachable in reference to spiritual things, and we shall soon have the joy of seeing others taking a light from us. We know people to whom no one would ever speak in the hour of trial; as well might they make a pillow of a thornbush. If people to whom they have never been introduced were to intrude their personal sorrows, they would be looked at with one of those searchers that read you from top to toe and at the same time wither you up. On the other hand, there are faces that are a living advertisement running thus: GOOD ACCOMODATION FOR MAN AND GRIEF. You are sure of a friend here. Certain persons are like harbors of refuge, to which every vessel will run in distress. When you want to ask your way in the street, you instinctively shun the stuck-up gentleman of importance, and you most readily put the question to the man with the smiling face and the open countenance. In our church we have friends who seem to say to everybody, "Take a light." May their number be greatly multiplied!

It should be a joy to hold a candle to another. It will not waste our own light to impart it. Yet holding a candle to another has a bitter meaning, as in these lines:

> *Some say compared to Buononcini*
> *That my lord Handel's but a ninny:*
> *Others aver that he to Handel*
> *Is scarcely fit to hold a candle.*

This candle is upside down, and it cannot be long before it puts itself out. When in our hearts the lower nature is uppermost and the animal dominates the spiritual, the flame of holy light cannot be long kept alight. When the world is uppermost and eternal things have a low place in the heart, the sacred life is in serious jeopardy. When the intellect crushes down the affections, the soul is not in an upright state. It needs that matters be quickly righted, or the worst consequences must ensue. Our prayer should rise to God that this happen not to ourselves; and when we see that it is so with others, we should be full of prayerful concern that they may be turned by the hand of God into a true and upright condition.

Some men who are not quite upright waste much of their influence. To such we might apply the old and almost obsolete word *candle-waster*. It is a pity to lose life in harmful or unprofitable ways.

Here is a very important-looking candle.

Its dimensions are aldermanic. You expect great flyings from so portly an illuminator. Look at the size of it. But when I light it, the illuminating power is very small. Can you see any light coming from it? It is a star of the smallest magnitude. We have here the maximum of tallow and the minimum of light. The fact is that only a little of the fat just near the center ever gets melted. This makes a little well of hot grease, but the rest is as hard and cold as if there were no burning wick in the middle. Thus it is with men of more talent than heart: The chief part of them is never used. Many a great and learned minister, with any quantity of Latin and Greek tallow, is but very little useful because his ability is not touched by his heart. He remains cold as to the bulk of him. Many a great rich man, with any amount of the fat of wealth, never gets warmed through: He is melted to the extent of a shilling or two, but his thousands are unaffected. Partial consecration is a very doubtful thing, yet how much we have of it! What is wanted is grace more abundant to fuse the whole man and make every part and parcel of him subservient to God's great design of light giving.

> When the world is uppermost and eternal things have a low place in the heart, the sacred life is in serious jeopardy. When the intellect crushes down the affections, the soul is not in an upright state.

The main business is to have plenty of heart. I have noticed that speakers produce an effect upon their audiences rather in proportion to their hearts than their heads. I was present at a meeting where a truly solid and instructive speaker succeeded in mesmerizing us all, so that in another half minute we should all have been asleep. His talk was as good as gold—and as heavy. A gentleman who was "all there" (what there was of him) followed him. He was so energetic that he broke a chair and made us all draw in our feet for fear he should come down upon our corns. How the folks woke up! The galleries cheered him to the echo. I do not know what it was all about and did not know at the time, but it was very wonderful. An express at sixty miles an hour is nothing to that orator. He swept past us like—well, like nothing at all. He meant it, and we felt that he deserved to be cheered for such zealous intentions. He was all ablaze, and we were willing for a season to rejoice in his light. I do not hold him up as an example, for in warfare we need shot as well as powder; but I could not help seeing that a warm heart and an energetic manner will carry the day, where a cold ponderosity effects nothing. My friend was like the second candle in our woodcut—the cobbler's candle with two wicks. His blaze was very large in proportion to the material that sustained it.

In our labor to do good, we must not let our learning remain cold and useless. Dr. Manton was one of the best of preachers, being both instructive and simple. On one occasion, however, he preached before an assembly of the great, and he very naturally used a more learned style than was his wont. He felt greatly rebuked when a poor man plucked him by the gown and lamented that, whereas he had often been fed under his ministry, there had been nothing for him on that occasion. The fire had not been so fierce as the tallow had been cold. It is a dreadful thing when hearers have more use for a dictionary than for a Bible under a sermon. A preacher may pile books on his head and heart till neither of them can work. Give me rather the enthusiastic Salvationist bearing a burning testimony than your cultured philosopher prosing with chill propriety.

Here is what your wise aunt in the country used to give you at night when you went down to the old farmhouse and time had come for bed.

You said, "Aunt, what is this cage for? Is this a mad candle, that it needs to be thus straitly shut up?"

"No," she said, "we have had young people here who have been so wicked as to read in bed, and you know how dangerous it is. Why, they might set all the bed curtains alight, and so the house might take fire, and all your uncle's ricks would soon be blazing, and soon the whole village would go like a bunch of matches. So I put the candle in a guard to prevent mischief."

Still, after all your aunt's lucid explanation, you did not like the look of this muzzled candle, and I should not wonder if you took it out of its prison and did a bit of reading by its naked light. Young people are so venturesome! Now, it is very proper to be on your guard in what you say and what you do. In all companies it is well to be guarded in your behavior. But is there not a way of being on your guard without diminishing the light of your cheerfulness? May you not be careful without being suspicious? Here is just as effectual a guard for a candle as that wire cage, but it is far brighter and more attractive. Let your prudence be always mated to your cheerfulness. Be on the watch, but don't look as if you had been drinking a quart of vinegar. Guard against sin, but do not check everything that would make life bright and happy. Don't put out the candle for fear of burning down the house.

In the matter of being on your guard against impostors who seek your charity, use common sense but not harshness. I had rather be taken in every now and then than be always suspicious. One does not care to go about in armor all day and all night; one is glad to get his head out of the helmet and lay it down on a pillow. It may be useful to us to be taken in sometimes, that we may see how weak we are—I mean the shrewdest of us.

This second guard, so pleasant and bright, is my ideal. Here you have care without anxiety and prudence without gloom. Be it so with us, that with a mortal hatred to all sin, we have a delight in all that is glad, joyous, and pure.

Here is a candle on a save-all—an invention that is scarcely ever thought of nowadays in this age of gas and general extravagance. Every prudent housewife had a save-all to burn up the smallest remnant of candle. Economy is necessary for the poor and salutary for the rich. He who would have much to give away should feel that he has nothing to waste. He who was heard to scold about a wasted match was found to be no miser but a greater giver than anyone else. Use the save-all to preserve every fragment of time. "Redeeming the time, because the days are evil" (Eph. 5:16 KJV). How much can be done in odd minutes! Many instances could be given to prove that it is so. Sanctify odd minutes, odd pence, and all sorts of oddments, and out of them you can bring glory to God.

Here is an hourglass and a candle. As the hourglass runs and the candle burns, we mark how the time passes away. In the old Puritan pulpits, there used to be an hourglass, and the preacher was expected to preach as long as the sand of the hourglass was running; which, of course, was just an hour. A witty preacher, having on one occasion only reached to "Eighteenthly" when the hourglass had run out, and having thirty heads to dilate upon, turned the machine over and cried, "Brethren, let us have another glass." When you hear of the length of time that your ancestors gave to hearing discourses, be ashamed at the grumbling about long sermons, and do try to take in every scrap of the poor pennyworth that we are allowed to give you in three poor quarters of an hour. Whether we preach or hear, time is hastening on. Our sands of life will soon run out. Just as we are being borne along irresistibly every moment as the earth speeds in her orbit, so are we being carried away by the resistless course of time. How it flies to a man of middle age! How exceedingly fast to the aged! We may say of the hours, as of the cherubim, "each one had six wings" (Isa. 6:2). If everything is made secure by faith in the Lord Jesus, we need not wish it to be otherwise; for the faster time passes, the sooner shall we be at home with our Father and our God.

(O)ur sands of life will soon run out. Just as we are being borne along irresistibly every moment as the earth speeds in her orbit, so are we being carried away by the resistless course of time.

We feel, as we watch the decreasing candle and the falling sand, that we, at least, have no time that needs killing. What we have is all too little for our high and holy purposes. We want not cards and dice and scenic displays for a pastime. Our time passes all too rapidly without such aids. Those who kill time will soon find that time kills them, and they would gladly give worlds, if they had them, to win back a single hour. Remember the story of Queen Elizabeth's last moments, and take care to spend each hour as carefully as if you had no other hour to follow it.

The next illustration is a warning, not an example. You have often heard it said of such and such a person, "He is burning the candle at both ends." Spendthrifts waste both capital and interest; and by both neglecting business and wasting their substance on expensive pleasures, they burn the candle at both ends. The vicious not only exhaust their daily strength, but they draw upon the future of their constitutions, so that when a few years have gone, they are old men before their time. Beware of burning the candle at both ends. It will go fast enough if you burn it only at one end, for your stock of strength and life is very limited. If there is anyone here who is sinning on the right hand and on the left, let him forbear and not be in such fearful haste to endless ruin. Let this candle cast a light upon the folly of prodigality, and may the prodigal hasten home before his candle is burned out. Did you ever see a candle used in that way? You do not live with folks so mad; but if you look abroad in the wide world, you may see how thousands are squandered and lives are cut short by burning the candle at both ends.

Some good people are unreasonable toward ministers and evangelists, and want them to be worked to death. Many a valuable man of God has been lost to the church by burning his candle at both ends.

This candle has fallen upon evil times. I have a bottle here full of a black material, which is to fall upon the flame of this candle. When I tell you that this bottle contains a quantity of steel filings, you will at once prophesy that the light will be put out.

Let us see what will happen! Why, well, instead of putting the candle out, I am making it display itself as candle never did before! Here we have fireworks, which if they do not quite rival those of the Crystal Palace, have splendor of their own. Do you not think that often when Satan tries to throw dust upon a Christian by slander, he only makes him shine the brighter? He was bright before, but now he coruscates and sends forth a glory and a beauty we could not have expected from him, for it never could have come from him if it had not been for the temptations, trials, and spiritual difficulties with which he has been assailed. God grant that it may be so with us in all time of our tribulation! May we turn the filings of steel into flashes of light!

The next illustration consists of two candles, and I am going to read, if I can, by the light of them. It may have happened to you at home, when you burned candles, that you required two of them. It needed some sense to arrange them if they were of unequal heights. I will place them here in this fashion, and I will sit down to read by their light. I cannot see, for I have put the tall candle in front and the shorter candle behind; the short one is envious and causes the tall one to cast an injurious shadow over my book. It seemed natural to put the greatest first, but I see that it will not work. I will put the shorter candle in front and put the longer one behind. Now I get the light of them both. Here is the lesson: Always put the weaker brother in the place of honor if you can, and thus make the best use of his light and prevent his creating a shadow through envy. Notice the order of marching in the Stockwell Orphanage when the children walk out to worship, or to the common. The rule is that the smallest boys and girls shall lead the way. In the old method the taller children blocked the vision of the little ones and also went along at a pace too great for the juniors; but on our plan the taller boys can see over the heads of the shorter ones, and the pace is toned down to suit little feet.

This is a suggestive rule for the young, and I trust that we who are older will not depart from it. Church members should make this the law of precedence in the house of the Lord, weaker brethren first considered. Let us not go our own pace, but consider their weakness, lest we cause any one of them to stumble. He who has only a little property, a little talent, a little position, and a little grace must be first thought of. It is not ours to strive for the first places, but in honor to prefer one another, looking more to the benefit of the whole body than to our own comfort or honor.

We will conclude as they do at open-air entertainments—with the greatest display of our fireworks.

Here are many candles uniting their brilliance; they all hang upon one support and shine by the same light. May they not represent the church of Christ in its multiplicity, variety, and unity? These candles are all supported upon one stem and giving forth the same light, yet they are of all manner of sorts, sizes, and colors. A great way off they would seem to be but one light. They are many yet one. I happened one evening to say that nobody could tell which was the "U.P." and which was the Free Church, or which was the Wesleyan or the Primitive or the Salvation Army or the Baptists, and so on; but one strong old Baptist assured me that the "Dips" gave the best light. Another said the Presbyterians were, on the whole, cast in the best mold; and a third thought the English church was made of the truest wax. I told them that some of the Baptists would be the better if they had another Baptism. The Free churches might be none the worse for being more established in the faith; and even the Methodists might improve their methods. The main question is possession of the one light and fire of God, the flame of divine truth. Those who shine by divine grace are all one in Christ Jesus.

What a glory will there be in the one church when all her members shine and all are one! May such a day come quickly! Amen.

Have I not proved that a world of illustration may be found in a candle?

AROUND THE WICKET GATE: A FRIENDLY TALK WITH
SEEKERS CONCEERNING FAITH IN THE LORD JESUS CHRIST

CONTENTS

"You are not far from the kingdom of God."
Mark 12:34

PREFACE

MILLIONS of men are in the outlying regions, far-off from God and peace; for these we pray, and to these we give warning. But just now we have to do with a smaller company who are not far from the kingdom but have come right up to the wicket gate that stands at the head of the way of life. One would think that they would hasten to enter, for a free and open invitation is placed over the entrance, the porter waits to welcome them, and there is but this one way to eternal life. He who is most loaded seems the most likely to pass in and begin the heavenward journey; but what ails the other men?

This is what I want to find out. Poor fellows! They have come a long way already to get where they are, and the King's Highway, which they seek, is right before them. Why do they not take to the Pilgrim Road at once? Alas! They have a great many reasons, and foolish as those reasons are, it needs a very wise man to answer them all. I cannot pretend to do so. Only the Lord Himself can remove the folly that is bound up in their hearts and lead them to take the great decisive step. Yet the Lord works by means, and I have prepared this little book in the earnest hope that He may work by it to the blessed end of leading seekers to an immediate, simple trust in the Lord Jesus.

He who does not take the step of faith, and so enter upon the road to heaven, will perish. It will be an awful thing to die just outside the gate of life. Almost saved but altogether lost! This is the most terrible of positions. A man just outside Noah's ark would have been drowned; a murderer close to the wall of the city of refuge yet outside of it would be slain; and the man who is within a yard of Christ yet has not trusted Him will be lost. Therefore am I in terrible earnest to get my hesitating friends over the threshold. "Come in! Come in!" is my pressing entreaty. "Why do you stand without?" is my solemn inquiry. May the Holy Spirit render my pleadings effectual with many who shall glance at these pages! May He cause His own almighty power to create faith in the soul at once!

My reader, if God blesses this book to you, do the writer this favor: either lend your own copy to one who is lingering at the gate or buy another and give it away, for his great desire is that this little volume should be of service to many thousands of souls.

To God this book is commended; for without His grace nothing will come of all that is written.

—*C. H. Spurgeon*

1

AWAKENING

GREAT numbers of persons have no concern about eternal things. They care more about their cats and dogs than about their souls. It is a great mercy to be made to think about ourselves and how we stand toward God and the eternal world. This is full often a sign that salvation is coming to us. By nature we do not like the anxiety that spiritual concern causes us, and we try, like sluggards, to sleep again. This is great foolishness; for it is at our peril that we trifle when death is so near and judgment is so sure. If the Lord has chosen us to eternal life, He will not let us return to our slumber. If we are sensible, we shall pray that our anxiety about our souls may never come to an end till we are really and truly saved. Let us say from our hearts:

> *He that suffered in my stead,*
> *Shall my physician be;*
> *I will not be comforted*
> *Till Jesus comfort me.*

It would be an awful thing to go dreaming down to hell and there to lift up our eyes with a great gulf fixed between heaven and us. It will be equally terrible to be aroused to escape from the wrath to come and then to shake off the warning influence and go back to our insensibility. I notice that those who overcome their convictions and continue in their sins are not so easily moved the next time: every awakening that is thrown away leaves the soul drowsier than before and less likely to be again stirred to holy feeling. Therefore our heart should be greatly troubled at the thought of getting rid of its trouble in any other than the right way. One who had the gout was cured of it by a quack medicine, which drove the disease within, and the patient died. To be cured of distress of mind by a false hope would be a terrible business. The remedy would be worse than the disease. Better far that our tenderness of conscience should cause us long years of anguish than that we should lose it and perish in the hardness of our hearts.

Yet awakening is not a thing to rest in or to desire to have lengthened out month after month. If I start up in a fright and find my house on fire, I do not sit down at the edge of the bed and say to myself, "I hope I am truly awakened! Indeed, I am deeply grateful that I am not left to sleep on!" No, I want to escape from threatened death, and so I hasten to the door or to the window that I may get out and may not perish where I am. It would be a questionable boon to be aroused yet not to escape from the danger. Remember, awakening is not salvation. A man may know that he is lost, yet he may never be saved. He may be made thoughtful, yet he may die in his sins. If you find out that you are bankrupt, the consideration of your debts will not pay them. A man may examine his wounds all the year around, and they will be none the nearer being healed because he feels their smart and notes their number. It is one trick of the devil to tempt a man to be satisfied with a sense of sin and another trick of the same deceiver to insinuate that the sinner may not be content to trust Christ, unless he can bring a certain measure of despair to add to the Savior's finished work. Our awakenings are not to help the Savior, but to help us to the Savior. To imagine that my feeling of sin is to assist in the removal of the sin is absurd. It is as though I said that water could not cleanse my face unless I had looked longer in the glass and had counted the dirty spots upon my forehead. A sense of need of salvation by grace is a very healthful sign; but one needs wisdom to use it aright and not to make an idol of it.

To be cured of distress of mind by a false hope would be a terrible business. The remedy would be worse than the disease.

Some seem as if they had fallen in love with their doubts, fears, and distresses. You cannot get them away from their terrors—they seem wedded to them. It is said that the worst trouble with horses when their stables are on fire is that you cannot get them to come out of their stalls. If they would but follow your lead, they might escape the flames, but they seem to be paralyzed with fear. So the fear of the fire prevents their escaping the fire. Reader, will your very fear of the wrath to come prevent your escaping from it? We hope not.

One who had been long in prison was not willing to come out. The door was open, but he pleaded even with tears to be allowed to stay where he had been so long. Fond of prison! Wedded to the iron bolts and the prison fare! Surely the prisoner must have been a little touched in the head! Are you willing to remain an awakened one and nothing more? Are you not eager to be at once forgiven? If you would tarry in anguish and dread, surely you, too, must be a little out of your mind! If peace is to be had, have it at once! Why tarry in the darkness of the pit, wherein your feet sink in the miry clay? There is light to be had, light marvelous and heavenly. Why lie in the gloom and die in anguish? You do not know how near salvation is to you. If you did, you would surely stretch out your hand and take it, for there it is; and it is to be had for the taking.

> *To believe that you have sinned and that your soul is forfeited to the justice of God is a very proper thing; but it will not save. Salvation is not by our knowing our own ruin, but by fully grasping the deliverance provided in Christ Jesus.*

Do not think that feelings of despair would fit you for mercy. When the pilgrim, on his way to the Wicket Gate, tumbled into the Slough of Despond, do you think that when the foul mire of that slough stuck to his garments it was a recommendation to him to get him easier admission at the head of the way? It is not so. The pilgrim did not think so by any means; neither may you. It is not what you feel that will save you, but what Jesus felt. Even if there were some healing value in feelings, they would have to be good ones; and the feeling that makes us doubt the power of Christ to save and prevents our finding salvation in Him is by no means a good one, but a cruel wrong to the love of Jesus.

Our friend has come to see us and has traveled through our crowded London by rail, or tram, or omnibus. On a sudden he turns pale. We ask him what is the matter, and he answers, "I have lost my pocketbook, and it contained all the money I have in the world." He goes over the amount to a penny and describes the checks, bills, notes, and coins. We tell him that it must be a great consolation to him to be so accurately acquainted with the extent of his loss. He does not seem to see the worth of our consolation. We assure him that he ought to be grateful that he has so clear a sense of his loss, for many persons might have lost their pocketbooks and have been quite unable to compute their losses. Our friend is not, however, cheered in the least. "No," says he, "to know my loss does not help me to recover it. Tell me where I can find my property, and you have done me real service; but merely to know my loss is no comfort whatever." Even so, to believe that you have sinned and that your soul is forfeited to the justice of God is a very proper thing; but it will not save. Salvation is not by our knowing our own ruin, but by fully grasping the deliverance provided in Christ Jesus. A person who refuses to look to the Lord Jesus but persists in dwelling upon his sin and ruin reminds us of a boy who dropped a shilling down an open grating of a London sewer and lingered there for hours, finding comfort in saying, "It rolled in just there! Just between those two iron bars I saw it go right down." Poor soul! Long might he remember the details of his loss before he would in this way get back a single penny into his pocket wherewith to buy himself a piece of bread. You see the drift of the parable; profit by it.

For Further Thought

1. *Romans 2:16 says that God will judge the secrets of men. In this verse, what is the standard of God's judgment?*
2. *Romans 3:23 says that all people have sinned. It also defines sin. What is that definition?*

2

JESUS ONLY

W E cannot too often or too plainly tell the seeking soul that his only hope for salvation lies in the Lord Jesus Christ. It lies in Him completely, only, and alone. To save both from the guilt and the power of sin, Jesus is all-sufficient. His name is called Jesus, because He shall save His people from their sins. The Son of man has power on earth to forgive sins. He is exalted on high to give repentance and forgiveness of sins. It pleased God from of old to devise a method of salvation that should be all contained in His only begotten Son. The Lord Jesus, for the working out of this salvation, became man, and being found in fashion as a man, became obedient unto death, even the death of the cross. If another way of deliverance had been possible, the cup of bitterness would have passed from Him. It stands to reason that the darling of heaven would not have died to save us if we could have been rescued at less expense. Infinite grace provided the great sacrifice; infinite love submitted to death for our sakes. How can we dream that there can be another way than the way that God has provided at such cost and set forth in Holy Scripture so simply and so urgently? Surely it is true that neither is there salvation in any other: for there is no other name under heaven given among men, whereby we are saved.

To suppose that the Lord Jesus has only half saved men, and that there is needed some work or feeling of their own to finish His work, is wicked. What is there of ours that could be added to His blood and righteousness? All our righteousnesses are as filthy rags. Can these be patched on to the costly fabric of His divine righteousness? Rags and fine white linen! Our dross and His pure gold! It is an insult to the Savior to dream of such a thing. We have sinned enough, without adding this to all our other offenses.

Even if we had any righteousness in which we could boast, if our fig leaves were broader than usual and were not so utterly fading, it would be wisdom to put them away and accept that righteousness which must be far more pleasing to God than anything of our own. The Lord must see more that is acceptable in His Son than in the best of us. The best of us! The words seem satirical, though they were not so intended. What best is there about any of us? There is none who does good, not one. I, who write these lines, would most freely confess that I have not a thread of goodness of my own. I could not make up so much as a rag, or a piece of a rag. I am utterly destitute. But if I had the fairest suit of good works that even pride can imagine, I would tear it up that I might put on nothing but the garments of salvation, which are freely given by the Lord Jesus out of the heavenly wardrobe of His own merits.

> *To suppose that the Lord Jesus has only half saved men, and that there is needed some work or feeling of their own to finish His work, is wicked.*

It is most glorifying to our Lord Jesus Christ that we should hope for every good thing from Him alone. This is to treat Him as He deserves to be treated, for as He is God, and beside Him there is none else, we are bound to look unto Him and be saved.

This is to treat Him as He loves to be treated, for He bids all those who labor and are heavy laden to come to Him, and He will give them rest. To imagine that He cannot save to the uttermost is to limit the Holy One of Israel and put a slur upon His power, or else to slander the loving heart of the friend of sinners and cast a doubt upon His love. In either case, we should commit a cruel and wanton sin against the tenderest points of His honor, which are His ability and willingness to save all that come unto God by Him.

The child, in danger of the fire, just clings to the fireman and trusts to him alone. She raises no question about the strength of his limbs to carry her or the zeal of his heart to rescue her, but she clings. The heat is terrible and the smoke is blinding, but she clings, and her deliverer quickly bears her to safety. In the same childlike confidence, cling to Jesus, who can and will bear you out of danger from the flames of sin.

The nature of the Lord Jesus should inspire us with the fullest confidence. As He is God, He is almighty to save; as He is man, He is filled with all fullness to bless; as He is God and man in one majestic person, He meets man in His humanity, and God in His holiness. The ladder is long enough to reach from Jacob prostrate on the earth to Jehovah reigning in heaven. To bring another ladder would be to suppose that He failed to bridge the distance, and this would be grievously to dishonor Him. If even to add to His words is to draw a curse upon us, what must it be to pretend to add to Him? Remember that He is the way; and to suppose that we must, in some manner, add to the divine road is to be arrogant enough to think of adding to Him. Away with such a notion! Loathe it as you would blasphemy, for in essence it is the worst of blasphemy against the Lord of love.

To come to Jesus with a price in our hand would be insufferable pride even if we had any price that we could bring. What does He need of us? What could we bring if He did need it? Would He sell the priceless blessings of His redemption? That which He wrought out in His heart's blood, would He barter it with us for our tears and vows or for ceremonial observances, feelings, and works? He is not reduced to make a market of Himself: He will give freely, as is suitable to His royal love; but He who offers a price to Him knows not with whom he is dealing, or how grievously he vexes His free Spirit. Empty-handed sinners may have what they will. All that they can possibly need is in Jesus, and He gives it for the asking; but we must believe that He is all in all, and we must not dare to breathe a word about completing what He has finished or fitting ourselves for what He gives to us as undeserving sinners.

> *He who believes on the Son has everlasting life because the ever-living God has taken him unto Himself and has given to him to be a partaker of His life.*

The reason why we may hope for forgiveness of sin and life eternal by faith in the Lord Jesus is that God has so appointed. He has pledged Himself in the gospel to save all who truly trust in the Lord Jesus, and He will never run back from His promise. He is so well pleased with His only begotten Son, that He takes pleasure in all who lay hold upon Him as their one and only hope. The great God Himself has taken hold on him who has taken hold on His Son. He works salvation for all who look for that salvation to the once-slain Redeemer. For the honor of His Son, He will not suffer the man who trusts in Him to be ashamed. He who believes on the Son has everlasting life because the ever-living God has taken him unto Himself and has given to him to be a partaker of His life. If Jesus only is your trust, you need not fear but what you shall effectually be saved, both now and in the day of His appearing.

When a man confides, there is a point of union between him and God, and that union guarantees blessing. Faith saves us because it makes us cling to Christ Jesus, and He is one with God and thus brings us into connection with God. I am told that years ago above the falls of Niagara, a boat was upset, and two men were being carried down by the current, when persons on the shore managed to float a rope out to them, which was seized by them both.

One of them held fast to it and was safely drawn to the bank; but the other, seeing a great log come floating by, unwisely let go the rope and clung to the great piece of timber, for it was the bigger thing of the two and apparently better to cling to. Alas! The timber with the man on it went right over the vast abyss, because there was no union between the wood and the shore. The size of the log was no benefit to him who grasped it; it needed a connection with the shore to produce safety. So when a man trusts to his works, to his prayers or almsgiving, to sacraments, or to anything of that sort, he will not be saved, because there is no junction between him and God through Christ Jesus. But faith, though it may seem to be like a slender cord, is in the hand of the great God on the shore. Infinite power pulls in the connecting line and thus draws the man from destruction. Oh, the blessedness of faith, because it unites us to God by the Savior, whom He has appointed, even Jesus Christ! Oh, is there not common sense in this matter? Think it over, and may there soon be a band of union between you and God through your faith in Christ Jesus!

For Further Thought

1. *Read Romans 3:10–12. What percentage of people understand God, seek God, or do good?*
2. *In Ephesians 2:8–9, what prevents us from boasting that we qualify for salvation?*

3

PERSONAL FAITH IN JESUS

THERE is a wretched tendency among men to leave Christ Himself out of the gospel. They might as well leave flour out of bread. Men hear the way of salvation explained and consent to it as being scriptural and in every way such as suits their case; but they forget that a plan is of no service unless it is carried out, and that in the matter of salvation their own personal faith in the Lord Jesus is essential. A road to York will not take me there; I must travel along it for myself. All the sound doctrine that ever was believed will never save a man unless he puts his trust in the Lord Jesus for himself.

Mr. MacDonald asked the inhabitants of the island of St. Kilda how a man must be saved. An old man replied, "We shall be saved if we repent and forsake our sins and turn to God."

"Yes," said a middle-aged female, "and with a true heart, too."

"Aye," rejoined a third, "and with prayer."

"And," added a fourth, "it must be the prayer of the heart."

"And we must be diligent, too," said a fifth, "in keeping the commandments."

Thus, each having contributed his mite, feeling that a very decent creed had been made up, they all looked and listened for the preacher's approbation, but they had aroused his deepest pity: He had to begin at the beginning and preach Christ to them. The carnal mind always maps out for itself a way in which self can work and become great, but the Lord's way is quite the reverse. The Lord Jesus puts it very compactly in Mark 16:16: "He who believes and is baptized will be saved." Believing and being baptized are no matters of merit to be gloried in; they are so simple that boasting is excluded and free grace bears the palm. This way of salvation is chosen that it might be seen to be of grace alone. It may be that the reader is unsaved. What is the reason? Do you think the way of salvation, as laid down in the text we have quoted, to be dubious? Do you fear that you would not be saved if you followed it? How can that be, when God has pledged His own word for its certainty? How can that fail which God prescribes and concerning which He gives a promise? Do you think it very easy? Why, then, do you not attend to it? Its ease leaves those without excuse who neglect it. If you would have done some great thing, be not so foolish as to neglect the little thing. To believe is to trust or lean upon Christ Jesus. In other words, it means to give up self-reliance and to rely upon the Lord Jesus. To be baptized is to submit to the ordinance that our Lord fulfilled at Jordan, to which the converted ones submitted at Pentecost, to which the jailer yielded obedience on the very night of his conversion. It is the outward confession that should always go with inward faith. The outward sign saves not, but it sets forth to us our death, burial, and resurrection with Jesus, and like the Lord's Supper, it is not to be neglected.

The great point is to believe in Jesus and confess your faith. Do you believe in Jesus? Then, dear friend, dismiss your fears; you shall be saved. Are you still an unbeliever? Then remember, there is but one door, and if you will not enter by it, you must perish in your sins. The door is there, but unless you enter by it, what is the use of it to you? It is of necessity that you obey the command of the gospel. Nothing can save you if you do not hear the voice of Jesus and do His bidding indeed and of a truth. Thinking and resolving will not answer the purpose; you must come to real business, for only as you actually believe will you truly live unto God.

I heard of a friend who deeply desired to be the means of the conversion of a young man, and one said to him, "You may go to him, and talk to him, but you will get him no further; for he is exceedingly well acquainted with the plan of salvation." It was eminently so. Therefore, when our friend began to speak with the young man, he received for an answer, "I am much obliged to you, but I do not know that you can tell me much, for I have long known and admired the plan of salvation by the substitutionary sacrifice of Christ." Alas! He was resting in the plan, but he had not believed in the person. The plan of salvation is most blessed, but it can avail us nothing unless we personally believe in the Lord Jesus Christ Himself. What is the comfort of a plan of a house if you do not enter the house itself? What is the good of a plan of clothing if you have not a rag to cover you? Have you never heard of the Arab chief at Cairo who was very ill and went to the missionary, and the missionary said he could give him a prescription? He did so, and a week later he found the Arab none the better. "Did you take my prescription?" he asked. "Yes, I ate every morsel of the paper." He dreamed that he was going to be cured by devouring the physician's writing, which I may call the plan of the medicine. He should have had the prescription made up, and then it might have done him good if he had taken the medicine. It could do him no good to swallow the recipe. So it is with salvation. It is not the plan of salvation that can save; it is the carrying out of that plan by the Lord Jesus in His death on our behalf and our acceptance of the same. Under the Jewish law, the offerer brought a bull and laid his hands upon it. It was no dream or theory or plan. In the victim for sacrifice, he found something substantial that he could handle and touch. Even so do we lean upon the real and true work of Jesus, the most substantial thing under heaven. We come to the Lord Jesus by faith and say, "God has provided an atonement here, and I accept it. I believe in the fact accomplished on the cross; I am confident that sin was put away by Christ, and I rest on Him." If you would be saved, you must get beyond the acceptance of plans and doctrines to a resting in the divine person and finished work of the Lord Jesus Christ. Dear reader, will you have Christ now?

> The great point is to believe in Jesus and confess your faith. Do you believe in Jesus? Then, dear friend, dismiss your fears; you shall be saved.

Jesus invites all those who labor and are heavy laden to come to Him, and He will give them rest. He does not promise this to their merely dreaming about Him. They must come. They must come to Him and not merely to the church, to baptism, to the orthodox faith, or to anything short of His divine person. When the brazen serpent was lifted up in the wilderness, the people were not to look to Moses or to the tabernacle or to the pillar of cloud, but to the brazen serpent itself. Looking was not enough unless they looked to the right object, and the right object was not enough unless they looked. It was not enough for them to know about the serpent of brass; they must each one look to it for himself. When a man is ill, he may have a good knowledge of medicine, yet he may die if he does not actually take the healing medicine. We must receive Jesus; for to as many as received Him, to those gave He power to become the sons of God. Lay the emphasis on two words: We must receive *Him*, and we must *receive* Him. We must open wide the door and take Christ Jesus in, for it is

Christ in you who is the hope of glory. Christ must be no myth, no dream, no phantom to us, but a real man and truly God; and our reception of Him must be no forced and feigned acceptance, but the hearty and happy assent and consent of the soul that He shall be the All-in-All of our salvation. Will we not at once come to Him and make Him our sole trust?

The dove is hunted by the hawk and finds no security from its restless enemy. It has learned that there is shelter for it in the cleft of the rock, and it hastens there on happy wings. Once wholly sheltered within its refuge, it fears no bird of prey. But if it did not hide itself in the rock, its adversary would seize upon it. The rock would be of no use to the dove if the dove did not enter its cleft. The whole body must be hidden in the rock. What if ten thousand other birds found a fortress there? That fact would not save the one dove that is now pursued by the hawk! It must put its whole self into the shelter and bury itself within its refuge, or its life will be forfeited to the destroyer.

What a picture of faith is this! It is entering into Jesus, hiding in His wounds.

> *Rock of Ages, cleft for me,*
> *Let me hide myself in Thee.*

The dove is out of sight; the rock alone is seen. Likewise, the guilty soul darts into the pierced side of Jesus by faith and is buried in Him out of sight of avenging justice. But there must be this personal application to Jesus for shelter; and this it is that so many put off from day to day till it is to be feared that they will die in their sins. What an awful word is that! It is what our Lord said to the unbelieving Jews, and He says the same to us at this hour. If you believe not that I am He, you shall die in your sins. It makes one's heart quiver to think that even one who shall read these lines may yet be of the miserable company who will thus perish. The Lord prevent it of His great grace!

I saw the other day a remarkable picture that I shall use as an illustration of the way of salvation by faith in Jesus. An offender had committed a crime for which he must die, but it was in the olden time, when churches were considered to be sanctuaries in which criminals might hide themselves and so escape from death. See the transgressor! He rushes toward the church; the guards pursue him with their drawn swords, athirst for his blood! They follow him even to the church door. He rushes up the steps, and just as they are about to overtake him and hew him in pieces on the threshold of the church, out comes the bishop, and holding up the cross, he cries, "Back, back! Stain not the precincts of God's house with blood! Stand back!" The fierce soldiers at once respect the emblem and retire, while the poor fugitive hides himself behind the robes of the bishop. It is even so with Christ. The guilty sinner flies straightaway to Jesus; and though justice pursues him, Christ lifts up His wounded hands and cries to justice, "Stand back! I shelter this sinner. In the secret place of my tabernacle do I hide him. I will not suffer him to perish, for he puts his trust in me."

Sinner, fly to Christ!

But you answer, "I am too vile."

The viler you are, the more will you honor Him by believing that He is able to protect even you.

"But I am so great a sinner."

Then the more honor shall be given to Him if you have faith to confide in Him, great sinner though you are.

If you have a little sickness, and you tell your physician, "Sir, I am quite confident in your skill to heal," there is no great compliment in your declaration. Anybody can cure a finger ache or a trifling sickness. But if you are sore sick with a complication of diseases that grievously torment you, and you say, "Sir, I seek no better physician; I will ask no other advice but yours; I trust myself joyfully with you," what an honor have you conferred on him, that you can trust your life in his hands while it is in extreme and immediate danger! Do the like with Christ; put your soul into His care. Do it deliberately and without a doubt. Dare to quit all other hopes. Venture all on Jesus; I say "venture" though there is nothing really venturesome in it, for He is abundantly able to save. Cast yourself simply on Jesus; let nothing but faith be in your soul toward Jesus; believe Him and trust in Him, and you shall never be made ashamed of your confidence, because he who believes on Him shall not be disappointed.

For Further Thought

1. *The people in Ephesus trusted the Lord after they heard the "word of truth" (Eph. 1:13). According to this verse, what happened to them after that?*
2. *According to 1 Timothy 4:10, why did the apostle Paul suffer reproach?*

4

FAITH VERY SIMPLE

To many, faith seems a hard thing. The truth is, it is only hard because it is easy. Naaman thought it hard that he should have to wash in the Jordan, but if it had been some great thing, he would have done it right cheerfully. People think that salvation must be the result of some act or feeling, very mysterious and very difficult; but God's thoughts are not our thoughts, neither are His ways our ways. In order that the feeblest and the most ignorant may be saved, He has made the way of salvation as easy as the ABCs. There is nothing about it to puzzle anyone; only, as everybody expects to be puzzled by it, many are quite bewildered when they find it to be so exceedingly simple.

The fact is, we do not believe that God means what He is saying; we act as if it could not be true.

I have heard of a Sunday school teacher who performed an experiment that I do not think I shall ever try with children, for it might turn out to be a very expensive one. Indeed, I feel sure that the result in my case would be very different from what I now describe. This teacher had been trying to illustrate what faith was, and as he could not get it into the minds of his boys, he took his watch and said, "Now, I will give you this watch, John. Will you have it?"

John fell thinking what the teacher could mean and did not seize the treasure, but made no answer.

The teacher said to the next boy, "Henry, here is the watch. Will you have it?"

The boy, with a very proper modesty, replied, "No, thank you, sir."

The teacher tried several of the boys with the same result, till at last a youngster who was not as wise or as thoughtful as the others, but rather more believing, said in the most natural way, "Thank you, sir," and put the watch into his pocket.

Then the other boys woke up to a startling fact: Their companion had received a watch that they had refused.

One of the boys quickly asked of the teacher, "Is he to keep it?"

"Of course he is," said the teacher, "I offered it to him, and he accepted it. I would not give a thing and take a thing. That would be very foolish. I put the watch before you and said that I gave it to you, but none of you would have it."

"Oh!" said the boy. "If I had known you meant it, I would have had it."

Of course he would. He thought it was a piece of acting, and nothing more.

All the other boys were in a dreadful state of mind to think that they had lost the watch. Each one cried, "Teacher, I did not know you meant it. I thought..."

No one took the gift, but everyone thought. Each one had his theory except for the simpleminded boy who believed what he was told and got the watch. Now I wish that I could always be such a simple child as literally to believe what the Lord says and take what He puts before me, resting quite content that He is not playing with me and that I cannot be wrong in accepting what He sets before me in the gospel. Happy should we be if we would trust and raise no questions of any sort. But alas! We will get thinking and doubting. When the Lord uplifts His dear Son before a sinner, that sinner should take Him without hesitation. If you take Him, you have Him; and none can take Him from you. Out with your hand, man, and take Him at once!

God's thoughts are not our thoughts, neither are His ways our ways. In order that the feeblest and the most ignorant may be saved, He has made the way of salvation as easy as the ABCs.

When inquirers accept the Bible as literally true and see that Jesus is really given to all who trust Him, all the difficulty about understanding the way of salvation vanishes like the morning's frost at the rising of the sun.

Two inquiring ones came to me in my vestry. They had been hearing the gospel from me for only a short season, but they had been deeply impressed by it. They expressed their regret that they were about to remove far away, but they added their gratitude that they had heard me at all. I was cheered by their kind thanks but felt anxious that a more effectual work should be wrought in them, and therefore I asked them, "Have you in very deed believed in the Lord Jesus Christ? Are you saved?"

One of them replied, "I have been trying hard to believe." This statement I have often heard, but I will never let it go by me unchallenged.

"No," I said, "that will not do. Did you ever tell your father that you tried to believe him?" After I had dwelt awhile upon the matter, they admitted that such language would have been an insult to their father. I then set the gospel very plainly before them in as simple language as I could and begged them to believe Jesus, who is worthier of faith than the best of fathers.

One of them replied, "I cannot realize it; I cannot realize that I am saved."

Then I went on to say, "God bears testimony to His Son, that whoever trusts in His Son is saved. Will you make Him a liar now, or will you believe His Word?"

While I thus spoke, one of them started as if astonished, and she startled us all as she cried, "O sir, I see it all; I am saved! Oh, do bless Jesus for me; He has shown me the way, and He has saved me! I see it all."

The esteemed sister who had brought these young friends to me knelt down with them while, with all our hearts, we blessed and magnified the Lord for a soul brought into light. One of the two sisters, however, could not see the gospel as the other had done, though I feel sure she will do so before long.

Did it not seem strange that, both hearing the same words, one should come out into clear light and the other should remain in the gloom? The change that comes over the heart when the understanding grasps the gospel is often reflected in the face and shines there like the light of heaven. Such newly enlightened souls often exclaim, "Why, sir, it is so plain; how is it I have not seen it before this? I understand all I have read in the Bible now, though I could not make it out before. It has all come in a minute, and now I see what I could never understand before." The fact is, the truth was always plain, but they were looking for signs and wonders, and therefore did not see what was nigh them. Old men often look for their spectacles when they are on their foreheads, and it is commonly observed that we fail to see that which is straight before us. Christ Jesus is before our faces, and we have only to look to Him and live, but we make all manner of bewilderment of it and so manufacture a maze out of that which is as plain as a pikestaff.

The little incident about the two sisters reminds me of another. A much-esteemed friend came to me one Sunday morning after service to shake hands with me. "For," said she, "I was fifty years old on the same day as yourself. I am like you in that one thing, sir; but I am the very reverse of you in better things."

I remarked, "Then you must be a very good woman, for in many things I wish I also could be the reverse of what I am."

"No, no," she said, "I did not mean anything of that sort: I am not right at all."

"What!" I cried. "Are you not a believer in the Lord Jesus?"

"Well," she said with much emotion, "I, I will try to be."

I laid hold of her hand and said, "My dear soul, you are not going to tell me that you will try to believe my Lord Jesus! I cannot have such talk from you. It means blank unbelief. What has He done that you should talk of Him in that way? Would you tell me that you would try to believe me? I know you would not treat me so rudely. You think me a true man, and so you believe me at once. Surely you cannot do less with my Lord Jesus."

Then with tears she exclaimed, "Oh, sir, do pray for me!"

To this I replied, "I do not feel that I can do anything of the kind. What can I ask the Lord Jesus to do for one who will not trust Him? I see nothing to pray about. If you will believe Him, you shall be saved; and if you will not believe Him, I cannot ask Him to invent a new way to gratify your unbelief."

Then she said again, "I will try to believe."

But I told her solemnly I would have none of her trying, for the message from the Lord did not mention "trying," but said she should believe on the Lord Jesus Christ and be saved.

I pressed upon her the great truth that he who believes on Him has everlasting life—and its terrible reverse: He who believes not is condemned already because he has not believed in the name of the only begotten Son of God. I urged her to full faith in the once crucified but now ascended Lord, and the Holy Spirit there and then enabled her to trust.

She most tenderly said, "Oh, sir, I have been looking to my feelings, and this has been my mistake! Now I trust my soul with Jesus, and I am saved." She found immediate peace through believing. There is no other way.

God has been pleased to make the necessities of life very simple matters. We must eat; and even a blind man can find the way to his mouth. We must drink; and even the tiniest babe knows how to do this without instruction. We have a fountain in the grounds of the Stockwell Orphanage, and when it is running in the hot weather, the boys go to it naturally. We have no class for fountain drill. Many poor boys have come to the orphanage, but never one who was so ignorant that he did not know how to drink. Now faith is, in spiritual things, what eating and drinking are in temporal things. By the mouth of faith we take the blessings of grace into our spiritual nature, and they are ours. O you who would believe but think you cannot, do you not see that, as one can drink without strength and as one can eat without strength and gets strength by eating, so we may receive Jesus without effort, and by accepting Him we receive power for all such further effort as we may be called to put forth?

Faith is so simple a matter that whenever I try to explain it, I am very fearful lest I should becloud its simplicity. When Thomas Scott had printed his notes upon *The Pilgrim's Progress*, he asked one of his parishioners whether she understood the book.

"Oh yes, sir," said she, "I understand Mr. Bunyan well enough, and I am hoping that one day, by divine grace, I may understand your explanations."

Should I not feel mortified if my reader should know what faith is and then get confused by my explanation? I will, however, make one trial and pray the Lord to make it clear.

I am told that on a certain highland road there was a disputed right of way. The owner wished to preserve his supremacy, and at the same time he did not wish to inconvenience the public: hence an arrangement that occasioned the following incident. Seeing a sweet country girl standing at the gate, a tourist went up to her and offered her a shilling to permit him to pass.

"No, no," said the child, "I must not take anything from you; but you are to say, 'Please allow me to pass,' and then you may come through and welcome."

The permission was to be asked for; but it could be had for the asking. Just so, eternal life is free; and it can be had, yea, it shall be at once had, by trusting in the Word of Him who cannot lie. Trust Christ, and by that trust you grasp salvation and eternal life. Do not philosophize. Do not sit down and bother your poor brain. Just believe Jesus as you would believe your father. Trust Him as you trust your money with a banker or your health with a doctor.

Faith will not long seem a difficulty to you or ought it to be so, for it is simple. Faith is trusting, trusting wholly upon the person, work, merit, and power of the Son of God. Some think this trusting is a romantic business, but indeed it is the simplest thing that can possibly be. To some of us, truths that were once hard to believe are now matters of fact that we should find it hard to doubt. If one of our great-grandfathers were to rise from the dead and come into the present state of things, what a deal of trusting he would have to do! He would say tomorrow morning, "Where are the flint and steel? I want a light"; and we should give him a little box with tiny pieces of wood in it and tell him to strike one of them on the box. He would have to trust a good deal before he would believe that fire would thus be produced.

We should next say to him, "Now that you have a light, turn that tap and light the gas."

He sees nothing. How can light come through an invisible vapor? Yet it does.

"Come with us, Grandfather. Sit in that chair. Look at that box in front of you. You shall have your likeness directly."

"No, child," he would say, "it is ridiculous. The sun takes my portrait? I cannot believe it."

"Yes, and you shall ride fifty miles in an hour without horses." He will not believe it till we get him into the train.

"My dear sir, you shall speak to your son in New York, and he shall answer you in a few minutes."

Should we not astonish the old gentleman? Would he not want all his faith? Yet we believe these things without effort because experience has made us familiar with them. Faith is greatly needed by you who are strangers to spiritual things; you seem lost while we are talking about them. But oh, how simple it is to us who have the new life and have communion with spiritual realities! We have a Father to whom we speak, and He hears us, and a blessed Savior who hears our heart's longings and helps us in our struggles against sin. It is all plain to him who understands. May it now be plain to you!

FOR FURTHER THOUGHT

1. In John 17:3, Jesus Christ defines eternal life. There are two aspects to this definition. What are these aspects?
2. In John 7:37, Jesus Christ invites people to come to Him. According to this verse, if a person responds to this invitation, what is he or she to do?

5

FEARING TO BELIEVE

IT is an odd product of our unhealthy nature—the fear to believe. Yet have I met with it often—so often that I wish I might never see it again. It looks like humility and tries to pass itself off as the very soul of modesty, yet it is an infamously proud thing. In fact, it is presumption playing the hypocrite. If men were afraid to disbelieve, there would be good sense in the fear, but to be afraid to trust their God is at best an absurdity, and in very deed it is a deceitful way of refusing to the Lord the honor that is due to His faithfulness and truth.

How unprofitable is the diligence that busies itself in finding out reasons why faith in our case should not be saving! We have God's Word for it, that whoever believes in Jesus shall not perish, and we search for arguments why we should perish if we did believe. If anyone gave me an estate, I certainly should not commence raising questions as to the title. What can be the use of inventing reasons why I should not hold my own house or possess any other piece of property that is enjoyed by me? If the Lord is satisfied to save me through the merits of His dear Son, assuredly I may be satisfied to be so saved. If I take God at His Word, the responsibility of fulfilling His promise does not lie with me, but with God who made the promise.

But you fear that you may not be one of those for whom the promise is intended. Do not be alarmed by that idle suspicion. No soul ever came to Jesus wrongly. No one can come at all unless the Father draw him; and Jesus has said, he who comes to me I will not cast out. No soul ever lays hold on Christ in a way of robbery; he who has Him has Him of right divine; for the Lord's giving of Himself for us and to us is so free that every soul that takes Him has a grace-given right to do so. If you lay hold on Jesus by the hem of His garment without leave and behind Him, yet virtue will flow from Him to you as surely as if He had called you out by name and bidden you trust Him. Dismiss all fear when you trust the Savior. Take Him and welcome.

He who believes in Jesus is one of God's elect.

Did you suggest that it would be a horrible thing if you were to trust in Jesus and yet perish? It would be so. But as you must perish if you do not trust, the risk at the worst is not very great.

I can but perish if I go;
I am resolved to try;
For if I stay away, I know
I must forever die.

Suppose you stand in the Slough of Despond forever; what will be the good of that? Surely it would be better to die struggling along the King's Highway toward the Celestial City than sinking deeper and deeper in the mire and filth of dark, distrustful thoughts! You have nothing to lose, for you have lost everything already; therefore make a dash for it, and dare to believe in the mercy of God to you, even to you.

If the Lord is satisfied to save me through the merits of His dear Son, assuredly I may be satisfied to be so saved.

But one moans, "What if I come to Christ and He refuses me?"

My answer is, "Try Him." Cast yourself on the Lord Jesus, and see if He refuses you. You will be the first against whom He has shut the door of hope. Friend, don't cross that bridge till you come to it! When Jesus casts you out, it will be time enough to despair, but that time will never come. This man receives sinners. He has not so much as begun to cast them out.

Have you never heard of the man who lost his way one night and came to the edge of a precipice as he thought, and in his own apprehension fell over the cliff? He clutched at an old tree and there hung, clinging to his frail support with all his might. He felt persuaded that, should he quit his hold, he would be dashed in pieces on some awful rocks that waited for him down below. There he hung, with sweat upon his brow and anguish in every limb. He passed into a desperate state of fever and faintness, and at last his hands could hold up his body no longer. He relaxed his grasp! He dropped from his support! He fell about a foot or so and was received upon a soft mossy bank, whereon he lay altogether unhurt and perfectly safe till morning. Thus, in the darkness of their ignorance, many think that sure destruction awaits them if they confess their sin, quit all hope in self, and resign themselves into the hands of God. They are afraid to quit the hope to which they ignorantly cling. It is an idle fear. Give up your hold upon everything but Christ, and drop. Drop from all trust in your works, prayers, or feelings. Drop at once! Drop now! Soft and safe shall be the bank that receives you. Jesus Christ, in His love, in the efficacy of His precious blood, in His perfect righteousness, will give you immediate rest and peace. Cease from self-confidence. Fall into the arms of Jesus. This is the major part of faith—giving up every other hold and simply falling upon Christ. There is no reason for fear: Only ignorance causes your dread of that which will be your eternal safety. The death of carnal hope is the life of faith, and the life of faith is life everlasting. Let yourself die that Christ may live in you.

> When Jesus casts you out, it will be time enough to despair, but that time will never come. This man receives sinners. He has not so much as begun to cast them out.

But the mischief is that, to the one act of faith in Jesus, we cannot bring men. They will adopt any expedient sooner than have done with self. They fight shy of believing and fear faith as if it were a monster. O foolish tremblers, who has bewitched you? You fear that which would be the death of all your fear and the beginning of your joy. Why will you perish through perversely preferring other ways to God's own appointed plan of salvation?

Alas! There are many, many souls who say, "We are bidden to trust in Jesus, but instead of that we will attend the means of grace regularly."

Attend public worship by all means, but not as a substitute for faith, or it will become a vain confidence. The command is, "Believe and live." Attend to that, whatever else you do.

"Well, I shall take to reading good books; perhaps I shall get good that way."

Read the good books by all means, but that is not the gospel. The gospel is, believe on the Lord Jesus Christ, and you shall be saved.

Suppose a physician has a patient under his care, and he says to him,

"You are to take a bath in the morning; it will be of very great service to your disease."

But the man takes a cup of tea in the morning instead of the bath, and he says, "That will do as well; I have no doubt."

What does his physician say when he inquires, "Did you follow my rule?"

"No, I did not."

"Then you do not expect, of course, that there will be any good result from my visits, since you take no notice of my directions."

> *L*ay hold on Jesus and keep hold on Jesus. Grow up into Him. Twist the roots of your nature, the fibers of your heart, about Him.

So we, practically, say to Jesus Christ, when we are under searching of soul, "Lord, You have bid me trust You, but I would sooner do something else! Lord, I want to have horrible convictions; I want to be shaken over hell's mouth; I want to be alarmed and distressed!"

Yes, you want anything but what Christ prescribes for you, which is that you should simply trust Him. Whether you feel or do not feel, cast yourself on Him that He may save you, and He alone.

"But you do not mean to say that you speak against praying, and reading good books, and so on?"

Not one single word do I speak against any of those things, anymore than if I were the physician I quoted I should speak against the man's drinking a cup of tea. Let him drink his tea, but not if he drinks it instead of taking the bath that is prescribed for him. So let the man pray—the more the better. Let the man search the scriptures, but remember that if these things are put in the place of simple faith in Christ, the soul will be ruined. Beware lest it be said of any of you by our Lord, "Search the scriptures, for in them you think you have eternal life; but you will not come unto me that you might have life."

Come by faith to Jesus, for without Him you perish forever. Did you ever notice how a fir tree will get a hold among rocks that seem to afford it no soil? It sends a tiny root into any little crack that opens; it clutches even the bare rock as with a huge bird's claw; it holds fast and binds itself to earth with a hundred anchorages. We have often seen trees thus firmly rooted upon detached masses of bare rock. Now, dear heart, let this be a picture of you. Grip the Rock of Ages, and with the tiny root of little faith hold to Him. Let that tiny feeler grow; and meanwhile send out another to take a new grasp of the same rock. Lay hold on Jesus and keep hold on Jesus. Grow up into Him. Twist the roots of your nature, the fibers of your heart, about Him. He is as free to you as the rocks are to the fir tree. Be you as firmly lashed to Him as the pine is to the mountain's side.

FOR FURTHER THOUGHT

1. *In Romans 5:2, into what does a person enter by faith?*
2. *Read 1 Corinthians 2:4–5. Why didn't Paul speak about human wisdom?*

6

DIFFICULTY IN THE
WAY OF BELIEVING

IT may be that the reader feels a difficulty in believing. Let him consider. We cannot believe by an immediate act. The state of mind that we describe as believing is a result, following upon certain former states of mind. We come to faith by degrees. There may be such a thing as faith at first sight; but usually we reach faith by stages. We become interested, we consider, we hear evidence, we are convinced, and we are so led to believe. If, then, I wish to believe, but for some reason or other find that I cannot attain to faith, what shall I do? Shall I stand like a cow staring at a new gate, or shall I, like an intelligent being, use the proper means? If I wish to believe anything, what shall I do? We will answer according to the rules of common sense.

If I were told that the Sultan of Zanzibar was a good man, and it happened to be a matter of interest to me, I do not suppose I should feel any difficulty in believing it. But if for some reason I had a doubt about it yet wished to believe the news, how should I act? Should I not hunt up all the information within my reach about His Majesty, and try, by study of the newspapers and other documents, to arrive at the truth? Better still, if he happened to be in this country and would see me, and I could also converse with members of his court and citizens of his country, I should be greatly helped to arrive at a decision by using these sources of information. Evidence weighed and knowledge obtained lead up to faith. It is true that faith in Jesus is the gift of God, yet He usually bestows it in accordance with the laws of mind, and hence the Word of God tells us that faith comes by hearing. If you want to believe in Jesus, hear about Him, read about Him, think about Him, know about Him, and so you will find faith springing up in your heart like the wheat that comes up through the moisture and the heat operating upon the seed that has been sown. If I wished to have faith in a certain physician, I should ask for testimonials of his cures, I should wish to see the diplomas that certified his professional knowledge, and I should also like to hear what he has to say upon certain complicated cases. In fact, I should take means to know in order that I might believe.

Be much in hearing concerning Jesus. Souls by hundreds come to faith in Jesus under a ministry that sets Him forth clearly and constantly. Few remain unbelieving under a preacher whose great subject is Christ crucified. Hear no minister of any other sort. There are such.

I have heard of one who found in his pulpit Bible a paper bearing this text, "Sir, we would see Jesus." Go to the place of worship to see Jesus; and if you cannot even hear the mention of His name, take yourself off to another place where He is more thought of and is therefore more likely to be present.

Be much in reading about the Lord Jesus. The books of scripture are the lilies among which He feeds. The Bible is the window through which we may look and see our Lord. Read over the story of His sufferings and death with devout attention, and before long the Lord will cause faith secretly to enter your soul. The cross of Christ not only rewards faith, but also begets faith. Many a believer can say:

> When I view You, wounded, grieving,
> Breathless, on the cursed tree,
> Soon I feel my heart believing
> You have suffered thus for me.

If hearing and reading suffice not, then deliberately set your mind to work to overhaul the matter and have it out. Either believe, or know the reason why you do not believe. See the matter through to the utmost of your ability, and pray God to help you to make a thorough investigation and to come to an honest decision one way or the other. Consider who Jesus was and whether the constitution of His person does not entitle Him to confidence. Consider what He did and whether this also must not be good ground for trust. Consider Him as dying, rising from the dead, ascending, and ever living to intercede for transgressors; and see whether this does not entitle Him to be relied on by you. Then cry to Him and see if He does not hear you. When Usher wished to know whether Rutherford was indeed as holy a man as he was said to be, he went to his house as a beggar and gained a lodging. He heard the man of God pouring out his heart before the Lord in the night. If you would know Jesus, get as near to Him as you can by studying His character and appealing to His love.

At one time I might have needed evidence to make me believe in the Lord Jesus; but now I know Him so well, by proving Him, that I should need a very great deal of evidence to make me doubt Him. It is now more natural to me to trust than to disbelieve. This is the new nature triumphing; it was not so at the first. The novelty of faith is, in the beginning, a source of weakness; but act after act of trusting turns faith into a habit. Experience brings to faith strong confirmation.

> Souls by hundreds come to faith in Jesus under a ministry that sets Him forth clearly and constantly. Few remain unbelieving under a preacher whose great subject is Christ crucified.

I am not perplexed with doubt, because the truth that I believe has wrought a miracle on me. By its means I have received and still retain a new life, to which I was once a stranger, and this is confirmation of the strongest sort.

I am like the good man and his wife who had kept a lighthouse for years. A visitor, who came to see the lighthouse, looking out from the window over the waste of waters, asked the good woman, "Are you not afraid at night when the storm is out and the big waves dash right over the lantern? Do you not fear that the lighthouse and all that is in it will be carried away? I am sure I should be afraid to trust myself in a slender tower in the midst of the great billows."

The woman remarked that the idea never occurred to her now. She had lived there so long that she felt as safe on the lone rock as ever she did when she lived on the mainland.

As for her husband, when asked if he did not feel anxious when the wind blew a hurricane, he answered, "Yes, I feel anxious to keep the lamps well trimmed and the light burning, lest any vessel should be wrecked." As to anxiety about the safety of the lighthouse or his own personal security in it, he had outlived all that. Even so it is with the full-grown believer. He can humbly say, "I know whom I have believed and am persuaded that He is able to keep that which I have committed unto Him against that day."

From henceforth let no man trouble me with doubts and questionings. I bear in my soul the proofs of the Spirit's truth and power, and I will have none of your artful reasoning. The gospel to me is truth. I am content to perish if it were not true. I risk my soul's eternal fate upon the truth of the gospel, and I know that there is no risk in it. My one concern is to keep the lights burning that I may thereby benefit others. Only let the Lord give me oil enough to feed my lamp so that I may cast a ray across the dark and treacherous sea of life, and I am well content.

> *If you would know Jesus, get as near to Him as you can by studying His character and appealing to His love.*

Now, troubled seeker, if it be so, that your minister and many others in whom you confide, have found perfect peace and rest in the gospel, why shouldn't you? Is the Spirit of the Lord straitened? Don't His words do good to them that walk uprightly? Won't you also try their saving virtue?

Most true is the gospel, for God is its author. Believe it. Most able is the Savior, for He is the Son of God. Trust Him. Most powerful is His precious blood. Look to it for pardon. Most loving is His gracious heart. Run to it at once.

Thus would I urge the reader to seek faith; but if he be unwilling, what more can I do? I have brought the horse to the water, but I cannot make him drink. This, however, be it remembered—unbelief is willful when evidence is put in a man's way and he refuses carefully to examine it. He who does not desire to know and accept the truth has himself to thank if he dies with a lie in his right hand. It is true that he who believes and is baptized shall be saved: It is equally true that he who believes not shall be damned.

For Further Thought

1. *According to Romans 10:17, how does faith come to a person?*
2. *Acts 13:39 says that there are ways in which the Law of Moses cannot make us just before God. What does this verse say is the way to justification?*

7

A Helpful Survey

To help the seeker to a true faith in Jesus, I would remind him of the work of the Lord Jesus in the room and place and stead of sinners. When we were without strength, "Christ died for the ungodly."

Upon one declaration of scripture, let the reader fix his eye: "By His stripes we are healed" (Isa. 53:5). God here treats sin as a disease, and He sets before us the costly remedy that He has provided.

I ask you very solemnly to accompany me in your meditations for a few minutes while I bring before you the stripes of the Lord Jesus. God resolved to restore us, and therefore He sent His only begotten Son that He might descend into this world to take upon Himself our nature in order to obtain our redemption. He lived as a man among men; and in due time, after thirty years or more of obedience, the time came when He should do us the greatest service of all, namely, stand in our stead and bear our chastisement. He went to Gethsemane, and there, at the first taste of our bitter cup, He sweated great drops of blood. He went to Pilate's hall and Herod's judgment seat and there drank drinks of pain and scorn in our room and place. Last of all, they took Him to the cross and nailed Him there to die—to die in our stead. The word *stripes* is used to describe His sufferings, both of body and of soul. The whole of Christ was made a sacrifice for us: His whole manhood suffered. As to His body, it shared with His mind in a grief that never can be described. In the beginning of His passion, when He emphatically suffered instead of us, He was in an agony, and from His bodily frame a bloody sweat distilled so copiously as to fall to the ground. It is very rarely that a man sweats blood. There have been one or two instances of it, and they have been followed by almost immediate death; but our Savior lived after an agony that, to anyone else, would have proved fatal. Before He could cleanse His face from this dreadful crimson, they hurried Him to the high priest's hall. In the dead of night they bound Him and led Him away. Quickly they took Him to Pilate and to Herod. These scourged Him, and their soldiers spit in His face, buffeted Him, and put on His head a crown of thorns. Scourging is one of the most awful tortures that can be inflicted by malice. It was formerly the disgrace of the British army that the "cat" was used upon the soldier: a brutal infliction of torture. But to the Roman, cruelty was so natural that he made his common punishments worse than brutal. The Roman scourge is said to have been made of the sinews of oxen, twisted into knots, and into these knots were inserted slivers of bone and hip bones of sheep, so that every time the scourge fell upon the bare back, "the plowers made deep furrows." Our Savior was called upon to endure the fierce pain of the Roman scourge, and this not as the end of His punishment, but as a preface to crucifixion. To this His persecutors added buffeting and plucking of the hair. They spared Him no form of pain. In all His faintness, through bleeding and fasting, they made Him carry His cross until another was forced, by the forethought of their cruelty, to bear it, lest their victim should die on the road. They stripped Him, threw Him down, and nailed Him to the wood. They pierced His hands and His feet. They lifted up the tree with Him upon it, and then dashed it down into its place in the ground, so that all His limbs were dislocated, according to the lament of the Twenty-second Psalm: "I am poured out like water, and all my bones are out of joint." He hung in the burning sun till the fever dissolved His strength, and He said, "My heart is like wax; it is melted in the midst of my bowels. My strength is dried up like a potsherd; and my tongue cleaveth to my jaws; and thou hast brought me into the dust of death" (Ps. 22:14–15 KJV). There He hung, a spectacle to God and men. His feet first sustained the weight of His body, till the nails tore through the tender nerves. Then the painful load began to drag upon His hands and rend those sensitive parts of His frame. How small a wound in the hand has brought on lockjaw! How awful must have been the torment caused by that dragging iron tearing through the delicate parts of the hands and feet! Now were all manner of bodily pains centered in His tortured frame. All the while His enemies stood around, pointing at Him in scorn, thrusting out their tongues in mockery, jesting at His prayers, and gloating over His sufferings. He cried, "I thirst" (John 19:28), and then they gave Him vinegar mingled with gall. After a while He said, "It is finished" (19:30). He had endured the utmost of appointed grief and had made full vindication to divine justice: Then, and not till then, He gave up the spirit. Holy men of old have enlarged most lovingly upon the bodily sufferings of our Lord, and I have no hesitation in doing the same, trusting that trembling sinners may see salvation in these painful stripes of the Redeemer.

> *God resolved to restore us, and therefore He sent His only begotten Son that He might descend into this world to take upon Himself our nature in order to obtain our redemption.*

To describe the outward sufferings of our Lord is not easy: I acknowledge that I have failed. But His soul sufferings, which were the soul of His sufferings, who can even conceive, much less express, what they were? At the very first I told you that He sweat great drops of blood. That was His heart driving out its life floods to the surface through the terrible depression of spirit that was upon Him. He said, "My soul is exceeding sorrowful, even unto death" (Matt. 26:38 KJV). The betrayal by Judas and the desertion of the Twelve grieved our Lord, but the weight of our sin was the real pressure on His heart. Our guilt was the olive press that forced from Him the moisture of His life. No language can ever tell His agony in prospect of His death; how little then can we conceive the death itself? When nailed to the cross, He endured what no martyr ever suffered; for martyrs, when they have died, have been so sustained of God that they have rejoiced amid their pain. But our Redeemer was forsaken of His Father, until He cried, "My God, My God, why have You forsaken Me?" (Matt. 27:46). That was the bitterest cry of all, the utmost depth of His unfathomable grief. Yet was it needful that He should be deserted, because God must turn His back on sin and consequently upon Him who was made sin for us. The soul of the great substitute suffered a horror of misery instead of that horror of hell into which sinners would have been plunged had He not taken their sin upon Himself and been made a curse for them. "It is written, 'Cursed is everyone who hangs on a tree'" (Gal. 3:13), but who knows what that curse means?

The remedy for your sins and mine is found in the substitutionary sufferings of the Lord Jesus, and in these only. These stripes of the Lord Jesus Christ were on our behalf.

Do you inquire, "Is there anything for us to do to remove the guilt of sin?"

I answer: There is nothing whatever for you to do. By the stripes of Jesus we are healed. All those stripes He has endured and left not one of them for us to bear.

"But must we not believe on Him?" Yes, certainly. If I say of a certain ointment that it heals, I do not deny that you need a bandage with which to apply it to the wound. Faith is the linen that binds the plaster of Christ's reconciliation to the sore of our sin. The linen does not heal; that is the work of the ointment. So faith does not heal; that is the work of the atonement of Christ.

"But we must repent," cries another.

Assuredly we must, and shall, for repentance is the first sign of healing; but the stripes of Jesus heal us, and not our repentance. These stripes, when applied to the heart, work repentance in us: We hate sin because it made Jesus suffer.

When you intelligently trust in Jesus as having suffered for you, then you discover the fact that God will never punish you for the same offense for which Jesus died. His justice will not permit Him to see the debt paid, first, by the Surety, and then again by the debtor. Justice cannot twice demand a recompense. If my bleeding Surety has borne my guilt, then I cannot bear it. Accepting Christ Jesus as suffering for me, I have accepted a complete discharge from judicial liability. I have been condemned in Christ, and there is, therefore, now no condemnation to me anymore. This is the groundwork of the security of the sinner who believes in Jesus: He lives because Jesus died in his place and stead; and he is acceptable before God because Jesus is accepted. The person for whom Jesus is an accepted substitute must go free; none can touch him; he is clear. O my hearer, will you have Jesus Christ to be your substitute? If so, you are free, because he who believes on Him is not condemned by God. Thus with His stripes we are healed.

Although it is by no means a difficult thing in itself to believe Him who cannot lie and to trust in the One whom we know to be able to save, yet something may intervene that may render even this a hard thing to my reader. That hindrance may be a secret, yet it may be nonetheless real. A door may be closed, not by a great stone that all can see, but by an invisible bolt that shoots into a deadlock quite out of sight. A man may have good eyes yet may not be able to see an object because another substance comes in the way. You could not even see the sun if a handkerchief or a mere piece of rag was tied over your face. Oh, the bandages men persist in binding over their own eyes!

A sweet sin, harbored in the heart, will prevent a soul from laying hold upon Christ by faith. The Lord Jesus has come to save us from sinning; and if we are resolved to go on sinning, Christ and our souls will never agree. If a man takes poison and a doctor is called in to save his life, he may have a sure antidote ready; but if the patient persists in keeping the poison bottle at his lips and will continue to swallow the deadly drops, how can the doctor save him? Salvation consists largely in parting the sinner from his sin, and the very nature of salvation would have to be changed before we could speak of a man's being saved when he is loving sin and willfully living in it. A man cannot be made white and yet continue black; he cannot be healed yet remain sick; neither can anyone be saved and be still a lover of evil.

> The betrayal by Judas and the desertion of the Twelve grieved our Lord, but the weight of our sin was the real pressure on His heart.

Believing in Christ will save a drunkard. That is to say, he will be saved from being a drunkard; but if he determines still to make himself intoxicated, he is not saved from it, and he has not truly believed in Jesus. A liar can by faith be saved from falsehood, but then he leaves off lying and is careful to speak the truth. Anyone can see with half an eye that he cannot be saved from being a liar and yet go on in his old style of deceit and untruthfulness. A person who is at enmity with another will be saved from that feeling of enmity by believing in the Lord Jesus; but if he vows that he will still cherish the feeling of hate, it is clear that he is not saved from it and equally clear that he has not believed in the Lord Jesus unto salvation. The great matter is to be delivered from the love of sin. This is the sure effect of trust in the Savior; but if this effect is so far from being desired that it is even refused, all talk of trusting in the Savior for salvation is an idle tale.

A man goes to the shipping office and asks if he can be taken to America. He is assured that a ship is just ready and that he has only to go on board and he will soon reach New York. "But," says he, "I want to stop at home in England and mind my shop all the time I am crossing the Atlantic."

The agent thinks he is talking to a madman and tells him to go about his business and not waste his time by playing the fool.

To pretend to trust Christ to save you from sin while you are still determined to continue in it is making a mockery of Christ. I pray my reader not to be guilty of such profanity. Let him not dream that the holy Jesus will be the patron of iniquity.

Consider a tree that has ivy growing all over it strangling it, sucking out its life, and killing it. Can that tree be saved? The gardener thinks it can be. He is willing to do his best. But before he begins to use his ax and his knife, he is told that he must not cut away the ivy. "Then," he says, "it is impossible. It is the ivy that is killing the tree, and if you want the tree saved, you cannot save the ivy. If you trust me to preserve the tree, you must let me get the deadly climber away from it." Is not that common sense? Certainly it is. You do not trust the tree to the gardener unless you trust him to cut away that which is deadly to it. If the sinner will keep his sin, he must die in it; if he is willing to be rescued from his sin, the Lord Jesus is able to do it and will do it if the sinner commits his case to Jesus' care.

> *A* man cannot be made white and yet continue black; he cannot be healed yet remain sick; neither can anyone be saved and be still a lover of evil.

What, then, is your darling sin? Is it any gross wrongdoing? Then very shame should make you cease from it. Is it love of the world or fear of men or longing for evil gains? Surely, none of these things should reconcile you to living in enmity with God and beneath His frown. Is it a human love that is eating like a canker into the heart? Can any creature rival the Lord Jesus? Is it not idolatry to allow any earthly thing to compare for one instant with the Lord God?

"Well," says one, "for me to give up the particular sin by which I am held captive would be to my serious injury in business. It would ruin my prospects and lessen my usefulness in many ways."

If it be so, you have your case met by the words of the Lord Jesus, who bids you to pluck out your eye and cut off your hand or foot and cast it from you rather than be cast into hell. It is better to enter into life with one eye, with the poorest prospects, than to keep all your hopes and be out of Christ. Better be a lame believer than a leaping sinner. Better be in the rear rank for life in the army of Christ than lead the van and be a chief officer under the command of Satan. If you win Christ, it will little matter what you lose. No doubt many have had to suffer that which has maimed and lamed them for this life, but if they have entered thereby into eternal life, they have been great gainers.

It comes to this, my friend, as it did with John Bunyan; a voice now speaks to you and says:

Will you keep your sin and go to hell?
Or,
Leave your sin and go to heaven?

The point should be decided before you quit the spot. In the name of God, I ask you, which shall it be—Christ and salvation or the favorite sin and damnation? There is no middle course. Waiting or refusing to decide will practically be a sure decision for the evil one. He who stands questioning whether he will be honest is already out of the straight line. He who does not know whether he wishes to be cleansed from sin gives evidence of a foul heart.

If you are eager to give up every evil way, our Lord Jesus will enable you to do so at once. His grace has already changed the direction of your desires. In fact, your heart is renewed. Therefore, rest on Him to strengthen you to battle with temptations as they arise and to fulfill the Lord's commands from day to day. The Lord Jesus is great at making the lame man to leap like a hart and enabling those who are sick of the palsy to take up their beds and walk. He will make you able to conquer the evil habit. He will even cast the demon out of you. Yes, if you had seven demons, He could drive them out at once; there is no limit to His power to cleanse and sanctify. Now that you are willing to be made whole, the great difficulty is removed. He who has set the will right can arrange all your other powers and make them move to His praise. You would not have earnestly desired to quit all sin if He had not secretly inclined you in that direction. If you now trust Him, it will be clear that He has begun a good work in you, and we feel assured that He will carry it on.

In these days, a simple, childlike faith is very rare, but the usual thing is to believe nothing and question everything. Doubts are as plentiful as blackberries, and all hands and lips are stained with them. To me it seems very strange that men should hunt up difficulties as to their own salvation. If I were doomed to die and I had a hint of mercy, I am sure I should not set my wits to work to find out reasons why I should not be pardoned. I could leave my enemies to do that: I should be on the lookout in a very different direction. If I were drowning, I should sooner catch at a straw than push a life belt away from me. To reason against one's own life is a sort of constructive suicide of which only a drunken man would be guilty. To argue against your only hope is like a foolish man sitting on a bough and chopping it away so as to let himself down. Who but an idiot would do that? Yet many appear to be special pleaders for their own ruin. They hunt the Bible through for threatening texts, and when they are done with that, they turn to reason, philosophy, and skepticism to shut the door in their own faces. Surely this is poor employment for a sensible man.

Many nowadays who cannot quite get away from religious thought are able to stave off the inconvenient pressure of conscience by quibbling over the great truths of revelation. Great mysteries are in the book of God of necessity; for how can the infinite God speak so that finite man can grasp all His thoughts? But it is the height of folly to get discussing these deep things and to leave plain, soul-saving truths in abeyance. It reminds one of the two philosophers who debated about food and went away empty from the table while the common countryman in the corner asked no question but used his knife and fork with great diligence and went on his way rejoicing. Thousands are now happy in the Lord through receiving the gospel like little children; while others, who can always see difficulties or invent them, are as far-off as ever from any comfortable hope of salvation. I know many very decent people who seem to have resolved never to come to Christ till they can understand how the doctrine of election is consistent with the free invitations of the gospel. I might just as well determine never to eat a morsel of bread till it has been explained to me how it is that God keeps me alive, and yet I must eat to live. The fact is that most of us know quite enough already, and the real want with us is not light in the head but truth in the heart; not help over difficulties but grace to make us hate sin and seek reconciliation.

Here let me add a warning against tampering with the Word of God. No habit can be more ruinous to the soul. It is cool, contemptuous impertinence to sit down and correct your Maker, and it tends to make the heart harder than the nether millstone. We remember one who used a penknife on his Bible, and it was not long before he had given up all his former beliefs. The spirit of reverence is healthy, but the impertinence of criticizing the inspired Word is destructive of all proper feeling toward God.

If ever a man does feel his need of a Savior after treating scripture with a proud, critical spirit, he is very apt to find his conscience standing in the way and hindering him from comfort by reminding him of his ill treatment of the sacred Word. It comes hard to him to draw consolation out of passages of the Bible that he has treated lightly or even set aside altogether as unworthy of consideration. In his distress the sacred texts seem to laugh at his calamity. When the time of need comes, the wells he stopped with stones yield no water for his thirst. Beware when you despise a scripture lest you cast away the only friend who can help you in the hour of agony.

A certain German duke was accustomed to call upon his servant to read a chapter of the Bible to him every morning. When anything did not square with his judgment, he would sternly cry, "Hans, strike that out."

At length Hans was a long time before he began to read. He fumbled over the book till his master called out, "Hans, why do you not read?"

Then Hans answered, "Sir, there is hardly anything left. It is all struck out!"

One day his master's objections had run one way, and another day they had taken another turn and another set of passages had been blotted, till nothing was left to instruct or comfort him.

Let us not, by carping criticism, destroy our own mercies. We may yet need those promises that appear needless; and those portions of holy writ that have been most assailed by skeptics may yet prove essential to our very life. Therefore let us guard the priceless treasure of the Bible and determine never to resign a single line of it.

What have we to do with obscure questions while our souls are in peril? The way to escape from sin is plain enough. The wayfaring man, though a fool, shall not err therein. God has not mocked us with a salvation that we cannot understand. "Believe and live" is a command that a little child may comprehend and obey.

> *Doubt no more, but now believe;*
> *Question not, but just receive.*
> *Artful doubts and reasonings be*
> *Nailed with Jesus to the tree.*

Instead of making a trivial objection to scripture, the man who is led of the Spirit of God will close in with the Lord Jesus at once. Seeing that thousands of decent, commonsense people—people, too, of the best character—are trusting their all with Jesus, he will do the same and have done with further delays. Then will he have begun a life worth living, and he may have done with further fear. He may at once advance to that higher and better way of living that grows out of love to Jesus, the Savior. Why shouldn't the reader do so at once? Oh, that he would!

A Newark, New Jersey, butcher received a letter from his old home in Germany, notifying that he had, by the death of a relative, fallen heir to a considerable amount of money. He was cutting up a pig at the time. After reading the letter, he hastily tore off his dirty apron and did not stop to see the pork cut up into sausages but left the shop to make preparations for going home to Germany. Do you blame him, or would you have had him stop in Newark with his block and his cleaver?

See here the operation of faith. The butcher believed what was told him and acted on it at once. Sensible fellow, too!

God has sent His messages to man, telling him the good news of salvation. When a man believes the good news to be true, he accepts the blessing announced to him and hastens to lay hold upon it. If he truly believes, he will at once take Christ, with all He has to bestow, turn from his present evil ways, and set out for the heavenly city, where the full blessing is to be enjoyed. He cannot be holy too soon or too early quit the ways of sin. If a man could really see what sin is, he would flee from it as from a deadly serpent and rejoice to be freed from it by Christ Jesus.

FOR FURTHER THOUGHT

1. *According to 1 Peter 3:18, why did Christ die for us?*
2. *Read Galatians 3:13. Why did God curse Jesus Christ as He hung on the cross?*

8

WITHOUT FAITH NO SALVATION

SOME think it hard that there should be nothing for them but ruin if they will not believe in Jesus Christ; but if you will think for a minute, you will see that it is just and reasonable. I suppose there is no way for a man to keep his strength up except by eating. If you were to say, "I will not eat again, I despise such animalism," you might go to Madeira or travel in all lands (supposing you lived long enough!), but you would most certainly find that no climate and no exercise would avail to keep you alive if you refused food.

Would you then complain, "It is a hard thing that I should die because I do not believe in eating"? It is not an unjust thing that if you are so foolish as not to eat, you must die. It is precisely so with believing. "Believe, and you are saved." If you will not believe, it is no hard thing that you should be lost. It would be strange indeed if it were not to be the case.

A man who is thirsty stands before a fountain. "No," he says, "I will never touch a drop of moisture as long as I live. Cannot I get my thirst quenched in my own way?"

We tell him no, he must drink or die.

He says, "I will never drink, but it is a hard thing that I must therefore die. It is a bigoted, cruel thing to tell me so."

He is wrong. His thirst is the inevitable result of neglecting a law of nature.

You, too, must believe or die; why refuse to obey the command? Drink, man, drink! Take Christ and live. There is the way of salvation, and to enter you must trust Christ; but there is nothing hard in the fact that you must perish if you will not trust the Savior.

Here is a man out at sea. He has a chart, and that chart, if well studied, will, with the help of the compass, guide him to his journey's end. The pole star gleams out amid the cloud breaks, and that, too, will help him. "No," says he, "I will have nothing to do with your stars; I do not believe in the

North Pole. I shall not attend to that little thing inside the box; one needle is as good as another needle. I have no faith in your chart, and I will have nothing to do with it. The art of navigation is only a lot of nonsense, got up by people on purpose to make money, and I will not be tricked by it." The man never reaches port, and he says it is a very hard thing—a very hard thing. I do not think so.

Some of you say, "I am not going to read the scriptures; I am not going to listen to your talk about Jesus Christ: I do not believe in such things." Then Jesus says he who believes not shall be damned.

"That's very hard," say you.

But it is not so. It is not harder than the fact that if you reject the compass and the pole star, you will not reach your port. There is no help for it; it must be so.

> *There is the way of salvation, and to enter you must trust Christ; but there is nothing hard in the fact that you must perish if you will not trust the Savior.*

You say you will have nothing to do with Jesus and His blood, and you pooh-pooh all religion. You will find it hard to laugh these matters down when you come to die, when the clammy sweat must be wiped from your brow and your heart beats against your ribs as if it wanted to leap out and fly away from God. O soul! You will find then that those Sundays and those services and this old book are something more and better than you thought they were, and you will wonder that you were so simple as to neglect any true help to salvation. Above all, what woe it will be to have neglected Christ, that pole star which alone can guide the mariner to the haven of rest!

Where do you live?

You live, perhaps, on the other side of the river, and you have to cross a bridge before you can get home. You have been so silly as to nurse the notion that you do not believe in bridges or in boats or in the existence of such a thing as water. You say, "I am not going over any of your bridges, and I shall not get into any of your boats. I do not believe that there is a river or that there is any such stuff as water." You are going home, and soon you come to the old bridge, but you will not cross it. Yonder is a boat; but you are determined that you will not get into it. There is the river, and you resolve that you will not cross it in the usual way, yet you think it is very hard that you cannot get home. Surely something has destroyed your reasoning powers, for you would not think it so hard if you were in your senses. If a man will not do the thing that is necessary to gain a certain end, how can he expect to gain that end?

You have taken poison, and the physician brings an antidote and says, "Take it quickly or you will die; but if you take it quickly, I will guarantee that the poison will be neutralized."

But you say, "No, doctor, I do not believe in antidotes. Let everything take its course; let every tub stand on its own bottom; I will have nothing to do with your remedy. Besides, I do not believe that there is any remedy for the poison I have taken; and what is more, I don't care whether there is or not."

Well, sir, you will die; and when the coroner's inquest is held on your body, the verdict will be, "Served him right!" So will it be with you if, having heard the gospel of Jesus Christ, you say, "I am too much of an advanced man to have anything to do with that old-fashioned notion of substitution. I shall not attend to the preacher's talk about sacrifice and blood-shedding."

Then, when you perish, the verdict given by your conscience that will sit upon the King's quest at last, will run thus: "Suicide: He destroyed his own soul." So says the old book—"O Israel, you have destroyed yourself!" Reader, I implore you, do not so.

For Further Thought

1. *Read John 20:24–29. What did Thomas say were the conditions for his believing in Jesus' resurrection? (See verse 25.)*
2. *In verse 29, what was Jesus' response to Thomas?*

9

To Those Who Have Believed

FRIENDS, if now you have begun to trust the Lord, trust Him out and out. Let your faith be the most real and practical thing in your whole life. Don't trust the Lord in mere sentiment about a few great spiritual things, but trust Him for everything forever, for time and eternity, for body and soul. See how the Lord hangs the world upon nothing but His own word! It has neither prop nor pillar. Yonder great arch of heaven stands without a buttress or a wooden center. The Lord can and will bear all the strain that faith can ever put upon Him. The greatest troubles are easy to His power, and the darkest mysteries are clear to His wisdom. Trust God to the hilt. Lean, and lean hard; yes, lean all your weight and every other weight upon the mighty God of Jacob.

The future you can safely leave with the Lord, who ever lives and never changes. The past is now in your Savior's hand, and you shall never be condemned for it, whatever it may have been, for the Lord has cast your iniquities into the midst of the sea. Believe at this moment in your present privileges. *You are saved*. If you are a believer in the Lord Jesus, you have passed from death unto life, and *You are saved*.

In the old slave days a lady brought her black servant on board an English ship, and she laughingly said to the captain, "I suppose if I and Aunt Chloe were to go to England she would be free?"

"Madam," said the captain, "she is now free. The moment she came on board a British vessel she was free."

When the Negro woman knew this, she did not leave the ship—not she. It was not the hope of liberty that made her bold, but the fact of liberty.

So you are not now merely hoping for eternal life, but he who believes in Him has everlasting life. Accept this as a fact revealed in the sacred Word and begin to rejoice accordingly. Do not reason about it or call it in question; believe it and leap for joy.

I want my reader, upon believing in the Lord Jesus, to believe for eternal salvation. Do not be content with the notion that you can receive a new birth that will die out, a heavenly life that will expire, a pardon that will be recalled. The Lord Jesus gives to His sheep eternal life, and do not be at rest until you have it. Now, if it is eternal, how can it die out? Be saved out and out, for eternity. There is a living and incorruptible seed that lives and abides forever; do not be put off with a temporary change, a sort of grace that will only bloom to fade. You are now starting on the railway of grace—take a ticket all the way through. I have no commission to preach to you salvation for a time. The gospel I am bidden to set before you is this: He who believes and is baptized shall be saved. He shall be saved from sin, from going back to sin, from turning aside to the broad road. May the Holy Spirit lead you to believe for nothing less than that.

> *Trust God to the hilt. Lean, and lean hard; yes, lean all your weight and every other weight upon the mighty God of Jacob.*

"Do you mean," says one, "that I am to believe if I once trust Christ I shall be saved whatever sin I may choose to commit?"

I have never said anything of the kind. I have described true salvation as a thorough change of heart of so radical a kind that it will alter your tastes and desires. And I say that if you have such a change wrought in you by the Holy Spirit, it will be permanent, for the Lord's work is not like the cheap work of the present day, which soon goes to pieces. Trust the Lord to keep you, however long you may live and however much you may be tempted, and according to your faith be it unto you. Believe in Jesus for everlasting life.

Oh, that you may also trust the Lord for all the sufferings of this present time! In the world you will have tribulation; learn by faith to know that all things work together for good, and then submit yourself to the Lord's will. Look at the sheep when it is being shorn. If it lies quite still, the shears will not hurt it; if it struggles, or even shrinks, it may be pricked. Submit yourselves under the hand of God, and affliction will lose its sharpness. Self-will and repining cause us a hundred times more grief than our afflictions themselves. So believe your Lord as to be certain that His will must be far better than yours, and therefore you not only submit to it, but even rejoice in it.

Trust the Lord Jesus in the matter of sanctification. Certain friends appear to think that the Lord Jesus cannot sanctify them wholly, spirit, soul, and body. Hence they willingly give way to such and such sins under the notion that there is no help for it, but that they must pay tribute to the devil as long as they live in that particular form. Do not basely bow your neck in bondage to any sin, but strike hard for liberty. Be it anger, unbelief, sloth, or any other form of iniquity, we are able, by divine grace, to drive out the Canaanite; and what is more, we must drive him out. No virtue is impossible to him who believes in Jesus, and no sin need have victory over him. Indeed, it is written that sin shall not have dominion over you: for you are not under the law, but under grace. Believe for high degrees of joy in the Lord and likeness to Jesus, and advance to take full possession of these precious things. For as you believe, so shall it be unto you. All things are possible to him who believes, and he who is the chief of sinners may yet be not a whit behind the greatest of saints.

> Believe for high degrees of joy in the Lord and likeness to Jesus, and advance to take full possession of these precious things. For as you believe, so shall it be unto you.

Often realize the joy of heaven. This is grand faith, yet it is no more than we ought to have. Within a very short time, the man who believes in the Lord Jesus shall be with Him where He is. This head will wear a crown; these eyes shall see the King in His beauty; these ears shall hear His own dear voice; this soul shall be in glory; and this poor body shall be raised from the dead and joined in incorruption to the perfected soul! Glory, glory, glory so near, so sure! Let us at once rehearse the music and anticipate the bliss!

But cries one, "We are not there yet."

No, but faith fills us with delight in the blessed prospect, and meanwhile it sustains us on the road.

Reader, I long that you may be a firm believer in the Lord alone. I want you to get wholly upon the rock and not keep a foot on the sand. In this mortal life, trust God for all things, and trust Him alone. This is the way to live. I know it by experience. God's bare arm is quite enough to lean upon.

I will give you a bit of the experience of an old laboring man I once knew. He feared God above many and was very deeply taught of the Spirit. He was great at hedging and ditching but greater at simple trust. Here is how he described faith:

> It was a bitter winter, and I had no work and no bread in the house. The children were crying. The snow was deep, and my way was dark. My old master told me I might have a bit of wood when I wanted it, so I thought a bit of fire would warm the poor children, and I went out with my chopper to get some fuel. I was standing near a deep ditch full of snow, which had drifted into it many feet deep—in fact, I did not know how deep. While aiming a blow at a bit of wood, my pruning hook slipped out of my hand and went right down into the snow, where I could not hope to find it. Standing there with no food, no fire, and the chopper gone, something seemed to say to me, "Will Richardson, can you trust God now?" and my very soul said, "That I can."

This is true faith—the faith that trusts the Lord when the pruning hook is gone; the faith that believes God when all outward appearances give Him the lie. The faith that is happy with God alone when all friends turn their backs upon you. Dear reader, may you and I have this precious faith, this real faith, and this God-honoring faith! The Lord's truth deserves it, His love claims it, and His faithfulness constrains it. Happy is He who has it! He is the man whom the Lord loves, and the world shall be made to know it before all is finished.

After all, the very best faith is an everyday faith: the faith that deals with bread and water, coats and stockings, children and cattle, house rent and weather. The superfine confectionery religion that is only available on Sundays and in living room meetings and Bible readings will never take a soul to heaven till life becomes one long conference and there are seven Sabbaths in a week. Faith is doing her very best when for many years she plods on, month by month, trusting the Lord about the sick husband, the failing daughter, the declining business, the unconverted friend, and such like things.

Faith also helps us to use the world and not abuse it. It is good at hard work and at daily duty. It is not an angelic thing for skies and stars; it is a human grace, at home in kitchens and workshops. It is a sort of maid-of-all-work and is at home at every kind of labor and in every rank of life. It is a grace for every day, all the year round. Holy confidence in God is never out of work. Faith's work is so valued at the heavenly court that she always has one fine piece of work or another on the wheel or in the furnace. Men dream that heroes are only to be made on special occasions, once or twice in a century; but in truth the finest heroes are homespun and are more often hidden in obscurity than observed on the public platform. Trust in the living God is the bullion out of which heroism is coined. Perseverance in well-doing is one of the fields in which faith grows not flowers, but the wheat of her harvest. Plodding on in hard work, bringing up a family on a few dollars a week, bearing constant pain with patience, and so forth—these are the feats of valor through which God is glorified by the rank and file of His believing people.

Reader, you and I will be of one mind in this: We will not have an intense longing to be great, but we will be eager to be good. For this we will rely upon the Lord our God, whose we are, and whom we serve. We will ask to be made holy throughout every day of the week. We will pray to our God as much about our daily business as about our soul's salvation. We will trust Him concerning our farm and our turnips and our cows, as well as concerning our spiritual privileges and our hope of heaven. The Lord Jehovah is our household God; Jesus is our Brother born for adversity; and the Holy Spirit is our Comforter in every hour of trial. We have not an unapproachable God: He hears, He pities, and He helps. Let us trust Him without a break, without a doubt, without a hesitation. The life of faith is life within God's wicket gate. If we have hitherto stood trembling outside in the wide world of unbelief, may the Holy Spirit enable us now to take the great decisive step and say, once for all, "Lord, I believe: Help my unbelief!"

For Further Thought

1. *How many conditions to salvation are there in John 6:47?*
2. *Of what and through what is a believer born again? (See 1 Peter 1:23.)*

The Greatest Fight in the World:
C. H. Spurgeon's Final Manifesto

CONTENTS

Fight the good fight of faith.
1 TIMOTHY 6:12

INTRODUCTION

MAY all the prayers that have already been offered up be answered abundantly and speedily! May more of such pleading follow that in which we have united! The most memorable part of past conferences has been the holy concert of believing prayer; and I trust we are not falling off in that respect, but growing yet more fervent and prevalent in intercession. On his knees the believer is invincible.

I am greatly concerned about this address for many months before it comes on: Assuredly it is to me the child of many prayers. I should like to be able to speak well on so worthy an occasion, wherein the best of speech may well be enlisted; but I desire to be, as our brother's prayer has put it, absolutely in the Lord's hands, in this matter as well as in every other. I would be willing to speak with stammering tongue if God's purpose could so be answered more fully; and I would even gladly lose all power of speech if, by being famished as to human words, you might feed the better on that spiritual meat that is to be found alone in Him who is the incarnate Word of God.

I may say to you, as speakers, that I am persuaded we should prepare ourselves with diligence and try to do our very best in our great Master's service. I think I have read that when a handful of lionlike Greeks held the pass against the Persians, a spy who came to see what they were doing went back and told the great king that they were poor creatures, for they were busied in combing their hair. The despot saw things in a true light when he learned that a people who could adjust their hair before battle had set a great value on their heads and would not bow them to a coward's death. If we are very careful to use our best language when proclaiming eternal truths, we may leave our opponents to infer that we are still more careful of the doctrines themselves. We must not be untidy soldiers when a great fight is before us, for that would look like despondency. Into the battle against false doctrine, worldliness, and sin we advance without a fear as to the ultimate issue; and therefore our talk should not be that of ragged passion, but of well-considered principle. It is not ours to be slovenly, since we look to be triumphant. Do your work well at this time that all men may see that you are not going to be driven from it.

The Persian said, when on another occasion he saw a handful of warriors advancing, "That little handful of men! Surely, they cannot mean fighting!" But one who stood by said, "Yes, they do, for they have burnished their shields and brightened their armor." Men mean business, depend upon it, when they are not to be hurried into disorder. It was the way among the Greeks, when they had a bloody day before them, to show the stern joy of warriors by being well adorned. I think, brethren, that when we have great work to do for Christ, and mean doing it, we shall not go to the pulpit or the platform to say the first thing that comes to the lips. If we speak for Jesus, we ought to speak at our best, though even then men are not killed by the glitter of shields or by the smoothness of a warrior's hair; but a higher power is needed to cut through coats of mail. To the God of armies I look up. May He defend the right! But with no careless step do I advance to the front; neither does any doubt possess me. We are feeble, but the Lord our God is mighty, and the battle is the Lord's rather than ours.

Only one fear is upon me to a certain degree. I am anxious that my deep sense of responsibility may not lessen my efficiency. A man may feel that he ought to do so well that, for that very reason, he may not do as well as he might. An overpowering feeling of responsibility may breed paralysis. I once recommended a young clerk to a bank, and his friends very properly gave him strict charge to be very careful in his figures. This advice he heard times out of mind. He became so extremely careful as to grow nervous, and whereas he had been accurate before, his anxiety caused him to make blunder after blunder till he left his situation. It is possible to be so anxious as to how and what you shall speak that your manner grows constrained and you forget those very points you meant to make most prominent.

Brethren, I am telling some of my private thoughts to you because we are alike in our calling; and having the same experiences, it does us good to know that it is so. We who lead have the same weaknesses and troubles as you who follow. We must prepare, but we must also trust in Him without whom nothing begins, continues, or ends aright.

I have this comfort, that even if I should not speak adequately upon my theme, the topic itself will speak to you. There is something even in starting an appropriate subject. If a man speaks well upon a subject that has no practical importance, it is not well that he should have spoken. As one of the ancients said, "It is idle to speak much to the point upon a matter which itself is not to the point." Carve a cherrystone with the utmost skill, and at best it is but a cherrystone, while a diamond if badly cut is still a precious stone. If the matter be of great weight, even if the man cannot speak up to his theme, yet to call attention to it is no vain thing. The subjects that we shall consider at this time ought to be considered, and to be considered just now. I have chosen present and pressing truths, and if you will think them out for yourselves, you will not lose the time occupied by this address. With what inward fervor do I pray that we may all be profited by this hour of meditation!

Happily the themes are such that I can exemplify them even in this address. As a smith can teach his apprentice while making a horseshoe, so can we make our own sermons examples of the doctrine they contain. In this case we can practice what we preach if the Lord be with us. A lecturer in cookery instructs his pupils by following his own recipes. He prepares a dish before his audience, and while he describes the viands and their preparation, he tastes the food himself, and his friends are refreshed also. He will succeed by his dainty dishes even if he is not a man of eloquent speech. The man who feeds is surer of success than he who only plays well upon an instrument and leaves with his audience no memory but that of pleasant sound. If the subjects that we bring before our people are in themselves good, they will make up for our want of skill in setting them forth. So long as the guests get the spiritual meat, the servitor at the table may be happy to be forgotten.

My topics have to do with our life work, with the crusade against error and sin in which we are engaged. I hope that every man here wears the red cross on his heart and is pledged to do and dare for Christ and for His cross and never to be satisfied till Christ's foes are routed and Christ Himself is satisfied. Our fathers used to speak of "the cause of God and truth," and it is for this that we bear arms, the few against the many, the feeble against the mighty. Oh, to be found good soldiers of Jesus Christ!

Three things are of the utmost importance just now, and indeed they always have stood, and always will stand in the front rank for practical purposes. The first is our armory, which is the inspired Word; the second is our army, the church of the living God, called out by Himself, which we must lead under our Lord's command; and the third is our strength, by which we wear the armor and wield the sword. The Holy Spirit is our power to be and to do, to suffer and to serve, to grow and to fight, to wrestle and to overcome. Our third theme is of main importance, and though we place it last, we rank it first.

1

Our Armory

WE will begin with *our armory*. That armory is to me, at any rate—and I hope it is to each one of you—the Bible. To us Holy Scripture is as "the tower of David builded for an armoury, whereon there hang a thousand bucklers, all shields of mighty men" (Song of Sol. 4:4 KJV). If we want weapons, we must come here for them, and here only. Whether we seek the sword of offense or the shield of defense, we must find it within the volume of inspiration. If others have any other storehouse, I confess at once I have none. I have nothing else to preach when I have got through with this book. Indeed, I can have no wish to preach at all if I may not continue to expound the subjects that I find in these pages. What else is worth preaching? Brethren, the truth of God is the only treasure for which we seek, and the scripture is the only field in which we dig for it.

We need nothing more than God has seen fit to reveal. Certain errant spirits are never at home till they are abroad. They crave for something which I think they will never find, either in heaven above, in the earth beneath, or in the water under the earth, so long as they are in their present mind. They never rest, for they will have nothing to do with an infallible revelation; and hence they are doomed to wander throughout time and eternity and find no abiding city. For the moment they glory as if they were satisfied with their last new toy, but in a few months it is sport to them to break in pieces all the notions they formerly prepared with care and paraded with delight. They go up a hill only to come down again. Indeed, they say that the pursuit of truth is better than truth itself. They like fishing better than the fish, which may very well be true, since their fish are very small and very full of bones. These men are as great at destroying their own theories as certain paupers are at tearing up their clothes. They begin again *de novo*, times without number. Their house is always having its foundation digged out. They should be good at beginnings, for they have always been beginning since we have known them. They are as the rolling thing before the whirlwind, or like the troubled sea when it cannot rest, whose waters cast up mire and dirt. Although their cloud is not the cloud that betokened the divine presence, yet it is always moving before them, and their tents are scarcely pitched before it is time for the stakes to be pulled up again. These men are not even seeking certainty; their heaven lies in shunning all fixed truth and following every will-o'-the-wisp of speculation: They are ever learning, but they never come to the knowledge of the truth.

As for us, we cast anchor in the haven of the Word of God. Here is our peace, our strength, our life, our motive, our hope, our happiness. God's Word is our ultimatum. Here we have it. Our understanding cries, "I have found it!" Our conscience asserts that here is the truth; our heart finds here a support to which all her affections can cling, and hence we rest content.

> Brethren, the truth of God is the only treasure for which we seek, and the scripture is the only field in which we dig for it.

If the revelation of God were not enough for our faith, what could we add to it? Who can answer this question? What would any man propose to add to the sacred Word? A moment's thought would lead us to scout with derision the most attractive words of men if it were proposed to add them to the Word of God. The fabric would not be of a piece. Would you add rags to a royal vestment? Would you pile the filth of the streets in a king's treasury? Would you join the pebbles of the seashore to the diamonds of Golconda? Anything more than the Word of God sets before us, for us to believe and to preach as the life of men, seems utterly absurd to us; yet we confront a generation of men who are always wanting to discover a new motive power and a new gospel for their churches. The coverlet of their bed does not seem to be long enough, and they would fain borrow a yard or two of linsey-woolsey from the Unitarian, the agnostic, or even the atheist. Well, if there be any spiritual force or heavenward power to be found beyond that reported of in this book, I think we can do without it. Indeed, it must be such a sham that we are better without it. The scriptures in their own sphere are like God in the universe—all-sufficient. In them is revealed all the light and power the mind of man can need in spiritual things. We hear of other motive power beyond that which lies in the scriptures, but we believe such a force to be a pretentious nothing. A train is off the lines or otherwise unable to proceed, and a breakdown gang has arrived. Engines are brought to move the great impediment. At first there seems to be no stir—the engine power is not enough. Hearken! A small boy has it. He cries, "Father, if they have not power enough, I will lend them my rocking horse to help them." We have had the offer of a considerable number of rocking horses of late. They have not accomplished much that I can see, but they promised fair. I fear their effect has been for evil rather than good: They have moved the people to derision and have driven them out of the places of worship they once were glad to crowd. The new toys have been exhibited, and the people, after seeing them for a little, have moved on to other toy shops. These fine new nothings have done no good, and they never will do any good while the world stands. The Word of God is quite sufficient to interest and bless the souls of men throughout all time, but novelties soon fail.

"Surely," cries one, "we must add our own thoughts thereto."

My brother, think by all means; but the thoughts of God are better than yours. You may shed fine thoughts, as trees in autumn cast their leaves, but there is One who knows more about your thoughts than you do, and He thinks little of them. Is it not written, "The LORD knows the thoughts of man, that they are futile" (Ps. 94:11)? To liken our thoughts to the great thoughts of God would be a gross absurdity. Would you bring your candle to show the sun or your nothingness to replenish the eternal all? It is better to be silent before the Lord than to dream of supplementing what He has spoken. The Word of the Lord is to the conceptions of men as a garden to a wilderness. Keep within the covers of the sacred book, and you are in the land that flows with milk and honey. Why seek to add to it the desert sands?

Try not to cast anything forth from the perfect volume. If you find it there, there let it stand, and be it yours to preach it according to the analogy and proportion of faith. That which is worthy of God's revealing is worthy of our preaching; and that is all too little for me to claim for it. By every word of the Lord does man live. "Every word of God is pure; He is a shield to those who put their trust in Him" (Prov. 30:5). Let every revealed truth be brought forth in its own season. Go not elsewhere for a subject. With such infinity before you, there can be no need that you should do so; with such glorious truth to preach, it will be wanton wickedness if you do.

The adaptation of all this provision for our warfare we have already tested. The weapons of our armory are the very best, for we have made trial of them and have found them so. Some of you, younger brethren, have only tested the scripture a little as yet; but others of us, who are now getting gray, can assure you that we have tried the Word, as silver is tried in a furnace of earth; and it has stood every test, even unto seventy times seven. The sacred Word has endured more criticism than the best-accepted form of philosophy or science, and it has survived every ordeal.

> *he Word of God is quite sufficient to interest and bless the souls of men throughout all time.*

As a living divine has said, "After its present assailants are all dead, their funeral sermons will be preached from this book—not one verse omitted—from the first page of Genesis to the last page of Revelation." Some of us have lived for many years, in daily conflict, perpetually putting to the proof the Word of God; and we can honestly give you this assurance—that it is equal to every emergency. After using this sword of two edges upon coats of mail and bucklers of brass, we find no notch in its edge. It is neither broken nor blunted in the fray. It would cleave the devil himself, from the crown of his head to the sole of his foot, yet it would show no sign of failure whatsoever. Today it is still the selfsame mighty Word of God that it was in the hands of our Lord Jesus. How it strengthens us when we remember the many conquests of souls that we have achieved through the sword of the Spirit! Have any of you known or heard of such a thing as conversion wrought by any other doctrine than that which is in the Word? I should like to have a catalog of conversions wrought by modern theology. I would subscribe for a copy of such a work. I will not say what I might do with it after I had read it, but I would, at least, increase its sale by one copy, just to see what progressive divinity pretends to have done. Conversions through the doctrines of universal restitution! Conversions through the doctrines of doubtful inspiration! Conversions to the love of God and to faith in His Christ by hearing that the death of the Savior was only the consummation of a grand example but not a substitutionary sacrifice! Conversions by a gospel out of which all the gospel has been drained!

They say, "Wonders will never cease," but such wonders will never begin. Let them report changes of heart so wrought and give us an opportunity of testing them; and then, perchance, we may consider whether it is worth our while to leave that Word which we have tried in hundreds, and some of us here, in many thousands of cases, and have always found effectual for salvation. We know why they sneer at conversions. These are grapes that such foxes cannot reach, and therefore they are sour. As we believe in the new birth and expect to see it in thousands of cases, we shall adhere to that Word of truth by which the Holy Spirit works regeneration. In a word, in our warfare we shall keep to the old weapon of the sword of the Spirit until we can find a better. "There is none like that; give it me," is at present our verdict.

How often we have seen the Word made effectual for consolation! It is, as one brother expressed it in prayer, a difficult thing to deal with broken hearts. What a fool I have felt myself to be when trying to bring forth a prisoner out of giant Despair's castle! How hard it is to persuade despondency to hope! How have I tried to trap my game by every art known to me; but when almost in my grasp, the creature has burrowed another hole! I had dug him out of twenty already and then have had to begin again. The convicted sinner uses all kinds of arguments to prove that he cannot be saved. The inventions of despair are as many as the devices of self-confidence. There is no letting light into the dark cellar of doubt, except through the window of the Word of God. Within the scripture there is a balm for every wound, a salve for every sore. Oh, the wondrous power in the scripture to create a soul of hope within the ribs of despair and bring eternal light into the darkness that has made a long midnight in the inmost soul! Often have we tried the Word of the Lord as the cup of consolation, and it has never failed to cheer the despondent. We know what we say, for we have witnessed the blessed facts: The scriptures of truth, applied by the Holy Spirit, have brought peace and joy to those who sat in darkness and in the valley of the shadow of death.

We have also observed the excellence of the Word in the edification of believers and in the production of righteousness, holiness, and usefulness. We are always being told in these days of the ethical side of the gospel. I pity those to whom this is a novelty. Have they not discovered this before? We have always been dealing with the ethical side of the gospel; indeed, we find it ethical all over. There is no true doctrine that has not been fruitful in good works. Payson wisely said, "If there is one fact, one doctrine, or one promise in the Bible that has produced no practical effect upon your temper or conduct, be assured that you do not truly believe it." All scriptural teaching has its practical purpose and its practical result; and what we have to say, not as a matter of discovery, but as a matter of plain common sense, is this: that if we have had fewer fruits than we could wish with the tree, we suspect that there will be no fruit at all when the tree has gone and the roots are dug up. The very root of holiness lies in the gospel of our Lord Jesus Christ; and if this be removed with a view to more fruitfulness, the most astounding folly will have been committed. We have seen a fine morality, a stern integrity, a delicate purity, and what is more, a devout holiness produced by the doctrines of grace. We see consecration in life; we see calm resignation in the hour of suffering; we see joyful confidence in the article of death, and these, not in a few instances, but as the general outcome of intelligent faith in the teachings of scripture. We have even wondered at the sacred result of the old gospel. Though we are accustomed oftentimes to see it, it never loses its charm. We have seen poor men and women yielding themselves to Christ and living for Him in a way that has made our hearts to bow in adoration of the God of grace.

We have said, "This must be a true gospel that can produce such lives as these." If we have not talked so much about ethics as some have done, we remember an old saying of the country folk: "Go to such a place to hear about good works, but go to another place to see them." Much talk, little work. Some have preached good works till there has scarcely been left a decent person in the parish, while others have preached free grace and dying love in such a way that sinners have become saints and saints have been as boughs loaded down with fruit to the praise and glory of God. Having seen the harvest that springs from our seed, we are not going to change it at the dictates of this whimsical age.

Especially we have seen and tested the efficacy of the Word of God when we have been by the sickbed. I was, but a few days ago, by the side of one of our elders who appeared to be dying; and it was like heaven below to converse with him. I never saw so much joy at a wedding as I saw in that quiet chamber. He hoped soon to be with Jesus, and he was joyful in the prospect.

He said, "I have no doubt, no cloud, no trouble, no want; nay, I have not even a wish. The doctrine you have taught has served me to live by, and now it serves me to die by. I am resting upon the precious blood of Christ, and it is a firm foundation." And he added, "How silly all those letters against the gospel now appear to me! I have read some of them, and I have noted the attacks upon the old faith, but they seem quite absurd to me now that I lie on the verge of eternity. What could the new doctrine do for me now?"

I came down from my interview greatly strengthened and gladdened by the good man's testimony; and all the more was I personally comforted because it was the Word that I myself had constantly preached that had been such a blessing to my friend. If God had so owned it from so poor an instrument, I felt that the Word itself must be good indeed. I am never so happy amid all the shouts of youthful merriment as on the day when I hear the dying testimony of one who is resting on the everlasting gospel of the grace of God. The ultimate issue, as seen upon a dying-bed, is a true test as it is an inevitable one. Preach that which will enable men to face death without fear, and you will preach nothing but the old gospel.

> Oh, the wondrous power in the scripture to create a soul of hope within the ribs of despair and bring eternal light into the darkness that has made a long midnight in the inmost soul!

Brethren, we will array ourselves in that which God has supplied us in the armory of inspired scripture, because every weapon in it has been tried and proved in many ways, and never has any part of our panoply failed us.

Moreover, we shall evermore keep to the Word of God, because we have had experience of its power within ourselves. It is not so long ago that you will have forgotten how, like a hammer, the Word of God broke your flinty heart and brought down your stubborn will. By the Word of the Lord, you were brought to the cross and comforted by the atonement. That Word breathed a new life into you; and when for the first time you knew yourself to be a child of God, you felt the ennobling power of the gospel received by faith. The Holy Spirit wrought your salvation through the Holy Scriptures. You trace your conversion, I am sure, to the Word of the Lord; for this alone is "perfect, converting the soul." Whoever may have been the man who spoke it, or whatever may have been the book in which you read it, it was not man's Word or man's thought upon God's Word, but the Word itself, which made you know salvation in the Lord Jesus. It was neither human reasoning, the force of eloquence, nor the power of moral suasion, but the omnipotence of the Spirit, applying the Word itself that gave you rest and peace and joy through believing. We are ourselves trophies of the power of the sword of the Spirit; He leads us in triumph in every place, the willing captives of His grace. Let no man marvel that we keep close to it.

How many times since conversion has Holy Scripture been everything to you! You have your fainting fits, I suppose. Have you not been restored by the precious cordial of the promise of the Faithful One? A passage of scripture laid home to the heart speedily quickens the feeble heart into mighty action. Men speak of waters that revive the spirits and tonics that brace the constitution, but the Word of God has been more than this to us times beyond count. Amid temptations sharp and strong and trials fierce and bitter, the Word of the Lord has preserved us. Amid discouragements that damped our hopes and disappointments that wounded our hearts, we have felt ourselves strong to do and bear, because the assurances of help that we find in our Bibles have brought us a secret, unconquerable energy.

> *I am never so happy amid all the shouts of youthful merriment as on the day when I hear the dying testimony of one who is resting on the everlasting gospel of the grace of God.*

Brethren, we have had experience of the elevation that the Word of God can give us—upliftings toward God and heaven. If you get studying books contrary to the inspired volume, are you not conscious of slipping downward? I have known some to whom such reading has been as a mephitic vapor surrounding them with the death-damp. Yes, and I may add, that to forgo your Bible reading for the perusal even of good books would soon bring a conscious descending of the soul. Have you not found that even gracious books may be to you as a plain to look down upon rather than as a summit which to aspire? You have come up to their level long ago and get no higher by reading them; it is idle to spend precious time upon them. Was it ever so with you and the book of God? Did you ever rise above its simplest teaching and feel that it tended to draw you downward? Never! In proportion as your mind becomes saturated with Holy Scripture, you are conscious of being lifted right up and carried aloft as on eagles' wings. You seldom come down from a solitary Bible reading without feeling that you have drawn near to

God. I say a solitary one, for when reading with others, the danger is that stale comments may be flies in the pot of ointment. The prayerful study of the Word is not only a means of instruction, but an act of devotion wherein the transforming power of grace is often exercised, changing us into the image of Him of whom the Word is a mirror. Is there anything, after all, like the Word of God when the open book finds open hearts?

When I read the lives of such men as Baxter, Brainerd, McCheyne, and many others, why, I feel like one who has bathed himself in some cool brook after having gone a journey through a black country, which left him dusty and depressed; and this result comes of the fact that such men embodied scripture in their lives and illustrated it in their experience. The washing of water by the Word is what they had and what we need. We must get it where they found it. To see the effects of the truth of God in the lives of holy men is confirmatory to faith and stimulating to holy aspiration. Other influences do not help us to such a sublime ideal of consecration. If you read the Babylonian books of the present day, you will catch their spirit, and it is a foreign one, which will draw you aside from the Lord your God. You may also get great harm from divines in whom there is much pretense of the Jerusalem dialect, but their speech is half of Ashdod. These will confuse your mind and defile your faith. It may chance that a book that is upon the whole excellent, which has little taint about it, may do you more mischief than a thoroughly bad one. Be careful, for works of this kind come forth from the press like clouds of locusts. Scarcely can you find in these days a book that is quite free from the modern leaven, and the least particle of it ferments till it produces the wildest error. In reading books of the new order, though no palpable falsehood may appear, you are conscious of a twist being given you and of a sinking in the tone of your spirit; therefore be on your guard. But with your Bible you may always feel at ease; there every breath from every quarter brings life and health. If you keep close to the inspired book, you can suffer no harm; say rather you are at the fountainhead of all moral and spiritual good. This is fit food for men of God; this is the bread that nourishes the highest life.

After preaching the gospel for forty years, and after printing the sermons I have preached for more than six and thirty years, reaching now to the number of twenty-two hundred in weekly succession, I am fairly entitled to speak about the fullness and richness of the Bible as a preacher's book. Brethren, it is inexhaustible. No question about freshness will arise if we keep closely to the text of the sacred volume. There can be no difficulty as to finding themes totally distinct from those we have handled before; the variety is as infinite as the fullness. A long life will only suffice us to skirt the shores of this great continent of light. In the forty years of my own ministry, I have only touched the hem of the garment of divine truth; but what virtue has flowed out of it! The Word is like its author, infinite, immeasurable, without end. If you were ordained to be a preacher throughout eternity, you would have before you a theme equal to everlasting demands. Brothers, shall we each have a pulpit somewhere amid the spheres? Shall we have a parish of millions of leagues? Shall we have voices so strengthened as to reach attentive constellations? Shall we be witnesses for the Lord of grace to myriads of worlds that will be wonderstruck when they hear of the incarnate God? Shall we be surrounded by pure intelligences enquiring and searching into the mystery of God manifest in the flesh? Will the unfallen worlds desire to be instructed in the glorious gospel of the blessed God? And will each one of us have his own tale to tell of our experience of infinite love? I think so, since the Lord has saved us "to the intent that now unto the principalities and powers in heavenly places might be known by the church the manifold wisdom of God" (Eph. 3:10 KJV). If such be the case, our Bibles will suffice for ages to come for new themes every morning and for fresh songs and discourses world without end.

> *Oh, that we might know the Spirit of Holy Scripture thoroughly, drinking it in, till we are saturated with it! This is the blessing that we resolve to obtain.*

We are resolved then, since we have this arsenal supplied for us of the Lord, and since we want no other, to use the Word of God only, and to use it with greater energy. We are resolved—and I hope there is no dissentient among us—to know our Bibles better. Do we know the sacred volume half as well as we should know it? Have we labored after as complete a knowledge of the Word of God as many a critic has obtained of his favorite classic? Is it not possible that we still meet with passages of scripture that are new to us? Should it be so? Is there any part of what the Lord has written that you have never read? I was struck with my brother Archibald Brown's observation, that he bethought himself that unless he read the scriptures through from end to end there might be inspired teachings that had never been known to him, and so he resolved to read the books in their order; and having done so once, he continued the habit. Have we, any of us, omitted to do this? Let us begin at once. I love to see how readily certain of our brethren turn up an appropriate passage and then quote its fellow and crown all with a third. They seem to know exactly the passage that strikes the nail on the head. They have their Bibles not only in their hearts, but also at their fingers' ends. This is a most valuable attainment for a minister. A good textuary is a good theologian. Certain others, whom I esteem for other things, are yet weak on this point and seldom quote a text of scripture correctly. Indeed, their alterations jar on the ear of the Bible reader. It is sadly common among ministers to add a word or subtract a word from the passage, or in some way to debase the language of sacred writ. How often have I heard brethren speak about making "your calling and salvation" sure! Possibly they hardly enjoyed so much as we do the Calvinistic word "election," and therefore they allowed the meaning; nay, in some cases contradict it. Our reverence for the great author of scripture should forbid all mauling of His words. No alteration of scripture can by any possibility be an improvement. Believers in verbal inspiration should be studiously careful to be verbally correct. The gentlemen who see errors in scripture may think themselves competent to amend the language of the Lord of hosts; but we who believe God and accept the very words He uses may not make so presumptuous an attempt. Let us quote the words as they stand in the best possible translation, and it will be better still if we know the original and can tell if our version fails to give the sense. How much mischief may arise out of an accidental alteration of the Word! Blessed are they who are in accord with the divine teaching and receive its true meaning as the Holy Spirit teaches them! Oh, that we might know the Spirit of Holy Scripture thoroughly, drinking it in, till we are saturated with it! This is the blessing that we resolve to obtain.

By God's grace we purpose to believe the Word of God more intensely. There is believing, and believing. You believe in all your brethren here assembled, but in some of them you have a conscious practical confidence, since in your hour of trouble they have come to your rescue and proved themselves brothers born for adversity. You confide in these, with absolute certitude, because you have personally tried them. Your faith was faith before; but now it is a higher, firmer, and more assured confidence. Believe in the inspired volume up to the hilt. Believe it right through; believe it thoroughly; believe it with the whole strength of your being. Let the truths of scripture become the chief factors in your life, the chief operative forces of your action. Let the great transactions of the gospel story be to you as really and practically facts as any fact that meets you in the domestic circle or in the outside world. Let them be as vividly true to you as your own ever-present body, with its aches and pains, its appetites and joys. If we can get out of the realm of fiction and fancy into the world of fact, we shall have struck a vein of power that will yield us countless treasures of strength. Thus, to become mighty in the scriptures will be to become mighty through God.

We should resolve also that we will quote more of Holy Scripture. Sermons should be full of Bible—sweetened, strengthened, and sanctified with Bible essence. The kinds of sermons that people need to hear are outgrowths of scripture. If they do not love to hear them, that is all the more reason why they should be preached to them. The gospel has the singular faculty of creating a taste for itself. Bible hearers, when they hear indeed, come to be Bible lovers. The mere stringing of texts together is a poor way of making sermons; though some have tried it, and I doubt not God has blessed them, since they did their best. It is far better to string texts together than to pour out one's own poor thoughts in a washy flood. There will at least be something to be thought of and remembered if the Holy Word be quoted; and in the other case, there may be nothing whatever. Texts of scripture need not, however, be strung together; they may be fitly brought in to give edge and point to a discourse. They will be the force of the sermon. Our own words are mere paper pellets compared with the rifle shot of the Word. The scripture is the conclusion of the whole matter. There is no arguing after we find that "It is written." To a large extent in the hearts and consciences of our hearers, debate is over when the Lord has spoken. "Thus says the Lord" is the end of discussion to Christian minds; and even the ungodly cannot resist scripture without resisting the Spirit who wrote it. That we may speak convincingly, we will speak scripturally.

We are further resolved that we will preach nothing but the Word of God. The alienation of the masses from hearing the gospel is largely to be accounted for by the sad fact that it is not always the gospel that they hear if they go to places of worship; and all else falls short of what their souls need. Have you never heard of a king who made a series of great feasts and bade many week after week? He had a number of servants who were appointed to wait at his table; and these went forth on the appointed days and spoke with the people. But, somehow, after a while the bulk of the people did not come to the feasts. They came in decreasing number; but the great mass of citizens turned their backs on the banquets. The king made enquiry, and he found that the food provided did not seem to satisfy the men who came to look upon the banquets; and so they came no more. He determined himself to examine the tables and the meats placed thereon. He saw much finery and many pieces of display that never came out of his storehouses.

He looked at the food and he said, "But how is this? These dishes, how came they here? These are not of my providing. My oxen and fatlings were killed, yet we have not here the flesh of fed beasts but hard meat from cattle lean and starved. Bones are here, but where is the fat and the marrow? The bread also is coarse, whereas mine was made of the finest wheat. The wine is mixed with water, and the water is not from a pure well."

One of those who stood by answered, "O King, we thought that the people would be surfeited with marrow and fatness, and so we gave them bone and gristle to try their teeth upon. We thought also that they would be weary of the best white bread, so we baked a little at our own homes, in which the bran and husks were allowed to remain. It is the opinion of the learned that our provision is more suitable for these times than that which Your Majesty prescribed so long ago. As for the wines on the lees, the taste of men runs not that way in this age; and so transparent a liquid as pure water is too light a draught for men who are wont to drink of the river of Egypt, which has a taste in it of mud from the mountains of the moon."

Then the king knew why the people came not to the feast. Does the reason why going to the house of God has become so distasteful to a great many of the population lie in this direction? I believe it does. Have our Lord's servants been chopping up their own odds and ends and tainted bits to make therewith a potted meat for the millions; and do the millions therefore turn away? Listen to the rest of my parable.

"Clear the tables!" cried the king in indignation. "Cast that rubbish to the dogs. Bring in the barons of beef; set forth my royal provender. Remove those gewgaws from the hall, and that adulterated bread from the table, and cast out the water of the muddy river."

They did so; and if my parable is right, very soon there was a rumor throughout the streets that truly royal dainties were to be had, and the people thronged the palace, and the king's name became exceeding great throughout the land. Let us try the plan. It may be that we shall soon rejoice to see our Master's banquet furnished with guests.

We are resolved, then, to use more fully than ever what God has provided for us in this book, for we are sure of its inspiration. Let me say that over again. *We are sure of its inspiration.* You will notice that attacks are frequently made against verbal inspiration. The form chosen is a mere pretext. Verbal inspiration is the verbal form of the assault, but the attack is really aimed at inspiration itself. You will not read far in the essay before you will find that the gentleman who started with contesting a theory of inspiration that none of us ever held winds up by showing his hand, and that hand wages war with inspiration itself. There is the true point. We care little for any theory of inspiration. In fact, we have none. To us the plenary verbal inspiration of Holy Scripture is fact and not hypothesis. It is a pity to theorize upon a subject that is deeply mysterious and makes a demand upon faith rather than fancy. Believe in the inspiration of scripture, and believe it in the most intense sense. You will not believe in a truer and fuller inspiration than really exists. No one is likely to err in that direction, even if error be possible. If you adopt theories that pare off a portion here and deny authority to a passage there, you will at last have no inspiration left worthy of the name.

If this book is not infallible, where shall we find infallibility? We have given up the pope, for he has blundered often and terribly; but we shall not set up instead of him a horde of little popelings fresh from college. Are these correctors of scripture infallible? Is it certain that our Bibles are not right but that the critics must be so? The old silver is to be depreciated, but the German silver that is put in its place is to be taken at the value of gold. Striplings fresh from reading the last new novel correct the notions of their fathers, who were men of weight and character. Doctrines that produced the godliest generation that ever lived on the face of the earth are scouted as sheer folly. Nothing is so obnoxious to these creatures as that which has the smell of Puritanism upon it. Every little man's nose goes up celestially at the very sound of the word *Puritan*; though if the Puritans were here again, they would not dare to treat them thus cavalierly, for if Puritans did fight, they were soon known as Ironsides, and their leader could hardly be called a fool, even by those who stigmatized him as a "tyrant." Cromwell and those who were with him were not all weak-minded persons—surely? Strange that these are lauded to the skies by the very men who deride their true successors, believers in the same faith.

But where shall infallibility be found? The depth says, "It is not in me," yet those who have no depth at all would have us imagine that it is in them; or else by perpetual change they hope to hit upon it. Are we now to believe that infallibility is with learned men? Now, Farmer Smith, when you have read your Bible and have enjoyed its precious promises, you will have, tomorrow morning, to go down the street to ask the scholarly man at the parsonage whether this portion of the scripture belongs to the inspired part of the Word, or whether it is of dubious authority. It will be well for you to know whether it was written by Isaiah, or whether it was by the second of the "two Obadiahs." All possibility of certainty is transferred from the spiritual man to a class of persons whose scholarship is pretentious but who do not even pretend to spirituality. We shall gradually be so bedoubted and becriticized that only a few of the most profound will know what is Bible and what is not, and they will dictate to all the rest of us. I have no more faith in their mercy than in their accuracy. They will rob us of all that we hold most dear and glory in the cruel deed. This same reign of terror we shall not endure, for we still believe that God reveals Himself rather to babes than to the wise and prudent, and we are fully assured that our own old English version of the scriptures is sufficient for plain men for all purposes of life, salvation, and godliness. We do not despise learning, but we will never say of culture or criticism, "These be your gods, O Israel!"

> Believe in the inspiration of scripture, and believe it in the most intense sense. You will not believe in a truer and fuller inspiration than really exists.

Do you see why men would lower the degree of inspiration in holy writ and would fain reduce it to an infinitesimal quantity? It is because the truth of God is to be supplanted. You may sometime go into a shop in the evening to buy certain goods that depend upon color and texture as to be best judged of by daylight. If after you have got into the shop, the tradesman proceeds to lower the gas or to remove the lamp and then commences to show you his goods, your suspicion is aroused, and you conclude that he will try to palm off an inferior article. I more than suspect this to be the little game of the inspiration depreciators. Whenever a man begins to lower your view of inspiration, it is because he has a trick to play, which is not easily performed in the light. He would hold a séance of evil spirits, and therefore he cries, "Let the lights be lowered." We, brethren, are willing to ascribe to the Word of God all the inspiration that can possibly be ascribed to it; and we say boldly that if our preaching is not according to this Word, it is because there is no light in it. We are willing to be tried and tested by it in every way, and we count those to be the noblest of our hearers who search the scriptures daily to see whether these things be so; but to those who belittle inspiration, we will give place by subjection, no, not for an hour.

Do I hear someone say, "But still you must submit to the conclusions of science?" No one is readier than we are to accept the evident facts of science. But what do you mean by science? Is the thing called "science" infallible? Is it not science "falsely so-called"? The history of that human ignorance that calls itself philosophy is absolutely identical with the history of fools, except where it diverges into madness. If another Erasmus were to arise and write the history of folly, he would have to give several chapters to philosophy and science, and those chapters would be more telling than any others. I should not myself dare to say that philosophers and scientists are generally fools, but I would give them liberty to speak of one another, and at the close I would say, "Gentlemen, you are less complimentary to each other than I should have been." I would let the wise of each generation speak of the generation that went before it—or nowadays each half of a generation might deal with the previous half generation, for there is little of theory in science today that will survive twenty years and only a little more that will see the first day of the twentieth century.

We travel now at so rapid a rate that we rush by sets of scientific hypotheses as quickly as we pass telegraph posts when riding in an express train. All that we are certain of today is this: that what the learned were sure of a few years ago is now thrown into the limbo of discarded errors. I believe in science, but not in what is called "science." No proven fact in nature is opposed to revelation. The petty speculations of the pretentious we cannot reconcile with the Bible and would not if we could.

I feel like the man who said, "I can understand in some degree how these great men have found out the weight of the stars and their distances from one another, and even how, by the spectroscope, they have discovered the materials of which they are composed. But," said he, "I cannot guess how they found out their names." Just so. The fanciful part of science, so dear to many, is what we do not accept. That is the important part of science to many—that part that is a mere guess for which the guessers fight tooth and nail. The mythology of science is as false as the mythology of the heathen, but this is the thing that is made a god of. I say again, as far as its facts are concerned, science is never in conflict with the truths of Holy Scripture, but the hurried deductions drawn from those facts and the inventions classed as facts are opposed to scripture, and necessarily so, because falsehood agrees not with truth.

Two sorts of people have wrought great mischief, yet neither of them is worth being considered a judge in the matter; both are disqualified. It is essential than an umpire should know both sides of a question, and neither of these is thus instructed. The first is the irreligious scientist. What does he know about religion? What can he know? He is out of court when the question is, Does science agree with religion? Obviously he who would answer this query must know both of the two things in the question. The second is a better man but capable of still more mischief. I mean the unscientific Christian, who will trouble his head about reconciling the Bible with science. He had better leave it alone and not begin his tinkering trade. The mistake made by such men has been that in trying to solve a difficulty, they have either twisted the Bible or contorted science. The solution has soon been seen to be erroneous, and then we hear the cry that scripture has been defeated. Not at all; not at all. It is only a vain gloss upon it that has been removed. Here is a good brother who writes a tremendous book to prove that the six days of creation represent six great geological periods; and he shows how the geological strata and the organisms thereof follow very much in the order of the Genesis story of creation. It may be so, or it may be not so, but if anybody should before long show that the strata do not lie in any such order, what would be my reply? I should say that the Bible never taught that they did. The Bible said, "In the beginning God created the heaven and the earth." That leaves any length of time for your fire ages and your ice periods and all that before the establishment of the present age of man.[1] Then, we reach the six days in which the Lord made the heavens and the earth and rested on the seventh day. There is nothing said about long ages of time, but on the contrary, "The evening and the morning were the first day," and "The evening and the morning were the second day," and so on. I do not here lay down any theory, but simply say that if our friend's great book is all fudge, the Bible is not responsible for it. It is true that his theory has an appearance of support from the parallelism he makes out between the organic life of the ages and that of the seven days, but this may be accounted for from the fact that God usually follows a certain order whether He works in long periods or short ones. I do not know, and I do not care, much about the question, but I want to say that if you smash up an explanation, you must not imagine that you have damaged the scriptural truth that seemed to require the explanation. You have only burned the wooden palisades with which well-meaning men thought to protect an impregnable fort that needed no such defense. For the most part, we had better leave a difficulty where it is, rather than make another difficulty by our theory. Why make a second hole in the kettle to mend the first—especially when the first hole is not there at all and needs no mending? Believe everything in science that is proved; it will not come to much. You need not fear that your faith will be overburdened. And then believe everything that is clearly in the Word of God, whether it is proved by outside evidence or not. No proof is needed when God speaks. If He has said it, this is evidence enough.

But we are told that we ought to give up a part of our old-fashioned theology to save the rest. We are in a carriage traveling over the steppes of Russia. The horses are being driven furiously, but the wolves are close upon us! Can you not see their eyes of fire? The danger is pressing. What must we do? It is proposed that we throw out a child or two. By the time they have eaten the baby, we shall have made a little headway; but should they again overtake us, what then? Why, brave man, throw out your wife! "All that a man has will he give for his life"; give up nearly every truth in hope of saving one. Throw out inspiration, and let the critics devour it. Throw out election and all the old Calvinism—here will be a dainty feast for the wolves. And the gentlemen who give us the sage advice will be glad to see the doctrines of grace torn limb from limb. Throw out natural depravity, eternal punishment, and the efficacy of prayer. We have lightened the carriage wonderfully. Now for another drop. Sacrifice the great sacrifice! Have done with the atonement!

Brethren, this advice is villainous and murderous; we will escape these wolves with everything or we will be lost with everything. It shall be "the truth, the whole truth, and nothing but the truth" or none at all. We will never attempt to save half the truth by casting any part of it away. The sage advice that has been given us involves treason to God and disappointment to ourselves. We will stand by all or none. We are told that if we give up something, the adversaries will also give up something; but we care not what they will do, for we are not in the least afraid of them. They are not the imperial conquerors they think themselves. We ask no quarter from their insignificance. We are of the mind of the warrior who was offered presents to buy him off, and he was told that if he accepted so much gold or territory, he could return home in triumph and glory in his easy gain. But he said, "The Greeks set no store by concessions. They find their glory not in presents, but in spoils." We shall with the sword of the Spirit maintain the whole truth as ours and shall not accept a part of it as a grant from the enemies of God. The truth of God we will maintain as the truth of God, and we shall not retain it because the philosophic mind consents to our doing so. If scientists agree to our believing a part of the Bible, we thank them for nothing; we believe it whether or no. Their assent is of no more consequence to our faith than the consent of a Frenchman to the Englishman's holding London, or the consent of the mole to the eagle's sight. God being with us, we shall not cease from this glorying, but will hold the whole of revealed truth even to the end.

> *It shall be "the truth, the whole truth, and nothing but the truth" or none at all. We will never attempt to save half the truth by casting any part of it away.*

But now, brethren, while keeping to this first part of my theme, perhaps at too great a length, I say to you that, believing this, we accept the obligation to preach everything we see to be in the Word of God as far as we see it. We would not willfully leave out any portion of the whole revelation of God, but we long to be able to say at the last, We "have not shunned to declare to you the whole counsel of God" (Acts 20:27). What mischief may come of leaving out any portion of the truth or putting in an alien element! All good men will not agree with me when I say that the addition of infant baptism to the Word of God—for it certainly is not there—is fraught with mischief. Baptismal regeneration rides in upon the shoulders of paedobaptism. But I speak now of what I know. I have received letters from missionaries, not Baptists, but Wesleyans and Congregationalists, who have said to me, "Since we have been here"—I will not mention the localities lest I get the good men into trouble—"we find a class of persons who are the children of former converts and who have been baptized and are therefore called

Christians, but they are not one whit better than the heathen around them. They seem to think that they are Christians because of their baptism, and at the same time, being thought Christians by the heathen, their evil lives are perpetual scandal and a dreadful stumbling block." In many cases this must be so. I only use the fact as an illustration. But suppose it to be either some other error invented or some great truth neglected, evil will come of it. In the case of the terrible truths known by us as "the terrors of the Lord," their omission is producing the saddest results.

A good man, whom we do not accept as teaching exactly the truth upon this solemn matter, has, nevertheless, most faithfully written again and again to the papers to say that the great weakness of the modern pulpit is that it ignores the justice of God and the punishment of sin. His witness is true, and the evil that he indicates is incalculably great. You cannot leave out that part of the truth that is so dark and so solemn without weakening the force of all the other truths you preach. You rob of their brightness and their urgent importance the truths that concern salvation from the wrath to come.

> *Keep you to the revelation of the Spirit. Remember, you will have to give an account, and that account will not be with joy if you have played false with God's truth.*

Brethren, leave out nothing. Be bold enough to preach unpalatable and unpopular truth. The evil that we may do by adding to or taking from the Word of the Lord may not happen in our own days; but if it should come to ripeness in another generation, we shall be equally guilty. I have no doubt that the omission of certain truths by the earlier churches led afterward to serious error, while certain additions in the form of rites and ceremonies, which appeared innocent enough in themselves, led up to ritualism and afterward to the great apostasy of Romanism! Be very careful. Do not go an inch beyond the line of scripture, and do not stay an inch on this side of it. Keep to the straight line of the Word of God, as far as the Holy Spirit has taught you, and hold back nothing that He has revealed. Be not so bold as to abolish the two ordinances that the Lord Jesus has ordained, though some have ventured upon that gross presumption; neither exaggerate those ordinances into inevitable channels of grace as others have superstitiously done. Keep you to the revelation of the Spirit. Remember, you will have to give an account, and that account will not be with joy if you have played false with God's truth. Remember the story of Gylippus, to whom Lysander entrusted bags of gold to take to the city authorities. Those bags were tied at the mouth and then sealed, and Gylippus thought that if he cut the bags at the bottom he might extract a part of the coin, and then he could carefully sew the bottom up again, and so the seals would not be broken, and no one would suspect that gold had been taken. When the bags were opened, to his horror and surprise, there was a note in each bag stating how much it should contain, and so he was detected. The Word of God has self-verifying clauses in it so that you cannot run away with a part of it without the remainder of it accusing and convicting you. How will you answer for it "in that day," if you have added to or taken from the Word of the Lord? I am not here to decide what you ought to consider to be the truth of God, but whatever you judge it to be, preach it all, and preach it definitely and plainly. If I differ from you or you from me, we shall not differ very much if we are equally honest, straightforward, and God-fearing. The way to peace is not concealment of convictions, but the honest expression of them in the power of the Holy Spirit.

One more word: We accept the obligation to preach all that is in God's Word, definitely and distinctly. Do not many preach indefinitely, handling the Word of God deceitfully? You might attend upon their ministry for years and not know what they believe. I heard concerning a certain cautious minister that he was asked by a hearer, "What is your view of the atonement?" He answered, "My dear sir, that is just what I have never told to anybody, and you are not going to get it out of me." This is a strange moral condition for the mind of a preacher of the gospel. I fear that he is not alone in this reticence. They say "they consume their own smoke"—that is, they keep their doubts for home consumption. Many dare not say in the pulpit what they say *sub rosa*[2] at a private meeting of ministers. Is this honest? I am afraid that it is with some as it was with the schoolmaster in one of the towns of a southern state in America. A grand old black preacher, one Jasper, had taught his people that the world is as flat as a pancake, and that the sun goes around it every day. This part of his teaching we do not receive; but certain persons had done so, and one of them, going to a schoolmaster with his boy, asked, "Do you teach the children that the world is round or flat?" The schoolmaster cautiously answered, "Yes." The enquirer was puzzled but asked for a clearer answer. "Do you teach your children that the world is round, or that the world is flat?" Then one American dominie answered, "That depends upon the opinions of the parents." I suspect that even in Great Britain, in some few cases, a good deal depends upon the leaning of the leading deacon or the principal subscriber or the gilded youth in the congregation. If it be so, the crime is loathsome.

But whether for this or for any other cause we teach with double tongue, the result will be highly injurious. I venture here to quote a story that I heard from a beloved brother. A cadger called upon a minister to extract money from him. The good man did not like the beggar's appearance much, and he said to him, "I do not care for your case, and I see no special reason why you should come to me."

The beggar replied, "I am sure you would help me if you knew what great benefit I have received from your blessed ministry."

"What is that?" said the pastor.

The beggar then replied, "Why, sir, when I first came to hear you, I cared neither for God or devil, but now, under your blessed ministry, I have come to love them both."

What marvel if, under some men's shifty talk, people grow into love of both truth and falsehood! People will say, "We like this form of doctrine, and we like the other also." The fact is, they would like anything if only a clever deceiver would put it plausibly before them. They admire Moses and Aaron, but they would not say a word against Jannes and Jambres. We shall not join in the confederacy that seems to aim at such a comprehension. We must preach the gospel so distinctly that our people know what we are preaching. If the trumpet gives an uncertain sound, who shall prepare himself for the battle? Don't puzzle your people with doubtful speeches. "Well," said one, "I had a new idea the other day. I did not enlarge upon it; I just threw it out." That is a very good thing to do with most of your new ideas. Throw them out, by all means, but mind where you are when you do it, for if you throw them out from the pulpit, they may strike somebody and inflict a wound upon faith. Throw out your fancies, but first go alone in a boat a mile out to sea. When you have once thrown out your unconsidered trifles, leave them to the fishes.

We have nowadays around us a class of men who preach Christ and even preach the gospel; but then they preach a great deal else that is not true, and thus they destroy the good of all they deliver and lure men to error. They would be styled "evangelical" and yet be of the school that is really anti-evangelical. Look well to these gentlemen. I have heard that a fox, when closely hunted by the dogs, will pretend to be one of them and run with the pack. That is what certain are aiming at just now: The foxes would seem to be dogs. But in the case of the fox, his strong scent betrays him, and the dogs soon find him out; and even so, the scent of false doctrine is not easily concealed and the game does not answer for long. There are extant ministers of whom we scarce can tell whether they are dogs or foxes, but all men shall know our quality as long as we live, and they shall be in no doubt as to what we believe and teach. We shall not hesitate to speak in the strongest Saxon words we can find and in the plainest sentences we can put together, that which we hold as fundamental truth.

Thus I have said all this while upon my first heading, and the other two must, therefore, occupy less time, though I judge them to be of the first importance.

FOR FURTHER THOUGHT

1. *What is the source of scripture according to 2 Timothy 3:16?*
2. *How does Ephesians 5:26 say that Christ sanctifies and cleanses the church?*
3. *According to 2 Timothy 1:13, whose words are we to hold fast?*

2

OUR ARMY

NOW we must review *our army.*

What can individual men do in a great crusade? We are associated with all the people of the Lord. We need for comrades the members of our churches; these must go out and win souls for Christ. We need the cooperation of the entire brotherhood and sisterhood. What is to be accomplished unless the saved ones go forth, all of them, for the salvation of others? But the question now is mooted. Is there to be a church at all? Is there to be a distinct army of saints, or are we to include atheists? You have heard of "the church of the future" that we are to have instead[3] of the church of Jesus Christ. It will be anything else you like, but not a church. When the soldiers of Christ shall have included in their ranks all the banditti of the adversary, will there be any army for Christ at all? Is it not distinctly a capitulation at the very beginning of the war? So I take it to be.

We must not only believe in the church of God, but also recognize it very distinctly. Some denominations recognize anything and everything more than the church. Such a thing as a meeting of the church is unknown. In some "the church" signifies the ministers or clergy; but in truth it should signify the whole body of the faithful, and there should be an opportunity for these to meet together to act as a church. It is, I judge, for the church of God to carry on the work of God in the land. The final power and direction is with our Lord Jesus, and under Him it should lie, not with some few who are chosen by delegation or by patronage, but with the whole body of believers. We must more and more acknowledge the church that God has committed to our charge; and in so doing, we shall evoke a strength that else lies dormant. If the church is recognized by Christ Jesus, it is worthy to be recognized by us, for we are the servants of the church.

Yes, we believe that there ought to be a church. But churches are very disappointing things. Every pastor of a large church will own this in his own soul. I do not know that the churches of today are any worse than they used to be in Paul's time, or any better. The churches at Corinth and Laodicea and other cities exhibited grave faults, and if there are faults in ours, let us not be amazed, but let us grieve over such things and labor after a higher standard. Albeit that the members of our church are not all they ought to be, neither are we ourselves. Yet if I went anywhere for choice company, I should certainly resort to the members of my church.

> *These are the company I keep:*
> *These are the choicest friends I know.*

O Jerusalem, with all your faults, I love you still! The people of God are still the aristocracy of the race. God bless them! Yes, we mean to have a church.

Now, is that church to be real or statistical? That depends very much upon you, dear brethren. I would urge upon you the resolve to have no church unless it be a real one. The fact is that too frequently religious statistics are shockingly false. Cooking of such accounts is not an unknown art in certain quarters, as we know. I heard of one case the other day where an increase of four was reported, but had the roll been amended in the least, there must have been a decrease of twenty-five. Is it not falsehood when numbers are manipulated? There is a way of making figures figure as they should not figure. Never do this. Let us not keep names on our books when they are only names. Certain of the good old people like to keep them there and cannot bear to have them removed. But when you do not know where individuals are or what they are, how can you count them? They are gone to America or to Australia or to heaven, but as far as your roll is concerned, they are with you still. Is this a right thing? It may not be possible to be absolutely accurate, but let us aim at it. We ought to look upon this in a very serious light and purge ourselves of the vice of false reporting, for God Himself will not bless mere names. It is not His way to work with those who play a false part. If there is not a real person for each name, amend your list. Keep your church real and effective, or make no report. A merely nominal church is a lie. Let it be what it professes to be. We may not glory in statistics, but we ought to know the facts.

But is this church to increase, or is it to die out? It will do either the one or the other. We shall see our friends going to heaven, and if there are no young men and young women converted and brought in and added to us, the church on earth will have emigrated to the church triumphant above; and what is to be done for the cause and the kingdom of the Master here below? We should be crying, praying, and pleading that the church may continually grow. We must preach, visit, pray, and labor for this end. May the Lord add unto us daily such as are saved! If there be no harvest, can the seed be the true seed? Are we preaching apostolic doctrine if we never see apostolic results? Oh, my brethren, our hearts should be ready to break if there be no increase in the flocks we tend. O Lord, we beseech You, send now prosperity!

If a church is to be what it ought to be for the purposes of God, we must train it in the holy art of prayer. Churches without prayer meetings are grievously common. Even if there were only one such, it would be one to weep over. In many churches the prayer meeting is only the skeleton of a gathering; the form is kept up, but the people do not come. There is no interest, no power, in connection with the meeting. Oh, my brothers, let it not be so with you! Do train the people to continually meet together for prayer. Rouse them to incessant supplication. There is a holy art in it. Study to show yourselves approved by the prayerfulness of your people. If you pray yourself, you will want them to pray with you; and when they begin to pray with you and for you and for the work of the Lord, they will want more prayer themselves, and the appetite will grow. Believe me, if a church does not pray, it is dead. Instead of putting united prayer last, put it first. Everything will hinge upon the power of prayer in the church.

> *O Jerusalem, with all your faults, I love you still! The people of God are still the aristocracy of the race. God bless them!*

We ought to have our churches all busy for God. What is the use of a church that simply assembles to hear sermons, even as a family gathers to eat its meals? What, I say, is the profit, if it does no work? Are not many professors sadly indolent in the Lord's work though diligent enough in their own? Because of Christian idleness, we hear of the necessity for amusements and all sorts of nonsense. If they were at work for the Lord Jesus, we should not hear of this.

A good woman said to a housewife, "Mrs. So-and-So, how do you manage to amuse yourself?"

"Why," she replied, "my dear, you see there are so many children that there is much work to be done in my house."

"Yes," said the other, "I see it. I see that there is much work to be done in your house, but as it never is done, I was wondering how you amused yourself."

Much needs to be done by a Christian church within its own bounds and for the neighborhood, for the poor and the fallen, for the heathen world, and so forth; and if it is well attended to, minds and hearts and hands and tongues will be occupied, and diversions will not be asked for. Let idleness come in, and that spirit that rules lazy people, and there will arise a desire to be amused. What amusements they are, too! If religion is not a farce with some congregations, at any rate they turn out better to see a farce than to unite in prayer. I cannot understand it. The man who is all aglow with love to Jesus finds little need for amusement. He has no time for trifling. He is in dead earnest to save souls, establish the truth, and enlarge the kingdom of his Lord. There has always been some pressing claim for the cause of God upon me; and that settled, there has been another and another and another, and the scramble has been to find opportunity to do the work that must be done. Hence I have not had the time for gadding abroad after frivolities. Oh, to get a working church!

The German churches, when our dear friend Mr. Oncken was alive, always carried out the rule of asking every member, "What are you going to do for Christ?" and they put the answer down in a book. The one thing that was required of every member was that he should continue doing something for the Savior. If he ceased to do anything, it was a matter for church discipline, for he was an idle professor and could not be allowed to remain in the church like a drone in a hive of working bees. He must do or go. Oh, for a vineyard without a barren fig tree to cumber the ground! At present most of our sacred warfare is carried on by a small body of intensely living, earnest people, and the rest are either in hospital or are mere camp followers. We are thankful for that consecrated few, but we pine to see the altar fire consuming all that is professedly laid upon the altar.

Brethren, we want churches that produce saints, men of mighty faith and prevalent prayer, men of holy living and consecrated giving, men filled with the Holy Spirit. We must have these saints as rich clusters, or surely we are not branches of the True Vine. I would desire to see in every church a Mary sitting at Jesus' feet, a Martha serving Jesus, a Peter, and a John; but the best name for a church is All Saints. All believers should be saints, and all may be saints. We have no connection with the Latter-day Saints, but we love everyday saints. Oh, for more of them! If God shall so help us that the whole company of the faithful shall, each one of them individually, come to the fullness of the stature of a man in Christ Jesus, then we shall see greater things than these. Glorious times will come when believers have glorious characters.

We want also churches that know the truth and are well taught in the things of God. What do some Christian people know? They come and hear, and in the plenitude of your wisdom, you instruct them; but how little they receive to lay by in store for edification! Brethren, the fault lies partly with us and partly with themselves. If we taught better, they would learn better. See how little many professors know: not enough to give them discernment between living truth and deadly error. Old-fashioned believers could give you chapter and verse for what they believed, but how few of such remain! Our venerable grandsires were at home when conversing upon "the covenants." I love men who love the covenant of grace and base their divinity upon it: The doctrine of the covenants is the key of theology. They that feared the Lord spoke often one to another. They used to speak of everlasting life and all that comes of it. They had a good argument for this belief and an excellent reason for that other doctrine; and to try to shake them was by no means a hopeful task. You might as well have hoped to shake the pillars of the universe, for they were steadfast and could not be carried about with every wind of doctrine. They knew what they knew, and they held fast that which they had learned. What is to become of our country, with the present deluge of Romanism pouring upon us through the ritualistic party, unless our churches abound in firm believers who can discern between the regeneration of the Holy Spirit and its ceremonial substitute? What is to become of our churches in this day of skepticism when every fixed truth is pointed at with the finger of doubt, unless our people have the truths of the gospel written in their hearts? Oh, for a church of out-and-out believers, impervious to the soul-destroying doubt that pours upon us in showers!

Yet all this would not reach our ideal. We want a church of a missionary character, which will go forth to gather out a people unto God from all parts of the world. A church is a soul-saving company, or it is nothing. If the salt exercises no preserving influence on that which surrounds it, what is the use of it? Yet some shrink from effort in their immediate neighborhood because of the poverty and vice of the people.

I remember a minister who is now deceased, a very good man he was, too, in many respects; but he utterly amazed me by a reply that he made to a question of mine.

I remarked that he had an awful neighborhood round his chapel. I said, "Are you able to do much for them?"

He answered, "No, I feel almost glad that we keep clear of them; for you see, if any of them were converted, it would be a fearful burden upon us."

I knew him to be the soul of caution and prudence, but this took me aback, and I sought an explanation.

"Well," he said, "we should have to keep them. They are mostly thieves and harlots, and if converted they would have no means of livelihood, and we are a poor people and could not support them!"

He was a devout man, and one with whom it was to one's profit to converse, yet that was how he had gradually come to look at the case. His people with difficulty sustained the expenses of worship, and thus chill penury repressed a gracious zeal and froze the genial current of his soul. There was a great deal of common sense in what he said, yet it was an awful thing to be able to say it. We want a people who will not forever sing:

> *We are a garden walled around,*
> *Chosen and made peculiar ground;*
> *A little spot enclosed by grace,*
> *Out of the world's wild wilderness.*

It is good verse for occasional singing, but not when it comes to mean, "We are very few, and we wish to be." No, no, brethren! We are a little detachment of the King's soldiers detained in a foreign country upon garrison duty, yet we mean not only to hold the fort, but also to add territory to our Lord's dominion. We are not to be driven out. On the contrary, we are going to drive out the Canaanites, for this land belongs to us. It is given to us of the Lord, and we will subdue it. May we be fired with the spirit of discoverers and conquerors, and never rest while there yet remains a class to be rescued, a region to be evangelized!

We are rowing like lifeboat men upon a stormy sea, and we are hurrying to yonder wreck, where men are perishing. If we may not draw that old wreck to shore, we will at least, by the power of God, rescue the perishing, save life, and bear the redeemed to the shores of salvation. Our mission, like our Lord's, is to gather out the chosen of God from among men that they may live to the glory of God. Every saved man should be, under God, a savior; and the church is not in a right state until she has reached that conception of herself. The elect church is saved that she may save, cleansed that she may cleanse, blessed that she may bless. All of the world is the field, and all the members of the church should work therein for the Great Husbandman. Wastelands are to be reclaimed and forests broken up by the plow till the solitary place begins to blossom as the rose. We must not be content with holding our own; we must invade the territories of the prince of darkness.

My brethren, what is our relation to this church? What is our position in it? We are servants. May we always know our place and keep it! The highest place in the church will always come to the man who willingly chooses the lowest, while he who aspires to be great among his brethren will sink to be least of all. Certain men might have been something if they had not thought themselves so. A consciously great man is an evidently little one. A lord over God's heritage is a base usurper. He who in his heart and soul is always ready to serve the very least of the family, who expects to be put upon, and willingly sacrifices reputation and friendship for Christ's sake shall fulfill a heaven-sent ministry. We are to be ministered unto, but to minister, as well. Let us sing unto our Well Beloved:

> *There's not a lamb in all Your flock,*
> *I would disdain to feed.*
> *There's not a foe before whose face*
> *I'd fear Your cause to plead.*

We must also be examples to the flock. He who cannot be safely imitated ought not to be tolerated in a pulpit. Did I hear of a minister who was always disputing for preeminence? Or of another who was mean and covetous? Or of a third whose conversation was not always chaste? Or of a fourth who did not rise, as a rule, till eleven o'clock in the morning? I would hope that this last rumor was altogether false. An idle minister—what will become of him? A pastor who neglects his office? Does he expect to go to heaven? I was about to say, "If he does go there at all, may it be soon." A lazy minister is a creature despised of men and abhorred of God.

"You give your minister only fifty pounds a year!" I said to a farmer. "Why, the poor man cannot live on it."

The answer was, "Look here, sir! I tell you what: We give him a good deal more than he earns."

It is a sad pity when that can be said; it is an injury to all those who follow our sacred calling. We are to be examples to our flock in all things. In all diligence, in all gentleness, in all humility, and in all holiness we are to excel. When Caesar went on his wars, one thing always helped his soldiers to bear hardships: They knew that Caesar fared as they fared. He marched if they marched, he thirsted if they thirsted, and he was always in the heart of the battle if they were fighting. We must do more than others if we are officers in Christ's army. We must not cry, "Go on," but "Come on." Our people may justly expect of us, at the very least, that we should be among the most self-denying, the most laborious, and the most earnest in the church, and somewhat more. We cannot expect to see holy churches if we who are bound to be their examples are unsanctified. If there be, in any of our brethren, consecration and sanctification evident to all men, God has blessed them, and God will bless them more and more. If these be lacking in us, we need not search far to find the cause of our nonsuccess.

I have many things to say to you, but you cannot bear them now, because the time is long and you are weary. I desire, however, if you can gather up your patience and your strength, to dwell for a little upon the most important part of my triple theme. Here suffer me to pray for His help, whose name and person I would magnify. Come, Holy Spirit, heavenly dove, and rest upon us now!

FOR FURTHER THOUGHT

1. *What three ways does 1 Corinthians 1:2 describe the people in the church of God?*

2. *According to Ephesians 4:14, what commonly happens to immature believers?*

3. *Acts 20:17–38 records Paul's last visit to the elders of the church in Ephesus. In verse 32, he commends them to two things. What are these?*

3

OUR STRENGTH

GRANTED that we preach the Word alone; granted that we are surrounded by a model church—which, alas, is not always the case; *our strength* is the next consideration. This must come from *the Spirit of God*. We believe in the Holy Spirit and in our absolute dependence upon Him. We believe, but do we believe practically? Brethren, as to us and our work, do we believe in the Holy Spirit? Do we believe because we habitually prove the truth of the doctrine?

We must depend upon the Spirit in our preparations. Is this the fact with us all? Are you in the habit of working your way into the meaning of texts by the guidance of the Holy Spirit? Every man who goes to the land of heavenly knowledge must work his passage thither; but he must work out his passage in the strength of the Holy Spirit or he will arrive at some island in the sea of fancy and never set his foot upon the sacred shores of the truth. You do not know the truth, my brother, because you have read *Hodge's Outlines* or *Fuller's Gospel Worthy of All Acceptation* or *Owen on the Spirit* or any other classic of our faith. You do not know the truth, my brother, merely because you accept the Westminster Assembly's Confession and have studied it perfectly. No, we know nothing till we are taught of the Holy Spirit, who speaks to the heart rather than to the ear. It is a wonderful fact that we do not even hear the voice of Jesus till the Spirit rests upon us. John says, "I was in the Spirit on the Lord's Day, and I heard behind me a loud voice, as of a trumpet" (Rev. 1:10). He heard not that voice till he was in the Spirit. How many heavenly words we miss because we abide not in the Spirit!

We cannot succeed in supplication except the Holy Spirit helps our infirmities, for true prayer is praying in the Holy Spirit. The Spirit makes an atmosphere around every living prayer, and within that circle prayer lives and prevails; outside of it prayer is a dead formality. As to ourselves, then, in our study, in prayer, in thought, in word, and in deed, we must depend upon the Holy Spirit.

In the pulpit do we really and truly rest upon the aid of the Spirit? I do not censure any brother for his mode of preaching, but I must confess that it seems very odd to me when a brother prays that the Holy Spirit may help him in preaching, and then I see him put his hand behind him and draw a manuscript out of his pocket, so fashioned that he can place it in the middle of his Bible and read from it without being suspected of doing so. These precautions for ensuring secrecy look as though the man was a little ashamed of his paper; but I think he should be far more ashamed of his precautions. Does he expect the Spirit of God to bless him while he is practicing a trick? And how can He help him when he reads out of a paper from which anyone else might read without the Spirit's aid? What has the Holy Spirit to do with the business? Truly, He may have had something to do with the manuscript in the composing of it, but in the pulpit His aid is superfluous. The truer thing would be to thank the Holy Spirit for assistance rendered and ask that what He has enabled us to get into our pockets may now enter the people's hearts. Still, if the Holy Spirit should have anything to say to the people that is not in the paper, how can He say it by us? He seems to me to be very effectually blocked as to freshness of utterance by that method of ministry. Still, it is not for me to censure, although I may quietly plead for liberty in prophesying and room for the Lord to give us in the same hour what we shall speak.

> *Results worth having come from that silent but omnipotent worker whose name is the Spirit of God. In Him, and in Him only, must we trust for the conversion of a single Sunday school child, and for every genuine revival.*

Furthermore, we must depend upon the Spirit of God as to our results. No man among us really thinks that he could regenerate a soul. We are not so foolish as to claim power to change a heart of stone. We may not dare to presume quite so far as this, yet we may come to think that, by our experience, we can help people over spiritual difficulties. Can we? We may be hopeful that our enthusiasm will drive the living church before us and drag the dead world after us. Will it be so? Perhaps we imagine that if we could only get up a revival, we should easily secure large additions to the church. Is it worthwhile to get up a revival? Are not all true revivals to be got down? We may persuade ourselves that drums and trumpets and shouting will do a great deal. But my brethren, "The LORD [is] not in the wind" (1 Kings 19:11). Results worth having come from that silent but omnipotent worker whose name is the Spirit of God. In Him, and in Him only, must we trust for the conversion of a single Sunday school child, and for every genuine revival. For the keeping of our people together, and for the building of them up into a holy temple, we must look to Him. The Spirit might say, even as our Lord did, "Without me ye can do nothing" (John 15:5 KJV).

What is the church of God without the Holy Spirit? What would Hermon be without its dew or Egypt without its Nile? Behold the land of Canaan when the curse of Elias fell upon it, and for three years it felt neither dew or rain; such would Christendom become without the Spirit. What the valleys would be without their brooks or the cities without their wells, what the cornfields would be without the sun or the vintage without the summer—that would our churches be without the Spirit. As well, think of day without light, or life without breath, or heaven without God, as of Christian service without the Holy Spirit. Nothing can supply His place if He be absent: The pastures are a desert, the fruitful fields are a wilderness, Sharon languishes, and Carmel is burned with fire.

Blessed Spirit of the Lord, forgive us that we have done You such despite by our forgetfulness of You, by our proud self-sufficiency, by resisting Your influences and quenching Your fire! Henceforth work in us according to Your own excellence. Make our hearts tenderly impressible, and then turn us as wax to the seal and stamp upon us the image of the Son of God. With some such prayer and confession of faith as this, let us pursue our subject in the power of the good Spirit of whom we speak.

What does the Holy Spirit do? Beloved, what is there of good work that He does not do? It is His to quicken, to convince, to illuminate, to cleanse, to guide, to preserve, to console, to confirm, to perfect, and to use. How much might be said under each one of these heads! It is He who works in us to will and to do. He who has wrought all things is God. Glory be unto the Holy Spirit for all that He has accomplished in such poor, imperfect natures as ours! We can do nothing apart from the life sap that flows to us from Jesus the vine. That which is our own is fit only to cause us shame and confusion of face. We never go a step toward heaven without the Holy Spirit. We never lead another on the heavenward road without the Holy Spirit. We have no acceptable thought, word, or deed apart from the Holy Spirit. Even the uplifting of the eye in hope or the ejaculatory prayer of the heart's desire must be His work. All good things are of Him and through Him, from beginning to end. There is no fear of exaggerating here. Do we, however, translate this conviction into our actual procedure?

Instead of dilating upon what the Spirit of God does, let me refer to your experience and ask you a question or two. Do you remember times when the Spirit of God has been graciously present in fullness of power with you and with your people? What seasons those have been! That Sabbath was a high day. Those services were like the worship of Jacob when he said, "Surely the LORD is in this place" (Gen. 28:16). What mutual telegraphing goes on between the preacher in the Spirit and the people in the Spirit! Their eyes seem to talk to us as much as our tongues talk to them. They are then a very different people from what they are on common occasions; there is even a beauty upon their faces while we are glorifying the Lord Jesus and they are enjoying and drinking in our testimony. Have you ever seen a gentleman of the modern school enjoying his own preaching? Our evangelical preachers are very happy in delivering what our liberal friends are pleased to call their *platitudes*; but the moderns in their wisdom feel no such joy. Can you imagine a Downgrader in the glow that our Welsh friends call the *Hwyl*? How grimly they descant upon the postexilic theory! They remind me of Ruskin's expression, "Turner had no joy of his mill." I grant you, there is nothing to enjoy, and they are evidently glad to get through their task of piling up meatless bones. They stand at an empty manger, amusing themselves by biting their crib. They get through their preaching, and they are dull enough till Monday comes with a football match or an entertainment in the schoolroom or a political meeting. To them preaching is work, though they don't put much work into it. The old preachers and some of those who now live but are said to be obsolete think the pulpit a throne or a triumphal chariot and are near heaven when helped to preach with power. Poor fools that we are, preaching our antiquated gospel! We do enjoy the task. Our gloomy doctrines make us very happy. Strange, is it not? The gospel is evidently marrow and fatness to us, and our beliefs—albeit, of course, they are very absurd and unphilosophical—do content us and make us very confident and happy. I may say of some of my brethren that their very eyes seem to sparkle and their souls to glow while enlarging upon free grace and dying love. It is so, brethren, that when we have the presence of God, then our hearers and we are carried away with heavenly delight. Nor is this all. When the Spirit of God is present, every saint loves his fellow saint, and there is no strife among us unless it be who shall be the most loving. Then prayer is wrestling and prevailing, and ministry is sowing good seed and reaping large sheaves. Then conversions are plentiful, restorations are abundant, and advances in grace are seen on every side. Hallelujah! With the Spirit of God all goes well.

But do you know the opposite condition? I hope you do not. It is death in life. I trust you have never, in your scientific experiments, been cruel enough to put a mouse under an air pump and gradually to exhaust the receiver. I have read of the fatal experiment. Alas, poor mouse! As the air gets thinner and thinner, how great his sufferings, and when it is all gone, there he lies—dead. Have you never yourself been under an exhausted receiver, spiritually? You have only been there long enough to perceive that the sooner you escaped, the better for you. Said one to me the other day, "Well, as to the sermon I heard from the modern-thought divine, there was no great harm in it, for on this occasion he kept clear of false doctrine, but the whole affair was so intensely cold. I felt like a man who had fallen down a crevasse in a glacier. I felt shut up as if I could not breathe the air of heaven." You know that arctic cold; and it may occasionally be felt even where the doctrine is sound. When the Spirit of God is gone, even truth itself becomes an iceberg. How wretched is religion frozen and lifeless! The Holy Spirit has gone, and all energy and enthusiasm have gone with Him. The scene becomes like that described in the "[The Rime of the] Ancient Mariner" when the ship was becalmed:

> *The very deep did rot,*
> *Alas, that ever this should be!*
> *Yea, slimy things did crawl with legs*
> *Upon the slimy sea.*

Within the ship all was death. And we have seen it so within a church. I am tempted to apply Coleridge's lines to much that is to be seen in those churches that deserve the name "congregations of the dead." He describes how the bodies of the dead were inspired and the ship moved on, each dead man fulfilling his office in a dead and formal fashion:

> *The helmsman steered, the ship moved on;*
> *Yet never a breeze up blew.*
> *The mariners all 'gan work the ropes,*
> *Where they were wont to do.*
> *They raised their limbs like lifeless tools—*
> *We were a ghastly crew.*

All living fellowship was lacking, for the ancient mariner says:

> *The body of my brother's son*
> *Stood by me, knee to knee:*
> *The body and I pulled at one rope,*
> *But he said nought to me.*

It is much the same in those "respectable" congregations where no man knows his fellow and a dignified isolation supplants all saintly communion. To the preacher, if he is the only living man in the company, the church affords very dreary society. His sermons fall on ears that hear them not aright.

> *Twas night, calm night, the moon was high;*
> *The dead men stood together.*
> *All stood together on the deck*
> *For a charnel-dungeon fitter:*
> *All fixed on me their stony eyes,*
> *That in the moon did glitter.*

Yes, the preacher's moonlight, cold and cheerless, falls on faces that are like it. The discourse impresses their stolid intellects and fixes their stony eyes. But hearts! Well, hearts are not in fashion in those regions. Hearts are for the realm of life, but without the Holy Spirit what do congregations know of true life? If the Holy Spirit has gone, death reigns, and the church is a sepulchre. Therefore we must entreat Him to abide with us, and we must never rest till He does so. O brothers, let it not be that I talk to you about this, and that then we permit the matter to drop, but let us each one with heart and soul seek to have the power of the Holy Spirit abiding upon him.

Have we received the Holy Spirit? Is He with us now? If so it be, how can we secure His future presence? How can we constrain Him to abide with us?

I would say, first, treat Him as He should be treated. Worship Him as the adorable Lord God. Never call the Holy Spirit "it" or speak of Him as if He were a doctrine or an influence or an orthodox myth. Reverence Him, love Him, and trust Him with familiar yet reverent confidence. He is God. Let Him be God to you.

See to it that you act in conformity with His working. The mariner to the east cannot create the winds at his pleasure, but he knows when the trade winds blow and takes advantage of the season to speed his vessel. Put out to sea in holy enterprise when the heavenly wind is with you. Take the sacred tide at its flood. Increase your meetings when you feel that the Spirit of God is blessing them. Press home the truth more earnestly than ever when the Lord is opening ears and hearts to accept it. You will soon know when there is dew about; prize the gracious visitation. The farmer says, "Make hay while the sun shines." You cannot make the sun shine; that is quite out of your power; but you can use the sun while he shines. "When you hear the sound of marching in the tops of the mulberry trees, then you shall advance quickly" (2 Sam. 5:24). Be diligent in season and out of season, but in a lively season be doubly laborious.

> *If the Holy Spirit has gone, death reigns, and the church is a sepulchre. Therefore we must entreat Him to abide with us, and we must never rest till He does so.*

Evermore, in beginning, in continuing, and in ending any and every good work, consciously and in very truth depend upon the Holy Spirit. Even a sense of your need of Him He must give you; and the prayers with which you entreat Him to come must come from Him. You are engaged in a work so spiritual, so far above all human power, that to forget the Spirit is to ensure defeat. Make the Holy Spirit to be the sine qua non of your efforts, and go so far as to say to Him, "If thy presence go not with me, carry us not up hence" (Exod. 33:15 KJV). Rest only in Him and then reserve for Him all the glory. Be especially mindful of this, for this is a tender point with Him: He will not give His glory to another. Take care to praise the Spirit of God from your inmost heart, and gratefully wonder that He should condescend to work by you. Please Him by glorifying Christ. Render Him homage by yielding yourself to His impulses and by hating everything that grieves Him. The consecration of your whole being will be the best psalm in His praise.

There are a few things that I would have you remember, and then I have done. Remember that the Holy Spirit has His ways and methods, and there are some things that He will not do. Bethink you that He makes no promise to bless compromises. If we make a treaty with error or sin, we do it at our own risk. If we do anything that we are not clear about, if we tamper with truth or holiness, if we are friends of the world, if we make provision for the flesh, if we preach halfheartedly and are in league with errorists, we have no promise that the Holy Spirit will go with us. The great promise runs in quite another strain: "Come out from among them and be separate, says the Lord. Do not touch what is unclean, and I will receive you. I will be a Father to you, and you shall be My sons and daughters, says the LORD Almighty" (2 Cor. 6:17–18). In the New Testament, only in that one place, with the exception of the book of Revelation, is God called by the name "the Lord God Almighty." If you want to know what great things the Lord can do, as the LORD God Almighty, be separate from the world and from those who apostatize from the truth. The title "LORD God Almighty" is evidently quoted from the Old Testament. "El Shaddai," God All-Sufficient, the many-breasted God. We shall never know the utmost power of God for supplying all our needs till we have cut connection once for all with everything that is not according to His mind. That was grand of Abraham when he said to the king of Sodom, "I will not take of you"—a Babylonish garment or a wedge of gold? No, no. He said, "I will take nothing, from a thread to a sandal strap" (Gen. 14:23). That was "the cut direct." The man of God will have nothing to do with Sodom, or with false doctrine. If you see anything that is evil, give it the cut direct. Have done with those who have done with truth. Then you will be prepared to receive the promise, and not till then.

Dear brethren, remember that wherever there is great love, there is sure to be great jealousy. "Love is as strong as death." What next? "Jealousy [is] as cruel as the grave" (Song of Sol. 8:6). God is love, and for that very reason

"The LORD your God is a jealous God" (Deut. 6:15). Keep clear of everything that defiles or that would grieve the Holy Spirit; for if He be vexed with us, we shall soon be put to shame before the enemy.

Note next that He makes no promise to cowardice. If you allow the fear of man to rule you and wish to save self from suffering or ridicule, you will find small comfort in the promise of God. He who saves his life shall lose it. The promises of the Holy Spirit to us in our warfare are to those who quit themselves like men and by faith are made brave in the hour of conflict. I wish that we were come to this pass, that we utterly despised ridicule and calumny.

> *Keep clear of everything that defiles or that would grieve the Holy Spirit; for if He be vexed with us, we shall soon be put to shame before the enemy.*

Oh, to have the self-oblivion of that Italian martyr of whom Foxe speaks! They condemned him to be burned alive, and he heard the sentence calmly. But, you know, burning martyrs, however delightful, is also expensive, and the mayor of the town did not care to pay for the fagots, and the priests who had accused him also wished to do the work without personal expense. So they had an angry squabble, and there stood the poor man for whose benefits these fagots were to be contributed, quietly hearing their mutual recriminations. Finding that they could not settle it, he said, "Gentlemen, I will end your dispute. It is a pity that you should, either of you, be at so much expense to find fagots for my burning, and for my Lord's sake, I will even pay for the wood that burns me, if you please." There is a fine touch of scorn as well as meekness there. I do not know that I would have paid that bill, but I have even felt inclined to go a little out of the way to help the enemies of the truth to find fuel for their criticisms of me. Yes, yes; I will yet be viler and give them more to complain of. I will go through with the controversy for Christ's sake and do nothing whatever to quiet their wrath. Brethren, if you trim a little, if you try to save a little of your repute with the men of the apostasy, it will go ill with you. He who is ashamed of Christ and His Word in this evil generation shall find that Christ is ashamed of him at the last.

I will be very brief on these points. Remember, next, that the Holy Spirit will never set His seal to falsehood. Never! If what you preach is not the truth, God will not own it. See ye well to this.

What is more, the Holy Spirit never sets His signature to a blank. That would be unwise on the part of man, and the holy Lord will not perpetrate such a folly. If we do not speak clear doctrine with plainness of speech, the Holy Spirit will not put His signature to our empty prating. If we do not come out distinctly with Christ and Him crucified, we may say farewell to true success.

Next, remember that the Holy Spirit will never sanction sin; and to bless the ministry of some men would be to sanction their evil ways. "Be clean, you who bear the vessels of the LORD" (Isa. 52:11). Let your character correspond with your teaching, and let your churches be purged from open transgressors, lest the Holy Spirit disown your teaching, not for its own sake, but because of the ill savor of unholy living that dishonors it.

> We ought to prepare the sermon as if all depended upon us, and then we are to trust the Spirit of God knowing that all depends upon Him.

Remember, again, that He will never encourage idleness. The Holy Spirit will not come to rescue us from the consequences of willful neglect of the Word of God and study. If we allow ourselves to go up and down all the week doing nothing, we may not climb the pulpit stairs and dream that the Lord will be there and then tell us what to speak. If help were promised to such, then the lazier the man the better the sermon. If the Holy Spirit worked only by impromptu speakers, the less we read our Bibles and the less we meditated on them, the better. If it be wrong to quote from books, "attention to reading" should not have been commanded (1 Tim. 4:13). All this is obviously absurd, and not one of you will fall into such a delusion. We are bound to be much in meditation and give ourselves wholly to the Word of God and prayer, and when we have minded these things, we may look for the Spirit's approbation and cooperation. We ought to prepare the sermon as if all depended upon us, and then we are to trust the Spirit of God knowing that all depends upon Him. The Holy Spirit sends no one into the harvest to sleep among the sheaves, but to bear the burden and heat of the day. We may well pray God to send more "laborers" into the vineyard, for the Spirit will be with the strength of laborers, but He will not be the friend of loiterers.

Recollect, again, that the Holy Spirit will not bless us in order to sustain our pride. Is it not possible that we may be wishing for a great blessing that we might be thought great men? This will hinder our success: The string of the bow is out of order, and the arrow will turn aside. What does God do with men who are proud? Does He exalt them? I think not. Herod made an eloquent oration, and he put on a dazzling silver robe that glistened in the sun, and when the people saw his vestments and listened to his charming voice, they cried, "The voice of a god and not of a man!" (Acts 12:22). But the Lord smote him, and he was eaten by worms. Worms have a prescriptive right to proud flesh, and when we get very mighty and very big, the worms expect to make a meal of us. "Pride goes before destruction, and a haughty spirit before a fall" (Prov. 16:18). Keep humble if you would have the Spirit of God with you. The Holy Spirit takes no pleasure in the inflated oratory of the proud. How can He? Would you have Him sanction bombast? Walk humbly with your God, O preacher! For thou canst not walk with Him in any other fashion; and if thou walk not with Him, your walking will be in vain.

As men alive from the dead, go forth in the quickening power of the Holy Spirit. You have no other strength.

Consider, again, that the Holy Spirit will not dwell where there is strife. Let us follow peace with all men, and especially let us keep peace in our churches. Some of you are not yet favored with this boon, and possibly it is not your fault. You have inherited old feuds. In many a small community, all the members of the congregation are cousins to one another, and relations usually agree to disagree. When cousins cozen their cousins, the seeds of ill will are sown, and these intrude even into church life. Your predecessor's high-handedness in past time may breed a good deal of quarreling for many years to come. He was a man of war from his youth, and even when he is gone, the spirits that he called from the vast deep remain to haunt the spot. I fear you cannot expect much blessing, for the Holy Dove does not dwell by troubled waters. He chooses to come where brotherly love continues. For great principles and matters of holy discipline, we may risk peace itself; but for self or party, may such conduct be far from us.

Lastly, remember the Holy Spirit will only bless in conformity with His own set purpose. Our Lord explains what that purpose is: "He will glorify Me" (John 16:14). He has come forth for this grand end, and He will not put up with anything short of it. If, then, we do not preach Christ, what is the Holy Spirit to do with our preaching? If we do not make the Lord Jesus glorious, if we do not lift Him high in the esteem of men, if we do not labor to make Him King of kings and Lord of lords, we shall not have the Holy Spirit with us. Vain will be rhetoric, music, architecture, energy, and social status if our one design be not to magnify the Lord Jesus. We shall work alone and work in vain.

This is all I have to say to you at this time. But, my dear brethren, it is a great all if first considered and then carried out. May it have practical effect upon us! It will, if the Great Worker uses it, and not else. Go forth, O soldiers of Jesus, with "the sword of the Spirit, which is the word of God" (Eph. 6:17). Go forth with the companies of the godly whom you lead, and let every man be strong in the Lord and in the power of His might. As men alive from the dead, go forth in the quickening power of the Holy Spirit. You have no other strength. May the blessing of the triune God rest upon you, one and all, for the Lord Jesus Christ's sake! Amen.

FOR FURTHER THOUGHT

1. *According to Ephesians 6:17, what is the sword of the Spirit?*
2. *Ephesians 6:18 speaks of prayer. In what, and in what ways are we to pray?*
3. *Read Galatians 5:16. How can we not fulfill the lusts of the flesh?*
4. *1 Kings 19:9–15 depicts Elijah hiding in a cave. While there, in what three places did Elijah not find the Lord? (See vv. 11–12.) Where did he find the Lord?*

NOTES

[1] Charles Spurgeon held to a version of "the gap theory," which is the idea that fire and ice ages fit into a gap between Genesis 1:1 and 1:2. Few evangelical scholars today hold to that view, but it was quite popular in Spurgeon's day.

[2] Privately.

[3] At this point, the audience could not be restrained, but stopped the speaker with cheers and laughter, to which he answered, "Nay, do not stop me in the middle of a sentence. My rule is not to mention names, and yet you have found a name hidden in a harmless word."

Scripture Index

Ruth
1:20—266

1 Samuel
3:5—906
3:9—906, 930
3:18—635
21:9—876
26:21—534

2 Samuel
5:24—437, 1386
22:47—378
23:5—341, 434, 450

1 Kings
5:9–11—617
10:21—730
19:9–15—1391
19:11—1382
19:18—1004

2 Kings
2:12—132
2:23—1001
5:1–14—859
18:4—819
20:1–6—121

1 Chronicles
4:9—454
16:32—753
17:23—449

Job
1:8—1204
5:9—1133
5:13—824
5:21—825
5:26—824
8:9—113
9:31—748
10:2—958
13:15—878
16:2—824
17:9—1202
18:6—1239
18:7—1239
19:25—365, 704, 1184
19:26—648
19:27—648
21:17—1239
23:12—905
25:6—863
29:2–3—1240
33:24—550
38:1—480
38:29—681
41:5—1140
41:31—433

Psalms
1:3—674
2:2—543
2:12—998
5:3—356

8:4—250
9:17—951
10:17—980
11:3—298
12:1—904
12:4—904
12:6—904, 908
17:6—1149
18:28—1240
18:29—775
19:7—550
19:10—703
22:14—707, 1324
22:15—1324
22:22—204, 217
22:27–28—134
24:7—264, 311
27:8—873
27:9—294
29:4—928
30:6–7—811
36:1—761
36:9—405
37:3—936
37:4—874
38:8—453
38:9—259, 453
39:12—322
40:2—544
42:5—294
42:6—714
42:7—301, 786
44:21—195

26:15—1074
29:1—432
29:15—1092
29:20—1091
30:5—1351
30:10—803
31:18—1241

Ecclesiastes
1:2—780, 932
3:1—130
8:4—933
9:7–8—292

Song of Solomon
1:4—995
1:7—703, 717, 720
4:4—1349
4:7—215
5:1—727
5:2—137
6:3—688
6:12—347
8:5—1209
8:6—1387
8:12—691

Isaiah
1:5—568
1:18—26, 1120
1:20—921, 923, 933
1:24—149
5:5–6—689
6:2—1284

7:1–17—280
7:14—279
7:15—279, 286
7:16—281
8:8—280
9:6—399
11:1–2—657
11:10—657
23:9—496
25:6—127
27:3—689
28:13—174
28:16—344, 349
30:33—194
31:2—906
33:17—648
40:8—912
40:15—193
40:22—129
41:1—928
41:9—1207
41:15—95
41:17—980
42:3—1222
43:4—348
43:25—1131
44:22—181
45:7—1008
45:10—1008
45:15—400
45:22—9, 27, 28,
  149, 356, 473,
  606, 621, 1133
46:4—373

48:22—439
52:11—1271, 1389
53:2—345
53:3—162, 309,
  325, 327
53:4—297
53:5—1323
53:6—297, 646
53:11—297, 689,
  753
53:12—311
54:13—509
55:1—498
55:3—928, 930
55:8—725, 970
55:9—970
55:10—547
56:11—671
57:15—268
62:1—327
62:4—215
63:16—155
64:6—1122
65:1—502

Jeremiah
1:17–19—925
2:3—216
3:14—1055
4:19—453
7:12—690
7:13—174
7:25—174
8:20—152

6:9—247
6:11—692
6:12—802
7:7—598
7:11—318
7:16—83
7:20—973
9:9—68, 1040, 1219
9:12—1124
9:13—1035
10:8—510
10:22—894
10:34–36—267
11:5—374
11:18—211
11:26—221
11:28—408, 863, 1177
12:20—718, 863
12:31—1132
13:30—826
16:13—406
16:16—406
16:17—406
17:5—215
17:20—580
18:22—804
19:6—908
20:15—218
20:16—1207
20:28—1021, 1022
21:19—854
22:14—1039
22:44—329
23:10—700

24:30—144
25:9—1095
25:21—367
25:23—965
25:41—191, 335,
  949
25:46—375, 934
26:38—1030, 1325
26:39—300, 447
27:22—1030
27:24—1195
27:25—1193, 1195
27:26—1195
27:42—335, 386,
  401
27:46—181, 211,
  293, 386, 460, 1325
27:54—387, 397
28:18—313, 365,
  473
28:19—365, 473
28:20—736

Mark
1:5—1035
2:27—525
5:19—447
5:36—1152
9:7—403, 1151
9:23—883
9:24—552
9:49—529
12:34—1291
13:20—1005

13:22—1005
13:27—1005
15:27—308
15:34—616, 1031,
  1137
15:35–36—707
16:15—25, 376,
  692
16:16—49, 119,
  231, 582, 862,
  919, 934, 1162,
  1303
16:20—701

Luke
1:46—284, 697
1:48—284
1:52—822, 1042
1:53—822, 982
2:1–4—278
2:14—173, 285
2:15—282
2:30—937
2:32—155, 1227
2:35—265
2:49—326
4:22—1248
4:29—322
5:1—1248
5:4—136
5:13—1132
7:44—98
7:48—1132
7:50—1160

13:26—374
13:36—11
13:39—1322
13:41—951
13:48—1006
16:6–8—461
16:9—449
16:14—1148
16:30—490, 1175
16:31—27, 34, 152, 541
16:37—1091
17:30–34—1184
19:20—494
20:17–38—1379
20:24—899
20:27—1367
20:28—471
20:32—1379
20:33–35—1102
24:15—640
26:17–18—1190
26:24—1212
24:29—1212

Romans
1:20—186
1:21—621
2:16—1298
3:9–19—564
3:10—1121, 1302
3:11—1302
3:12—1302
3:21—1135

3:22—1135
3:23—1135, 1298
3:24—511, 1135
3:25—1135
3:26—1135
4:5—584, 590, 1121
4:22–25—579
5:1—34, 514, 560, 589, 590, 788, 823, 1096, 1158
5:2—589, 788, 823, 1096, 1318
5:3—589, 813, 823, 1096
5:4—813, 823, 1096
5:5—813, 823, 1096
5:6—765, 805, 936, 1128, 1165, 1169, 1174
5:8–9—1174
5:18—581, 590, 1128
5:19—569, 581
5:20—1114
6:3—771
6:4—574, 771, 869
6:8—308
6:14—315, 1203
6:15—526
6:23—498
7:12—762
7:14—762
7:18—1164

7:19—950
7:21—41
7:24—41, 566, 811, 1145
8:1—797
8:2—1145
8:14—445
8:15—136, 257, 261, 527
8:17—155, 249, 254, 524
8:26—445, 461, 883
8:27—445
8:28—331, 1096
8:29—1007, 1020
8:30—120, 575, 1007, 1020, 1039, 1130, 1207
8:31—1007
8:32—214, 1007
8:33—209, 499, 630, 797, 1007, 1129, 1132, 1138
8:34—43, 499, 797, 1138
8:35—891, 1134, 1209
8:37—630
8:38–39—805, 1134
9:6—271
9:8—769
9:10–13—122
9:11—122, 1007
9:12—122, 1007

2:11—335
2:13—217
3:3—156
3:10—394
3:12—764, 771,
  899, 976
3:13—764, 771
3:14—764, 771
3:20—887, 899,
  903
3:21—331, 887,
  903
4:1—887, 892,
  903
4:4—245
4:7—634

Colossians
1:2—154
1:10–11—1209
1:12–13—999
1:15—292
1:19—881
1:28—577
2:9—399
2:10—159, 577,
  650, 755
2:12—768
2:15—309
3:2—1108
3:3—877, 1108
3:4—630, 831
3:5—1269
3:9–10, 161

3:11—154, 1195
3:13—161, 805
3:14–15, 162
3:16—162
3:17—162

1 Thessalonians
2:19—755
4:17—828, 839
5:9—1008

2 Thessalonians
2:13–14—1000
3:7–9—1080
3:10—442, 1077,
  1080, 1102
3:11—1080, 1099
3:12—1080, 1099
3:13—1080

1 Timothy
1:12—798, 823
1:13—798, 823,
  1111
1:14—1111
1:15—860, 1033,
  1036, 1125
2:5—292, 342
2:6—1034
2:8–10—1088
3:15—737
3:16—204, 217, 362,
  399, 919
4:10—1307
4:13—1389

5:8—83
5:14—1099
6:12—1343
6:16—311

2 Timothy
1:9—1050
1:12—704, 755, 817,
  942
1:13—1371
2:10—558
2:17—737
2:18—737
2:19—83, 721, 722,
  733, 737
2:20—721
2:21—721, 733
3:2—840
3:3—840
3:5—840
3:8—853
3:10–12—1096
3:13—841
3:15—149
3:16—1000, 1371
4:2–3—1212
4:7—839
4:8—839

Titus
2:8—80
2:11—869, 1145
2:12—869
2:13—334

Hebrews
1:3—331
1:5—249
1:8—166
2:11—892
2:17—286
3:1—603
3:15—1118
4:12—199, 201
4:15—306
6:4—1051, 1066
6:5—1051, 1066
6:6—1051
6:7-8—1062
6:18—118
7:3—543
7:21—166
7:25—331, 591, 605, 1151
8:6—232
8:12—798
9:27—827
9:28—353
10:11—325
10:12—325, 326, 329, 335, 387
10:13—325, 335
10:14—329
10:17—499
10:31—119
11—124
11:1—788, 1152
11:5—542
11:6—528, 1149

11:32—534
11:37—642
12:2—753
12:3—397
12:6—956
12:14—768, 1203
13:5—296, 718, 964
13:7—368, 373, 381
13:8—368, 373, 933
13:9—373

James
2:6—78
3:2—1098
4:13—612

1 Peter
1:3—249
1:8—140
1:23—1181, 1340
2:4—343
2:6—351
2:7—336, 351
2:24—297, 503
3:3—1088
3:4—860, 1088
3:18—1332
3:21—768
4:14—657
5:8—752
5:10—46

2 Peter
1:1—581

1:4—629
1:10—944
2:10–20—855
2:17—852
3:4—145
3:15—144

1 John
1:7—488, 1033, 1150
2:2—654
2:15—654
2:19—894
2:23—406
3:1—206
3:2—254
3:5—1141
3:9—630
3:10—206
3:14—625, 637
3:16—213
3:18—711
4:1—1001, 1105
4:2—1105
4:6—908
4:7—704
4:19—720
4:20—802
5:1—406, 573, 624
5:2—625
5:3—626
5:7—627
5:9—628, 1150
5:11—629
5:13—622

5:16—177
5:18—630, 1204
5:19—1035
5:20—399

Jude
1:1—1269
1:5—742
1:6—742
1:7—743
1:12—855
1:13—744
1:18—952
1:21—888
1:24—88, 331, 738,
  755, 1205
1:25—738, 755

Revelation
1:5—375, 471
1:6—375
1:10—1380
1:18—398
2:23—196
3:9—850
3:15–16—758
3:20—759, 1120
3:21—166
4:11—965
5:10—333
5:12—331
7:16–17—324
11:15—166, 654
14:4—350, 387

18:7—609
18:21–23—1243
19:7—166
22:1—166
22:3—166
22:5—1245
22:12—365, 389
22:14—123
22:17—64